The Palgrave Handbook of Small Arms and Conflicts in Africa

Usman A. Tar · Charles P. Onwurah
Editors

The Palgrave Handbook of Small Arms and Conflicts in Africa

palgrave
macmillan

Editors
Usman A. Tar
Nigerian Defence Academy
Centre for Defence Studies and
Documentation
Kaduna, Nigeria

Charles P. Onwurah
Nigerian Defence Academy
Centre for Defence Studies and
Documentation
Kaduna, Nigeria

ISBN 978-3-030-62182-7   ISBN 978-3-030-62183-4 (eBook)
https://doi.org/10.1007/978-3-030-62183-4

© The Editor(s) (if applicable) and The Author(s) 2021
This work is subject to copyright. All rights are solely and exclusively licensed by the Publisher, whether the whole or part of the material is concerned, specifically the rights of translation, reprinting, reuse of illustrations, recitation, broadcasting, reproduction on microfilms or in any other physical way, and transmission or information storage and retrieval, electronic adaptation, computer software, or by similar or dissimilar methodology now known or hereafter developed.
The use of general descriptive names, registered names, trademarks, service marks, etc. in this publication does not imply, even in the absence of a specific statement, that such names are exempt from the relevant protective laws and regulations and therefore free for general use.
The publisher, the authors and the editors are safe to assume that the advice and information in this book are believed to be true and accurate at the date of publication. Neither the publisher nor the authors or the editors give a warranty, expressed or implied, with respect to the material contained herein or for any errors or omissions that may have been made. The publisher remains neutral with regard to jurisdictional claims in published maps and institutional affiliations.

Cover credit: zabelin/Getty Images

This Palgrave Macmillan imprint is published by the registered company Springer Nature Switzerland AG
The registered company address is: Gewerbestrasse 11, 6330 Cham, Switzerland

To the victims of small arms and their families for bearing the brunt of armed violence.

To all the selfless individuals and organizations working tirelessly to get rid of small arms in Africa and across the world.

Acknowledgements

In the course of working on this book project, we have incurred debts of appreciation to a number of people and organizations who provided selfless support. First, our employers—the Nigerian Ministry of Defence (MOD) and Nigerian Defense Academy (NDA)—granted us exceptional institutional support to see this manuscript completed. In particular, the Commandant of NDA General Sagir Yaro and the Academy Provost, Professor Isa Garba proved to be highly understanding and visionary leaders that spearhead a vibrant culture of intellectual enterprise, and cordial civil–military relations both within and outside the Academy. Their relentless push on us to finish this book project has indeed paid off. We are also grateful to the professoriate, academic and non-academic staff of NDA for providing a collegial atmosphere to finish this Handbook.

Sincere appreciations to the following external colleagues, some of who read portions of this volume and made valuable suggestions: Prof. Alfred Zack-Williams (University of Central Lancashire, UK), Prof. Kenneth Omeje (University of Johannesburg South Africa); Prof. Rita Abrahamsen (University of Ottawa, Canada); Prof. Ebenezer Obadare (University of Kansas, USA), Prof. Cyril Obi (Social Science Research Council, USA); Marc-Antoine Pérouse de Montclos (*Institut de recherche pour le développement* [IRD] Paris); Prof. Celestine Oyom Bassey (University of Calabar, Nigeria), Prof. Rauf Ayo Dunmoye (ABU, Zaria, Nigeria); Prof. Habu Mohammed and Prof. Umar Pateh (Bayero University of Kano, Nigeria); Prof. Albert Isaac Olawale (University of Ibadan, Nigeria), and Prof. Yusuf Zoaka, Prof. Kabiru Mato and Prof. Abdulhamid Suleiman-Ozohu (all of the University of Abuja, Nigeria); Ambassador Abdu Zango, Country Director of United States Institute for Peace (USIP), Nigeria; and Dr. Usman Bugaje of the Arewa Research and Development Programme, Kaduna.

A number of very senior colleagues, serving and retired, guided us and challenged our thoughts on issues of defence and security: Prof. Tijjani

Muhammad-Bande, President of the UN General Assembly; Air Marshal SB Abubakar, Nigeria's Chief of the Air Staff; General Tukur Yusuf Buratai, Chief of Army Staff; Major General Babagana Monguno, the National Security Advicer; General Garba A Wahab, Director General of Nigeria's Army Resource Centre (NARC); General Ibrahim Manu Yusuf, Commander of the Joint Multinational Joint Task Force (MNJTF) of the Lake Chad Basin Commission; Rear Admiral Sanmi Alade, former Commandant of the National Defence College, Nigeria; Major General C Ofoche, former Commandant of the Army War College Nigeria (AWCN); Air Vice Marshall AS Liman, Commandant of the Armed Forces Command and Staff College, Jaji, and his predecessor Air Vice Marshall LS Alao.

Prof. Tar's colleagues at the Presidential Committee to Review Nigeria's National Defence Policy—in particular, Chairman of the Committee Air Vice Marshal MN Umaru and Secretary Brigadier General Alaya—were extremely supportive. In addition, Prof. Tar's colleagues at the Presidential Think Tank on Threats to National Security deserve sincere appreciation. The Chairman Major General AM Jibril, Secretary Major General AT Umaru, Alternate Secretary Captain Ahmed Chiroma and members were delightful to work with. Prof. Tar appreciates Major General Garba Ayodeji Wahab, Major General Ahmed Mohammed (Bandit), Major General Adamu Abubakar, Major General Chumkwuemeka Osita Onwamaegbu former Commandant at NDA and his successors Major General Mohammed Inuwa Idris, Major General Mohammed Tasi'u Ibrahim and Major General Adeniyi Oyebade.

We appreciate the National Foundation for the Support of Victims of Terrorism (Victims Support Fund, VSF) who funds national research consortium to conduct research on the root causes of terrorism in Nigeria coordinated by Prof. Tar and domiciled at NDA's Centre for Defence Studies and Documentation. The Fund provided a platform to engage peers and stakeholders who work on Countering Violent Extremism. In addition, Prof. Tar deeply appreciates the Alumni Association of NDA Regular Combatant Course 26 who endowed him as a Chair in Defence and Security Studies. The endowment enabled Prof. Tar to take time out to conduct primary and archival research, and desk work for this Handbook.

We owe a debt of gratitude to Prof. Tar's research assistants and associates—Dr. Abdullahi Yusuf Manu, Mr. Samuel Ayeba and Mr. Yekini Bello—provided auxiliary support to execute this project, especially the compilation of list of abbreviations, muster of contributor contracts and formatting of tables and figures.

Members of Prof. Tar's extended family were incredibly supportive during my regular absence to work on the manuscript. My wife, Fatima and children—Mustapha, Abubakar, Aisha, Maryam and Amaal—have been my pillar of support. Prof. Tar's parents and siblings prevailed on him to keep going: Hajja Yakaka Mohd Tar, Alhaji Maina Tar, Alhaji Abubakar Akirga (*Galadiman Afoland*), Hajja Yagana Abubakar, Mustapha Tar, Hajja Fanta, Ya Fanta Mohd Tar, Momodu Mohd Tar, Jibrin Mohd Tar, Isa Mohd

Tar, Architect Yusuf Abubakar, Prof. Prince Sanusi Ibrahim, Dr. Halimatu Sadiya Ibrahim, Dr. Aisha Kana, Sub-Lieutenant Faruk Ahmed, Barrister Hauwa Faruk Ahmed and ASC Kabiru Yakubu. Charles thanks his wife Mrs. CP Onwurah, his mother Mama Onwurah and siblings for their wonderful support.

Words cannot convey our gratitude to folks at Palgrave Macmillan Publishers. We missed several deadlines but they encouraged us to keep going. In particular, Alina Yorova, our Commissioning Editor, and Editorial Assistants Mary Fata and Anne-Kathrin Birchley-Brun were profoundly patient and understanding.

Finally, to those whose names are inadvertently omitted, we extend our sincere apologies.

Contents

1. Introduction: The Frontiers of Small Arms Proliferation and Conflicts in Africa ... 1
   Usman A. Tar

Part I Theory and Concepts

2. Background: Small Arms, Violent Conflicts, and Complex Emergencies in Africa—A Fatal Combination ... 17
   Usman A. Tar

3. The Theoretical Parameters of the Proliferation and Regulation of Small Arms and Light Weapons in Africa ... 41
   Usman A. Tar and Sunday Adejoh

4. The Political Economy of Small Arms and Light Weapons Proliferations in Africa ... 69
   Moses Eromedoghene Ukpenumewu Tedheke

5. (En)Gendering the Small Arms Discourse: Women and the Management of Violent Conflicts in Africa ... 95
   Caroline Obiageli and Agnes Okorie

Part II Topographies and Contexts

6. The Context of Small Arms Proliferation in Africa: State Fragility and Management of Armed Violence ... 113
   Chris M. A. Kwaja

7. Mapping of Conflicts and Small Arms and Light Weapons Proliferations in Africa ... 133
   Taiye Oluwafemi Adewuyi and Mwanret Gideon Daful

8	External Influence, Failed States, Ungoverned Spaces and Small Arms Proliferation in Africa Muhammad Dan Suleiman, Hakeem Onapajo, and Ahmed Badawi Mustapha	161
9	Borderland Security and Proliferation of Small Arms and Light Weapons in Africa Anthony Israel Rufus	187
10	Urban Dynamics and the Challenge of Small Arms and Light Weapons in Africa Enoch Oyedele	207
11	Forests, Ungoverned Spaces and the Challenge of Small Arms and Light Weapons Proliferation in Africa Usman A. Tar and Yusuf Ibrahim Safana	223
12	"Resource Curse" and "Resource Wars" and the Proliferation of Small Arms in Africa Otoabasi Akpan and Ubong Essien Umoh	245
13	Armed Conflicts, SALWs Proliferation, and Underdevelopment in Africa Aliyu Mukhtar Katsina, Mubarak Ahmed Mashi, and Mohammed Abdullahi	265
14	Civil Wars, Complex Emergencies, and the Proliferation of Small Arms in Africa Hussaini Jibrin and Umar Aminu Yandaki	285
15	Poverty, Greed and the Proliferation of Small Arms in Africa Ubong Essien Umoh and Otoabasi Akpan	299
16	Personality, Arms and Crime: The Psychological Dynamics of Small Arms and Light Weapons Proliferation in Africa Philemon A. Agashua, David M. Shekwolo, and Orkuugh L. Lawrence	323
17	Socialization, Culture of Violence and Small Arms and Light Weapons Proliferation in Africa Aminu Umar and Nachana'a Alahira David	345
18	Youth Bulge and Small Arms Proliferation in Africa: Guns, Generations and Violent Conflicts John Tor Tsuwa	373
19	Gendered Construction of Conflict and Small Arms Proliferation in Africa Omotola A. Ilesanmi	393

20	Guns, Arms Trade and Transnational Crime in Africa Adewunmi J. Falode	411

Part III Institutional Framework and Dynamics

21	Military, Arms Monopoly and Proliferation of Small Arms and Light Weapons in Africa Al Chukwuma Okoli	429
22	Legislation, Institution-Building and the Control of Small Arms and Light Weapons in Africa Shuaibu A. Danwanka	453
23	Police and the Control of Firearms in Africa Dawud Muhammad Dawud and Tukur Abdulkadir	473
24	Civil Society and Arms Control in Africa Abdulmalik Auwal and Moses T. Aluaigba	501
25	Traditional Institutions and Firearms in Africa: The Politics and Historiography of Small Arms and Conflict Management Muhammad Sanusi Lawal and Bem Japhet Audu	517
26	Customs, Contrabands and Arms Control in Africa Mubarak Ahmed Mashi and Habu Mohammed	539
27	Transport Networks and the Proliferation of Small Arms in Africa Terzungwe Nyor	567
28	Multinational Corporations, Trafficking of Small Arms and Intractable Conflicts in Africa Emmanuel Ukhami and Lassana Doumbia	585
29	Private Security Companies and the Proliferation of Small Arms and Light Weapons in Africa Jonathan S. Maiangwa and Usman A. Tar	609
30	Economics of Armed Violence in Africa: Supply and Demand Sides of Small Arms and Light Weapons Proliferation Suleiman Sa'ad and Blessing Idakwoji	627
31	Information Communication Technology, CyberSecurity and Small Arms in Africa Francisca Nonyelum Ogwueleka	647

Part IV National Experiences

32 **Central African Republic: The Contagion of Identity-Linked Sectarian Violence, Internally Displaced Populations (IDPs) and Small Arms Proliferation** 681
Wendy Isaacs-Martin

33 **Egypt: Arab Spring, Regime Crisis and the Proliferation of Small Arms** 707
Audu Nanven Gambo

34 **Ethiopia: Political Volatility and Small Arms Proliferation** 721
Roy Love

35 **Libya: The Proliferation of Small Arms Post-Ghaddafi** 739
Dauda Abubakar and Sharkdam Wapmuk

36 **Mali: The Ecology of Insurgency, Terrorism and Small Arms Proliferation** 761
Jude Cocodia

37 **Nigeria: Militancy, Insurgency and the Proliferation of Small Arms and Light Weapon** 777
Freedom Chukwudi Onuoha, Joachim Chukwuma Okafor, and Osinimu Osebeba Femi-Adedayo

38 **Niger Republic: Small Arms and Asymmetric Warfare in a Volatile Neighborhood** 803
David Omeiza Moveh

39 **South Africa: Xenophobia, Crime and Small Arms Proliferation** 819
Dorcas Ettang

40 **Sierra Leone: Civil War, Democratic Collapse and Small Arms Proliferation** 847
Sharkdam Wapmuk

41 **Somalia: State Collapse and the Proliferation of Small Arms and Light Weapons** 863
Mala Mustapha and Haruna Yerima

42 **Uganda: Protracted Conflict, Insurgency and SALWs Proliferation** 879
David Andrew Omona and Samuel Baba Ayegba

Part V Regional Perspectives

43 West Africa: Regional Control of Small Arms and Light Weapons Proliferation 909
Oluwafisan Babatunde Bankale
and Chukwuzitara Juliet Uchegbu

44 Lake Chad Basin: Transnational Insurgency, Counter-Insurgency and the Proliferation of Small Arms 927
Bashir Bala and Usman A. Tar

45 The Manor River Region: Volatility and Proliferation of Small Arms and Light Weapons 951
Uchenna Simeon

46 Southern Africa: Regional Dynamics of Conflict and the Proliferation of Small Arms and Light Weapons 983
Pamela Machakanja and Chupicai Shollah Manuel

Index 1003

Editors and Contributors

About the Editors

Usman A. Tar, Ph.D. is Professor of Political Science and Defence Studies, and Endowed Chair of Defence and Security Studies (26RC Endowment) at the Nigerian Defence Academy. He is the Director of the Academy's flagship Centre for Defence Studies and Documentation, and a member of the Board of Social Science Research Council's African Peacebuilding Network (SSRC/APN), New York, USA. He was formerly an Associate Research Fellow at Africa Centre for Peace and Conflict Studies, University of Bradford, UK. He has authored several books including *The Politics of Neoliberal Democracy in Africa* (London/New York: I B Tauris, 2009); *Globalization in Africa: Perspectives on Development, Security and the Environment* (Lanham, MD, Lexington Books, 2016); *New Architecture of Regional Security in Africa* (Lanham, MD, Lexington Books, 2020); and *Routledge Handbook of Counterterrorism and Counterinsurgency in Africa* (London, Routledge, 2020). Prof. Tar has consulted for the United Nations Development Programme (UNDP), Nigeria; Konrad Adaneur Stiftung (KAS, German Development Fund); and the Westminster Foundation for Democracy (WFD), Nigeria. Prof. Tar is a member of Nigeria's Presidential Think Tank on National Defence and Security, and has served as a member of Nigeria's Presidential Committee to review the national defence policy in 2015.

Charles P. Onwurah is a Research Associate at the Centre for Defence Studies and Documentation, Nigerian Defence Academy. He is a candidate for Ph.D. in Defence and Strategic Studies at the Department of Political Science and Defence Studies, Nigerian Defence Academy. He has published on globalisation, private security companies, small arms, and civil militias in Africa.

Contributors

Tukur Abdulkadir, Ph.D. is an Associate Professor at the Department of Political Science at Kaduna State University, Nigeria. He obtained Ph.D. in Political Science from Ahmadu Bello University, Zaria (2015) and M.Sc. in International Relations and Strategic Studies from the University of Jos, Nigeria. His areas of research interest include international relations, strategic studies, political Islam, religious fundamentalism, terrorism, democracy, and development.

Mohammed Abdullahi is a lecturer in the Department of Political Science Federal University, Gashua. He graduated with a bachelor degree in political science from Ahmadu Bello University Zaria and he is currently undergoing his M.Sc. Degree in Political Science at Kaduna state university.

Dauda Abubakar, Ph.D. received his doctorate degree from the University of Wisconsin-Madison. He taught at the University of Maiduguri in the Department of Political Science where he was also the Head of Department; and coordinator of Graduate programs. From 2003 to 2009, Dr. Abubakar taught in the Department of Political Science at Ohio University-Athens, USA. He is a tenured faculty in the Department of Political Science and African Studies at the University of Michigan-Flint, and also the Chair of Africana Studies Department. He is the co-editor (with Caroline Varin) of *Violent Non-State Actors in Africa: Terrorists, Rebels and Warlords* (Palgrave Macmillan: London, 2017), and has contributed numerous chapters to edited volumes on Africa and global politics. His current research agenda examines the intersection of identity politics, securitization, and intervention in postcolonial Africa.

Sunday Adejoh, Ph.D. is a Lecturer with the Department of Defence and Security Studies, Nigerian Defence Academy, Kaduna. He lectured at the Department of Political Science and Diplomacy, Veritas University Abuja. He obtained Ph.D. in Defence and Strategic Studies (NDA) and Ph.D. in International Relations (University of Abuja). His has interest in global governance, strategic studies, and international development. He is one of the leading and pioneer scholars of Islamophobia in Nigeria. He is a member of the Nigerian Political Science Association (NPSA) and has published widely in both local and international journals and book chapters.

Taiye Oluwafemi Adewuyi, Ph.D. is a Professor in the Department of Geography, Nigerian Defence Academy, Kaduna, and the Business Manager of Academy *Journal of Defence Studies* and a formal Head of Department. His teaching and research interests focus on the application of Geographic Information Systems (GIS) and Remote Sensing Environmental Resources Management and Socio-economic issues. He has contributed several dozen articles and essays in reputable local and international journals and books, encompassing a wide variety of subjects such as mapping, environmental degradation (land, vegetation, and water), agroforestry, flooding, change analysis, crime assessment, and resource allocation.

Philemon A. Agashua, Ph.D. is a retired Air Commodore of the Nigerian Air Force and Professor of Clinical, Military and Practicing Psychology in the Department of Psychology, Nigerian Defence Academy Kaduna. He is also a Visiting Professor at the Benue State University, Makurdi, Nigeria as well as External Examiner to a number of Universities in Nigeria and Overseas. His teaching and research interests span across the areas of clinical psychology, military/aviation psychology, forensic psychology, development of general and vocational aptitude tests, psychotherapy, management of PTSD and psychological disorders. Professor Agashua received the *USA President Lifetime Achievement Award* for lifelong commitment to building a strong nation through Volunteer Service-2016 and *Leadership Award* by the Nigerian Association of Clinical Psychologists in recognition of his excellent service to the development of the profession of Clinical Psychology in Nigeria-2012. He has published widely in reputable local and international journals, encompassing areas such as Promoting resilience among Military Personnel and Families, Aviation Psychological Practice, Cadets Adjustment to Training, Personality Assessment of Military Pilots, Military Psychology as a Veritable Tool for Combat Readiness, Psychological Bases of Corruption in the Nigerian Society, Psychological imperatives of Defence Transformation in the Armed Forces of Nigeria, and Internally Displaced families in Nigeria.

Otoabasi Akpan, Ph.D. is a Professor of History of Ideas and International Security Studies, with more than 100 publications in his areas of specialization. He has a B.A. in History from the University of Calabar, Calabar; M.A. in History of Ideas from the University of Ibadan, Ibadan; M.Sc. in International Relations and Strategic Studies from the University of Jos, Jos; and Ph.D. in Diplomatic Studies from the University of Port Harcourt, Port Harcourt. He is domiciled in Akwa Ibom State University, Nigeria, where he has served as Head, Department of History and International Studies; Dean, Faculty of Arts; and since 2018, as Director, Collaboration and Linkages.

Moses T. Aluaigba, Ph.D. is an Associate Research Professor at Mambayya House, Aminu Kano Centre for Democratic Studies, Bayero University, Kano, Nigeria. He obtained his Ph.D. in Political Economy and Development Studies from the University of Abuja, Nigeria in 2011. He has authored *Ethnic Conflicts in Nigeria: Insight Into the Tiv-Jukun Ethnic Crisis* (2015); edited *Land Resource-based Conflicts in Nigeria* (forthcoming); co-edited *The Nigerian Youth: Political Participation and National Development* (2010); *Corruption, Governance and Development in Nigeria: Perspectives and Remedies* (2012); *Insurgency and Human Rights in Northern Nigeria* (2015) and is the Managing Editor of *Mambayya House Journal of Democratic Studies* (MHJDS). His other contributions on various areas of Political Economy are published as book chapters and as articles in national and international journals such as *Journal of African Elections, African Conflict and Peace-Building Review, The Researcher: An Interdisciplinary Journal, Childhood in Africa: An Interdisciplinary Journal, Time Journals, Bayero Journal of Political Science, FAIS Journal of Humanities*, etc. He was a Fulbright Visiting Scholar at the Center for African Studies, Ohio University Athens, USA, 2008–2009. He is also an alumnus of the APSA Africa Workshop 2013. Dr. Aluaigba is a member of the Nigeria Political Science Association (NPSA), the American Political Science Association (APSA), and the West African Research Association (WARA). His areas of research interest include democracy, democratization in Nigeria, ethnic conflicts, conflict resolution, and research methods.

Bem Japhet Audu, Ph.D. is a Lecturer in the Department of History and War Studies, and Head of the Centre for the Study of Leadership and Complex Military Operations, Nigerian Defence Academy, Kaduna, Nigeria. He earned his Ph.D. in History (International Studies) at the Nigerian Defence Academy, Kaduna in 2016. He also studied M.A. History (2012) and M.A. International Relations and Strategic Studies (2007) as well as B.A. History (2003) at Benue State University, Makurdi. He has published many scholarly articles in local and international journals and contributed chapters in books. He also has two published books to his credit: *Leadership and Development: The Media Involvement* (2010), and *Wars and Changing Patterns of Inter-Group Relations in the Middle Benue Valley, c.1300–1900* (2018).

Abdulmalik Auwal, Ph.D. is an Associate Professor in the Department of Political Sciene, Bayero University, Kano, Nigeria and the immediate past Deputy Dean of the Faculty of Social and Management Sciences, Bayero University, Kano. He is the Secretary General of Fulbright Alumni Association of Nigeria (FAAN) in addition to being a member of Social Science Council of Nigeria (SSCN); Society for Peace Studies and Practice (SPSP); Nigerian Political Science Association (NPSA); among many others. He was a Fulbright Visiting Scholar at the Centre for African Studies, University of Massachussetts, Boston, USA, 2010–2011. Mr Auwal has contributed in several journal articles, book chapters, and co-edited conference proceedings in Conflict and Peace-Building; Violence and Security; Civil Society; Democracy and Democratization; Gender; Party Politics and Electoral Process. His areas of research is Political Economy.

Samuel Baba Ayegba is a Lecturer in the Department of Defence and Security Studies, Nigerian Defence Academy, Kaduna, and a Research Fellow at the Centre for Defence Studies and Documentation (CDSD), Nigerian Defence Academy, Kaduna. He has completed M.Sc. in Defence and Strategic Studies from the Nigerian Defence Academy, Kaduna. He completed his dissertation on "Food and National Security in Nigeria: A Case Study of Adamawa State", and has published on several peer review platforms. He is currently a Doctoral Candidate in Defence and Strategic Studies, Nigerian Defence

Academy, Kaduna. His thesis title is *Gender and Violent Extremism in Nigeria*. His area of specialization includes Security and Strategic Studies, Gender Studies, Environmental Politics, Peace and Conflict Studies.

Bashir Bala is a Doctoral researcher in Defence and Security Studies at the University of Exeter, UK, and a Captain in the Nigerian Army. Bala graduated from the Nigerian Defence Academy (NDA), commissioned at the Royal Military Academy Sandhurst, United Kingdom, and thereafter, attended Shijiazhuang Mechanized Infantry Academy for Basic and Advanced Special Operations Courses, China. Capt. Bala is a Research Fellow, Centre for Defence Studies and Documentation, Nigerian Defence Academy (NDA). He is now a Doctoral Candidate for Ph.D. in Strategy and Security Studies at the University of Exeter, United Kingdom. Formerly a tactical commander in several critical Counter-Insurgency Operations in the Northeast region of Nigeria, he is the Co-author of *Insurgency and Counter-Insurgency in Nigeria: Perspectives on the Nigerian Army Operation Against Boko Haram* (Nigerian Defence Academy Publishers, 2019) and the Co-editor of *New Architecture for Regional Security in Africa: Perspectives on Counter-Terrorism and Counter-Insurgency in the Lake Chad Basin* (Lanham, MD, Lexington Books, USA). He has published widely on terrorism, insurgency, CT-COIN, security and development, cattle rustling, and armed banditry.

Oluwafisan Babatunde Bankale was the Head of Advocacy in the Small Arms Division of the ECOWAS Commission and Representative of the President of the Commission on the International Advisory Board on Small Arms for 7 years (2006–2012); Adviser on Advocacy/Gender and Head of the National Programme Advisory Unit at the United Nations Population Fund's Nigeria Country Office; Chief Executive/Editor-in-Chief between 1999 and 2001 at Sketch Press Limited. Since 2006, Mr. Bankale has been providing policy advice to stakeholders at national, regional, and global levels in the fight against proliferation of Small Arms Light Weapons (SALW). Between 1993 and 2001 Mr. Bankale was a Consultant to various UN agencies including the UNDP, UNICEF, UNAIDS, among others. He has advised governments and intergovernmental organisations on public policy in thematic areas as varied as education, democracy and good governance, gender equity/equality, conflict prevention, management and resolution, poverty eradication, sustainable human development, population, reproductive health/rights, media/communication. Mr. Bankale is an alumnus of the University of Ife, University of Ibadan, where he is currently enrolled as a Ph.D. student, the University of Wales, Cardiff and the United Nations University.

Jude Cocodia, Ph.D. is a Senior Lecturer and an Acting Head of the Department of Political Science, Niger Delta University, Nigeria. He has an M.Sc. in International Relations from the University of Benin, Nigeria (1999), an M.A. in Philosophy from Erasmus University Netherlands (2004), and a Ph.D. from the University of Nottingham, UK (2016). He is a recipient of the International Peace Research Association Foundation award and an Associate Fellow of the Higher Education Academy, UK (2016). He is the Secretary of the Nigeria Political Science Association South-South Zone. His research interests are in the areas of peace, conflict, security, and democracy in Africa. His publications include *Peacekeeping in the African Union: Building Negative Peace* (Routledge, 2018). Outside academics, Jude worked with Everyone Counts International Charity, a London-based NGO as the Project Coordinator in Yenagoa, Nigeria (2011–2012) and London, UK (2013–2016).

Mwanret Gideon Daful is a Ph.D. student with the Department of Geography, Nigerian Defence Academy, Kaduna. His teaching and research interests focus on the application of Geographic Information Systems (GIS) and Remote Sensing in Environmental Resources Management, Military mapping, and Socio-economic issues. He has contributed a number of articles in reputable local and international journals and book chapter.

Shuaibu Abdullahi Danwanka, Ph.D. is a specialist in Legislative Drafting, Bill Scrutiny/Analysis, Parliamentary Strengthening, Constitutionalism, Legal Research, Corporate Reconstruction, and Legislative Practice and Procedure. He holds a Doctorate, Master's, and Bachelor Degrees in Law and Barrister at Law (BL) from University of Jos, Bayero University Kano, and Nigerian Law School Lagos, respectively. He was a Senior Lecturer in the Law Faculty, University of Jos, Nigeria. In 2008, he joined the erstwhile Policy Analysis and Research Project (PARP)–National Assembly, Abuja–Nigeria as legal expert Legislative Drafting and Deputy Director–Bills and Legislative Drafting, Department of Legislative Support Services, National Institute for Legislative and Democratic Studies (NILDS). Danwanka is a Director, Legal Services at the National Institute for Legislative and Democratic Studies (NILDS)–National Assembly, Abuja–Nigeria.

Nachana'a Alahira David is an Associate Professor in the Department of Political Science and Defence Studies at the Nigerian Defence Academy, Kaduna. She obtained a Ph.D. in Political Science from Ahmadu Bello University, Zaria (Nigeria) and has held a sabbatical position at the Adamawa State University, Mubi. David's research interest covers international organization, security studies, gender, and rural livelihood.

Dawud Muhammad Dawud is a Nigerian Police Officer and a Doctoral researcher in the Department of Political Science and Defence Studies, Nigerian Defence Academy (NDA), Kaduna, Nigeria. His area of research interest is terrorism, foreign policy, and security sector reform. He has also contributed a chapter in the book titled *New Architecture of Regional Security in Africa: Perspectives on Counter-Terrorism and Counter Insurgency in the Lake Chad Basin*, published by Lexington Publishers, Lanham, Maryland, USA.

Lassana Doumbia is an Army Senior Colonel in Malian Armed Forces, and the Director General of National Early Warning and Response Center, Mali. He served as Defense Attache in the Embassy of Mali in Abuja, Nigeria, Head of military and security staffs to the Prime minister, consultant for various national and international think tanks, lectures at various institutions and a private University (Sup'Management) in Mali, and has participated in local and international conferences, seminars, workshops, and dialogues. He also has participated in the redaction on national DDR strategy. His research interests cut across irregular threats (insurgency, organized crime, and terrorism), international relations, security, cooperation, and integration. He is a member of scholarly bodies.

Dorcas Ettang, Ph.D. is a Senior Lecturer in Political Science in the School of Social Sciences, University of KwaZulu-Natal, Pietermaritzburg, South Africa. She teaches undergraduate and postgraduate modules while supervising Masters and Ph.D. students in International Relations and Conflict Transformation and Peace Studies. She holds a Ph.D. in Conflict Transformation and Peace Studies from the University of KwaZulu-Natal, South Africa, and a Masters in Political Science from the University of Windsor, Canada. She has previous experience as a Programme Officer and an Analyst with the African Centre for the Constructive Resolution of Disputes (ACCORD) in Durban. Her areas of research include conflict prevention, peacebuilding, identity politics, migration, and non-violence with a grassroots focus. She has published in journals including *Africa Development, Journal of African Elections, Communication and Gender and Behaviour.*

Adewunmi J. Falode, Ph.D. is a Senior Lecturer in the Department of History and international Studies, Lagos State University. He earned his Ph.D. (2012) in History and Strategic Studies from the University of Lagos, Akoka, Lagos. His areas of interest are international relations, strategic studies, war studies, terrorism studies, cybersecurity studies, and Nigerian history. Dr. Falode has published extensively in local and international peer-reviewed journals. He is an international reviewer for reputable journals like *Behavioural Sciences of Terrorism and Political Aggression, Canadian Journal of African Studies* and *African Security Review.* Dr. Falode is a member of the Nigeria Institute of International Affairs (NIIA).

Osinimu Osebeba Femi-Adedayo is a Research Fellow with the Centre for strategic Research and studies, National Defence College, Abuja. She is a graduate of English Language and International studies from Benue state University Makurdi, Benue State and Nigerian Defence Academy, Kaduna, respectively. Her research interests include but not limited to conflict analysis and management. Her other areas of interest centre around leadership structure, nation building, and governance policy.

Audu Nanven Gambo, Ph.D. is a Professor of International Relations and Strategic Studies in the Department of Political Science, University of Jos,

Nigeria. He holds a Ph.D. degree in International Relations and Strategic Studies from the University of Jos. He was the Director of Centre for Conflict Management and Peace Studies, University of Jos, between 2010 and 2015. He was a Fulbright Fellow for the Study of United States Foreign Policy at the University of South Carolina in 2006. He was also a Visiting Scholar at the University of Amsterdam, The Netherlands, in 2011. His scholarship focuses on national defence, Conflict and peace studies, foreign policy, and security studies and he has published nationally and internationally in these areas. Among his recent publications is *Peace Architecture for Jos City, Nigeria* (2013), published by John Archers Publishers in Ibadan.

Blessing Idakwoji is a postgraduate student at the Department of Economics, Nigerian Defence Academy. Her research interest includes the economics of violence, economic security, and development studies.

Omotola A. Ilesanmi, Ph.D. holds her doctorate in Political Science from Babcock University, Ilishan-Remo Ogun State, Nigeria. She is a Research Fellow in the Department of Research and Studies of the Nigerian Institute of International Affairs, Lagos, Nigeria. Dr. Ilesanmi is a specialist on women and peacebuilding processes, gender and security, security sector reforms, and peace and conflict studies. She also teaches courses in the areas of foreign policy analysis, diplomacy, and international law. She is an alumnus of the Kofi Annan International Peacekeeping Training Centre Accra Ghana, and has published widely in local and foreign journals and books.

Wendy Isaacs-Martin, Ph.D. is a Research Associate with the Archie Mafeje Research Institute at the University of South Africa. She has published in several peer-reviewed journals and book chapters on the themes of identity and conflict in Africa. Currently she is working on a narrative on the future of state formation. Her research on scapegoating, identity formation and maintenance, and violence is viewed through the lens of nation-state ideologies and state-formation theories.

Hussaini Jibrin is a Senior Lecturer in the Department of History and War Studies, NDA Kaduna, Nigeria. He obtained his B.A. History from Bayero University Kano, M.A. Military History, NDA, Kaduna, and Ph.D. Military History, Usmanu Danfodio University, Sokoto, respectively. He has been teaching various courses and has supervised research at both undergraduate and postgraduate levels. Dr Hussaini has attended and presented papers at many conferences within and outside Nigeria. These include; Regional Conference on Peace Building and Reconstruction in the Chad Basin organized by Centre for Peace and Security Studies, Modibbo Adama University of Technology, Yola, in collaboration with the Nigerian Army (September, 2016); Postgraduate Conference on Changing Land Use, Resource Conflicts and Environmental Implications on African organized by the Department of History, University of Dar es Salam, Tanzania, in collaboration with the Department of History, University of Warwick, England Landscapes (August,

2015); and the 1st International Conference on First World War and Africa 1914-2014, organized by the Department of History, University of Cape Coast, Ghana (October, 2005), among others. Similarly, he has contributed a number of articles and chapters in peer- reviewed journals and book projects. With a career spanning over a decade, he has held different academic and administrative responsibilities in Nigerian Universities. He edited two books *Readings on Peace Studies and Conflict Resolution* (2016); and (with AM Ashafa) *The Nigeria Army in a Democracy Since 1999: A Professional Demonstration of Military Subordination to Civil Authority: Essays in Honor of Lieutenant General T.Y. Buratai* (2017)

Aliyu Mukhtar Katsina, Ph.D. graduated with a Bachelor of Science degree in Political Science from Usmanu Danfodio University Sokoto, Nigeria. Later he obtained a Postgraduate Diploma in Education (PGDE) from the same university and a Master of Science degree in Defence and Strategic Studies from the Nigerian Defence Academy (NDA), Kaduna. At the Universiti Islam Antrabangsa Malaysia (UIAM) where he obtained his Ph.D. in Political Science, Aliyu Katsina was the recipient of the prestigious *Best Ph.D. Graduating Award* at the Faculty and University levels. He currently teaches research methodology, political parties and party politics, political economy, and Nigerian Foreign Policy to undergraduate and postgraduate students of the Department of Political Science of Umaru Musa Yar'adua University (UMYU) and Al-Qalam University (AUK), Katsina. Until June 2020, Aliyu Katsina was also the Dean of Faculty of Social and Management Sciences (FSMS) of UMYU. His previous book, *Party Constitutions and Political Challenges in a Democracy: Nigeria in the Fourth Republic*, was published by IIUM Press, Kuala Lumpur, Malaysia. Aliyu Katsina was the *Editor-in-Chief* of the *Social and Administrative Sciences Review*—a peer review bi-annual *Journal of the Faculty of Social and Management Sciences*, UMYU.

Chris M. A. Kwaja, Ph.D. *fspsp* is currently a Senior Lecturer and a Researcher at the Centre for Peace and Security, Modibbo Adama University of Technology, Yola, Adamawa State, Nigeria. He is also the Chairperson-Rapporteur of the United Nations Working Group on Mercenaries. He is also an International Fellow at the Centre for Human Rights and Humanitarian Studies, Watson Institute of International Affairs, Brown United States, as well as Visiting Researcher at the Centre for Democracy and Development (CDD), Abuja, Nigeria. He was formerly the Director General of Research and Planning, Governor's Office, as well as the Honourable Commissioner for Local Governments and Chieftaincy Affairs, Plateau State, Nigeria. His research focuses on the security sector reform in transition societies; the privatization of security; the politics of identity in Africa; civil society, elections, and democratization, as well as conflict, peace, and security analysis.

Mohammed Sanusi Lawal, Ph.D. is a Senior Lecturer in the Department of Political Science and Defence Studies (PSDS), Nigerian Defence Academy. He joined the services of the Academy in 1997 as a Graduate Assistant. He was the Programme Director of the Academy's Masters in Security Studies and Administration (MASSA) from 2013 to 2015, PGDPA from 2015 to date. Dr. Lawal attended the Ahmadu Bello University Zaria where he obtained his B.Sc. in Political Science and Masters in Public Administration in 1994 and 2004, respectively. He then obtained his Ph.D. in Defence and Strategic Studies from the Nigerian Defence Academy in 2018. He has since been promoted to the rank of Senior Lecturer in the same department. His areas of research interests include peace and conflict studies, gender, development, and security studies.

Orkuugh L. Lawrence, Ph.D. is a Senior Lecturer in the Department of Psychology, Nasarawa State University, Keffi and the immediate past Head of Department. Dr. Lawrence is an Industrial/Organizational Psychologist. Beside this, he is a member of professional bodies including the Nigerian Psychological Association (NPA). He has contributed articles and essays in reputable local and international journals and books, encompassing a wide variety of subjects such as statistical techniques for the measurement of human behaviour, psychology of vocational and career choice, psychology of social change, political psychology, environmental psychology, industrial and organizational psychology.

Roy Love, Ph.D. is an Economist who has published regularly on *Ethiopia* and the *Horn of Africa* since 1979 and has lectured at the Universities of Addis Ababa, Botswana, Lesotho, and Sheffield Hallam (in the UK). He has also in recent years been engaged in consultancy on African projects, including Ethiopia, for the European Union, World Bank, UK Department for International Development, and USAID. He is currently attached, as an associate staff, to the Centre for Lifelong Learning at the University of York in Britain, with current research on the economics of modern slavery in Ethiopia and the Horn of Africa.

Pamela Machakanja, Ph.D. is a Professor of Peace, Leadership, and Security Studies and the Dean in the College of Business, Peace Leadership, and Governance at Africa University, Zimbabwe. She holds a Ph.D. in Peace, Conflict, and Security Studies from the University of Bradford in the United Kingdom; a Master of Arts degree in Peace and Conflict Resolution; a Diploma in Research Methods in Social Sciences; and a Diploma in Leadership and Policy Development all from the University of Bradford in the United Kingdom. She also holds a Masters degree in Educational Psychology and a Bachelor of Education degree from the University of Zimbabwe; a Diploma and Advanced Diploma in Negotiation Skills from the International Negotiation Academy in South Africa. Her expansive multidisciplinary research interests include peace and conflict issues, gender equality, state capture and corruption, human security and the rights of vulnerable groups including minority groups; democratisation processes in post conflict transitional societies, gender and post-colonial discourses, and transitional justice processes. Prof. Machakanja has written three books, fourteen book chapters, and twenty-four journal articles in international peer reviewed journals. Over the years Pamela has developed skills in innovative competency-based curriculum development that integrate technological content knowledge that facilitate innovative e-pedagogical models in peace, human rights, gender, and development.

Jonathan S. Maiangwa, Ph.D. is a Senior Lecturer at the Department of Political Science, University of Maiduguri, Borno State, Nigeria. His research interests are in terrorism, counterterrorism/counterinsurgency, local security institutions, private military and security companies, governance, and development studies. He has published in referred journals and contributed chapters to edited books. He is the author of *The Concept of Terrorism in Africa* (Kaduna, Nigeria: Pyla-mak Publishers, 2015) which enjoys*a* wide readership and circulation.

Chupicai Shollah Manuel is a Ph.D. Candidate in Governance and Political Transformation, with a Masters in Peace and Governance, Master in Intellectual Property Law, and Bachelor of Social Sciences in Sociology and Economics. Currently, he is affiliated to Africa University as a Lecturer in the area of Peace and Security, Governance, Human Rights, and International Relations.

Mubarak Ahmed Mashi is a Lecturer at the Department of Political Science, Umaru Musa Yar'adua University, Katsina, Nigeria. His research interest focuses on security and political economy. His research interest focuses on the security of internally displaced women and children, rural banditry and cattle rustling, and electoral violence. Some of his published works include: *Critique of Development and Underdevelopment Theories: Lessons for Africa* (2018), *The Military and the Socio-economic Development of Nigeria; A Study of General Yakubu Gowon and General Murtala/Obasanjo Military Regimes* (2019), *Small and Light Weapons Proliferation and the Growing Challenges of Insecurity in Nigeria* (2019), *The Political Economy of African Security in the State of Underdeveloped Capitalism* (2019), Boko Haram and the Challenge of Development in Nigeria, Youths violence and the credibility of the 2019 General Elections in Nigeria.

Habu Mohammed, Ph.D. is a Professor at the Department of Political Science, Bayero University, Kano, Nigeria. Prof. Mohammed is biased in Politics of Development, Peace and Conflict Resolution, Federalism and National Question, Civil Society, and Democratisation in Africa. He is a co-editor of *Readings in Social Science Research* (2006), the editor of *Concepts and Issues in Peace Studies and Conflict Resolution* (2006), a co-editor of *Poverty in Nigeria, Causes, Manifestations and Alleviation Strategies* (2008), the author of a book titled: *Civil Society Organizations and Democratization in Nigeria: The Politics of Struggles for Human Rights* (2010), and the editor of *Nigeria's Convulsive Federalism: Flash-points of Conflicts in Northern Nigeria* (2012) and *The Patterns and Dynamics of Party Politics in Nigeria's Fourth Republic*

1999–2015 (2017). Mohammed served in various Departmental, Faculty, and University committees. He has contributed several articles on Nigerian politics and political economy of development in both local and international books and journals. In all, he has more than forty (40) publications thus far: One (1) published book; three (3) edited books on Nigerian Politics; three (3) co-edited books; and more than five (5) technical reports for UNDP, DFID, CODESRIA, CRD, and Mambayya House, among others. He was a Fulbright Visiting Scholar at Programme of African Studies (PAS), Northwestern University, Illinois, U.S.A. (2003/2004).

David Omeiza Moveh, Ph.D. is a Senior Lecturer in the Department of Political Science and International Studies, Ahmadu Bello University, Zaria, Nigeria. Dr. Moveh's research interests are in the areas of insurgencies and counter insurgencies, elections management, party politics, and the democratization process in Africa. Moveh has published extensively in local and international journals. He is also presently coordinating a research network in the areas of peace and conflict management in Africa.

Ahmed Badawi Mustapha, Ph.D. is a Research Fellow at the Institute of African Studies, University of Ghana. His research focused on militant organisations, political violence, terrorism, radical ideologies, counter-extremism, Islam in Africa and in global affairs, and International Security. He had his Ph.D. in International Relations with focus on International Security at the Middle East Technical University (METU), Ankara. Ahmed had his B.A. (Hons) and M.A. degrees in Political Science from the University of Ghana and the National University of Singapore (NUS), respectively.

Mala Mustapha, Ph.D. is a Reader and Head at the Department of Political Science University of Maiduguri, Nigeria. He obtained his M.A. in International Politics and Security Studies at Bradford University, UK, in 2003 and was awarded a Ph.D. in Conflict Resolution and Peace Studies by the University of Central Lancashire, UK in 2013. His research interests are security in the Lake Chad region, the Horn of Africa, and regional security in Africa focusing on themes of resource conflicts, political economy, globalisation and human security, democracy and democratisation in Africa, and terrorism studies. Recently his research focuses on internal displacements (refugee/IDP), humanitarian crisis, and counter-terrorism and counter-insurgency studies in the Northeast part of Nigeria and Somalia. He has published widely in peer-reviewed journals and books including the *Review of African Political Economy* and *CODESRIA*. Since 2019 Mustapha is a Senior Research Fellow at the Centre for Democracy and Development Abuja, Nigeria.

Terzungwe Nyor, Ph.D. is an Accountant and Logistician, a Professor of Accounting, and the present Head of Department of Logistics and Supply Chain Management at the Nigerian Defence Academy, Kaduna. He was Head of Department of Accounting and Management for two consecutive tenures from 2013 to 2017. A man of great interdisciplinary skills and a member of the Institute of Chartered Accountants of Nigeria (ICAN), he is a practising Company Secretary, a Tax Consultant, a Management Consultant, an Accounting System Designer, an Auditor, and a Researcher. He holds B.Sc. in Accounting from Bayero University Kano (1989), M.Sc. in Accounting also from Bayero University Kano (2008), and Ph.D. in Accounting from the Nigerian Defence Academy (2011). As a Lecturer, Professor Nyor has taught at different undergraduate levels spanning a period of over twenty (20) years. At postgraduate level, he lectures in the Postgraduate Diploma in Accounting, Postgraduate Diploma in Management, Master's in Business Administration, Master's in Financial Economics, Master's in Security Management, Master's in Disaster and Risk Management, M.Sc. in Accounting, and Ph.D. in Accounting classes till date. He has also delivered lectures and seminars at different training workshops and conferences over time. As a researcher, Prof. Nyor has over thirty-five (35) publications to his credit, in both national and international journals. He is a Visiting Professor, an External Examiner, and a member of the NUC and MBTE Accreditation Teams to some Nigerian Tertiary Institutions. His hobbies include travelling, watching football, and swimming.

Caroline Obiageli, Ph.D. is a Senior Lecturer in Department of Languages, on secondment to the Centre for Critical Thinking, Teaching and Learning (CCTTL) and also a Resource Person to Centre for the Study of Leadership and Complex Military Operations in Nigerian Defence Academy, Kaduna, Nigeria. Her scholarly specialization focuses on critical emancipatory practice which is keenly based on the philosophies of Critical Theory. In this regard her academic work spans the areas of Critical Thinking, Critical Emancipatory Education, Entertainment Education for Social and Behaviour Change, Critical approaches to Gender Parity, and Critical Security Studies. She has made scholarly contributions in these areas in both national and international journals and books and has served as Guest Lecturer to various military and non-military institutions. Dr. Obiageli is an Associate Fellow of UK Higher Education Academy and a Fulbright Visiting Scholar Awardee.

Francisca Nonyelum Ogwueleka, Ph.D. is a Professor of Computer Science in Nigerian Defence Academy, Kaduna, Nigeria. She is currently the Dean of Faculty of Military Science and Interdisciplinary Studies. Her research focuses on big data, artificial intelligence, cloud security, data mining techniques, steganography, penetration testing solutions, and information security. She has nine published books, two book chapters, and ninety-two original articles in international and national journals. She is a member of numerous professional bodies, editorial board, and conference technical program committee. She has been a keynote speaker and conference session chair in several international and national conferences. She has received many academic and professional awards. Professor Ogwueleka is an External Examiner for Ph.D. dissertation and M.Sc. thesis evaluation for national and international universities. She was a Resource

Person for the development of Nigeria Undergraduate Curriculum in Cyber Security and Information Technology programmes for National Universities Commission. She has held different academic and administrative positions in the university. She is happily married with children.

Joachim Chukwuma Okafor is a Lecturer in the Department of Political Science, University of Nigeria, Nsukka, and a doctoral student in International Relations with research interest in global environmental governance, peace, security and strategic studies, governance, foreign policy analysis, energy politics, and international political economy. He obtained his B.Sc. degree from Ebonyi State University, Abakaliki, and M.Sc. degree from University of Ibadan, Nigeria. He has published widely in reputable journals and books.

Al Chukwuma Okoli, Ph.D. is an expert in Defence and Strategy. He is a Senior Lecturer in Political Science at Federal University of Lafia, Nigeria. He has consulted for *UN Women, The Conversation*, Centre for Democracy and Development, National Open University of Nigeria. He is a Double Laureate of CODESRIA (GI: 2018; HEPI: 2019) as well as a Research Fellow of IFRA-Nigeria. He specializes in Liberal Political Ecology, Security Studies, and Gender & Development.

Agnes Okorie, Ph.D. is a Senior Lecturer and Head of the Department of Psychology, Nigerian Defence Academy, Kaduna. She has a Ph.D. in Psychology and is a member of the Psychological Assessment Committee of the Armed Forces Selection Board, Nigerian Defence Academy. She is a member of Nigerian Psychological Association (NPA). She has published many articles in local and international journals, as well as contributed to book chapters.

David Andrew Omona, Ph.D. is a Senior Lecturer and the Head of Department at Uganda Christian University, a National Coordinator for Religious Leaders' Justice and Peace Network, a Researcher, a Transitional Justice Fellow, and a Trainer of Trainers in Peace-building and Conflict Resolution in the East and Greater Horn of Africa. He holds a Ph.D. in Political Studies/International Relations and Diplomacy, M.A. in International Relations and Diplomacy, M.A. in Theology, B.A. with Education, and several specialized Diplomas and Certificates. He has done extensive research on conflicts in Africa, the Great Lakes Region, and Uganda in particular. His current research interest is in transitional justice, peace building and conflict resolution, and ethics. He has done collaborative research with people from across the world and still looks forward to getting researchers to collaborate with in his areas of expertise.

Hakeem Onapajo, Ph.D. is a Lecturer in the Department of Political Science and International Relations at Nile University of Nigeria, Abuja. Hakeem Onapajo holds a Ph.D. in Political Science from the University of KwaZulu-Natal, South Africa. He has held teaching and research positions at the

University of KwaZulu-Natal and the University of Zululand, in South Africa. Dr. Onapajo researches in the areas of elections and democratisation in Africa, conflict, and terrorism. His publications have appeared in reputable international journals and other publishing outlets.

Freedom Chukwudi Onuoha, Ph.D., fdc is a Senior Lecturer in the Department of Political Science, University of Nigeria, Nsukka. He is also the Coordinator of the Security, Violence and Conflict (SVC) Research Group at the University. Prior to joining the University, Dr. Onuoha worked for over a decade as a Research Fellow at the Centre for Strategic Research and Studies, National Defence College, Nigeria. Dr. Onuoha received his Ph.D. from the University of Nigeria, Nsukka, with specialty in political economy. He has published extensively in the broad area of security and strategic studies, covering diverse subjects such as terrorism, maritime security, radicalisation, violent extremism, kidnapping, civil-military relations, infrastructure protection, election, and globalisation, among others. His recent co-edited books include *Security in Nigeria: Contemporary Threats and Responses* (Bloomsbury, 2020) and *Internal Security Management in Nigeria: Perspectives, Challenges and Lessons* (Palgrave Macmillan, 2019).

Enoch Oyedele, Ph.D. is a Historian and a Fellow of the Historical Society of Nigeria (FHSN) and a Professor of History at Ahmadu Bello University (ABU), Zaria. He was the Head of Department and the Director of the Institute for Development Research (IDR) both at ABU. He was also a one time Secretary of the Historical Society of Nigeria. He was also a member of the Board of Governors of Arewa House, Kaduna. Professor Oyedele has published widely. Some of these publications are: "Quantity Surveying in Nigeria: NIQS at 50"; and *Africa* (edited). His research interest is social and economic history, with specialisation in Urban History. He has also served as External Examiner for Undergraduate programmes of several departments of several Masters and Doctoral candidates across the country. He is happily married with five children.

Anthony Israel Rufus, Ph.D. obtained his Ph.D. in Defence and Strategic Studies from the Nigerian Defence Academy, Kaduna. He taught at the University of Maiduguri in the Department of Political Science from 2007 to 2016, Dr. Rufus is the North Central Zonal Coordinator of the Administrative Staff College of Nigeria (ASCON). He has written and published several articles at both local and international journals as well as book chapters especially on issues relating to border security and national security.

Suleiman Sa'ad, Ph.D. is an Associate Professor and the former Head of the Department of Economics at the Nigerian Defence Academy. He was also the former Head of Centre for Energy and Environment NDA (CEENDA) in the Academy. He obtained his Ph.D. in Economics from the University of Surrey, United Kingdom. In 2013/2014, Dr. Sa'ad was at the University of Cambridge, UK, as a Visiting Research Fellow. During a sabbatical year at the Kaduna State University in 2017–2018, Dr. Sa'ad pioneered in the establishment of the Centre for Energy Studies at the University.

Yusuf Ibrahim Safana is a senior staff with State Universal Education Board, Katsina, Nigeria. He is currently a Desk Officer Global Partnership for Education, Safana Local Government Education Authority. He has NCE in Islamic/Social Studies, B.Sc. in Political Science, M.Sc. in Defence and Strategic Studies, and undergoing a Ph.D. in International Relations under the Department of Political Science, Federal University, Dutsin-Ma. His research focuses on forest management and National Security. He is interested in rural violence and environmental security studies. He is a member of numerous professional bodies and one time a Resource Person to Katsina State Ministry of Education on School Records Keeping. He held different academic and administrative positions in the Safana Local Government Education Authority.

David M. Shekwolo, Ph.D. is a Lecturer in the Department of Psychology, Nigerian Defence Academy, Kaduna. He holds a Ph.D. in Forensic and Correctional Psychology. He is a member of Nigerian Psychological Association; the Secretary General of Nigerian Association of Forensic Psychologists; and a member of Association of Practicing Psychologists in Nigeria. He has been a member of Psychological Assessment Committee, Armed Forces Selection Board since 2017 to date. His areas of research focus on specific areas of Forensic and Correctional Psychology of global status appraisal. His work cut across other fields in Psychology which encompasses forensic, clinical, police, organizational, cognitive, psychological assessment, criminal and investigation, terrorism, radicalization, legal, military, prisons, and gradually developing the ideas and perspectives in the practice and development of Psychology programs. He has been a resource person to many security organizations. He has participated in several conferences with conference proceedings, book chapters, as well as international and national journal publications. He is happily married to Mrs. Mercy D. Markus with a daughter.

Uchenna Simeon a Lecturer in the Department of Political Science, Federal University, Lafia, Nasarawa State where he is saddled with the responsibilities for teaching at the undergraduate level, research, administration, and community service. His research interests include international affairs, security, peace and conflict studies as well as defence and strategic studies. Prior to his foray into academia, Uchenna had worked in various capacities in the organized private sector in Nigeria which include Hallmark Bank PLC (defunct), Nigerian Association of Small and Medium Enterprises (NASME) Abia State Chapter, Ecobank Nigeria PLC, Fidelity Bank PLC, and Oceanic Bank International PLC (defunct). He is a member of the Chartered Institute of Bankers of Nigeria (CIBN) and a registered student of the Chartered Institute of Administration.

Muhammad Dan Suleiman, Ph.D. holds a Ph.D. in Political Science and International Relations from the University of Western Australia (UWA),

Perth, where he is a Research Fellow at the university's Africa Research & Engagement Centre. He researches on state-society relations in Africa, Islamist movements and security in Western Africa and the Sahel, and the international politics of Africa. He is a Fellow of the UWA Centre for Muslim States and Societies, the West Africa Centre for Counter-Extremism (Ghana), and writes as an Africa geopolitical risk analyst for a few think tanks. At UWA, Dr. Dan Suleiman teaches units on Africa's international politics, and peace and security in Africa.

Moses Eromedoghetne Ukpenumewu Tedheke, Ph.D. is a Professor at the Department of Political Science and Defense Studies, Nigerian Defense Academy. Tedheke was formerly the Head of Department. He obtained a Ph.D. in Political Science from Ahmadu Bello University, Zaria, Nigeria and an M.Sc. in Political Economy from the University of Jos, Nigeria. Prof Tedheke is a Resource Person to the National Institute for Policy and Strategic Studies (NIPSS), National Defence College (NDC), Armed Forces Command and Staff College (AFCSC), and External Examiner to several universities in Nigeria. He has carried out research on the interface between capitalism and security.

John Tor Tsuwa, Ph.D. is a Senior Lecturer in Political Science at Benue State University, Makurdi, Nigeria. He has been a Resource Person for the Air Force War College, National Institute for Policy and Strategic Studies, and National Open University of Nigeria. He is the Chairman, Nigerian Political Science Association, North Central Zone, Nigeria, and the Editor of two Faculty-based journals. He is a Research Fellow of IFRA-Nigeria and member, Society for Peace Studies and Practice. He specializes in Peace and Conflict Studies, Inter-Group Relations and Gender Studies, Governance and Development Studies.

Chukwuzitara Juliet Uchegbu is pursuing Ph.D. in Defence and Strategic Studies at the Nigerian Defence Academy, Kaduna. She had worked with the civil society as a Programme Officer with the West Africa Action Network on Small Arms (WAANSA) in Nigeria before joining the National Defence College (NDC), Nigeria, as a Research Fellow at the Centre for Strategic Research and Studies, NDC.

Emmanuel Ukhami is a candidate for Ph.D. in Defence and Strategic Studies at the Nigerian Defence Academy, Kaduna. He has authored and co-authored books, several journal articles, and book chapters in Nigeria and overseas. His major area of research interest includes international politics, security, defence, and strategic studies.

Aminu Umar, Ph.D. specializes in Political Economy, Public Policy, Corporate Management, and Parliamentary Strengthening. He holds a Doctorate and Master's Degrees in Political Science from Ahmadu Bello University, Zaria and B.Sc. in Sociology & Anthropology from the University of Maiduguri,

Nigeria, alongside Professional Certificates in Research Methods & Project Planning, Monitoring/Evaluation from London Graduate School/Albion College, London, respectively. Umar began his career as a Lecturer with Kaduna Polytechnic where he rose to the rank of a Senior Lecturer at the Department of Social Sciences. He served as Senior Legislative Aide through the Sixth and early Seventh Nigerian National Assembly in Nigeria and later joined the erstwhile National Institute for Legislative Studies (NILS), (now, National Institute for Legislative and Democratic Studies, NILDS), and participated in the NILS/University of Benin Post Graduate Studies Progamme in Legislative Studies. In 2017, Umar joined the Department of Political Science, Faculty of Social Sciences, National Open University of Nigeria (NOUN) as a Senior Lecturer and later served as its Head of Department. He is a Certified Management Consultant, Fellow of the Institute of Management Consultant, and member of numerous professional bodies. Umar is an External Examiner to several tertiary institutions and facilitator to capacity development bodies within and outside Nigeria. He is currently the Director, Kaduna Study Centre, NOUN.

Ubong Essien Umoh, Ph.D. is an Associate Professor of Military History in the Department of History and International Studies, University of Uyo, Nigeria. He earned a Ph.D. in Military History from the Department of History and War Studies, Nigerian Defence Academy (NDA), Kaduna. Between 2015 and 2016, he was part of the research team of the National Institute of Policy and Strategic Studies (NIPSS) consulting for the Presidential Committee (PRESCOM) on Small Arms and Light Weapons in Nigeria. Since 2017 he has been part of the joint research team on the *Boko Haram* insurgency carried out by the Centre for Defence and Documentation, Nigerian Defence Academy (NDA), Kaduna, and the Victims Support Fund (VSF), Abuja. He serves as a Senior Research Fellow at the Centre for the Study of Leadership and Complex Military Operations (CSLCMO), NDA, Kaduna, and has been a Visiting Scholar to the Air Force War College (AFWC), Makurdi and the National Defence College (NDC), Abuja.

Sharkdam Wapmuk, Ph.D. is an Associate Professor in the Department of Defence and Security Studies, Nigerian Defence Academy (NDA) Kaduna. He serves as a consultant for international organizations and think tanks, lectures at various institutions in Nigeria, and participates in local and international conferences, seminars, workshops, and dialogues. His research interests cut across the thematic fields of Afro-Asian relations, security, cooperation, and integration. His articles have been published in local and international journals and books. He is a member of scholarly bodies, including the Nigerian Political Science Association (NPSA) and Nigerian Society of International Affairs (NSIA).

Umar Aminu Yandaki is a Lecturer at the Department of History, Usmanu Danfodiyo University, Sokoto, Nigeria. He graduated in 2018 with Bachelor

Degree in History as the overall best student, and for the first time in 33 years (since 1985), with a First Class Honor. He is a writer with academic articles on African Historiography, Cultural History, and African Gender Studies, variously published in refereed journals and books. Yandaki is a researcher, essayist and analyst on literary and development issues in developing nations through media and strategic communications.

Haruna Yerima, Ph.D. is an Associate Professor at the Department of Public Administration, Ahmadu Bello University, Zaria, Nigeria. He obtained Ph.D. in Public Administration from the University of Maiduguri. Dr. Yerima has worked as a Distinguished Lecturer at the Ramat Polytechnic Maiduguri. He was a member of Nigeria's Federal House of Representatives (2003–2007) representing Biu-Shani-Kwayakusar Federal Constituency. Yerima has published extensively on governance, public sector management, public policy, public service, and democracy. He is a member of the Nigerian Political Science Association (NPSA).

ABBREVIATIONS

ABA	Adaka Boro Avengers
ACLED	Armed Conflict Location and Event Data Project
ACMS	African Centre for Migration & Society
ADB	African Development Bank
ADF	Allied Defence Forces
ADF	Allied Democratic Forces
ADFB	African Development Bank
ADFND	Asawana Deadly Force of Niger Delta
AEFJN	Africa Europe Faith and Justice Network
AFCONE	African Commission on Nuclear Energy
AfD	Arms for Development
AFL	Armed Forces of Liberia
AFRC	Armed Forces Revolutionary Council
AMISOM	African Union Mission in Somalia
AMU	Arab Maghreb Union
ANC	African National Congress
APB	Armaments Production Board
APC	All People's Congress
APC	All Progressive Congress
APD	Academy for Peace and Development
APV	Africa and the Psychology of Violence
AQIM	Al Qaeda in the Islamic Maghreb
ARMSCOR	Armaments Corporation of South Africa
Art.	Article
ATT	Arms Trade Treaty
AU	African Union
AUPSC	African Union Peace and Security Council
BH	Boko Haram
BBC	British Broadcasting Corporation
BCR	Bureau of Counter Terrorism
BFI	Big Five Inventory
BICC	Bonn International Centre for Conversion

BIS-II	Barrett Impulsiveness Scale- II
CAC	Control Arms Campaign
CACD	Community Arms Collection and Destruction Program
CAPP	Community Action for Popular Participation
CAR	Central African Republic
CAR	Conflict Armament Research
CASA	Coordinating Action on Small Arms
CBOs	Community Based Organizations
CD	Campaign for Democracy
CDCAC	Chief Directorate Conventional Arms Control
CDF	Civil Defence Force
CDHR	Committee for the Defense of Human Rights
CECORE	Centre for Conflict Resolution
CEDAW	Convention on the Elimination of All Forms of Discrimination Against Women
CEMAC	Economic and Monetary Community of Central Africa/*Communauté économique et monétaire de l'Afrique central*
CERT	Computer Emergency Response Team
CFCR	Citizen's Forum for Constitutional Reform
CISLAC	Civil Society Legislative Advocacy Centre
CISO	Chief Information Security Officer
CLO	Civil Liberty Organization
CML	Concerned Militant Leaders
CMRRD	Commission for the Management of Strategic Mineral Resources, National Reconstruction and Development
CNDP	National Congress for the Defence of the People
COGWO	Coalition for Grassroots Women Organizations
COMA	Coalition for Militant Action
CoU	Church of Uganda
CPA	Comprehensive Peace Agreement
CPALD	Centre for Policy Advocacy and Leadership Development
CPI	California Personality Inventory
CSOs	Civil Society Organizations
CSS	Critical Security Studies
DBD	Disruptive Behaviour Disorder
DDR	Disarmament, Demobilization and Reintegration
DDRR	Disarmament, Demobilization, Reintegration and Rehabilitation
DICON	Defence Industries Corporation of Nigeria
DIRCO	Department of International Relations and Cooperation
DoD	Department of Defense
DP	Democratic Party
DPIC	Directorate for Priority Crime Investigation
DR	Democratic Republic
DRC	Democratic Republic of Congo
EAC	East African Community
EAPCCO	East African Police Chief Cooperation Organization
EAPCO	East African Police Chiefs Organization
EC	Electoral Commission
ECCAS	Economic Community of Central African States

ECOMOG	Economic Community of West African States Monitoring Group
ECOSAP	ECOWAS Small Arms Control Programme
ECOSOC	Economic and Social Council
ECOWAS	Economic Community of West African States
ECPF	ECOWAS Conflict Prevention Framework
EFCC	Economic and Financial Crime Commission
ELG	Ekpeye Liberation Group
EO	Executive Outcomes
EPI	Eysenck Personality Inventory
EPLF	Eritrean People's Liberation Front
EPRDF	Ethiopian People's Revolutionary Democratic Front
ERC	Education Rights' Campaign
ESO	External Security Organization
EU	European Union
EUFOR	EU Force
EUMAM	EU Military Advisory Mission
EUTM	EU Training Mission
FAO	Food and Agricultural Organization
FAS	Federation of American Scientists
FCA	Firearms Control Act
FCT	Federal Capital Territory
FDLR	Democratic Forces for the Liberation of Rwanda
FDRE	Federal Democratic Republic of Ethiopia
FDS	Forces de Securite
FEDEMU	Freedom Democratic Movement
FFP	Fund for Peace
FOBA	Force Obote Back Again
FOMAC	Multinational Force in the Central African Republic/*Force multinationale en Centrafrique*
FPI	Front Populaire Ivoirien
FRONASA	Front for National Salvation
FUNA	Former Uganda National Army
GB	Great Britain
GBV	Gender Based Violence
GDP	Gross Domestic Product
GFSA	Gun Free South Africa
GFZ	Gun Free Zone
GIABA	Inter-Governmental Action Group against Money Laundering in West Africa
GIS	Geographic Information System
GLR	Great Lake Region
GNP	Gross National Product
GoG	Gulf of Guinea
GOSA	Gunowners Association of South Africa
GoU	Government of Uganda
GPI	Global Peace Index
GPMG	General Purpose Machine Guns
GPS	Global Positioning System
GTI	Global Terrorism Index

GTZ	German Technical Cooperation International Services
GWOT	Global War on Terror
HDI	Human Development Index
HIV/AIDS	Human Immunodeficiency Virus/Acquired Immunodeficiency Syndrome
HMIC	Her Majesty's Inspectorate of Constabulary
HRW	Human Rights Watch
HSM/A	Holy Spirit Movement/Army
IACP	International Association of Chiefs of Police
IANSA	International Action Network on Small Arms
IARMS	Interpol's Illicit Arms Record and Tracing Management System
IATG	International Ammunition Technical Guidelines
IBIN	INTERPOL Ballistics Information Network
ICGLR	International Conference on Great Lakes Region
ICRC	International Committee of the Red Cross
ICT	Information Communication and Technology
ICU	Islamic Courts Union
IDPs	Internally Displaced Persons
IEDs	Improvised Explosive Devices
IFRT	INTERPOL Firearms Reference Table
IGAD	Inter-Governmental Agency for Development
IGNU	Interim Government of National Unity
IGP	Inspector General of Police
IHL	International Humanitarian Law
IHRL	International Human Rights Law
ILO	International Labour Organization
INPFL	Independent National Patriotic Front of Liberia
INTERPOL	International Criminal Police Organization
IPCR	Institute for Peace and Conflict Resolution
IPOB	Indigenous People of Biafra
IQ	Intelligence Quotient
IRIN	Integrated Regional Information Networks
ISACS	International Small Arms Control Standards
ISIL	Islamic State in the Levant
ISIL	Islamic State of Iraq and Levant
ISO	Internal Security Organization
ISS	Institute for Security Studies
ISWAP	Islamic State in West Africa Province
IT	Information Technology
ITI	International Tracing Instrument
IYC	Ijaw Youth Council
JEM	Justice and Equality Movement
JNDLF	Joint Niger Delta Liberation Front
JTF	Joint Task Force
KM	Kikosi Maalum
KY	Kabaka Yeka
KZN	KwaZulu Natal
LAS	League of Arab States
LCB	Lake Chad Basin

LECs	Least Developed economies (LECs)
LFN	Laws of the Federation of Nigeria
LRA	Lord's Resistance Army
LSE	London School of Economics
LURD	Liberians United for Reconciliation and Democracy
MANPADs	Man Portable Defence Systems
MARWOPNET	Mano River Women Peace Network
MASSOB	Movement for the Actualization of the Sovereign State of Biafra
MB	Moslem Brotherhood
MDGs	Millennium Development Goals
MEC	Member of the Executive Council
MENA	Middle East and North Africa
MEND	Movement for the Emancipation of the Niger Delta
METEC	Metal and Engineering Corporation
MICOPAX	Mission to Consolidate Peace in the Central African Republic/*Mission de consolidation de la paix en Centrafrique*
MINUSCA	United Nations Multidimensional Integrated Stabilisation Mission in Central African Republic
MISCA	African-led International Support Mission to the Central African Republic/*Mission international de soutien à la Centrafrique sous conduit africaine*
MJP2	Mouvement pour la justice et la paix
MMPI-2	Minnesota Multiphasic Personality Inventory 2
MNCs	Multinational Corporations
MNJTF	Multinational Joint Task Force
MNLA	National Movement for the Liberation of Azawad
MNLA	Movement for the Liberation of Azawad
MNOCs	Multinational Oil Companies
MODEL	Movement for Democracy in Liberia
MOSIEND	Movement of the Survival of the Ijaw Ethnic Nationality in the Niger Delta
MOSOP	Movement for the Survival of the Ogoni People
MoU	Memorandum of Understanding
MPA	Azawad People's Movement
MPIGO1	Mouvement Populaire Ivoirien du Grand Ouest
MPLA	Movimento Popular de Libertacao de Angola
MPQ	Multi-dimensional Personality Questionnaire
MRA	Media Rights Agenda
MRU	Mano River Union
MUJAO	Movement for the Unity and Jihad in West Africa
MUJAO	Movement for Oneness and Jihad in West Africa
NACS	National Arms Control Strategy
NACTEST	National Counter Terrorism Strategy
NAGAAD	Somali for "Peaceful Resting Place"
NALU	National Army for the Liberation of Uganda
NAP	National Arms Policy
NatCom	National Commission on the Control of Small Arms and Light Weapons
NATCOM	National Committee on the Control of Small Arms and Light Weapons

NATO	North Atlantic Treaty Organisation
NCACA	National Conventional Arms Control Act
NCACC	National Conventional Arms Control Committee
NCIIPC	National Critical Information Infrastructure Protection Centre
NCIS	Nigeria Police Central Information Centre
NCPSALW	National Commission for the Proliferation of Small Arms and Light Weapons
NCRRR	National Commission for Reconstruction, Resettlement and Rehabilitation
NCS	Nigerian Customs Service
NDA	National Democratic Army
NDA	Niger Delta Avengers
NDE	National Directorate of Employment
NDFF	Niger Delta Freedom Fighters
NDJM	Niger Delta Greenland Justice Mandate
NDLEA	National Drug Law Enforcement Agency
NDM	Niger Delta Militants
NDPVF	Niger Delta People's Volunteer Force
NDRS	Niger Delta Red Squad
NDV	Niger Delta Vigilantes
NFPs	National Focal Points
NGOs	Non-Governmental Organisations
NISAT-PRIO	Norwegian Initiative on Small Arms Transfer-Peace Research Institute Oslo
NLC	Nigerian Labour Congress
NOM	Ninth October Movement
NOREF	Norwegian Peacebuilding Resources Centre
NPFL	National Patriotic Front of Liberia
NRA	National Resistance Army
NRA/M	National Resistance Army/Movement
NRC	National Resistance Council
NRCC- SALW	National and Regional Commissions on Combatting Small Arms and Light Weapons
NSA	Non-State Actors
NSCDC	Nigeria Security and Civil Defence Corps
NST	Neighbourhood Security Teams
NTC	National Transitional Council
NTR	Not Tax Revenue
NWLR	Nigerian Weekly Law Reports
OAU	Organization of African Unity
OCSE	Organization for Co-operation and Security in Europe
OECD	Organization for Economic Co-operation and Development
OHCHR	Office of the United Nations High Commissioner for Human Rights
OLF	Oromo Liberation Front
ONLF	Ogaden National Liberation Front
ONSA	Office of the National Security Adviser
ONUCI	United Nations Operation in Cote d' Ivoire
OPC	Oodua People's Congress

OPC	Organ on Peace and Security
OSCE	Organization for Security and Co-operation in Europe
OSSREA	Organization for Social Science Research in Eastern and Southern Africa
PAP	Presidential Amnesty Programme
PCASED	Program for Coordination and Assistance for Security and Development in Africa
PCASED	Programme for Coordination and Assistance for Security and Development
PDF	Popular Defence Force
PDSALWP	Psychological Dynamics Small Arms and Light Weapons Proliferation in Africa
PDU	Protocol Data Units
PEW	Psychological Effects of Weapons
PF	Parliamentary Forum
PLAC	Policy and Legal Advocacy Centre
PLO	Palestinian Liberation Organization
PMSCs	Private Military and Security Companies
PoA	UN Programme of Action
PPP	Purchasing Power Parity
PRA	Peoples Redemption Army
PRB	Population Reference Bureau
PRESCOM	Presidential Committee on Small Arms and Light Weapons
PSA	Peace and Security Architecture
PSC	Peace and Security Council
PSCs	Private Security Companies
PSIRA	Private Security Industry Regulatory Authority
PWD	People with Disability
R2P	Responsibility to Protect
RAP	Research and Production Directorate
RCC	Regional Coordinating Committee
RDR	Reassemlement des Republicairies
REC	Regional Economic Corporations
REC/s	Regional Economic Community
RECA	Regional Centre on Small Arms
RECSA	Regional Centre on Small Arms
RENAMO	Mozambican National Resistance Movement
REWL	Red Egbesu Water Lions
RFDG	Reassemblement des forces democratiques de Guinea
RLP	Refugee Law Project
RMCS	Royal Military College of Science
RO	Regional Organisation
RPF	Rwanda Patriotic Force
RPGs	Rocket Propelled Grenades
RSC	Regional Security Community
RUF	Revolutionary United Front
SADC	Southern Africa Development Community
SADCC	Southern African Development Coordination Conference
SADF	South African Defence Force

SAGA	South African Gunowners Association
SAHRC	South African Human Rights Commission
SALWs	Small Arms and Light Weapons
SANDF	South African National Defence Force
SAPS	South African Police Service
SARPCCO	Southern African Regional Police Chiefs Cooperation Organization
SAS	Small Arms Survey
SASCO	South African Students Congress
SATCRA	Small Arms Transparency and Control Regime in Africa
SDGs	Sustainable Development Goals
SEMG	Somalia and Eritrea Monitoring Group
SIPRI	Stockholm Peace Research Institute
SLA	Sierra Leone Army
SLM/A	Sudan Liberation Movement/Army
SLPP	Sierra Leone People's Party
SNG	Save Nigeria Group
SNM	Somali National Movement
SPLA	Sudan People's Liberation Army (SPLA)
SPLA/M	Sudan People's Liberation Army/Movement
SPRI	Stockholm International Peace Research Institute
SSDF	Somali Salvation Democratic Front
SSR	Security Sector Reform
SWAPO	Southwest African People's Organization
TAH	Trans-African Highway
TMG	Transition Monitoring Group
TNG	Transitional National Government
TOC	Transnational Organised Crime
UNSC	United Nations Security Council
UNODC	United Nations Office on Drugs and Crime
TPA	Terrorism Prevention Act
TPLF	Tigre Peoples' Liberation Front
TSG	The Security Group
TUC	Trade Union Congress
TUT	Tshwane University of Technology
TV	Television
UAE	United Arab Emirates
UFF	Uganda Freedom Fighters
UGS	Ungoverned Spaces
UJCC	Uganda Joint Christian Council
UK	United Kingdom
ULIMO	United Liberation Movement of Liberia for Democracy
UN	United Nations
UN Comtrade	United Nations Commodity Trade Statistics Database
UN PoAIM	UN Small Arms Programme of Action Implementation Monitor
UNAMSIL	United Nations Assistance Mission in Sierra Leone
UNBCPR	United Nations Development Programme, Bureau for Crisis Prevention and Recovery
UNCTAD	United Nations Conference on Trade and Development
UNDDR	United Nations Disarmament, Demobilization and Reintegration

UNDFW	United Nation Development Fund for Women
UNDP	United Nations Development Programme
UNECA	United Nations Economic Commission for Africa
UNFPA	United Nations Population Fund
UNGA	United Nations General Assembly
UNHCR	United Nations High Commissioner for Refugees
UNHRC	United Nations High Commission for Refugees
UNICEF	United Nation International Children's Education Fund
UNIDIR	United Nations Institute for Disarmament Research
UNIDO	United Nations Industrial Development Organization
UNITA	National Union for the Total Independence of Angola
UNLA	Uganda National Liberation Army
UNLF	Uganda National Liberation Front
UNMAS	United Nation Mine Action Service
UNMIL	United Nations Mission in Liberia
UNODA	United Nations Office for Disarmament Affairs
UNODC	United Nations Office of Drugs and Crime
UNOMIL	United Nations Observer Mission
UNOMSIL	United Nations Observer Mission in Sierra Leone
UNOWA	United Nations Office for West Africa
UNOWAS	United Nations Office for West Africa and Sahel
UNPoA	UN Programme of Action to Prevent, Combat and Eradicate the Illicit Trade in Small Arms and Light Weapons in All Its Aspects
UNREC	United Nations Regional Centre for Peace and Disarmament
UNRF I	Uganda National Rescue Front I
UNSC	United Nations Security Council
UNSCAR	United Nations Trust Facility Supporting Cooperation on Arms Regulation
UNSCR	United Nations Security Council Resolution
UNSD	United Nations Statistics Division
UNSMIL	United Nations Support Mission for Libya
UNSOM	United Nations Assistance Mission in Somalia
UPC	Uganda People's Congress
UPDA	Uganda People's Democratic Army
UPDF	Uganda People's Defence Forces
UPF	Uganda Police Force
UPF/A	Uganda People's Front/Army
UPM	Uganda Patriotic Movement
US	United States
USA	United States of America
USC	United Somali Congress
USD	United States Dollar
USDS	United States Department of States
USSR	Union of Soviet Socialist Republic
UWA	Uganda Wild Life Authority
UWND	Ultimate Warriors of Niger Delta
VNSAs	Violent Non-State Actors
VOA	Voice of America
WAANSA	West Africa Action Network on Small Arms

WACD	West Africa Commission on Drugs
WAFF	West African Frontier Force
WAM	Weapons and Ammunition Management
WANJSD	West African Network of Journalists on Security and Development
WAPCCO	West African Police Chiefs Committee
WCO	World Customs Organization
WED	Weapons in Exchange for Development
WfD	Weapons for Development
WHO	World Health Organization
WMD	Weapons of Mass Destruction
ZANU-PF	Zimbabwe African National Union - Patriotic Front
ZCC	Zero Corruption Coalition

List of Figures

Fig. 2.1	Armed conflict and associated violence in postcolonial Africa (*Source* Author 2020)	32
Fig. 3.1	Circles of Arms proliferations (*Source* International Action Network on Small Arms [IANSA])	45
Fig. 3.2	Theoretical matrix on Small Arms and light weapons proliferation in Africa (*Source* Authors 2020)	46
Fig. 7.1	Types of conflicts in Africa	140
Fig. 7.2	Duration of conflicts in Africa	141
Fig. 7.3	Major actors of conflicts in Africa	142
Fig. 7.4	Ownership of conflicts in Africa	143
Fig. 7.5	Reasons for conflicts in Africa	144
Fig. 7.6	Types of SALWs in Africa	145
Fig. 7.7	Sources of weapons in Africa	146
Fig. 7.8	Purpose of acquisition of SALWs	147
Fig. 7.9	Countries destabilized by weapons	148
Fig. 7.10	Countries cleared of weapons	149
Fig. 8.1	North and Western Africa: emerging and potential ungoverned spaces (Source *The Guardian (UK)*. Available http://image.guardian.co.uk/sys-files/Guardian/documents/2013/01/21/Africa_Turmoil_WEB.pdf. Accessed 11 November 2019; *Le Monde diplomatique*, Celeste Hicks)	166
Fig. 8.2	Rate of conflict in Sahel with fatalities (*Source* Raleigh and Dowd 2013: 5)	168
Fig. 8.3	Cocaine flows through West Africa (*Source* UNODC 2017)	169
Fig. 8.4	Connection between drug smuggling and organised crime, illicit financial flows, corruption and terrorism (*Source* UNODC 2017: 13)	169
Fig. 8.5	Documented flows of weapons and non-state armed personnel in the Sahel, 2011–2020 (*Source* Conflict Armament Research Report 2016: 8)	178
Fig. 9.1	Reported craft production of small arms in Africa, 2011–2018 (*Source* UNREC 2016: 21)	195

Fig. 11.1	Kamuku Forest, Nigeria: the Hideout of Armed Criminal Gangs (*Source* Uwe Dedering - Own work, CC BY-SA 3.0, available: https://commons.wikimedia.org/w/index.php?curid=12256786)	226
Fig. 13.1	Major conflict hotspots in Africa, 2000—Present (*Source Prio Armed Conflict Dataset,* 2012)	272
Fig. 13.2	Sources of Africa's Weapons (*Source SIPRI* 2013)	274
Fig. 14.1	Conflict zones in Africa as at 2018 (*Source* The African Military blog. Available: https://www.africanmilitaryblog.com/2018/07/african-conflict-map-acomprehensive-guide?v=65d8f7baa677, Accessed 05 July 2020)	288
Fig. 17.1	Agents/institution of socialization (*Source* Herzog 2020)	349
Fig. 17.2	Social influence in socialization (*Source* Adapted from Herbert. *Social influence chart-social psychology.* Available https://socialpsychoproject.weebly.com. Accessed 6 July 2020)	350
Fig. 17.3	The environment, demography, and conflict (*Source* Spielmann et al. 2020)	352
Fig. 17.4	Dimensions of social change (*Source* Adopted from Lonside et al. 2015)	353
Fig. 17.5	Forces of social change (*Source* Adopted from Alfred North Whitehead https://courses.lumenlearning. Accessed 7 July 2020)	353
Fig. 17.6	Areas affected by armed conflicts in Nigeria (*Source* https://www.google.com. Accessed 6 July 2020)	357
Fig. 17.7	Global sources of SALWS in Nigeria (*Sources* Abubakar et al. 2020; (ONSA) (UNREC) Experts)	359
Fig. 17.8	Small arms intercepted by the Nigerian Police Force (*Source* www.guardian.ng/opinion/unbodies)	360
Fig. 17.9	Homemade guns in Nigeria (*Source* www.guardian.ng/opinion/unbodie)	360
Fig. 17.10	Zones of violence: Nigeria's six geopolitical zones (*Source* Akande 2015)	363
Fig. 18.1	a-d Age distribution of the population, aggregate and country examples % (*Source* Yifu 2011)	377
Fig. 18.2	Spread of guns in the hands of youth (*Source* Child Soldier International Index 2018 and modified by the author 2019)	380
Fig. 18.3	Reasons for vulnerability of youths for Recruits in child soldiers (%) (*Source* Tsuwa 2019)	382
Fig. 21.1	Categories of Small Arms and Light Weapons (SALWs) (*Source* UNDP 2008: 2)	432
Fig. 21.2	Arms flows in Africa's Maghreb, Sahel and Sub-Sahara (*Source* Libya Tribune, July 27, 2019)	437
Fig. 26.1	Pathways of illegal proliferation SALWs in West Africa (*Source* United Nations Office on Drugs and Crime [2013: 33])	551
Fig. 27.1	Map of Trans-African highways *Source* Wikimedia Commons, Available: https://commons.wikimedia.org/wiki/File:Map_of_Trans-African_Highways.PNG	573

Fig. 27.2	Transport network in Africa *Source The Economists*. Avialable: https://www.economist.com/business/2008/10/16/network-effects	576
Fig. 30.1	Demand for SALWs in Africa (*Source* Authors [2020])	634
Fig. 30.2	Supply of SALWs in Africa (*Source* Authors [2020])	636
Fig. 30.3	Equilibrium in demand and supply of SALWs (*Source* Authors [2020])	637
Fig. 30.4	The economic trajectories and consequences of SALWs proliferation in Africa (*Source* Authors [2020])	638
Fig. 31.1	Conflicts in Africa by their intensity, 2011–2015 (*Source* Heidelberg conflict barometer, 2011–2015)	665
Fig. 31.2	High-Intensity Conflicts in Africa 2013–2015 (*Source* Heidelberg conflict barometer, 2013–2015)	665
Fig. 32.1	Internally displaced persons in the Central African Republic (CAR) in 2017 (*Source* Internal displacement Monitoring centre: Central African Republic. www.internal-displacement.org)	693
Fig. 32.2	Civilian and deaths by armed groups between 2017 and 2018 (*Source* United Nations, World population prospects 2017 Revision. https://esa.un.org/unpd/wpp/)	694
Fig. 34.1	Expansion of Abyssinia under Emperor Menelik II (*Source* File_Ethiopia_shaded_relief_map_1999,_CIA. University of Texas Libraries, Perry-Castañeda Library Map Collection, available https://legacy.lib.utexas.edu/maps/ethiopia.html)	723
Fig. 34.2	Horn of Africa with major urban centres (*Source* https://globalbiodefense.com/wp-content/uploads/2013/05/horn_of_africa_map.jpg)	730
Fig. 35.1	Top eight arms exporters to Libya, 1970–1991 (*Source* SIPRI Arms Transfer Database 2015)	747
Fig. 35.2	States with confirmed Libyan SALWs proliferation (*Source* SIPRI Arms Transfer Database 2015)	750
Fig. 36.1	Conflict in the north and central regions of Mali (*Source* The organisation for world peace)	765
Fig. 37.1	Trend of pipeline vandalisation in the Niger Delta region, 1999–2018 (*Source* Authors' compilation from NNPC Annual Statistical Bulletin for the various years)	782
Fig. 37.2	Incidents and casualties from the Boko Haram insurgency, 2011–2019 (*Source* Allen 2019)	787
Fig. 37.3	Average cost of an illegally acquired AK-47 on the black market in US dollars (*Source* Adapted from Global Financial Integrity [2017: 14])	791
Fig. 37.4	SALWs proliferation, armed violence and human (in)security dynamics (*Source* Onuoha and Ezirim [2020: 76])	792
Fig. 37.5	Killings by violent groups in Nigeria, January to September 2019 (*Source* Adapted from Mac-Leva and Ibrahim [2019])	794
Fig. 38.1	Trafficking routes of illicit SALWs in Niger Republic (*Source* Tessieres [2017])	812
Fig. 39.1	Illegal possession of firearms and ammunition: trend over ten years, SAPS (2019)	820

Fig. 39.2	Illegal possession of firearms and ammunition by province for 2017/2018 and 2018/2019 (*Source* SAPS [2019])	821
Fig. 39.3	The ten most common instruments used nationally to commit murder 2018/2019 (*Source* SAPS [2019: https://www.saps.gov.za/services/april_to_march2018_19_presentation.pdf])	824
Fig. 39.4	Causative factors of murder and attempted murder (April 2018–March 2019) (*Source* SAPS [2019: https://www.saps.gov.za/services/april_to_march2018_19_presentation.pdf])	827
Fig. 39.5	South Africa murder statistics April 1, 2018–March 31, 2019 (*Source* SAPS [2019: https://www.saps.gov.za/services/april_to_march2018_19_presentation.pdf])	830
Fig. 41.1	Political map of Somalia (*Source* Google Map [2019])	865
Fig. 42.1	Maps of Uganda showing some of the Postcolonial Conflict Hotspots (*Sources* Adopted from Ogenga, Otunu (2002), Causes and Consequences of the War in Acholiland, ACCORD, p. 15; cf. Omona, A. D. (2015), Management of postcolonial intrastate conflicts in Uganda: A case of northern Uganda, Nairobi: Kenyatta University—Ph.D. Thesis, p. 26)	885
Fig. 43.1	Movements of SALWs in West Africa (*Source* UNODC, TOC in West Africa)	915

LIST OF TABLES

Table 2.1	Summary of PRIO Conflict Trends in Africa, 2017	21
Table 2.2	Small arms and ammunition manufacturing capacities in Africa	31
Table 2.3	Estimated African subregional distribution of civilian firearms, 2017	33
Table 3.1	Estimated African sub-regional distribution of civilian firearms 2017	59
Table 3.2	Regional and Sub-Regional approaches to the control of SALWs in Africa	62
Table 6.1	Taxonomy of arms control	115
Table 6.2	Mapping of ongoing production of arms and ammunition in Africa	116
Table 6.3	Firearms data for selected African countries	119
Table 6.4	Regional instruments and conventions on arms control in Africa	123
Table 6.5	UN Programme of action on common norms and principles of SALWs	126
Table 7.1	Estimated African subregional distribution of civilian firearms, 2017	138
Table 8.1	Largest exporters of arms to sub-Saharan Africa (in USD million), 2013–2015	170
Table 8.2	Main importers for the five largest exporters to sub-Saharan Africa, 2013–2015	171
Table 9.1	Small arms, light weapons, ammunition and explosives	192
Table 9.2	Estimated African sub-regional distribution of civilian firearms, 2017	196
Table 10.1	African countries categorised by extent of urbanisation, 2014	212
Table 12.1	Civil wars linked to resource wealth, 1990–2002	255
Table 12.2	Armed conflicts in Africa and the rest of the world, 1989–2001	255
Table 13.1	Sub-regional distribution of SALWs in civilian hands in Africa in 2017	271
Table 13.2	Concentration of SALWs in Africa as at 2018	275

Table 17.1	Nigeria Police Force (NPF) stock of small arms and ammunition	358
Table 18.1	Post-Cold War US arms transfer to governments involved in the Congo War, 1989–1998 (in 1998 constant Million Dollars)	381
Table 18.2	IDPs and Refugees in Africa	387
Table 21.1	Types and patterns/manifestations of ungoverned spaces	435
Table 21.2	World's large and small arms importers (Comtrade data, 2014)	437
Table 21.3	Firearms data for some African countries (by 2016)	439
Table 21.4	Regional prevalence of SALWs proliferation in Africa	442
Table 21.5	Some patterns of SALWs-driven criminality and violence in Africa	443
Table 21.6	Africa's top 10 fragile states (2017)	446
Table 23.1	Estimated African sub-regional distribution of civilian firearms, 2017	482
Table 26.1	Destinations, types, origin and routes of SALWs in West Africa	552
Table 31.1	Countries with ongoing conflicts or incidences of Insecurity in Africa	664
Table 31.2	Legal and illegal spread and possession of firearms in Africa	670
Table 32.1	Weapons and ammunition of origin located in the Central African Republic during the period 2000–2017	697
Table 34.1	Indicative data on Arms Regulation in the Horn of Africa	725
Table 35.1	Transfers of major conventional weapons to Libya, 1951–2008 (In Million US$)	746
Table 37.1	Some reported cases of Boko Haram attacks and looting of security posts in Nigeria	789
Table 38.1	Frequencies of definitional elements in 109 definitions of terrorism	808
Table 38.2	Types, sources and estimated number of SALWs in Niger Republic	811
Table 38.3	Terrorists organizations and types of SALWs used in Niger Republic (2013–2017)	813
Table 39.1	Highest femicide rates in the world	822
Table 39.2	Categories of victimisation of xenophobic violence from January to September 2019	829
Table 40.1	Estimate of illicitly acquired funds from unrecorded diamond export in Sierra Leone, 2001–2006	853
Table 40.2	Estimates of West African SALW in or out of circulation (2000–2010)	856
Table 41.1	Existing mechanisms for arms control	873
Table 43.1	ECOWAS/EU arms collection project	920
Table 45.1	Classifications of small arms and light weapons (SALWs)	956
Table 45.2	Proliferation of SALWs in liberian civil war	966
Table 45.3	Proliferation of SALWs in Sierra Leonean civil war	968
Table 45.4	Proliferation of SALWs in Guinean conflict	970
Table 45.5	Western-standard ammunition calibre and related arms in Cote d'Ivoire	972

Table 45.6	Eastern Bloc-standard ammunition calibres and related arms in Cote d'Ivoire	972
Table 46.1	Estimated African subregional distribution of civilian firearms, 2017	993

CHAPTER 1

Introduction: The Frontiers of Small Arms Proliferation and Conflicts in Africa

Usman A. Tar

The proliferation of Small Arms and Light Weapons (SALWs) has transformed Africa's political, economic, demographic, and sociocultural landscapes in spectacular, but gory ways. SALWs constitutes one of the key factors in the escalation of conflict and instability in Africa's *zones of violence*. Even in relatively peaceful parts of Africa—such as Botswana, Seychelles, Comoros—and in "pockets of peace" *within* conflict-prone states—such as Nigeria, South Africa, Kenya, and Tanzania, there are fears of diffusion of SALWs to fuel dormant conflicts and criminality. Africa is a continent of paradoxes and extremes. On the one hand, it is depicted as the home of ancient civilizations and steeped in history, rich in mineral resources, endowed with amazing flora and fauna and home to hospitable people. Media adverts—for instance by the Kenyan Tourism Board—show Africa as a grandiose paradise with an evergreen scenery and a thriving wildlife—an ideal getaway and a dream destination for tourists and adventurers. On the other hand, Africa also carries the label as the home of civil wars, failing states, communal strife, and feuding communities, of farmer–herders conflict, spiraling insurgency and violent extremism, and senseless killings of vulnerable citizens. There is some truth in either extreme. Africa's democratic and developmental footprint has improved over the years, relatively speaking. At the same time, it is easier to commit crime in African countries than perhaps anywhere in the world. The proliferation and misuse of small

---

U. A. Tar (✉)
Nigerian Defence Academy, Centre for Defence Studies and Documentation
Nigerian Defence Academy, Kaduna, Nigeria

© The Author(s), under exclusive license to Springer Nature Switzerland AG 2021
U. A. Tar and C. P. Onwurah (eds.), *The Palgrave Handbook of Small Arms and Conflicts in Africa*,
https://doi.org/10.1007/978-3-030-62183-4_1

arms and light weapons (SALWs) pose one of the greatest risks to the survival and development of African continent. To be sure, every continent and every country around the world is faced with the challenges of SALWs. However, Africa's load of the dangers of SALWs is disturbing. Domiciling many weak states, impoverished citizens and highly divided communities—particularly in the rural areas and urban fringes who now enjoy unfettered access to drugs, guns and violent images from the net—Africa sits on a tinderbox of violence and destruction. Small arms have become a cheap, affordable, accessible, and portable, and they litter the political, economic, social, and communal spaces. There is gun addiction in Africa, and all over the continent guns are traded, transferred, and projected as the most efficient means of transaction, and in display of power and might. In remote communities, there is increasingly dependence on sophisticated weapons as a means of livelihood and survival. In urban areas, small arms have become the weapon of choice in the hands of criminal gangs and "area boys."

At the state level, most African countries are faced by crisis of security and contest over state power and legitimacy between divergent factions of the elites and society. In many cases, the state has failed to provide security, thus allowing citizens and communities to take the law into their hands. Many African states, including the relatively stable, as well as weak and collapsing ones, enjoy unfettered access to arms from the global arena through official bilateral and multilateral transfers and local sources. There has been poor accountability in the management of official stockpiles, and in wrongful application of the state's arsenals: in many states, such as Nigeria, Congo DR, CAR, South Africa, and Kenya, the armed forces and paramilitaries have been alleged for unethical and extrajudicial use of arms against citizens. At the same time, the theft of arms from official stockpiles have allowed members of the society—including criminal gangs, insurgents, and communities—to access arms for purposes that threaten the very existence of the state. In many African states, terrorists, insurgents and local criminal gangs—all armed to the teeth with weapons obtained from local and external sources—have emerged and blossomed, and are increasingly challenging the host state, confronting law enforcement agents, attacking vulnerable communities, inducing fear in society and creating "ungoverned spaces." Rather than normalcy, criminality seems to hold sway as the most thriving vocation in Africa. It is easier to make it in life by resorting to criminality, than through legitimate livelihood. The motivations for crime and violence are higher than deterrence from the state and law enforcement officials. At the regional level, African regional organizations are beset by a motley of challenges ranging from transborder skirmishes between local states, to the rise of transnational crime and terrorism which require collective action. The continental and regional protocols for small arms control and conflict management have resulted in providing transnational mechanisms for addressing conflicts and criminality, but there remain hurdles in enforcement, and ensuring cooperative regional security among African states.

This *Handbook* provides a critical discussion of the theory and practices of small arms proliferation and organized violence in Africa. The *Handbook* examines the terrains, institutions, factors and actors that drive armed conflict and arms proliferation in Africa. The volume examines the nature, scope, and dynamics of small arms proliferation and its impact on conflict flashpoints across the continent. The *Handbook* displays the wide experience and perspectives of scholars and practitioners who are acquainted with the formal and informal structures of arms proliferation and control, and its impact across the continent. The Handbook presents a collection of original essays from scholars, development practitioners, defense and security professionals, and civil society activists who share a common vision of dissecting the challenges of SALWs in Africa with a view to understanding its root causes and drivers, and generating a fresh body of analyses that will add value to the existing conversation on conflict management and peacebuilding in Africa. It will also serve as a pool of resource for students, researchers, and policy makers on SALWs proliferation, control, and regulation in Africa, with a view to understanding the root causes and drivers of conflicts and insecurity on the continent.

AIMS OF THE *HANDBOOK*

There are five driving aims of this *Handbook*: first, to explore the depth of, and linkages between, the theory and empiricism of SALWs proliferation and its impact on conflict, security, and peacebuilding in Africa. A cursory view of the literature reveals some imbalances. For instance, most of the mainstream literature are steeped in theory-making than in advancing ethnographic analyses (or real-life reflections) that illuminate the reality in Africa. In addition, some of the literature are based on "armchair analysis", while some are developed by opportunists who lack a sound ethnographic knowledge of Africa. In addition, there is a sizeable array of analyses that are shallow in scope and bereft of local perspectives. Secondly, the volume aims to provide a fresh multidisciplinary and comprehensive resource material for scholars and practitioners. We reckoned that it was impossible, even counterintuitive, to quarantine this volume to a single-lens analysis, or to restrict the contributors to any specific discipline or professional enclave. Therefore, this *Handbook* is designed to serve the needs of diverse disciplines, institutions and communities of practice. Thirdly, the volume aims to cast the net wider and deeper by engaging scholars and practitioners to take a voyage on specific topics that are located within the five component-scope of the volume—theory and context; terrain analysis; institutional and actor analysis; state-centered analysis; and transnational analysis. We hope that the 46 chapters contained in this volume will quench the appetite of those seeking a fresh, but in-depth analysis, of a wide-ranging thematic groundswell of analysis. Fourthly, in this volume, we seek to break away from disciplinary cocoons and offer a robust compendium that draws from the perspectives of scholars and practitioners drawn from diverse communities of practice. The *Handbook* aims to pull together a hybrid and multiplex perspectives of scholars, development practitioners, security personnel, and other stakeholders both within and outside Africa to offer critical reflections on the problems of small arms and implications for African conflict and security. Finally, the contributors of this volume were recruited on ground of their passion for scholarship and policy discourse on Africa.

SCOPE AND LIMITS OF THE EXISTING LITERATURE

A cottage industry has blossomed on issues surrounding the proliferation, regulation, and control of small arms—and their implications for conflicts, insurgencies, and criminality—around the world and in Africa.[1] The literature on small arms and conflicts in Africa is rich but not without some limitations—thus providing the justification for this volume. In this section, a selected mixture of the literature is reviewed to demonstrate the scope and limitations of the existing literature.[2] We focus on the global and local genres of the literature, without prejudice to the fact that the boundaries between the global and local discourses can be blurry.

Global Dimensions

To start with, an analysis of the global and comparative experiences in arms proliferation, and global best practice in norm-setting[3] is offered by Garcia (2006) in *Small Arms and Security: New Emerging International Norms*. This volume examines the challenges posed to the world by the production and circulation of SALWs; regimes put in place to manage arms production and distribution; as well as the applicability of these regimes across states, regions, and international organization. The volume depicts these arms control regimes as norms setters or "common understanding", and advances a creative framework for assessing the emergence of arms proliferation and the growing challenges of violence associated to SALWs. The volume advances solid analogies and solutions for reducing arms circulation and arms-related violence. However, the volume is characterized by some pitfalls, among them are: it mainly focuses on common understanding and collaboration among states and regions for joint effort at checkmating arms circulation; and it only treated Africa as a case in point rather than a dedicated case study. This *Handbook* provides a robust examination of the processes of arms proliferation in Africa, as well as the regimes and infrastructure of arms control and disarmament. Another global volume is Michael Bourne's *Arming Conflict: The Proliferation of Small Arms* published in 2007. This volume argues that across the globe, "the arming of conflict is complexly structured and highly dynamic." The volume unpacks and describes the construction and interaction of structures and dynamics at global and regional levels, which shape the arming patterns of both state and non-state actors. The nine chapters of this book deal with specific issues—for instance, in Chapter 2 titled "Structure and Dynamic in Weapons Spread: The Trade and Proliferation of Weapons in Comparative Perspective," Bourne captures the complexity of arms proliferation:

> weapon spread may occur through the manufacture of weapons and through import of weapons...the spread of most types of weapons occur through a combination of the two... Within each method of acquisition, a number of different channels may be used to obtain weapons or the technology to produce weapons. The nature and structure of these channels varies according to the type of weapons concerned and are reflected in the three images of spread. There are three main images of spread are weapons spread, each of which portrays the process through which a given actor obtains a particular type of weapon. These three images are proliferation, diffusion and trade. While these three images overlap and the boundary between them are blurred, the applicability to the spread of a particular type of weapon relates to the structures of their availability and the implications of those structures for the process of acquisition. (Bourne 2007: 15)

Bourne also explores, in fine details, the "The Foundations and Construction of Global SALW Trade" (Chapter 3); "Global Structures and SALW Flows to Conflict" (Chapter 4); Regional Facilitation and the Construction of Networks (Chapter 5); Structures and Dynamics of Intra-regional SALW Spread to Conflicts (Chapter 6); Arming Conflict from the Bottom-Up: SALW Spread at the Conflict level (Chapter 7) and Constructing Top-Down Arming Patterns: Sovereignty, Money, Networks, and the Cumulative Impact of Structures and Dynamics of SALW Spread (Chapter 8). Each of these chapters provided fineline analysis, steeped in data of the complex networks of interest and institutions that drives weapons proliferation. In the concluding chapter, Bourne (2007) argues that:

> When viewed through a reflection of structures and dynamics of the spread of other weapons ... current understanding of SALWs spread are revealed not only as emphasizing the relative breadth and complexity of SALW spread, but as framing it in an amorphous image ... [which] implies that there is no non-state threshold in SALW spread, but rather that SALW to conflicts is a function of a vast global stock of arms, available in a viable globalized illicit market and accessed through a shadowy array of nefarious brokers. The amorphous image is inaccurate, it obscures structures and dynamics rather than reflecting the essence. (Bourne 2007: 238)

In *Weapon of Choice: Small Arms and the Culture of Military Innovation*, Ford (2017) examines the nature and scope of Western military technological innovation and production in the twentieth century. The volume offers solid insights into the social and political constructions of small arms. The text exposes the mechanics of power across the military-industrial complex. This in turn reveals how power relations between soldiers and scientists, bureaucrats and engineers, innovators and producers have allowed the private sector to exploit infantry anxiety and shape soldiers' weapon preferences. The book provides an exhilarating analysis of the international dynamics of arms politics, production and transfer but mainly outside the context of Africa. However, it is worth noting that a significant fraction of the small arms produced globally end in fuelling conflicts across Africa. Therefore, the present Handbook beams the searchlight on African reality of SALWs proliferation—including imports as depicted by Ford (2017) and local production and supply—as well as the role of local political, bureaucratic, and military actors in supporting or obstruction the proliferation of small arms on the continent.

In 2002, the *Brown Journal of World Affairs*[4] published a special issue on Small arms. This volume offers a global painting of small arms proliferation and control, and their implications on several issues such as violence, human rights, regimes security around the world, and in Africa. A section of the journal "At Gunpoint: The SALWs trade" contains thirteen relevant articles which discussed the collapse of the Cold War and the privatization of conflict especially in the global south; illicit arms trade, arms brokers and their consequences on Africa and her nascent democracy; foreign and global public policy on small arms; and multilateral cooperation in checkmating the menace of arms proliferation. It examines the impact of SALWs on public health, the weak, especially children, and clandestine re-armament on peace process. In particular, specific articles deal with "multilateral cooperation on SALWs" with particular reference to "collective response" (Dhanapala 2002: 163–171); "illicit arms brokers" and their role in "aiding and abetting atrocities" (Austin 2002: 203–216); and "the legal and illegal trade in small arms" (Marsh 2002: 217–228). Together, these articles illuminate the conspiracies and weaknesses of the global small arms fraternity. Further, three specific articles on Africa (Montague 2002: 229–237; Musa 2002: 239–249; and Eavis 2002: 251–260) critically examine the challenges of small arms proliferation and how African countries are coping with local and foreign challenges. The Brown Journal offers a very robust attempt at exploring the challenges of small arms, and pay sufficient attention to the African reality at the time of publication. And, nearly two decades on, the analysis contained in this journal strikes a chord with the poignant realities in Africa and around the world.

Beyond understanding the dynamics of arms proliferation, arms control and disarmament has received significant attention in the literature. For instance, the United Nations Report (2010) on the emerging practices of DDR explores field practices and innovations implemented by DDR practitioners in Afghanistan, Cote d'Ivoire, Haiti, and Liberia with the aim of acquainting practitioners with robust and contemporary practices that are capable of addressing future challenges of DDR. The volume illuminates the challenges and frustrations that are faced by mediators in disarmament. The volume privileges two strands of disarmament: "Traditional DDR" and "Second Generation or Interim Stabilization." While the Traditional DDR model is centered on the classical categories of DDR and targets military encamped combatants, the later (that is, the interim stabilisation model) moves from military control to need-based DDR which is broader and supportive in nature with sufficient room for local participation and ownership of the DDR process. On weapons management and reduction approaches, the report posits that the term weapons should not be limited to sophisticated mechanics like guns, rather, should include objects such as machetes. At regional level, the report highlighted efforts made by the Brahimi Report of 2000 and UN Security Council at broadening peace process; checking leakages from military depots; diversion of genuinely imported weapons; checking local production; cross-border trafficking on SALWs and repatriation of foreign combatants in West Africa as a perennial challenge in the region. This report is robust and comprehensive, but it has been overtaken by time and suffers from diffused attention. Similarly, in *UN DDR in the Era Violent Extremism: Is it Fit for Purpose?*, Cockayne and O'Neil (2015) examine the rationale, purposes, changing roles, and applicability of DDR in the contemporary conflicts; the challenges faced by the UN in peace operations. Based on the experiences of AMISOM in Somalia, ISAF in Afghanistan and Operation Serval in Mali, the volume posits that it is futile for UN alone to address the challenges of DDR without support from national or regional government; this is necessary as successful DDR exercises have been collaborative in nature. The volume also cautiously observed the role of criminal actors in keeping rebel fighters in business; and concludes that due to multidimensional nature of the challenges in post-conflict environment, there may be need to apply peace enforcement approach in disarmament.

In *Security Beyond the State: Private Security in International Politics*, Abrahamsen and Williams (2011) examined the role of private security companies and defense contractors in discharging security functions—these roles are in the traditional domain of the state. Since security cannot be provided without weapons, the new international regimen has "weaponized" private security service providers. The authors observe that since the end of the Cold War, there has been increasing involvement of private military contractors and mercenaries in international politics; and these have focused on global political discourse around conventional and nonconventional security. To the authors, since the 9/11 attack on the United States of America, there has been paradigm shift aimed at identifying, containing, and managing danger or risk if the pattern of contemporary attack must be averted. With wide acceptance, security became an industry that admits hundreds of operators and thousands of employees in the world, with their services transcending borders. They find presence around capital, defending it irrespective of the hostile nature of the environment. A good instance was presented with oil fields in Nigerian Niger Delta, diamond mining sites of Sierra Leone and urban security in general. The authors argue that the role of private security companies in extractive industries and conflict management is yet to get the needed attention, it is on record that is one of the fastest growing businesses in Africa. This volume provides a refreshing and data-based analysis of the performance of private security companies in Africa. Despite that, it failed to mention or discuss the acquisition, proliferation and use of SALWs especially by private security companies and mercenaries who are hired to carry out specific duties in host states. This Handbook contains a chapter that not only investigates the performance of private security companies in Africa, but also their sources of weapons and the risk they carry as vectors of SALWs proliferation.

Regional and Local Dimensions

The volumes of work on the regional context of SALWs in Africa is legion. This could be divided into those covering *proliferation* and *regulation*. On proliferation, two texts are worth consideration. First, in *Proliferation of Small Arms and Light Weapons in West Africa: Implications for Subregional Security*, Okoro (2012) examines the impacts of socioeconomic and structural imbalances in West Africa and how this has affected regional development and security. The text argues that arms-related conflicts spill across boundaries and political divides, and are driven by the prevailing climate of insecurity in the sub-region. This text is narrow in context, focusing on the cross-border crime and violation of security within the sub-region. The deeper dimensions of SALWs proliferation such as the impact of globalization, and information and communication technologies which have challenged traditional boundaries of the state and allowed non-state actors to participate, almost freely, in regional arms trade and proliferation have not received sufficient attention. Second, in *Proliferation and Illicit Trafficking of Small Arms and Light Weapons in the Great Lakes and Horn of Africa*, Kiugu (2012), appraises the techniques, ways, and means through which countries of the Great Lakes and Horn of Africa are confronting the challenges of SALWs proliferation, with special interest on Kenya, Uganda and Ethiopia. It recounts the negative impacts of SALWs proliferation on economic growth and development in the Great Lakes Region and the Horn of Africa (GLHA) within the period of 2000 to the recent past as well as looked into the regional and sub-regional initiatives and efforts like Nairobi and Bamako declarations on the "African Common Position on the Illicit Proliferation, Circulation and Trafficking of Small Arms and Light Weapons" in March and December 2000, respectively. This *Handbook* offers a robust analysis of the challenges confronting the state and sub-regional organizations in addressing these challenges.

With regard to SALWs *regulation and control*, the mechanisms for regional architectures for managing SALWs—legislation, local institutional framework, law enforcement, multilateral protocols, and non-governmental organizations—have received significant attention in the literature. In *Combating the Proliferation of Small Arms and Light Weapons in West Africa: Handbook for the Training of Armed and Security Forces*, Ayissi and Sall (2005) offer some constructive insights on local capacity building of armed forces and law enforcement personnel, and citizen participation in ensuring local ownership of arms control protocols. This text was borne out of collaborative effort by United Nations Institute for Disarmament Research (UNIDIR), Program for Coordination and Assistance for Security and Development (PCASED), and Economic Community of West African States (ECOWAS) on the need to mobilize, institutionalize, and enhance local capacities in West Africa in combating SALWs proliferation. This is in view of the adverse effects of small arms on peace, security, and development in the region and the need to make an impression of its mission (UNIDIR)—that is, research and dissemination of information on peace building across the region. The volume emphasies robust training of the armed and security forces on the necessary measures for disarmament as indispensable in the pursuit of its mission as well as impacting on the moral, ethical, civic, and professional values conducive to making them reliable and efficient partners that populations can depend upon. Thus, the volume stresses the need for the international community to be educated on the local and regional methods for addressing the challenges of arms proliferation as primers to conflict transformation and peace building. This volume is written by scholars, experts, and practitioners in the subject area, and presents a rich blend of local experiences and regulatory frameworks available within the specific region of West Africa. The present *Handbook* advances wider themes and comparative cases across Africa to provide a more robust analysis of the continental, sub-regional and municipal experiences in the proliferation of small arms, the legal and regulatory mechanisms adopted in these contexts, and collaborative initiatives in managing armed violence across the continent of Africa. Another pertinent text considered is *Trafficking of Small Arms and Light Weapons (SALW) in West Africa*, edited by Asoba and Glokpor (2014). This volume provides illuminating perspectives on arms proliferation and management in West African countries of Ghana, Togo, Benin, and Nigeria. With insightful contributions by a group of seasoned scholars and development practitioners—Ohene-Asare; Aklavon; Moussou & Ikelegbe—the volume provides perspectives on artisanal manufacturers of illicit weapons, strategies of arms concealment adopted by actors in the small arms value chain, network of arms circulation, border control services, and drivers of arms trafficking. This volume reports that importation, local manufacturing and circulation of SALWs provides as much money to ordinary citizens as death to the larger population in the region (Knight and Özerdem 2004). Despite this the volume only focuses on West Africa and, as a matter of fact, it covered only 4 out of 16 states of West Africa. The present *Handbook* offers broader, national, comparative, and transnational perspectives of SALWs proliferation and its impacts on conflict, security, and peacebuilding in Africa.

Methodology and Rationale

This *Handbook* is based on multidisciplinary methodologies. First, the contributors were drawn from diverse disciplines and granted freedom to write from their disciplinary perspectives, but in a manner that ensures a synergy between these diverse methodologies—this is especially the case for coauthored chapters. In this volume, we deployed a curious mix of scholars deliberately drawn from different disciplines—Political Science; International Relations; Defense

Studies; History; Economics Psychology; Geography; Sociology; Accounting; Law; Education; Transport and Logistics; and Gender Studies, among others. Even for chapters that were developed by single authors with their disciplinary biases, we ensured that the editorial oversight instilled disciplinary and methodological variety. Several chapters were actually developed by teams of scholars—or a mixture of scholars and practitioners—from diverse disciplines with divergent perspectives such that the final outcome is, we hope, more versatile and richer outcome. Secondly, each chapter contributor(s) was/were granted the liberty to deploy the methodologies that they were conversant with, so long as the quality of analysis and integrity of data are not compromised. For instance, some authors applied mixed methodology, others relied heavily or partially on secondary data, while quite a few recalled ethnographic and experiential data to support their arguments—the latter applied to contributors with background in development practice and field experience, as well as those involved in providing consultancies for diverse clients in the public sector, private sector, or NGOs. However, the editorial team insisted that contributors present analyses that are steeped in literature and empirical data—and strictly adhere to the principles of research ethics with regard to confidentiality, authenticity, validity, reliability, and applicability of data source. Furthermore, we realized that there exists an impressive body of empirical data produced by reputable think tanks that needed to be exposed to proper multidisciplinary analysis, and thus encouraged authors to tap from these sources in the form of constructive engagement, adoption of short quotes, adaptation of tables, models, and figures with due acknowledgement for all sources of data. In themselves, the raw and anecdotal data emerging from databases would not yield the desired outcome unless they are applied to critical thinking and policy analysis. Another methodological feature of this *Handbook* is that contributors tried to blend theory with empirical praxis; abstract analogies with ethnographic evidence; existing data with newly generated data; the aim is to generate a new ground for constructive engagement on managing armed violence and insecurity in Africa. In addition, while reviewing the literature, we realized that the frequency of new materials on small arms in Africa is relatively lower, albeit rich and intense, than other variables such as democracy, elections, development, and globalization. This is without prejudice to the intricate connection that exists between SALWs on these variables. We also realized that small arms research in Africa is driven by a cottage industry comprising a small body of scholars and development institutions: we envisioned the need to open up the field and recruit more analysts who will take a fresh and detached look at the subject matter. However, we noted that though some of the materials that are so far produced by scholars are of very high quality, they appeared to be heavily concentrated in specific periods, context, and themes. What we did was therefore, to craft a more comprehensive compendium whose shelf life, we hope, will be longer than a typical volume on a specific theme, specific period, or specific context within Africa. The three variables that frame this *Handbook*—small arms, conflict, and Africa—granted us sufficient latitude to craft contributions that provide in-depth analyses of those variables in themselves, and as they relate to each other and in the wider context of Africa.

STRUCTURE OF THE HANDBOOK

This handbook is divided into five sections each complementing the others. *Section I* of this *Handbook* titled *Theory and Concepts* contains 5 chapters that broadly explore and problematize the theoretical (and empirical) parameters of SALWs and conflict in Africa. The first chapter examines the frontiers of small arms and conflicts in Africa. The second traces the historical and contemporary trajectories of "conflict" and "small arms" in Africa. The chapter reveals the dynamics, spread, and intensities of conflict and small in Africa. Chapter 3 explores the major theoretical perspectives to explain the problematics of small arms and conflict in Africa; the chapter also traces the empirical parameters to add flesh on the different theories identified in the chapter. Chapters 4–5 deal with political economy, and gendered analysis of SALWs and conflict in Africa, respectively.

Section II of this Handbook titled *Topographies and Contexts* contains 15 chapters dealing with diverse context and conflict scenarios in Africa. These topographies are carefully chosen to provide periscopic accounts that complement one another. These scenarios include state fragility as a compelling background to the proliferation and mismanagement of SALWs (Chapter 6); geographic mapping of conflict and SALWs in Africa (Chapter 7); the function of external interventions in creating failed states and ungoverned spaces in Africa (Chapter 8); borderland s and transborder security (Chapter 9); urban dynamics (Chapter 10); forest governance and ungoverned spaces (Chapter 11); resource wars versus resource curse (Chapter 12); armed conflict and developmental deficits (Chapter 13); civil wars and complex emergencies (Chapter 14); poverty, greed, and arms proliferation (Chapter 15); personality and psychological dynamics (Chapter 16): sociological dynamics and cultures of violence (Chapter 17); youth bulge and generational dynamics (Chapter 18); the gendered construction of conflict and armed violence (Chapter 19); and arms trade and transnational crime (Chapter 20).

Section III tiled *institutional framework and dynamics* contains 11 chapters that deal with legal, institutional, and bureaucratic dimensions of SALWs and conflicts in Africa. To avoid state-centric scoping which is often the bane of many of the existing literature, the chapters deal with diverse institutional actors from state and non-state actors, as well from local state and international organizations. These include the military as a driver of both armament and disarmament (Chapter 21); legislation (Chapter 22); the policing of arms control (Chapter 23); civil society and constructive engagement on arms control and disarmament (Chapter 24); traditional institutions, firearms and conflict management (Chapter 25); customs, contraband and arms control (Chapter 26); transport networks and logistic governance (Chapter 27); multinational corporations and the trafficking of small arms (Chapter 28); private security companies and the proliferation of small arms (Chapter 29); the economics of small arms proliferation, particularly demand and supply sides (Chapter 30); and the role of information communication technologies in small arms control and management (Chapter 31).

Section IV titled *national experiences* contains case experiences from 11 African countries. The country analyses are drawn from *all* regions of the continent. These includes 2 chapters on North Africa (Egypt, Chapter 33 and Libya, Chapter 35); 3 chapters on East Africa (Ethiopia [Chapter 34]; Somalia [Chapter 41]; and Uganda [Chapter 42]); one chapter on Central Africa (CAR Chapter 32); 3 chapters on West Africa (Mali [Chapter 36]; Niger [Chapter 38]; Nigeria [Chapter 37]; and Sierra Leone [Chapter 40]); and finally one chapter on Southern Africa (South Africa, Chapter 39). Together, these chapters provide sufficient representative samples for the entire continent. Finally, *Section V* titled *regional perspectives* contains 4 chapters from regional unions and regional security platforms in Africa—West Africa (Chapter 43); Lake Chad Basin (Chapter 44); Mano River region (Chapter 45); and Southern Africa (Chapter 46). These regional samples focus on the regional challenges of, and structures for, small arms and conflict. They complement the state-centered analyses contained in Section IV of this Handbook, but specifically focus on regional architectures rather than municipal mechanism therein per se.

NOTES

1. In the lead are the *Small Arms Surveys* with a solid base nourished by exponential field data and commissioned research. See for instance, Small Arms Survey (2005), *Small Arms Survey 2005: Weapons at War* (Oxford: Oxford University Press); Small Arms Survey (2006), *Small Arms Survey 2006: Unfinished Business* (Cambridge: Cambridge University Press, p. 263; Small Arms Survey (2007), *Small Arms Survey 2007: Guns and the City* (Cambridge: Cambridge University Press, 2007). For more recent work of the Small Arms Survey, see Small Arms Survey (2018), *Global Firearms Holdings Database*. Geneva: Small Arms Survey. Available: http://www.smallarmssurvey.org/weapons-and-markets/tools/global-firearms-holdings.html; and Small Arms Survey (2019). *Weapons Compass: Mapping Illicit Small Arms Flows in Africa*. Geneva: Small Arms Survey and Addis Ababa: African Union. Available: http://Hwww.smallarmssurvey.org/fileadmin/docs/U-Reports/SAS-AU-Weapons-Compass.pdf. Other institutions have also done substantial work on advancing the frontiers of SALWs research especially as they pertain to conflict analysis, national, human, regional, and global security. For instance, the Peace Research Institute Oslo (PRIO) deserves a special mention for the amazing flow of fresh data and in-depth analysis on many aspects of armed violence and conflict in Africa and across the world (see e.g., Rustad and Bakken 2019; Bakken and Rustad 2018).
2. There is a vast array of volumes and journals that deal with the subject of small arms and conflict, and security in Africa, and globally. Many research

think tanks in Africa and across the world—for instance, United States Institute for Peace, Washington, DC; The Royal United Services Institute (RUSI), London, UK; the Peace Research Institute, Oslo (PRIO); the Centre for Security Studies (ISS), Pretoria, South Africa—have produced copious literature and databases on the subject matter. A good example is the *Small Arms Survey*, a "global centre of excellence, the Small Arms Survey generates evidence-based, impartial, and policy-relevant knowledge and analysis on small arms and armed violence issues for governments, policy-makers, researchers, and civil society. The Survey is a project of the Graduate Institute of International and Development Studies in Geneva, Switzerland" (available: http://www.smallarmssurvey.org/). Another example is the *Small Arms Defence Journal*, "a bimonthly publication that focuses on small arms, accessories, gear for the soldier, new products, industry news, and defense trade shows. The first issue of *SADJ* was Spring 2009, which launched at the LAAD show in Rio de Janeiro, Brazil. *SADJ* (pronounced 'sage') is targeted toward military, law enforcement, and defense industry professionals. Our job is to reach these groups and tailor content to their interests while producing a publication that is applicable to an international audience" (available: http://www.sadefensejournal.com/wp/sample-page/). For this section, we scan a representative sample of the literature and policy discourses.
3. An understanding of the global framework is pertinent in setting the tone for this volume. Such analysis would provide a clear picture of the situation across with world, and provide a searchlight for the African perspectives which this volume seeks to provide.
4. The *Brown Journal of World Affairs* is published in Providence, USA by Brown University Press.

References

Abrahamsen, R., & Williams, M. C. (2011). *Security Beyond the State: Private Security in International Politics*. Cambridge: Cambridge University Press.

Asoba, S., & Glokpor, R. (Eds.). (2014). *Trafficking of Small Arms and Light Weapons (SALW) in West Africa: Routes and Illegal Arm Caches Between Ghana, Togo, Benin and Nigeria*. Friedrich Ebert Stiftung: Abuja.

Austin, K. (2002). Illicit Arms Brokers: Aiding and Abetting Atrocities. *Brown Journal of World Affairs, 9*(1 Spring), 203–216.

Ayissi, A., & Sall, I. (2005). *Combating the Proliferation of Small Arms and Light Weapons in West Africa: Handbook for the Training of Armed and Security Forces*. Geneva: United Nations Institute for Disarmament Research (UNIDR).

Bakken, I. V., & Rustad, S. A. (2018). *Conflict Trends in Africa, 1946–2017, PRIO Paper*. Oslo: Peace Research Institute Oslo.

Bourne, M. (2007). *Arming Conflict: The Proliferation of Small Arms*. Basingstoke: Palgrave.

Cockayne, J., & O'Neil, S. (2015). *UN DDR in the Era Violent Extremism: Is it Fit for Purpose?* Costa Rica: United Nations University.

Dhanapala, J. (2002). Multilateral Cooperation on Small Arms and Light Weapons: From Crisis to Collective Response. *Brown Journal of World Affairs, 9*(1 Spring), 163–171.

Eavis, P. (2002). SALW in the Horn of Africa and the Great Lakes Region: Challenges and Ways Forward. *Brown Journal of World Affairs, 9*(1 Spring), 251–260.

Ford, M. (2017). *Weapon of Choice: Small Arms and the Culture of Military Innovation*. London: Oxford University Press.

Garcia, D. (2006). *Small Arms and Security: New Emerging International Norms*. New York: Routledge.

Kiugu, A. A. M. (2012). *Proliferation and Illicit Trafficking of Small Arms and Light Weapons in the Great Lakes and Horn of Africa*. BiblioScholar.

Knight, M., & Özerdem, A. (2004). Guns, Camps and Cash: Disarmament, Demobilisation and Reinsertion of Former Combatants in Transitions from War to Peace. *Journal of Peace Research, 41*(4), 499–516.

Marsh, N. (2002). Two Sides of the Same Coin? The Legal and Illegal Trade in Small Arms. *Brown Journal of World Affairs, 9*(1 Spring), 217–228.

Montague, D. (2002). The Business of War and the Prospects for Peace in Sierra Leone. *Brown Journal of World Affairs, 9*(1 Spring), 229–237.

Musa, A-F. (2002). Small Arms: A Time Bomb Under West Africa's Democratization Process. *Brown Journal of World Affairs, 9*(1 Spring), 239–249.

Okoro, V. U. (2012). *Proliferation of Small Arms and Light Weapons in West Africa: Implications for Subregional Security*. BiblioScholar.

Rustad, S. A., & Bakken, I. V. (2019). *Conflict Trends in Africa, 1989–2018, Conflict Trends, 6*. Oslo: Peace Research Institute Oslo.

UN (United Nations). (2010). *DDR in Peace Operations: A Retrospect*. New York: United Nations.

Usman A Tar is Professor of Political Science and Defence Studies, and Endowed Chair of Defence and Security Studies (26RC Endowment) at the Nigerian Defence Academy. He is the Director of the Academy's flagship Centre for Defence Studies and Documentation, and a member of the Board of Social Science Research Council's African Peacebuidling Network (SSRC/APN), New York, USA. He was formerly, Associate Research Fellow at Africa Centre for Peace and Conflict Studies, University of Bradford, UK. He authored several books including *The Politics of Neoliberal Democracy in Africa* (London/New York: I B Tauris, 2009); *Globalization in Africa: Perspectives on Development, Security and the Environment* (Lanham, MD, Lexington Books, 2016); *New Architecture of Regional Security in Africa* (Lanham, MD, Lexington Books, 2020); and *Routledge Handbook of Counterterrorism and Counterinsurgency in Africa* (London, Routledge, 2020). Prof Tar has consulted or consults for the United Nations Development Programme (UNDP), Nigeria; Konrad Adaneur Stiftung (KAS, German Development Fund); and the Westminster Foundation for Democracy (WFD), Nigeria. Prof Tar is a member of Nigeria's Presidential Think Tank on National Defence and Security, and served as a member of Nigeria's Presidential Committee to review the national defence policy in 2015.

Part I

Theory and Concepts

CHAPTER 2

Background: Small Arms, Violent Conflicts, and Complex Emergencies in Africa—A Fatal Combination

Usman A. Tar

INTRODUCTION

The proliferation SALWs in Africa is both a cause and manifestation of diverse conflicts that are internal and/or external to the continent, and are driven by the forces of demand and supply, predicated on weak structures that sabotage preemptive conflict management mechanisms. In particular, arms control enables governments and institutions to mobilize and enhance their capacities in addressing the free flow of arms among unauthorized persons. Such mechanisms have been adopted in several instances in the continent with little or no gains. Rather, states, organizations, and charities working on Disarmament, Demobilization, and Reintegration (DDR) among other exercises pay for new weapons as ex-combatants practically use the proceeds of old weapons submitted to exchange for newer ones waiting outside the arena (Caleb and Okafor 2014; Cockayne and O'Neil 2015).

Africa represents a major front in the global proliferation of SALWs which has fueled a host of conflict flashpoints on the continent. On February 5, 2020, the UN reports that globally, "half of all violent deaths involve small arms and light weapons," and that "one billion small arms are in circulation worldwide, and that their use in lethal violence is prevalent from the Americas, to Africa and Southern Europe … The illicit flow of small arms is

---

U. A. Tar (✉)
Centre for Defence Studies and Documentation, Nigerian Defence Academy, Kaduna, Nigeria
e-mail: uatar@nda.edu.ng

© The Author(s), under exclusive license to Springer Nature Switzerland AG 2021
U. A. Tar and C. P. Onwurah (eds.), *The Palgrave Handbook of Small Arms and Conflicts in Africa*,
https://doi.org/10.1007/978-3-030-62183-4_2

having a serious impact, including in relation to violent extremism, throughout the African Sahel region, and parts of Central Africa, warned the disarmament chief. This is a cause for serious concern in war-torn Libya and South Sudan, both of which are seeing a steady influx of weapons and ammunition" (United Nations News 2020: paras. 1, 3 and 4). By all accounts, Africa experiences the worst trend in global arms transfer and proliferation of small arms, with disastrous consequences on national, regional, and global security. Worse still, Africa seems to be at the receiving end of a complex global arms economy as captured in the following accounts:

> The global small arms and light weapons (SALW) market size was valued over USD 18.70 billion in 2015. The increasing civilian interest in various sports such as shooting and self-defense are expected to boost market growth for small arms weapons. The rising incidents of armed violence and terrorism has led the civilians to procure the weapons for self-defense purposes. Various law enforcement and military agencies have also invested heavily in the industry globally for acquiring advanced weapon systems which include pistols, rifles, and shotguns. (*Grand View Research* 2017)

> Although proliferation of small arms generates a lot of money for those who manufacture and trade them, African people pay a heavy price due to a lack of accountability or international regulations to address the abuses those products cause… nations such as France, Russia, China, UK and USA – the five permanent members of the UN Security Council—together account for 88 percent of the world's conventional arms exports. These exports contribute regularly to gross abuses of human rights in Africa and elsewhere. (*Africa Faith and Justice Network* 2020)

The cessation of Cold War has confronted Africa with increase in trade and circulation of Small Arms and Light Weapons (SALWs) from the stockpile of arms at the disposal of weak states, at the end of the hostility between the two power blocs. These weapons gained entrance into Africa's conflict hotspots through unlicensed exports, clandestine gun-running, criminal organizations, private (security) entrepreneurs/companies, or through the activity of local blacksmiths within the continent (Asoba and Glokpor 2014; Garcia 2006; Abrahamsen and Williams 2011). Myriad of unwavering conflicts and instabilities have bedeviled the global South as a whole and the continent in particular. Governments, institutions as well as individuals within the continent periodically report of deaths linked to SALWs but the fact remains that, since 1990, Africa has lost count of death, destruction of property and crimes associated with SALWs (UNICEF 2001; Fleshman 2011). With the possibility of all entry points into Africa being the trafficking routes, the Inter-Governmental Action Group Against Money Laundering in West Africa—GIABA reported in 2013 that over 4,364,690 SALWs are in circulation within and outside West Africa alone outside known interceptions by security agencies at various entry points (Ayissi and Sall 2005; UN Report 2010). The porous nature of

African borders, including the continents ancient and modern transit countries and routes; limited intelligence, record, and control by governments on the activities of their citizens within and outside Africa; collaboration between small arms racketeers and criminally minded law enforcement agents and disparaging incrimination of illegal possessors provided a franchise for these weapons as items in shrouded trades and used in the consummation of violence, intimidation, conflicts, scores, and wars (Lumpe et al. 2000; Marsh 2002).

SALWs proliferation is a phenomenon that exists at communal, national, regional, and international levels, and needs to be tackled at all levels simultaneously. African states have through these levels keyed into arms control regimes such as: Program for Coordination and Assistance for Security and Development in Africa (PCASED) of the United Nations; Interstate Defence and Security Committee (ISDSC) of the Southern Africa Regional governments; and Ghana National Commission on Small Arms (GNCSA) of the Ghanaian national government in places where ideas on non-proliferation of arms; gun-licensing; and arms destruction revolve around local initiative on containing the entry, acquisition, and circulatory rate of weapons in the continent without any tangible result (Ayissi and Sall 2005; Okoro 2012).

This chapter aims to provide a broad overview of the nature and dynamics of conflicts and complex emergencies in Africa, and illuminate the role of SALWs in exacerbating Africa's conflicts. The chapter argues that the nature of the state and the character of Africa's elites define the root causes and complexities of conflicts on the continent. It is argued that crisis of governance and legitimacy provide the fillip for structural imbalances in political, economic, sociocultural, and behavioral spheres, thus creating lack of confidence on the formal state. By extension, when pushed to the precipice of poverty and marginalization, marginal elites and citizens challenges the state—including through armed rebellion—as a show of political expression. The chapter is divided into three broad parts. The introduction is followed by sect. "Africa's Terrains of Conflicts, Complex Emergencies and Insecurity" which provides a broad analysis of the nature, scope, and dynamics of conflict, complex emergencies, and insecurity in Africa. Section "Small Arms and Conflicts in Africa" conducts a root and branch analysis of the problematics of SALWs proliferation in Africa.

AFRICA'S TERRAINS OF CONFLICTS, COMPLEX EMERGENCIES, AND INSECURITY

> Africa has earned a negative niche as the region of civil wars, lawlessness and dictatorships. Though the all-too familiar derogatory metaphors ... are slightly reversed, particularly since 2000s following substantial democratic transformation, the continent continuous to experience spates of intra- and inter-state wars

with impact on the prospects of peace, stability and security in the continent. (Abdulrahman and Tar 2008: 185)

Armed violence has defined the politics and nation-building in postcolonial Africa (Anderson and Øystein 2014). A recent study by the Peace Research Institute, Oslo (PRIO) conducted 2018–2019, based on data covering 1989–2018, reveals the complexity of Africa's conflicts:

> In the past five years, there has been an increase in the number of conflicts in Africa. This holds for state-based conflicts,[1] non-state conflicts,[2] and one-sided violence.[3] While the number of civil wars and conflict-affected countries have increased in 2018, the number of battle deaths have decreased considerably. In 2018, the conflict over the Ambazonia in Cameroon escalated dramatically [adding a new candidate to the conflict scenarios on the continent]. Although conflict numbers are high, it is important to note that most of these conflicts are geographically restrained. First, the number of countries experiencing conflict is lower than the number of conflicts. Second, within conflict-affected countries, conflict takes place in limited geographical areas and rarely throughout the whole country. (Rustad and Bakken 2019, emphasis in parenthesis added)

The PRIO report shows a mixture of disturbing and consoling trends. On the one hand, it reveals that "the number of conflict countries has previously been comparably low, in 2018 the number reached an all-time high." On the other hand, "the high number of conflicts has not been followed by a substantial increase in number of battle-related deaths; rather, 2018 has seen a substantial decrease, suggesting that the level of intensity remains relatively low." Therefore, the report concludes, "many countries on the African continent struggle with several parallel conflicts. However, the picture indicated by these conflict trends is by no means straightforward." The report further advises that "when discussing recent conflict trends, policy makers, scholars, civil society and media should be aware of the nuances and avoid simplifying. Indeed, the decrease in battle deaths and the stabilizing of the number of non-state conflicts suggests that the level of conflict in most countries is low. Furthermore, the ceasefires data suggests that there is a high level of dialogue and attempts to solve conflicts" (Rustad and Bakken 2019). An earlier study of the PRIO covering a longer period, 1946–2017 (Bakken and Rustad 2018) sheds some finer details (see Table 2.1).

Africa is a home of complex emergencies, defined as a situation characterized by precipitous and violent contest over state power, breakdown of law and order, humanitarian crisis and, in extreme circumstances, total collapse of the state as exemplified by Somalia in 1990s (Aboagye 2009). Africa is often depicted as "ground zero" in global spread of complex emergencies, a situation that was heightened from the end of the Cold War onward (de Souza 2016). Africa's chronic display of complex emergencies was painted by the former UN Secretary General's report to the United Nations Security Council (UNSC) of 1998 titled *the causes of conflict and the promotion of durable peace*

Table 2.1 Summary of PRIO Conflict Trends in Africa, 2017

Serial	Factor	Key observations
1.	State-based conflicts	• Decrease in conflicts in the mid-2000s, followed by a dramatic increase in the past few years, with an all-time high of 21 conflicts in 2016 (20 civil wars and 1 interstate war) • In 2017, Africa had 18 state-based conflicts, all which were civil conflicts. However, a feature of the new conflicts in 2015, 2016, and 2017 is that many of them are related to the rise of IS. Moreover, IS is gaining traction in already ongoing Islamic conflicts, such as the conflicts around Lake Chad. Thus, the conflict in Northern Nigeria is no longer just a conflict between the Nigerian government and Boko Haram, but also between the Nigerian government and IS • Five of the state-based conflicts in Africa were related to IS (Chad, Libya, Mali, Nigeria, Niger). The fact that an external actor like the IS is able to gain this much traction in internal conflicts is a very worrisome development • Nigeria, Somalia and DR Congo account for 70% of all the battle-related deaths in state-based conflict. Both Nigeria and DR Congo have two conflicts each, i.e. two rebel groups fighting the government
2.	Non-state conflicts	• The number of non-state conflicts has increased dramatically over the last five to six years, peaking in 2017 with 50 conflicts • In 2017, only 11 countries experienced non-state conflict in Africa, which was the same number as in 2016. Among these, Nigeria, South Sudan, and the Central African Republic had the highest number of non-state conflicts
3.	On-sided conflicts	• A large peak in fatalities in 1994, which reflects the genocide in Rwanda • A peak around 1995 and 1996, which is related to the conflicts in DR Congo and Burundi • A substantial increase in one-sided violence since 2012. By far the worst perpetrator during this period was Boko Haram in Northeastern Nigeria

(continued)

Table 2.1 (continued)

Serial	Factor	Key observations
4.	Geographical extent of conflicts	• Most conflicts are geographically limited … in most cases, only a small part of a country is directly affected by conflict
		• Conflicts do not affect the entire country, and are often geographically limited to a relatively small area. Only in a few countries, like Somalia, do we see that the conflict covers large parts country
5.	State failure and Coup D'etat	• The number of failed states seems to have been decreasing during the past three decades. Even if we see a slight increase toward the end of the 2000s, this dropped again in 2016
		• The number of coups d'état, both failed and successful. In general, there is a downward trend, from the early 1990s until today
		• The number of states categorized as extremely fragile in Africa has decreased from 1995 to 2016. The pattern also reveals that some countries have improved slightly, while the number of moderately fragile states has increased. However, most African countries still score relatively high on this indicator, with countries with low or little fragility remaining at a very low number
6.	Conflict incompatibility	• This covers two types of incompatibilities: conflicts over government and conflicts over territory
		• Until 2015, the share of governmental conflicts was higher than the share of territorial conflicts in most years
		• In recent years, however, we see a sharp increase in territorial conflicts, and the share of territorial conflicts compared to governmental conflicts is approximately a 1:1 relationship
		a peak of territorial conflicts in 2015. The number declined in 2016 and 2017, but the number of conflicts is still higher in 2017 than during the period 1989–2014

Source Bakken and Rustad (2018: 1–28)

and sustainable development in Africa. In that Report, Mr Kofi Annan stated that "… 14 of the continent's 53 countries were afflicted by armed conflict in 1996 alone, and over 30 wars have occurred … since 1970, mostly within states. These accounted for more than half of all the war-related deaths worldwide and caused over 8 million people to become refugees, returnees and displaced persons" (UN 1998, para. 4, page 3). The 2014 report of the UN Secretary General to the 69th Session of General Assembly painted a slightly different—but no less grim—picture. This time, the report noted a mixture of economic growth, democratic peace, and precipitous descent to conflicts in some African countries:

> African countries have made tangible progress in reforming their economies, boosting economic growth, improving governance and respect for the rule of law, and managing and resolving conflicts …While these positive trends have created a favourable climate for investment and a new spirit of optimism about Africa's prospects, there have also been some reversals. In the Central African Republic, Libya, Mali, Nigeria, Somalia and South Sudan, renewed hostilities and threats from growing acts of terrorism, violent extremism and transnational organized crime have resulted in challenges to both peace and development. (UN 2014: 3/21)

Worse still, the 2019 report of the UN Secretary General provides an even more grim reality:

> The overall security situation across the continent also remained a serious concern, owing to growing threats from insurgency, extremism, terrorism, transnational organized crime and intercommunal violence, exacerbated by the effects of climate change and environmental degradation, especially in the Sahel and the Horn of Africa… Insurgency, terrorism and violent extremism remained persistent threats to peace and security, human rights protection and sustainable development in Africa… There was an increase in the geographical scope and frequency of the activities of insurgent, extremist and terrorist groups … Upticks in intercommunal violence and individual, group, social and structural vulnerabilities were also exploited to advance their causes. Their expansion and sustainment was, and continues to be, enabled by the malicious use of new technologies and links to organized criminal networks that provide financing and logistical support. (UN 2019: 5–6/19)

Thus, the UN reports (1998, 2014, 2019) have consistently painted a gloomy picture of the conflict situation in Africa. In all the reports mentioned earlier, there is consistent reference to the failure of the state and its governing institutions to provide the basis for good governance, accountability, and due process as baseline conditions for institution-building, equitable distribution of power and resource, and conflict management and resolution. The nature of the state, and the performance of the local comprador elites account for Africa's grotesque flurry of conflicts on the continent. With few exceptions, most African states and elites have failed to build the basis for national legitimacy, patriotism and integration. Instead, certain demographic constituencies are spurred by their marginalized elites to confront the state. In the first instance, African states are not cast in the mold of their counterparts in Europe, Eurasia, Nordic region, Baltics, or North America. They are new creations facing structural challenges:

> The modern state system in Sub-Saharan Africa … is relatively new; only Ethiopia, Liberia, and South Africa were recognized as independent states prior to 1950 and most states in the region only gained their independence since 1960. For the most part, the economies of the African states at the time of their ascensions to independent status were primarily extractive and mainly directed toward trade with the extra-regional system. There was little or no industrial or service economic capacities in place at independence, except in South Africa. (Marshall 2005: 1)

A key dilemma confronting most African states is the capture of national power by an elite base that has failed to provide a broad-based structure of governance, development, and security. Instead, over time the state became an instrument for patronage and marginalization—especially of real and perceived enemies who are deprived of access to basic constitutional rights and privileges. Marginalized elites found it expedient to challenge the state with a view to either seceding from the state or, use marginal politics—described by Celestine Monga as "anthropology of anger"—as a bargaining chip for negotiation for power (Monga 1996; see also Poroma and Iwuoha 2018; Onuoha 2011). In the case of secessionist politics, the elites have set up guerilla movements or a "parallel state"—as in the case of South Sudan (1958–2011), South East Nigeria (1967–1970), and Cameroon (1980 to present)—to divide and distabilise the formal state. On the other hand, in some African countries—such as Zimbabwe (2000s) and Kenya (2000s)—the marginalized elites opted for negotiated arrangements that only provided tokenistic palliative and defer the conflicts for another day (Knight and Özerdem 2004). In any case, African elites and the states that they control have conspired to ensure that conflicts remain a permanent feature of politics and nation-building (Fearon and Laitin 2003; Gurr and Marshall 2000). This reality brings into the questions the pacifist and patriotic content of the African elites: "the circumstance of African history conspired to produce an elite which could not function because it had no sense of identity or integrity and no confidence, did not know where it was coming from or where it was going" (Ake 1985: 1212).

Africa's experience in democratic experiment is fuzzy, as democratic practice has not significantly reversed the volumes and intensities of conflict on the continent: "experiments in democratic forms of governance in Africa were relatively rare and short-lived during the Cold War period… In the late 1980s, over eighty-five percent of African countries were governed by personalistic, bureaucratic, or military dictatorships... By 1992, the number of autocracies in Africa had fallen by half and continued to decline through the 1990s, reaching a low of five in 2000" (Marshall 2005: 8). Though African countries experienced sustained period of continuous democratic rule the 1990s and 2000s, the risk of relapse remained high, while quite a few states have experienced real relapse and collapse of established democratic structures—such as Congo Brazaville (1990s), Central African Republic (2000s), Rwanda (1994), Cape Verde (2000s), and Sierra Leone (1990s). While many African democracies are improving in terms of their capacities for managing conflicts, the objective reality and structural imbalances in most states have not significantly yielded the so-called "democratic peace" (Musa 2002). For instance, Nigeria returned to democratic rule in 1999 after nearly two decades of military rule. The instrumental character of the state has not changed even after return to democracy. If anything, the democratic system was captured by a toxic combination of elites drawn from the military, professional politicians, the bureaucracy technocrats, private sector financiers who have conspired to control power and usurp the state of its social provisioning potentials. The restoration of democracy, it seems, actually resulted in increased intensification of existing conflicts (Niger Delta, communal clashes) and efflorescence of newer forms of conflicts and insurgencies—violent extremism in the Northeast, organized criminal gangs in the Northwest, farmer–herders conflict in the Benue Trough, and virulent strands of successionist movements (such as Niger Delta Avengers, Ooduwa Peoples Congress). The key factors that underpin the failure of the democratic state in Nigeria to provide democratic peace include: the failure of the elite to provide the dividend of democracy as a result of the failure of the three arms of the government to achieve cooperative separation of power; corruption in public service and the armed forces especially with regard to procurement of arms and ammunition; and alleged support for violence and insurgency by external actors who are hostile to the Nigerian State. Elsewhere in the Horn of Africa, the Kenyan example shows that a stable democracy may be handicapped in enforcing peace in a violent neighborhood, with significant implications for democratic stability: a daring raid by the Kenyan armed forces named *Operation Linda Nchi* to upstage and "liquidate" Al-Shabaab in neighboring Somalia, which received parliamentary approval, only achieved momentary success, as Al-Shabaab was soon back on its feet to cause mayhem and fear in the horn of Africa (Anderson and McKnight 2015: 1–27).

The rise of *violent extremism* presents a new sinister front of conflicts and wars in Africa. Africa is home to a bevy of terrorist groups which are affiliated to cells in the Middle East and elsewhere. Africa's experience in terrorism and violent extremism is not unconnected with the structural imbalance in state: the failure of the state to provide a solid base for national patriotism; the imbalances in distribution and power and resources; failure in the management of religion and proselytization in the public domain; and failure in public infrastructure—especially education, health, agriculture, water, and transport—have created general apathy and anger in society. So, when violent ideologies surfaced in Africa with promise of mundane and afterlife promises, there was a large reserve of angry and poverty-stricken citizens waiting to join up the jihadi movements. A recent study by the United Nations Development Programme Regional Bureau for Africa reveals the complexity of factors that underpin citizens' recruitment to violent extremist platforms in Africa:

> Long-standing realities of 'centre/periphery' divides have, if anything, been exacerbated by the recent economic growth enjoyed overall in Africa…a sense of grievance towards, and limited confidence in, government is widespread in the regions of Africa associated with the highest incidence of violent extremism. This may be an inevitable corollary of the life experience of growing up in the context of acute and relative multidimensional poverty, neglect and political marginalization affecting these areas… The *Journey to Extremism* research unequivocally underscores the relevance of economic factors as drivers of recruitment. The grievances associated with growing up in contexts where multidimensional poverty is high and far deeper than national averages, with the lived reality of unemployment and underemployment, render 'economic factors' a major source of frustration identified by those who joined violent extremist groups. (UNDP 2017: 4–5)

A number of violent extremist groups have transformed from benign preaching bands and sleeper cells into formidable armed insurgency and terrorist platforms. Key examples include in *Boko Haram* (Nigeria) whose splinter has expressed alliance with ISIS and adopted the austere name of Islamic State in West African Province (ISWAP); *Al-Shabaab* (Horn of Africa); and *Al-Qaeda in the Maghreb* (north Africa). These groups have challenged the host states and, in some cases, conquered state's territory and converted them into caliphates. Though most of these groups operate as highly mobile and nebulous armed groups relying on guerilla tactics of hit and run, but tarrying awhile to steal and plunder before escaping back to the jungle, some are bold enough to organize themselves into prolific organizations with command and control; steady flow of arms and terror finances from local and foreign sources; and secure permanent staging camps and forward operating bases for keeping the host states on their toes. The armed forces of many African countries have developed local and regional architecture for counterterrorism and counterinsurgency (CT-COIN), but so far this has proved to be a herculean task (Tar and Bala 2020; Tar 2021).

Box 1. Drivers of Conflicts in Africa
Instability associated with state formation

1. *Political Factionalism*, distinct political, and/or social identity groups polarize and promote incompatible or uncompromising political platforms prioritizing parochial interests and creating a contentious atmosphere in which negotiated solutions to policy differences are difficult to achieve; political deadlock, coercive practices, and inequitable policy outcomes are common under such circumstances (in more democratic systems),
2. *Elite Ethnicity, or Ethnic Group Capture of the State*, ethnicity is politically salient among ruling elites and members of the ruling ethnic group(s) are strongly favored in the distribution of political positions and, especially, in command positions in the military, often including restrictions on political access and activities of other constituent ethnic groups (in more autocratic systems)

Instability associated with post-formation—that is, postcolonial—era:

3. *Dependency*, governments that are overly dependent on foreign aid and foreign trade for operating revenues (foreign aid as a percent of gross capital formation; foreign aid per capita; trade openness; high export duties, low government revenues, low investment);
4. *Polarization*, societies that have politicized and mobilized social identity constituencies through inequitable use of public policies, particularly in regard to ethnic differences (official policies of political discrimination or repression of constituent ethnic groups; ethnic group capture of the state; political factionalism);
5. *Unmanageability*, countries that must manage large territories, particularly those with substantial forested regions; concentrated, high density, populations; or contentious social divisions institutionalized during conflicts over the original terms of state formation (state formation instability; high population density; large land area; high percentage of forest cover);
6. *Leadership Succession*, states where the political process is overly dependent on key personalities are highly susceptible to succession struggles, leading to instability (top ranking political leader in power for twenty years or more);
7. *Neighborhood Effects*, weak states not only have trouble managing internal political dynamics, they are highly vulnerable to negative external influences from repressive or unstable neighboring countries (less democratic neighbors; societal war in at least one neighboring country); and
8. *Islamic Countries* (countries with Muslim populations comprising forty or more percent of the country's population), only one-third of Islamic countries in Africa experienced state formation instability

> but seventy percent have experienced post-formation instability; on the other hand, sixty-four percent of non-Islamic countries experienced state formation instability with only one-third experiencing post-formation instability.
>
> *Source* Marshall (2005: 21–23).

SMALL ARMS AND CONFLICTS IN AFRICA

The persistence and the complication of wars in Africa are partially due to small arms proliferation. The consequences of small arms on African people due to international conflicts within Africa, rebel group activities, mercenary groups, and armed gang activities have yet to be fully measured. (*Africa Faith and Justice Network* 2020)

There are guns everywhere. We don't produce guns here. They are all smuggled into our community. Guns are cheap. It can be easily hidden. The insurgents, kidnappers and militant can lay their hands on them. Anyone with a gun can do whatever he wants. The insurgents were spurred by the possession of guns and other dangerous instruments. We are displaced. Our farms have been mined. We cannot farm or feed ourselves any more. We are at the mercy of the insurgents, poverty and hunger. (Kyari 2020)

The frontiers of small arms proliferation and conflicts in Africa are highly interconnected, contested, and volatile (Eavis 2002; Kiugu 2012). Small arms have changed the terrain, dynamism, and intensities of conflicts, and blurred the potentials for managing conflict across Africa. For instance, in northern Kenya, the proliferation of small arms changed local dynamics among nomadic and farming communities within a short time:

> ... in less than a generation the pastoral Pokot people and their neighbours have gone from protecting their herds with spears to outfitting their young men with cheap, reliable and deadly automatic rifles from the war zones of Somalia, Ethiopia and Sudan. The impact of modern military weapons on the Pokot and surrounding communities was brought tragically home in early 2001, when Pokot youth opened fire on a rival settlement, killing 47 people, burning down the village and transforming the almost-ceremonial tradition of cattle raiding into an occasion for human slaughter. (Fleshman 2011, para. 1)

For the most part, Africa's conflicts are propelled by imported small arms. However, some countries have had local technological capacity for producing small arms, but these arms have always been low grade, some are even archaic, while some are produced in small quantities. Again, it is important to note the variation between precolonial, colonial, and postcolonial era. During the precolonial era, African societies relied on a mixture of improvised and imported firearms mainly for survival, but also for conducing raids and invasion of vulnerable communities. Further, the precolonial political formations in Africa—such as the Buganda kingdom in modern-day Uganda; Zulu Kingdoms in southern African; Kanem-Bornu Empire, and the Sokoto Caliphate in modern-day Nigeria—relied heavily on local production and usage of small arms for empire building. Wars were fought or lost on the strength of arms stockpile and the men to deploy them (see Chapter 25 in this *Handbook*). During the colonial era, modern and far more lethal variations of small arms were introduced by the European colonial powers—Britain, Belgium, France, Italy, Germany, Portugal, Spain—with the aim of colonizing the kingdoms and acephalous states of Africa. African kingdoms were easily subdued using a mixture of foreign firearms and locally recruited forces. Thus, all that the Europeans powers did was to dispatch sufficient catches of arms and ammunition under the care of a small detachment of colonial regiments to Africa. Paradoxically, the colonial state raised its armed forces within the African tribal formations and deployed them to capture or subdue African kingdoms. It could thus be argued that the proliferation of small arms constituted the single most important factor in the colonial conquest of Africa (see Chapters 4 and 25 in this volume). The colonial basis of African conflicts is captured by Cohen (1995: 11): "the modern African state was created by colonial powers out of ethnic and regional diversities, and rendered conflictual by gross inequities in power relations and in uneven distribution of national wealth and development opportunities."

Box 2. Recent Trends in Small Arms Flow in African States 2019

Recent study jointly conducted by the African Union and Small Arms Survey revealed the following findings:
- AU member states identify the trafficking of arms and ammunition across land borders as the main type of illicit flow they are confronted with. Armed groups, including terrorist organizations, have demonstrated their capacity to move weapons across borders or carry out attacks.
- While the pool of illicit weapons in Africa remains dominated by old, often cold war era models and makes, seizures of recent models of varied origins point to new and emerging sources of small arms for the armed and criminal actors active on the continent.
- External sources of illicit small arms include embargo-breaking transfers from the Middle East and Eastern Europe, the trade in readily convertible imitation firearms, and the diversion of recently authorized

> imports of both arms and ammunition. Some of this equipment is diverted quickly to armed groups after reaching African soil.
> - Regional sources of illicit weapons include the trafficking of already illegal weapons across borders; the diversion of national stockpiles—including stockpiles held by peacekeeping forces—and civilian holdings through theft, loss, or corruption; and the production of craft or artisanal firearms. Craft-produced firearms on the continent range from rudimentary pistols and shotguns to sophisticated assault-type rifles.
> - Because data on illicit weapons holdings is scarce, currently the magnitude of the phenomenon can at best only be very roughly estimated. It is, however, better understood in a limited number of countries that have undertaken nationwide assessments and that rely on multiple sources of information and methods for gathering data.
> - As both the AU Roadmap and the relevant subregional conventions exemplify, AU member states have showed strong political will to tackle the scourge of illicit weapons flows. The practical steps identified in the AU Roadmap, notably capacity building for states in the areas of stockpile management, record keeping and tracing, and the destruction of illicit firearms, can contribute to reducing the threat. An important challenge lies in prioritizing, coordinating, and implementing these commitments and initiatives.
> - AU member states' participation in international information-sharing platforms that can help to provide critical weapons-trafficking intelligence has been very limited to date. Prioritizing this area has the potential to provide the continent with timely and actionable information on new and emerging trends in illicit firearms trafficking.
> - The continent has hosted innovative interventions, notably in the areas of weapons collection in (post-)conflict settings, joint border initiatives, and end-user controls, that merit further dissemination and development into practical guidelines.
>
> *Source* Small Arms Survey (2019: 16)

After independence in 1960s,[4] African states—which by then were a contested assemblage of ethnic nationalities wielded together as citizens or "strange bed fellows" in newly formed and arbitrarily named states[5]—experienced the problems of fragmentation and armed conflicts in profound ways, both in the state and non-state sectors. As Achankeng (2013) argues, "the concern of the colonial masters at independence and beyond, for the most part, was to hand power to a group of cronies whose mission was always not to 'govern their people well' but to protect the interest of the metropole. In this regard, many political leaders of Africa, especially those in in the former French colonies, were and continued to be imposed on upon the people with almost no consideration for good governance." The crisis of legitimacy associated with the state and the rise of civil wars and domestic insurrections meant that both the state and violent non-state actors (VNSAs) have had to resort to armament to engage in war of attrition. These wars are essentially intra-state, and asymmetric in nature, and there is little or no accountability both on the conduct of the wars, as well as the usage of arms and ammunition. Lack of accountability meant that all sides of conflict are not willing to subject themselves to wars of armed conflict, or the legitimate use of arms. As the experiences of Sierra Leone and Liberia in the 1990s have shown, total collapse of law and order allowed the state armed forces and VNSAs to operate with relative impunity and, in the process, cause maximum havoc on the economy and society (Collier and Hoeffler 2004; Montague 2002). The carnage unleashed in most of African conflict zones is largely perpetrated with the use of small arms (Table 2.2).

Throughout the Cold War (especially 1960s–1990s), African countries engaged in proxy battles on behalf of global superpowers—but too often such conflicts were glazed in local nuances and elites struggles for power. Such battles were played out using free flow of arms and ammunition supplied clandestinely by the superpowers (Duffield 1991, 1994). According to Fleshman (2011):

Table 2.2 Small arms and ammunition manufacturing capacities in Africa

Subregion	AU member states with reported ongoing or recent production of small arms or ammunition	
	Small arms	Ammunition
Northern Africa	Algeria Egypt Sudan	Algeria Egypt Sudan
Western Africa	Nigeria	Cameroon Mali Nigeria
Middle Africa	Democratic Republic of the Congo (DRC)[a]	Angola Chad[a] DRC Republic of Congo
Eastern Africa	Ethiopia[a] Kenya[a] Tanzania Uganda[a] Zimbabwe	Ethiopia Kenya Madagascar Tanzania Uganda Zimbabwe
Southern Africa	South Africa	Namibia South Africa

[a] Unconfirmed/uncertain
Source Small Arms Survey (2019: 27)

Millions of light arms – lightweight, highly portable, and devastatingly effective in the hands of even young or poorly trained users – were shipped to Africa during the Cold War to equip anti-colonial fighters, newly independent states and superpower proxy forces alike. The collapse of the Soviet bloc saw a new flood of small arms entering Africa as manufacturers put additional millions of surplus Cold War-era weapons on the international arms market at cut-rate prices. (Fleshman 2011: para. 4)

Several violent scenarios could be discerned: *interstate wars* (such as Uganda–Tanzania in 1980s); *civil wars* (such as the Nigerian civil war of 1967–1970; Chadian civil war of 1980–1990s); *communal violence*; and *violent extremist wars* (see Fig. 2.1). In the post-cold war era (1990s–2020s), the spectrum of armed violence and small arms proliferations have assumed a more dynamic and macabre dimension. The participants in African conflicts have increased and diversified—for instance, foreign mercenaries are increasingly visible in conflicts in Nigeria, Somalia, and Mali. At the same time, the volume of small

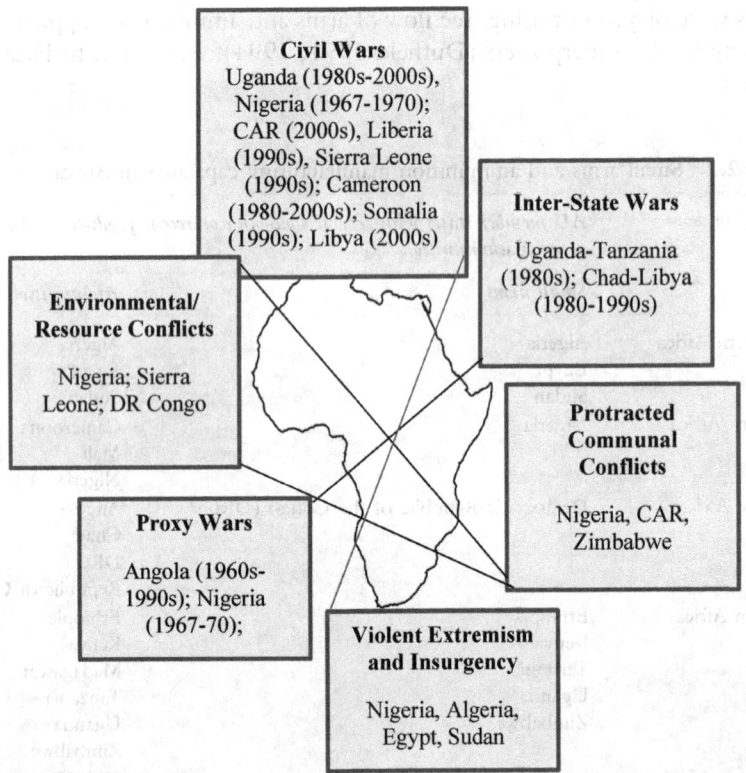

Fig. 2.1 Armed conflict and associated violence in postcolonial Africa (*Source* Author 2020)

arms coming into African conflict spots, or those produced within the continent, have exponentially diversified, while the level of transparency in reporting stockpiles have been below global thresholds. As a recent joint study of the Small Arms Survey and African Union reveals:

> … data on both licit and illicitly held weapons is hard to come by both globally and – notably so – in Africa. Of the 21 states that responded to the Small Arms Survey–AU questionnaire, only 9 provided an official count of registered firearms, while 4 offered estimates of registrations. Eight countries provided estimates of illicitly held firearms elaborated by national authorities, subregional organizations, or research institutions such as the Small Arms Survey … This means that among the responding states, fewer than half were able to provide any figures or estimates on the licit and illicit firearms held by civilian actors in their countries. (Small Arms Survey 2019; see also Table 2.3)

In addition to artisanal production—which accounts for a tiny fraction of stockpile in Africa—current data shows that majority of Africa's stockpile of small arms emanate from imports from USA, China, Brazil, Russia, and Ukraine, and local production. This is largely because of the efficiency, affordability, portability, concealability, and sophistication of foreign-made small arms relative to local variants: "In some parts of Africa, a Soviet-designed AK-47 assault rifle, coveted for its simplicity and firepower, can be purchased for as little as $6, or traded for a chicken or sack of grain. In 1999 the Red Cross estimated that in the Somali capital of Mogadishu alone, the city's 1.3 million residents possessed over a million guns – among an estimated 550 mn small arms in circulation worldwide" (Fleshman 2011). Table 2.2 reveals a number of glaring facts: first, across Africa there is significant capacity for local production, which appears to be underpinned by lucrative profits that accrues from such production. There is a flurry of arms production facilities in every region of the continent, but this is often under-reported: foreign sources and "merchants of violence"[6] are often pointed for the problems of SALWs in Africa. Secondly, most of these production facilities are owned by

Table 2.3 Estimated African subregional distribution of civilian firearms, 2017

Subregion	Population	Number of civilian-held firearms	Civilian-held firearms per 100 population
Africa total	1,246,505,000	40,009,000	3.2
Eastern Africa	416,676,000	7,802,000	1.9
Middle Africa	161,237,000	4,981,000	3.1
Northern Africa	232,186,000	10,241,000	4.4
Southern Africa	63,854,000	6,012,000	9.4
Western Africa	372,551,000	10,972,000	2.9

Source Small Arms Survey (2018)

the state-owned military-industrial complexes. For instance, in Nigeria, the Defence Industry Corporation of Nigeria (DICON) enjoys monopoly of arms production solely for the consumption of the national military and paramilitary forces. In addition, Nigeria's Office of the National Security Adviser (ONSA) is empowered to monitor and regulate inflow of armament by issuing end-user certificates for arsenals that are imported into the country, thus putting a steep obstacle on import and local use. However, in spite the appearance of a rigid national regulation on the local production or control of small arms, loopholes in state bureaucracy—especially the existence of corrupt officials and theft from state armouries—have created a situation in which large quantities of SALWs find their way into wrong hands, including local criminal gangs, armed militias, insurgents and other VNSAs who challenge the state. Thirdly, globalization has created an added layer in the foggy scenario of SALWs and conflict in Africa. By breaking down political, economic, and territorial boundaries, globalization has provided easy access to SALWs, mercenaries and terror finance. Through clandestine means of terror finance and "black markets," (Austin 2002) armed militias and criminal gangs can bypass state restrictions to procure arms and ammunitions (Shettima 2021; Osiki 2021; Delmas 1997).

Notes

1. This is defined as "conflict where at least one of the actors is state government." For instance, violent conflict between the Boko Haram Insurgents and the Nigerian state which commenced in 2009 and continues to intensify. "In 2018, Africa experienced 21 state-based conflicts. This is a return to the all-time high in 2015 and 2016. Globally, we saw a decrease from 2017 to 2018…In 2018, the number of conflict-affected countries rose from 14 in 2017 to 17 in 2018. This is the second highest number since 1946, only surpassed by 2016 with 18 countries. This suggests that while the conflict areas are still geographically limited […], there is an increasing number of conflict-affected countries." (Rustad and Bakken 2019).
2. This is defined as defined as a "conflict fought between two organized groups, neither of which is related to the state" (Rustad and Bakken 2019). For instance, conflict between splinter factions of the Boko Haram Sect in Northeast Nigeria. "In Africa, the number of non-state conflicts has increased dramatically over the last five to six years, peaking in 2017 with 50 non-state conflicts, compared to 24 in 2011. In 2018, the number has decreased to 46. This makes Africa the continent with the highest number of non-state conflicts. The levels of battle deaths in non-state conflicts is stable from 4609 in 2017 to 4649 in 2018" (Rustad and Bakken 2019).
3. This refers to "violence against civilians by a formally organized group, which can be either the state or a non-state actor" (Rustad and Bakken 2019). This happens where civilians become victims of extrajudicial killings by either or both factions of fighting forces. "There has been substantial increase in the number of actors carrying out one-sided violence since 2012. The worst perpetrator by far during this period was Boko Haram in Northeastern Nigeria. We see a quite

substantial decrease in one-sided violence from 2017 to 2018 (3850 to 2350)" (Rustad and Bakken 2019).
4. Most African countries achieved their independence in 1960s described by many as the "year of Africa" with sixteen countries achieving their independence in this year alone. However, some achieved their independence before that year (e.g., Egypt, Ghana), while many more achieved their sovereignty in the subsequent years (e.g. Zimbabwe, 1980, Namibia 1990). The Sahrawi Arab Democratic Republic which was relinquished by her erstwhile colonialist, Spain in 1975 and later conquered by her neighbor Morocco, has not yet secured her independence. For recent reflection on 60 years of independence in Africa, see *New York Times* (2020) "Reflections on 1960: The Year of Africa." Available: https://www.nytimes.com/interactive/2020/02/06/world/africa/africa-independence-year.html accessed 10 July 2020.
5. For instance, Nigeria was derived from "Niger Area" and named so by Lady Flora Shaw the spouse of Lord Frederick Luggard. Nigerians were never consulted in inventing this austere name for them. Similar arbitrary stories abound in almost all African countries.
6. There is a network of arm sellers both within Africa and overseas who participate in the business of arms supply to African conflict hotspots. The value chain of arms sellers is perpetuated by clandestine support and patronage of state officials who profit from the network, but also use them as a conduit for supply of the arms and ammunition to state armories. Africa's merchants of violence are not driven by any ethical standards, and lack of transparency in governance have ensured a brisk business for these networks.

REFERENCES

Abdulrahman, I., & Tar, U. A. (2008, June). Conflict Management and Peacebuilding in Africa: The Role of State and Non-State Agencies. *Information, Society and Justice, 1*(2), 185–202.

Aboagye, F. B. (2009). *Confronting Complex Emergencies in Africa Imperatives of a Search for a New Doctrine of Humanitarian 'Security' Interventions* (Institute for Security Studies Paper #204). Available https://www.files.ethz.ch/isn/111693/P204.pdf. Accessed 20 April 2020.

Abrahamsen, R., & Williams, C. M. (2011). *Security Beyond the State: Private Security in International Politics*. New York: Cambridge University Press.

Achankeng, F. (2013). *Conflict and Resolution in Africa: Engaging the Colonial Factor*. IJCR 2013/2. Available https://www.accord.org.za/ajcr-issues/conflict-and-conflict-resolution-in-africa/. Accessed 10 July 2020.

Africa Faith and Justice Network. (2020, June). *Impact of Small Arms Proliferation on Africa*. Available https://afjn.org/impact-of-small-arms-proliferation-on-africa/. Accessed 17 June 2020.

Ake, C. (1985). Why Is Africa Not Developing? *West Africa, 1985*, 1212–1212.

Anderson, D. M., & McKnight, Jacob. (2015). Kenya at War: Al-Shabaab and Its Enemies in Eastern Africa. *African Affairs, 114*(454), 1–27.

Anderson, D. M., & Øystein, R. H. (2014). Violence as Politics in Eastern Africa, 1940–1990: Legacy, Agency, Contingency. *Journal of Eastern African Studies, 8*(4), 539–557.

Asoba, S., & Glokpor, R. (Eds.). (2014). *Trafficking of Small Arms and Light Weapons (SALW) in West Africa: Routes and Illegal Arm Caches Between Ghana, Togo, Benin and Nigeria*. Friedrich Ebert Stiftung: Abuja.

Austin, K. (2002, Spring). Illicit Arms Brokers: Aiding and Abetting Atrocities. *Brown Journal of World Affairs, 9*(1), 203–216.

Ayissi, A., & Sall, I. (Eds.). (2005). *Combating the Proliferation of Small Arms and Light Weapons in West Africa: Handbook for the Training of Armed and Security Forces*. Geneva: United Nations.

Bakken, I. V., & Rustad, S. A. (2018). *Conflict Trends in Africa, 1946–2017* (PRIO Paper). Oslo: Peace Research Institute Oslo.

Caleb, A., & Okafor, G. (2014). The Role of Small Arms and Light Weapons in African Conflicts. *African Journal of Political Science and International Relations, 9*(3), 76–85.

Cockayne, J., & O'Neil, S. (2015) (Eds.). *UN DDR in the Era Violent Extremism: Is it Fit for Purpose?* New York: United Nation University.

Cohen, H. J. (1995). What Should We Do When Nations Get Angry? *Nexus Africa, 1*(2), 11–14.

Collier, P., & Hoeffler, A. (2004). Greed and Grievance in Civil War. *Oxford Economic Papers, 56*(4), 563–595.

Delmas, P. (1997). *The Rosy Future of War*. New York: Free Press.

De Souza, A. N. (2016). Between East and the West: The Cold War's Legacy on Africa. *Feature Africa*. Available https://www.aljazeera.com/indepth/features/2016/02/east-west-cold-war-legacy-africa-160214113015863.html. Accessed 10 July 2020.

Duffield, M. (1991). *War and Famine in Africa* (Oxfam Research Paper 5). Oxford: Oxfam Publications.

Duffield, M. (1994). The Political Economy of Internal War: Asset Transfer, Complex Emergencies, and International Aid. In A. Zvi (Ed.), *War and Hunger: Rethinking International Responses to Complex Emergencies*. London: Zed Books.

Eavis, P. (2002, Spring). SALW in the Horn of Africa and the Great Lakes Region: Challenges and Ways Forward. *Brown Journal of World Affairs, 9*(1), 251–260.

Fearon, J. D., & Laitin, D. D. (2003). Ethnicity, Insurgency, and Civil War. *American Political Science Review, 97*(1), 75–90.

Fleshman, M. (2011). Small Arms in Africa: Counting the Cost of Gun Violence. *Africa Renewal* (Magazine). Available https://www.un.org/africarenewal/magazine/december-2011/small-arms-africa. Accessed 20 July 2020.

Garcia, D. (2006). *Small Arms and Security: New Emerging International Norms*. New York: Routledge.

Grand View Research. (2017). Small Arms and Light Weapons (SALW) Market Analysis by Type (Small Arms, Light Weapons), By Application (Military, Law Enforcement), By Region (North America, Europe, Asia Pacific, Rest of the World), and Segment Forecasts, 2018–2024. Available https://www.grandviewresearch.com/industry-analysis/small-arms-light-weapons-salw-market. Accessed 10 July 2020.

Gurr, T. R., & Marshall, M. G. (2000). Assessing the Risks of Future Ethnic Wars (chapter 7). In T. R. Gurr (Ed.), *Peoples Versus States*. Washington, DC: United Stated Institute of Peace Press.

Kiugu, M. A. (2012). *Proliferation and Illicit Trafficking of Small Arms and Light Weapons in the Great Lakes and Horn of Africa*. BiblioScholar.

Knight, M., & Özerdem, A. (2004). Guns, Camps and Cash: Disarmament, Demobilisation and Reinsertion of Former Combatants in Transitions from War to Peace. *Journal of Peace Research, 41*(4), 499–516, p. 501.

Kyari, M. (2020, January 10). Author's Interview with Mallam Kyari, a Displaced Farmer and Community Leader, Maiduguri, Nigeria.

Lumpe, L., Meek, S., & Naylor, R. T. (2000). Introduction to Gun-Running. In Lumpe (Ed.), *Running Guns: The Global Black Market in Small Arms* (pp. 1–12). London: Zed Books.

Marsh, N. (2002, Spring). Two Sides of the Same Coin? The Legal and Illegal Trade in Small Arms. *Brown Journal of World Affairs, 9*(1), 217–228.

Marshall, M. G. (2005). *Conflict Trends in Africa, 1946–2004: A Macro-Comparative Perspective*. Report prepared for the Africa Conflict Prevention Pool (ACPP) Government of the United Kingdom. Available https://africacenter.org/wp-content/uploads/2016/01/Conflict-Trends-in-Africa-1946-2004.pdf. Accessed 20 June 2020.

Monga, C. (1996). *The Anthropology of Anger: Civil Society and Democracy in Africa*. Boulder, Co: Lynne Rienner.

Montague, D. (2002, Spring). The Business of War and the Prospects for Peace in Sierra Leone. *Brown Journal of World Affairs, 9*(1), 229–237.

Musa, A.-F. (2002, Spring). Small Arms: A Time Bomb Under West Africa's Democratization Process. *Brown Journal of World Affairs, 9*(1), 239–249.

New York Times. (2020). Reflections on 1960: The Year of Africa. Available https://www.nytimes.com/interactive/2020/02/06/world/africa/africa-independence-year.html. Accessed 10 July 2020.

Okoro, U. V. (2012). *Proliferation of Small Arms and Light Weapons in West Africa: Implications for Subregional Security*. BiblioScholar.

Onuoha, B. (2011). *Power, Conflict and Consensus-Building in Africa: Ideology Revisited*. AJCR 2011/2. Available https://www.accord.org.za/ajcr-issues/power-conflict-and-consensus-building-in-africa/. Accessed 12 July 2020.

Osiki, O. M. (2021). The global war on terror and its African front. In U. A. Tar (Ed.), *The Routledge Handbook of Counterterrorism and Counterinsurgency in Africa*. London: Routledge.

Rustad, S. A., & Bakken, I. V. (2019). *Conflict Trends in Africa, 1989–2018*. Conflict Trends, 6. Oslo: Peace Research Institute Oslo.

Poroma, C. L., & Iwuoha, P. P. (2018). Power Struggles and Crisis in Africa: Implications for Foreign Direct Investment. *International Journal of Advanced Academic Research, 4*(10), 33–41.

Shettima, A. G. (2021). Global Roots of Local Problems: Globalisation, Terrorism and Counterinsurgency in Africa. In U. A. Tar (Ed.), *The Routledge Handbook of Counterterrorism and Counterinsurgency in Africa*. London: Routledge.

Small Arms Survey. (2018). *Global Firearms Holdings Database*. Geneva: Small Arms Survey. Available http://www.smallarmssurvey.org/weapons-and-markets/tools/global-firearms-holdings.html. Accessed 10 July 2020.

Small Arms Survey. (2019). *Weapons Compass: Mapping Illicit Small Arms Flows in Africa*. Geneva: Small Arms Survey and Addis Ababa: African Union. Available http://www.smallarmssurvey.org/fileadmin/docs/U-Reports/SAS-AU-Weapons-Compass.pdf. Accessed 10 July 2020.

Tar, U. A (2021) (Ed.). *Routledge Handbook of Counterterrorism and Counterinsurgency in Africa*. London and New York: Routledge Publishers.

Tar, U. A., & Bala, B. (2020) (Ed.). *New Architecture of Regional Security in Africa: Perspectives on Counterterrorism and Counterinsurgency in the Lake Chad Basin*. London and New York: Routledge Publishers.

UNDP (United Nations Development Programme). 2017. *Journey to Extremism in Africa: Drivers, Incentives, and the Tipping Point for Recruitment*. New York: UNDP.

UNICEF. (2001). *No Guns, Please. We Are Children!* New York: UNICEF. Available http://www.unicef.org/emerg/files/Emergencies_No_guns_please_leaflet.pdf. Accessed 28 June 2020.

United Nations. (1998, April 16). *The Causes of Conflict and the Promotion of Durable Peace and Sustainable Development in Africa*. Report of the Secretary-General to the 52nd Session of the General Assembly, New York. Available https://documents.wfp.org/stellent/groups/public/documents/eb/wfp000065.pdf. Accessed 17 January 2020.

United Nations. (2010). *Second Generation Disarmament, Demobilization and Reintegration (DDR) Practices in Peace Operations: A Contribution to the New Horizon Discussion on Challenges and Opportunities for UN Peacekeeping*. New York: United Nations Publication.

United Nations. (2014). *Causes of Conflict and the Promotion of Durable Peace and Sustainable Development in Africa*. Report of the Secretary-General to the 69th Session of the General Assembly. File Number A/69/162–S/2014/542. New York: United Nations.

United Nations. (2019). *Causes of Conflict and the Promotion of Durable Peace and Sustainable Development in Africa*. Report of the Secretary-General to the 74th session of the General Assembly, File No. A/74/301–S/2019/645. New York: United Nations.

United Nations News. (2020). *Half of All Violent Deaths Involve Small Arms and Light Weapons*. Available https://news.un.org/en/story/2020/02/1056762. Accessed 10 July 2020.

Zartman, I. W. (1995). *Collapsed States: The Disintegration and Restoration of Legitimate Authority*. Boulder: Lynne Rienner.

Usman A. Tar is Professor of Political Science and Defence Studies, and Endowed Chair of Defence and Security Studies (26RC Endowment) at the Nigerian Defence Academy. He is the Director of the Academy's flagship Centre for Defence Studies and Documentation, and a member of the Board of Social Science Research Council's African Peacebuilding Network (SSRC/APN), New York, USA. He was formerly, Associate Research Fellow at Africa Centre for Peace and Conflict Studies, University of Bradford, UK. He authored several books including *The Politics of Neoliberal Democracy in Africa* (London/New York: I B Tauris, 2009); *Globalization in Africa: Perspectives on Development, Security and the Environment* (Lanham, MD: Lexington Books, 2016); *New Architecture of Regional Security in Africa* (Lanham,

MD: Lexington Books, 2020); and *Routledge Handbook of Counterterrorism and Counterinsurgency in Africa* (London: Routledge, 2020). Prof Tar has consulted or consults for the United Nations Development Programme (UNDP), Nigeria; Konrad Adaneur Stiftung (KAS, German Development Fund); and the Westminster Foundation for Democracy (WFD), Nigeria. Prof Tar is a member of Nigeria's Presidential Think Tank on National Defence and Security, and served as a member of Nigeria's Presidential Committee to review the national defense policy in 2015.

CHAPTER 3

The Theoretical Parameters of the Proliferation and Regulation of Small Arms and Light Weapons in Africa

Usman A. Tar and Sunday Adejoh

INTRODUCTION

The global system is a reflection of networks of relationships between several state and non-state actors. Among other issues, the proliferation of SALWs is a major threat to the international system. As far as this threat is concerned, no country or continent is left out from Europe to America and from Asia to Africa. The post-Cold War era compounded the proliferation of small arms because many of the weapons were sold at very cheap prices by the major military powers in the world as they reduced their Cold War stockpiles and/or modernized their armed forces (Stohl and Hogendoorn 2010). The end of the Cold War also generated global cautious optimism regarding global peace and security because of the shift from super-power-initiated proxy wars in developing countries towards the seemingly viable project of social and economic growth. These hopes were shattered by the outbreak of many civil wars during the post-Cold War era (Kingazi 2006: 3).

As part of its contribution to the discourse on the proliferation SALWS and its implications for national and international security, the Small Arms Survey

U. A. Tar (✉)
Centre for Defence Studies and Documentation, Nigerian Defence Academy, Kaduna, Nigeria
e-mail: uatar@nda.edu.ng

S. Adejoh
Department of Defence and Security Studies, Nigerian Defence Academy, Kaduna, Nigeria

© The Author(s), under exclusive license to Springer Nature Switzerland AG 2021
U. A. Tar and C. P. Onwurah (eds.), *The Palgrave Handbook of Small Arms and Conflicts in Africa*,
https://doi.org/10.1007/978-3-030-62183-4_3

estimates that of the one billion firearms in global circulation as of 2017, 857 million (85%) are in civilian hands, 133 million (13%) are in military arsenals, and 23 million (2%) are owned by law enforcement agencies. The new studies suggest that the global stockpile has increased over the past decade, largely due to civilian holdings, which grew from 650 million in 2006 to 857 million in 2017 (Small Arms Survey 2011). Illegal possession and use of small arms and light weapons (SALW) cause hundreds of thousands of deaths across the globe each year. In order to address these problems, action needs to be taken at many different levels. At the international level, more robust regulatory mechanisms are needed to better control the production, sale and movement of SALW between and within different countries. And at the national and sub-national level, a comprehensive approach is needed to address the reasons why so many civilians regard it as necessary to own a firearm (Saferworld 2012).

The post-colonial state in Africa is beset by crises of legitimacy and insecurity: the contested nature of the state and the centralization of power and resources in the hands of the state has increased the premium on elite capture and control of power. Elites struggle to capture the state by all means. In doing so, they engage in fatal alliances, including establishment of armed militias and proliferation of SALWS, as a means for acquiring, maintaining and perpetuating power. The proliferation of SALWs is part of a motley of symptoms that bedevil Africa: the continent is grappling with issues of ethno-religious conflicts, armed banditry, militancy, terrorism/insurgency, human trafficking, smuggling, drugs and other trans-border crimes which are not unconnected to the political instability and the inchoate nature of leadership and governance in Africa.

The proliferation of SALWs on the African continent poses a threat to the security of lives and properties of Africans. The control of its spread by national, regional and international governments, the collection and destruction of surplus weapons, co-operation in effective intelligence, communication, etc., have been carried out with less success (Johnson et al. 2012). Badmus (2005) maintains that SALWs have become so wide spread that not only do they threaten security across the world but also undermine the peace and stability of civil society. Musah (2002) contends that a major source of its proliferation remains the stockpiles that were pumped into Africa in the 1970s and 1980s by the Soviet Union, the USA and their allies to fan proxy interstate wars.

Although many African countries have adopted regional and global policies on arms control, the continued illicit proliferation of small arms and light weapons is an indication of wider transnational organized crime on the continent that calls for more attention. Criminal networks exploit gaps in the regulatory systems, porous borders and weak law enforcement procedures (Alusala 2018). As states are making efforts so also are the perpetuators coming up with new strategies to continue the proliferation of SALWs within the continent. It is important to note that one cannot completely rule out the role of corruption particularly among security agents especially the customs service and immigration personnel.

This chapter therefore conceptualizes SALWs, looked at several theoretical basis associated with the proliferation of SALWs in Africa, identified several precipitators of SALWs and also examined several regional and sub-regional approaches in addressing the proliferation of SALWs in Africa.

Conceptualizing Small Arms and Light Weapons (SALWs)

The concept of SALWs is amenable to different definitions advanced by scholars, policy makers and practitioners in the areas of defence, international relations and strategic studies. The Organization for Security and Co-operation in Europe (OSCE 2012: 2) defines small arms as:

> Small arms and light weapons are man-portable weapons made or modified to military specifications for use as lethal instruments of war. Small arms are broadly categorized as those weapons intended for use by individual members of armed or security forces. They include revolvers and self-loading pistols; rifles and carbines; sub-machine guns; assault rifles; and light machine guns. Light weapons are broadly categorized as those weapons intended for use by several members of armed or security forces serving as a crew. They include heavy machine guns; hand-held under-barrel and mounted grenade launchers; portable anti-aircraft guns; portable anti-tank guns; recoilless rifles; portable launchers of anti-tank missile and rocket systems; portable launchers of anti-aircraft missile systems; and mortars of calibres less than 100 mm.

Michael (2001) views small arms as weapons that can be carried by an individual. This includes everything from revolvers and pistols to machine guns, light anti-tank weapons and shoulder fired surface-to-air missiles. Small arms are weapons that can be carried and used by an individual, for example, revolvers, pistols, rifles, shotguns, sub-machine guns and assault rifles. Light weapons are weapons designed for use by two or three persons serving as a crew, although some may be carried and used by a single person. Light weapons include heavy machine guns, hand-held under-barrel and mounted grenade launchers, portable anti-aircraft guns, portable anti-tank guns, recoilless rifles, portable launchers of anti-tank missile and rocket systems, portable launchers of anti-aircraft missile systems, and mortars of a calibre of less than 100 mm (Saferworld 2012).

Article 1 of the ECOWAS Convention on SALW defines Light Weapons as Portable arms designed to be used by several persons working together in a team and which include notably:

    i. Heavy machine guns;
    ii. Portable grenade launchers, mobile or mounted;

iii. Portable anti-aircraft cannons;
iv. Portable anti-tank cannons, non-recoil guns;
v. Portable anti-tank missile launchers or rocket launchers;
vi. Portable anti-aircraft missile launchers;
vii. Mortars with a calibre of less than 100 millimetres.

The same Article 1 of the ECOWAS Convention on SALW also defined Small Arms as Arms used by one person and which include notably: firearms and other destructive arms or devices such as an exploding bomb, an incendiary bomb or a gas bomb, a grenade, a rocket launcher, a missile, a missile system or landmine:

a. Revolvers and pistols with automatic loading;
b. Rifles and carbines;
c. Machine guns;
d. Assault rifles;
e. Light machine guns.

While appreciating the divergent opinions on the concepts of SALWs, Ochoche (2002) identities some common elements that reoccur in so many definitions of SALW as follows:

> First, the focus is on lethal equipment, i.e. weapons and their ammunition, generally used by military and paramilitary forces, excluding items such as knives and hunting rifles. Second, the emphasis is on weapons that are man-portable or transportable by light vehicles, i.e. on the weight and size of the equipment. Third, this equipment is easy to maintain, can function without much logistical back-up and requires light training for use. Fourth, to be militarily and politically relevant, the definition comprises weapons that are in frequent use, i.e. weapons that really kill.

Proliferation on the other hand indicates degree of circulation in terms of quantity. Some researchers have attributed the proliferation of arms to arms race between nations. The increasing rate of arms race precipitated by the idea of national defence/security and role of power in global politics is a major factor as far as the proliferation of arms in concerned. Proliferation of weapons can be defined as their spread from one group of owners or users to another. This can be horizontal, which refers to the acquisition of weapons systems by states not previously possessing them, or vertical, which refers to increases in the arsenals of these states already possessing particular weapons (Obasi 2001). Figure 3.1 shows Arms proliferation within the context of process and stages:

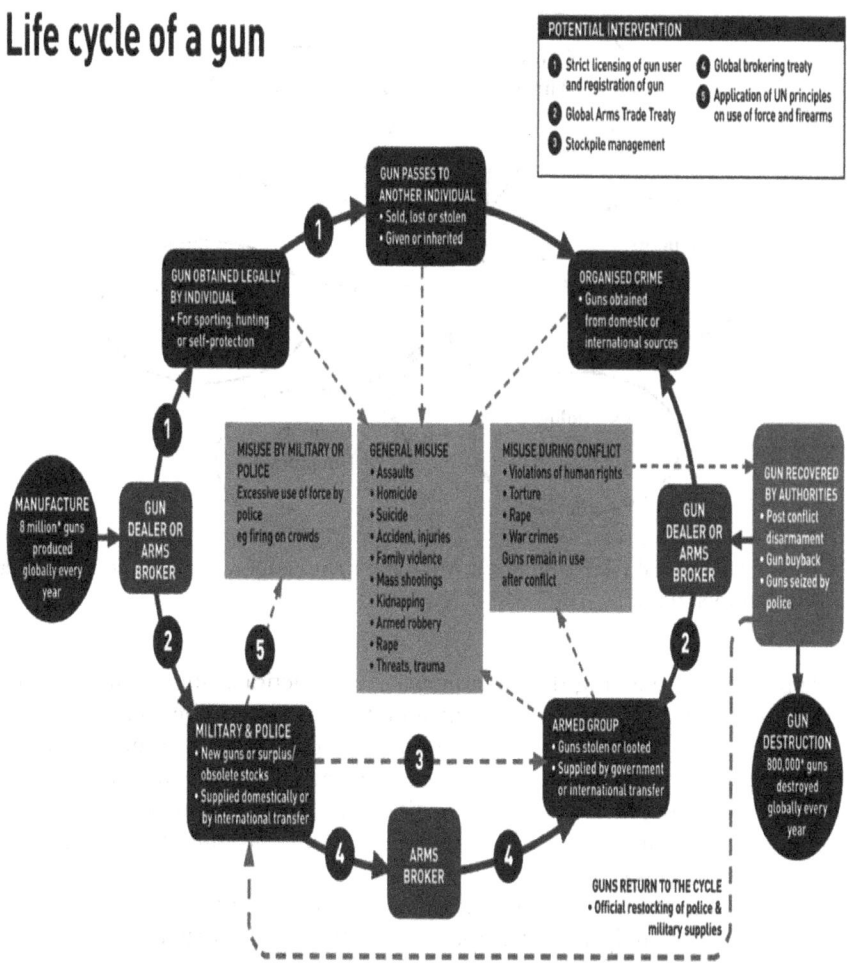

Fig. 3.1 Circles of Arms proliferations (*Source* International Action Network on Small Arms [IANSA])

Theoretical Dimensions of Small Arms and Light Weapons Proliferations in Africa

The importance of theories in social science research cannot be overemphasized. It is the fulcrum for research and investigations since it situates a research in proper perspectives, concept and context by providing a concrete conceptual scaffold for carrying out investigations and emerging with an informed analysis. Kerlinger (1977) sees theory as a set of interrelated constructs (concepts) and propositions that presents a systematic view of phenomena by specifying relations among variables, with the purpose of

Fig. 3.2 Theoretical matrix on Small Arms and light weapons proliferation in Africa (*Source* Authors 2020)

explaining and predicting the phenomena. The functional superiority of theories as guideposts in all fields of human endeavour lies in the fact that rather than base action on judgement derived from mere experience, guesswork or speculations, theories enable a chosen line of action to be anchored in and guided by evidence derived from scientific research, which makes the consequences of such an action fall as close in line with the intended direction as possible (Onah 2003: 128–129).

Even though studies in arms control and of related subjects abound, there have been surprisingly few attempts to construct a general theory of arms control In fact, only few texts pay considerable attention to extensive theorization of small arms (e.g. Morgan 2012). However, there exist galaxies of theoretical underpinnings that can shed light on the issues around SALWs proliferation in Africa. For the purpose of this chapter, the following theories, by no means exhaustive, will be considered: the theory of Geopolitics; the Security Dilemma Theory; Behavioural Theories; The Theory of State Collapse; Marxist Conflict Theory; The Theory of Anomie; and Frustration-Aggression Theory. These theories will be employed to analyze the nature, reasons, dimensions and impact of SALWs in Africa (Fig. 3.2).

THE THEORY OF GEOPOLITICS

The Theory of Geopolitics emphasizes the intersection between Geography and Politics as the "cross-hair" underpinning the proliferation of small arms. Also, interchangeably used with "political geography", geopolitics provides the concept-context balance in which territoriality and power define the behaviour of states towards one another, and in their domestic posturing. Friedrich Ratzel, Halford Mackinder, Rudolf Kjellen, and Karl Haushofer are the major proponents of the theory of geopolitics. The German geographer Friedrich Ratzel, whose—*Politische Geographie* (1897) and paper *Laws on the Spatial Growth of States* (1896)—laid the concrete foundation for the conceptualisation of geopolitics (see Ratzel 2011). Ratzel developed the organic theory of the state, which treated the state as a form of biological organism—territory being its body and alleged that states behaved and lived in accordance with biological laws. Thus,

> Political geography is the study of the effects of political actions on human geography, involving the spatial analysis of human phenomena. Traditionally political geography was concerned with the study of states—their groupings and global relations (geopolitics) and their morphological characteristics, i.e. their frontiers and boundaries. In the last twenty years increasing interest has been shown in smaller political divisions, i.e. those within states, involving an appreciation of the interaction between political processes and spatial organization, e.g. the nature and consequences of decision-making by urban government, the relationship between public policy and resource development, the geography of public finance and electoral geography (Dodds 2000).

The Theory of Geopolitics illuminates the proliferation SALWs in Africa. The African continent is a volatile "geopolity" populated, as it were, by a bunch of failed or failing states who have failed to ensure domestic law and order leading to "crisis of security"—defined as the failure of the state to create the prevailing condition for securing governmental assets as well as lives and property of citizens. Understanding the proliferation of SALWs within the context of geopolitical theory reflects the nature of trans-border and trans-human activities within the continent of Africa. Issues of trans-border crimes occasioned by porous borders and poor border management reaffirms the reason why borderlines are characterized with crimes. For instance, in the Lake Chad Basin, the porous nature of boundaries, the existence of smuggling networks, suspicion among countries of region (as a result of the influence of France against Nigeria), etc., have all conspired to bring about massive proliferation of SALWs to sustain Boko Haram insurgency in the region. Similarly, in the Horn of Africa, State collapse in Somalia and the rise of warlords across the region have led to proliferation of SALWS and, by extension, the transcendent rise of Al-Shabab insurgency in neighbouring countries of Kenya and Uganda. In addition, it has given rise to civil militias and warlords who curved out huge tracts of land and rule by violence.

Like every theory, the theory of geopolitics has its own weaknesses and limitations. The evolution of geopolitics as a concept and subsequently as a theory is such that reflects the politics of superpowers relations especially in relations to annexation of and territorial expansions. Hence, the issue of bias is a major criticism of this theory. Throughout the Cold War, both super powers developed geopolitical strategic lenses that guided and legitimized their actions as they began to develop their roles as world powers. Their geopolitical views aimed at commanding the world and took the form of ideologies. Government statements assumed the status of theories, and hence took on the authority of objective truths (Flint 2006). In short, "critical geopolitics is an aspect of a politicized debate, rather than the product of an academic culture as classically understood (Black 2009). Both classical geopolitics and critical geopolitics are political movements that use geopolitics to advance their social agendas. Each school has an underlying political agenda that blinkers their world views (Terrence et al. 2014).

STATE COLLAPSE THEORY

This theory is hinged on the assumption that the state that fails to secure territorial integrity and internal security is invariably underpinned by the breakdown of the basic functions of the state—in defence, security, social welfare etc.—leading to general discontent within society and dearth of loyalty and commitment on the part of public servants, and eventual disintegration of the structures of the state. States succeed or fail across all or some dimensions such as security, economic development, political representation, income distribution and so on. But it is according to their performance, according to the levels of their effective delivery of the most crucial political goods that strong states may be distinguished from weak ones, and weak states from failed or collapsed states. Political goods are those intangible and hard to quantify claims that citizens once made on sovereigns and now make on states. They encompass expectations, conceivably obligations, inform the local political culture, and together give content to the social contract between rulers and ruled that is at the core of regime/government and citizenry interactions (Pennock 1966).

In most strong states unlike weak and failed states, the state has monopoly of the means of violence, the state is devoid of political crisis/instabilities, economically developed, strong and stable economy, adequate infrastructural development and income distribution among others. Strong states like the USA, China, Russia, United Kingdom, France and Germany among others have manifested these characteristics. Weak states like Nigeria, Liberia, South Africa, Niger, Venezuela, Brazil and Kenya are characterized by some deficiencies in terms of the state having monopoly of power and enjoying stable economy. One major indices of weak state is the increasing rate of internal conflicts which could be politically motivated of precipitated by socioeconomic issues especially since these states reflect some degree of plurality. Failed states reflect total collapse of state institutions and increase in non-state actors who challenge state monopoly of coercion. Such states are unable to exert authority and ensure its territorial integrity. Failed states are characterized by economic underdevelopment, gross deficiency of basic amenities with increasing rate of unemployment and in most cases the state is unable to provide basic human needs for her citizenry. States like Somalia, Afghanistan, Iraq, etc., are typical examples of failed states.

In the dominant literature, state "collapse" refers to the crumbling of institutions while state "failure" is defined by the non-performance of key state functions (Zartman 1995). State collapse is a situation where the structure, authority, law and political order have fallen apart. State failure, on the other hand, begs the question of what the core functions of the state actually are, and these may vary from minimal concern with basic security to respect for the rights of citizens, and even the provision of welfare (Clapham 2002). Failed states are tense, deeply conflicted, dangerous and contested bitterly by warring factions. In most failed states such as Somalia, Afghanistan, Iraq, Yemen, Darfur, the state elites and its bureaucracy have failed in defence and security management: in spite of drawing generous budget and security votes, the military, police and paramilitary forces have largely failed to confront insurgent and terrorists, or ensure general low, order and security. Occasionally, the official authorities in a failed state face two or more insurgencies, varieties of civil unrest, different degrees of communal discontent, and a plethora of dissent directed at the state and at groups within the state (Rotberg 2004). The failure of the state to provide law and order, control arms and mediate contradiction in society. Loss of state legitimacy and the rise of armed militia and complex emergencies are attributes of state collapse.

Drawing from the above, it is obvious that the failure of states to provide necessary political goods can snowball into the proliferation of Small Arms and Light Weapons which will further degenerate into series of political crises. The use of force is the exclusive preserve of states. However, the emergence of militias, insurgents, terrorist, bandits' militants, etc., in several African countries clearly indicates state failure. The proliferation of SALW has further encouraged the activities of these groups. The Democratic Republic of the Congo, Angola, Sierra Leone, Uganda, Nigeria, Sudan, South Sudan, Libya, Kenya, Somalia just to mention but a few countries in Africa indicate that the failure of the state has increased the rate of illicit weapons in circulation.

This theory has suffered several criticisms particularly in relations to the concept and context of its application. The term "failed state" has faced criticism along two main strands. The first argues that the term lends itself to overgeneralization, by lumping together different governance problems among diverse countries, and without accounting for variations of governance within states (Woodward 2017). The second is concerned with the political application of the term in order to justify foreign military interventions and state-building based on a Western model of the state (Grimm et al. 2016).

Security Dilemma Theory

It is an interesting theory that contributes to the understanding of SALWs proliferation. Security dilemma theory describes a phenomena that influence all human relations: a deep-seated uncertainty and fear of others intentions caused by the essential insecurity of human nature, that in the worst case may lead to a logic of "kill first or risk being killed" leading two parties to try to pre-empt each other even though both parties did not harbour any harmful intentions to begin with (Roe 1999: 3). According to the theory, dilemma is caused by a tragic combination of a desire growing out of uncertainty for actors to prepare for the worst, coupled with a failure to realize how threatening their own security measures appear to others around them. Applied to the security space, it means that states more often than not prepare for eventualities that they envisage either based on threat analysis their environment or the global system at large. However, such eventualities may occur or not. Like Clausewitz will say "if you want peace, prepare for war". This phenomenon is described by Booth and Wheeler as the "Security Paradox", where a concern for one's own security leads to an overall decrease in security. Uncertainty is therefore at the heart of the SD. Booth and Wheeler define the SD as consisting of two interrelated dilemmas: the "dilemma of interpretation"—knowing whether the other's motives are defensive or offensive; and the aspect of response—how one should respond to the other's actions (Booth and Wheeler 2013: 139).

In the context of Africa, the proliferation of SALWs is also a result of the feelings of insecurity and the lack of confidence in state institutions to guarantee security. Hence a lot of individuals would prefer to protect themselves from would-be or perceived enemies. Thus, private individuals are tempted to acquire small arms as a means of self defence. The risk, however, is that this private acquisition of SALWs may spiral out control as criminals gangs and insurgents may exploit the same avenues to acquire arms and wreak havoc on the state and society. The increasing rate of kidnapping, cattle-rustling, armed robbery, resource war; political thuggery in Africa has further worsened the situation. Hill takes this argument further by suggesting that SDs in an anarchical intrastate context may even be more acute than its international counterpart, since individuals are much more vulnerable relative to states, meaning that even a small influx of arms may provoke dramatic results, increasing the risk of civil war (Hill 2004: 14).

Theory of Deviance

Deviant behaviour is any behaviour that is contrary to the dominant norms of society. There are different theories that explain how behavior comes to be classified as deviant and why people engage in it, including biological explanations, psychological explanations and sociological explanations (Crossman 2019). There are several theorists that seek to explain deviant behaviour. Examples include Emile Durkheim's *Theory of Anomie*, Edwin Sutherland's *Theory of Differential Association*, Walter Reckless's *Control Theory*, William Chambliss's *Labelling theory* and Robert Merton *Theory of Anomie*. However Merton's theory is the subject of discussion.

Robert K. Merton's theory of anomie argued that certain groups participate in criminal behaviour because they are "responding normally to the social situation in which they find themselves" (Tierney 2006). Borrowing a term sociologically introduced by Durkheim (1997), Merton adopts the anomie concept as part of his effort to suggest that biological explanations of deviant behaviour are inadequate to explain social reality and that, instead, structural conditions should be considered as inducing deviation from prescribed patterns of conduct. Thus, according to Merton, crime and deviance are caused by an imbalance in social order, when individuals utilize the most efficient and convenient means, including crime, to achieve their goals (Cullen and Agnew 2006). This imbalance, in which some individuals (particularly those of the lower- and lower-middle social classes) are disadvantaged and have few prospects of reaching goals, produces a strain (Gomme 2007). There are five types of deviance based upon these criteria: conformity, innovation, ritualism, retreatism and rebellion.

The illicit proliferation of SALWs in Africa by terrorist, militias, rebels and bandits reflects anomie. It is only the state that has the exclusive preserve for coercion and force and so any group or groups within a state in possession of firearms to the point of challenging the authority of the state are retreaters, nonconformist and rebellious to the state because their goals and means of achieving them are contrary to the laid down principles of the state. When the coercive state fails to meet its expectations, it loses its legitimacy in the eyes of the citizens who resort to challenging the state and its authority.

Merton's theory of deviance has also been a subject of several criticisms. Some scholars have argued that that Merton's use of anomie is enshrined in ambiguity and confusion. Conceptual ambiguity over Merton's anomie concept is at least partly a result of Merton's own inconsistent use of the term. As Levine (1985) argues, Merton's various formulations of anomie demonstrate "a pattern of steadily increasing semantic confusion". Featherstone and Deflem (2003), argued that in his contributions on social structure and anomie, Merton forwarded two distinct theories that he did not always clearly distinguish. First, he presents a theory of anomie, referring to deinstitutionalization of norms that occurs when there is a disjunction between the emphasis on cultural goals and institutional means (Merton 1938). Second, he presents a strain theory of deviant behaviour that holds that people are more likely to pursue illegitimate means to attaining culturally prescribed goals when they are blocked from accessing the institutionalized means to these goals (Merton 1938).

QUEER LADDER THEORY (QLT)

This theory accounts for the rise of crime and deviance as a result of the failure of the formal to provide legitimate grounds for self-actualization. Daniel Bell (1964) who wrote one of the most famous sociological assays on organized crimes in America referred to organized crime as providing the queer ladder for social mobility in America in an attempt to explain the instrumental essence of organized crime as a desperate means of economic empowerment and social climbing. Although the theory was used by Bell to explain the behavioural pattern of Italian migrants in America in relation to organized crime, it is now widely used in contemporary security studies. Often ascribed to this theory is the notion that organized crime thrives in contexts where the government's capacity to dictate, sanction and deter crime is poor; where public corruption is endemic; and where prospects for legitimate livelihood opportunities are slim (Nwoye 2000; Lyman 2007; Okoli and Orinya 2013). QLT can be highlighted thus: (i) Organized crime is an instrumental behaviour; it is a means to an end. (ii) It is an instrument of social climbing and/or socio-economic advancement (iii) It is a means to accumulate wealth and build power (Mallory 2007; Okoli and Orinya 2013).

Applied to the proliferation of SALWs in Africa, the Queer Ladder Theory illuminate how insurgent and criminals acquire small arms as a means of "getting rich quick" or "foisting their way" through crime and criminality. It is clear that people who carry arms do so because they have lost hope in the prospects of achieving their dreams using the conventional ladder. Thus, small arms provide an alternate route to arriving at their dream destination. Organized crime is made possible by the availability of illicit weapons in the hands of non-state actors. Armed robbery, kidnapping, militancy and piracy are all means of climbing the social ladder. It is also pertinent to note that rate of unemployment within the continent has hindered young people from achieving their dreams of social mobility. Hence the increasing rate of organized crime.

This theory has however been criticized for being stereotypic and bias for viewing organized crime from an ethnic dimension as though certain ethnicities are known for and inherently associated with crime.

Marxist Conflict Theory

The Marxist conflict theory is situated within the context of human society and social relations of production vis-a-vis the dialectical characteristics of every society. Class differentiation is an important attribute of states; the class of the haves (bourgeois) and that of the have not (proletariat). The contradictory relationships between the classes are the basis of conflict. Conflict is a product of human material condition.

Marx claims that society is in a state of perpetual conflict because of competition for limited resources. It holds that social order is maintained by domination and power, rather than consensus and conformity. According to conflict theory, those with wealth and power try to hold on to it by any means possible, chiefly by suppressing the poor and powerless. A basic premise of conflict theory is that individuals and groups within society will work to maximize their own benefits (Chappelow 2019).

Small arms are a mechanism for power grab and access to power. Elites use small arms to outdo one another. Also, the whole range of conflict and contradictions that underpin society kidnapping, cattle-rustling, armed robbery, resource war, political thuggery—are spawned by the struggle for power and wealth. Communal conflicts, ethno-religious and the farmers–herders conflict in different parts of Africa is a reflection of the struggle for material possessions. These conflicts are made possible with the aid of SALWs. One major limitation of the Marxist theory is its so much emphasis on conflict/revolution and social relations as though change cannot be achieved except through conflict alone.

Frustration–Aggression Theory

This theory explains the proliferation of SALWs from the perspectives of anger and discontent associated with state failure and crisis of security. The theory is propounded and developed by John Dollard and his research associates in 1939. The original formulation of the frustration–aggression hypothesis by Dollard et al. (1939) stated that "the occurrence of aggressive behavior always presupposes the existence of frustration and, contrariwise, that the existence of frustration always leads to some form of aggression". The theory seems to be the most common explanation for violent behaviour stemmed from inability to fulfil needs (Dollard et al. 1939). In attempts to explain aggression, Dollard points to the difference between what people feel they want or deserve, to what they actually gets, the want get-ratio and difference between expected need satisfaction and actual need satisfaction (Davies 1962).

Revisions of the theory have pointed at nuanced elements of the frustration and agression theory. For instance, Berkowitz (1989) reformulated the theory, arguing that frustrations are still defined as aversive events but that they "generate aggressive inclinations only to the extent that they produce negative affect". It is important to understand that, within this reformulated theory, not the frustration but negative affect is the proximal cause of aggressive responses, and frustrations are just one of many potential sources of negative affect (Berkowitz 1988). When an individual is frustrated, there is a tendency for aggression to set in. In real terms, the proliferation of terrorism, rebels and militias in Africa vis-à-vis the proliferation of SALWs in Africa is sometimes linked to frustration and aggression against the state. The proliferations of SALWs in Africa can also be viewed as the failure of states institutions and agencies to perform their statutory functions. The failure and inability to provide basic human needs will usually elicit frustration on the side of the citizens. When state fails to guarantee the security of lives and properties, individuals are then forced to resort to self-help by acquiring arms to protect themselves. Individuals and groups who feel marginalized or disadvantaged by lopsided state policies do resort to armed rebellion as a means of pursuing their individual or collective aspirations.

One major criticism of the theory is on the grounds of its theoretical rigidity and overgeneralization which also accounted for Berkowitz (1989) reformulation of the theory.

EMPIRICAL DIMENSIONS: PRECONDITIONS AND PRECIPITATORS OF SALW PROLIFERATION IN AFRICA

It is imperative to buttress the empirical contexts of SALWs proliferation in Africa, if to further buttress the abstract theories mentioned above. Illuminating theories with empirical data will reveal the material conditions behind the proliferation of SALWs which the various theories seek to explain. To squarely understand why and how Africa is bedevilled with the threat of SALWs, one needs to situate this discussion within the context of the socio-economic, political and geopolitical architecture of Africa vis-à-vis the international contradictions within the continent. There are a bevy of factors encouraging and facilitating the proliferation of SALWs in Africa and this section will attempt an analysis of some of these variables. These variables are identified as follows:

Political Instability

The uncontrolled proliferation and widespread availability of small arms is a development that is affecting virtually every African country and poses threats to domestic and regional security. The problems posed by small arms proliferation are complex and multidimensional in character. They are entangled with other broad security and societal issues such as conflict prevention and resolution, poverty, gender, cultures of violence, governance issues, criminal activity and links to terrorism. They also portend serious implications for human rights and humanitarian activities (Ogaba 2005: 9–10).

The nature of political instability in Africa has manifested in forms of ethno-religious conflicts, militancy, terrorism and electoral and post-elections conflicts which are springboards for the proliferation of Small Arms and Light Weapons in Africa. Galadima (2006) admits that Africa, since the eve of the twenty-first century, has been challenged by a variety of complex political, economic, environmental and social upheaval in degrees and intensity that is unprecedented in the continent. These challenges have launched the continent into a series of devastating intrastate conflicts ever experienced in a single continent anywhere in the world in the last decade and a half. In the 1990s and 2000s, conflicts erupted into ethnic warfare in Central African Republic (CAR), Democratic Republic of Congo (DRC), Burundi and Rwanda. There were/are armed uprisings in Northern Uganda: civil wars in the Republic of Sudan and Southern Sudan; and border conflicts between Ethiopia and Eritrea. In fact, the Republic of Sudan is encountering humanitarian catastrophe arising from a bitter intrastate conflict between rebel groups in western sudan and the central government in Khartoum (Galadima 2006). In 1994,

Rwanda witnessed a mass genocide carried out by the majority Hutu ethnic group against a minority Tutsis. The genocide was executed using basic small arms such as knives, matchetes and cudgels and engulfed nearly one million innocent lives.

Instead of realizing sustainable security and development, civil wars have resulted in state disintegration, complex political emergencies and gross human rights violations. In many of the brutal conflicts in Africa, there were reported cases of mass destruction, genocides and extra-judicial killings against unarmed civilians carried out by all sides of these wars; collapse of state authority, law and order; internal displacement; and exodus of refugees to neighbouring states—examples include, Mozambique in the 1980s; Angola and Somalia in the early 1990s; Nigeria, Sierra-Leone in the early 2000s; Central African Republic, Cote d'Ivoire, and Liberia in the late 1990s; and Sudan, Democratic Republic of Congo (DRC) and Libya from 2011 to the present; Small arms play a key role in these conflicts (Stohl and Hogendoorn 2010: 3).

Sharing their views on the relationship between arms proliferation and conflict, Johnson et al. (2012: 4) note:

> Conflict may be regarded as a characteristics feature of the political process Africa. There is scarcely any part of Africa without its share of major conflicts in the past four decades. African conflicts exhibit some features that seem particular to them. There are conflicts of secession, conflicts of ethnic sub-nationalism, conflicts of self-determination, conflicts of military intervention and political legitimacy, conflicts of national liberation, conflicts over religion and over territory or boundaries. These conflicts can be intractable lasting for up two decades resulting in loss of lives and property, slow pace of development and insecurity.

Similarly, as Francis (2008) notes, during conflicts, some states in West Africa have liberalized gun possession laws in order to stimulate civilian arming and self-defence. Also, arms were directly distributed to paramilitary groups by governments in order to fight rebel forces during the civil wars in Côte d'Ivoire, Liberia and Sierra Leone, but legislation was also liberalized, and proved a major driver of small arms diffusion. The member states of the Economic Community of West African State (ECOWAS) started from the premise that to reach the organization's initial objective of economic development would require a stable and peaceful environment, which the West Africa of the 1990s certainly did not provide. Civil wars, notably in Liberia and Sierra Leone, plunged the sub-region into a situation of endemic insecurity which was all the more difficult to combat because it was brought about not by regular armies but by factions or rebellious forces, that is, by groups that are difficult to control (Francis 2008). Further, Oluyemi-kusa Dayo (2006) posits that armed conflicts today are more likely to occur within states than across national borders. Since the collapse of the Soviet Union, the number of intrastate conflicts has proliferated and even more pronounced in Africa due to the level of poverty and weak democratic institutions as a result of the long period of military rule in most of these countries. Thus, economic disintegration, political upheaval and competition for scarce resources have opened a Pandora's Box of long-suppressed ethnic, religious and regional tensions that have erupted into violent conflict.

Poor Border Management and Illicit Arms Transfers

Apart from the issues of size and landmass, every country in Africa is bordered by several other countries; hence the management of mobility of humans, goods and services becomes a major issue. Several borders in Africa are either unmanned or poorly managed thus supporting the proliferation of SALWs on the continent and other trans-border crimes because borders are easily crossed. In West Africa, as elsewhere in Africa, borders are not only arbitrarily demarcated, but they are also easy to cross. Thus, there need only be unrest in one state for the repercussions—particularly through the influx of refugees—to be felt in other states, especially neighbouring states. Unregulated movements of people facilitate the circulation of weapons. Indeed, in the 1999 Protocol, ECOWAS draws a very clear link between cross-border crime and arms proliferation (Alusala 2018: 54).

In West Africa, some scholars have also argued that the ECOWAS Protocol on free movement of persons, goods and service has further increased the level of insecurity and threat within the Sub-region. Armed groups and militias are able to cross borders easily in conflict zones, and cross-border shipment of arms and ammunition is generally on the increase. Smugglers also exploit irregular sea and land routes in an effort to bypass the law in the transportation of weapons, making it difficult for security forces to detect the movements of illegal arms and other contrabands. Terrorist and violent extremist groups, such as Boko Haram and al-Shabaab, also operate across borders using irregular routes and taking advantage of poorly secured border points to smuggle weapons (Onuoha 2013).

Some international borders in Africa pose a considerable challenge to law enforcement. These constitute borders located in ungoverned spaces, and which are therefore prone to corruption, conflict and political instability. Weak state capacity also makes it difficult to monitor cross-border proliferation of arms, which occurs insidiously (Alusala 2018: 6).

In West Africa, the evidence of proliferation is an extreme concern. Out of the 650 million SALW circulating globally, some estimated 7 million are in West Africa, and 77,000 small arms are in the hands of major West African insurgent groups (Small Arms Survey 2003: 82). The inability of states and security agencies in Africa to manage and regulate the use of and spread of SALWs has further aggravated the threat to national security. The continent has become so unsecured that one begins to wonder whether states still reserve the sovereignty and their coercive powers.

In terms of arms transfer diversions in Africa, the data indicates that the largest cases of transfer diversions have been directed to Libya, and notably before the strengthening of the arms embargo on that country in mid-2014. For example, the UN Panel of Experts on Libya revealed that an Albanian broker and a Ukrainian company organized the transfer of 800,000 cartridges of 12.7 × 108 mm calibre from Albania to Libya in 2011 (UNSC 2013).

In relation to the above and identifying the role played by Africans, the UN Monitoring Group on Eritrea, posits that:

> A Sudanese national organized the shipment by boat of 25,000 readily convertible blank-firing pistols from Turkey to Eritrea in January 2017. According to shipping documentation, the intended final consignee was an Eritrean state-owned import and export company based in Asmara. While the ship transporting the consignment initially docked at the port of Massawa, Eritrea, it was seized two weeks later at the port of Kismayo in Somalia. The Sudanese owner stated that he had wanted to offload the weapons in Eritrea to transfer them by land for sale to retailers in Sudan. While a large market for such firearms appears to exist in Sudan, the Sudanese government imposes restrictions on the number of items that can be imported and applies strict licensing laws to importers, which the broker in this case may have sought to evade by attempting to smuggle the guns by land through Eritrea. Yet the Monitoring Group was unable to confirm that the weapons were destined for Sudan and not Eritrea or Somalia, and did not report on the reasons why the shipment continued on to Somalia after docking in Eritrea. (United Nations 2017: 14–17)

State Failure and Efflorescence of Ungoverned Spaces

There are countries in Africa where non-state actors are challenging the authority and policies of the state because they have as much fire-power as the state and in some instance can encounter the state effectively in the event of war. In Nigeria for instance, the military has been unable to effectively and efficiently counter Boko Haram terrorist group for over a decade. The Niger Delta militants, too, have also challenged the Nigeria Military in several occasions. In Darfur, South Sudan, Congo, Rwanda, Uganda, and Somalia, militias, rebels, bandits and militant groups have curved large swathes of "ungoverned spaces" and constituted "state within a state". Some states in Africa have been described as "failed states" because of the inability of the state to exert its powers.

Mass proliferation of small arms, and access to smalls arms and other weapons of mass destruction by violent non-state actors are often cited as the main reason for state collapse and state disintegration in Africa. This is the moreso in a situation where the host state faces a crisis of legitimacy and a jaundiced armed forces and policing architecture that is inadequately resourced and, therefore, unable to contain existential threats against the state and its citizens. In this vein, Francis (2008) posits that the fragmentation of the political and economic space in West Africa has shaped the availability and circulation of SALWs in private hands. The deterioration of many West African states' capacity to enforce the rule of law has blurred the boundaries between legal and illicit markets, enabling a thriving trade in SALW. Politicians have even been known to acquire weapons from illegal dealers to arm security personnel during election season. This largely explains the proliferation of private security companies, vigilante groups, etc., these go to show how the failure of the state can propel the spread and proliferation of illicit arms and weapons.

Stockpiling and Diversions of Arms and Ammunitions

Stockpiling of arms by state actors, state-authorized private sector players, and military industrial complexes constitute another springboard for the spread of SALWs in Africa. Stockpiling of SALWs can be interrogated within different context and different perspectives. One factor that has over the years encouraged the stockpiles of arms and weapons is tied to the states' innate and existential desire to preserve sovereignty and territorial integrity. The size of a country's stockpile is an indicator of the state's level of preparedness to confront external aggression and internal rebellion. Further, Arms race between States within the international system has encouraged stockpiling. States believe that their security is determined by the sophistication, variety and volume of arms at their disposal, even where they lack the capacity to maintain or deploy such armament. There is however a nexus between legal and illegal stockpiling of arms and weapons. Licit stockpiles are one of the main sources of illicit arms flows in Africa.

In Africa, much attention has been paid to the effects of the 2011 armed conflict in Libya, which led to the loss of state control over and the looting of the large national weapons stockpile accumulated under the rule of Muammar Qaddafi (UNODC 2013). During the period 2012–2014, weapons of Libyan origin were reportedly trafficked to a number of neighbouring countries in West Africa, the Sahel, Lake Chad Basin and, possibly, as far as the Central African Republic and Somalia (UNSC 2014). The spike in civil wars, insurgencies and organised violence in many states within these regions may be associated with the inflow of large stockpiles of arms and ammunitions from Libya.

The Small Arms Survey (2018) suggests that African civilian actors, which include private individuals, registered businesses such as private security companies, and non-state armed groups, hold more than 40 million—or almost 80%—of all small arms on the continent. In contrast, the continent's armed forces and law enforcement agencies hold less than 11 million small arms. Among the 40 million civilian-held firearms in Africa, 5,841,200 are recorded as being officially registered, while 16,043,800 are unregistered, with the status of the remainder remaining unclear (see Table 3.1).

Related to the issue of stockpile is the diversion of arms. Diversion of legal arms refers to the clandestine entry of arms and ammunitions in the armouries of state armed forces and paramilitaries into the illicit market as a result of sharp practices within the defence and security establishment. Diversion may

Table 3.1 Estimated African sub-regional distribution of civilian firearms 2017

UN Subregion	Population	Number of civilian held Firearms	Civilian-held firearms per 100 population
Africa total	1,246,505,000	40,009,000	3.2
Eastern Africa	416,676,000	7,802,000	1.9
Middle Africa	161,237,000	4,981,000	3.1
Northern Africa	232,186,000	10,241,000	4.4
Southern Africa	63,854,000	6,012,000	9.4
Western Africa	372,551,000	10,972,000	2.9

Source Small Arms Survey (2018)

also occur as a result of the unauthorized use or re-export of arms or ammunition without the consent of the legitimate owner or original exporting state (UNSCAR and MAG 2015). Diversions from national stockpiles' refer to the loss of arms and ammunition that are under the control of a state's defence and security forces. They can take several forms, including theft by personnel and by external actors at storage facilities or during combat operations, and are often facilitated by weak oversight and poor physical security measures (Parker 2016).

In Africa, this diversion of weapons occurs in several ways. One way is for armed militias or rebels to overrun government forces and raid government arsenals. Another is the case where rogue soldiers trade arms opportunistically with rebels. The latter is most rampant in cases where the state's forces are poorly paid (*The Guardian*, October 2nd, 2014). A second method of diversion, mentioned earlier, is the unauthorised sale of arms and ammunitions from state armouries to unauthorised persons and groups by greedy state officials. This method is often difficult to detect because of the existence of secret code of practice between compromised state officials, arms merchants and local consumers (insurgents, gangs and politicians). A third method of diversion is the illegal-cross-jurisdictional importation of weapons from states whose security regimens are compromised. A good example is the behind-the-scene merchandising of illegal arms from Libya to many parts of western and central Africa.

Weapons that were diverted from national stockpiles, such as the post-2011 outflows of looted Libyan national stockpiles. Shotgun ammunition smuggled from Cameroon to the Central African Republic in 2014, some of which had been imported from Europe shows how authorized transfers can be quickly diverted and reach conflict actors through the ant trade (UNSC 2014).

Illicit Arms Market

The illicit arms market or "black market" involves various actors, from the manufacturer to the end user, and usually a number of illicit brokers along the supply chain, who often conceal their activities in a highly complex transnational criminal network (Rothe and Collins 2011). Examining the rate of illicit arms flow in relations to markets, Alusala (2018: 5) claimed that: "it is evident that the licit and illicit arms markets are separated by a very thin line. Several factors enable weapons to enter the illicit supply chain. To help prevent this, there is need for greater transparency at three critical points—the manufacturing, brokering and end-user (recipient) markets. Arms traffickers use various processes to abet illicit arms flows" (Alusala 2018: 5). According to Potter (2017) syndicates exploit the "grey market" by disguising themselves as "employees" of legitimate corporations, or by fronting entities that pass themselves off as those corporations. This way, they are able to make grey-market transactions using a false flag. This is why most grey-market arms transactions are dominated and controlled by large, legitimate companies.

REGIONAL AND SUB-REGIONAL PROTOCOLS FOR CONTROL OF SALWs IN AFRICA

Beyond theorizing the roots of SALWs, it is apposite to trace the pragmatic problem-solving approach adopted by African countries to address the proliferation of SALWs. In this Handbook, Danwanka examines the national legislation and strategy for gun control in Nigeria, while Mashi and Mohammed attempt an analysis of the effort by African countries to control small arms and contrabands from the standpoint of customs union. In this chapter, we attempt to trace the broader context of the regulations of SALWs from the perspectives of regional, sub-regional, national, bilateral/multilateral and non-governmental perspectives.

Recognizing the impact and implications of SALWs proliferation in Africa, Many African countries have adopted a number of regional and global policies on arms control. Despite this, arms destined for conflicts continue to be trafficked in Africa in defiance of these measures. The fact that small arms and light weapons (SALWs) continue to proliferate on the continent can be seen as a symptom of wider organized crime (Alusala 2018: 6).

There have been attempts and measure put in place in Africa to fight against proliferation of illicit Small Arms and Light Weapons (SALW) this include; Bamako Declaration on an African Common Position on the Illicit Proliferation, Circulation and Trafficking of Small Arms and Light Weapons (2000) as well as signing, ratification and implementation of legally binding protocols or conventions at the regional level, such as, the SADC Protocol on

The Control of Firearms, Ammunition and Other Related Materials, 2001; the Nairobi Protocol on the Control, Prevention and Reduction of Small Arms and Light Weapons in the Great Lakes Region, the Horn of Africa and Bordering States, 2004; the Economic Community of West African States (ECOWAS) Convention on Small Arms and Light Weapons, their Ammunitions and Other Related Materials 2006; and the Central Africa Convention for the Control of SALW, their Ammunition and Parts and Components that can be used for their Manufacture, Repair or Assemblys, 2010 are some of such effort (AU 2013).

The African Union strategy on the control of illicit proliferation, circulation and trafficking of SALWs is to prevent, combat and eradicate the illicit proliferation, circulation and trafficking of small arms and light weapons in an integrated and holistic manner across all regions of Africa (see Table 3.2). The specific objectives of the Strategy are to:

i. Promote a culture of peace by carrying out education and public awareness programmes on the problems of the illicit proliferation, circulation and trafficking of small arms and light weapons;
ii. Address comprehensively the problem of the illicit proliferation, circulation and trafficking of SALW through mainstreaming SALW control as a cross-cutting and multidimensional issue in achieving peace, security, development and stability in the Continent;
iii. Strengthen the capacity of AU Member States, RECs and Regional Bodies, and the African Union Commission, to implement measures against the illicit proliferation, circulation and trafficking of SALW;
iv. Promote cooperation, coordination and exchange of information between relevant stakeholders at national, regional, trans-regional and continental levels;
v. Enhance international cooperation and assistance in the fight against proliferation of SALW at the national, regional and continental levels.

In relation to the AU strategy on the proliferation of SALWs is another sub-regional and bilateral approach to combating the menace of illicit arms which addresses sub-regional peculiarities and threats. All these approaches as seen in Table 3.2 are complementary and create a mutually reinforcing disarmament and arms control network across the continent. For instance, one unique addition of the ECOWAS protocol is its emphasis on National Database and Registers of SALWs. All these mechanisms notwithstanding, the continent seems not to have recorded remarkable success as far as combating the proliferation of SALWs is concerned as it is one thing to make policies and another thing to ensure efficient and effective implementation. The challenge with most African countries has never been the formulation of policies but effective implementation. Despite the efforts of the African Union (AU) and other regional initiatives and reduction strategies, SALWs have

Table 3.2 Regional and Sub-Regional approaches to the control of SALWs in Africa

S/N	Regional/Sub-Regional entity	Approach/Protocol	Effective date
1.	African Union	i. Bamako Declaration on an African Common Position on the Illicit Proliferation, Circulation and Trafficking of Small Arms and Light Weapons	2000
		ii. African Union Strategy on the Control of Illicit proliferation, Circulation and Trafficking of Small Arms and light Weapons	2013
		iii. Silencing the Guns Plan of Action on Controlling Illicit SALW	2018
2.	Southern Africa Development Community (SADC)	SADC Protocol on The Control of Firearms, Ammunition and Other Related Materials	Adopted on 14 August 2001 and entered into force on 8 November 2004
3.	Economic Community of West African States (ECOWAS)	Convention on Small Arms and Light Weapons, their Ammunitions and Other Related Materials	Adopted on 14 June 2006 and entered into force on 29 September 2009
4.	Economic Community of Central African States (ECCAS)	Central Africa Convention for the Control of SALW, their Ammunition and Parts and Components that can be used for their Manufacture, Repair or Assembly	Adopted on 30 April 2010 in Kinshasa, Democratic Republic of the Congo
5.	East African Community (EAC)	The Nairobi Protocol for the Prevention, Control and Reduction of Small Arms and Light Weapons in the Great Lakes Region and the Horn of Africa and bordering	Signed in April 2004 and entered into force in 2006

Source Compiled by Authors 2020

remained the sustenance and promoter of the culture of conflict in Africa (Weiss 2003). Even with sub-regional initiatives and moratorium implemented a by the Economic Community of West African States (ECOWAS), East Africa Community (EAC), and the Southern African Development Community (SADC), all towards limiting arms proliferation, but little or no success was recorded (Oche 2005).

Shading light on the above argument, the AU Silencing the Guns Plan of Action on Controlling Illicit SALW (2017: 2) did not only examine the nexus between SALWs proliferation and conflicts but also agrees that several policies on combating illicit flow of arms are in place without efficient and effective implementation when it maintained that:

> The Roadmap (AU Silencing the Guns Plan of Action on Controlling Illicit SALW) aims to address the root causes of conflict, prevent relapse into violence, and create the conditions required for sustainable peace and development across the continent…It recognizes that while several instruments have been developed at the international and regional levels, progress in controlling illicit SALWs is often undercut by an implementation deficit caused, in part, by limited human and financial resources, absence of political will, and inadequate coordination among stakeholders.

Thus, it is proper and expedient to put in place approaches and mechanism to curb the proliferation of SALWs in Africa but it is more appropriate to address the remote and immediate precipitators of SALWs in the continent among which is the failure of African political leadership to guarantee the delivery of political goods to their citizens. Good governance is apposite if Africa must counter the proliferations of SALWs. The theory of state collapse clearly presents the nexus between state failure and the flow of illicit weapons in Africa.

There is a need for an efficient management of African borders through collaborations among states that are especially contiguous with the use of modern technology. The geopolitical architecture of the continent is critical to understanding and addressing the proliferation of SALWs. Apart from geographical size, the topography and the network between and among states in Africa, there has been serious deficiency in border management. The increasing rate of illicit arms markets in Africa is made possible courtesy of poor border management in the continent. Apart from the fact that these borders are porous and unmanned, the continent is yet to employ the use of remote sensing, aerospace and geo-spatial technology to ensure effective and efficient border management.

There is a need for a re-evaluation of not only the African Union's strategy on the control of illicit proliferation, circulation and trafficking of SALWs, but institutionalizing robust strategies in all other sub-regional frameworks with a view to identifying its successes and failures as a way to re-strategize. The African Union should put in place sanctions against states the overtly or covertly encourage the proliferation of SALWs. The lack of political will vis-à-vis the inability of the AU to sanction member states is a serious issue that needs to be looked into. The issue of national interest and mutual suspicion has made some countries and sub-regions not to subscribe to some of these approaches. A case in point is North Africa where it has been impossible to develop a sub-regional approach to regulate the proliferation of SALWs.

Conclusion

The proliferation of Small Arms and Light Weapons in Africa is a major threat to the continent as far as security, peace and development is concerned. Postcolonial Africa has been grappling with this challenge regardless of several measures put in place at the regional and sub-regional levels to combat the spread of illicit arms. This chapter examined the theoretical and contextual parameters of the proliferation of SALWs. It further identified issues, examined perspectives and interrogated approaches put in place in Africa to address the challenge of SALWs proliferation. It examined several factors such as state failure, stockpiling, trans-border crimes, poor border management, arm race, illicit arm markets, and conflicts, etc., as major precipitators of the proliferation of SALWs in Africa. It also put forward and analysed SALWs using several theoretical frameworks such as the theory of geopolitics, Security Dilemma theory, State failure theory, Frustration aggression theory, etc., to shed more light on the proliferation of SALWs in Africa.

References

African Union. (2013). *African Union Strategy on the Control of Illicit Proliferation, Circulation and Trafficking of Small Arms and Light Weapons*. Addis Ababa: African Union Commission.

African Union. (2017). *Silencing the Guns Plan of Action on Controlling Illicit SALWs*. Addis Ababa: African Union Commission.

Alusala, N. (2018). *Africa and Arms Control: Challenges and Successes*. Policy Brief 03 / April. Available: https://reliefweb.int/report/world/africa-and-arms-control-challenges-and-successes-issue-03-april-2018. Accessed 20 June 2020.

Ayissi, A. N., & Sall. I. (2005). *Combating the Proliferation of Small Arms and Light Weapons in West Africa: A Handbook for the Training of Security Force*. Geneva: United Nations Institute for Disarmament Research (UNIDIR) Publications.

Badmus, I. A. (2005). Small Arms and Light Weapons Proliferation and Conflicts: Three African Case Study. *Nigerian Journal of International Affairs, 31*(2), 34–56.

Bell, D. (1953). Crime as an American Way of Life. *The Antioch Review, 13*(2), Summer, 133–151.

Bell, D. (1964). *Crime as an American Way of Life in the End of Ideology*. Glenceo, IL: Free PRESS.

Berkowitz, L. (1988). Frustrations, Appraisals and Aversively Stimulated Aggression. *Aggressive Behavior, 14*(1), 3–11.

Berkowitz, L. (1989). Frustration-Aggression Hypothesis: Examination and Reformulation. *Psychological Bulletin, 106*(1), 59–73.

Berlowitz, L. (1962). *Aggression: A Social Psychological Analysis*. New York, NY: McGraw-Hill.

Booth, K., & Wheeler, N. J. (2013). Uncertainty. In P. D. Williams (Ed.), *Security Studies: An Introduction* (pp. 135–154). New York, NY: Routledge.

Black, J. (2009). *Geopolitics*. London: The Social Affairs Unit.

Crossman, A. (2019). *Sociological Explanations of Deviant Behavior*. Available: https://www.thoughtco.com/sociological-explanations-of-deviant-behavior-3026269. Accessed 13 May 2020.

Chappelow, J. (2019). *Conflict Theory*. Available: https://www.investopedia.com/terms/c/conflict-theory.asp. Accessed 13 May 2020.

Clapham, C. (2002, November). The Challenge to the State in a Globalized World. *Development and Change, 33*(5), 775–795.

Cullen, F. T., & Agnew, R. (Eds.). (2006). *Criminological Theory: Past to Present*. Roxbury: Los Angeles.

Davies, J. C. (1962). Towards a theory of revolution. *American Sociological Review, 27*(1), 5–18.

Dodds, K. (2000). *Geopolitics in a Changing World*. Edinburg: Pearson Education Limited.

Dollard, J., Doob, L., & Miller, I. (1939). *Frustration Aggression Theory*. New Heaven CT: Yale University Press.

Dollard, J., Miller, N. E., Doob, L. W., Mower, O. H., & Sears, R. R. (1939). *Frustration and Aggression*. New Haven, CT: Yale University Press.

Durkheim, E. (1997). *The Division of Labor in Society*, translated by W.D. Halls. New York: Simon and Schuster.

ECOWAS. (2006). *ECOWAS Convention on Small Arms and Light Weapons, their Ammunition and other Relate Materials*. Abuja: ECOWAS Secretariat.

Featherstone, R., & Deflem, M. (2003). Anomie and Strain: Context and Consequences of Merton's Two Theories. *Sociological Inquiry, 73*(4), 471–489.

Flint, C. (2006). *Introduction to Geopolitics*. London: Routledge.

Francis, L. K. (2008). *Small Arms and Light Weapons Transfer in West Africa: A Stock Taking*. Available at: https://www.unidir.org/files/publications/pdfs/the-complex-dynamics-of-small-arms-in-west-africa-en-329.pdf. Accessed 13 May 2020.

Galadima, H. (2006). Peace Support Operations in Africa. In G. S. Best (Ed.), *Introduction to Peace and Conflict Studies in West Africa*. Ibadan: Spectrum Books Ltd.

Grimm, S., Lemay-Hebert, N., & Nay, O. (2016). *The Political Invention of Fragile States: The Power of Ideas*. London: Routledge.

Encyclopædia Britannica. (2019). *Geography*. Online, http://www.britannica.com/EBchecked/topic/229637/geography. Accessed 15 December.

Gomme, I. M. (2007). *The Shadow Line: Deviance and Crime in Canada*. Toronto, ON: Thomson Nelson.

Goodall, B. (1987). *Dictionary of Human Geography*. London: Penguin Books.

Hill, S. M. (2004). *United Nations Disarmament Processes in Intra-State Conflict*. New York, NY: Palgrave Macmillan.

International Action Network on Small Arms. (2006). *Bringing the Global Gun Crisis Under Control*. https://reliefweb.int/sites/reliefweb.int/files/resources/DB2973EEAE4DDF94C1257172002DD392-IANSA.pdf. Accessed 12 November 2019.

Johnson, N. N, Pabon, B. G, & Nkoro, F. (2012). Arms Proliferation and Conflicts in Africa: The Sudan Experience *IOSR Journal of Humanities and Social Science (JHSS), 4*(4) (Nov.—Dec. 2012), 31–39.

Kerlinger, F. N. (1977). *Foundations of Behavioural Research*. New York, NY: Holt, Rinehart and Winston.

Kingazi, L. (2006). *Enhancing Human Resource Capability in the Tanzania Peoples Defence Force (TPDF)*. Master's Thesis. Monterey, California: US Naval Postgraduate School.

Levine, D. (1985). *The Flight From Ambiguity*. Chicago: University of Chicago Press.

Lyman, P. M. G. (2007). *Organized Crime*. Prentice Hall, NJ: Person Education. Inc.

Mallory, S. L. (2007). *Theories on the Continued existence of Organized Crime*. Sudbury, MA: Jones and Bartlet Publishers.

Merton, R. (1938). Social structure and anomie. *Americana Sociological Review, 3*(5), 672–684.

Michael, F. (2001). Counting the Cost of Gun Violence. *Africa Recovery, 14*(4), 231–253.

Morgan, P. M. (2012). Elements of a General Theory of Arms Control. In R. E. Williams & P. R. Viotti (Eds.), *Arms Control: History, Theory and Policy* (pp. 15–41). Santa Barbara, CA: ABC-CLIO LCC.

Musah, A.-F. (2002). Small Arms: A Time Bomb Under West Africa's Democratization Process. *Brown Journal of World Affairs, 9*(1) (Spring), 239–249.

Nwoye, K. (2000). *Corruption, Leadership, and Dialectics of Developments in Africa*. Enugu: Associated printers.

Obasi, N. K. (2001). *Small Arms and Sustainable Disarmament in West Africa: Progress and Prospects of ECOWAS Moratorium*. Abuja: Apophyl Productions.

Oche, O. (2005). *The Proliferation of Small and Light Weapons*. Nigeria: Nigerian Institute of International Affairs.

Ochoche, S. A. (2002, November). *Civil-Military Cooperation in the Fight against the Proliferation of Small Arms and Light Weapons*. A Paper Presented at a Seminar on the Establishment of Culture of Peace, organized by NATCOM, Abuja.

Ogaba, D. O. (2005). *The Proliferation of Small Arms and Light Weapons*. Lagos: FOG Ventures.

Okodolor, Cletus Omo-Afeh. (2005). *Arms Control and Disarmament*. Nigeria: DeCafé Ventures.

Okoli, A. C., & Orinya, S. (2013). Oil Pipeline Vandalism and Nigeria's Sational Security. *Global Journal of Human Social Sciences, 13* (3:1.0), 65–75.

Oluyemi-kusa Dayo. (2006). Gender, Peace and Conflict in Africa. In G. S. Best (Ed.), *Introduction to Peace and Conflict Studies in West Africa*. Ibadan: Spectrum Books Ltd.

Onah, F. O. (2003). *Human Resource Management*. Enugu: Fulladu Publishing Company.

Onuoha, F. C (2013, 8 September 8). *Porous Borders and Boko Haram's Arms Smuggling Operations in Nigeria, Aljazeera*. Avialable: http://studies.aljazeera.net/en/reports/2013/09/201398104245877469.html. Accessed 2 May 2020.

Organization for Security and Co-operation in Europe. (2012). *Document on Small Arms and Light Weapons*. Adopted at the 686th Plenary Meeting of the Forum for Security Co-operation on 20 June 2012.

Pennock, J. R. (1966). Political Development, Political Systems, and Political Goods, *World Politics, XVIII* (1966), 420–426, 433.

Parker, S. (2016). *The Arms Trade Treaty: A Practical Guide to National Implementation. Handbook*. Geneva: Small Arms Survey.

Potter, G. (2017). *Globalization and the Illicit Trafficking in Arms*. http://uprootingcriminology.org/essays/globalization-illicit-traffic-arms/. Accessed 15 September 2019.

Ratzel, F. (1897). Studies in Political Areas: The Political Territory in Relation to Earth and Continent. *The American Journal of Sociology, 3*(3), 297–313.

Ratzel, F. (2011). *The Structure of Political Geography*. London: Routledge.

Roe, P. (1999). The Intrastate Security Dilemma: Ethnic Conflict as a 'Tragedy'? *Journal of Peace Research, 36*(2), 183–202.

Rotberg, R. (2004). *When States Fail: Causes and Consequences*. Princeton, NJ: Princeton University Press.

Rothe, D., & Collins, V. (2011). An Exploration of Applying System Criminality to Arms Trafficking. *International Criminal Justice Review, 2*(1), 141–163.

Saferworld. (2012). *Small Arms and Light Weapons Control: A Training Manual Small Arms Survey (2017)*. Available: http://www.smallarmssurvey.org/fileadmin/docs/Weapons_and_Markets/Tools/Firearms_holdings/SAS-Press-release-global-firearms-holdings.pdf. Accessed 22 May 2020.

Small Arms Survey. (2003). *Development Denied*. Oxford: Oxford University Press.

Small Arms Survey. (2011). Ethos of Exploitation: Insecurity and Predation in Madagascar. In *Small Arms Survey 2011: States of Security* (pp. 167–191). Cambridge: Cambridge University Press.

Small Arms Survey. (2018). *Global Fire arms Holdings Database*. Geneva: Small Arms Survey.

Small Arms Survey and African Union. (2018). *Country Responses to the Questionnaire on Mapping Illicit Arms Flows in Africa*. Geneva: Small Arms Survey.

Stohl, R., & Hogendoorn, E. J. (2010). *Stopping the Destructive Spread of Small Arms: How Small Arms and Light Weapons Proliferation Undermines Security and Development*. Washington, DC: Centre for American Progress.

Terrence, W. H., Kevin, M. B., & Brandon, A. M. (2014). The Three Critical Flaws of Critical Geopolitics: Towards a Neo-Classical Geopolitics. *Geopolitics, 19*(1), 19–39.

The Guardian. (2014, October 2). *Africa's Arms Dump: Following the Trail of Bullets in the Sudans*. Available: https://www.theguardian.com/world/2014/oct/02/-sp-africa-armsdump-. Accessed 15 January 2020.

Tierney, J. (2006). *Criminology: Theory and Context*. Essex: Longman.

United Nations. (1997). *Report of UN Panel of Group of Governmental Experts on Small Arms*. New York, NY: United Nations.

United Nations. (2017). *Eritrea Report of the Monitoring Group on Somalia and Eritrea Submitted in Accordance with Resolution 2317 (2016)*. S/2017/925 of 6 November.

United Nations Office on Drugs and Crime. (2012). *The Flows: Firearms Trafficking in West Africa*. Vienna: UNODC.

United Nations Office on Drugs and Crime. (2015). *UNODC Study on Firearms 2015: A Study on the Transnational Nature of and Routes and Modus Operandi Used in Trafficking in Firearms*. Vienna: UNODC.

United Nations Security Council. (2014). *Final Report of the Panel of Experts Established Pursuant to Resolution 1973 (2011) Concerning Libya*. S/2014/106 of 19 February.

UNSC (United Nations Security Council). (2013). *Final Report of the Panel of Experts Established Pursuant to Resolution 1973 (2011) concerning Libya*. S/2013/99 of 9 March. New York: United Nations.

UN Trust Facility Supporting Cooperation on Arms Regulation and MAG. (2015, April). *Practical Disarmament Initiative: Stockpile Management & Diversion Prevention*. Dakar. http://www.file.com///C:/Users/User/Downloads/practicaldisarmament-initaitive%20(1).pdf. Accessed 27 September 2019.

Yacubu, J. G. (2005). Cooperation Among Armed Forces and Security Forces in Combating the Proliferation of Small Arms. In A. Anatole & S. Ibrahima (Eds.), *Combating the Proliferation of Small Arms and light Weapons in West Africa*. Switzerland: United Nations Institute for Disarmament Research, Geneva.

Yale, A. J. (1962). *Frustration and Conflict*. London: Matheun.

Weiss, T. (2003). A Demand-Side Approach to Fighting Small Arms Proliferation. *Africa Security Review, 12*(2), 5–16.

Woodward, S. (2017). *The Ideology of Failed States*. Cambridge University Press.

Zartman, W. (1995). *Collapsed States: The Disintegration and Restoration of Legitimate Authority*. Boulder, CO: Lynne Rienner.

Usman A. Tar is a Professor of Political Science and Defence Studies, and Endowed Chair of Defence and Security Studies (26RC Endowment) at the Nigerian Defence Academy. He is the Director of the Academy's flagship Centre for Defence Studies and Documentation, and a member of the Board of Social Science Research Council's African Peacebuilding Network (SSRC/APN), New York, USA. He was formerly, Associate Research Fellow at Africa Centre for Peace and Conflict Studies, University of Bradford, UK. He authored several books including *The Politics of Neoliberal Democracy in Africa* (London/New York: I. B. Tauris, 2009); *Globalization in Africa: Perspectives on Development, Security and the Environment* (Lanham, MD, Lexington Books, 2016); *New Architecture of Regional Security in Africa* (Lanham, MD, Lexington Books, 2020); and *Routledge Handbook of Counterterrorism and Counterinsurgency in Africa* (London, Routledge, 2020). Prof Tar has consulted or consults for the United Nations Development Programme (UNDP), Nigeria; Konrad Adenauer Stiftung (KAS, German Development Fund); and the Westminster Foundation for Democracy (WFD), Nigeria. Prof Tar is a member of Nigeria's Presidential Think Tank on National Defence and Security, and served as a member of Nigeria's Presidential Committee to review the national defence policy in 2015.

Adejoh Sunday is a Lecturer with the Department of Defence and Security Studies, Nigerian Defence Academy Kaduna. He lectured at the Department of Political Science and Diplomacy, Veritas University Abuja. He obtained his Ph.D. in Defence and Strategic Studies (NDA) and Ph.D. in International Relations (University of Abuja). He has published extensively on Global Governance, Strategic Studies and International Development. He is one of the leading and pioneer scholars of Islamophobia in Nigeria. He is a member of the Nigerian Political Science Association (NPSA) and has published widely in both local and international journals and book chapters.

CHAPTER 4

The Political Economy of Small Arms and Light Weapons Proliferations in Africa

Moses Eromedoghene Ukpenumewu Tedheke

INTRODUCTION

The dynamics of the proliferations of small arms and light weapons (SALWs) in Africa is a historical outcome of the integration of Africa into the emergent racialised World capitalist system at the close of the Middle Ages, at the defeat of feudalism by the various European revolutions prior to the birth of classical capitalism. If we agree that globalisation is not a new phenomenon, it equally follows that the proliferations of SALWs which were and are the "violent drivers" of globalisation are not equally new to the "civilisation" that succeeded feudalism, the racialised world capitalist system. To understand the dynamics of the global empire of capital and its "blood lettings strategies" we have to get grips with its mode of birth and expansions out of its enclaves in Western Europe and North America and indeed later Japan. Capital's dictum is accumulate or perish and everything was done and is being done to actualise capital's dream by the very few, the bourgeoisie who held and are holding the reigns of power of the racialised classical capitalist states. This is what is known in Marxian circle as pervasive commodification. Europe had its mirror from the conquest of ancient African Egypt by Alexander the Great of Macedonia in 332 BC whose massive loots profited Athens and its philosophers who have always denied Africa's very valuable contributions to Euro-American civilisations with their lives and blood. African scholars who fail to examine this *long*

M. E. U. Tedheke (✉)
Department of Political Science and Defence Studies, Nigerian Defence Academy, Kaduna, Nigeria

© The Author(s), under exclusive license to Springer Nature Switzerland AG 2021
U. A. Tar and C. P. Onwurah (eds.), *The Palgrave Handbook of Small Arms and Conflicts in Africa*,
https://doi.org/10.1007/978-3-030-62183-4_4

view of history will fall prey to Western intellectual romanticism and will not be able to grasp the political economy of the African security question not to talk of its small arms and light weapons proliferations in this age of high technology imperialism (Tedheke 2016).

The political economy of SALWs proliferations was originally a product of nascent racialised mercantilist capitalist imperialism of Atlantic Chattel Slavery and later of matured capitalism of its home economy of over production and under consumption which led to armed invasions of Africa and the European militarisation of the continent. This was a product of post-industrial revolution of Western European expansionism to Africa resulting eventually into colonisation. The first colonisation wave was of the Americas and the Indian sub-continent and East Indies followed which were of the pre-industrial revolution periods and the second was massively the invasions of Africa by post-industrial revolution Europe. Capitalism of post-industrial revolution was a very virulent and violent one, of colonial conquest in order to realise surplus value (surplus value is made of profits, rents and dividends) created by labour that is always given necessary labour (peanuts as wages and salaries) by the capitalists. In this respect, therefore, the contradictions of alienations of labour power of concrete labour and socialising it resulted into over production and under consumption in the classical metropolitan capitalist countries which always results in over production and under consumption in the homes of racialised capital. They, therefore, needed to realise surplus value which led to wars of colonisations in Africa. Wars cannot happen without arms flowing in society, as such Africa was awash with arms of various degrees that were used to conquer the continent. Hell was let loose on the continent and new global division of labour was being sown in which Africa became the junior partner in the emerging international division of labour by providing slaves through wars that were orchestrated in Europe, executed in Africa and its products of captures were sold in the Americas (Inikori 2003; Jalata 2012, Martin 2005). These various wars for slave captures were the beginnings of SALWs proliferations in the continent.

The African continent has been a battle ground of history, of so many wars that were fought for the soul of the continent which were always wars of outside invasions and conquests. It has always been a very fertile ground for SALWs proliferations taking a departure from Atlantic Chattel Slavery, though small arms and light weapons seem to outperform the other segments of capitalist global expansionism depending on the lethality and the sophistications of the weapons of the age. In the age of Atlantic Chattel Slavery, Martin (2005) said estimated 600 million Africans were taken into slavery out of which 500 million were killed through tortures and 100 million survived that built Europe and North America. The figures of those who died by the bullets were not given but Adam Hochschild's accounts in the Congo in which King Leopold was said to have killed 10 million Congolese in his rubber wars (Hochschild 1998: 297) is a pointer to the brutalities of the emergent racialised European capitalism. Martin (2005) accounting for about 30 million

Africans killed during colonisation is another pointer that should make Africans and the rest of the World outside Europe and North America not to doubt the figures of African deaths to arms in racialised Atlantic Chattel Slavery. In his work titled; *King Leopold's Ghost: A Story of Greed, Terror and Heroism in Colonial Africa*, Adam Hochschild stated that "The Congo offers striking example of the politics of forgetting…" (Hochschild 1998: 294). The West emphasising the current SALWs proliferations in Africa is equally a part of politics of forgetting imposing group amnesia on Africans so that Europe and indeed all of the Western Capitalist societies criminal political economy will be covered up with politics of forgetting so that Africans will not catch historically that SALWs proliferations has been an agenda of the racialised world capitalist system.

There are two forces working for this merchandise of death currently which are endogenous and exogenous, products of the evolution of decolonisation in Africa unlike the period of Atlantic Chattel Slavery and colonisation in which they were completely exogenous. The outcome of the so-called second World War that weakened the colonial powers resulting in the defeat of French colonial enterprise in Vietnam at the Battle of Dien Bien Phu in 1954, the second strongest colonial power in Africa was a pointer to the future expectations of this deadly developments of predatory capital of Western imperialism which shot itself into World domination by predatory accumulation resulting into capital accumulation creating the Atlantic killing machines which Thomas Hobbes calls *the Great Leviathan* or Hobbesian state (Reyna and Downs 1999) which was not a product of the state of nature in crises after all as Hobbes would make us believe but of the seventeenth and eighteenth centuries Great Revolutionary crises in Western Europe, the crises that resulted in the overthrow of feudalism at the end of the Middle Ages. Citing Mann (1986) *The Sources of Social Power*, Reyna and Downs (1999: 17) infers that, "The capitalist states that had developed in Atlantic Europe by the eighteenth century were killing machines. Roughly seventy to eighty percent of their budgets were spent to pay the expenses of ongoing wars and debts of past wars." These war economies of Western Europe that turned the rest of the world outside Europe into *killing fields* are the beginnings of the political economy of SALWs proliferations in Africa starting from Atlantic Chattel Slavery through the so-called Legitimate Commerce to Colonialism and Neo-colonialism or Imperialism and Neo-imperialism are products of deliberate construction of antagonistic identities by political leaders seeking to control these states with connivance of agents of advanced industrial racialised capitalist states.

The Politics of "Collective Amnesia"

Decolonising the African mind is to reason critically in theoretical and historically conceptions in the analysis of issues relating to the continent. Africans were decolonised into believing that they have achieved independence when it is not but only a paper independence as a periphery of advance racialised capitalism and has to be maintained under the jackboot of imperialism of Europe and North America. Theorising the issues concretely is to reinsert Africans into their history in order to overcome imperialist politics of collective amnesia. According to Reinert (2007: 18), colonialism was a system where development was not intended to take place and failure to understand the connections between colonialism and poverty is a significant barrier to the understanding of poverty. One would like to add that it equally becomes a barrier in understanding the present situation of things in Africa that are causing crises in the continent resulting in civil wars aiding SALWs proliferations. It must also be scientifically stated that colonialism, neocolonialism anchored in imperialism or racialised monopoly financial capital and its post-Cold War form of neo-imperialism aided by their local collaborators, the comprador bourgeoisie are the fuels for the African continental crises and SALWs proliferations.

> The theory of capitalism and uneven development, therefore, is the anchor of this study which will elaborate on the forgoing key features of capitalism as they impact on the African crises. According to Reyna and Downs (1999: 3), "Most capital accumulation in the early modern period (c 1415-c 1760) resulted from the maximisation of profits of mercantile enterprises. After this time, capital accumulation increasingly resulted from the maximisation of profits of manufacturing enterprises that utilised machine technologies. These two varieties of capitalism have been respectively called "commercial" and "industrial." A "capitalist state" is one in which either of the two forms of capitalist enterprise dominate the civil society." The processes of accumulations in these different capitalist states which made some few states of high technologies rich and the rest of low technologies poor (Reinert 2007) and the relations of global dependency forcing the later to depend on the former for its developmental processes is the problem of the relations between the two different approaches to capitalist development (Tedheke 2014). Marx and Engles (1977: 289) remarked on the impact of the crises always generated at the core of capital (industrial) but always magnified at the periphery of capital (commercial dependencies) thus: While, therefore, the crises first produce revolutions on the continent, the foundation for this, nevertheless was always laid in England. Violent outbreaks must naturally occur rather in the extremities of the bourgeois body than in its heart, since the possibility of adjustment is greater here than there.

Not seeing the forgoing as the inner kernel of African crises underpinning the SALWs proliferations is to miss the point and succumb to the propaganda of imperialism or its politics of human rights violations turning Africans into culprits in collective amnesia instead of the victims of imperialist political economy. The crises in the extremities of bourgeoisie body were the case of mainland Europe, especially in France in which they fought and killed each other for 91 years from 1789 to 1891 but which became a lesson to others to take the right path to socio-economic development. History is repeating itself today in Africa as the capitalist crises of uneven and spasmodic development of capital is playing itself out today in the continent in its harvests of crises, civil wars calling for endemic peace keepings and peace support operations across the continent since decolonisation (Tedheke 2012a). According to Ekekwe (2019: 19–20) " …on account of the social formation being suspended between two opposing modes of production, informal mode of behaviour from the pre-capitalist era often collide with, and overwhelm, the formal rules of engagement embedded in the bureaucracy, producing clouds of chaos and confusion in the economy, politics and society generally." As such one has to view the crises that have led to the African condition that have resulted into SALWs proliferations beyond the analytical glasses being painted by Western imperialists giving vent to politics of group amnesia so as not to get to the roots of the African crises (Lenin 1978). These crises are products of inter and intra-class struggles in the process of class formation and accumulation of capital in the redistribution question in a continent not prepared for industrial capitalist development but restricted to merchant capitalism dependent on the political economy of raw material dependence which is the nexus of the African crises. Turner (1982: 158) succinctly said that the forgoing produces crises in a commercial capitalist social formation. The struggles for material interests by what she calls the "commercial triangle" involving international capital, the state officials and the middlemen always create and intensify internal crises. Thus she said:

> The political economy of commercial capitalist society is defined largely by effort to establish these triangular relationships and to operate them profitably. Instability is endemic in the struggle among middlemen for state patronages, and in the competition among officials of state for control of decisions. In these circumstances, politics is a form of business through which actors seek influence in the state, not in order to make and apply general rules but in order to secure advantages.

The centrality of the state in the distribution of patronages becomes crucial and therefore the intensification of struggles for state power increases, especially in the periods of state and world economic down turn or meltdown. Since the coming into the stage of racialised industrial capitalism as a global phenomenon, it has always given birth to crises in its periphery which we have conceptualised as commercial capitalism because of its lack of industrial base necessary for its rejuvenation in its periods of crises of accumulation in the redistribution question. As the backward societies lack industrial base and their commercial bourgeoisie mostly dependent on the state and foreign linkages for their sustenance, politics becomes a do-or-die affair or a life and death matter and thus is turned into a battle ground. According Turner (1982: 160):

> Since governments are responsible for a great deal of expenditure in poor countries, the full pressure of an oligopolistic market is brought to bear on state

affairs. Local intermediaries and foreign businessmen who are unable to gain access to the decision-makers of the moment look forward to their replacement. State officials who cannot obtain positions which allow them to influence decision-making similarly seek to unseat those in power. In this conflict-ridden context, the power of guns and money plays an everyday role.

In the foregoing context, two forces identified by Terisa Turner and S. P. Reyna coalesced to play a destabilising role in African and indeed most Third World politics. Thus the struggles for political power so as to gain access to public till and access foreign businessmen to their economies becomes a daily life-and-death struggles where guns and money must play an everyday role. We have to place these *deadly developments* at the feet of capitalism of the two shades—the commercial and industrial capitalism which are products of the division of labour of industrial capitalism between its core and its periphery. It gave birth to capitalism of uneven development as capitalism is not a welfare scheme but a mode of production attuned to the maximisation of surplus value (profits, rents and dividends), more surplus value if the capitalist is to maintain his stead and advance in the cut throat competition in its dictum of the *survival of the fittest*. As a result of the urge for more surplus value in order to accumulate in response to the eternal logic of capital, it is only profitable ventures that naturally attract the capitalist and hence he has no moral obligation for even development.

The emergence of capital from the womb of feudalism took plunder anchored in its killing machine as its point of departure in its primitive accumulation of capital through Atlantic Chattel Slavery that first defined the geography of nascent racialised merchant capitalism transformed into racialised industrial capital from fifteenth to nineteenth centuries that later metamorphosed into matured racialised industrial capitalism after the industrial revolution of the seventeenth and eighteenth centuries Western Europe. The dog often wipes its lips with its tong savouring the aroma of the sweet meal it previously consumed and capital from its nascent stage of merchant capital or mercantilism to industrial revolution like the dog has always remembered the sweet meals of conquests in its previous styles of preying and would always want a re-enactment in one form or the other. The sweet memories of Alexander the Great's conquest of ancient African Egypt that was practiced later in Europe against themselves, resulting in the emergence of the Roman Empire and later its breakup at the tail end of the Middle Ages resulting in Austro-Hungarian Empire and later the Spanish Empire among others were schoolings for Europeans and their later extractions in North America, Australia and New Zealand to always see as a mirror for the emergent Euro-American civilisation. For capitalism, Marx (1984: 113) posited that it is the tendency of capitalist mode of production to transform all production as much as possible into commodity production, when the dictates of profits have prevailed for their commodification. This is what is regarded in Marxian circles as the process of pervasive commodification. In the capitalists' quests for accumulation through subjugation and conquest, Marx (1984: 202–203) wrote:

> Conquest may lead to either of three results. The conquering nation may impose its own mode of production upon conquered people-or it may refrain from interfering in the mode of production and may be content with tribute-or interaction may take place between the two, giving rise to a new system as a synthesis... in any case, it is the mode of production brought about by merging of the two that determines the new mode of distribution employed.

In most of the underdeveloped world, racialised capitalism penetrated, left the old structures intact but converted them to serve the interests of accumulation of capital for metropolitan capitalism through the enthronement of capitalist relations of production. From the British experiences in its North American colonial experiment in which their kits and kens expelled them from the very lucrative colony, a new strategy of satellisation or divide-and-rule was put into action to safeguard the later days colonies for effective hegemonic control by the British colonial masters. All the various forms of satellisation conglomerated in the later day colonial enterprises. They ranged from cultural satellisation to industrial satellisation, educational satellisation and also satellised national consciousness based on secondary variables of analysis such as ethnicity, religion, sectionalism among others which are products of both internal and external capital accumulation in a dependent capitalist social formation or a political economy of raw material dependency. The forgoing processes according to Nnoli (1978: 22–23) give vent to uneven development inherent in imperialist global relations which imbalances deepen the antipathies between ethnic groups which today is the hallmark of African societies giving the continent the harvest of conflicts enhancing SALWs proliferations. There was a Dass Portuguese gun belonging to the Zeggi family which was not thrown down from the sky or heaven by some angels but a product of European expansionism, and one can guess from its age manufactured in the eighteenth century that it was a part of the guns for Atlantic Chattel Slavery.

Overcoming Collective Amnesia in the Narratives of SALWs Proliferations

The narratives of SALWs proliferations all over the world seem to have a disregard for its political economy which is the economy of racialised predatory capital, imperialism and neo-imperialism that is always after accumulation or perish in which anything goes for accumulation hence the capitalist dictum of *the survival of the fittest*. This barbaric urge for accumulation resulted in the taking into slavery estimated 600 million Africans in which 500 million were killed through tortures and 100 million survived that build Europe and North America (Martin 2005; Jalata 2012, 2013). This dastardly act could not have taken place without SALWs proliferations into the bargain as history has it that this was the era of the invention of the Maxim Gun and the Gatling Gun which played major roles in the massive kidnappings of Africans that were taken into Atlantic Chattel Slavery. In Dass town in Bauchi state of Nigeria, the Zeggi family still has one of such guns produced by the Portuguese in the eighteenth century perhaps used for slave captures. This was one of the proofs of the first point of departure of SALWs proliferations in Africa. Chattel Slavery was a triangular activity which was planned in Western Europe executed in Africa and its harvests disposed off in the Americas as slaves (Inikori 2003). We have noted earlier that Atlantic Europe or states of industrial revolution were *killing machines that they took upon themselves to kill humans for capital accumulation* in hundreds of millions to realise their goal. This was what brought about the so-called Hobbesian theory of the Great Leviathan, the central sovereign or the modern capitalist state (Reyna and Downs 1999).

Throughout the history of father rights societies of Northern Cradle which Europe has been a part, wars have always been a vocation. Since the defeat of mother rights societies of the Southern Cradle which was black African Egypt under the jack booths of Alexander the Great invading army in 332 BC (Diop 1989), war games have assumed critical dimensions especially in Europeans' empire building and capital accumulation. Frederick Engels gave the fact and character of the military of the emergent historical states of Europe from ancient Greece through medieval Europe to the time of the birth of capitalism. He said that the transformation of the primitive communal system from a naturally grown democracy to a hateful aristocracy was a product of division of labour that breached the gentile constitution of egalitarianism prior to the emergence of civilisation. Equally, their security strategy which was based on *the strategy of the armed people* an institution of class power or the state and of plunder. As such Engels (1977: 160–161) gave us the dialectics of the transformations from the gentile constitution to civilisation in which, war, once waged to avenge aggression or as a means of enlarging territory that had become inadequate, was now waged for the sake of plunder, and became a regular profession.

This culture of plunder that informed the dynamics of Euro-American civilisation has been carried through post primeval times, through Medieval Europe, through Atlantic Chattel Slavery to industrial revolution to the age of racialised monopoly financial capital or imperialism and in the twenty-first century to globalisation or neo-imperialism's gun boat diplomacy. The fact that some SALWs proliferations from the former Soviet Union which epicenter is Russia, including the Chinese and a part of Eastern Europe under defunct Warsaw Pact is not the matter. As has been the historical practices of capital, the principle of capitalist pervasive commodification is taking place and this became enhanced with the collapse of the former Soviet Union, the Euro-American supports for Mujahidin in Afghanistan, the Taliban that succeeded them that developed into Al-Qaeda, the American and her allies' invasions of Afghanistan, Iraq, Libya, Syria and a host of others are cases in point in in the twenty-first-century's gun boat diplomacy spreading SALWs proliferations. The crises of accumulation must force capital always into very dangerous ventures outside its core and its foreign policy based on so-called theory of realism or power politics forces the World always into global arms race. Is this an African or Third World affair? Not at all! It was first of all an intra-imperialist affair resulting in colonisations from which intra-imperialist greed caused the so-called First and Second World Wars. And at the end of the Second World War it turned ideological between the East and the West (Communism versus Capitalism) which turned Africa into Cold War camps resulting in coups and counter coups across the continent giving into excessive SALWs proliferations.

The various anti-colonial and neo-colonial liberation wars in Africa, Indo-China and Latin America with imperialism trying to maintain its' stranglehold on the South resulted in various ways in SALWs proliferations across the globe. After all Africans are not the producers of these SALWs and their proliferations is an agenda of imperialist financial capitals' realisation problem which turned the European Atlantic states into killing machines giving birth to the so-called Great Leviathan which we were told was a project to avoid the state of nature in which *life was nasty, brutish and short* but which case was not and is not true. The fact remains that these Atlantic states, the lithospheres of Europe emerged as great states after their killing sprees on the South in the first, second and third phases of Euro-American capital accumulation. The eliminations of the American Indians and their replacements by Chattel Slaves from Africa in the first phase of colonisation, followed by the spices and cotton trading in the second phase of colonisation of the East Indies prior to industrial revolution and thirdly the pressures of industrial revolution resulting in the third phase of colonisation of Africa which was in order to solve the problems of the realisation of surplus value for the emergent racialised monopoly financial capital or imperialism were all stages that gave birth to the so-called Great Leviathan. In all of these stages in the historical and geographical spread of capital, the proliferations of the Maxim Guns and the Gatling Guns were to the rescue of the emergent Atlantic European states globalised racial capitalism. Reyna and Downs (1999: 16) in Reyna and Downs has educated us on the armaments build-up by capitalist states resulting in the emergence of the modern slaughter states with its distinctive quality having evolved between 1415 and 1763 as a military-capitalist-complex-in military institutions in governments co-dependent with those of capitalism in civil society that warred to assist in capital accumulation, and then used this capital to increase military capabilities, i.e., to facilitate predatory accumulation. Reyna and Downs (1999: 17) conclude thus: "Structural and subjective factors found in, or associated with capitalist states help to determine or accelerate the types of war found in modern world. This means that any representation of capitalist states as pacific is delusional." We are pointing our fingers as regards SALWs proliferations at imperialism and their creations in Africa, *the abnormal states generating crises* resulting into state failures in the peripheries of capitalism.

Imperialism and the Creation of the Abnormal States Through SALWs Proliferations

The spates of SALWs proliferations as we have seen in the forgoing is a product of racial capitalism of Western Europe and its spread across the globe in the past 500 years from the fifteenth century to date. In its processes of capital accumulation, capitalism has no option but to spread violence across the globe as a killing machine and as it incorporates societies outside its traditional home states, wars became and have become its eternal interests hence its dictum of *the survival of the fittest*. There is no fitting description to what is happening today in the capitalist world than Engels' (1983) statement thus; "Naked greed has been the moving spirit of civilisation from the first day of its existence to the present time; wealth, more wealth and wealth again; wealth not of society, but of...the shabby individual was its sole and determining aim." As such the cut throat competitions among and between capitalists and also in intra-capitalist nations' rivalries; issues in ideological confrontations have spiralled arms race. These have always been very serious issues prior to and since the two destructive capitalist intra-European, inter-tribal wars which they have wrongly conceptualised as World Wars but were rather intra-capitalist wars of greed. Greeds have been features of societies governed by private property from the classical slave epoch through the feudal epoch of the Middle Ages or Medieval Europe now giving it to us in more deadly forms as capitalist killing machines of Western Europe, North America, Australia and Japan.

These killing sprees which began with nascent capital were products of the historical carryover from classical slave states of European antiquity through their Middle Ages to present day capitalism of Euro-American and Japanese imperialism which have been the consequences of greeds of societies of private property. This political economy of blood and guns has been the traditions of all European civilisations. This *naked greed being the moving spirit of Euro-American civilisation* has strengthened the culture of guns and violence with which Euro-American imperialism has destroyed other societies outside Europe and North America to cushion their primitive capital accumulation drive from the fifteenth to nineteenth centuries and since then spurred by imperialist's realisation problem. The primitive accumulation of capital, especially from Atlantic Chattel Slavery of greed capitalism created the surpluses that generated the industrial revolution in Atlantic Europe and later the United States.

The primitive capital accumulation that occurred was with very massive blood lettings from the fifteenth century on prior to their industrial revolution and indeed post-industrial revolution giving birth to bloody colonisation. These brutal activities by what Jalata (2011) calls racialised capitalism have not been addressed regarding its horrors on humanity, specifically the African people, a holocaust, that can be classified as the greatest crime against humanity in its Atlantic Chattel Slavery on African human cargoes merchandise from the fifteenth century to the nineteenth century. It never ended there but was carried to the post-industrial revolution colonisation of Africa. Jalata (2011: 2) went further to talk about the inadequacies of critical thinkers like Karl Marx, Andre Gunder Frank, Immanuel Wallestein and others who have studied the emergence, development and expansion of the racialised capitalist world system who have primarily focused on trade, the international division of labour, exploitation, capital accumulation, political structures, development and underdevelopment, and social inequality and ignored the role of terrorism in creating and maintaining it. This is why Africans must have to reinvestigate history and such endeavours must abandon the partial and percellised history (Tedheke 2019) given to us as history to enforce group amnesia on Africa and the Third World.

The most problematic of this racialised capitalist world system is its lack of dialectical approaches anchored on ahistoricism so as to cover-up its crime against humanity on the global South not to expose the evolution of how nascent capitalism became imperialism that is now neo-imperialism or globalisation which have become the key in understanding the *national question* of these former colonised societies. The national question writ large are those issues preventing the national/continental socio-economic transformation thus intensifying the centrifugal forces in the dependencies which always give vent to destructive ethnic and sectional politics now taking the central stage in today's African crises resulting in SALWs proliferations across the continent.

On the development or evolution of the world capitalist system Karl Marx put an icing on the cake by exposing an inkling leading to the truth with a veil of Eurocentric spicing nevertheless bringing the truth to the fore. In this respect, any intellectual or academician that is serious minded can piece through the veil and arrive at the scientific truth. The liberal scholars and their ideological masters rather buried the cake which is the truth as such putting on us a blindfold permitting only the maggots of capital to access it, preventing the rest of us, the colonised peoples from getting at the root of our problems including causes of SALWs proliferations in Africa and other dependencies. Thus the origin of capital has been anchored on killing sprees which are always covered up. Marx (1978: 11) exposed the truth about the birth of capitalist nations thus: "But unheroic as bourgeois society is, nevertheless it took heroism, sacrifice, terror, civil wars and the battles of nations to bring it into being." According to Jalata (2011: 2–3) "Even critical scholars that studied the emergence, development, and expansion of the racialised capitalist world system have primarily focused on trade, the international division of labour of racialised capital." However he cited Marx (1967: 753–754) thus:

> The colonies secured a market for the budding manufacturers and, through the monopoly of the market, an increasing accumulation.... As a matter of fact, methods of primitive accumulation are anything but idyllic. In actual history it is notorious that conquest, enslavement, robbery, murder, briefly force, played the great part. In fact, the veiled slavery of the wage workers in Europe needed

for its pedestal, slavery pure and simple in the new world. Capital comes [into the world] dripping from head to foot, from every pore, with blood and dirt.

The fact that Karl Marx did not study the forgoing in detail tells the Eurocentric nature of his scholarship that one has set under criticism of Marxian and Liberal theories of the state in another write-up as such exposing their inadequacies in addressing the issue. Nevertheless Karl Marx has given an inkling into what transpired during the emergence and development of racialised capitalist world system that it has been a killing machine indeed. These killing machines of capital were to distort states formations in the peripheries of capital (mercantile capitalist social formations) causing endemic crises in these extremities of capital or mercantilist capitalist states such as Nigeria and other Third World states giving birth to abnormal state structures lacking the capacity for autonomous capitalist development.

THE CONTINENTAL QUESTION, WARS OF LIBERATION AND SALWs PROLIFERATIONS

The continental question is an embodiment of the thwarted African history as a result of its subjugation by Euro-American racialised world capitalist system since 500 years now. It is very important that the tragedies resulting in the current African condition must be properly focused on if we are to overcome its imposed crises. In most cases, the issues involved are always addressed midstream thus putting them in obscurantism and agnosticism turning Africans into acqiutience of collective amnesia. According to Hochschild (1998: 293–235), Jalata (2013: 2) the West has relied on politics of forgetting deliberately encouraged to hide their crimes against humanity in Africa from Atlantic Chattel Slavery to colonialism to date which have been the traditions of both the right and left scholars of Euro-American descent. This pervasive great forgetting, according to Adam Hochschild is not something passive but an active deed which is universally evident as recorded in early white conquistadors in Africa from which one can catch the act of forgetting at the very moment it happens. In several publications, Asafa Jalata and Guy Martin differently detailed the atrocities of the globalised racial capitalist world system visited on Africa which the West and their African adherents have consciously and criminally decided to forget. Is it not anti-history which the *Groundwork of Nigerian History* is anchored and indeed the main stream of Nigerian History in percellised broken up into various components not dialectically linked? This politics of deliberate forgetting the African past tragedies, is it now consciously being weaved into the narratives of SALWs proliferations in Africa today without linking such to the racialised world capitalist system since the fifteenth century? This politics of deliberate forgetting, is it not to excuse the globalised culprit of capitalist racialised system and blame the victims? Answers to the forgoing will open to us why the African condition in

SALWs proliferations is being intensified since the anti-colonial struggles and indeed the Cold War period to post-Cold War.

As has been progressively stated in this work that SALWs proliferations in Africa and other colonised societies have been the agenda of the racialised world capitalist system from its mercantile stage of Atlantic Chattel Slavery through the so-called legitimate commerce, through colonialism to date. The strategies were in various forms of brutalities against Africans and other colonised peoples. It is very wrong to have the view that SALWs proliferations in Africa is as a result of primordial sentiments or ethnic irredentism or identity politics forgetting the merchants of blood of death, imperialism and its military-industrial-complex being the perpetrators with their African accomplices (Tedheke 2012a, 2014). It is equally wrong to rope in the Russians and the Iranians as the anchors of post-Cold War SALWs proliferations which is the propaganda of the West. The various acts of the brutalities of the globalised racial world capitalist system have been set out in theoretical romanticism of advance capitalist societies, theories that were born out of the genocidal holocaust against the subjugated peoples of the global South, such as realism, gunboat diplomacy, the survival of the fittest, Darwinism, the military-industrial-complex among others which have forced on the South as "very important" academic fields in international relations, defence and strategic studies but which are rather fallouts from the practices of the racialised world capitalist system of Western Europe, North America, Japan and English pogrom against aborigines of Australia. These theories encouraged blood merchandise from the citadel of capital and their harvests in Africa and other colonised peoples resulted in the harvests of SALWs proliferations across the global South today.

Arising from the forgoing are the perpetual conditions imposed on the Africans that amount to the continental question which is a summation of the national questions of the various African states calling for urgent resolution without which Africa will continue in the endemic crises spiralling SALWs proliferations for the military-industrial-complex to sell their weapons to advance its global agenda. Thus a very clear understanding of the causes of conflicts require differentiating the primary from the secondary/intervening variables which would place us at the verge of getting at the fundamentals of peace, democracy and security (Tedheke 2013). This will make us to put the proper socio-economic infrastructures in place for real peace building because it is impossible to create peace and disarm when the irreconcilable contradictions of racialised world capitalist system are still there and we seem not to understand them. There are internal and external causes of these conflicts and wars. The external sources are what Tandon (Echoes17 2000) located in his work titled "The Violence of Globalisation." He said:

> On causes of conflict and violence there are two major lines of thought. The mainstream or dominant theory tends to emphasize the internal factors within a nation as the root causes. The corresponding solutions are economic growth

and good governance. Whilst there is much that may be accepted in this analysis, its principal fault is that it does not adequately analyse the international or global dimension of conflicts, and does not connect various factors in a holistic manner. This is so because of its stake in the preservation of the existing value system. Thus the very factors that have impoverished a region namely: exploitation by foreign capital under conditions of free market-are the ones offered by mainstream thinkers as solutions to that region's economic woes.

The forgoing mainstream theoretical representation of conflicts blame the ethnic irredentism or primordial sentiments as the causes of African crises, especially the proliferations of small arms and light weapons(SALWs) across the continent. The imperialists are equally shifting the blames on Russia and Iran which the gullible South and Africans are equally buying. There is a purpose by the prevailing dominant global racialised capitalist system and the forces behind it to make such issues in the Third World look as if they are completely internal or locate the external on their enemies—Russia, Turkey and Iran. In the view of Nnoli (1978: 13), "By diverting attention from imperialist exploitation and the resultant distortions of African economic and social structures, ethnicity preforms the function of mystification, and militates against the imperatives of revolutionary struggles by hampering the development of a high level of political consciousness of its victims." This is the case of the so-called ECOWAS Moratorium on SALWs proliferations which only stated the historical background as the humanitarian disasters in Sierra Leone, Liberia and Cote d'Ivoire claiming to have been occasioned by internal conflicts. The moratorium took effect from November 1998, for a renewable period of three years (Lodgaard and Fung 1998) but it is faulted on limiting causations of the West African regional conflicts only to internal factors.

On the Nigerian Civil War which can go for all of Africa crises, Nafziger (1983: 19) said that the political economy model asserts that "...the probability of political violence is partly a function of internal domestic factors,- regional economic rivalries, conflicts among elite groups, class conflicts, economic inequality and domestic economic policy-all of which depend, (to a large extent-my emphasis) on international variables. And the explanations of the relationship rely in part on economic analysis ..." However, he failed to address the historical dynamics of the evolution of the situation being analysed. Thus without stating the particular political economy combined with its historical settings as in the case of Africa, the African condition resulting in the SALWs proliferations will be hard to comprehend and therefore an exercise in confusion or obscurantism. When we use the non-dialectical historical eclectic approach, we will continue to blame victims of global racial capitalist imperialist violence on the global South or the perpetrators will direct our attention on imagined enemies. Socrates said that the first rule of discourse is the clarification of concepts and without understanding the primary causal variables of the African crises both internal and external, it will be difficult to get at the root causes of these conflicts and why the proliferations of SALWs all over the continent. We have stated the historical roots right from Atlantic Chattel Slavery through the so-called Legitimate Commerce through Colonialism and as we shall see in next section, it has continued to post-Cold War of racialised advanced capitalist neo-imperialist globalisation.

We have to call on the denied but authentic historical records to our aid in the very vast revamped historical materialist analysis, deeper than Eurocentric versions of this criminal World Order of racialised capitalist holocaust on the global South for the past 500 years now, which has not abated despite denials by its perpetrators. We have given account citing Guy Martin in this work earlier who estimated that 600 million Africans were taken into slavery out of which 500 million were killed through brutalities of European slavers and 100 million survived that built Europe and North America which no source has countered. We have equally cited Chinweizu who said that the entire holocaust of Atlantic Chattel Slavery was a product of war planned in Europe, executed in Africa and the proceeds disposed off in the Americas. Since even radical Eurocentric scholarship has not gone deep enough to expose in-depth the criminalities of this racialised global capitalist political economy, it is incumbent on all true humanists, especially Africans, to remove the scaffold inhibiting the truth about this criminal world order since its birth in Western Europe in the fifteenth century. Neglecting how SALWs proliferations was criminally encouraged from that time is nothing but obscurantism and agnosticism in the global historical dynamics of this phenomenon which has been engrained in the global military-capitalist-complex and now military-industrial-complex.

According to Jalata (2013: 163), "Enslaving some young Africans involved warfare, trickery, banditry, kidnapping, burning villages, raping, torturing, dividing and destroying communities, facilitating civil wars, and destroying existing leadership and cultures." He went further to say that they were in alliance with some Africans, recruited African mercenaries for warfare and terrorism to break the will of the Africans (Jalata 2013: 164). Wilkinson (1979: 45) cited by Jalata (2013: 4) said, "We really understand very little about the origins and causes of human violence in its daunting variety.... There is no substantial theoretical literature in social science concerned specifically with terrorist phenomena." But Jalata (2013: 4) countered the foregoing remarks by Paul Wilkinson thus:

> Nevertheless, since the frequency, intensity, and the volume of terrorism have increased with the emergence and development of global capitalism, a definition and a theory of terrorism cannot be adequately developed without considering terrorism as an aspect of the racialised capitalist world system. Beginning in 1492, European colonialists engaged in terrorism, genocide, and enforced servitude in the Americas and extended their violence into Africa through racial slavery. Then in the sixteenth, seventeenth, eighteenth and nineteenth centuries, they incorporated other parts of the world into this system through colonial terrorism and genocidal wars.

Despite both right and left philosophers of the goodness of racialised global capitalist system, various records in the historical process have denounced the encomiums always poured on this Euro-American phenomenon called capitalism, that it is nothing but holocaustal blood capitalism in its historical trajectory which it accomplished through arms proliferations and warfares. According to Reyna and Downs (1999: 16) "...what gave the modern state (classical capitalist states-my emphasis) its distinctive quality was the evolution between 1415 and 1763 of a military-capitalist complex-military institutions in governments co-dependent with those of capitalism in civil society-that warred to assist in capital accumulation, and then used this capital to increase military capabilities, i.e., to facilitate predatory accumulation." Also Mann (1986) was cited by Reyna and Downs (1999: 17) who said that the capitalist states that had developed in Atlantic Europe by the eighteenth century were killing machines. Roughly seventy to eighty per cent of their budgets were spent to pay the expenses of ongoing wars and the debts of past wars. This is the historical origin of the military-industrial complex that African intellectuals think can be replicated in Africa or in other former colonies which is not possible.

As always with the case of the chameleon called capitalism, capital accumulation has evolved to other forms of deadly developments. In collaboration with their dependent capitalists of the global South they have deliberately been constructing antagonistic ethnic identities in order to control the neo-colonial states. This suggests that those marketing ethnic essentialism—dreaming that all ethnic groups hate each other as the savage Other—peddle a phantasmagoria (Reyna and Downs 1999: 16). This is the problem with Africa. We have to point out the flaws properly situating the crises spiralling SALWs proliferations in the continent so as to show us that the capitalist "angel" is indeed the devil hence the continental question or condition starting from colonial conquests. One is always at great pains when African intellectuals cannot piece through the collective amnesia that has been imposed by Euro-American scholarship. Since we have sufficiently elaborated on the pre-colonial stage of Atlantic Chattel Slavery, we now have before us the brutalities of colonisations SALWs proliferations spiralling into neo-colonialism, the age of high-tech imperialism now the heart of the matter before us.

Post-Cold War Africa and SALWs Proliferations: Neo-imperial Globalising Agenda?

Capital accumulation is the key project of the racial globalised Euro-American world system that began in the fifteenth century to date. It has always prospered with blood on the global South which has become its mainstay. The crises of accumulation have become increasingly compounded with the emergence of the East Asia as the store houses of global non-racialised productive centres now overtaking the racialised global world capitalist system. The accumulation question of racialised Euro-American world capitalist system that has always been based on might is right has suddenly woken up as a wounded lion to the realities before it by the economic might of the East and they have to fall on a plan of sustenance of imperialist onslaught on the weaker other half of the South. What is the strategy? Destabilisations of the other half of the South that have not developed to become nations or that have been unable to resolve their national questions to become real nations in relative economic autonomy. If they are able to resolve their national questions, it will be a minus for Euro-American imperialism and a plus for the other half of the global South. For imperialism, this is *death sentence* hence the type of decolonisation that kept the global South in bondage but with eternal struggles some parts of this South have began the process of having their second independence or economic independence. Africa, however, is not moving in this direction because of imperialists' machinations of divide-and-rule strategies supported by the comprador bourgeoisie that were born in the colonial political economy of raw material dependency. According to Nkrumah (1973) in his book *Class Struggles in Africa*, during anti-colonial struggles there were two liberation movements, the pro-imperialists and the anti-imperialists. The pro-imperialists were the Monrovian/Brazzaville Groups and the anti-imperialists were made up of the Casablanca Group. Nigeria was the head of the Monrovia/Brazzaville Groups that became the majority that founded the Organisation of African Unity (OAU) in 1963 hence decolonisation into state failures and crises in neo-colonial Africa.

The forgoing was in the interest of Euro-American imperialism. How was imperialism able to manipulate Africa as usual? It was through the processes of decolonisation through which the colonialists snatched the rearguards of the nationalist movements and planted stooges to dissipate the victories won. The processes of decolonisation split Africa between imperialist interests and African interests as such the seeds of crises were sown between patriots and traitors. The pace was set for a neo-colonial political economy of raw material dependency in which when Europe and North America (imperialism) sneezes Africa will always catch cold or collapse. The imperialists always employ different strategies in each turn in the crises of their historical processes. For decolonisation they foresaw their weaknesses and decided to manipulate the processes. According to Fanon (1980: 55): This encompassing violence does not work upon the colonised people only; it modifies the attitude of the colonialists hence the colonial wars of liberation.

Thus imperialism kept Africa divided through neo-colonialism in which crises of development and insecurity have been entrenched. We have cited earlier that anytime there is crisis of accumulation in the core of capital there are always revolts, conflicts and wars in the periphery of capital. Now the periphery of capital is narrowing down on Africa as the New Industrialising countries are catching on very fast. What are the consequences of this global relations? Internecine conflicts and wars to fulfil one agenda for neo-imperialism which is the drastic reduction of African population. Are Africans surprised at the flow of SALWs proliferations into the continent in the post-Cold War era? Our dubious acceptance of over population theory and that the problem is that our people are producing children like rats has become the booze ideology, preventing Africans, especially, the conventional scholars from deeper investigations on imperialist roots of SALWs proliferations in the continent. Rather they say that the so-called population explosion is the problem and that we must depopulate to que into growth and development according to imperialist and neo-imperialist agenda.

The battles to reduce African population is being waged on many fronts through African neo-colonialist and neo-imperialist despots who cause crises, conflicts and wars. It is equally being waged by African Eurocentric academicians who propagate the Euro-American view of over population and also the military-industrial-complex that is interested in the supersonic profitability of light weapons sales, equally working in tandem with the ideology of family planning and biological terrorism on Africa and the global South. All these are working towards one goal which is the reduction of the African population, an agenda that was started from Atlantic Chattel Slavery through imperialist colonisation to neo-colonialism and now neo-imperialist globalisation. This agenda of population reduction in Africa is not new but has been since Atlantic Chattel Slavery from the fifteenth century to date, a project first anchored by the Portuguese, followed by the Spanish, the Dutch or the Netherlands, the English, the French, the Belgians and the Germans. In both the West coast and the East coast of Africa, whether by the Europeans or Arabs, Chattel Slavery and the depopulation of Africa was for European plantations in both the East Indies and the Americas (Rodney 1972: 105–106). African intellectuals that lose sight of this will always give us half baked facts whether in the Social Sciences or History. We have stated earlier that what emerged from Europeans exploitation of the global South has been the killing machine (Reyna and Downs 1999).

What we have been taught to see in parts, S. P. Reyna and R. E. Downs made us to see in the whole and the secrets are no longer hidden that the Atlantic Killing Machines was the origin of the so-called *Great Leviathan or the Stately Whale/Crocodile* which Thomas Hobbes called *the State*. This Atlantic Killing Machines continue to date based on the *criminal theories of realism, gunboat diplomacy, the survival of the fittest anchored on power politics*. These theories of the racialised global capitalist system were the inklings giving away the terrorisms of the Euro-American civilisations. Despite its chameleonic movements can the tiger change its spurs as its killing weapons? Not at all! Bah (2004: 1) gave humanity very frightening figure of SALWs in circulations world-wide 500 million illicit weapons. He estimated the ones in circulation in sub-Saharan Africa to be 100 million and 8–10 million concentrated in West Africa alone. In stating the obvious, Alhaji M. S. Bah said that "small arms and light weapons destabilise regions; spark, fuel and prolong conflicts; obstruct relief programmes; undermine peace initiatives; exacerbates human rights abuses; hamper development; and foster culture of violence." The scenario painted by this author is awesome and horrifying because of the interests involved that are not amenable to international treaties or legal instruments for dealing with these types of weapons. More awesome and horrifying is the fact that M. S. Bah said in a footnote that, "Of the 49 major conflicts in the 1990s, 47 were waged with small arms as weapons of choice. Small arms are responsible for over half a million deaths a year, including 300,000 in armed conflicts and 200,000 from homicides and suicides."

There are other angles to the conflicts in Africa which are in the agenda of neo-imperialism through the strengthening of neo-colonialism by weakening the African states which are policies that encourage conflicts. It was Kwame Nkrumah who rightly said that there were two movements in the anti-colonial struggles. One was pro-imperialism and the other was anti-imperialism. As a result there was no really coherent Pan-Africanist Front against imperialism. One suspects that Nkrumah might have seen this fissure hence he recommended African High Command which the Monrovia Group led by Nigeria, being the majority shot down. It nevertheless pointed at what to expect in the emergent African continent with the birth of the Organisation of African Unity (OAU) at its inception in May 1963. We are into this deeper analysis because in introduction to Karl Marx Class Struggles in France 1848–1850 Engels said, "A clear survey of economic history of a given period can never be obtained contemporaneously, but only subsequently after collecting and sifting of the materials have taken place. Hence, the materialist method has often to expound its focus in tracing political conflict back to the struggles between existing social classes and fractions of classes created by economic development." Engels confirms Karl Marx discovery thus:

> That the world trade crisis of 1847 has been the true mother of the February and March revolutions, and that the industrial prosperity, which had been returning gradually since the middle of 1848 and attained full bloom in 1849 and 1850, was the revitalizing force of the newly strengthened European reaction that were decisive. (Marx 1983: 9)

Many traps set for Africa in the population question have found a more reliable option in SALWs proliferations in order to eliminate the African population by Africans themselves. There is also the quest for minerals in Africa by Euro-American imperialism, as a result the African population growth would put a strain on the easy access to the mineral resources for the advance industrial societies. This was what the Americans in official policy circles referred to as a thermo-nuclear bomb in the early 1960s if not checked. Now that all the arsenal marshalled against the relatively growing African population have not been very effective, the most effective one based on instigating conflicts but which can be tied to ethnic irredentism anchored on accusatory slants of bad governance, bad leadership and corruption slangs of neo-liberalism or neo-imperialism for a relief to the racialised global capitalist system became handy in post-Cold War Africa. As regards the inner kernel of the African conflicts, most analysts, especially, the conventional security analysts because of ideological orientation would not focus on the structural contradictions plaguing the continent (Tedheke 2016: 317). Bowen (1996: 5–6) said that Euro-American view of African violence has been clouded with "ancient tribal hatred" that it becomes impossible for a Western reporter on the Rwandan massacre to hear the other view. As an African UN official at that time, ever so politely demurred, repeatedly reminding the reporter that mass conflict began when Belgian colonial rulers gave Tutsis a monopoly of state power but the reporter pressed on ancient tribalism (sic) as the cause of the Rwandan crisis.

These issues of so-called tribalism or ethnic irredentism are a fallout from *modernisation* and *development administration* schools of thought, that were theorised to turn our attention from the realities to frivolities setting Africans and the Third World against themselves in what Klein (2008) calls *Disaster Capitalism* in which imperialist capital creates the disaster and offers a helping hand to its victims for the interests of capital accumulation even in capital's home base. Capital has gone so haywire that it equally does this on its home citizens. What about the global South, its sphere of historical holocaust? This is the dilemma of Africa in the continental historical connections with Europe and later North America, all for the interests of capital accumulation. The more the contradictions of accumulations intensify, the more capital employs *deadly developments* on its prey to conform, such as the *Structural Adjustment Programmes* (SAP) that crippled the global South by imperialist capital that intensified conflicts in these areas and its harvests in post-Cold War Africa thus spreading SALWs proliferations. The foregoing is a process of justifying the status quo and to invite humanitarianism when conflicts and crises have been enthroned by structural violence of imperialism and neo-imperialism but which humanitarian interventions are justified using medieval just war theory (Manokha 2008: 13–14).

It was not surprising that the soucerer prevaricates when the need to douse its spell on its victim is being suggested in order to end the vampires fangs into its victim's arteries, hence the just war theory in global capitalist terrorism. This was the case of the ECOWAS Moratorium and indeed the Convention by the controllers of the merchandise of death that they being given notices of shipment would only be for information and would have no force of law. It specifically stated that where legal advice is required exporters should make their own arrangements (de Beer 2001). This business of blood from Atlantic Chattel Slavery to date with its holocaust on Africa has been a veritable source of Euro-American capital accumulation and indeed the source of the industrial revolution. In the *modernisation* and *development administration* paradigms the soucerers locate the crises in the domain of the internal dynamics of the former colonised peoples, thus extricating themselves from their own criminal activities of the merchandise of blood and death. This is to turn reality upside down and prepare the ground for humanitarian intervention should SALWs proliferations boil over to wars and humanitarian disasters. This has been the cases of the post-Cold War Africa and the near East in which imperialism has employed the theory of *a just war* to maintain its hegemony (Manokha 2008: 13) in arms trade disasters and indeed the uneven-development imposed on the global division of labour by capital giving birth to conflicts and wars in the global South spiralling SALWs proliferations. It is not surprising that the crises in the Mano River Basin, the Niger Delta Militancy and indeed Boko Haram are the results of the merchandise of death due to the profitability of the SALWs trade. Also the proliferations of SALWs in conflict areas is being compounded by imperialists' hunger for raw materials especially minerals for their industries (Tedheke 2016: 318). According to Smith (2006: 13) …the crisis in the Great Lakes region of Africa attracted the world looters to the mining in the Congo (DRC). In Angola, DRC and Sierra Leone "blood diamond" was the case and also with other strategic minerals.

From "blood diamond" in the Great Lakes to "blood oil," the political economy of SALWs proliferations gained both ways. The merchandise of blood and death profits from strategic minerals for Euro-American strategic industries. It is a very conscious effort by imperialism right from in the 1950s as the US confessed that it had no minerals to sustain its civilisation. Lenin (1974: 1880) said …to understand the fundamental economic question, that of economic essence of imperialism, for unless this is studied, it will be impossible to understand and appraise modern war and modern politics. African leaders and conventional academics have little or no inklings of the dialectics of small arms and light weapons proliferations as a capitalist project. This lack of scientific approach to the issue at hand poses a very serious challenge to African Union as did to its predecessor in resolving the issues of SALWs proliferations. The second very serious challenge is the gluttonous appetite of capital for strategic raw materials and minerals, particularly those of Africa that is at the back water of capitalist world civilisation. According to Dean (1979: 146) it was only in 1952 that the USA became disturbed whether she has the mineral means to sustain her civilisation; having discovered that her mineral wealth may not suffice. This is the fear that strengthens imperialism of the entire North Atlantic Treaty Organisation (NATO), the military arm of global capital. The need to dominate global resources has given vent to the sustenance of NATO after the demise of the Warsaw Pact in the 1990s (Tedheke 2016: 325). Are Africans surprised at what is happening in the Great Lakes region and can Africans link it to the murder of Patrice Lumumba in the early 1960s? This is the continental question! It is there till today manifesting in various forms of continental security questions!! We have noted earlier the co-incidence between strategic resources and war prone regions in Africa. War is being used to extract strategic raw materials from parts of Africa by multinational corporations of the advanced capitalist countries (Tedheke 2016: 325).

There are other build-ups towards post-Cold War conflicts in Africa anchored on the restrictions of the space of exploitation to Africa by imperialism with the socio-economic transformations of the Far East and Latin America. These were the cases of national liberation movements in the

Portuguese colonial territories, Southern Africa and indeed the non-integrative political economy that separated communities in colonial enclave economies which worked for centrifugal forces instead of centripetal forces. The foregoings were the forces that coalesced to fuel the post-Cold War conflicts resulting in the spiralling of SALWs proliferations in Africa since the close of the Cold War. The wars in the Great Lakes, Mano River Basin, the Darfur-Sudan conflict, the secession of South Sudan, the secession of Eritrea, the Somalian conflict, and agricultural policies which encouraged crops needed in the advanced industrial societies pitted herders against farmers in the Sahel worked to instigate conflicts and wars spiralling SALWs proliferations in the continent (Bah 2004; Reyna and Downs 1999; Tedheke 2016; Smith 2006). Any one who fails to link all the foregoings to imperialism as the underpinnings of the African condition in SALWs proliferations and only restricts the issues to internal factors alone anchors his analysis on complete reductionism and anti-history.

Conclusion: What Africans Must Do

The political economy of SALWs proliferation is an agenda of Euro-American imperialism which has been on since Atlantic Chattel Slavery from the late fifteenth century to date. The idea has been a carryover from the Northern Cradle's Father Rights societies which were anchored in wars and looting of vanquished societies on their way. The defeat of ancient African Egypt by Alexander the Great was the mirror that pointed to the future of societies of private property that became the focus and fundamental interests of such societies that were accidentally European which became the slogans for national interests of modern racialised global capitalist states since Atlantic Chattel Slavery, colonialism, neo-colonialism and now neo-imperialism or globalisation. The expansions of European empires since Atlantic Chattel Slavery were based on SALWs proliferations anchored on what Reyna and Downs (1999) conceptualised as predatory accumulation and capital accumulation giving rise to Thomas Hobbes' so-called Great Leviathan liken to the stately crocodile or whales. They also liken it as the Atlantic Killing Machines in which Atlantic Europe visited holocaust on the global South for capital accumulation that built Europe and North America which was done through SALWs proliferations (Jalata 2013; Reyna and Downs 1999; Martin 2005). This project extended to latter day Euro-American imperialism which has festered into neo-imperialism of the post-Cold War Africa and the near East in SALWs proliferations across these zones giving rooms to endemic conflicts and wars. This very dangerous encirclement and suppression campaigns on the global South by Euro-American and Japanese imperialism is the greatest undoing of the African people and must be challenged through the philosophy of Pan-Africanism which has to be the unity of the continent against imperialism and neo-imperialist globalisation.

Africans must have to get it very clear that the racialised capitalist world system has imposed its racialised political economy on the global South through arms violence of SALWs proliferations. The USA was speaking for the entire Western racialised capitalist world when she discovered in 1952 that she had no minerals to sustain its civilisation and the strategy employed has been encirclement and suppression campaigns by opening up many fronts to hinder the global South from historical movement. Oblivious of the lessons of the dialectics of history, the dominant classes of racialised global capitalist system are confident that they can continue their brigandage of the "civilising mission" visiting holocaust on the global South into eternity but they are losing out in the game as East Asia and Latin America are beginning to realise their history. This is an indication that nothing is permanent that the only thing that is permanent is change which is the logic of dialectics. Africans must move against the global forces of racialised capitalist world system by taking to Robert McNamara's invaluable advice that security is development and that without development there can be no security. McNamara (1968) correctly stated that:

> In a modernising society, security means development, security is not military force though it may involve it, security is not traditional military activity, though it may encompass it, security is not military hardware though it may include it. Security is development and without development there can be no security.

The crises of underdevelopment have exposed Africa to myriads of crises that the racialised greedy world capitalist system has been catching on to dispose off its armament production, especially its SALWs resulting in their proliferations across the continent. The inner logic of capital creates uneven and spasmodic development. It would be surprising if the contrary is the case. It is doubly surprising that African political personalities seek the aid of the racialised global capitalist system for continental economic development. Cabra (1980: 116) thus warned "…so long as imperialism is in existence, any independent African government must be a liberation movement in power or it will not be independent." How time has proved Amilcar Cabral right. In most of the underdeveloped world, capitalism has penetrated, left the old structures intact and converted them to serve the interests of metropolitan racialised capital through the enthronement of capitalist relations of production (Marx 1984: 202–203). Karl Marx thus confirmed the dynamics of capital, that of uneven and spasmodic development which engenders unequal trade relations, unequal exchange which is the root cause of African conflicts (Tandon 2004). Such impose infrastructures of insecurity which agrees with McNamara (1968: 150) who said: …any country that seek to achieve adequate military security against the background of acute food shortages, population explosion, and low level economic development, inadequate and inefficient public utilities and chronic problem of unemployment has a false sense of security.

The racialised capitalist West has multiple strategies in its encirclement and suppression campaigns against the global South, now increasingly narrowing on Africa. They are ideologically making population culpable hence so many battle fronts have been and are being opened to attack this so-called culprit called population explosion from acquired immune deficiency syndrome (AIDS) to Ebola, now genetically modified organism (GMO) which are meant to reduce the African population for the greed for minerals by Euro-American imperialism. The SALWs proliferations have added to the foregoing of the killing machine scenario that has been the handmaiden of the West or the racialised capitalist global system. Africa must pose a challenge to this global onslaught on the continent by the forces of Western imperialism. The first step is to identify the enemy and face the crises it is generating so as to deal with issues involved which is underdevelopment fuelling of the African crises. Africa must put onstream and stand up for a second independence-economic independence. From what we have learnt from Robert McNamara, security is development and without development there can be no security. Africa cannot rely on the producers of these SALWs to help to stop their sales. Africa must have to develop a counter strategy of *Defence Industrialisation* as the *New Industrialising countries* are doing to enhance their security. Can we see the wisdom in Kwame Nkrumah's *African High Command*?

Africans must also make sure that the best sons and daughters of the land must lead in order to enthrone centripetal forces instead of the centrifugal forces in vogue now which results in primordialism, conflicts and wars giving rise to the escalations of SALWs proliferations across the continent. We have to advise ourselves about the dangers in the game of pro-imperialist outlook of most African leaders that is why we need Pan-Africanism so as to understand the harm we are doing to ourselves and future generations by the lack of good leadership to pilot continental affairs. This is because we have been schooled into collective amnesia anchored on the poverty of history. *We Africans are however to blame and we must be properly informed hence we have endeavoured to go the Long View of History.* Because eclectic approach cannot help matters unless we locate the historical evolution of the issue and that is exactly what we have done in this matter of the political economy of SALWs proliferations in Africa. The records are now here for us to see and judge, to know where the blames should go.

REFERENCES

Bah, M. S (2004). Micro-Disarmament in West Africa: The ECOWAS Moratoriun on Small Arms and Light Weapons . *Africa Strategic Review,13*(3), 33–46.

Bowen, J. R. (1996, October). The Myhts of Global Ethnic Conflict. *Journal of Democracy, 7*(4), 3–14.

Cabra, A. (1980). *Unity and Struggle*. London: Henineman Educational Books Limited.

de Beer, D. (2001). Official. *Journal for European Community.* www.eurlexeuropa. eu/legal-content/eng. Accessed 20 January 2016.

Dean, H. (1979). Scarce Recources: The Dynamics of American Imperialism. In A. Mark, D. Plant, and U. Doyce (Eds.), *Intervention and Development*. London: Croom Helm Ltd.

Diop, C. A. (1989). *The Cultural Unity of Black Africa: The Domain of Matriarchy and Patriarchy in Classical Antiquity*. London: Karnak House.

Ekekwe, E. N. (2019). *Valedictory Lecture*. Nigeria: University of Porharcourt.

Engels, F. (1977). *Origin of the Family, Private Property and the State*. Moscow: Progress Publishers.

Engels, F. (1983). *The Origin of the Family, Private Property and the State* (with Introduction by Pat Brewer). Chippendale, NSW, Australia: Resistance Publishers. Available: https://readingfromtheleft.com/PDF/EngelsOrigin.pdf.

Fanon, F. (1980). *Wretched of the Earth*. Harmonworth Middlesex, England: Pengium Books Ltd.

Hochschild, A. (1998). *The Ghost of King Leopold*. New York, NY: Houghton Mufflin Company.

Inikori, J. E. (2003). The Struggle against the Trans-Atlantic Slave Trade. In A. Diouf (Ed.), *Fighting the slave trade: West African strategies*. Athens, Ohio: Ohio University Press.

Jalata. A. (2011). *Indigenous Peoples in the Capitalist World System: Researching, Knowing, and Promoting Social Justice*. http://trace.tennessee.edu/uk_socopubs/82.

Jalata, A. (2012). Gadaa (Oromo Democracy): An Example of Classical African Civilisation. *Journal of Pan-African Studies*, 126. http://trace.tennessee.edu/utk_socopubs.

Jalata, A. (2013, March). Colonial Terrorism, Global Capitalism and Africa Underdevelpoment: 500 Years of Crime Against African People. *Journal of Pan African Studies, 5*(9), 1–43.

Klein, N. (2008). *The Shock Doctrine: The Rise of Disaster Capitalism*. New York, NY: Henry Holy and Company.

Lenin, V. I. (1974). *Collected Works* (Vol. 29). Moscow: Progress Publishers.

Lodgaard, S., & Fung, I. (1998, May). A Moratorium on Small Arms. In S. Lodgaard & C. F. Roondfeldt (Eds.), *A Moratorium on Light Weapons in West Africa*. Oslo: Norwegian Initiative on Small Arms Trasfers.

Lenin, V. I. (1978). *Imperialism the Highest Stage of Capitalism*. Moscow: Progress Publishers.

Manokha, I. (2008). *The Political Economy of Human Rights Enforcement*. London and New York, NY: Palgrave Macmillan.

Martin, G. (2005). The West, Natural Resources and Population Control in Africa in Historical Perspective. *Joournal of Third World Studies, 22*(1), 69–107.

Marx. K. (1967). Cited by Jalata, A (2011) *Capital* (F. Engeis, Ed). New York, NY: New York International Publishers.

Marx, K. (1978). *The Eighteen Brumaire of Louis Bonaparte*. Peking: Foregin Languages Press.

Marx, K. (1983). *The Class Struggles in France 1948 to 1950*. Moscow: Progress Publishers.

Marx, K. (1984). *Contribution to the Critique of Political Economy*. Moscow: Progress Publishers.

Marx, K., & Engles, F. (1977). *Selected Works* in 3 (Vol. 1). Moscow: Progress Publishers.

McNamara, R. (1968). *The Essence of Security*. New York, NYH: Harper and Row.

Nafziger, E. W. (1983). *The Economics of Political Instability-The Nigerian-BAiafran War*. Boulder, CO: Westview Press.

Nkrumah, K. (1973a). *Class Struggles in Africa*. London: Panaf Books Ltd.

Nkrumah, K. (1973b). *Towards Colonial Freedom*. London: Panaf Books.

Nnoli, O. (1978). *Ethnic Politics in Nigeria*. Enugu: Fourth Dimension Publishers.

Reinert, E. (2007). *How Rich Countries Got Rich and Why Poor Countries Stay Poor*. New York: PublicAffairs.

Reyna, S. P., & Downs, R. E. (1999). *Deadly Developmrnts Capitalism, States and War*. London: Gordon and Breach Publishers.

Rodney, W. (1972). *How Europe Underdeveloped Africa*. London: Bougle L'Overture Publications.

Smith P. (2006, April–June). Free for all DR Congo's Wealth has Never Been Used for the Nation's Benefits. *BBC Focus on Africa*.

Tandon, Y. (2000). The Violence of Globalization. *Echoes: Journal of World Council of Churches, 17*.

Tedheke, M. E. U. (2012a). Africa, Theoretical Contradictions and Development Problematiques–The Tyranny of Received Paradigm. *Journal of Law and Social Sciences, 2*(1), 32–45.

Tedheke, M. E. U. (2012b). The Arab Revolts and the Dialectic of the Global Redistribution Question-Lessons for Sub-Saharan Africa . *International Affairs and Global Strategy, 6*, 2224–8951.

Tedheke, M. E. U. (2013). Politics, Democracy and the Military-A Materialist Analysis in *International Journal of Humanities and Social Sciences, 2*(1).

Tedheke, M. E. U. (2014). Youth Crises and Conventional Policing: A political Economy Analysis. In E. Alemika & O. Tangban (Eds.), *Bassey, R.* Policing and Crime Prevention in Nigeria Jos: The African Council on Narcotics.

Tedheke, M. E. U. (2016). Globalisation and the Political Economy of Small Arms and Light Weapons Prolifcerations in Nigeria: Beyond the Ratification of ECOWAS Convention. In U. A. Tar, M. E. U. Tedheke, & E.B. Mijah (Eds.), *Readings on Globalisation and Development in Africa*. Kaduna: Nigerian Defence Academy Press.

Tedheke, M. E. U. (2019). *History versus Anti-History-The Place of the Crises of Historiography*. Being a Paper Delivered at the Faculty of Arts and Social Sciences, Nigerian Defence Academy, Kaduna.

Turner, T. (1982). Commercial Capitalism in Nigeria: The Partern of Competition. In D. L. Cohen & J. Daniel (Eds.), *Political Economy of Afruca-Selected Readings*. Longman Group Ltd: Harlow Essex, UK.

Moses Eromedoghene Ukpenumewu Tedheke (Ph.D.) is a Professor at the Department of Political Science and Defense Studies, Nigerian Defense Academy. Tedheke was former Head of Department. He obtained a Ph.D. in Political Science from Ahmadu Bello University, Zaria, Nigeria and MSc in Political Economy from the University of Jos, Nigeria. Prof Tedheke is a resource person to the National Institute for Policy and Strategic Studies (NIPSS), National Defence College (NDC), Armed Forces Command and Staff College (AFCSC) and External Examiner to several universities in Nigeria. He has carried out research on the interface between capitalism and security.

CHAPTER 5

(En)Gendering the Small Arms Discourse: Women and the Management of Violent Conflicts in Africa

Caroline Obiageli and Agnes Okorie

Introduction

Small Arms and Light Weapons (SALW) proliferation portends great danger to all societies. The lethal consequences of indiscriminate possession and use of illicit SALW has had devastating effects on societies so affected by the menace of the proliferation. This also, in many ways, undermines sustainable peace and continental integration in Africa and contributes to the exacerbation of conflict and increased lethality of violence in the numerous violent hotspots in the continent. For this reason, African states, with the support of donor governments and organizations, have actively taken actions in initiating efforts to counteract this menace. Some of such initiatives include the Bamako Declaration on an African Common Position on the Illicit Proliferation, Circulation and Trafficking of Small Arms and Light Weapons, which was compiled by member states of the Organization of African Unity in Bamako, Mali in the year 2000. This impressively predates the premier international SALW control framework, titled the UN Programme of Action to Prevent, Combat and Eradicate the Illicit Trade in Small Arms and Light Weapons in All Its Aspects,

---

C. Obiageli (✉)
Centre for Critical Thinking Teaching and Learning, Nigerian Defence Academy, Kaduna, Nigeria
e-mail: coemekaogbonna@nda.edu.ng

A. Okorie
Department of Psychology, Nigerian Defence Academy, Kaduna, Nigeria
e-mail: aookorie@nda.edu.ng

© The Author(s), under exclusive license to Springer Nature Switzerland AG 2021
U. A. Tar and C. P. Onwurah (eds.), *The Palgrave Handbook of Small Arms and Conflicts in Africa*,
https://doi.org/10.1007/978-3-030-62183-4_5

which was initiated by UN members in 2001. These documents specifically recommend that "signatory states establish National Focal Points that synchronize the government bodies responsible for devising a national arms control action plan, facilitating small arms control research, monitoring arms control activities and formulating policy and legislation" (Lamb and Dye 2009: 77). In furtherance to these efforts, the discourse around the norms and policies on preventing the proliferation and misuse of SALW has continued to receive impetus in the academic and policy circle and is becoming more informed and complex.

However, despite the efforts by institutions and agencies responsible for the control of SALW at national, regional and international levels; and the complexity of the discourse within the contemporary field of human security, there has remained a noticeable gap in this discourse which is the absence of "a discussion of how gender ideologies, which shape and constrain the behaviour of women and men, might influence people's attitudes to small arms" (Schroeder et al. 2005c: 3). There has also been little consideration of research into the "gender differences in approaches to and use of small arms" such that "inadequate data has been collected on how males and females are differently impacted by prolific weapons" (Schroeder et al. 2005c: 3). African nations are no exception in this regard especially with the predominant existential perceptions held around gender and violence in the continent. Working from a critical perspective therefore, this chapter seeks to proffer new approaches that would mainstream gender considerations and maintain objectivity in the management and control of violence resulting from SALW proliferation.

GENDERED PERSPECTIVES ON VIOLENT CONFLICT AND (IN)SECURITY

The perspective adopted in approaching discourse issues always determine, to a large extent, possible outcome in such endeavour. Various perspectives have been identified to serve as guiding principles for approaches to the conceptualization of gendered construction of violence and (in)security. In her work on gender equity in disarmament demobilization and reintegration programme participation, Obiageli (2017) discussed extensively the feminist theoretical analysis of violence and security as well as the implication of the varied theoretical perspectives to beliefs and practices around the handling of men and women's propensity for militarization, capacity for perpetration of violence, participation in conflicts, and skills of peace building. Three broad categories of feminist theories, along their postulation of relationship between body and behaviour, were identified as *Essentialism, Constructivism* and *Post-structuralism*. Essentialist feminist security scholars believe that insecurity arises out of the norm of male dominance over female (of masculinity over femininity). Hence they construe security from the perspective that men have power while women don't. Therefore their analysis of violence and armed conflict rarely assumes women to be combatants or active participants in violence. They consider women as specific targets of war and violence and in specifically gendered ways. Scholarly studies of international security within this logic "document differential impact of armed conflict on women and girls as compared to men and boys" (Whitworth 2013: 112) with focus on the impact of armed conflict on women and girls such as in heightened sexual violence, including its use as a weapon of war; killing and maiming of women as direct targets of violence; physical assault and exploitation of women by "men" working as peacekeepers, aid workers, guards and police who are meant to be protecting them; social and economic impacts on women as IDPs who had lost their means of livelihood in the conflict, etc. Whitworth (2013) concludes that even though some analysts with this perspective could rarely recognize women as combatants in armed conflicts, their analytical perspectives consider women's particular experiences generally not worthy of specific or sustained study, or in any way important in determining how we might understand both security and insecurity (Whitworth 2013). Working from this perspective could therefore, easily mislead scholars and policy makers to lose sight of mainstreaming gender logics and ideologies in the conflict and small arms proliferation discourse. This is because women are essentially considered as victims of violence and would have no active role in conflict and illicit arms movement, brokering and misuse.

The constructivist feminist security scholars also consider insecurity as one of the ways in which power inequalities are enacted but however, with the consideration that both men and women can be victims and perpetrators of violence and thus consider insecurity as Gender Violence. Through this lens gendered logic assumes that both men and women can be actors and victims of violence either as perpetrators of violence or participants in peace process (Obiageli 2017). The security scholars of this approach interrogate the traditional understanding and assumptions of men as combatants and women as victims of violence. Hence they highlight in their researches, the varied (both negative and positive) impacts of the gendered perception of men and women in security such as: women's greater freedom in organizing informal peace campaigns since they would not be viewed as having served as combatants; women's exclusion from formal peace-tables and from Disarmament, Demobilisation and Reintegration (DDR) programmes which give former combatants access to educational, training and employment opportunities; men being at higher risk as targets for violence as they are considered to have been combatants and instigators of conflict; men's effort to initiate peace is always received with doubt since they are considered as active combatant actors in conflict even though this wins them the opportunity of participating in formal peace efforts (Whitworth 2013). This perspective therefore summarily considers the actual threat to security as the prevailing understanding and assumptions about men and women and considers that this can significantly shape and limit the people's experiences of (in)security in profoundly positive or negative ways (Obiageli 2017).

This therefore suggests that the absence of, or little reference to, gendered discourse around issues of conflict and small arm proliferation portends the real danger and threat of properly understanding the subject matter. This is because, despite all efforts at policy formulation and plans of action around the management and control of conflict and small arm proliferation, as long as attention is not paid to the reality of both men and women being equal potential perpetrators as well as victims, some portion of active participants (mostly of women) in this dreadful menace would continue to go unnoticed or undetected while they intensify their illicit actions in movement, brokering and misuse of SALWs in the society. This is exemplified in a recent case of the arrest of 3 women for concealment of 818 rounds of live ammunition in a bag of rice for the purpose of transportation from Kano state to Bayelsa state of Nigeria (AIT 2020). The case is that of a clearly thought out plan by a Lance Corporal in Nigerian Army who uses his wife, niece and sister to move ammunition across the country under the cover of the social perception of women as victims of violence who most likely are incapable of illicit small arms brokering. Such abuse of the perception therefore leads to our consideration of the critical perspective on gendered construction of conflict and small arms proliferation as the most recommended approach to this discourse.

The critical perspective draws from its traditional theoretical base of post-structuralism. Post-structuralism is a theory of critique which emphasizes plurality of meaning and instability of concepts which structuralism used to define society. Hence, Post-structural feminist security scholars present (in)security as a part of gender performance; one of the ways in which gender identity is forcibly materialized through time. Hence, they consider (in)security as violent reproduction of gender. This means that the core explanatory factor of insecurity is gender logic itself; the way in which societies reward and punish different forms of behaviours depending on the body that perform that kind of behaviour (Obiageli 2017). Thus the stereotypical identification of specific gender roles with specific sexes should be considered the cause of insecurity since acts out of the constructed gender role within a particular society would attract disapproval for the individual.

Therefore, feminist scholars in this tradition focus on the ways in which gender is constructed through (in)security and on the ways in which (in)security is constructed through gender. It highlights ways in which symbolic dimensions of weapons and foreign policy decisions can impact decision makers in ways clearly tied to their own sense of masculinity (Whitworth 2013) since society has constructed the use and misuse of weapons as masculine traits. But because critical perspective considers that there is nothing inherent in the body to give it any meaning prior to its emergence into a particular discursive context, Shepherd (2013: 15) argues that "the body is not ontologically prior to gendered discourses but rather is gendered as/through part of those discourse". Hence as the society has generally constructed a normative masculinity for the possession and misuse of SALW in conflicts, this masculinity should not be stereotypically fixated as traits to be associated only with men but that could possibly be displayed by men and women as well as boys and girls. By implication therefore the discourse around the norms and policies on preventing and controlling the proliferation and misuse of SALW should freely explore the realities of these issues as they manifest in all human actors in any given context, and not focus mainly on male actors with little or no attention paid to the female actors. This is because both males and females in procession of SALW, either legitimately or illegitimately, portend the same and equal level of threat to the people within their immediate space or in the larger society.

Background: Small Arms Proliferation and Conflict in Africa

The African region is confronted with the challenges of both dealing with socio-economic reconstruction in post-conflict societies and containing various internal conflicts. The uncontrolled availability of SALWs is not only fuelling such conflicts but is also exacerbating violence and criminality (Minnaar 1996). This undermines the State's ability to govern effectively, thereby threatening the stability and security necessary for socio-economic development (Nnamdi 2002). Porous borders, lack of resources and the absence of detailed and comprehensive data on the extent of this phenomenon are inhibiting the region's ability to effectively deal with the problem of proliferation.

The weapons proliferated and available in West Africa are not newly produced but left over from several civil wars of the recent past. This proliferation is enhanced by particularly long and unmanned borders. This destabilizing factor has forced some states in the sub-Saharan region to ask for and receive assistance from the United Nations (Minnaar 1996). Insurgency and terrorism remain as factors in the destabilizing use of small arms, light weapons or explosives. Other factors are drug trafficking and criminality (Remar 1997). The link between terrorism and such weapons has been referred to by several international fora. When the State loses control over its security functions and fails to maintain the security of its citizens, the subsequent growth of armed violence, banditry and organized crime increases demand for weapons by citizens seeking to protect themselves and their property.

Inter-communal violence remains a serious concern in Nigeria, the most populous country in Africa. Since the end of military rule in 1999, fighting in several regions of the country has claimed thousands of lives. Plateau State in central Nigeria has been particularly badly affected, as well as Boko Haram in the North East and Armed Bandits in the North West (DFID 2000). Hundreds of people have been killed and thousands displaced by this conflict, which has seen an increasing use of SALW. Nigeria's illicit light weapons trade can be traced back to the failure to execute a comprehensive arms collection programme after the 1967-70 civil war (Dokubo 2003). It has subsequently been fuelled by growing crime, endemic corruption and ethnoreligious conflicts. There have also been widespread leakages from government Armouries.

In fact, small arms, which include rifles, pistols and light machine guns, are filling African graves in ever-increasing numbers from the killing fields of Burundi and the Democratic Republic of Congo to the North East and North West of Nigeria, and Johannesburg. While the international community searches, so far unsuccessfully, for agreement on the regulation of the global trade in small arms, a growing number of African countries, UN agencies and non-governmental organizations are grappling with the human and development consequences of gun violence and seeking to reduce both the supply and the demand for what Secretary-General Kofi Annan has called "the weapons of choice for the killers of our time" (UN 2008).

Reducing the availability and use of small arms in places where fighting has ended has become increasingly important to Africa's development prospects as the number of conflicts has increased over the past decade. The widespread abuse of weapons diverts scarce government resources from health and education to public security, discourages investment and economic growth, and deprives developing countries of the skills and talents of the victims of small arms. Years later, these durable killing machines fight on in the hands of insurgents, local militias, criminal organizations and ordinary people left vulnerable to violence by ineffective policing and simmering civil conflict. In some parts of Africa, a Soviet-designed AK-47 assault rifle, coveted for its simplicity and firepower, can be purchased for as little as $6, or traded for a chicken or sack of grain (Osaghae 1991). In 1999 the Red Cross estimated that in the Somali capital of Mogadishu alone, the city's 1.3 million residents possessed over a million guns—among an estimated 550 m small arms in circulation worldwide (Chandre and Lamb 2004).

As Ms. Virginia Gamba, the former director of the Arms Management Programme of the South African Institute for Security Studies (ISS) noted, "the proliferation of light weapons in Africa poses a major threat to development". Their low cost, ease of use and availability "may escalate conflicts, undermine peace agreements, intensify [the] violence and impact of crime, impede economic and social development and hinder the development of social stability, democracy and good governance" (Minnaar 1996: 23). In July 2001 the US government estimated that small arms are fuelling conflicts in 22 African countries that have taken 7–8 million lives (Vines 2005). In Africa guns are not just the weapons of choice but also weapons of mass destruction.

The illicit proliferation and misuse of small arms and light weapons rank among today's most pressing security threats. Tens of thousands of people are killed or wounded each year in conflicts that are fought primarily with these weapons and in crime-ridden areas outside of conflict zones. They are also the weapons of choice for many terrorists. Approximately half of the international terrorist incidents documented in the 2003 Department of State report on global terrorism were perpetrated with small arms and light weapons (Vines

2005). Yet, there is still much more to be done. Reports of lost, stolen and diverted small arms and light weapons are daily reminders of the continued prevalence of weak export controls, poor stockpile security practices, and inadequate or nonexistent border security. Particularly disheartening are arms shipments to war zones and dictators. Since 2001, UN investigators have documented numerous violations of arms embargoes on governments and armed groups in Liberia, Sierra Leone, the Sudan, the Democratic Republic of Congo, the Somalia and Nigeria.

Where wars have officially come to an end, the presence of small arms makes sure that physical insecurity persists through banditry and violent settlement of scores. In the context of Africa, many countries could be described as nominally at peace. But even in these societies—South Africa, Nigeria, and Ghana—armed robbery is rampant and coercive, protection and vigilante justice are replacing the incapacitated state security rackets. As long as the small arms pipelines remain open, the prospects for disarmament and peaceful conflict management, reigning in crime and promoting human rights will be greatly undermined. This has dire consequences for the process of democratization and fostering secure livelihoods.

In Nigeria, the oil-rich Niger Delta remains the scene of recurring violence between members of different ethnic groups competing for political and ethnic power, and between security and militia groups. This crisis has been aggravated by the theft of crude oil, known as "illegal bunkering", and the availability of light weapons (Ladipo 1985).

Gender and Violent Conflicts

As stated earlier, the lethal consequences of indiscriminate possession and use of illicit SALWs has had devastating effects on societies so affected by the menace of the proliferation. In the same vein, "the wide presence of guns in all societies, be they peaceful, at war, or somewhere in between, has an impact on men and women in all kinds of communities" (Schroeder et al. 2005b: 19). However, a general attitude to small arm is a consideration of gun culture as closely linked to notions of masculinity and male identity. Therefore, even though violence is not exclusively practiced by males, it is linked, along with guns, to masculine identity. This could have been intensified by the conventional notions of masculinity which ascribes the role of protector and defender to men, and in many cultures this role has become symbolized by and synonymous with the possession of a gun (Schroeder et al. 2005b). Nevertheless, the association of masculinity with small arms possession and violent behaviour is socially constructed. Young boys are sometimes given toy guns to play with, or they make their own in order to emulate characters they have seen in violent films, music-videos or video-games, or in real-life gangs or militias. Small arms are sometimes implicated in rites of passage from boyhood to manhood. Young men are not merely passive receptors of social norms. They participate actively in internalizing, reframing and reproducing norms that they receive from their social settings, their families and their peers (Cialdini and Goldstein 2004). A young man's gender is not the sole determinant of his association with or willingness to perpetrate armed violence. His understanding of social and cultural ideologies of masculinity will influence whether a young man turns to armed violence or not.

In exploring the relationship between small arms, culture and violence with particular emphasis on gender dimensions with Africa Schroeder et al. (2005b: 19) argue that "cultural norms are both contributors to and consequences of violence, and small arms usage and proliferation sometimes figures largely into this culture". They insist that the association between masculinity and guns has been (re)produced by a variety of global cultural practices as represented in entertainment, video and commercial adverts, with particular intensity by media which is one of the principal conduits of culture. They site American media, in particular, as tending to portray heroes as using violence as a justified means of resolving conflict and prevailing over others. Thus many in the society perceive guns more as a status symbol than as a killing device—"to command respect and show that the person who holds it has a certain amount of power, wealth or sex appeal in the community" (Schroeder et al. 2005b). Hence young men could often consider the "tough and macho" image that would facilitate impressing girls as a big motivator to obtaining a gun.

As a result of this cultural dominance, most small arms owners and users are males. Additionally, men dominate the military and the police; men also dominate domestic firearms ownership. However, women occupy different roles and participate directly or indirectly in gun-related violence, such as hiding drugs or guns for others, or using guns themselves in criminal activities—they can be both victim and active supporter of gun possession. Their support can also go beyond encouragement of male gun ownership since women represent a very small proportion of gun owners, though they tend disproportionately to be victims of gun violence (Schroeder et al. 2005b).

On impact of violent conflict, Christopher (1995) points out that armed conflict and violence take a terrible human toll and seriously perturb social and economic order of the entire society. He argues that most direct victims of small arms violence are male. Young men (aged 15–29) are especially vulnerable as they are the primary victims of violence in general, and account for an even greater proportion of victims of small arms violence. Young men are also more likely to use a small arm when carrying out a crime than any other demographic group.

However, both during and after armed conflict, women and girls are exposed to many forms of gender-based violence as direct and indirect consequences of the availability and misuse of small arms and light weapons—including rape, forced pregnancy, sexual exploitation, sexual abuse, enforced prostitution, sexual servitude/slavery and forced sterilization, as well as secondary violence against survivors of sexual violence, such as so-called "honour killing" and disfigurement. Most of the world's displaced people are women, children and the elderly. In refugee camps displaced women must contend with armed violence as they care for their families.

Women and girls are affected disproportionately by small arms in a number of ways. For example, their rate of death by gunshot is disproportionate to (i.e. lower than) their share of the population (since more men than women are killed with small arms) and is also disproportionate to (i.e. higher than) the extent to which they are owners or users of small arms—i.e. women are many times more likely to be a victim of armed violence, usually at the hands of men, than a perpetrator of it. The very fact that almost all small arms are owned, used and misused by men puts women in a vulnerable position. Small arms play an important role in lethal violence generally, and in violence against women specifically. In the context of domestic violence, women are affected differently by small arms. Some women are most at risk from their intimates: partners, fathers, brothers, sons. The brandishing of a small arm in order to intimidate, threaten or coerce is a predictor of its actual use. Women who fall victim to femicide often have previously reported being threatened with a small arm as part of a broader pattern of coercive, controlling violence perpetrated against them by their male partners. This imbalance has been one of the arguments advanced by feminists for positioning the gun control debate in the context of human rights and equity, which asserts women's equal right to live in safety.

GENDER AND SMALL ARMS PROLIFERATION

In a study of three voluntary approaches to small arms collection as conducted across three countries—Albania, Cambodia and the African country of Mali—Schroeder et al. (2005a) examined disarmament approaches known as "weapons for development" (WfD) or "weapons in exchange for development" (WED) programmes in which they argue that "the capacities of women as actors in small arms collection programs are not fully recognized nor utilized by relevant stakeholders, and that women have much more potential to contribute to such projects" (Schroeder et al. 2005a: 8). This is largely due to the fact that existing data and research on small arms are usually gender insensitive and tend to focus only on men as the only possible owners and users of small arms. In another study conducted by Somaliland Academy for Peace and Development (APD), UNDP and Small Arms Survey (SAS) for baseline assessment in Somaliland, Schroeder et al. (2005b) report that only male heads of household were interviewed. It is observed that the survey design itself suggests that all respondents were presumed to be males since one of the questions, for instance, which reads: "Who do you turn to for protection?" presented answer options without the likely choices for women, such as "husband". The all men team of local researchers who conducted the assessment had reasoned that "women did not need to be included in the interviews, as women did not have access to small arms and, therefore, did not know much about them. Moreover, it was claimed that it would be culturally inappropriate to interview women" (Schroeder et al. 2005b: 26). This clearly illustrates the degree of masculinity associated with small arms procession and use or misuse.

However, Schroeder et al. (2005b) further note that at a UNDP-sponsored workshop of the women umbrella organization NAGAAD (Somali for "peaceful resting place") in Hargeisa, Somali, women themselves reported on their involvement in the small arms trade. This indicates that academic and policy discourse might be erroneously undermining the role of women in small arm proliferation and possible misuse. With the instance of the three women arrested in connection with the movement of ammunition from Kano to Bayelsa states in Nigeria, it cannot be ascertained that the incident was their first time just as the impact of the small arm brokering would have been extremely destructive if not that they ran out of luck. This particular case could be considered a representational case of several such instances when law enforcement agents have made several arrests of women trying to broker small arms concealed in food stuffs. As a result, it is pertinent to draw attention to the critical perspective on conflict and small arm proliferation which would promote the disregard of the bodies/sexes of humans and focus rather in the observations for actions or behaviours that could portend an indication of engagement in any illicit act. It has therefore been suggested that "strategies need to be developed on how to respond to local resistance to the inclusion of women in professional research, and how to support women in their own attempts to participate in a societal dialogue on security issues" (Schroeder et al. 2005b: 26) which include small arms proliferation.

In terms of participation and impact, it is considered that marginalized young men frequently perceive violence especially small arms violence as a way to attain positions of social and economic status to which they feel entitled but which are otherwise closed off to them. Musa (1999), points out that by offering empowerment in the face of exclusion from socially defined masculine roles, small arms can represent potent symbols of power for marginalized young men. Small arms can enable marginalized young men, who would otherwise have little influence in their communities, to exert considerable control, even over traditional figures of authority. Small arms make it easier for young men to seize authority through violence, while in the process reversing or destroying the existing social order and its traditional structures and customs of authority.

Although only a small share of small arms-related misuse is committed by women, who also represent a minority of SALW owners, women do also engage in violent behaviours, including with small arms, but tend to do so less frequently and for different reasons (UNBCPR 2002). Female combatants and women or girls associated with non-State armed groups are common in armed conflicts throughout the world. In addition to engaging directly in armed conflict, women and girls also fulfil essential support functions in such groups (e.g. as sex objects, spies, smugglers, paramedics, teachers, couriers, mechanics, drivers, etc.). Like men and boys, women and girls sometimes join armed groups voluntarily and sometimes are forcibly recruited. Forcibly recruited female combatants are especially vulnerable to gender-based violence, including rape, forced marriage and sexual slavery. Women and girls engaged in armed conflict can thus find themselves in a position of being simultaneously perpetrators and victims of human rights violations (UNIFEM 2004).

While armed gang violence mainly involves men, women who are involved in gangs can occupy a number of roles, including as perpetrators (who participate in gang violence alongside male gang members), victims (i.e. partners, sisters and mothers of gang members who are targeted by other gangs) and associates (i.e. women and girls who occupy support roles). Women and girls (like men and boys) join gangs for a variety of reasons, including for protection following a history of physical and sexual abuse, the desire for a family structured environment, to obtain money and respect, to secure a means of livelihood, or because they have been forced to join. According to Brown (2006), factors that seem more to affect girls' delinquent behaviours include early puberty (which can lead to increased conflict with parents and associations with older boys or men), sexual abuse or maltreatment, depression and anxiety.

Women are severely under-represented in professions that use small arms (e.g. law enforcement, military and private security). When small arms that are used by men at work are brought into the home, they heighten the risk of injury and death to family members, especially women and children. Male soldiers and police officers suffering from post-traumatic stress are much more likely to use psychological and physical aggression against their intimate partners than those not suffering from the disorder and are also at higher risk of turning small arms against themselves. Female soldiers and police officers suffering from post-traumatic stress are more likely to turn lethal violence against themselves (Litz 2004).

Towards a Gendered Palliative to Conflict Resolution and Arms Control in Africa

Small arms and light weapons control is not the exclusive domain of men. Women should participate meaningfully in all aspects of control initiatives, from assessments and design, through planning and implementation, to monitoring and evaluation; and women's participation should permeate all levels, including policymaking, programming and budgeting. Gender-sensitive programmes or projects are simply more effective in addressing the adverse impacts of the illicit trade and misuse of small arms and light weapons than those that do not take a gender perspective into account. As such, ensuring that gender is adequately integrated into all stages of a small arms control initiative is essential to assuring its overall quality.

It is also the primary responsibility of the government to ensure that gender equality and the empowerment of women are mainstreamed across all government departments and that women and men, especially those in decision-making positions, are included in gender-related awareness raising, education, advocacy and capacity building initiatives. In order to ensure that gender perspectives are fully integrated, the national coordinating mechanism should include, the government department(s) responsible for women's affairs, as well as for health, education and social policy; civil society organizations that work on gender and women's issues; ensure that small arms and light weapons controlling issues, in particular those affecting demand, brokering and misuse, are analysed and addressed from a gender perspective; train police on their roles and responsibilities under relevant national law regarding the presence and use of small arms in the context of intimate partner and domestic /family-related violence, including, where relevant, informing victims of their rights, e.g. regarding protection orders, firearms seizure, etc (ECOSOC 2016).

In an attempt to achieve a global impact, the UN small arms meetings have begun to connect small arms control to the broader UN agenda on women, peace and security. This is to help national stakeholders to identify and take advantage of implementation synergies between the UN small arms and Sustainable Development Goals processes. By so doing, the need to promote the participation of women in small arms related policymaking, planning and implementation processes would be foregrounded. Hence, in broad terms, institutions and governments would underline the importance of gender distinctions ('women, men, girls and boys'), gender-disaggregated data, and gender equality to the fight against illicit small arms (UN 2018). A gendered perspective permeating all aspects of policy making and implementation on the issues of peace building and security would raise and sustain institutional sensitivity towards equal and objective treatment for men and women especially in relation to violent conflict and small arms proliferation.

Conclusion

SALWs largely constitute a major domestic and public security threat to men and women, boys and girls across all ages and societies. Irrespective of the sex or gender of whose interest these weapons are in service, SALW constitutes equal threat and could wreck the same degree of destruction when misused. As a result national, regional and international governments and organizations or agencies have variously made concerted efforts at managing the movement, possession and use of SALW. However, national, regional and international efforts at control of small arm related violence and small arm proliferation seem to have so far lost sight of the participation of men as well as women in especially the illicit sector of possession, use/misuse and brokering of these SALW. With a gendered construction of masculinity around the concepts of arm possession and usage, discourse on arm related violent conflicts and small arms proliferation have shown to be prevalently skewed towards men and boys as perpetrators and women and girls as victims. There is therefore, a relaxed approach to the consideration of the involvement of women in researches and programmes in this area to the extent of some total exclusion.

In identifying this shortfall in the approaches for the control of SALW, we have highlighted in this chapter the need for policy makers and implementers on control of conflict and small arm proliferation to embrace a conceptual perspective that analyses people's actions beyond their bodies/sexes. Policies and plans of actions in relation to violent conflicts and small arms proliferation should be targeted at all human actors - men and women, boys and girls, who participate in any way immediately and remotely whether legitimately or illegitimately. We are of the opinion that if policies and strategies designed for the control of SALW proliferation and violence were to adopt the critical perspective on gender and violence, then all institutions and governments would comprehensively address not only the participation in SALW brokering and use but also the possible becoming of a victim by all men, women, boys and girls to the misuse of SALW. By so doing, such measures would be ensuring that gender is adequately integrated into all stages of small arms control initiative as an essential process to assuring its overall quality and impact.

References

AIT (Writer). (2020). Kano Crime: Police Nab Female Armourers With Live Ammunition. In *News Hour*. Nigeria: Official AIT Live.

Brown, J. D. (2006). *Social Psychology*. New York: McGraw-Hill.

Chandre, G., & Lamb, G. (2004). "Hide and Seek: Taking Account of Small Arms in Southern Africa." Institute for Security Studies/Centre for Conflict Resolution/Gan free.

Christopher, L. (1995). *The Social Impact of Light Weapons Availability and Proliferation*. A Discussion paper of UNIDAR: International Alert.

Cialdini, R. B., & Goldstein, N. J. (2004). Social influence: Compliance and Conformity. *Annual Review of Psychology, 55*, 591–621.

Dokubo, C. (2003). *Small Arms as a Threat to National Security*. A Nigerian Case Study: University of Ilorin press.

ECOSOC Main Streaming a Gender Perspective into all Policies and Programmes in the United Nations systems. Economical and Social Council, Resolution, E/RES/2016/2, 15 July, 2016.

DFID. (2000). "Improving the Knowledge Base on Small Arms in Northern and Central Nigeria". Unpublished Report for DFID, Nigeria, 22 febuary, 2000.

Ladipo, A. (1985). *The fall of the Second Republic*. Ibadan, Nigeria: Spectrum.

Lamb, G., & Dye, D. (2009). African Solutions to an International Problem: Arms Control and Disarmament in Africa. *Journal of International Affairs, 62*(2), 69–83. Retrieved from http://www.jstor.com/stable/24358195.

Litz, B. T. (2004). *Early Intervention for Trauma and Traumatic Loss*. New Yolk: Guilford Press.

Minnaar, T. (1996). *Small Arms Proliferation and Control in South Africa*. Broamfontein: South Africa Institute of International Affairs.

Musa, A. (1999). "Small Arms and Conflicts Transformation in West Africa." In Abdel- Fatau Musa and Niobe Thompson, Over a Barrel: Light Weapons and Human rights in the Common Wealth (London).

Nnamdi, O. (2002). *Small Arms Proliferation and Disarmament in West Africa: Progress and Prospect of the ECOWAS Moratium*. Abuja: Apophyl Productions.

Obiageli, C. (2017). Gender Equity in Disarmament Demobilisation and Reintegration Programme Participation: A Theoretical Insight In C. C. C. Osakwe & M. T. Ibrahim (Eds.), *Studies in Disarmament, Demobilisation and Reintegration* (pp. 31–44). Kaduna: NDA Press.

Osaghae, E. (1991). A Re-examination of the Conception of Ethnicity in Africa as Idealogy of Inter-Elite Competition. African Studies Monographs.

Remar, M. (1997). "Small Arms Big Impact" The Challenge of Disarmament. World Watch Paper 137. World Watch Institute, Washinton DC.

Schroeder, E., Farr, V., & Schnabel, A. (2005a). *Gender Perspectives on Small Arms and Light Weapons Collection Programs*. Retrieved from http://www.jstor.com/stable/resrep11088.7.

Schroeder, E., Farr, V., & Schnabel, A. (2005b). *Gender Perspectives on Small Arms and Light Weapons in Society*. Retrieved from http://www.jstor.com/stable/resrep11088.9.

Schroeder, E., Farr, V., & Schnabel, A. (2005c). *Introduction*. Retrieved from https://www.jstor.org/stable/resrep11088.6.

Shepherd, L. J. (2013). Feminist Security Studies. In L. J. Shepherd (Ed.), *Critical Approaches to Security: An Introduction to Theories and Methods* (pp. 11–23). New York: Routeledge.

UN. (2008). Small Arms: Report of the Secretary General. S/2008/258 of 17 April, 2008.

UN. (2018). *Ways Forward: Conclusions of the Small Arms Symposia* Retrieved from Geneva: http://www.jstor.com/stable/resrep20051.

UNBCPR (United Nations Development Programme, Bureau for Crisis Prevention and Recovery). (October, 2002). *Gender Approaches in Conflict and Post Conflict Situations*.

UNIFEM. (2004). Getting it Right, Doing it Right: Gender and Disarmament Demoblilization and Reintegration. United Nation Development Fund for Women.

Vines, A. (2005). Combating Light Weapons Proliferation. Journal of International Affairs, *81*(2), 341–360.

Whitworth, S. (2013). Feminism. In P. D. Williams (Ed.), *Security Studies: An Introduction* (2nd ed., pp. 107–119). Oxon: Routledge.

Caroline Obiageli is a Senior Lecturer in Department of Languages Director of the Centre for Critical Thinking, Teaching and Learning (CCTTL) and also Resource Person to Centre for the Study of Leadership and Complex Military Operations in Nigerian Defence Academy, Kaduna—Nigeria. Her scholarly specialization focuses on critical emancipatory practice which is keenly based on the philosophies of Critical Theory. In this regard her academic work spans the areas of Critical Thinking, Critical Emancipatory Education, Entertainment Education for Social and Behaviour Change, Critical approaches to Gender Studies, and Critical Security Studies. She has made scholarly contributions in these areas in both national and international journals and books and has served as Guest Lecturer to various military and non-military institutions. Dr. Obiageli is an Associate Fellow of UK Higher Education Academy and a Fulbright Visiting Scholar Awardee. She is married with children.

Agnes Okorie is a Senior Lecturer in the Department of Psychology, Nigerian Defence Academy, Kaduna. She has a Ph.D. in Psychology and is a member of the Psychological Assessment Committee of the Armed Forces Selection Board, Nigerian Defence Academy. She is a member of Nigerian Psychological Association (NPA). She has published many articles in local and international journals, as well as contributed to book chapters.

Part II

Topographies and Contexts

CHAPTER 6

The Context of Small Arms Proliferation in Africa: State Fragility and Management of Armed Violence

Chris M. A. Kwaja

INTRODUCTION

Armed conflicts remain a challenging aspect of Africa's growth, development and peace (Murshed 2018). Conflict escalation in different parts of Africa is amplified by several factors, including governance, corruption, historical antecedence of different wars and a quest for significance by various conflicts actors. However, the proliferation of arms and different weapons have deepened the conflicts, creating political economies and collapse of social structures that could support peace across different societies. Illicit arms trade in Africa is amorphous; thus, creating increased illegal presence and accessibility to arms in virtually every country in the region. Also, the clandestine nature of illicit arms trade affects societal progress, impeding developmental on many fronts. The impacts of arms proliferation in conflicts in Africa is complex and challenging to resolve because of the complacency of some political and state actors/regimes across the continent, in addition to other factors.

The spate of insurgency in the continent is escalated by these clandestine arms trade, enabling the proliferation of small arms and light weapons (SALWs), which then affects economic and social growth, inter-communal/social cohesion, increases radicalization, violent extremism and inter-communal tension, promotes gun culture, and fosters inter-generational

---

C. M. A. Kwaja (✉)
Centre for Peace and Security Studies, Modibbo Adama University of Technology, Yola, Adamawa State, Nigeria
e-mail: chris-kwaja@mautech.edu.ng

© The Author(s), under exclusive license to Springer Nature Switzerland AG 2021
U. A. Tar and C. P. Onwurah (eds.), *The Palgrave Handbook of Small Arms and Conflicts in Africa*,
https://doi.org/10.1007/978-3-030-62183-4_6

hate because of the destructions and human suffering that accompany these violent conflicts. The Economic Community of West African States (ECOWAS) Convention on SALW defined it as:

> Small arms' refers to arms used by one person, and which include firearms and other destructive arms or devices such as exploding bombs, incendiary bombs or gas bombs, grenades, rocket launchers, missiles, missile systems or landmines; revolvers and pistols with automatic loading; rifles and carbines; machine guns; assault rifles; and light machine guns. 'Light weapons' are portable arms designed to be used by several persons working together in a team, and which include heavy machine guns, portable grenade launchers, mobile or mounted portable anti-aircraft cannons; portable anti-tank cannons, non-recoil guns; portable anti-tank missile launchers; and mortars with a calibre of less than 100 millimetres.[1]

Post-colonial Africa's complex history of armed conflicts, coupled with porous borders, weak state institutions and trans-border criminal activities continue to provide fertile ground for the production and flow of arms in the continent. This involves a complex mix of armed actors within and outside the continent that are driven or motivated by both ideological and financial gains. The porosity of many African borders (Vorath 2017), the presence of institutional corruption that facilitates illicit arms and political economies, weak implementation and evaluation of regional arms trade legislations, and poor operationalization of peace and security architectures and other models for arms monitoring are major factors that have supported the continuous spread of arms from one part of Africa to another.

Protracted armed conflicts contribute to the presence of arms in many societies because of the non-retrieval and/or abandonment of these weapons by soldiers and other fighters that waged some of these conflicts. Increased proliferation of arms in Africa holds grave implications for the future of the region and its overall stability. Hence, this chapter submits that strengthening the capacity of the regional arms monitoring structures and other (sub-) mechanisms that have mandates to contribute to conflict de-escalation in the different parts of Africa will put the continent on a trajectory towards reduced armed conflicts, growth and progress, and overall harmony across the continent. The dependence of the African continent to the international capitalist economy has also been linked to huge amount of capital flight away from the continent, under the premise of arms purchase or importation, which in turn has led to the militarization of the African states. This situation of armament-underdevelopment as captured by Ochoche (2002), is one in which the deployment of resources for the importation of arms takes precedence over issues that bothers on economic growth and development. The reality today in Africa is that despite the fact that many of the economies of its states are weak or non-functional, such states are spending heavily on arms importation under the guise of responding to many of their security challenges as evident in

Table 6.1 Taxonomy of arms control

Type of control	Key focus
Horizontal control	Controlling the proliferation of some weapon types to the existing group of states who have such technology
Numerical control	This involves caps on weapons, usually by type
Technological control	This involves mutual agreement to forgo a technology deemed to threaten balance of power, as well as stipulating a blanket ban on weapons of a certain type
Confidence building measures	This involves transparency, sharing knowledge about escalation/procedure, as well as communication/verification and compliance
Geographic control	Agreements surrounding the placement and targeting of weapon systems

Source Griffiths et al. (2007: 12)

countries such as Mali, Nigeria, Niger, Chad, Libya, South Sudan, Democratic Republic of Congo, Ethiopia, Eritrea among others.

Though arms control and disarmament might look similar as revealed by the United Nations Institute for Disarmament Research (UNIDIR), there are variations: while the former focuses on how best to limit the flow and circulation of arms, the latter is aimed at the physical elimination of some agreed types or categories of arm (UNIDIR 2001). In the context of this paper, the notion of disarmament has to do with the collection, documentation, control and disposal of small arms, ammunition, as well as small arms. It also represents a strategy or programme of action that seeks to minimize both the flow of arms, as well as the costs and dangers of arms races (Schelling and Halperin 1985). Within this frame of understanding, a taxonomy of arms control and restrictions was developed, with a view to locating the different forms and shape that it takes, as shown in Table 6.1.

Factors Contributing to Arms Proliferation in Africa

The proliferation of SALWs is one of the most immediate challenges to human and national security in Africa. The presence of arms in any society increases insecurity and criminality, and can contribute to the emergence of full-scale civil wars. The emergence of insecurity in any society prevents development and collective harmony of the society and its members. Also, the proliferation of arms contributes to state fragility, creating further constraints on state actors to effectively use available state resources to manage the social welfare of citizens and service machineries of war at the same time. These arms, and their subsequent use in violent conflicts, forcefully displaces civilian population, promotes and increases extractive and political economies, and truncate

Table 6.2 Mapping of ongoing production of arms and ammunition in Africa

UN subregion[a]	AU member states with reported ongoing or recent production of small arms or ammunition	
	Small arms	Ammunition
Northern Africa	Algeria, Egypt, Sudan	Algeria, Egypt, Sudan
Western Africa	Nigeria	Cameroon, Mali, Nigeria
Middle Africa	Democratic Republic of the Congo (DRC)[b]	Angola, Chad[b], DRC, Republic of Congo
Eastern Africa	Ethiopia[b], Kenya[b], Tanzania, Uganda[b], Zimbabwe	Ethiopia, Kenya, Madagascar, Tanzania, Uganda, Zimbabwe
Southern Africa	South Africa	Namibia, South Africa

Available in https://raytodd.blog/2019/07/19/african-union-and-the-small-arms-survey-release-first-ever-continental-study-mapping-illicit-arms-flows-in-africa/, accessed 20 June 2020
[a]This refers to UN Statistics Division (UNSD)-designated African subregions. This classification refers to Middle Africa as a subregion, although generally the more familiar term Central Africa is used
[b]Unconfirmed/uncertain

any actions aimed at building peace. Arms proliferation also enables different forms of armed attacks and terrorism, degenerating society into chaos and discord (Stohl and Hogendorn 2010). Apart from the factor discussed below, Table 6.2 shows specific cases of countries within Africa that are involved in the production of arms and ammunition.

Porosity of African Borders

While the proliferation of SALWs could partially be a challenge of governance, it also reveals the gaps of immigration and arms trade policies and institutional weakness of border agencies. Although it is difficult to isolate these gaps from the overall governance of particular states, regional (African) governance and its efforts at tackling violence emergence, escalation and protraction also contribute to conflict. While the promotion of regional free trade aims to broaden the African market and "ease of doing business", the poor implementation of sanctions to prevent further illegal economies, especially for arms trade, hinders conflict reduction regionally. According to the Small Arms Survey, there are more than 1200 companies in 90 countries that produce small arms (Small Arms Survey 2011). Increase in small arms manufacturing and poor monitoring mechanisms for their distribution creates uncertainties of safety, and facilitates broader proliferation of criminality and armed conflicts, due to the transnational character of the criminal groups and networks that are responsible for the flow of these arms within the continent (Alusala 2018).

Poor border regulations and security, the absence of sophisticated technologies for arms detection at the borders, poor capacity of human resource at the border, and complicity of some border security have fuelled the easy entrance of many illegal arms into different countries, enabling their accessibility to armed groups and rebels. Although some of these weapons are transported through large shipments and the airspace, "merchants of deaths", especially from the West, have capatilized on poor inspection of shipments due to corruption and inefficient facilities to sustain their arms trade in many parts of Africa, especially conflict zones. Schroeder and Lamb (2018) account that many traffickers of arms capitalize on the porous and poorly patrolled land borders to systematically transport small arms through trucks or by foot. Also, they transport some of these arms through rivers in many coastal regions in Africa. Small Arms Survey (2019) revealed that "arms smugglers pack small arms into waterproof sacks, attach them to the bottom of boats, and run them up the Niger River. In the Horn, the smugglers that ply the Gulf of Aden often use dhows to deliver large quantities of small arms from Yemen to Somali warlords". While the size and length of some land borders contributes to the proliferation of small arms and light weapons, the weak implementation of border regulations and the laws associated with the inter-state (bi-literal) trade increases the susceptibility of conflict protraction because of arms proliferation.

Corruption and Illicit Arms Economy

Another method through which illegal arms proliferate in many African societies is through collusion between rebels/criminals and legitimate states security actors. Badmus (2009) argues that several arms that are used to facilitate conflicts are stolen from actors that work in state security services and government armouries. These activities are often aided and abetted by greedy and corrupt law enforcement personnel. In some cases, when weapons are stolen from legitimate security services, domestic artisans and illegal arms manufacturing industries are engaged to produce prototypes of these weapons to enable large-scale proliferation and increased violent conflicts. Some of these illegal arms manufacturing industries have been in existence across the sub-region, including in Senegal, Guinea, Ghana and Nigeria (Bah 2004).

The desire by some heads of security institutions and government officials to illegally enrich themselves instigates the development of conspiracy theories that support the diversion of arms legally acquired by state authorities into black markets, and subsequently into the hands of rebels and other insurgents. In most cases, some security and state actors unlawfully provide these arms to local groups, especially youths, to perpetrate crime and cause chaos. For instance, some members of Boko Haram enjoyed patronage from the Borno State Governor, Ali Modu Sheriff, due to the funding he provided to them as part of his political thugs, which later emboldened them to challenge state authority in the long run (Seiyefa 2017). Also, many conflicts in Africa transform into regional insurgency because governments of neighbouring countries provide weapons and material supports to parties (insurgents or security forces) engaged in the conflicts (Schroeder and Lamb 2018). The proliferation and availability of arms in different societies and the presence of protracted armed conflict have further facilitated a "gun culture" in many African societies.

The perpetuation of corruption at both individual and institutional levels, especially in relation to illegal arm deals with conflict entrepreneurs, affects overall improvement of security in society. The investments made in arms purchase (and its illegal proliferation) increases the financial burden of states as more state resources will be invested into servicing security machineries for combating armed conflicts and other forms of criminalities. When arms proliferation and conflict gains prominence in society, the tendencies that state and individual assets are lost is high. Also, development rate (human capital and structural) becomes slowed, paving way for new forms of conflicts associated with development and a "contest for the survival of the fittest". For instance, Liberia's economy collapsed during its civil war. The GDP of the country declined between 1989 and 1995 to one-tenth. This decline affected economic activities, causing a collapse of social welfare, infrastructure and security. Also, it hindered diverse forms of humanitarian aid and rehabilitation efforts that could focus on transforming human suffering (Malam 2014).

Also, the influx of arms from some countries in the West who fund "regime change" in certain African countries, especially during the Arab Spring, contributed to regional insurgency across Africa. The impact of some of these insurgencies created threats (including no-go-areas in certain parts of sovereign states) and red tapes in places like Libya, Somalia, South Sudan, etc. In Libya, for instance, despite the killing of Gadhafi and his removal as military leader for over seven years, armed conflicts have protracted in the country, thereby making the country a shadow of itself.

Mercenaries, Warlords, Armed Groups and a Thriving War Economy

Mercenaries, warlords and armed groups still pose serious challenge for West Africa's security.[2] The easy access to arms by these non-state actors is responsible for the sustained conflicts, violence, insurgency and criminality that have besieged the region since the early 1990s. Resolution 1467 of the United Nations Security Council drew attention to the link between the proliferation of arms and the activities of mercenaries and other non-state actors in West Africa.[3] Though many of the African states are signatories to the Organisation of African Unity (OAU) convention on mercenary, they have not done much in containing the threats posed by mercenaries, in the light of the access to arms they have (Organisation of African Unity 1972).

By virtue of their capacity to sustain conflict and exacerbate violence in the region, these violent non-state actors (VNSAs) and other remnants of war economies in post conflict countries such as Cote d'Ivoire, Liberia and Sierra Leone still pose serious threats to security. The situation is not different n countries such as Chad, Mali, Niger and Nigeria where insurgent groups continue to hold the countries siege. The collapse of the regime of Muammar

Table 6.3 Firearms data for selected African countries

Country	Privately owned firearms (licit and illicit)	Country civilian firearms possession per 100 population
Algeria	1,900,000	7.6
Angola	2,800,000	17.3
CAR	40,000	1.0
Cote d'Ivoire	400,000	2.4
DRC	800,000	1.4
Ghana	2,300,000	8.55
Libya	900,000	15.5
Mali	143,000	1.1
Mozambique	1,000,000	5.1
Nigeria	2,000,000	1.5
South Africa	3,400,000	6.61
South Sudan	3,000,000	28.23
Sudan	2,000,000	5.5
Somalia	750,000	9.1
Uganda	400,000	1.4

Source Adeniyi (2017: 11)

Gadhafi led to the uncontrolled proliferation of arms and an upsurge in mercenary activities in the region, particularly in Mali, Chad and Nigeria (see chapter on Libya in this Handbook).

Within the Gulf of Aden and Gulf of Guinea, the activities of pirates and other criminal groups have led to the huge flow of arms flow into Africa. These threats have evolved in ways that made these geostrategic spheres to be among the most dangerous and major source of insecurity in the continent, against the backdrop of the series of armed attacks that were carried out by pirates on the sea. The phenomenon of hijacking ships loaded with oil is not one that can be easily undertaken without access to arms, which end of in the hands. As observed by the United Nations (2011), the consequences of piracy are far-reaching, to the extent that proceeds from such acts can be used to arm rebels and pirates. In fact, the activities of these mercenaries, warlords and gangs, which have contributed to the striving of the war economy in the continent has been responsible for the spread of arms in the African continent on a large scale (Table 6.3).

PMSCs and the Market for Force for Arms Use in Africa

Since the 1990s, the African continent has witnessed the influx of Private Military and Security Companies (PMSCs) corporate actors under contract for direct combat operations (Kwaja 2014; Gwatiwa 2016). In Sierra Leone, Libya, Democratic Republic of Congo among others, the proliferation of these entities has had serious consequences for the security of the countries where they operate, coupled with the porous nature of the borders. As observed by the United Nations Working Group on the Use of Mercenaries: "...the trans-border activities of PMSCs illustrate the reality that most of these actors operate within porous borders, which have allowed for the free movement of individuals as well as illicit weapons and arms that have perpetuated conflicts and violence in certain countries".[4]

In the light of the fact that the contracts involve the use of light, heavy duty and sophisticated weapons, they have been responsible for the movement of such weapons into these locations. Though the existing African Union policy framework for Security Sector Reform (SSR) abhors the use of PMSCs (African Union 2006), the weakness associated with the AU's inability to address this situation has made the continent to be a dumping ground for weapons, as well as its use these entities.

With respect to the activities of PMSCs in Africa, most scholarly and policy related work has paid more attention to the western-based companies located in Europe and North America, against the backdrop of their involvements in African conflicts both in the context of combat and non-combat operations (Kwaja 2015). In recent times, Russia and China have become dominant actors that are shaping the conflict and security landscape of Africa. The Russian based Wagner group was linked to the conflict in Libya, with a personnel strength of 800–1000, as well as their involvement in Madagascar and the Central African Republic (British Broadcasting Corporation 2020). Apart from the establishment of a military base in Djibouti, there is also strong evidence of the presence of Chinese Private Security Companies (PSCs), providing guarding and Very Important Persons (VIPs) services in the continent (Arduino 2020). As a consequence of these realities, there are strong indications that the spread of SALWs in the continent is bound to burgeon in the face of Africa's fragile institutional capacities to checkmate these situations.

Weak Implementation and Evaluation of Arms Trade Legislations/Operationalization of Regional Peace and Security Architecture

SALWs create a myriad of challenges to society and increase the sophistication of conflicts. However, beyond the physical efforts to curb arms proliferation and conflict escalation, the operationalization of mechanisms that can support this effort in Africa is pertinent. The AU's mechanism for checking arms control within member states and across the region is relatively weak or ineffective; thus, increasing the effectiveness of illegal arms trade and conflict proliferation and escalation in the region. Although the government of each independent member state has a role to play in combating illegal arms trade and the proliferation of small weapons, the complacency of some of these actors and their refusal to nudge impedes comprehensive attempts to address the menace.

The checking of unauthorized and illegal arms production industry as a substantial source of illicit small arms in some areas is not operational. In Ghana, blacksmiths are identified to be manufacturing firearms with relative sophistication. Some of these guns are prototypes of original versions retrieved through illegal means; either from security actors or through raiding/robbery of security armouries. Such industries are identified to exist but weakly operationalized and coordinated regional mechanisms enable the sustainability of these industries. In addition, many state authorities leverage these companies to produce and circulate illegal arms to facilitate conflicts that are politically motivated (Schroeder and Lamb 2018; Stohl and Hogendorn 2010).

The weakness of a comprehensive arms control mechanism also affects the likelihood to curb illegal arms trade and proliferation. This dilemma is further complicated by the absence of political will by the government of some countries to adequately implement regional mandates (and referendum) on the issue. For instance, the Bamako Declaration (2000) represents the African Union's position on illicit arms trafficking and proliferation. This Declaration recommends that each African state establishes a National Focal Points (NFP), which will be the coordination mechanism for devising a national arms control action plan and facilitate small arms control research, monitoring and policy formulation on issues related to arms trade and control.

However, these NFPs have not been established by the governments of some African countries, while in some that have set-up this mechanism, they are quite ineffective. Only countries like Botswana, Kenya, Namibia and Rwanda have effectively working NFPs (Schroeder and Lamb 2018). In West Africa, ECOWAS designed National Commissions (NATCOMS) to handle illicit arms proliferation in the West African region. The essence of its establishment was to encourage regional and national initiatives intended to control illegal arms trade and curb its contribution to conflict in the region significantly. Malam (2014: 264) summarized that Natcoms have the mandate to:

> …formulate strategies, policies, and programs to counter the proliferation of small arms; Sensitize public on the need to turn in illegally held weapons to security forces; update arms registers and transmission to ECOWAS Secretariat; provide appropriate recommendations to ECOWAS Secretariat on exemptions to be granted to the Moratorium for weapons covered by the agreement; mobilise resource for program expenditures; liaise on a permanent basis with ECOWAS and PCASED Secretariats on issues relevant to the Moratorium as well as on the proliferation of SALW in general; and initiate and developed an exchange of information and experience with the other national commissions…

Although this mechanism had a mandate that would contribute to arms control in the region, especially by achieving considerable progress in the areas of compliance by member nations, its capacity to deliver its mandates is weak. The presence of weak institutional capacity is further complicated by lack of funds and political support from ECOWAS member states.

Thefts, Diversions from Government Stockpiles and Local Production

Government stockpiles represents one of the most available means of access to arms in Africa. Though such stockpiles are supposed to be well protected, there has been instance where rebels, insurgents and other criminal groups invade, overran and loot from state armouries, leading to huge loss of arms and attendant insecurities. There are reported cases of complicity of situation where high-ranking military personnel were involved in the supply of arms and ammunition to rebel groups. For instances, President Joseph Kabila of the Democratic Republic of Congo had to sack the commander of the land forces, General Gabriel Amasi over allegation that he was involved in the supply of arms to the M23 rebels, which led to their victory over the government forces in Goma.[5] One of the major drawbacks in Nigeria's counter insurgency operation against Boko Haram was the accusation against some military personnel that were reported to have been involved in the sale of arms and ammunition to the insurgents. The insurgents were also linked to series of attacks and theft of arms and ammunitions from government stockpile (Campbell 2014). With the fall of the regime of Colonal Muammar Ghadafi of Libya, there were reports that the large cache of arms in his amouries were overran by rebels with no trace, which are now in circulation within the continent and beyond (Adeniyi 2017). For instance, it was reported that two rebel groups fought to gain access to 22 containers of arms, also bearing in mind the fact that much of the arms were linked to some of the conflicts and insurgencies in Nigeria, Mali, Somalia and Syria (Basar 2012).

The activities of gun-smiths have come under focus in Africa, against the backdrop of their role in the production of arms. The shift from inter-state to intra-sate conflicts in the continent, has no doubt expanded the market of gun-smiths. Since the import of arms is becoming a bit difficulty, most of the local actors have turned to gun-smiths for the production of arms that are quite sophisticated. It was reported that the local manufactures of arms in Ghana have the capacity of producing over 200,000 arms annually (Aning 2005), while in the case of Nigeria, over 60 per cent of the illicit arms in the south-east of the country are locally manufactured (Nwaiwu 2015).

REGIONAL AND CONTINENTAL EFFORTS TOWARDS ARMS CONTROL AND DISARMAMENT IN AFRICA

Across the African continent, there have been series of initiatives and responses to the growing menace of arms both at the national, regional and continental levels. At the national levels, the issue of disarmament has been used as a basis for reasserting state control and monopoly over the use of arms as evident in the series of coordinated approaches to disarmament and demobilization of rebels and other non-state armed groups as witnessed in Liberia, Sierra Leone, Nigeria, among others. Within the continent, there are several regional initiatives, instruments and frameworks that have been designed to complement some of the continental and global responses to arms control and other weapons. Table 6.4 provides a snap-shot of such instruments.

Though the initiatives on arms control highlighted above have been operational across the regions that make up the African continent, each of these regions has had to confront huge security threats. These threats are increasingly perpetuated and sustained by the illicit flow of arms and their use by non-actors. In line with the provisions of the Arms Trade Treaty (ATT), which many of the member states of the regional organizations ratified, they are expected to implement public reporting standards. Unfortunately, many of the

Table 6.4 Regional instruments and conventions on arms control in Africa

Region	Regional organisation	Year	Instrument/Convention
West Africa	Economic Community of West African States (ECOWAS)	1998	Declaration of a Moratorium on Importation, Exportation and Manufacture of Light Weapons in West Africa (ECOWAS Moratorium)—It was renewed in 2001 and 2004
		2006	ECOWAS Convention on Small Arms and Light Weapons, Their Ammunition and Other Related Materials[a]
Central Africa	Economic Community of Central African States (ECCAS)	2010	Central African Convention for the Control of Small Arms and Light Weapons, Their Ammunition, Parts and Components that Can Be Used for Their Manufacture, Repair or Assembly (also known as the Kinshasa Convention)[b]
Southern African	Southern African Development Community (SADC)	2001	Protocol on the Control of Firearms, Ammunition and Other Related Materials in the SADC Region (SADC Protocol)[c]
North Africa	League of Arab States (LAS)	2002	LAS Arab Model Law on Weapons, Ammunition, Explosives and Hazardous Material

(continued)

Table 6.4 (continued)

Region	Regional organisation	Year	Instrument/Convention
		2004	LAS Resolution 6447: Arab Coordination for Combating the Illicit Trade in Small Arms and Light Weapons
		2006	LAS Resolution 6625: Arab Coordination for Combating the Illicit Trade in Small Arms and Light Weapons[d]
Great Lakes and the Horn of Africa	Regional Centre on Small Arms (RECSA) in the Great Lakes Region, the Horn of Africa and Bordering States	2000	Nairobi Declaration on the Problem of the Proliferation of Illicit Small Arms and Light Weapons in the Great Lakes Region and the Horn of Africa
		2004	Nairobi Protocol for the Prevention, Control, and Reduction of Small Arms and Light Weapons in the Great Lakes Region and the Horn of Africa[e]

Source Berman and Maze (2016: 22–59)
[a]ECOWAS (2006) ECOWAS convention on small arms and light weapons, their ammunition and other related materials, Abuja: ECOWAS Secretariat
[b]ECCAS (2010) Central African convention for control of small arms, light weapons, their ammunition, parts and components that can be used for their manufacture, repair or assembly, Libreville: ECCAS Secretariat
[c]SADC (2001) Protocol on the control of firearms, ammunition and other related materials in the SADC region, Gaborone: SADC Secretariat
[d]LAS (2006) Arab coordination for combating the illicit trade in small arms and light weapons, Cairo: LAS Secretariat
[e]RECSA (2004) Nairobi protocol for the prevention, control, and reduction of small arms and light weapons in the Great Lakes Region and the Horn of Africa, Nairobi: RECSA Secretariat

countries have not been transparent in this regard, in the light of the opaque nature of their military and defence related dealings.

Silencing the Guns by 2020: Policy Implications for Africa

Concerned by the devastating impact of violent conflicts that have been fuelled and sustained by arms flow within and into the continent, at the 50th Anniversary of the OAU/AU IN 2013, the African Union adopted the policy on "Silencing the Guns in Africa by the Year 2020". This represents a flagship project agenda for 2063, which is focused on creating a conducive environment for development in the continent (African Union 2019). Though the policy was lauded as an important roadmap towards durable peace, security and stability in the continent, not much has been achieved in terms of addressing many of the drivers of insecurity in the continent, which to a large extent are more internal to the member states of the AU. For several decades now, much of the conflict witnessed in the continent have been intra-state, rather than inter-state, with the exception of cases of cross border crimes, insurgency and terrorism in the Lake Chad, Sahel, Gulf of Aden, Gulf of Eden, Great Lakes region among others. The silencing the guns by the year 2020 initiative reinforces Goal 14 and Target 4 of the Sustainable Development Goals (SDGs) of the United Nations, which calls on all countries to take deliberate actions towards the significant reduction of illicit financial and arms flows (United Nations 2017).

The African Union policy framework on Security Sector Reform as it relates to the use of PMSCs in SSR needs to be reviewed with a view to capturing the reality of their operations, which is linked to the proliferation of arms in the continent. In this sense, there is a need to enact national, regional and continental regulatory frameworks requiring the registration and licencing of PMSCs, with clearly defined mechanisms for oversight and accountability, including provisions for effective monitoring and reporting in relation to the use of arms. Despite the commitment of the AU in the pursuit of its agenda on silencing the guns by the year 2020, the continent does not have any legally binding instruments that can be used to checkmate the activities of states and non-states actors who violate any of the provisions regarding arms in the continent (Berman and Maze 2016). There is no doubt that this situation serves as a major enabler for the ease with which arms flow or are trafficked in and out of the continent. Furthermore, the continent is still witnessing the involvement of PMSCs in both combat and non-combat operations (Kwaja 2015), with little or no attempt by the AU to checkmate them. With the exception of South Africa there is no African country that has been able to effectively put in place measures to regulate the activities of PMSCs. Most of the countries have only succeeded in regulating the activities of local entities involved in the provision of security related services.

United Nations Arms Control/Disarmament Measures in Africa

Within the United Nations system, there are several initiatives and programmes that have been designed and implemented in response to the threats posed by the proliferation of arms on a global scale. Africa has featured prominently here against the backdrop of the spate of conflicts and organized crimes that threatens national, regional and continental peace, security and stability. Arms embargo have also been used as instruments for arms control in the African continent. Though such embargoes were imposed by

Table 6.5 UN Programme of action on common norms and principles of SALWs

Area of commitment	Focus
Transfer	States to establish proper standards, and checks and balances in relation to the import, export, transit and transfer of SALWs
Brokering	States should establish proper mechanism for registration, authorization and international cooperation with respect to arms brokers and their activities
Stockpile, Management and Destruction	States to establish adequate standards and procedures for stockpile management and destruction as a basis for preventing the theft and diversion of SALWs from the stockpile of the states to the black markets
Disarmament	States should disarm soldiers and civilians in the aftermath of war through Disarmament, Demobilisation and Reintegration (DDR), and voluntary civilian disarmament programme
Marking and Tracing	States should ensure the adequate marking and record-keeping of SALWs and to cooperate with other states in tracing weapons found in the illegal sphere
Cooperation, Assistance and Transparency	States should submit annual report on the implement of the agreement as contained in the PoA

Source Parker and Green (2012)

the United Nations, the African Union in the interest of peace and stability of the continent, the AU is expected to monitor the implementation of such UN decisions. Unfortunately, some African states were reported to have circumvented them in favour of countries they might have had some friendly relations with. For instance, Ethiopia, Eritrea and Djibouti were alleged to have circumvented the arms embargo imposed against Somalia. In the case of the embargo against the Democratic Republic of Congo (DRC), Uganda and Rwanda were linked to bursting the embargo (Lamb 2006). The two countries were accused by a panel of experts of the United Nations Security Council of providing direct military support and arms to the M23 rebels in their fight against the Congolese government (Charbonneau and Nichols 2012). Though there have been attempts by countries to violate arms embargo, it is still viewed as a viable option that can be used to address global concerns around the proliferation and diversion of arms (United Nations 2019), in a world where it is estimated that there are also one billion arms currently in circulation (United Nations 2020).

The United Nations firearms protocol of 2001 represents one of the globally recognized legally binding decisions that was designed to promote, facilitate and strengthen cooperation among states parties as a basis for preventing, combating and eradicating the illicit manufacturing of and trafficking of firearms, their parts, components and ammunitions. States were requested to put in place national laws that criminalizes the illegal production of firearms, strengthen the procedures for gun licencing, as well as establish measures for the effective marking and tracing of firearms in order to prevent or reduce the diversion of such firearms to the black market.

Though not a legally binding decision, the 2001 United Nations Programme of Action (UN-PoA) established some common norms and principles for preventing the illicit sale of Small Arms and Light Weapons (SALWs) as shown in Table 6.5.

African Nuclear-Weapons-Free-Zone Treaty

In line with its vision of denuclearizing the African continent, the African Nuclear-Weapons-Free-Zone treaty, otherwise known as the Pelindaba Treaty, was signed by member states of the defunct Organisation of African Unity (OAU) in 1996 and it came into effect in 2009. The Treaty prohibited the research, development, manufacture and stockpile, acquisition, testing, possession, control or stationing of nuclear explosive devices, as well as dumping of radioactive wastes in the territory of parties to the treaty (Scott et al. 2008). The treaty, which principally targets disarmament and non-proliferation, does not prohibit African states from enhancing their nuclear capabilities for peaceful purposes, which in recent time have witnessed several African countries signing nuclear deals in this regard.

Under Protocol I and II of the treaty, some countries such as China, France, Russia, United Kingdom, United States were called upon not to use or threaten to use a nuclear explosive devise against any member part to the treaty within the African continent. They were further called upon to agree not to test, assist or encourage the testing of a nuclear explosive device anywhere within the African zone (Foy 2015). Though Article 12 of the treaty called for the establishment of the African Commission on Nuclear Energy (AFCONE) as a mechanism for compliance, not much has been achieved with respect such decision, which is supposed to provide a broader continental framework for cooperation among African states on the nuclear weapons that are currently one of the biggest threats to international peace, security and stability. One of the highlights of the recent Russia–Africa summit was the signing of nuclear deals between Russia and some African countries such as Rwanda, with the goal of nuclear enrichment for energy related purposes, similar to the ones already signed with Egypt, Uganda and the Democratic Republic of Congo (DRC) (Schepers 2019). This is in line with the vision of the AFCONE in ensuring that nuclear enrichment by member states of the AU are strictly for peaceful purposes as highlighted above. The key problematic here has to do with the extent to which the AU is able to put in place mechanisms to ensure compliance among member states, against the backdrop of its consistent inability to take decisive decision against its members.

In line with its vision of support war to peace transitions processes in the continent, the AU established the Disarmament, Demobilisation and Reintegration (DDR) in 2012. Despite this show of commitment towards disarmament, most of the disarmament programmes undertaken in the continent have been designed and implemented by the United Nations as the lead entity, particularly in Liberia, the Great Lakes region of Central Africa, Democratic Republic of Congo, Burundi, Somalia, Sierra Leone (Hanson 2007). The only exception was Nigeria's oil rich Niger Delta region where the Nigerian government launched and implemented a comprehensive disarmament and amnesty programme for repentant militant youths in the region. Unlike the other countries where the disarmament programmes were externally driven, that of Nigeria was home grown, with a significant part of the strategy and resources provided by the Nigerian government under Musa Yar'adua (Ushie 2013).

Conclusion

Curbing the menace of arms proliferation and its contribution to conflicts escalation in Africa is an enormous task. Hence, it is important that individual state governments in Africa and the Africa Union improve actions towards positively transforming arms proliferation and conflict. Governments in the region must decisively respond to any form of violation of arms embargoes, including the continuous illegal arms trades. Violations of such provisions should be followed by sanctions on individuals and companies engaged in illicit trafficking of arms. To this end, the African Union (AU), regional bodies (such as ECOWAS, SADC, IGAD), and other member governments should implement various legislations and provisions in different agreements that focus on the control of arms and arms trades.

Notwithstanding the continental response to arms in Africa, each country reserves the right to also define rules applicable to the acquisition, retention and use of arms by their citizens. Though the rules may vary from country to country, they should be defined in ways that reinforce or compliment the continental efforts towards arms control and disarmament. These actions will strengthen arms regulation mechanisms and improve their effectiveness towards delivering their various mandates. Also, ensuring political and economic integration, and addressing the factors that increases inequality, under-development, poverty and impedes human development is vital to prevent the perpetuation of illicit arms economy.

There is a sense in which the African countries have demonstrated immense capacity and commitment to support initiatives and seek to address the challenges posed by the proliferation of arms and their use in the continent. The major drawback has been the fact that such commitments are not seen when it comes to the domestication and implementation of the treaties, conventions or agreements as evident in the weakness associated with their implementation. Going forward, any road map that seeks to reduce the flow of arms as part of a broader initiative of silencing the guns in the continent, should be predicated on a robust implementation strategy that goes beyond lip-service to a more proactive approach.

Notes

1. ECOWAS Convention on Small Arms and Light Weapons, Their Ammunition and Other Related Materials (June, 2006).
2. The discourse on mercenarism as a security challenge for the state in Africa has been on for decades. See Musah, A.F. and Fayemi, J.K. eds. (2000). *Mercenaries: An African Security Dilemma*, London: Pluto Press.
3. The United Nations Security Council adopted resolution 1467 in 2003.
4. United Nations (2018) Report of the United Nations Working Group on the Use of Mercenaries as a Means of Violating Human Rights and Impeding the Rights to Self Determination, 73rd Session, available in https://www.securitycouncilreport.org/atf/cf/%7B65BFCF9B-6D27-4E9C-8CD3-CF6E4FF96FF9%7D/a_73_303.pdf, p. 13 accessed 20 June 2020.
5. See DRC army chief suspended for smuggling arms, available in www.aljazeera.com/news/africa/2012/11/2012112355224852821.html.

References

Adeniyi, A. (2017, March). *The Human Cost of Uncontrolled Arms in Africa* (OXFAM Research Report). United Kingdom: OXFAM.

African Union. (2006). *African Union Policy Framework on Security Sector Reform*. Addis Ababa: African Union.

African Union. (2019). *Silencing the Guns by 2020*. Available in https://au.int/en/flagships/silencing-guns-2020. Accessed 21 June 2020.

Alusala, N. (2018). *Africa and Arms Control: Challenges and Successes* (ENACT: Policy Brief). Issue 3.

Aning, K. E (2005). The Anatomy of Ghana's Secret Arms Industry. Available in www.works.bepress.com/kwesi_aning/17/. Accessed 20 June 2020.

Arduino, E. (2020). *The Footprints of Chinese Private Security Companies in Africa* (China-Africa Research Initiative, Working Paper: no. 35).

Bah, H. (2004). *Implementing the ECOWAS Small Arms Moratorium in post-War Sierra Leone*. Ottawa: Canadian Peacebuilding Coordinating Committee.

Badmus, I. A. (2009). *Managing Arms in Peace Processes: ECOWAS and the West African Civil Conflicts*, WP/CEAUP/2009.

Basar, E. (2012). *Report Update: Unsecured Libyan weapons—Regional Impact and Possible Threats*. Available in www.reliefweb.int/sites/reliefweb.int/files/resources/20121031%Libya%Weapons%20Update_Final.pdf.

Berman, G. E., & Maze, K. (2016). *Regional Organisations and the UN Programme of Action on Small Arms (PoA)*. Switzerland: Small Arms Survey.

British Broadcasting Corporation. (2020). *Wagner, Shadowy Russian Military Group, Fighting in Liberia*. Available in https://www.bbc.com/news/world-africa-52571777. Assessed 21 June 2020.

Charbonneau, L., & Nichols, M (2012). *Exclusive: Rwanda, Uganda Arming Congo Rebels, Providing Troops*. Available in https://in.reuters.com/article/us-congo-democratic-rwanda-uganda/exclusive-rwanda-uganda-arming-congo-rebels-providing-troops-u-n-panel-idUSBRE89F1CM20121016. Accessed 16 June 2020.

Campbell, J (2014). *Nigeria's Boko Haram and Heavy Weapons*. Blog Post. Washington, DC: Council on Foreign Relations (CFR).

Foy, K. H. (2015, April 28). *Five Years After Entry-into-Force of the Treaty of Pelindaba on the African—Nuclear-Weapon-Free-Zone: Progress, Challenges and Next Steps*. Background Paper Prepared for the Nuclear Non-Proliferation Treaty, New York.

Griffiths, M., O'Callaghan, T., & Roach, S. (2007). *International Relations: Key Concepts*. London: Routledge.

Gwatiwa, T. T. (2016). Private Military and Security Companies Policy in Africa: Regional Policy Statis as Agency in International Politics, Scientia Militaria. *South African Journal of Military Science*, 44(2), 68–86.

Hanson, S. (2007). *Disarmament, Demobilization and Reintegration (DDR) in Africa, Backgrounder*. Washington, DC: Council on Foreign Relations.

Kwaja, A. M. C. (2014). The Private Military and Security Sector and African Conflicts: The Case Study of Sierra Leone. *Journal of African Foreign Affairs*, 1(1), 83–110.

Kwaja, A. M. C. (2015). From Combat to Non-Combat Action: Private Military and Security Companies and Humanitarian Assistance Operations in Darfur, Sudan. *African Security Review*, 27(2), 153–161.

Lamb, G. (2006). The Illicit Arms Trade in Africa. *African Analyst*, Third Quarter (1), 69–78.

Malam, B. (2014). Small Arms and Light Weapons Proliferation and Its Implication for West African Regional Security. *International Journal of Humanities and Social Science*, 4(8), 260–269.

Murshed, M. S. (2018). Conflict, Civil War and Underdevelopment: An Introduction. *Journal of Peace Research*, 39(4), 387–393.

Nwaiwu, C. (2015). *60% of Illicit Arms in S/East Produced Locally*. Available in www.vanguardngr.com/2015/10/60-of-illegal-arms-seast-produced-locally-presidential-cttee/.

Ochoche, A. SS. A. (2002, May 14–15). The Nigerian Military as an Institution for Peace and Stability in Africa. In *The African Union and the Challenges of Cooperation and Integration*. Proceedings of the National Seminar, Organised by the Ministry of Cooperation and Integration in Africa: The Presidency, Abuja, Nigeria.

Organisation of African Unity. (1972). *Convention for the Elimination of Mercenaries in Africa*. Addis Ababa: Organisation of African Unity.

Parker, S., & Green, K. (2012). *A Decade of Implementation of the United Nations Programme of Action on Small Arms and Light Weapons: Analysis of National Reports*. Geneva: United Nations.

Schelling, T., & Halperin, M. (1985). *Strategy and Arms Control*. London: Pergamon-Brassley.

Schepers, N. (2019, February). *Russia's Nuclear Energy Exports: Status, Prospects and Implications* (Non-Proliferation and Disarmament Papers, No. 61).

Schroeder, M., & Lamb, G. (2018). The Illicit Arms Trade in Africa: A Global Enterprise. *African Analyst*, Third Quarter, 1, 69–78.

Scott, N., Rand, D. A., & Preez, D. J. (2008). *A Brief Guide to the Pelindaba Treaty: Towards Entry into Force of the African Weapon Free Zone Treaty*. Pretoria: Institute for Security Studies (ISS).

Seiyefa, E. (2017). Elite Political Culture—A Link to Political Violence: Evidence from Nigeria. *African Security, 10*(2), 103–130.

Small Arms Survey. (2011). *Small arms survey 2011: States of security*. Geneva: Graduate Institute of International and Development Studies.

Small Arms Survey. (2019). *The West Africa—Sahel connection: Mapping cross-border arms traffickign, Briefing Paper*. Geneva: Graduate Institute of International and Development Studies.

Stohl, R., & Hogendorn, E. J. (2010). *Stopping the Destructive Spread of Small Arms: How Small Arms and Light Weapons Proliferation Undermine Security and Development*. Available in https://www.americanprogress.org/wp-content/uploads/issues/2010/03/pdf/small_arms.pdf.

UNIDIR. (2001). *Coming to Terms with Security*. UNIDIR/2001/16. Geneva: United Nations.

United Nations. (2011). *Emerging Security Threats in West Africa*. Special Research Report. New York: United Nations.

United Nations. (2017). *The Sustainable Development Goals 2015–2030*. New York: United Nations.

United Nations. (2019). *Small Arms and Light Weapons: Report of the Secretary-General*. S/2019/1011. New York: United Nations.

United Nations. (2020). *Spread of 1 Billion Small Arms, Light Weapons Remains Major Threat Globally*. SC/14098. Report of the High Representative for Disarmament. New York: United Nations.

Ushie, V. (2013). Nigeria's Amnesty Programme as a Peacebuilding Infrastructure: A Silver Bullet? *Journal of Peacebuilding and Development, 8*(1), 30–44.

Vorath, J. (2017). *Containing Illicit Flows at African Borders: Pithfalls for Europe*. Berlin: German Institute for International and Security Affairs.

Chris M. A. Kwaja is a Senior Lecturer and Researcher at the Centre for Peace and Security, Modibbo Adama University of Technology, Yola, Adamawa State, Nigeria. He is also the Chairperson-Rapporteur of the United Nations Working Group on Mercenaries. He is also an international fellow at the Centre for Human Rights and Humanitarian Studies, Watson Institute of International Affairs, Brown United States, as well as Visiting Researcher at the Centre for Democracy and Development (CDD), Abuja, Nigeria. He was formerly Director General, Research and Planning, Governor's Office, as well as Honourable Commissioner for Local Governments and Chieftaincy Affairs, Plateau State, Nigeria. His research has focused on the security sector reform in transition societies; the privatization of security; the politics of identity in Africa; civil society, elections and democratization; as well as conflict, peace and security analysis.

CHAPTER 7

Mapping of Conflicts and Small Arms and Light Weapons Proliferations in Africa

Taiye Oluwafemi Adewuyi and Mwanret Gideon Daful

INTRODUCTION

In recent years, many studies have shown interest in the mapping of location of features or phenomena (Adewuyi and Olofin 2014; Musa et al. 2019). This has increased even more with the advancement in the information technology. There are new softwares that can plot locations and subsequently analyze the locations and patterns of distribution. Geographical mapping has been of great interest because it forms the basis for understanding of the distribution of things, establishment of their patterns, the modeling of future trends and the establishment of relationships between different features. As a result, geographical mapping is the creation of database on a given subject and therefore the more comprehensive it is, the better the analysis, and the better the subsequent applications to real situations. In that light, this chapter maps conflicts and the proliferation of Small Arms and Light Weapons (SALWs).

The proliferation of SALWs is an issue of concern at all levels of governance (local, state, national, regional and global community) because of its consequences on lives, property, economy, social norms and the environment (UNDP 1994). Further reasons for concern are the complexity of the actors involved (both state and non-state), the types of conflicts they are used for, the nature of the business, the duration of the conflicts and their effects on the environment.

T. O. Adewuyi (✉) · M. G. Daful
Department of Geography, Nigerian Defence Academy, Kaduna, Nigeria

© The Author(s), under exclusive license to Springer Nature Switzerland AG 2021
U. A. Tar and C. P. Onwurah (eds.), *The Palgrave Handbook of Small Arms and Conflicts in Africa*,
https://doi.org/10.1007/978-3-030-62183-4_7

There is no doubt that the proliferation of arms in Africa has contributed directly and indirectly to several crises which bedevil the continent in the forms of militancy, terrorism, genocide, human trafficking, armed robbery, cattle rustling and politically motivated violence and killings. A good example is the Boko Haram activities in the north east of Nigeria. All of these affect different components of the environment (climate, soil, water and vegetation) at different scales and stages of the conflicts (Laurance 1998).

As of 2018, more than a dozen of countries in Africa are destabilized by civil wars with the proliferation SALWs playing a prominent role as conflict multiplier. Even countries that are thought to be politically, economically and socially stable (such as Kenya) are experiencing various levels of danger and unrest which can be directly or indirectly attributed to the proliferation of small arms and light weapons (NOREF 2013). Consequently, some political and cultural issues that should ordinary correct themselves through peaceful means, are now escalating to new and higher conflict dimensions. Some of these issues are conflicts emanating from elections, appointment, locations and control of markets. Therefore, easy movement of SALWs through very porous borders has created protracted conflicts like the cases of Central Africa Republic and South Sudan just to mention a few.

The dynamic nature of the quantity of SALWs in the hands of non-state actors who got them through smugglers of arms and the paucity of records on the legal production, exports, imports and storage because they are not officially acquired and they do not pass through custom at the point of entrance makes it very difficult to assess the status of SALWs in Africa. Added to this is the fact that the modern manufacturing process has changed them to modular designs making them more difficult to trace, and ultimately more popular among civilian (Jenzen-Jones 2016).

More importantly, a good number of exporters (contractors of arms) are not the major producers of small arms, but middle men, with substantial numbers of legally acquired arms entering the illicit market through corruption, seizure and loss during operation and from storage facilities. Therefore, to have a long-lasting solution to most of the problems facing Africa, there is the urgent need to mitigate this small arms and light weapon proliferation. It is clear that when the SALWs challenges are addressed, the problems they constitute to the nations and environment will also be automatically eliminated (AEFJN 2010).

A number of questions are pertinent to this chapter: Where and what are the quantities of SALWs in various countries and regions of Africa? what are the categories and flow of SALWs in Africa, especially, in countries that undergo violent conflicts? What is the pattern of acquisition and distribution? To provide answers to these questions, this chapter aims to establish and maps the location of SALWs in Africa, as a basis for tackling of this enormous problem and its impacts on lives and the environment.

The novelty of this study is in the creation of an up to date maps on SALWs in Africa, characterize the conflicts as well as established the likely relationship between SALWs proliferation and conflicts in Africa. Consequently, assessment will be carried out which will then form a platform for future global assessment and analysis. As a result, this chapter comprises of the following sections: staring with introduction, conceptual framework, materials and methods and the results which include, characterization of conflicts in Africa, proliferation of SALWs, discussion, implications and conclusion.

CONCEPTUAL AND THEORETICAL FRAMING

The following provide operationalization of some concepts as used in this chapter:

Small arms: These include, but not limited to revolvers and self-loading pistols, squad automatic weapons, rifles and carbines, assault rifles, sniper rifles, battle rifles, submachine guns and light machine guns. "Small arms" are, broadly speaking, weapons designed for individual used, they are firearms designed to be carried and fired by a single person; often held in the hand, and that can expel or launch a shot, bullet, or projectile by action of explosive (United Nations 2006; Small Arms Survey and the African Union (AU) Report 2019).

Light weapons: are, broadly speaking, infantry weapons firing explosive munitions, designed for use by two or three persons serving as a crew, although some may be carried and used by a single person. These include heavy machine guns, mounted grenade launchers and hand-held under-barrel, portable anti-tank and anti-aircraft guns, recoilless rifles, mobile containers with missiles or portable launchers of anti-tank and anti-aircraft missile systems, shells and missiles for light weapons, and mortars of calibers of less than 100 mm (United Nations 2006; Small Arms Survey and the African Union (AU) Report 2019).

Conflict mostly arises as a result of solemn disagreement between two parties (two people or groups) over an interest, idea or beliefs, and finds it impossible to reach an agreement. it is normally characterized by antagonism and hostility. The most common conflicts in Africa are conflict over land border, natural resources, power and religious conflicts. Conflict is generally a specific status of relationship between states or rival factions within a state which implies subjective hostilities or tension manifested in subjective economic or military hostilities. Conflicts could, however, be violent or uncontrollable, dominant or recessive, resolvable or insolvable. This presupposes that violence is not an inherent aspect of conflict but rather a potential form that conflict may take (Holsti 1983; Adedeji 1999; Adeyemo 2000; Aremu 2010).

Mapping: the art and science of providing a symbolic representation of selected characteristics of a place, usually drawn on a flat surface. In this chapter the characteristics of SALWs in Africa are mapped. Maps are graphic representation, drawn to scale and usually on a flat surface, and are used to illustrate specific or detail features of an area. maps generally represent the real world on a much smaller scale. It helps organize and present information about a place, which is vital for decision-making.

Deviance Theory: an action that is perceived as violating a society's or group's cultural norm. Norms dictate what is considered acceptable and unacceptable behavior across cultures. One category of deviance is crime, which occurs when someone violates a society's formal laws. Criminal deviance spans a wide range of behavior, from minor traffic violations to arson to murder. This idea is also closely related to the statistical approach to definite abnormality which rests on the idea that differences in human behavior tend to fall into a normal distribution curve (Nwankwo 2006). A particular behavior is not acceptable or is antisocial if any of these three criteria are seen; the behavior does not allow a person to function effectively with others as a member of society, if the behavior does not permit the person to meet his or her own needs and the behavior has a negative effect in the wellbeing of others (Roberts 1981). Deviant behavior goes against the rules they have created to bring order to their society. Breaking one results to negative social reaction. By specifying the causes of deviance, the theories reveal how aspects of the social environment influence the behavior of individuals and groups.

THE STUDY AREA, MATERIALS AND METHODS

The Context—Mapping the Environmental Fundamentals of SALWs and Conflict

The temporal scope for this study is 2017 while the spatial extent is Africa, with a geographical coordinate of latitude 27° N – 38° S and longitude 18° W – 58° E. This continent has 56 independent states (with South Sudan being the newest addition), and with a combined population of 1.250 billion as of 2017. 41% of the population is less than 15 years old, with the majority living in sub-Saharan Africa (1.021 billion), while the East African region has the highest population (422 million) followed by West African region (371 million) and Nigeria having the highest population of 190 million and Sao Tome and Principe the least with 200,000 people. Africa has a land mass of 30,335,000 km^2 translating to a population density of 41 per km^2, with 41% of the population living in urban area and 534,000 persons per square kilometer of arable land (PRB 2017).

Africa has diverse natural vegetation that is influenced by climate (rainfall and temperature) and the type of soil. The vegetation ranges from barren desert of the Sahara Desert to the north, grassland (savanna), to the rain and mangrove forest along the equatorial zone, with each type being well adapted to the regions in which they are found. The continent has boundaries with the Atlantic Ocean to the west, Indian Ocean to the east and Mediterranean Sea to the north.

The continent of Africa is blessed with many geographical features such as Mount Kilimanjaro in Tanzania at 5895 m above mean sea level; the largest desert, the Sahara with an approximate size of 9 million km^2; and massive forest areas that cut across west, central and east Africa. The continent also has the River Nile of 6695 km length, Lake Victoria having a size of 68,800 km^2; Victoria Falls at 128 m, and Lake Chad. These are just a few of the natural endowments of Africa, which has also been said to be the cradle of civilization (Adewuyi 2016).

Most of the land is used for agriculture in the form of crop farming and animal husbandry, but the African vegetation also provides thick forests that serve as hideout of terrorist, insurgents and common criminals. Other uses are mining, forestry and infrastructure in forms of road, rail, settlements and a few spaces for recreation. The economy revolves around the land use with majority in the continent practicing subsistence agriculture which most of the countries are attempting to modernize to commercial farming. There exists some level of industrial complex across the continent but it is nothing compared to what exists in America, Europe and China in terms of scale, density, percentage contributed to GDP, employment and level of automation.

The systems of government are a mixture of parliamentary and presidential with the characteristic of a sit-tight democracy where many of the heads of government stay in power for many years (as it is in Sudan, Cameroon, Uganda and Angola) with only a few like Botswana and Ghana having more of a semblance of true democracy. Consequently, most of the countries usually have serious political crises before, during and after elections.

According to Small Arms Survey (2018) Sub-Saharan Africa suffers excessively from the undesirable impacts of small arms and ammunition flows on peace, security, stability and development, yet it only accounts for less than five percent of the estimated value of the authorized global small arms trade. Due to historically low levels of openness regarding sub-Saharan African small arms production and transfers, identifying major African importers and exporters as well as suppliers remains a challenge.

Holtom and Pavesi (2018) *Sub-Saharan Africa in Focus* uses multiple open sources to tentatively map major sub-Saharan African producers, exporters and importers of small arms as follow:

   i. The Small Arms Survey (2007) identified that at least 15 sub-Saharan African states industrially produce small arms and/or ammunition, namely: Angola, Cameroon, Chad, the Democratic Republic of the Congo, the Republic of Congo, Ethiopia, Kenya, Madagascar, Mali, Namibia, Nigeria, South Africa, Tanzania, Uganda, and Zimbabwe.
  ii. Official data indicates that South Africa was the largest sub-Saharan African exporter and importer of small arms during 2013–2015. Significant importers during this period include: Angola, Cameroon, Côte d'Ivoire, Malawi, Namibia, Niger, Nigeria, and Uganda.
 iii. The largest transparent small arms exporters to sub-Saharan Africa for 2013–2015 appear to be Bulgaria, Serbia, France, Spain, and Italy, in descending order of importance. Exporters such as China, the Russian Federation, and Turkey also concluded significant deals to supply small arms to sub-Saharan Africa during this period. These countries recorded

low scores for transparency in the 2018 Barometer, and have delivered small arms to the region in this period in quantities that would suggest that they are also important sources of supply.

Small Arms Survey and the African Union (AU) Report (2019) report that AU member states identify the trafficking of arms and ammunition across land borders as the main type of illicit flow they are confronted with. Armed groups, including terrorist organizations, have demonstrated their capacity to move weapons across borders or carry out attacks.

Existing estimates provide a sense of the scale and subregional distribution of small arms in Africa (Table 7.1). They suggest that African civilian actors, which include private individuals, registered businesses such as private security companies, and non-state armed groups, hold more than 40 million (almost 80 percent) of all small arms on the continent. In contrast, the continent's armed forces and law enforcement agencies hold less than 11 million small arms. Among the 40 million civilian-held firearms in Africa, 5,841,200 are recorded as being officially registered, while 16,043,800 are unregistered, with the status of the remainder remaining unclear (Small Arms Survey 2018).

In absolute terms, Western Africa has the largest number (about 11 million) of—licit and illicit civilian-held firearms on the continent, followed by Northern Africa (10.2 million) and Eastern Africa (7.8 million) (Table 7.1). When applied to population distribution, Southern Africa is the subregion with the highest number of civilian-held firearms per 1000 people (94), followed by Northern (44) and Middle (31) Africa (Small Arms Survey 2018). The large volume of civilian-held firearms in Africa might be responsible for the different kinds of conflicts in the region, such as border conflicts, headers farmer's conflicts, insurgencies, banditry and so on (Babalola 2017; Gaddo 2017).

This study engaged documentary data of which Small Arms in Africa (Sall 2011) and PRB (2017) plays a major role. Several other databases like UNDP (1994); Jekada (2005); Anders (2009); AEFJN (2010); Sall (2011) and

Table 7.1 Estimated African subregional distribution of civilian firearms, 2017

UN subregion*	Population	Number of civilian-held firearms	Civilian-held firearms per 1000 population
Africa total	1,246,505,000	40,009,000	32
Eastern Africa	416,676,000	7,802,000	19
Middle Africa	161,237,000	4,981,000	31
Northern Africa	232,186,000	10,241,000	44
Southern Africa	63,854,000	6,012,000	94
Western Africa	372,551,000	10,972,000	29

Source Small Arms Survey (2018). Adopted from Small Arms Survey and the African Union (AU) Report (2019)

NOREF (2013) were consulted to augment these two. Information on location of conflicts, time of occurrence, types of conflicts and nature of arms used were extracted and georeferenced for maps creation and subsequent analysis. The Geographic Information System (GIS) (ArcGIS 10.5 version) provided the environment for mapping, statistical analysis and presentation of findings, and discussions of the implications. This platform utilized tables and maps to summarize the result.

Mapping of Conflicts and Small Arms and Light Weapons Proliferations in Africa

Characterization of Conflicts in Africa

Of the 57 nations in Africa, this chapter assessed and mapped 51 countries on the main land, for the proliferation of small arms and light weapons. This was done for two reasons, scale of presentation, pattern of distribution of both SALWs and conflicts and their significance in the study. The remaining six (6) islands are considered insignificant to the study. On the whole, Africa has 1.25 billion people at the end of 2017 with majority of the population in the sub-Saharan region (1.02b). When this number is further characterized, East Africa with twenty (20) countries has 422 m people, followed by West Africa with sixteen (16) nations with 371 m. North Africa has seven (7) nations and 230 m people. Central Africa has nine (9) countries and 163 m people and the least is Southern Africa both in terms of number of countries (5) and population of 65 m people (PRB 2017). Appendix 1 at the end of this paper provided a concise summary of the database established for this study.

In order to gain an in-depth perspective on the issues of small arms and light weapon proliferation in Africa, the first attempt made was to examine the nature of conflicts in Africa. This was very important because the issues of conflicts and arms are like Siamese twins, if there is no conflict there will be no need for arms, since it is small arms and light weapon that are mostly used in such crises situation (Ero and Ndinga-Muvumba 2004; Edeko 2014). The review of the types of conflicts in Africa revealed that most of the conflicts are internal (amounting to about 62% of all conflicts) while countries with both internal and external conflicts account for 34%. Figure 7.1, further revealed that internal conflicts spread across all the regions while countries with both internal and external did not occur in the southern Africa region.

Examining the conflicts from the view of length of the crisis is indicative of how long the small arms and light weapons are required to pursue the fighting. The survey revealed in Fig. 7.2, that most of the countries in east, west and central Africa (17) experienced conflicts that lasted between 11 and 15 years. Fourteen countries (mainly in West and North Africa) had their countries' conflicts lasting between 6 and 10 years. Eight countries (mainly in central and West Africa) had durations less than 5 years. Two nations ranged between 16 and 20 years. Six countries had conflicts for more than 20 years, and only 3

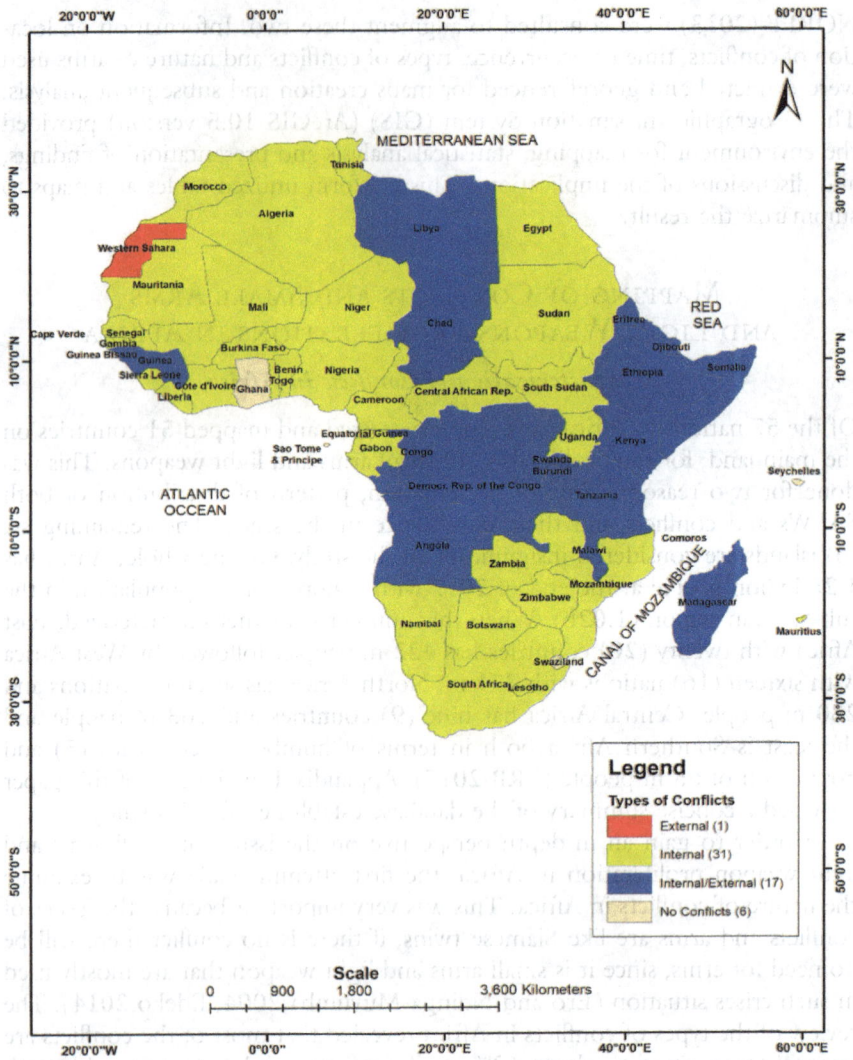

Fig. 7.1 Types of conflicts in Africa

without any major conflicts. Again, this statistics show the widespread distribution of conflicts in Africa and for how long this continent has been subjected to conflicts by those who profited from the proliferation of small arms and light weapons (Bekoe 2010).

Another major area of our investigation was to identify the major actors (stakeholders) of these numerous conflicts on the continent. Without knowing them, it would be difficult to tackle this menace. The survey revealed most of the conflicts (30%) are political in nature and are mainly situated in central, east and southern Africa; 20% are religious which are dominant in west and North

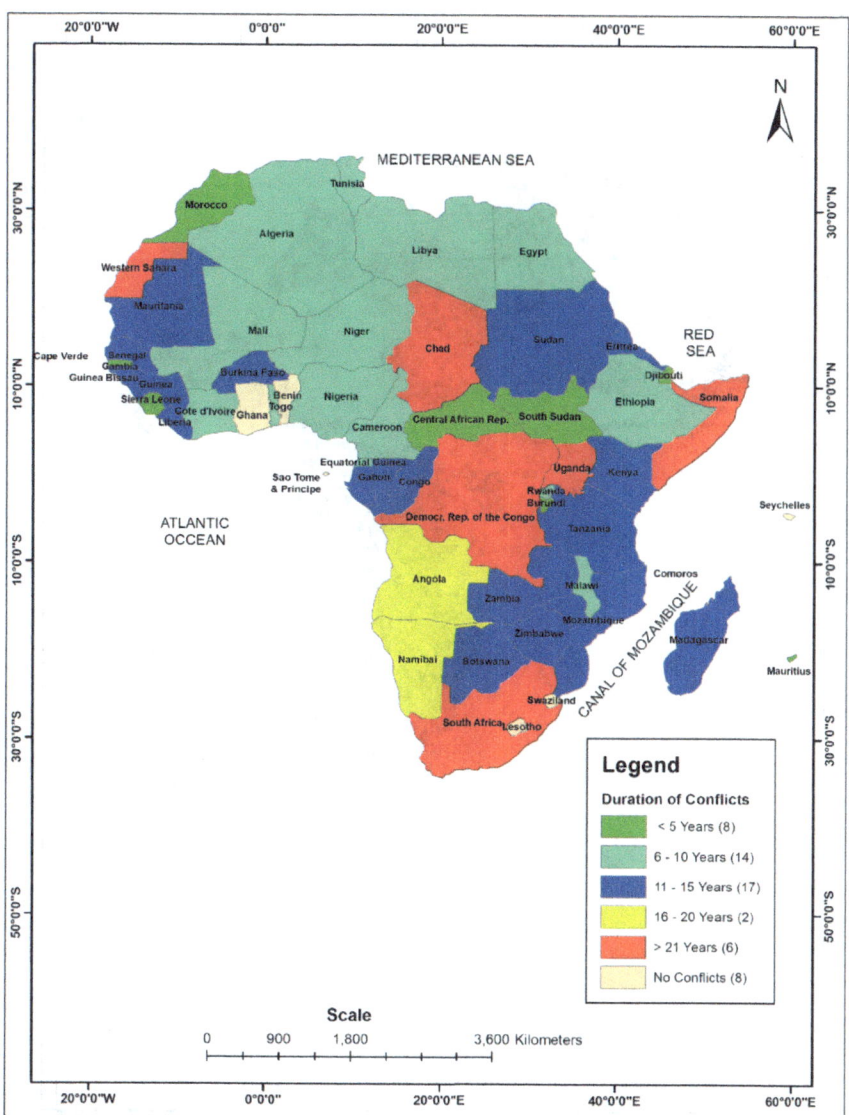

Fig. 7.2 Duration of conflicts in Africa

Africa (Fig. 7.3). For the rest of the continent, conflict is influence by the combined forces of ethnic factors, economic factors, banditry and crime. This implies there are different actors in the numerous conflicts on the continent.

Furthermore, most of the conflicts (80%) which cut across all the regions as displayed in Fig. 7.4 are owned by combinations of individuals and groups which may be the reasons why most of the conflicts extend for a long time. Clearly it is more difficult to resolve issues that have so many individuals as

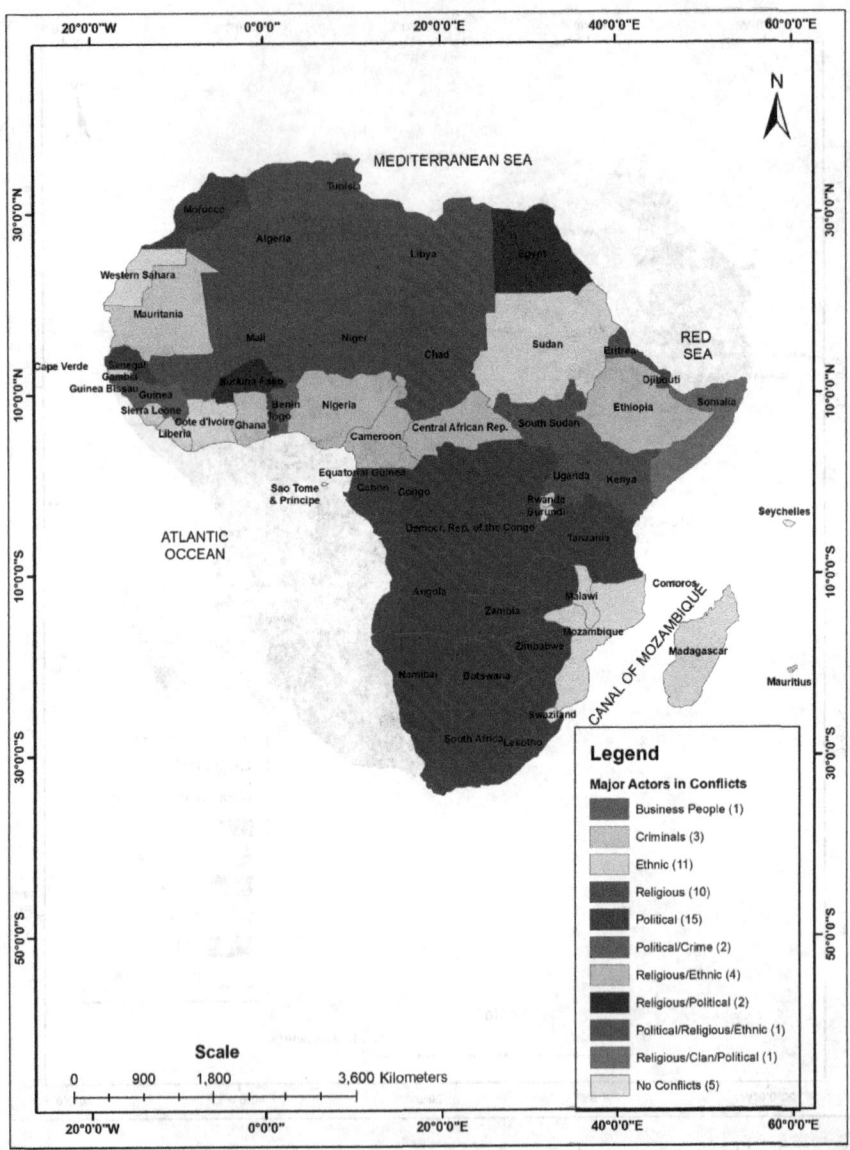

Fig. 7.3 Major actors of conflicts in Africa

stakeholders, as evidenced by the protected crises in Somalia and Congo DRC, which have proven quite intractable to resolve. Also, it was noticed that the timing of the conflicts are usually just before independence or immediately after independence (as with the case with South Sudan, which is the youngest country in the continent and many other countries like Nigeria and Angola). Although, several conflicts occurred long after independence, like the case of

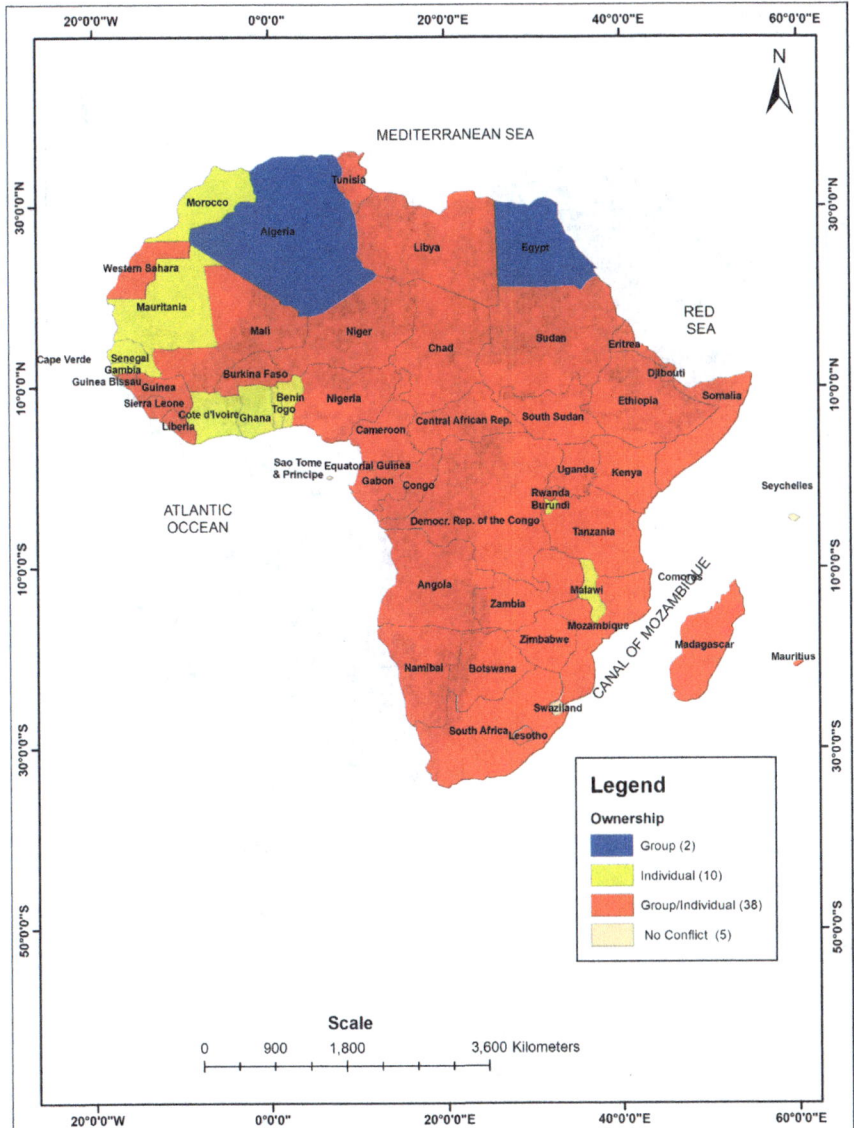

Fig. 7.4 Ownership of conflicts in Africa

Liberia and Sierra Leone which may be attributed to post-cold war dynamics. More than 80% of the countries which spread across all the regions suffered from conflicts that are in form of political uprising and religious fighting (as currently is the case in Libya, Tunisia and Central Africa Republic (Fig. 7.5). These twin factors have caused most of the crises in the continent.

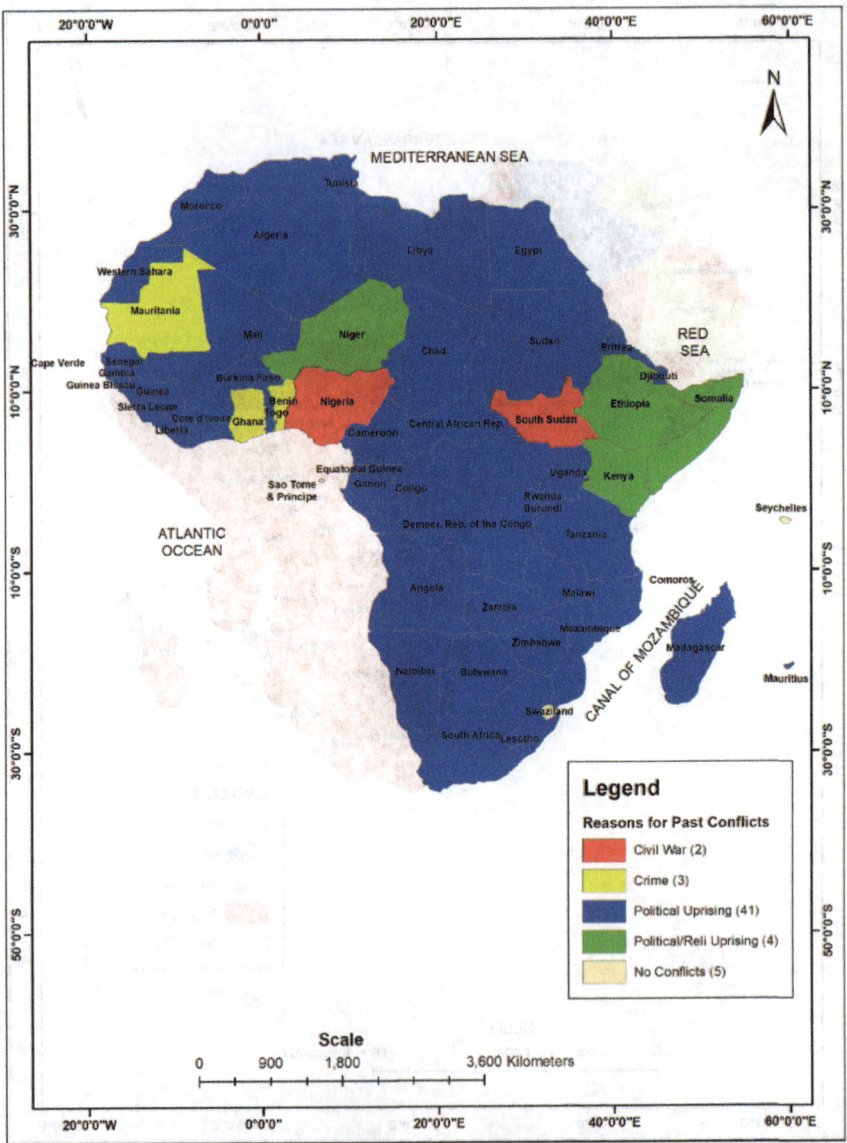

Fig. 7.5 Reasons for conflicts in Africa

Proliferation of Small Arms and Light Weapons (SALWs)

Africa is perpetually at war as revealed from the characterization of conflicts in Africa using different colors. The immediate consequence of that is the prevalence, spread and ownership of SALWS across the continent Our survey revealed that 27 countries predominantly located in the northern and central

Africa regions have small arms (portable guns) and light weapons (mortars), while the remaining countries (23), mainly in the southern, western and east Africa areas have only small arms in the form of rifles (Fig. 7.6).

However, 96% of these arms are sourced from a mixture of foreign and domestic producers with only two countries depending exclusively on domestic production (Fig. 7.7). Most, if not all the countries in Africa still

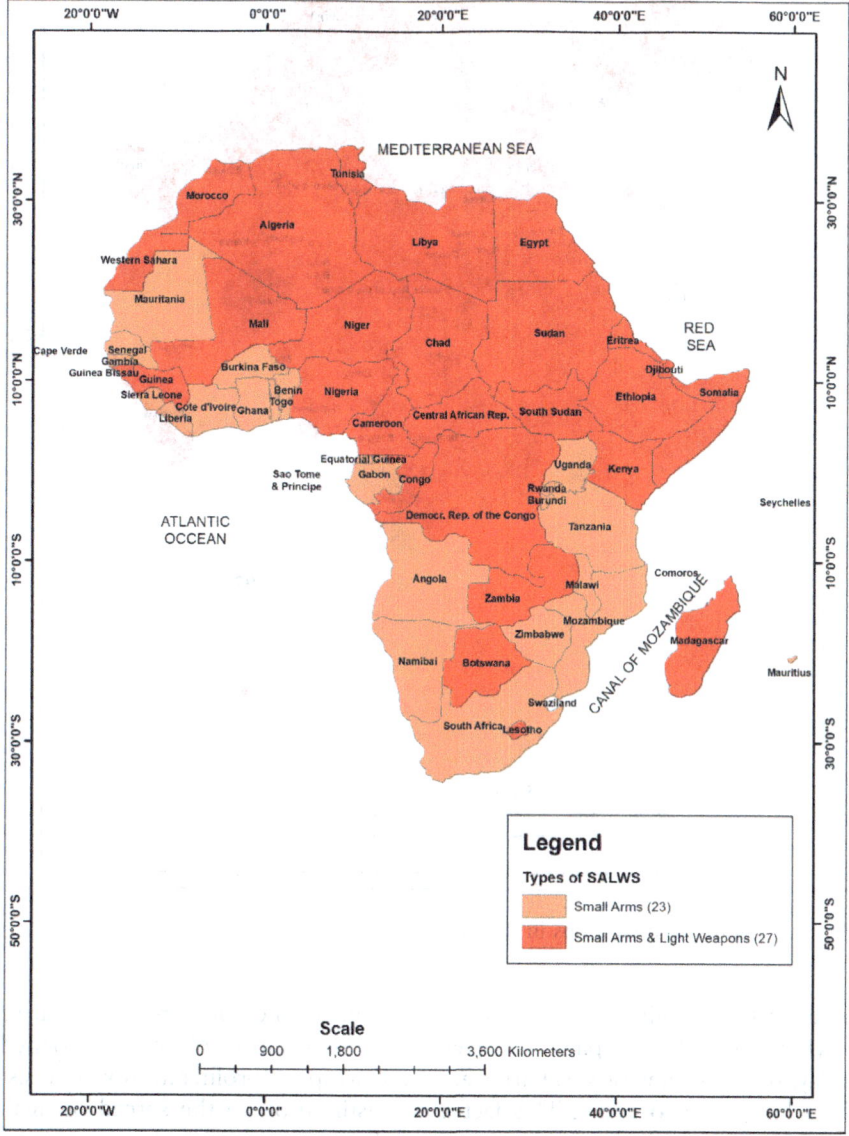

Fig. 7.6 Types of SALWs in Africa

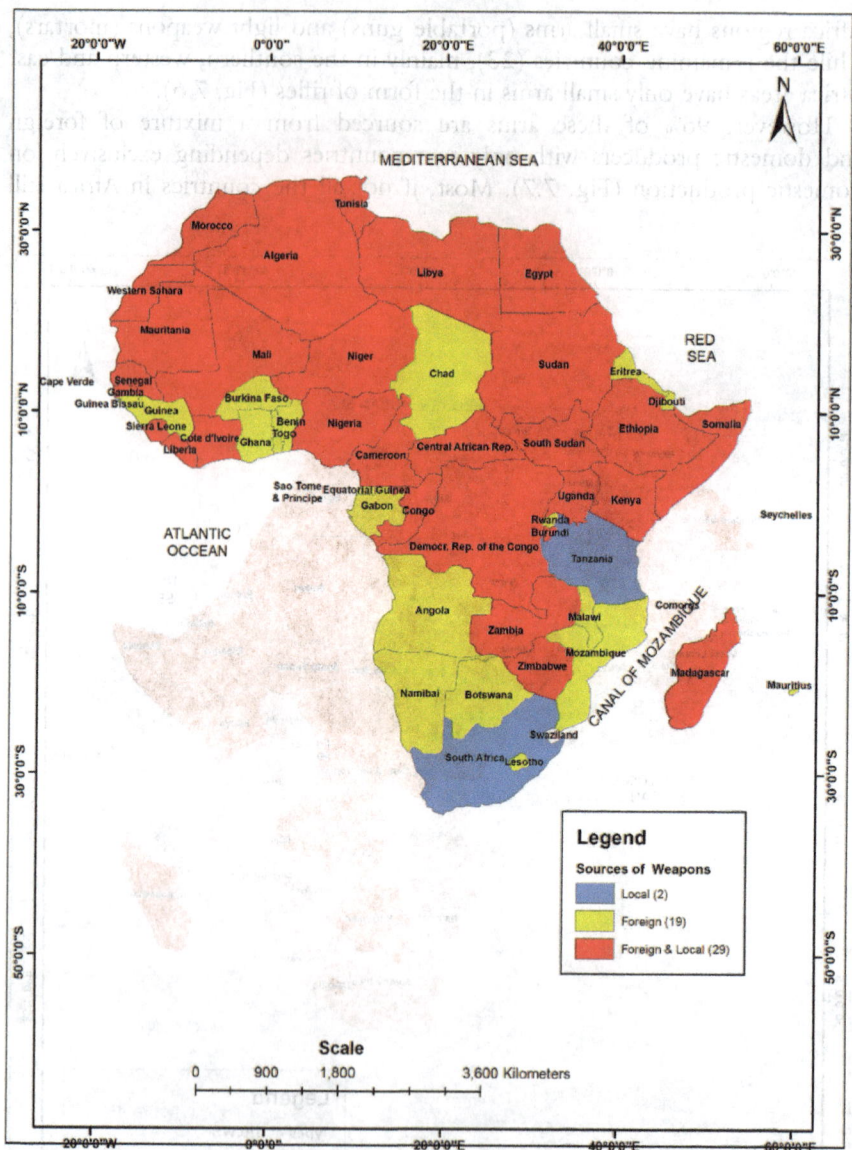

Fig. 7.7 Sources of weapons in Africa

have local blacksmiths contributing substantially to the numbers of small arms in circulation. This implies that even if the importation of arms is stopped today, the problems of small arms and light weapons proliferation will persist for a long time to come. This fact gives justification to the spread of small arms and light weapons in the continent. It further explains the reason why both individuals and groups in the continent have easy access to small arms in particular to propagate conflicts of whatever type and at whatever scale. It is also the reason for the easy movement of the same across countries and regions (as is the case with herdsmen and cross border bandits, criminals and human traffickers in west, central and east Africa) taking advantage of porous border (Fig. 7.8).

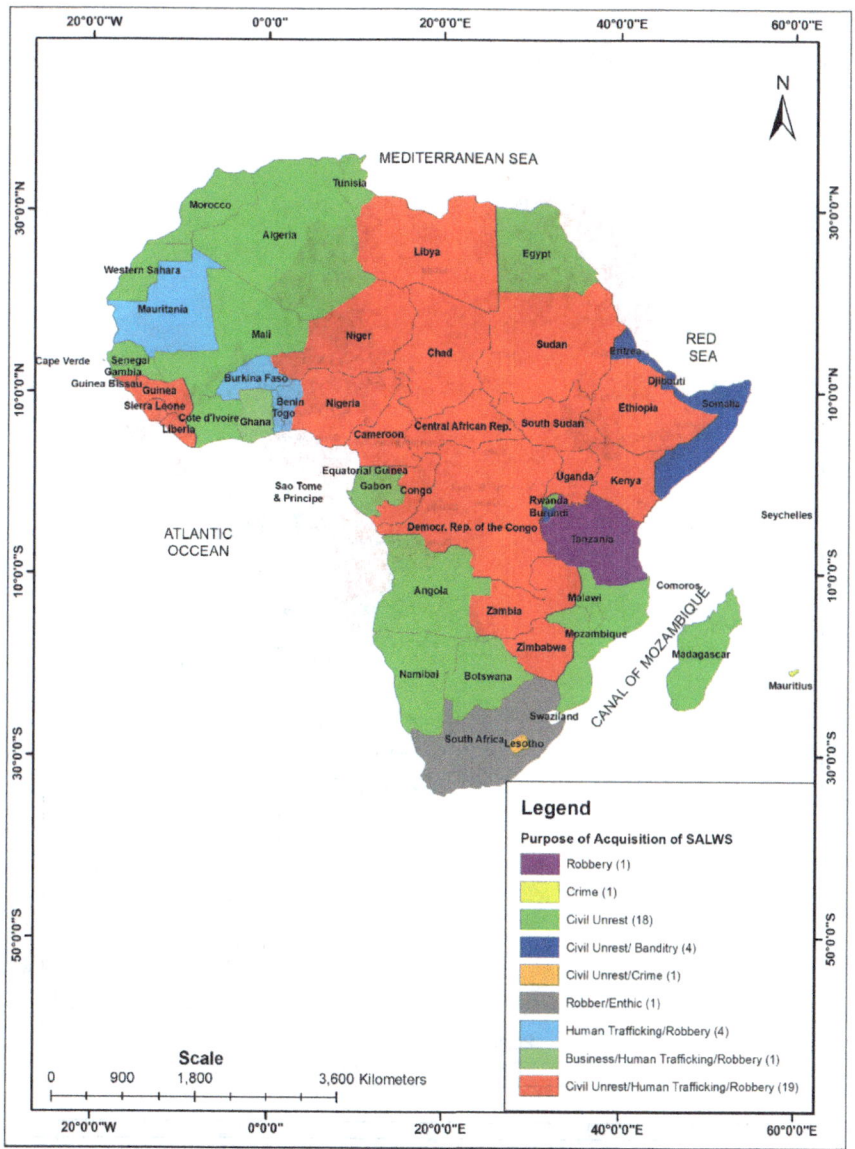

Fig. 7.8 Purpose of acquisition of SALWs

The frequent and easy reoccurrence of conflicts in Africa on one hand, and the presence of strong, well-established syndicates in arms trafficking on the other, has made efforts to clear any country of small arms and light weapons nearly impossible. This study discovered that 96% of the countries are not cleared (Fig. 7.9) of assorted weapons. It has led to 70% of the countries

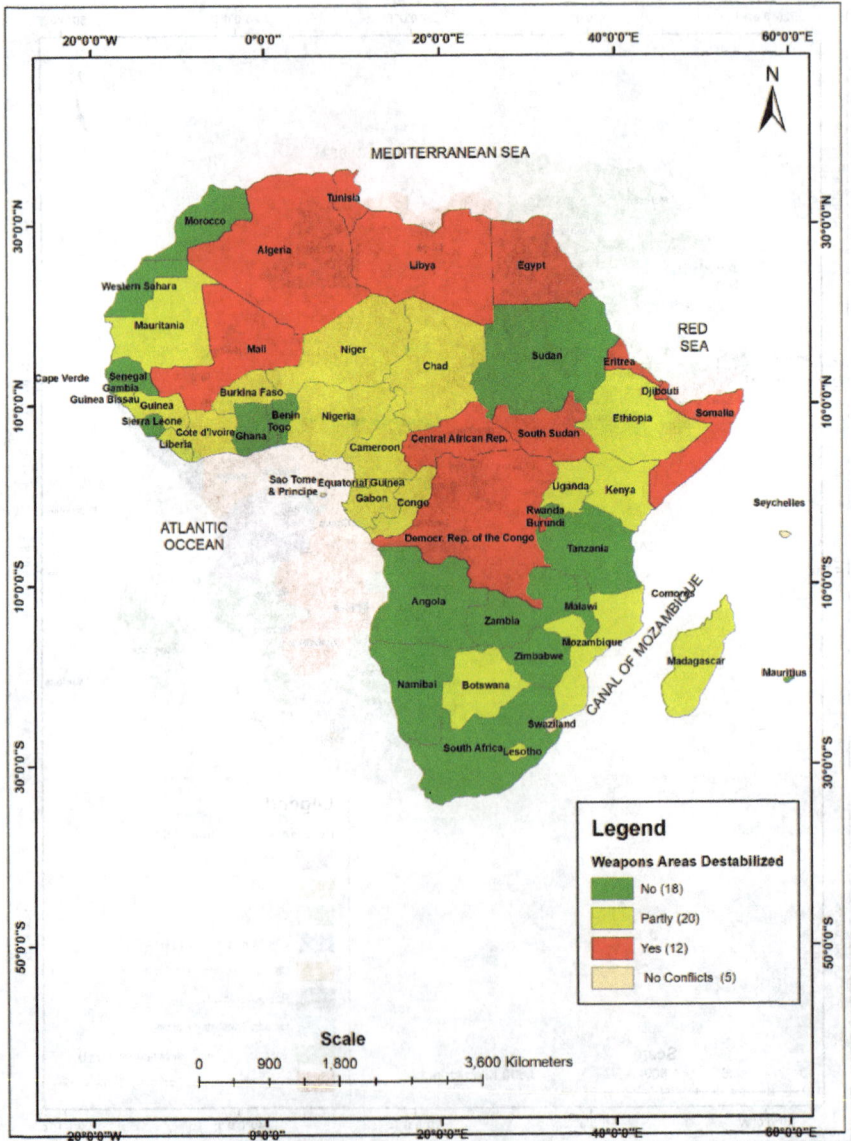

Fig. 7.9 Countries destabilized by weapons

being full or partly unstable (Fig. 7.10) and at any slightest provocation, these countries may return to full blown uprising, chaos and even war in the worst-case scenario.

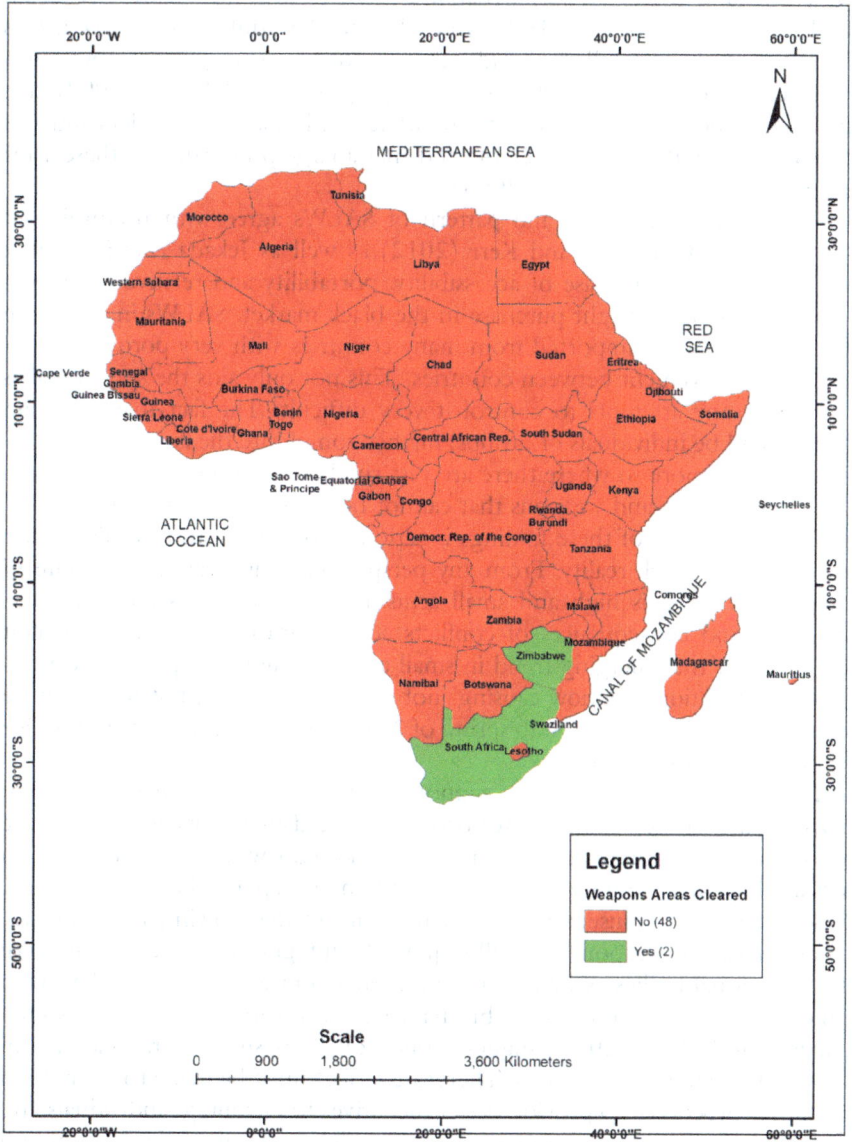

Fig. 7.10 Countries cleared of weapons

What Is Peculiar About Africa's Topography of Conflicts and Small Arms?

The spatial pattern of conflicts occurrence in terms of type, duration, actors, ownership and nature is very dynamic across the continent and it reflected similar outcome (Osaghae 1994; Adesola and Anyaduba 2017). So also is the proliferation of small arms and light weapons in Africa, being more internally generated, as postulated by Kamiwesiga (2016), and Anders (2009), it is increasingly becoming complex and multifaceted in nature to understand and handle appropriately (Malam 2014) and that a large proportion of these arms are produced in Africa (Aning 2003).

Findings on the nature and pattern of SALWs agree with Boutwell and Klare (2000), Grimmeth and Kerr (2012) as well as Jekada (2005), that it is partly attributed to ease of accessibility, portability and relatively low cost of production or outright purchase in the black market. SALWs in Africa are produced as well as imported from many countries with very porous borders facilitating movement between countries. This not only aids the spread makes but makes any attempts to control it very difficult. The fact that the main actors could be individuals or groups, further complicate the issues of disarmament. This is more so where there are vast rural areas with several settlements and assorted arms and weapons that cannot be accounted for (King 2014).

The implication of these findings is serious, not merely to raise alarm, but to present the stark reality. From any perspective, it is clear that the rate of arms proliferation is high and small arms and light weapons are now both the cause and consequences of conflicts across Africa. The most important side effect of the emerging trend in small arms and light weapons in Africa is the destabilization it is now causing, not only to countries, but to the entire region. North Africa since Arab spring of 2011, and east Africa in the rift valley region are cases in point.

The emergence of new socio-economic crimes such as human trafficking, cross border crime, banditry, terrorism and herdsmen/farmer conflicts are introducing new dimensions to small arms and light weapons proliferation in Africa which may require a paradigm shift in the approaches to addressing these challenges. Consequently, it is most likely that solving the proliferation of arms and weapons will still require the integration and cooperation of states, regional bodies as well as the continental and world bodies. The Africa Union and United Nations exist but have not been very effective, and as such Ganesan and Vines (2004) suggest conditionalities such as transparency in dealing with countries in Africa. Therefore, effort must be made to strengthen existing protocols or to provide better incentives to encourage individuals and groups to turn in their weapons. This will require the absolute political and financial commitment of all the stakeholders, as well as confidence building that the conflicts will not reoccur. On past evidence, such assurance has not been guaranteed.

CONCLUSION

This chapter maps the contours of conflicts and small arms and light weapons proliferation in Africa. The chapter revealed that Africa has been a continent rife with conflicts, from the years of colonization, right through to post-independence. The conflicts are in various forms, have lasted for different durations, with politics, ethnicity and religion as the major drivers, and with vested interests mostly by individual and groups resulting to different patterns and trends across Africa. These crises which are often prolonged have resulted to the proliferation of small arms and light weapons. These arms are imported or produced in Africa. The problem is exacerbated by very porous borders across all the countries, gang violent, the portability of the weapons, and low cost of purchase. This has resulted in the wide spread of these weapons, leading to the destabilization of several countries, and causing death, poverty, economic exploitation, famine and environmental degradation. Ending conflicts in Africa will of course address the proliferation of small arms and light weapons considerably. It will however, require an integrated approach that will involve nations, regional groups and the continental body as a whole. It will also entail cooperation of international organization since most of the arms and weapons are imported. Devising new approaches to conflict resolution without necessarily resorting to violence and the use of small arms and light weapons is also necessary.

The chapter has established that there exist serious conflicts and proliferation of small arms and light weapons in Africa as revealed from several maps generated that revealed the characteristics of SALWs, despite several attempts by different organizations in many countries in Africa and the world at large. These conflicts have continued to manifest in the form of political uprising, religion intolerance, ethnic domination and recently terrorism and crime. Small arms and light weapons proliferation therefore become both the cause and effect of conflicts in most African countries. Without any doubt or contradictions, conflicts and proliferations of small arms and light weapons in Africa are closely intertwined and have many effects and implications for the entire world. It is sufficing to say that SALWs is responsible for increase in the frequency, intensity and spatial spread of the conflicts that occur in Africa. It is hoped that the awareness this paper will generate on the scope and scale of these problems will mark a turning point on how the challenges of perennial conflicts in Africa (which have increased the proliferations of small arms and light weapons) among other challenges are tackled head long. As a result, there is need for African countries to be proactive and cooperate with one another in the management of conflicts, in order to minimize the negative consequences that arise both in the short, medium and long term.

APPENDIX 1: DYNAMICS OF CONFLICTS AND PROLIFERATION OF SMALL ARMS AND LIGHT WEAPONS IN AFRICA

S/No	Sub-region	Country	Conflicts Types	Duration of last conflict (Years)	Actors	Ownership	Past conflicts
1	North Africa	Algeria					
2		Egypt	Internal	7	Religious/political	Group	Political uprising
3		Libya	Internal/external	7	Religious	Group/Individual	Political uprising
4		Morocco	Internal	3	Political	Individual	Political
5		Sudan	Internal	15	Ethnic	Group/Individual	Political uprising
6		Tunisia	Internal	7	Religious	Group/Individual	Political uprising
7		Western Sahara	External	25	Ethnic	Group/Individual	Political uprising
8	Western Africa	Benin	Internal	–	Business people	Individual	Crime
9		Burkina Faso	Internal	15	Religious/Political	Group/Individual	Political
10		Cape Verde	–	–	–	–	–
11		Cote d'Ivoire	Internal	10	Ethnic	Individual	Political uprising
12		Gambia	Internal	2	Ethnic	Individual	Political uprising
13		Ghana	–	–	Criminals	Individual	Crime
14		Guinea	Internal/external	15	Political/Crime	Group/Individual	Political uprising
15		Guinea-Bissau	Internal/external	15	Political/Crime	Group/Individual	Political uprising
16		Liberia	Internal	13	Ethnic	Group/Individual	Political uprising
17		Mali	Internal	10	Religious	Group/Individual	Political uprising
18		Mauritania	Internal	15	Criminals	Individual	Crime
19		Niger	Internal	10	Religious	Group/Individual	Political/Religious Uprising
20		Nigeria	Internal	10	Religious/Ethnic	Groups/Individual	Civil war
21		Senegal	Internal	15	Political	Individual	Political
22		Sierra Leone	Internal	5	Ethnic	Group/Individual	Political uprising
23		Togo	Internal	10	Political	Individual	Political
24	Eastern Africa	Burundi	Internal/External	5	Ethnic	Individual	–
25		Comoros	–	–	–	–	–
26		Djibouti	Internal/External	5	Religious	Group/individual	Political uprising

(continued)

(continued)

S/No	Sub-region	Country	Conflicts Types	Duration of last conflict (Years)	Actors	Ownership	Past conflicts
27		Eritrea	Internal/External	15	Religious	Group/individual	Political uprising
28		Ethiopia	Internal/External	10	Religious/Ethnic	Group/Individual	Political/Religious uprising
29		Kenya	Internal/External	15	Religious	Group/Individual	Political/Religious uprising
30		Madagascar	Internal/External	15	Ethnic	Group/Individual	Political uprising
31		Malawi	Internal/External	10	Ethnic	Individual	Political uprising
32		Mauritius	Internal	5	Criminal	Group/Individual	Political uprising
33		Mayotte	–	–	–	–	–
34		Mozambique	Internal	15	Ethnic	Group/individual	Political uprising
35		Reunion	–	–	–	–	–
36		Rwanda	Internal/External	10	Ethnic	Group/Individual	Political uprising
37		Seychelles	–	–	–	–	–
38		Somalia	Internal/External	25	Religious/Clan/Political	Group/individual	Political/Religious uprising
39		South Sudan	Internal	5	Political/Religious/Ethnic	Group/Individual	Civil war
40		Tanzania	Internal/External	15	Political	Group/Individual	Political uprising
41		Uganda	Internal	25	Religious	Group/Individual	Political uprising
42		Zambia	Internal	15	Political	Group/Individual	Political uprising
43		Zimbabwe	Internal	15	Political	Group/Individual	Political uprising
44	Central Africa	Angola	Internal/External	20	Political	Group/individual	Political uprising
45		Cameroon	Internal	10	Religious/Ethnic	Group/Individual	Political uprising
46		Central Africa Republic	Internal	5	Ethnic/Religious	Group/individual	Political uprising
47		Chad	Internal/External	25	Religious	Group/Individual	Political uprising
48		Congo	Internal/External	15	Political	Group/individual	Political uprising

(continued)

(continued)

S/No	Sub-region	Country	Conflicts				Ownership	Past conflicts
			Types	Duration of last conflict (Years)	Actors			
49		Congo Democratic Republic	Internal/External	25	Political		Group/Individual	Political uprising
50		Equatorial Guinea	Internal	10	Political		Group/Individual	Political uprising
51		Gabon	Internal	15	Political		Group/Individual	Political uprising
52		Sao Tome and Principe	–	–	–		–	–
53	Southern Africa	Botswana	Internal	15	Political		Groups/Individual	Political uprising
54		Lesotho	Internal	–	Political		Groups/Individual	Political uprising
55		Namibia	Internal	20	Political		Group/Individual	Political uprising
56		South Africa	Internal	60	Political		Group/Individual	Political uprising
57		Swaziland	–	–	–		–	–
Total	5	57						

S/No	Sub-region	Country	Weapons			Areas	
			Types—Small arms or light weapons	Purpose of acquisition	Sources—Foreign or local	cleared	Destabilized
1	North Africa	Algeria	Both	Civil unrest	Both	No	Yes
2		Egypt	Both	Civil unrest	Both	No	Yes
3		Libya	Both	Civil unrest/Human trafficking/Robbery	Both	No	Yes
4		Morocco	Both	Civil Unrest	Both	No	No
5		Sudan	Both	Civil unrest/Human trafficking/Robbery	Both	No	No
6		Tunisia	Both	Civil unrest	Both	No	Yes

(continued)

(continued)

S/No	Sub-region	Country	Weapons		Purpose of acquisition	Sources—Foreign or local	Areas	
			Types—Small arms or light weapons				cleared	Destabilized
7		Western Sahara	Both		Civil unrest	Both	No	No
8	Western Africa	Benin	Small Arms		Human trafficking/Robbery	Foreign	No	No
9		Burkina Faso	Small arms		Human trafficking/Robbery	Foreign	No	Partly
10		Cape Verde	–		–	–	–	–
11		Cote d'Ivoire	Small arms		Civil unrest	Both	No	Partly
12		Gambia	Small arms		Civil unrest	Both	No	No
13		Ghana	Small arms		Business/Human trafficking/Robbery	Foreign	No	No
14		Guinea	Both		Civil Unrest/Human trafficking/Robbery	Foreign	No	Partly
15		Guinea-Bissau	Both		Civil unrest/Human trafficking/Robbery	Foreign	No	Partly
16		Liberia	Small Arms		Civil unrest/Human trafficking/Robbery	Both	No	Partly
17		Mali	Both		Civil unrest	Both	No	Yes
18		Mauritania	Small Arms		Human trafficking/Robbery	Both	No	Partly
19		Niger	Both		Civil unrest/Human trafficking/Robbery	Both	No	Partly
20		Nigeria	Both		Civil unrest/Human trafficking/Robbery	Both	No	Partly
21		Senegal	Small arms		Civil unrest	Both	No	No
22		Sierra Leone	Small Arms		Civil unrest/Human trafficking/Robbery	Both	No	No

(continued)

(continued)

S/No	Sub-region	Country	Weapons Types—Small arms or light weapons	Purpose of acquisition	Sources—Foreign or local	Areas cleared	Destabilized
23		Togo	Small arms	Human trafficking/Robbery	Foreign	No	No
24	Eastern Africa	Burundi	Small arms	Civil unrest/Banditry	Both	No	Yes
25		Comoros	–	–	–	–	–
26		Djibouti	Both	Civil unrest/Banditry	Foreign	No	Yes
27		Eritrea	Both	Civil unrest/Banditry	Foreign	No	Yes
28		Ethiopia	Both	Civil unrest/Human trafficking/Robbery	Both	No	Partly
29		Kenya	Both	Civil unrest/Human trafficking/Robbery	Both	No	Partly
30		Madagascar	Both	Civil unrest/	Both	No	Partly
31		Malawi	Small arms	Civil unrest	Foreign	No	No
32		Mauritius	Small arms	Crime	Foreign	No	No
33		Mayotte	–	–	–	–	–
34		Mozambique	Small arms	Civil unrest	Foreign	No	Partly
35		Reunion	–	–	–	–	–
36		Rwanda	Small Arms	Civil unrest	Foreign	No	No
37		Seychelles	–	–	–	–	–
38		Somalia	Both	Civil Unrest/Banditry	Both	No	Yes
39		South Sudan	Both	Civil unrest/Human trafficking/Robbery	Both	No	Yes
40		Tanzania	Small Arms	Robbery	Local	No	No
41		Uganda	Small Arms	Civil unrest/Human trafficking/Robbery	Both	No	Partly
42		Zambia	Both	Civil unrest/Human trafficking/Robbery	Both	No	No

(continued)

(continued)

S/No	Sub-region	Country	Weapons Types—Small arms or light weapons	Purpose of acquisition	Sources—Foreign or local	Areas cleared	Destabilized
43		Zimbabwe	Small Arms	Civil unrest/Human trafficking/Robbery	Both	Yes	No
44	Central Africa	Angola	Small Arms	Civil unrest	Foreign	No	No
45		Cameroon	Both	Civil Unrest/Human trafficking/Robbery	Both	No	Partly
46		Central Africa Republic	Both	Civil unrest/Human trafficking/Robbery	Both	No	Yes
47		Chad	Both	Civil unrest/Human trafficking/Robbery	Foreign	No	Partly
48		Congo	Both	Civil unrest/Human trafficking/Robbery	Both	No	Partly
49		Congo Democratic Republic	Both	Civil unrest/Human trafficking/Crime	Both	No	Yes
50		Equatorial Guinea	Small arms	Civil unrest	Foreign	No	Partly
51		Gabon	Small Arms	Civil unrest	Foreign	No	Partly
52		Sao Tome and Principe	–	–	–	–	–
53	Southern Africa	Botswana	Both	Civil unrest	Foreign	No	Partly
54		Lesotho	Both	Civil unrest/Crime	Foreign	No	Partly
55		Namibia	Small Arms	Civil unrest	Foreign	No	No
56		South Africa	Small arms	Robbery/Ethnic	Local	Yes	No
57		Swaziland	–	–	–	–	–
Total	5	57					

Source Small Arms Survey (2018)

References

Adedeji, A. (1999). *Comprehending and Mastering African Conflicts: The Search of Sustainable Peace and Good Government.* London: Zed Books.

Adesola, A., & Anyaduba, C. A. (2017). Rethinking Violence in Africa. *Peace Review, 29*(3), 275–281.

Adewuyi, T. O. (2016). Globalisation, Ecology and Land Degradation in Africa. In U. A. Tar, B. E. Mijah, & M. E. U. Tedheke (Eds.), *Globalisation in Africa: Perspective on Development, Security and the Environment* (pp. 345–362). Lanham, MA: Lexington Books.

Adewuyi, T. O., & Olofin, E. A. (2014). Spatio-Temporal Analysis of Flood Incidence in Nigeria and Its Implication for Land Degradation and Food Security. *Journal of Agricultural Science, 6*(2), 100–109. ISSN: 1961-9752, Canadian Centre of Science and Education, Canada.

Adeyemo, F. O. (2000). *Conflicts, Wars and Peace in Africa, 1960–2000.* Lagos: Franc Soba Nig. Ltd.

Africa Europe Faith and Justice Network. (AEFJN, December). (2010). Arms Export and Transfer: From Sub-Saharan Africa to Sub-Saharan African.

Anders, H. (2009). *Ammunition Stockpile Management in Africa: Challenges and Scope for Action, note d' Analyze.* Brussels: GRIP.

Aning, K. (2003, July 7–13). Home Made and Imported Guns. *West Africa.* London.

Aremu, J. O. (2010). Conflicts in Africa: Meaning, Causes, Impact and Solution. *African Research Review, 4*(4), 549–560.

Babalola, Y. (2017, Wednesday, November 22). Illegal Arms Imports: Nigeria to Clampdown on Shipping Firms. *Leadership Newspaper,* page 25.

Bekoe, D. (2010). *Trends in Electoral Violence in Sub-Saharan Africa.* US Institute of Peace.

Boutwell, J., & Klare, M. J. (2000). A Scourge of Small Arms. *American Academy of Arts and Social Sciences, 282,* 6.

Edeko, S. E. (2014). The Proliferation of Small Arms and Light Weapons in Africa: A Case Study of the Niger Delta in Nigeria. *International Journal of Humanity and Social Science, 4*(8), 8–10.

Ero, C., & Ndinga-Muvumba. (2004). Small Arms and Light Weapons. In A. Adebajo & I. Rashid (Eds.), *West Africa's Security Challenges: Building Peace in a Troubled Region.* London: Lynne Rienner Publisher.

Gabdo, H. H. (2017, Wednesday, November 22). Adamawa: Uneasy Calm in Numan Over Killing of 44 Person. *Leadership Newspaper.* Page 12.

Ganesan, A., & Vines, A. (2004, January 1). *Engine of War: Resources, Greed and the Predatory State, Human Rights Watch.* World Report 2004: Human Rights and Armed Conflict.

Grimmett, R. F. & Kerr, P. K. (2012, August 24). *Conventional Arms Transfers to Developing Nations 2004, 2011.* Congressional Research Services.

Holsti, K. J. (1983). *International Politics, A Framework for Analysis* (4th ed.). London: Prentice Hall.

Holtom, P., & Pavesi, I. (2018). *Trade Update: 2018, Sub-Saharan Africa in Focus.* A publication of the Small Arms Survey, with support from the Department of Foreign Affairs and Trade of Australia.

Jekada, E. K. (2005). *Proliferation of Small Arms and Ethnic Conflicts in Nigeria: Implication for National Security.* Dissertation for the award of the degree of

Doctor of Philosophy in International Relations and Strategic Studies, St Clements University.

Jenzen-Jones, N. R. (2016). *A Tale of Two Rifles: The Proliferation of F2000 and AK 103 Self-Loading Rifles Exported to Libya in 2006–2009*. Armament Research Services (ARES) RESEARCH REPORT No. 5. 38 pp.

Kamiwesiga, P. K. (2016). *Small Arms Proliferation and Homegrown Terrorism in the Great Lakes Region: Uganda's Experience*. Naval Postgraduate School, Monterey, USA.

King, B. (2014, April 1–16). *Excess Arms in South Sudan: Security Forces and Surplus Management* (Small Arms Survey: Issue Brief, Number 6).

Laurance, J. (1998). Small Arms and Light Weapons as a Development and Disarmament Issue: An Overview. In BICC Report 12; Converting Defense Resources to Human Development: *Proceeding of the International Conference*, 9–11 November, 1997.

Malam, B. (2014, June). Small Arms and Light Weapons Proliferation and Its Implication for West African Regional Security. *International Journal of Humanities and Social Science, 4*(8), 260–269.

Musa, S., Ezeamaka, C. K., Adewuyi, T. O., & Daful, M. G. (2019). Spatio-Temporal Assessment of Quarry Sites in Mpape, Abuja, Nigeria. *Journal of Remote Sensing and GIS, 8*(1), 1–12.

Norwegian Peacebuilding Resources Centre (NOREF) Report. (2013, April). The Regional Impact of the Armed Conflict and French Intervention in Mali. D. J. Francis (Eds.). NOREF Publication.

Nwankwo, H. (2006). *Youth Deviant Behaviour in West Africa*. Haven: Yale.

Osaghae, E. E. (1994). Persistent Conflict in Africa: Management Failure or Endemic Catastrophe? *South Africa Journal of International Affairs, 2*(1), 85–103.

Population Reference Bureau (PRB). (2017). *2017 World Population Data Sheet*. Washington, DC, USA.

Roberts, J. K. (1981). *Effect of Poverty on Youths in African Continent*. London: OUP.

Sall, E. (2011). *Small Arms Survey 2011: States of Security*. Small Arms Survey. Geneva, Cambridge University Press.

Small Arms Survey. (2007). *Small Arms Survey 2007: Guns and the City*. Cambridge: Cambridge University Press.

Small Arms Survey. (2018). *Global Firearms Holdings Database: Civilians*. Geneva: Small Arms Survey.

Small Arms Survey and the African Union (AU) Report. (2019). *Weapons Compass: Mapping Illicit Small Arms Flows in Africa*. A joint publication of the Small Arms Survey and the African Union (AU) Commission, with financial support from the German Federal Foreign Office and AU Member State.

United Nations. (2006). Small Arms Review Conference 2006, International Instrument to Enable States to Identify and Trace, in a Timely and Reliable Manner, Illicit Small Arms and Light Weapons.

United Nations Development Programme (UNDP). (1994). *Human Development Report 1994*. New York: Oxford University Press.

Dr. Taiye O. Adewuyi is a Professor of Geographic Information System in the Department of Geography, Nigerian Defence Academy, Kaduna, the Business Manager of Academy's *Journal of Defence Studies* and a formal Head of the Department of Geography. His teaching and research interests focus on the application of Geographic Information Systems (GIS) and Remote Sensing, Environmental Resources Management and Socio-economic issues. He has contributed several dozen articles and essays in reputable local and international journals and books, encompassing a wide variety of subjects such as mapping, environmental degradation (land, vegetation and water), agroforestry, flooding, change analysis, crime assessment and resource allocation.

Dr. Mwanret Gideon Daful is a PhD holder at the Department of Geography, Nigerian Defence Academy, Kaduna. His teaching and research interests focus on the application of Geographic Information Systems (GIS) and Remote Sensing in Environmental Resources Management, Military mapping and Socio-economic issues. He has contributed a number of articles in reputable local and international journals and book chapters.

CHAPTER 8

External Influence, Failed States, Ungoverned Spaces and Small Arms Proliferation in Africa

Muhammad Dan Suleiman, Hakeem Onapajo, and Ahmed Badawi Mustapha

Introduction

The search for solutions to the challenges of governance in Africa is characteristically encumbered by geopolitical constructs that disempower, rather than empower, African actors. Constructs such as "failed states" and "weak states", "arc of instability" and "Africanistan" (Lecocq 2013) are only a few examples of such constructs. Apart from obscuring the reality of the challenges of governance in the continent, these constructs also aid in apportioning or avoiding blame for geopolitical expediency. Clionadh Raleigh and Catriona Dowd thus argue that some of these constructs "have become coterminous and common because they benefit various state and international powers [...] who avoid responsibility for the geopolitical and economic processes within these spaces" (Raleigh and Dowd 2013: 1). In this chapter, we agree with this conclusion and assert that what many actors call "ungoverned spaces"—hence their relationship to conflicts and the proliferation of small arms and light weapons (SALWs) in Africa—is a geopolitical constructs whose conception remains incomplete.

M. Dan Suleiman (✉)
University of Western Australia, Perth, WA, Australia

H. Onapajo
Nile University of Nigeria, Abuja, Nigeria

A. B. Mustapha
University of Ghana, Accra, Ghana

© The Author(s), under exclusive license to Springer Nature Switzerland AG 2021
U. A. Tar and C. P. Onwurah (eds.), *The Palgrave Handbook of Small Arms and Conflicts in Africa*,
https://doi.org/10.1007/978-3-030-62183-4_8

Our understanding of SALWs follows the one given by the United Nations (UNGA 1997), and describes small arms to include "revolvers and self-loading pistols, rifles and carbines, sub-machine guns, assault rifles, and light machine guns" and light weapons to include "heavy machine guns, grenade launchers, portable anti-tank and anti-aircraft guns, recoilless rifles, portable anti-tank missile and rocket launchers, portable anti-aircraft missile launchers, and mortars of less than 100 mm calibre" (Florquin et al. 2019: 24). The proliferation of these weapons has multilevel (national, regional and global) and multifactorial manifestations. In relative terms, however, due to incomplete geopolitical representations, the global and historical dimensions of the phenomena or processes surrounding SALWs are usually treated as peripheral whereas the national and regional geopolitical dimensions are forcefully highlighted. Consequently, current understanding of the threat posed by "ungoverned spaces" and SALWs in Africa belittles, if not removes, the complicity of global actors in creating a decadent political geography out of African places and spaces.

This chapter takes the view that such tangential treatment of the global geopolitics of the phenomenon does not allow for a holistic appreciation of the problem of SALWs in Africa's ungoverned spaces. We argue that to better understand the nature and spread of SALWs in Africa—how they start or change the dynamics of violent conflicts in the continent, and how to possibly curb or regulate the situation—the geopolitics of global actors must be brought to the centre of analysis. Drawing mainly from the Sahel region of Africa as our primary referent, we illustrate how global actors have historically facilitated the existence and perpetuation of "ungoverned spaces" over time. Contemporarily, we cite the role of global actors in the 2011 Libyan revolution and how the removal of the then President Ghaddafi by NATO and its allies armed and endangered the ungoverned spaces of the Sahel-Sahara, through the proliferation of SALWs into the hands of unregulated people, organisations and places. Accordingly, as a follow-on argument from this, to address the challenges of ungoverned spaces in Africa—including the proliferation of SALWs and the conflicts they cause or inflame or protract—the role of global actors must be acknowledged and addressed. This will lead to a holistic conception of the problem, hence a progressive solution.

Analytically, we make this argument through a Critical Security Studies (CSS) and via a human security approach. Briefly, the principles of critical theory that apply to this chapter include a refusal to identify freedom with any set of institutions or system of thought; exploring the underlying assumptions and purposes of existing theories and forms of practice; that thought must respond to new challenges confronting humanity; thought must be emancipatory; and skepticism of existing traditions and all absolute claims (Bronner 2011: 1). CSS is thus an intellectual tradition that criticises and challenges conventional wisdom about security. Yet, we do not criticise orthodox tropes for the sake of it. We do so to privilege human security through which the chapter focuses on individual human beings as opposed to the State or the geostrategic interests of actors in the international system. It is also "an attempt to transcend the state and national security as the locus of the political in the contemporary global order" (Van Munster 2007: 235), focusing instead on the fear of ordinary people from threats to their lives and livelihoods (Hutchful 2008).

In making our argument through the CSS and human security lenses, we do not deny the agency of local elements in the subsistence of ungoverned spaces and SALWs. Indeed, the activities of global actors in Libya survived with the support of local disgruntled, marginalised and greedy elements within the local ruling elites (Campbell 2013). Historically, even the colonial project in Africa largely survived on partnerships between, on one hand, marginal elites and criminal fraternities who pursued localised interests, and global actors on the other. Yet, while African national governments and localised elements have played significant roles in overseeing and enforcing the existence of ungoverned spaces, this chapter focuses primarily on the role of global actors with colonial history in Africa who, either as individual actors or via their membership of intergovernmental organisations, continue to feature on the geopolitical landscape of Africa. The chapter's overarching theoretical starting point is the role of global coloniality in the transhistorical creation of ungoverned spaces and related problems of SALWs, conflicts and "failed" states in Africa. Global coloniality highlights the "long-standing patterns of power that emerged as a result of colonialism, but that [continue to] define culture, labour, intersubjective relations, and knowledge production well beyond the strict limits of colonial administrations" (Maldonado-Torres 2007: 243). Thus, we focus on the complicity of powerful global actors in creating adverse geopolitical forms in Africa. Such emancipatory and progressive approach brings important perspectives to the debate on ungoverned spaces in Africa beyond the tropes of orthodox geopolitical and strategic analysis.

With this clarification, the next section presents a general conceptualisation of the ungoverned spaces-arms proliferation nexus in the Sahel, focusing on how they impact on conflict dynamics and ecologies. This is followed by a section which highlights the historical and contemporary roles of global actors in the creation, arming and endangering of ungoverned spaces in Africa. This section is further divided into two parts: first part revisits colonialism and illustrates how European, mainly French, colonialism played a role in creating the security threat that ungoverned spaces are; while the second part focuses on the role of global actors in the 2011 Libyan civil war and how that geopolitical event endangered the Sahel arc, through facilitating the unleashing of arms into the region. This is followed by a summary of our arguments.

"Ungoverned Spaces", SALWs and Conflicts in Africa

The terminology of "ungoverned spaces" has crept into the security and conflict literature to push the frontiers of knowledge on the concept of failed state. The terminology is used to describe a physical territory as well as non-physical policy space in which "there is an absence of effective state sovereignty and control" (Raleigh and Dowd 2013: 1). The reference to "effective state sovereignty and control" suggests that the authority whose absence qualifies a region as "ungoverned" is the State. This means there could be other forms of government or governance present in regions we call "ungoverned". Ungoverned spaces are therefore not necessarily ungoverned (see Keister 2014), since there are always localised, even traditional, forms of governance in these spaces. Only that the Eurocentric international system does not recognise these localised forms of governance.

Thus, ungoverned space is not about the absence of state control in an area but more about the way certain areas are governed. This argument suggests that no area is ungoverned (Ottaway 2002); it can either be governed by recognised state authorities or non-state authorities including terrorist organisations, rebel groups, criminal gangs or traditional chiefs. While the former may guarantee conventional security for its people as well as its neighbours, the latter may represent a major security threat for most people under its governance or control, although this is not always the case. Thus, this chapter understands "ungoverned spaces" to be ungoverned only in the orthodox sense of the terminology. The same usage equally applies to our conceptualisation of "failed" and "failing" states.

Conjointly, these concepts and terminologies offer useful analyses on the multiple threats inherent in situations when the state is no longer able to effectively perform its fundamental functions—the provision of public/political goods. Most especially, they articulate a situation when the state has lost its capacity to guarantee adequate security and safety for its citizens, and cannot guarantee human and economic development for the progression of the state or parts thereof. In this case, it is almost certain that the government consequently loses control of its geographical parts to non-state actors. Such states also become vulnerable to the encroachment of its borders because there is no effective control of movement across those borders. In this context, ungoverned spaces play crucial roles in facilitating the spread of SALWs, prolonging violent conflicts to their potential as precursor to the development, and storage of Weapons of Mass Destruction (WMD) (Piombo 2008).

In Africa, ungoverned spaces remain one of Africa's threats to state and human security, and a major character of "failed" state is the existence of ungoverned spaces or territories (Olaniyan 2018; Whelan 2006). The easy access to weapons by clandestine, transnational groups, and even by private citizens, in parts of the continent is facilitated by the presence of stateless spaces and porous borders. This has significantly contributed to protracted and prolonged conflicts across the continent. However, ungoverned spaces may not be exclusive to failed or weak states but could exist in stronger or viable states, where spaces could become "ungoverned" due to a lack of political will for governance in the relevant area. Indeed, some governments wilfully neglect certain geographical areas because of economic reasons (less productive nature of the other areas) or less political patronage from those areas (Piombo 2008).

Africa has the largest concentrations of ungoverned spaces. To highlight the connection between ungoverned spaces and state weakness, the 2019 report of the Fund for Peace's (FFP) index of fragile states shows that Africa represents 74% of countries discovered as most fragile in the world under the categories of "Very High Alert", "High Alert" and "Alert" (FFP 2019). In all the geographical regions of Africa, it has been established that there are areas outside effective control of State authorities, and they pose a great danger for both Africa, neighbouring regions and the international community. A prominent example of an ungoverned spaces in Africa is the Sahel region of Western Africa. The Sahel is a 3860-kilometre arc-like land mass lying to the immediate south of the Sahara Desert and stretching east-west across the breadth of the African continent (Dan Suleiman 2017b). A largely semi-arid belt of barren, sandy and rock-strewn land, the Sahel marks the physical and cultural transition between the continent's more fertile tropical regions to the south (Dan Suleiman 2017b).

Along with the Sahara Desert to its north, the Sahel-Sahara has expansive ungoverned areas, which have become a haven for criminal and terrorist activities. As Fig. 8.1 shows, the Sahel has been a major source of conflict and human trafficking in the West African sub-region and beyond. A useful study has given a sufficient demonstration of the many atrocities that occur in the largely ungoverned Sahara Desert (Wehrey and Boukhars 2013). The Horn of Africa in East Africa has also for a long time been in the spotlight for notorious piracy, conflicts and terrorism as there has been a total collapse of governments in many states in the region (Whelan 2006). Conflicts in The Great Lakes Region have rendered the government weak and incapable to govern many territories in Uganda, Democratic Republic of Congo, Burundi, and even Kenya (Whelan 2006). In the Southern African region, there has been a record of ineffective monitoring of the Indian Ocean which has led to environmental crisis around the coastal areas (Whelan 2006).

The lack of governance in many areas in Africa has obviously created room for easy movement and smuggling of arms by conflict entrepreneurs, thereby increasing human insecurities across the continent. Reports indicate that an estimated 100 million of the total 875 million global small arms are in Africa (GRIP, n.d.). Mohammed Ibn Chambas, the Special Representative of the Secretary-General and Head of the United Nations Office for West Africa and the Sahel (UNOWAS) has revealed that USD 35 million worth of SALWs find their way into West Africa each year. These arms are mainly smuggled into the sub-region by non-state actors, and Nigeria alone provides destination for 70% of the arms smuggled into Africa (Agbajileke 2017). A major source of the spread of SALWs is cross-border trafficking given the very poor governance structures at state borders. SALWs including rifles, machine guns, handguns, explosives, handguns, etc. are commonly available in Africa because of the porosity of the borders and extremely weak policing of territories. It

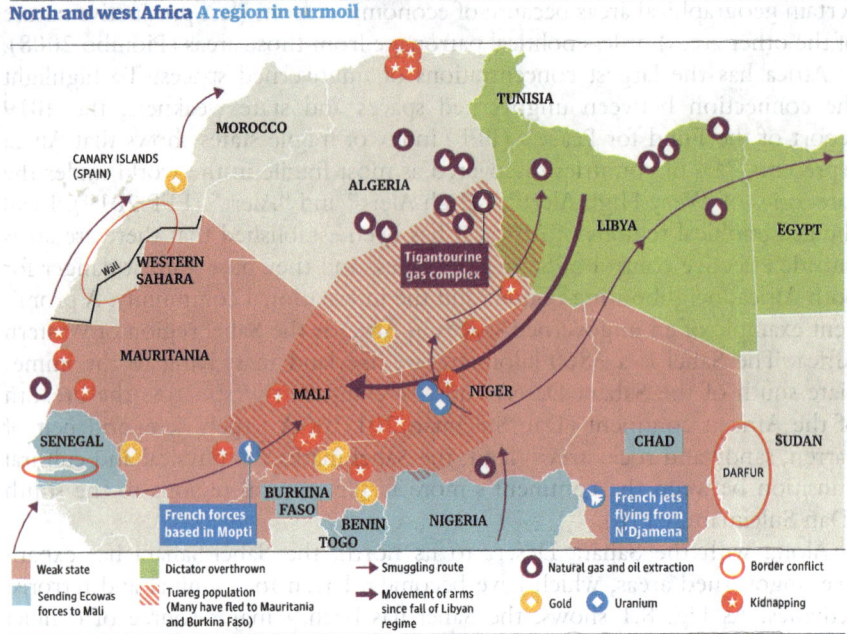

Fig. 8.1 North and Western Africa: emerging and potential ungoverned spaces (Source *The Guardian (UK)*. Available http://image.guardian.co.uk/sys-files/Guardian/documents/2013/01/21/Africa_Turmoil_WEB.pdf. Accessed 11 November 2019; *Le Monde diplomatique*, Celeste Hicks)

is reported that in the West African sub-region arms trafficking and exchanges amongst rebels in Liberia, Cote d'Ivoire and Mali were a popular practice across the borders (Schroeder and Lamb 2006).

In addition to porous land borders, ungoverned rivers and coasts also represent a major source of arms smuggling. This has been reported in the Western and Eastern Africa where arms are smuggled from Mali through Niger River, while in East Africa, arms are usually smuggled by warlords through the Gulf of Aden (Schroeder and Lamb 2006). Furthermore, arms have been smuggled into Africa via the less regulated air spaces. Several of these illegal weapons have been ferried into the continent from other foreign countries. In a United Nations (UN) report on transnational crime in West Africa (UNODC 2013), one can deduce that the sources of illegal firearms in the continent are: weapons from past and on-going conflicts in the region; weapons from corrupt security officials; weapons from sympathetic governments; and weapons from international sources.

Indeed, an Oxfam Research Report shows that poor regulation of local arms production also represents a major source of the spread of illegal SALWs across the continent (Adeniyi 2017). The United Nations and the Small Arms

Commission of Ghana also disclosed in June 2017 that about 2.3 million unregistered arms are in circulation in Ghana (Dan Suleiman 2017a: 319). Ghana also has flourishing artisanal arms manufacturing industry which, owing to weak governance of West Africa's borders, get smuggled to Togo, Benin, and Nigeria for criminal purposes (Aning 2005). The point we are making here, therefore, is that while the origins of SALWs in West Africa are not always outside of the region, it is mainly international arms traffickers who find African markets especially lucrative and easy to penetrate. Schroeder and Lamb (2006), for example, find that most of the smuggled arms into Africa come from foreign countries including China, Israel and over 20 European countries. Thus, how weapons manufactured in developed countries constitute a most important decider of violence in Africa ought to be a central concern. Looked differently, and as we shall illustrate later, how the activities of Western actors in Africa compound conflicts also ought to be considered, especially in the context of the rise of religious and related violence in Africa.

As a Small Arms Survey show, conflicts in North Africa have further escalated arms smuggling in Africa (Anders 2018). The Libyan refugees fleeing the civil war and the revolution against Ghaddafi in 2011 who needed cash brought all their valuables including gold, firearms—especially AK47 and handguns—and other valuables in exchange for money at their destinations (Kartas 2013). The UN has noted that whereas "[t]he scale of Ghaddafi's arsenal is still being evaluated by the United Nations, but all indications are that it was vast and sophisticated" (UNODC 2013: 33). This large arsenal of arms has found their way into the hands of rebel leaders and terrorists including Al Qaeda in the Islamic Maghreb (AQIM), Ansar al Dine (Mali), the Movement for Unity and Jihad in West Africa (MUJAO) (Mali), Nigerien Movement for Justice (Niger) and Boko Haram (Nigeria) etc. Thus, the increasing rise of religious terrorism and conflicts in Africa has been further compounded by the problem of SALWs smuggling. Nigeria and Somalia appear in the first 10 countries with the highest number of casualties on the GTI (www.statista.com). In fact, Nigeria's Boko Haram was in 2015 declared the world's most deadly terrorist group in the GTI following a record of 300% increase in terrorism in terrorism deaths (IEP 2015). It is not surprising therefore that, as Fig. 8.2 shows, violence across the Sahel has seen a geometric rise since 2011.

No doubt, the escalating rate of smuggling of SALWs into Africa has intensified conflicts on the continent, and in some cases fuelling newer ones. As usefully noted by Adeniyi (2017), citing different reliable sources, 52% of the global conflict incidents in 2014 was recorded in Africa, even though the continent has just 16% of the world's population. Africa also recorded 87 of 236 incidents between 2011 and 2015. Given that most of the conflicts are closely associated with non-state actors, it is safe to argue that the spread of SALWs based on ineffective governance of territories has significantly contributed to the rise in violence. In the end, ungoverned spaces have been responsible for the intensification of conflicts in Somalia, DRC, Nigeria, Mali,

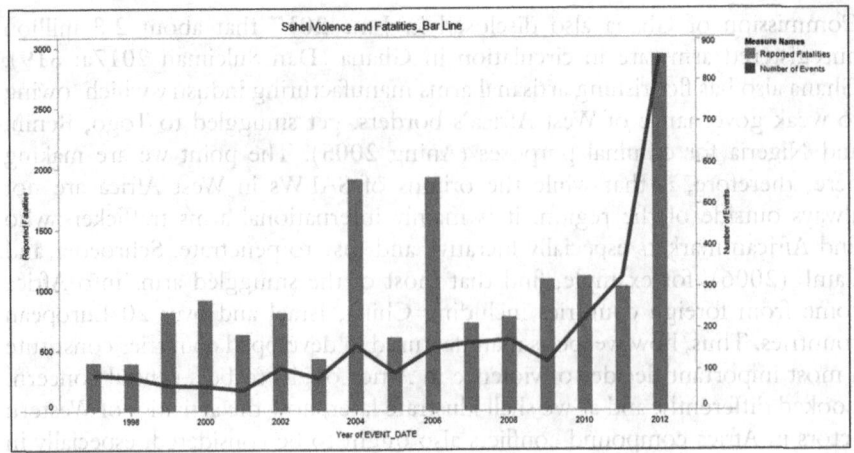

Fig. 8.2 Rate of conflict in Sahel with fatalities (*Source* Raleigh and Dowd 2013: 5)

Libya, Burundi, Central African Republic, South Sudan, and many other under-reported cases.

Across West Africa, while the threat of religious terrorism is metastasizing, other forms of conflicts such as between farmers and herders are fast overwhelming the sub-region. In Nigeria, between 2011 and 2016, an estimated 2000 annual fatalities are being recorded from the conflict (Tall 2018). Whereas many factors can be argued as being responsible for their outbreak including politics, climate change, historical factors or weak state response, it cannot be disputed that the easy access to SALWs has facilitated a long duration of the conflicts. This may substantiate persistent claims by Nigeria's President Muhammadu Buhari at international forums that the growing farmer–herder violence in his country cannot be disconnected from the influx of arms from Libya after the fall of Ghaddafi (see works such as Maiangwa 2017 for a brief historicity of the farmer–herder conflicts in Nigeria). While farmer–herder conflicts predate the geopolitical vacuum across the Sahel-Sahara following the removal of Ghaddafi, the proliferation of SALWs post-Ghaddafi has come to complicate pre-existing ungoverned spaces (Olaniyan and Yahaya 2016) (Fig. 8.3).

Similarly, the rising cases of crime unfolding in Africa cannot be separated from the problem of SALWs and drugs smuggling. In 2018, the Executive Director of UNODC reported that his organisation "is registering new alarming trends on drug trafficking in West and Central Africa" (UN News 2018). In 2014, the West Africa Commission on Drugs (WACD) concluded that not only is the sub-region a transit point for drugs trafficking to Europe but that local consumption is also on the rise (WACD 2014). The 2017, World Drug Report identifies the strong connections between drug trafficking and organised crime (such as armed robbery and murders) and even terrorism (UNODC 2017), as Fig. 8.4 shows. It is not a mere coincidence therefore

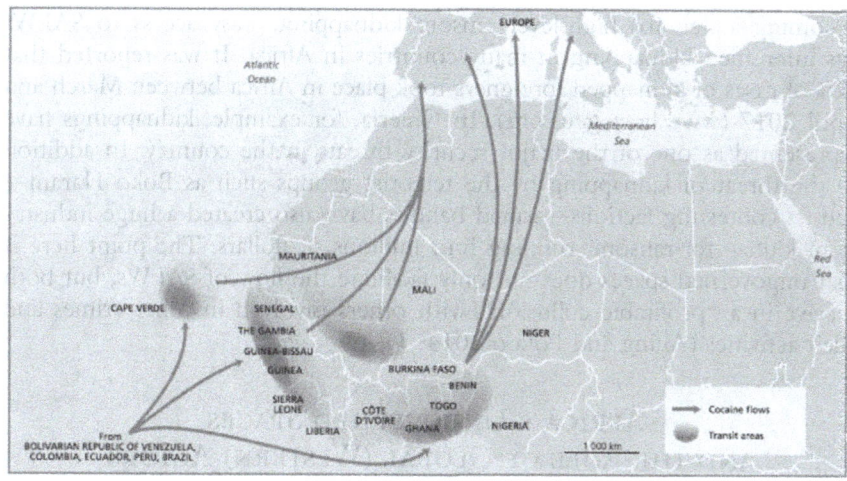

Fig. 8.3 Cocaine flows through West Africa (*Source* UNODC 2017)

Fig. 8.4 Connection between drug smuggling and organised crime, illicit financial flows, corruption and terrorism (*Source* UNODC 2017: 13)

that the UNODC also reported in 2014 that Africa and Latin America have the highest number of countries with homicide incidents with Lesotho and South Africa in the top 10 countries in the world (Ser 2016).

In South Africa alone, 34 murders per 100,000 people were reported between 2015 and 2016, whereas at least a murder was recorded on an average of 51.2 times in a day (https://africacheck.org/). Increasingly, Africa is also becoming a den for high-level ransom kidnapping. Easy access to SALWs has intensified kidnapping in many countries in Africa. It was reported that 72% of cases of kidnapped foreigners took place in Africa between March and April 2017 (www.hostageus.org). In Nigeria, for example, kidnappings have represented as one of the major security threats in the country. In addition to the threat of kidnapping by the terrorist groups such as Boko Haram—and its contesting factions—armed bandits have also created a huge industry from kidnap-for-ransom, running into millions of dollars. The point here is that ungoverned spaces does not only facilitate the flow of SALWs, but both survive in a "profitable collusion" with others involved in other crimes and illicit activities (Aning and Pokoo 2014: 1).

Africa's Ungoverned Spaces and the Role of Global (Western) Actors

As stated earlier, one cannot deny the complicity of national governments, and local and marginalised elites in the scourge of SALWs. Yet, while the regional geopolitical complications that aid the sale and transfer of arms are also accounted for, what seldom receives a robust account in the relationship between ungoverned spaces and SALWs is the role of global actors—acting as Western governments such as the US, the UK and France, or as Western-dominated intergovernmental organisations such as the NATO or even the UN. It is crucial to note, as Tables 8.1 and 8.2 show, that the five largest exporters of small arms to Sub-Saharan Africa are mostly powerful Western actors. These actors not only maintain geopolitical interests in the region contemporarily, but most of them also had colonial ties to Africa. Herein lies our argument that to get to the root of the problem of SALWs we must also consider the geopolitical aftermaths of oppressive globalism, in their historical and contemporary forms. This consideration, in the present case, should involve how these actors endanger ungoverned spaces through the proliferation of SALWs.

Table 8.1 Largest exporters of arms to sub-Saharan Africa (in USD million), 2013–2015

Exporting country	2013	2014	2015	Total
France	12.3	17.9	48.4	78.6
United States	13.6	18.2	35.7	67.5
Spain	8.3	11.5	13.3	33.1
Italy	10.1	6.6	8.0	24.7
Turkey	5.7	8.6	9.4	23.7

Source Holtom and Pavesi (2018: 65)

Table 8.2 Main importers for the five largest exporters to sub-Saharan Africa, 2013–2015

Exporter	Largest importer, %	2nd largest importer, %	3rd largest importer, %
France	Côte d'Ivoire 63	Niger 26	Cameroon 3
United States	South Africa 58	CAR 23	Ghana 5
Spain	Ghana 33	Cameroon 16	South Africa 12
Italy	South Africa 73	Ghana 8	Cameroon 8
Turkey	Mali 49	South Africa 16	Burkina Faso 10

Source Holtom and Pavesi (2018: 65)

We argue, firstly, that the geopolitical equation that multiply the danger of ungoverned spaces through the proliferation of SALWs has historical and contemporary dimensions. Secondly, we argue that this assertion puts global actors at the centre of the analysis of the problem of and solutions to SALWs and ungoverned spaces in Africa. We make these arguments referring primarily to the Sahel-Sahara region. To do so, it is crucial to reiterate the earlier point that ungoverned spaces as understood in this chapter is in the conventional sense while at the same time trying to challenge that conception. West Africa and the Sahel for example had some of the most organised empires in the pre-colonial world. Remnants of such empires exist till today. What we call ungoverned spaces is therefore the absence of Westphalian state authority, being the most pervasive unit of analysing contemporary international relations.

The Historical Role of Global Actors in "Creating" Africa's Ungoverned Spaces

Without assuming any strict departure from the coloniality of "guns-for-slaves" practices of earlier period of the slave trade (see Northrup 2002), we start our argument with the historical role of colonialism from the late nineteenth century. There are three processes in which the colonial project in Africa created or facilitated the problem of ungoverned spaces and the related problem of SALWs, namely; the cartographic violence registered on the African continent through the Treaty of Berlin in 1984–1985, the colonial model of governance by convenience, and the continuation of colonial governance traditions by the post-independence state. To begin, the Treaty of Berlin "created a border issue in Africa" because "it did not take into consideration the political and social reality of each area, leading to nations being separated and rival peoples being united, regardless of the consequences and long-term impact of these decisions" (Galito 2012: 141). This action of post-Berlin colonial powers has meant that "80% of African borders follow latitudinal or longitudinal lines and many scholars believe these artificial divisions are the roots for the African economic tragedy" (Galito 2012: 141).

The second process through which colonialism facilitated the problem of ungoverned spaces concerns how respective colonial governments governed different geographical regions in Africa differently, after the initial creation of artificial nationalities at Berlin. The colonial state created armed forces and police, equipped them with small arms and low calibre weapons to execute the project of colonial conquest. Once they captured territory, they concentrated resources for governance on population centres and lucrative territories, thus abandoning large swathes of rural formations as tributaries for the colonial economic value chain. The colonial state concentrated resources in the urban areas at the expense of rural areas. In the end, the rural areas became economically exploitable but politically expendable. Thus, many African countries are steeped in the politics of "wet" and "dry" development, as a legacy of colonial administrators governing by concentrating development along the coast (wet development), leaving hinterlands mostly dry of development. This colonial model of "governance by convenience", conjoined with the initial arbitrariness in drawing colonial borders, facilitated what we now call "ungoverned" spaces.

The third process in the making of ungoverned spaces has taken place in the post-colonial period. Governments in African countries have perpetuated the developmental inequity created and sustained by the colonial government. By keeping the pre-existing colonial borders for the the postcolonial state, "African countries also kept the conditions to consolidate the power conditions from the colonial period" (Schneider 2008: 14). In this stead, ungoverned spaces or territories have come to exist because of governments' lack of political will for governance in the area. Thus, some governments wilfully neglect certain geographical areas because of economic reasons (less productive nature of the areas) or less political patronage from those areas (Piombo 2008). Azeez Olaniyan's (2018) work demonstrates how large swathes of forests in Nigeria have been left ungoverned, which has been responsible for kidnappings, armed robberies and terrorism.

Crucially, in consonance with the arguments of this chapter, the colonial and post-colonial states used SALWs as the key coercive instrument. Here, apart from the importation of weapons into Africa throughout the era of the slave trade (see Richards 1980; Inikori 1977), both the colonial and post-colonial governments relied on SALWs as instruments of governance. In Nigeria for example, the maintenance of colonial hegemony involved an "effective engagement with the manifold deployment of arms" (Aderinto 2018: 16). Post-independence, the presence of arms facilitated activities such as coup d'états and armed robberies not due to, as Aderinto acknowledges (2018: 261), the fact that the leadership of post-colonial states have been unable to effectively control the activities of security officers, but mainly because leaders within Africa's "fragile" independent states have been primarily concerned with forcibly holding the colonially inherited country together (Aderinto 2018: 261), through the effective deployment of armed force.

In most cases, due to the rigidity of the inherited colonial structures in the post-colonial, "these new countries did not have enough state capacity, which led to power being concentrated in the capital cities and economic enclaves, leaving the rest of the country unattended" (Schneider 2008: 14). For example, colonialism rendered the Sahel regions so uneconomical that "even after independence the ghost of French colonial law which did not recognise pastoralism as a legitimate trade still held sway" (Schneider 2008: 14). Elsewhere, Brigitte Thébaud and Simon Batterbury show how in contemporary Western Sahel regions, structural-institutional legacies of colonialism persist till today, whereby legal and institutional interpretations of the tenure and use of pastoral range and how to secure formal rights to pastures and water resources are rendered to disempower herders (Thébaud and Batterbury 2001: 71). Ultimately, post-independent governance, continuing that colonial structural-institutional legacy, has also preferred that South-North bifurcation and structural injustice by colonialism.

Perhaps, the most enduring legacy of colonialism's arbitrary creation of borders in Sahelian Africa, as elsewhere, is that those borders have become inherently and rigidly "absent" or, in contemporary geopolitical parlance, porous. This is because arbitrary colonial borders only destabilised geo-cultural homelands. In many cases, linguistic and cultural bonds and traditions continued, beyond borders and beyond the limits set by the contemporary state system. This continuation created a condition in which ethnic groups become scattered across many countries. For example, the Fulani are scattered across some five countries in the Sahel arc where they remain significant demographic components of local populations. Yet, as Eghosa Osaghae (2017: 57) notes, "the Fulani have maintained their (separate) identities of ethnicity, language, faith, livelihood methods and land-use patterns peculiar to their Sahel belt, which they kept apart from host communities". What emerges from the perpetuation of bifurcated governance structures and the parallel proliferation and malregulation of arms in the post-colony is the incidence of secessionism and other violent anti-state encounters involving peripherised peoples and communities.

Relatedly, continuation of linguistic and cultural bonds and traditions in the context of arbitrary colonial borders created quasi-statelessness for some ethnic groups in which indigenous people were denied their pre-colonial ethnic homelands but not completely "accepted" by post-colonial homelands. This point goes to the core of why the Tuareg in Mali have rebelled against Malian state four times—and two times against Niger—since independence in pursuit of their "State of Azzawad" (Raleigh and Dowd 2013; Ronen 2013; Shaw 2013). Tuareg people are ethnic Berber nomads who are spread across the Sahel-Sahara region, and who have been involved in self-determination campaigns for the last many decades. Through successive rebellions, the Tuareg have destabilised the local state and often carved out ungoverned spaces which were later recaptured by the local state with the support of France and other international partners. Crucially, it was the harsh repression of the Malian state of one of their revolts in 1963 that pushed many Tuareg to flee to Libya (Ronen 2013: 549), an event that would become one of the decisive factors in the geopolitical aftereffects of post-Ghaddafi Libya since 2011. Consequently, for cultural groupings such as the Fulani or the Tuareg or their derivative groups, cultural connections continue despite their geographical destabilisation by the post-colonial state.

The point here is that whereas history created, facilitated or enforced divisions of colonial convenience among Sahelian peoples, and while post-independent governments appropriated and empowered these divisions, ethnic and cultural factors remain bonds that bind people beyond the combined might of both colonial history and contemporary geopolitics. How does this relate to ungoverned spaces and consequently the proliferation of SALWs? As people, including state officials, retain cultural bonds and connections to local communities—bonds stronger than the trust and confidence in the State—it becomes difficult to track arms flow and criminal activity: people would not usually give up their brother (or sister) who is involved in illegal activity in such culturalised spaces.

In the context of such strong culturally binding ties beyond colonial creations, the original Tuareg who fled to Libya and Algeria would come back to bite, after NATO's 2011 intervention in Libya. It is instructive from the above that structural and geopolitical legacies of colonialism continue to infect the post-colonial state such that the post-colonial state still fails "to create viable structures that unite its multiple constituent populations" (Wai 2014: 486).

Despite the persistent negative fallouts from colonial decisions and imperial policies in the colonial and post-colonial era, some suggest that Africans and their governments should ignore the past and focus on the responsibility of the present. It is argued, for example, that perhaps there was "the end of the post-colonial state" (Young 2004) in Africa by the end of the Cold War—an end to the state in which the State frequently ties its present ontology to its colonial antecedent. Yet what we see from the brief historiography of governance above, and how the colonial project set African spaces up for contemporary threats, suggests all but a disconnect between the past and the present. The above history illustrates that global colonial powers are central to what ungoverned spaces have become to governance in Africa. Still, after facilitating, if not creating, the threat that ungoverned spaces have become in the colonial period, contemporary geopolitical actions of these powers continue to arm these spaces. A recent example is the 2011 NATO/UN intervention in Libya.

NATO, Libya and Proliferation of SALWs

NATO's "Operation Unified Protector" intervention in Libya in July 2011 evokes mixed reactions regarding the results of that event and its impact on the current geopolitics of the Sahel-Sahara region. With the leading role of France and Britain armed with a UN Resolution 1973, and a lot of weapons and a globalist dose of a saviour's resolve, along with some curious actors including Qatar, Jordan and the United Arab Emirates, the operation was regarded as very successful and worthy of emulating: to some it was "the right way to run an intervention" which must be "rightly hailed as a model intervention" (Daalder and Stavridis 2012: 2). To such commentaries on this NATO's intervention, the intervention was justifiable due to the invocation of the Responsibility to Protect (R2P) principle. They argue that peaceful protestors were being crushed by the then Ghaddafi regime denying citizens their basic rights to express their political discontent, and NATO therefore "responded rapidly to a deteriorating situation that threatened hundreds of thousands of civilians rebelling against an oppressive regime" (Daalder and Stavridis 2012: 2). Eventually, "Western media and politicians praised the intervention as a humanitarian success for averting a bloodbath in Libya's second largest city, Benghazi, and helping replace the dictatorial Ghaddafi regime with a transitional council pledged to democracy" (Kuperman 2013: 105). In this sense, NATO's intervention was timely, and commendable. Its success, it appears, lies in the fact that it ousted Ghaddafi from power and prevented catastrophic mass killings of Libyans.

However, such early validations rarely stood the test of time, not only after been subjected to critical analysis on both the legal and geopolitical levels (see Campbell 2013; Forte 2012; Malito 2017). Indeed, to many Libyans today, what their country has become makes a heaven of Libya under Ghaddafi. What Libya has become today is testimony that that intervention failed in two crucial requirements for a pragmatic humanitarian intervention: namely; a viable intervention plan that guarantees low casualties from intervening forces, and a viable reconstruction strategy that would guarantee lasting peace and human security (Pape 2012). Through a similar lens of critique—and in the context of ungoverned spaces and the proliferations of SALWs—we also argue here that that intervention further armed and endangered the Sahel-Sahara regions ex post facto. We are not, by making this argument, reducing the outcome of the Libyan revolution to one decisive factor: NATO's intervention. There were many other decisive factors such as the decades-long rule of Ghaddafi and, of course, the connivance between dissident elites in Libya and the NATO fraternity to unseat Ghaddafi. Evidently, these dissident groups which constitute the leadership of the rebellion and allies of external powers appear to make the masses into pawns in a more complex geopolitical game. Most importantly, reducing the demise of Ghaddafi to the geopolitical machinations of NATO alone would amount to disrespecting the political and human agency of Libyans who felt, legitimately or not, that Ghaddafi must go, and revolted accordingly. Indeed, these group of Libyans relied on their alliance with NATO to achieve their objective.

Similarly, we are not arguing that the current state of insecurity in the Sahel region is singularly caused by NATO's intervention in Libya, but that that geopolitical event was almost singular in the security dynamics of the Sahel-Sahara post-Ghaddafi. Indeed, as we have stated above, there were ungoverned spaces with pockets of conflicts, militia groups, terror networks, and SALWs movements across the region long before that intervention. However, these conditions were under limited but reasonable control and regulation by state and regional authorities. Particularly, Libya under Ghaddafi played two key roles, starting with his ability to control national borders through tribal alliances along the border.

The southern part of Libya has the longest and the most porous of its borders of about 2700 km owing to this part of the country linking it to the three countries (Sudan, Niger and Chad) (Chivvis and Martini 2014). Whereas Ghaddafi's regiobal control had its challenges, at least it served some form of control over the porousness of the long border (Bøas and Utas 2013). Secondly, Libya had significant economic leverage over its neighbours due to its oil resources. This attracted a lot of migrants from sub-Saharan Africa, with the onward effect of creating income for families in sub-Saharan Africa through remittances. Under Ghaddafi, Libya was then a security and economic bulwark especially for the regions to its south. These roles played by Libya under Ghaddafi in terms of security and economy somewhat maintained a level of stability in the region. Subsequently, the "ungoverned" spaces across the Sahel-Sahara were relatively peaceful and secure prior to Ghaddafi's overthrow. In other words, prior to 2011, Libya, despite Ghaddafi been regarded as a dictator, was a key stabilising factor in many respects for the region.

By making especially Libya's southern borders more porous and dangerous, the removal of Ghaddafi with NATO's help eased Libya's move to becoming a part of the already "ungoverned" swath of lands across the region. Francesco Strazzari and Simone Tholens note that during and after NATO's intervention "a process of fragmentation occurred, there were obstacles hindering efforts to build mechanisms that would allow control of the direction of the revolutionary armed movement" (Strazzari and Tholens 2014: 343). Two ways in which the intervention affected the region were, firstly, the facilitation of the start of new conflicts or the aggravation of existing ones (Strazzari and Tholens 2014). Indeed, Scott Shaw (2013: 199) notes that "the conflict in Mali is explained by a combination of escalation and diffusion/contagion from Libya". Related to this, the second impact of Ghaddafi's overthrow is its endangering the Sahel-Sahara through the release of unregulated SALWs into the region. Libya then became a spot from where clandestine and criminal agents operated across its porous borders into the greater Sahel-Sahara, blurring the lines between refugee and fugitive. These unregulated movements of people were to be rendered more dangerous through easy access of arms.

Ghaddafi's regime was conspicuously an enormous purchaser of ammunitions, perhaps, because he was a leader with many powerful enemies (he feared possible internal or external overthrow). It is estimated that at the time of Ghaddafi's overthrow, the Libyan armed forces had about 250,000–700,000 firearms most of which assault rifles (Chivvis and Martini 2014: 8). According to another estimate, Libya's weaponry was more than that of the entire British army at the time Ghaddafi's overthrow (Chivvis and Martini 2014). There were reports about the vestiges of Ghaddafi's botched nuclear weapon programme. These included remnants of 2000 MANPADS (Man-Portable Air-Defence Systems) acquired from Russia, 6400 barrels of yellowcakes (partially processed uranium), and about 24 metric tons of mustard gas (Chivvis and Martini 2014: 8). Additionally, at the peak of the conflict France, Qatar and other NATO allies supplied the rebels with large amounts of weapons, while Qatar alone supplied about 20,000 tonnes of weapons including rocket-propelled grenades, assault rifle and small arms (Chivvis and Martini 2014: 8). These large concentration of arms poses threats to the countries of sub-Saharan Africa.

Therefore, what the NATO intervention did achieve was the unseating of the existing regime of control, hence aggravating the situation. Ghaddafi's removal led to a geopolitical vacuum, proportionate to the huge stabilising role he played in the region. Thus, while the fall of Ghaddafi could be considered mission accomplished by NATO and its allies, the vacuum created within Libya was to be filled by various splinter groups who shared unsteady alliances and motivations in regards to the overthrow of the Libyan leader. But outside of Libya, Ghaddafi's assorted arsenal, and the huge stockpiles of weapons brought into Libya as part of NATO's intervention, became up for grabs by clandestine elements, and by any novice and genius who cared to have one. Consequently, the long history of ungoverned spaces across the broader Sahel in the colonial and post-colonial periods, Libya's mainly southern borders potentially "absent", and the harsh and treacherous geography of the Sahel-Sahara region conjointly provided free space for various elements and criminal trades to fester. With sophisticated weapons in the hands of suspect individuals and organisations in a volatile region rendered even more volatile by removing almost all remaining state control, the terrorist organisations operating in the broader Sahel-Sahara as well as operations of banditry and illicit trade had the right conditions to ply their trade. Figure 8.5 provides a picture of weapons flows from Libya and across the Sahel from 2011 to the present.

Most citizens from the neighbouring countries who had migrated to Libya either permanently or temporary were forced by the outbreak of the Libyan conflict and the subsequent disintegration of the country to return home. With the sudden economic and geopolitical downturn, whatever these migrants had were lost along with Ghaddafi. The idea of arms sales therefore became lucrative to returnees pursuing survival (Murray 2017: 15). For example, the refuge sought by the quasi-stateless Tuareg dissidents who fled from Mali to Libya in the 1970s and 80s were forced to return after the demise of Ghaddafi,

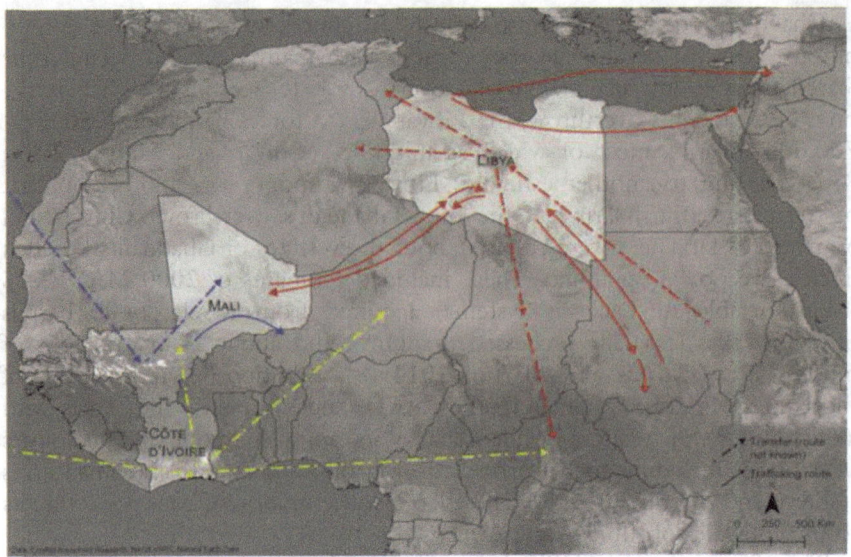

Fig. 8.5 Documented flows of weapons and non-state armed personnel in the Sahel, 2011–2020 (*Source* Conflict Armament Research Report 2016: 8)

their erstwhile generous host (Klute 2013). Ghaddafi had sought a consolidation of his power by utilising his Tuareg guests by giving them key and strategic posts in the army (Ronen 2013). With his demise, the Tuareg became objects of pursuit for persecution by anti-Ghaddafi elements. These armed and well trained returnee Tuareg—also known as "orphans of the Sahara" (from a 2014 Al Jazeera documentary by the same title) because they have no home to return to—served as tools for the transfer of SALWs from Libya: the Tuareg know the geopolitical value of these weapons and are well versed in the geographical terrain of the Sahara Desert, their home (*Conflict Armament Research Report* 2016).

As we would expect, Mali was the first country to feel the blowback of mass Tuareg return from post-Ghaddafi Libya—they returned to support the National Movement for the Liberation of Azzawad (MNLA) for the creation of their homeland of Azzawad (Klute 2013: 55). The NMLA is a Tuareg group that has been demanding separate autonomous territory of Azzawad in northern Mali around Timbuktu, Kidal and Gao (Gaasholt 2013; Klute 2013). Tuareg elements of Ghaddafi's army returned to Mali to champion the course of the MNLA (Atallah 2012). Notably, prior to their return, the NMLA and the Malian government were enjoying over two years of cease-fire. Thus, the returnees however tilted the balance of MNLA-Malian government relations in favour of a full-blown campaign against the government. Soon, what may be an understandable, if not legitimate, quest for self-determination by the Tuareg would merge into an unholy acquaintance with militant Islamist groups such as al-Qaida in the Maghreb (AQIM), Ansar al Dine and the Movement for Unity and Jihad in West Africa (MUJAO) (Atallah 2012: 66). This merge was possible because of a harmony of interest—leaders and members of these Islamists groups had a Tuareg ethnicity. Thus, ethnic Tuareg and Islamist Tuareg became united in the singularity of their Tuareg harmony.

The return of Tuareg militia to Azzawad, within the context of the geopolitical destabilisation of Libya by NATO, became a threat to human security in the Sahel-Sahara in the form of increased violence against civilians and a threat to state building. That intervention is central to the 2013 Islamist takeover of parts of Mali. The immediate aftermath of the Libyan intervention within the country and across the Sahel region especially Mali, informed UN's decision to send in about 12000 of its peacekeeping force. Earlier in 2013, at the request of Mali, France launched *Operation Serval* in the northern desert territories of Mali which was believed to have succeeded in pushing back and dispersed militia and jihadist groups like AQIM, Ansar Deen, and the MUJAO (Boeke and Schuurman 2015). In 2014, *Operation Barkhane* was launched to operate across the Sahel. This later operation would lead to the G5-Sahel Joint Force—a regional response initiative made up of Burkina Faso, Mauritania, Mali, Niger and Chad, and a plethora of security actors.

Yet the greater Sahel-Sahara continues to be in the state of acute insecurity. In many respects, the porosity of the region, further unsettled by NATO's removal of Ghaddafi, has aided the protracted nature of many conflicts in the region. The 2016 Conflict Armament Report concludes that although there is no direct link between late Ghaddafi-era Libyan arms in the civil war in the Central African Republic (CAR), Libyan arms arrived in the CAR through Chad and Sudan between 2013 and 2014 (*Conflict Armament Research Report* 2016: 21), to further protract the conflicts involving the Anti-Balaka and Séléka groups and their splinters groups and alliances. There are reports of Malian (potentially Tuareg) rebels fleeing to the western Sudan region of Darfur. Niger also served as a conduit for the transportation of ammunitions from the Libyan conflict to Mali. In the immediate aftermath of the conflict in Libya, Nigerien authorities captured three convoys believed to be carrying Tuaregs and weapons (Marsh 2016). In the process of serving as a passage some of the weapons made it to the illicit weapons market in Niger.

Beyond the Sahel-Sahara, there are reports of inflows of Libyan weapons to the conflict region of Sinai in Egypt, some making their way to the Gaza strip in the Palestinian territories. There are even reports of the Libyan ammunition making its way to Syria. Indeed, as Francesco Strazzari and Simone Tholens (2014: 353) note,

> since the onset of the 'February 17 Revolution', warnings came from many quarters about how assault rifles, ammunitions and sophisticated weapons systems diverted from Libyan depots could rekindle Tuareg violent mobilisation in the Sahel, fuel armed Jihadism in the Maghreb and Nigeria, destabilise the Sinai peninsula and Gaza, and potentially affect the military balance in Syria.

However, the point about making the above analysis is that, as Georg Klute (Klute 2013: 56) notes, the war in Libya and the removal of Ghaddafi by NATO and its allies have had enormous, overwhelmingly negative, geopolitical impact, even if inadvertently, on Sahelian countries in general, and on Mali in particular.

All the above is proof that the NATO intervention lacked a plan to control movements of humans and goods within and across Libyan borders during and after the intervention. The NATO mission in Libya was poorly executed, with no entry or exit strategies. This shows that Western-led interventions in Africa either have little respect for local conditions or lack a carefully planned intervention programme and a clearly thought-out reconstruction programme and their consequences. NATO's Libya operation lacked any viable reconstruction plan for Libya and the region beyond the "geopolitical rash" which led to the adrenaline-urge to overthrow Ghaddafi. Given the geostrategic and military sophistication of bodies such as NATO, and the military capacity of countries such as the UK, US and France etc., it becomes very difficult to agree that these intervenors in the Libyan case could not foresee the geopolitical meltdown that removal and killing of a decades-long leader like Ghaddafi would cause, after Ghaddafi had somehow become the economic and security bulwark of the region for decades.

Even more importantly, if we consider the connection between the geostrategic interests of NATO members and that intervention then we can further argue that the pursuit of geopolitical interests by global actors such as France, Britain and the US in the Sahel region played a role in removing Ghaddafi. Campbell (2013) for example refers to the pursuit of oil and the fact that the revolution in Libya presented a one-time opportunity for some Western countries to remove a man they have always wanted removed. This evokes a clairvoyance that immediately connects the present to the past: it was these same global actors who—acting as colonial powers in the nineteenth and twentieth centuries—facilitated the political-institutional process that created or enforced ungoverned spaces in the Sahel-Sahara to begin with.

Therefore, whereas the institutional-normative foundations of the contemporary international system may not allow us to explain the NATO-Libya intervention in terms of imperial indiscretion as we may do in regard to historical colonial decisions and policies, a question remains: if there was an agreement that an intervention was inevitable because of the invocation of R2P, why must the primary intervener be NATO and not a regional body like the African Union (AU)? It is reasonable to argue, therefore, that the NATO intervention lacked local content and challenges the AU's paradigm of seeking "African solution to Africa's problems". This is especially so given that the AU rejected NATO's intervention and called for mediation and dialogue instead. The AU's Peace and Security Council also had a concrete road map to solving the Libyan crisis (Akuffo 2014: 119) whilst former South African president Jacob Zuma visited Libya and indicated Ghaddafi's willingness to accept AU negotiated truce (Kedze 2015: 19). Nonetheless, in disregard for relatively peaceful and reconciliatory efforts by regional bodies like the AU to resolve the crisis in Libya, NATO felt obligated to intervene without the same commitment to the obligation to consider the consequences of such intervention. In fact, after the Resolution 1973 intervention had begun, Russia, China and South Africa raised objections to NATO's interpretation of the Resolution, arguing that the NATO intervention had crossed the line between civilian protection and regime change (Chivvis and Martini 2014: 5). This reiterates Mahmood Mamdani's questioning of whether R2P stood for "Right to Punish", instead of "Responsibility to Protect" (see Mamdani 2010).

Conclusion

What this chapter set out to address is the less acknowledged role of global coloniality or what Zubeiru Wai (2014: 486) calls "oppressive imperial globalism and its regimes of violence" in the creation, facilitation and arming of Africa's ungoverned spaces. The chapter has drawn attention to the historical role of the global powers of the colonial period in Africa in creating ungoverned spaces by cutting African lands and territories without recourse to pre-existing cultural and ethnic ties. In the contemporary sense, the NATO intervention in Libya, which removed Ghaddafi from power in 2011, created a dangerous alchemy of geopolitical events that released and facilitated the transfer of SALWs into the Sahel-Sahara. In the normative-institutional sense, this intervention was conducted with disregard for regional bodies such as the African Union, in whose primary domain the Libyan conflict lied.

Interestingly, the central players in that NATO intervention happen to be the colonial powers of old, who, on taking control of these regions after the Berlin conference of 1884/5 rolled out governance programmes and motives that would eventually widen the institutional-developmental divide of the Sahel-Sahara to create what is now "ungoverned spaces". These colonial powers of old—now operating from the vantage point of global coloniality via their control of intergovernmental organisations such as NATO and UN— have thus played key roles in endangering the ungoverned spaces of the Sahel-Sahara. The aim of drawing the above parallel between NATO's role in Libya and insecurity in the Sahel-Sahara is not because NATO and its allies caused all the said insecurity. Rather, their actions facilitated a process of endangerment of geopolitical spaces and activities that have become threats to human and state security. Yet, despite this central role of global actors in the creation and endangering of the Sahel-Sahara's ungoverned spaces, discourses on the role of powerful global actors in this geopolitical challenge to governance in Africa is not always acknowledged as much as local factors are. Thus, this chapter has argued that global actors must be brought back into the centre of the analysis along with the national and regional dimensions of the problem of ungoverned spaces and SALWs. It is only through this that a comprehensive conception of the problem, hence a sustainable solution, can be achieved.

References

Adeniyi, A. (2017). *The Human Cost of Uncontrolled Arms in Africa: Cross-National Research on Seven African Countries*. Oxford: Oxfam. Retrieved from https://policy-practice.oxfam.org.uk/publications/the-human-cost-of-uncontrolled-arms-in-africa-cross-national-research-on-seven-620205. Accessed 16 June 2018.

Aderinto, S. (2018). *Guns and Society in Colonial Nigeria: Firearms, Culture, and Public Order*. Bloomington, IN: Indiana University Press.

Agbajileke, O. (2017). *$35m Authorised Small Arms Enter West Africa Yearly—UN*. Retrieved from http://www.businessdayonline.com/news/article/35m-authorised-small-arms-enter-west-africa-yearly-un/.

Akuffo, E. A. (2014). The Politics of Interregional Cooperation: The Impact of NATO's Intervention in Libya on Its Relations with the African Union. *African Conflict and Peacebuilding Review, 4*(2), 108–128.

Anders, H. (2018). Monitoring Illicit Arms Flows: The Role of UN Peacekeeping Operations. In M. Johnson (Ed.), *SANA Briefing Paper*. Geneva: Small Arms Survey.

Aning, E. K. (2005). The Anatomy of Ghana's Secret Arms Industry. In N. Florquin & E. G. Berman (Eds.), *Armed and Aimless: Armed Groups, Guns, and Human Security in the ECOWAS Region* (pp. 79–102). Geneva: A Small Arms Survey Publication.

Aning, E. K., & Pokoo, J. (2014). Understanding the Nature and Threats of Drug Trafficking to National and Regional Security in West Africa. *Stability International Journal of Security and Development, 3*(1), 1–13.

Atallah, R. (2012). The Tuareg Revolt and the Mali Coup. *ASPJ Africa & Francophonie, 4*(1), 66–79.

Bøas, M., & Utas, M. (2013). Introduction: Post-Ghaddafi Repercussions in the Sahel and West Africa. *Strategic Review for Southern Africa, 35*(2), 3–15.

Boeke, S., & Schuurman, B. (2015). Operation 'Serval': A Strategic Analysis of the French Intervention in Mali, 2013–2014. *Journal of Strategic Studies, 38*(6), 801–825. https://doi.org/10.1080/01402390.2015.1045494.

Bronner, S. E. (2011). *Critical Theory: A Very Short Introduction*. Oxford: Oxford University Press.

Campbell, H. G. (2013). *Global NATO and the Catastrophic Failure in Libya*. New York: New York University Press.

Chivvis, C. S., & Martini, J. (2014). *Libya After Qaddafi: Lessons and Implications for the Future*. Santa Monica, CA: Rand Corporation.

Conflict Armament Research Report. (2016). London: Conflict Armament Research.

Daalder, I. H., & Stavridis, J. G. (2012). NATO's Victory in Libya: The Right Way to Run an Intervention. *Foreign Affairs, 91*(2), 2–7.

Dan Suleiman, M. (2017a). Global Insecurity and Conflict Dynamics in Ghana. *Peace Review: A Journal of Social Justice, 29*(3), 315–324. https://doi.org/10.1080/10402659.2017.1344759.

Dan Suleiman, M. (2017b). The Sahel Region. *Countries to Watch in 2017*. Retrieved from The Conversation website https://theconversation.com/sahel-region-africa-72569. Accessed 30 June 2018.

Florquin, N., Lipott, S., & Wairagu, F. (2019). *Weapons Compass: Mapping Illicit Small Arms Flows in Africa*. Retrieved from http://www.smallarmssurvey.org/fil

eadmin/docs/U-Reports/SAS-AU-Weapons-Compass.pdf. Accessed 25 November 2019.
Forte, M. C. (2012). *Slouching Towards Sirte: NATO's War on Libya and Africa*. Montreal: Baraka Books.
Fund for Peace. (2019). *Failed States Index Annual Report 2019*. Washington, DC: Fund for Peace.
Gaasholt, O. M. (2013). Northern Mali 2012: The Short-Lived Triumph of Irredentism. *Strategic Review for Southern Africa, 35*(2), 68.
Galito, M. S. (2012). Terrorism, Ethnicity and Islamic Extremism in Sahel. *JANUS. NET, 3*(2), 139–152.
GRIP. (n.d.). *Small Arms and Light Weapons*. Retrieved from Group for Research and Information on Peace and Security (GRIP) https://www.grip.org/en/node/948.
Holtom, P., & Pavesi, I. (2018). *Trade Update 2018: Sub-Saharan Africa in Focus*. Geneva: Small Arms Survey.
Hutchful, E. (2008). From Military Security to Human Security. In J. Akokpari, A. Ndinga-Muvumba, & T. Murithi (Eds.), *The African Union and Its Institutions* (pp. 63–84). Sunnyside: Jacana Media.
IEP. (2015). *Global Terrorism Index 2015*. Retrieved from http://economicsandpeace.org/wp-content/uploads/2016/11/Global-Terrorism-Index-2016.2.pdf. Accessed 7 June 2018.
Inikori, J. E. (1977). The Import of Firearms into West Africa 1750–1807: A Quantitative Analysis. *The Journal of African History, 18*(3), 339–368.
Kartas, M. (2013). *On the Edge? Trafficking and Insecurity at the Tunisian-Libyan Border*. Graduate Institute of International and Development Studies, Geneva: Small Arms Survey.
Kedze, D. T. (2015). The 2011 Libyan Crisis: Would the African Solution Have Been Preferred? *Conflict Trends, 2015*(1), 18–24.
Keister, J. (2014). *The Illusion of Chaos: Why Ungoverned Spaces Aren't Ungoverned, and Why That Matters*. Retrieved from https://ssrn.com/abstract=2563431.
Klute, G. (2013). Post-Ghaddafi Repercussions in Northern Mali. *Strategic Review for Southern Africa, 35*(2), 53–67.
Kuperman, A. J. (2013). A Model Humanitarian Intervention? Reassessing NATO's Libya Campaign. *International Security, 38*(1), 105–136.
Lecocq, B. (2013). Mali: This Is Only the Beginning. *Georgetown Journal of International Affairs, 14*(Summer/Fall), 59–69.
Maiangwa, B. (2017). "Conflicting Indigeneity" and Farmer–Herder Conflicts in Postcolonial Africa. *Peace Review, 29*(3), 282–288.
Maldonado-Torres, N. (2007). On the Coloniality of Being: Contributions to the Development of a Concept. *Cultural Studies, 21*(2–3), 240–270.
Malito, D. V. (2017). The Responsibility to Protect What in Libya? *Peace Review, 29*(3), 289–298.
Mamdani, M. (2010). Responsibility to Protect or Right to Punish? *Journal of Intervention and Statebuilding, 4*(1), 53–67.
Marsh, N. (2016). Brothers Came Back with Weapons: The Effects of Arms Proliferation from Libya. *Prism: A Journal of the Center for Complex Operations, 6*(4), 78–96.
Murray, R. (2017). *Southern Libya Destabilized: The Case of Ubari*. Geneva: Small Arms Survey.

Northrup, D. (2002). *Africa's Discovery of Europe: 1450-1850*. New York: Oxford University Press.

Olaniyan, A. (2018). Foliage and Violence: Interrogating Forests as a Security Threat in Nigeria. *African Security Review, 27*(1), 88–107.

Olaniyan, A., & Yahaya, A. (2016). Cows, Bandits, and Violent Conflicts: Understanding Cattle Rustling in Northern Nigeria. *Africa Spectrum, 51*(3), 93–105.

Osaghae, E. E. (2017). Conflicts Without Borders: Fulani Herdsmen and Deadly Ethnic Riots in Nigeria. In P. Aall & C. A. Crocker (Eds.), *The Fabric of Peace in Africa: Looking Beyond the State* (pp. 49–66). Waterloo: Centre for International Governance Innovation.

Ottaway, M. (2002). Rebuilding State Institutions in Collapsed States. *Development and Change, 33*(5), 1001–1023.

Pape, R. A. (2012). When Duty Clls: A Pragmatic Standard of Humanitarian Intervention. *International Security, 37*(1), 41–80.

Piombo, J. (2008). *Ungoverned Spaces and Weapons of Mass Destruction in Africa: Exploring the Potential for Terrorist Exploitation* (ASCO 2008-016).

Raleigh, C., & Dowd, C. (2013). Governance and Conflict in the Sahel's "Ungoverned Space". *Stability: International Journal of Security and Development, 2*(2). http://doi.org/10.5334/sta.bs.

Richards, W. A. (1980). The Import of Firearms into West Africa in the Eighteenth Century. *The Journal of African History, 21*(1), 43–59.

Ronen, Y. (2013). Libya, the Tuareg and Mali on the Eve of the 'Arab Spring' and in Its Aftermath: An Anatomy of Changed Relations. *The Journal of North African Studies, 18*(4), 544–559.

Schneider, L. G. (2008). *As causas políticas do conflito no Sudão: Determinantes estruturais e estratégicos*. Retrieved from http://www.lume.ufrgs.br/bitstream/handle/10183/16012/000685618.pdf?sequence=1. Accessed 7 June 2018.

Schroeder, M., & Lamb, G. (2006). The Illicit Arms Trade in Africa: A Global Enterprise. *African Analyst Quarterly, 1*, 69–78.

Ser, K. (2016). *Map: Here Are Countries with the World's Highest Murder Rates*. Retrieved from https://www.pri.org/stories/2016-06-27/map-here-are-countries-worlds-highest-murder-rates. Accessed 15 July 2017.

Shaw, S. (2013). Fallout in the Sahel: The Geographic Spread of Conflict from Libya to Mali. *Canadian Foreign Policy Journal, 19*(2), 199–210.

Strazzari, F., & Tholens, S. (2014). 'Tesco for Terrorists' Reconsidered: Arms and Conflict Dynamics in Libya and in the Sahara-Sahel Region. *European Journal on Criminal Policy and Research, 20*(3), 343–360.

Tall, O. (2018). Herders vs Farmers: Resolving deadly conflict in the Sahel and West Africa. *OECD Insights*. Available at: http://oecdinsights.org/2018/04/16/herders-vs-farmers-resolving-deadly-conflict-in-the-sahel-and-west-africa/. Accessed 12 November 2019.

Thébaud, B., & Batterbury, S. (2001). Sahel Pastoralists: Opportunism, Struggle, Conflict and Negotiation: A Case Study from Eastern Niger. *Global Environmental Change, 11*(1), 69–78.

UN News. (2018). *Crime and Drugs in West and Central Africa: Security Council Highlights 'New Alarming Trends*. Retrieved from https://news.un.org/en/story/2018/12/1029011. Accessed 19 November 2019.

UNGA (United Nations General Assembly). (1997). *Report of the Panel of Governmental Experts on Small Arms* (A/52/298 of 27 August (annexe)). New York: United Nations.

UNODC. (2013). *Firearms Trafficking in West Africa: What Is the Nature of the Market?* United Nations Office on Drugs and Crime (UNODC). Vienna published online at https://www.unodc.org/documents/toc/Reports/TOCTAW estAfrica/West_Africa_TOC_FIREARMS.pdf.

UNODC. (2017). *The Drug Problem and Organised Crime, Illicit Financial Flows, Corruption and Terrorism* (World Drug Report 2017). Vienna: United Nations Office on Drugs and Crime.

Van Munster, R. (2007). Review Essay: Security on a Shoestring: A Hitchhiker's Guide to Critical Schools of Security in Europe. *Cooperation and Conflict, 42*(2), 235–243.

Wai, Z. (2014). The Empire's New Clothes: Africa, Liberal Interventionism and Contemporary World Order. *Review of African Political Economy, 41*(142), 483–499.

Wehrey, F., & Boukhars, A. (2013). *Perilous Desert: Insecurity in the Sahara.* Washington, DC: Carnegie Endowment for International Peace.

West Africa Commission on Drugs (WACD). (2014). *Not Just in Transit Drugs, the State and Society in West Africa.* WACD. Retrieved from http://wwwwacommiss ionondrugs.org/report/. Accessed 19 November 2019.

Whelan, T. (2006). Africa's Ungoverned Space. *Nação E Defesa, 114*(3), 61–73.

Young, C. (2004). The End of the Post-Colonial State in Africa? Reflections on Changing African Political Dynamics. *African Affairs, 103*(410), 23–49.

Muhammad Dan Suleiman holds a Ph.D. in Political Science and International Relations from the University of Western Australia (UWA), Perth, where he is a Research Fellow at the university's Africa Research & Engagement Centre. He researches on state–society relations in Africa, Islamist movements and security in Western Africa, and the international politics of Africa. He is also a fellow of the UWA Centre for Muslim States and Societies, and teaches units on Africa's international politics, and peace and security in Africa.

Hakeem Onapajo is a Lecturer in the Department of Political Science and International Relations at Nile University of Nigeria, Abuja. Hakeem Onapajo holds a Ph.D. in Political Science from the University of KwaZulu Natal, South Africa. He has held teaching and research positions at the University of KwaZulu-Natal and The University of Zululand, in South Africa. Dr. Onapajo researches in the areas of elections and democratisation in Africa, conflict and terrorism. His publications have appeared in reputable international journals and other publishing outlets.

Ahmed Badawi Mustapha is a Research Fellow at the Institute of African Studies, University of Ghana. His research focuses on militant organisations, political violence, terrorism, radical ideologies, and counter-extremism, Islam in Africa and in global affairs and International Security. He had his Ph.D. in International Relations with focus on International Security at the Middle East Technical University (METU), Ankara. Ahmed had his B.A. (Hons) and M.A. degrees in Political Science from the University of Ghana and the National University of Singapore (NUS), respectively.

CHAPTER 9

Borderland Security and Proliferation of Small Arms and Light Weapons in Africa

Anthony Israel Rufus

INTRODUCTION

Borderland security has come to assume heightened importance in the world of realism today, with emphasis on territoriality and sovereignty. However, the security of border is source of worry even for advanced garrison states, like China, Russia and USA. This is so because a range of factors—including the proliferation of Small Arms and Light Weapons (SALWs), smuggling and human trafficking—have contributed to the growing incidence of border violation and insecurity. In particular, the need to understand the dynamic nature of SALWs proliferation is imperative because of the growing sophistication and lethality of these weapons in international criminal activities. The proliferation of SALWs has been attributed to the Cold War (1945–1989) during which SALWs were generously supplied by the superpowers to fight proxy wars in Africa and other parts of the world. Even in the post-Cold War era (1990 to date), the trade in, and proliferation of, SALWs have flourished as many "rogue state", organized syndicates and individual "merchants of death" have continued to supply SALWs to conflict zones in Africa. The flourishing global trade in SALWs as well as the effects of globalization makes it easy for unhindered movement of criminals and SALWs across the borders. The transfer of SALWs among non-state actors in Africa have increased the possibility of diverse security challenges and undermined greatly the ability of governments in Africa to fulfill their constitutional mandate of securing their frontiers or

A. I. Rufus (✉)
Administrative Staff College of Nigeria, Badagry, Nigeria

© The Author(s), under exclusive license to Springer Nature Switzerland AG 2021
U. A. Tar and C. P. Onwurah (eds.), *The Palgrave Handbook of Small Arms and Conflicts in Africa*,
https://doi.org/10.1007/978-3-030-62183-4_9

borders and ensuring the safety of lives and property as well as promoting the welfare of their citizens. Consequently, the proliferation of SALWs across the borders has increased criminal and other terrorist's activities in much of the borderland areas of Africa.

There is nothing new about the selling of SALWs in the global marketplace, but this trade has changed and evolved over the years in many ways. For example, in the decades immediately following the Second World War, developed nations trade in SALWs with the developing world often consisted of supplying already outdated SALWs left over from the preceding conflicts. By the 1980s, states in developing world were demanding and receiving some of the most sophisticated SALWs available, as they do today. Another important development is that the expansion in SALWs trade in recent times has been greatly facilitated by the twin trends of globalization and economic liberalization. Just as barriers and restrictions in other areas of economic activity have been lowered and eased as part of a global trend towards embracing free markets and deregulation, the same is true in relation to the SALWs trade. Similarly, advances in information and communications technology have enabled transactions to be conducted faster and more easily, and improvements in transportation—land, sea and air—have greatly aided the physical delivery of SALWs (Pilbeam 2015: 136).

The problem posed by SALWs proliferation is complex and multidimensional in character. They are entangled in broad security and societal issues—such as civil wars, communal conflicts, resource wars, criminality, insurgency and terrorism—which have spawned and exacerbated cultures of violence and crisis of governance with serious implications for human rights and humanitarian crisis (Oche 2005: 9–10). The United Nations Development Programme (UNDP) Report in 2018, observed that we are living in a complex world, people, nations and economies are more connected than ever, and so are the global development issues we are facing. Inequality and conflicts are on the rise in many places, poverty and exclusion is persisting, climate change and other environmental concerns are undercutting development now and for future generations. These issues span borders, straddle social, economic and environmental realms, and can be persisting or recurring (UNDP 2018). This is in addition to its earlier Report on Human security, which identified some of the new security concerns to include environmental degradation; large scale refugee movements and migrations; widespread destructive epidemic, including HIV/AIDs and even more recently, malaria; growth of religious fundamentalism; increased cases of intra-state violence, armed conflicts and increasing civil wars, with resultant incidents of state collapse. Still others are, rising unemployment; deepening poverty; gross human rights violations and increased cases of genocide and ethnic cleansing; massive trade and transfer of illegal surplus SALWs and their cross-border implications; globalization and its resultant discontents; terrorism; sales of drugs and persons across borders (drug and human trafficking); economic and financial crimes and adverse consequences on good governance; among many others.

The proliferation of SALWs has become a very lucrative business worldwide. This may be attributable to their physical characteristics of being compact, portable, cheap, highly destructive and easy to operate, as well as being easy to conceal and transport (Oche 2005: 2). The Small Arms Survey, an independent research project, observed that there are approximately 875 million SALWs in the world today (Small Arms Survey 2014). The United Nations estimates that these SALWs are responsible for 350,000–500,000 deaths a year, as well as over a million non-fatal injuries. Not all of these deaths and injuries occur in armed conflicts, since large numbers are the result of criminal activity and suicides. Regardless, globally over 90% of civilian casualties resulting from acts of violence can be attributed to SALWs. Over three-quarters of SALWs are possessed by non-state actors. The majority of these are private individuals, but this category also includes militias, insurgents, criminal gangs and private military and security companies (Pilbeam 2015). The fact that these weapons have brought devastation and destruction of millions of people, primarily women and children in various parts of Africa, shows the lethal and damaging capabilities of SALWs.

The fundamental questions however are: to what extent have these movements and treaty/treaties been able to curtail the global proliferation of SALWs? What are the challenges confronting the global reduction and management of SALWs. What are the security implications of SALWs proliferation in the borderlands of Africa? It is against the background of this and other related issues that this Chapter examines the security implications for SALWs proliferation on borderland security in Africa. The Chapter is structured into five major sections: introduction; conceptualizing borderlands and small arms proliferation; the nature and impact of SALWs proliferation on borderland security in Africa; border security management in Africa: challenges and solutions and conclusion.

Conceptualizing Borderlands and Small Arms Proliferation

Before we delve into the conceptualizations of borderlands, SALWs, it is vital to state from onset that the historical evolution of borderlands/boundaries in Africa could be traced to the Berlin Conference which took place between November, 1884 and February, 1885. The Conference was the colonial initiative that gave legal backing to the acquisition of territories and effective colonization by European powers (see Asiwaju 1984). After independence, African states were left with no alternative, but to accept these inherited artificial lines of demarcations as boundaries on the attainment of political independence. Thus, Onuoha (2013b) observed that the porosity of the borders owe as much to the way the colonialists carved up the African continent as to the nature of their management by post-colonial states. The original intention of the colonialists in the balkanization of Africa was not to create a boundary per se, but to create a sphere of influence driven by political and economic motives. These boundaries—defined in terms of latitudes, longitudes, geometric circles and straight lines—split several ethnic and cultural communities. As a result, most African governments find it extremely difficult to administer international boundaries that sliced through cultural and ethnic groups.

Borders and borderlands in Africa are spaces where the nexus of security, development, crime, conflict and politics is often at its most dynamic. In theory, borders serve to demarcate states' territory, and the movement of goods and people across them are managed in the interest of national trade and security. In practice, African borders are often little more than notional lines across huge stretches of land or water. A crucial feature of borderlands in Africa is the difference in how they are perceived by local people (border inhabitants) and the central government. For locals, the border or borders they live on or near are frequently hypothetical, without physical markers or regulatory presence; for business people, border present economic opportunities in trade routes, goods and markets. For central governments, on the other hand, borderlands are often viewed as a place where their control over citizens is weak, illegal trade occurs and security threats from insurgent groups can enter their territory. In sum, borderlands in Africa are typically characterized by low state presence, mistrust between local communities and the state and high levels of crime, insecurity and poverty (Naish 2016). Ekoko (2013) posit that it is generally acknowledge that "frontiers", "borders", "boundaries" and sometimes borderlands connote nearly the same thing and therefore used interchangeably. A border is the political and geographical area that demarcates and defines the territoriality of the state and limits of legitimate government control. Nigerian external boundaries, like those of other African States originated from the colonial experience, not clearly defined, un-demarcated and porous. This makes borderlands in Africa to be susceptible to smuggling activities, influx of illegal immigrants and the proliferation of SALWs used by armed bandits, terrorists and other transnational criminal gangs. According to Asiwaju (1984) since Lord Curzon attempted his admittedly highly qualified distinction of the terms in his very influential Romanes Lecture at Oxford in 1907, it has been fashionable in texts, written mostly by geographers and some scholars in International Law, to describe as "Artificial" all boundaries other than those made up of natural features such as oceans, seas, lakes, swamps, forests, deserts and mountains. Boundaries marked by such features are the ones categorized as "Natural".

Accordingly, artificial boundaries are defined as those lines of geopolitical demarcations which, not being dependent upon natural features of the surface of the earth for their selection, have been artificially or arbitrarily created by men. Imobighe (1993: 15) opined that the issue of "natural" and "artificial" boundaries came up as an attempt by boundary experts and statesmen to classify boundaries. Even though boundaries could be classified in a number of ways, the above two types are undoubtedly the most popular. It should be further emphasized that though all boundaries are man-made and, therefore, have a touch of artificiality and at times arbitrariness, some boundary lines could be deliberately drawn to conform to natural features like rivers, lakes, mountain ranges, etc., or with existing ethno-cultural and political groupings. Where this happens such boundaries are said to be natural because they follow what could be regarded as natural gradients. To sum up therefore, natural boundaries are boundaries which follow natural physical features like rivers, lakes, mountain ranges, etc., or which separate homogenous territories or communities. Artificial boundaries on the other hand, refer to boundaries that are drawn to follow lines of latitude and longitude with little or no regard for the existing ethno-cultural or political groupings and loyalties. Africa's international boundaries and the internal boundaries of some African states represent good examples that could be cited. This is because the boundaries were drawn by Europeans who had little or no knowledge of the topography of the Continent, neither were they familiar with the existing ethno-cultural or political groupings and loyalties prevailing in Africa at the time (Imobighe 1993: 15–16).

It is apparent that Africa's inherited boundaries reinforced conflict and disharmony in the post-colonial period. For instance, in 1960s, Morocco and Algeria resorted to war in order to maintain their boundaries. In many African states, there is an uneasy stirring of irredentist claims kept alive by the clamour of groups whose traditional frontiers have apparently been outraged by the international boundaries. Somalia makes territorial claims against Ethiopia and Kenya. Togo, the home of the Ewe groups, insists that Ghana should return to her the portion of Ewe country incorporated into Ghana (Anene 1970). The Nigeria—Cameroun contention over the Bakassi Peninsula, the war between Libya and Chad over the Aozon strip, the Tanzania—Uganda war, the war between Ethiopia and Eritrea over their common borders are but a few cases out of the many border conflicts with bitter experiences in Africa. The point therefore is that the causes of border-related conflicts, such as the illicit proliferation of SALWs, armed incursions, smuggling of contraband products as well as human and drug trafficking among other crimes in Africa are to be found partly in the very nature of the boundaries themselves. Furthermore, such boundaries were never clearly defined nor demarcated properly, thereby making it difficult for people to know when they were crossing them. The combination of these elements provided a general background or laid the foundation for fluid and porous boundaries, a situation which is reinforced by more specific factors such as social and economic activities between the border communities.

The proliferation of SALWs has become one of the most endemic problems of our time and generally accounts for a greater proportion of human mortality in the world. Armed conflicts have led to the loss of lives of tens of thousands of innocent civilian population each year, while the number of wounded and disabled people resulting from the consequences of SALWs proliferation and misuse is thirteen (13) times greater than those killed by other means (Small Arms Survey 2003: 57). Small arms proliferation is simply the undue increase in the number of arms and munitions. According to the United Nations (2008 & 2010), small arms are dominant tools of criminal violence; cheap, light and easy to handle, transport and conceal. The International Action Network on Small Arms (IANSA) see SALWs as capable of facilitating a vast spectrum of human rights violations including killing, maiming, and all forms of sexual violence, enforced disappearance, torture and forced recruitment of children by armed groups (IANSA 2006). The Royal Military College of Science (RMCS) in 1993, defines small arms as, "man portable, largely shoulder controlled weapons of up to 12.7mm (0.5") caliber; such weapons generally have a flat trajectory and an effective operational range of 0-800m, although this varies considerably with caliber and weapon type, certain weapons can also provide neutralizing fire up to 1800m" (RMCS 1993: 4). SALWs are revolvers and semi-automatic pistols, rifles and carbines, automatic rifles and sub-machine guns which are designed for personal use and can usually be carried and operated by one individual. Light weapons are heavy machine guns, hand-held and mounted grenade launchers, man-portable anti-tank and anti-aircraft guns, recoilless rifles, portable anti-tank and anti-aircraft missile systems, and mortars of less than 100 mm bore. Despite the nomenclature, "light weapons" are usually too heavy for one person to carry and require a small team to operate (Ebo 2003: 138).

In terms of SALWs, Table 9.1 presents a list from a 1997 United Nations (UN) Report that shows the range of weapons that might be considered to belong to the category often labeled SALWs, together with associated ammunition and explosives, encompassing weaponry from revolvers and rifles to grenades and landmines. Yet even this list has some crucial absences, as

Table 9.1 Small arms, light weapons, ammunition and explosives

Small arms	Light weapons	Ammunition and explosives
Revolvers and self-loading pistols	Heavy machines guns	Cartridges (rounds)for small arms
Rifles and carbines	Hand-held under-barrel and mounted grenade launchers	Shells and missiles for light weapons
Sub-machine-guns	Portable anti-aircraft guns	Mobile containers with missiles or shells singles-action, anti-aircraft and anti-tank systems
Assault rifles	Portable anti-tank guns, recoilless rifles	Anti-personnel and anti-tank hand grenades
Light machine guns	Portable launchers of anti- tank missile and rocket systems	Landmines
	Portable launchers of anti-aircraft missile systems	Explosives
	Mortars of calibres of less than 100 mm	

Source UN Report of the Panel of Governmental Experts on Small Arms (1997)

it includes only distinctively modern weapons. This overlooks the fact that there are many other sorts of weapons that may be wielded by individuals which have been used throughout human history, including clubs, knives and machetes, and which continue to be significant even in conflicts today, especially in the developing world (Pilbeam 2015: 134). SALWs offer distinct advantage over alternative means of violence because they are cheap, light, durable, powerful and easy to operate; they work with compelling accuracy from a great distance to the target (Brauer and Muggah 2006: 6). The fact is that SALWs are capable of facilitating a vast spectrum of human rights violations including killing, maiming, and all forms of sexual violence, enforced disappearance, torture and forced recruitment of children by armed groups. Where the use of armed violence becomes a means for resolving grievances and conflicts legal and peaceful approach to resolution of conflicts suffer set back while it becomes difficult to uphold the rule of law. According to Ebo (2003: 139) human security is a major casualty of SALWs, and the damage done by small arms is deep. SALWs have been aptly described as holding development hostage and the ransom is often paid in lives and livelihoods. SALWs proliferation causes great damage. Even though it is widely acknowledge that SALWs do not by themselves cause war, but they do have a catalytic effect such as intensifying violence and armed crime, and hindering stability, democracy and good governance. The atmosphere of insecurity created by SALWs proliferation lessens the prospects for stability and order.

When a border is not managed properly, it gives room for a conducive environment to the trade in drugs for precious minerals or SALWs and vice versa. A United Nations Security Council (UNSC) Report practically highlighted the need for arms embargo on Somalia, because it was observed that in wartime, members of armed groups are sometime a vector for transporting SALWs across borders to sell them in exchange for food or other commodities of need (UNSC 2008). This scenario was captured succinctly by Oche (2005: 13) when he argued that in some parts of Africa, such as Horn, a Soviet-designed AK-47 assault rifle, which was coveted for its simplicity and firepower, can be purchased for as little as $6, or traded for a chicken or sack of grain. Individuals involved in SALWs trafficking often use the same routes and itineraries as those used to transport other illicit goods across borders. SALWs do not proliferate by themselves, there are many sources of SALWs proliferation. Jekada, observed that even though there is a legal trade in small arms, legally purchased weapons may end up in criminal hands or be used by state security personnel for illegal acts. Africa itself can boast of countries that are SALWs manufacturers-South Africa, Zimbabwe, Egypt, Morocco and Nigeria, are among other countries that are dotted with growing SALWs cottage industries (Jekada 2005: 55). Be that as it may, the growing proliferation of SALWs in Africa can only be properly understood when we examine the nature and its increasing impact on borderland security in Africa.

The Nature and Impact of SALWs Proliferation on Borderland Security in Africa

The proliferation of SALWs in Africa has gradually developed to an alarming rate and has made the African continent unsecure and unstable. Terrorist groups, criminal gangs and other non-state actors have used SALWs to inflict violence on people living in the borderland areas of Africa; thereby reducing the capacity of the state to fulfill its constitutional mandate of securing the borders as well as enhancing the welfare of the people. The proliferation of SALWs could be attributed to a number of factors, prominent among them were the surplus SALWs that were provided during the Cold War by the opposing super powers (United States and Soviet Union), these SALWs were pumped to serve proxy inter-state conflicts; massive flow of SALWs from Central and Eastern Europe and the loosening control of small arms industry as a result of the collapse of Soviet Union (Mallam 2014). Following the end of the Cold War, the SALWs in circulation lost their way into the hands of illegal SALWs dealers, security entrepreneurs, ethnic militia groups, private military companies and local smugglers thereby fuelling on-going wars and facilitating the commencement of new ones in Africa. Also, the accelerated pace of globalization in the same period facilitated both legal and illegal cross-border transfers of SALWs, while a sudden upsurge in intra-state conflicts created an overwhelming demand for SALWs, making them weapons of choice in majority of recent conflicts and in non-war settings such as sectarian violence (ethnic, religious, communal and chieftaincy conflicts), suicides, murders, homicides and accidental discharges. Another important factor responsible for the widespread availability of SALWs is the intractable supplies from current and past conflict zones; other sources are stolen SALWs from the state security service, and leakage from government armories in which corrupt law enforcement and military personnel selling SALWs and growing domestic artisan production scattered across the continent (Badmus 2009; Bah 2004).

Figure 9.1 shows countries in Africa where SALWs are manufactured locally. The weapons being produced are low-grade by global standards, and range from rudimentary traditional hunting weapons to more sophisticated firearms, including copies of assault rifles, as well as home-made ammunition (UNREC 2016: 35). Irrespective of the source of SALWs, whether licit or illicit, SALWs do not portend anything positive in continental or national histories especially for a continent grappling with the negative index of extremely entrenched incidence of poverty; widening gaps in standards of living, lower incomes and consumption capacities, poor health services, low quality education and technology, low people's self-esteem, unstable political and economic systems and less freedom for the choice of goods and services (South Commission 1983; Rajagopal 2000). Since the African continent staggeringly trudged out of the throes of a dehumanizing colonial experience in the 1960s, the African narrative has been characterized by the debilitating occurrences of violent conflicts and wars—a condition occasioned by the acquisition of SALWs by criminal

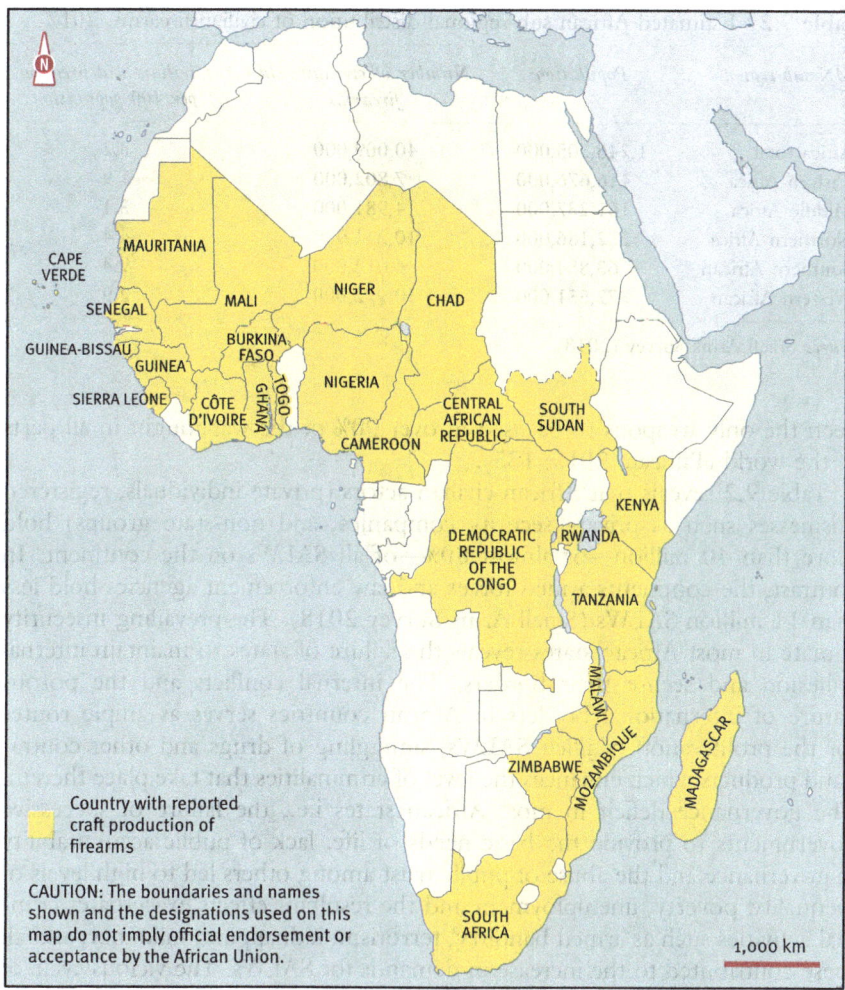

Fig. 9.1 Reported craft production of small arms in Africa, 2011–2018 (*Source* UNREC 2016: 21)

and non-state actors and national governments. Resources that should be directed at infrastructure and sustainable growth and human development were, and still are, increasingly channeled to SALWs purchase (Ayuba and Okafor 2015). The most direct predicaments caused by SALWs proliferation lies in the realm of conflicts, the primary reason that explains the acquisition of the vast majority of SALWs in the first place. The proliferation of SALWs does not directly cause conflict; it is nevertheless irrefutable that the presence of large concentrations of arms tends to prolong conflicts, increase their lethality and render the process of reconciliation between conflicting groups a much more difficult task. This axiom can be gleaned from the fact that SALWs have

Table 9.2 Estimated African sub-regional distribution of civilian firearms, 2017

UN sub-region	Population	Number of civilian-held firearms	Civilian-held firearms per 100 population
Africa total	1,246,505,000	40,009,000	3.2
Eastern Africa	416,676,000	7,802,000	1.9
Middle Africa	161,237,000	4,981,000	3.1
Northern Africa	232,186,000	10,241,000	4.4
Southern African	63,854,000	6,012,000	9.4
Western African	372,551,000	10,972,000	2.9

Source Small Arms Survey (2018)

been the only weapons to be used in over 90% of the war fought in all parts of the world (Pilbeam 2015: 135).

Table 9.2 reveals that African civilian actors (private individuals, registered businesses such as private security companies, and non-state groups) hold more than 40 million—or almost 80%—of all SALWs on the continent. In contrast, the continents armed forces and law enforcement agencies hold less than 11 million SALWs (Small Arms Survey 2018). The prevailing insecurity climate in most African states reveals the failure of states to maintain internal cohesion and secure their borders. The internal conflicts and the porous nature of international borders in African countries serves as ample routes for the proliferation of illicit SALWs, smuggling of drugs and other contraband products which enhances the level of criminalities that take place therein. The governance deficit in most African states i.e., the failure of successive governments to provide the basic needs of life, lack of public accountability in governance and the abuse of public trust among others led to high levels of inequality, poverty, unemployment and the resultant effects exacerbates criminal activities such as armed banditry, terrorism, kidnapping, militancy; and all these contributed to the increase in demands for SALWs. The vicious cycle of low salaries and corruption creates breeding grounds for the proliferation of SALWs among the civilian population. Customs officers are bribed by small arms dealers, while soldiers, police officers and security forces are known to have sold government SALWs to criminals (Ayissi and Sall 2005: 68).

The civil war in the Democratic Republic of Congo (DRC), for instance has been fought almost entirely with SALWs. Vast quantities of SALWs that were already in the country after years of violence and turbulence preceding and following Mobutu's death were enlarged by new supplies brought in by militias and foreign armies that became embroiled in conflict. This had rendered the achievement of a lasting peace in the DRC very difficult. The Somali civil war is another case in point. At a point, about one out of every four Somali males possessed a light weapon. The fact that such weapons could be readily obtained at the arms market in Mogadishu at a cost equal to a chicken reflected its availability and affordability (see Oche 2005). The Great

Lakes region, including the eastern part of the vast territory that is today the DRC, has been one of Africa's most unstable and insecure regions. This instability has its origins in a multiplicity of factors, including the colonial legacy of arbitrary borders, and unviable states on the one hand and poorly managed politics and governance in the post-independence years on the other. While the DRC is one of Africa's larger and potentially more viable states, the neighbouring states of Rwanda and Burundi are tiny pieces of territory that are hardly viable economically. Moreover, colonial machinations resulted in the blind fusion of two seemingly incompatible "nations", the Hutu and Tutsi ethnic groups, into the territories of both states. The fact that elements of these groups are also found across their borders in a number of other states in the region, including the DRC, has tended to complicate the security situation and facilitate the regionalization of the conflicts (Ikome 2012: 6). The African Great lakes region is one of marked contrasts and striking continuities. Beset by destructive conflicts, it also possesses extraordinary potential for peace and development. From biodiversity to solid minerals and human talents, this geopolitical space is endowed with abundant natural and cultural resources. Some of the world's most ecologically diverse freshwater systems, subtropical rainforests, savannah grasslands and temperate highlands with immense extractive, agricultural and touristic value are found in the Great Lakes region. (Omeje and Hepner 2013). While the above depicts a general feature of the region, the Great Lakes region has indeed been characterized by conflicts.

The fact is that the root causes and dynamics of conflict in the Great Lakes region are multiple and complex. Inequitable access to state and natural resources, a lack of equal opportunities to access political power and the proliferation of SALWs are just a few of the factors that perpetuate conflict in the region. Often, these issues underline actual or perceived inequalities and grievances between identity groups, which can lead to, among other outcomes, the violent expression of these grievances. These factors also relate to structural problems of weak governance and economic mismanagement such as an unaccountable security sector, debt burdens, unpopular macro-economic policies, the collapse of social services and poor terms of trade. The border troublesomeness in the Horn has been evidenced not only in the extremely high incidence of deadly border conflicts (Somalia and Ethiopia; Ethiopia and Eritrea; Somalia and Djibouti; Somalia and Kenya; Eritrea and Djibouti; Sudan and South Sudan); the ease of escalation into terrorism, so easily illustrated in the case of the Republic of Somalia vis-à-vis the intractable Al-Shabaab militants, has been particularly affected by the location of the entire sub-region in the fragile environment of the eastern Sahel, prone to periodic disasters of droughts, floods and famine (Asiwaju 2015). Similarly, in the Horn of Africa, all the cases for complex and paradoxical issues of borderlands can be found. However, much a central government insists on securing the border, the idea of a hard border regime (wall, fence, or Berlin or Korean-type division) is not feasible. It is an illusion to believe that any country in Africa or elsewhere would have the capacity to fully secure and monitor its borders (Weber 2012).

Therefore, only localized border administration is a realistic option. However, the tendency to outsource security to proxy militias and to instrumentalist borderland populations in the interest of the central government constitutes a risk and must be critically reflected upon when localizing border issues and disputes.

The Horn of Africa has experienced a peculiar pattern of state formation, quite distinct from state building processes in the rest of the continent. Rather than states and boundaries being the exclusive result of European imperialism as elsewhere on the continent, in the Horn region, Ethiopia has played a major role in shaping state borders and has therefore tended to be perceived as a colonial and expansionist state by some of its neighbours. This has had far-reaching implications on inter-state relations in general and border relations in particular. (Ikome 2012). Somalia's claim over Haud and Ogaden amounts to a continuation of the struggle for decolonization, rather than a boundary review. This position has resulted in wars between Ethiopia and Somalia from 1977 to 1978 and 1987 to 1989, and partly explains Ethiopia's intervention in Somalia. The weaponization of the African continent has led to the phenomenon of state collapse or failed states in many countries among which are Somalia, Central African Republic (CAR), Rwanda, Burundi, Liberia, Sierra Leone and DRC, to mention but a few. The civil strife experienced by these countries had greatly influenced the successive security irritants across the continent due largely to cross-border militia activities armed with SALWs. These weapons provided leverages to Militia movements in Nigeria and other parts of the continent particularly, the Central African sub-region (which is arguably the most volatile part of Africa since independence). The democratic (electioneering campaigns), competition in Rwanda during the 1990s led to genocide. The Hutu-Tutsi massacres in the Great Lake region accentuated militia movement throughout the region. This is not unconnected with the alliance of militias that toppled then President Mobutu Sesse Seiko of Zaire, now DRC. However, in spite of their success in regime change, they could not find a compromise among themselves. The government of Joseph Kabila is faced numerous challenges from militia groups such as Banya Malinge, the M23, the Lord Resistance Army (LRA) which operates in Uganda with its base in the CAR, and neighbouring Sudan. They move either way when faced with overwhelming state firepower. The militia group based in Chad/Nigeria borders led by Francois Bozize who was also toppled by the Seleka militia (an alliance of rebel movements with different nationalities as its members). Republic of Congo was also polarized along two powerful militias; the Cobras and the Ninjas (Umara 2014). Chad is also facing similar problem due to threats of attacks by different militia groups. These militia groups could be hired by any personality on contractual basis and have over the years becomes a colossus that conflagrated relatively peaceful Nigeria from both the Atlantic seabed and the Lake Chad region. The weaponization and, of course, militia maneuvers across borders of the Central and Western African sub-regions. The flow of these weapons to the non-state constellations has completely mortgaged the state institutions in charge of security, making everybody unsafe.

The illegal SALWs smuggling is a common feature in West Africa, involving some transnational networks. These SALWs are sourced from within West Africa and also from world supply of arms through the collaboration of Nigerians and foreigners. Other possible sources may include pilfering of weapons by unscrupulous peacekeepers in the conflicts in West Africa. Also, the proximity of some of the conflict zones in West and Central Africa to Nigerian land and sea borders has aggravated the illicit flows of SALWs. The official position in Nigeria is that virtually all the border entry points in the country are being used for drug trafficking, illegal migration, trafficking in persons and illicit SALWs transfer into the country. (Adetula 2015). Another factor facilitating trafficking (especially SALWs) across borders is the proximity of cross-border communities particularly in Africa where the borders were partitioned in the nineteenth century, without taking into cognizance ethnic considerations.

In many cases, ethnic or economic ties existed before the borders were imposed and the local communities have often developed formal and informal cooperation in a variety of areas, irrespective of the restrictions linked to the existence of a political border (Marenin 2010). Moreover, when times are difficult for survival, small scale trafficking is seen as a means of survival for the local community. As an integral part of informal cross-border economies, small scale trafficking can become normalized. This helps no doubt to explain the reluctance displayed by local communities with regards to cooperating with the authorities in fighting against cross- border trafficking activities (Adejo 2003). The report of the UN panel of Governmental Experts on SALWs (1997), established that irregular forces such as guerillas and terrorist groups not only posses little regards for the norms of international law but also do not distinguish between combatants and non-combatants. As a result, vulnerable groups such as women and children are increasingly becoming targets. A further consequence of the proliferation of SALWs is the increase in terrorist activities. Terrorism no doubt constitutes a major threat to domestic, as also to regional and international security. Security report on international terrorist networks identifies the presence of active terrorist cells in parts of Africa, particularly within Djibouti, Somalia, Ethiopia, Eritrea, Liberia, Algeria, Kenya, Sudan and Tanzania. The other apprehension of the vulnerability of Africa to terrorism is the prevalence of poverty, famine, conflicts and instability, which offers terrorists opportunities to insert themselves into the region, to develop support systems and to recruit new members into their groups (Ochoche 2006: 155–156).

Today no single issue had dominated the global strategic landscape as terrorism. The battle against terrorism is led by the United States and conducted across the globe. Terrorist activities in Afghanistan, Palestine in the Middle East and Chechnya in Eastern Europe had led to the destruction of towns, cities and even refugee settlements and, of course, the elimination of innocent lives (Imobighe 2006). In the same vein, Nigeria has been making international news headlines over the past few years for acts of terror perpetrated by groups within her borders. The attention is focused on the series of violent attacks on diverse civilian, police and military targets in Nigeria by the *Jama'atu Ahlissunnah Lidda'awati Wal Jihad* (JAL) otherwise known as Boko Haram, using SALWs, improvised explosive devices (IEDs), and other dangerous weapons to launch their violent attacks. The wanton destruction of lives and property as well as the humanitarian crises caused by the Boko Haram insurgents has led to the displacement of hundreds of thousands of people both within the country and neighbouring Cameroun, Chad and Niger Republics for their safety (Onuoha 2013a). Terrorism thrives on SALWs: for instance, in Nigeria, the Boko Haram insurgency is known to have acquired, through clandestine means, a large number of assault rifles, rocket propelled grenades (RPG's), mortars and improvised bombs and shells in its stockplile. The group possesses a limited anti-aircraft capability, and a large number of pickup trucks that have been adapted as improvised fighting vehicles to carry heavy machine guns (Steve and Chris 2015). In March 2015, Boko Haram declared allegiance to Islamic State proclaiming itself Islamic State's "West African Province" (ISWAP). Increased flows of SALWs from North Africa through Lake Chad's unsecured borders have solidified the group ties with other radicalized Islamist groups (Oputu and Lilley 2015). Therefore, one of the effects of conflicts fuelled by the spread of SALWs is that of Internally Displaced Persons (IDPs), and cross-border refugees. The problem of refugees and IDPs mainly stem from the proliferation of inter-and- intra-state conflicts. The point is that apart from the refugee flows themselves, there is the possibility of refugee camps being used to conceal SALWs and the likelihood of the refugees wanting to arm themselves for reason of personal security (Ladan 2004).

Thus, the proliferation and availability of SALWs has enabled militant and criminal groups to perpetrate cross-border terrorism (Adetula 2015). The crime-border combination or, more specifically, the terrorism-border partnership is especially demonstrable in Africa in view of the widespread identification of borders and borderlands in the continent as notoriously "porous", "ungoverned" and "ungovernable" locations and spaces, which allow for easy permeation of SALWs. The problem is underscored in the literature on "failed states", failed on account of, among other critical factors, the deplorable inability to exercise effective control on the entirety of claimed territory, notably at the adjoining borders and border areas of the national peripheries (Asiwaju 2015). The linkage between terrorism and other scourges, such as the illicit proliferation of SALWs cannot be over-emphasized. Many scholars believe that proliferation of SALWs increases the level and perhaps the frequency of violence between and within countries. Thus, the crisis in Libya, Sudan, Liberia, Sierra Leone and Somalia among others has greatly contributed to the proliferation of SALWs, thereby increasing the frequency of violence in Africa. Rebels in these countries are desperate to exchange small arms for money to "insurgents", their financiers and network of collaborators who are often affiliated to global terror fraternity (Sagir 2013). This has added to the overwhelming challenge of the influx of illegal aliens, arms and ammunitions, given the porous nature of international borders along this region with so many illegal entry points. Studies on the proliferation of SALWs conclude that the consequences of the flow of weapons, especially to the developing countries are likely to be severe. These studies note that while no one can predict that the growing availability of modern weapons will lead to an increased frequency of armed conflict, there is a high correlation between growing diffusion of war-making material and the increased tempo of insecurity (Klaire and Lumpe 2000; Parker 1999; Sanjian 1999; Hashim 1998). From the foregoing, it is clear that the proliferation of SALWs is a major issue of regional and global security concern. It is therefore imperative for us to examine initiatives in addressing the phenomenon.

BORDER SECURITY AND MANAGEMENT OF SMALL ARMS IN AFRICA: CHALLENGES AND SOLUTIONS

The growing incidence of violence across the globe, particularly in Africa as a result of SALWs proliferation, underscores the need to have a credible arms control programme that will make the world and indeed the African continent safer and peaceful. African states need to pay serious attention to border security and management with a view to understanding the dynamics of security in the borderlands of Africa. Considering the fact that international boundaries and borderlands in Africa are characteristically distinct peripheries where a wide range of criminal activities such as terrorism, armed banditry, illicit trafficking of SALWs; drug and human trafficking among other violent criminal offences take place regularly (Asiwaju 2015), it is necessary to advocate for a broad base regional integration in order to consolidate on the existing framework of the African Union (AU), as it relates to the promotion of good governance and in particular border governance in Africa. In West Africa for instance, the international borders are hospitable to smugglers of illicit SALWs, drug and human traffickers and sundry criminal networks (Eselebor 2013). Therefore, the Economic Community of West African States (ECOWAS) Treaty as well as other arms control protocols that have been signed and institutionalized should be strengthened. The 1979 ECOWAS Protocol relating to free movement of Persons, Residence and Establishment has liberalized freedom of movement within the Community for all ECOWAS citizens. Criminal gangs have equally exploited the enormous decline in security regulations, lessened border controls and the resultant greater freedom of movement, to expand their activities across borders. The influx of illegal and undesirable immigrants is a potential source of threat to the security of the sub-region. Hence, member states of ECOWAS should educate and re-educate their nationals on the Protocol on freedom of movement. In other words, such freedom of movement of Community citizens as contained in the ECOWAS Treaty should not be abused by anyone willing to move or settle in a foreign country. ECOWAS Governments on their part should not spare any person, group of persons that are found contravening the Treaty. Accordingly, other countries in Africa should cooperate with their neighbours in their respective sub-regions in order to promote regional integration as a people-centered development strategy.

The governance deficit in the borderlands of Africa is a major factor responsible for the insecurity that characterized the continent. This has led to the rise of militia groups, terrorists and insurgents who through the illicit proliferation of SALWs are challenging their home governments and other neighbouring governments. The violent nature of their attacks constitutes a huge security challenge to the continent. The recent conflict in Mali between the government forces and the Tuareg separatist, the crises in the Horn of Africa and the insurgency by the Boko Haram sect in Nigeria and the spillover effects on other countries are but a few examples of such conflicts. Therefore, the illicit inflow of SALWs, terrorists and other transnational criminals in the borderlands of Africa are a serious threat to the economic and security interests of the continent. Since modern criminals are highly mobile and sophisticated, no one nation may be in a position to fight them successfully, more so when porous and long border areas are involved. It is necessary to put in place a joint communication system with neighbouring countries in order to effectively track down criminal positions and movements along the border areas. In line with the globalization process, borderlands in Africa should have access to communication network for quick facilitation of security information as regards cross-border criminal activities. A dynamic information service and a good and effective communication system would boost security in the borderlands areas of Africa.

On the whole, the overall socio-economic development of the borders will go a long way in reducing to the bearest minimum the activities of violent criminal networks within the borderland areas of Africa. Africa is said to be one of the most backward in terms of socio-economic development and the most vulnerable as far as peace, security and stability are concerned. Studies have shown that one of the highest concentrations of SALWs is in Africa and this is perhaps connected with the poverty situation ravaging border areas. What this implies is that people tend to arm themselves with a view to challenging their socio-economic conditions or the perceived exploitation and injustice of their respective governments. The summary from the discussion above is that most conflicts in sub-Saharan Africa have been attributed to lack of development or struggle over limited or scarce resources. Another popular explanation of the escalation of violent conflicts points to cultural or ethnic differences. It is certainly true that conflicts have a tinge of both economic and cultural dimensions; hence socio-economic development question is a vital requirement for peace, security and stability in the borderland areas of Africa.

CONCLUSION

The illicit proliferation of SALWs have contributed significantly to the growing incidence of violent conflicts globally (especially in Africa), which have brought death, sexual violence and poverty to tens of millions of people across Africa. The widespread proliferation of SALWs has become one of the most urgent security and development challenges in the borderland areas of Africa. The uncontrolled proliferation and availability of SALWs is a development that is affecting virtually every African country and constitutes a threat to domestic and regional security. The United Nations estimates that SALW are responsible for 350,000–500,000 deaths a year, as well as over a million non-fatal injuries. The fact that these weapons have brought devastation and destructions of millions of people, primarily women and children in various parts of Africa, shows the lethal and damaging capabilities of SALWs. The proliferation of SALWs has undermined socio-economic and political development of most countries in Africa. The weaponization of the African continent by the industrialized nations of the world has led to the phenomenon of state collapse or failed states in many countries among which are Rwanda, Burundi, DRC, Somalia and CAR to mention but a few. The activities of militia groups and terrorists networks have over the years disrupted the peace, security and stability of the continent due to the spillover effects it has on neighbouring countries. The porous nature of the borderland areas of Africa facilitates the trafficking of illicit SALWs, drugs, human as well as terrorists activities.

In addition to the porous nature of international boundaries and borderlands in Africa, the governance deficit is also a major factor responsible for the insecurity that characterized the continent, with disastrous repercussions on border security. This has led to the rise of militia groups, terrorists and sundry transnational criminals who through the illicit proliferation of SALWs are challenging their home and neighbouring governments: the situation in the borderland where development and governance are scant, is worse, with militias opening brandishing arms and engaging in clandestine activities. The violent nature of their attacks constitutes a huge security challenge to the continent. In view of these, it is necessary for the borderland areas of Africa to take the socio-economic development question serious. Since modern criminals are highly mobile and sophisticated, no one nation may be in a position to fight them successfully, more so when long and porous borders are involved. Therefore, it is important to put in place a joint communication system with neighbouring countries in order to effectively track down criminal positions and movement along the border areas. In other words, a dynamic information service and a good and effective communication system between and among neighbouring countries would boost security in the borderland areas of Africa and by extension socio-economic as well as political development of the borderlands of Africa.

REFERENCES

Adejo, P. Y. (2003). Crime and Cross-Border Movement of Weapons: The Case of Nigeria. In A. Ayissi & S. Ibrahima (Eds.), *Combating the Proliferation of Small Arms and Light Weapons in West Africa*. United Nations: Handbook for the Training of Armed and Security Forces.

Adetula, V. A. O. (2015). Governance Deficit, Violence and Insecurity in African Border Areas. In *Reflections on Nigeria's Foreign Policy: The Challenges of Insurgency*. Society for International Relation Awareness (SIRA). Friedrich-Ebert-Stiftung, Nigeria: Abuja, 4(1), 43–64.

Anene, J. C. (1970). *The International Boundaries of Nigeria, 1885-1960: The Framework of an Emergent African Nation*. London: Longman.

Asiwaju, A. I. (1984). *Artificial Boundaries*. Lagos: University Press, Lagos.

Asiwaju, A. I. (2015). Terrorism and African Border Governance. In *Reflections on Nigeria's Foreign Policy: The Challenges of Insurgency*. Society for International Relation Awareness (SIRA). Friedrich-Ebert-Stiftung, Nigeria: Abuja, 4(1), 15–42.

Ayissi, A., & Sall, I. (2005). *Combating the Proliferation of SALWs in West Africa: Handbook for the Training of Armed Security Forces*. United Nations Institute for Disarmament Research (UNIDIR), Geneva, Switzerland.

Ayuba, C., & Okafor, G. (2015). The Role of Small Arms and Light Weapons Proliferation in African Conflicts. *African Journal of Political Science and International Relations*, 9(3), 76–85.

Badmus, I. A. (2009). *Managing Arms in Peace Process: ECOWAS and the West African Civil Conflicts*. Retrieved from http://www.africanos.eu.

Bah, A. (2004). *Implementing the ECOWAS Moratorium in Post-War Sierra Leone*. Paper Prepared for the Working Group of the Peace Building Coordination Committee in Support of the Peace Building and Human Security: Development of Policy Capacity of the Voluntary Sector Project.

Brauer, J., & Muggah, R. (2006). Completing the Circle: Building a Theory of Small Arms Demand. *Contemporary Security Policy*, 27(1), 138–154.

Ebo, A. (2003). Combating Small Arms Proliferation and Misuse After Conflict. In I. O. Albert, N. Danjibo, O. O. Isola, & S. A. Faleti (Eds.), *Democratic Elections and Nigeria's National Security* (pp. 127–140). Ibadan: John Archers (Publishers).

Ekoko, A. E. (2013). *Secure Frontiers and National Security in Nigeria: Issues and Prospects*. Being a Paper Presented at a Conference of the National Defence College, Abuja.

Eselebor, W. A. (2013). Security and Development in the Context of Borderless Border in West Africa. In I. O. Albert & W. A. Eselebor (Eds.), *Managing Security in a Globalised World* (pp. 171–193). Ibadan: John Archers (Publishers).

Hashim, A. S. (1998). Revolution in Military Affairs Outside the West. *Journal of International Affairs*, 5(1), 431–446.

IANSA. (2006). *A Thousand People Die Every Day: Bringing the Global Gun Crisis under Control*. London: International Action Network on Small Arms.

Ikome, F. N. (2012). Africa's International Borders as Potential Sources of Conflict and Future Threats to Peace and Security. *Institute for Security Studies*, 233(1), 1–14.

Imobighe, T. A. (1993). Theories and Functions of Boundaries. In B. M. Barkindo (Eds.), *Management of Nigeria's Internal Boundary Questions* (pp. 13–25). Lagos: Joe-Tolalu and Associates (Nigeria).

Imobighe, T. A. (2006). Rethinking Terrorism and Counter-Terrorism. In T. A. Imobighe & A. N. T. Eguavoen (Eds.), *Terrorism and Counter-Terrorism: An African Perspective* (pp. 7–28). Ibadan: Heinemann Educational Books (Nigeria) Plc.

Jekada, E. K. (2005). *Proliferation of Small Arms and Ethnic Conflicts in Nigeria: Implication for National Security*. Ph.D. Dissertation, St. Clements University.

Klaire, M. T., & Lumpe, L. (2000). Fanning the Flames of War: Conventional Arms Transfer in the 1990s. In *World Security: Challenges for a New Century* (3rd ed.). New York: St. Martines.

Ladan, M. T. (2004). *Migration, Trafficking, Human Rights and Refugees Under International Law: A Case Study of Africa*. Zaria: Ahmadu Bello University Press.

Mallam, B. (2014). Small Arms and Light Weapons Proliferation and Is Implication for West African Regional Security. *International Journal of Humanities and Social Science, 4*(8), 260–269.

Marenin, O. (2010). *Challenges for Integrated Border Management in the European Union*. Geneva: Centre for the Democratic Control of Armed Forces Occasional Paper.

Naish, D. (2016). *Security and Conflict Management in the African Borderlands: A People-Centred Approach Danish Demining Group*. Retrieved from http://www.accord.org.za/conflict-trends/security-conflict-management-africanborderlands.

Oche, O. D. (2005). *The Proliferation of Small Arms and Light Weapons*. Lagos: FOG Venture Surulere.

Ochoche, S. A. (2006). Terrorism and Counter-Terrorism: The African Experience In T. A. Imobighe & A. N. T. Eguavoen (Eds.), *Terrorism and Counter-Terrorism: An African Perspective* (pp. 155–177). Ibadan: Heinemann Educational Books (Nigeria) Plc.

Omeje, K., & Hepner, T. K. (2013). *Conflict and Peace-Building in the African Great Lakes Region*. Indiana: Indiana University Press.

Onuoha, F. C. (2013a). Boko Haram: Evolving Tactical Repertoire and State Responses. In O. Mbachu & U. M. Bature (Eds.), *Internal Security Management in Nigeria: A Study in Terrorism and Counter-Terrorism* (pp. 407–434). Kaduna: Medusa Academic Publishers.

Onuoha, F. C. (2013b). *Porous Borders and Boko Haram's Arms Smuggling Operation in Nigeria*. Retrieved from https://www.studies.aljazeera.net/en/reports.

Oputu, D., & Lilley, K. (2015). *Boko Haram and Escalating Regional Terror*. Retrieved from http://www.soufangroup.com/tsg-intelbrief-boko-haram-and-escalating-regional-terror.

Parker, C. S. (1999). New Weapons for Old Problems: Conventional Proliferation and Military Effectiveness in Developing States. *International Security Journal, 23*(1), 119–147.

Pilbeam, B. (2015). The International Arms Trade in Conventional Weapons. In P. Hough, S. Malik, A. Moran, & B. Pilbeam (Eds.), *International Security Studies: Theory and Practice* (pp. 133–149). New York: Routledge.

Rajagopal, B. (2000). Locating the Third World in Cultural Geography. *Third World Legal Studies, 15*(1), 18–26.

RMCS. (1993). *Handbook on Weapons and Vehicles*. Sweden: Shrivenham.

Sagir, M. (2013). *Nigeria's Military List Factors That Hinders Efforts to Combat Boko Haram*. Retrieved from www.premiumtimesng.com.

Sanjian, G. S. (1999). Promoting Stability or Instability? Arms Transfers and Regional Rivalries 1950-1991. *International Studies Quarterly, 43*(1), 641-670.
Small Arms Survey. (2003). *Development Denied.* Geneva: Graduate Institute of International Studies, Oxford University Press.
Small Arms Survey. (2014). *Weapons and Markets.* Retrieved from http://www.smallarmssurvey.org/weapons-andmarkets.
Small Arms Survey. (2018). *Global Firearms Holdings Database.* Geneva: Small Arms Survey.
Steve, H., & Chris, A. (2015). *Intelligence Brief: Reducing the Supply of Weapons to Boko Haram.* Retrieved from http://www.openbriefing.org.
The South Commission Report. (1983). New York: UN Publications.
Umara, I. (2014). *National Interest and Foreign Policy Options for Nigeria in the Central African Sub-region.* Kaduna: Joyce Publishers.
UN Report of the Panel of Government Experts on Small Arms. (1997). Retrieved fromhttp://www.disarmament.un.org.
UNDP. (2018). *Human Development Indices and Indicator, Statistical Update.* Geneva: UNDP.
United Nations. (2008 & 2010). *Secretary-General Report on Small Arms.* Retrieved from http://www.un.org/disarmament/convarms/SALWs.
United Nations Security Council. (2008). *Documentation Research Guide: Meeting Records.* New York: Dag Hammarskjold Library.
UNREC. (2016). *Assessment Survey on Small Arms in the Sahel Region and Neighbouring Countries.* Geneva.
Weber, A. (2012). *Boundaries with Issues: Soft Border Management as a Solution.* Retrieved from http://www.fes.de/afrika.

Anthony Israel Rufus obtained a Ph.D. in Defence and Strategic Studies from the Nigerian Defence Academy, Kaduna. He taught at the University of Maiduguri in the Department of Political Science from 2007 to 2016, Dr. Rufus is the North Central Zonal Coordinator of the Administrative Staff College of Nigeria (ASCON). He has written and published several articles at both local and international journals as well as book Chapters especially on issues relating to border security and national security.

CHAPTER 10

Urban Dynamics and the Challenge of Small Arms and Light Weapons in Africa

Enoch Oyedele

INTRODUCTION

African development against the background of colonialism and within the context of globalisation has acquired certain characteristics that make it somewhat different from the pattern of development experienced in most advanced countries of the world. Essentially, African development occurs as a dependent phenomenon that is vulnerable to influences from external forces, inputs and institutions. Urban dynamics in Africa are not an exception to this fact. This chapter explores the manner in which urban areas have developed in Africa, and the accompanying institutional malaise that provided for the proliferation of Small Arms and Light Weapons (SALWs) as instruments for inter-group interactions among the different human formations that emerged in the processes of Urbanisation in Africa.

The chapter first attempts a conceptual clarification of the concepts of urbanisation and SALWs; then it goes on to explain the process and nature of urbanisation together with the ensuing institutions for socio-economic and political governance; it also examines the implications of these urban dynamics on the socio-economic and political conditions of urban dwellers, especially the proliferation of SALWs and other similar phenomena; and then explores relationship between these urban dynamics and the challenge of SALWs. The

E. Oyedele (✉)
Department of History, Ahmadu Bello University, Zaria, Nigeria

study concludes with a note on how to build governance, political economic and social institutions that will contain the challenge of SALWs in whatever form it manifests.

Conceptual Clarification
Urbanisation

Urbanisation is a concept that has been defined in various ways by scholars—Economists, Political Scientists, Historians, Urban and Regional Planners, Sociologists, Geographers, etc.—from several viewpoints to suit their interests. Besides, some of the definitions are simplistic and vague. In our view, urbanisation is a continuing process of increasing functional or structural social differentiation and specialisation in human society. It is a social process involving people in social relationships within a new kind of physical environment. This process involves agglomeration, increasing transformation of the economy from agriculture to a predominantly non-agricultural one, and a structural change in the form of settlements. The process entails spatial, social and temporal phenomena and, thus by definition, requires an interdisciplinary approach (Oyedele 1987; Onyemelukwe 1997). This process is characterised by the concentration of population in urban centres, hence the growth of towns and cities. An urban centre is defined as a large settlement of people of whom a significant proportion is engaged in specialised and non-agricultural activities.

Urbanisation has also been described as the process of change in the situs of population due to changing conditions in society associated with economic, social and technological processes of development. Therefore, changes associated with urbanisation can, if well managed, be veritable instruments of national development. Thus urbanisation is one of the major changes that occurred in man's march for progress and development (Sada 1986).

Small Arms and Light Weapons (SALWs)

The term small arms and light weapons (SALWs) have been defined in various ways. The International Committee of the Red Cross (ICRC) define small arms as the weapons which are light, extremely durable and require little upkeep, logistical support and above all minimal maintenance (Matson 2011). The North Atlantic Treaty Organisation (NATO) defines SALWs as all crew portable direct fire weapons of calibre less than 50 mm and which include a secondary capability to defeat a higher armour and helicopters (Akaenyi and Osuagwu 2013). The NATO definition describes SALWs in terms of crew portability and weapon capability. However, it limits the calibre to a maximum of 50 mm. it therefore did not take into cognisance advancements in technology which has afforded the use of lightweight materials for making weapons with longer range and more lethal effect.

The most commonly used definition is that put forward by the 1997 United Nations (UN) Panel of Government Experts, which consider portability of small arms as the defining characteristics. The Panel Report categorised small arms to include the following: revolvers and self-loading pistols, rifles and light machine guns. The Panel Report also has a category slightly different called light weapons; this category of weapons include: heavy machine guns, recoilless rifles, portable anti-tank missile and rocket launchers, portable anti-aircraft missile launchers and mortars of less than 100 mm calibre (UN General Assembly 1997; African Union, (AU) 2019). These definitions are adopted in this discussion.

There are two other terms related and relevant to the discussion that requires definition, namely fire arms, illicit small arms and proliferation. The term firearm is used to refer to the types of weapons belonging to the following categories only: revolvers and self-loading pistols, rifles and carbines, shotguns, sub-machine guns, and light and heavy machine guns. On the other hand, illicit small arms refer to weapons that are produced, transferred, held or used in violation of national or international laws. This definition acknowledges the many different forms that illicit arms flow can take, and includes both in-country and cross-border flows of small arms and ammunition (AU 2019).

Singh (2003) defines proliferation as "the sudden increase in the number and amount of something. This definition is simplistic. On his part, Obasi (2001) defines proliferation as the spread of weapons from one grow of owners to others. This could be horizontal or vertical: horizontal proliferation refers to the acquisition of weapons system by states not previously possessing them, while vertical proliferation refers to increase in the arsenal of states already possessing partial weapons. This definition however restricts proliferation to states alone and did not take into account other channels of possible proliferation (Ayuba 2009).

Urbanisation in Africa

It is imperative to state from the onset that urbanisation is not a new phenomenon in Africa, as colonial historiography will want us to believe. In fact, some of the world's earliest and oldest cities such as Memphis, Rabat and Kumbi Saleh, to mention only a few, were found in Africa. In view of the long history of the urbanisation process in Africa, it can be divided into three major phases: the Pre-Colonial phase which can be further divided into two, namely the Pre-1800 and the nineteenth Century phases; the Colonial phase and the Post-Colonial phase. It is important to state that the context, pace and pattern of the urbanisation processes vary widely across the continent from one century to the next. The varying trend of the process has been categorised into five groups of countries based on three indicators: their current level of urbanisation and their degree of structural transformation from low-productivity economic activities like traditional farming to high-productivity ones such as manufacturing. The five categories are:

1. *Diversifiers*, such as Egypt, South Africa and Tunisia. These have reached the most advanced stage of each process.
2. *Agrarians*, such as Chad, Niger and Malawi. These are at the early stage of the process.
3. *Early urbanisers*, such as Cote d'Ivoire, Ghana and Senegal. Though not showing a lot of progress in their structural transformation, they are generally more urbanised and have low fertility ratios.
4. *Late urbanisers*; this category includes Ethiopia, Kenya and Tanzania. They have begun urbanising but are still predominantly rural with high fertility ratios and generally low income levels.
5. *Natural resource-based countries*, such as Congo, Nigeria and Zimbabwe. They are generally more urbanised, particularly around a single prime city. Fertility rates remain generally high and income levels vary widely depending on what natural resources they produce (UrbanAfrica.Net 2016).

One of the biggest drivers of urbanisation is the growth of towns. This trend is continuing to the present. Meanwhile, a handful of countries, including Cote d'Ivoire, Mali and Zambia, have actually seen drops in the urban share of their populations.

However, the structural transformation is not keeping pace with urbanisation. Historically, there has been a link between urbanisation and/structural transformation: the emergence of cities brings a rise in incomes and living standards but this appears to not always be the case in Africa. Many countries that are more than 50% urbanised still have low income levels. In some places, urbanisation has become synonymous with overcrowded informal settlements, congestion, overloaded infrastructure and high costs of living. Also, many states have failed to industrialise as they urbanise, especially within Sub-Saharan Africa.

Importantly, African cities have high rates of poverty and inequality. Poverty is a major problem in African cities, as most population of Sub-Saharan Africa live in slums. Africa also has some of the world's most unequal cities, such as Johannesburg, South Africa. Inequality leads to an unequal provision of services and limited access to opportunities for the urban poor, to high crime rates and levels of insecurity.

In addition, majority of Africa's middle class live in cities and this class drives sustainable economic growth. As much as a third of the population is considered middle class in *diversifier* countries such as South Africa. Meanwhile, in late *urbanizers* such as Kenya and *Agrarians* such as Niger, as little as 5% of the population is middle class. Three reasons why the middle class can contribute to growth are: first, people with more income are more inclined to pursue entrepreneurial activities that may create employment and productivity growth. Second, those who do not become entrepreneurs can provide labour or investment for those who do. And thirdly, a growing middle class means of growing demand for consumer goods.

Finally, although Africa has contributed relatively little to the world's greenhouse gas emissions, its cities increasingly feel the impacts of a changing climate. Flooding, changing rain patterns and extreme heat waves may leave most African countries poorer than they are today (urbanAfrica.Net 2016) (Table 10.1).

UN Economic Commission for Africa 2017 Economic Report on Africa. Urbanisation and Industrialisation for Africa's Transformation. p. 78.

The first stage of the urbanisation process witnessed the gradual development of settlements into large urban centres, especially from the fifteenth Century. The urban centres were important for their economic, political, religious and military functions. These urban centres continued to expand in the seventeenth and eighteenth Centuries. But as a result of some revolutionary changes that took place in most parts of Africa in the nineteenth Century, rooted in the socio-economic and political structures of the society, the nature and tempo of the process was radically transformed. These forces of the transformation include movements like the Jihads in West Africa—Sokoto, Masina, the Mfecane in Southern Africa, the decline and consequent collapse of powerful kingdoms like the Oyo Alafinate and the Buganda Kingdom coupled with their aftermath, the emergence of Mohammed Ali Pasha in Egypt and the increasing European penetration from the coast.

A major feature of the Pre-Colonial urban centres is that they were centres of production; this placed them in direct contrast to Colonial and Post-Colonial cities. In addition, the cities and their surrounding agricultural areas were tightly integrated into a series of basically self-sufficient regional economies. Thus the economies were essentially self-reliant, wherein most members of the society were involved in productive activities, and the economic connections between the cities and the countryside were organic and showed interdependence of all sectors of the economy. Traders functioned as linkages in the system and trade itself was intimately connected with production (Oyedele 1987).

Dependent Urbanisation

The next two phases of the process, Colonial and Post-Colonial urbanisation, are characterised by domination and dependency—that is, urbanisation within a dependent economy. And by "dependency" is meant the situation in which the economy of a country is conditioned by the development and expansion of another economy to which it is subjected. The relationship of interdependence ensures that while the dominant economies can expand and can be self-sustaining, the dependent enclave can do this only as a reflection of that

Table 10.1 African countries categorised by extent of urbanisation, 2014

Category	Urban Population As % of Total Population	Number of Countries	Countries[a]		Average Per Capita GNI (2011 PPP$)
			Resource-Rich	Non-Resource-Rich	
I	>60	10	Algeria, Libya (NA); Djibouti (EA); Rep. of Congo, Gabon (CA); South Africa (SA)	Morocco, Tunisia (NA); Cabo Verde (WA); Sao Tome and Principe (CA)	9201
II	51–60	7	Mauritania (NA); Cote d'Ivoire (WA); Ghana (WA); Cameroon (CA); Botswana (SA)	Seychelles (EA); Gambia (WA)	7834
III	41–50	10	DRC (EA); Benin, Liberia, Nigeria (WA); Angola, Namibia, Zambia (SA)	Egypt (NA); Guinea-Bissau, Senegal (WA)	4263
IV	31–40	13	Sudan (NA); Madagascar, Tanzania (EA); Guinea, Mali, Sierra Leone, Togo (WA); Central African Republic, Equatorial Guinea (CA); Mozambique, Zimbabwe (SA)	Somalia (EA); Mauritius (SA)	4590
V	<30	14	Eritrea, Rwanda, South Sudan, (EA); Burkina Faso, Niger (WA); Chad (CA); Lesotho (SA)	Burundi, Comoros, Ethiopia, Kenya, Uganda (EA); Malawi, Swaziland (SA)	1937
		54	36	18	5031

Source Data on urban population as a percentage of total population and average per capita GNI from UNDP (2015); country classification from UNECA (using the criteria specified below).
Note [a]Resource-rich countries are those that have 20% or more of exports of either oil or minerals. CA-Central Africa, EA-East Africa, NA-North Africa, SA-South Africa and WA-West Africa

expansion of the former, which can have either positive or negative effects on the latter's immediate development. African countries and other developing countries are suffering, in various degrees, from domination and dependency in a world of increasing interdependence and, lately, globalisation, wherein the relationships among nations are highly asymmetrical.

As the capitalist mode of production gathered momentum in the West and as the process of industrialisation accelerated, the effects were felt in the spatial organisation of both developed and developing societies. The political economy of urbanisation in its aim to understand the social production of space and spatial reproduction of society, as well as unravel the relationship between the dynamics of capital accumulation and the built environment, was led to establish the link between locational behaviour, changing patterns of employment and development of the level of the process of capital accumulation. Thus, it contends that capital, in its search for profit, is both a creative and destructive force. It *creates* and *recreates* new landscapes, new divisions of labour and new social relations (Short 1996). The analysis linked social changes and economic restructuring in particular places to the rhythm and beat of capital. It also *destroys* by wiping away existing norms and structures and replacing them with variants that do not necessarily represent those of the host culture or sub-culture.

It must be emphasised that capital responds to the uneven distribution of investment opportunities in the socio-spatial landscape. Land beyond the city edge, for example, provides opportunity for speculative development. This investment involves new transport routes and new spatial divisions of labour. The transformed spatial structure in turn guides the flow of successive waves of capital investment. Patterns of fixed capital investment provide the decision-making context for successive waves of investment. Space is not only continually structured, but also shapes the basis for subsequent capital restructuring (Gordon et al. 1983; Harvey 1985).

In the case of developed societies, the Industrial Revolution involved spatial reorganisation as well as an economic reorganisation of society. Urbanisation went hand in hand with industrialisation and economic development. The new industrial order was also the new urban order in which social classes replaced social rank and modernity replaced tradition. The industrial cities were the crucible in which classes and class identity were shaped and formed. For Marx and Engels, the creation of an urban working class was the creation of an agent of social change (Castells 1977; Harvey 1978).

In Africa and other developing countries, not only is urbanisation taking place at a low level of economic development, it is also proceeding much rapidly than in the industrial nations in the heyday of their urban growth. For Amilcar Cabral (1966) has argued, the essential characteristics of imperialist domination, Colonialism and Neo-Colonialism remain the same: "The negation of the historical process of the dominated people by means of the violent usurpation of the freedom of the process of development of the productive forces of the dominated socio-economic whole".

The Atlantic Slave Trade and Colonialism are the principal agencies responsible for the stunted development of Africa or underdevelopment (Rodney 1972). The economic incorporation of Africa into the world capitalist system was achieved through the political domination of the continent from about 1900. The change was structurally very different from the one that established the domination of the capitalist mode of production in metropolitan Europe. The existing productive forces were not smashed but extended and encapsulated to meet the requirements of metropolitan capital, in such a way as to block the transition to autonomous capitalist development. For instance, using their traditional farming methods, farmers were manipulated, sometimes directly ordered into production of specific cash crops at the expense of food crops production. Rodney stated that "Africa went into Colonialism with a hoe and came out with a hoe".

An important factor in the process of Colonial urbanisation was the new transport system of port and railway road network throughout the continent. The transport system disrupted the existing North–South and East–West trade routes and commerce of most societies. The commercial system and the urban centres that supported it were related to internal concerns of the economy rather than external. Thus, all the urban centres whose prosperity depended on this system were replaced by urban centres that sprang up as Colonial capitals and administrative centres, mining towns, on the coast and along the railway networks (as terminals or junction towns) as a result of their location in areas with very high agricultural potentials.

Colonialism also affected established urban centres on several other ways: indigenous industries were decimated as a result of importation of manufactured goods from Europe; hence, many craft industries declined severely while others closed shop completely. The decline in urban manufacturing was accompanied by a parallel shift in the orientation of the rural economy, which was compelled to move away from production of foodstuffs and raw materials for internal needs to production of cash crops for export. Meanwhile, agriculture became neglected as people moved massively into the urban centres. The rural areas became more deprived and impoverished. The migrants do not leave the rural areas because their labour has been replaced by better machines, nor do they move into cities because there are industries for them to be gainfully employed. This lack of industrial employment means the migrants remain largely outside the productive sector of the urban economy and engage in the informal sector—marginal retailing and servicing. The longer they remain at this subsistence level, the longer it takes them to shed their rural lifestyles and beliefs, thus the persistently high rates of natural increase in Nigerian cities.

Thus it became more profitable to leave farming, in view of fluctuating prices of cash crops, and move to the cities where one could earn some wages as unskilled labour in the processing industries or get a job as messenger, gateman, cook, steward, etc. There was no question of anybody with minimum educational qualification going back to the rural areas and to farming. Such people found work as office clerks in government provincial offices, Colonial companies, etc. Hence, the irreversible process of rural–urban migration began.

Most African states secured political independence in the 1960s, but this only marked the end of direct administration because domination and dependency continued in a different form—capitalist commercial or economic domination. The basic trade terms and patterns established in the Colonial period continued in the Post-Colonial period. African cities continued to play the role of collection and marketing of agricultural and mining raw materials, which were the largest earners of foreign exchange. These products, whose prices fluctuated downwards most of the time, are exchanged for industrial manufactured goods from Europe. It became increasingly more difficult for the rural population to stay on the land, as the urban centres continued to be sustained as centres of high consumption of imported industrial goods, at the expense of the rural countryside.

With the emergence of mining and minerals—oils, diamond, gold, copper, etc.—as the major foreign revenue earner of most African states, the nations embarked on giant industrial projects aimed at raising the Gross National Product (GNP) and creating employment for the urban populations. The nature and tactics of domination and dependency changed; the characteristics of the new strategy are speculative investments and the creation of local industries. At first, these industries were merely branch companies with head offices somewhere in Europe, and they operated under the blanket cover of "import substitution" while they followed a strategy of profit appropriated by international trusts throughout the world market. Much of the investible surplus needed in the various countries were moved to accounts abroad; they appear in the companies' accounts under all sort of heading, disguised as inflated head office charges, management and consultancy fees, machinery cost and commission.

Meanwhile, agriculture became neglected as people migrated in large numbers into urban centres. The rural areas became deprived and impoverished, while so much wealth abounded in the urban centres. Moreover, so much wealth of the nation like oil money in Nigeria was pumped into *urbanscapes* as they became more tuned to the latest trends on the international business map to the total alienation of the surrounding rural areas. Growth centres are isolated because there are no backward linkages to the rural areas, and the traditional system has remained largely outside the influence of market forces. The nature and dimensions of the urbanisation process in Africa is dependent urbanisation rooted in dependent capitalism. In other words, there was a situation of "exploding" cities in "un-exploding" economies. This development in turn has led to urban crisis in the continent manifest in the problems of urban violence and insecurity, urban poverty, unemployment, poor housing, inept administration, decaying transportation, inadequate infrastructure and utilities (water, power, road s), and problems of urban waste disposal.

Summatively, urbanisation in Africa is rooted more in the economic preferences of both Colonial governments and Post-Colonial political elites, rather than in the socio-economic and political realities of the peoples that make up African countries. Therefore, the urbanisation process has been driven by politics more than any other force, such that political imperatives, underscored by profit and other economic motives, induced the emergence and growth of urban centres. As aforementioned, urban centres eventually became hubs that attracted people of different backgrounds, including unskilled rural inhabitants, leading to a build-up of ethnic and other forms of plurality in those centres. This development would normally require the setting of corresponding institutions such as laws, agencies, infrastructures and processes to manage the growing urban variables—activities, interactions, changes/dynamics, shocks, conflict resolution, etc. It is such institutions that can ensure and insure/guarantee the socio-economic and political stability and enhance the advancement for urban inhabitants and processes.

What can be deduced from the foregoing is the fact the urban centres in Africa emerged to serve the interests of those who govern the society, whether directly or indirectly. The peoples that populate these urban centres were not taken into consideration either at the initial or the successive stages of their developments. Consequently, the urbanisation process in most of Africa, driven by political imperatives, focused more on structural developments and the growth of establishments that serve politically defined goals, than on the formation of relevant institutions. These institutional deficits in the urbanisation process provided loopholes for the build-up of urban vices and threats to socio-economic and political stability of urban inhabitants. Invariably, SALWs proliferation, among other social vices prevalent in urban centres, is a consequence of institutional deficits in the process of urbanisation in Africa. The following section discusses some of the socio-economic and political implications of urban dynamics in Africa.

URBAN DYNAMICS AND SOCIO-ECONOMIC AND POLITICAL IMPLICATIONS

All human beings have a deep psychological need for a sense of security which comes from knowing where you are. But 'knowing where you are' is a matter of recognising social as well as territorial position.
- Edmund Leach, *Culture and Communication*, 1976

The division of society is embodied in space and place. The urban centre separates out different types of people; it also acts to bring certain types of people together. Part of the differences between people is in the spaces they occupy, the places they inhabit. Part of the similarities among peoples is in their shared spaces and common places. Thus it is important to consider some of the relationships between urban space and the social order. There are three major sources of social differentiation: class, ethnicity and gender (Short 1985).

Class is concerned with the world of work, the realm of production and people as workers. It is however observed that it ignores differences between men and women, young and old, black and white. It is a useful concept that helps us to understand the nature and dimensions of urban conflicts. Most urban centres in Africa have three major classes: the upper, ruling class made up of the wealthy who are generally a small group, and live behind walls patrolled by armed guards; the middle class comprising workers, businessmen and professionals; and the lower class made up of the urban poor, the lumpen proletariat and the unemployed. They are marginalised by society and the economy, and are regarded as the source of social disruption. Though the three classes live in the same space, the differences between the qualities of their lives and wealth is always growing (Gugler 1988).

Ethnicity is a complex term. It has been used to refer to religious denomination, racial category and nationality. This shifting usage is part of its nature; there is no simple definition because it is a provisional, historically conditioned and a socially constructed term. People are not born with an ethnic identity as much as they are given one, or socialised into one. The issue here is: the role of space and place is crucial to ethnic identity. Ethnic conflicts are common in urban Africa, and they are expressive of more general relations of power. Ethnicity is tied to power; indeed, the social construction of ethnicity is an expression of both the exercise of power and the lack of power.

Gender is also an important issue of concern in urban dynamics; it is a social construction as well as a biological fact. People are born either males or females—this is a biological fact. But the roles that men and women perform and what it means to be a man or woman are social constructs. And space is crucial to these social constructions. The need to make women's lives more visible has spurred feminist and gender researches. The researches, among other things, have shown that the bulk of domestic labour is performed by women who also have primary responsibility for child bearing and child care. This imposes enormous burdens on women who work both at home and in paid employments. The design and organisation of urban space reinforces the sexual division of labour. The term "man-made city" is indicative of the social construction of urban space, the male domination of the design and planning professions. There are also significant differences in the way women and men experience the city. Women's use of urban space, for example, is more constrained than men's because of the fear of male violence. And when urban conflicts occur, women and children are mostly affected.

Urban Dynamics and Challenge of the Proliferation of SALWs

The proliferation of SALWs is regarded as the most immediate security challenge to individuals, societies and states worldwide, fuelling civil wars, organised criminal violence, insurgency and terrorist activities, and posing great obstacles to sustainable development. Importantly, most times small insurgencies tend to develop into larger civil wars and even destabilise entire regions. This trend, especially in Africa, is attributed to weakness and fragile nature of states and their attendant failure to deliver good governance. Even though there is no accurate data on the quantity of SALWs in Africa, several attempts have been made to measure it. For instance, the African Union (2019) has provided some useful statistics.

In Africa, over 100 million SALWs are reported to be in circulation, with a significant quantity held in urban enclaves in the hands of urban criminals, warlords, political thugs and civil militias. Most of them are also in use in conflict areas of the continent such as Chad, Somalia, Sudan, South Sudan, Ethiopia and Eritrea in the horn of Africa. In Eastern and Central Africa, large quantities of arms are in use in Central African Republic, Uganda, Rwanda, Burundi and the Democratic Republic of Congo (DRC). In West Africa, countries like Mali, Guinea, Liberia, Sierra Leone, Cote d'Ivoire, Senegal (Casamas) and Nigeria are centres of SALWs. With specific reference to urban centres, studies have shown that wielding of a weapon gives power to coerce, and small arms are known to be used for a wide range of crimes such as cultism, gangsterism, kidnapping, rape and robbery, among others (Adedeji 2007).

Generally, there are several factors that contribute to the proliferation of SALWs in the continent, including the nature of SALWs, internal factors and structural factors. First, there is a general lack of transparency around the arms trade, and most states in the world consider their arms policies to be top secret, which makes them hard to assess. Second, SALWs are characteristically very attractive to paramilitary and irregular forces, and even untrained civilians, thereby assisting in their proliferation. Apart from governments' increasing demand for SALWs to counter political insurgency and suppress domestic opposition movements, a number of different factors account for their "high desirability" on the region. Their simplicity makes them easy to operate even by people who have had very little or no military training. This explains their use by untrained combatants and child soldiers, as it was the case in many armed conflicts in Congo DRC, Rwanda, Liberia, Sierra Leone, Mali, Cote d'Ivoire and Nigeria, among others. They are often sold with little domestic and international regulation by weapon producers, from surplus military stockpiles and by private arms dealers (Mallam 2014).

There are still other factors responsible for the proliferation of SALWs, with significant implications for urban dynamics. A prominent one is the porous and poorly defined nature of land and sea borders with several entry points, which is a factor of the size of the continent; this has contributed to the easy movement of SALWs in Africa. Furthermore, the forces of globalisation with its opportunities and challenges, the elimination of state-enforced restrictions on exchanges across borders and the increasingly integrated and complex global system of production and distribution further complicate the challenge of containing the proliferation of SALWs in Africa. The linkage of banks with the internet has also posed a new form of challenge in combatting illegitimate activities in the financial sector. In addition, the expansion of commercial airlines and freight industries, making transportation cheaper and easier, is instrumental in the increased penetration of arms in conflict zones. The growth of global communication in the past two decades has enhanced the ability of arms dealers to freely communicate internationally through the internet at cheaper rates and in untraceable ways. The urban areas constitute the hub for online and offline transaction and proliferation of SALWs, not only to meet the "violent demands" of the urban enclaves but also to service the needs of rural herdsmen, farmers, cattle rustlers, armed robbers and insurgents.

Movement of SALWs from countries that have been war zones like Syria, Libya and Sudan into other African has been very easy. And, as mentioned earlier, globalisation has contributed immensely to this easy transfer of arms from manufacturing countries to recipient countries (UN Arms Treaty 2013/2014 Domesticated by ECOWAS Commission. It requires certification to be endorsed by all member states). The transactions and transfers are mainly done by arms brokers who often operate contrary to national and international laws regulating arms. This non-compliance with the law has made SALWs proliferation a global phenomenon, and the impact is manifest in ethno-religious, communal, sectional, political and other forms of conflicts that are always rife in urban centres that lack strong institutional frameworks for stabilising socio-economic and political interactions. In some cases, some of the arms are locally produced through illegal manufacturing activities that thrive in countries where government institutions for socio-economic and political control are generally weak.

Civil wars, ethno-religious crises, socio-economic problems, unemployment, boundary disputes, agitations for better control of national resources and political disputes are some of the conditions that encourage the proliferation of SALWs in Africa, especially in urban centres. The inefficiency of security agents, coupled with corruption has also contributed to the problem. In the same poor implementation of laws prohibiting the possession of SALWs is another unique, institutional factor in the proliferation. At the international level, there is the factor of a lack of or poor inter-state co-operation among countries to combat the proliferation of SALWs in Africa, especially the lack of proper inspection equipment at cargo terminals and trans-shipment points (UN 2005).

The aforementioned factors and conditions that encourage the proliferation of SALWs are usually found in urban centres which host people who have conflicts of interests, people who have the financial and other means to acquire the weapons, people who have the technical know-how to take advantage of modern technology and opportunities provided by globalisation, and people who know how to find a way around laws prohibiting the illicit use of SALWs. Thus, the institutional deficits of the urban framework predispose urban centres to the tendency for survival of the fittest, thereby making the stronger, albeit richer, powerful, positioned and influential persons or groups of persons to always overcome and subdue the weaker ones, especially their opponents, because of their access to means for acquiring what they need, including SALWs. The effects of this have been and can be quite devastating, as Kofi Anan (2000) noted:

> The toll from small arms dwarfs that of all other weapons systems – and in most years greatly exceeds the toll of the atomic bombs that devastated Hiroshima and Nagasaki. In terms of carnage...small arms, indeed, could well be described as "weapons of mass destruction"...small arms proliferation is not merely a security issue; it is also an issue of human rights and of development. The proliferation of small arms sustains and exacerbates armed conflicts. It endangers peacekeepers and humanitarian workers. It threatens legitimate but weak governments and it benefits terrorists as well as the perpetrators of organised crime.

Most of these small arms are in the hands of non-state actors operating without regard for human rights as entrenched in international humanitarian laws. These weapons have caused heavy losses to human lives, with women and children accounting for nearly 80% of the casualties (Ochogwu and Aku 2011).

Concluding Remarks

The proliferation of SALWs in Africa is generally rooted in institutional deficits that accompanied the process of urbanisation. Urban centres therefore grew to attract different kinds of people with different interests, who came and experience different conditions that predispose them to different behaviours in their interactions with others, including negative vices and security-threatening actions for which little or no conscious institutional arrangement is made to address. These urban dynamics have given room for the proliferation and use of SALWs as instruments for social interaction, resulting in socio-economic and political destabilisation in many urban settlements. Therefore, focusing attention towards the formation of viable institutions to serve the social, economic and political needs of urban dwellers should be the crux of governance and administration, including the use of participatory processes that includes people in decisions on issues and areas that affect them directly or indirectly. This is one way to minimise the challenges of SALWs in urban centres with their changing dynamics.

REFERENCES

Adedeji, E. (2007). An overview of Small Arms Control Initiatives in West Africa. *Africa Strategic Review, 1*(1), 66.

African Union. (2019). *Weapons Compass: Mapping Illicit Small Arms Flows in Africa*. Switzerland: Small Arms Survey.

Akaenyi, I. W., & Osuagwu, O. E. (2013). Deploying Electric Roadside Vehicle Identification Technology to Intercept Small Arms and Ammunition on Nigerian Roads. Retrieved from www.ajol.info/index.php/wajiar/article/download/86899/76692.

Anan, K. (2000). We the people: The Role of the UN in the 21st Century. Geneva: United Nations, 52–53. Retrieved from http://www.un.org/millennium/sg/report/full.htm.

Ayuba, A. O. (2009). *Small Arms and Light Weapons Proliferation in the West African Sub-region: Implications for National Security*. Abuja: National Defence College.

Cabral, A. (1966). *The Weapon of Theory*.

Castells, M. (1977). *The Urban Question*: A Marxist Approach., London: Edward Arnold.

Gordon, D. M., Weisskopf, T. E., & Bowles, S. (1983). Long Swings and the Non-reproductive cycle. *American Economic Review, 73,* 152–157.

Gugler, J. (1988). *The Urbanisation of the Third World*. Oxford: Oxford University Press.

Harvey, D. (1978). The Urban Process Under Capitalism. *International Journal of Urban and Regional Research, 2*(1), 101–131.

Harvey, D. (1985). *The Urbanisation of Capital*. Oxford: Blackwell.

Leach, E. (1976). Culture and Communication, cited in Short J. R. 1996. *The Urban Order: An Introduction to Cities, Cultures and Power*. Cambridge: Blackwell Publishers.

Mallam, B. (2014). Small Arms and Light Weapons Proliferation and Its Implication for West African Regional Security. *International Journal of Humanities and Social Sciences, 4*(8), 260–269.

Matson. (2011). Towards Checking the Proliferation of Small Arms and Light Weapons in West Africa. *American Journal of Law and Public Policy, 1*(4), 14.

Obasi, N. (2001). *Small Arms and Sustainable Disarmament in West Africa: Progress and Prospects of ECOWAS Moratorium*. Abuja: Apophl Productions.

Ochogwu, J., & Aku, D. (2011). Small Arms and Light Weapons Proliferation and Violent Crime in Nigeria. *African Strategic Review, 10*(2), 92.

Onyemelukwe, J. C. O. (1977). Urbanisation in a Development Context: Patterns, Problems and Prospects in Nigeria. In Urbanisation and Nigeria Economic Development, Proceedings of the 1977 Annual Conference of the Nigerian Economic Society.

Oyedele, E. (1987). *Colonial Urbanisation in Northern Nigeria: Kaduna 1913–1960*. Unpublished PhD Thesis, Ahmadu Bello University, Zaria.

Rodney, W. (1972). *How Europe Underdeveloped Africa*. Dar es Salaam: Tanzania Publishing House.

Sada, P. O. (1986). The Nigerian City. Occasional Papers: Urban Studies Series, 1(3), National Institute for Policy and Strategic Studies.

Short, J. R. (1985). Human Geography and Marxism. In Z. Baranski & J. R. Short (Eds.), *Developing contemporary Marxism*. London: Macmillan.

Short, J. R. (1996). *The Urban Order: An Introduction to Cities, Culture, and Power.* Cambridge: Blackwell.

Singh, J. (2003). *Light Weapons and International Security.* Puguish: Wazhing Press.

United Nations. (2005). *Combating the Proliferation of Small Arms and Light Weapons: Handbook for the Training of Armed and Security Forces.* Geneva, Switzerland: United Nations Institute for Disarmament Research, 56–61.

United Nations General Assembly. (1997). Report of the Panel of Governmental Experts on Small Arms, A/52/298, 27 August (Annex).

UrbanAfrica.Net. (2016). "Five Trends in Africa's Rapid Urbanisation". 15th Edition of the African Economic Outlook, Published by the African Development Bank (AfDB), the Organisation for Economic Co-operation and Development (OECD), and the United Nations Development Programme (UNDP). Citiscope, Gabriela Rico.

Enoch Oyedele, Ph.D a historian and a fellow of the Historical Society of Nigeria (FHSN), is a Professor of History at Ahmadu Bello University (ABU), Zaria. He was Head of Department and Director of the Institute for Development Research (IDR) both at ABU. He was also a one time secretary of the Historical Society of Nigeria. He was also at some point, a member of the Board of Governors of Arewa House, Kaduna. Professor Oyedele has published widely. Some of these are: "Quantity Surveying in Nigeria: NIQS at 50; and "Africa: National Unity, Stability and Development" (edited). His research interest is social and economic history, with specialisation in Urban History. He has also served as external Examiner for Undergraduate programmes of several Departments of History and has examined several Masters and Doctoral candidates across the country. He is happily married with five children.

CHAPTER 11

Forests, Ungoverned Spaces and the Challenge of Small Arms and Light Weapons Proliferation in Africa

Usman A. Tar and Yusuf Ibrahim Safana

INTRODUCTION

Forests in Africa have emerged as marginal spaces that are susceptible to capture by criminal and clandestine elements who seek shelter and hideout to carry nefarious activities. Insurgents, armed bandits and kidnappers who would normally be rejected in society find solace in forests and use them as staging posts to conduct their terror activities. Unless the state takes adequate control of those forests, they are bound to become a permanent safe haven for criminals and terrorist organizations. In Africa, the quantum of ungoverned forest is increasing. Forests in the continent are increasingly becoming bases for rebels that launch attacks, hideouts for armed robbers, thieves, kidnappers, ritual killers, bandits, cattle rustlers, camping sites for insurgents and a base from which non-state armed actors organize guerrilla attacks against the state and/or its economic interests. Typical examples are most of the Forests in Central African Republic (CAR), Democratic Republic of Congo (DRC), Southern Sudan, Kenya, Niger, Chad, Cameroon, Nigeria, etc. the ugly nature of those forests is largely associated with uncontrolled flow of illicit

---

U. A. Tar (✉)
Centre for Defence Studies and Documentation, Nigerian Defence Academy, Kaduna, Nigeria
e-mail: uatar@nda.edu.ng

Y. I. Safana
Department of Political Science, Al-Kalam University, Katsina, Nigeria

© The Author(s), under exclusive license to Springer Nature Switzerland AG 2021
U. A. Tar and C. P. Onwurah (eds.), *The Palgrave Handbook of Small Arms and Conflicts in Africa*,
https://doi.org/10.1007/978-3-030-62183-4_11

Small arms and light weapons through porous borders, forest policy inconsistency coupled with government's negligence to effectively deter criminal activities. The management of forest through proper surveillance and patrol is key to taking ownership of these forests and depriving violent elements from accessing them or challenging national security. According to Kankara (2010) the measures should be a government effort to introduce subsidiary laws in form of policies and programmes that aimed at achieving sustainable utilization of forest products and the outcome should also be economically viable, ecologically sound and socially just.

As part of many sovereign Nation states source of internally generated Revenue, African Nation states have existing forest policies, programmes and institutions that regulate the conservation of timber and non-timber products, grazing, eco-tourism, mining and indeed other human activities taking place on daily bases. Generally, forest holds both beneficial and nuisance values, depending on its structure and motive of its exploitation. The beneficial value of it has to do with legitimate economic and socio-ecological exploitation of forest resources that include grazing, conservation of Wild animals, hunting and gathering, ecological conservation, eco-tourism, scientific research and military trainings/simulation. It is against this background that nation states especially in the Sahel and Sudan Savannah regions demarcated certain areas as Forest Reserves, National Parks, Game Reserves and Grazing Reserves with the aim to manage natural resources, stimulate rainfall, reduce wind erosion, stem the tide of desertification and halt its encroachment, eco-tourism, preserve livestock, conservation of both human and natural resources, etc. The operational behaviours and conducts of the Areas are moreover, guided by policies, programmes and institutions particularly in countries like Burkina Faso, Malawi, Algeria, Democratic Republic of Congo, Tanzania, Kenya, Libya and Nigeria (*Daily Trust* 2015 February). On the other hand, the nuisance value of the forest refers to the untoward use of the forest environment by criminals, insurgents and terrorist towards advancing their nefarious activities.

Over the years, efficient management of forestlands in Africa has increasingly proved problematic due to the expanse and density of these forests coupled with lack governments' capacity to cover large swathes of forests. In effect, most of the forestlands in the continent have become centres of illicit and criminal activities such as illegal exploitation of forest resources, Human Trafficking, Drugs Trafficking, Ritual killing, Rape, Armed Robbery, Cattle Rustling, Kidnapping, Armed Banditry, Small Arms and Light Weapons Proliferation and above all centres for training and recruitment of Non-State armed Actors that launched incessant attacks to Government Institutions, Security Personnel and defenceless Communities Bordering the Areas. In fact, some of the forests have degenerated into safe havens for criminality, militancy and insurgency (Ladan 2014). The nature and criminal activities taking place in most of the forests in Cambodia, Burma, Congo DR, Nigeria, Cameroon, Chard, Niger, Liberia, Sierra Leone, etc. are clear evidence (Albert 2017;

Edeko 2011). For instance, the difficult nature of the Niger Delta regional forests in south-south part of Nigeria conferred on the militants some degree of strategic advantage over the government troops, who were not sufficiently conversant with the terrain (Okoli 2016). Besides, the forests also afforded the militants with an enabling 'political economy of war' by providing them with an enabling environment for the exploitation and expropriation of petroleum resources through oil theft and artisanal refining. This opportunistic strategy boosted the operational efficacy and sustainability of the Niger Delta militancy in the focal era. Such a strategy has since been adopted and perfected by the Boko Haram insurgents who capitalize on their stranglehold in the Sambisa forest to sustain their operations through Bomb blast, cattle rustling, hostage taking and arms smuggling (Okoli and Atelhe 2014). The Forest provides the insurgents with a space for organizing their prayer sessions, interrogating and executing abductees, producing media instruments and undertaking military trainings (Okoli 2017b: 13).

In northwestern Nigeria, Kamuku, Kuyanbana and Rugu Forests are also recently overrun by criminal elements and being converted to safe haven for criminal activities (see Fig. 11.1). As a result, forests have provided operational, logistical and technical infrastructure of Armed Bandits that lunched attacks in Katsina, Kaduna, Zamfara, Niger and some part of Niger Republic. They jointly became safe abode to Kidnappers, Rustlers, Assassins and Armed Robbers, armoury, training, detention and execution camps, landmines, artisanal bomb-making factories, military and civilian supplies, loots and livestock. Also the destination for abductees, sex slaves, and those kidnapped for ransom. The situation has so far proven a hard nut for the Nigerian troops to neutralize and challenges naturally emanate from the uncontrolled flows of Small Arms and light Weapons proliferation in the continent coupled with vast nature of the forests and security policies gaps characterized by poorly policed borderlines (Okoli 2017a). Reports have shown that out of 10 million illicit small arms in West Africa one to three million are in circulation in Nigeria (Vines 2005). Onouha (2012) has in the same vein revealed that, over 70% of the total illegal small arms in West Africa are in Nigeria, and further laments that, it is worrisome that there is regular interception of illegal small arms trafficking within and across the border by security agencies in Nigeria (Onouha 2012).

Forests and Ungoverned Spaces in Africa

Forests are ecological communities or *flora and fauna* consisting predominantly of animals, trees and other woody vegetation occupying an extensive area of land for wildlife. Forests make up one of the earth's greatest reservoirs of renewable resources. There are two types of forest regime in Africa. These are wild woods and protected forests. Wild woods are naturally growing forests that are open to primitive and unregulated exploitation while protected forests are woodlands controlled and regulated by the government (Federal Republic of Nigeria 2010; Imaseun *et al* 2013). Garg *et al* (2006), posit

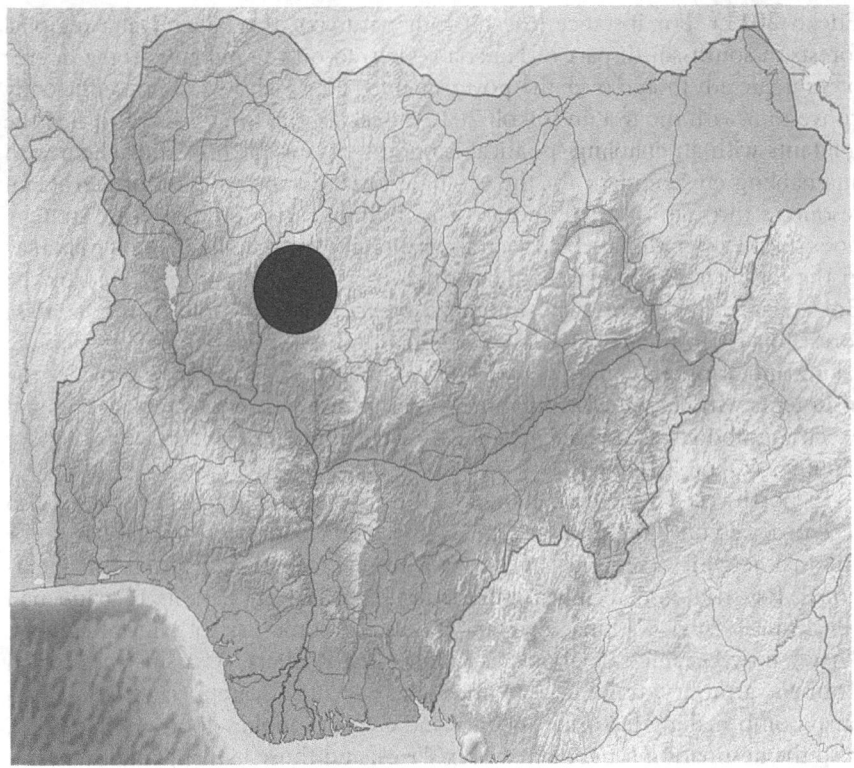

Source: Uwe Dedering - Own work, CC BY-SA 3.0, available: https://commons.wikimedia.org/w/index.php?curid=12256786

Fig. 11.1 Kamuku Forest, Nigeria: the Hideout of Armed Criminal Gangs (*Source* Uwe Dedering - Own work, CC BY-SA 3.0, available: https://commons.wikimedia.org/w/index.php?curid=12256786)

that, forests are the next most important resources of nature on earth after air and water. They essentially support life on earth by absorbing carbon dioxide and releasing oxygen, thereby maintaining balance in the gaseous atmosphere and also in completion of hydrological cycle to cause rainfall. It is based on above importance that the United Nations mandated that 25% of the surface area of every country should be conserved under permanent forest cover as the minimum ecological requirement for the socio-economic survival of the country (Bugaje 2007). In compliance to the above mandate, many countries across the globe established forests. In Africa and other part of the world however, the areas (forests) have presently become security threats. For decades the areas have been a base for insurgents to launch attacks, Hideouts for armed robbers who launch attacks on travellers/traders, hideouts for criminals and camping sites for unknown gunmen that launch attacks on local people. In DRC, various armed groups having their bases in the forests fought the national army and United Nations (UN) forces for many years. The armed groups from their forest bases ambush government troops and also launch attacks on the civilian population in the vast forests of the country. Besides, the series of armed conflict and insurgencies waged in the country have sapped the coercive machinery of the state from decisively dealing with any one of these security challenges. As a result, armed group took control of national parks which are characterized by remoteness and dense vegetation, with little or no human presence. About the only government presence in most these forests are the forest rangers who are often kicked out by the armed gangs. The armed groups also engaged in the deforestation to produce charcoal to finance their illegal activities that serve as security threat to the country. According to Okoli (2015), the Garamba forest has been a rebel stronghold for nearly two decades which has negatively affected the plants and animals that are found there (Okoli 2016). In Kenya gunmen believed to be members of Al-shabab hiding in two forests in Lamu County carried out attacks that killed 60 people, destroyed people's houses and farmlands in July 2014 from Gorji and Balasange forests (*Daily Nation* 2014).

The security question is largely influenced by high influx of illegal weapons. Usually, the demand for illegal weapons comes from bandits or rebel groups that operate outside the effective control of the central authorities. The North Caucasus, the Afghan-Pakistani frontier, portions of the Arabian Peninsula, and large swatches of Africa share this attribute.

Forest Management and Ungoverned Space in Nigeria

Forest Management literally refers to the practical application of the legal, scientific, technical and economic principles governing the forest activities. It also refers to the structure and processes by which officials and institutions acquire and exercise authority in the sustainable management of forest resources (Innes and Tikina 2017). Contemporary forest management emphasizes issues that are critical to the safety, security and sustainability of forests (Yale School of Forest and Environmental Studies, n.d). This includes measures geared towards reducing illegal and subversive activities in forested areas (cf. FAO, n.d.; Kishor and Rosenbaum 2012). Nigeria and other African Nations formulate and execute certain policies and programmes to regulate and manage the formation and operations of forest community. The process covers the overall administrative, economic, legal and social aspects and in strict sense with technical and scientific aspects, especially silviculture.

Historically, Nigeria and 37 other African nations signed the African Convention for the Conservation of Nature and Natural Resources in 1968 (Innes and Tikina 2017). This development gave rise to the formation of protected areas as Forest reserves and Game Reserves from which the present generation National Parks and grazing reserves eventually emerged. In 1988 under the Federal Ministry of Agriculture a new Policy of forestry was established. The major concerns of the policy were on forest planning, monitoring and enforcing various forest uses, including conservation and ecological uses, community uses, commercial and extractive uses. The policy succeeded in producing management plans for the different forest formations in the country (Balogun and Daramola 2014). In later time however, the forests witnessed attempts by several governments to put in place programmes that would ensure its efficient management. These include the introduction of Production of perspective plan for the period 1990–2005 and formulation of a Nigerian Forest Action Program in 1997.

Despite all the efforts, successive governments both at state and federal recorded very minimal success. Because the policies gaps have turned many forests in the country particularly in the North-west, North-east and South-South regions of Nigeria into ungoverned spaces. The areas are now controlled by non-state actors and other criminal elements that carryout notorious activities against defenceless communities, security agencies and travellers and the Government efforts to arrest the situation has been abortive. According to Ladan (2014), gaps of Nigerian forest policies, population increase and corruption in governance have favoured non-state actors to camp and conduct their activities freely inside Forests. In fact, Nigerian forestlands have been grossly under-regulated and under-policed. Apart from the various extant frameworks for forest control, the only existing mechanism for forest policing in Nigeria is the 'forest-guard system' (Federal Republic of Nigeria 2010). Forest guards are paramilitary personnel trained to oversee forest reserves and National Parks. They are expected to ensure that untoward exploitation of the forest reserves is hindered. They are also expected to forestall acts of encroachments within and around the protected areas of the forest reserves. This is in addition to monitoring and controlling human trespasses in the reserves (Odutan et al. 2013). They are however limited in training and resourcing. They are exposed to elementary paramilitary training and are equipped with more or less 'rudimentary' weapons. Moreover, they are limited in number, compared to the criminal activities that required military approach. Given the above, they are only fit for routine conventional policing that does not entail military sophistication.

Contemporary indicators of forest-based criminality in Nigeria indicate that criminals bear sophisticated modern arms and ammunitions (Okoli and Okpaleke 2014). They also operate with enhanced tactical efficiency, enabled by functional syndication. For instance, Idu and Gwagwa Forest Reserves in Federal Capital Territory (FCT) Abuja are fast becoming haven for criminals. Many residents who lived around these reserves feel insecure as the reserves become places where criminals occasionally come through the forest to attack residents of the area, especially at night (Aduge-Ani 2014). People who pass by roads are also not left out of these attacks as they are frequently waylaid by criminals who have turned the reserves into their abode. It has now become risky to live in residential areas around the reserves due to the fear of being attacked by criminals who have taken over the areas. Even when the police were called, the criminals always escape through the two forests without being caught (Aduge-Ani 2014).Similarly, Balmo Forest in Bauchi and Jigawa States is also used by Boko Haram insurgents as bases and hideouts for launching attacks. For example from their base in the forest the insurgents launched an attack on the Bauchi township prison on 7 September July, 2010 and freed 721 inmates some of who were their captured members awaiting trial (TV360 Nigeria 2014). On 5–6 July 2014, Nigerian military raided Balmo forest and discovered a stockpile of weapons at underground armouries, motorcycles, motor vehicles, communication equipment, food stuff and kitchen utensils (TV360 Nigeria 2014). During this raid, a senior member of the group believed to be the 'chief butcher' was arrested while fleeing from the intensive counter insurgency operations. Falgore forest in Kano State has over the years been used by robbers who launch attack on travellers and traders travelling to or from Jos to the commercial city of Kano (Musa 2010). In 2012, an armed group attempted to rob a filling station at Tudun Wada of the sum of N2.65 million.

Forests have acquired the coinage of 'ungoverned spaces' when they cease to be under the reach and surveillance of the state and, by extension, become a safe haven for criminals. The Kamuku National Park in Eastern Kaduna State posed security threat particularly to the people who travel along the Funtua-BirninGwari-Kagara road. This is due to frequent armed robbery attacks on defenceless travellers which resulted in many people fearing to travel through the road. The gang of armed robbers set up road blocks to rob and terrorize unfortunate travellers along this federal highway as they have ample cover to hide in the forest. Rugu Grazing reserve also in Katsina state has for many years become a camp for thieves, armed robbers and cattle rustlers who attack nearby villages and travellers that pass through the forest along the Safana-Batsari road. The robbers attack especially on Thursdays which are market days for Batsari and along Batsari-Kurfi road on Saturdays for those travelling to Yargamji market. The security threats arising from the activities of criminals in the forest have limited government forest protection and conservation efforts. Fuel wood collectors from the reserve faced serious threats from the criminals as they also rob them of their money, cooked food and cell phones. On 17 November 2014, criminals fought and burnt the trucks of the wood and charcola transporters as they realized that cutting the trees exposed them to surveillance of the security agencies. These attacks were carried out in multiple locations along the roads, at the markets on market days, and even at homes in the towns and villages. The frequency of attacks is almost every day, and the valuables lost include money, domestic animals such as cattle and sometimes food stuffs. In addition, stored grains were burnt, or destroyed and young women were taken away and used as bargaining chips for ransome. In these attacks, people also lost their lives when they fled, or attempted to defend themselves or their properties as the attackers are well armed.

Ungoverned Forests, Small Arms and Light Weapons Proliferation

Out of the 640 million small arms circulating globally, it has been estimated that 100 million are found in Africa about 30 million in sub-Saharan Africa and 8 million in West Africa, alone. African countries spent over 300 billion dollars on armed conflict between 1990 and 2005 equalling the sum of international aid that was granted to them within the same period. An estimated 79% of small arms in Africa are in the hands of civilians (Ibrahim 2003; Nte 2011). Between 2000 and 2013, there were over 40 communal clashes, sectarian violence and ethno-religious conflicts with each claiming hundreds of lives and properties, and internal displacement of women and children. Hence, problems of armed violence and proliferation of Small Arms Light Weapons (SALW) worsened by the inability of the government or unwilling to reduce organized crimes and perhaps, ensure law and order through adequate security measures in countries Forests. The major causes/sources of uncontrolled flow of arms in most African countries are as follows: The first cause is diversion from state stockpiles of arms and ammunition. The diversion of legally acquired arms by African countries is a common source of uncontrolled and illicit arms. This occurred in several forms, including the illegal sale of official arms by corrupt officials to non-state actors. For instance, official reports showed that most of the illicit small arms in Nigeria are stolen arms from the government armouries and stockpile. Others are arms brought by the security forces who returned from peace-keeping operations, the remaining guns used during the civil war, local manufactured, smuggled arms and arms from war and conflict zones in other African countries (Okoro 2007; Obuoforibo 2011; Edeko 2011; Onouha 2012; Okeke and Oji 2014). Ethiopian and Ugandan soldiers serving with the African Union Mission in Somalia (AMISOM) were accused of selling weapons from their stockpiles to traders in Somalia's illicit arms market. The conspiracy is facilitated by the poor welfare conditions of uniformed personnel, weak governance and lack of oversight over arms procurement and accountability of weapons stockpiles. Soldiers in most African countries are underpaid, and their salaries are often delayed for several months. This has reportedly led to riots, sexual violence, looting and involvement of security personnel in corrupt practices, as has been reported across Africa especially in Mali, Guinea Bissau, Sudan and South Sudan (Obi 2012; Ping 2012). In some cases, official acquisitions are either undeclared or unreported by buyers and suppliers in order to bypass extant procedures, thereby complicating official tracing and accountability. In short, poor stockpile management, and limited transparency and accountability in arms procurement, aid the illegal sale of state weapons by their custodians.

The second source of poor forest management is illicit trafficking of small arms. The number of conflicts in Africa illustrates the thriving scope of the illicit arms trade in the continent. Locally made arms and diverted stocks are traded in parallel arms markets also known as "black markets". Smuggling constitutes a lucrative source of arms trade. Being ungoverned spaces, many forests in Africa provide a cover for smuggling and other nefarious activities. In 2013, Cameroonian security forces arrested a man who was transporting 655 guns to Nigeria, and another 5400 AK-47 rifles were intercepted in Maroua, in the northern region of Cameroon (Small Arms Survey 2014). The smugglers used the thick vegetation between Nigeria-Cameroon borders to carryout their activities without detection. The collapse of the Gaddafi regime in Libya also provided a new market for illegal arms trade. Libya shares vast territories with several African countries. Based on the Small Arms Survey assessment of Libya's illicit arms market, SALW such as heavy machine guns, shoulder-fired recoilless weapons, rocket launchers, anti-tank guided missiles, man-portable air defence systems, grenade launchers and different types of rifles can be bought online (Small Arms Survey 2016).

The third cause is the poor regulation of local arms production at both industrial and artisanal levels. Several unauthorized local arms producers exist across Africa, and the limited regulation of their activities contributes to the ready availability of SALWs. In Ghana for instance, as of 2005, local gunsmiths have the capacity to produce over 200,000 weapons annually, including pistols, single- and double-barrel guns, traditional guns and pump-action shotguns. Over 60% of illegal arms in southeast Nigeria are locally made. In Mali, locally made weapons are widespread, and are used to commit crimes. This led to the enactment of law 040-50/ANLM to regulate the manufacture, use and trade in locally made weapons, and the promulgation of decree -441/P-RM for the enforcement of the law.

The fourth challenge stems from external inflow of illegal arms. Although most of the proliferated uncontrolled arms in circulation in Africa are being trafficked and transferred within the continent, weapons are initially shipped into conflict zones from outside the continent. For example, the UN Panel of Experts on Sudan identified certain countries, including Ukraine, China, Canada, Israel, Bulgaria and Slovakia, Iran and Russia as major suppliers of large stockpiles of arms and other materiel to South Sudan. Somalia and Eritrea Monitoring Group (SEMG) also noted that one of al-Shabaab's supply lines originates in Yemen, with weapons delivered through multiple receiving points on the Somali coast.

The fifth and key factor is poor management of forest and other ungoverned spaces. Most of the policies of African states on Forest management are on operational aspects of planning, monitoring, grazing, tourism, conservation and ecological uses, community uses, commercial and extractive uses. Associated with this is the worsened economic situation of most African countries in the past 20 years that further eroded their capacity to address pressing developmental challenges such as poverty, unemployment and poor infrastructure. 2016 World Bank African Poverty Report confirms that poverty levels among Africans are higher than in the 1990s. When provided, employment opportunities and infrastructure are mainly concentrated in urban centre or constituencies that are loyal to ruling political parties, thus fuelling or compounding inequality. As such, many deprived or excluded groups express grievances through the use of illicit arms against the state. The widespread poverty and limited economic opportunities in Nigeria's northeast region were exploited by Boko Haram to recruit and radicalize poor, uneducated and vulnerable young people. One of the group's recruitment strategies involved the provision of cash loans to potential recruits (Okoli and Ochim 2016). The underdevelopment of Mali's northern regions, relative to the South, has been identified as a major reason why the Tuaregs decided to bear arms against the Malian state.

Sixthly, the struggle for political power in Africa often takes violent dimensions, which are underscored by the use of arms in the competition for power. Conflicts often break out when power is manipulated to include or exclude certain individuals, communities, groups, religions or regions. Those excluded resort to extreme measures such as violent protests or armed rebellion with the use of illicit arms. Illicit weapons were used in electoral violence in various parts of the continent. A long history of the militarization of society has also contributed to the problem of SALW in Nigeria. The military has ruled for the majority of the period following independence from Britain in 1960. During the Biafran Civil War (1967–1970), large numbers of SALW passed into general circulation. Civil–military relations have worsened since the transition to civilian rule in 1999, and most of the population see the armed forces and police as coercive and corrupt.

The seventh challenge is associated with poor management of natural resources: the control, access and distribution of natural resources has triggered, sustained or exacerbated conflicts in many resource-rich countries in Africa. Illicit arms have contributed to the escalation and deadliness of such conflicts in recent years. This includes conflicts over hydrocarbons, mineral deposits or grazing land. For example, illicit arms are a key factor in the militancy and insecurity in the Niger Delta region of Nigeria, Katanga areas of DRC and the gold-rich Tibesti region in northern Chad. In fact, the gold mines in Tibesti have become a theatre of war fuelled primarily by SALW from Gaddafi-era SALW stockpiles. South Sudan led to over 2000 deaths and 34,000 displacements in Pibor in January 2012. Similarly, illicit arms have increased the spate of violent clashes and casualties between herders and farmers in Mali and Nigeria, Bororo in CAR, as well as Barara in Chad. In fact, herdsmen in Sudan and South Sudan openly display SALW, and cattle raids, involving the use of SALW, in rural areas of South Sudan led to over 2000 deaths and 34,000 displacements in January 2012.

The eighth reason has to do with the rise of violent extremism and their craving for small arms and other deadly weapons to carry out their insurgent activities. The growth and activities of religious groups that espouse radical extremist ideologies have contributed to the spread and use of illicit arms in Africa. The existence and possession of SALW by violent extremist groups have negatively impacted security in West and North Africa. The open display of SALW is a requisite element in the identity of violent extremist groups, and extremist groups appear deadlier as their access to and quantity of SALW increases. For instance, radical Tuareg militias and Al-Qaeda in the Islamic Maghreb (AQIM) in northern Mali have initiated and sustained armed insurgencies because of their access to and use of SALW. Islamist militancy has garnered the most attention as a consequence of the violent attacks of Boko Haram, (AQIM), Al-Shabaab and other similar groups operating across Africa. Based on United Nations Development Program (UNDP) estimates, 24,771 people were killed and 5507 wounded between 2011 and 2015, with most of the fatalities recorded in Nigeria and Somalia.

Security Implications of Ungoverned Forests and Illicit SALW Proliferation

African countries have experienced both direct and indirect consequential impacts of poorly managed forests and illicit weapons proliferation (Olaniyan 2018). Thousands of people, both civilians and combatants are killed or injured on a daily basis in the continent. The threat and use of small arms has undermined development, prevented the delivery of humanitarian and economic aid and contributions to refugee and internally displaced persons (IDP) populations in Africa (Okoro 2007; Ayissi and Sall 2005). Since the end of military rule in 1999, fighting in several regions of the country has claimed thousands of lives. Plateau State in central Nigeria has been particularly badly affected (Vines 2005).Thus, the key consequences of the poorly managed forests and SALWs Proliferation are discussed as follows.

Cattle Rustling and Rural Banditry

Cattle rustling has been defined to mean forceful stealing of cattle from their legal owners. Precisely, it means the planning, organizing, attempting, aiding or supporting the stealing of livestock by any person from any country or community. Cattle rusl123 is characterised by the use of dangerous weapons and/or violence (Olaniyan and Yahaya 2016). In addition, cattle rustlers are emboldened by inefficient forest management and porous borders allow for easy circulation of stolen cattle, arms trade and the weak governance that indicates government's lack of capacity and authority to curb the practice. The extent and seriousness of cattle rustling in Africa has largely been attributed to the availability of illicit Small Arms and Light Weapons (SALW). Reports by the Regional Center on Small Arms (2018) identify a number of drivers of proliferation of illicit SALWs: porous borders, sociocultural perceptions, weak legislations and inadequate presence of state security personnel in the African forests. As a result of these factors, there were heightened incidences of cattle rustling and criminality in pastoral areas along the border regions of Kenya, Uganda, South Sudan and Ethiopia, Nigeria, Niger, Cameroon,

Mali and Chad. The incessant attacks by cattle rustlers on herding communities tend to set them at loggerheads with their ecological neighbours (native farmers). In some instances, the farmers are arbitrarily accused by the herders as the culprit and masterminds of their cattle raids. This engenders ill-feelings that exacerbate the already conflictive herder/farmer inter-group relations, leading ultimately to vicious circle of violence. The situation goes with repercussions that do not portend well for the collective wellbeing of the herding communities. It creates a sense of insecurity which has the capacity to hamper the productivity of the herding enterprise. The loss of cattle to rustlers means depletion of household income and communal resource of the herding community (Gueye 2013). Cattle rustling in Kenya is common in eastern, north eastern and North Rift regions (Baringo, Samburu, Isiolo, West Pokot, Turkana and Marsabit). In Ethiopia and South Sudan, it is predominantly common in the southern parts of these countries. In Uganda, it is more prevalent in north-eastern region, commonly referred to as the Karamoja cluster. In Somalia, the prolonged nature of armed conflicts has overshadowed any other form of conflict, albeit livestock theft continues to pose serious threats to security in the Southern and Northern regions of the country. Livestock exports account for up to 40% of the Growth Domestic Product (GDP) of Somalia. This means that livestock theft has become very lucrative given the ready market for meat abroad and within the region. Thus, cattle rustling in Africa are largely associated with a number of predisposing and causative factors, among which are the following:

a. Proliferation of SALW and ammunition in Africa that placed enormous weaponry in the hands of criminal elements some of whom perpetrate cattle rustling.
b. Terrorism and armed rebellion in the sub-Saharan Africa have promoted cattle rustling as a franchise dedicated to funding of group struggles.
c. The remoteness of grazing fields makes effective surveillance and policing of cattle herd problematic.
d. The itinerant pattern of grazing in Africa predisposes cattle rustling.
e. Absence of effective legal framework for mandatory cattle identification and/or registration has obstructed the fight against cattle rustling.
f. The porous nature of inter-state borderlines in Africa makes trans-border cattle rustling conducive and thriving.
g. The criminal impunity of the people, arising from the apparent lethargy of the government to deter crime through drastic penalty News24 (2013) and Gueye (2013).

Herdsmen Militancy

Herdsmen militancy is defined as heightened hostility and criminality exhibited by herdsmen—especially against farmers—who enjoy access of SALWs under the guise of 'self-defence' but eventually use the small arms to engage in nefarious activities. It is essentially a forest-based violence driven by acute knowledge of the rural and forested terrain, underlying economic motivations and, in some instances, clan rivalry. It is the latest complication in the farmer–herder crisis in Nigeria. It is essentially a post-2000s development that precipitated around 2015/16. Hitherto, there had been cases of 'low-intensity' skirmishes or clashes between native farming communities and pastoral herdsmen over competitive land use—especially over claims of farmland and rangeland trespasses. Such clashes were largely restricted to peak planting and harvesting periods in northern Nigeria. At worst, they involved the use of rudimentary arms and ammunition such as dane guns, machetes, spears and arrows and amulets. In the mid-2010s, however, there was a dramatic turn in the farmer–herder crisis in Nigeria. This is evident in the advent of organized and militarized onslaughts orchestrated by migrant herdsmen—or their mercenaries—on native farming communities, under the pretext of the farmers' unwarranted provocation. A typical instance of this aggression takes the form of a well-coordinated village raid, conducted with warlike brutality, lethality and destructiveness. Modern, sophisticated weapons such as AK-47s are employed to inflict maximum collateral destruction on the targeted community. In some cases, whole villages are razed, looted and dislodged in an overnight or day-long campaign of obscene violence.

Transformation of the farmer–herder crisis into a pattern of agrarian militancy reflects the contemporary dynamics of armed conflict in Nigeria in the present era of heightened arms proliferation and criminal impunity. Since its escalation in 2016, herdsmen militancy has prospectively competed with the Boko Haram insurgency as the dominant national security challenge in contemporary Nigeria. The militancy in Nigeria festers in a volatile, precarious public security ambience characterized by communal strife, arms proliferation, rural banditry, and insurgency. The perpetrators of this violence plan their attacks from their improvised camps in the forest from where they proceed to hit their target communities. This pattern of rural violence has been pervasive in the North-central region of Nigeria with Benue, Nasarawa and Plateau States as veritable critical flash-beds (Okoli and Atelhe 2014; Okoli 2015; Okoli and Okpaleke 2014). Contemporary indicators of herdsmen militancy are fast degenerating into a national emergency virtually witnessed in all the geo-political zones of Nigeria. It has led to mass killing and human displacements in places likeAgatu and Guma in Benue state, Obi and Lafia East in Nasarawa state and BarkinLadi and Wase in Plateau state (Okoli and Ayokhai 2015).

The prevalence of herdsmen militancy is not restricted to Nigeria. It also occurs in varying degrees in other African states, such as CAR and Mali. Global Terrorism Index (GTI 2015), identifies such militancy as the fourth deadliest instance of organized terror in the world. The Report indicates that Africa is a critical flashpoint of the occurrence. According to the Report, causalities associated with herdsmen militancy in the various States of Nigeria rose from

80 in 2012 to 2013 period to 1229 in 2014 alone (GTI 2015: 49). The above threat has led to dire socioeconomic and humanitarian consequences, including loss of livelihoods, population displacement, loss of life and property and decline in rural productivity and agricultural output. Loss of livelihoods in turn exposes the affected population to material hardships, exemplified in hunger, disease and malnutrition.

The humanitarian consequences of herdsmen militancy point to the fact that it is a threat to human security and, by extension, to the national security of Nigeria. By displacing farmers from their productive bases, it has led to decrease in agricultural productivity and output, to the detriment of food security. These episodic occurrences of herdsmen militancy in Nigeria have also worsened rural insecurity in the country. To ward off possible attacks by herdsmen, local farming communities have often mobilized for self-defence through the instrumentality of self-help vigilantism. The activities of the vigilantes vis-à-vis the herdsmen have more often than not led to multiple reprisals in a manner that plunges the affected communities into a circle of mutual violence and vendetta. In the report of the committee set up to find solutions to banditry in Zamfara State, supervised by the erstwhile Inspector-General of Police, Mohammed Abubakar, reported a total of 6319 deaths including women and children between June 2011 and May 2019 in the State. Additionally, an estimated 4983 women were widowed, 25,050 children orphaned and 190,340 others internally displaced between June 2011 and May 2019 in Zamfara State. In Katsina State, over 2000 people have been killed, 500 communities destroyed and over 33,000 people displaced. Further reports also revealed that over 10,000 cattle were lost, while 2688 hectares of farmlands and 10,000 houses destroyed within 2011 and mid-2018 in Zamfara State. Also, the State recorded the loss of 147,800 vehicles and motorcycles from June 2011 to May 2019. In November 2019, an estimated 4000 people were also internally displaced in Shiroro LGA of Niger State alone.

Kidnapping and Hostage-Taking for Ransom

Kidnapping for ransom is a prevalent pattern of violent crime in Nigeria and other African States. Perpetrators of the act have resorted to use SALWs and established base camps in the forests which double as a sanctuary for safe keeping of their abductees as they negotiate for ransom. Mercantile kidnapping has been most prevalent in the south eastern and South-South parts of Nigeria. In these regions, kidnapped persons are often held hostage in the forests by their abductors while ransom negotiations or 'tactical suspense' lasts. Between 2008 and 2010, the Nigeria Police Force recorded 887 cases across the country (Action on Armed Violence 2013). Statistics appear to support the views of analyst. In December 2009, Police Affairs Minister, disclosed that 512 cases of kidnapping had been recorded from January 2008 to June 2009 against 353 recorded in 2008. Rundown of the statistics indicates that Abia State led the pack with a total of 110 kidnapping incidents: Imo: 58,109 arrests, 41 prosecution and one is dead, Delta recorded 44 kidnap cases, 43 releases, 27 arrests, 31 prosecuted and one death, and Akwa Ibom recorded 40 kidnap cases, 418 arrests and 11 prosecutions. The report added that between July/September 2008 and July 2009, over 600 million was lost to kidnappers. But beyond statistics being available, it is a known fact the most kidnap cases are never reported to the police authority for the fear of murder of the victims hence most families prefer to pay ransom to losing one of its own. For instance, in Kano, N80 million ransom was allegedly paid to kidnappers for the release of a Kano-based multi-millionaire businessman, without a recourse to the police authorities; an industrialist in Nnewi paid 70 million to regain his freedom from his captors; another multi-millionaire businessman was kidnapped and released after he allegedly paid a ransom without recourse from the police. In the same vein, kidnapping for ransom increased from 290 fatalities in 2017 to 358 in 2018, mainly in Bauchi, Benue, Cross River, Ebonyi, FCT, Jigawa, Kaduna, Kebbi and Kwara. Kaduna maintained its status as the most dangerous state in respect to kidnapping, with a record of 23 deaths in 15 incidents. Abuja-Kaduna expressway and Birnin Gwari LGA via Kamuku National Park also remained hotspots for kidnapping activities (see Fig. 11.1). A special military operation in the zone, Operation Whirl Punch, was not able to eradicate kidnapping in the state. It, however, curbed the ease of operation and the frequency of abductions. Between September and October, 2018, about 30 kidnappers were killed by soldiers in Kamuku forest, Kidandan, Unguwan Bilya, Sofa and UnguwanNakuli areas along Abuja-Kaduna Expressway. The victims of high-profile kidnap included foreigners, prominent politicians, traditional rulers and religious leaders.

Highway Robbery

Robbers stage their attacks from their base camps in the adjoining forests and in turn, make their way back into the forests after an operation. This threat is often experienced by many commuters using Nigerian roads. Armed robbery is a prevailing social phenomenon that negatively affects the lives and social functioning of a significant number of people in contemporary Nigerian society. It involves stealing, during which force and violence or the threat of violence are employed. In Nigerian daily newspaper reports, Television news headlines and radio announcements have shown that the activities of armed robbers are increasing at an alarming rate. Both the rich and the poor are always in a perpetual state of fear because nobody really knows where and when they will strike. Meanwhile, there are some hotspots where the incidence of highway robbery frequently takes place—for instance, Katari and Jere axis along Kaduna-Bwari-Abuja road. One of such spots is Abuja-Lokoja road where several passengers and travellers have been robbed or/and injured or/and killed by suspected highway robbers. A pathetic case was the incident of highway robbery that happened recently where many victim passengers were crushed to death by an oncoming trailer, which was on top speed while trying to avoid being pinned down by the robbers. The ugly incident happened when the victim passengers were asked by the robbers to lie face down, and many of the victims never suspected that the trailer approaching would crush them. The Okene-Lokoja, Akwanga-Nasarawa Eggon, Benin-Ore and Zaria-Funtua highways have been notorious for such attacks. The highway robbers operate with wartime arms and commando-like brutality. In most incidents, they kill and maim people in their scores. The rampant cases of armed robbery on the Abuja-Kaduna expressway have forced some regular travellers on that route to defect to the use of rail services to commute to and from their destinations in order to safeguard themselves. The killing and shooting of people most especially the youth by armed robbers reduce the size of the Nigerian working population. This automatically led to the loss of human resources (affects human resources). Many resources are channelled to physical and psychological treatment of victims of armed robbery. The resources that would have been used to stimulate the growth of other sectors of economy are also invested in security to enable the security agents curtail the activities of robbery. Another significant effect of armed robbery is on the reduction of the rate or level of development. As a result of high prevalence incidences of armed robbery in Nigeria, many foreign investors are afraid of committing their resources to operate in industries that would employ many millions of the unemployed Nigerians. This consequently retards the development of the Nigerian society.

Insurgency and Militancy

Nigeria is currently bedevilled with profound threat of violent extremism, armed militancy and terrorism, especially in the North-Eastern part of the country. Since 2011, the country has witnessed the heightened vulnerability of terror, criminality and instability. The disheartening phenomena include, but not limited to the devastation and annihilations of several towns, villages, churches, mosques, police stations, schools and other public institutions with Improvised Explosive Devices (IED) bombs planted and small arms and light weapons (SALW) by the Boko Haram insurgents in Niger, Bornu, Adamawa, Kano, Bauchi, FCT Abuja, Kaduna, Plateau and Yobe states, respectively (Okoli and Iortyer 2014; Otegwu 2015).

The proliferation of these small arms and light weapons and the new emergent trend in armed violence in Nigeria put to question the efficacy and total commitment of the Nigerian government in combating the menace. The alarming rate of SALW spread poses a serious threat and challenge to Nigeria"s internal security. However, the outbreak of Islamic extremism and domestic terrorism in the North-East Nigeria, has unleashed the growing audacity of the Boko Haram sect. With easy access to small arms and improvised explosive devices, Boko Haram has intensified its attack on both civilian and military targets in Nigeria. Key incidents include their attacks on the Eagle Square, Abuja during Nigeria's 50th Independence Day anniversary on 1 October,

2010 in which no fewer than 12 people were killed; the Nyanya Motor Park bombing on 14 April 2014 which claimed more than 75 lives and injured several dozen others; the bombing of the UN Building in the FCT Abuja; and abduction of about 216 girls of in Chibok, Borno State the next day leaving the country in a state of insecurity. Small arms is the game changer in the increaasing audacity of the Boko Haram sect: if small arms could be knocked off the scale, it would be easy for Nigeria's counterinsurgency forces to win the battle against militant insurgency in the Northeast region.

Conclusion

Security challenges, including the proliferation of small arms and light weapons have been a global concern for a very long time, however, the negative impacts of this and other security threats can be largely minimized and their effects on both individuals and the country reduced. The war against SALWs—as well as their illegal manufacture, sale and transfer—can only be close to success when sincere and responsible leadership, responsible followership, coupled with realistic policies and strategies that reflect the needs and aspirations of the citizens become characteristics of the country. Though it is very difficult to completely eradicate the illegal proliferation of SALWs in Africa, especially because of the very nature of the continent with regard to tribal conflict, militancy, secessions, insurgency, armed banditry, etc (Onuoha 2011; Onouha 2012).

Moreover, ungoverned forests have appeared to be the major security challenge to African States. Most of defence and national security policies of African nations are silent over the measures on criminal activities taking place in the forest. This by implication has favoured non-state actors that evidently challenged the sovereignty of the African nations. Through porous borders that mostly situated around forests is now control by criminals that engaged on treasonable activities. In Nigeria Boko Haram insurgent, Fulani Militia, militancy in the Niger Delta, Smugglers that supply arms uses forest as a safe home, Al-Shabbab extremist Islamic sect in Somali and Kenya also resides and lunch attacks from forest. Therefore, effective legislations and programmess need to be put in place to amend forest policy and SALWs proliferation in the continent.

References

Action on Armed Violence. (2013). *The Violent Road: An Overview of Armed Violence in Nigeria*. London: Action on Armed Violence.

Aduge-Ani, D. (2014). FCT Forest Reserves Becoming Haven for CriminalActivities www.leadership.ng/…/fct-forest-reserve-becoming-haven-forcriminal-activities Accessed 10 october 2019.

Albert, I. O. (2017). *Beyond Nigeria's Sambisa: Forests, Insurgency and Counterinsurgency in Africa*. Ibadan: Ibadan University Press.

Ayissi, A., & Sall, I. (eds) (2005). Combating the Proliferation of Small Arms and Light Weapons in West Africa: Handbook for the Training of Armed and Security Forces, Geneva: United Nations Institute of Disarmament Research (UNIDIR).
Balogun, I. I., & Daramola, A. O. (2014). Mainstreaming Socio-economic Realities into National Forest Policy. *JORIND*, *12*(2), 28–38.
Bugaje, U. (2007). Policy Document for Democratic Transformation of Katsina State Action Congress (AC) Gubernatorial Campaign Organization. Katsina: Action Congress Party.
Chuma-Okoro, H. (2011). Proliferation of Small Arms and Light Weapons in Nigeria: Legal Implications. *Law and Security in Nigeria*. https://nairametrics.com/wp-content/uploads/2013/02/legal-implication-of-small-arm1.pdf. Accessed 19 July 2020.
Daily Nation. (2014). Military Jets Hunts Down Attackers in Lamu Forest. www.nation.co/< e/news/military. Accessed 10 october 2019.
Daily Trust. (2015 February). Investigation: 322 Herders Killed, 60,000 Cattle Rustled in 2013. *Daily Trust* online at http://dailytrust.info/likked-60,000-cattle-rustled-in-2013. Accessed 19 July 2020.
Edeko, S. E. (2011). The Proliferation of Small Arms and Light Weapons in Africa: A Case Study of the Niger Delta in Nigeria. *Sacha Journal of Environmental Studies*, *1*(2), 55–80.
FAO. (n.d.) *Forest Governance Assessment and Monitoring*. Retrieved from: http://www.fao.org/forestry/governance/monitoring/en/ (link is external).
Federal Republic of Nigeria. (2010). *Fourth National Biodiversity Report*. Nigeria: Abuja.
Garg, S. K., Garg, R., & Garg, R. (2006). Environmental Science and Ecological Studies, Khanna Publishers, New Delhi, India.
Global Terrorism Index. (GTI, 2015). *Measuring and Understanding the Impact of Terrorism*. New York: Institute for Economics and Peace. Available https://reliefweb.int/sites/reliefweb.int/files/resources/2015%20Global%20Terrorism%20Index%20Report_0_0.pdf. Accessed on 20 August 2020.
Gueye, A. B. (2013). Organized crime in the Gambia, Guinea-Bissau and Senegal. In E.E.O. Alemika (Ed.), *The Impact of Organized Crime on Governance in West Africa*. Abuja: Friedrich-Ebert-Stiftung. (Abuja Regional Office, Nigeria).
Ibrahim, M. (2003). Democracy and the Menace of small Arms of Small Arms proliferation in Nigeria, Lagos: Centre for Democracy andDevelopment.
Imaseun, O. I. Oshodi, J. N., & Onyeobi, T. U. S. (2013). Protected Areas of Environmental Sustainability in Nigeria. *Journal of Applied Sciences, Environment Management*, *17*(1), 53–58.
Innes, J. L., & Tikina, A. V. (2017). *Sustainable forest management: From concept to practice*. London: Routledge.
Kankara, A. I. (2010). "Forests as Catalyst for Industrial Growth: Their Distribution and Disappearances in Katsina State http://www.taskarmammanshata.blogspot.com.
Kishor, N., & Rosenbaum, K. (2012). *Assessing and monitoring forest governance: A user's guide to a diagnostic tool*. Washington, DC: Program on Forests (PROFOR).
Ladan, S. I. (2014). An Appraisal of the Status and Consequence of Encroaching Into Forest Reserves in Katsina Urban Environment, Katsina State. *Danmarna International Journal of Multi-Disciplinary Studies*, *5*(1), 91–101.
Musa, H. (2010). Nigeria: Kano Traders Protest Withdrawal of Army onTrade Route. www.allafrica.com/stories/20100620252.htm. Accessed 2 october 2018.

News24. (2013, October) Rebel kill 44 in South Sudan Cattle Raid. http://www.news24.com.ng/Africa/News/Rebels-kill-41-south-sudan-cattle-raid-20131021-2. Accessed 24 March 2016.

Nte, N. D. (2011a) The Changing Patterns of Small and Light Weapons (SALW) Proliferation and the Challenges of National Security inNigeria. *Global Journal of Africa Studies 1*(1), 5–23.

Nte, N. D. (2011b). The Changing Patterns of Small and Light Weapons (SALW) Proliferation and the Challenges of National Security in Nigeria. *Global Journal of Africa Studies, 1*(1), 523.

Obi, C (2012). *Conflict and Peace in West Africa*. Uppsala, Sweden: The Nordic Africa Institute.

Obuoforibo, G. I. (2011). *Small Arms and Light Weapons (SALW) Proliferation and Instability in the Niger Delta: An analysis of the Disarmament, Demobilization, and Reintegration (ddr) Process* (p. 49). SPECIAL ISSUE: THE NIGER DELTA.

Oduntan, O. O., Soaga, J. A. O., Akinyemi, A. F., & Ojo, S. O. (2013). Human Activities, Pressure and Its Threat on Forest Reserves in Yewa division of Ogun State, Nigeria. *Journal of Environmental Research and Management, 4*(15), 0260–0267.

Okere, V. O., & Oji, R. O. (2014). The Nigerian State and the Proliferation of Small Arms and Light Weapons in the Northern part of Nigeria. *Journal of Educational and Social Research, 4*(1), 41–58.

Okoli, A. C. (2015). Pastoral Transhumance and Dynamics of Social Conflict in Nasarawa state, North-central Nigeria. Paper prepared for Center for Democracy and Development (CDD), Abuja, Nigeria.

Okoli, A. C. (2016). *Petroleum Pipeline Vandalism and National Security in Nigeria, 2001–2012*. Ph.D. thesis submitted to the School of Post-graduate Studies, Nigerian Defence Academy, Kaduna (August).

Okoli, A. C. (2017a). Nigeria: Volunteer Vigilantism and Counter-insurgency in the North—East. *Conflict Studies Quarterly, 20*, 34–55.

Okoli, A. C. (2017b). *Cows, Cash and Terror: How Cattle Rustling Proceeds Fuel BokoHaram Insurgency in Nigeria*. Paper presented at International Policy Dialogue Conference on money, security, and democratic governance in Africa, organized by CODESRIA and UNOWAS on October 1th to 23rd, 2017 at Blu Radisson Hotel, Bamako, Mali.

Okoli A. C., & Atelhe, G. A. (2014). Nomads Against Natives: A Political Ecology of Herder/Farmer Conflicts in Nasarawa state, Nigeria. *American Journal of Contemporary Research, 4*(2), 76–88.

Okoli, A. C., & Ayokhai, F. E. F. (2015). Insecurity and Identity Policies: A Study of Fulani Militancy in North Central Nigeria in the Fourth Republic. *Studies in Politics and Society, 3*(1), 288–142.

Okoli, A. C., & Iortyer, P. T. (2014). Terrorism and Humanization Crisis in Nigeria: Insights from the Boko Haram insurgency. Global Journal of human social science (F: Political Science) 14(1:1.0), 39–50.

Okoli, A. C., & Ochim, F. I. (2016). Forestlands and National Security in Nigeria: A Threat-Import Analysis. *IIARD International Journal of Political and Administrative Studies, 2*(2), 43–53.

Okoli, A. C., & Okpaleke, F. N. (2014). Cattle Rustling and the Dialectics of Security in Northern Nigeria. *International Journal of Liberal Arts and Social Science, 2*(1), 109–117.

Okoro, V. U. (2007). Proliferation of Small Arms and Light Weapons in West Africa: Implications for Sub-Regional Security: Army Command and General Staff Coll Fort Leavenworthks.

Olaniyan, A. (2018). Foliage and Violence: Interrogating Forests as a Security Threat in Nigeria. *African Security Review,* 27(1).

Olaniyan, A., & Yahaya, A. (2016). Cows, Bandits and Violent Conflicts: Understanding Cattle Rustling in Northern Nigeria. *African Spectrum,* 3, 93–105.

Onuoha, F. C. (2011). Small Arms and Light Weapons Proliferation and Human Security in Nigeria. *Conflict Trends,* (1), 50–56.

Onouha, F. C. (2012). Proliferation of Small Arms and Light Weapons in West Africa: Implications for Sub-Regional Security: Army Command and General Staff College Fort Leavenworth's.

Otegwu, I. O. (2015). *Insurgency in West Africans: A critical assessment of federal government response to the Boko Haram insurgency in Nigeria (2009–2013).* Ph.D. Thesis submitted to the Post-graduate school, Ahmadu Bello University, Zaria (September).

Ping, J. (2012). African Union Report on Guinea-Bissau, Mali, Sudan and South Sudan. *Pan-African News Wire,* April 25, 2012.

Small Arms Survey. (2014). *Small Arms Survey 2014: Women and Guns.* Geneva: Small Arms Survey. Available http://www.smallarmssurvey.org/?small-arms-survey-2. Accessed on 19 July 2020.

Small Arms Survey. (2016). Measuring Illicit Arms Flow: Somalia. Research Notes, Number 61, October 2016. http://www.smallarmssurvey.org/fileadmin/docs/H-ResearchNotes/SAS-Research-Note-61.pdf.

Small Arms Survey. (2018). *Global Firearms Holdings Database. Geneva: Small Arms Survey.* Available http://www.smallarmssurvey.org/weapons-andmarkets/tools/global-firearms-holdings.html. Accessed on 10 July 2020.

Stohl, R. J., & Hagedorn, E. J. (2010). Stopping the Destructive Spread of Small Arms: How Small Arms and Light Weapons Proliferation Undermines Security and Development. Centre for American Progress.

Stohl, R., & Tutle, D. (2009). The Challenges of Small Arms and Light Weapons in Africa. *Conflict Trends Issue,* 1, 2009.

Stott, N. (2016). Small Arms Proliferation in Southern Africa: Reducing the Impact of real Weapons of Mass Destruction.

TV360Nigeria. (2014). More Weapons Discovered in Balmo Forest Raid Army. www.tv360nigeria.com/more-weapons-Accessed 2 october 2014.

Vines, A. (2005). "Combating Light Weapons Proliferation in West Africa".

Yale School of forestry and Environmental Studies. (n.d.). Forest Governance Monitoring; https://globalforestatlas.yale.edu/forest-governance.

Usman A. Tar is Professor of Political Science and Defence Studies, and Endowed Chair of Defence and Security Studies (26RC Endowment) at the Nigerian Defence Academy. He is the Director of the Academy's flagship Centre for Defence Studies and Documentation, and a member of the Board of Social Science Research Council's African Peacebuidling Network (SSRC/APN), New York, USA. He was formerly, Associate Research Fellow at Africa Centre for Peace and Conflict Studies, University of Bradford, UK. He authored several books including *The Politics of Neoliberal Democracy in Africa* (London/New York: I.B. Tauris, 2009); *Globalization in*

Africa: Perspectives on Development, Security and the Environment (Lanham, MD, Lexington Books, 2016); *New Architecture of Regional Security in Africa* (Lanham, MD, Lexington Books, 2020); and *Routledge Handbook of Counterterrorism and Counterinsurgency in Africa* (London, Routledge, 2020). Prof Tar has consulted or consults for the United Nations Development Programme (UNDP), Nigeria; *Konrad Adaneur Stiftung* (KAS, German Development Fund); and the Westminster Foundation for Democracy (WFD), Nigeria. Prof Tar is a member of Nigeria's Presidential Think Tank on National Defence and Security, and served as a member of Nigeria's Presidential Committee to review the national defence policy in 2015.

Yusuf Ibrahim Safana is an adjunct lecturer at Department of Political Science, Al-Kalam University, Katsina, Nigeria. He is also a senior staff with State Universal Education Board, Katsina, Nigeria. He is currently a Desk Officer Global Partnership for Education, Safana Local Government Education Authority. He has NCE Islamic/Social Studies, B.Sc. Political Science, M.Sc. Defence and Strategic Studies and undergoing a Ph.D. on international Relations under the Department of Political Science, Federal University, Dutsin-Ma. His research focuses on forest management and National Security. He is interested on Rural Violence and Environmental Security Studies. He is a member of numerous professional bodies and one time a resource person to Katsina State Ministry of Education on School Records Keeping. He held different academic and administrative positions in the Safana Local Government Education Authority. He is happily married with children.

CHAPTER 12

"Resource Curse" and "Resource Wars" and the Proliferation of Small Arms in Africa

Otoabasi Akpan and Ubong Essien Umoh

INTRODUCTION

Natural resource wealth holds prospects of both blessings and curse for a people. The United States of America and a few countries in Europe are countries that have derived lots of blessings from natural resources but not so for majority of developing nations with natural resources. Indeed, for such countries with abundant natural resources like Australia, Canada and the United States of America, they have even outgrown these resources and are no longer dependent on them overwhelmingly unlike their counterparts in the developing world. For the developing countries with natural resources, it is observed that majority depends on them for practically all their socioeconomic needs. For these categories of countries, natural resource discoveries have been found to be, more often than not, a challenge, rather than a blessing. This is a typical situation of resource curse which in turn has resulted in resource conflicts and wars necessitating excessive use of Small Arms and Light Weapons (SALWs). In other words, resource curse is presented as the cause and resource wars and proliferation of SALWs as the effects. This cause–effect phenomenon

O. Akpan (✉)
Department of History and International Studies, Akwa Ibom State University, Uyo, Nigeria

U. E. Umoh
Department of History and International Studies, University of Uyo, Uyo, Nigeria
e-mail: ubongumoh@uniuyo.edu.ng

has indeed led to a vicious cycle where resource curse produces resource wars and resource wars produce proliferation of SALWs and proliferation of SALWs produces resource curse. In Africa, which has a third of the natural resources of the world and especially in the sub-Saharan Africa region where natural wealth dominates a staggering figure of 50% of total wealth, it is highly paradoxical that the resources do not constitute natural resource blessing but natural resources curse with a high risk of contracting the "Dutch Disease," resource wars and the use of SALWs to sustain the vicious cycle of resource curse and resource wars.

In this chapter, the issues of resource curse, resource wars and the proliferation of SALWs in Africa are explored alongside the causative factors.

Paradoxical Considerations and Analysis of "Resource Curse" Phenomenon

Natural resource-rich countries are endowed with abundant natural wealth, but most of them advertise poverty, unemployment, and inequality (Seers 1969). Africa is a continent that has experienced the paradox such that instead of being the most developed continent of the world on account of being the most naturally endowed continent of the world, it is the most poverty-unemployment-and inequality-ridden continent of the world with no meaningful development in any sector of its economy.

This state of affairs stands two logical considerations on the head. The first concerns the natural capacity and promise of economic geography for a people with natural resource endowment. From the very beginning the promise of economic geography was that natural resource-rich countries were the ones to be powerful and developed. This much has been argued thus by Thorvaldur Gylfason (2011: 7):

> Economic geography is no longer what it used to be. For a long time, economic geographers studied raw materials and their distribution around the world and assigned crucial roles to natural resource wealth and raw materials, their ownership, and trade routes. Ownership of those important resources tended to be equated with economic and political strength. The European powers' scramble for Africa that began in 1881 – this was when France occupied Tunis with Germany's consent – was mainly a scramble for the great continent's resources. The slave trade from the mid-15th century onward can be viewed the same way. It wasn't long before it became clear that natural resources do not always confer widely shared benefits on the people from whose territory they are extracted. Even after the end of colonial rule in Africa and elsewhere, many resource-abundant countries – Congo is a case point – remained in dire straits. Countries that discovered their natural resources after independence, such as Nigeria, also do not make rapid economic progress for reasons that seem to be related in part to poor management of their natural resources. In the same vein, Russia's former president and now Prime Minister Vladimir Putin has said "our country is rich, but our people are poor." Even so, some natural-resource-rich countries

have made impressive progress. Botswana, Chile, and Mauritius will be singled out in what follows. Meanwhile, several resource-poor countries have managed to become rich, including Hong Kong, Japan, and Singapore.

These three countries in Asia without natural resources—Hong Kong, Japan, and Singapore—have outclassed Africa with abundance of natural resources. This implies that the new economic geography emphasizes other factors other than natural resources in the growth and development of a people.

The second logical consideration concerns still the role of old economic geography in today's advanced economies that started out with the use of, and dependence on, natural resources which evidently turned out to be resource blessing rather than curse. This is a contrasting position in the cases of such European and American countries as Finland, Sweden, Norway, Australia, Canada, and the United States of America. Without doubt, these countries used natural resources to promote economic growth and development and consequentially industrialization. Take Norway as example. As argued by Ragnar Torvik (2011), Norway was one of the poorest countries in Europe at the beginning of the twentieth century but the narratives changed such that at the end of that century she was one of the richest countries not only in Europe but also in the world. In his words, Torvik underlines the rare and inconvertible facts in the following way:

> ...today, Norway is one of the richest countries in the world. This remarkable transition has been driven by the exploitation of natural resources. It started with fish, timber, and minerals, continued with hydroelectric power, and since the 1970s has developed oil and natural gas as key sectors. It is obvious that natural resources have been a blessing for Norway. Economic historians...have pointed out that looking back in time, resource abundance has been a main driver of growth rather than the opposite.

These contrasting positions on economic geography and indeed economic history as well take us the need to examine the properties of resource curse.

There exists extensive literature on the phenomenon of resource curse. To start with, resource curse concerns the state of paradox in which countries with superfluous quantity and quality of non-renewable natural resources experience stagnant economic growth and economic contraction. Ross (1999) calls this sad state of affairs *resource curse*, Karl (1999) calls it *paradox of plenty*, Auty (2001) calls it *natural resource curse*, Akpan (2003) calls it *tragedy at mid-day*, Collier and Hoeffler (1998, 2004); Elbadawi and Sambanis (2000); Lujala et al. (2005) all call it *the spoils of nature*, and Umoh (2010) calls it *crisis of abundance*. Indeed, a whole body of literature called the "resource curse literature" has been developed by scholars in peace and conflict studies to analyze the relationship between natural resources and conflicts in natural resource-endowed states. The resource curse literature "argues that heavy dependence on natural resources can be detrimental to state capacity not only in the case of oil, but also for other energy resources such as natural gas and, indeed, for mineral resources" (de Soysa and Neumayer 2007: 205).

A number of factors have been stressed by scholars as responsible for resource curse. They range from the sublime to the ridiculous. In this Chapter, three critical ones would be examined and they are Dutch disease, absence of tangible capital, and lack of functional institutions.

Dutch Disease

Dutch disease owes its origin to economic developments in the Netherlands as a result of discovery of oil which made it to depend overwhelmingly on it to the neglect of other sources of revenue and the consequences of this decision. The Netherland condition found its way into economics where it is described as the apparent causal relationship between the increase in the economic development of a specific sector and a decline in other sectors. Put differently, the Dutch disease is a phenomenon of large commodity exports leading to an appreciation of the real exchange rate, which in turn slows productivity growth in other sectors of the economy. This in effect weakens competitiveness and holds back economic diversification thus leaving the economy highly dependent on the natural resource sectors. On account of the fact that the Dutch disease makes tradable goods less competitive in the international markets, productivity suffers alongside manufacturing capabilities of the countries that are victims of the disease.

The term was coined by *The Economist Magazine* in 1977 to describe the decline of the manufacturing sector of the Netherland's economy after the discovery of the large Groningen natural gas field in 1959. The country began to depend absolutely on huge profits from gas and neglected other sectors of the economy. That means that it was not able to compete against other countries' exports. Even though its currency appreciated substantially, the appreciated level of the currency had the effect of hurting the Dutch economy and the red flag in form of recession was hoisted in the country. In a sentence, the boom on gas exports had detrimental effects in other sectors of the economy and invited economic recession and hence the Dutch disease.

There is hardly any resource-rich country in Africa that has not been seriously affected by the Dutch disease. As a result of overdependence on natural resources which are very cheap and rather lootable, the traditional agricultural sector of African economies is neglected; same with the budding manufacturing sector. As a consequence, the state of underdevelopment persists in the continent. Additionally, many of African economies had either been threatened by recession or had experienced recession once and had come out of it. Those which have not had recession yet are on the verge of experiencing it as a result of over reliance on natural resources with their high rate of volatility.

Absence of Tangible Capital

For an economy to grow and develop capital is very essential. The centrality of capital can be seen in its analysis by Otoabasi Akpan (2019: 148) in the following way:

> Capital is the pre-condition of wealth and, indeed, the principal part of the economic whole. For the past three centuries or more, it is one subject that has fascinated thinkers and philosophers. The fundamental role of capital in the affairs of men and nations cannot be overemphasized. Such phrases as *capital* importance, *capital* punishment and *capital* city of a country shows capital as the nerve centre of everything. Indeed, for governments, capital (city) functions as the seat of government or administrative centre of a region; capital letters begin sentences and names; for an offence or charge, capital offence leads to death penalty, and for the human beings, capital is the location of the organs for procreation. In all particulars, *capital* is essential in human endeavours and without it nothing can succeed excellently.

In point of fact, capital is one of the missing gaps in the aspirations of the Third World to develop. Walt W. Rostow (1960), the American Economic Historian, emphasized it in his famous book, *The Stages of Economic Growth*. Rostow argued among other things that developing economies need capital to grow and develop. Providing a rather penetrating analysis of the role of capital in development and the consequences of its absence, especially in the Third World is Hernando de Soto (2000: 5), who concluded in his book, *The Mystery of Capital*, that:

> The major stumbling block that keeps the rest of the world from benefiting from capitalism is its inability to produce capital. Capital is the force that raises productivity of labour and creates the wealth of nations. It is the lifeblood of the capitalist system, the foundation of progress, and the one thing that the poor countries of the world cannot seem to produce for themselves, no matter how eagerly their people engage in all the other activities that characterize a capitalist economy.

African states with mineral resources have not been able to transform the natural resources that they have in abundance into other fundamental capital(s) for diversification of their economies and development. Thorvaldur Gylfason (2011: 10) has examined six of the several different types of capital that are necessary for growth and development especially in resource-rich nations. These are:

1. Real Capital: saving and investment to build up *real capital* – physical infrastructure, roads and bridges, factories, machinery, equipment, and such;
2. Human Capital: education, training, health care, and social security to build up *human capital*, a better and more productive work force;

3. Foreign Capital: exports and imports of goods, services, and capital to build up *foreign capital*, serving among other purpose to supplement domestic capital;
4. Social Capital: democracy, freedom, equality and honesty – that is, absence of corruption – to build up *social capital*, to strengthen the social fabric, the glue that helps hold the economic system together and keep it in good running order;
5. Financial Capital: economic stability with low inflation to build up *financial capital*, or liquidity, which lubricates the wheels of the economic system and helps keep it running smoothly; and
6. Natural Capital: manufacturing and service industries that permit diversification of the national economy away from excessive reliance on low-skill-intensive primary production, including agriculture, based on *natural capital*.

These six types of capital are quite essential and the most essential one, which the developing states lack in quality and quantity, is the human capital. As Thorvaldur Gylfason (2011: 19) aptly remarks "more and better education at all levels of schooling is conducive to diversification, because a good education attracts workers to well-paying jobs in services and manufacturing. Education and diversification go hand in hand." This is an incontrovertible fact.

Lack of Functional Institutions

A number of works point out that it is the differences in the quality of institutions that "are at the root of the diverging growth paths of successful and less successful resource rich countries" (Gelb 2011: 66). Mehlum et al. (2006) argues that the quality of institutions is critical in determining whether countries are affected by resource curse. Therefore, natural resources can only have a negative impact on growth performance of nations with inferior institutions. Lipschitz (2011) emphasizes that the existence of natural resources tend to distort the allocation of talents and that especially in states with weak institutions; talents tend to shift out of private entrepreneurial areas into more lucrative rent-seeking sectors, with harmful implications for sustainable growth. Drawing typical examples from strong and reliable property rights, Lipschitz contends that these rights can foster financial sector development thus allowing the financial system to play a more active and strategic role in moderating resources to help build small-and-medium-size enterprises in the non-resource-rich sectors of the economy. This is a case of functional diversification of the economy which resource curse acts as constraint. Finally, Lipschitz asserts that checks and balances and greater transparency in managing natural resource revenues can help tremendously in counteracting the misallocation of talent into unproductive activities.

On the question of checks and balances, Collier (2007) argues persuasively that without effective checks and balances on power, competition for natural resource rents can make democracies, for instance, malfunction with dire consequences. This is because competition for rent, unlike taxation, does not invite public scrutiny and financial accountability and to that extent, encourages the emergence of patronage politics. Research by Acemoglu et al. (2003) on long-term growth has significantly emphasized the strategic importance of institutions and the implication is that without effective institutions in natural resource-rich nations, resource curse is the end state.

This is also the conclusion of Mehlum and others (2006), and Robinson et al. (2006). They all argue that resource-rich countries need not experience lower growth as long as they are equally endowed with good institutions. For them, whether natural resource abundance increases or decreases economic growth depends more on the institutional architecture. Augustine Kwasi Fosu and Anthony Owusu Gyapong (2011) have examined the effects of effective institutions and governance on Nigeria and Botswana and concluded that "Botswana displays good institutions that gave rise to ... relatively high governance measures ... Nigeria stands in stark contrast with Botswana on all governance measures..." (Fosu and Gyapong 2011: 261). Both Nigeria and Botswana earn substantial revenues from natural resource wealth: oil in Nigeria and diamond in Botswana. Oil has provided more than 90% of foreign exchange earnings and about 80% of Nigeria's budgetary revenues. In the case of Botswana, diamonds have provided about 80% of export earnings and about 40% of the government's revenues.

The cases of Finland, Sweden, Norway, Australia, Canada, and the United States of America have been touted as clear examples of the relationship between effective institutions and economic growth through natural resources. This had led to one hypothesis that an eventual change in the growth effect of natural resources has been found on account of the fact that countries with different degrees of institutional quality industrialized at different times (Torvik 2011). Arising out of this hypothesis, Acemoglu et al. (2001, 2002) point out that those countries that industrialized first were the ones that had the best quality of institutions by stating that: "...the countries that industrialized early had an institutional apparatus in place that prevented the negative growth effects of resources, while those that first utilized their resources at a later stage did not have such institutions in place." It is little wonder to note that Karl (1997) had since the twentieth century warned that a resource discovery is worse for any country that has not yet developed its institutions. Outside Botswana, all resource-rich countries in Africa are affected by resource curse and are limping in pains, reflected principally in resource wars and the proliferation of SALWs to compete for "the spoils of nature."

Resource Wars

Resource wars are straightforwardly wars waged on account of resources by combatants who may be government agents or merchants of violence for the control of locations, production, distribution and marketing of natural resources. Resource wars are unique in that they involve the control of natural resources by armed groups. There is a body of research on the triggers and consequences of resource wars. According to Michael Ross (2003) one of the most surprising and important findings is that natural resources play a significant role in triggering, prolonging and financing these conflicts. To be sure, no monocausal approach can sufficiently explain any cause of war, as wars by their nature occur as a result of complex sets of events. However, the point to note is that natural resources facilitate occurrences of resource wars, especially in resource-rich countries that lack effective institutions for governance and are burdened by challenges of ethnicity, racism, poverty, and inequality.

Most scholars in conflict studies argue that natural resource wealth is a major cause of civil war (Berdal and Malone 2000; Klare 2001; Ballentine and Sherman 2003; Collier et al. 2003; Fearon and Latin 2003; Ross 2003, 2004; Fearon 2005; de Soysa and Neumayer 2007). Two models are often used to explain why natural resource is a major determinant of civil war. First is the "looting rebels" model and the second is the "state capacity model" (de Soysa and Neumayer 2007; Braithwaite 2010; Sobek 2010; Hendrix 2010). The looting rebels model concerns a situation where resource wealth provides finance and motive for rebels to fight governments whereas the state capacity model argues that the political Dutch disease weakens state capacity and makes governments easy prey for social actors. According to Indra de Soysa and Eric Neumayer (2007: 202):

> Natural-resource-dependent countries have a lower level of bureaucratic capacity than their level of per capita income would suggest and, in extreme cases, suffer from socioeconomic and political breakdown. This could be either because dependence on natural resources weakens states or because natural resource abundance allows states to become rentier economies, with few incentives for the ruling elites to develop the broader economy as would rulers of natural-resource-poor economies that are forced to provide broad public goods in order to raise productivity. Natural resource abundance might induce leaders to foster corruption, patronage and rent-seeking behaviour rather than effectiveness, efficiency, and competence.

Natural resources are triggers for secessionist rebellions for at least three reasons:

(i) They are not found in all regions of a country, but in a particular region of it;
(ii) The question of ownership arises as to who owns it - the whole nation or the lucky region; and
(iii) If it is managed by the central government, are the proceeds evenly distributed with special consideration to the lucky region?

On account of these reasons, the World Bank Policy Research Report (2003: 60) argues that: "statistically, secessionist rebellions are considerably more likely if the country has valuable natural resources, with oil being particularly potent." Typical examples include Cabinda in Angola, Katanga in the DR Congo, Aceh and West Papua in Indonesia, Scotland in Great Britain, and the Niger Delta in Nigeria.

There is hardly a resource-rich country in Africa that has not had experiences of resource wars. Nigeria, for example, has since the 1990s been having resource wars in its Niger Delta region (Akpan 2011; Akpan and Umoh 2016). A glance at Table 12.1 compiled by Michael Ross (2003) on wars linked to resource wealth between 1990 and 2002, shows that of the 16 resource-related wars, 9 were in Africa.

The above data do not tell the entire story. It is contended that these wars in Africa show complex and worrisome trends. It cannot be anything else when the number of armed conflicts outside Africa had dropped by half between 1992 and 2001 but not so in Africa as captured in Table 12.2. Conversely, resource wars in Africa had become extremely complex and rather severe. In 1996, for instance, the Congo Democratic Republic engaged itself in Africa's Second World War, which claimed 6 million of its citizens (Akpan 2013a). Though ethnicity, unstable government, and poverty played some roles, natural resource wealth was implicated in this very war.

The economic profile of the DR Congo is both impressive and unimpressive. It is impressive in the sense that on account of its resources, mostly natural resources, it is easily the richest country in the world and it is unimpressive in the fact that the years of armed conflicts have killed more than six million people and instituted warlordism, leaving the country as one of the poorest states in the world. The value of the mineral resources of the DR Congo is worth about $30 trillion which is in excess of the GDP of the American continent (Akpan 2013a). Minerals which are available in the country in superfluous quality and quantity include cadmium, copper, cobalt, industrial and gem-quality diamonds, gold, silver, zinc, tin, manganese, radium, uranium, coal, bauxite, iron ore, cassiterite, platinum, germanium (a brittle element used as a semi-conductor), and palladium (a metallic element used as a catalyst and in alloys), columbotantalite (a natural oxide), wolframite (a source of tungsten), cassiterite, beryl (a mineral containing beryllium and aluminum), and monazite (a phosphate of the cerium metals and thorium). It is instructive to note that mineral resources in the DR Congo are found in almost all regions.

Most of these minerals are strategic and critical to the industrial economies. Take cobalt for example. It has both industrial and military uses. Used as superalloys, cobalt is very critical in the making of jet engine parts. It is also used in magnetic alloys and in cutting and wear-resistant materials such as cemented carbides. In the chemical industry, cobalt is used as catalysts for petroleum and chemical processing, drying agents for paints and inks, ground coat for porcelain enamels, decolorizers for glass and ceramics, and pigments for ceramics, paints, and plastics. Cobalt therefore is critical to the establishment of many industries and creation of millions of jobs. DR Congo has over 80% of the world's reserves of cobalt. The country also has 70% of the world's coltan and about 50% of the world's diamond reserves. Coltan is a mineral used in the manufacture of mobile phones. DR Congo is the second largest producer of colobine-tantalite which is a key raw material in the manufacture of satellite and telecommunications products.

Sadly, these minerals, as typical lootable wealth, are largely looted by warlords. Since independence, they have been providing powerful incentives for irredentist and secessionist conflicts. These local problems have always been fuelled by industrial nations and neighboring states; each aspiring for a share in the Kinshasha scramble (Akpan 2013a). These states are the US, Russia, Britain, Japan, India, Brazil, China, France, Rwanda, Uganda, and South Africa. Regardless of the unfortunate state of the country's mining business, it still accounts for 70% of the national budget and about 80% of total exports.

By the time that the DR Congo achieved independence in 1960, it was obviously the second most industrialized economy in Africa after South Africa. It had a productive mining sector and a growing agricultural sector but resource wars have consigned it to the lowest rank in the continent. Its second position has been taken over by Nigeria. In the agricultural sector, the DR Congo has a lot of export crops. They include coffee, rubber, cotton, cocoa, sugar, tea, palm oil, plantain and groundnuts. DR Congo is the fourth largest producer of rubber in the world. Food crops include corn, cassava, legumes, plantain and groundnuts. There are forest products that are of economic value in the DR Congo. They include timber of various shapes, sizes and quality. The country's forest reserves cover about 60% of the DR Congo and constitute the largest in Africa.

Nigeria is another typical case of a country in Africa that has been experiencing resource wars. Between 1967 and 1970 the country had a civil war which, *strictu* sensu, was Africa's First World War with more than 1 million deaths. The war was partly triggered by oil-resource in the Niger Delta region of the country. Africa's world wars refer to wars in Africa in which major powers in all the continents of the world are either direct or indirect participants.

A number of major natural resources that are incentives for resource wars in Africa have been identified (Ross 2003). They are largely oil and hard-rock minerals and they include coltan, diamonds, gold, gemstone, timber, and some categories of drugs. In the Table 12.1, eight of the resource wars were triggered by gemstones, six by oil and gas, five by illicit drugs, and three by timber. Diamonds have had the rare notoriety of being designated as *blood diamonds* and, *conflict diamonds*. Excepting Botswana which has diamonds and an excellent record of using same for economic growth and development, diamonds elsewhere in Africa have been conflict resource causing civil wars and the destructions of lives and property. In both Sierra Leone and Angola,

Table 12.1 Civil wars linked to resource wealth, 1990–2002

Country	Duration	Resource s
Afghanistan	1978–2001	Gems, opium
Angola	1975–2002?	Oil, diamonds
Angola (Cabinda)	1975–	Oil
Cambodia	1978–97	Timber, gems
Colombia	1984–	Oil, gold, coca
Congo, Rep. of	1997	Oil
Congo, Dem. Rep. of	1996–97, 1998–	Copper, coltan, diamonds, gold, cobalt
Indonesia (Aceh)	1975–	Natural gas
Indonesia (West Papua)	1969	Copper, gold
Liberia	1989–96	Timber, diamonds, iron, palm oil, cocoa, coffee, marijuana, rubber, gold
Morocco	1975–	Phosphates, oil
Myanmar	1949–	Timber, tin, gems, opium
Papua New Guinea	1988–	Copper, gold
Peru	1980–95	Coca
Sierra Leone	1991–2000	Diamonds
Sudan	1983	Oil

Source Michael Ross. The Natural Resource Curse: How Wealth can make you Poor. In I. Bannon and P. Collier. Natural Resources and Violent Conflicts: Options and Actions. Washington, DC: The World Bank, 2003: 18

diamonds were conflict commodities that were used to finance all manners of rebellions and wars (Collier 2000a, b).

Table 12.2 Armed conflicts in Africa and the rest of the world, 1989–2001

Year	Africa	Rest of World
1989	14	33
1990	17	32
1991	17	34
1992	15	40
1993	11	35
1994	13	29
1995	9	26
1996	14	22
1997	14	20
1998	15	22
1999	16	21
2000	15	19
2001	14	20

Source Michael Ross. The Natural Resource Curse: How Wealth can make you Poor. In I. Bannon and P. Collier. *Natural Resources and Violent Conflicts: Options and Actions.* Washington, DC: The World Bank, 2003: 18

A number of factors responsible for this state of affairs have been examined by scholars. Four of such economic effects concern a reduction in economic growth, increase in poverty, insatiable appetite for natural resources by advanced countries and resources as finances to rebellion. Already, it has been pointed out that resource-dependent states grow rather slowly than resource-poor states. It has also been pointed out that resource-dependent economies are struck with Dutch disease. The implications of all of these are economic stagnation or depression and in an atmosphere of economic stagnation there is a reduction in growth and development. Taken together, there is a high likelihood that youth unemployment would occur and because youth are by nature restless, reckless and careless, they would engage in protest, rebellion and insurgencies which in most cases snowball into full-scale resource wars.

Closely related to the above is the issue of poverty. Poverty is highly implicated in the occurrence of resource wars in Africa. On account of overdependence on natural resources and consequential occurrence of Dutch disease, most resource-dependent economies experience absolute poverty. Absolute poverty takes place where a population or a section of a population is, at most, able to meet only its bare subsistence essentials of food, clothing and shelter to maintain minimum levels of living (Todaro and Smith 2004). In some resource-rich states like Nigeria, Angola, Gabon, and Sierra Leone, the level of poverty is far beyond absolute; many do not have food to eat or shelter to accommodate themselves. Indeed, many have been forced to migrate to many countries to eke out a living. In situations such as these, many believe that the revenues from natural resources should ordinarily meet their needs and where they do not, they opt to engage in resource wars in order to have a piece of the cake.

It is observed that many advanced countries scramble for natural resources in Africa and this provokes resource wars. A typical example is the Sudanese case. The civil war in Sudan which eventually led to its dismemberment was equally fuelled by China and the United States of America. China is all over Africa investing in minerals, especially critical minerals and many other advanced countries do not want China to benefit from the spoils alone or to have advantage over them. Overall, in many mineral-rich economies in Africa, there exists small wars (Osakwe et al. 2016) that are rather proxy in nature and the overall aim is to control the resources.

With regard to the finances of rebels in natural resources-rich countries, it has been found out that as they do not control territories on a permanent basis and unlike governments cannot tax the population, they rely extensively on funding from illicit control of the natural resources. This point has been well sharpened by Ian Bannon and Paul Collier (2003: 4) thus:

> Unless a successful rebel organization is bankrolled by another country or an extensive and willing diaspora, it must generate income by operating some business activity alongside its military operation. The question then becomes the type of business activity in which a rebel group is likely to be competitive.

Unfortunately, the obvious answer is that the rebel groups' only competitive advantage is their large capacity for organized violence and mayhem. Since, for military reasons, rebel groups tend to be based in rural areas, they turn to business activities such as various forms of extortion and the exploitation of primary commodities. Where rural areas produce primary commodities with high economic rents, generally for export, it is a relatively simple matter for rebel groups to run an extortion racket, levying protection charges on producers or carrying out some of the trades themselves. The best-known example are the conflict diamonds of Angola and Sierra Leone. Alluvial diamonds are particularly well suited as a business line for rebels because the technology is so simple that the group can directly enter the extraction process and diamonds are a small, high-value commodity that is easy to hide and transport and has a readily accessible international market.

Interestingly, rebel groups have devised new methods of sustaining themselves in locations of natural resources that require extensive and expensive technology for exploitation of the resources. The rebel groups simply target the multinational oligopolies by threatening their expensive equipment and infrastructure such as oil and gas pipeline and their expatriates through kidnapping and murder. In return they are paid handsomely to ward them off. An additional observation and, indeed, incentive is that the rebel groups often raise finance by selling the advance rights to the extraction of minerals that they do not control, but that they intend to control. Called booty futures by Michael Ross, it is a method of financing the tools of war through the sale of extraction rights (Bannon and Collier 2003).

All of these uncanny tactics and strategies by rebel groups prolong resource wars, make peace efforts elusive, and inspire both governments and the rebel groups to engage in procurement of weapons. The end state of these efforts is the proliferation of SALWs.

"Resource Curse" and "Resource Wars" as Triggers of the Proliferation of SALWs in Africa

SALWs are without doubt instruments of security, conflicts, conflict resolution, crimes, and foreign policies (Akpan 2011; Akpan and Afaha 2017). As instruments of security, they are used by the security forces of states to maintain law and order and to defend the territorial integrity of a state when threatened; as instruments of conflicts, SALWs are used by parties to conflicts to seek competitive advantage; as instruments of conflict resolution, SALWs are equally used by governments and violence entrepreneurs to convey advantages in relation to their adversaries or challengers; as instruments of crimes, SALWs are fitting weapons to easily commit various types of crimes; and as instruments of foreign policies, they are used by nations for diplomatic leverage, diplomatic blackmail, and tools for peace keeping operations.

In most cases, SALWs are used for the wrong purposes and mostly by warlords to perpetrate crimes. Although many nations are menaced by availability of SALWs, resource-rich nations experience exponential numbers of SALWs because of the roles they can play in conflicts. The 1997 Report of the United Nations Panel of Government Experts on Small Arms provides the most widely accepted definition of SALWs. According to the Panel:

- The category of small arms includes: revolvers and self-loading pistols, rifles and carbines, assault rifles, sub-machine guns and light machine guns.
- Light weapons include heavy machine guns, hand-held under-barrel and mounted grenade launchers, portable anti-tank and anti-aircraft guns, recoilless rifles, portable launchers of anti-tank missile and rocket systems, portable launchers of anti-aircraft missile systems, and mortars of calibers less than 100mn.

On a more fundamental note, small arms are seen as kinetic projectile firearms designed to be used by individuals. Arms of these categories include revolvers and pistol (handguns), machine pistols, shotguns, rifles, carbines, submachine guns, personal defense weapons, assault rifles, battle rifles, designated marksman rifles, sniper rifles, squad automatic weapons, and light machine guns. On the other hand, Light weapons are, generally speaking, either crew-served kinetic weapons or any infantry weapons firing explosive munitions. These categories of guns include anti-materiel rifles, general-purpose machine guns, medium machine guns, heavy machine guns, grenades, rifle grenades, grenade launchers, under-slung grenade launchers, automatic grenade launchers, anti-tank rifles, recoilless rifles, rocket-propelled grenades, man-portable anti-tank missiles, man-portable air-defense systems, and mortars of a caliber of less than 100 mm. Small arms and Light Weapons also include ammunition, explosives, hand grenades, land mines, and any other man-portable weapons not listed already.

Small arms are not just smaller and less powerful variants of major weapons system—they are a distinct class of weapons with unique properties and advantages that distinguish them from other types of weapons by their low capital, availability, portability, minimum infrastructure and training, concealability, lethalness, and suitability. In an environment which is strange to even the basic issues of human security, SALWs have institutionalized human insecurity.

As to the number of SALWs in Africa, no one or organization can pronounce with exactitude the actual number. Figures range from 100 million. All engage in what Okon Uya (2005) calls *numbers game*. Regardless, in one estimate it is indicated that the world has about 640 million SALWs and that an estimated 100 million are located in Africa, 30 million of which are found in sub-Saharan Africa (Method 2018). But Otoabasi Akpan has asserted that the world has in excess of 1 trillion SALWs and Africa has in excess of 50 million of these weapons (Akpan 2013a). According to the UN, only 3% of these arms are used by governments, military or paramilitary forces (Naim 2003); the rest are in illegal hands especially in conflict-prone areas. Outside outright sales and military programs, SALWs are stretched through covert and "gray market" channels especially in Africa (Akpan 2007). Their low cost nature, portability, ease of maintenance, and operations make them perfect instruments for use by insurgents, criminal bands, separatist groups, and other sub-and non-state actors. In fact, the increasing sophistication and lethality of some of these weapons have given these social actors a firepower that often exceed that of any nation's security operatives.

With such weapons capable of firing up to 300 rounds a minute, one individual can threaten a society in no small measures. Besides, the simple nature of SALWs can be demonstrated with the use of AK 47. The assault rifle has about 30 moving parts and is so simple that it can be used and maintained by teenagers. Most of these weapons require few hours of training for users to be highly skilled in using them. Consequently, the phenomenon of child soldiers in Africa is structured on SALWs.

Conflicts and SALWs have turned the continent of Africa into one risky region. The risk index for the inhabitants, visitors, governments, and investors is extremely high especially in the natural resources endowed areas. For the multinational companies that extract minerals, the prospects of jumbo profits have made them to endure the risk. Even so, most of them have engaged the services of Private Military Companies (PMCs) to provide them with security thus constituting themselves into governments within governments in the region (Akpan 2013a).

This situation takes place in almost all resource-rich states in Africa because they are all fragile or quasi state burdened by the weak state insecurity dilemma. The nature of insecurity dilemma confronting weak states is largely a function of the structural conditions of their existence. They lack the most fundamental of state attributes which concern the existence of effective institutions, a monopoly on the instruments of violence and consensus on the idea of the state (Jackson 2007).

Essentially, one enduring issue triggering the weak state dilemma in Africa has to do with oil (Akpan 2003). Chaudhry (1997); Karl (1997); Herbst (2000); Klare (2001); Synder (2002); Fearon and Latin (2003); Ross (2004); Smith (2004); de Soysa and Neumayer (2007) and Lujala and Thieme (2007), also argue that oil is generally regarded as the resource most directly associated with the weak state capacity and the "resource curse" phenomenon discussed earlier. Indra de Soysa and Eric Neumayer (2007: 202) forcefully emphasize that:

> ...dependence on natural resources weakens states ... because natural resource abundance allows states to become rentier economies, with few incentives for the ruling elites to develop the broader economy as would rulers of natural-resource-poor economies that are forced to provide broad public goods in order

to raise productivity. Natural resource abundance might induce leaders to foster corruption, patronage and rent-seeking behaviour rather than effectiveness, efficiency, and competence.

Utilizing the analyses of Collier and Hoeffler (1998, 2004) and Fearon and Latin (2003) and Fearon (2005) on the subject matter of the relationship between natural resources and the weak state syndrome, de Soysa and Neumayer (2007: 204) further state that:

> ...state strength is weaker under conditions of oil extraction ... because of "political Dutch disease" working through negative effects of resource wealth on state institutions. Apparently, oil, unlike most other resources, has special, corrosive effects on state institutions, allowing patterns of patronage and weak political control. Without strong institutions, the base of taxation remains small and focused on natural resource extraction, the provision of public goods is low and the state's ability to weather temporary economic and political shocks is weak.

Anybody with a nodding acquaintance of Africa's political economy, especially the political economy of mineral-rich states, will readily admit that the countries in the continent have weak capacity for resource extraction particularly in the key area of taxation. Added to the woes of the country is the phenomenon of weak institutions.

Conclusion

In this chapter, the challenges of resource curse, resource wars, and proliferations of SALWs in Africa have been examined and it has been documented that states that are rich in natural resources have not benefited from those resources because of the peculiar manner that the resources have been managed. Poor management of the resources and especially lack of effective institutions to oversee the management of the resources are the reasons that the mineral-rich states in Africa are not experiencing resource blessings.

It has been demonstrated in the chapter that the resources in themselves do not lead to resource curse but its management. Evidences have been drawn from the management of natural resources in Finland, Australia, Canada, Norway, and the United States of America to aid the conclusion that resource curse is not a natural state of affairs but a contrived one by the resource-rich states.

On account of the mismanagement of the resources, Africa is confronted with deadly resource wars and the free use of SALWs. The impact of the wars and the proliferations of SALWs in the continent, especially in natural wealth countries has been examined. It is contended in the chapter that resource curse provokes a vicious cycle of resource curse and the foundation leading to resource wars, the use of SALWs and eventually strengthening the base of the resource curse phenomenon, which started the vicious cycle in the first place.

REFERENCES

Acemoglu, D., Johnson, S., & Robinson, J. A. (2001). The Colonial Origins of Comparative Development: An Empirical Investigation. *American Economic Review, 91,* 1369–1401.

Acemoglu, D., Johnson, S., Robinson, J. A., & Thaicharoen, Y. (2003). Institutional Causes, Macroeconomic Symptoms: Volatility, Crises and Growth. *Journal of Monetary Economics, 50,* 49–123.

Akpan, O. (2003). "Tragedy at Midday: Oil and Underdevelopment of Nigeria." In Akpan O. E. 2003. The Art and Science of Politics Essays in Honour of Alhaji Ghali Umar Na'Abba. Port Harcourt. Footsteps Publications.

Akpan, O. E. (2007). *Globalization and Arms Trafficking: The Role of Small Arms and Light Weapons (SALWs) in Conflicts and Crimes in Africa.* Paper Presented at the Historical Monthly Seminar of the Department of History and International Studies, University of Uyo, Uyo, on August 31.

Akpan, O. (2011). *The Niger Delta and the Peace Plan.* Ibadan: Spectrum Books.

Akpan O. (2013a). *An Introduction to the Modern Gulf of Guinea: People, History, Political Economy & Strategic Future.*

Akpan O. (2013b). "The Sovereign Wealth Funds (SWFs) and International Political Economy." In Akpan, O. E. and A. Ekpe (eds). 2013. *Readings in International Political Economy.* Yaounde: Book House: 154–177.

Akpan, O. (2019). "Building a Stable Society Through Infrastructures For Peace." *Lecture Delivered at the University of Uyo During the Official Launching of PayForphan Foundation and Amathy Peace Pheremones Foundation* on September 20.

Akpan, O., & Afaha, P. (2017). "Globalization and Arms Trafficking: The Role of Small Arms and Light Weapons (SALWs) in Conflicts and Crimes in Africa". Abuja Journal of Humanities, Vol. 5. *Num, 3,* 191–205.

Akpan, O., & Umoh, U. E. (2016). Nigeria: State Capacity and Insurgency in the Niger Delta Since the 1990s. *Conflict Studies Quarterly,* (14), 92–110.

Auty, R. M. (2001). *Resource Abundance and Economic Development. UNU/WIDER Studies in Development Economics.* Oxford: Oxford University Press.

Ballentine, K., & Sherman, J. (2003). *The Political Economy of Armed Conflict: Beyond Greed and Grievance.* Boulder, CO: Lynne Rienner.

Bannon, I., & Collier, P. (2003). "Natural Resources and Conflict: What We Can Do." In Bannon, I. and P. Collier (eds). 2003. *Natural Resources and Violent Conflict: Options and Actions.* Washington DC: The World Bank: 1–16.

Berdal, M., & Malone, D. M. (Eds.). (2000). *Greed & Grievance: Economic Agendas in Civil Wars.* Boulder Co: Lynne Rienner.

Braithwaite, A. (2010). Resisting Infection: How State Capacity Conditions Conflict Contagion. *Journal of Peace Research, 47*(3), 311–319.

Chaudhry, K. A. (1997). *The Price of Wealth: Economies and Institutions in the Middle East.* Ithaca, New York: Cornell University Press.

Collier, P. (2000a). "Rebellion as Quasi-Criminal Activity." *Journal of Conflict Resolution, 44*(6), 839–853.

Collier, P. (2000b). "Doing Well Out of War." In M. Berdal and D. Malone (eds). *Greed and Grievance: Economic Agendas in Civil Wars.* Boulder, CO: Lynne Rienner.

Collier, P. (2007). *The Bottom Billiom: Why the Poorest Country are Failing and What Can Be Done About It*. London: Oxford University Press.
Collier, P., et al. (2000). *Breaking the Conflict Trap: Civil War and Development Policy*. London: Oxford University Press.
Collier, P., & Hoeffler, A. (1998). On the Economic Causes of Civil War. *Oxford Economic Papers*, 50(4), 563–573.
Collier, P., & Hoeffler, A. (2004). Greed and Grievance in Civil War. *Oxford Economic Papers*, 56(4), 563–595.
Collier, P., Elliott, V. L., Hegre, H., Hoeffler, A., Reynal-Querol, M., & Sambanis, N. (2003). *Breaking the Conflict Trap: Civil War and Development Policy*. Washington, DC: The World Bank and Oxford University Press.
de Soysa, I., & Neumayer, E. (2007). Resource Wealth and the Risk of Civil War Onset: Results from a New Dataset of Natural Resource Rents, 1970–1999. *Journal of the Peace Science Society*, 24(3), 201–218.
Elbadawi, I., & Sambanis, N. (2000). *How Much War Will We See? Estimating the Incidence of Civil War in 161 Countries*. Washington, DC: World Bank.
Fearon, J. D. (2005). Primary Commodities Exports and Civil War. *Journal of Conflict Resolution*, 49(4), 483–507.
Fearon, J. D., & Latin, D. D. (2003). Ethnicity, Insurgency, and Civil War. *American Political Science Review*, 97(1), 1–16.
Fosu, A. K., & Gyapong, A. O. (2011). "Terms of Trade and Growth of Resource Economies: Contrasting Evidence from Two African Countries." In Areki, R, Gylfason, T & A. Sy (eds). 2011. *Beyond the Curse: Policies to Harness the Power of Natural Resources* (pp. 257–272). Washington DC: International Monetary Fund, Publication Services.
Gelb, A. (2011). "Economic Diversification in Resource-Rich Countries." In Areki, R, Gylfason, T & A. Sy (eds). 2011. *Beyond the Curse: Policies to Harness the Power of Natural Resources* (pp. 55–78). Washington DC: International Monetary Fund, Publication Services.
Gylfason, T. (2011). "Natural Resources Endowment: A Mixed Blessing?" In Areki, R, Gylfason, T & A. Sy (eds). 2011. *Beyond the Curse: Policies to Harness the Power of Natural Resources* (pp. 7–33). Washington, DC: International Monetary Fund, Publication Services.
Hendrix, C. S. (2010). Measuring State Capacity: Theoretical and Empirical Implications for the Study of Civil Conflict. *Journal of Peace Research*, 49(3), 273–285.
Herbst, J. (2000). Economic Incentives, Natural Resources and Conflict in Africa. *Journal of African Economies*, 9(3), 270–294.
Jackson, R. (2007). "Regime Security." In A. Collins (Ed.). *Contemporary Security Studies*. London: Oxford University Press.
Karl, T. (1997). *The Paradox of Plenty: Oil Booms and Petro-States*. Berkeley: CA: University of California Press.
Karl, T. L. (1999). The Perils of the Petro-State: Reflections on the Paradox of Plenty. *Journal of International Affairs*, 53(1), 31–48.
Klare, M. T. (2001). *Resource Wars: The New Landscape of Global Conflict*. New York: Henry Holt and Company.
Lipschitz, L. (2011). "Overview." In Areki, R, Gylfason, T & A. Sy (Eds.), *Beyond the Curse: Policies to Harness the Power of Natural Resources* (pp. 1–4). Washington DC: International Monetary Fund, Publication Services.

Lujala, P. J. K., & Thieme, N. (2007). Fighting Over Oil: Introducing a New Dataset. *Journal of Peace Science Society, 24*(3), 239–256.

Lujala, P., Gleditsch, N. P., & Gilmore, E. (2005). A Diamond Curse? Civil War and a Lootable Resource. *Journal of Conflict Resolution, 49*(4), 538–562.

Mehlum, H., Moene, K., & Torvik, R. (2006). Institutions and Resource Curse. *Economic Journal, 116*, 1–20.

Mehlum, H., Moene, K., & Torvik, R. (2006). Cursed by Resources or Institutions? *World Economy, 29*, 1117–1131.

Method, S. (2018). "Stemming the Tide: African Leadership in Small Arms and Light Weapons Control." *African Security*, August 6: 5.

Naim, M. (2003, January/February). Five Wars We're Losing: Why Governments Can't Stop the Illegal Trade in Drugs, Arms, Ideas, People and Money. *Foreign Policy*, 28–37.

Osakwe, C. C. C., Akpan, O., & Umoh, U. E. (2016). Globalization and "Small Wars" in Africa: The Case of Niger Delta, Nigeria. In A. U. Tar, E. B. Mijah, & M. E. U. Thedheke (Eds.), *Globalization in Africa: Perspectives on Development, Security and the Environment*. London: Lexington Books.

Robinson, J. A., Torvik, R., & Verdier, T. (2006). The Political Foundation of the Resource Curse. *Journal of Development Economics, 79*, 447–468.

Ross, M. (1999). *The Political Economy of the Resource Curse*. World Politics, 51(2), 297–332.

Ross, M. (2003). "The Natural Resources Curse: How Wealth Can Make You Poor." In I. Bannon & P. Collier (Eds.), *Natural Resources and Violent Conflict: Options and Actions* (pp. 17–42). Washington DC: The World Bank.

Ross, M. (2004). What Do We Know About Natural Resources and Civil War? *Journal of Peace Research, 41*(3), 337–356.

Rostow, W. W. (1960). *The Stages of Economic Growth*. London: Cambridge University Press.

Seers, D. (1969). "The Meaning of Development." *Paper Presented at the Eleventh World Conference of the Society for International Development*. New Delhi.

Smith, B. (2004). Oil Wealth and Regime Survival in the Developing World, 1960–1999. *American Journal of Political Science, 48*(2), 232–246.

Sobek, D. (2010). Masters of their Domains: The Role of State Capacity in Civil Wars. *Journal of Peace Research, 47*(3), 267–271.

Soto, H. (2000). *The Mystery of Capitalism: Triumphs in the West and Fails Everywhere Else*. New York: Basic Books.

Synder, R. (2002). "Does Lootable Wealth Breed Civil War? Resource Extraction and Political Order in Comparative Perspective." Boston: Paper Presented at the American Political Science Association (APSA) Annual Meeting.

Todaro, P. M., & Smith, S. C. (2004). *Economic Development*. Singapore: Pearson Education.

Torvik, R. (2011). "The Political Economy of Reform in Resource-Rich Countries." In R. Areki, T. Gylfason & A. Sy (Eds.), *Beyond the Curse: Policies to Harness the Power of Natural Resources* (pp. 237–254). Washington DC: International Monetary Fund, Publication Services.

Umoh, U. E. (2010). *The Crisis of Abundance and the Challenge of Nation Building in Nigeria*. Paper Presentation in the Department of History and International Studies, University of Uyo, Nigeria.

United Nations Office on Drugs and Crime. (2015). *International Instrument to Enable States to Identify and Trace in a Timely and Reliable Manner, Illicit Small Arms and Light Weapons* (PDF). *unodc.org.United Nations Office on Drugs and Crime.* February 2013. Retrieved October 9, 2019.

Uya, O. E. (2005). *African Diaspora and the Black Experience in New World Slavery.* Calabar: Clear Lines Publications.

Otoabasi Akpan is a Professor of History of Ideas and International Security Studies, with more than 100 publications in his areas of specialization. He has a B.A. in History from the University of Calabar, Calabar; M.A. in History of Ideas from the University of Ibadan, Ibadan; M.Sc in International Relations and Strategic Studies from the University of Jos, Jos; and Ph.D. in Diplomatic Studies from the University of Port Harcourt, Port Harcourt. He is domiciled in Akwa Ibom State University, Nigeria, where he has served as Head, Department of History and International Studies; Dean, Faculty of Arts; and since 2018, as Director, Collaboration and Linkages.

Ubong Essien Umoh is an Associate Professor of Military History in the Department of History and International Studies, University of Uyo, Nigeria. He earned a Ph.D. in Military History from the Department of History and War Studies, Nigerian Defence Academy (NDA), Kaduna. Between 2015 and 2016, he was part of the research team of the National Institute of Policy and Strategic Studies (NIPSS) consulting for the Presidential Committee (PRESCOM) on Small Arms and Light Weapons in Nigeria. Since 2017 he has been part of the joint research team on the *Boko Haram* insurgency carried out by the Centre for Defence and Documentation, Nigerian Defence Academy (NDA), Kaduna, and the Victims Support Fund (VSF), Abuja. He serves as a Senior Research Fellow at the Centre for the Study of Leadership and Complex Military Operations (CSLCMO), NDA, Kaduna, and has been a Visiting Scholar to the Nigerian Air Force War College, Makurdi, and the National Defence College, Abuja.

CHAPTER 13

Armed Conflicts, SALWs Proliferation, and Underdevelopment in Africa

Aliyu Mukhtar Katsina, Mubarak Ahmed Mashi, and Mohammed Abdullahi

INTRODUCTION

Proliferation of small arms and light weapons (SALWs) is a serious and clear danger to the national security and economies of states in the twenty-first century. The gravity of this danger, however, differs with less developed countries (LDCs) of Africa, Asia, and Latin America suffering the worst consequences. Weak political and economic institutions, poor social infrastructure, and low gross domestic product (GDP) have combined to give most of these states, especially in Africa the appearance of failure. The emergence and activities of armed groups, therefore, introduced competitors in the use of violence and made its application to achieve objectives, not necessarily public ones, quite more frequent. In fact, in most cases, non-state armed groups possess the capability and wherewithal to significantly affect the political and economic trajectories of their communities and even beyond. Boutwell and Klare (2000) note that because SALWs are widely available, cheap, effective, portable, and easy to handle, they have become a strategic game changer in the politics of the developing world, especially Africa. Essentially, it is their effectiveness from combat point of view as well as the ease with which they could be operated and maintained made them quite attractive to armed groups. SALWs

---

A. M. Katsina (✉) · M. A. Mashi
Department of Political Science, Umaru Musa Yar'adua University, Katsina, Nigeria
e-mail: aliyu.mukhtar@umyu.edu.ng

M. Abdullahi
Department of Political Science, Federal University Gashua, Gashua, Nigeria

© The Author(s), under exclusive license to Springer Nature Switzerland AG 2021
U. A. Tar and C. P. Onwurah (eds.), *The Palgrave Handbook of Small Arms and Conflicts in Africa*,
https://doi.org/10.1007/978-3-030-62183-4_13

incentivize the use of violence by different types of armed groups to achieve specific political or other forms of agenda. Expectedly, their usage has led to escalation in crimes such as kidnapping for ransom, banditry in rural areas, and armed robberies. It has also been connected with rise in revolts and rebellions; subversion and sabotage; violent communal and ethno-religious conflicts; insurgency and terrorism; and other forms of urban crimes. Of particular interest are the circumstances and factors that aid proliferation. Scholars, notably Stohl and Tuttle (2009) blamed proliferation on porous borders that facilitates smuggling, and racketeering and corruption among law enforcement agencies.

Because of its nature with figures and consignments shrouded in secrecy, trade in small arms is difficult to estimate with any degree of accuracy. Much of it is carried illegally via black markets and other arms merchants. Still, the *Small Arms Survey* (2019) estimates that there are no less than eight hundred and seventy five million (875,000,000) SALWs in the world with about one thousand two hundred (1200) in ninety (90) countries producing them. With these weapons, between 500,000 and 750,000 people are killed annually in circumstances as varied as they are wide—urban violence, drug-related killings, terrorism, piracy, banditry, etc. In essence, availability and affordability of SALWs not only contribute to armed conflicts, displacement of people, organized crimes and terrorism, but also undermined social cohesion, harmony, reconciliation, peace, and sustainable social and economic development (Mallam 2014; Geneva Declaration Secretariat 2011). Several examples from places such as Libya, Mali, Nigeria, Niger, Sudan, and Burkina Faso exist to support this position (Malhotra 2011). As alarming as this appears, it does not come as a surprise since in the sub-Saharan Africa alone there are over thirty (30) million illegal SALWs in the hands of several armed groups (Abiodun et al. 2018).

A valid question at this juncture is: how does this proliferation in SALWs impact the African economic landscape since the dawn of the twenty-first century; what experiences and lessons could be constructed from how widespread use of illegal SALWs in the hands of armed groups in Africa contributed to an atmosphere of instability, insecurity, and economic stagnation, if not collapse? There are no easy answers to these questions, but by focusing on the connection between proliferation on one-hand and security challenges such as insurgency, militancy, and banditry in different parts of Africa, this chapter hopes to answer these questions. Before proceeding further, it is important to address two important issues here. The first relates to the significance of an investigation such as this, which the chapter tackles. Hopes and aspirations around democratization, good governance, social stability, and economic development heralded the dawn of the twenty-first century in Africa. Two decades into this century, these hopes have been dashed. In fact, for many the preceding century was a better alternative. In Nigeria, Africa's largest democracy, hope has turned into despair and killings and pillaging of properties have become quite rampant. Thus, any effort designed to deepen our understanding of the underlying factors responsible for the seemingly unending crisis of development and security facing Africa such as which this chapter aims at is welcome. The second issue is methodological and revolves around source materials for this chapter. Substantial chunk of the data for this chapter is derived from online databases of international research groups and think tanks such as SIPRI. We use other sources notably scholarly articles to supplement and complement these sources. In the end, we succeeded in presenting proliferation of SALWs as a great inhibitor to economic development of Africa in this century.

Proliferation of SALWs and Economic Performance: A Conceptual Review

The dawn of the twenty-first century saw the emergence of new issues, trends, and challenges related to the questions of political development, economic performance, and general security of Africa and its people. Proliferation of SALWs is one of the issues that has managed to remain a dominant one in both security and economic development discourse. An explanation for this situation is not difficult to determine. The impact which SALWs have on political stability, social cohesion, economic development, and national security of states in Africa and even beyond ought not to be a question for debate. Before proceeding any further, it is important to start by offering some conceptual clarifications at this juncture. Although small arms and light weapons have been used in different forms and by different groups for different purposes for generations, the concept of SALWs and its application in security discourses is a relatively recent one. In fact, emerging understanding of SALWs is influenced by changing dynamics of the weapons' technologies in contemporary period. Industrialization and advancement in armaments technology means that SALWs could be produced and traded on massively unprecedented scale. The Best Practice Guidelines for the Implementation of the Nairobi Declaration and Nairobi Protocol on Small Arms and Light Weapons (2005) define small arms as weapons designed for personal use and generally include light machine guns, machine pistols, fully automatic rifles, assault rifles and semi-automatic rifles (Best Practice Guidelines 2005). The United Nations General Assembly defines SALWS as any portable lethal weapon that expels or launches, is designed to expel or launch, or may be readily converted to expel or launch a shot, bullet or projectile by the action of an explosive (Heinrich 2006).

According to Nte (2011), small arms are smaller infantry weapons, such as firearms that an individual soldier can carry. It is usually limited to revolvers, pistols, submachine guns, shotguns, carbines, assault rifles, rifle squad automatic weapons, light machine guns, general-purpose machine-gun, medium machine guns and hand grenades. However, it can also include heavy machine guns, as well as smaller mortars, recoilless rifles, and some rocket launchers, depending on the context. Other portable arms and weapons which could be operated by one person such as landmines, bombs, grenades, rocket launchers, and even small machine-operated projectiles all fall within the ambit of SALWs. Distinction is sometimes made between small arms and light weapons with the latter encompassing much more complicated weapon systems requiring more than a single person to operate such as heavy machine guns, portable grenade launchers, mobile anti-aircraft cannons, non-recoilless guns, portable anti-tank missile launchers, and mortars (SADC Firearms Protocol 2004: Article 1.2). It is, however, important to note that large mortars, howitzers, cannons, vehicles, and larger pieces of equipment are not considered small arms (Nte 2011).

The technology that allows for the production of SALWs on a mass scale goes hand in hand with the circumstances that lead to their proliferation on a global scale. In its own right, proliferation is not a contentious concept. It refers to the sudden increase in the spread of weapons, generally, from one country to another. It defines the transfer of arms from one group of owners and users to other groups. Acquisition of small arms can be transacted through official channels or through covert, clandestine, or black market networks. In general, certain intermediaries based on legal or illegal demands coming from particular lawless or restricted environments facilitate proliferation of arms. This means that, there is "licit and illicit proliferation of arms." This last point requires some elaboration here. States as legitimate wielders of instruments of violence do not fall within the scope of actors that partakes in illicit acquisition of SALWs. This distinction, apparently, is only applicable to non-state actors, notably armed groups, who under municipal and international laws have no legitimate claim to use of violence or its instruments in pursuance of their objectives. Proliferation, therefore, is the situation which obtains when these types of groups have easy access to cheap, portable, and easy to handle and easy to maintain weapons occasioned by the presence of large markets, usually black markets, and other sources, usually clandestine, of these SALWs. But black markets are not necessarily the only source of SALWs. States are known to have sponsored, trained, and most importantly, equipped several armed groups for different national security interests. For instance, at the height of the Cold War, USA was an important source and supplier of these weapons to various armed groups in Africa, Asia, Middle East, and Latin America. And even today, there are intelligence agencies which as part of counter-insurgency (COIN) strategies supply arms and weapons to armed groups in different parts of the world.

Violent Conflict and War Economy

The consequences of proliferation on security, internal stability, and economic development of states in Africa and elsewhere are clear and manifest in many forms. Of course, the most visible is the violent conflicts which availability, affordability, and portability of SALWs fosters. The impacts of these conflicts on the economy are quite devastating. They appear in the form of deaths and injuries of active and productive segment of the populace in conflict zones.

In most cases, majority of participants in these conflicts—both as combatants and victims—are youths. The attendant decline and even total collapse in productive vocations have severe implications on national GDP. But this is not the only manner in which violent conflicts impact economies. Even in situations where killings were relatively low, displacement and or mass migrations significantly affect the upward progress of the economy. As conflicts intensify, insecurity becomes more widespread. Industries and other critical sectors of the economy all close down and investments dry up.

Perhaps the greatest impact which violent conflicts have on national economies in Africa and elsewhere is the forced transformation in their economies—and the efflorescence of "war economies." An evident shift could be discerned with most states making efforts to accommodate this shift in the new form which their economies assume. Precisely, they shift toward what could be described as the war economy. This concept denotes the organization of a country's productive and distributive capacities during times of conflicts in order to accommodate defence production needs. In a war economy, governments usually prioritize resource allocation in order to achieve military victory while also meeting vital domestic consumer demands (Kenton 2019). A war economy prioritizes the production of goods and services that support war efforts, while also seeking to support other critical sectors. During times of conflict, governments may take measures to prioritize defence and national security expenditures, including rationing, in which the government controls the distribution of goods and services, as well as resource allocation. In times of war, each country approaches the reconfiguration of its economy in a different way and some governments may prioritize particular forms of spending over others. Kenton (2019) provides three conditions for war economy. One, a war economy happens when a country is at war and it affects its capacity to produce and distribute goods. Two, governments must decide on how to allocate resources to provide defence needs. Three, war economies generally use hard currency for defence spending.

Armed Conflicts, SALWs Proliferation and Underdevelopment in Africa

> Legal arms sales have flagged in recent years, but illegal and semi legal traffic has kept weapons flowing steadily to world trouble spots (Klare 1988: 16)

There is some justification in describing Africa as a continent steeped in violence. For many decades after the wave of decolonization of the 1950s and 1960s had subsided, the continent found itself in the grip of different forms of violent conflicts. In fact, the last four decades of the twentieth century represented a mosaic of Africa in which the most prominent feature was violent conflicts with racial, political, religious, and economic undertones. We can still recall the tragic civil wars of Sudan, Somalia, Nigeria, Rwanda, Burundi, Algeria, Angola, Liberia, Libya, Chad, and Sierra Leone, not to talk of war in places such as Ethiopia and Eritrea (Olaosebikan 2010). Africa has been prone to inter and intra-state wars and conflicts. Most pathetic about these conflagrations is that they have defied any meaningful solution and their negative impacts have retarded growth and development in Africa while an end to them seems a bit distant. According to Cohen (1995), modern African states were created by colonial powers out of ethnic and cultural diversities, and rendered conflictual by gross inequities in power relations, and in the uneven distribution of national wealth and development opportunities. Both Cohen (1995, in Achankeng 2013) and Achankeng (2013) blamed the process of decolonization that took place in many countries andin how the inherent contradictions of the colonial state were passed on to the post-colonial states through institutions and structures established by the colonizers as being partly responsible for the conflicts in Africa. Cohen (1995, in Achankeng 2013) further argues, the instability and bad governance in Zaire, Rwanda, and Burundi can be attributed to the unprepared granting of independence to these countries by Belgium in 1960.

For Arriola (2009), political instability caused by what he called the sit-tight syndrome of most political leaders in Africa is a substantial contributor to outbreaks of conflicts in several parts of Africa. Leaders across Africa have the propensity to hold onto office by purchasing support through the distribution of state resources; as such, any conflict over their allocation is thought to degenerate into a struggle over control of the state. Violence erupts when the political elites take over large chunks of the spoils controlled by the leader or because those outside the leader's patronage-based coalition struggling to have access to state resources, to which they have been denied or blocked from such access. According to a United Nations report on conflict in Africa, the nature of political power in many African States, together with the real and perceived consequences of capturing and maintaining power, is a key source of conflict across the continent (Arriola 2009). Zaire under Mobutu, Libya under Gaddafi, and Egypt under Mubarak represent some of these cases.

In East Africa, the war in South Sudan, the collapse of the state in Somalia, and the conflicts in Rwanda and Burundi, the situation in Ethiopia as well as the conflict in former Zaire, are some instances of prolonged conflicts. These conflicts were only addressed superficially, their intensity notwithstanding (Achankeng 2013). In spite of all the urgency concerning the conflict in Burundi, the focus was mainly on diplomatic interventions by several agencies and actors. These interventions ended up with the establishment of war crime tribunals with none of the actors giving any consideration for the need to address the deep concerns of the parties in the conflict. The tribunals seem to have been intended for punishing individuals seen to have participated in the conflicts rather than in unearthing the causes of the conflict that remain deeply rooted in the structures and institutions of governance in these societies (Achankeng 2013). An interesting feature of all these conflicts was in how parties appeared able to obtain weapons from different sources and suppliers. Indeed, the ability of the markets to meet the demands for SALWs by parties to the conflict must have substantially nurtured, sustained, and elongated the conflicts in many places.

The proliferation of SALWs in Africa has developed over the years to a rate that is currently quiet alarming and has put the security and stability of the entire African continent on the precipice. It is estimated that non-state actors including private citizens, registered private security companies, and other armed groups possess about 40 million SALWs or about 80% of all SALWs in the continent. In contrast, the whole of the continent's armed forces and other law enforcement agencies hold less than 11 million SALWs. Out of the 40 million SALWs held by civilians in Africa, 5,841,200 are recorded as being officially registered, while 16,043,800 are unregistered, with the status of the rest being unclear (Small Arms Survey 2019).

From Table 13.1, it is clear that West Africa has the highest number with about 11 million, followed by Northern Africa with 10.2 million and Eastern Africa with 7.8 million SALWs. Most of these as noted are being held illegally by private citizens. Expectedly, they made the continent vulnerable to conflict and instability. SALWs have, evidently, become weapons of choice in

Table 13.1 Sub-regional distribution of SALWs in civilian hands in Africa in 2017

Sub-region	Population	Number of firearms held by civilians	Civilian-held firearms per 100 population
Eastern Africa	416,676,000	7,802,000	1.9
Middle Africa	161,237,000	4,981,000	3.1
Northern Africa	232,186,000	10,241,000	4.4
Southern Africa	63,854,000	6,012,000	9.4
Western Africa	372,551,000	10,972,000	2.9
Africa total	1,246,505,00	40,009,000	3.2

(*Source* Small Arms Survey 2019)

the hands of terrorist groups and other non-state players to inflict considerable damage on the state and, more importantly, on citizens who the state has the responsibility of protecting. According to Keili (2008: 6),

> SALWs are extreme tools of violence in Africa for several reasons. Small arms are durable, highly portable, easily concealed, simple to use, extremely lethal and possess legitimate military, police and civilian uses. In Africa, these weapons are cheap and widely available; they are also lightweight, and so can be used by child soldiers, who have played such a significant role in recent conflicts in Africa. SALW have been used to grossly violate human rights, to facilitate the practice of bad governance, to subvert constitutions, to carry out coups d'état and to create and maintain a general state of fear, insecurity and instability.

Similarly, the United Nations Security Council asserts that the destabilizing accumulation and uncontrolled spread of SALWs in many regions of the world increases the intensity and duration of armed conflicts, undermines the sustainability of peace agreements, impedes the success of peace building and hinders efforts aimed at preventing the escalation of armed conflicts (Laurence and Stohl 2002; United Nations Security Council 2001). Furthermore, Laurance (1998) notes that the proliferation of SALWs in Africa is one of the major factors directly responsible for the frequency and intensity of the prevailing conflicts in the continent. And for good measure we can add that this proliferation at global level accounts for the high number of insurgencies the world is presently witnessing (Fig. 13.1).

The collapse of the Berlin Wall in 1990 and the subsequent ending of the Cold war heralded a new international order. However, the collapse of the Eastern bloc and the disintegration of the Soviet Union was not without severe

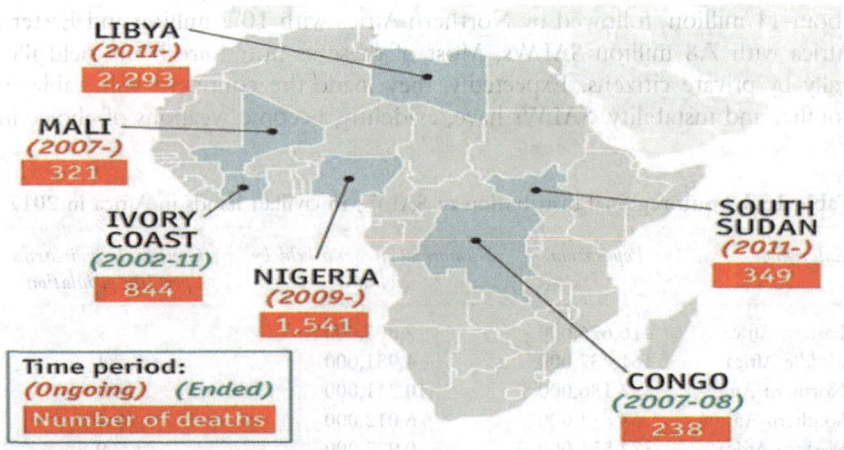

Fig. 13.1 Major conflict hotspots in Africa, 2000—Present (*Source Prio Armed Conflict Dataset*, 2012)

implications on SALWs market and security discourse, especially in Africa. The disintegration of the Soviet Union left behind an alienated and impoverished populace in possession of the world's largest collection of unregistered arms stockpiled in places such as Ukraine. Under the KGB millions of these weapons disappeared from the Soviet arsenals to the Asian, African, and North American black markets in exchange for hard currency. As noted earlier, this significantly helped to alter the course of violent conflicts by redirecting the waves of smuggled SALWs into Africa. Local warlords now have unfettered access to small but deadly weapons with which to wage wars against their states (Eloma et al. 2014). For instance, arms found their way into West Africa and helped fuelled and executed some of the most violent human conflicts of the twentieth century in states such as Liberia and Sierra Leone. Nigeria itself became a huge illegal trading post for smuggled arms (GIABA 2013).

The Arab spring which swept most dictatorships and autocracies of the Middle East and North Africa (MENA) equally confounded the problem of SALWs into sub-Saharan Africa. SALWs, generously provided by Western powers in toppling autocratic leaders such as Gaddafi in Libya, later found their ways through various clandestine routes and corridors from North to West Africa. In fact, some studies even suggested that the arsenals of Gaddafi that were overran by rebels were later used in waging other violent conflicts including piracy in Somalia, Boko Haram in Nigeria, and the Azwadi rebellion in northern Mali (Katsina 2012). Practically, the successful overthrow of these erstwhile leaders led to the retention of weaponry in the hands of rebels who in most cases were mercenaries hired to help either in shoring up the government's support base as was the case in Libyan *Mujahiddeens* who joined the struggle to dislodge the governments. These weapons were later smuggled into many African countries, which were used in perpetuating criminal or terrorist activities (Katsina 2012). They also fuelled kidnappings, insurgency, armed robbery, banditry, and other security challenges in the region (Mashi, et al. 2019).

Official corruption and racketeering among border security forces is another enabler of proliferation of SALWs in Africa. Illicit arms often enter Africa without passing examination or screening as a result of collusion between arm dealers and corrupt border officials. Porous nature of African borders and vast ungoverned territories provide great incentives not just for trafficking in arms but also for effective movements of men and materials and the uncontested operations of numerous armed groups (GIABA 2013). The experience of Sudan, Congo, and Chad—three of the largest countries in the sub-Sahara—supports this observation. All of them have had to fight a vicious civil war and contend with various armed groups. No doubt, their size and porous borders have contributed in facilitating weapons smuggling thereby inflaming violence (Ngang 2007). Lastly, the forces of globalization come with several opportunities and challenges—the removal of state enforced restrictions on exchanges across borders allows for free movement of people and goods across national frontiers. This idea of free movement or at least with minimum legal barriers provides ground for licit trade in SALWs by minimizing custom regulations and border control which has made trafficking of SALWs easier (Mallam 2014) (Fig. 13.2).

According to SIPRI (2020), the five largest exporters of arms from 2015–2019 were the United States, Russia, France, Germany and China. The five largest importers were Australia, India, Saudi Arabia, China and Egypt. Between 2010–2014 and 2015–2019, there were increases in arms transfers to the Middle East (by 61%) and to Europe (3.2%), while there were decreases in the transfers to Africa (−16%), the Americas (−40%) and Asia and Oceania (−7.9%).

In Africa, North Africa accounted for 74% of arms imports in 2015–2019. Algeria accounted for 79% of North African arms imports. Algeria's arms imports were up by 71% from 2010 to 2014, making it the sixth-largest arms importer in the world in 2015–2019 and the sub-Saharan African states accounted for 26% of African arms imports in 2015–2019. The five largest arms importers in sub-Saharan Africa were Angola, Nigeria, Sudan, Senegal and Zambia which accounted for 63% of all arms imports to the sub region (SIPRI 2020).

The Africa Europe Faith and Justice Network (2010) reports that selling and transferring arms to the African market is a very profitable enterprise for many European countries and companies. For example, Russia, the second largest arms exporter after the United States, sell 14% of its arms and weapons exports in African markets. From 2005 to 2009, South Africa and the North African countries of Algeria, Morocco, Libya, and to a lesser extent, Egypt and Tunisia, are the largest arms importers in Africa. It is imperative to know

Fig. 13.2 Sources of Africa's Weapons (*Source SIPRI* 2013)

that it was during this period that Egypt, Tunisia, and Libya experienced civil-unrest, which eventually unseated Hosni Mubarak, Zine El Abidine Ben Ali, and Muammar Gaddafi. In terms of arms manufacturing capacity of African states, the AEFJN reports that only few African countries have the capacity to manufacture arms and ammunition with South Africa topping the list on the continent, followed by Nigeria, and other states, like Kenya, Uganda, Tanzania, and Zimbabwe (AEFJN 2010) (Table 13.2).

Small arms have continued to constitute a serious challenge to African development and have led to the loss of millions of lives, which would have formed part of the work force needed to drive the development of the continent. The genocide in Rwanda, the civil wars in Liberia, Sierra Leone, the Democratic Republic of Congo, and Mali as well as the Boko Haram insurgency in Nigeria have all shown the significance of SALWs in fuelling and sustaining violent conflict over an extended period (Eloma et al. 2014). According to Renner (2006), over six million lives were lost in Africa alone over the last fifty years due largely to violent conflicts enabled by proliferation of SALWs. According to Ero and Ndinga-Muvumba (2004), in West Africa alone, over 30,000 people have been killed by SALWs in low-intensity conflicts annually since the end of the Cold War. For instance, between 1999 and 2003, there were over 30 communal clashes, sectarian violence, and ethno-religious conflicts with each claiming hundreds of lives and properties, disruption of livelihood and internal displacement of women and children in Nigeria alone.

Table 13.2 Concentration of SALWs in Africa as at 2018

S/N	COUNTRIES	POPULATION (2017)	SALWs
1.	Libya	6,409,000	851,000
2.	Somalia	9,225,000	1,145,000
3.	South Africa	55,436,000	5,351,000
4.	South Sudan	13,096,000	1,255,000
5.	Ghana	28,657,000	2,280,000
6.	Sudan	42,166,000	2,768,000
7.	Morocco	35,241,000	1,690,000
8.	Mozambique	29,538,000	1,337,000
9.	Ivory Coast	23,816,000	1,049,000
10.	Egypt	95,215,000	3,931,000
11.	Nigeria	191,836,000	6,154,000
12.	Algeria	41,064,000	877,000
13.	Cameroon	24,514,000	510,000
14.	Kenya	48,467,000	750,000
15.	DR Congo	82,243,000	946,000
16.	Tanzania	56,878,000	427,000
17.	Ethiopia	104,345,000	377,000

(*Source* Small Arms Survey 2018)

Overall, available data suggest that there had been about 15,874 cases of armed conflicts in Africa in 2018 and 21,600 in 2019. It is remarkable to note how the figure jumped upward within a span of a single year (Allison 2020). As pointed, a significant portion of the blame for these violent conflicts and their accompanying fall-out including refugee problem, mass internal displacement of people, kidnappings, rape, and killings could directly be traced to the cheap weapons that abound in hundreds of black markets in Africa. Terrorism, ethno-religious violence, armed robbery, cattle rustling, and insurgency in many other parts of Africa were also linked to proliferation of SALWs.

SALWs Proliferation and the Dwarfing of the African Economy

One of the tragedies associated with the influx of SALWs into Africa is that their production and exportation create employment opportunities and boost national economies of Western powers, while leaving African economy weak and gasping for breath. This paradox is clear and requires little elaboration. It suffices to point that influx of SALWs into Africa poses not just a severe security challenge but also create conditions that negatively affect economies of most African states. African countries have experienced direct and indirect consequences of weapons proliferation. Millions of people have lost their lives in several violent conflicts. Yet, even when death or injury can be averted, small arms proliferation and misuse can affect economic, political and social sphere of a country. The threat and use of small arms undermine development, prevent the delivery of humanitarian and economic aid, and contribute to problems of refugees and internally displaced persons (Stohl and Tuttle 2009). The top five African countries facing humanitarian crisis in 2020 are Democratic Republic of Congo, Nigeria, Burkina Faso, Burundi and Chad. There are about 18 million internally displaced persons around the world with more than 12.5 million being in Africa due to conflicts and violence. Majority of these IDPs are women and children under the age of eighteen living in serious humanitarian crisis (United Nation 2010).

Williams (2019) opines that, more than 1.6 million Africans are faced with forceful displacement annually since 2014. The record of 25 million African refugees, internally displaced persons (IDPs), and asylum seekers documented in 2018 represents an almost five-fold increase since 2005, when just 5 million Africans were displaced (Williams 2019). 84% of the 25 million forcibly displaced on the continent come from 8 conflict-affected countries of South Sudan, the Democratic Republic of the Congo (DRC), Somalia, Sudan, Ethiopia, Nigeria, the Central African Republic (CAR), and Cameroon. In the process of displacement, these people face serious challenges. Problems such as sexual abuse, malnutrition, poverty, diseases, and squalor are quite rampant in affected communities and in IDP camps. The economic implication of this misadventure manifests itself in how a significant portion of the populace becomes unproductive and dependent on the goodwill of the state and donor agencies. For IDPs, serving as workers, producers, consumers, and taxpayers are no longer on the menu of options available to them (IDCM 2018). This greatly affects the level of economic development which African states could be able to attain.

There are other implications besides those outlined in the preceding paragraphs. Trade and investment, long accepted as great catalysts to economic development and social prosperity also suffered. Violent conflicts in Africa have created an atmosphere of instability and conditions of insecurity which encourage kidnappings of expatriates, for instance, in many parts of the continent. Militancy in the Nigeria's Niger-Delta and high-sea piracy in the Horn of Africa are two excellent examples that buttress our argument here. Activities of militants in the Delta area, especially kidnappings of expatriate oil workers and vandalization of oil pipelines resulted into dramatic fall in Nigeria's oil output, drying up of investment into critical infrastructure to support crude oil production, and generally worsening Nigeria's revenue. As an important and key indicator for economic development, the flow of foreign direct investment has therefore, dropped sharply in many countries because of the prevailing insecurity. Foreign investors are generally unwilling to risk their investments in unsecured environments. For instance, in 2017 the FDI flow to Africa dropped to 6.3% from 12.3% in 2012 (UNCTAD 2018). In 2018, FDI flow to Africa rose to $46 billion, an increase of 11%. This could be as a result of improved security situation in some parts of Africa. These 2018 figures of the FDI flow excludes Nigeria (UNCTAD 2019). This type of situation must have been the cause, at least in the past, of the closure of some portions of Nigeria's oil industry, unemployment rates rose, poverty became even more pronounced, and the whole Niger-Delta became militarized.

According to Olaosebikan (2010), conflicts and violence have aggravated the problem of unemployment in the continent. In Africa, high rate of unemployment, especially among youths, is a serious menace. It has continued to grow at 10% annually, a major security threat in the region. In post-conflict countries, many among the youths lack not only employment opportunities but also even more disturbing have no prospects of ever acquiring meaningful education, because critical social infrastructure have either been disrupted or altogether destroyed. It is imperative to state that, without other economic means to support these unemployed youths, there will be serious security threats, especially among former or repentant combatants, who may resort to crime as a means of livelihood (Olaosebika 2010). When we ponder on the tens of millions of unaccounted SALWs in various corners of Africa the prospects of having teeming youths as unemployed becomes quite frightening.

Other important examples could be drawn from other crucial aspects. One of these is the Sustainable Development Goals (SDGs), an initiative of the United Nations, which aims at combating poverty, providing affordable healthcare, improving the wellbeing of the poor and vulnerable, providing quality education, ensuring safe water, reviving industries, promoting innovation, and construction of social infrastructure to the LDCs by 2030. The success of this initiative, it is increasingly becoming apparent, is not feasible in the face of on-going violent conflicts in many parts of Africa. Needless to stress, the currency of these conflicts is ensured by the proliferation of SALWs (Safer World 2012). For instance, between 2017 and 2018, Boko Haram, an insurgent group operating in Nigeria's northeast, killed about 15,952 people and occupy a vast stretch of land around the Lake Chad area bordering Chad, Cameroon, and Niger Republic (Global Terrorism Index 2019). Of course, all of these significantly hamper effective implementation of SDGs in these areas and many more.

Huge amount of monies that are supposed to be used for developmental purposes in Africa have been diverted to addressing problems of insecurity, thereby neglecting other vital sectors critical to economic development. In some countries, as much as 25% of their annual gross domestic product is being spent on addressing the problems of insecurity (Saferworld 2012). Huge spending in this direction is, however, not a new development. Available data suggest that African countries have spent over 300 billion dollars on armed conflicts between 1990 and 2005. These figures equal the total international aid grant to Africa within the same period (Jekada 2005). According to SIPRI (2018), the military expenditure of sub-Saharan Africa in 2017 was $19.6 billion. Nigeria being the largest spent $1.7 billion in 2017, making it the fourth-largest spender behind Sudan, South Africa and Angola. In April 2018, the Nigerian head of state, President Muhammadu Buhari, approved a sum of $1 billion for the purchase of security equipment to fight the Boko Haram insurgents. In spite of these huge expenditures, the group still operates and threatens regional stability and economic development (GTI 2019). According to a 2016 World Bank Report, Borno State, the epicenter of Boko Haram activities, had suffered property damage, since the beginning of the insurgency, worth $5.9 billion (Sule 2016). Onuoha (2013) observes how telecommunication companies spent over 75 billion naira in fixing critical communication infrastructure destroyed by Boko Haram. The Borno State Commissioner of Health laments how important health facilities and infrastructure worth over 4.5 billion naira were destroyed due to the activities of Boko Haram (*Premium Times* 2017).

Conclusion

This chapter studied the proliferation of SALWs in Africa since the dawn of the twenty-first century. The objective as explained in the introduction was to link proliferation with violent conflicts that ravage different parts of Africa and show that these significantly retard the upward progression of African economy. We argued that SALWs have, due to their nature which made them simple to operate, easy to maintain, cheap to obtain, portable to carry, and deadly effective, emerged as strategic game changer in the security landscape of Africa over the last five decades. The various conflicts that broke out in different parts of Africa—the civil wars, insurrections, insurgencies—and bourgeoning urban and rural criminal enterprise all serve as a clear evidence of how proliferation aids and facilitates conflicts and insecurity on a grand scale. The implications of these, we argued, on African economy are clear represent imminent danger to its performance. SALWs ensured the sustainability of violent conflicts and other forms of crimes on a grand scale. This situation creates an atmosphere of insecurity with significant impact on economic productivity, in-flow of investments, particularly FDI, and the security of social infrastructure. Drawing from rich datasets, we illustrate using several cases of conflict how SALWs facilitate and sustain conflicts thereby aggravating problems of economic development in Africa. In the final analysis, it is our position that the question of economic development in Africa in the twenty-first century could only be addressed in the context of the proliferation of SALWs that exacerbate conflicts, increases crime rates, create insecurity, and give Africa the appearance of a continent in perpetual conflict and violence.

REFERENCES

Abiodun, T. F., Ifeoluwa, A., Oluwasolape, O., & Chukwuyere, N. (2018). Small Arm and Light Weapons Proliferation and Its Threat to Nigeria's Internal Security. *International Journal of Social Science and Humanities Research, 6*(3), 34–45.

Achankeng, F. (2013). Conflict and Conflict Resolution in Africa. Retrieved from:www.accord.org.za/ajcr-issues/conflict-and-conflict-resolution-in-Africa/. Accessed 13 January 2020.

Africa Europe Faith and Justice Network. (AEFJN). (2010). Arms Exports and Transfers: Europe to Africa, by Country. Retrieved from: http://www.gunpolicy.org. Accessed 4 July 2020.

Allison, S. (2020). Conflict is Still Africa's Biggest Challenge in 2020. Institute for security studies. Retrieved from: http://www.issafrica.org/iss-today/conflict-is-still-africas-biggest-challenge-in-2020. Accessed 6 July 2020.

Armed Conflict Dataset. (2012). African Civil Wars and Internal Armed Conflicts Beginning from 2002–2012, Highest Combatant Death Tolls. Retrieved from: http://www.prio.org. Accessed 4 July 2020.

Arriola, L. (2009). Patronage and Political Stability in Africa. *Comparative Political Studies, 42*(10), 1339–1362. Retrieved from: http://online.sagepub.com. Accessed 19 January 2020.

Boutwell, J., & Klare, M. (2000). A Scourge of Small Arms. *American Academy of Arts and Science, 282*(6), 48–53.

Best Practice Guidelines. (2005). Best Practice Guidelines for the Implementation of Nairobi Declaration and the Nairobi Protocol on Small Arms and Light Weapons. Retrieved from: www.poa-iss.org. Accessed 13 December 2019.

Eloma, U., Ugwumba, N., & Abang, E. (2014). Effect of Proliferation of Small Arms and Light Weapons on the Development of the Niger Delta Region of Nigeria. *Journal of Developing Country Studies, 4*(10), 60–72. Retrieved from: http://www.iiste.org. Accessed 6 July 2020.

Ero C., & A. Ndinga-Muvumba (2004) Small Arms and Light Weapons.In AdekeyeAdebajo and Ismaail Rashid *West Africa's Security Challenges: Building Peace inTroubled Region*, London: Lynne Rienner Publishers.

Declaration, Geneva. (2008). *Dimensions of Armed Violence: Global Burden of Armed Violence*. Geneva: Geneva Declaration on Armed Violence and Development Secretariat.

GIABA (Inter-Governmental Action Group Against Money Laundering in West Africa). (2013). The Nexus Between Small Arms and Light Weapons and Money Laundering and Terrorist Financing in West Africa. Retrieved from: http//gaiba.org. Accessed on 22 June 2019.

Global Terrorism Index (GTI). (2019). Measuring the impact of terrorism. Retrieved from http://www.visionofhumanity.org/reports.

Heinrich, M. (2006). Small Arms and Development: The Results of the UN Small Arms Review Conference 2006 and Their Policy Implications. Retrieved from: http://www.ipb.org. Accessed 27 March 2020.

Jekada, E. K. (2005). *Proliferation of Small Arms and Ethnic Conflicts in Nigeria: Implication for National Security*, Dissertation for the award of the degree ofDoctor of Philosophy in International Relations and Strategic Studies, St. Clements University.

Kenton, W. (2019). War Economy. Retrieved from: http://www.investopedia.com/terms/w/war-economy. Accessed 3 June 2020.

Klare, M. (1988). Secret Operatives, Clandestine Trades: The Thriving Black Market for Weapons. Retrieved from: http://www.books.google.com.ng/books?id=qgYAAAMBAJ&pg. Accessed 6 June 2020.

Karp, A. (2007).*Completing the count: civilian firearms small arms survey 2007: Guns and the City*, Cambridge: Cambridge University Press.

Katsina, A. M. (2012, May). Islamist Threat in sub-Sahara: Arab Spring in North Africa and Regional Security in West Africa [Seminar Presentation]. 23rd Seminar Series of the Department of Political Science, International Islamic University Malaysia (IIUM), Kuala Lumpur, Malaysia.

Keili, F. L. (2008). Small Arms and Light Weapons Transfer in West Africa: Stocktaking, Disarmament Forum. Retrieved from: http://www.ssrnetwork.net/. Accessed 23 December 2019.

Kenton, W. (2019). War Economy. Retrieved from:www.investopedia.com/terms/w/war-economy.asp. Accessed 29 June 2020.

Laurance, J. (1998). Small Arms and Light Weapons as a Development and Disarmament Issue: An Overview. In: BICC Report 12; *Converting DefenseResources to Human Development: Proceedings of an International Conference*, held 9–11 November 1997.

Laurence, J., & Stohl, R. (2002). Small Arms Survey: Making Global Public Policy, the Case of Small Arms and Light Weapons. Retrieved from http://www.smallsurvey.org/2002/.Accessed 4 July 2020.

Malhotra, A. (2011). Globalization and the Illicit Trade of Small Arms and LightWeapons. The Eurasia Review. Retrieved from: http://www.eurasiareview.com/201009017600/globalisation-andthe-illicit-trade-of-small-arms-and-light-weapons.html. Accessed June 2018.

Mallam, B. (2014). Small Arms, Light Weapons Proliferation and Its Implication for West African Regional Security. *International Journal of Humanities and Social Science*, 4(8), 260–269.

Mantzikos, L. (2014). Boko Haram Attacks in Nigeria and Neighbouring Countries: A Chronology of Attacks. Retrieved from:http://www.terrorismanalysts.com/pt/index.php/pot/article/view/391/. Accessed 6 June 2020.

Mashi, A. M., Shani, B., & Jibril, M. (2019). The Nexus Between Small and Light Weapons Proliferation and the Growing Challenges of Human Security in Nigeria. *Journal of Social and Administrative Sciences Review*, 5(2), 155–169.

Ngang, C. (2007). *Small Arms and Light Weapons, Africa's True Weapons of Mass Destructions: the Role of SALWs in African Sub-Saharan Conflicts and Insecurity*, M.A Dissertation, Submitted to the European University, Centre for Peace Studies, Austria. Retrieved from: https://www.academia.edu/4221688/proliferation_of_small_arms. Accessed 27 June 2020.

Nte, N.D. (2011). The Changing Patterns of Small and Light Weapons (SALW) Proliferation and the Challenges of National Security in Nigeria.*Global Journal of African Studies, 1* (1), 5–23. Retrieved from: http://www.researchgate.net/publication/221448493. Accessed 11 January 2020.

Olaosebikan, (2010). Conflicts in Africa: Meaning, Causes, Impact and Solution. *An International Multi-Disciplinary Journal, Ethiopia*, 4(4), 549–560. Retrieved from: www.ajol.info. Accessed 16 January 2020.

Onuoha, F. (2013). The costs of Boko Haram Attacks on Critical Telecommunication Infrastructure in Nigeria. Retrieved from: http://www.e-ir.info/2013/11/03/the-cost-of-boko-haram-attacks. Accessed 6 July 2020.

Premiums times (2017, August 10). Boko Haram destroyed 267 hospitals, clinics in Borno. Retrieved from: http://premiumtimesng.com/health-news/239869-boko-haram-destroyed-267-hospitals-clinics-in-Borno.

Premiumtimes. (2020, 10 August). Boko Haram Destroyed 267 hospitals, clinics in Borno- Commissioner. Retrieved from: http://www.premiumtimes.com/health-news/. Accessed 6 June 2020.

Renner, M. (2006). Curbing the Proliferation of Small Arms. Retrieved from: www.worldwatch.org/node/3738. Accessed 23 June 2018.

SaferWorld, (2012). Small Arms and Light Weapons Control: A Training Manual. Retrieved from: http://www.saferworld.org.uk. Accessed 6 June 2020.

Stohl, R., & Tuttle, D. (2009). The Challenges of Small Arms and Light Weapons in Africa. conflict trend.

Sule, I. (2016). Nigeria: World Bank report- Borno lost N1.9 trillion to Boko Haram. Retrieved from: http://www.allafrica.com/stories/201603210101. Accessed 6 June 2020.

Stockholm International Peace Research Institute (SPRI). (2020).Trends in International Arms Transfers, 2019. Retrieved from: http://www.sipri.org/2020. Accessed 29 July 2020.

Stockholm International Peace Research Institute (SPRI). (2018). Military Expenditure Transparency in sub-Saharan Africa. Retrieved from: http://www.sipri.org/2018. Accessed 4 June 2020.

South African Development Community (SADC). (2004). Protocol on the Control of Firearms, Ammunition and Other Related Materials in South African Development region 2001/2004. Retrieved from: http://www.sadc.int/int/index.php.protocol-_firearms. Accessed 22 June 2019.

Strohmeyer, H. (1999), *The Humanitarian Implications of Small Arms and Light Weapons*, Background Paper, United Nations Office for the Coordination of

Humanitarian Affairs, 25 January 1999. Retrieved from: http://www.unocha.org. Accessed 27 March 2019.
Small Arms Survey (2001). Weapons Compass: Mapping Illicit Small Arms Flows in Africa. Retrieved from: http://www.smallarmssurvey.org. Accessed 4 April 2018.
Small Arms Survey, (2004). *Rights at Risk*. Oxford, Oxford University Press. Retrieved from: http://www.smallarmssurvey.org. Accessed June 2018.
Small Arms Survey, (2007). Weapons Compass: Mapping Illicit Small Arms Flows in Africa. Retrieved from: http://www.smallarmssurvey.org. Accessed 21 June 2019.
Small Arms Survey. (2011). *Shadow of War*. Cambridge: Cambridge University Press.
Small Arms Survey. (2019). Weapons Compass: Mapping Illicit Small Arms Flows in Africa. Retrieved from: http://www.smallarmssurvey.org. Accessed 2 July 2020.
UNCTAD. (2019). Foreign Direct Investment to Africa Defies Global Slump, Rises 11%. Retrieved from http://www.unctad.org/news/foreign-direct-investment-africa-defies-global-slump-rises-11.
UNDP. (2004). *Human Development Report 1994*. New York: Oxford University Press.
United Nations Security Council. (2001). Statement by the President of the United Nation Security Council 2001 Press Release. Retrieved from: http://www.un.org/securitycouncil/content/notes-president-security-council-2001. Accessed 28 June 2020.
United Nations. (2002). Program of Action to Prevent, Combat and Eradicate the Illicit Trade in Small Arms and Light Weapons in all Its Aspects. Retrieved from: http://www.un.org. Accessed April 2 2019.
United Nations Conference on Trade and Development (UNCTAD). (2018). World Investment Report 2018. Retrieved from: http://www.unctad.org/diae. Accessed 6 June 2020.
United Nations. (2010). Africa's Displaced People: Out of the Shadows. Retrieved from: http://www.un.org/africarenewal/magazine/april-2010/africa's-displaced-people-out-shadows. Accessed 6 June 2020.
Williams, W. (2019). Shifting Borders: Africa's Displacement Crisis and its Security Implications. Retrieved from: http://africacenter.org/wp-content/uploads/2019/10/ARP08EN-Shifting-Borders-Africas-Displacement-Crisis-and-its-Implications.pdf. Accessed 7 June 2020.

Aliyu Mukhtar Katsina graduated with a Ph.D. in Political Science from the *Universiti Islam Antrabangsa Malaysia* (UIAM). Dr Katsina was the recipient of the prestigious *Best PhD Graduating Student Award* at the Faculty and University levels at UIAM. He currently teaches research methodology, political parties and party politics, political economy, and Nigerian Foreign Policy to undergraduate and postgraduate students of the Department of Political Science of Umaru Musa Yar'adua University (UMYU) and Al-Qalam University (AUK), Katsina. Until June 2020, Aliyu Katsina was also the Dean of Faculty of Social and Management Sciences (FSMS) of UMYU. His book, *Party Constitutions and Political Challenges in a Democracy: Nigeria in the Fourth Republic*, was published by IIUM Press, Kuala Lumpur, Malaysia. Aliyu Katsina was the *Editor-in-Chief* of the *Social and Administrative Sciences Review*—a peer review bi-annual Journal of the Faculty of Social and Management Sciences at UMYU.

Mubarak Ahmed Mashi graduated with a Master's degree in defence and strategic studies from Nigerian Defence Academy Kaduna, Nigeria. He is currently a Lecturer at the Department of Political Science, Umaru Musa Yar'adua University, Katsina, Nigeria. His research interest focuses on security and political economy.

Mohammed Abdullahi is with the Department of Political Science Federal University Gashua. He graduated with a bachelor degree in political science from Ahmadu Bello University Zaria and he is currently undergoing his M.Sc Degree in Political Science at Kaduna State University, Nigeria

CHAPTER 14

Civil Wars, Complex Emergencies, and the Proliferation of Small Arms in Africa

Hussaini Jibrin and Umar Aminu Yandaki

INTRODUCTION

Civil Wars and Complex Emergencies in most modern African countries are an offshoot of the legacies bequeathed to such countries by colonial rule. This is because the colonial powers that created the modern African countries had little regard for Africans' cultural affinities and the political structures that existed in Africa before their arrival. Large nationalities or ethnic groups were split between states, while others, who related on the basis of warfare and endless enmity, were drawn together to share new state boundaries (Odunuga 1999). This no doubt created situations that made these conflicts inevitable in Africa. It is widely accepted that civil wars and complex emergencies were and are still the major hindrances to the development of Africa. They inflict human sufferings through deaths, destruction properties, constant displacements, and general insecurity. Undoubtedly, these menaces disrupted the processes of production, created conditions for the pillage of many African countries' resources and diverted the application of such resources from development purposes to servicing war. Violent conflict is thus, responsible for perpetuating misery and underdevelopment in the continent (Awori 1999).

H. Jibrin (✉)
Department of History and War Studies, Nigerian Defence Academy, Kaduna, Nigeria

U. A. Yandaki
Department of History, Usmanu Danfodiyo University, Sokoto, Nigeria

Since the euphoric decade of Africa's independence in 1960s,[1] the continent could be described by the trinity of diversity, heterogeneity, and complexity, across all imaginable divides. Made up of five major regions, namely, "West, Southern, East and Central, Horn and the Northern Maghreb," each housing "various peoples, cultures, ecological settings, historical experiences, and political and socio-economic geographies" (Francis 2008: 4), Africa presents a microcosm of conflicts and contradictions of epic proportion. This is not unconnected to the colonial history of the continent. At the eve of the colonial project in nineteenth century, the whole of Africa was an asset owned by seven European powers (Belgium, Britain, France, Germany, Italy, Portugal, and Spain), who agreed to arbitrarily divide it into their fiefs without recourse to the existing political, linguistic, and cultural formations within the continent. Therefore, a typical spectacle in most African states is that peoples of diverse and irreconcilable ethno-demographic and cultural mix were foisted into artificially constructed states by the erstwhile colonial masters. As such, the Post-Colonial African countries are not more than rickety, heterogeneous, and puzzlingly complex ex-colonial formations, each bedeviled by challenges of forging national integration among its citizens whose loyalties are shared between the formal state and informal entities such as tribes, religions, and traditions. No wonder, socio-economic and political situations in most of the countries in the contemporary times are not only faulty (resulting from a range of internal and external factors), but also provide fertile grounds for the eruption of violent conflicts, especially civil wars and complexemergencies. Essentially, these violent conflicts were and are still triggered, perpetuated, and toxified by the proliferation and misuse of Small and Light Weapons (SALWs) within the continent.

The recurrence and gradual increase in the number of violent conflicts in forms of civil wars and complex emergencies, particularly owing to the proliferation of SALWs, continued to consume not only the resources of various African countries combating insecurity, but the lives and properties of people. It, thus, deserves serious academic attention. This is more so because Africa's peace, security, and development, which the Afro-optimists envisaged during the early years of independence, are seemingly becoming elusive. In their stead, violent conflicts and economic underdevelopment took over. Already, considering the worrying nature of the happenings within the continent, some sorts of stereotypical images have been created by the international media to depict Africa. Therefore, today, by mere mentioning of the continent's name, the images that conjure in people's minds are those of "famine in Ethiopia, civil war in Somalia, and ethnic genocide in Rwanda," among many other dark images associated with lush jungles and wild life, poverty, famine,

---

[1]The period of 1960s is referred to as the decade of Africa's independence not because all the countries in the continent obtained their political independence within that decade, but because most of the nations got the independence between 1960 and 1970.

ethno-religious conflicts and deadly diseases. This eventually moulds Afro-pessimism—"a belief that grinding poverty, outbreaks of devastating diseases and intensifying conflicts will remain staples of the African landscape for the foreseeable future" (Schraeder 2004: 14). This chapter assesses how civil wars and complex emergencies were caused, toxified, perpetuated, and even made frequently recurrent in Africa due to the proliferation of SALWs. This is with a view to explain the devastating effects of such weapons on peaceful coexistence, without which sustainable development will continue to evade Africa.

Civil Wars and Complex Emergencies in Post-Colonial Africa

Simply put, a *civil war* is a war that is fought between the citizens of the same country, often between a government and rebel forces who seek to dismantle the formal state. Civil war is closely associated with *civil unrest*, but the two can be mutually exclusive. A civil unrest is the eruption of mass violence in a state or society as a result of irreconcilable difference between the constituent elements of that state. The unrest can be caused by cultural and religious differences, resource conflicts, or struggle for power. On its own side, *complex emergency* is a term used to refer to "any major humanitarian crisis owing to a combination of factors resulting from political instability, conflict and violence, social inequalities, natural hazards, devastating diseases and underlying poverty" (FAO 2020). Among the devastating effects of complex emergencies is the general erosion of societal stability across all divides. Civil wars and other humanitarian crisis associated with armed conflicts have been recurrent in Africa. This is so pervasive to the extent that such violent acts "dominated the presentation and international media coverage in the continent because of the high incidence of political violence and frequency and multiplicity of wars and armed conflicts" (Francis 2008: 7). As reported by the Uppsala University conflict database, more than any other region around the world, Africa is conflict-ridden. In fact, between 1946 and 2006 alone, about 74 conflicts erupted in different parts of Africa, the highest number when compared to Asia, which had 68; the Middle East, 32; Europe, 32; and the Americas, 26 (Francis 2008: 7). Nevertheless, to adequately provide a general picture of the civil wars and complex emergencies in Post-Colonial Africa, one needs to classify them into two major, albeit overlapping categories: those that occurred before the end of the Cold War (i.e., from 1960s to 1990) and those that followed, after the collapse of the Soviet Union and the end of the Cold War (from 1990 to date). Although these two major categories are not mutually exclusive, each has some distinctive features (Fig. 14.1).

To begin with the first category, it is worthy of note that in the period that immediately followed independence, Africans more than ever before, felt

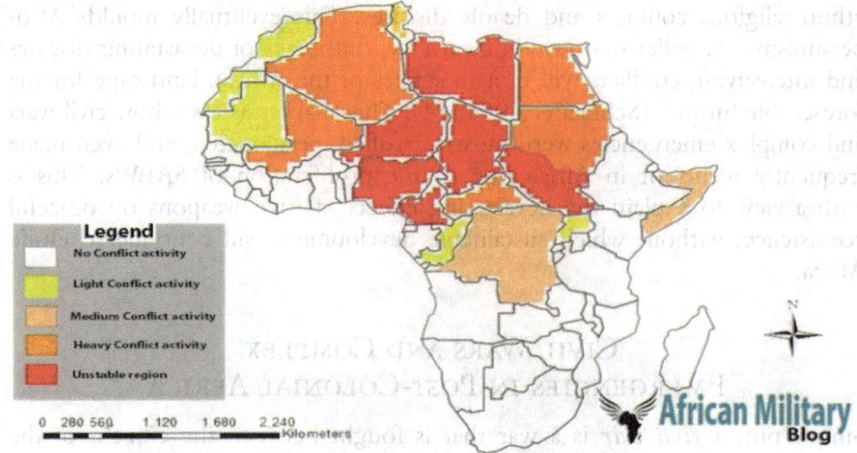

Fig. 14.1 Conflict zones in Africa as at 2018 (*Source* The African Military blog. Available: https://www.africanmilitaryblog.com/2018/07/african-conflict-map-acomprehensive-guide?v=65d8f7baa677, Accessed 05 July 2020)

relieved of the parasitic nature of colonialism, the only good thing associated with which, Rodney cautioned, was when it ended (Rodney 2009: 320). Though highly complicated with the "deep economic crisis that had been the end-product of almost a century of colonial misrule and exploitation" (Yandaki 2015: 187), as well as neo-colonialism and the uncertain world order characterized by the Cold War period, the expectations of Africans during the early years of independence were extremely high as regards to attaining an all-round development and prosperity. Nonetheless, these external forces, coupled with the puzzles of politics, regionalism, ethnicity, and class, especially those associated with the rough interlude of the military rule—in the late 1960s and throughout the 1970s and 1980s—combined to plunge the newly independent countries in Africa into civil wars, complex emergencies, and other serious humanitarian crises. In Nigeria, for example, it were the bombs of regionalism, ethnicity, political instability as well as military coups that combined to throw the country into a thirty months civil war, during which the Igbo people of the South-eastern part of the country fought the Federal Government with a view to secede and create an independent Republic of Biafra (Faruk 2011).

In southern Sudan also, a revolt against the northern rule, which began in the late 1950s and early 1960s, continued between 1972 and 1983 (Reid 2012: 333). In the same parlance, Eritreans fought a prolonged war against Ethiopia, fighting independence against Ethiopian occupation right from 1961. The war was only ended in 1991 when Eritreans gained victory under the Eritrean People's Liberation Front (EPLF). This particular war went through some bitter internal twists, including an intermittent civil war during the 1970s. Other insurgencies that took place in Ethiopia were in Tigray, among the Oromo, in the Somali Ogaden and along the Sudanese borderlands. In fact, it was a coalition of some of these various forces under the rubric—the Ethiopian People's Revolutionary Democratic Front (EPRDF) that collaborated with the EPLF to ousted the Marxist dictatorship in the country (Ried 2012: 333). In Uganda, the National Resistance Army (NRA) under the leadership of Yoweri Museveni, fought Milton Obote in the early 1980s, before capturing Kampala in 1986. In the same vein, the Rwandan Patriotic Front (RPF) advanced gradually from the north of Rwanda through the early 1990s and finally seized power during the Rwandan genocidal chaos (Ried 2012: 333).

Indeed, a wide range of politically and socially induced violence and insurgencies had taken place between mid-1960s and early 1990s. These violent conflicts had gulped enormous resources of the various African countries. They also pauperized many Africans, and even cost many others their lives. Nevertheless, this first category of civil wars and complex emergencies in Africa, when compared to those that ensued after the end of the Cold War, were generally characterized by less destructions and minimal mortality rates. Indeed, the end of Cold War ushered in a New World Order, characterized by the triumph of the West, especially the United States of America and its attendant values of capitalism and democracy. This period, which was described by "Huntington as a global 'third wave' of democratization" (Kaarsholm 2006: 1), gathered momentum in Africa, resulting to the quadrupling of the number of African countries that hold competitive legislative elections from 9, to 38, out of a total of 47 countries in the sub-Saharan region (Kaarsholm 2006: 1). Indeed, this "third wave" added significance in African political development as it contributed to other forces that eventually combined to make realistic, the "events of negotiated and 'pacted' transition of South Africa from apartheid state to majority rule," "making Nelson Mandela proclaim democracy to be "our national soul" (Kaarsholm 2006: 1–7).

Simultaneously, however, this New World Order ignited violent conflicts and other forms of social tensions in forms of civil wars and complex emergencies in Africa. This is basically as a result of the resurgence of ethnically based nationalism on a global scale, owing to the disintegration of the Soviet Union into numerous independent republics (Reid 2012: 333), and the faulty nature of democracy as practiced in the African countries. Following the end of the Cold War, the practice of democracy proved to be faulty in Africa as "the actual modes of conducted governance in individual countries have indicated serious difficulties in arriving at 'consolidated' forms of democracy or peaceful regulation of differences and contestations" (Kaarsholm 2006: 1). This is because, although, most of these conflicts are ethno-religious and social, they are basically politically induced. As such, many analysts have for long viewed the democratization of Africa as not a way forward, but rather, a means to violent conflicts:

the weight of the evidence—and it is, indeed, very weighty to suggest that democratic openings have often aggravated communal tensions in divided societies... Free party-based competitive elections in heterogeneous societies... encourage leaders to manipulate latent regional, ethnic, or religious animosities as a way to mobilize electoral support. (Kaarsholm 2006: 2)

All these problems, coupled with many others associated with the puzzles of religious fundamentalism and neoliberal globalization—too numerous to be mentioned in this overview—made the rise of violent conflicts in Africa to be overly glaring. No wonder, the Uppsala University conflict database suggested that the period from 1990 to 2002 witnessed the intensification of what is often described as "post-Cold War wars" in Africa (Francis 2008: 7). This became even more intensified in the twenty-first century, following the rapid spread of violent horrors of terrorism and insurgencies in the continent (Kaarsholm 2006: 3).

Most of the violent conflicts in the post-Cold War Africa can summarily be said to be caused by "political, ethic and cultural oppressions, economic marginalization, and straightforward greed, or at least restless ambition" (Reid 2012: 349). Indeed, right from the beginning of the 1990s, the devastating effects of civil wars and complex emergencies began to be felt by Africans in various parts of the African continent. In Rwanda, the age-old underlying ethnic mutual distrust between the Tutsi and Hutu became intensified, eventually erupting into genocide in 1994. This civil war did not only lead to the deaths of over 800,000 people from among the Tutsi and Hutu, but also seriously destabilized the Great Lakes region (Reid 2012: 349). This is because similar devastating effects were suffered in the neighboring Burundi, following the unpopular pogrom against Hutu in 1989 and Hutu's ascension of power after the 1993 elections. According to Daley (2008: 1), an approximate number of 300,000 people lost their lives in Burundi between 1994 and 2006. The same war extended into the Democratic Republic of Congo (DRC) as a result of the overthrow of Mobutu, which was strongly aided by the Ugandan and Rwandan forces. All these, combined to turn DRC into a landscape of violence and security entrepreneurism (Reid 2012). Unfortunately, over 3.8 million lives were lost in the DRC between 1998 and 2005 (Daley 2008: 1).

In Somalia, instability nearly became integrated into the people's lives in the region. The regime of General Siad Barre failed to wield together the various clans inhabiting the country, or to provide an egalitarian state that meets the wishes and aspirations of the people. By 1990s, Somalis have become highly discontented with the Barre Regime. This, coupled with the end of the superpower politics in 1989 (Somalia was a proxy of the defunct Soviet Union), emboldened dissident groups in Somalia to confront the regime and expel General Barre out of the country (he went on exile to Lagos, Nigeria). In 1990s and 2000s, Somalia became a collapsed state and an ungoverned territory. Even the US-led intervention under the banner "Operation Restore

Hope" unfortunately ended in abyss (Reid 2012: 349). In Liberia and Sierra Leone, there were massive efflorescence of armed militias and "war lords" who confronted and ousted the governing regimes—a similar group of notorious gangsters that were also found in Somalia and Congo. These war lords were a group of "traumatized young men" that squarely engaged in security entrepreneurship. These sorts of criminals inflicted enormous sufferings to defenseless populations. A good example of these groups of insurgents could be cited with the Lord's Resistance Army (LRA) in the northern part of Uganda, "where the insurgents brutalized local people in the name of an idiosyncratic amalgamation of Old Testament and indigenous spiritualism" (Reid 2012: 350). In Sudan also, racial tensions and religious confrontations culminated into a lengthy civil war, which partially persisted even after the South's secession. Even then, the intricacies associated with the conflicts in the western Sudanese province of Dafur are beyond enormous. These included fighting rebel movements yearning for autonomy and rights, backed by Khartoum. This Khartoum-supported violence have, itself, been classified, variously, as genocidal (Reid 2012: 349–350). The Niger Delta region in Nigeria was also nearly shattered by the activities of militants, which became intensified during the first decade of the twenty-first century (Obi and Rustad 2011). The Libyan Civil War of 2011, which cost the country's leader, Gaddafi his life, was also devastating (Encyclopedia Britannica 2020). Meanwhile, a pocket of other conflicts associated with "Islamic resurgence" had distressed various African countries including Tunisia with its Al-Ghanoushi's Islamic Trend Movement, Egypt with its Ikhwan al Muslimeen (Muslim Brotherhood), and Nigeria with its Boko Haram insurgency (Fineman 2018).

The foregoing is a depiction of the dynamics of civil wars and complex emergencies that have been bedeviling Africans since the ending of colonial rule. Indeed, quite many of these conflicts tend to persist despite the enormous wealth expunged by the various African countries, International Organizations, and other humanitarian groups to tame them. Among the major reasons behind the failure of these efforts is the proliferation of Small and Light Weapons in the continent. The sources of SALWs and their proliferation in Africa are discussed in the next section of this chapter.

Sources of SALWs and Their Proliferation in Africa

SALWs are "weapons designed for personal use and include light machine guns, pistols, fully automatic and assault rifles such as the AK-47 and M16 series, and semi-automatic rifles. These arms are such that they are easy to move, hide, trade, steal, are durable, portable and light such that adults, children and security use them across the globe" (Ehiane and Uwizeyimana 2018: 70). It is important to note that during the colonial period in Africa, most of the available weaponry (as regards modern sophisticated weapons) in most colonies was squarely monopolized by the colonial governments and their security agents. Therefore, the proliferation of SALWs during this period was very minimal. Indeed, this form of strict control of weapons was inherited, albeit in a futile effort, by the various sovereign African countries after independence; thus, nearly all weapons were under strict control of the independent countries through the agencies of their respective militaries and paramilitaries. However, arms restrictions are easily prone to violation in Africa. The artificial nature of the state—characterized by officials and citizens who habour allegiance to other entities such as tribe and religion apart from the state, coupled with the zero-sum nature of state politics—meant that arms restriction were not rigid, or even totally enforceable. This was exacerbated by the eventual politicization of the military—the hitherto, sole repositories of the moral and physical order during the early Post-Colonial years (Reid 2012).

Essentially, in just few years of African decade of independence, the proliferation of SALWs began to take an ugly shape in the continent. SALWs, which are largely manufactured in Europe, North America, the defunct Soviet Union, and Asian countries, began to find their ways into Africa through both legal and illegal means. There are many illegal ways in which they were, and still are, transported into Africa and moved from one "trouble spot" to another in the continent. In fact, these forms of weapons are particularly found handy by criminals and other rebel groups within the continent because of their low price, portability, and technical plainness. They are also easy to conceal and be transferred, and they proved to be highly effective in causing mass bodily harm and mass destruction (Jekada 2015). These weapons have also contributed to the escalation, perpetuation and toxifying of civil wars and complex emergencies, especially where they meet underlying triggers in form of growing misunderstandings and mistrusts, or even existing tensions. Just like the categorization of civil wars and complex emergencies in Africa, the proliferation of SALWs in Africa can equally be categorized thus: those that found their ways into Africa amidst the tensions of the Cold War and those that proliferated resulting from the new sources of SALWs created by the end of the Cold War and the collapse of the Soviet Union.

Indeed, right from the later years of the African decade of independence, the influences, intrusions, and political tensions associated with the Cold War, saw a massive influx of automatic weapons, with which the two contending powers: the USA and the Soviet Union, used to fight by proxy on the African continent (Malam 2014). Also, the Cold War created a brisk business for arms manufacturers and importers in Africa. A very good instance of this early proliferation of SALWs in Africa, especially as affected by the Cold War, has been vividly seen during the Nigerian Civil War, from 1967 to 1970. The Nigerian Civil War (1967–1970)—which, as earlier stated, was triggered by an ethnically induced military coup that resulted to further mistrust and tensions among the major tribesmen in the country—saw heavy importation of foreign arms and ammunition from the global arms manufacturers: both sides of the war (federal government and the Biafran secessionists) openly purchased arms from their foreign allies. This marked the earliest instance in which the proliferation of SALWs was recorded in Nigeria, and perhaps, Africa at large. This is conspicuous, considering the summary of Nigeria's arms import by the federal government, which dramatically rose from an average of £250,000 between 1963 and 1966 to about £10,533,036 in 1967, as a result of the outbreak of the war (Fyanka 2013: 2). Indeed, throughout the civil war, which was largely "fought on ground by foot soldiers that were well armed with small and light weapons," there had been a massive influx of such type of weapons, variously as war aid, to support the two contending parties in the conflict. For example, in line with the Cold War tensions, Britain, Nigeria's erstwhile colonial master, which was initially reluctant to support any of the contending parties, eventually aided the Federal Government with enormous weapons, being an apprehension over USSR's intervention in support of the Federal Government. There was also a massive, albeit secret inflow of weapons into the South-eastern part of the country as war aids to the Biafrans, especially through the agencies of France and other Francophone African countries of Ivory Coast and Gabon, all of whom recognized the autonomy of the Biafran secessionists (Fyanka 2013).

Moreover, during this period (1967–1970), local crafts and production of small arms was effectively utilized to supplement the weapons that were being imported. In 1967, for example, the Biafran Science group was inaugurated in Enugu. This later metamorphosed into the Research and Production Directorate (RAP). Its membership comprised scientists, engineers, and technicians who combined the knowledge they acquired from their respective fields of endeavors to invent different kinds of weapons. While the chemical group worked on incendiaries, smoke signals, detonators, bombs, etc., engineers produced grenades, bullets, rocket casting, etc. Others constructed armored cars out of tractors and trucks. In fact, one of the best weapons made by the RAP was called *Ogbunigwe* (mass killer or destroyer) (Fyanka 2013: 6–9). The locally made weapons, though, instrumental in the intensification of wars, also had their own limitations.

Indeed, this illustration through the Nigerian example provides a general image not only on how SALWs were massively imported into Africa during the Cold War, but how the manufacturing of small weapons for the sole aim of intensifying violent conflicts began. Unfortunately, during the civil wars and complex emergencies that took place before the end of the Cold War, huge amounts of weapons got into the hands of individuals and other non-state actors. Moreover, there was a general failure of ensuring proper implementation of Disarmament, Demobilization, and Reintegration (DDR) programs after the cessation of hostilities. This further compounded the proliferation of SALWs throughout the continent, impeding the various porous African borders and recycled for other criminal uses, long after the end of the civil wars they were originally used to fight (Malam 2014).

The proliferation of SALWs in Africa became unprecedented, during the post-Cold War period (1990 to present). This was owing to a number of reasons. The collapse of the Soviet Union witnessed a huge flood of small arms into Africa, at a time when the former Eastern bloc countries were grappling for markets in the "Third World" to dump the surplus manufactures of their industries, especially the arms industries (Reid 2012: 333). Unfortunately, a huge number of these arms in circulation became lost in the hands of illegal arm dealers, security entrepreneurs, ethnic militia groups, local smugglers, etc., who in turn used them to toxify ongoing civil wars and complex emergencies and even precipitate new ones. Here, the example of the Somali militias, who according to UN investigators, regularly buy and sell arms to each other on the local black market, is instrumental (Schroeder and Lamb 2006: 70). There were also established networks of transferring SALWs from current and past war zones. SALWS are also seized or stolen from government security agents and state's armories. They are also purchased from corrupt security personnel and private owners. In the instances of wars, also, peacekeepers are severally relieved of their small arms that often end up in the rebels' possession. Here, a good example is the ambush of Guinean peacekeepers in 2002, which netted Sierra Leonean rebels with more than 550 weapons (Schroeder and Lamb 2006: 69). Moreover, the unauthorized production of firearms by local craft producers is another major source of SALWs and a chief way through which arms proliferation is being intensified in Africa. In Ghana alone, unlicensed gun producers have the collective capacity of manufacturing over 200,000 firearms in a year, with some of these likened to industrially produced guns in terms of quality (Schroeder and Lamb 2006: 70). In Nigeria, local craft industries in small arms grew especially in Awka, in Anambra State, where assorted firearms such as Dane guns, revolvers, and semi-automatic rifles are invented (Fyanka 2013: 8). The proliferation of SALWs in Africa, as pointed out earlier, did not only perpetuate the frequent recurrence of civil wars and complex emergencies in Africa, but also toxify them; and the apparent expansion in the sources and proliferation of SALWs in the post-Cold War Africa informs the reason why, as pointed out in the previous section, civil wars, and complex emergencies became overly terrible and continued to mutate across the continent from 1990s to date. This, in turn, has many devastating effects on the security, peaceful coexistence, and the overall development of most African countries. This is briefly discussed in the following section of the chapter.

EFFECTS OF THE PROLIFERATION OF SALWS IN AFRICA

The proliferation of SALWs in Africa has seriously devastating effects on the continent. The widespread availability of SALWs in Africa did not only affects peace and security in the continent, but also contributed to the level of violence and the intractability of conflicts. As it is conspicuous from the foregoing discourse, the number and level of violence in the various cases of civil wars and complex emergencies that took place in Africa during the Cold War were less when compared with those that followed in the post-Cold War period. This was due to the increasingly expanding sources of SALWs in Africa, since the end of the Cold War, which has resulted to the massive increase in the number of weapons in the possession of ethnic militias, insurgents, and terrorists, among other criminals. For example, armed conflicts in Sierra Leone, DRC, Uganda, etc., all witnessed the toxic integration of children as combatants, using small arms with ease. This alerts us not only on the abundance, but illegal use of SALWs in intensifying violent conflicts. In Nigeria also, the Niger Delta militants surrendered 2760 arms, 287,445 ammunition, 18 gunboats, 76 explosives, 1090 dynamite caps, and 3155 magazines during the 2009 Amnesty Program of President Umaru Yar'adua's administration (Fyanka: 16). In July 2013, soldiers on patrol arrested a truck in Kebbi State. The truck was fully loaded with AK-47 rifles, one rocket-propelled grenade (RPG), nine AK-47 magazines, two bombs, three RPG chargers, and 7.6 mm special ammunition which was suspected to be Boko Haram supplies (Ehiane and Uwizeyimana 2018: 69). These few examples of surrendered and arrested weapons also signifies the huge number of firearms in the possession of criminals, which have neither been surrendered nor arrested by security agents throughout the continent; more so, considering the number of casualties victimized by criminal activities in the continent on daily basis.

Due to the unholy relationship between civil wars, complex emergencies and arms proliferation, there is presently an unprecedented mutation of armed conflicts and criminal activities, both in numbers and level of violence, leading to the deaths and victimization of thousands of Africans. This is in addition to enormous wealth gulped by individual states' and collective (regional and continental) efforts at combating these menaces, alongside their byproducts including robbery, kidnapping and the rapidly increasing nature of banditry and the raiding of small villages, as well as the vicious criminal activities knotted with the puzzles of electoral processes, leading to electoral violence. Essentially, small arms are responsible for 60–90% of total conflicts deaths in Africa. In South Africa, for example, SALWs is the principal cause of unnatural deaths (close to 30% of the total) (Schroeder and Lamb 2006: 72). Additionally, the unhealthy romance between violent conflicts and the proliferation of SALWs in Africa had precipitated other inter-communal tensions and conflicts over scarce resources. This, for example, was occasioned by the rise of highly toxic cattle rustling, which has for long, been bedeviling some parts of Kenya and Uganda. As a result of cattle rustling, hundreds of people have been killed and numerous others displaced, with the Karamojong and the Pokot nomadic cattle herders been the principal perpetrators. In April 2003 alone, over 2000 Pokot cattle rustlers from Kenya killed 28 people and displaced thousands in Ugandans through the use of illicit firearms (Schroeder and Lamb 2006: 74). Furthermore, cattle rustling, armed banditry and their devastating effects, have since the closing years of the first decade of the twenty-first century, been bedeviling the inhabitants of North-West Nigeria, leading to the loss of properties, deaths and displacement of many people (Rufa'i 2018).

The availability of small arms among private individuals and other non-state actors, coupled with the experience of frequent armed conflicts, also made many African countries to embrace a kind of "gun culture," under which the ownership of small arms is linked to identity and social prestige. This has been particularly rampant in the eastern provinces of DRC and Somalia. Finally, the general insecurity caused by all these, weakens the already shaky economic base of most African countries, thus, hindering any meaningful development in the continent (Schroeder and Lamb 2006).

CONCLUSION

This chapter examines the nexus between civil wars, complex emergencies and the proliferation of SALWs in Africa. The chapter provided a brief analysis of the major cases of civil wars and complex emergencies in the Post-Colonial history of Africa. Essentially, this brief analysis laid bare, the fact that civil wars and complex emergencies could be broadly divided into two major categories: those that occurred during the Cold War and those that followed after the collapse of the Soviet Union and the end of the Cold War. It was also identified that the civil wars and complex emergencies that followed the end of the Cold War were comparatively proportional both in number and in terms of fatality rate. Interestingly, this was justified by the discourse made on the sources and proliferation of SALWs in Africa; because it was posited that the proliferation and illegal use of small arms, which became massive during the post-Cold War period, has been instrumental in the complication, intensification, perpetuation and the massive increase in fatality rates of the various civil wars and complex emergencies they were used in.

Moreover, the seriously devastating effects of the unhealthy intersections between civil wars, complex emergencies and the proliferation of SALWs have been glanced. It has been established that the lack of proper DDR after civil wars, along with other factors have resulted in the free circulation of arms among criminals which often lead to the escalation of new inter-communal clashes, rebellions, kidnappings, banditry, and cattle rustling among others. In order to curb this menace, there is a serious need to begin an all encompassing movement toward the disarmament of private individuals and other non-state actors in the continent. While this is being pursued, however, the deadlier scourges of illiteracy, cultural arrogance, corruption, poverty, etc., needs to be tackled in order to neutralize the root causes of violent conflicts in Africa.

BIBLIOGRAPHY

Awori, T. (1999). Forward. In A. Adedeji (Eds.), *Comprehending and Mastering African Conflicts: The Search for Sustainable Peace and Governance*. London: Zed Books.

Daley, P. O. (2008). *Gender and Genocide in Burundi: The Search for Spaces of Peace in the Great Lakes Region* (First Paperback ed.). Kampala: Fountain Publishers.

Encyclopedia Britannica. (2020). *Libya Revolt of 2011*. Available: www.britannica.com/event/Libya-Revolt-of-2011. Accessed 24 June 2020.

Ehiane, S. O., & Uwizeyimana, D. D. (2018). Challenges in Combating the Proliferation of Small Arms and Light Weapons (SALWs) in Nigeria: A Human Security Perspective. *Journal of African Foreign Affairs, 5*(3), 65–85.

FAO (Food and Agriculture Organisation. (2020). *Complex Emergency*. Available www.fao.org/emergencies/emergency-types/complex-emergencies/en/, Accessed 24 June 2020.

Fineman, G. G. (2018). Nigeria's Boko Haram and its Security Dynamics in the West African Sub-Region. *Journal of Language, Technology and Entrepreneurship in Africa, 9*(1), 102–131.

Faruk, U. (2011). *The Victors and the Vanquished of the Nigerian Civil War, 1967–1970: Triumph and Valour over Greed and Ambition*. Zaria: ABU Press.

Francis, D. J. (2008). Introduction: Understanding the Context of Peace and Conflict in Africa. In D. J. Francis (Ed.), *Peace and Conflict in Africa*. New York, NY: Zed Books Ltd.

Fyanka, B. B. (2013). From Civil War to the Age of Terror: A Historical Analysis of Patterns of Small Arms Proliferation in Nigeria. *Journal of Defence Studies, 18*, 39–59.

Jekada, E. K. (2015). *Proliferation of Small Arms and Ethnic Conflicts in Nigeria: Implication for National Security*. Ph.D. International Relations and Strategic Studies, St. Clement University, United Kingdom.

Kaarsholm, P. (2006). States of Failure, Societies in Collapse? Understandings of Violent Conflict in Africa. In P. Kaarsholm (Ed.), *Violence, Political Culture and Development in Africa*. Anthens, OH: Ohio University Press.

Malam, B. (2014). Small Arms and Light Weapons Proliferation and Its Implication for West African Regional Security. *International Journal of Humanities and Social Sciences, 4*(8), 260–269.

Obi, C., & Rustad, S. A. (2011). *Oil and Insurgency in the Niger Delta: Managing the Complex Politics of Petro-violence*. London: Zed Books.

Odunuga, S. (1999). Nigeria: 'A Victim of its Own Success.' In A. Adedeji (Ed.), *Comprehending and Mastering African Conflicts: The Search for Sustainable Peace and Governance*. London: Zed Books.

Reid, R. J. A. (2012). *History of Modern Africa 1800 to the Present* (2nd ed.). London: Wiley-Blackwell.

Rodney, W. S. (2009). *How Europe Underdeveloped Africa* (2009th ed.). Abuja: Panaf Publishing Inc.

Rufa'i, M. A. (2018). Vigilante Groups and Rural Banditry in Zamfara State. *International Journal of History and Social Sciences, 7*(6).

Schroeder, M., & Lamb, G. (2006). *The Illicit Arms Trade in Africa: A Global Enterprise* (pp. 69–78). Third Quarter: African Analyst.

Schraeder, P. J. (2004). *African Politics and Society: A Mosaic in Transformation* (2nd ed.). Montreal, QC: Wadsworth.

Yandaki, A. I. (2015). *The State in Africa: A Critical Study in Historiography and Political Philosophy*. Zaria: Gaskiya Corporation Ltd.

Hussaini Jibrin is a senior lecturer in the Department of History and War Studies, Nigerian Defence Academy, Kaduna. Dr. Hussaini has attended and presented papers at many conferences within and outside Nigeria. He has contributed a number of articles and chapters in peer reviewed journals and book projects. With his career spanning over a decade, he has held different academic and administrative responsibilities in Nigerian Universities. He edited two books: *Readings on Peace Studies and Conflict Resolution*, (2016); and (with AM Ashafa) *The Nigeria Army in a Democracy Since 1999: A Professional Demonstration of Military Subordination to Civil Authority: Essays in Honor of Lieutenant General T.Y. Buratai* (2017).

Umar Aminu Yandaki is an alumni of the Department of History, Usmanu Danfodiyo University, Sokoto, Nigeria. He graduated in 2018 with a Bachelors Degree in History, as the overall best student, and for the first time in thirty three years (since 1985), with a First Class Honors. He is a writer with academic articles on African Historiography, Cultural History and African Gender Studies, variously published in refereed journals and books. Yandaki is a researcher, essayist and analyst on literary and development issues in developing nations, especially through media and strategic communications.

CHAPTER 15

Poverty, Greed and the Proliferation of Small Arms in Africa

Ubong Essien Umoh and Otoabasi Akpan

INTRODUCTION

Small arms and light weapons (SALWs) combine to make armed conflicts in Africa cheap, frequent and sustainable. The relationship between SALWs and armed conflicts in Africa is often represented as interdependent where SALWs provide the temptation for armed conflicts and armed conflicts in turn feed upon SALWs. The chapter engages in the effort to integrate poverty and greed as a co-efficient of the existing equation of SALWs proliferation and armed conflicts. Poverty and greed combine to lure actors in armed conflicts, providing both attraction and invitation that comes with the consequences of displacement and devastation. Indeed, central to the analysis of the manifestation of armed conflicts in Africa has been the presentation of poverty short of greed and greed dressed in poverty. A vicious cycle is observed where poverty and greed sustain armed conflicts, and such armed conflicts, in turn, sustain the proliferation of SALWs; and the proliferation of SALWs reinforces the enduring permanence of armed conflicts. While poverty appeared necessary to initiate armed conflicts in Africa, greed appeared sufficient to sustain such

U. E. Umoh (✉)
Department of History and International, University of Uyo, Uyo, Nigeria
e-mail: ubongumoh@uniuyo.edu.ng

O. Akpan
Department of History and International Studies, Akwa Ibom State University, Ikot Akpaden, Nigeria

© The Author(s), under exclusive license to Springer Nature Switzerland AG 2021
U. A. Tar and C. P. Onwurah (eds.), *The Palgrave Handbook of Small Arms and Conflicts in Africa*,
https://doi.org/10.1007/978-3-030-62183-4_15

armed conflicts. The chapter carries this out in a relative chronological slide through the pre-colonial, colonial and post-colonial period in Africa, identifying poverty and greed as causal continuities for interpreting the phenomenon of SALWs proliferation in Africa.

Proliferation of SALWs in Pre (Colonial) Africa: Did Poverty and Greed Matter?

For Africa, the phrase SALWs is arguably recent. Its dated companion, firearms, have occupied a venerable subject in the field of African Military History. Lacking a viable armament industry, significant quantity of firearms made an early entry into Africa from the industrial West as the most important item of Euro-African trade (see, Ajayi 1989). Debatably, the first firearms to the West African coast were brought in by the Portuguese during their explorations in the fifteenth century (Aderinto 2018: 30). While Portuguese trading records with Africa appear silent on the subject of firearms (Alpern 1995: 18), by the sixteenth century when the slave trade—a trade that greatly exploited the poverty and greed of Africans—had sprouted, the Portuguese inaugurated arms traffic with Kwaland in the Lower Guinea and Elmina in the Gold Coast which grew in leaps and bounds that by the turn of the eighteenth century, 20,000 guns were being absorbed by Kwaland per annum (Alpern 1995: 18–19). However, Britain overtook Portugal, leading the slave trade project which made for a dominant theme in Hatch's (1969) "History of Britain in Africa." For instance, an English cargo headed for Ghana's Cormantin in 1658 included 1550 muskets and the warehouse at Cape Coast Castle contained 1397 snaphances and 4107 matchlocks in 1680 (Kea 1971: 195). Between 1701 and 1704, the Royal African Company (RAC) sent 32,954 arms to West Africa (Davies 1957: 177) and the Dutch West India Company had in 1704 stocked 7741 guns at its Gold and Slave Coast posts (Kea 1971: 195).

These descriptive statistics combine to validate Northrup's (2002: 90) view that "firearms were arguably the most significant technical innovation to arrive from the Atlantic." Indeed, firearms were so significant that they made for an integral component of the military history of African slavery (Hacker 2008). Northrup (2002: 90–91) notes that "the importation of guns was the principal reason for warfare within Africa and that it was by means of such wars that gun-toting Africans supplied the Atlantic economy with slaves." This was carried out mostly through the commercial valve of European multinational companies such as the Royal African Company, the Dutch West India Company, among others. Indeed, firearms largely remained a European monopoly until the eighteenth century (White 1971; Hacker 2008: 66). The outcome was suggestive—the general destabilization of the African continent.

In West Africa, Inikori (1977) and Richards (1980) established a correlation between the massive quantity of firearms imports and the flourishing of the slave trade. So bountiful was the inflow of firearms in the rivers,[1] creeks,[2] rivulets and coasts of the Niger Delta that its official designation as a slave coast and oil rivers, would easily substitute for an unofficial designation of a gun coast and a firearms river. More so, firearms with its contemporary nomenclature as small arms, induced several small wars in the Niger Delta (Osakwe et al. 2016), distinguished as slave wars, especially during the height of the transatlantic slave trade abolition effort (Afigbo 2006; Umoh 2017b). Indeed, firearms were central in promoting warfare in Atlantic Africa and supplying African armies (Thornton 1999). This picture made it difficult to disagree with Hacker's (2008: 62) submission that "the slave trade out of Africa resembled in many respects a prolonged series of small-scale military actions." Given that poverty and greed were central in the smooth operations of the slave trade (Akpan 2011), and the slave trade in turn depended on firearms, the indulgence and attraction of African states to arms and wars became sealed and was to outlive the period.

It is of note that Bonny was not only famous as the most important slave-exporting part of West Africa, but also the notoriety as the largest importer of firearms (Inikori 1977: 351) which accounted for the Bonny civil wars in 1869 argued in the context of crisis of adaptation inherent in commercial transition of coastal trading states from slave trade to trade in agricultural staples (Hopkins 1968: 580–606; 1973: 125–126, 135–164) as well as capability distribution among the canoe houses in the Niger Delta (Wariboko 1998). Indeed, the Niger Delta state in the period transiting the slave and non-slave trade, were able to indulge in power asymmetry (Kugler and Lemke 1996), power transition (see, Organski 1958; Organski and Kugler 1980), the Thucydides war trap (Allison 2017; Chan 2020) as well as the Ecclesiastes trap (Musgrave 2019), given the relative preponderance of SALWs at their disposal. Dike (1956) provided this backbone thought in his authoritative submission that guns provided unparallel assistance for the slave trading and slave raiding states of the Niger Delta coastal states to economically dominate and oppress the slave raided states in the hinterland.

These all weave to make valid the "slave-gun cycle" thesis which posits, using econometric models, that the arming of Africans was the principal reason for wars in Africa and the supply of slaves to the Atlantic world (Pilossof 2010; Whatley 2012). This meant that Africans conducted wars with weapons to supply the slave trade, and sold slaves chiefly to obtain the weapons that allowed them to seize more slaves, thereby making the rise in slave exports directly proportional to the quantity of firearms imported (Hacker 2008: 66). The trans-Atlantic slave trade period thus portrayed an armed conflict economy where poverty combined with greed, assumed epidemic proportions. As war clearly resulted from the efforts to control the slave trade (Hacker 2008), firearms combined to sustain the "slave-gun cycle" both as a motivation and a cause (Akpan 2011; Imbua 2013). However, this view has been challenged by Richards (1980) who notes that firearms were being imported well before the heyday of the slave trade and their importation continued to rise in many key slaving areas after its abolition.

Firearms also featured as items of ransom, reflecting the manifestation of greed in the context of a prevailing war economy. For instance, in the early 1860s, two hundred kegs of gunpowder and two hundred guns were among the items requested by Ogunmola, an Ibadan warrior, for the release of Edward Roper of the Church Missionary Society whom he had detained (Johnson 1956: 353). Firearms were very useful in the armed resistance of African states, kingdoms and potentates to European buccaneering imperial invasion. The armed resistance from King Jaja of Opobo (1887), King Nana of Olomu of Itsekiri (1892), King Ibanichuka of Okrika (1896), Oba Ovanrenwem of Benin (1897), and King Koko of Brass to European rule in the Niger Delta utilized resourceful amounts of firearms. The Akassa Small War of 1895 and the Ekumeku Small Wars between 1898 and 1911 in Ibusa (1898), Onicha-Olana (1902, 1903–1904 and 1909–1910), Ubulu-Uku (1904) and Ogwashi-Uku (1910–1911), all relied almost exclusively on small arms (Osakwe et al. 2016). However, it was reluctantly sufficient in the face of a larger cache of European firearms to neither resist Nigeria's British invaders (Asiegbu 1984) nor prevent the fall of Nigeria (Ikime 1977). It bears emphasizing that European colonialism in Africa was a violent enterprise achieved through the barrel of a gun and sustaining it was "forcibly carried out through the deployment of superior violence with the aid of highly lethal weapons," making for the proliferation of firearms (Aderinto 2018: 16).

In East Africa, firearms were significant for Ethiopia's power and the evolution of its army (Caulk 1972; Dunn 1994). Up North, aggressive European colonialism in the Maghrib between 1830 and 1914 witnessed the proliferation of SALWs (Abun-Nasr 1975: 235). The violent and rapid changes in African societies were significantly induced by the horde of firearms that thronged predominantly from Europe. Bialuschewski (2010) has shown how the European trade in slaves for firearms with indigenous communities accounted for the transformation of Malagasy society. European intrusion into Africa through the doors of the slave trade, imperialism, pacification, colonialism and neocolonialism brought in impressive volumes of firearms and these firearms accounted for the success of these enterprises. For instance, firearms were overwhelmingly significant in the pacification, annexation and colonialization of a great landscape of African societies including the extermination of a number of African people. Consequently, Aderinto (2018) identified small arms as enduring symbols of European imperialism. Ajayi (1968) and Roberts (1980) show how firearms created and sustained warrior-states in West Africa, while Kaba (1981) and Thornton (1998) have shown how firearms were implicated in inter-state warfare, regional conflict and state formation. Guy (1971) establishes a similar parallel for Southern Africa using the Zulu, and Storey (2008) interrogates the role that firearms played in conflicts in South Africa, extending the frontiers of the discussion of firearms beyond their military uses.

The extant literature has shown the breath of thoughts on the spread of SALWs in Africa. Fisher and Rowland (1971), Smaldone (1972, 1977) and

Inikori (1977) have examined the small arms trade in Central Sudan and the Sokoto Caliphate. Ubah (1994) showed how firearms aided the staggering caving in of the Sokoto Caliphate to British colonial domination. Smith (1976) attributed to West Africa the notorious designation of an armament zone in Africa. Subsequent research by Inikori (1977) and Eltis and Jennings (1988) made it difficult to disagree with Smith's assertion. For instance, Inikori (1977: 341) made an estimate of 45% as the proportion of English firearms in the total annual West African import of between 283,000 and 394,000 guns per annum in the second half of the eighteenth century, while Eltis and Jennings (1988: 950–951) submitted that the number of guns into sub-Saharan Africa surged to 200,000 annually in the 1860s from 190,000 annually in the 1780s. Aderinto (2018) went further to deploy firearms as a window into a broader political, social, cultural and economic history of colonial Nigeria. Despite the pre-colonial and colonial proliferation of firearms, Aderinto (2018: 7) argues that what pre-twentieth-century Africa had was a gun culture, not a gun society when measured in terms of "the level of interaction between a society and a gun." The outcome was an African society under the tight squeeze of militarism and militarization.

Explaining Poverty and Greed in SALWs Proliferation: The Deprived Actor and the Rational Actor Debate

Having established the relationship between SALWs and armed conflicts in Africa, it suffices to infer that that poverty and greed explain the proliferation of SALWs the same way it explains the manifestation of armed conflicts. Social actors in armed conflicts across Africa have displayed a combination of grievance or greed. This agrees with Jakobsen (2011) contention that in the literature on civil conflict, the deprived actor (DA)—which emphasizes grievances—and the rational actor (RA)—which emphasizes greed resource mobilization (McCarthy and Zald 1977) and opportunity structures (Collier and Hoeffler 1998; Korf 2011)—make for the two main theoretical schools for explaining collective armed violence. The DA approach emphasizes deprivation, grievance and frustration (DGF) as essential motivating factors for armed conflict and consequently the acquisition of SALWs. The RA approach, originally springing out from an economic theory (Jakobsen 2011), shifts from the DGF and emphasizes greed, opportunity and cost-benefit (GOC) as factors explaining armed conflicts and hence, proliferation of SALWs. Central to the RA is the expectation of a reward (Muller et al. 1991) where the expected utility of armed conflict is greater than the expected utility of keeping their daytime job (Collier and Hoeffler 1998: 517–518; Jakobsen 2011: 27–28).

Poverty and greed provide academic analyses of the drivers behind the proliferation of SALWs. The poverty-greed explanation provides a comprehensive challenge to the arms dynamics *cum* defense trade explanation. Buzan and Herring (1998: 790) defined the arms dynamics as "the entire set of pressures that make actors" pander toward arms in terms of increase in its quantity and quality. Those "set of pressures" that drive the arms dynamics have been identified by Spear and Cooper (2007: 312) as the action-reaction factors, domestic factors, technological imperative and the symbolic meaning. The arms dynamics drive vertically downward from top (the global north) to Collier's (2007) "bottom billion"—the biggest recipients of these arms. In most cases, such arms selling to the poorer developing countries have been "dressed as foreign aid" (Sampson 1977). This has spiraled dependency of the third world, of which Africa is located, on the "first world", a drain on the economy of the third world and a bleed on their development. However, the arms dynamic explanation has appeared too state-centric, narrowed to embrace the utility of the increase in the quantity and quality of arms on national influence (Schelling 1966) and the might of nations (Stoessinger 1992) or even why nations go to war (Stoessinger 2010). Apart from ignoring the overwhelming indulgence of non-state actors in the arms trade, the arms dynamic argument appears to consider all kinds of arms and not the exclusive limits of SALWs.

Toward the end of the twentieth century, economists made renewed and more vicious intervention into the theoretical and empirical understanding of a distinct subset of war—civil wars. This buccaneering invasion of social science scholars into the sub-disciplines of military history and economic history, was informed by the policy need to manage the antithetical relationship between civil wars and development. The idea and progress were needful to challenge the prevailing position that exclusively placed explanation for the initiation, duration and intensity of civil wars on the cold war geopolitical matrix (see, Newman 2014). First presented as a model, and later tested empirically using Africa as one of the distinguished geographical experiment, grievance (and its underbelly, poverty) and greed have thrived as viable explanations for civil wars in Africa, Americas, Europe and Asia. For instance, Bredal and Keen (1997) examined the policy implications of violence and economic agendas in civil wars. Collier and Hoeffler (1998) utilizing the platform provided by the *Oxford Economic Papers* ventilated their seminal contention "On the Economic Causes of Civil Wars." The ripples of their incisive contribution to the field of economic studies in general, and military studies in particular, had hardly settled when Collier (2000) employed econometric and statistical tools to explain rebellion as a quasi-criminal activity using the outlet of the *Journal of Conflict Resolution*. Berdal and Keen (1997) as well as Berdal and Malone (2000), capture greed and grievance as economic agendas in civil wars. Building upon bourgeoning literature on the subject, Collier (2001) proceeded to examine comprehensively an economic analysis of the implications of ethnic diversity. Collier and Hoeffler (2002), eventually identified greed and grievance as *explanans* of civil wars, drawing a significant empirical data for their fateful conclusion from Africa.

Furthermore, in Collier and Hoeffler's (2002) exposé, greed in civil wars concerned the ability to finance rebellion; and grievance concerned ethnic and religious divisions, political repression, inequality, poverty and bad governance. This added healthy justifications to why Collier (2000) had earlier dismissed rebellion as "quasi criminal activity." Ross (2003, 2004a, b, 2006) on his part, using evidences from 13 cases, has showed how natural resources influence civil wars and create what is called "booty futures"—exploitation rights to natural resources that they hope to capture in battle. Ross (2005: 28) further adds that "the market for booty futures, thus far, seems to be limited to Africa," explaining "why Africa has been the site of a growing fraction of the world's civil wars." Sorens (2011) made a bold case for the relationship between mineral production and ethnic rebellion incorporating Africa into the equation. Collier et al. (2004) extended the frontiers of knowledge to explain the duration of civil wars using grievance and greed. Fearon (2004) on his part used the dual *explanans* to explain why some civil wars enjoyed longer duration compared to other subset of wars. In all, grievance and greed has been utilized to provide causal explanations for the relationship between natural causes and natural resources as it affects the initiation, continuation, duration, intensity, inhibition and termination of civil wars in Africa, Americas, Europe and Asia (see, Collier and Hoeffler 1998; Klare 2001; Le Billon 2001; Fearon 2004, 2005; Collier et al. 2004). Indeed, grievance and greed served as utilities for rebellion. However, the enduring debate on greed and grievance (Collier and Hoeffler 2004) has been revisited by Bodea and Elbadawi (2007) as well as Collier et al. (2009) but falls outside the responsibility of this chapter.

In order to execute armed conflicts, both conflict labor and conflict capital are needed. The payment of conflict labor and the maintenance of conflict capital is made easy by the presence of what Synder (2002), as well as Lujala et al. (2005), call "lootable resources" such as diamonds in Angola and Sierra Leone, timber in Cambodia and Liberia, cocaine in Columbia, crude oil in Nigeria, among others. These resources, unfortunately have been the bane of poverty in these countries as well as point to the concentration of armed conflicts in states rich in natural resource. Conflict capital has been known to be sufficiently generated from the exponential rents accrued from the exploration and exploitation of primary commodities (de Soysa and Neumayer 2007). SALWs have enjoyed the conflict capital of states in armed conflict.

SALWs proliferation explains the strategic domain of armed conflicts, while poverty and greed combine to explain socio-economic motivations in armed conflicts. Besides SALWs proliferation, other strategic explanations for the incidence and duration of armed conflicts in Africa include terrain (Collier and Hoeffler 2004; Korf 2011; Umoh 2017a), ungoverned spaces (Rabasa 2007; Clunan and Trinkunas 2010; Umoh 2017a), skills, geographic dispersion of population (Herbst 2000), military advantage, state capacity (Englehart 2009; Fjelde and de Soysa 2009; Thies 2010; DeRouen et al. 2010; Hendrix 2010; Sobek 2010; McBride et al. 2011; De Juan and Jan 2015; Akpan and Umoh 2016), location and loss of strength gradient (Buhaug 2010), failure of the democratic peace project (Bodea and Elbadawi 2007; Collier 2009; Umoh 2012, 2015a) and even colonial and decolonizing experiences (Schmidt 2013). Ferguson (2006) went further to argue convincingly that the Third World War actually took place as the Third World's wars. Buhaug and Rod (2006) proceeded to compile the local determinants of African civil wars.

As Klare (2014) attempted to show, the importance of grievance over greed in armed conflict is eminent:

> While ethnic and religious divisions may provide the political and ideological fuel for these battles, it is the potential for mammoth oil profits that keeps the struggles alive. Without the promise of such resources, many of these conflicts would eventually die out for lack of funds to buy arms and pay troops. So long as the oil keeps flowing, however, the belligerents have both the means and incentive to keep fighting.

Such interest in profit does not coincide with neither Kaldor's (1998) and Münkler's (2004) "New Wars" nor Hoffman's (2007) "Hybrid Wars." From Julius Ceaser to Otto von Bismark, stretching through the conquistadores, the feudal barons and the condottiere, interest in profit had always been common (Lewison 1936). Whether explained in terms of greed or grievance, civil wars in Africa attract heavy reliance on the environment.

POVERTY AND GREED IN AFRICA'S POST-COLONIAL SALWs PROLIFERATION

The field of armed conflicts in Africa became more extensive and expensive in the post-colonial period, providing a more fertile arena where SALWs were deployed. Such armed conflicts follow an irregular bandwidth morphing and overlapping as the subsets of civil wars such as insurgencies, separatism, irredentism, militancy, as well as religious clashes, inter-communal wars, election wars, banditry, violent social movements, violent extremism, terrorism, among others. The basic heritage of these armed conflicts became a repetition *cum* continuation, laying credence to Stern's (2003) official submission that "the chief legacy of a civil war is another war." This reality in turn sustained the proliferation of SALWs in Africa. In the post-colonial period, SALWs were used to facilitate cross-border drug trafficking, smuggling, child theft and a general culture of violence. As the number of armed conflicts increased in Africa, so did the quantity of SALWs; and as the quantity of SALWs surged, so did armed conflicts endure. As colonial Africa gradually receded and gave way to the post-colonial period, it appeared that armed conflicts rapidly grew more intense and the availability of SALWs increased in epidemic proportions. For instance, Ross (2005: 28) notes that during the 1970s and 1980s, half of all intrastate armed conflicts in Africa could be classified as civil wars and in the 1990s, two-thirds of Africa's intrastate armed conflicts were civil wars. Debatably, such civil wars were mere effects made possible by a cause behind the causes—SALWs proliferation which received an exponential leap in Africa's post-colonial period. Aderinto (2018: 256–257) worked out a plausible explanation thus:

> The proliferation of guns in postcolonial Nigeria, as elsewhere in Africa, can also be explained in terms of the changes in the physical and political geography of the world following the collapse of European imperialism after World War II. In the first half of the twentieth century, European nations respected mutual agreements about the international sale of prohibited firearms to their colonies. But after granting independence to their former colonies, they flooded the continent with weapons of war in the global struggle against Soviet influence, supporting one armed group against another during civil wars and other Cold War–inspired conflicts. Lack of proper disarmament and demobilization after each major domestic conflict meant that firearms remained in circulation decades after wars and were recycled for use in subsequent strife.

The drawing up of the curtains upon the Cold War in the 1990s made the supply of SALWs overwhelm demand, thereby resulting in low cost weapons appealing to an array of violent social actors and giving rise to what Boutwell and Klare (1999) call "the killing grounds of the 1990s." Thus, the proliferation of SALWs in Africa coincided with a collapse in its cost in Europe. SALWs enjoyed remarkable proliferation in the anti-colonial insurgencies and revolutions in Angola, Mozambique, Guinea Bissau, Rhodesia, Algeria, among others, in the 1960s and 1970s as well as post-colonial interstate wars such as Ethiopia and Eritrea and even separatism attempts such as Nigeria and Biafra. The events in apartheid South Africa also attracted a swarth of SALWs for the festival of violence that ensured. Fleshman (2011) notes that in the 1970s, the apartheid government ensured the supplying of thousands of tons of arms and ammunition to its domestic and regional allies for the defense of white minority rule. The anti-apartheid government also smuggled in an estimated 30 tons of guns and explosives such as was sufficient to overwhelm domestic law enforcement efforts.

The tripartite of poverty, greed and the proliferation of SALWs has not featured as a wholesale attraction to scholars on African conflict. Kaplan (1994) for instance, neither considered poverty nor greed in the causal mix of the "coming anarchy" in West Africa. He rather considered "overpopulation, tribalism, drugs and environmental decline" as subsets of West Africa's violent future, leaving behind the manifestation of the proliferation of SALWs. However, a swarth of scholarship on African conflict overwhelmingly point to the manifestation of greed and grievances. For instance, Collier (1997), Collier and Hoeffler (1998), Gamba (1998), Reyneke (2000) have all shown how the proliferation of SALWs enhanced the phenomenon of armed conflicts in Africa. Gleditsch et al. (2002) noted that in 1992, 27% of the world's armed conflicts occurred in Africa. By 2001 when Salopek (2001) had estimated that over 100 million SALWs were circulating in Africa, Africa's share of the world's armed conflicts had risen to 41% (see, Wallensteen and

Sollenberg 2001). Building upon this empirical data, Ross (2005: 28) noted that while the number of armed conflicts outside of Africa had dropped by half between 1992 and 2001, within Africa, a drop in frequency of armed conflicts was hardly noticed. In 2006, the West Africa Action Network on Small Arms (WAANSA) estimated that 8 million small arms and light weapons were transiting through the sub-region (Ndiaye 2008: 3) making West Africa "the most unstable subregion on the continent" (Keili 2008: 5). Accordingly, the stark reality of armed conflicts in Africa in that period attracted the ink of a host development scholars.

The vast majority of SALWs—perhaps 95%—that sustain armed conflicts in Africa, come from outside Africa (Hillie 2007: 2). With an estimated quantity of over 550 million small arms in circulation globally (SAS 2001: 59) and nearly 300 companies in over 50 countries worldwide actively manufacturing small arms and its complementary equipment and accessories (Rana 1995: 7), there is a geographical pressure on sustaining violence in Africa. Uncontrolled SALWs in Africa has sustained the concentration of armed conflicts in Africa, consolidated crisis ridden zones, and shaped the socio-political and security concerns across the African continent (Adeniyi 2017: 11, 28).

The proliferation of SALWs (both legitimate and illicit) in post-colonial Africa appeared to have followed an assumed parabola which touched the axes of production, distribution and consumption. Undeniably, the proliferation of SALWs is not barren of a political-economy argument, especially as it concerns its demand and supply parabola. In this curve, the global, national and local interface. Weak state capacity which produces the triple realities of governance capacity, vulnerability quotient and ungoverned spaces (Umoh 2017a), are often prioritized in the explanation of the proliferation of SALWs in Africa. State fragility, as noted by Barlow (2020), contributes in creating an ever-increasing demand for small arms and light weapons. Howbeit, the incidences of poverty and greed are overshadowed by these dominant *explanans*.

Poverty in Need of SALWs

The proliferation of SALWs for the purpose of a range of armed conflict, mirrors the degree of grievances against the state. In grievance, military and political objectives appear to provide the obvious rationale for fighting. Such grievances have been identified to be induced by relative poverty in the context of relative deprivation (Gurr 1970; Abeles 1976; Gurney and Tierney 1982), rank disequilibrium (Hernes 1969), basic human needs (Maslow 1943; Burton 1990), rising expectations (Davies 1962; Obershall 1968; Davies 1969; Gurr 1970; Taylor 1982) frustration (Dollard et al. 1939; Miller et al. 1941; Galtung 1964; Berkowitz 1969), among others. All these grievance spin-offs point to deprivation as their common denominator; and deprivation, according to Narayan et al. (2000: 4), represents a multidimensional view of poverty. Such poverty-driven grievances bridged the economic and the political. While Sen (1973) asserted that the relationship between economic inequality and rebellion is a closed one, Renal-Querol (2002) restricted armed conflict initiation to ethnicity and political systems; and Collier and Hoeffler (2004) broadened it to encompass four "objective" variables: ethnic or religious hatred, political repression, political exclusion and economic inequality.

As Collier et al. (2003: 53) noted, "war causes poverty, but the more important reason for the concentration is that poverty increases the likelihood of civil war." The armed conflict-development scholar and his team empirically showed how poverty tends to cause armed conflicts by revealing that civil wars are heavily concentrated in the poorest countries. Africa with exceptionally high poverty rates, provides an easy explanation for the incidences of armed conflicts in Africa. It is suggestive then that poverty inscribes and describes need modeled in the context of grievance.

Given the development determinants of African countries which is arguably ascertained by Seers' (1969) core development variables of poverty, unemployment and inequality; the argument for poverty and greed in the acquisition of SALWs for the prosecution of armed conflicts for both survival and commercial gains becomes almost complete. Armed rebellion in Africa appeared to have provided a safety valve out of poverty. In most conflict zones, like witnessed in the Niger Delta of Nigeria, it provided armed groups and its leaders with an industry to employ an impressive number of youths who, with minimum academic qualifications, lacked monthly paid jobs (see, Tangban and Umoh 2014; Umoh 2015b). Consequently, poverty and unemployment— a twin status that measures inequality—are often addressed in a convoluted environment of violence in Africa. Seers' (1969) variables of poverty, unemployment and inequality also make for composite arguments for grievances, compressing the relationship between grievance and greed into a lump.

GREED IN NEED OF SALWs

The political economy of natural resource curse (Ross 1999) in unique ways interfaces the political economy of SALWs proliferation through the political economy of violence. Armed conflicts circumscribe a political economy of destruction (see, Collier 2009) with SALWs being the basis of that political economy. Greed makes for the proliferation of SALWs in Africa on the basis of marketing of local resources and procurement of SALWs. As greed sustains the duration of armed conflicts, it sustains the proliferation of SALWs. Such armed conflicts are hardly fought to be won but rather fought to sustain the profits garnered from the manipulation of violence in a war economy. In Africa's post-colonial armed conflict environment, shooting became sustained through looting, and looting became uninterruptedly carried out in the atmosphere of shooting. Indeed, as long as the shooting is sustained, the looting goes unhindered. Consequently, a criminal economy is sustained and SALWs stand out as the basic feature and outcome of that economy. Keen (1998: 11) for instance had observed that:

Conflict can create war economies, often in the regions controlled by rebels or warlords and linked to international trading networks; members of armed gangs can benefit from looting; and regimes can use violence to deflect opposition, reward supporters or maintain their access to resources. Under these circumstances, ending civil wars becomes difficult. Winning may not be desirable: the point of war may be precisely the legitimacy which it confers on actions that in peacetime would be punishable as crimes.

Greed has also been implicated in African armed conflicts. Rebels, warlords and insurgents have not been the only perceived "deviant" set to passionately indulge in the proliferation of arms for war-economy profits in Africa, but also mercenaries, and the array of private securities (see, Cilliers and Mason 1999). Difficulties permeate the attempt to entirely discountenance greed from natural resource secession (Collier et al. 2003: 64). Commenting on the commercial dimension of rebellion, Collier et al. (2003: 82) enthused thus: "Greed perhaps fares a little better as an explanation, as secessionist rebellions seem to be linked to the desire to appropriate valuable resources and some rebel leaders appear more committed to a person than to a social agenda."

The extent to which these resources make conflict actors vulnerable to contention by means of armed fighting has attracted appellations with elastic connotations such as: "paradox of plenty" (Karl 1997), "natural resource curse" (Auty 2001; Caselli and Cunningham 2009), "natural resource wars" (Klare 2001; Le Billon 2005), "tragedy of endowment" (Alao 2007), "fighting over oil" (Lujala et al. 2007), "oil-civil war link" (Di John 2007), "honey pot thesis" (Collier 2009), "spoils of nature" (Lujala 2010), "crisis of abundance" (Umoh 2010), "oiling and spoiling", "oil wars" (Tamuno 2011), "oil and blood" (Klare 2014) "energy wars" (Klare 2014), among others. Using Nigeria's Niger Delta as a research experiment, Oyefusi (2008) made a detailed examination of the multiplicity of factors that present rebels with opportunity, thereby adding to the theoretical explanations for rebel motivation in resource-based societies. He notes elsewhere that while a grievance-based explanation appears to be obvious, it lacks a high statistical effect to make it sufficient compared with perceived benefits, and opportunity cost of participation in violence such as low-income level, low-education attainment and abysmal social infrastructure (Oyefusi 2010).

The "greed" thesis mirrors the rent-seeking theory, which, posits that the existence of a valuable "prize" such as mineral resource rents, induces individuals with motivation to devote time and resources to appropriate the "prize" by trying to capture the state and finance rebellion (see, Di John 2007). The more so, when the state, in de Soysa and Fjelde's (2010: 290) phrase, is "the only game in town." Armed groups motivated by greed hardly strive for defeat and the subsequent termination of armed conflicts, but the continuity thereof. In Liberia (1990–1997) and Sierra Leone (1997–2002) for instance, battlefield intensity and duration meant profit. Liberia, Sierra Leone, Angola, and the DRC, made for classic instances where armed groups sold natural resources to fund their war efforts. Indeed, the flow of SALWs and low-cost military equipment into Liberia during its civil war years made warfare rather cheap attracting Muntschick's (2008) description of the outcome as "greedy and grievous." Mateos (2010) attempt to interface greed and grievance in armed conflicts in Sierra Leone was further strengthened by Feinstein's (2011) use of Sierra Leone and Liberia to establish the relationship between diamonds and SALWs. Feinstein (2011: 98) blamed the "whirlwind of human brutality" in the two neighboring states on the "shadow world of a network of arms dealers, diamond smugglers and timber merchants." This view incorporates and accommodates greed dressed as grievance. These combine to show that SALWs have fueled the illicit trafficking of natural resources such as oil, diamonds, timber and coffee in many parts of Africa. Keili (2008: 8) puts it in a rather organized and convincing narrative thus: "the local oil boom also facilitates proliferation, as rebel groups carry out oil bunkering to arm themselves. Much of West Africa's mineral wealth is being diverted to aid small arms proliferation in West Africa, and ..., these arms in turn are ensuring that this diversion of resources persists, to the detriment of development."

Congo, a resource domain for over 80% of the world's reserves of cobalt, 70% of the world's coltan and about 50% of the world's diamond reserves (Thomson 2004: 217–225; Meredith 2006: 93–100) has been an armed conflict zone in Africa since the 1960s given the need for violent entrepreneurs to actualize what Ross (2005) calls "booty future." The argument of Berdal and Malone (2000) point to this reality: "what is usually considered to be the most basic of military objectives in war - that is, defeating the enemy in battle - has been replaced by economically driven interests in continued fighting and the institutionalization of violence at what is for some clearly a profitable level of intensity."

As Arson (2005: 4) observes, "defeating the enemy or bringing the fighting to an end appears to have become less important for key parties involved than securing the benefits from the continuation of conflict." Thus, continuity defines the violence space in Africa, suggesting the permanence of war. Such permanence is sustained by an enduring proliferation of SALWs. The use, misuse and abuse of SALWs made it easy and tempting for children to participate in the armed conflicts of Liberia, Sierra Leone, Mozambique, Angola, Sudan, Tanzania, Rwanda, Burundi, Congo (see, Singer 2005; Honwana 2006) and even Nigeria.

An extension of the greed argument is that the benefits of war are closely linked to the presence of, and access to, natural resources in the area of conflict. Indeed, various armed groups and governments have funded armed conflicts in Africa and financed the purchase of SALWs by illegally exploiting various resources such as timber, coltan, diamond, gold, ivory, among others, or engaged in drug trafficking and other such illegal activities. Relying on quantitative analysis, de Soysa (2000) argues that "an abundance of mineral wealth is positively and significantly related to armed conflict." The Angolan

Civil War, for instance, provided the National Union for the Total Independence of Angola (UNITA) about 70% of Angola's diamond production, creating conditions for regional commanders, cross national middlemen, local gold artisans and traders to accumulate substantial national wealth. As the Angolan civil war dragged on, the belligerency in the war became even more questionable given the observed collusion between the Popular Movement for the Liberation of Angola (MPLA) and UNITA in the aspect of sales of SALWs. UNITA also depended heavily on the diamond trade having outlets in Israel, Belgium and South Africa. These three conflict actors appeared to be more concerned about enriching themselves through black market logging activities and gems trading than in ensuring, through decisive battles, that the war came to an end. Ellis (1999) notes also that during the Liberian Civil War between 1989 and 1997, factions avoided real time battle engagement but rather simulated military engagements designed solely to facilitate looting. In Sierra Leone the sale of diamonds and gold on the global market partly explained the prolonged duration of the war. As the war continued, it generated wealth for elite officials, warlord commanders and various international companies and businesses, thereby giving war the proxy notion as the trade of kings.

While poverty and greed combine to circumscribe the economic causes and commercial schemas in wars (Berdal and Malone 2000), greed is directly linked to the "attempt to benefit materially from war, through looting or other forms of violent accumulation" (Berdal and Malone 2000: 3). Attempts at bilateral and multilateral cooperation, border surveillance and patrols, judicial cooperation, intelligence sharing on curtailing the flow of SALWs in Africa, and even the regulation of local arms production, appear to have all collapsed under the weight of poverty and greed.

Conclusion

The proliferation of SALWs is tied to both poverty and greed alike and this has left behind huge footprints of ruins. Poverty and greed suffice as its causes, while proliferation of SALWs as its effects. The experience of African states has shown that need combines with greed to make the proliferation of SALWs inevitable. Africa's post-colonial period attracted an overwhelming interest in the consideration of poverty and greed as explanations for armed conflicts and by extension, the utility and spread of SALWs. The security guarantee from SALWs in Africa has produce insecurity and fear. Armed conflicts were neither a function of ignorance nor fear but of poverty and greed. The fragmentation of Africa's political and economic space from the colonial into the post-colonial shaped the availability, circulation and utility of SALWs. Neither the intensity of poverty nor the passion of greed can sustain armed conflicts without the sustained supply of SALWs. The unavoidable intersection of poverty and greed largely determine the proliferation of SALWs in Africa's armed conflicts.

NOTES

1. Such as the Benin, Escravos, Forcados, Nun, Brass, Adoni, Opobo, Brass, Ramos, Ethiope and Sangara Rivers, among others.
2. Such as the Jones, Brass, Bodo, Nwaja, Clough, and Robbins creeks, among others.

REFERENCES

Abeles, R. P. (1976). Relative Deprivation, Rising Expectations and Black Militancy. *Journal of Social Issues, 32,* 119–137.

Abun-Nasr, J. M. (1975). *A History of the Maghrib.* Cambridge: Cambridge University Press.

Adeniyi, A. (2017). *The Human Cost of Uncontrolled Arms in Africa: Cross-National Research on Seven African Countries* (Oxfam International Research Reports).

Aderinto, S. (2018). *Guns and Society in Colonial Nigeria: Firearms, Culture, and Public Order.* Bloomington: Indiana University Press.

Afigbo, A. E. (2006). *The Abolition of Slave Trade in Southeastern Nigeria, 1885-1950.* New York: University of Rochester Press.

Ajayi, J. F. (1968). Professional Warriors in Nineteenth Century Yoruba Politics. *Tarikh, 1,* 72–81.

Ajayi, J. F. (1989). Africa at the Beginning of the Nineteenth Century: Issues and Prospects. In J. F. Ajayi (Ed.), *UNESCO General History of Africa VI: Africa in the Nineteenth Century Until the 1880s.* Los Angeles, CA: University of California Press.

Akpan, O. (2011). *The Niger Delta Question and the Peace Plan.* Ibadan: Spectrum Books.

Akpan, O., & Umoh, U. E. (2016). State Capacity and Insurgency in the Niger Delta of Nigeria Since the 1990s. *Conflict Studies Quarterly, 14,* 92–110.

Alao, A. (2007). *Natural Resources and Conflict in Africa: The Tragedy of Endowment.* New York: University of Rochester Press.

Allison, G. (2017). *Destined for War: Can America and China Escape Thucydides's Trap?* Boston: Houghton Mifflin Harcourt.

Alpern, S. B. (1995). What Africans Got for Their Slaves: A Master List of European Trade Goods. *History in Africa, 22,* 5–43.

Arson, C. (2005). The Political Economy of War: Situating the Debate. In C. Arson & W. Zartman (Eds.), *Rethinking the Economics of War: The Intersection of Need, Creed and Greed* (p. 4). Washington, D.C: The Woodrow Wilson Centre Press.

Asiegbu, U. J. (1984). *Nigeria and Its British Invaders, 1851-1920.* London: Nok Publishers International.

Auty, R. (2001). *Resource Abundance and Economic Development.* World Institute for Development Economics Research, London: Oxford University Press.

Barlow, E. (2020). A Plague of Greed and Illegality. *Africa in Fact.* Issue 52.

Berdal, M., & Keen, D. (1997). Violence and Economic Agendas in Civil Wars: Some Policy Implications. *Millennium: Journal of International Studies, 26*(3), 795–818.

Berdal, M., & Malone, D. M. (2000). *Greed and Grievance: Economic Agendas in Civil Wars.* Boulder and London: Lynne Rienner.

Berkowitz, L. (1969). *Roots of Aggression: A Re-Examination of the Frustration-Aggression Hypothesis*. New York: Atherton Press.

Bialuschewski, A. (2010). Firearms and Warfare in Late Seventeenth and Early Eighteenth Century Madagascar. In T. Falola & R. C. Njoku (Eds.), *War and Peace in Africa* (pp. 57–71). Durham, NC: Carolina Academic Press.

Bodea, C., & Elbadawi, I. (2007). *Riots, Coups and Civil Wars: Revisiting the Greed and Grievance Debate* (World Bank Policy Research Working Paper 4397). New York: World Bank.

Boutwell, J., & Klare, M. (1999). *Light Weapons and Civil Conflict: Controlling the Tools of Violence*. New York: Carnegie Corporation.

Buhaug, H. (2010). Dude, Where Is My Conflict? LSG, Relative Strength, and the Location of Civil War. *Conflict Management and Peace Science, 27*(2), 107–128.

Buhaug, H., & Rod, J. K. (2006). Local Determinants of African Civil Wars, 1970-2001. *Political Geography, 253,* 315–335.

Burton, J. (1990). *Conflict: Human Needs Theory*. London: Palgrave Macmillan.

Buzan, B., & Herring, E. (1998). *The Arms Dynamics in World Politics*. London: Lynne Rienner.

Caselli, F., & Cunningham, T. (2009). Leader Behaviour and the Natural Resource Curse. *Oxford Economic Papers, 61*(4), 628–650.

Caulk, R. A. (1972). Firearms and Princely Power in Ethiopia in the Nineteenth Century. *Journal of African History, 13*(4), 609–630.

Chan, S. (2020). *Thucydides's Trap? Historical Interpretation, Logic of Inquiry, and the Future of Sino-American Relations*. Ann Arbor, MI: University of Michigan Press.

Cilliers, J., & Mason, P. (Eds.). (1999). *Peace, Profit or Plunder: The Privatisation of Security in War-Torn African Societies*. Johannesburg: Institute for Security Studies.

Clunan, A., & Trinkunas, H. A. (2010). *Ungoverned Spaces: Alternatives to State Authority in an Era of Softened Sovereignty*. Stanford, CA: Stanford University Press.

Collier, P. (1997). *The Role of the State in Economic Development: Cross Regional Experience*. Plenary Paper presented at the AERC Research Workshop, Harare, Zimbabwe, 6–11 December.

Collier, P. (2000). Rebellion as Quasi-Criminal Activity. *Journal of Conflict Resolution, 44*(6), 839–853.

Collier, P. (2001). Ethnic Diversity: An Economic Analysis of Its Implications. *Economic Policy, 32,* 129–166.

Collier, P. (2007). *The Bottom Billion: Why the Poorest Countries Are Failing and What Can Be Done About It*. London: Oxford University Press.

Collier, P. (2009). *Wars, Guns and Votes: Democracy in Dangerous Places*. London: The Bodley Head.

Collier, P., Elliott, V. L., Hegre, H., Hoeffler, A., Reynal-Querol, M., & Sambanis, N. (2003). *Breaking the Conflict Trap: Civil War and Development Policy*. Washington, DC: The World Bank and Oxford University Press.

Collier, P., & Hoeffler, A. (1998). On the Economic Causes of Civil War. *Oxford Economic Papers, 50,* 563–573.

Collier, P., & Hoeffler, A. (2002). *Greed and Grievance in Civil War* (CSAE Working Paper WPS 2002-01). Oxford University.

Collier, P., & Hoeflfer, A. (2004). Greed and Grievance in Civil War. *Oxford Economic Papers, 56,* 563–595.

Collier, P., Hoeffler, A., & Rohner, D. (2009). Beyond Greed and Grievance: Feasibility and Civil War. *Oxford Economic Papers, 61*(1), 1–27.

Collier, P., Hoeffler, A., & SÖderbom, M. (2004). On the Duration of Civil War. *Journal of Peace Research, 41,* 253–273.
Davies, G. (1957). *The Royal African Company.* London: Longmans, Green & Co.
Davies, J. C. (1962). Toward a Theory of Revolution. *American Sociological Review, 27*(1), 5–19.
Davies, J. C. (1969). The J-Curve of Rising and Declining Satisfactions as a Cause of Some Great Revolutions and a Contained Rebellion. In H. D. Graham & T. R. Gurr (Eds.), *Violence in America: The History of Violence in America: Historical and Comparative Perspectives* (pp. 690–730). New York: Praeger.
De Juan, A., & Jan, H. (2015). Manpower to Coerce and Co-Opt: State Capacity and Political Violence in Sudan 2006-2010. *Conflict Management and Peace Science, 32*(2), 175–199.
de Soysa, I. (2000). The Resource Curse: Are Civil Wars Driven by Rapacity or Paucity? In M. Berdal & D. M. Malone (Eds.), *Greed and Grievance: Economic Agendas in Civil Wars* (p. 113). Boulder: Lynne Rienner Publishers, Inc.
de Soysa, I., & Fjelde, H. (2010). Is the Hidden Hand an Iron Fist? Capitalism and Civil Peace, 1970-2005. *Journal of Peace Research, 47*(3), 287–298.
de Soysa, I., & Neumayer, E. (2007). Resource, Wealth and the Risk of Civil War Onset: Results from a New Dataset of Natural Resource Rents, 1970-1999. *Conflict Management and Peace Science, 24*(3), 201–218.
DeRouen, K., Ferguson, M., Norton, S., Park, Y., Lea, J., & Streat-Bartlett, A. (2010). Civil War Peace Agreement Implementation and State Capacity. *Journal of Peace Research, 47*(3), 333–346.
Di John, J. (2007). Oil Abundance and Violent Political Conflict: A Critical Assessment. *Journal of Development Studies, 43*(6), 961–986.
Dike, K. O. (1956). *Trade and Politics in the Niger Delta, 1830-1885: An Introduction to the Economic and Political History of Nigeria.* London: Clarendon Press.
Dollard, J., Miller, N. E., Doob, L. W., Mowrer, O. H., & Sears, R. R. (1939). *Frustration and Aggression.* New Haven, CT: Yale University Press.
Dunn, J. (1994). "For God, Emperor, and Country!" The Evolution of Ethiopia's Nineteenth-Century Army. *War in History, 1*(3), 278–299.
Ellis, S. (1999). *The Mask of Anarchy.* London: Hurst and Company.
Eltis, D., & Jennings, L. C. (1988). Trade Between Western Africa and the Atlantic World in the Pre-Colonial Era. *American Historical Review, 93*(4), 936–959.
Englehart, N. (2009). State Capacity, State Failure and Human Rights. *Journal of Peace Research, 46*(2), 163–180.
Fearon, J. (2004). Why Do Some Civil Wars Last so Much Longer Than Others? *Journal of Peace Research, 41*(2), 275–301.
Fearon, J. (2005). Paradigm in Distress? Primary Commodities and Civil War. *Journal of Conflict Resolution, 49*(4), 483–507.
Feinstein, A. (2011). *The Shadow World: Inside the Global Arms Trade.* London: Hamish Hamilton.
Ferguson, N. (2006). The Next War of the World. *Foreign Affairs, 85*(5), 61–74.
Fisher, H. J., & Rowland, V. (1971). Firearms in Central Sudan. *Journal of African History, XII,* 215–239.
Fjelde, H., & de Soysa, I. (2009). Coercion, Co-optation, or Cooperation? State Capacity and the Risk of Civil War, 1961-2004. *Conflict Management and Peace Science, 26*(1), 6–25.

Fleshman, M. (2011, December). Small Arms in Africa: Counting the Cost of Gun Violence. *Africa Renewal*.
Galtung, J. (1964). A Structural Theory of Aggression. *Journal of Peace Research*, 1(2), 95–119.
Gamba, V. (Ed.) (1998). *Society Under Siege: Licit Responses to Illicit Arms*. Pretoria, South Africa: Institute for Security Studies.
Gleditsch, N. P., Strand, H., Eriksson, M., Sollenberg, M., & Wallensteen, P. (2002). Armed Conflict 1946-99: A New Dataset. *Journal of Peace Research*, 38(5), 615–637.
Gurney, J. N., & Tierney, K. J. (1982). Relative Deprivation and Social Movements: A Critical Look at Twenty Years of Theory and Research. *The Sociological Quarterly*, 23(1), 33–47.
Gurr, T. R. (1970). *Why Men Rebel*. Princeton, NJ: Princeton University Press.
Guy, J. (1971). A Note on Firearms in the Zulu Kingdom with Special Reference to the Anglo-Zulu War, 1879. *Journal of African History*, 12(4), 557–570.
Hacker, B. C. (2008). Firearms, Horses, and Slave Soldiers: The Military History of African Slavery. *Icon*, 14, 62–83.
Hatch, J. (1969). *The History of Britain in Africa: From the Fifteenth Century to the Present*. London: André Deutsch.
Hendrix, C. (2010). Measuring State Capacity: Theoretical and Empirical Implications for the Study of Civil Conflict. *Journal of Peace Research*, 47(3), 273–285.
Herbst, J. I. (2000). *State and Power in Africa: Comparative Lessons in Authority and Control*. Princeton: Princeton University Press.
Hernes, G. (1969). On Rank Disequilibrium and Military Coups D'Etat. *Journal of Peace Research*, 6(1), 65–72.
Hillie, D. (2007). *Africa's Missing Billions: International Arms Flows and the Cost of Conflict* (Oxfam International, IANSA and Saferworld Briefing Paper 107). UK.
Hoffman, F. (2007). *The Rise of Hybrids Wars*. Arlington, VA: Potomac Institute for Policy Studies.
Honwana, A. (2006). *Child Soldiers in Africa*. Philadelphia: University of Pennsylvania Press.
Hopkins, A. G. (1968). Economic Imperialism in West Africa, Lagos 1880–92. *Economic History Review*, 21(2), 580–606.
Hopkins, A. G. (1973). *An Economic History of West Africa*. London.
Ikime, O. (1977). *The Fall of Nigeria: The British Conquest*. London: Heinemann Publishers.
Imbua, D. L. (2013). Slavery and Slave Trade Remembered: A Study of the Slave History Museum in Calabar, Nigeria. *Journal of the Historical Society of Nigeria*, 22, 112–136.
Inikori, J. E. (1977). The Import of Firearms into West Africa 1750-1807: A Quantitative Analysis. *Journal of African History*, 18(3), 339–386.
Jakobsen, T. G. (2011). Theories of Collective Violence: The Continuing Rational Actor Versus Deprived Actor Debate. In T. G. Jakobsen (Ed.), *War: An Introduction to Theories and Research on Collective Violence* (pp. 19–34). New York: Nova Science Publishers.
Johnson, S. (1956). *The History of the Yorubas: From the Earliest Times to the Beginning of the British Protectorate*. Lagos: CMS (Nigeria) Bookshop.

Kaba, L. (1981). Archers, Musketeers and Mosquitoes: The Moroccan Invasion of the Sudan and the Songhay Resistance (1591–1612). *Journal of African History, 20*(4), 457–475.

Kaldor, M. (1998). *New and Old Wars: Organized Violence in a Global Era*. Oxford: Blackwell Publishers.

Kaplan, R. D. (1994). *The Comming Anarchy: Shattering the Dreams of the Post Cold War*. New York: Random House.

Karl, T. (1997). *The Paradox of Plenty: Oil Booms and Petro-States*. Los Angeles: University of California Press.

Kea, R. E. (1971). Firearms and Warfare in the Gold and Slave Coast from the Sixteenth to the Nineteenth Centuries. *Journal of African History, 12*(2), 185–213.

Keen, D. (1998). *The Economic Functions of Violence in Civil Wars* (Adelphi Paper 320). Oxford: Oxford University Press for the International Institute for Strategic Studies.

Keili, F. L. (2008). Small Arms and Light Weapons Transfer in West Africa: A Stock-Taking. *Disarmament Forum, 4*, 5–12.

Klare, M. T. (2001). *Natural Resource Wars: The New Landscape of Global Conflict*. New York: Metropolitan Books.

Klare, M. T. (2014). *Twenty-First Century Energy Wars: How Oil and Gas Are Fueling Global Conflicts*. http://energypost.eu/twenty-first-century-energy-wars-oil-gas-fuelling-global-conflicts/. Date accessed and retrieved 16 September 2019, 9:54 a.m.

Korf, B. (2011). Resources, Violence and the Telluric Geographies of Small Wars. *Progress in Human Geography, 35*(6), 733–756.

Kugler, J., & Lemke, D. (1996). *Parity and War: Evaluations and Extensions of the War Ledger*. Ann Arbor, MI: University of Michigan Press.

Le Billon, P. (2001). The Political Ecology of War: Natural Resources and Armed Conflicts. *Political Geography, 20*(5), 561–584.

Le Billon, P. (2005). Geographies of War: Perspectives on 'Resource Wars'. *Geography Compass, 1*(2), 163–182.

Lewison, R. (1936). *The Profits of War Through the Ages*. London: George Routledge and Sons Ltd.

Lujala, P. (2010). The Spoils of Nature: Armed Civil Conflict and Rebel Access to Natural Resources. *Journal of Peace Research, 47*(1), 15–28.

Lujala, P., Gleditsch, N. P., & Gilmore, E. (2005). A Diamond Curse? Civil War and a Lootable Resource. *Journal of Conflict Resolution, 49*(4), 538–562.

Lujala, P., Rod, J., & Thieme, N. (2007). Fighting Over Oil: Introducing a New Dataset. *Conflict Management and Peace Science, 24*(3), 239–256.

Maslow, A. H. (1943). A Theory of Human Motivation. *Psychological Review, 50*(4), 370–396.

Mateos, O. (2010). Beyond Greed and Grievance: Towards a Comprehensive Approach to African Armed Conflicts—Sierra Leone as a Case Study. In R. Bowd & A. B. Chikwanha (Eds.), *Understanding Africa's Contemporary Conflicts: Origins, Challenges and Peacebuilding*. A Monograph for the Africa Human Security Initiative, Addis Ababa.

McBride, M., Milante, G., & Skaperdas, S. (2011). Peace and War with Endogenous State Capacity. *Journal of Conflict Resolution, 55*(3), 446–468.

McCarthy, J. D., & Zald, M. N. (1977). Resource Mobilization and Social Movements: A Partial Theory. *American Journal of Sociology, 82*(6), 1212–1241.

Meredith, M. (2006). *The State of Africa: A History of Fifty Years of Independence*. London: Free Press.
Miller, N. E., et al. (1941). The Frustration-Aggression Hypothesis. *Psychological Review*, 48(4), 337–342.
Muller, E. N., Dietz, H. A., & Finkel, S. E. (1991). Discontent and the Expected Utility of Rebellion: The Case of Peru. *American Political Science Review*, 85(4), 1261–1282.
Münkler, H. (2004). *The New Wars*. Cambridge: Polity Press.
Muntschick, J. (2008). The 'Great War' in Liberia as Classic Example for Persistent Armed Conflicts and War-Economies in Africa. *Columbia Internacional*, 67, 38–59.
Musgrave, P. (2019). Asymmetry, Hierarchy and the Ecclesiastes Trap. *International Studies Review*, 21(2), 284–300.
Narayan, D., Patel, R., Schafft, K., Rademacher, A., & Schulte, S. K. (2000). *Voices of the Poor: Can Anyone Hear Us?* New York: Oxford University Press.
Ndiaye, N. (2008). Special Comment. *The Complex Dynamics of Small Arms in West Africa* (Disarmament Forum No. 4). United Nations Institute for Disarmament Research.
Newman, E. (2014). *Understanding Civil Wars: Continuity and Change in Intrastate Conflict*. New York: Routledge.
Northrup, D. (2002). *Africa's Discovery of Europe*. Oxford: Oxford University Press.
Obershall, A. (1968). Rising Expectations and Political Turmoil. *Journal of Development Studies*, 6(1), 5–23.
Organski, A. F. K. (1958). *World Politics*. New York, NY: Knopf.
Organski, A. F. K., & Kugler, J. (1980). *The War Ledger*. Chicago, IL: University of Chicago Press.
Osakwe, C. C. C., Akpan, O., & Umoh, U. E. (2016). Globalization and 'Small Wars' in Africa: The Case of Niger Delta, Nigeria. In U. A. Tar, E. Mijah, & M. E. U. Tedheke (Eds.), *Globalization in Africa: Perspectives on Development, Security and Environment* (pp. 271–288). Lanham: Lexington Books.
Oyefusi, A. (2008). Oil and the Probability of Rebel Participation Among Youths in the Niger Delta of Nigeria. *Journal of Peace Research*, 45(4), 539–555.
Oyefusi, A. (2010). Oil, Youths, and Civil Unrest in Nigeria's Delta: The Role of Schooling, Educational Attainments, Earnings, and Unemployment. *Conflict Management and Peace Science*, 47(4), 326–346.
Pilossof, R. (2010). 'Guns Don't Colonise People …': The Role and Use of Firearms in Pre-Colonial and Colonial Africa. *Kronos*, 36, 266–277.
Rabasa, A. (2007). *Ungoverned Territories: Understanding and Reducing Terrorism Risks*. Santa Monica: RAND Corporation.
Rana, S. (1995). *Small Arms and Intra-State Conflicts*. New York: UNIDIR.
Renal-Querol, M. (2002). Ethnicity, Political Systems and Civil War. *Journal of Conflict Resolution*, 46, 29–54.
Reyneke, E. (2000). *Small Arms and Light Weapons in Africa: Illicit Proliferation, Circulation and Trafficking*. Proceedings of the OAU Experts Meeting and International Consultation, May–June 2000. Pretoria, South Africa: Institute for Security Studies.
Richards, W. A. (1980). The Import of Firearms into West Africa in the Eighteenth Century. *Journal of African History*, 21(1), 43–59.

Roberts, R. L. (1980). Production and Reproduction of Warrior States: Segu Bambara and Segu Tokolor, c. 1712-1890. *International Journal of African Historical Studies, 13*(3), 389–419.

Ross, L. (1999). The Political Economy of the Resource Curse. *World Politics, 51*(2), 297–332.

Ross, L. (2003). Oil, Drugs and Diamonds: The Varying Role of National Reserves and Civil War. In B. Karenand & J. Sherman (Eds.), *The Political Economy of Armed Conflict: Beyond Greed and Grievance* (pp. 47–60). Boulder, CO: Lynne Reiner.

Ross, M. (2004a). What Do We Know About Natural Resources and Civil War? *Journal of Peace Research, 41*(3), 337–356.

Ross, L. (2004b). How Do Natural Resources Influence Civil War? Evidence from Thirteen Cases. *International Organisations, 58*(2), 489–516.

Ross, M. (2005). *Booty Futures*. Los Angeles: Mimeo, University of California.

Ross, L. (2006). A Closer Look at Oil, Diamonds, and Civil War. *Annual Review of Political Science, 9*, 265–300.

Salopek, P. (2001, December 23). Leftover Arms Fuel Continent's Ruinous Wars: Cold War Surplus Wreaks Havoc. *Chicago Tribune*.

Sampson, A. (1977). *The Arms Bazaar: The Companies, The Dealers, The Bribes—From Vickers to Lockheed*. Hodder and Stoughton: Coronet Books.

Schelling, T. C. (1966). *Arms and Influence*. New Haven: Yale University Press.

Schmidt, E. (2013). *Foreign Intervention in Africa: From the Cold War to the War on Terror*. Cambridge: Cambridge University Press.

Seers, D. (1969). The Meaning of Development. *International Development Review, 11*(4), 3–4.

Sen, A. (1973). *On Economic Inequality*. Oxford: Clarendon Press.

Singer, P. W. (2005). *Children at War*. New York: Pantheon Books.

Smaldone, J. P. (1972). Firearms in Central Sudan: A Revaluation. *Journal of African History, XIII*(IV), 591–607.

Smaldone, J. P. (1977). *Warfare in the Sokoto Caliphate: Historical and Sociological Perspectives*. Cambridge: Cambridge University Press.

Small Arms Survey (SAS). (2001). *Profiling the Problem*. Oxford: Oxford University Press.

Smith, R. S. (1976). *Warfare and Diplomacy in Pre-Colonial Africa*. Madison: University of Wisconsin Press.

Sobek, D. (2010). Masters of Their Domains: The Role of State Capacity in Civil Wars. *Journal of Peace Research, 47*(3), 267–271.

Sorens, J. (2011). Mineral Production, Territory, and Ethnic Rebellion: The Role of Rebel Constituencies. *Journal of Peace Research, 48*(5), 571–585.

Spear, J., & Cooper, N. (2007). The Defence Trade. In A. Colins (Ed.), *Contemporary Security Studies*. London: Oxford University Press.

Stern, N. (2003). Foreword. In P. E. Collier, L. Hegre, H. Hoeffler, A. M. Reynal-Querol, & N. Sambanis (Eds.), *Breaking the Conflict Trap: Civil War and Development Policy* (p. x). New York: Word Bank & Oxford University Press.

Stoessinger, J. G. (1992). *The Might of Nations*. New York: McGraw Hill.

Stoessinger, J. G. (2010). *Why Nations Go to War* (11th ed.). New York: Cengage Learning.

Storey, W. K. (2008). *Guns, Race, and Power in Colonial South Africa*. New York: Cambridge University Press.

Synder, R. (2002). *Does Lootable Wealth Bring Civil War? Resource Extraction and Political Order in Comparative Perspective.* Paper Presented at the American Political Science Association (APSA) Annual Meeting, Boston.

Tamuno, T. N. (2011). *Oil Wars in the Niger Delta, 1849-2009.* Lagos: Stirling-Horden Publishers.

Tangban, O. E., & Umoh, U. E. (2014). A Political Economy of the Niger Delta Insurgency, 1999-2009. In G. Ichimi (Ed.), *Perspectives on Contemporary Nigeria: Essays in Honour of Professor A. Bolaji Akinyemi, CFR* (pp. 39–58). Salwin Nig: Abuja.

Taylor, M. C. (1982). Improved Conditions, Rising Expectations, and Dissatisfaction: A Test of the Past/Present Relative Deprivation Hypothesis. *Social Psychology Quarterly, 45*(1), 24–33.

Thies, C. (2010). Of Rulers, Rebels and Revenue: State Capacity, Civil War Onset and Primary Commodities. *Journal of Peace Research, 47*(3), 321–332.

Thomson, A. (2004). *An Introduction to African Politics.* New York: Routledge.

Thornton, J. K. (1998). The Art of War in Angola, 1575-1680. *Comparative Studies in Society and History, 30*(2), 360–378.

Thornton, J. K. (1999). *Warfare in Atlantic Africa, 1500-1800.* London: Routledge.

Ubah, C. N. (1994). The British Occupation of the Sokoto Caliphate: The Military Dimension, 1897-1906. *Paideuma, 40*, 81–97.

Umoh, U. E. (2010, September 21). *The Crisis of Abundance and the Challenge of Development in the Niger Delta of Nigeria.* Paper Presented to the Department of History and International Studies, University of Uyo, Nigeria.

Umoh, U. E. (2012). Armed Conflicts in Post-Colonial Africa and the Democratic Peace Theory. *Nasarawa Journal of General Studies, 1*(2), 7–25.

Umoh, U. E. (2015a). Cameroon, Nigeria and the Bakassi Conflict: Building Blocks for a Non-Democratic Peace Theory. *Journal of International Relations and Development, 18*(2), 227–247.

Umoh, U. E. (2015b). *The Joint Task Force and Insurgency in the Niger Delta of Nigeria, 1999–2009.* Ph.D. Thesis, Department of History and War Studies, Nigerian Defence Academy, Kaduna, Nigeria.

Umoh, U. E. (2017a). Maritime Domain Awareness and Coastal Insurgency in Nigeria's Southeast. *AKSU Journal of History and Global Studies, 3*(1), 62–75.

Umoh, U. E. (2017b, May 11–12). *The Niger Delta and the Trans-Atlantic Slave Trade, 1433 – 1833: A Copenhagen School Securitization Model Representation of External Threats.* Paper presented at the International Workshop on Representation of External Threats in History (Medieval World to 19th Century), Madrid, Spain.

Wallensteen, P., & Sollenberg, M. (2001). Armed Conflict 1989–2000. *Journal of Peace Research, 38*, 629–644.

Wariboko, N. (1998). Capability Distribution and Onset of the 1869 Bonny War. *Nordic Journal of African Studies, 7*(2), 1–26.

Whatley, W. (2012). *The Gun-Slave Cycle in the 18th Century British Slave Trade in Africa* (MPRA Paper 44492). University Library of Munich, Germany.

White, G. (1971). Firearms in Africa: An Introduction. *Journal of African History, 12*(2), 173–184.

Ubong Essien Umoh is an Associate Professor of Military History in the Department of History and International Studies, University of Uyo, Nigeria. He earned a Ph.D. in Military History from the Department of History and War Studies, Nigerian Defence Academy (NDA), Kaduna. Between 2015 and 2016, he was part of the research team of the National Institute of Policy and Strategic Studies (NIPSS) consulting for the Presidential Committee (PRESCOM) on Small Arms and Light Weapons in Nigeria. Since 2017 he has been part of the joint research team on the *Boko Haram* insurgency carried out by the Centre for Defence and Documentation, Nigerian Defence Academy (NDA), Kaduna, and the Victims Support Fund (VSF), Abuja. He serves as a Research Fellow at the Centre for the Study of Leadership and Complex Military Operations (CSLCMO), NDA, Kaduna, and has been a Visiting Scholar to the Nigerian Air Force War College (AFWC), Makurdi and the National Defence College (NDC), Abuja.

Otoabasi Akpan is a Professor of History of Ideas and International Security Studies, with more than 100 publications in his areas of specialization. He has a BA in History from the University of Calabar, Calabar; MA in History of Ideas from the University of Ibadan, Ibadan; MSc in International Relations and Strategic Studies from the University of Jos, Jos; and Ph.D. in Diplomatic Studies from the University of Port Harcourt, Port Harcourt. He is domiciled in Akwa Ibom State University, Nigeria, where he has served as Head, Department of History and International Studies; Dean, Faculty of Arts; and since 2018, as Director, Collaboration and Linkages.

CHAPTER 16

Personality, Arms and Crime: The Psychological Dynamics of Small Arms and Light Weapons Proliferation in Africa

Philemon A. Agashua, David M. Shekwolo, and Orkuugh L. Lawrence

Introduction

The definition of Psychology has undergone some evolution over the years. In its early years, leading up to about 1920, Psychology was defined as the science of mental life. Then, from about 1920 to 1960, American behavioural Psychologists redefined Psychology as the science of behaviour, referring particularly to observable behaviour (Myers 1986). But from the 1960s, with encouragement from increasingly successful researches on how the mind processes and retains information, Psychology recaptured its interest in mental processes, while at the same time acknowledging that behaviour is an important channel for the scientific study and understanding of Psychology for human behavioural measurements.

The aim of this chapter is to broadly explore the nature of the Psychological dynamics of small arms and light weapons proliferation in Africa and Nigeria in particular. Accordingly, our concerns explored in great detail the dynamics of the Psychological influences of the phenomena. The outcome of the review indicated that across Africa and Nigeria in particular regardless of regional, ethnic or religious peculiarities, a major cause of violent conflict

---

P. A. Agashua (✉) · D. M. Shekwolo
Department of Psychology, Nigerian Defence Academy, Kaduna, Nigeria

O. L. Lawrence
Department of Psychology, Nasarawa State University, Keffi, Nigeria

© The Author(s), under exclusive license to Springer Nature Switzerland AG 2021
U. A. Tar and C. P. Onwurah (eds.), *The Palgrave Handbook of Small Arms and Conflicts in Africa*,
https://doi.org/10.1007/978-3-030-62183-4_16

was the overt acts of discrimination meted to citizens who have been classified as non-indigenes or settlers in different parts of their country (Golwa and Ojiji 2008). This conflict has continued to grow both in prevalence, incidence, intensity including the proliferation of small arms and light weapons with rising cost to the society (Akwash et al. 2016). As product of British colonial conquest, the Nigerian state is still grappling with challenges of political instability and socio-economic crisis. No doubt, conflicts—in particular, citizenship-related conflict represent a major threat to the nation's developmental aspiration (Orkuugh and Godiya 2010). Moreover, a nation of 250 ethnic linguistic groups the challenges of weaving together divergent groups is further compounded by the relentless assault on the right of citizens as a result of dichotomy between the notion of citizenship and indigeneship.

The psychological dynamics of small arms and light weapons proliferation, circulation and use in Africa have exacerbated insecurity, organized violence, illicit acts and criminality. Unravelling this phenomenon requires total human and financial resources, strong institutions and governments, psychosocial intervention and proactive engagement of civil society actors. Woven together to combat the small arms problem, these deviant and criminal elements offer both optimism and concrete security challenges to finding solutions for lasting peace and stability in the subregion. Efforts by sub-regional governments, civil societies, regional institutions and agreements such as the African Convention and other organizations like the Millennium Development Goals (MDGs) are interlinked, their efforts synergistic, and together are aimed at building a stronger and more secure region UNIDIR (2008). Regrettably, these have not so far produced tangible results. Without any doubt, the results of this ongoing work assessment will provide a psychological dimension to the proliferation of small arms and light weapons in the African subregion and proffer ways of control. In particular, we already know that the availability of small arms accounts for a considerable number of deaths and injuries in the military and civilian population, allowing interpersonal and inter-communal tensions to escalate into small and eventually full-fledged conflicts which affect the overall physical, economic social and psychological well-being of African States and its people (United Nations (1997).

BACKGROUND: AFRICA AND THE PSYCHOLOGY OF VIOLENCE

The continent of Africa was from its inception plagued by violence, conflicts, wars, instability and general underdevelopment, mainly as a result of Europe's colonization of Africa and slave trade. The Berlin conference of 1884–1885 had left a legacy of continuing tension even after Europe's formal withdrawal from colonial jurisdiction in Africa. The entire colonial period was an experience in state building based on official violence, and a phase in the growth of the modern African State. During colonial era, the state monopolized the use of arms; but peasants and dissenting groups developed clandestine means of bearing arms and challenging the state. As noted by Mazrui (1986), it was soon clear that the post-colonial African State was inherently fragile, domestically as well as in relation to the outside world. Externally, a few European mercenaries could at times play havoc with political order in an African State. Domestically the African State has lacked legitimacy and popular acceptance. Moreover, some African States were even unable to assert a monopoly of the legitimate use of physical force as they were regularly confronted by common criminals and violent nationalist movements—each bearing arms secured through local production and clandestine means. The partitioning of Africa left a new tradition of violence in the post-colonial era. Furthermore, scramble for and partitioning of Africa has put both kith and kin into artificial colonial dividing lines. For example, the Ewes spread from Badagry in Nigeria to HO in Ghana but broke up into four nations. Mazrui (1986) has argued that violence in pursuit of private economic gain is more a consequence of the impact of the Western colonization on Africa than of anything else. Indigenous culture can be violent for ethnic reasons; Islam can be violent for religious reasons; while Westernism in Africa is often violent for economic reasons. The majority of major civil wars in Africa including those in Sudan, Nigeria, Chad, Eritrea and Uganda have had an Islamic component. All civil wars in Africa have been substantially ethnic including those listed above. With the addition of Angola, Zimbabwe and Zaire, the West has provided those artificial borders which have enclosed the battlegrounds the boarders inherited from Africa's partition. The West has also produced and supported white settlers communities in Southern Africa. The most racist component of the triple heritage is the Western Legacy. Thus, racial conflict in Southern Africa is part of the triple heritage of violence, as argued by Mazrui (1986). Several devastating conflicts have persisted in sub-Saharan Africa for the past five decades. Some countries are still emerging from the era of cold war politics, while debilitating internal struggles continue to plague others. They are Ethiopia, Namibia, South Africa and Uganda. More recently, Angola and Mozambique are examples of the first group. The Second and later groups are illustrated by the situations in Liberia, Sierra Leone and Sudan. The scenarios in Rwanda and South Africa show sordid situations from the historical, political and psychological perspectives. Nigeria as the giant of Africa is still grappling with problems of Boko-Haram insurgency in the North East of the country, Fulani Herdsmen and Farmers crises in the Middle Belt zone and terrorism in the South-West zone.

In all the debates on Africa, one issue that stands out above the others is the issue of violence—particularly state-sponsored violence and, by extension, violence orchestrated by militant groups—its root causes and its self-destructive impact (Olowu 2010). As noted by Olowu (2010) nearly a third of Africa's 53 States suffer from conflict situations and often the destabilizing consequences of civil war in one country will spill across borders (Liberia civil war, Sairalone, Sudan civil war, Congo DR civil war in the 90s and Boko Haram, Kidnapping and Banditry in Nigeria, etc.) and affect whole regions of the continent. War in Africa eats up scarce resources and destroys development. Moreover, it contributes to a chronic loss of confidence and morale in the continent, not least from foreign investors and with serious attendant psychological consequences.

CONCEPTUAL PARAMETERS: SMALL ARMS AND PSYCHOLOGY OF VIOLENCE

SALWs had sometimes been referred to as "weapons of mass destruction" in Africa because of its long-term and widespread pernicious effects. Even when conflicts have been officially terminated, small arms have remained illicitly, in the post-conflict zones of Mali, Sierra Leone, Niger, Senegal and Liberia, making it easy for fighting to continue and instigate more serious problems in the society (Michael 2001). Also, while further combat is avoided, the easy availability of small arms has become common tools of violence, used in criminal activities such as ethnic and political rivalries. Armed ex-combatants may become affiliated with local gangs, warlords or militias (Michael 2001). This enduring climate of violence has often resulted in refugees and displaced persons fearing to return home after conflicts have ended. The insidious nature and impact of these weapons affects all aspects of society. Small arms, especially firearms, are the primary tools used to kill, maim, threaten and intimidate civilian populations in Africa (Michael 2001). In Nigeria in particular, the use of Small arms plays a significant role in many abuses, including rape, kidnapping, torture, forced displacement and enforced recruitment of child soldiers. When crimes have been committed with machetes, the victims were often initially rounded up with small arms. Heavily armed individuals create an environment in which atrocities can be committed at will and with impunity. Even small numbers of small arms confer great power on those that bear them. It is estimated that more than 50% of the weapons that proliferate in Africa are used illicitly in trafficking, armed robbery, terrorism and organized crime (Michael 2001). The proliferation of small arms has also encouraged fear in countries where the state uses small arms to quell political opposition.

The control of small arms became a collective endeavour within the African States with the adoption of the Declaration of a Moratorium on the Importation, Exportation and Manufacture of Small Arms and Light Weapons in Africa by the Conference of Heads of State and Government in Abuja on 31 October 1998. Implementing this political framework to combat small arms proliferation very quickly proved to be impossible without adopting joint measures and institutional arrangements for its operationalization and monitoring (Small Arms Survey 2004).

Over the last decade, the links between SALW proliferation, conflict, security and development have become better recognized and understood within the sub-region. It is now accepted that sustainable development is seriously threatened by recurrent violent armed conflict. The proliferation of small arms has erased decades of development and progress; indeed, it has further entrenched poverty within Africa. The interdependence of small arms control, security and development speaks to the core development mandates of poverty eradication, enhanced human security, inclusion and governance (Small Arms Survey 2004). Communities affected by small arms violence have become socially and economically marginalized. This has all grossly undermined progress towards West Africa meeting the targets of the Millennium Development Goals. It is clear that Africa desperately needs the rapid ratification and comprehensive implementation of the Convention on Small Arms in Africa (Small Arms Survey 2004).

Therefore, the proliferation of SALWs in Africa is a criminal activity so the Psychological dynamics of the menace can be appreciated by looking at the paradigm shift of crime in Psychology. That is when we talk about the Psychological traits of the perpetrators of these criminal acts in which Psychology view their characteristics or features of being antisocial, mood disorders, paranoid and schizoid ideation. While, behavioural perspective anchored on social learning, family socialization, environmental influence and the mass media, cognitive perspectives also have a lot to contribute, personality of an individual too is a factor, the intelligence of one, whether low or high, our culture, etc. They are discussed beneath.

Another conceptual issue is personality and criminal behaviour provided by Swiss Psychologist Sigmund Freud (1856–1939). Freud believed that as human beings we all have left over one important aspect of emotional attachment when we were children which guide our interpersonal relationship in future as we grow up. They believe that our instinctive drives contribute a lot in making us to be who we are in life. Emphasis is laid on personality as being anchored on three part structure, the Id, the Ego and Super ego.

The Id: the Id is the primitive part of an individual mental makeup which is present at birth. This represents the unconscious biological drives for food, sex and other necessities over the life span. Most important is the idea that the Id is concerned with instant pleasure or gratification while disregarding concern for others. This is known as the pleasure principle and it is often paramount when discussing criminal activities or behaviour. With all these proliferations of SALWs in African countries, the people concerned have no concern for anyone but themselves. It is possible that these people are driven by instant gratification. They are controlled by unconscious mental processes that are grounded in early childhood. Carrying SALWs to them is a normal and ideal thing to do in the society, so no matter what government, society do to stop them they will not listen because they are already lacking consciousness and are more inclined to indulge in self-gratification on obsessive compulsive neurotic disorder.

The Ego: the Ego is the second element of the human personality according to Psychodynamics which is thought to develop early in a person's life. This is a moment when children begin to learn that their wishes cannot be gratified instantaneously they often throw a tantrum. The ego compensates for the demands of the Id helping the individual guide his/her actions or behaviour to keep him/her within the boundaries of society. The ego is guided by reality principle which takes into account what is practical and conventional by societal norms or standards. Individuals with weak and undeveloped ego are prone to obsessive compulsive delinquent behaviours which manifest into gross commission of criminal acts such as arson, gang robbery, rape, gun-running, drug trafficking, etc.

The Super ego: this third element develops as the person incorporates the moral standards and values of the community: parents and significant others, such as friends and clergy members. It is the moral aspect of the individual which passes judgement on behaviour and action of individual. One can assume that young adults as well as adults understand right from wrong. However, when a crime is committed especially like in this context the SALWs proliferation advocates of psychodynamic theory would suggest that an individual committed a crime because he/she has an underdeveloped super ego. They also suggest that criminals are frustrated and aggravated and are constantly drawn to past events that occurred in their early childhood. It may be because of negligent, unhappy or miserable childhood, which is most often characterized by a lack of love/nurturing. They are also seen as having a weak (or absent) ego which may be linked with poor or absence of social etiquette, immediately and dependence on others and these individuals may be more likely to engage in SALWs proliferation, drug abuse, trafficking in persons, etc.

Another theorist, Alfred Adler (1870–1937) a neo-Freudian linked criminality to antisocial behaviour which is seen as abnormal mental states produced by early childhood trauma. The work of Alfred Adler (1870–1937) who founded individual Psychology and went ahead to describe individuals who have feelings of inferiority and compensate for them with a drive for superiority as inferiority complex. They commit crime because they have difficulty understanding the consequences of their action (Aichorn 1935).

Some of these SALWs actors according to this perspective manifest feelings of oppression and their inability to develop the proper Psychological defense and rationale to keep that feeling under control by so doing because they are seen as been oppressed the best way for them is to handle SALWs as compensation for low self-esteem, and cause problem in the society (James 1994).

Criminal violence has its beginning in the abuse, neglect, loss of parents, and exposure to violence in early childhood resulting in disruptions in attachments. Those with disrupted attachments fail to reach pro-social maturity interpersonally, in affect regulation and self-control, and in moral development. They may not understand human reciprocity. Relationships are superficial. They may have little or no empathy or remorse. To them the world is not safe and they must always be on the offensive in order to be safe. Generations of war and violence in the Middle East and Africa continue to produce more terrorists. Children are not safe after they become orphaned. They are exposed to violence daily during times of conflict and always have the fear of a new attack. The effect of this environment on everyone, especially young children can be psychologically devastating. They need someone to take them in and take care of them. Thus, if a terrorist organization, like Boko Haram or a gun-running and drug-trafficking gang takes advantage of that vulnerability, they have recruited new, loyal members for their group.

A recent report revealed that more than 100,000 children have been abducted, tortured and sexually abused before being recruited to fight in Africa's long-running civil wars in the past three years. Teenage boys and girls forced to join militaries are being subjected to psychological torture so that they can be indoctrinated. The Democratic Republic of Congo has more than 30,000 child soldiers fighting in militias and acting as body guards for government army commanders. Girls are also kidnapped and gang-raped by soldiers using them as entertainment and rewards for bravery (Purwar et al. 1996).

A disorder called Disruptive Behaviour Disorder (DBD) is associated to SALWs proliferation especially among adolescents who are frequently uncooperative and hostile and are more difficult than other children (Krueger et al. 1996). These children manifest an abnormal and hostile behaviour towards society or authority because of the frequent loss of temper and constant argument with their elders. They tend to carry SALWs with them any time because they know that the society is always against them. They do not want anybody to control them, give them rules and regulation or orders. They are antisocial and they can also be involved in other activities as bullying, fighting and committing sexual aggression (Oimette 1977). Crime also provide them with the promise of positive gain by allowing them to blame others for their predicament (for Example, the police and gives them a chance to rationalize their sense of failure.

Similarly, a behavioural theorist J. B Watson (1878–1958) and other scholars who came after him like Albert Bandura (1973) believes that human behaviour is developed via learning by experience or from others in the society. As we live in a society with one another we tend to learn some behaviours from each other either good or bad ones. According to this school of thought, people alter their behaviour according to the reactions they receive from others. If a behaviour is non-rewarding then we tend to quit. That is to say behaviour is supported by rewards and extinguished by negative reactions or punishments. This theory also encompasses social learning, family interaction, environmental experience s and mass media in looking at crime or violence in the society.

The social learning theorists believe that any behaviour can be learned in society especially those that are rewarding. For example, in the African context it is believed that anybody that is ahead of you must be given his respect and if possible, learn some things from him/her. With what is going on in Nigeria especially the criminals are celebrated, of course these behaviours are learned that when you steal either government, money nobody cautions you rather you are clapped and celebrated. People will steal money and go into politics and they are voted into power and nobody cares.

A boy who grows up and sees his father repeatedly strike his mother with impunity is the one most likely to grow up to become a battering parent and husband. With these behaviours exhibited in our society and are encouraged the younger ones learn and the outcome may be proliferation of SALWs in our society. The specific forms that aggressive behaviour takes the frequency with which it is expressed, the situations in which displaced and the specific targets selected for attack are largely determined by social learning.

The case of Boko Haram in Nigeria, Niger, Cameroon, Chad is a motivational paradigm based on social learning. The youths from north eastern Nigeria, for example, are into Boko Haram because they learn that it pays and is rewarding and being sponsored by some of these politicians who provide easy access to firearms and as such they tend to join the group for destruction not minding what it may cause them, their families, relatives and the society.

Social learning perspectives view this as a behaviour learned via a process called behaviour modelling which are modelled into these three principles; Family interaction, Environmental experiences and Mass media.

Family Interaction: Family is the primary social group comprising parents, their offspring, and in some societies other relatives sharing the same house hold or more generally any group of individuals related to blood or descended from an identifiable common ancestor. This is the first agent of socialization in the society. If a child or member of a family learns a particular behaviour which is not good it may be aggressive, behaviour, violence behaviour, stealing will tend to grow with it and also exhibit in the family. If their fathers were (is) a SALWs dealer, the children may learn from that and it goes on from generation to generation which will continue to affect the society.

Environmental Experience: The continent of Africa has places and boarders that are too porous and where SALWs proliferations are seen as normal. It is expected that one will learn the business of the day and adapt to the style of the environment. People who reside in an environment in which violence is the order of the day are more likely or prone to act violently than those in a crimeless environment and have learned discipline. In addition to making the ability to kill far easier, the technology now being employed by light weapons, and particularly small arms, represents a greater capacity for destroying societal cohesion. The rapidity of firepower and the ability to expend more ammunition in a shorter space of time offer a new set of tactical options, as killing capabilities become more efficient, subsequently resulting in a greater sense of civilian terror.

The trauma experienced by societies in which violence is rife is a consequence of the deep fears that become entrenched in the communal psyche and result from the process of proliferation of small arms and the unchecked use of weapons. The undermining of traditional communal values in Africa has partly been a result of the empowerment of individuals and groups through weapons diffusion and the dynamics of local arms resulting to conflicts. It can be argued that widespread societal trauma is, therefore, a result of weapons proliferation in an unstable environment. One of the more destructive effects of this societal dynamics is the communal division which results, particularly in agrarian societies, whose viability is largely dependent on unity (Jeffrey 2002).

Mass Media: mass media is another agent of socialization which we learn many things from. A child who learned a violent act, aggressive act, war will act more violently than a child who always watches cartoons and nonviolence programmes. In our media on violence, uses of SALWs are often portrayed as an acceptable behaviour especially for heroes who are not to face any legal consequences for their behaviours. All these and many more when learned in the society especially in Africa, leave us so vulnerable to trafficking in arms.

The acquisition of values favouring law violation, including violence, SALWs proliferation, occurs through repeated exposure not only to unlawful behaviour itself but also to the values underlying it that are entrenched in action social milieus. Agents within an individual's social context, such as peers, the family and neighborhood residents, convey normative protocols regarding illegal conduct. An actor's reaction to verbal threats, physical threats, his or her strategy of response to economic distress and his/her adherence to formal legal mandates are artifacts of the normative complex that blankets the actor's daily life and that is procured via social interaction either in the family, society violence-conducive value orientations are thus effectively transmitted throughout local collectivities over time and sustained spatially.

Participating in physical fights, bullying and carrying of weapons are the risk behaviours. The rate of violent injuries tends to increase dramatically in youth in Africa. A survey of families in South Africa found that 52.3% of victims of violence were among youths. Another one conducted in Kenya, Jamaica, also showed high rate of violent crimes among youths. This was attributed to a learned behaviour from the society (Mike 1994).

The cognitive school of psychology focus on mental processes and how people perceive and mentally represent the world around them and solve problems. The moral development perspective as propounded by Witheln Wundt (1832–1920) is concerned with the way and manner people morally represent and reason about the world. The humanistic sub-disciplines developed by Edward Titchener (1867–1920) stress self-awareness and getting in touch with feelings. The information processing discipline by William James (1842–1920) focuses on the way people process, store, encode, retrieve and manipulate information to make decisions and solve problem. The cognitive intellectual self, with its moral and ethical structure, is important in decision making, so the effective state of an individual, with its variations, may influence human behaviour. At times fluctuations of a person's mood, not clearly pathological but limited to a feeling of sadness, joy may bring about changes in conduct in relation to the people within his/her usual habitat. Occasionally when this affective fluctuation becomes gradually exaggerated and not controlled by the powers of objectivity, discrimination, and the anticipation of future consequences, the individual may not be strong enough to hold back the negative instinctual, impulsive drives. This can also be seen among the characteristics traits of individuals who commit crimes is an inability to exercise the effective will power necessary to control their behaviour when under the influence of instinctual negative emotions or alcohol and drugs.

In addition to the impulsivity found among the major personality characteristics of the criminals are restlessness and hostility. A propensity to rage and destructive violence are characteristics of many of them. This can graduate to handling of arms in the society and causing trouble. That may include the criminals' proneness, rage, humiliation and guilt. The information we process as individual have a role to play in the way we view the society or environment. When people make decisions in their lives, they involve succession of cognitive thought process (Michael 2001).

Conflict has ceased to become the struggle between states or ideologies but has become the struggle between peoples and cultural identities. With some level of weakness prevalent in most societies, the degree to which human security has been eroded has become linked to the propensity for violence. Modern weapons have made the ability to kill, more than ever before, a utilitarian act, restrained neither by age nor gender; it was estimated that in 1988 there were at least 200,000 child soldiers under the age of 15 years fully participating in conflicts around the world. The introduction of small calibre weapons has, according to military historian John Keegan, changed modern warfare (Kohlberg 1969).

The moral and intellectual development perspectives believe that people passes through different stages of moral development, and that their decisions and judgements on issues of right and wrong are made for different purposes. When these decisions are not made rightly, they tend to lead them in deviation to the laws of the society and are seen as deviants. So behaving in a manner that they do not regard anybody in the society and violation of law and order will be the order of the day. Kohlberg (1969) categorized people according to the stages on the line of continuum at the point where their moral development refused to grow. He found that the criminals in the society are suffering from low moral development of stage 1 and 2 than non-criminals whose level of moral development has grown to level 3 and 4. Of course, looking at people that have developed their morals in the society, they are always aware, conscious and afraid of going contrary against the law because of the fear of being sanctioned and tarnishing their integrity. But for the low moral development persons, their thought has not gotten to that so they tend to do anything anyhow in the society including trafficking in arms without counting the cost and the repercussions. Those at higher stages of moral reasoning tend to sympathize with the rights of others.

The development of the personality and later of character is greatly determined by the way a young child resolves internal object relations and in later years, in adolescence and early adulthood, how he or she relates to and incorporates parental models and those people he encounters in life in the society. Studying individual and certain traits in him/her and comparing it with psychological problems and development of antisocial behaviour is of paramount importance here.

Looking at personality and crime is significant to this chapter. People's outcome of attitudes, interests and needs that stem from a complex of unconscious and conscious biological factors, Psychological drives, and emotions that form the self, unique and distinct from others with its affectivity and intelligence. As individuals move into the world at different stages of maturity, they develop feelings, drives and emotions and will attempt, successfully or not, to repress their instincts they will become aware of anger, fear, love, humiliation, joy and disappointment. Such emotions will interplay within the self as they relate to others, at times in a passive or aggressive manner, especially when their personality will be able to control his/her negative emotions and get along with others (Hans 1985). It is when the personality traits become exaggerated that he may become disorganized and what is termed a personality disorder and crime can be observed. The behaviour of a person suffering from a personality disorder is pertinent to the understanding of personality, aggression and criminal manifestations and often in the latter ascertaining of criminal responsibility.

Connecting this with Sheldon's discovery of personality traits which characterized antisocial behaviour in the society such as self-assertiveness, deviance, extroversion, ambivalence, impulsiveness, narcissism, suspicion, destructiveness, sadism, lack of concern for others, feeling unappreciated, distrust of authority, poor personality skills, mental instability, hostility and resentment, etc. These personality traits are linked to crime. It is possible that people who have these traits are prone to committing crime and or these traits interact with our environment to prone the behaviour. Sheldon (1950) gave an example with kids who have low conscientiousness that will most likely have poor educational and occupational histories which limit their opportunity for advancement and render them crime prone.

Although many criminals with personality disorder may belong to low economic groups and are without any basic training for a rewarding job in a competitive society, economic poverty cannot be subscribed to as the only determinant of their offensive behaviours. A sense of lost power is also often the basis of the antisocial behaviour of people with personality disorders. Many of them offend because they feel powerless, overwhelmed by and unable to face up to their duties and social demands. Their frustration brings about their acting out, their hostility may be directed towards the self—a self that is hated because it is not responsive to what is demanded of it, a self that the offender believes must have no value because no one seems to accept him/her, a self that feels deeply rejected.

Most criminals are classified as suffering from some type of personality disorder as mentioned above. Their criminal behaviour has been defined as intentional act that is committed without defence or excuse in violation of the criminal law and penalized by the law. Basic to such behaviour is impulsivity which can be observed in the severe personality disorders, especially the antisocial personality disorder, the borderline personality disorder. Among the psychosis, the paranoid delusional type is more prone to cause an individual to act out impulsively and suddenly. However, only a minimal percentage of psychotics, whether schizophrenic, bipolar or delusional paranoid, act out. More so, people commit crime or engage in violent behaviour for a multitude of reasons that will need to be uncovered. A group of individuals who are at risk repetitively engage in criminal and violent behaviour, who show little remorse for their actions and are therefore poor to be rehabilitated and these are described as psychopaths or individuals with antisocial personality disorder. This discussion focuses on personality characteristics rather than overt behaviour, highlighting the motivating factors behind criminal acts.

Hare (1993) described psychopaths as people who "charm, manipulate and ruthlessly plow their ways through life". They are always selfish, disregarding the right and happiness of others. The Psychopaths look out for him/herself, seem to lack a conscience, and show little empathy towards the pain of others. In addition, to identify traits in an individual, some specific test can be used to trace a person with psychopathy. Thorough assessment that includes widely used global measures of personality such as Minnesota Multiphasic Personality Inventory—2 (MMPI-2), California Personality Inventory (CPI), Multi-dimensional Personality Questionnaire (MPQ), Big Five Inventory (BFI), Eysenck Personality Inventory (EPI) are use. Assessment can be supplemented and information can be extracted through trait specific test that may appear less threatening and less likely to be faked by the respondents. This can include measures of traits conceptually associated with the core characteristics of psychopath such as impulsivity measured with Barrett Impulsiveness Scale-II (BIS-II) personality traits of an individual predicts crime and violence. The root cause of crime can be found in the forces that influence human development at an early stage of life. This is because one is born and brought up in the environment and there are forces that either support him/her to grow positively or negatively. If he/she is affected positively, he/she tend to grow with morals, if is negatively, then he/she will become a deviant in the society. So to curb these menace, the control efforts should be geared towards helping the family, society to raise moral children that will be reasonable and responsible in future.

In the study of intelligence and crime, the issue of high and low intelligence is the centre point to note. Criminals were believed to have low IQ compared to non-criminals with high IQ. This can be examined in nature vs nurture controversy.

The Nature Perspective: This perspective stressed that intelligence is determined genetically via ancestral genes and that low intelligence is linked to criminal behaviour. Argument here is that when newly developed IQ test was administered to inmates of first decade, the position of nature was strongly supported that inmates scored low in IQ test (Henry 1920). These and other early studies took a position that low IQ scores identified potentially delinquent children and that a correlation existed between inmates' low intelligence and deviant behaviour.

This school believed that anybody that is born is endowed genetically with inherited gene from his/her parents as such whether low or high IQ it is an inheritance from one's biological parents. So, one inherits criminal behaviour from his/her parents which is genetically in nature and begin to act in an abnormal way and because it is in blood, he/she will continue to transmit the same to his/her biological offspring.

The Nurture Perspective: this school believed in the cultural modelling of a person. Argument is that intelligence though biological is primarily sociological. That intelligence is not inherited, low IQ parents do not necessarily produce or give birth to low IQ children, rather the society in which they live affect and shape their IQ and behaviour. They discredited the fact that people commit crime because of low IQ. Instead they posit that environmental stimulation from parents, relatives, social contacts, schools, peers create a child's IQ and that low IQ results from an environment that also motivates delinquent and criminal behaviour. It is what children see happening in the society that they copy to grow with, which at long run become part of their behaviour in life. If a society is moral, a child will grow up with the morals of the society as he/she interacts and associates with different kinds and types of people in that society he/she inculcates some morals. On the other hand, if the society has low morals, it also tend to affect him/her negatively and the issue of criminality in that child will be paramount because that is what he/she grows up to know in the society. The society becomes the impetus for socialization of the child and anything he/she found rewarding and people are doing he/she learns from them. So proliferation of SALWs in our African society is seen as a learned behaviour which people exhibit in the society and the young ones copy or grow up to learn and model after.

THE PSYCHOLOGICAL EFFECTS OF SMALL ARMS IN AFRICA

Social disintegration, linked to gun-culture is most clearly reflected in areas most severely affected by small arms proliferation. It is poignantly illustrated in the behaviour and response of children. The militarization of future generations which have known little else, other than processes of brutalization and conflict, makes the rejuvenation of societies an even greater task to achieve. In Uganda, "some children had spent the whole of their formative years carrying a gun. When the war ends, they have never been to school. All they know is how to shoot. You can't just expect them to put down the guns and start being kids again". With a crisis of sovereignty, civilians have been placed at the heart of modern conflict, the nature of which has been profoundly influenced by the development and diffusion of modern light weapons (John 1920).

Following their statements, the president of the Côte d'Ivoire chapter of the West Africa Action Network on Small Arms, Karamoko Diakité, recounted the terror he experienced after an electoral dispute led to the anarchic distribution of small arms and ammunition by some political and district leaders, after those weapons had entered his country in violation of the arms embargo. Thousands were killed and the total cost was beyond estimation. "We were terrorized for days, hunted like animals, without food, without water, without receiving help, constantly living in fear of being killed", he said (Lumpe 2000). Groups of young, lawless offenders in possession of arms would not hesitate to take a life or to indulge in all forms of abuse on a terrorized and paralyzed population, particularly on women and girls. Arms had also poured into the region after the fall of Muammar Qadhafi in Libya and were feeding terrorist movements in Mali, Niger, Nigeria, Chad and Cameroon, he said. Advocating mechanisms to stem the flow of such weapons, he, too, urged accession to the Arms Trade Treaty (ATT) (Lumpe 2000).

Just as weapons are recycled from conflict to conflict in Africa, so too are some of the fighters. There is a thriving trade in mercenaries in Africa, aiding the circulation and proliferation of small arms in the region. Levels of youth unemployment are high and there are many able-bodied, disgruntled persons available, ready and willing to be trained and armed to fight. As the same ethnic groups live in different states, shared identity can motivate individuals to become future mercenaries in the society (Lumpe 2000).

The extent to which small arms and light weapons have proliferated throughout societies has been consistent with and reflected changes in the nature of conflict, and the security priorities which determine modern trends in human development. However, what remains clear is that the scope for killing is not subject to the caliber of weapons possessed, neither is the inclination to kill predetermined by the possession of such weapons. The nature of modern warfare and the weaponry used has had an increasingly detrimental effect on civilians. Since World War II, over 23 million people have been killed in the developing world as a result of war, 90% of them civilians. During World War I, 90% of those killed were soldiers. The easy availability of modern weapons and the changed nature of the use of violence have polarized ethnic, religious, economic and political differences in regions of spiraling structural collapse and blurred the distinction between civilian and combatant. The marriage of technology, firepower and convenience has facilitated the non-discriminatory use of immensely powerful weapons, putting military hardware in the hands of civilian constituencies. Advances in light weapons technology have led to increased lethality and destructiveness. Modern assault rifles, for instance can fire a burst of 30–35 rounds with one pull of the trigger (rather than one round, as with older bolt action rifles). Fear and attempts at self-preservation have split many such communities around the world. In Cambodia, the sense of mistrust which accompanied the war was extremely divisive; collaboration with the enemy and the reporting of neighbours contributed to the destruction of co-operative structures in many communities.

Malignant Anxiety is a culture-bound syndrome that manifests into fullblown crimes such as gun-running, kidnapping and political violence among marginal and pressure groups in the African subregion. Malignant Anxiety is characterized by chronic anxiety, tension, hostility, moodiness, restlessness, a preoccupation with witchcraft and confusion, excitement, social desirability, homicide and suicide. It is also marked by impaired perception, fear of bewitchment, confusion, disorganization and occasionally, ritual homicide or suicide (Lambo 1962). Malignant anxiety is seen most commonly in marginal Africans, in western contact areas such as labour camps, new industrial settlements and artificial villages. The recent epidemics of it in Kenya, Eastern Nigeria and the Congo have generally been initiated by abnormal individuals with social position and authority or aggressive power, who have intimidated some weak individuals into joining antisocial secret societies (Kiev 1972). Unlike Manic depressive disorders, malignant anxiety is not phasic; it may occur without excitement, there is no flight of ideas, by contrast with the situation among catatonic patients, genuine schizophrenic symptoms do not emerge after the excitement. These disorganized individuals are prone to committing crime in our society; they lack insight and do things without control which make them to violate the rules and regulations of the society. Also, they easily fell prey as agents of foreign imperial forces and mercenaries that work to destabilize legitimate governments.

The family is the foundation of human society. Families are the strongest socializing forces of life. They teach children to eschew unacceptable behaviour, to delay gratification and to respect the right of others. Conversely, families can teach children aggressive, antisocial and violent behaviors. Also, children who are rejected by their parents, who grow up in homes with considerable conflicts or who are inadequately supervised are at the greatest risk of becoming delinquent (Green 2001). Adolescence is a time of expanding vulnerabilities and opportunities that accompany the widening social and geographical exposure to life beyond the school or family, but it starts with the family.

During the past century, significant changes in family environment have occurred, modern family structures vary widely. Its form is diversifying with, for example, the increase in one-parent families and non-marital unions as well as extended family arrangements. Differing family structures may directly impact on the stability of the family, home and the functioning of children and adolescents.

Green (2001) indicates that various exposures to violence within the family or outside the family are important sources of delinquencies. In other words, if violence encompasses all emotional environmental aspects of the juvenile's life, he is more likely to engage in delinquent activities (Hare 1993). Families' behaviours particularly parental monitoring and disciplining seem to influence association with delinquent peers throughout the juvenile period (Cashwell and Vacc 1994). A long history of research has further linked family dysfunction with future criminal offending, in part because parents monitor and provide nurturance to children. It is thought that the loosening of bonds among family members may result in more criminal involvement, including gangsterism, cultism, drug trafficking, robbery and trading in arms.

Studies have shown that weapons are themselves aggression eliciting cues. In one of such early studies, Leonard Berkowitz showed this more clearly when he had subjects given an electric Shock to people who were apparently getting a research task wrong (Brekowitz 1967). In some cases a gun happened to be present on the table of the experimental room. Berkowitz found that when the gun was there, the subjects administered a stronger, longer shock than when no gun was present. This suggests that a soldier or policeman is likely to be more aggressive when carrying a gun than when he is not, as events at Chicago Democratic convention in 1968 proved. Police with truncheons and guns were highly likely to use their truncheons, whereas police without guns were unlikely to use any other weapon. We can perhaps cautiously extrapolate from these findings, and suggest that by possessing a nuclear capability, a nation is more likely to use less devastating weapons, while, at the same time, by possessing a whole range of weapons, from the so-called less-lethal to nuclear missiles, a nation is more likely to move towards a nuclear engagement. Further studies have revealed that in many countries, guns are closely linked to identity and culture, and to perceptions of masculinity. For example, in parts of Latin America, gun ownership is a sign of strength and power, particularly among young men. Thus, changing the perception of weapons can be done in many innovative ways (Small Arms Survey 2004).

Conclusion

The phenomenon of Small Arms and Light Weapons proliferation seems to know no borders or bound in Africa. Weapons are circulating at all levels—from the smuggling of individual weapons to large shipments. Recent research assessing the border threat noted the patterns of arrival and circulation of small arms within the Mano River Union (Guinea, Liberia and Sierra Leone) (Small Arms Survey 2004). Communities interviewed disclosed that during the civil wars in Liberia and Sierra Leone, illicit trade in small arms and light weapons, particularly AK-47s, RPGs, FM light machine guns, M16 rifles, two-barrel Berettas, pistols, bazookas and mortars, increased along the Koinadugu-Kailahun axis of Sierra Leone. Some of these arms and ammunition are still being trafficked into Sierra Leone from Guinea and Liberia and vice versa. The assessment report identified the Guinea Forest and the Parrot Beak regions as the most prominent routes for trafficking arms within the Mano River Basin. The borders between West Africa's states are long and full of footpaths, which are poorly patrolled. More than 150 illegal crossing points were identified to and from Sierra Leone and Guinea and Liberia (Small Arms Survey 2004). Over 85% of crossing points were covered by fewer than 11% of the customs, immigration and security officials identified. The Sierra Leone Border Threat Assessment Report established that smuggling of SALW can be a real threat to stability in the Mano River Basin. In mid-2003, while conflict raged in Liberia, the government of Guinea imported mortar rounds and other ammunition from Iran. These were declared on cargo documents as "detergent" and "technical equipment". From Guinea, the weapons were forwarded to allied rebels inside Liberia who had just launched two offences on the capital, Monrovia. The rebels of Liberians United for Reconciliation and Democracy used these weapons to fire indiscriminately on civilian areas of Monrovia.

During conflict, the structures of SALW circulation have integrated into economic structures. SALWs have an economic value to the fighters that receive them: they enable combatants to engage in predatory violence against civilian populations, stealing goods to sell on the local black market, which is the easily accessible illicit medium of transaction, for personal sustenance and enrichment. In some sub-regional conflicts, such "bottom-up" war economies have generated a degree of informal cooperation between the combatants of governments and insurgent forces that sometimes included the trading of SALW (Small Arms Survey 2004). Thus in Sierra Leone, in a new form of co-operative predation, government forces would withdraw from a town, leaving SALW behind. The RUF rebels would take control, collect the arms, and extract cash from the civilian population before retreating. Government forces would then reoccupy the town, looting property that the rebels found more difficult to sell, and engage in illegal mining. But the threats to peace and security in the sub-region are changing, and this is one of the major challenges Africa faces in its efforts to achieve the twin objectives of security and the MDGs. A new generation of threats is emerging, which is giving rise to a range of compound challenges that the sub-region is as yet ill-equipped to deal with. For example, West Africa is increasingly cited as one of the hubs of hard drug (cocaine) trafficking from Latin America to Europe, and this has several consequences relating both to small arms proliferation and to the MDGs. The criminal gangs that control illicit drug trafficking are causing a new wave of small arms proliferation in Africa, and there are countries, Guinea-Bissau for example, where these gangs will soon have taken over some areas, making them dangerous for agriculture (MDG) (Small Arms Survey 2004). Already weak states are being further weakened by the trade in illicit narcotics (and by corruption in particular), making them less able not only to promote the MDGs at the national level but also to work effectively towards regional integration strategies.

Small Arms and Light Weapons proliferation had affected Africa, including the destabilization of the Sahel region after the pillaging of Libya's arsenals, which contained the world's largest accumulation of man-portable air defence systems. The only way forward was to secure arms and provide capacity-building for border guards and police while bolstering regional cooperation.

The Psychological trauma caused by illegal circulation of weapons of mass destruction in the African continent including Nigeria had left indelible scars on the psyche of individuals, families and groups which are now difficult to erase. Almost on daily bases, horrendous stories and scenes of gruesome killing, arson, kidnappings, robbery, wars, suicidal bombing and communal conflicts with wanton destruction of lives and properties are reported in the contemporary newspapers and electronic media for which the governments and security agencies including the military are helpless to prevent or control. Regardless of how many people a crisis affects, their effects are often quite similar. They paralyze the power of will, disassemble the cognitive system, cause emotional breakdowns and induce weird behaviours. Many of these effects appear once a crisis begins manifesting itself with strong power, hence quickly affecting the way certain people behave and their resilience to cope.

This is an area in which the psychological dynamics of this study can address by proposing measures to minimize incidences and consequences of SALW proliferation in Africa. The following proposals are submitted as measures to tackle the psychological impact of SALW proliferation in the African subregion. The implementation of these measures will require concerted efforts by all stakeholders in the subregion and the international communities:

1. Governments and Stakeholders in the subregion should embark on credible policies and programmes of rehabilitation which is a process that uses educational, social, vocational and scientific methods to nurture their violent youths, adult and aged persons back to their highest levels of functional ability. The Nigerian government for example, has not applied these basic methods which include using Internationally Standardized Assessment/Treatment and Rehabilitation Schedule like the Comprehensive Mental, Psychological, Physical and Treatment Schedule for rehabilitation and re-integration of the ex-militants and repentant insurgents. Rehabilitation is not just vocational training and skill acquisition using government institutions like SMEDAN, NAPEP and NDE. There is a need to thoroughly assess/examine the personality of the persons, especially those with abnormal personality traits and disorders, because some conducts and behaviours of militants and insurgents can be traceable to some types of disordered personality. Thus, this scientific process is capable of bringing about change, modification of attitudes, values, behaviours and skills of persons in order to encourage transmission into a new way of life.
2. African States should have credible governments and security apparatus that is well trained, well-motivated and remunerated which would service the people with integrity. They can leverage the states and society out of poverty and violence with the determination to overcome problems of poor governance.
3. All political office holders should be thoroughly screened and assessed to ensure they are free from criminal tendencies, personality disorders and are well-motivated to serve the nation with integrity.
4. Social scientists, educators and other professionals in numerous communities across the States of Africa and the International Organisations should come together in search of ways to promote peace, social and economic development of African States.

REFERENCES

Aichorn, A. (1935). *Wayward Youth*. New York, NY: Viking Press.
Akwash, F. B. A., & Zamani, E. A., & Nweze, A. (2016). Terrorism Militancy and the Nigerian State. *Central Nigerian Journal of Psychology, 1* (1), 31–40.
Bandrura, A. (1973). *Aggression: A Social Learning Analysis*. Englewood Cliffs, N J: Prentice Hall.
Brekowitz, L. (1967). Weapons as Aggression-Eliciting Stimuli. *Journal of Personality and Social Psychology, 7* (2), 202–207.
Cashwell, C., & Vacc, N. (1994). Family Functioning and Risk Behaviours: Influence on Adolescent Delinquency. *School Counselor, 4*, 105–114.
Freud, S. (1923 [1961]). The Ego and the Id. In J. Strachey (Ed. & Trans.), *The Standard Edition of the Complete Psychological Works of Sigmund Freud* (283–387). London: Hogarth Press.
Golwa, P. H. J., & Ojiji, O. O. (2008). *Dialogue on Citizenship in Nigeria*. Abuja: Institute for peace and conflict resolution.
Green, D. (2001). Why Protect Private Arms Possession. *Notre Dame Law Review, 84*(1), 131–137.
Hans, E. (1985). *Personality and Individual Differences*. New York, NY: Plenum.
Hare, R. (1993). Psychopaths and their Nature. In A. Raine & J. Sanmartín (Eds.), *Violence and Psychopathy*., Boston, MA: Springer.
Henry, G. (1920). *Efficiency and Levels of Intelligence*. Princeton, NJ: Princeton University.
James, G. (1994). Domestic Violence an Emerging Health Issue. *Social Science and Medicine, 39*(9), 1181–1188.
Jeffrey, B. (2002). Oppositional Conduct Disorder: Review of the Past 10 Years, Part II. *Journal of the American Academy of Child and Adolescent Psychiatry, 41*, 1275–1294.
John, S. (1920). Self and Peer Perception and Attributional Biases of Aggressive and non Aggressive Boys in Dyadic Interaction. *Journal of Consulting and Clinical Psychology, 55*, 404–410.
Kiev, A. (1972). *Culture-Bound Disorders, in Tran cultural Psychiatry*, p. 100. London: Penguin.
Kohlberg, L. (1969). *Stages in the Development of Moral Thought and Action*. New York: Holt.
Krueger, R., Caspl, A., Silver, P., & Mc Gee, R. (1996). Personality Traits are Differentially Linked to Mental Disorders: A Multitrait-Multi-diagnosis Study of an Adolescent Birth Cohort. *Journal of Abnormal Psychology, 105*, 299–312.
Lambo, T. A. (1962). Malignant Anxiety. *Journal of Mental Science, 108*, 256–264.
Lumpe, L. (2000). *Curbing the Proliferation of Small Arms and Light Weapons*. Retrieved April 12, 2019, from http://www.nisat.org/publications/curbingthepfoliferationofsma.html.
Mazrui, A. (1986). The Africans: A Triple Hertage. London: BBC Publications.
Michael, F. (2001). Counting the Cost of Gun Violence. *Africa Recovery, 14*(4), 56–67.
Mike, D. (1994). *Facts About Fiction: In Defence of TV*. Los Angeles, LA: Violence.
Myer, R. J. (1986). *Introduction to Psychology* (9th ed.). New York, NY: McGraw-Hill.
Oimette, P. C. (1977). Psychopathology and Sexual Aggression in Nonincareated Men. *Violence and Victimization, 12*, 389–397.

Olowu, A. A. (2010). The Psychology of Violence and its Managements. In H. O. Osinowo, O. E. Akinnawo, G. E. Abikoye, A. O., & Oguiyi (Eds.), *Violence*, (pp. 5–16) Ibadan, Nigeria: Publication of the Nigerian Association of Clinical Psychologists.

Orkuugh, L. L., & Godiya, A. (2010). *Urban Violence.* An Evolutionary Social and Mental Health Problem in Nigeria.

Purwar, E., Dhaban, S., & Chakravar, T. (1996). *Conflict Resolution: Building Bridges.* Newbery Park, CA: Corwin Press.

Small Arms Survey. (2004). *Rights at Risk.* Oxford: Oxford University Press.

Sheldon, G. (1950). *Unraveling Juvenile Delinquency.* Cambridge, UA: Harvard University Press.

UNIDIR. (2008, 31 March–1 April). *Security in Space: The Next Generation.* Conference Report 2008.

United Nations. (1997). *Report of UN Panel of Group of Governmental Experts on Small Arms.* New York, NY: United Nations.

Watson, J. B. (1878). *Handbook of Experiential Psychotherapy.* New York, NY: Guilford.

Philemon Atume Agashua Professor of Clinical, Military and Practicing Psychology and Head of Department of Psychology, Nigerian Defence Academy Kaduna. He is also a Visiting Professor at the Benue State University, Makurdi, Nigeria and some overseas Universities. His research interests span across the areas of Clinical Psychology, Military/Aviation Psychology, Forensic Psychology, Development of General and Vocational Aptitude Tests, Psychotherapy, Management of PTSD and Psychological disorders. He has published widely in reputable local and international journals. He is a member of numerous professional bodies, editorial boards and have attended several national and international conferences where in some instances he served as the keynote speaker and has also chaired some technical sessions. He has received many academic and professional awards such as Member of the National Institute (mni), the USA President Lifetime Achievement Award, Leadership Award by the Nigerian Association of Clinical Psychologists. Professor Agashua has been external examiner for PhD candidates as well as MSc in some Universities in Nigeria and overseas. He has held numerous academic and administrative positions, and has been a member of the Armed Forces Selection Board since 1985 to date. He is a Fellow of Institute of Management Consultants and Certified Management Consultant (FIMC CMC).

David M. Shekwolo is a Lecturer in the Department of Psychology, Nigerian Defence Academy, Kaduna. He holds a Ph.D. in Forensic and Correctional Psychology. He is a Member of Nigerian Psychological Association, Secretary General, Nigerian Association of Forensic Psychologists and member, Association of Practicing Psychologists in Nigeria. He has been a member, Psychological Assessment Committee, Armed Forces Selection Board since 2017 to date. His areas of research focus on specific areas of Forensic and Correctional Psychology of global status appraisal. His work cut across other field in Psychology which encompasses Forensic, Clinical, Police, Organizational, Cognitive, Psychological assessment, Criminal and Investigation, Terrorism, Radicalization, Legal, Military, Prisons, and gradually developing the ideas and perspectives in the practice and development of Psychology programmes. He has been a resource person to many security organizations. He has participated in several conferences with conference proceedings, book chapters, as well as international and national journal publications. He is happily married to Mrs. Mercy D. Markus with a daughter.

Orkuugh L. Lawrence is an Industrial/ Organizational Psychologist and a Senior Lecturer in the Department of Psychology, Nasarawa State University, Keffi. He is the immediate past Head of Department of Psychology, Nasarawa State University, Keffi. Beside this, he is a member of professional bodies including the Nigerian Psychological Association (NPA). He has contributed articles and essays in reputable local and international journals and books, encompassing a wide variety of subjects such as statistical techniques for the measurement of human behaviour, psychology of vocational and career choice, psychology of social change, political psychology, environmental psychology, industrial and organizational psychology.

CHAPTER 17

Socialization, Culture of Violence and Small Arms and Light Weapons Proliferation in Africa

Aminu Umar and Nachana'a Alahira David

INTRODUCTION

Africa experiences some of the most violent forms of conflict in the world, and most of these conflicts are perpetuated using basic weapons of violence. Here, it is not ballistic missiles or other sophisticated warheads that are the weapons of choice for the perpetuation of violence. Instead, Small Arms and Light Weapons (SALWs) are used to cause mayhem and destructions of epic proportions. This chapter recalls evidence from Nigeria to explore and establish the tenuous relationship between socialization, violent (sub) culture and the proliferation of Small Arms and Lights Weapons (SALWs) in Africa. Violent conflicts in Africa can be noticed across the continent with disturbing consequences or deaths. These conflicts have become more complex as the numbers of conflict actors have increased over the years (Cilliers 2018). This is evident from the activities of groups such as the ISIS, Rebels (and extremist), the Boko Haram, ISWAP, and Al-Shabab. Today, conflict in Africa generally takes place within states (rather than war between countries), although a number of armed groups operate regionally, such as the Boko Haram, Al-Shabab, ISWAP,

A. Umar (✉)
Department of Political Science, National Open University of Nigeria, Abuja, Nigeria

N. A. David
Department of Political Science and Defence Studies, Nigerian Defence Academy, Kaduna, Nigeria

© The Author(s), under exclusive license to Springer Nature Switzerland AG 2021
U. A. Tar and C. P. Onwurah (eds.), *The Palgrave Handbook of Small Arms and Conflicts in Africa*,
https://doi.org/10.1007/978-3-030-62183-4_17

Lord's Resistance Army, etc. as well as the emerging xenophobic and anti-immigrant attacks in countries such as South Africa and retaliation in some African countries.

According to some reports, fatality rates from armed conflicts are decreasing; the conflicts are concentrated in a relatively small number of countries, with particularly large burden of non-state conflict which explains greatly the nature of SALWs used. Disturbingly, the numbers of riots and protests are increasing across the continent as reported incidents of political violence such as riots, and violence against civilians are escalating and have recently been responsible for significantly more incidents and higher levels of casualties than in the past (Cilliers 2018). The impacts of insecurity and other problems attributed to the use of SALW are evident in most parts of Africa, with negative consequences on the economic development of the continent. This is so as the as the high levels of insecurity continue to affect economic development initiatives with the attendant effects of increased military spending which affects the use of scarce resources for developmental purposes.

The continent of Africa is a major trans-shipment point for the international trade, as well as a major producer of local arms. Likewise, the proliferation of SALW in Africa is increasing in proportion and making violent conflict a daily routine on the continent. It is reported that The Institute for Security Studies (ISS) of South Africa reports that Africa alone has suffered 5,994,000 fatalities in the past 50 years, due mostly to SALW. Estimates of the number of small arms and light weapons in circulation range from 100 to 500 million, with 50 to 80 million being AK-47 assault rifles (Knight 2008). These small arms being the remnants of conflicts in Mozambique, Angola, Somalia, Liberia, Sudan, Sierra Leone, etc. as well as licensed weapons being stolen or lost, have played a major role in exacerbating crimes and armed violence in countries such as Nigeria (Francis et al. 2018). Whereas in 2010 only five countries experienced sustained activity from violent religious extremism (i.e., Algeria, Mali, Niger, Nigeria, and Somalia) that number has grown to 12 countries (Algeria, Burkina Faso, Cameroon, Chad, Egypt, Kenya, Libya, Mali, Niger, Nigeria, Somalia, and Tunisia) (Cilliers 2018).

It is worthy to note that the borders inherited by Africans are badly demarcated; hence, they are easily crossed. These boundaries inherited by African states, were arbitrarily drawn by European imperialists who colonized almost the entire continent making conflict and proliferation of SALW an easy endeavor (Imobighe 1989). For example, it was observed that Liberia and its neighbors do not produce arms, but the major entry points of illicit armsarms and drugs were more than 170 border points with Guinea, Sierra Leone, and the Ivory Coast. Thus, small arms and light weapons are spread as a result of the influx of refugees from especially other neighboring countries. In other words, unregulated movement of people facilitates the circulation of such illegal weapons (Diarra 2005) and encourages conflict on the continent. This position seems a little narrow as most states in Africa have immigration laws but the level of corruption or poor management of the borders across the continent makes it easy to move arms and promote violence or culture of violence across the continent.

Narrowing the above estimate of the consequences of violence due to SALW to West Africa, it was estimated that 30,000 people have been killed by SALW in conflict each year since the end of the Cold War (Renner 2006). Illicit trade in firearms generates vast sums of money both directly and indirectly, with an estimated annual value of $53 million. This trade inflicts immeasurable human costs throughout the world. West Africa is one of the most unstable regions in Africa and the world. Accordingly, the United Nations has not only deployed four missions to the sub-region, but also created the United Nations Office for West Africa (UNOWA) with the mandate of enhancing the contributions of the UN toward regional peace and security (UNOWA, n.d.). There are an estimated eight million small arms and light weapons (SALW) in the hands of state and non-state actors in the West African sub-region. In fact, illicit trafficking in SALW is considered a lucrative business because of the high demand and the relative ease with which illicit weapons are brought into the region and moved across the ECOWAS Member States. (Florquin and Berman 2005). Underpinning illicit trade in SALW in the region are several factors, including porous borders between ECOWAS countries, existence of large swathes of ungoverned or unmonitored territory, weak and often nonexistent capacities of law enforcement institutions, largely informal and cash-based nature of economic transactions, to mention but a few (GIABA 2013). In the specific context of Nigeria, a tour of the country's border in September 1984 by Nigerian Immigration officials in Sokoto revealed that there were over 1500 illegal entry points along Nigeria's border with Benin and Niger (Imobighe 2003). This shows that as people move with arms from one part of the continent to another, so also the movement of their violent habit/culture or tradition or attitudes which in some instances negate peaceful co-existence and promote conflict among the African communities. Thus, there is a strong relationship between levels of violence and modifiable factors such as poverty, extremism, drug use and abuse, gender inequality, the absence of safe, stable, and nurturing relationships between children and parents, etc. It implies that there is a growing concern to culture of violence among the communities in Africa. This is especially so taking into consideration the rising rate of child abuse, ethno-religious crisis, arrogance of power, hate speech, and xenophobic attacks across the continent.

This chapter appraises the sociological foundations of armed violence in Africa, and draws attention to crisis of value systems, and failure of the institutions of socialization as the bases for the disturbing scenarios of violent conflicts and proliferation of SALWs in the continent. The chapter traces the social and societal foundations of the existence of armed violence and associated proliferation of SALWs based on the quality of socialization (i.e., culture of violence) or education (formal and informal) in our communities toward understanding the lingering violent atrocities on the continent.

Conceptual Framework—Socialisation and Culture

Socialization entails the complex process through which every society trains its members to imbibe the cultures, mores and values of the community so that a person's behavior will be meaningful in terms of the group norms. It is simply defined here as the internalization of societal norms and values. From the popular point of view, socialization is the way through which society transmits its culture from generation to generation and maintains itself. From the point of view of the individual, socialization is the process by which the individual learns social behavior, develops his personality. In the course of socialization, the individual learns the reciprocal responses of the society. According to Crisogen (2015), depending on various criteria, the specialized literature defined several types of socialization, i.e., primary socialization and secondary socialization (and continues). According to the assessment of society there are positive or negative socialization, and as awareness of how socialization process is distinguished there is formal or informal socialization. Depending on the objective pursued by already created effects, we have anticipatory or adaptive socialization. Also, depending on the intervention of legitimate power we can talk about associative or institutional socialization after as contents and the results expressed in statuses and roles, etc. These types of socialization are not individualized in an amorphous environment, but they intermingle, they complement and, by correlation, manage to describe the complex phenomenon of socialization. The contribution of those who have defined numerous types of socialization should not be approached holistically, nor in opposition with each other, but as a complement to the comprehensive and specialized understanding of socialization. It is with this in mind that this piece adapts an African perspective to collective good to define socialization on the continent. The average African cultural milieu upholds the virtues of respect for others and promote hospitality to strangers and collective good. Every member of society is conditioned to be acutely conscious of these virtues, without prejudice to their individual perception on what is good or bad. Simply put, one is expected to show love, kindness, hard work, dedication to common good, respect for elders, commitment to duty, and honesty as a matter of deep-rooted communal value (Fig. 17.1).

Traditionally, society apportions the task of socialization of children to the institutions and pivotal individuals (such as community leaders, teachers, and elders) that nurture the individual, safeguard group cohesion or collective interest. This implies that socialization is a function of a process normally carried out through social institutions or agents. That is, any individual, group, act, event or a process that has influence in molding the behavioral pattern of the individual can be labeled as an agent of socialization. In reality these groups, acts which are intentionally trying to socialize an individual are labeled as agents of socialization. Typically, school, peer group, mass media, educational institutions, religion, and agencies of the state are among the agents of

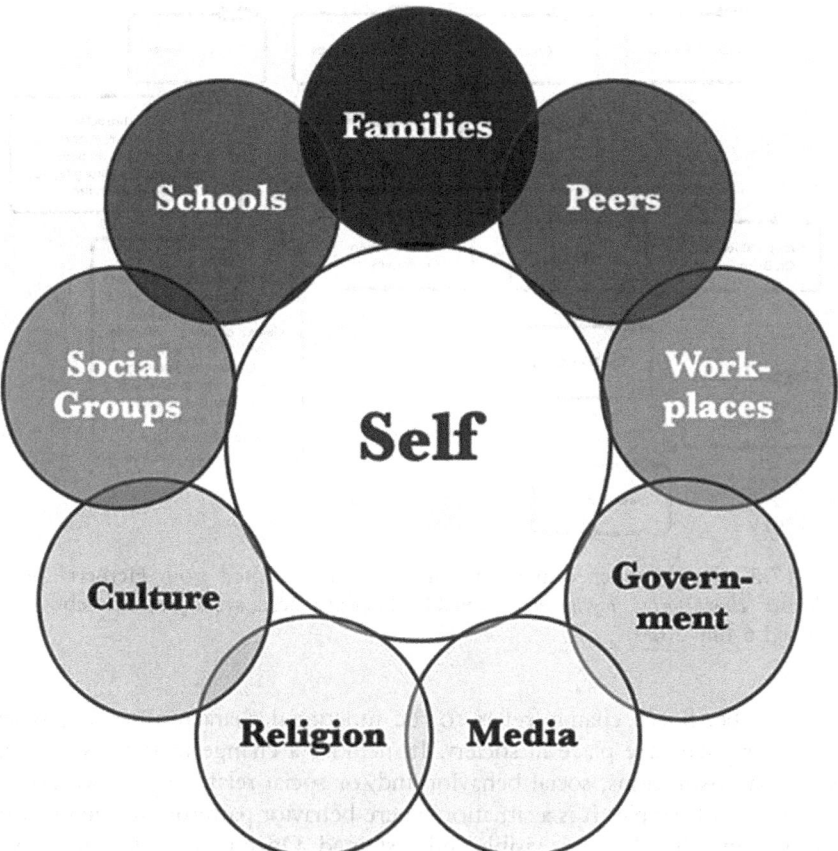

Fig. 17.1 Agents/institution of socialization (*Source* Herzog 2020)

socialization. These agents based on the degree of social relationship or intimacy or serve as the medium for the socialization process or behavioral change that reflect in one's conformity in the society (Fig. 17.2).

Socialization is a process in which a human being is changed into a social being, a process where the younger generation learns the dos and don'ts of a society into adulthood (Cole 2018). According to Horton and Hunt (1984), socialization is the process whereby one internalizes the norms of his groups, so that a distinct "self emerges, unique to this individual." Through the process of socialization, the individual becomes a social person and attains his personality. To Cole (2018), socialization serves as the process by which the child acquires a cultural content, along with selfhood and personality. Simply put, it leads to social change of the individual as he/she moves from one stage to another or from the younger age to the old. Therefore, socialization is expected to lead to social change or social transformation as the

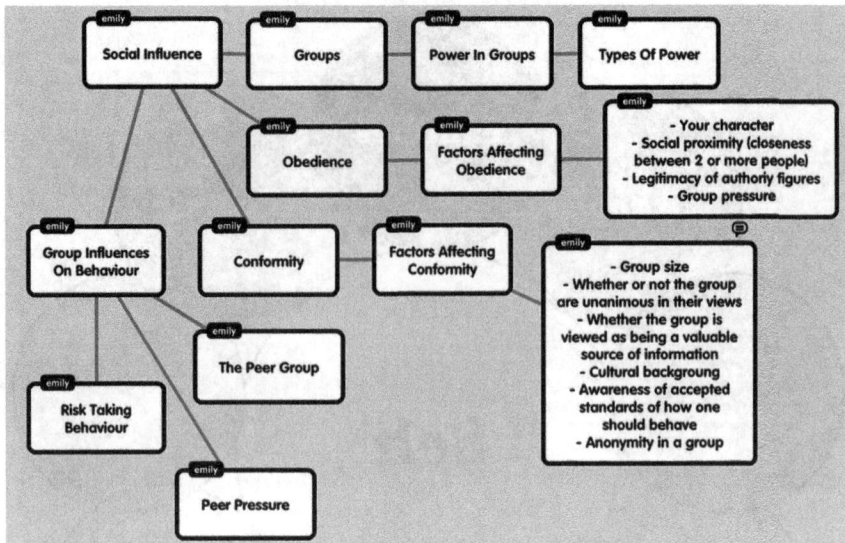

Fig. 17.2 Social influence in socialization (*Source* Adapted from Herbert. *Social influence chart-social psychology*. Available https://socialpsychoproject.weebly.com. Accessed 6 July 2020)

case may be. Social change refers to the functional characteristics and types of changes that take place in society. It includes a change in social structure i.e., social institutions, social behavior and/or social relations of a society or community of people. It is a situation where behavior patterns change in large numbers and this change is visible and sustained. Once there is deviance from culturally inherited values, rebellion against the established system may result, resulting in a broad change in the social order or SALWs as the experience in most African countries.

Social Transformation, Social Change and Culture of Violence

Social transformation refers to complete change in the nature and nurture of a person due to factors such as physical environment, demography, science and technology, political, social or cultural, economic and ideational structures. For example, scientific inventions and new technologies provide an easy access or capacity to develop weapons or improvised devices which greatly influence the social life or socio-political order. It brings changes in the economic structure and relations. This leads to a transformation of old values, norms, and ideals into newer ones. Likewise, it brings about changes in the physical environment and the material culture of each society which in turn gives birth to social change or transformation. In the context of this chapter, the society is viewed as an entity that must experience transformation as it moves from one epoch to another: this includes, perverse and violent transformation characterized by culture of violence and the proliferation of SALWS across society. In this sense, transformation can be seen as a social process involving social change in attitude, action, or norm toward a new state.

Social change is the significant alteration of social structures and cultural patterns through time. These structures or patterns are made up of an enduring network of social relationships in which interaction between people or groups has become constant. Social change can affect everything from education, population, politics, culture, law, and administration to the economy and international affairs. Social change often happens alongside other major changes such as industrialization. It is a process whereby the values, attitudes, or institutions of society (such as education, family, religion, and industry) are modified and includes both natural processes and action programs initiated by members of the affected community (Ololube 2011). Such changes can slowly and over time lead to the rise or fall of political systems or ideologies, economic growth or recession, and "cultures of peace" or "cultures of violence." The resultant effect of social change can be positive or negative i.e., it can enhance love, affection, development, or hatred, hate speech, violence, to mention but a few. Social change can refine communal values to a more cherished level or retard same to destructive position as experience through the use of SALWs to perpetrate violence or evil by some elements in Africa.

Scholars have argued that the ways in which parents socialize children depend on the parents' social class and on their child's biological sex (e.g. Kohn 1965, 1977; Shelton 2008; Wood 2009). Schools socialize children by teaching them both the formal curriculum and a hidden curriculum. Peers are an important source of emotional support and companionship, but peer pressure can induce individuals to behave in ways they might ordinarily regard as wrong. The mass media is another important agent of socialization, and scholars are divided on the effect the media has on violence in society. In considering the effects of religion on socialization, we need to distinguish between religious preference and religiosity. Thus, the agents of social change are not without multi-dimensional interpretations as it relates to the development of personality or negative or positive cultural/societal values.

Social change, as a continuous and evolving feature of societal development, is characterized by change relationships with/between sectors of the society. Changes that take place in one sector of a society often affect others, which imply that it has a "transfer effect." Social changes have a rate and are not uniform; they can be fast or slow, and the rate of change in societies, institutions, and organizations vary in relation to nature of the society or environmental factors (Ololube et al. 2013). No one society, institution, or organization can claim to have the same pace of development as any other. Likewise, growth or change in one sector of society does not mean the same rate of growth or change in other sectors. Impliedly, social change or transformation is a function of norm or culture.

Figure 17.3 shows the interaction between the environment and demography and impact especially with regard to land use and resource conflict. The impact of religious and political institutions, settlement pattern and climate is highlighted. The point is, the social world is underpinned by the complex universe of demography, environment, politics, religion, etc., and how the interface between these variables impact on conflict and peace in society.

Figure 17.4 depicts internal and external dimensions of social change, with US as focal unit of emphasis, but the rubric of analysis can be universal. Similarly, Fig. 17.5 shows the internal and external forces of social change. It shows that change requires a fair balance of the internal and external influence to occur.

Culture has multiple meanings in different disciplines and contexts; cultures are subject to change as defined by internal and external factors (Fig. 17.4). For example, some view it as a collective set of meanings, beliefs, and behavioral norms that guide the individual in a closed group (Jahoda 2012). Others view culture as a memory and control mechanism for society (Baecker 1997). It may be conceived of as providing the distinction of correct versus incorrect behavior. But who decides on the correctness or incorrectness of this distinction? Sociological thinking takes off where the cultural and the social are distinguished. As early as 1952, a review of the anthropological literature revealed 164 different definitions of the word culture (Samovar et al. 2009). Culture is a set of human-made objective and subjective elements that in the past have increased the probability of survival (Baldwin et al. 2005).

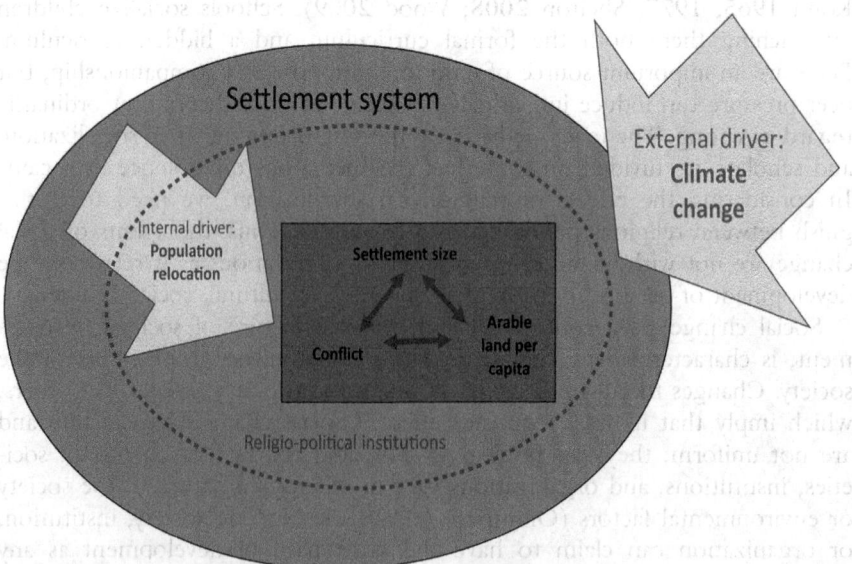

Fig. 17.3 The environment, demography, and conflict (*Source* Spielmann et al. 2020)

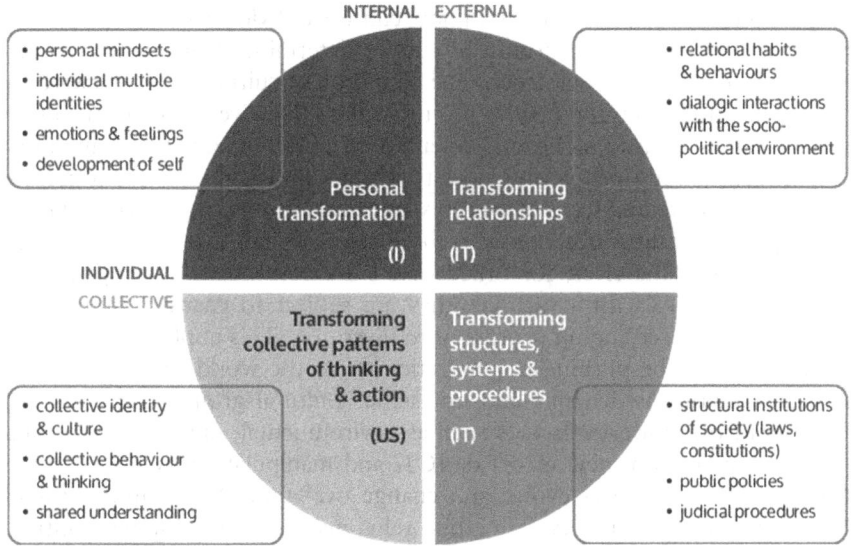

Fig. 17.4 Dimensions of social change (*Source* Adopted from Lonside et al. 2015)

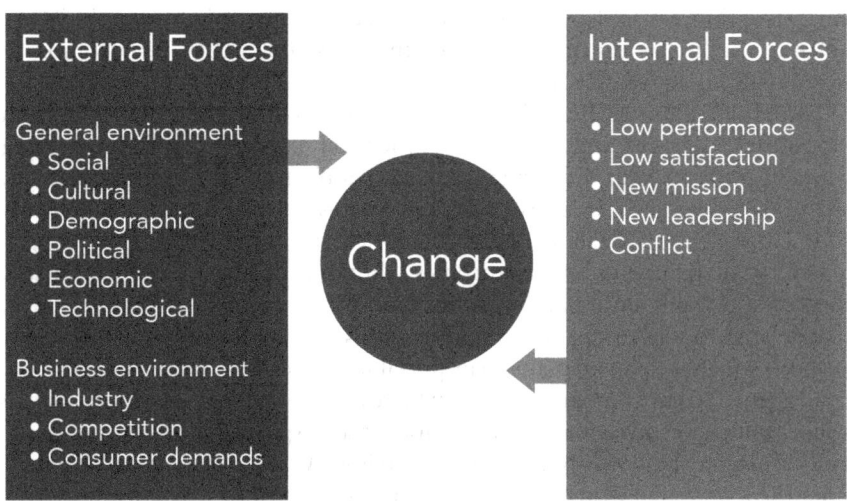

Fig. 17.5 Forces of social change (*Source* Adopted from Alfred North Whitehead https://courses.lumenlearning. Accessed 7 July 2020)

Culture seeks to inform members of a community what to expect from life, and therefore reduces confusion and helps to predict what to expect from persons. Culture is learned, shared, and transmitted from one generation to another based on symbols, dynamic and integrated systems. Culture is a function of history, religion or belief, values, social organization, and language. For our purpose, we are concerned with how culture and violence are linked. This implies that the subjective notion of culture determines largely the relationship between culture and violence. The definition of culture as put forward by Harrisson and Huntington (2007) posit that the subjective elements of culture such as values, attitudes, beliefs, orientations, and underlying assumptions are prevalent among people in a society. Philipsen (1997) notes that culture involves transmitted patterns of symbols, meanings, premises, and rules. Greek Philosopher Heraclitus observed two thousand years ago that you cannot step twice into the same river, for other waters are continually flowing in. i.e., cultures do not exist in a vacuum, they are subject to change. Simply put, cultures are in never ending process of re-invention. This implies that cultural change seems to be pushing communities across the world relentlessly. This is because culture is dynamic and not static. Cultural groups face continual challenges from powerful factors such as environmental, upheavals, wars and conquests, migration, new media or ICT, and manipulation by power elites, which is making cultures evolve and change over time. For example, values toward materialism as reflected in ethno-religious crisis, land disputes, cultural superiority, to mention but few, have changed the nature and character of most communities across Africa or specifically Nigeria; elections are rigged through violence, ethnic sentiments are erroneously projected to reflect group interests and corruption covered by ethno-religious sentiments or hate speech. These and many more lay the foundation of the quest for SALW proliferation in most countries across Africa.

The proliferation of SALWs is a marker of a "culture of violence" which weaponizes "culture" and unleashes mayhem on innocent people, destroying lives and property, and displacing innocent people from their natural habitat. SALWs is a term used in arms control protocols to refer to two main classes of weapons. First, is small arms e.g., hand-held small caliber firearms, usually consisting of handguns, rifles, carbines, shotguns, manual, semi-automatic, burst mode, and automatic weapons and man-portable machineguns. It includes the locally made guns in Africa or Nigeria. Secondly, we have light weapons which is defined as any man-portable weapon that expels or launches, it is designed to expel or launch or may be readily converted to expel or launch a shot, bullet, or projectile by the action of an explosive, excluding antique small arms and light weapons or their replicas (Weaponslaw, n.d.). Furthermore, SALWs range from clubs, knives, and machetes to those weapons just below those covered by the United Nations Register of Conventional Arms. SALWs have unique characteristics which make them attractive for irregular warfare, terrorism, and criminal activities. They are cheap, easy to handle, transport, conceal, and can cause heavy casualties (IPB 2018). In this chapter, small arms and light weapons are used interchangeably as the focus is not on weapons categorization but how "negative socialization" aids "culture of violence" marked by violent conflicts, crime, criminality, and proliferation of SALWs in Africa, with specific focus on Nigeria. The lesson from Nigeria is not far-fetched, it is the most populous, and perhaps the most violence-prone country on the continent characterized by Boko Haram insurgency in the Northeast, communal clashes in the Northcentral, resource conflict and rural banditry in the Northwest, succession movements in the South east, and environmental militancy in the Niger Delta, among others.

Although much of the cultural socialization research has focused on ethnic identity development of the youths, there is an emerging literature, suggesting cultural socialization is also associated with better academic engagement and achievement during adolescence (Huynh and Fuligni 2008; Smalls 2010; Wang and Huguley 2012), as well as better cognitive, behavioral, and academic outcomes during pre-school and early elementary school (Brown et al. 2009; Caughy et al. 2006). Theories regarding how cultural socialization may contribute to the nurturing of a culture of violence are particularly underdeveloped. Taking the case of Nigeria into cognizance, issues of informal social transformation or peer influence, effects of the media, can raise more concern in understanding the high level of hate speech, violence, crime, in the polity. This is because increased violent behaviour can weaken societal co-existence, increased the use of violent tools or the proliferation of SALW in communities. This prompted the need to examine how socialization or social change often happens alongside other changes that breed the culture of violence and SALW proliferation in the country. The central question that lies at the root of this piece is the extent to which socialization or social transformation or change serves to mitigate or accelerate the degree of the culture of violence and the proliferation of SALW in Africa. It is in this respect that the piece examines social transformation in Africa's most populous country (Nigeria) to serve as a baseline for the generalization of the subject matter of this chapter.

Culture of Violence and SALWs Proliferation in Nigeria

Cultural and social norms are rules or expectations of behavior within specific cultural or social groups. Often unspoken, these norms offer social standards of appropriate and inappropriate behavior, governing what is (and is not) acceptable and co-coordinating our interactions with others. Cultural and social norms persist within society because of individuals' preference to conform, given the expectation that others will also conform. A variety of external and internal pressures are thought to maintain cultural intolerance, intense dislike, and stereotyping of "different" groups within society e.g., xenophobic or racist violence and homophobic violence are best achieved with some level of protection through the use of SALW (WHO 2009). It shows that the root cause of the desire for violence or use of SALWs to achieve personal or group interests may not be unconnected with life style or learned cultural traits or influence that reinforces violence.

Nigeria is Africa's most populous country whose population grew substantially from 17.3% in 1967 to 49.4% in 2017 and comprised of approximately

198 million people (Adeyemo 2018), with undaunted challenges of enculturation or departure from the once peaceful path of social cohesion to phenomenal culture of violence and proliferation of SALW. Strategically located in the West Africa region with 770 km of shared land border with the Republic of Benin, around 1500 km with the Republic of the Niger, 1700 km with the Cameroon and 90 km with Chad and 850 km of maritime border with the Atlantic Ocean (ibid.), Nigeria is characterized by multi-ethnic and religious affiliations amidst rich cultural heritage that can stand out among the best in the world. This rich cultural heritage which used to be a source of inspiration as encapsulated with values that bred discipline, hard work, group cohesion, brotherhood, and, supported the citizenry to internalize norms or values that promotes esprit de corps and peaceful co-existence have transformed into bitterness and acrimony among the populace. Paradoxically, the country has continued to be confronted by religious intolerance, ethnic crisis, militia movements, communal land disputes, rural banditrybanditry, oil pipe line vandalism, pastoralist-agronomist skirmishes; making one to wonder why are these manifesting with "speed" at a time when the country deserves peaceful co-existence and development. Hence, the question of what is wrong with Africa's socialization or processes of internalizing "positive" cultural norms and values for the society? (Fig. 17.6).

The United Nations has raised alarm over proliferation of illicit small arms and light weapons (SALW) in Nigeria, with over 350 million illicit weapons. The UN observes that, 70% of estimated 500 million of such weapons said to be circulating in West Africa is domiciled in the country. Nigeria is among the countries experiencing some of the devastating effects of the proliferation of SALW as a result of spillover effects of the recent crises in the sahel region alongside numerous unresolved internal conflicts in different parts of the country, especially in the North East, Niger Delta and Southern regions. While reliable data on the numbers of these weapons circulating freely in the country is unavailable, analysts have estimated that out of the about 500 million weapons that may be circulating in West Africa in 2010, some 70% of these could be found in Nigeria (Ayissi and Sall 2005).

The spread of SALWs has resulted in endemic occurrence of violence at both public and private spaces, and increasing militarization of society. For instance, the Boko Haram insurgency in Northeast region has resulted in "normalization of violence" and erosion of pacifist societal values as militants regularly invade towns, villages, churches, mosques, police stations, schools and other public institutions with Improvised Explosive Devices (IED) (Abiodun 2016). The Boko Haram insurgents have justified their violent action by resorting to grandstanding and blaming the state that failed to follow God's way. In reality, however, members of the Boko Haram are victims of societal neglect in terms of access to education, job opportunities, and social welfare. This, raised concerns as regards to the root cause of the situation or cultural values or reorientation of most communities in the country. It implies that nature and character of the state—in particular, the policies of

Fig. 17.6 Areas affected by armed conflicts in Nigeria (*Source* https://www.google.com. Accessed 6 July 2020)

the state and behavior of the elites toward the masses—seemed to have influenced public perception of the state and mass resort to collective violence by those who feel marginalized by the state. Thus, violent social change is a function of a process whereby the values, attitudes, or institutions of society (such as education, family, religion, and industry) are subversively modified by structural violence (Ololube 2011). The culture of violence is thus a form of protest against that state. On the other hand, pacifist cultural socialization—for instance, through formal education—yields a better behavioral and cognitive outcome because of improved child self-esteem (Hughes et al. 2006).

Nature of Violent Conflicts and SALWs Proliferation in Nigeria

In Nigeria, as in much of Africa, there is a phenomenal efflorescence of a national pathology of violence. Throughout the country and across historical periods, violence has emerged as the new norm: for instance, insurgency in the Northeast, kidnappings in the North central, environmental militancy in the South-South, political assassinations during elections and farmers-herders conflicts. In April 2018, UNICEF reported that Boko Haram had abducted more than 1000 children since 2013, including 276 girls from Chibok in Borno state and 113 from Dapchi in Yobe state (UNICEF 2018). In 2015, the Nigeria Police Force reported 886 kidnappings. A recent Bulwark Intelligence threat analysis indicated that kidnapping figures remained relatively stable in 2017 and 2018. Likewise, about 630 people were reportedly abducted between May 2016 and May 2017 (Assano and Okereke 2018). The situation has more to do with the socialization and economic variables than religious inclinations as pointed out by President Muhammadu Buhari (Ogundipe 2018). However, the nature of transformation in Nigeria seems to show that the processes of internalizing societal norms and values have suffered set back owing to the increasing rate of violence and the proliferation of arms or dangerous weapons across the country e.g., the religious riots in Kano, Bauchi and Kaduna; conflicts in Jos, the Tiv-Junkun uprising, Ijaw-Ilaje, Ijaw-Itsekiri, Urhobo-Itsekiri and Ijaw-Urhobo crises; kidnapping and cattle rustling in Northern Nigeria, etc. are various crises faced as a result of the proliferation of arms in the country. These crises or the use of SALWs across most African countries look ambiguous as some of the communities are a predominantly homogenous social setting that raises a lot of concerns as to the rationale behind the use of arms against one another.

Table 17.1 on the Nigerian Police Force Small Arms and Ammunition shows that additional requirements are needed for effective internal security

Table 17.1 Nigeria Police Force (NPF) stock of small arms and ammunition

Type of arms	Present holdings	Estimated additional requirements over next five years
Pistols (various models): Revolver 38 mm, revolver chief special shot, Browning 9 mm, revolver 38 mm, chief long Browning DA, Browning 32 mm, Beretta 9 mm	8524	20,000
Rifles (various models): K2, FWC, SMG Model 12, SMG Beretta, Sterling, Beretta pump-action shotgun, submachine gun, AK-47	65,000	510,500
Ammunition:	(Rounds)	(Rounds)
5.56 mm for rifles	650,000	5,000,000
9 mm for rifles	434,000	100,000

Source Okeke and Orji (2014: Table 3.1)

operations. However, while the internal security agent is in dare need of additional arms and ammunition in Nigeria there is a growing concern that at least 350 million (three hundred and fifty million) illegal weapons are in circulation in Nigeria. The image below depicts the types of weapons in circulation in Nigeria's political environment (Figs. 17.7, 17.8 and 17.9).

Nigeria's precipitous descent to collective violence is underpinned largely by the proliferation of SALWs which comes from two main sources i.e. import of sophisticated SALWs from North America, South Asia, and Eurasia, as well as smuggled weapons from conflict zones such as Libya and Somalia; and, local fabrication, residues of guns used during the civil war, and thefts from government armouries or stolen arms from the state security service, and leakage from government armories' which corrupt law enforcement agents and military personnel sell for personal gains. Also the growing regional network of artisan production scattered across the ECOWAS sub-region. The recent reform of the ECOWAS protocol to allow movement of peoples and goods has made it possible for smugglers to illegally import artisanal weapons into Nigeria (Musa 2002; Bah 2004; Badmus 2009).

The bulk of these SALWs, whether imported or locally produced, goes into the hands of armed militias, insurgents and organized criminals (Adejo 2005). The affordability of these arms, poor licencing policy and connivance of government personnel have made it easy to transact SALWs. Armed conflict across Nigeria has made trading in, and smuggling of, SALWs a brisk, albeit risky, business. It appears a new war economy lubricated by sale of SALWs and hired mercenaries has emerged in Nigeria. A chief source of supply is the large

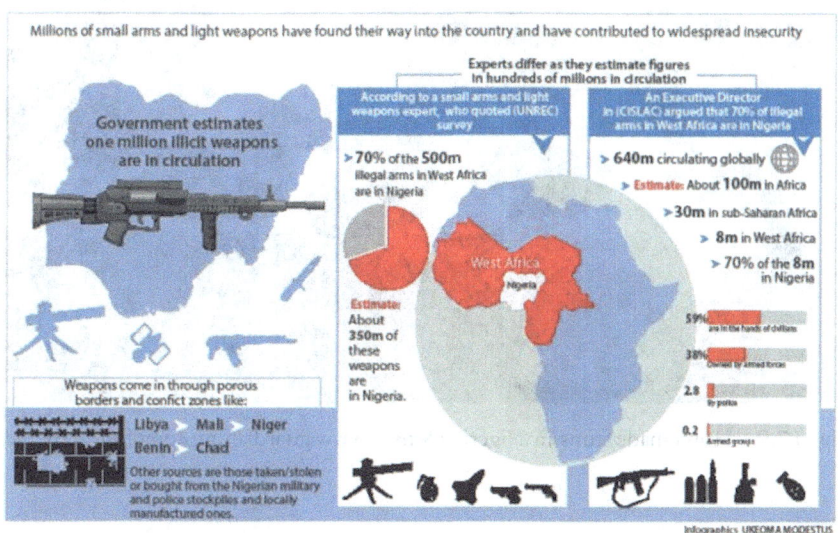

Fig. 17.7 Global sources of SALWS in Nigeria (*Sources* Abubakar et al. 2020; (ONSA) (UNREC) Experts)

Fig. 17.8 Small arms intercepted by the Nigerian Police Force (*Source* www.guardian.ng/opinion/unbodies)

Fig. 17.9 Homemade guns in Nigeria (*Source* www.guardian.ng/opinion/unbodie)

stockpile of stray arms from Libya—whose regime led by Col Gaddafi collapsed in 2012. Libyan SALWs have found their way into the country and are being used to fuel killings in the Northeast, Northwest, and North-Central regions of the country. In addition to the small arms for sale—but often working in tandem—is the influx of armed mercenaries for hire from Libya, Niger, and Mali into the country. These mercenaries are hired by willing buyers like Boko Haram. Thus the influx of armed gunmen from the Sahel region into different parts of the West African sub-region has further compounded the intensity of conflict in the region. It is generally believed that most of these gunmen and mercenaries were trained and armed by Muammar Gaddafi to achieve personal and regime security. When Gaddafi was killed by the NATO-backed Libyan rebels in 2012, the gunmen escaped with their arms and become "mercenaries for hire" across the Sahel region: some were encountered fighting with Boko Haram (Ogundibe 2018).

Nigeria's political and electoral space has grown to be fertile ground for the proliferation of SALWs (Campbell and Page 2018; Campbell 2020). This proliferation was attributed to the rise of electoral violence, ethnic bigotry and the rise of successionist movements in the South East and South South region of the country. There is also the rise of armed criminality especially highway robbery, kidnapping, and hostage taking—which is underpinned by the mass proliferation of SALWs. The rise of armed criminality cannot be dissociated from the "youth buldge," high level of poverty and unemployment that exist in the country (Campbell and Page 2018). The nature of SALWs proliferation can as well be attributed to the accelerated pace of the rise of violent subculture mediated by epochal development in ICT and new technologies of virtual crime. Sudden upsurge in communal violence and hate speech have created an overwhelming demand for the SALW, thereby making them weapons of choice in majority of recent conflicts (Malam 2014; IPCR 2017).

Media reports have illuminated the foregoing analysis and paint a grim picture of the endemic nature of SALWs proliferation in Nigeria. On 18 September 2013, *ThisDay* Newspaper reported that Nigerian Customs impounded a cargo from United States, which smuggled Arms concealed in house hold cargo. Prior to this incidence on 13 April 2013, the *Daily Trust* Newspaper reported that Nigeria Police detectives from Anambra and Delta States have uncovered arms factories in three communities in Delta State. Similarly, the *Newswatch* (Nigeria) on 9 May, 2013 carried a grim headline: "Police Confirm 1 Million Illegal Guns in Nigeria." At the same time, the Nigeria Customs Service too intercepted 49 boxes with 661 pieces of pump-action rifles in a 40ft container along Mile 2 Apapa Road, Lagos; concealed with steel doors and other merchandise goods, which came in through Lagos port (Malam 2014). The News Agency of Nigeria reported that the consignment was cleared from Lagos port (NAN 2017). The rifles were under absolute prohibition list in Nigeria. The consignment was reported to have originated from Turkey, with a mix-up in the document which finally revealed that the consignment originated from China. The report further explains that both

Turkey and China have taken over from Europe and North America as the net importer of legitimate goods, they appear to be net importers of illegal arms too. Deducing from the above, one can notice that the situation reflects negative signal on the poor attitude of the citizenry to safeguard the country from the purchase and proliferation of SALW.

THE GEO-SPATIAL DYNAMICS OF SMALL ARMS PROLIFERATION AND CULTURE OF VIOLENCE IN NIGERIA

It is a fact that each of Nigeria's six geopolitical zones have experienced varying manifestations of armed violence, especially since the return of the country to democratic rule in 1999. For example, the South-South Zone which comprises Bayelsa, Cross-Rivers, Rivers, Delta, Edo, and Akwa Ibom States has experienced violent political/environmental agitations by armed youths through oil pipeline vandalism, kidnapping and hostage taking, arm conflict by gangs/cult groups, inter and intra-community strife, armed robbery and oil bunkering (Inokoba and Imbua 2010). The South-East Zone comprising Ebonyi, Imo, Enugu, Abia, and Anambra States has experienced violent conflicts of kidnapping, armed robbery, intra-community cleavages and crises (e.g. Aguleri/Umuleri crises, the Okija Shrine mystery, and the Ezza-Ezilo fratricidal war) (Mbah and Nwangwu 2014), Pro-Biafra agitation and attacks on policemen and innocent citizens, etc. The South-West Zone which comprised of Osun, Ondo, Ekiti, Ogun, Lagos, and Oyo States, respectively, has suffered security breaches and incidences of the use of SALW via intra-ethnic crises (e.g., the Ife/Modakeke land disputes), armed robbery, political unrest/political killings such as that of the late Bola Ige, attack on judges and disruption of court proceedings by a serving Governor in Ekiti State, the Shagamu Hausa/Yoruba clash and kidnapping among others.

The North-East Zone (shaded green in map/Fig. 7.10) which is the epicenter of the Boko Haram comprises of Adamawa, Bauchi, Borno, Gombe, Taraba, and Yobe States, is also known for violence and heightened use of SALWs which includes the use of IEDs for suicide bombings, indiscriminate killings, kidnapping, cattle rustling, cultism and students uprising (e.g., the killing of students in Mubi-Adamawa State), attack on banks, law enforcement agents, attacks on traditional rulers or institutions (e.g., Emir of Fika & El Kanemi of Borno), assassinations of retired or serving public officials such as the late Comptroller General of the Nigerian Immigration Service Ibrahim Jarma, the military veteran General Shuwa, etc.; ethnic clash such as Tiv/Jukun, Tiv/Kuteb, Jukun/Kuteb, Bachama/Fulani; violent community upheavals such as the Tingno-Waduku crisis in Adamawa State, ethno-religious crisis in Mambila, Wukari, Takum, to mention but a few. The North Central Zone (shaded brown in map/figure above) comprises Benue, Kogi, Kwara, Nasarawa, Niger, Plateau and the FCT, Abuja. Incidences of suicide bombings, killings and destruction of property have occurred in the zone since return to democracy in 1999. Further, the region has experienced ethno-religious crisis,

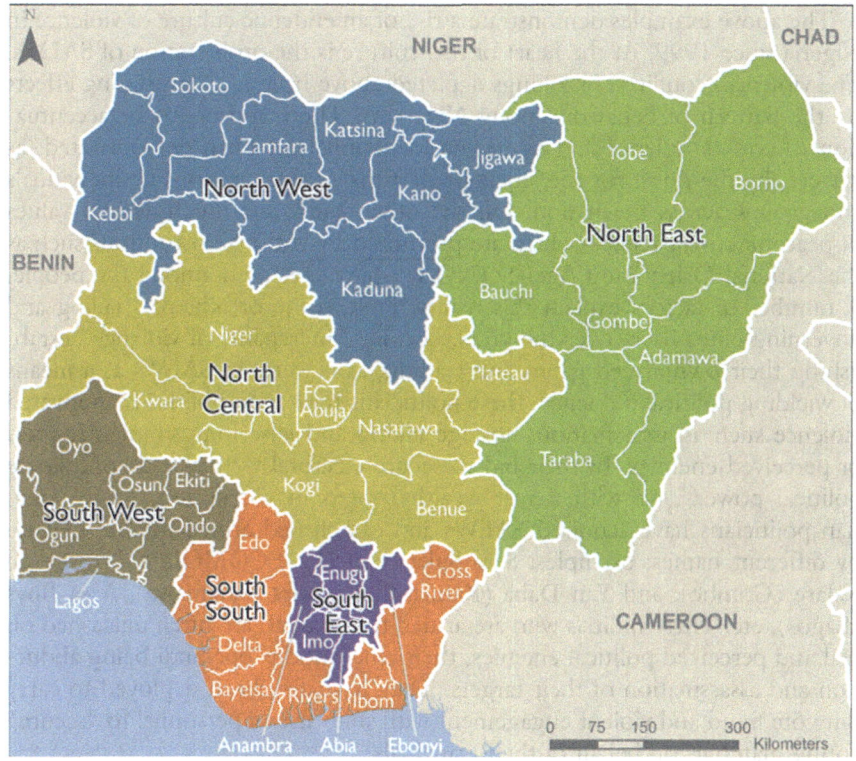

Fig. 17.10 Zones of violence: Nigeria's six geopolitical zones (*Source* Akande 2015)

indigene/settler violent conflicts in Plateau State, Bombing of United Nations and the Police Headquarters in Abuja, attack on *Thisday* Newspapers, bank robbery in Ankpa local government area of Kogi and Kwara States, killing of policemen/officers in an ambush by the Ombatse worshippers in Nassararwa State, farmers/herdsmen clash, kidnapping, and communal conflict (Obahopo and Obateru 2012).

The North-West Zone which stands legendry for banditry comprises of Sokoto, Zamfara, Jigawa, Kebbi, Katsina, Kano, and Kaduna States. The zone has witnessed coordinated attacks on places of worship in Zaria, Kaduna, etc.; post 2011 election riots in Kano, Kaduna, Katsina; violent ethno-religious crises in Kaduna, Kafanchan and environs, alongside kidnapping/rescue operation that led to the death of Edgar Fritz Raupach (a German) in the city of Kano, killing of British citizen Chris McManus and fellow Italian hostage, Franco Lamolinara by gunmen in Sokoto, cattle rustling and kidnapping by armed gangs along the Birnin Gwari axis, the Shiites/military clash in Zaria (Umoru et al. 2015) and Abuja, kidnapping for ransom, rape, to mention but a few.

The above examples demonstrate a rise of an endemic culture of violence in Nigeria since 1999. At the heart of this culture is the proliferation of SALWs. The violence, conflicts, or killings depicted above have had devastating effects on the pattern of behavior among Nigerians. There appears to be accentuation of armed violence and crime into a national art form demonstrated, as it were, by the quest for the stockpile of arms or ammunitions by individuals and groups across the nation. On the other hand, the much-desired values of peaceful co-existence—which are promoted by national institutions such as the National Orientation Agency (NOA)—have collapsed among the people. A number of factors explain this reality. First, some of Nigeria's ruling and governing elites have, over the years, become "merchants of violence" establishing their own armed gangs and trading, as it were, in SALWs as a means of wielding political influence: these politicians have used politically motivated violence such as assassination, hostage taking and false imprisonment of real or perceived enemies. In their bid to secure electoral victory and consolidate political power, and with a vast wealth rooted in corruption, some Nigerian politicians have acquired SALWs and established armed militias that go by different names: examples, Sara Suka (Bauchi); ECOMOG (Borno); Yan Kalare (Gombe); and Yan Daba (Kano), Shilla Boys (Adamawa), Area Boys (Lagos), etc. These militias who are armed to the teeth are often unleashed on real and perceived political enemies, their chief modus operandi being abduction and assassination of their targets. They have also been deployed to carry out vote fraud and violent engagement with state armed personnel to "secure" voting materials on behalf of their principals.

Another key factor that underpins the culture of violence in Nigeria is the rise of ethnographic contradiction spawning from the so-called indigene-settler dichotomy. Though the Nigerian constitution recognizes the right of every citizen to settle in any part of the country, in reality in every state of the federation, the indigenous tribes are not ready to accept the legitimacy of the so-called settlers—these are Nigerian citizens who are considered citizens of another state but settling in a particular state as a result of work, business, or marriage. It is often argued that the political elites manipulate the indigene-settler dichotomy for their material political ambitions. Specifically, they employ ethnicity to achieve their divisive aims. As Nnoli (2003) argued, the problem of Nigeria is not that of cultural differences among the various ethnic groups; neither is it geographical differences, nor their social and economic differences. The difference among the various ethnic groups in Nigeria, rather, ethnic question arises from the degree to which this emergent identity has been manipulated by unpatriotic politicians. Disturbingly, in geopolitical regions, Nigeria experiences an endemic culture of violence and intolerance which has threatened Nigeria's unity and corporate existence. At the heart of this reality is the massive accumulation and deployment of SALWs in politically motivated incendiary conflicts. For instance, the conflict in Taraba State between the Jukun and the Tiv proves the fact that differences in ancestral origin and history are not the main problem in the State, but the manipulations of these issues by the political elites—that is, the elites used settler-indigene antics to divide the people for their political benefits (Akintola and Yabayanze 2017). This was also supported by Usman (1987) who asserts that settler-indigene question in Nigeria is the manifestation of the manipulative skills of the elites in the country. In most cases, the ethnic crises or indigene/settler conflicts constitute a new trend in religious crises, tending to obscure the religious dimension and transform the situation into a political crisis. Related to the indigene-settler dichotomy is the politics of contestation over land and scarce natural resources. The farmers-herders violence in North-Central Nigeria, which involve the mass deployment of SALWs, is actually inflamed by the elites to increase their political and electoral gains.

A third factor underpinning the endemic culture of violence in Nigeria is the rise of violent extremism and fundamentalism. The state's exit of the religious space through poor management of preachers and contents of proselytization have given rise to violent extremists and fundamentalist groups that seek to challenge the state, and wrestle for parallel power. Through foreign and local support, these groups have successfully combatted with the armed forces and police and curved out "ungoverned spaces" wherein they seek to mount theocratic structures. The Boko Haram insurgency is an example of an extremist group which emerged in the Northeast in 2009 as a result of poor handling of disagreement between a funeral party and the Police. Boko Haram's antecedents date back to 2000s when a group of young preachers, led by Muhammad Yusuf, commenced vile preaching against the secular state, and mustered a group of young ideologues to resist the "heretic state" (*Zindiq*). The group was forced by constant police raids to migrate from Maiduguri to Kanama, Yobe State where they set up a base camp. They later returned back to Maiduguri and established Albani Islamic Centre in Bayan Kwata (Railway Quarters) of Maiduguri. In the course of time, the followers of Boko Haram movement were able to muster SALWs through clandestine means and unleash into a full blown militant organization that was able to overwhelm the Police and, following declaration of state of emergency in 2013, government deployed the armed forces to help contain the insurgency. As at 2015, the group was able to capture seven out 27 local government areas in Borno State. Boko Harams stockpile of arms and ammunitions comes from diverse sources—including theft and invasion of government armouries, purchase from local and foreign suppliers, alleged support from unknown foreign sources. Thus, in Nigeria religion has been converted into an institution for violent struggle, rather than peacemaking.

Conclusion

The problem of SALWs proliferation in Africa is centrally rooted in the rise of emergent cultures of violence that permit, or at least tolerate, the use of arms as a means of social or political expression and a new form of "bloody livelihood" for newly emerging "war economies" across the continent. Across Africa, young peoples are perniciously internalized into violent "uncivil norms" that privilege the use of small arms. To overcome this challenge, a reconstruction to a pacific culture is necessary through positive enculturation to address the spate of culture of violence and proliferation of SALW in Africa. Owing to the multi-cultural nature of the African communities, options to address the menace should be innovative, people-oriented and community-driven initiatives spearheaded by the government which should institutionalized inter-agency collaboration to co-ordinate and engage communities on the declining or negative trends of socialization. This can be achieved via value reorientation activities and sustainable public enlightenment programs. The state social services and orientation agencies across the continent need to redefine their role in sensitizing the citizenry on the need for a stable and nurturing relationship between children and their parents and caregivers. Efforts should be strengthened in developing life skills in children and adolescents. Likewise, juvenile institutions or Borstal home should be adequately funded to cater for the correctional care of deviant youths. This should be backed by legislation that will enrich the reorientation of youths. To this effect, legislations to support value reorientation should be of paramount attention to National and State/Counties Assemblies in the continent. E.g., issues related to victims of violence, identification, care and support should be backed by legislations to mitigate the negative effects of retaliation or more violence in the communities. Laws and policies that make violent behavior an offence send a message to the society that it is not acceptable.

Mass media campaigns, including education through entertainment to challenge norms supportive of violence are a good way to counteract and contain the culture of violence and SALW proliferation. In addition, African countries should invest in legislation and law enforcement to limit and regulate the possession, sale, and transfer of SALWs and engagement in acts of violence and criminality. Furthermore, traditional institutions should be accorded recognition as it stands acceptable to most communities across the continent, and establish some level of accountability and community inclined intelligence gathering mechanisms which, if properly harnessed may help the state to identify culprits involved in the abuse or use of SALW, and exposed notorious parents that undermine cultural and social norms i.e., not committed to "positive" child rearing practices for community or state intervention. Finally, given that civilians constitute the overwhelming majority not only of gun owners, but also of the victims and perpetrators of gun violence (UN Chronicle 2009), the civil population should be at the heart of arms control Africa initiatives. African governments should create incentives for disarmament and arms control. For example, the efforts shown in the case of Nigeria's Niger Delta is a model that should be emulated and improved upon. However, beyond the surrendering of weapons, there is need for training programmes for reintegration into the society; provision of basic necessities of life to discourage a rethink to violence or recidivism. Likewise, psychological or trauma lessons to victims of violence, youth's engagement in skills acquisition programmes, counselling/mentoring, and sustained monitoring/evaluation of intervention activities towards the mitigation of the proliferation of SALWs or violence in African societies.

References

Abiodun, T. (2016). An Appraisal of Nigeria's Counter-Terrorism Policy: The Case of Boko Haram. In Akinwunmi and Olaniyan (Eds.), *Global Perspectives in Education: A Book in Honour of Late Prof. Mobolaji Ogunsanya*. Ibadan: Department of Educational Management, Faculty of Education, University of Ibadan and His Lineage Publishing House.

Abubakar, A. I., Ronald, M., & Simon, E. S. (2020, February 17). *How Illicit Weapons Fuel Nigeria's Insecurity*. https://www.dailytust.com.ng/how-illicit-weapons-fuel-nigerias-insecurity.html. Accessed 8 July 2020.

Adejo, P. Y. (2005). Crime and the Cross-Border Movement of Weapons: The Case of Nigeria. In A. Ayissi & I. Sall (Eds.), *Combating the Proliferation of Small Arms and Light Weapons in West Africa*. UNIDIR/2005/7. Geneva: UNIDIR. Available at https://www.researchgate.net/publication/331639338_Small_Arms_and_Light_Weapons_Proliferation_and_Its_Threats_to_Nigeria's_Internal_Security. Accessed 19 November 2019.

Adeyemo, I. (2018). *Nigeria's Population Now 198 Million—NPC*. Available at https://www.premiumtimesng.com/news/top-news/264781-nigerias-population-now-198-million-npc.html. Accessed 15 November 2019.

Akande, N. O. (2015). *Geo-Political Zones of Nigeria*. https://www.researchgate.net/figure/Geo-political-zone-nigeria-of-all–.

Alfred, N. W. (2020). *Force of Change and Organizational Behaviour*. https://courses.lumenlearning.com/vm-organisational. Accessed 7 July 2020.

Akintola, E. O., & Yabayanze, A. J. (2017). Settlers-Indigenes Question in Nigeria: Much Rhetoric, No Answers. *European Scientific Journal, 13*, 365–378.

Assano, W., & Okereke, D. (2018). *Nigerian Kidnappings Crisis*. Available at https://enactafrica.org/enact-observer/nigerias-kidnapping-crisis. Accessed 25 October 2019.

Ayissi, A., & Sall, I. (Eds.). (2005). *Combating the Proliferation of Small Arms and Light Weapons in West Africa: Handbook for the Training of Armed and Security Forces United Nations Institute for Disarmament Research*. Geneva, Switzerland: United Nations Institute for Disarmament Research.

Badmus, I. A. (2009). *Managing Arms in Peace Processes: ECOWAS and the West African Civil Conflicts*. Available at https://trove.nla.gov.au/work/236494359. Accessed 12 January 2018.

Baecker, D. (1997, November). *The Meaning of Culture*. Article in Thesis Eleven. Available at https://www.researchgate.net/publication/240706335. Accessed 10 October 2019.

Bah, A. (2004). *Implementing the ECOWAS Moratorium in Post-war Sierra Leone*. A Report prepared for the Working Group of the Peace-building Coordination Committee in support of the Peace-building and Human Security: Development of Policy Capacity of the Voluntary Sector Project.

Baldwin, J. R., Faulkner, S. L., Hecht, M. L., & Lindsley, S. L. (Eds.). (2005). *Redefining Culture: Perspectives Across the Disciplines*. London: Lawrence Erlbaum Associates.

Brown, T. N., Tanner-Smith, E. E., & Lesane-Brown, C. L. (2009). Investigating Whether and When Family Ethnic/Race Socialization Improves Academic Performance. *Journal of Negro Education, 78*(4), 385–404.

Campbell, J. (2020). *Graph 1: Death Over Time*. Nigeria Security Tracker. Available at https://www.cfr.org/nigeria/nigeria-security-tracker/p29483. Accessed 1 June 2020.

Campbell, J., & Page, T. M. (2018). *Nigeria: What Everyone Needs to Know*. Oxford: Oxford University Press.

Caughy, M. O., O'Campo, P. J., Nettles, S. M., & Lohrfink, K. F. (2006, September–October). Neighbourhood Matters: Racial Socialization and the Development of Young African American Children. *Special Issue on Race, Ethnicity, and Culture in Child Development, 77*(5), 1220–1236.

Cilliers, J. (2018). *Violence in Africa Trends, Drivers and Prospects to 2023* (Africa Report). Institute for Security Studies. Available at https://www.alnap.org/system/files/content/resource/files/main/ar-12.pdf. Accessed 18 December 2019.

Cole, N. L. (2018). *Understanding Socialization in Sociology: Overview and Discussion of a Key Sociological Concept*. Retrieved from https://www.thoughtco.com/socialization-in-sociology-4104466. Accessed 10 October 2019.

Crisogen, D. T. (2015). Types of Socialization and Their Importance in Understanding the Phenomena of Socialization. *European Journal of Social Sciences, 2*(4), 331–336.

Diarra, C. O. (2005). The Economic Community of West African States (ECOWAS) as the Institutional Framework for Efforts to Combat the Proliferation of Arms in Africa. In A. Anatole & S. Ibrahima (Eds.), *Combating the Proliferation of Small Arms and Light Weapons in West Africa*. Geneva, Switzerland: UNIDIR.

Florquin, N., & Berman, E. G. (2005). *Armed and Aimless: Armed Groups, Guns, and Human Security in the ECOWAS Region* (p. xiv). Geneva: Small Arms Survey.

Francis, T. A., Ifeoluwa, A., Oluwasolape, O., & Chukwuyere, N. (2018). Small Arms and Light Weapons Proliferation and Its Threats to Nigeria's Internal Security. *International Journal of Social Science and Humanities Research* (online), *6*(3), 34–45. Available at www.researchpublish.com. Accessed 23 March 2020.

GIABA Report. (2013). *The Nexus Between Small Arms and Light Weapons and Money Laundering and Terrorist Financing in West Africa*. Ponty Dakar, Senegal: GIABA Publications.

Harrisson, E., & Huntington, S. P. (2007). *After 40 Years, Inter-Racial Marriage Flourishing*. http://msnbc.msn.com/id/18090277. Accessed 15 December 2018.

Herbert, K. *Social Influence Chart-Social Psychology*. Available socialpsychproject.weebly.com. Accessed July 2020.

Herzog, P. S. (2020, January). *Multiple Dynamic Agents of Socialisation*. https://www.researchgate.net/figure/multiple-and-dynamicagent-of-socialisation. Accessed July 2020.

Horton, P. B., & Hunt, C. L. (1984). *Sociology*. London: McGraw-Hill.

Hughes, D., Smith, E. P., Stevenson, H. C., Rodriguez, J., Johnson, D., & Spicer, P. (2006). Parents' Ethnic-Racial Socialization Practices: A Review of Research and Directions for Future Study. *Developmental Psychology, 42,* 747–770.

Huynh, V. W., & Fuligni, A. J. (2008). Ethnic Socialization and the Academic Adjustment of Adolescents from Mexican, Chinese, and European Backgrounds. *Developmental Psychology, 44,* 1202–1208.

Imobighe, T. (1989). *The OAU, African Defence and Security.* Benin and Owerri: Adena Publishers, p. 16.

Imobighe, T. (2003). *Nigerian's Defence and National Security Linkages.* Ibadan: Heineman Educational Book Nigerian Plc.

Inokoba, P., & Imbua, D. L. (2010). Vexation and Militancy in the Niger Delta: The Way Forward. *Journal of Human Ecology* (Delhi, India), *29*(2), 101–120. Available at https://www.researchgate.net/publication/228672550_Vexation_and_Militancy_in_the_Niger_Delta_The_Way_Forward. Accessed 10 February 2020.

International Peace Bureau—IPB. (2018). *Small Arms and Light Weapons.* International Peace Bureau. Retrieved from http://www.ipb.org/small-arms-and-light-weapons/. Accessed 10 November 2018.

IPCR. (2017). *2016 Strategic Conflict Assessment of Nigeria: Consolidated and Zonal Reports.* Dugbe, Ibadan, Nigeria: Institute for Peace and Conflict Resolution (IPCR) and John Archers (Publishers).

Jahoda, G. (2012). Critical Reflections on Some Recent Definitions of "Culture". *Culture & Psychology, 18*(3), 289–303. Available at https://citeseerx.ist.psu.edu/viewdoc/download?doi=10.1.1.946.8338&rep=rep1&type=pdf. Accessed 15 January 2020.

Knight, W. A. (2008). Disarmament, Demobilization, and Reintergration and Post Conflict Peacebuilding in Africa: An Overview, *African Security, 1*(1), 24–52, https://doi.org/10.1080119362200802285757.

Kohn, M. (1965). Social Class and Parent-Child Relationships: An Interpretation. *American Journal of Sociology, 68,* 471–480.

Kohn, M. (1977). *Class and Conformity.* Homewood, IL: Dorsey.

Lonside, K. G., Patrick, P., & Turner, B. (2015). *Dimensions of Social Change.* https://www.researchgate.net/figure/dimension-of-social-change-redrawn-from-fig-293823090-download. Accessed 6 July 2020.

Malam, B. (2014, June). Small Arms and Light Weapons Proliferation and Its Implication for West African Regional Security. *International Journal of Humanities and Social Science, 4*(8), 260–268 Available at https://www.researchgate.net/publication/327288413_Small_Arms_and_Light_Weapons_Proliferation_and_Its_Implication_for_West_African_Regional_Security. Accessed 22 March 2020.

Mbah, P., & Nwangwu, C. (2014). Sub-Ethnic Identity and Conflict in Nigeria: The Policy Option for the Resolution of the Conflict Between Ezza and Ezillo in Ebonyi State. *Mediterranean Journal of Social Sciences, 5*(2), 681–688.

Musa, A. (2002). Small Arms: A Time Bomb Under West Africa's Democratization Process. *Brown Journal of World Affairs, 9*(1), 239–250.

New Agency of Nigeria—NAN. (2017). *Nigerian Authorities Intercept 661 Pump-Action Rifles Imported Through Lagos Port* (Agency Report). Available at https://www.premiumtimesng.com/news/headlines/222039-nigerian-aut

horities-intercept-661-pump-action-rifles-imported-lagos-port.html. Accessed 29 November 2018.

Nnoli, O. (2003). *Ethnic Violence in Nigeria: A Historical Perspective*. Retrieved from www.indiana.edu/~workshop/papers/nnoli_021003.pdf. Accessed 23 December 2018.

Obahopo, B., & Obateru, T. (2012). 10 Die in Kogi Banks Robbery, as Gunmen Kill Policeman, 4 Ohers in Yobe. *Vanguard Newspapers*. Available at http://www.vanguardngr.com/2012/04/10-die-in-kogi-banks-robbery. Accessed 19 September 2018.

Ogundipe, S. (2018). *Buhari Blames Gaddafi for Killings Across Nigeria*. Available at https://www.premiumtimesng.com/news/top-news/264764-buhari-blames-gaddafi-for-killings-across-nigeria.html. Accessed 12 April 2018.

Okeke, V. C., & Orji, R. O. (2014). Nigerian State and the Proliferation of Small Arms and Light Weapons in the Northern Part of Nigeria. *Journal of Education and Social Research*. https://doi.org/105901/jers.2014v4n1p415-428.

Ololube, N. P. (2011). *Education and Society: An Interactive Approach*. Owerri: SpringField Publishers.

Ololube, N. P., Uriahii, O. A., & Agbor, N. C. (2013). The Nature of Social Change and Its Implication for Educational Management and Planning. *International Journal of Educational Foundation Management*, 1(1), 49–58. Available at https://www.researchgate.net/publication/283081698. Accessed 19 December 2019.

Philipsen, G. (1997). A Theory of Speech Codes. In G. Philipsen & T. Albercht (Eds.), *Developing Theories in Communication*. New York: Albany State University of New York Press.

Renner, M. (2006). *Curbing the Proliferation of Small Arms*. www.worldwatch.org/node/3738. Accessed 14 November 2006.

Reuters. (2012). *Suicide Car Bombs Hit Nigerian Newspaper Offices*. Reuters. Available at http://www.reuters.com/article/us-nigeria-bomb-idUSBRE83P0NR20120426. Accessed 10 October 2018.

Samovar, L. A., Porter, R. E., & McDaniel, E. R. (2009). *Communication Between Cultures*. Wadsworth Cengage Learning. Boston, USA: Monica Eckman.

Shelton, J. E. (2008). The Investment in Blackness Hypothesis: Toward Greater Understanding of Who Teaches What During Racial Socialization. *Du Bois Review: Social Science Research on Race*, 5(2), 235–257.

Smalls, C. (2010). Effects of Mothers' Racial Socialization and Relationship Quality on African American Youth's School Engagement: A Profile Approach. *Cultural Diversity and Ethnic Minority Psychology*, 16, 476–484.

Spielmann, K. A., Matthew, A. P., Glowack, D. M., & Andrew, D. (2020). *Early Warning Signals of Social Transformation: A Case Study of US South West*. https://journals.plo.org/plosone/article?id=10,1371/journal.pone.0163685. Accessed July 2020.

Umoru, H., Binniyat, L., Erunke, J., & Etim, M. (2015). Army/Shiite Clash: I Escaped by the Will of God—Buratai. *Vanguard Newspapers*. Available at http://www.vanguardngr.com/2015/12/armyshiite-clash-i-escaped-by-the-will-of-god-buratai/. Accessed 21 December 2019.

UNICEF. (2018). More Than 1,000 Children in Northeastern Nigeria Abducted by Boko Haram Since 2013. Four Years on from Chibok Abduction. *UNICEF Continues to Call for Children's Release and Immediate End to Attacks on Schools*.

Available at https://www.unicef.org/wca/press-releases/more-1000-children-nor
theastern-nigeria-abducted-boko-haram-2013. Accessed 26 June 2019.
UN Chronicle. (2009). *Small Arms: No Single Solution*. United Nations. Available at https://www.un.org/en/chronicle/article/small-arms-no-single-solution. Accessed 10 November 2019.
UNOWA. (n.d.). *United Nation Office for Africa*. Available at https://unowa.unmiss ions.org/mandate. Accessed 25 March 2020.
Usman, Y. B. (1987). *The Manipulation of Religion in Nigeria*. Lagos: Vanguard Printers and Publishers.
Wang, M. T., & Huguley, J. P. (2012). Parental Racial Socialization as a Moderator of the Effects of Racial Discrimination on Educational Success Among African American Adolescents. *Child Development, 83*, 1716–1731.
Weaponslaw. (n.d.). *Small Arms*. Available at http://www.weaponslaw.org/glossary/small-arms. Accessed 14 March 2020.
WHO. (2009). *Changing Cultural and Social Norms Supportive of Violent Behaviour*. Geneva: WHO Press.
Wood, J. T. (2009). *Gendered Lives: Communication, Gender, and Culture*. Belmont, CA: Wadsworth.

Aminu Umar research interest covers Political Economy, Public Policy, Corporate Management, Parliamentary Strengthening and Small Arms and Light Weapons Proliferation in Africa. He holds a Doctorate and Master's Degrees in Political Science from Ahmadu Bello University, Zaria and B.Sc. in Sociology and Anthropology from the University of Maiduguri, Nigeria, and Professional Certificates in Research Methods and Project Planning, Monitoring/Evaluation from London Graduate School/Albion College-London. He served as Senior Legislative Aide through the Sixth and early Seventh Nigerian National Assembly, and Research Fellow/Lecturer at the erstwhile National Institute for Legislative Studies (NILS), National Assembly, (now, National Institute for Legislative and Democratic Studies, NILDS), and participated in the NILS/University of Benin Post Graduate Studies Progamme in Legislative Studies. In 2017, Umar joined the Department of Political Science, Faculty of Social Sciences, National Open University of Nigeria (NOUN) as Senior lecturer and served as its Head of Department. He is a Certified Management Consultant, Fellow of the Institute of Management Consultant, Nigeria; and member of numerous professional bodies. Umar is an external examiner to several tertiary institutions and facilitator to capacity development bodies within and outside Nigeria. He is currently the Director, Kaduna Study Centre, NOUN.

Nachana'a Alahira David is an Associate Professor in the Department of Political Science and Defence Studies at the Nigerian Defence Academy, Kaduna. She obtained a Ph.D. in Political Science from Ahmadu Bello University, Zaria (Nigeria) and has held a sabbatical position at the Adamawa State University, Mubi. David's research interest covers international organization, security studies, gender, and rural livelihood.

CHAPTER 18

Youth Bulge and Small Arms Proliferation in Africa: Guns, Generations and Violent Conflicts

John Tor Tsuwa

INTRODUCTION

One of the central challenges of conflict and security discourse of post-independence Africa has been to explain how to mitigate the proliferation of small arms and light weapons and to prevent underage acquisition and usage of the same. This is because most of the post-independence African leaders as Tsuwa (2015) argues have constructed security in terms of the availability of physical arms and as such have moved to accumulate them and use them at any slight provocation by perceived enemies. This agrees with what Collier (2010) had earlier observed that, African leaders and governments have always conceived that the government next door has guns, their government needs guns and a government without guns cannot defend its citizens against a neighbour with guns. The implication of this he argues is in three-fold. One, cheap and plentiful guns may increase the risk of violence. Two, they make violence so dangerous than to reduce the gravity, and three, guns are plentiful where there is a lot of violence. This we can argue has increased military spending in African countries and has increased the propensity of conflict on the continent because government arms usually leak into non-government hands with militia and rebellious interest through official lines. As Collier further argues, African governments import arms during war times. This creates room where poorly paid soldiers either sell their guns or steal them from stockpiles and sell to non-state actors. This menace is facilitated by

J. T. Tsuwa (✉)
Department of Political Science, Benue State University, Makurdi, Nigeria

© The Author(s), under exclusive license to Springer Nature Switzerland AG 2021
U. A. Tar and C. P. Onwurah (eds.), *The Palgrave Handbook of Small Arms and Conflicts in Africa*,
https://doi.org/10.1007/978-3-030-62183-4_18

the porous nature of African boarders and the rise in private security outfits and militia groups with illegal finances to acquire and use arms.

What we can deduce from the above is that, SALWs by their nature are relatively cheap and easy to carry or move around, it has become possible for both state and non-state actors to possess and use them relatively easily. These illicit proliferations and misuse of SALW have severe effects on conflict, security and human development on the African continent. It is wont to observe that the availability of SALW on a continent with diverse sense of disunity based on ethnic, indigenous and identity issues exacerbated by external interest over resources and the militarization of the democratization process in African states with weak political institutions and unreliable legal systems has made the continent vulnerable to cases of conflicts without easy control. Consequently, the spread of uncontrolled arms increases mutual suspicion, distrust and encourages retaliatory measures and worsens social divides and disagreements among different groups over the desire for peaceful cooperation and response to conflictual issues involving groups.

Central to the acquisition and usage of these arms and the intensity of conflict on the continent is the age of the users. According to Bellamy (2001: 23) "the spread of small arms creates a serious global problem and requires equally urgent response because the lives and future of children are at stake. Suffice to say here that, in African societies where SALWs are commonly used in disputes, children come to regard the weapon as necessary for safety and security, a condition that has fueled the culture of violence. To strengthen the above assertion, Amos (2017: 5) reported that, "in some countries in Africa such as Chad, Niger, Central African Republic, DRC, Somalia, Burundi and South Sudan among others where there is rebellion, SALW weapons have become like pure water or bread, so people from there see it as normal to hang AK 47" and to use it effortlessly. According to UNICEF report (1999) "Children are uniquely vulnerable to military recruitment because of their emotional and physical immaturity. They are easily manipulated and can be drawn into violence that they are too young to resist or understand". According to the Child Soldier International Index (2018), the boys and girls who are recruited to serve as soldiers are very young, some as young as seven years, they serve in government forces and armed opposition groups. The report argues that, many are abducted or recruited by force, while others join out of desperation, believing that these armed groups offer their best chance for survival.

In view of the above, youth bulge, small arms proliferation and conflict are themes which cumulatively delineate a vast tract of inquiry concerning security studies in Africa in the twenty-first century. This is the crux of this chapter as it seeks to investigate guns and its age usage in African conflict and suggest strategies of not only reducing the age usage of guns but also a reduction of conflicts on the African continent in order to stimulate growth and development.

Conceptual and Theoretical Framing

Conflict

Human existence and the needs of humans situated within their environment and their access to resources to facilitate the achievement of these needs based on their capacity has made conflicts inevitable in human interaction. This is because these resources are scarce. As diverse as the perspectives on conflicts are, so is the definition of what actually constitutes conflicts. Tsuwa (2014) had earlier viewed conflict as opposition among social entities directed against one another. This describes conflicts as centring on mutually exclusive social forces of pursuing incompatible goals that can only be achieved by one party at a time. The argument here is that, conflict is essentially about needs, interests, positions and goals, which are not only scarce but also often fiercely competed for by citizens in a society. Due to the scarce nature of these tangible and or intangible resources, competition becomes inevitable and tense. This tense competition usually degenerates into violent conflict especially when the parties involved brazenly abuse the prescribed rules. This is why Coser's (1956) argument that people or groups who engage in conflicts are even prepared to neutralize or eliminate the opponent is linked with Gross's (1966) argument which viewed conflict as the escalation of antagonism involving mustering of forces and preparation for a direct clash of adversaries is considered appropriate in this work. Whatever dimension conflicts take, whoever is or are the actors involved in conflicts or the stages a conflict takes, the functionality or dyfunctionality of conflict, what is central to conflict is that it takes place in stratified societies either at individual, group or societal levels over scarce and highly cherished goals that the actors involved who may be state or non-state actors are prepared to use any means available including the use of arms to achieve favourable results at the expense of the other competing Parties.

Small Arms and Light Weapons

Conceptualizing SALWs is as problematic as other concepts in the social sciences. This is because some scholars or practitioners conceptualize it in terms of their carriage, while others conceptualize it base on their weight, impact and availability. For instance, Collier (2010) used the simplicity of the usage of weapon and the name of the manufacturer of the weapon to conceptualize what he considered as SALWs. To him, SALWs are the Kalashnikov's. This is because they have their origin from the Russian General, Kalashnov who was the first to design and produce the AK-47 which has now become highly available. He argues that, this has become a weapon of choice for every self-respecting rebel based on the fact that they are simple and seldom go wrong, need little maintenance and can be used by people with little knowledge of weapons. They are also cheap and available and can be used by both the young and illiterates. This definition however is considered to be too specific to a particular weapon, the AK-47 and its Russian origin without bearing in mind other weapons that fall within this category.

The United Nations General Assembly on 8 December 2005, defines SALWs as:

any man-portable lethal weapon that expels or launches, is designed to expel or launch, or may be readily converted to expel or launch a shot, bullet or projectile by the action of an explosive, excluding antique small arms and light weapons or their replicas. Antique small arms and light weapons and their replicas will be defined in accordance with domestic law. In no case will antique small arms and light weapons include those manufactured after 1899.

To the UN General Assembly (2005: 12), these arms are categorized into:

a. "Small arms" are, broadly speaking, weapons designed for individual use. They include, inter alia, revolvers and self-loading pistols, rifles and carbines, sub-machine guns, assault rifles and light machine guns;
b. "Light weapons" are, broadly speaking, weapons designed for use by two or three persons serving as a crew, although some may be carried and used by a single person. They include, inter alia, general-purpose or universal machine guns, medium machine guns, heavy machine guns, rifle grenades, under-barrel grenade launchers and mounted grenade launchers, portable anti-aircraft guns, portable anti-tank guns, recoilless rifles, man-portable launchers of anti-tank missile and rocket systems, man-portable launchers of anti-aircraft missile systems, and mortars of a calibre of less than 100 millimetres.

The International Community on the Red Cross (2006) defines small arms as "major weapons which are quite light extremely durable and require little upkeep, logistic support and above all, with minimal maintenance". The import of these definitions is that, SALWs are easy in acquisition, usage and maintenance. The market for small arms and light weapons includes both unauthorized transfer of SALWs or illegal trafficking of small arms and their parts, accessories and bullets. Underwood (2009) argues that, these arms are usually used by armed groups outside the official authority of the state. His argument is that, armed groups who use these arms fall into three basic categories along a spectrum, ranging from poorly organized, disjointed and motivated by greed, to highly organized, coordinated and motivated by ideology. What we can deduce here is that, the trade in SALWs occur globally, but is concentrated in areas of armed conflict, violence and organized crime. It also shows that, these weapons are not only the choice for majority of armed groups involved in criminality and conflicts today, but also for many terrorist or acclaimed liberation groups operating round the world.

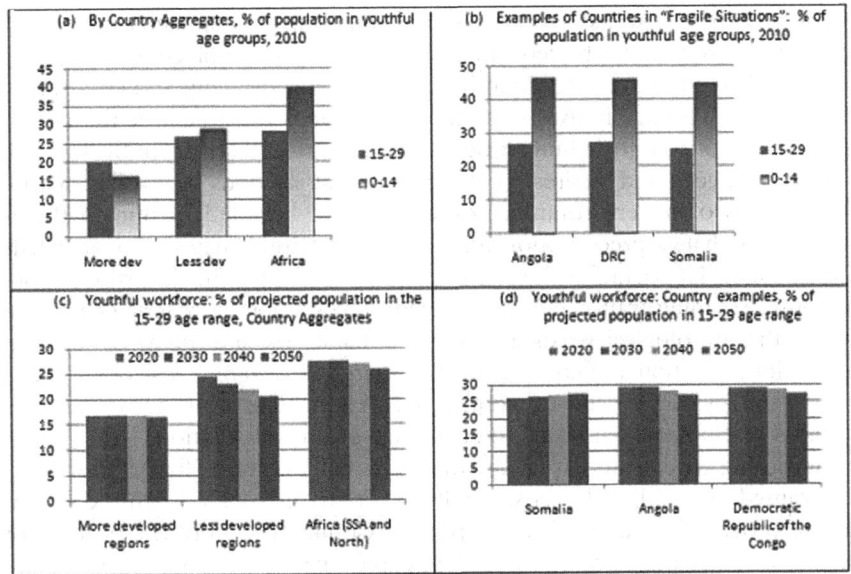

Fig. 18.1 a-d Age distribution of the population, aggregate and country examples % (*Source* Yifu 2011)

Youth Bulge

Youth bulge is a common phenomenon in many developing countries, and in particular, in the least developed countries. It is often due to a stage of development where a country achieves success in reducing infant mortality but mothers still have a high fertility rate. The result is that a large share of the population is comprised of children and young adults. In Africa, about 40% of the population is under 15, and nearly 70% is under 30. The diagram below shows the description of a typical youth bulge analysis.

Figure 18.1 (a-d) shows that, in majority of African societies, there is a high level of youth bulge that is characterized by a high percentage of unskilled and unemployed youth. The consequence of this is that majority of the youth bulge have become a demographic bomb as they become frustrated in their bid to meet their needs. Consequently, they become a potential source of social and political instability as they are easily manipulated and conscripted into taking up arms.

Theoretical Framing

This chapter adopts human needs theory whose arguments are closely related with those of frustration and aggression theory to analyse the causality factors of conflicts in Africa and the involvement of the youths in the conflict and their usage of SALWs (Burton 1979, 1990). To Burton, human behaviour is conditioned by needs. He argues that, there are fundamental drives and motivations that cannot be repressed; these are based on universal and genetic basic needs such as needs for identity, development, meaning and consistency in response. To him, individuals and social groups regardless of the consequences will pursue their human needs. This is to say that, the individual will pursue his needs and desires to the extent that he finds it possible within the confines of his environment, experience and knowledge. Burton therefore argues that, a precondition for peace is that fundamental human needs must be met. He identifies the need for control, security, Justice, stimulation, response, meaning, rationality and esteem/recognition as crucial needs. He argues that ontological needs are non-negotiable which if alienated leads to frustration, agitation and conflict. Burton therefore recommends cooperation-based strategy for peace—or conflict resolution. This cooperative strategy focusses on fundamental needs to encourage a win-win solution.

According to the human needs' theory, conflict emerges from the frustration caused by unfulfilled needs. Conflict becomes inevitable when the system fails to provide for the needs of its people. Conflict therefore is a product of alienation. Alienation occurs when the people's needs for recognition, participation in the governance process and their identity are denied. Supporting Burton, Lewin (1997: 67) sees conflict as a situation of tension that is caused by a number of factors including the degree to which the needs of a person are in a state of hunger or dissatisfaction, which include the needs of sex and security. It can therefore be argued that, human needs are a powerful source of explanation of human behaviour and social interactions. All individuals have needs that they strive to satisfy, by using the system, acting on the fringes, or acting as a reformist or revolutionary group. Given this condition, a social system must be responsive to individual needs or be subject to instability and forced change, possibly through violence or conflict.

This theory is applicable here because, the situation in Africa is that which has deprived and crippled the achievements of human needs in many societies. Factors such as slave trade and colonial policies have divided, exploited and dehumanized majority of Africans despite their huge natural endowment. Neocolonial policies of capitalist exploitation and globalization which has reduced the production and purchasing power of most Africans. The struggle by African societies to liberate themselves and enshrine social justice over the colonial and post-colonial forces had made some African countries to engage in conflicts. Issues of military rule and democratic dictatorship, poverty and general underdevelopment have also contributed in establishing conflict enclaves on the African continent. The consequence of this is the acquisition of SALWs and their usage which the youth have became ready constrictors.

Age, Guns and Conflicts in Africa

The African continent is dotted with conflicts around, power, indigeneship, citizenship and identity issues. The nature and character of African conflicts as of recent extended to issues of criminality, rural banditry, kidnapping, cattle rustling, land resource and boundary contestation. As Coning et al. (2016) argues, African conflicts have become highly complex and dynamic and have moved from resulting to the menace of internally displaced persons to devastations caused by coordinated operations of terrorist groups like the Janjaweed, Al-Shabab and Boko Haram. Central to these conflicts is the availability of SALWs which will be used interchangeably in this chapter as guns. The nature and dimension of conflicts in Africa are becoming more local with local impact on local individuals and communities. This has made mobilization towards executing conflicts to also change to local sources of recruits to fight in the conflicts. These local sources are largely militias recruited from in house groups based on their identity contestation and interest in the causality factor of the conflict. Group elites in Africa are found both within the political authority and criminal gangs and they usually rely on the youths who are more vulnerable for conscription, manipulation and indoctrination to carryout arms during these conflicts. This is not to say that militias are not outsourced. They are, but the majority of the armed groups that are easily available to be mobilized along identity lines are the locals. As Tsuwa (2019) argues, African elites and leaders have constructed their ideology of governance and security around the ideology of acquiring and utilizing guns as they seek to legitimize, retain and use indefinitely their power of office utilizing the youth who are already frustrated. For instance, John Garang of South Sudan had told the passing out batch of the Sudanese People Liberation Army combatants in Bonga Training Centre that; through this AK-47, you will get all you want—food, women and any other thing that accompany good life (Nyaba 2019). This ideology therefore created a culture of producing robots armed with AK-47 who have been trained only to kill both their friends and enemies.

As the political elite acquire arms to enable them access to power, local community elites also acquire arms towards what they call liberation struggle or access to their community resources, territories and militia groups, pirates, terrorists and other criminal groups as acquired arms to achieve their various goals. With government and community elites needing power and particularly power through the barrel of the gun, the youths whose needs are deprived and have nothing to lose rather assuming that taking up arms will earn them a living become ready instruments to be used. Nyaba (2019) pointed out that in many parts of Africa, the desire of the youth is to join either the state or militia armed groups, collect arms then return home to *settle* local conflicts stimulated by community elites. The cases of child soldiers in DRC, Sudan, Sierra Leone, Somalia and Liberia among others have remained classical examples of guns in the hands of underage. According to the Child Soldier International index 2018, all conflicts in the world today are replete with high rate of guns in the hands of the young population. The figure below shows the dimension of guns in the hands of the young in the world.

Figure 18.2 demonstrates what can be referred as preponderance of the youth bulge in Africa and global conflicts. According to the figure, in the 18 identified conflicts in the world, a total of 240 million youths are conscripted either by state or non-state groups to fight in these conflicts. This attest to the fact that, there cannot be conflicts without youth, as combatants in any conflict in any part of the world are made up primarily of young people. We can argue that, in the case of Africa, there is a connection between youth bulge, uncontrolled arms and conflict. This is because the post-colonial state formations, the nature and character of the predatory post-colonial elites, group contestations over perceived scarce resources and general acts of criminality clothed into the garments of indigeneship, citizenship and identity have exacerbated the situation. This situation has been fueled by external manipulations especially in the sale of arms to the African continent.

It has been documented that, between 1990 and 2002, US alone supplied arms to Africa worth $608,912,899 (Kuna 2005). This projection is aside

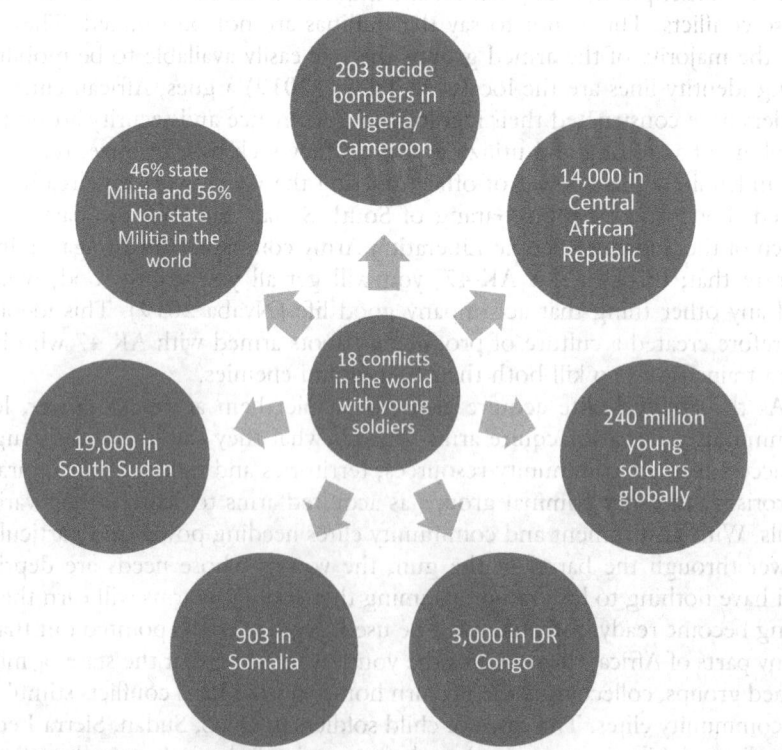

Fig. 18.2 Spread of guns in the hands of youth (*Source* Child Soldier International Index 2018 and modified by the author 2019)

Table 18.1 Post-Cold War US arms transfer to governments involved in the Congo War, 1989–1998 (in 1998 constant Million Dollars)

Country	Foreign military sales	Commercial sales	Total (Million)
Angola	Nil	31,000	31,000
Burundi	74,000	312,000	386,000
Chad	21,767,000	24,677,000	46,444,000
DRC	15,151,000	218,000	15,369,000
Namibia	2,311,000	1,934,000	4,245,000
Rwanda	324,000	0	324,000
Sudan	30,258,000	1,815,000	32,073,000
Uganda	1,517,000	9,903,000	11,420,000
Zimbabwe	567,000	828,000	1,395,000
Total	71,969,000	39,718,000	111,687,000

Source Kuna (2005: 17)

from other countries such as Russia, France, Germany, UK, Italy, Canada and Japan. Kuna has given graphic details of some of the scenario of arms supply to Africa which tended to encourage African conflicts (see, for instance, Table 18.1 which shows the US arms transfer to governments involved in the Congo war between 1989 and 1998).

Thus, Kuna (2005) further notes:

> The links between arms sales and transfers on the one hand and conflicts on the other are nowhere most clearly demonstrated as in the conflict in the Great Lakes Region. This hydra-sided war has a large array of combatants involving states, militias, criminal groups and multinational mining concerns from at least eight countries. On the side of the Congolese state, are the armed forces of Zimbabwe, Namibia, Chad, and to some certain extent some reported level of Sudan and Libyan support. On the opposing side is an alliance of Rwanda, Uganda, Burundi and Congolese opponents of Kabira. (Kuna 2005: 14)

Kuna (2005) also indicates that it is however not just in the Great Lakes Region that arms are fueling conflicts. Some of the largest arms sales and transfer according to him have been to countries that were either in conflict, or which became embroiled in conflicts shortly after. The susceptibility of Africa's peace and security arising from the sales and transfer of arms by the producer countries, to her territories has been very aptly captured in the following words; these arms fueled internal repression and military conflicts that led to the deaths of many hundreds of thousands of people, most of whom were civilians (Kuna 2005).

SMALL ARMS, YOUTH BULGE AND THE CAUSALITY OF CONFLICTS IN AFRICA

The problematic conflicts in Africa and the causality factors are no longer new. Figure 18.3 shows the basic causality factors of age and guns in Africa and by extension conflicts.

From the foregoing, we can explain further these factors as follows.

High Rate of Unemployment

According to the UNDP (2006) Sub-Saharan Africa offers a telling example of youth bulge and conflict increasingly seen as a cause of societal crisis. The states have not been able to create the jobs: there are fewer job vacancies that require millions of young people to compete for. Thus, they are prone to criminal behaviour, petty theft, drugs, drunkenness and gross indiscipline (Abdullah 1998). In similar vein, Bangura (1997) argued that young people in Sierra Leone reacted to exclusionary neopatrimonial practices and state decay in form of armed rebellion. Far from being mindless or random, youth violence resulted from the alienation of young people because of failures in the educational system and death of employment opportunities. According to Inyatullah (2016) the youth are not only unemployed, but they are disempowered. The post-colonial state in Africa has shown a habit of the old leaders recycling themselves into offices and patronize their loyalist base on old held affinities without giving room to the young generation without old "connections". This has created a sense of emptiness and economic discrimination as

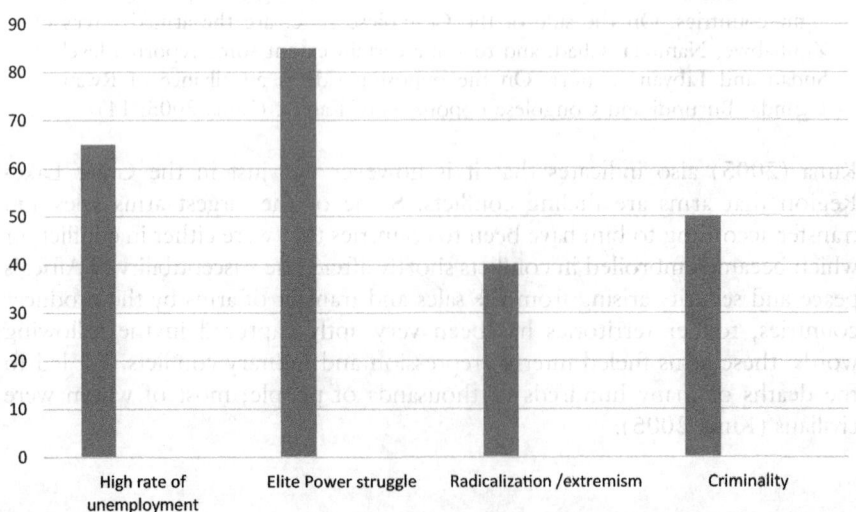

Fig. 18.3 Reasons for vulnerability of youths for Recruits in child soldiers (%) (*Source* Tsuwa 2019)

they get a feeling of a raped future. With this kind of feeling, they become increasingly restive and disruptive. A study conducted by Huba (2014) shows that "youth bulge makes countries, most especially the Least Developed economies (LECs), more unstable in general and thus more susceptible to armed conflict – especially under the conditions of economic stagnation and discrimination". In light of the above, Igbhobor (2017) quoted the International Labour Organization (ILO) to have reported in 2016 that up to 70% of Africa workers—a significant fraction of who are young were "working poor", the highest rate globally. The organization added that "the number of poor working youth has increased by as much as 80% for the past (25) years". This has become a major source of recruits of youths in the use of guns and the re-enforcement of conflicts in Africa. Africa's population of largely young and high susceptible to violence and gun violence.

Elite Power Struggle

The struggle for power in Africa often takes violent dimensions, which are underscored by the use of arms in the competition for power. Conflict often breaks out when power is manipulated to include or exclude certain individuals, communities, groups, religions or regions. Those who control power and wish to retain it sometimes resort to the acquisition and use of guns and those who feel excluded also resort to extreme measures such as violent protests or armed rebellion with the use of illicit arms. This trend percolates the entire African continent where political elites mobilize the pool of unemployed youths, often along ethnic, religious and party affiliation, as a vital political resource. It is alleged that incumbents of power, before and during elections aided the proliferation of small arms in Africa by arming youths and political things to manipulate electoral outcomes by kidnapping or killing political opponents, threatening and intimidating electorates, destroying lives and properties, and disrupting election campaigns (Jeremy and Ismail 2005). In the build up to the 2019 general elections in Nigeria, Mudiaga (2018) reported that, "armed thugs played the ignoble role of disrupting the electoral process. He further observed that Rivers State recorded widespread violence as armed political thugs' unleashed mayhem on various communities leading to the death of several persons".

Radicalization and Extremism

The growth and activities of religious groups that espouses radical extremist ideologies have contributed to the spread and use of illicit arms in Africa by the youth. The open display of SALWs is a requisite element in the identity of violent extremist groups, and extremist groups appear deadlier as their access to and quality of small arms increases. In Nigeria, when Boko Haram started in Nigeria, many poor Muslim families and neighbouring countries sent their children to the school to get a proper Islamic education. However, the Centre had ulterior political goals to create an Islamic state and impose sharia laws, and it soon became recruiting ground for future Jihadis to fight the state". Hundreds of impoverished young northerners, students and professionals, many of whom are unemployed are recruited. Islamic militancy has garnered the most attention as a consequence of the violent attacks of Boko Haram, Al-Qaeda in the Islamic Maghreb, Al-Sharaha and other similar groups operating across Africa because of their access to and use of SALWs. Based on UNDP (2015) estimates, 24,771 people were killed and 5507 wounded between 2011 and 2015, with most of the fatalities in Nigeria and Somalia. To buttress on the above, in Kano, there was a discovery of a catch of arms and ammunition at a bunker in a house belonging to a Lebanese national in 2013 by security operatives. According to Egbuta (2019), "a total of 11,50 mm anti-tank weapons two, two 122 mm artillery gun ammunition, four anti-tank landmines, 21 rocket-propelled grenades, 16 rocket-propelled grenade charger, one rocket-propelled grenade tube and 76 military grenade, one SMG riffle, nine pistols, 17 AK 47 riffles, 44 magazines, 11,433 rounds of 7.62 mm special ammunition and 103 packet of slap TNT were among the weapons". These were all meant for the Nigeria young people to help prosecute one form of conflict or crime.

Criminality

The flow of uncontrolled arms plays a crucial role in the activities of organized crime networks across Africa. They are either the object of illicit trafficking and/or used to protect the infrastructures used for criminal activities. There is a convergence of organized crime and small arms proliferation and armed conflict, in places such as the Sahel, Libya and Somalia. Privates use illicit arms in the Horn of Africa and the Gulf of Guinea region to attack and seize ships and to kidnap crew for ransom. Similarly, South American drugs heading for Europe are trafficked through West Africa and the Sahel, and SALWs are used to protect the trafficking routes (Adeniyi 2017). In support of the argument above, Fritz (2012)φ presented a clear picture of the issue of youth bulge and armed conflict or criminality in Africa. He posits thus "in March 2011, an Indian vessel captured sixty-one pirates, twenty-five of whom were under the age of fifteen and at least four of whom where under the age of eleven at the time of apprehension". He further said, "high levels of poverty define the lives of many Somali children who often seek more to support themselves and their families". This explains that the large presence of youths on the street of Somalia breeds criminality and "gangsterism" which requires the use of small arms.

AGE, GUNS AND IMPLICATIONS ON AFRICA'S DEVELOPMENT

The implications of large number of idle youths with access to uncontrolled arms cannot be overemphasized. The negative impact ranges from erosion of social cohesion and trust, internal displacement and refugee problem, decline in socio-economic activities, growth of private security and militarization of society.

Erosion of Social Cohesion

State formation has remained one of the problematics of African cohesive existence. Colonial manipulations had foisted on majority of African nations a diverse and disunited state that promoted issues of divisions centred on the questions of ethnicity, indigeneship and identity. These issues have not only assumed the primacy of social expressions in African but as Nwogbaga et al. (2017) argued, they have become conditions and principles through which rights and privileges are shared. The implication of this is that, African societies have jettison the nationalistic and patriotic disposition that was inscribed on the hearts of the independent nationalist and have embraced ethnic, cultural and identity nationalism that its primary goal is inclusivity of their group rather than the collectivity that served the national goals. The apartheid region and its policies in South Africa, the ethnic contestations that led to the Nigerian civil war, the Hutu–Tutsi conflicts in Rwanda, the white and black struggled and conflict over land in Zimbabwe, the Ivorian conflict and the conflict in South Sudan are few cases were identity formations, indigeneship and ethnicity have replaced national cohesion. It is argued here that, the acquisition and usage of arms by factional groups pursuing the individual interest has become central to achieving the objectives of these groups. The extensive possession and use of uncontrolled arms and the attendant explosion in armed violence has eroded Social cohesion and trust across many countries in Africa. The possession and usage of illicit arms reduce the use and effectiveness of challenges and negotiated settlement of disputes; uncontrolled arms contribute to the choice of violence to settle disputes. The spread of uncontrolled arms increased mutual suspicion and mistrust, encourage retaliatory measures and worsens social divides among different groups. Long years of peaceful coexistence and flourishing socio-economic ties between different ethnic, religious, political, communal and even individuals have given way to bitter armed confrontation. In Nigeria, South Sudan, Central Africa Republic and South Africa targeted killings with uncontrolled arms have fragmented communities and countries along ethnic, religious and political links.

More generally, the widespread possession of guns in Nigeria has led to a state of fear and mistrust. According to Sale Bayari, as reported by Tajudeen (2012), "the Fulani man lives in a hostile environment. He has to be hostile as the environment for him to survive. There must be a balance of terror for you to survive in the jungle". When members of a society begin to see their environment in the form of jungle, then, possession of uncontrolled arms becomes the alternative to provide their security. In South Sudan, the consistent access to weapons has worsen the dire situation and mistrust among the Dinka, Jonglei and Nile ethnic groups. According to Mueller (2013: 12) "where there is conflict arms will flow". The demand for weapons in South Sudan is enormous, and outside suppliers have had no problem meeting the demands. This is to say, a gun culture has been deeply entrenched fuelling the fragmentation.

Growth of Private Security and Militarization of Society

The availability of uncontrolled weapons has resulted in the militarization of the African states. The states no longer enjoy the monopoly of the use of free or violence. From criminal gangs, to ethnic militias and community vigilante, everybody owns a gun to protect his/herself. According to Heinrich (2006: 23) "before, we considered the gun a weapon for the military. But now it is common. Today, so many people are killed (by them). They circulate everywhere. You can find them in any hand". Jean-Charles a humanitarian officer in the Democratic Republic of Congo was also quoted by Heinrich to have said. "There are so many weapons here that each person makes his own law. There is practically complete impunity. Anyone who holds a weapon has authority over anyone and can threaten anyone". The situation has deteriorated such that, people resort to self-help. Some people feel that they and/or their families are made more secure by owning a weapon, particularly in situations where governments cannot protect their citizens.

Civil Wars and State Collapse

In most civil wars in Africa, the youth constitute the bulk of the fighting force in all sides of the conflict. They also constitute the bulk of the casualty of the conflict. Child soldiers add a gorier layer to the "infantilizations of violent conflicts in Africa". The resultant state collapse in African countries such as Somalia (1991), Libya (2012) led to massive displacement of youth and increase in violence and crime. This is closely related to the next factor of humanitarian crisis.

Upsurge of Internally Displace Persons and Refugees

Humanitarian crisis such as displacement from once original home is also one of the problems caused by growing population of youth in a society that cannot provide for their basic needs, yet are in possession of illicit arms. While internal displacement and refugee are common features of armed conflict in Africa, enforced population movements are generally motivated by the need to avoid injuries and deaths from uncontrolled arms. Although, the date on refugees and internal displaced persons are fluid and varied from one country

Table 18.2 IDPs and Refugees in Africa

Central Africa		
Country	Number of IDPs	Number of refugees to other countries
DRC	4.5 million	Rwanda—219,000
		CAR—182,000
		South Sudan—91,000
Central Africa	1.9 million	568,000
Burundi	169,000	430,000 (Burundi within the region)
East Africa		
South Sudan	1.8 million	2.5 million South Sudanese within the region
Somalia	2.65 million	820 in Yemen and within region
Ethiopia	2.8 million	
West Africa		
Nigeria	2.4 million	227,000 in Cameroun, Chad and Niger
Mali	51,800	130,000 in Mauritania and Niger B/Faso
Burkina Faso	15,000	7000 in Mali

Source Update of UNHCR's Operations in Africa, 2018

to another, they point to massive displacement of people due to the increased deadliness of armed groups and conflicts. Available data from the International Crisis Group (2019) posits thus, "over 65 million people have been forced from their homes and almost 74 million face acute hunger due primarily to uncontrolled arms and conflict. The Boko Haram insurgency in Nigeria has forced over 2.3 million people to abandon their homes, and has left nearly 11 million people in need of emergency aid. A study by Adeniyi (2017) indicated that, "466,000 and 434,174 represented the refugees and internal displaced persons from Central African Republic". In addition, United Nation Humanitarian Commission on Refugees (UNHRC) reports of 2016–2018 shows that, by the end of 2017, there were an estimated 24.2 million people of concern in the region, an increase of 4.6 million since 2016 in the first half of 2018, the numbers increased, with some 170,000 new refugees and over two million now IDPS mainly from Nigeria, Central Africa Republic, Democratic Republic of Congo (DRC), Somalia and South Sudan. Table 18.2 shows the distribution of IDPs and refugees in Africa. It is important to note that a significant fraction of these displaced persons are the youth, with serious implications for spike in of poverty, crime and substance abuse in the host state or community.

Disruption of Socio-Economic Activities

There is massive disruption of socio-economic activities across Africa. Most displaced people lose their businesses to looting and their homes are often destroyed. They become dependent on assistance and many sink into poverty (Ginifer and Olawole 2005). The recurring spate of small armed weapons and conflict that is now a feature of life in Africa engenders an atmosphere of insecurity that discourages formal and informal economic activities. This situation derives from threat and actual unleashing of violence. According to UNDP (2017: 23) report, the "spate of Islamist Militant Al-Shabaab attack has affected Kenya's tourism sector. It declined from about $500 million annually to US$1 million. The African society has a high youth bulge with a bleak future and also harbours massive small armed that have continued to exacerbate armed violence. This kind of environment discourages investment".

Conclusion

A greater percentage of the world's youthful population resides in Africa. Resolving the critical challenges facing them is an urgent need of the states in Africa if socio-economic development is to be achieved. The problem facing the youth in Africa is essentially a societal crisis. These issues range from youth unemployment, lack of economic opportunities, lack of educational opportunities, high poverty rate and health challenges. Youth bulge could be associated with armed conflicts. This is as a result of the increase in the population of educated youths confronted with bleak future for its survival. The contradiction in Africa where there is abundance of human and natural resource yet, there is prevalence of poverty simply put the society on time bomb.

There is no doubt that the accumulation of SALWs and their diffusion into the larger African society are simply an expression of the erosion of good governance. The impact of SALWs is more than just individual well-being; they typically have the potential to challenge the very existence of the state. Many countries have collapsed, failed and disintegrated (Somalia, Liberia and Sudan) respectively with the use of SALWs. Although the manifestation of violence appears irrational, its reasons such as economic underdevelopment faced by the youth are fully rational.

It is recommended that governments of African States should stop paying lip services to issues of governance, they should formulate and sustain policies that would address the socio-economic problems confronting the increasing youthful population. Harnessing the youth bulge productively and effectively could lead to prolonged economic growth and substantial poverty reduction. The youth bulge presents great potentials for economic opportunities for all African states through active participation in labour market, engender innovation and support governance. This will reduce inequality, thereby enhancing the prospects for social cohesion and stability. It is also recommended that sources of guns to the youth should be blocked and those found violating such provisions which be prosecuted as well as youth found with SALWs.

REFERENCES

Abdullah, I. (1998). Bust Path to Destruction: The Origin and Character of the Revolutionary United Front. *The Journal of Modern African Studies, 36*(2), 223.

Adeniyi, A. (2017). *The Human Lost of Uncontrolled Arms in Africa*. Oxfam International Policy Papers. Retrieved March 4, 2020, from, https://www.cdn.oxfam.org> rr-human-lost-of-uncontrolled-arms-in-africa.

Amos, T. (2017, February 10). Porous Border Responsible for Frequent Fulani/Farmers Attacks. *Daily Post*, p. 1.

Bangura, Y. (1997). Understanding the Political and Cultural Dynamics of the Sierra-Leone War: A Critique of Paul Richards *Fighting for the Rain Forest*. *Africa and Development, XXII*, ¾. Retrieved March 4, 2020.

Bellamy, C. (2001). *No Guns, Please We are Children*. New York: UNICEF Division of Communication United Nations Plaza.

Burton, J. (1979). *Deviance, Terrorism, and War: The Process of Solving Unresolved Social and Political Problems*. Canberra: Australian National University Press.

Burton, J. (1990). *Conflict: Resolution and Prevention*. New York: St. Martin's Press.

Child Soldier International World Index, 2017–2018 Annual Report.

Coser, L. (1956). *The Functions of Social Conflict*. In Onigu & Otite (Eds.), *Community Conflicts in Nigeria*. Ibadan, Nigeria: Spectrum Ltd.

Coning, C. D., Gelot, L., & Karlsrud, J. (2016). *The Future of African Peace Operations: From the Janjaweed to Boko Haram*. London: Zed Books.

Collier, P. (2010). *Wars, Guns and Votes: Democracy in Dangerous Places*. London: Vintage Publishers.

Egbuta, O. (2019). Conflicts and Communication in Complex Place. In *Journal Social Inquiry, A Publication of the Faculty of Social Sciences*, Vol. 2 No. 1. Makurdi: Benue State University.

Fritz, D. (2012). Child Pirates from Somalia: A Call for the International Community to Support the Further Development Juvenile Justice System in Portland and Somaliland. *Western Journal of International Law, 44*(3), 891–919.

Ginifer, J., & Olawole, I. (2005). *Armed Violence and Poverty in Nigeria: Centre for International Cooperation and Security*. University of Bradford Press.

Gross, F. (1966). *World Politics and Tension Areas*. London: London University Press.

Heinrich, M. (2006). *Small Arms and Development: The Result of UN Small Arms Review Conference 2006 and Their Policy Implications*. Geneva: International Peace Bureau.

Huba, J. (2014). SALWs Proliferation in Nigeria's Niger Delta Region. *Studies in Politics and Society, a Journal of the Nigerian Political Science Association (NPSA), 5*(1), 4–5.

Igbhobor, K. (2017). *Africa's Jobless Youth Cast Shadow Over Economic Growth: African Renewal*. https://wwwun.org/africa-renewal/magazine/special-edition-youth-2017/africa-jobless-youth-cast-shadow-over-economic-growth.

International Committees of Red Cross. (2006). Unregulated Arms Availability, Small Arms Light Weapons, and the UN Process. Retrieved March 21, 2020, from icrc.org.

International Crisis Group. (2019). Report on 10 Selected Conflicts. Retrieved from https://www.crisisgrop.org. January 2019.

Inyatullah, S. (2016). Youth Bulge: Demographic Dividend, Time Bomb and Other Futures. *Journal of Future Studies, 21*(2), 21–34.

Kuna. (2005). Arms and Daggers in the Heart of Africa: Globalization and Africa's New Conflicts. In *African Conflict profie, A Journal of the Centre for Ethnic and Conflict Studies*, Vol. 1. No. 2, University of Portharcut.

Lewin, K. (1997). *Resolving Social Conflicts & Field Theory in Social Science*. Washington, DC: American Psychological Association.

Mudiaga, A. (2018, December 23). Influx of Illegal Arms Ahead of 2019 Elections. *The Punch Newspaper*. https://punchng.com/influx-of-illegal-arms-ahead-of-2019-elections.

Mueller, K. (2013). Disturbing the Peace: SALW in Post-Conflict Sudan and South Sudan. *Independent Study Project (ISP) Collection* 2525. Retrieved March 5, 2020, from https://digitaledelection.sit.edu/isp-collection/25/25.

Nwogbaga, D. E. M., Amadi, I. G., & Onwa, D. O. (2017). Social Pluralism as a Major Threat to Security and Development in Africa: A Study of the Ivorian Conflict 2000–2011. *Studies in Politics and Society, a Journal of the Nigerian Political Science Association (NPSA)*, 5(1).

Nyaba, P. A. (2019). *South Sudan: Elites, Ethnicity, Endless Wars and the Stunted State*. Dar-Es-salaam: Mkuki Na Nyota.

Tajudeen, S. (2012, November 26). The Cattle Mean More to the Fulani. *Tell Magazine*, p. 51, No. 47.

Tsuwa, J. T. (2014). *Ethnic Conflicts and the Challenge of Development: A Study of the Tiv and Their Neighbours*. Unpublished PhD thesis submitted to the post graduate School, Benue State University, Makurdi.

Tsuwa, J. T. (2015). Retrogressing Africa: Failed State or Failed Leadership. *Wukari Journal Humanities and Management Science*, 1(2), 8–9.

Tsuwa, J. T. (2019, October 24). Africanizing Poverty and Insecurity: Interrogating the Ideology of Governance in Nigeria, Being a Paper Presented at the 3rd ASAA Conference at the USIU- Nairobi, Kenya.

Underwood, P. T. (2009). Pirates, Vikings and Teutonic Knights. In J. H. Norwitz (Ed.), *Pirates, Terrorist and Warlords: The History, Influence and Future of Armed Groups Around the World*. New York: Skyhorse Publishing.

UNDP. (2006). *Youth and Violent Conflict: Society and Development in Crisis?* New York, USA: Bureau for Crisis Prevention and Recovery. www.undp.org/bcpr.

UNDP. (2015). *Preventing and Responding to Violent Extremism in Africa: A Development Approach*. Retrieved February 12, 2020, from https://www.undp.org/content/dom/undp/library.

UNDP. (2017). *Articulating the Pathways of the Impact of Terrorism and Violent Extremism on the Kenyan Economy*. Retrieved February 13, 2020, from https://www.undpurg>SPAN.

UNHCR. (2018). *Operations in Africa*. Retrieved February 12, 2020, from https://reliefweb.int/representworld/update-unchr-s-operations-africa-14-september-2018.

UNICEF. (1999). *Children and Armed Conflict Office of the Special Representative for Secretary General*. Retrieved February 12, 2020, from https://childrenandarmedconflict.un.org/wp-content/uploads/2016/08/Children-in-Conflict_WEB.pdf.

United Nations General Assembly Resolution on Small Arms and Light Weapons (A/RES/60/250), 2005, December 8.

Yifu, L. J. (2011, September). New Structural Economics: A Framework for Rethinking Development. *World Bank Research Observer*, 26(2), 193–221.

John Tor Tsuwa is a Senior Lecturer in Political Science at Benue State University Makurdi, Nigeria. He has been a resource person for the Airforce War College, National Institute for Policy and Strategic Studies and National Open University of Nigeria. He is the Chairman, Nigerian Political Science Association, North Central Zone-Nigeria and Editor of two Faculty based journals. He is a research fellow of IFRA-Nigeria and member of Society for Peace Studies and Practice. He specializes in Peace and Conflict Studies, Inter-Group Relations and Gender Studies, Governance and Development Studies.

CHAPTER 19

Gendered Construction of Conflict and Small Arms Proliferation in Africa

Omotola A. Ilesanmi

INTRODUCTION

Africa is disproportionately affected by armed conflict. Several countries on the continent,—and within states, as well as among different categories of people—experience armed conflict and violence on recurring basis. This situation has negative implication for its development, peace and stability. Africa continues to experience widespread violence and armed conflict in the form of civil wars, insurrections among state actors and non-state actors. The debilitating consequences of armed conflict on the continent are multiple ranging from poverty, infrastructural deficit, refugees and internal displacements, unemployment among others. The pervasiveness of conflicts in Africa has been linked to the proliferation, easy availability and acquisition of small arms and light weapons on the continent. In this regard, small arms and light weapons which include rifles, pistols and light machine guns remain a major contributor to the prevalence, lethality and longevity of conflicts and violence globally, as they facilitate the commission of gross violation of human abuses by armed groups. The linkage between the proliferation of Small Arms and Light Weapons (SALWs) and other vices including transnational organized crimes, illicit arms trafficking, terrorism and cybercrime have become apparent (Alemika 2013; UN Secretary General Report 2019).

O. A. Ilesanmi (✉)
Department of Research and Studies, Nigerian Institute of International Affairs, Lagos, Nigeria

© The Author(s), under exclusive license to Springer Nature Switzerland AG 2021
U. A. Tar and C. P. Onwurah (eds.), *The Palgrave Handbook of Small Arms and Conflicts in Africa*,
https://doi.org/10.1007/978-3-030-62183-4_19

Furthermore, it has been acknowledged that almost all violent deaths worldwide are caused by firearms and the level of firearm-related homicides in post-conflict countries are more than battlefield deaths (Cukier 2001). Approximately 500,000 people are killed each year with small arms: 300,000 of these die in "conflict" situations and 200,000 in murders, suicides and accidents (Cukier 2001). The uncontrolled nature of small arms, their illicit acquisition and transfer has been identified as a major contributor to the widespread nature of armed conflict and violence on the continent. Africa's estimated 100 million uncontrolled SALWs in conflict zones and other crises regions contributes to the prevalence of conflicts on the continent (Adeniyi 2017). Africa is disproportionately affected by the negative impact of small arms on security, development, peace and stability, this is in spite of the fact that it accounts for less than 5% of the estimated value of the international trade in small arms (Holtom and Pavesi 2018). Alluding to this, Amao (2012) maintains that several countries in West Africa have experienced armed conflicts including Liberia, Sierra Leone, Guinea Conakry, Côte d'Ivoire and Niger, while Mali is in the forefront of SALWs proliferation, with extremist groups operating in the north of the country. Recent conflicts in Sudan, South Sudan, Cameroun, Burundi have been aided by small arms which remains the choice tool for unleashing mayhem. Similarly, Northeast Nigeria with the presence of the Boko Haram terrorists and the Islamic State in West Africa Province (ISWAP) has seen widespread proliferation of small arms employed by these groups in their dastardly acts. Other parts of the continent are enmeshed in conflicts as small arms and light weapons remain pervasive. And despite measures by the African Union to "silence the guns" by 2020 and end conflicts in its Agenda 2063 framework, easy availability and misuse of licit and illicit arms continue to promote conflicts in many African countries, from petty crime to insurgencies and terrorist activities.

Armed conflict affects men, women, boys and girls in a multiplicity of ways. While more men are victims of gun-related deaths, torture, displacements, women are more majorly victims of sexual violence, rape, forced prostitution, sexual slavery perpetrated against them as a strategy of war. However, this analogy is not absolute—in rare circumstances, men can be victims of rape and domestic violence, while women can be victims of torture and gun-related death (Mazurana and Proctor 2013). A binary categorization of men and women as victims of small arms violence tends to becloud the nuances of other vulnerable demographic categories such as the physically challenged, the elderly and children. Therefore, it is fair to note that the victims of small arms violence cuts across gender, class and generational categories. The proliferation of SALWs has gendered consequences for men, boys, women and girls—as well as other social and economic categories—both in conflict and post-conflict situations. Aside from vulnerability, the perpetration of small arms violence yields another layer to the discourse on small arms: men account for the majority of the owners and user of SALWs since they are mostly represented in state security services and rebel militia groups, and women account for the majority of victims. Although more men and boys are killed from gun-related violence, more women are subjected to acts of sexual violence and mass rapes aided by the use of SALWs. It is noteworthy that women also engage in the use of SALWs particularly through their membership of state security forces and rebel forces. The ubiquitous nature of acts of sexual violence and rape perpetrated against women and girls as well as the systematic targeting of women's bodies in armed conflict is effectively facilitated through the easy availability and widespread misuse of the weapon. Galace (2010) argues that men are the primary owners, users and traders of arms and while women suffer from the lack of controls over SALWs and are at risk of gender-based violence. Similarly, the licit and illicit transfer and ownership of SALWs in post-conflict periods and times of peace also greatly contributes to the prevalence of domestic and intimate partner violence worldwide. However, beyond their role as victims in armed conflict, women also assume roles as perpetrators of violence through their participation in rebel and militia groups. Women and girls who are either forcibly recruited or voluntarily join rebel groups assume different roles in these groups as sex slaves, rebel wives, spies, porters. In another vein, women also transcend their roles as victims and perpetrators of violence to act as mobilizers and advocates for peace. As peace agents, women and women groups play critical roles in conflict prevention and conflict resolution globally. Armed conflict also results in reversal of gender roles for women as they assume new leadership roles as heads of households due to the death of husbands or them going to fight wars (Arostegui 2013). Armed conflict exacerbates the vulnerability of women and the existing power inequality between men and women. Globally and in Africa's patriarchal societies, men and women are placed in different positions of power as men occupy superior positions in the public sphere of decision-making while women are too often constrained to the private sphere of domestic responsibilities hereby placing women in subordinate positions of power.

Within the sphere of peace and security, attention has been placed on the critical contributions of women to conflict prevention and resolution. To this end, the United Nations Security Council Resolution 1325 formally recognized women's contribution to maintaining international peace and security, the disproportionate impact of violence on women and girls and therefore called for the full and equal participation of women in peacekeeping and peacebuilding processes (UNSCR 1325, 2000). Building on the 1979 Convention on the Elimination of All Forms of Discrimination Against Women CEDAW, and the 1995 Beijing Declaration and Platform of Action, UNSCR 1325 and its follow up resolutions namely UNSCR 1820 (2008), UNSCR 1888 (2009), UNSCR 1889 (2009), UNSCR 1960 (2010), UNSCR 2106 (2013), UNSCR 2122 (2013), UNSCR 2242 (2015), UNSCR 2467 (2019), and UNSCR 2493 (2019) (PeaceWomen 2020) that make up the Women, Peace and Security Agenda are employed by women's groups and civil society in Africa to advocate for the increased participation of women in peace and security and the ending of impunity for sexual violence. Within the sphere of small arms, women and women's groups have also been critical to the control, transfer and illegal use of SALWs, as well as the development of legal and policy instruments nationally, regionally and internationally with a view to achieving effective and sustainable small arms control. Arms control laws and policies reduce the violence committed against women in situations of armed conflict and in "peace" time. The control of small arms and light weapons remain critical to conflict prevention and women are key resources to achieving this goal. In this regard women can play multifarious roles such as campaign for safe storage of weapons to avoid theft; campaign for weapons destruction; educate the public on the risks of having guns at home; work towards breaking the perceived link between guns and manliness, security, power and prestige; lobby for and participate in the crafting of more restrictive policies on the possession and carrying of firearms and other small arms policy and programmes; work towards the abolition of political dynasties and private armed groups; and lead in the use of indigenous peaceful conflict resolution methods to settle conflicts (Galace 2010). The Arms Trade Treaty ATT remains the first-ever global legal binding international instrument on conventional arms trade under the auspices of the United Nations. The ATT prohibits the export of arms and ammunition that violates United Nations Security Council embargoes or arms that can be used against civilians in the commission of violations of International Law (Parker 2014).

Gendered Impact of Conflict in Africa: An Exposition

It has been widely established in the literature that armed conflict is gendered and that conflicts affect men, women, boys and girls in different ways (Myrttinen et al. 2014; Kirsten 2008). A gender analysis of conflict thus highlights the different experiences of conflict by men and women in terms of their needs, acquisition, and control of resources, and access to decision-making processes in post-conflict situations (UNDP 2002). According to the Centre for Humanitarian Dialogue (2006), a large proportion of violence including firearm violence is overwhelmingly perpetrated by men and boys while they are also victims of firearm-related deaths in most parts of the world. Women on the other hand suffer widespread sexual violence in addition to other forms of violence they experience in armed conflict. Armed conflicts reinforce gender stereotypes that contribute to the subordination of women in societies. War is a time when men are made out of boys, and being a good solider is synonymous to being a "real man" (Cohn 2013). While women are saddled with the responsibility of reproducing and socializing the next generation of male soldiers as wives and mothers, men are regarded as the defenders of the nation wherein women reside as weaker vulnerable demographic constituency (Enloe 2000: El Jack 2002, 2018). Such phenomena rely on a familiar discourse that stresses masculinity in terms of encouraging men to defend their nation while having control over "their women", and emphasizes femininity in terms of "raising warriors" and "needing protection" (Enloe 2000).

The end of the Cold War saw an unprecedented shift in the nature of conflicts globally. The world witnessed a reduction in wars and conflict between and among sovereign states and an increase in wars occurring within states. The intra-state wars which became pervasive at the end of the Cold War in the 1990s took the nature and form of civil wars, rebellions to mention a few, and fought by both state and non-state actors including the state military and security forces, rebel groups, warlords, child soldiers, militants and terrorists (Abdi 2007; Mazurana and Procter 2013). A key feature of these new forms of war is the high rate of civilian casualties including men, women, boys and girls, the widespread use of sexual violence against women and girls, and the gendered experiences of men and women in conflict (ICRC 1999). While men account for the majority of deaths from gun violence, women on the other hand suffer widespread gender-based violence and sexual violence such as rape, enforced prostitution, abduction, sexual slavery in conflict periods. It is estimated that close to 45.6% of African women have experienced GBV as a result of armed conflict, compared to 35% globally, and that most African women and girls will experience a form of GBV in their lifetime (Adeniyi 2017).

Alluding to the foregoing, Abdi (2007) and Campbell (2005) argue that armed conflict and political instability affects the lives of women in adverse ways while gender inequalities are exacerbated in Africa's patriarchal societies during such periods. Plumber and Neumayer (2006) in a study of 14 ethnic conflicts and four non-ethnic conflicts that lasted for 10 years found that interstate and civil wars (in particular ethnic conflicts and conflicts in failed states) negatively impacts women more than men. Similarly, numerous studies have underscored how conflicts and wars emblematizes women as victims, with women experiencing rape, sexual violence, gang rape (Rehn and Sirleaf 2002; Dietrich and Quain 2014). For instance, in the ongoing conflict in Central African Republic, it was reported that armed groups that are parties to the conflict use sexual violence as a tactic of war, with widespread rape of majority of women and girls on their way to their farms or when fleeing for safety. In the United Nations Secretary General's Report to the Security Council (S/2019/280) in March 2019, The United Nations Multidimensional Integrated Stabilisation Mission in Central African Republic (MINUSCA) reported 239 cases of rape or attempted rape, 14 forced marriages, one case of sexual slavery and five other forms of sexual violence. 101 cases were attributed to ex-Seleka groups, 62 to Fulanis, 45 to Anti-Balaka group, two to the Lord's Resistance Army, three to Armed forces of the Central African Republic CAR to mention a few (UN 2019). Alluding to this, Buchowska (2016) avers that rape and sexual violence against women and girls is employed as a strategy to break and humiliate women, men, families and communities. A survey of 991 households in a study in Sierra Leone revealed that 94% reported one or more human rights abuses and 13% reported some war-related sexual violence (Cukier et al. 2002).

However, moving beyond the stereotyping of men as aggressors and perpetrators of violence, feminist scholars have established that men also suffer as victims of sexual violence (El Jack 2018) although at a lower proportion compared to women, and that women transcend beyond the victim in armed conflict. Feminist scholars argue that women transcend beyond the role of victims in armed conflict to assume multifarious roles during conflicts such as spies, cooks, fighters, peace agents, sex slaves, couriers. Furthermore, armed conflicts provide opportunities for social transformation of and reversal of gender roles with women assuming leadership roles as heads of households owing to their husbands being killed or going to war (Arostegui 2013; Moser and Clark 2001; El-Bushra 2000). The participation of women in armed conflict as combatants and violence perpetrators has been brought to the spotlight by feminist scholars. The stereotypical depictions of women as victims and peace advocates have occupied a large proportion of writings on women and armed conflict, while women's role as agents of violence perpetrators have been less recognized in the literature. Feminist scholars have however drawn attention to the roles of women and girls during periods of armed conflict in the unleashing violence and terror as a result of their membership in armed groups and as liberation fighters. Women's direct participation as fighters and combatants in armed conflicts and wars in several parts of Africa such as Egypt, Ethiopia, Liberia, Rwanda, Sudan, Sierra Leone, Tunisia have been documented (Abdelzaher and Abdelzaher 2019; El Jack 2003; Hitman 2018). In South Sudan, women have been active and powerful agents of war in their capacities as recruited combatants in the Sudan People's Liberation Army (SPLA), as well in their association with armed groups and forces (El Jack 2007). Women and girls become members of armed groups and rebel militias as a result of their being forcibly recruited into such groups and through voluntary recruitment (El Jack 2018). This lack of acknowledgement of women participating in violence has been attributed to stereotypes of women as being innately peaceful and hence incapable of unleashing violence, while women who engage in such violent acts are stigmatized and regarded as deviants (Henshaw 2013; Sjoberg and Gentry 2015). In Sierra Leone, women who were combatants, and resistors were branded as "rebel women", "monsters" and "barbarians" (Coulter 2008), while female protesters in Egypt and Libya, were labeled as "drunkards" and "prostitutes", and subjected to virginity tests (Johansson-Nogués 2013). However, in spite of women's involvement in logistics, strategy and combat in armed groups, their participation and experience as ex-combatants in post-conflict interventions particularly, disarmament, demobilization and reintegration programmes DDR have been limited. A lot of DDR programmes have not adequately taken into account and addressed the specific needs of female ex-combatants, hereby shutting them from the benefits associated with such programmes (Tarnaala 2016). Consequently, gender sensitive policies have been advocated for to effectively address the vulnerabilities of female ex-combatants.

Women also assume roles as peace advocates mobilizing for in their communities during periods of armed conflict. African women have been actively involved in entrenching peace in their war-torn communities although this is majorly at the grass root and informal as they are largely absent from formal peace processes. In Liberia, where women were involved in ending the civil war mobilizing under the slogan "We Want Peace: No more War", Liberian women clad in white t-shirts demanded for an end to the war in 2003. While meeting with the then Liberian President Charles Taylor, they demanded for unconditional ceasefire, dialogue for a negotiated settlement and an external intervention force. And using the platform of the Mano River Women Peace Network (MARWOPNET) these women were able to further influence the negotiations (Women & Peacebuilding in Africa 2005). In several other parts of Africa women contribute to conflict prevention and resolution using different strategies.

Gendered Dimensions of Small Arms and Light Weapons in Africa

Research has shown that the proliferation of small arms and light weapons SALWs has a direct bearing on violence against women and men including sexual violence in conflict and post-conflict situations (El Jack 2018; Cukier et al. 2002; Farr 2002). Deriving from this is the recognition that small arms and light weapons are gendered in nature, affecting men, women, boys and girls in different ways (Cukier 2000). Gender is relevant to understanding the impact of conflict aided by small arms because the experience of violence is different for men and women. Furthermore, SALWs play a central role in maintaining male dominance over women and exacerbates existing power inequality between men and women as majority of the violence perpetrated against women in conflict and post-conflict situations are through the use of a gun. SALWs changes the balance of power in a relationship, as they are used to instill fear, kill, intimidate, rape, coerce women into sexual slavery, and to perpetrate other forms of sexual violence (Amnesty International 2012). Cukier et al. (2002) and Barr (2011) maintain that women represent a smaller proportion of users and abusers of small arms than men. Women also constitute the majority of victims of SALWs and are more likely to be involved in developing strong measures for reducing its proliferation and usage. In reality, the processes aimed at curbing the proliferation of small arms are dominated by men.

The debilitating effects of the proliferation of small arms worldwide cannot be overemphasized. Anton (2016) maintains that roughly 200,000 people are killed each year by small arms and light weapons, and that SALW's effects contributes to migration flows of thousands of people, destabilization of entire regions and devastating humanitarian crises. Others include death, injury, displacement and reduced access to and quality of health services, different forms of violence including sexual violence. Additionally, proliferation of SALWs contributes to widespread domestic violence and intimate partner deaths in peacetimes. Akatsa-Bukachi (2012) argues that the presence of firearms can significantly increase the risk that domestic violence results in fatalities. Research has shown that the unrestrained availability of small arms is directly linked to levels of lethal violence in both conflict and non-conflict contexts. With global efforts focussed on achieving the Sustainable Development Goals by 2030, specifically goal five which calls for achieving gender equality and goal 16 which calls for a significant reduction in illicit arms flow and its resultant violent deaths. The international community has recognized the implicit relationship and linkage between both goals, and the critical need to achieving the two goals with a view to creating peaceful and more equal societies.

Conflicts are pervasive in Africa, and its debilitating effects on Africa's growth and development indices cannot be overemphasized. This has resulted in widespread poverty, underdevelopment, insecurity and infrastructural deficit on the continent. The proliferation of SALWs has significantly contributed to armed conflict and violence in Africa. Indeed, SALWs have been identified as primary tools and enablers of violence and conflict including crime, insurgencies and terrorism in Africa (Florquin et al. 2019; Mangan and Nowak 2019; Mules 2019). Referred to as "Africa's weapon of mass destruction" by the former UN Secretary General Mr. Kofi Annan and former President of the Commission of the Economic Community of West African States (ECOWAS) Dr. Mohammed Ibn Chambas. SALWs proliferation is a major contributor to the widespread nature of conflicts in Africa since the decolonization era of the 1950s, with an estimated 100 million uncontrolled SALWs in crisis zones and other security-challenged environments (Adeniyi 2017). The proliferation of SALWs fosters armed conflict which affects men and women in different ways. While women account for a large proportion of victims of small arms and light weapons violence and a small proportion of its users and owners, ownership and utilization of arms is profoundly attached to perceptions of masculinity in many cultures (Cukier 2000). Alluding to this, El Jack (2018) maintains that some African societies see the gun as a sign of masculinity or male power such that a man without a gun in some African war zones is often not considered "a real man" (El Jack 2018). In Southern Sudan, since the 1980s, small arms have played an increasingly important symbolic role as "complementary symbols of wealth, physical strength' and a strong symbol of masculine identity and marriage worthiness" for young men (Hutchinson 1996). In most societies, violent behaviour and possession of small arms are strongly associated with cultures of violence and notions of masculinity (Cukier et al. 2002). In South Africa a culture of violence prevails in which the gun remains a key feature of South Africa's landscape and marker for male identity (Kirsten 2008). The proliferation of guns in South Africa contributes to the high rate of criminality including sexual violence and intimate partner violence in the country. The estimated number of illicit and licit guns in the possession of civilians in South

Africa as of 2017 was 5,351,000 (Karp 2018), while annual deaths resulting from firearms totaled 5, 622 in 2015 (WHO 2016).

Myrttinen (2006) states that "Weapons systems are designed mostly by men, marketed mostly for men and used mostly by men- and in many parts of the world, they are the primary source of death for men". Similarly, it has been discovered that globally over 90% of victims of homicide are men, with men accounting for 88% of gun-related suicide victims in 2010 (IANSA Women's Network 2011). Furthermore, men account for the majority of owners and users of small arms either as majority members of state security sector including armed forces, police and para-military forces or as members of non-state actors including rebels, militia groups and dissidents (Barr 2011). The easy availability of small arms and its widespread possession by civilians remain a key challenge. A major difference between small arms, and other types of weapons such as nuclear weapons or landmines—is the fact that there are many more in civilian possession than in the hands of states, police or paramilitaries (ICRC 1999). A consequence of this is the easy availability and proliferation of these weapons in the hands of individuals, criminals and members of armed groups and which are used to unleash violence and for criminal purposes. In December 2009, it was estimated that Sudan and South Sudan contained some 2.7 million small arms and light weapons, more than two-thirds of which were in the hands of non-state actors, including civilians, rebel groups and tribal militias, and this has been identified as a major causal factor in the outbreak and escalation of armed violence and conflict in Sudan and South Sudan (Small Arms Survey 2009). Akatsa-Bukachi (2012) avers that SALWs are durable in nature with a long life span which means that they continue to present a serious risk in a country for as long as they remain in circulation in a country from conflict to peace periods when they are used by criminal gangs, vigilante groups and individuals.

Women, men, boys and girls are confronted with multifarious forms of violence deriving from the direct and indirect consequences of small arms prevalence and misuse including rape, domestic and sexual violence, injury, and murder (Bastick and Valasek 2014). Women are often targets of certain types of violence involving small arms, particularly domestic violence and rape which are mostly perpetrated by men. Alvazzi del Frate (2011) avers that the rate of femicide—which is the deliberate killing of a woman because of her gender—are high in countries where other forms of violence are widespread, firearms are widely available, and the investigation and prosecution of gender-based violence is weak. In conflict situations small arms increase the lethality of conflicts, as they are widely used against enemy camps, and used majorly to perpetrate different forms of violence against women and girls particularly sexual assault, enforced pregnancy and mass rape. As women's bodies are systematically targeted in armed conflict with the aim of denigrating and dishonouring the enemy nation, rape and sexual violence have remained pervasive and indeed ubiquitous in conflict periods (Cukier 2001;

Rehn & Sirleaf 2001; Bakoru 2002). Examples abound in numerous countries including Rwanda, former Yugoslavia, Liberia, Cambodia, Haiti, South Sudan to mention a few (Farr 2002). The consequences of sexual violence and rape against women and girls are multifarious including HIV/AIDS and other sexually transmitted diseases, unwanted pregnancy, psychological and emotional trauma, social stigmatization and rejection by close family members. These negative consequences linger on into post-conflict periods even when the conflict has ended.

In a similar vein, SALWs results in an increase in domestic violence perpetrated majorly by men against women in post-conflict situations which occur as a result of the transfer of the violence in the conflict period to the domestic sphere (Barr 2011; Farr 2002). This was demonstrated in a study in Cambodia, where it was discovered that failure to remove small arms at the end of conflicts may result in such weapons directed against the civilian population or used in interpersonal violence (ICRC 1999). Domestic violence and intimate partner violence remains a feature of countries transiting from conflicts to peace as a result of the availability of small arms in the communities. Farr (2002) avers that domestic violence prevalence is high in conflict situations and increases in post-conflict situations and women are at the receiving end of such violence. It was revealed that during the war in Cote d'Ivoire rates of reported domestic violence rose by 43% (International Rescue Committee 2012). Women are disproportionately affected by domestic violence and intimate partner violence, with women accounting more from intimate partner violence-related deaths. Myrttinen (2006) notes that, "The tragic irony of the concept of the armed male as a defender of the weak and helpless is that often women and children are far more likely to be killed by the male protector of the family and his weapon than by an outside intruder". In a study by Abraham and others carried out in 2010, it was reported that globally South Africa has the highest reported rate of female murdered through gun violence in a country not at war.

REGIONAL AND INTERNATIONAL POLICY AND LEGAL FRAMEWORK ON SALWs CONTROL AND REGULATION

Measures for controlling and regulating SALWs trade and transfer is a major issue globally. Several international legal framework and policies have been adopted at the national, regional, continental and international levels to control and regulate SALWs. At the global level, the UN has initiated a Programme of Action in 2001 to tackle the illicit trade in SALWs, to which member states have agreed to adhere. Recently, in 2013 the UN adopted the Arms Trade Treaty as a measure to regulate the transfer of SALWs. The UN has played a key role in adopting these frameworks in collaboration with other stakeholders including civil society organizations and women groups. Women groups and civil society organizations have been actively involved in ensuring the recognition of the linkage between SALWs and violence against women and girls in conflict and post-conflict zones. Africa continues to engage in a range of initiatives to control the misuse of arms including participation in the implementation of international agreements such as the United Nations (UN) Programme of Action on Small Arms and Light Weapons UNPoA, the Arms Trade Treaty (ATT), among other efforts. In Africa, relevant regional instruments and Protocols include: Action Plan for the Implementation of the African Union Strategy on the Control of Illicit proliferation, Circulation and Trafficking of Small Arms and Light Weapons;

The Bamako Declaration on an African Common Position on the Illicit Proliferation, Circulation and Trafficking of Small Arms and Light Weapons (2000); *The Nairobi Protocol for the Prevention, Control and Reduction of Small Arms and Light Weapons in the Great Lakes Region and the Horn of Africa* (2004); and *The Nairobi Declaration on the Problem of the Proliferation of Illicit Small Arms and Light Weapons in the Great Lakes Region and the Horn of Africa* (2000). In a similar vein, African Regional Economic Communities RECs have also established legal framework for the regulation and control of SALWs, these include *Central African Convention for the Control of Small Arms and Light Weapons, Their Ammunition and All Parts and Components that Can Be Used for Their Manufacture, Repair or Assembly* (2010), *ECOWAS Convention on Small Arms and Light Weapons, Their Ammunition and Other Related Materials (2006), and the Protocol on the Control of Firearms, Ammunition and Other Related Materials in the Southern African Development Community (SADC) Region*. It is noteworthy that Sub-Saharan countries were among the earliest countries to achieve progress in developing regional small arms control instruments, with the Regional Economic Communities RECs assisting member states in meeting their small arms commitments (Small Arms Survey 2013). Nevertheless, the success of these initiatives lies ultimately in their implementation at the national and sub-regional levels, and this requires significant commitment from governments, non-state actors and donors to act cooperatively to achieve the changes required.

Till date the Women, Peace and Security framework consisting of seven United Nations Security Council Resolutions including UNSCR 1325 (2000), UNSCR 1820 (2008), UNSCR 1888 (2009), UNSCR 1889 (2009), UNSCR 1960 (2010), UNSCR 2106 (2013), UNSCR 2122 (2013) form the major international policy framework that recognizes the link between women's role, participation and contribution to global peace and security. UNSCR 1325 which was adopted in October 2000 recognizes the disproportionate impact of armed conflict on women and girls, and calls for the full and equal participation of women in peace and security including peacekeeping, and peacebuilding measures. Specifically, the resolutions within the women peace and security framework focus on three major thematic areas: the protection of women's right in armed conflict and post-conflict settings, in particular sexual violence; the full and equal participation of women in peace and security; and gender mainstreaming in UN peacekeeping and peacebuilding (Bastick and

Valasek 2014). Although the women peace and security agenda constitute a major international policy framework linking women and peace and security, the 1979 (CEDAW) and the 1995 Beijing Declaration and Platform for Action remain the foundation of the women peace and security framework. The CEDAW is a legally binding instrument that requires states to adopt appropriate legislation and other measures to prohibit discrimination against women and to establish legal protection for the equal rights of women. In this regard, countries are to regularly report on their progress on the implementation to the CEDAW Committee. Patten (2012) states that CEDAW Committee members have highlighted the need for states to regulate small arms if states are to prevent violence such as domestic violence and sexual violence as required under Article 2 and to ensure women's participation in public life as required under Article 7. The CEDAW Committee's work on small arms underscores its role in preventing discrimination and violence against women within the sphere of arms control. In a similar vein, the 1995 Beijing Declaration and Platform of Action building on the CEDAW focuses on the promotion of women's equal rights and women empowerment. The Beijing Declaration and Platform for Action focuses on 12 key areas and provides a list of actions to be undertaken by countries, financial and development institutions among others. Furthermore, the chapter on Women and Armed Conflict of the Beijing Declaration and Platform for Action links women and disarmament, acknowledges women non-government organizations' call for reduction in the international trade, trafficking and proliferation of weapons. It also recognizes that women living in poverty particularly rural women suffer as a result of the use of arms, and that the negative impact of excessive military expenditure, arms trade and investment on arms production and acquisition on development must be addressed (UN 1995, Art. 138).

In their contribution, Bastick and Valasek (2014) maintain that of the seven United Nations Security Council resolutions within the women peace and security agenda, only the last two namely UNSCR 2106 (2013) and UNSCR 2122 (2013) make specific references to small arms, arms trade treaty and importance of women's participation in disarmament. Specifically, UNSCR 2106 (2013) making explicit reference to the Arms Trade Treaty in its preamble states: "the provision in the Arms Trade Treaty that exporting Sates Parties shall take into account the risk of covered conventional arms or items being used to commit or facilitate serious acts of gender-based violence or serious acts of violence against women and children" (UN 2013).

Similarly, the United Nations in an effort to highlight the linkage between small arms and violence against women and girls adopte d the UN Programme of Action on Small Arms and Light Weapons in 2001. The UN Programme of Action in its preamble underscored the negative impact of the illicit trade in small arms and light weapons on women, children and the elderly (UN 2001, Preamble, para 6). However, it was the adoption of the Arms Trade Treaty ATT in 2013 that formalized the linkage between SALW and gender-based violence. The ATT remains the only international agreement on the sale, or transfer of conventional weapons globally. The ATT which was adopted by the UN General Assembly in April 2013 and came into force in 2014 is the world's only legally binding international treaty that formally recognizes the relationship between arms trade and gender-based violence (Cobar and Maletta 2019). The adoption of the ATT with the inclusion of the clause on gender-based violence has been attributed to advocacy effort by several stakeholders including women's groups such as the IANSA Women Network that lobbied for the ATT to include binding measures to prevent gender-based violence and encourage women's participation in the implementation of the treaty (Amnesty International 2012). Article 7(4) of the ATT highlights the need for State Parties to consider the risk that SALWs is being used to commit acts of gender-based violence against women and children when exporting SALWs to states (UNGA 2013, Art. 7[4]). Furthermore, states are to deny arms export if there is an "overriding risk of any of the negative consequences" listed in Article 7(1) including serious violations of international humanitarian and human right laws (UNGA 2013, Art. 7).

However, in spite of the lofty provisions of the ATT particularly with reference to gender-based violence, several criticisms have trailed the treaty with regards to its implementation. Some concepts and terms used in the text of the treaty such as "overriding", "gender" have been identified as open to several interpretations as there is a lack of agreement on such terms. Furthermore, Hutchinson (2019) avers that state parties may face challenges with the ATT's provision on gender-based violence, for instance the possibility of measuring the prevalence of gender-based violence in an importing country maybe problematic as such violence is normally underreported as a result of the social stigma attached to it. And in situations where prevalence of gender-based violence can be detected, exporting states must then determine if such prevalence provides sufficient grounds to deny arms export to the receiving state (Cobar and Maletta 2019; Hutchinson 2019). Notwithstanding the likely challenges states may encounter in implementing the ATT's provisions on gender-based violence, the treaty remains a veritable instrument in curbing sexual violence.

Conclusion

Women and women groups remain an important resource on the control and regulation of small arms and light weapons. Their participation becomes even more important considering the gendered dimension of SALWs and the fact that women and men are affected differently by small arms. While men are direct victims of gun violence, women experience gender-based violence including rape, domestic violence and intimate partner violence and other forms of vices aided by the use of small arms. It therefore becomes pertinent that women have full and equal participation in measures to control them. UNSCR 1325 on Women, Peace and Security recognizes the role of women in conflict prevention and resolution, and calls for the full and equal participation on issues of peace and security at various levels. However, scholars have bemoaned the low participation of women in the control of SALWs and lack of adequate mainstreaming of gender in SALWs policies and legislation. It has been recognized that integrating a gender perspective in small arms control initiatives are more effective in addressing the adverse impact of the illicit trade and misuse of SALWs. In Africa, women have involved in the prevention of misuse of small arms and remain agents of change although men continue to dominate formal measures that are put in place. Women play important roles in the disarmament and mobilization against small arms through several means. For instance, in Mozambique, "The Tools for Arms Project" involved the collection and destruction of weapons, the exchange of weapons for tools among others. Their experiences of how small arms actually increased their insecurity compelled women to hand in weapons belonging to their husbands or relatives, and persuade their family members (Masters 2010). Furthermore, women civil society organizations such as members of the IANSA Women's Network are also leading the way in micro-disarmament projects including awareness-raising and weapons collection components (Masters 2010). In Libya the UN Mine Action Service, in cooperation with the Small Arms Survey, has supported women who are raising awareness in their communities of small arms-related risks and control measures through risk education sessions, the distribution of risk awareness material and radio programmes (UNSMIL 2017). There is however need for more robust studies to be conducted on the gendered nature of small arms and light weapons control and regulation, and how women can effectively participate in the control and regulation of small arms and light weapons in Africa.

References

Abdelzaher, A., & Abdelzaher, D. (2019). Women on Boards and Firm Performance in Egypt: Post the Arab Spring. *The Journal of Developing Areas, 53*(1), 225–241.

Abdi, C. (2007). The New Age of Security: Implication for Refugees and IDPs in the Horn of Africa. *Development, 50*(4), 75–81.

Abraham, N., Jewkes, R., & Mathews, S. (2010). Guns and Gender-Based Violence in South Africa. *South Africa Medical Journal, 100*(9), 586–588.

Adeniyi, A. (2017). *The Human Cost of Uncontrolled Arms in Africa: Cross-National Research on Seven African Countries*. Oxfam Research Reports.

Akatsa-Bukachi, M. (2012). Gender and Violence: Small Arms—A Human Security Issue. *New Routes, 4*, 17–19.

Alemika, E. O. (2013). Organized Crime and Governance in West Africa: An Overview. In E. O. Alemika (Ed.), *The Impact of Organized Crime on Governance in West Africa* (pp. 15–33). Abuja: Friedrich-Ebert-Stiftung.

Alvazzi del Frate, A. (2011). When the Victim Is a Woman. In Geneva Declaration Secretariat. *Global Burden of Armed Violence 2011: Lethal Encounters*. Cambridge: Cambridge University Press.

Amao, B. (2012, November 22–25). *Africa Struggles with Impact of Small Proliferation*. World Council of Churches (WCC) Consultation Organized by Commission of the Churches on International Affairs (CCIA) in Addis Ababa, Ethiopia. http://www.oikoumene.org/en/press-centre/news/africa-struggles-with-impact-of-small-arms-proliferation. Accessed 5 October 2019.

Amnesty International. (2012). *If You Resist We'll Shoot You: The Democratic Republic of Congo and the Case for an Effective Arms Trade Treaty*. https://www.amnesty.org/en/library/asset/AFR62/007/2012/en/cdd8cdd9-913f-4de-5-84/8-71d/2eedhddefc/afr620072012en.pdf. Accessed 30 September 2019.

Anton, C. (2016). *Small Arms and Light Weapons: The Road to the 2018 Review Conference*. United Nations Office for Disarmament Affairs. https:/un.org/disarmament/updates/the-road-ahead-for-small-arms-and-light-weapons-the-2018-review-conference.

Arostegui, J. (2013). Gender, Conflict and Peacebuilding: How Conflict Can Catalyse Positive Change for Women. *Gender and Development, 21*(3), 533–549. https://doi.org/10.1080/13552074.

Bakoru, Z. (2002). Personal Reflections of Small Arms and Light Weapons. In V. Farr & K. Gebre-Wold (Eds.), *Gender Perspectives on Small Arms and Light Weapons: Regional and International Concerns* (24). Germany: Bonn International Centre for Conversion (BICC).

Barr, C. (2011). *Why Women? Effective Engagement for Small Arms Control*. International Action Network on Small Arms (IANSA).

Bastick, M., & Valasek, K. (2014). Converging Agendas: Women, Peace, Security and Small Arms. *Small Arms Survey: Women and Guns* (pp. 34–63). Small Arms Survey: Switzerland.

Beijing Declaration and Platform for Action. Fourth World Conference on Women. 15 September 1995. A/CONF177/20(1995) and A/CON/F177/20/Add/(1995).

Buchowska, N. (2016). Violated or Protected: Women's Right in Armed Conflict After the Second World War. *International Comparative Jurisprudence, 92*, 72–80.

Campbell, P. (2005). Gender and Post-conflict Civil Society: Eritrea. *International Feminist Journal of Politics, 7*(3), 377–399.

Centre for Conflict Resolution & UN Development Fund. (2005, October 27–28). *Women and Peacebuilding in Africa*. Seminar Report, Policy Seminar in Cape Town South Africa.

Centre for Humanitarian Dialogue. (2006). *Hitting the Target: Men and Guns*. RevCon Policy Brief. https://www.reliefweb.int/sites/reliefweb.int/files/resources/0EEDEB71D81C2BD9852571FF00698B66-hd-men-jun2006.pdf.

Cobar, J., & Maletta, G. (2019). *The Inclusion of Gender-Based Violence in Arms Transfer Decisions: The Case of the Arms Trade Treaty*. https://www.sipri.org/commentary/blog/2019/inc;ision-gender-based-violence-concerns-arms-transfers-decisions-case-arms-trade-treaty.

Cohn, C. (Ed.). (2013). *Women and Wars: Contested Histories, Uncertain Futures*. Hoboken, NJ: Wiley.

Coulter, C. (2008). Female Fighters in the Sierra Leone War: Challenging the Assumptions? *Feminist Review, 88*, 54–73. https://doi.org/10.1057/palgrave.fr.9400385.

Cukier, W. (2000). *Gender and Small Arms*. A Special Report for the Small Arms Yearbook Project.

Cukier, W. (2001). Firearms: Licit/Illicit Links. *Criminologie, 43*(1), 24–41.

Cukier, W., Kooistra, A., & Anto, M. (2002). Gendered Perspectives on Small Arms Proliferation and Misuse: Effects and Policies. In V. Farr & K. Gebre-Wold (Eds.), *Gender Perspectives on Small Arms and Light Weapons: Regional and International Concerns*. Brief 24. Germany: Bonn International Centre for Conversion (BICC).

Dietrich, C., & Quain, C. (2014). Gender in Conflict. *European Union Security Studies*. https://www.iss.europa.eu/publications/detoul/article/gender-in-conflict.

El Jack, A. (2002). Gender Perspectives on the Management of Small Arms and Light Weapons In V. Farr & K. Gebre-Word (Eds.), *Gender Perspectives on Small Arms and Light Weapons: Regional and International Concerns*. Brief 24. Germany: Bonn International Centre for Conversion (BICC).

El Jack, A. (2003). *Gender and Armed Conflict: Overview Report*. Brighton: Institute of Development Studies.

El Jack, A. (2007). Gendered Implications: Development-Induced Displacement in Sudan. In *Development's Displacements: Ecologies, Economies, and Cultures at Risk* (pp. 61–81). Vancouver: UBC press.

El Jack, A. (2018). Wars and Conflicts in Sub-Saharan Africa/the Middle East and North Africa (MENA): A Gender-Relational Perspective. *Journal of Global Peace and Conflict*, 6(2), 19–26.

El-Bushra, J. (2000). Transforming Conflict: Some Thoughts on a Gendered Understanding of Conflict Processes. In S. Jacobs, R. Jacobson, & J. Marchbank (Eds.), *States of Conflict: Gender, Violence & Resistance*. London: Zed Books.

Enloe, C. (2000). *Maneuvers: The International Politics of Militarizing Women's Lives*. Berkeley: University of California Press.

Farr, V. (2002). A Gendered Analysis of International Agreements on Small Arms and Light Weapons. In V. Farr & K. Gebre-Word (Eds.), *Gender Perspectives on Small Arms and Light Weapons: Regional and International Concerns*. Brief 24. Germany: Bonn International Centre for Conversion (BICC).

Florquin, N., Lipott, S., & Wairagu, F. (2019). *Weapons Compass: Mapping Illicit Small Arms Flow in Africa*. African Union Commission and Small Arms Survey Report. Switzerland: Graduate Institute of International and Development Studies.

Galace, J. (2010). *1325 and the Violent World of Small Arms*. https://www.opendemocracy.net/en/5050/1325-and-violent-world-of-small-arms/.

Henshaw, A. (2013). Why Women Rebel: Understanding Female Participation in Armed Rebel Groups (1990–2008). *International Feminist Journal and Politics*, 18(1), 39–60.

Hitman, G. (2018). Arab Spring Era: Winds of Change in the Direction of Gender Equality for Tunisian Women. *Digest of Middle East Studies*, 27(2), 168–184.

Holtom, P., & Pavesi, I. (2018). *Trade Update 2018: Sub-Saharan Africa in Focus*. Small Arms Survey, Graduate Institute of International and Development Studies, Switzerland: Small Arms Survey.

Hutchinson, S. (1996). *Nuer Dilemmas: Coping with Money, War, and the State*. Berkeley, CA: University of California Press.

Hutchinson, S. (2019). Gender-Based Violence and the Arms Trade Treaty. *The Interpreter*. https://www.lowyinstituteorg/the-interpreter/gender-based-violence-and-arms-trade-treaty.

IANSA Women's Network. (2011). *Voices of Survivors: The Different Faces of Gun Violence*. https://www.iansa-women.org/sites/default/files/newsviews/iansa_wn_voices_of_survivors_2011_web_o.pdf.

International Committee for Red Cross. (1999). *Arms Availability and the Situation of Civilians in Armed Conflict*. Geneva: ICRC. https://www.icrc.org/eng/assets/files/other/icrc_002_0734_arms_availability.pdf.

International Rescue Committee. (2012). *Let Me Not Die Before My Time: Domestic Violence in West Africa*. New York: IRC. https://www.rescue.org/sites/default/files/resource-files/IRC_Report_DomVioWAfrica.pdf.

Johansson-Nogués, E. (2013). Gendering the Arab Spring? Rights and (in) Security of Tunisian, Egyptian and Libyan Women. *Security Dialogue, 44*(5–6), 393–409.

Karp, A. (2018). *Civilian Firearms Holdings, 2017, Estimating Global Civilian-Held Firearms Numbers*. Geneva: Small Arms Survey, Graduate Institute of International and Development.

Kirsten, A. (2008). *Guns and Roses: Gender and Armed Violence in Africa*. Background Paper Swiss Confederation. Government of Republic of Kenya, UNDP, Geneva Declaration on Armed Violence and Development, Small Arms Survey.

Mangan, F., & Nowak, M. (2019). *The West Africa- Sahel Connection: Mapping Cross-Border Arms Trafficking*. Briefing Paper. Small Arms Survey. https:/smallarmssurvey.org/fileadmin/docs/t-briefing-paper/SAS-BP-West-Africa-Sahel-Connection.pdf.

Masters, S. (2010). *UN Business: Women, Guns and Small Arms Control*. https://www.opendemocracy.net/en/5050/un-business-women-guns-and-small-arms-control/50.50.

Mazurana, D., & Proctor, K. (2013). *Gender, Conflict and Peace*. Occasional Paper. World Peace Foundation.

Moser, C., & Clark, F. (2001). *Victims, Perpetrators or Actors: Gender, Armed Conflict and Political Violence*. London: Zed Books.

Mules, I. (2019). *Stemming the Flow of Illicit Arms in Africa*. https://www.dw.com/en/stemming-the-flow-of-illicit-arms-in-africa/a-49761552.

Myrttinen, H. (2006). Disarming Masculinities. *Disarmament Forum: Women, Men, Peace and Security, 4*, 37–46.

Myrttinen, H., Naujoks, J., & El-Bushra, J. (2014). *Rethinking Gender in Peacebuilding: Understanding Conflict, Building Peace*. International Alert.

Parker, S. (2014). Breaking New Grounds: The Arms Trade Treaty, In *Small Arms Survey 2014: Women and Guns*. https://www.smallarmssurvey.org/fileadmin/docs/A-Yearbook/2014/en/small-Arms-Survey-2014-Chapters-3-EN.pdf.

Patten, P. (2012). *Women's Human Right: The Arms Trade Treaty and CEDAW*. Paper presented at a panel discussion by International Alliance of Women.

PeaceWomen. (2020). *The Resolutions*. https://www.peacewomen.org/why/solutions/resolutions.

Plumber, T., & Neumayer, E. (2006). The Unequal Burden of War: The Effect of Armed Conflict on the Gender Gap in Life Expectancy. *International Organization, 60*(3), 723–754.

Rehn, E., & Sirleaf, E. J. (2002). *Women, war, peace: The independent experts' assessment on the impact of armed conflict on women and women's role in peace building*. New York: UNIFEM.

Sjoberg, L., & Gentry, C. (2015). *Mothers, Monsters, Whores: Women's Violence in Global Politics*. London: Zed Books.

Small Arms Survey. (2009). *Supply and Demand: Arms Flows and Holdings in Sudan*. Sudan Issue Brief. Human Security Baseline Assessment No. 5. Retrieved from https://www.smallarmssurveysudan.org/filesadmin/docs/issue-briefs/HSBA-IB-15-arms-flows-and-holdings-in-Sudan.pdf.

Small Arms Survey. (2013). Efficacy of Small Arms Measures and National Reporting: Learning from Africa. *Research Notes, 33,* 1–2.

Tarnaala, E. (2016). *Women in Armed Groups and Fighting Forces: Lessons Learned from Gender-Sensitive DDR Programmes.* The Norwegian Peacebuilding Resource Centre https:/reliefweb.int/sites/reliefweb.int/files/resources/03ec67e9de77d98612373f974b54909c.pdf.

UN. (2001). *Programme of Action to Prevent, Combat and Eradicate the Illicit Trade in Small Arms and Light Weapons in All Its Aspects.* United Nations General Assembly; A/CONF.192/15. New York, NY: UN General Assembly

UNDP (United Nations Development Programme). (2002). *Gender Approaches in Conflict and Post-Conflict Situations.* https://www.undp.org/erd/ref/gendermanualfinal.pdf.

UNGA (United Nations General Assembly). (2013). The Arms Trade Treaty. Resolution/234B, adopted 2 April 2013. A/RES/67/234B of 11 June 2013.

United Nations. (1995). The Beijing Declaration and the Platform for Action: Fourth World Conference on Women, Beijing, China, 4–15 September 1995. New York: Department of Public Information, United Nations.

United Nations. (2013). UN Security Council Resolution 2106 (S/RES/2106) 2013. https://www.securitycouncilreport.org/atf/cf/%7B65BFCF9B-6D27-4E9C-8CD3-CF6E4FF96FF9%7D/s_res_2106.pdf.

United Nations. (2019). Report of the Secretary-General to the Security Council (S/2019/280) March 2019. https://www.un.org/sexualviolenceinconflict/countries/central-african-republic/.

United Nations Secretary General. (2019, December). *Small Arms and Light Weapons.* UN Security Council. https://www.securitycouncilreport.org/atf/%7B65BFCF9B-6D27-4E9C-8CD3-CF6E4FF96FF9%7D/s_2019_1011.pdf.

UNSMIL. (2017). *UN Complete Third Training on Small Arms and Light Weapons Risk Awareness and Control Measures for Libyan Women.* https://unsmil.unmissions.org/un-complete-third-training-small-arms-and-light-weapons-risk-awareness-and-control-measures-libyan.

WHO (World Health Organisation). (2016). *Inter-Country Comparison of Mortality for Selected Causes of Death.* WHO Mortality Database, Geneva: World Health Organisation.

Omotola A. Ilesanmi holds a Ph.D. in Political Science from Babcock University, Ilishan-Remo Ogun State, Nigeria. She is a Research Fellow in the Department of Research and Studies of the Nigerian Institute of International Affairs, Lagos, Nigeria. Dr. Ilesanmi is a specialist on women and peacebuilding processes, gender and security, security sector reforms, peace and conflict studies. She also teaches courses in the areas of foreign policy analysis, diplomacy and international law. She is an alumnus of the Kofi Annan International Peacekeeping Training Centre Accra Ghana, and has published widely in local and foreign journals and books.

CHAPTER 20

Guns, Arms Trade and Transnational Crime in Africa

Adewunmi J. Falode

INTRODUCTION

Transnational crimes are crimes that are committed across the national boundaries of states (Sheptycki and Wardack 2003: 146). Such crimes are sometimes committed by individuals or groups in one state across the borders of several others (Brown 2020: 1–12). This has come to define the nature of most crimes committed across borders in Africa in the twenty-first century. Transnational crime is diverse and it includes: drug trafficking, human and people trafficking, advanced fee and internet fraud, maritime piracy, illegal manufacture of firearms, trafficking in firearms, banditry, theft and smuggling of oil and cattle-rustling (United Nations Office on Drugs and Crime [UNODC] 2005: ii). Most of these transnational crimes are carried-out using small arms and light weapons (SALWs). Small arms and light weapons refer to those weapons that can be carried by one or two persons, mounted on a vehicle, or lugged by an animal from one place to the other (Kumar 2008: 787). These weapons include revolvers, rifles and sub-machine guns. The use of SALWs has contributed to the breakdown of law and order, institutions, and socio-economic and political life across the African continent. The major impacts of transnational crime in Africa has been the collapse of state, institutions, civil

A. J. Falode (✉)
Department of History and International Studies,
Lagos State University, Lagos, Nigeria
e-mail: adewunmi.falode@lasu.edu.ng

© The Author(s), under exclusive license to Springer Nature Switzerland AG 2021
U. A. Tar and C. P. Onwurah (eds.), *The Palgrave Handbook of Small Arms and Conflicts in Africa*,
https://doi.org/10.1007/978-3-030-62183-4_20

wars, ethnic–religious crisis, piracy, banditry and farmers/herders' conflicts across the continent (Reitano 2018: 23–35).

Conceptual Clarification

Transnational Crime

Transnational crime covers virtually all profit-motivated criminal actions of an international nature where more than one country is involved (UNODC 2012). A crime is transnational if it is perpetrated in more than a state and has substantial effect in more than one state. Transnational crime threatens peace and human security, leads to human rights being violated and undermines the economic, social, cultural, political and civil development of societies all over the world (UNODC 2012). Although, there is no universal definition of transnational crime, researchers have agreed that it has some basic discernible features: perpetrators, object, motive, digital signal and subject (Stoica 2016: 14). The perpetrators are those who carry-out the crime across national boundaries; the object is the illicit good that is traded across national borders—this could be manufactured within the country or the country could be used as a transit hub; the subject is the foreign element that is engaged in the illicit act; and the motive refers to the gains to be had from such acts—this could be monetary, political, economic or religious; and the digital signals refer to the use of electronic means to steal or wire money from financial institutions. For example, an unholy alliance now exists between transnational organized criminal actors in West Africa and Latin America. State embedded-actors in Nigeria, Ghana, Guinea Bissau and Guinea have turned the subregion to major transit shipment hub for drugs like cocaine, heroin and methamphetamine that are usually supplied by non-state actors like the Sinaloa Cartel in Mexico (Ogunniyi and Akpu 2019: 29–49; Organised Crime Index 2019: 8–19). Transnational crime has three distinct features (Stoica 2016: 14): (a) extensive transborder connections (b) capacity to challenge national and international authorities; and (c) it operates at both regional and global levels.

These three features, as will be shown, have been displayed in the nature of the transnational crime that is obtainable in Africa. Different theoretical models have been used to explain the occurrence of transnational crime (Stoica 2016: 14–15). However, two of these models, Realism and Liberal theories, that are applicable to Africa will be explained here. The Realism model argues that transnational crime at its core is a continuation of economic activities using illicit method like violence, blackmail and intimidation. The Liberal model argues that globalization and economic liberalization, which are the cores of the paradigm, have encouraged and enabled transnational crime to flourish. The ease of transborder communications and multilateral trading agreements between and among states have made it possible for perpetrators to carry-out their illicit activities. This is particularly true for Africa where regional arrangements like the Economic Community of West African States

(ECOWAS) have made it possible for SALWs to proliferate unchecked in the subregion. These two major models provide the theoretical rationale for the high incidence and successes of transnational crime that has been recorded in Africa.

Small Arms and Light Weapons (SALWs)

Most transnational crime in Africa are carried-out with the aid of SALWs. Civil wars in both Nigerian and the Democratic Republic of the Congo in the 1960s were fought with SALWs. Maritime piracy on both the Gulf of Guinea and the Horn of Africa are carried-out using SALWs. Small arms and light weapons have aided and enabled the spread and commission of transnational crime on the continent (Bourne 2005). It facilitates and enables armed conflict, terrorism and transnational crime in Africa. So, what is SALWs? Small arms are those weapons that can be carried by one or two persons that is mounted on a vehicle or carried by a pack animal from one place to the other (Kumar 2008: 787). The term is used for three major subdivisions of weaponry: small arms, light weapons and ammunition and explosives (Kumar 2008: 787). Examples of small arms are revolvers, self-loading pistols, rifles, submachine guns and light machine guns. All these weapons, it should be noted have featured regularly in the transnational crime that has ravaged Africa since the 1960s. For example, in the West African states of Nigeria, Cameroon, Chad and Niger, Boko Haram has used submachine guns, light machine guns and explosives in its various criminal attacks. Al-Shabaab has used small arms like explosives, submachine guns, rifles and light machine guns in its attacks against East African states like Somalia and Kenya. Heavy machine guns, hand grenades and mounted grenade launchers, anti-tank guns and portable launchers of anti-aircraft missile system are good examples of light weapons. Light weapons have been used by various terrorist groups in East, Central and West Africa. Such weapons have aided and prolonged the duration of civil conflicts that have ravaged different countries on the continent. Small arms and light weapons are used by various groups across Africa: militaries, insurgents, terrorists, vigilantes, herders, bandits and transnational criminals. Such weapons have some basic characteristics that make them appealing to perpetrators who carry-out transnational crime in Africa (Jeffrey and Klare 1998):

1. They are of low cost and widely available. The porous nature of Africa's borders make it easier for such weapons to be transferred from one state to the other
2. They are easy to use and maintain. The maintenance requires little or no technical skill. This characteristic of the SALWs is significant in the African setting because most of those that use such weapons in transnational criminal enterprises are from the unskilled or educationally disadvantaged section of the society.
3. They are concealable and easy to carry from one location to the other.

The foregoing characteristics show why SALWs has been the weapon of choice for perpetrators like terrorists, bandits, herders and criminals that have been involved in such transnational crime like maritime piracy, human trafficking, cattle rustling, drug trafficking and mineral trafficking across the borders of some states in Africa.

Arms Trade

The global conventional arms trade, that is worth billions of dollars, is engaged in by every country in the world (Stohl 2017: 1; Holstom and Pavesi 2018: 10). The clandestine nature of the trade, especially the unconventional type dominated by non-state actors from within and outside the continent, has made it impossible to put an accurate figure on its overall cost in Africa. Schroeder and Lamb (2006: 69) have argued that the trade in SALWs in Africa is over $1 billion United States (US) dollars or at 10–20% of the global trade. Sources of such trade on the continent are both internal and external. African states like South Africa, Namibia, Kenya and Cote d'Ivoire, and non-state actors like rebel groups are usually the internal sources of such trade (Holstom and Pavesi 2018: 53). Externally, arms are trafficked into the continent via ships and planes from countries as far afield as China, Israel and member states of Organisation for Security and Cooperation in Europe (OCSE) (Schroeder and Lamb 2006: 70). Available statistics suggest that the overall SALWs imports into Africa between 2001 and 2015 was approximately $82–$257 million dollars (Holstom and Pavesi 2018: 57). In total, Africa has approximately over 50 million of these SALWs floating around on the continent in the hands of both state and non-state actors (Small Arms Survey 2019). The breakdown shows that Western Africa has the highest concentration of both licit and illicit SALWs (about 11 million), followed by Northern and Eastern Africa (about 10.2 and 7.8 million), and Southern and Middle Africa (about 6 and 4.9 million) respectively (Small Arms Survey 2019). The arms trade in Africa can be divided into two, licit and illicit. These arms are usually trafficked by both state and non-state actors. Arms that are traded on the continent can be divided into five categories (Levine et al. 1997: 340): weapons of mass destruction (WMD), major weapons systems, light weapons, dual-use equipment and services. Weapons of mass destruction cover nuclear, biological and chemical weapons and long-range missiles. Major weapons systems cover things like tanks, large-calibre artillery, armoured personnel carriers, warships, combat aircrafts and attack helicopters. Light weapons (SALWs) include traditional small arms like rifles, submachine guns, pistols, but also land mines and small mortars. Dual-use equipment serves both military and civilian purposes. For example, the Global Positioning System (GPS) developed by the military for combat use is now widely deployed in the civilian sector. Military services range from training in the use of the weapons sold to its maintenance and direct provisioning of the military.

Of the five categories of arms, the light weapons (SALWs) have been the most problematic for Africa. Nearly all conflicts in Africa are either fuelled or carried-out by SALWs. SALWs have also been the favourite weapons of transnational criminals engaged in illicit and criminal activities on the continent.

Background: Arms Trade and Transnational Crime in Africa

The arms trade in Africa are a double-edged sword. On the one hand, countries on the continent needs the trade to protect themselves and at the same time generate sorely needed revenue. For instance, South Africa, Kenya, and Cot d'Ivoire have been using this legitimate aspect of the trade to export arms to countries in both Africa and Eastern Europe. At the other extreme, the illegitimate aspect of the trade is an important source of revenue for transnational criminals in both Europe and Africa, and this had played an outsize role in the outbreak, intensity and duration of conflicts on the continent. The argument here is that the arms trade, especially the trade in SALWs is not just a lucrative business but that it also fuels and prolong conflicts in the subregions. In other words, there is a direct link to the arms trade, unchecked proliferation of SALWs, transnational crime and conflict on the continent.

Two major defining features of the twenty-first century are market liberalization and political democracy (Lloyd et al. 2012: 153–180). The Market liberalization aspect that guarantees a more open and almost borderless trading environment among the different states on the continent is a major factor responsible for the exponential growth of transnational crime in Africa. As transaction costs have fallen, the opportunities for illicit traders to operate unrestricted across borders has also grown (Mystris 2019: 482–487). Transnational crime in turn creates growing challenges for national authorities at all levels, from foreign policy and security establishments to law enforcement authorities and border control officials (Lloyd et al. 2012: 153). This has constituted a serious threat to good governance and state sovereignty across the continent. The major transnational crime in Africa are drug trafficking, human trafficking, environmental crime, artefact trafficking, financial crimes, counterfeit goods, counterfeit pharmaceuticals, cyber-attacks and hacks on financial institutions, maritime piracy and automobile trafficking (Interpol 2018). The connection between these transnational crimes and guns is that SALWs enables the commission of some of the more egregious of the crimes and further makes it difficult for the various national security agencies on the continent to combat them.

The African continent is both a growing global transit hub for the trafficking of illegal drugs en route to other continents and a market where drugs are abused. Drugs like cocaine, heroin, cannabis and synthetic drugs like Tramadol and methamphetamines are trafficked within and outside the continent. For example, Western, Eastern and Northern Africa are transit regions for cocaine and other drugs from South America (UNODC 2017). For example, the Sinaloa drug Cartel in Mexico uses the West African states of Guinea and Guinea Bissau as an important staging and repacking points for drugs destined for Europe and the United States (Organised Crime Index 2019: 8–19). Africa is also the transit hub for heroine destined for Europe and coming from Asia. Indeed, Kenya is an important transit hub for cocaine and heroin coming in from Southern America and Asia. At least ten major international drug trafficking networks are embedded in the country (Miraglia et al. 2012). Likewise, cannabis is both trafficked within and outside the continent. In 2016, Nigeria was discovered to be the main hub for the production and distribution of methamphetamine in the subregion (NDLEA 2016). The link between drug trafficking and SALWs is that the transnational criminals would need such weapons to protect their merchandise during transit across the different African borders. In the process, such weapons can proliferate unchecked across the continent's borders.

Africa is also known as a hub of human and people trafficking. These are two important transnational crime that occur across Africa. Women (for labour and sex), men (for labour) and boys and girls (for labour, sex and child soldiers) are trafficked across different borders on the continent; and at other times trafficked to Western Europe and the Middle East. The International Labour Organization (ILO) claims that human trafficking generates US$150.2 billion dollars and that Africa accounts for approximately US$10.5 dollars out this (ILO 2014: 17; May 2017: 21). For example, Cameroon is an important collation and transit point for women and girls from Western Africa destined for Europe (USDS 2017). Ivorian nationals are trafficked to North Africa, especially, Tunisia to be exploited as labour and sex slaves (Victims of Trafficking 2019). Almost all African countries are affected by these particular crime due to the labour-intensive extractive industries, porosity of the borders and poverty (Interpol 2018: 14). This particular transnational crime also contributed to the proliferation of SALWs on the continent due to the fact that the perpetrators require such weapons to protect their subjects from one African border to the other. Additionally, the subjects are sometimes killed and their organs are harvested and trafficked across the continent's borders.

Africa is also a major stage for environmental crimes which is divided into two: exploitation of natural resources and wildlife crimes (Interpol 2018: 18). Exploitation of natural resources covers illegal lumbering and that of wildlife covers that of poaching of different species of animals. Illegal lumbering not only leads to deforestation with serious environmental consequences, it also leads to the loss of tax revenue and economic opportunities that will further entrench poverty. This is an important transnational crime with serious deleterious ramifications for the countries in Africa. For example, over 120 companies were found to be guilty of illegal logging activities in Mozambique alone in March 2017 (Agence France Press 2017, April 27). Cameroon made close to 97,000 Dollars in 2016 from the fines of companies found culpable of violating the country's forestry law (FLEGT 2016). Interestingly, terrorist groups like Al-Shabaab in Somalia (East Africa) and rebel groups like anti-Balaka Movement (Central Africa) embarked on this kind of resource trafficking to generate sorely needed revenue (United Nations Publication 2017). In the process of committing such transnational crime, these groups use SALWs to protect the movement of their goods from one border location to the other. It is via this means that such weapons are allowed to proliferate across the borders and are then used to destabilize states and create insecurity in the different regions on the continent.

Another layer of trafficking is stolen motor vehicle trafficking. They are of two types: intra- and inter-continental trafficking. Intra-continental deals with stolen vehicles that are trafficked within the continent from one border region to the other. This affects almost all the regions on the continent. The inter-continental dimension deals with those cars that are brought from Europe, North America and Asia into Africa. Different models of stolen cars, trucks and buses are trafficked within the continent. Stolen cars are driven across several borders for resale in final destination countries. For example, cars stolen in Uganda have been recovered in the Democratic Republic of the Congo and those stolen in Kenya and South Sudan were recovered in Uganda (Daily Monitor 2017). In West Africa, ECOWAS, the regional economic arrangement that has encouraged the free movement of people, goods and services across borders in the region has aided this kind of transnational crime in the region. Trafficking in stolen vehicles has aided the proliferation of SALWs in West Africa because such weapons are sometimes smuggled through the porous borders into the countries in the region. Nigeria has been negatively impacted by this kind of crime. Stolen vehicles coming in from Benin Republic and Ghana have been used to smuggle SALWs into Nigeria at various times.

Yet another layer of trafficking in Africa is that of maritime crimes and piracy which occur in the Gulf of Guinea in West and Central Africa, and the shores of the Gulf of Aden and Horn of Africa countries in the East. Piracy is particularly deadly on the continent because it not only leads to disruption in intra- and intercontinental maritime trade, it also drives the proliferation of SALWs. Indeed, pirates on the continent have become very adept at kidnapping for ransoms, attacks on oil tankers and vessels, and hijacking and boarding of cargo vessels. To this mix has been added the trafficking of illicit SALWs. In almost all the attacks, the weapon of choice of the perpetrators has always been SALWs. The easy accessibility and portability of SALWs on the continent have facilitated and enabled the high incidence of piracy on the waters in Africa. In 2017, there were seven incidents involving a vessel coming under fire in the Gulf of Guinea (Times Live 2018). In the Niger Delta of Nigeria, pirates attack oil tankers to steal the crude which are then sold to refineries in both the country and the West African subregion (International Chambers 2016). The proceeds from oil bunkering provide the fund for the purchase of SALWs in the region and at the same time the presence of more SALWs leads to more bunkering. This is a vicious circle. This explains the influx of sophisticated SALWs like Russian Ak-47, German G-3, Czech machine guns and Serbian rocket propelled grenades into the region during the height of Niger-Delta insurgency between 2006 and 2009 (Keili 2008: 7). Indeed, a Nigerian arms dealer cum oil-bunker, Chris Ndidi Njoka was arrested with an arms cache that included G-3s, AK-47s and Beretta auto rifles by the Nigerian authorities during the period (Keili 2008: 7). Maritime pirates in all the regions in Africa rely heavily on the SALWs in carrying out their nefarious transnational activities.

The spate of transnational crimes in Africa is caused by a number of factors. The first factor is *Relative Deprivation*: most economies in Africa are poor and the governments on the continent have done a poor job of lifting the citizen out of the poverty trap. Unemployment, that is rife in most cities on the continent, has created a high level of social inequality and disparity. The desire to escape the poverty trap is a major driver for such transnational crime like maritime piracy, human trafficking, drug trafficking and arms trafficking on the continent (May 2017: 85). Indeed, in a study that was carried out by the European Union-sponsored project, "Organised Crime Index Africa 2019", it was discovered that poverty sometimes predisposes certain set of population in a country to engage in transnational crime (Organised Crime Index 2019: 90–95). The conclusions of the study hold true for the high incidence of transnational crime in countries like Nigeria, Somalia, Guinea and Central African Republic. This explains the high incidence of transnational crime in both West and East Africa. The second factor is associated with the repercussions of *globalization*, characterized by the break down of borders among states and economic interdependence that is devoid of any serious artificial barrier to trade (Rahim et al. 2014: 1–8). This is in itself a good thing. But, then it becomes a problem when the perpetrators put the free movement of people and capital to nefarious uses. These include human trafficking, arms trafficking and other illegal and illicit activities. Countries like Nigeria, Somalia, Kenya and Libya have experienced these aspects of transnational crime in one form or the other. These have contributed to political and economic instability in the sub-regions.

The third factor is the pull and push of Demand and Supply Cycle. Africa is riven with pockets of conflicts that range from civil wars to ethno-religious conflicts, from terrorism to boundary disputes and farmers–herders conflicts. These conflicts require that the combatants have adequate resources (weapons) to prosecute their wars. This is the demand aspect of the cycle. The perpetrators now step-in to provide the needed weapons. This is the supply aspect of the cycle. Of course, the more the demand is met, the more the conflict rages and the more the combatants demand for more weapons from the supplier. This has led to an unending circle of violence on the continent (Adeniyi 2017: 7–11). For instance, it has been argued that the unfettered sale and availability of SALWs like Duska 108 mm heavy machine gun and the PKM general-purpose machine gun in Mogadishu's Bakara market is a major cause of instability in the country (Cilliers 2015). Moreover, such conflicts that have been enabled by the proliferation of SALW will further ensure the commission of other transnational crime like drug trafficking and human trafficking, and the violation of human and international rights. This point shows the important connection between guns (SALWs) and transnational crime on the African continent. The guns aid the commission of these crimes on a greater and larger scale. This is the experience of Somalia in the Horn of Africa and Nigeria in West Africa.

Finally, regionalization has, while aiding free movement of goods and services within the continent, fortuitously aided the spread of transnational crime on the continent. Most countries on the continent belongs to various regional and continental organizations. For example, there is ECOWAS in the West and Southern African Development Commission (SADC) in the South. By virtue of their memberships of these economic unions, African states have little or no barrier to the free flow of goods, services and capital in the subregions. Since borders security checks have been relaxed, or with some being poorly manned, perpetrators have found it easier to move illicit goods in the regions from one state to another (OECD 2018). This has been the experience of Nigeria with its neighbours such as Benin, Chad and Niger in West Africa. Illegal weapons have flowed through Nigeria's borders because its membership of ECOWAS made it compulsory for her to grant unimpeded access to goods entering from the neighbour.

IMPACTS OF GUN TRAFFICKING AND TRANSNATIONAL CRIME IN AFRICA

Transnational crime has affected socio-economic and political development in Africa. In its various formats, transnational crime has ensured that the issues of governance, security, socio-economic and political development have become intractable on the continent. The following is the analysis of how transnational crime has retarded social, economic and political growth and development in Africa. First is the impact on Governance. Transnational crime has made the issues of governance and legitimacy onerous for the different governments in Africa. The proliferation of SALWs has aided the growth and spread of transnational criminals on ungoverned spaces in countries on the continent. For example, Al-Shabaab, a Somali jihadi group was able to wrest effective control of vast swathes of that country that includes Diinsor, Barawe and Mogadishu from the legitimate government in the 2000s (Falode 2018: 159). Al-Shabaab turned to piracy and other criminal acts such as transborder smuggling to generate revenue for the group and sustain its campaigns against the state in the ungoverned space that it controlled. The conflict in that country, that is still ongoing, has been facilitated by the proliferation of both SALWs and the engagement of non-state actors in transnational criminal enterprise. This same trend was noticeable in the northeast of Nigeria where Boko Haram took effective control of more than 10 local government areas in the three states of Adamawa, Yobe and Borno (Falode 2016). To sustain its campaign against the Nigerian state, Boko Haram has turned to criminal activities such as cattle rustling, human trafficking and fish smuggling to generate fund and prolong the insurgency in its ungoverned space. Therefore, these ungoverned spaces, usually in the border regions, have allowed transnational criminal enterprises such as human, arms and drug trafficking to fester and flourish. In some cases, these transnational criminal enterprises have been responsible for the economic survival and sustenance of most communities and towns in the periphery of the states. This means that such communities' allegiances will not be to the states but to the perpetrators of such transnational criminal enterprises that were responsible for their socio-economic survival. Once any of these transnational criminal enterprises has been sufficiently developed, it will affect the relationship between the constitutionally recognized authority in the state and the citizens in this border region. In the long-term, this will affect the overall ability of the government to exercise control over all the regions in the state since its legitimacy will now be in doubt. This impact of transnational crime is being felt in West African countries like Nigeria, Chad, Mali and Niger and in Somalia in East Africa.

Secondly, transnational crime and gun trafficking have compounded the spectres of conflict in Africa: the trafficking of SALWs has affected both the duration, character and intensity of conflicts in Africa. The proliferation and portability of SALWs has made the phenomenon of child soldiers to become a permanent feature of conflicts on the continent. For example, civil conflicts in Liberia, Sierra Leone, Uganda and the Democratic Republic of the Congo have witnessed the use of children as active combatants using SALWs like pistols, AK-47 and rifles. Being the first weapons of choice for both state and non-state combatants on continent, SALWs has made it possible for non-state actors like militants, terrorists and herders to effectively challenge states in conventional engagements. This is true for the conflict situation in the West African state of Nigeria in its confrontation with the terrorist group known as Boko Haram. For instance, due to the availability of vast quantities of SALWs at its disposal, Boko Haram has been able to overrun fortified military installations in Nigeria at different periods. This happened in March 2014 when Boko Haram, in a show of force, overran and sacked Giwa Barracks, the HQ of the 21 Brigade of the Nigerian Army in Maiduguri (Omeni 2018). Moreover, it has made it possible for the group to engage Nigerian security forces in conventional combats rather than the asymmetric ones that would naturally have been the preference of similar jihadi groups. This is also true for the long-running conflict between the Lord's Resistance Army (LRA) and the Ugandan security forces in East Africa. The point here is that the easy access to SALWs and its trafficking across the different porous borders on the continent is a major factor responsible for the high incidences and long duration of conflicts on the continent. Thirdly, and closely associated with aiding and abetting conflict, the proliferation and trafficking of SALWs and transnational crimes have impacted adversely on regional and national security in Africa. The widespread availability of trafficked SALWs on the continent has created serious human security challenges. This is because the presence of such weapons has encouraged state and non-state actors to readily resort to violence and force rather than negotiation, diplomacy and persuasion to resolve their differences (UNDDR 2006). The unregistered nature of such weapons makes it easier for both state and non-state actors to use such to violate human rights and international humanitarian law. Additionally, since most states in Africa did not have credible and viable disarmament and demobilization programmes at the end of any major conflict, SALWs in the hands of the erstwhile combatants then become a tool that enables the commission of transnational crime like hijacking, piracy, arms, drug and human trafficking.

Finally, transnational crime and the proliferation of SALWs has had tsunamic effect on socio-economic development on the continent. Poverty, social and economic inequality in the different societies in Africa encourages perpetrators to engage in transnational crime to the detriment of the states. It has also encouraged the proliferation of SALWs that has the multiplier effect of the commission and enablement of other transnational crime like piracy, human and drug trafficking. The long-term costs of SALWs in terms of human and economic development affect societies as a whole; and the adverse effects on armed violence on poverty, social spending and economic development perpetuates human suffering (Shaw and Wannenburg 2005: 368–386). For example, the Civil War in Sierra Leone, where SALWs was the main engine of violence, killed some 50,000 people, 30,000 had their limbs amputated and between 215,000 and 257,000 became victims of sexual violence (Keili 2008: 9). Such conflicts generally impact human development, knowledge and education, income, standard of living and community participation (BICC 2006).

Conclusion

Transnational crime is not a uniquely African phenomenon. It is felt in the different continents of the world in varying degrees. However, a combination of factors such as a dysfunctional political system, poverty, ill-equipped security forces, well organized criminal groups and porous borders have conspired to make the effects of SALWs to be more pronounced in Africa. In the same vein, the easy access, unregulated nature and portability of SALWs have made it possible for perpetrators to commit the different variants of the crime in Africa. Small arms and light weapons have both enabled and ensured the commission of transnational crime like human and drugs trafficking, maritime piracy and arms trafficking in Africa. Guns like SALWs are not just used to commit transnational crime but they also enable it. Moreover, governments on the continent will have to expand foreign aid programmes that target the illicit arms trade, crackdown on violations of UN arms embargoes, strengthen arms control legislation and address the factors that fuel the illicit transnational crime economy. In other for Africa to be able to escape its unending transnational crime and conflict traps, concerted effort is needed to tackle the problem of the proliferation of SALWs holistically and effectively. Tackling the problems and dangers posed by transnational crime will require a two-pronged targeted approach from policy makers on the continent. The first measure will be directed towards using security agencies and legal provisions to tackle transnational crimes in their respective domains. The legislations are there already but they will have to be fully and rigorously implemented. Since transnational crime by definition traverses borders, it will mean that the security agencies on the continent will have to establish an institution that can coordinate law enforcement response to the menace across states. The second targeted measure will be designed to address the root causes of those factors that push people in a given country to engage in transnational crime. Since poverty and political insecurity are important drivers that fuel the illicit trade, governments on the continent will have to embark on massive social and economic programmes.

REFERENCES

Adeniyi, A. (2017, March). The Human Cost of Uncontrolled Arms in Africa: Cross-National Research on Seven African Countries. *Oxfam* (pp. 7–12). https://www-cdn.oxfam.org/s3fs-public/file_attachments/rr-human-cost-uncontrolled-arms-africa-080317-en.pdf.

Agence France Press. (2017, April 27). Mozambique Battles Illegal Logging to Save Tropical Forests. *Agence France-Presse*. https://www.news24.com/Africa/News/mozambique-battles-illegal-logging-to-save-tropical-forests-20170426.

Bonn International Centre for Conversion (BICC). (2006). *People Safe from Guns in South Sudan: A Training for Local Stakeholders*. Bonn International Centre for Conversion (BICC). www.bicc.de/uploads/pdf/publications/other/salw_booklet_sudan/salw_booklet_sudan.pdf.

Bourne, M. (2005). The Proliferation of Small Arms and Light Weapons. In E. Krahmann (Ed.), *New Threats and New Actors in International Security* (p. 45). New York: Palgrave Macmillan.

Brown, S. S. (2020). Introduction: Setting the Stage. In S. S. Brown & M. G. Hermann (Eds.), *Transnational Crime and Black Spots: Rethinking Sovereignty and Global Economy* (pp. 1–12). London, UK: Palgrave Macmillan.

Cilliers, J. (2015, October). (Im)Perfect Future? Mapping Conflict, Violence and Extremism in Africa, ISS paper 287. https://issafrica.s3.amazonaws.com/site/uploads/Paper287-1.pdf.

Daily Monitor. (2017, August 6). Interpol Recovers Seven Stolen Motor Vehicles. *Daily Monitor*, 6. http://www.monitor.co.ug/News/National/Interpol-recover-seven-stolen-motor-vehicles/688334-4047128-23jpjr/index.html.

Falode, J. A. (2016). The Nature of Nigeria-Boko Haram War, 2010–2015: A Strategic Analysis. *Perspectives on Terrorism, 10*(1), 44. http://www.terrorismanalysts.com/pt/index.php/pot/article/view/488.

Falode, J. A. (2018). Terrorism 4.0: A Global and Structural Analysis. *Open Political Science, 1*(1), 159. https://doi.org/10.1515/openps-2018-0013.

FLEGT. (2016, August 8). Cameroon Publishes Data on Illegal Logging Cases and Fines. *FLEGT*. http://www.flegt.org/news/content/viewItem/cameroon-pub lishes-data-on-illegal-logging-cases-and-fines/08-08-2016/22.

Holstom, P., & Pavesi, I. (2018). Trade Update 2018: Sub-Saharan Africa in Focus. *Small Arms Survey*. Geneva. http://www.smallarmssurvey.org/fileadmin/docs/S-Trade-Update/SAS-Trade-Update-2018.pdf.

International Chambers of Commerce. (2016, February 2). *Maritime Piracy Hotspots Persist Worldwide Despite Reductions in Key Areas*. International Chambers of Commerce. https://www.icc-ccs.org/index.php/1154-imb-maritime-piracy-hot spots-persist-worldwide-despite-reductions-in-key-areas.

International Labor Organization (ILO). (2014). *Profits and Poverty: The Economics of Forced Labour*. International Labor Organization. Geneva, p. 17. http://www.ilo.org/wcmsp5/groups/public/---ed_norm/-declaration/doc uments/publication/wcms_243391.pdf.

Interpol. (2018). Overview of Serious and Organized Crime in Africa 2018. *Interpol*, pp. 10–28. https://www.interpol.int/content/download/12850/file/Overview%20of%20Serious%20and%20Organized%20crime%20in%20Africa-EN.pdf.

Jeffrey, B., & Klare, M. (1998). Small Arms and Light Weapons: Controlling the Real Instruments of War. *Arms Control Today*. https://www.armscontrol.org/act/1998_08-09/mkas98.

Keili, F. L. (2008). Small Arms and Light Weapons Transferrin West Africa: A Stock-Taking. The Complex Dynamics of Small Arms in West Africa. *Disarmament Forum*, p. 7. http://nisat.prio.org/misc/download.ashx?file=7470.

Kumar, S. (2008, October–December). Small Arms and Light Weapons: A Global Health to Human Security and Development. *The Indian Journal of Political Science, 69*(4), 787. http://www.jstor.org/stable/41856469.

Levine, P., Smith, R., Reichlin, L., & Ray, P. (1997, October). The Arms Trade. *Economic Policy, 12*(25): 335–370. http://www.jstor.com/stable/1344683.

Lloyd, P., Simmons, B., & Stewart, B. (2012). Combating Transnational Crime: The Role of Learning and Norm Diffusion in the Current Rule of Law Wave. In A. Nolkaemper, M. Zurn, & R. Peerenboom (Eds.), *The Dynamics of the Rule of Law* (pp. 153–180). Cambridge: Cambridge University Press.

May. C. (2017). Human Trafficking (pp. 21, 85). Transnational Crime and the Developing World. *Global Financial Integrity*. https://www.gfintegrity.org/wp-content/uploads/2017/03/Transnational_Crime-final.pdf.

Miraglia, P., Ochoa, R., & Briscoe, I. (2012). *Transnational Organised Crime and Fragile States*. Organisation for Economic Cooperation and Development. https://www.oecd.org/dac/accountable-effective-institutions/WP3%20Transnational%20organised%20crime.pdf.

Mystris, D. (2019). Transnational Crime in the African Union. V. Mitsilegas, S. Hufnagel, & A. Moiseienko (Eds.), *Research Handbook on Transnational Crime* (pp. 482–488). Cheltenham: Edward Elgar Publishing.

National Drug Law Enforcement Agency (NDLEA). (2016). *Super Laboratory: NDLEA Arraigns 4 Mexicans, 5 Nigerians*. National Drug Law Enforcement Agency. https://ndlea.gov.ng/new-and-event/super-laboratory-ndlea-arraings-4-mexicans-5-nigerians/.

Ogunniyi, O. J., & Akpu, J. O. (2019). The Challenge of Drug Trafficking to Democratic Governance and Human Security in West Africa: A Historical Reflection.

Africa Development, XLIV(4), 29–49. https://www.jstor.org/stable/10.2307/268 73443.

Omeni, A. (2018). Boko Haram's Increasingly Sophisticated Military Threat. *Small Wars and Insurgencies, 29*(5), 886–915. https://doi.org/10.1080/09592318. 2018.1519299.

Organisation for Economic Cooperation and Development (OECD). (2018). West-Africa: Regional Context and Susceptibility in Criminal Economies. In *Illicit Financial Flows: The Economy of Illicit Trade in West Africa*. OECD Publishing. https://www.oecd-library.org/development/illicit-financial-flows_9789264268418-en.

Organised Crime Index 2019. (2019). *Enhancing Africa's Response to Transnational Organised Crime (Enact)* (pp. 50–100). European Union. https://ocindex.net/assets/downloads/enact_report.pdf.

Rahim, H. L., Abidin, Z. Z., Ping, S. D., Alias, M. K., & Muhamad, A. I. (2014). Globalization and Its Effect on World Poverty and Inequality. *Global Journal of Management and Business, 1*(2), pp. 8–13. http://repository.upenn.edu/bepp_papers/70.

Reitano, T. (2018). Organized Crime as a Threat to Sustainable Development: Understanding the Evidence. Comolli, V. (Ed.), *Organized Crime and Illicit Trade: How to Respond to This Strategic Challenge in Old and New Domains* (pp. 23–35). New York: Palgrave Macmillan.

Schroeder, M., & Lamb, G. (2006). The Illicit Arms Trade in Africa. *African Analyst*, Third Quarterly, pp. 69–78. https://fas.org/asmp/library/articles/SchroederLamb.pdf.

Shaw, M., & Wannenburg, G. (2005). Organized Crime in Africa. In P. Reichel (Ed.), *Handbook of Transnational Crime and Justice*. Thousand Oaks, CA: Sage.

Sheptycki, J., & Wardack, A. (Eds.). (2003). *Transnational and Comparative Criminology*. London: Glasshouse.

Small Arms Survey. (2019). Assessing the Scale and Availability of Illicit Small Arms in Africa (pp. 21–30). *Weapons Compass: Mapping Illicit Small Arms Flows in Africa*. Small Arms Survey 2019. Geneva. http://www.smallarmssurvey.org/fileadmin/docs/U-Reports/SAS-AU-Weapons-Compass.pdf.

Stohl, R. (2017, November 15). Understanding Conventional Arms Trade. In *AIP Conference Proceedings 1898* (pp. 1–9). https://doi.org/10.1063/1.5009220.

Stoica, I. (2016). Transnational Organized Crime: An International Security Perspective. *Journal of Defence Resources Management, 7*(2), 4–15. http://journal.dresmara.ro/issues/volume7_issue2/02_stoica_vol7_issue2.pdf.

Times Live. (2018, March 7). Off West Africa, Navies Team Up in Fight Against Piracy. *Times Live*. https://www.timeslive.co.za/news/africa/2018-03-07-off-west-africa-navies-team-up-in-fight-against-piracy.

United Nations Disarmament, Demobilization and Reintegration (UNDDR). (2006, August 1). *Integrated Disarmament, Demobilization and Reintegration Standards: Module 4.11 SALW Control, Security and Development*. United Nations Inter-Agency Working Group on Disarmament, Demobilization and Reintegration (UNDDR). www.unddr.org/iddrs/04/download/IDDRS_411.pdf.

United Nations Office on Drugs and Crime (UNODC). (2005). *Transnational Organized Crime in the West African Region*. United Nations Office on Drugs and Crime. New York: United Nations. https://www.unodc.org/pdf/transnational_crime_west-africa-05.pdf.

United Nations Office on Drugs and Crime (UNODC). (2012). *Transnational Organized Crime—The Globalized Illegal Economy*. United Nations Office on

Drugs and Crime (UNODC). New York: United Nations. http://www.europarl. europa.eu/document/activities/cont/201207/20120717ATT49047/20120717A TT49047EN.pdf.

United Nations Office on Drugs and Crime (UNODC). (2017). *World Drug Report 2017*. United Nations Office on Drugs and Crime. United Nations. https://relief web.int/report/world/unodc-world-drug-report-2017.

United Nations Publication. (2017, November 14). *Extending Arms Embargoes on Somalia, Eritrea, Security Council Adopts Resolution 2385 (2017) by 11 votes in Favour, 4 Abstentions*. United Nations Publication. https://www.un.org/press/en/2017/sc13065.doc.htm.

United States Department of States (USDS). (2017). 2017 *Trafficking in Persons Report—Cameroon*. United States Department of State. United States. https://cm.usembassy.gov/official-reports/trafficking-persons-report-cameroon/.

Victims of Trafficking in the Central Mediterranean Route: Focus on Women from Cote d'Ivoire, from the Trafficking in Tunisia to the Risk of Re-trafficking in Italy. (2019, September 30). *IOM Briefing*. https://italy.iom.int/sites/default/files/news-documents/IOM_Briefing_Victims_of_Trafficking.pdf.

Adewunmi J. Falode is a Senior Lecturer in the Department of History and International Studies, Lagos State University. He earned his Ph.D. (2012) in History and Strategic Studies from the University of Lagos, Akoka, Lagos. His areas of interest are international relations, strategic studies, war studies, terrorism studies, cybersecurity studies and Nigerian history. Dr. Falode has published extensively in local and international peer-reviewed journals. He is an international reviewer for reputable journals like Behavioural Sciences of Terrorism and Political Aggression, Canadian Journal of African Studies and African Security Review. Dr. Falode is a member of the Nigeria Institute of International Affairs (NIIA).

Part III

Institutional Framework and Dynamics

CHAPTER 21

Military, Arms Monopoly and Proliferation of Small Arms and Light Weapons in Africa

Al Chukwuma Okoli

INTRODUCTION

The modern state is an institutionalized territorial force characterized, above all, by military sovereignty. By military sovereignty is meant the supreme authority of the state in wielding monopoly on legal use of force within its jurisdictional spheres. The Weberian conception holds that a state's monopoly on legitimate coercion is a sine qua non for its existence and persistence (Weber 1946). In other words, any state that fails to guarantee her military sovereignty on a sustainable basis can only exist in dysfunctionality. The military is an indispensable institution of the state. It is rightly referred to as the custodian of national security in view of its strategic role in safeguarding the territorial integrity and sustainability of the state. Through the military, the state makes good her command-ship of monopoly on violence. In effect, the state relies on the institution of the military in order to live up to the demands of national sovereignty and territoriality (Krahmann 2009; Okoli and Anjide 2015). Reference 'Acemoglu et al. (2019)' is cited in the text but not provided in the reference list. Please provide the respective reference in the list or delete this citation.

Contemporary dynamics and trajectories of the global security sector tend to have queried the traditional assumptions regarding state's monopoly of legitimate force. The territoriality of the state has been significantly eroded by

A. C. Okoli (✉)
Department of Political Science, Federal University of Lafia, Lafia, Nasarawa State, Nigeria

© The Author(s), under exclusive license to Springer Nature Switzerland AG 2021
U. A. Tar and C. P. Onwurah (eds.), *The Palgrave Handbook of Small Arms and Conflicts in Africa*,
https://doi.org/10.1007/978-3-030-62183-4_21

the untoward forces of globalization: cybercrime, digital espionage, transnational terrorism, and the like. Likewise, the emergence and proliferation of non-state armed actors at the national and international levels have persistently disputed the Weberian orthodoxy of military sovereignty in the context of the state. Indeed, non-state forces have not only negotiated the state's monopoly over legal coercion, they have, worse still, contended with the state in terms of exclusive territoriality (Ayissi and Sall 2005; Whelan 2006; Okoli 2017a). Hence, the hitherto acclaimed "exclusive jurisdiction" of state-military control is nowadays being incrementally eroded, infiltrated and subverted—for instance, by violent non-state actors (VNSAs) (Nna et al. 2012; Tar and Mustapha 2017; Varin and Abubakar 2017).

It is against the backdrop of the above that this chapter reflects on the issue of military arms monopoly against the backdrop of the proliferation of Small Arms and Light Weapons (SALWs) in Africa. What is the role of the state's armed forces vis-a-vis defense management and arms monopoly? Why has the proliferation of SALWs persisted in spite of the acclaimed state-military control of the arms sector? What are the challenges confronting the Westphalian state as the custodian of force and enforcer of order? Given the emergence of VNSAs in many developing states, resulting in the creating of "ungoverned/undergoverned spaces", what are the implications for the state's claim to sovereignty and territorial integrity in Africa? How are non-state actors sourcing their arms and ammunition to challenge the state at local, regional and global levels? And how does the scenario affect regional and continental stability in Africa? These questions are explored in some detail in this chapter.

In situating the above analytical posers, the chapter posits that SALWs proliferation in Africa is symptomatic of the dysfunctionality of the state in that context, especially as it relates to functional its capabilities and will to govern. This governance deficit has given rise to swathes and pockets of ungoverned and undergoverned spaces that conduce to violence and criminality, which undermine sustainable stability in the continent. The remainder of the chapter is structured thematically along the following broad sections: conceptual and theoretical framework; nature and incidence of SALWs proliferation; SALWs, armed conflicts, violent non-state actors (VNSA) and organized crime; the state-military arms control, ungoverned spaces and SALWs proliferation (strategic implications); conclusion and recommendations.

Understanding the Threshold Terminologies

Seven key terms constitute the conceptual thrust of this paper, namely military, arms monopoly, SALWs, SALWs proliferation, VNSAs and ungoverned/undergoverned spaces. For the purpose of shared scientific understanding, it is germane to operationalize these concepts vis-a-vis their contextual meanings within this chapter. This forms the concern of the subsections that follow forthwith.

The Military refers to an institutionalized system of legal violence. As an institution of the state, the purpose of the military is to ensure the safeguard of territorial integrity of the state through the exercise of legitimate armed violence. According to Johnson (1990: 1) "the business of the military is violence. The military must be ready and able to use violence to protect national interest when it is called upon to do so. The effectiveness of military violence hinges, in large measure…on proper deployment of trained personnel".

The military comprises, traditionally, the Army, Navy, Air Force and territorial guards. The military exists pari passu with, and is often complemented by, allied para-military forces. While the regular military (Army, Navy, Air Force, territorial guards, coast guards) is charged with the responsibility of protecting the sovereignty and territoriality of the state, the informal para-military are military-like bodies that may be called up by the state to reinforce the regular armed forces (Okoli and Anjide 2015).

Arms Monopoly refers to the exclusive power of the state in respect of legitimate use of physical violence, or simply, state's monopoly on violence. The principle derives from the Weberian conception of the state as a political organization that wields exclusive right to use, threaten or authorize physical force within its territorial domain. Max Weber's classic definition of the state holds that the state is that "human community that claims the monopoly of the legitimate use of physical force within a given territory" (Weber 1946: 78). Arms monopoly is exercised by the military at the instance of the state. Its efficiency, however, does not lie with military might or effectiveness. It rather, more fundamentally, depends on the ability of the state to foster sustainable legitimacy through good governance (Keister 2014).

The principle of monopoly on violence does not presuppose exclusive restriction of legal violence to the military machinery in absolute terms. Private individuals and groups can exercise some forms of armed physical force provided that they are warranted by the legal instrumentalities of the state. This has been variously justified on the basis of self-defence, community policing and military volunteering (Okoli 2017b). The abusive side of this is when these non-state actors wield such violence against the government or citizenry in outright usurpation of rule of law.

Small Arms and Light Weapons (SALWs) refers to "any man-portable lethal weapon that expels or launches, is designed to expel or launch, may be readily converted to expel or launch a shot, bullet or projectile by the action of an explosive" (UNGA 2005). SALWs are by nature "small" and "light". Hence, they are easy to use, to carry, and to conceal (UNODA 2017: 1). SALWs consist of two distinct categories, namely small arms and light weapons (see Fig. 21.1). They are weapons of choice in the context of civil wars, organized crimes, gang warfare and terrorist attacks (UNODA 2017). Apparently, this is by virtue of their easy availability, affordability, portability and manageability.

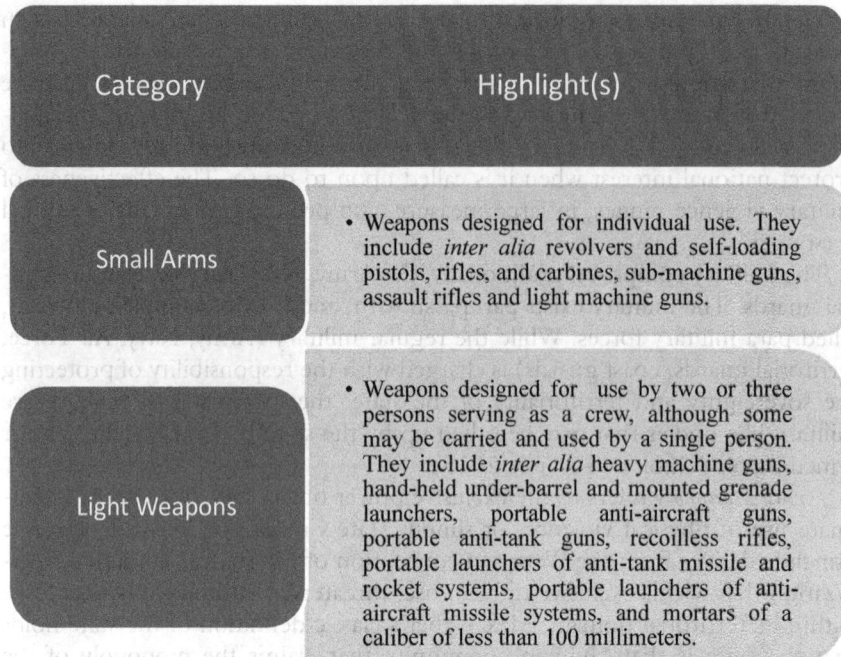

Fig. 21.1 Categories of Small Arms and Light Weapons (SALWs) (*Source* UNDP 2008: 2)

Expert analyses have ascribed a number of characteristics to SALWs. These include low cost and wide availability, increasing lethality, simplicity and durability, portability and military–civilian use (UNDP 2008: 6). SALWs have often been simply referred to as "small arms", especially in studies dealing with the effects of these weapons in conflicts (Grip 2017). More specific and elaborate details concerning the nature of SALWs are highlighted in Box 21.1.

SALWs proliferation refers to illicit, subversive and destructive circulation of SALWs within the civilian population (UNGA 2005). It involves all facets of illegal transaction, transfer, acquisition, possession and use of SALWs. SALWs proliferation has been principally engendered by illicit arms trade, arms diversion and armed conflicts (Malam 2014; Adeniyi 2017; Tessieres 2007; Parliamentary Forum 2017). Much of illicit SALWs trade results from poor or lack of regulation of legal transfers. Symptomatic of this is the twin issue of arms smuggling and trafficking, which has been a critical driver of arms proliferation in the contemporary world (Tessieres 2007). Allied to this is the diversion of arms and ammunition to the illicit market, "in the form of theft or unlawful transfers from civilian and national stockpiles" (Parliamentary Forum 2017: 2). SALWS proliferation has been, arguably, the "cause" and "effect" of organized crime and violence, as well as armed conflicts in Africa (Ogu 2008: 1).

Violent Non-State Actors (VNSAs) refers to armed individual and organizations that espouse violence and seek to challenge, upstage, unsettle, dismantle or replace the formal state authority (Varin and Abubakar 2017; Finucane 2012). They include militias, insurgent groups, organized bandits and large-scale cultists. The activities of these groups have often threatened the survival of the state in many parts of Africa. These actors have often festered on the faultlines of "ungoverned/undergoverned spaces" where the coercive powers of the state are hardly existent or grossly limited.

Un(under) Governed Spaces (UGS) refers to the territorial space of the state—land, air, marine or terrestrial—that are conquered, usurped, annexed or controlled by VNSAs or foreign powers, physically or virtually, thus depriving the owner-state from exercising sovereignty over the space. Undergoverned spaces are spheres of limited or competitive control where state authorities and non-state forces compete for influence. The state's loss of control in this regard can be as a result of its inability to exercise developmental, security, judicial or administrative functions within that territorial sphere. Essentially, UGS refers to "a physical or non-physical area where there is an absence of state capacity or political will to exercise control" (Whelan 2006: 65). The extreme of ungoverned spaces syndrome is *state failure or collapse*. This is defined as the functional or structural sliding of the state in terms of its relative capability to assume territorial control and perform its traditional functions. The functional and structural dimensions of the state collapse/failure problematic is situated shortly herewith.

Our exposition of the conceptual frame of the chapter would not be complete without the consideration of *conflict–crime nexus*. This refers to the correlational relationship between crime and conflict in the context of protracted armed violence (Boer and Bosetti 2015). The logic of this is that actors in such conflict overtime resort to opportunistic survival tactics, including indulging in petty or organized crime. The Niger Delta militants have capitalized on oil bunkering to sustain their violent campaign. This is akin to Boko Haram's (B/H) resort to cattle rustling and other forms of rural banditry as a means of funding its operations (Okoli 2017c).

Box 21.1: Definition of SALWs

SALWs are any man-portable lethal weapon that expels or launches, is designed to expel or launch, or may be readily converted to expel or launch a shot, bullet or projectile by the action of an explosive, excluding antique small arms and light weapons or their replicas. Antique small arms and light weapons and their replicas will be defined in accordance with domestic law. In no case will antique small arms and light weapons include those manufactured after 1899:

(a) "Small arms" are, broadly speaking, weapons designed for individual use. They include, inter alia, revolvers and self-loading pistols, rifles and carbines, sub-machine guns, assault rifles and light machine guns;

> (b) "Light weapons" are, broadly speaking, weapons designed for use by two or three persons serving as a crew, although some may be carried and used by a single person. They include, inter alia, general purpose or universal machine guns, medium machine guns, heavy machine guns, rifle grenades, under-barrel grenade launchers and mounted grenade launchers, portable anti-aircraft guns, portable anti-tank guns, recoilless rifles, man portable launchers of anti-tank missile and rocket systems, man portable launchers of anti-aircraft missile systems and mortars of a calibre of less than 100 millimetres
>
> *Source* UNODC (2013: 3).

SMALL ARMS PROLIFERATION, VIOLENT CONFLICT, "UN(UNDER) GOVERNED SPACES" AND STATE COLLAPSE

The chapter appropriates the "ungoverned spaces" (UGS) hypothesis as its theoretical anchor. This analytical construct is an attempt to situate the threat-import of "under-governed, ill-governed, contested, and exploitable areas" in contemporary state systems (Taylor 2016: 2). Deriving from the counterterrorism/insurgency cum state-failure literature of the post-9/11 era, the framework posits that the existence and prevalence of ungoverned spheres within the territories of states have provided safe havens for criminal and subversive activities, often orchestrated by organized criminals and terrorist/insurgent groups (Rabasa et al. 2007). Ungoverned spaces may include land areas, maritime spheres and cyberspace (see Table 21.1).

As Table 21.1 would readily indicate, ungoverned spaces are "areas of limited or anomalous governmental control inside otherwise functional states" (Keister 2014: 1). More elaborately, the United States Department of Defense (DoD) conceptualizes ungoverned spaces as:

> A place where the state or central government is unable or unwilling to extend control, effectively govern, or influence the local population, and where a provincial, local, tribal, or autonomous government does not fully or effectively govern, due to inadequate governance capacity, insufficient political will, gaps in legitimacy, the presence of conflict, or restrictive norms of behavior. (DoD 2007: 15)

Although ungoverned spaces are occupied and exploited by criminal and subversive non-state elements and VNSAs, they are, in the first instance, created by the state through its failings or inadequacies in terms of functional capacities and legitimacy (Keister 2014). The inability or failure of the state to hold sway in terms of governance and security has often created "governmentality gaps", which are exploited by aggrieved, disgruntled or criminally motivated elements to perpetrate violence and criminality. This is the case with

Table 21.1 Types and patterns/manifestations of ungoverned spaces

Serial	Type	Patterns/manifestations
1.	Ungoverned territories	Maritime, forestial, littoral or desert areas bereft of significant government presence and authority; e.g. Nigeria's Sambisa forests occupied by Boko Haram insurgents
2.	Areas of competing governance	Places where government is unable or unwilling to exercise effective control/authority, thereby ceding such to outside elements; e.g. Northern part of Mali occupied and ruled by the jihadists
3.	Exploitable legal pretexts/principles	Areas of disputed sovereignty, where, for instance, a self-determination struggle, supported by international laws, is being waged against the state
4.	Opaque areas	Spheres of illicit transactions/activities undetected and/or uncontrolled by the state; e.g. the cyberspace

Source Adapted from Whelan (2006: 65–66)

the phenomenon of arms proliferation in contemporary Africa (Gofwan et al. 2019).

Against the backdrop of the ungoverned spaces hypothesis, therefore, it is posited herein that the problem of SALWs proliferation in Africa is symptomatic of the state's fragility syndrome. A veritable indicator of this malaise is the erosion of the state-military arms monopoly through the emergence, prevalence and proliferation of non-state armed groups which contend with the military sovereignty of the state. So, while the existence and prevalence of swathes of ungoverned spaces stands implicated in Africa's state dysfunctionality question, SALWs proliferation remains symptomatic of that pathology.

In the ungoverned spaces theorizing, it is recognized that the ability or inability of the state to assume territorial and coercive control is significantly relative. In effect, state failure or collapse could be a matter of degree or relativity. In any case, the failure/collapse could be functional or structural. The former occurs when structures of the state are intact but it lacks the requisite capacity to perform its traditional functions. On the other hand, it is a structural failure where the "edifice" of the state itself is equally collapsing. A case in point of the structural failure is Somalia that deteriorated from a territory of competitive governance to one of virtual ungovernability in the 1990s–2000s. The crux of matter is that an existing state may nominally retain its monopoly of violence whereas in reality such a state has lost ground and even collapsed either as a result of poor management of arms or armed confrontation with assertive VNSAs.

Nature and Incidence of SALWs Proliferation in Africa: Is the State Loosing Out?

SALWs are, by definition, armaments that are produced, transferred, held or used in violation of national and international law (Schroeder 2013: 284). In Africa, the two main sources of SALWs proliferation are illicit production and transfers. The problem of illicit manufacturing of arms derives essentially from poor regulation of the bourgeoning local artisanal arms industry. Local gunsmiths in Ghana, Nigeria, Mali and elsewhere have been famous for the production of assorted small arms that are used to perpetrate violent crimes (Adeniyi 2017).

The problem of illicit transfer of arms has been bolstered by the prevalence of arms smuggling and trafficking in the continent. This is reinforced by the phenomenon of arms diversion from the state stockpiles (Adeniyi 2017). Diverted arms and ammunition are not virtually missing; they ultimately find their way in conflict situations where they fall into the hands of fighters and their criminal cohorts. There have been instances where the state armories have been invaded and plundered by criminals or insurgents who were motivated by arms expropriation drive (Okoli and Iortyer 2014). Insurgents affiliated to Boko Haram and Al-Shabaab have capitalized on this approach to sustain their terrorist agenda.

Available data indicate an incremental trend in Africa's small arms profile over the recent years (see Table 21.2). According to Holtom and Pavesi:

> Although the African region had the lowest value for documented small arms imports in 2001-14, the value almost tripled, from USD 82 million to USD 237 million. Thirteen African states imported more than USD 10 million worth of small arms at least once during this period. Egypt is the only African state that qualified as a top importer in 2001-14 with USD 148 million worth of small arms importers in 2014, mostly from the Czech Republic. (2017: 24)

Seven African countries (Egypt, Morocco, South Africa, Botswana and Cote d'Ivoire) made the list in Table 21.2, indicating the arrival of the continent in terms of global SALWs profile. Apart from Egypt that is listed among the major importers, the rest of the African states in Table 21.2 are categorized as minor importers. That notwithstanding, all African states are arms-dependent. They depend on European and Asian states for the bulk of their national arms supplies. SALWs imported into African states often find themselves transferred from one destination to another via irregular and illicit avenues. While some countries are known to be important destinations of SALWs, others have played the role of transit states. A veritable case in point for the latter within the West African region is Niger which has served as a transit-point for illicit arms transfer to Nigeria and Mali (Adeniyi 2017; see also Fig. 21.2).

Table 21.2 World's large and small arms importers (Comtrade data, 2014)

Category		Import value (USD)	Importers (in descending order of import value per million: 5000 m to 10 m)
Top Importers	Tier 1	500 million	United States
	Tier 2	100–499 million	Canada, Indonesia, Saudi Arabia, Germany, Australia, Iraq, France, Netherlands, United Kingdom
Major Importers	Tier 3	50–99 million	Israel, Mexico, Norway Philippines, United Arab Emirates, Belgium, Italy, Thailand, Colombia, Russian Federation, Turkey, **Egypt**, Denmark, Switzerland
Minor importers	Tier 4	10–49 million	Portugal, Spain, Japan, Austria, **South Africa**, Poland, Finland, Oman, Czech Republic, Sweden, South Korea, New Zealand, Pakistan, Kuwait, Luxemburg, **Malawi**, Singapore, Qatar, Slovakia, Chile, Kazakhstan, Estonia, Ukraine, **Cote d'Ivoire**, Argentina, Paraguay, Hungary, Afghanistan, **Morocco**, Bulgaria, **Algeria**, Peru, Greece, Malaysia, Guatemala, **Botswana**

Source Adapted from Holtom and Pavesi (2017: 21)

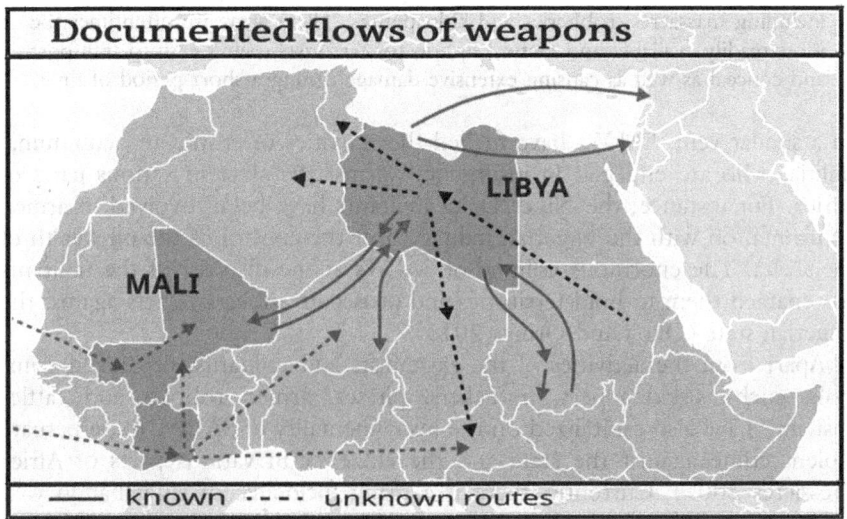

Fig. 21.2 Arms flows in Africa's Maghreb, Sahel and Sub-Sahara (*Source* Libya Tribune, July 27, 2019)

The prevalence of SALWs proliferation in Africa has been principally complicated by state or regime collapse, violent conflict and organized crime. The failure of the Somalia state and the reign of Al-Shabaab, for instance, led to the escalation of SALWs proliferation in the Horn of Africa and the adjoining Great Lakes region (African Peace Forum 2006). Similarly, the fall of Qadhafi regime in Libya in 2011 occasioned a dramatic explosion in SALWs proliferation within the entire Sahel, Maghreb and the Sub-Sahara (Holtom and Pavesi 2017). Figure 21.2 is indicative of the arms flows in the regions.

The activities of extremists groups such as Al Qaeda in the Maghreb (AQIM), the Movement for Unity and Jihad in West Africa (MUJAO), Al Murabitam in Mali, Boko Haram in Nigeria, and the like, have added a convolution to the challenge of SALWs proliferation. As Fig. 21.2 suggests, arms flow from the hotbed of post-Qadafi's Libya to volatile areas such as Mali and the Lake Chad axis, where they end up in the hands of jihadists and allied violent groups operating in the regions. AQIM and Boko Haram fighters have capitalized on the volume of arms available in their operational areas to wage protracted insurgency/terrorism against state authorities in Mali, Burkina Faso, Niger, Chad, Cameroon and Nigeria. Generally, the use of SALWs as instruments of terrorism has been well noted. According to the Parliamentary Forum [PF] (2017: 1):

> SALW are used by terrorists in a wide range of activities supporting their cause, including massacres, robberies and kidnappings. These arms are oftentimes the most readily available and tactical option for terrorists, being easy to transport and conceal as well as causing extensive damage during a short period of time.

In a similar vein, SALWs have fuelled the activities of ethnic and communal militias who are engaged in insurgency against the state in various parts of Africa. For instance, the Niger Delta militants have been involved in armed confrontation with the Nigerian military over the control of the oil wealth of the Delta. The enormous volume of SALWs at the disposal of the militants has enabled them to hold territories and prosecute subversive acts against the Nigerian state (Okoli and Orinya 2013).

Apart from the activities of the extremists and militants, organized criminals—such as kidnappers, traffickers, pirates, armed robbers and cattle-rustlers—have also capitalized on the instrumentality of SALWs to perpetuate violent crime against the state and the citizenry in various parts of Africa (Tessieres 2007). Currently, there is a rising incidence of rural banditry in Nigeria's north-central and north-western regions, where transnational clans of bandits terrorize communities in the frontiers and hinterlands with utmost criminal impunity.

According to Adeniyi (2017: 14), "The flow of uncontrolled arms plays a crucial role across Africa; they are either the object of trafficking and/or used to protect the infrastructures used for criminal activities". This trend has often degenerated into a crime-insecurity complication. In this regard, Adeniyi (2017: 14) further observes:

> There is a convergence of organized crime SALW availability and armed conflict, includingviolent extremism, in places such as the Sahel, Libya and Somalia. Pirates use illicit arms in the Horn of Africa and the Gulf of Guinea region to attack and seize ships and to kidnap crews for ransom. Similarly, South American drugs heading for Europe are trafficked through West Africa and the Sahel, and SALW are used to protect the trafficking routes.

Following the logic of "crime-conflict nexus" (Boer and Bosetti 2015: 1), SALWs proliferation has fuelled armed conflicts in various parts of Africa by sustaining, prolonging and complicating them (SIPRI 2017). A case in point is the situation in DRC where "conflict and insecurity are fuelled by continued inflow… of illicit arms traced to stockpiles from past conflicts and new supplies from a variety of sources" in the Great Lakes region (Adeniyi 2017: 19).

Generally, the incidence of SALWs proliferation in Africa has been alarming (see Table 21.3). This is also true of its consequences, which have often plunged nations into cycles of complex humanitarian situations. As rightly observed by a UNDP document:

> Small arms proliferation has been particularly devastating in Africa. Grenades, pistols and other small arms have killed and displaced many civilians across the continent. These weapons have been used in deadly conflict in Sudan,

Table 21.3 Firearms data for some African countries (by 2016)

Country	Privately owned firearms (licit and illicit)	Civilian firearms possession per 100 population
Algeria	1,900,000	7.6
Angola	2,800,000	17.3
CAR	40,000	1.0
Cote d'Ivoire	400,000	2.4
DRC	800,000	1.4
Ghana	2,300,000	8.55
Libya	900,000	15.5
Mali	143,000	1.1
Mozambique	1,000,000	5.1
Nigeria	2,000,000	1.5
South Africa	3,400,000	6.61
South Sudan	3,000,000	28.23
Sudan	2,000,000	5.5
Somalia	750,000	9.1
Uganda	400,000	1.4

Source Adeniyi (2017: 11)

Uganda, Sierra Leone, Rwanda, Angola, the Democratic Republic of Congo, Somalia and other African countries. They are frequently recycled from country to country, and their ownership is transferred among fighters, security forces and war profiteers. (UNDP 2008: 4)

Table 21.3 indicates, among other things, that enormous volumes of arms are in the hands of private citizens. These arms are committed to both licit and illicit purposes by criminals and violent non-state groups to foment crisis. The table also indicates a significant high concentration of arms in conflict-ridden countries such as the Democratic Republic of Congo (DRC), Libya, Somalia, and Algeria. The quasi-narcotic states of Angola and Mozambique also have a disproportionate share of the arms distribution. This situation holds ominous implications for sustainable peace and stability in Africa.

The incidence of SALWs proliferation in Africa speaks volume of the declining coercive powers of the state in that context. Some African states have become increasingly helpless in terms of territorial security. In these states, tonnes of arms and ammunition are freely at the disposal of various armed groups that control swathes of the national territorial sphere in the frontiers and hinterlands. Militias operating in the creeks and inlands of the Niger Delta have engaged the Nigerian state in a protracted violence since the late 1990s. This is also the case with the Boko Haram insurgency in the country's North East. Elsewhere in northern Mali and some parts of Burkina Faso, the Jihadists have also confronted the state authorities in a sort of competitive territorial contestations. Furthermore, there are worse case scenarios, such as Somalia and DRC where the activities of organized militant groups led to virtual collapse of the state. In the face of this scenario, the state along with its territorial integrity and military monopoly has merely become hoax.

SALWs, Armed Violence and Organized Crime

There is an ongoing debate among scholars as to whether SALWs are the cause, symptom, effect or complication of armed conflict in Africa (Adeniyi 2017). The consensus seems to be that SALWs constitute a veritable predictor and a driver of armed conflict. Thus, it is apposite to add that SALWs double as the cause and consequence of armed conflict in the continent. This is evidenced in the spate of aggravated armed violence in places such as DRC, Sudan, Somalia, Mali, Libya, Nigeria and the adjoining Lake Chad axes. Situating this line of thought, Adeniyi (2017: 11) poignantly opines:

> The problem of uncontrolled arms, as well as their illicit acquisition and transfer, is a recurring security challenge in Africa. While they do not directly cause conflict, their concentration in crisis zones often sustains or prolongs them. Uncontrolled arms also fuel civil wars, empowering non-state armed groups to launch attacks against governments and local communities.

The complications of SALWs have been so dire in conflict situations in parts of Africa. This is evident in the overt degeneration of low-intensity conflicts into lethal sophistication and immensity (Rabasa et al. 2007). A case in point is the famer–herder conflicts which has since assumed the posture of asymmetric violence in Nigeria, Mali, Burkina Faso and other parts of West and Central Africa (Gaye 2018a). This is also true of incidences of ethnic, communal, cult and electoral violence in various parts of contemporary Africa (see Table 21.4).

Much as SALWs proliferation has complicated the prevalence of armed conflict, it has also accentuated the occurrence of organized crimes in Africa (see Table 21.5). SALWs have been implicated in the violent crimes, such as cattle rustling, rural banditry, piracy, kidnapping, drug trafficking and arms trafficking. SALWs trafficked to Boko Haram insurgents have been used to perpetuate rural banditry in northern Nigeria. Organized criminal syndicates have resorted to the use of SALWs to further and protect their criminal enterprises (Gaye 2018b). In conflict-ridden zones of Africa, violent groups have often taken to hostage-taking, substance and human trafficking, cattle rustling and banditry as a means of survival and sustenance (Gaye 2018a; Okoli 2017c). These criminal activities have been facilitated by arms bearing and brutality.

Curiously, there seems to have been a tactical synergy between organized criminals and extremists/insurgents in the Sahel and the adjoining fringes of the Sahara. According to Gaye:

> Intrinsic links exist between terrorist groups and organized crime rings, which work together to maximize their business. These networks develop with the complicit or participation of local actors, who profit from these illicit dealings. Drug traffickers also have connections with jihadist groups that totally or partially control certain major cross-border roads. There is therefore a real interweaving of issues, actors, and networks in the Sahel to control local resources and drug trafficking in areas where state representation in terms of administration and defence and security is limited or virtually inexistent. (Gaye 2018b: 6)

Underlying the above conflict–crime collusion is the opportunistic appropriation of SALWs towards subversive ends (Boer and Bosetti 2015). This scenario has created and sustained a scepter of virtual territorial ungovernability in the affected areas, given rise to subregional and regional instability in dire cases (see Table 21.5).

The State, State Collapse, Un(Under) Governed Spaces and SALWs Proliferation in Africa

African states can be classified as thriving, weak/fragile or failed states. Thriving states are those that can appreciably perform its primary functions while upholding their territorial integrity and sovereignty reasonably. Typical

Table 21.4 Regional prevalence of SALWs proliferation in Africa

Region	Some historical drivers	Some contemporary indicators/complications	Some critical hotbeds (country wise)
East Africa	Regime-borne organized violence Uganda; genocidal wars in Rwanda and Burundi; armed conflict in Djibouti and Sudan; Ethiopia-Eritrea war; Al-Shabab's insurgency in Somalia	Transnational terrorism orchestrated by Al-Shabab; sundry armed violence and criminality on the Great Lakes region; electoral violence in Kenya	Ethiopia, Eritrea, Sudan, Somalia, Kenya
Central Africa	Regime-borne organized violence in Congo, DR (Zaire) and Central African Republic (CAR); Guerilla warfare in northern Congo	Transnational terrorism; Islamist uprising in CAR; armed trafficking	Cameroon, Chad, CAR
North Africa	Anti-colonial armed resistance in Algeria; Arab nationalism in the Maghreb; regime-borne organized violence in Qadhafi's Libya	Post-Arab Spring neo-Islamist uprising in the wider Maghreb; fall of Qadhafi's regime and its regional repercussions; armed smuggling and trafficking across the Mediterranean	Egypt, Morocco, Algeria, Libya, Tunisia
Southern Africa	Anti-colonial armed resistance in South Africa, Mozambique, Namibia and Zimbabwe; Cold war contingency armed supplies	Urban violence occasioned by armed robbery and gang brigandage	South Africa, Zimbabwe, Angola, Namibia, Malawi
West Africa	Civil wars in Nigeria, Sierra Leone, Liberia and Cote d'Ivoire; ethno-religious conflicts in Nigeria	Armed smuggling and trafficking, piracy on the Gulf of Guinea; rural and urban banditry; armed militancy; Islamist insurgencies; communal conflicts; electoral violence in Nigeria and Cote d'Ivoire; cult violence	Nigeria, Niger, Mali, Cote d'Ivoire, Burkina Faso

Source Authors' compilation from sundry sources (UNDP 2008; Adeniyi 2017; Gaye 2018b)

Table 21.5 Some patterns of SALWs-driven criminality and violence in Africa

	Organized Crime	Armed conflict
1.	**Piracy**, e.g. high sea robbery and killings on the continental waters of the Gulf of Guinea in western Africa, and Gulf of Eden in Eastern Africa	1. **Insurgency**, e.g. the activities of Boko Haram in Nigeria, Al-Shabab in the Horn of Africa and sundry extremist jihadist movements in the Sahel and West Africa
2.	**Kidnapping/Hostage-taking**, e.g. the scepter of ransom-driven human kidnapping in the pre-Amnesty Niger Delta	2. **Ethnic/Communal conflict**, e.g. the Ombatse uprising in Nasarawa State, Central Nigeria
3.	**Cattle rustling**, e.g. Prevalence of armed cattle theft in Nigeria, Burkina Faso and Mali	3. **Farmer-herder crisis**, e.g. the orgy of violent confrontation between crop/settled farmers and nomadic/migrant herdsmen in Nigeria
4.	**Drug trafficking**, e.g. incidence of substance and human trafficking in Northern Mali	4. **Cult violence**, e.g. resurgence of cult activism and disturbances in the Niger Delta
5.	**Banditry**, e.g. spate of rural banditry in North West Nigeria	5. **Electoral violence**, e.g. the 2007 post-electoral violence in Kenya

Source Author's original compilation

instances include Ghana, South Africa and Botswana. Thriving states are characterized by affirmative indicators of political stability, democratic consolidation and economic development. These states have been often referred to as emerging democracies in Africa (Okoli and Anjide 2017).

Fragile or weak states are those that are besought with instability arising from armed conflicts as well as governance and development failures. Important attribute of a fragile state is contested territoriality and sovereignty. This is instantiated by the existence of non-state/sub-state armed groups which contend the authority of the state, seeking to subvert it. Fragile states lack effective territorial control (Finucane 2012). They often exist at the mercy of insurgents, militias, and armed criminal networks. Cases in point include Nigeria, DRC, Mali, CAR, South Sudan and a host of others.

Failed states are states whose central authority has literally collapsed, giving rise to the prevalence of an interregnum whereby two or more armed groups lay malignant claim to state power. A typical instance of this scenario played out in Somalia in the aftermath of Al-Shabab's takeover in 2000s. Another relevant instance is the Libyan state in the immediate aftermath of the fall of Qadhafi in 2011 (Okoli and Atelhe 2018). Apart from lacking a credible central authority, failed states are bereft of the virtues of constitutionality and legitimacy. They exist only in name, apparently in the fashion of what Finucane (2012: 35) has designated "fictitious states".

The common feature of African state system in the contemporary era is its relative dysfuntionality. Most of the existing African states fall within the typology of fragile or weak states, while a few are either failing or failed. In view of the fact that the best of the contemporary African states is merely thriving, none of these states could rightly appropriate the standing of a typical effective state (see Box 21.2). To be sure, the functionality and effectiveness of these states are highly circumscribed. Expectedly though:

> A weak, failed or collapsed state performs none of its governance functions effectively in a given area, freeing illicit actors to pursue threatening activities. All ungoverned areas have the potential to become safe havens, but not all of them do; of those ungoverned areas that do not become safe havens, many are exploited not by transnational illicit actors but by groups whose activities and interests remain strictly local. (US Department of Defence 2007: 15)

The point being emphasized in the foregoing is that the incapacity of the state to hold effective sway creates ungoverned spaces which are exploited by the political and criminal underworld to perpetrate subversions against the state (Taylor 2016). This is the case with SALWs proliferation which has been most pronounced among the fragile and failed states of Africa over the years (Whelan 2006). Suffice it, therefore, to note that the phenomenon of SALWs proliferation obtains in an enabling socio-political ambience. Typifying this environment is the prevalence of ungoverned spheres, which are, in turn, reflective of the structural and/or functional failure of the state in that context.

Box 21.2: Nature and Character of Contemporary Weak and Failed States
Weak States are characterized by the penetration of crime into politics. You cannot tell where politics leaves off and crime begins. The government does not have the strength to fight lawlessness, drug trafficking, corruption, poverty and breakaway movements. Justice is bought. Democracy is preached more than practiced and elections often rigged. Little is collected in taxation. Revenues from natural resources, such as Mexico's and Nigeria's oil, disappear into private pockets. Much of Asia, Africa and Latin America are weak states.

Failed States have essentially no national government, although some pretend they do. Warlords, militias and opium growers do as they wish. There is no law besides the gun. Territorial breakup threatens. Education and health standards decline (as in the increase of HIV/AIDS). Afghanistan, Iraq and Somalia could be counted as failed states. Only outside assistance and pressure keep them from disappearing altogether.
Source Roskin et al. (2010: 60).

THE MILITARY AND SALWs CONTROL IN AFRICA: WITHER THE STATE MONOPOLY OF ARMS?

The traditional notion of state monopoly of violence comprehends three fundamental aspects, to wit (Krahmann 2009: 2):

i. It determines who is permitted to use force, namely the democratic state and its agencies;
ii. It involves all agreement on what is considered the legitimate use of violence and on what basis, such as the outlawing of torture and the proportionality of force;
iii. The definition prescribes under which circumstances and for what purposes state actors may employ force, including public security and national defense.

Central to the norm of state monopoly on violence is the question of who is permitted to bear and/or use armed force. The norm prohibits privatization of armed force and mandates the military to wield and exercise monopolistic control thereof. In order to ensure that this monopolistic control is not usurped by any civilian agency, the military needs to be strong enough to overcome possible domestic and international territorial threats. In the views of Krahmann (2009: 2–3):

> The norm of the state monopoly violence rests on the assumption that a general expectation of peaceful cooperation and conflict resolution can only develop among citizens if individuals are prohibited from using armed force to further their own interests. At the same time, it contends that the state needs to retain a minimum of force in order to protect its citizens against domestic actors who ignore this prohibition as well as international threats.

The problem of SALWs proliferation in Africa to a large extent reflects the failure of the state in that context to exhibit monopoly of violence (Acemoglu et al. 2013). This is oftentimes resulting from protracted armed conflict or sudden regime collapses that weakens the coercive might of the central government. More fundamentally, it also adumbrates the incapability of the military to make good the "arms monopoly" principle. The failure of the state to establish such monopoly has been attributed to a variety of factors including difficult geography, rough terrain, poverty, and interstate competition and warfare (Acemoglu et al. 2013: 6). This is often complicated by gross governance and development deficits which negate the structural and functional essences of the state and its basic institutions. The dysfunctionality of the state in such context often begets violent anti-state pressures that undermine the military sovereignty of the state. Amidst the volatile existential scenario such as this, the essence and end of the state apropos of its monopoly of violence remain patently precarious.

SALWs and State's (De)Monopoly of Arms: Strategic Implications

The basic quality of the state from the standpoint of traditional security is its effectiveness. This refers to the ability of the state to hold sway within its

Table 21.6 Africa's top 10 fragile states (2017)

Rank	Country
1	Ethiopia (32.26)
2	Burundi (8.56)
3	Chad (27.91)
4	Libya (26.57)
5	Eritrea (23.07)
6	Congo DR (22.64)
7	Central African Republic (21.85)
8	Sudan (18.53)
9	South Sudan (14.41)
10	Somalia (13.35)

Source In On Africa (2013, para 9)

jurisdictional sphere. State effectiveness comprises coercive and social capabilities (Finucane 2012: 41). Coercive capability refers to effective control of territory, including the state's capacity to checkmate the activities of non-state armed groups. This is contingent on the strength and efficacy of the police and military in relation to non-state actors (Finucane 2012).

Social capability has to do with affective control of, or authority over, people. This is vitally contingent upon "legitimacy" and "shared identity" (Finucane 2012: 41). These capabilities are mutually reinforcing. For instance, abiding coercive control forecloses the emergence of abusive non-state and private armed groups, just the same way effective control of people would. Conversely, a state's legitimacy boosts its coercive capabilities by leveraging affective hold of the state on the civil population. The reverse is also the case. The phenomenon of SALWs proliferation negates the very essence of state-military effectiveness. Its prevalence in Africa has fundamentally eroded military sovereignty of states, making nonsense of the doctrine of monopoly of violence. The implication of this scenario is that states infested with the pathology of SALWs proliferation are merely states in name, not in fact.

The foregoing point to the fact that African state system is to a large extent functionally challenged. The dysfunctionality of African state system, however, goes beyond the question of security governance wherein SALWs proliferation is implicated. In effect, it affects all facets of governance at all levels. The inability of the government to ensure basic social provisioning has equally created a huge governance deficit that often engenders anti-state/military antipathies. In any case, it suffices to reiterate that the problem of SALWs proliferation in Africa is fundamentally reflective of the dysfunctionality of the state in that context, especially in respect of security and development governance.

Nothing situates the dysfunctionality of African states better than the fragility/stability index. Table 21.6 lists the least stable countries in Africa in descending order based on 2017 data. It is deducible from the table that most of these countries also rank among the worst-performing countries in terms of SALWs proliferation (see Fig. 21.2 and Tables 21.3 and 21.5). The implication of this is that SALWs proliferation is a veritable factor in Africa's state fragility (failure) syndrome. Among these countries are war-torn states where government's capability to assume coercive control has been whittled down by forces of insurrection. Others belong to the apocalyptic axis of doom where SALWs proliferation and state failure has mutually reinforced themselves to produce and reproduce a dynamic of virtual instability.

Conclusion

The military is an indispensable institution of the modern state. It is an established coercive authority by which the territorial integrity of the state is maintained and sustained. Through the instrumentality of the military, the state ensures its survival against the threats of internal insurrection or external aggression.

The military is the custodian of national security. It is, indeed, the last resort in the times of dire national territorial emergency. To make good its strategic role, the military wields authoritative exclusive control over the issue of arms at the instance of the state. It ultimately superintends the arms sector in such a manner that upholds the state's monopoly of the legal use of coercion. This includes the production, circulation, possession, acquisition and use of arms.

The emergence and proliferation of non-state military actors on the global security terrain has questioned the traditional notion of monopolistic military control of arms. Beyond questioning this conventional assumption, the trend implies that individuals and groups other than the military now manufacture, acquire, circulate, wield, use and abuse different kinds of arms, often in asymmetric contention with the military. This underscores the problematique of arms proliferation in the contemporary world.

While the problem of arms proliferation is a global phenomenon, its incidence and prevalence have been so alarming in Africa. As has been argued and illustrated in the course of the chapter, the dysfunctionality of the African state coupled with its gross governance deficits has created multiple ungoverned spaces where criminalities such as SALWs proliferation fester. To mitigate the challenges, therefore, there is a need for a pragmatic statecraft that prioritizes matters of security and sustainability, viz:

i. Transformative state-building and security sector reform: The basic step towards ameliorating the menace of SALWs proliferation in Africa is transformative state-building. This entails reinvigorating the state's capacity and resilience to rule through a conscientious institutional cum procedural adjustments designed to promote the efficiency of governance, especially in the aspects of security and social welfare provisioning. Effective security governance, for its part, requires a pragmatic effort at security sector reform. There is a need to overhaul the national security philosophy and architecture of African states to make them amenable to the realities of the contemporary times. The military formation should be repositioned for more operational efficiency through training and retraining of personnel. The substructure of the military sector should be strengthened via an enabling viable military–industrial complex system that guarantees a high level of technical and logistical resourcing. More importantly, there is a need for the demilitarization and deweaponization of the civil society through a conscious Demobilization, Disarmament and Rehabilitation (DDR) programme, especially in post-conflict situations. Above all, the human security component of security provisioning must be prioritized through people-oriented policies and programmes geared towards empowering the masses.

ii. Optimization of deliverables of governance and development: Ungoverned and undergoverned spaces obtain and prevail because of failure of governance. Therefore African states/governments should strengthen their capacity to govern, especially in relation to conflict management, peacebuilding, democratization, economic development and human security. When governance deficits in these areas are addressed, the state regains its functionality in such a manner that forecloses the mushrooming of exploitable safe havens within its domain.

iii. Devolved security regimen: There is a need for the Nigerian government to strengthen its security capabilities and strategies. The current approach to national security that favours hard-military reconnaissance and combat-operations should be substituted for a model based on intelligence and civil–military collaboration. A mechanism for border/frontier, forestlands and hinterlands security based on strategic civil–military synergy and community volunteering is needed to fill the vacuum of territorial security in the countrysides so as to mitigate the activities of VNSAs.

iv. Evolving regional and subregional security and defense architectures: The prevailing national security architectures in various African states have proven inadequate in dealing with the exigencies of SALWs proliferation and allied criminalities. The increasing transnational dimensions and complications of such occurrences have necessitated an equally transnational framework of security governance. The prospects and challenges of that framework in the context of West Africa have been vigorously interrogated in Volume 42(3) of the flagship journal of Council for the Development of Social Science Research in Africa (CODESRIA) (see for instance Tar and Mustapha 2017). Such a strategy will ensure a functional synergy and solidarity among states in a fashion that makes for collective security.

REFERENCES

Acemoglu, D., Santos, R., & Robinson, J. (2013). The Monopoly of Violence: Evidence from Colombia. *Journal of the European Economic Association, S1,* 5–44.

Adeniyi, A. (2017, March). *The Human Cost of Uncontrolled Arms in Africa: A Cross-National Research on Seven African Countries.* Oxfam Research Reports. https://www-cdn.oxfam.org/s3fs-public/file_attachments/rr-human-cost-uncontrolled-arms-africa-080317-en.pdf. Accessed 20 June 2020.

Ayissi, A., & Sall, I. (Eds.). (2005). *Combating the Proliferation of Small Arms and Light Weapons in West Africa: Handbook for the Training of Armed and Security Forces.* Geneva: United Nations Institute for Disarmament Research.

Boer, J., & Bosetti, L. (2015, July). *The Crime-Conflict "Nexus": State of the Evidence.* London: United Nations University of Conflict Resolution, Occasional Paper 5.

Department of Defence (DoD). (2007). *Ungoverned Areas and Threat from Safe Havens.* Washington, DC: United States Department of Defense.

Finucane, B. (2012). Fictitious States, Effective Control, and the Use of Force Against Non-State Actors. *Berkeley Journal of International Law, 30*(1), 35–93. Available: http://scholarship.berkeley.edu/bjil/vol30/iss1/2. Accessed 23 December 2019.

Gaye, S. (2018a). *Conflicts Between Farmers and Herders Against a Backdrop of Asymmetric Threats in Mali and Burkina Faso.* Dakar: Friedrich Ebert Stiftung.

Gaye, S. (2018b). *Connections Between Jihadists Groups and Smuggling and Illegal Trafficking Rings in the Sahel.* Dakar: Friedrich Ebert Stiftung.

Gofwan, D., Ishaya, J., & Muhammad, D. (2019). Small Arms and Light Weapons Proliferation and Insecurity in Nigeria: Nexus and Implications for National Stability. *IOSR Journal of Humanities and Social Science (IOSR-JHSS), 24*(2), 34–39.

Grip, L. (2017, May). *Small Arms Control in Africa.* Unpublished M.Sc. dissertation, Faculty of Social Sciences, the University Porthania.

Holtom, P., & Pavesi, I. (2017). *Trade Update 2017: Out of the Shadows. A Publication of the Small Arms Survey, with Support from the Department of Foreign Affairs and Trade of Australia.* Graduate Institute of International Development Studies, Geneva.

In On Africa (IOA). (2013). *Africa's Top Most Stable Countries.* https://www.inonafrica.com/2018/02/08/africas-top-5-politically-stable-countries/. Accessed 20 June 2020.

Johnson, R. (1990). *Institutional Violence: Organizational and Psychological Issues in Military Context.* United States Army Research Institute for the Behavioral and Social Sciences, American University.

Keister, J. (2014). The Illusion It Chaos: Why Ungoverned Spaces Aren't Ungoverned and Why That Matters. *Policy Analysis, 777,* 1–24.

Krahmann, E. (2009). *Private Security Companies and the State Monopoly on Violence: A Case of Norm Change?* Frankfurt: Peace Research Institute, Frankfurt.

Malam, B. (2014). Small Arms and Light Weapons Proliferation and Its Implication for West African Regional Security. *International Journal of Humanities and Social Science, 4*(8), 260–269.

Nna, N., Pabon, B., & Nkoro, F. (2012). Arms Proliferation and Conflicts in Africa: The Sudan Experience. *IOSR Journal of Humanities and Social Science (JHSS), 4*(4), 31–39.

Ogu, Michael. (2008, April 30–May 2). *Proliferation of Small Arms and Light Weapons in Africa: Cause or Effect.* Paper presented at the International Political

Science: New Theoretical and Regional Perspectives Conference Organized by the International Political Science Association, Montreal.

Okoli, A. C. (2017a). Understanding the State: A Typological Refresher. *FULafia Journal of Contemporary Political Studies, 1*(1), 206–217.

Okoli, A. C. (2017b). Nigeria: Volunteer Vigilantism and Counter-Insurgency in the North-East. *Conflict Studies Quarterly, 20,* 34–55.

Okoli, A. C. (2017c). *Cows, Cash and Terror: How Cattle Rustling Proceeds fuel Boko Haram Insurgency in Nigeria.* Paper presented at International Policy Dialogue Conference on Money, Security, and Democratic Governance in Africa, Organized by the Council for the Development of Social Research in Africa (CODESRIA) and United Nations Office in West Africa (UNOWAS) on October 19th to 23rd, 2017 at Blu Radisson Hotel, Bamako, Mali.

Okoli, A. C., & Anjide, S. (2015). Of Democratic Backsliding and Neo-praetorianism: Evaluating the Resurgence of Military Intervention in West Africa. *Journal of History and Military Studies, 1*(2), 112–124.

Okoli, A. C., & Atelhe, G. (2018). Libya's Foreign Policy Under Muammar Qadhafi: A Historical and Contextual Overview. *Lafia Journal of History and International Development, 1*(2), 136–151.

Okoli, A. C., & Iortyer, P. (2014). Terrorism and Humanitarian Crisis in Nigeria: Insights from Boko Haram Insurgency. *Global Journal of Human Social Sciences, 14*(1:1.0), 39–50.

Okoli, A. C., & Orinya, S. (2013). Oil Pipeline Vandalism and Nigeria's National Security. *Global Journal of Human Social Sciences, 13*(3:1.0), 37446.

Parliamentary Forum [PF]. (2017). Policy Statement on Illicit Small Arms and Light Weapons and Terrorism. In *Board of the Parliamentary Forum on Small Arms and Light Weapons Meeting on the 23rd of November, 2017.*

Rabasa, A., Boraz, S., Chalk, P., Gragin, K., Karajik, T., Monroney, J., et al. (2007). *Ungoverned Territories: Understanding and Reducing Terrorism Risks.* Santa Monica, CA: RAND Project Air Force.

Roskin, M., Cord, R., Medeiros, J., & Jones, W. (2010). *Political Science: An introduction* (11th ed.). New York: Pearson/Longman.

Schroeder, M. (2013). *Captured and Counted: Illicit Weapons in Mexico and Philippines.* In Small Arms Survey. Small Arms Survey 2013: Everyday Dangers: Cambridge.

Stockholm Peace Research Institute (SIPRI). (2017). "Armaments, Disarmament and International Security" (Summary). SIPRI Yearbook 2017. Stockholm International Peace Research Institute, Stockholm.

Tar, U. A., & Mustapha, M. (2017). The Emerging Architecture of a Regional Security Complex in the Lake Chad Basin. *Africa Development, 42*(3): 99–118.

Taylor, A. (2016). Thoughts on the Nature and Consequences of Ungoverned Spaces. *SAIS Review of International Affairs, 36*(1), 5–15.

Tessieres, S. (2007, March). *Measuring Illicit Arms Flows: Niger.* Briefing Paper, Small Arms Survey, Geneva.

United Nations Development Programme [UNDP]. (2008). *How to Guide the Establishment and Functioning of National Small Arms and Light Weapons Commissions.* Bureau for Crisis Prevention and Recovery, United Nations Development Programme, New York.

United Nations General Assembly (UNGA). (2005). International Instrument to Enable States Identify and Trace, in a Timely and Reliable Manner, Illicit Small Arms and Light Weapons (A/60/88); adopted by the United Nations General Assembly, New York.

United Nations Office on Drug and Crime (NODC). (2013). *International Instrument to Enable States to Identify and Trace, in a Timely and Reliable Manner, Illicit Small Arms and Light Weapons.*

United Nations Organization's Office for Disarmament (UNODA). (2017). *Fact Sheet: Small Arms and Light Weapons.* New York: United Nations Office for Disarmament Affairs.

Varin, C., & Abubakar, D. (Eds.). (2017). *Violent Non-State Actors: Terrorists, Rebels, and Warlords.* London: Palgrave Macmillan.

Weber, M. (1946). Politics as a Vocation. In *From Max to Weber: Essays in Sociology* (H. H. Gerth & C. Wright Mills, Trans.). Oxford: Oxford University Press.

Whelan, T. (2006). Africa's Ungoverned Space. *Nacao Defenca, 114*(3), 61–73.

Al Chukwuma Okoli holds a Ph.D. in Defence and Strategic Studies. He is a Senior Lecturer in Political Science at Federal University of Lafia, Nigeria. He has consulted for UN Women, The Conversation, Centre for Democracy and Development, and National Open University of Nigeria. He is a double laureate of CODESRIA (GI: 2018; HEPI: 2019) as well as a research fellow of IFRA-Nigeria. He specializes in Liberal Political Ecology, Security Studies, and Gender and Development.

CHAPTER 22

Legislation, Institution-Building and the Control of Small Arms and Light Weapons in Africa

Shuaibu A. Danwanka

Introduction

The mounting insecurity in Africa is a direct consequence of proliferation of SALWs. An issue that is not amenable to agreement among scholars is whether possession of SALWs is an immediate or remote cause of insecurity. However, there is a consensus that it expedites militancy, insurgency and various forms of unrest with the attendant negative consequences, including loss of lives and property (Oguche 2013). Highlighting the challenges of SALWs in Africa, a former Secretary General of the United Nations (UN), in his popular 2000 Millennium Report to the UN General Assembly, noted that:

> The death toll from small arms dwarfs that of all other weapons systems—and in most years greatly exceeds the toll of the atomic bombs that devastated Hiroshima and Nagasaki. In terms of the carnage they cause, small arms, indeed, could well be described as "weapons of mass destruction" ... Small arms proliferation is not merely a security issue; it is also an issue of human rights and of development. The proliferation of small arms sustains and exacerbates armed conflicts. It endangers peacekeepers and humanitarian workers. It undermines respect for international humanitarian law. It threatens legitimate but weak governments, and it benefits terrorists as well as the perpetrators of organised crime. (Anan 2000: 52–53)

S. A. Danwanka (✉)
National Institute for Legislative and Democratic Studies, Abuja, Nigeria

© The Author(s), under exclusive license to Springer Nature Switzerland AG 2021
U. A. Tar and C. P. Onwurah (eds.), *The Palgrave Handbook of Small Arms and Conflicts in Africa*,
https://doi.org/10.1007/978-3-030-62183-4_22

There is a direct link between the law (or lack of it) and the proliferation of small arms in Africa. The illegal and indiscriminate proliferation of SALWs is presently one of the main security challenges confronting Africa and indeed the entire world (Uwa and Anthony 2015). The availability and trafficking of these weapons fuel and strengthen political instability, communal clashes (e.g. Fulani/herdsmen clashes), terrorism, insurgency, kidnapping, militancy and other forms of crime. It is also detrimental not only to national security but also to achieving sustainable development. Proliferation denotes a rapid increase in the number or amount of something, growth, multiplication, spread, escalation, expansion or excessive spread. Proliferation when used within the context of SALW means the rapid increase, multiplication or spread of biochemical, nuclear and other weapons of mass destruction to countries not initially involved in developing them (Araromi et al. 2017). Firearms as seen earlier in the chapter cover a wide range of weapons which are basically utilized for warfare and defence either acquired for legal or illegal purposes by state and non-state actors for security, local and private reasons. These reasons could be for safety, hunting, national security, self-defence, crime, etc (ibid.). However, for the purpose of this chapter, it used in the light of illegal multiplication of SALWs to perpetuate crime and other vices.

The existence of wide and porous borders with several unauthorized routes has made it almost impossible and difficult for Security personnel at border checkpoints to effectively intercept such arms trafficking. A number of Security agencies lack the requisite skills and facilities to adequately monitor and clamp down the operations of arms dealers. Also, corruption and bribery among security personnel drives illegal SALW trade. The lack of a comprehensive legal framework has also contributed to and escalated the ongoing trend (Osoba and Ohene-Asare 2014). This is because the proliferation of illegal arms will continue to thrive in the absence of proactive laws to put in place checks against illegal production and trafficking of arms and similarly ensure effective investigation and prosecution of such heinous acts. The role of fully equipped and disciplined security personnel can also not be over-emphasized.

Therefore, this chapter addresses the increasing and alarming proliferation of SALWs in Nigeria and the underlying threat it poses to national security and sustainable development. The chapter argues that in order to effectively reduce proliferation of arms, there is a need to have proactive laws and policies such as the whistle-blowing policy on corruption. The chapter recommends an extension of the policy in dealing with proliferation of SALW as has been done in corruption, trafficking in persons and kidnapping in some States. Effective policing by security agencies will also go a long way in the fight against proliferation of arms. The chapter shall thus look at key terms such as proliferation and small arms and light weapons. It will also examine the historical development of SALWs in Nigeria, the increasing trend of proliferation of SALWs: causes and implications for Nigeria, existing legal framework and policies on SALWs in Nigeria and thereafter conclude with recommendations which are imperative in addressing, preventing, combating and exterminating the proliferation of SALWs.

Conceptual Clarification of Terms

Small Arms and Light Weapons (SALWs)—A Legal Perspective

There is no universally accepted meaning of SALWs. Any reference to SALWs basically refers to basic infantry weapons, such as firearms that an individual could carry and is generally restricted to revolvers, pistols, submachine guns, shotguns, carbines, assault rifles, rifle squad automatic weapons, light machine guns, general purpose machine gun, medium machine guns and hand grenades (Okeke and Oji 2014). Depending on the context in which it is used, it could also include heavy machine guns, as well as smaller mortars, recoilless rifles and some rocket launchers (Okeke and Oji 2014). Furthermore, the terms, SALWs are sometimes used interchangeably with weapons, guns, arms, ammunitions' and firearms. For instance, Article 3 of the UN Illicit Firearms Protocol[1] defines firearms to include 'any portable barreled weapon that expels, is designed to expel or may readily be converted to expel a shot, bullet or projectile by the action of an explosive antique firearms or their replicas. Antique firearms and their replica shall be defined in accordance with domestic law'.

From the foregoing, it can be stated unequivocally that small arms are firearms which are manufactured to expel shots or could easily be transformed for that particular purpose. According to the ECOWAS Convention on Small Arms and Light Weapons, their Ammunition and other Related Materials, 2006,[2] Small arms is defined as arms destined for personal use and include: firearms and other destructive arms or devices such as an exploding bomb, an incendiary bomb or a gas bomb, a grenade, a rocket launcher, a missile, a missile system or a mine; revolvers and pistols with automatic loading; rifles and carbines; machine guns; and assault rifles.

Section 2 of the Firearms Act Cap F28, LFN 2004 which is the Interpretation section of the Act also incorporates the meaning of Firearm. It provides thus: 'firearms means any lethal weapon of any description from which any shot, bullet or other missile can be discharged, and includes a prohibited firearm, a personal firearm and a muzzle-loading firearm of any of the categories referred to in Parts I, II and III respectively of the Schedule hereto, and any component part of any such firearm'. The Act goes further to define ammunition in the same section as any firearm and any component of any such ammunition, but does not include gun powder or trade powder not intended or used as such a component part.

The aforementioned definition was reproduced in the case of *Olatunji v State*, [2003] 14 NWLR (Pt. 839) 138 at pp. 165–166 where the appellant was charged with the unlawful possession of a hand grenade. Thus, SALWs include any weapon that can be handled and, manipulated by one or two persons. 'Light weapons' consist of heavy machine guns, mortars of up to 100mm, and portable anti-craft/aircraft systems, while 'small arms' connotes a sub-category of SALWs consisting of automatic/semi-automatic weapons of up to 20mm, for instance, self-loading pistols, revolvers, carbines, rifles and machine guns. Ammunition and explosives are also listed under this term (Thom-Otuya 2009).[3]

BACKGROUND: PROLIFERATION OF SALWS IN NIGERIA—AFRICA'S WORSE CASE SCENARIO?

Nigeria presents a disturbing case of SALWs proliferation in Africa. The United Nations, for instance, recently raised alarm over the proliferation of illegal SALWs in Nigeria which is estimated at over 350 million. 70% of estimated 500 million of such trafficked weapons in West Africa is allegedly stored in Nigeria according to the Organisation (*Gun Policy* 2016). The late President Musa Yar'Adua embarked on policies aimed at suppressing militancy. One of those policies that received wide commendation was the Presidential Amnesty Programme that suppressed militancy and saved oil exploration activities in the Niger Delta- the mainstay of the country's economy. It was however, disheartening that the surrendering exercise witnessed mopping up of unimaginable number of SALWs; this being a condition precedent for the grant of presidential amnesty (Eno-Abasi and Sulaimon 2017).

Discovery of SALWs continued in October 2016 when 22, 430 militants, agitators, criminals, cultists, etc., embraced the amnesty offer of Rivers State government, leading to the surrender of about 1000 firearms, 7661 rounds of ammunition and 147 explosives. Nevertheless, many continue to be incredulous because of the fact that there is abundance of SALSs for surrender to the appropriate authorities during each amnesty programme. This raises a serious concern about the SALWs in the hands of non-state actors such as the Boko Haram fighters, Fulani herdsmen, kidnappers, etc. The inevitable question is how unlicenced and authorized users lay hands on SALWs in addition to the complicit role of security personnel at the country's borders and ports, resulting in the proliferation of illegal SALWs in the country (Eno-Abasi and Sulaimon 2017). Small arms basically first came into use towards the end of the fourteenth century. Hitherto, what existed were merely handful cannons, fired by placing a lighted match at the touch hole. A stock was added much later- the match lock and the first real handgun (Okeke and Oji 2014).

Non-state actors have been in the act of possession of guns in Nigeria from the pre-colonial era, thereby removing such possession from the realm of a new phenomenon. They were introduced by the Europeans before colonialism to carry out legal and illegal trade of persons (slave) in Africa. Afterwards, guns, ammunition, weapons and other arms were utilized by Europeans to actualize their imperial desires when they conquered and forced Africans into colonialism. The gunboat diplomacy was readily used by the British to coerce

African chiefs into entering several treaties with them. The West African Frontier Force (WAFF) was set up and used by the British to fight the British-Aro War of (1901–1902), and suppress other acts of resistance in Nigeria, West Africa and Africa generally. These antique weapons or arms especially locally made guns and gun powder were subsequently utilized by the locals for hunting purposes and traditional festivities (Araromi et al. 2017). They soon became signs of strength and power, and were exhibited at funerals, burials, ceremonies and customary festivals, etc., among the locals. Some of these practices still exist until date.

In contemporary times, guns and other types of SALWs have undergone some transformation as regards functionality, lethality, sophistication, ubiquity and motive behind ownership. They are now weapons used to perpetuate all forms of crime as opposed to their previous perception as just ornaments of prestige, or utilized solely for hunting and other mundane missions. The 1959 Firearms Act was apparently passed to control the alarming rate of arms proliferation in Nigeria towards independence. The Nigerian police records after the civil war revealed a disturbing upsurge in occurrences of violent misconducts linked with SALWs as opposed to the era before the war (Araromi et al. 2017). The inability of the Nigerian government to implement a robust disarmament and arms destruction programme after the civil war (1967–1970) intensified the proliferation of guns and illegal arms trafficking. It has however been observed that there were growing concerns regarding the proliferation of arms which dates back to the period before the civil war and the passage of the Firearms Act but become more intensified after the civil war (Okoro 2014). Also, proliferation of SALWs has been associated with returnee peace-keeping forces from across the world—but this matter is under-reported. Guns from returnee soldiers from peace-keeping missions and unrecorded rifles from the collapsed strike force under the command of Al-Mustapha during General Sani Abacha's military administration were reabsorbed into the society (Araromi et al. 2017).

On the overall, evidence abounds of the proliferation of SALWs in Nigeria. As far back as 2002, the amount of SALWs in Nigeria was projected by several reports and studies at approximately 1 and 3 million as well as arms in lawful possession of the military, the police and those that were in the hands of members of the public. 80% of SALWs in civilian possession were illicitly acquired given the stringent regulations (Okeke 2014). At the National Consultation on Physical Security and Stockpile Management which was organized under the auspices of the United Nations Regional Centre for Peace and Disarmament and the Presidential Committee on Small Arms and Light Weapons (PRESCOM) in 2016, it was noted that 350 million out of 500 million SALWs in West Africa are domiciled in Nigeria. A considerable amount of these arms are not only unlawfully possessed but are also acquired to carry out criminal activities (Araromi et al. 2017).

The Increasing Trend of Proliferation of SALWs in Nigeria

Generally, the proliferation of small arms and light weapons around the world and particularly in Africa has over time developed at an alarming rate which has put the security and stability of the entire African continent in jeopardy. SALWs have become useful instruments in the hands of terrorist groups, vicious groups and other non-state actors to wreak havoc on the state and more significantly on citizens whom the state ordinarily owe a duty to protect by reducing the ability to fulfil its security mandate. The United Nations Security Council in 2002 opined that:

> the destabilizing accumulation and uncontrolled spread of small arms and light weapons in many regions of the world increases the intensity and duration of armed conflict, undermines the sustainability of peace agreements, impedes the success of peace building, frustrates efforts aimed at the prevention of armed conflict, hinders considerably the provision of humanitarian assistance and compromises the effectiveness of the Security Council discharging its primary responsibility for the maintenance of international peace and security.[4]

Proliferation of SALWs has been one issue that has formed part of the international agenda since 1998 when the journey to the Fourth Republic began. Across the world, SALWs has become a security challenge that is threatening the existence of emerging nations especially in Africa—a phenomenon that is undermining their peace and development. The horrid intrastate wars that destroyed several developing countries in the 1990s were fought mainly with small arms and light weapons. For instance, in Rwanda's genocide, approximately a million people were killed in less than a month with machetes and AK-47 guns. Also in Liberia where the civil war lasted for more than a decade, over 250,000 people were killed with small arms and light weapons which also displaced nearly half of the population (Schroeder and Stohl 2006). Nigeria is not also left out as the activities of the infamous Boko Haram sect, Fulani herders-farmers conflicts and general criminality have led to the death, destruction of property and internal displacement of so many Nigerians throughout the country.

Kofi Anan, the former UN Secretary General in his 2000 Millennium Report to the United Nations (UN) General Assembly, described the proliferation of SALWs thus:

> The death toll from small arms dwarfs that of all other weapons systems—and in most years greatly exceeds the toll of the atomic bombs that devastated Hiroshima and Nagasaki. In terms of the carnage they cause, small arms, indeed, could well be described as "weapons of mass destruction" ... Small arms proliferation is not merely security issue; it is also an issue of human rights and of development. The proliferation of small arms sustains and exacerbates armed conflicts. It endangers peacekeepers and humanitarian workers. It undermines

respect for international humanitarian law. It threatens legitimate but weak governments and benefits terrorists as well as the perpetrators of organised crime. (Okoro 2014)

The foregoing problems have become manifest in many conflicts in Africa, and they have continued in spite of concerted efforts at the international and regional level to assuage it, culminating in the loss of many lives and destruction of properties in many African States. These existing security challenges, as well as small arms proliferation, and their effects stagnates the development of the continent.

Since 1999, following the restoration of democracy after several decades of continuous military rule (1966–1979 and 1984–1999), Nigeria has particularly been overwhelmed with violent conflicts as well as inter-communal and intra-communal, ethnic conflicts, inter-regional tensions, religious riots, political conflicts, e.g. agitations from the Indigenous people of Biafra (IPOB), Niger Delta Avengers and Movement for the Emancipation of Niger Delta (MEND). Recently, the activities of the Boko Haram Sect in the Northeast, Fulani herdsmen/farmers conflict and Northwestern parts of the country, as well as armed robbery, kidnapping and hostage-taking have become more endemic. Nigeria has become a huge market for local, regional and international arms dealers and syndicates, a primary destination of SALW flows and the centre of illegal trafficking (Yahaya 2020). The Government's inability to provide adequate security has culminated in people resorting to self-help by taking up arms and consequently driving the largest proliferation and use of SALW (Osoba and Ohene-Asare 2014). Proliferation and misuse of SALWs no doubt threatens personal security, weakens good governance, contributes to human rights violations and undermines social justice, development and peace all over the world. SALWs have become the main source of the breach of security and violation of human rights entrenched in International, regional Instruments, as well as the Constitutions of various States. For instance, killing people with firearms or SALWs obviously deprives them of their right to life whether at the hands of State actors or via extra-judicial killings or use of excessive force, or through criminals, vigilantes or rioters (Okoro 2014). The killings in Niger Delta as a result of the activities of the Niger Delta Avengers, MEND, in the North East through the activities of the Boko Haram Sect, Fulani herdsmen/farmers conflicts, etc., are all typical illustrations of the failure of the State to protect its citizenry in contravention of the provisions of section 14(2) of the 1999 Constitution which provides that the security and welfare of the people shall be the primary responsibility of government.

The proliferation and misuse of SALWs has some connection with the prevailing intra-state armed conflicts and violence and could thus be regarded as the immediate cause of conflicts. As observed in the forward to the Report of the Panel of Experts, 'while not themselves causing the conflicts in which they are used, the proliferation of small arms and light weapons affects the intensity and duration of violence and encourages militancy rather than a peaceful resolution of unsettled differences'. This undoubtedly creates a rancorous circle where insecurity leads to an increased demand for arms by both State and non-state actors (Okoro 2014).

SALWs raise serious concerns in conflict situations, the most obvious being the high death toll. This comprises deaths directly caused by the use of SALWs and indirect causes of armed conflict resulting in diseases, malnutrition, starvation and displacement. There are also socio-economic problems like poverty, trauma and health care crisis. The devastating effect of SALWs is also seen in the lives of people in situations of non-conflict (Okoro 2014). Between June 2006 and September 2015, an overall 4268 deaths occurred in 1682 armed robbery incidents nationwide (*Nigeria Watch* Database).

Crisis in public sector governance—which has weakened the institutional base for arms control—contributes significantly to the rise of prevailing conditions for the proliferation of SALWs in Nigeria. Corruption, uneven distribution of resources, violence and unemployment provides a fertile ground for criminal activities that threatens the peace, security and economic development to thrive. These factors create a situation where possession of arms becomes vital and is also perceived as a source of empowerment and means of livelihood. Several reports of lost, stolen and diverted small arms and light weapons are all pointers to the continued existence of weak export regulations/controls, poor stockpile security practices and porous borders (Abdul'aziz 2011; Oji 2011). This is even more disheartening where these arms are shipped to war zones and political dictators. For instance, on 11 September 2017, the Operatives of the Tin-Can Island Command of the Nigeria Customs Service, NIS recently intercepted a syndicate that specializes in smuggling weapons into the country. In the course of the raid, 1100 pump action riffles loaded in a 20 foot container was discovered (Usman and Oritse 2017). This brings to question how these weapons found their way into Nigeria in the first place and what they were intended for. It would seem that poor licencing regimes for small arms, smuggling of contraband through Nigeria's porous borders, corrupt tendencies of security operatives and regulatory agencies who can be compromised by criminal gangs to allow shipment of dangerous materials into the country, as well as weak enforcement framework for legislation have all conspired to create a fertile ground for the proliferation of SALWs in Nigeria. In particular, the ineffective management of Nigerian borders and the stockpile mismanagement by security agencies whereupon weapons intended for government are hired out or sold to criminals and other non-state actors needs to be seriously looked into in order to address this misnomer.

Perhaps, the worst factor in the proliferation of SALWs is weak governance infrastructure and the crisis of leadership. In Nigeria and some other parts of Africa, politicians subvert governance protocols, undermine security agencies, and resort to violence and other unconventional means to acquire or retain power and amass wealth and these nefarious acts are carried out with SALWs. In pursuing their political interests, armed groups, governments and political leaders are all involved one way or the other in the creation and arming of non-state actors (Osoba and Ohene-Asare 2014). The availability of SALWs may possibly prolong fighting, increase human and material loses, diminish the willingness of warring parties to find a middle ground or solutions to their differences, thwart the efforts of international and non-governmental organizations from engaging in conflict prevention, management and resolution, may cause severe challenges for the nations within the conflict milieu, and probably activate regional violence, and seriously undermine global security.

MULTILATERAL LEGAL AND INSTITUTIONAL FRAMEWORK ON SALWs

The International community has made concerted efforts, mapped out strategies geared towards addressing the issue of SALWs which are implemented both at the international, regional and national levels. They have also in addition articulated detailed guidelines and rules to assist nation states to develop effective legal framework to address the phenomenon of SALWs. Although these Instruments expressing these standards lack legal impetus, there are still persuasive as States are obliged to respect them. The obligations imposed by these international laws with regard to SALWs involve developing proactive laws for combating SALWs and also ensuring effective enforcement.

It is important to point out that Nigeria has ratified some of these international and regional instruments regulating the proliferation of SALWs and as such is morally or legally bound by them. Because of the humanitarian issues connected with SALWs, it therefore becomes a matter of international interest for Nigeria to tackle the issue of SALW proliferation and misuse. The various laws, policies and regulations on SALWs shall now be examined hereunder and this will be done in no particular order.

The United Nations Arms Trade Treaty

The United Nations Arms Trade Treaty to which Nigeria is also a state party is the first global, legally binding instrument to regulate the transfer of conventional arms. It was adopted by the United Nations General Assembly on 2 April 2013 and entered into force on 24 December 2014. The Treaty outlines a robust scope which includes the types of conventional arms and transfers it covers; prohibition on the transfers of these conventional arms in certain circumstances and the requirement on states parties to establish a formal control regime to regulate transfers at the national level as well as the requirement on state parties to report on the exports and imports that take place or that was authorized.

The International Instrument to Enable States to Identify and Trace Illicit Small Arms and Light Weapons

This Instrument was adopted in recognition of tracing which is crucial to preventing, combating and eradicating illegal SALWs. Articles 1 and 2 stipulate the purpose of the Instrument. It provides that the objective of the Instrument is to enable States to identify and trace, in a timely and reliable manner, illicit small arms and light weapons which is intended to help States establish a mechanism to facilitate the identification and tracing of illicit SALWs. Also, this Instrument seeks to promote and facilitate international cooperation and assistance in marking and tracing and to enhance and complement the effectiveness of existing bilateral, regional and international agreements to prevent, combat and eradicate the illicit trade in small arms and light weapons in all its aspects. Article 24 obliges state parties in accordance with their constitutional process to put in place laws, (where there are none) regulations and administrative procedures needed to ensure the effective implementation of the Instrument.

UN Protocol Against the Illicit Manufacturing of and Trafficking in Firearms

The Protocol which was adopted in 2001 and came into force on 3 July 2005 is a supplementary Protocol to the United Nations Convention against Transnational Organized Crime, 2000. Article 4 stipulates that the Protocol shall apply to the prevention of illicit manufacturing of and trafficking in firearms and ammunition as well the investigation and prosecution of offences specified in Article 5. Nigeria being a party to the Protocol is committed to preventing and combating the illegal trafficking in firearms and also obliged to put in place effective control, security and disposal mechanisms to prevent theft, diversion into illegal circles, adopting a system of licencing to guarantee effective manufacturing, trafficking, marking, record and tracing of firearms within the confines of the Law.

The United Nations Programme of Action on Small Arms and Light Weapons (UNPOA), 2001

The UNPoA was adopted by all UN member states in 2001. It is one of the earliest international instruments on SALWs. It provides a framework to counter illicit trade in SALWs. Since its adoption, the UN has worked towards supporting its enforcement at national, regional and international levels. As stated in its Preamble, the UNPoA seeks to address the uncontrolled spread of SALW, which have 'a wide range of humanitarian and socio-economic consequences and poses a serious threat to peace, reconciliation, safety, security, stability and sustainable development'. Article II (2) enjoins nation states to put in place 'adequate laws, regulations and administrative procedures to exercise effective control ...over the export, import and transit of small arms' (Okoro 2014). It has however been observed that the Instrument does not specifically stipulate what constitutes 'adequate laws' or 'effective control' of SALWs. It is also not legally binding as it is merely persuasive or a moral obligation on nation states. It nevertheless provides an important international standard for evaluating the adequacy or otherwise of any national regulatory framework for SALWs.

The ECOWAS Moratorium

The Moratorium which was signed on 31 October 1998 was the first initiative or attempt at the sub-regional level to combat the proliferation of SALWs. Its adoption was as a result of the devastating effect of SALWs proliferation in the sub-region and the threat to peace and security of the sub-region. Accordingly, the focus of the Moratorium was to solicit the assistance of the Organistion of African Unity (now African Union), the United Nations and the international community in implementing the Programme for Coordination and Assistance for Security and Development (PCASED). Consequently, it directed the Executive Secretary to, in collaboration with PCASED, convene a meeting of Ministers of Foreign Affairs to assess and evaluate the moratorium at the end of the initial three-year period.

The ECOWAS Protocol Relating to the Mechanism for Conflict Prevention, Management and Resolution, Peace-Keeping and Security

The Protocol which was adopted in Lome (Togo) on 10 December 1999 is aimed at assisting the regional body to ensure peace and security within the West African sub-region. The Protocol in Articles 50 and 51 underscores the responsibilities of ECOWAS in controlling small arms and light weapons to maintain sub-regional security. They include establishing effective measures to control the importation, exportation, manufacture as well as eradicating the flow of small arms, registering and controlling the movement and use of legitimate arms stock, detecting, collecting and destroying all illicit weapons and also encouraging member states to collect and destroy all surplus weapons. Furthermore, under the Protocol, ECOWAS is also expected to take all the necessary measures towards combating illicit trafficking and circulation of small arms. These measures include developing a culture of peace, training for military, security and police forces, enhancing weapons control at border posts, establishing a database and regional arms register, collecting and destroying surplus illegal weapons, facilitating dialogue with producers and suppliers, reviewing and harmonizing national laws and administrative procedures.

The Bamako Declaration, 2000

In 1998, the Economic Community of West African States (ECOWAS) of which Nigeria is a party State approved a moratorium on the manufacture, importation and exportation of small arms to the sub-region. This move by a regional organization was exceptional and consequently propelled the African Union (AU) to adopt a common African position on the proliferation of small arms. This was done in December 2000 and the Declaration is popularly known as the Bamako Declaration, 2000 (Araromi et al. 2017). Under the Declaration, States are enjoined to put in place specific laws with definite structures and machinery to handle the issue of SALWs. It also encourages them to boost the capacity of their national law enforcement mechanisms and security outfits and personnel.

The ECOWAS Convention on Small Arms and Light Weapons, Their Ammunition and Other Related Materials

The ECOWAS Convention (a regional instrument) which was adopted on 14 June 2006 is a legally binding Instrument regulating the manufacture, trade, possession and disposal of small arms and light weapons, firearms, ammunition as well as landmines, bombs and missile systems. It builds on an earlier 1998 Moratorium on the importation, Exportation, and Manufacture of SALWs in West Africa. In its preamble, the Convention makes reference to a number of Instruments, specifically the ECOWAS Protocol Relating to the Mechanism for Conflict Prevention, Management and Resolution, Peace-Keeping and Security that was adopted in Lome on 10 December 1999. The Convention also refers to the Wassenaar Arrangement which calls for cooperation from arms producers in implementing the Convention. The Convention similarly institutionalizes the National Commission to synchronize the fight against the proliferation of illegal SALWs at the national level. The Convention covers small arms and light weapons on the basis of the 1997 UN Panel of Governmental Experts definition, but adds firearms in the category on small arms, as well as 'other destructive arms or devices such as an exploding bomb, an incendiary bomb or a gas bomb, a grenade, a rocket launcher, a missile, a missile system or landmine' (Art. 1[2]). In addition, it covers ammunition (Art. 1[3]) and 'other related materials', defined as components, parts or spare parts and chemical substances (Art. 1[4]).

The Convention prohibits arms transfers generally, and bans transfers of weapons to non-state actors not explicitly authorized. However, exemptions can be granted for legitimate national defence and security needs, and participation in peace support operations (Art. 4[1]), and such exemptions are required to be requested from the ECOWAS Executive Security, and will be refused under certain circumstances, which are if not all states directly concerned by the transfer have authorized it; if the transfer would violate principles of international law; if the weapons would be used to violate international humanitarian law or worsen the internal situation of the country of final destination; if they would be used in violent crime, unduly divert human and economic resources, or involve corrupt practices; or if they are likely to be diverted (Art. 6).

Under the Convention, member states are to establish computerized national registers and databases of firearms, combining information on firearms, their owners and any international transfers (Art. 9) and control the activities of weapons manufacturers, who must be listed and registered, and the information shared with ECOWAS. The Convention lays down conditions under which a request for manufacture of small arms and light weapons will be denied, such as when information related to marking has not been shared A database is also to be established by ECOWAS at sub-regional level. Weapons and ammunition must be marked at the point of manufacture, and member states must exchange information on manufacturers and marking systems.

Under the Convention, possession, use and sale of light weapons by civilians must be prohibited, while possession, use and sale of small arms is to be regulated (Art. 14). In addition, member states can impose a limit on the number of weapons covered by a licence, and impose a delay of 21 days before authorization is granted (Art. 14[5]). Weapons in the hands of individuals and dealers must be safely stored. Article 14(5) provides that licences must have an expiry date and must be reviewed periodically. In ensuring full compliance, Article 21 requires member states to review their legislation for compliance with the Convention.

It will appear from the foregoing that what all the International and Regional Instruments examined—to which Nigeria is a state party—have certain features in common: for instance, that they all enjoin state parties to put in place national laws and an effective enforcement machinery to fight proliferation of small arms and light weapons. The following sections deal with municipal legislation and institution-building for on SALWs in Nigeria. It should be stressed, however, that Nigeria has not taken elaborate measure in enacting any proactive law and implementing any action plan/policy on SALWs. Rather it has recycled old laws to serve modern realities.

MUNICIPAL INSTRUMENTS ON SALWS IN NIGERIA

Alongside the international instruments, local instruments have been promulgated in Nigeria granting the state sweeping powers to control the proliferation and abuse of SALWs in the country. These instruments are contained in the Laws of the Federation of Nigeria (LFN) promulgated in 2004.

The Firearms Act, Cap F8 LFN 2004

The Firearms Act which was enacted in 1959 is the principal national law regulating SALWs. It prohibits illegal possession, transfer, manufacture, assembly, repair, shortening and trading as well as import and export of firearms as contained in Sections 3, 4, 5, 8, 9, 17, 18, 22 and 26 of the Act. The Act prescribes punishment for the said offences under section 27 of the Act. With respect to section 3 which prohibits possession of firearms, section 17 which prohibits importation and exportation of firearms and ammunition other than through prescribed ports, section 18 which is still on importation and exportation and section 22 which prohibits the manufacture, assembly or repair of firearms, a minimum of ten years is prescribed as sentence. While regarding sections 4 & 8 on restriction of possession of personal and certain firearms, section 9 (on any dealing in arms or ammunition), section 19 (on importation of personal firearms) and section 26, the term of imprisonment is for a period not exceeding five years. For other offences under the Act, the punishment is a paltry sum of one thousand naira as fine or imprisonment for a term of two years or both.

It is worthy of note that the Firearms Act is an outdated law which was enacted in 1959 (with no substantive amendment to it since then) can no longer deal with the current realities on SALWs given the light penalties prescribed under the Act for dealing in arms and ammunition. Enacting a new law/policy to adequately tackle or reduce incidences of theft, loss, diversion, importation/exportation of SALWs has thus become imperative. The Firearms Regulations is a complementary regulation made pursuant to section 32 of the Firearms Act. It provides among other things for the duration and renewal of licences (section 3), marking and stamping of firearms (sections 7 and 42) revocation of licence (section 9), application for registration as a dealer (section 12), procedure for the grant of the relevant licences, sale and transfer of weapons by a registered dealer, etc. Section 27 outlaws acts violating certain provisions of the Regulations and consequently provide penalties.

The Criminal Code Act, Cap C38 LFN 2004

The Criminal Code is the extant substantive law on criminal law in Nigeria. Even though the term 'small arms and light weapons' cannot be found in the Code, it however defines 'firearms' which is not any different from the definition of firearms in the Firearms Act. It also contains some penalties for unlawful possession of arms. Under section 428, the punishment for unlawful possession of arms belonging to the Nigerian armed forces is a fine of 40 naira (less than half of $1US) and also payment of double the value of all or any of the several articles in the person's possession. It has been argued that this weakens any reasonable attempt or effort towards fighting the plague of proliferation of SALWs (Okoli 2014) given the penalty which is not commensurate with the offence. The Penal Code, which has the same effect as the Criminal Code, is operational in Northern Nigeria. In view of its similar content with the Criminal Code, no further discussion is required of it here.

The Robbery and Firearms (Special Provisions) Act, Cap R11 LFN 2004

The Act similarly bothers on firearms possession and provides punishment for gun-related offences. Illegal possession of firearms under the Act attracts a fine of N20, 000 or a minimum of ten years imprisonment, or both. The Act also prescribes a death penalty by hanging or firing squad as punishment for armed robberies, and life imprisonment for attempted robbery which involves the use of firearms.

The Police Act, Cap P19 LFN 2004

The Act provides for the organization, discipline, powers and duties of the police. Section 4 of the Act provides for employment of the police the prevention and detection of crime, the apprehension of offenders, the preservation of law and order, the protection of life and property and the due enforcement of all laws and regulations with which they are directly charged. Furthermore, section 23 empowers any police officer may conduct in person all prosecutions before any court whether or not the information or complaint is laid in his name. In addition to the above powers, section 24 (1) of the Act empowers any police officer to arrest without warrant any person whom he finds committing any felony, misdemeanour or simple offence, or whom he reasonably suspects of having committed or of being about to commit any felony, misdemeanour or breach of the peace; (b) any person whom any other person charges with having committed a felony or misdemeanour; any person whom any other person- (i) suspects of having committed a felony or misdemeanour; or (ii) charges with having committed a simple offence, if such other person is willing to accompany the police officer to the police station and to enter into a recognizance to prosecute such charge.

Similarly, under section 28 (1), a superior police officer may by authority under his hand authorize any police officer to enter any house, shop, warehouse or other premises in search of stolen property, and search therein and seize and secure any property he may believe to have been stolen, in the same manner as he would be authorized to do if he had a search warrant, and the property seized, if any, corresponded to the property described in such search warrant. The Act makes robust provisions, empowering the police to combat illegal use of arms and other general crimes in Nigeria.

Defence Industries Corporation of Nigeria Act, Cap D4 LFN 2004

This Act establishes a Corporation to operate, maintain and control factories for the manufacture, storage and disposal of ordnance and material capable of being used by the Armed Forces. Under section Every ordnance factory under the control of the Corporation shall, for the purposes of the Firearms Act, be deemed to have been recognized as a public armoury without further authority than this Act; but firearms and ammunition therein may be held by the Corporation for such period as it thinks fit, anything in the Firearms Act to the contrary notwithstanding. Under section 9(1) of the Act, the provisions of the Firearms Act shall be construed to preclude the importation by the Corporation of any firearm as therein defined or ammunition, or the manufacture, assembly, repair or disposal of any such firearm or ammunition in an ordnance factory.

Small Arms Bill

Apart from the above, a bill to provide for the establishment of the National Commission against the Proliferation of Small Arms and Light Weapons, is currently before the National Assembly. The bill, which is sponsored by Hon. Mohammed Monguno, is seeking to establish a Commission to be principally responsible for the collection, storage, destruction, management and stockpiling of small arms and light weapons; registration of arms for peace operations, and control as well as manufacture of small arms and light weapons. The Bill, among others, provides that, the National Commission shall collect: small arms, which are surplus to the national needs or have become obsolete, seized weapons, unmarked light weapons, illicitly held light weapons, small arms collected in the implementation of peace accords or programmes for the voluntary handing in of weapons.

In summary, the key import of the foregoing national framework of laws examined is that Nigeria's key statutes on firearms are flexible enough to cover the types of weapons envisaged as SALWs. They are notwithstanding insufficient in terms of scope, application and penalties/fines for dealing with the present day menace of proliferation of SALWs. They also fall below the accepted International standards for combating proliferation of illegal arms, implementation of the provisions is inhibited by corrupt practices and ill-equipped institutional/enforcement machinery as shown by the low success rate in the prosecution of persons caught with illegal weapons. The laws do not similarly reflect some of the important measures considered germane by the International/Regional community in the fight against unlawful arms proliferation (Okoro 2014).

National Institutional Mechanisms on the Control of SALWs

The national institutional framework for implementing these legislations are National Committee on the Control of Small Arms and Light Weapons (NATCOM), the Police, the Presidential Committee on Small Arms and Light Weapons (PRESCOM) and the Courts for the prosecution of offenders. The National Committee, which was inaugurated in 2001, is composed of representatives of the Ministries of Defence, Internal Affairs and Integration and Cooperation in Africa (MICA), Defence Industries Corporation of Nigeria (DICON), the National Orientation Agency, the Immigration Service, the Police, the State Security Services and the National Drug Law Enforcement Agency, among others. The composition of the Committee is flawed due to non-representation of the Ministry of Justice and the Ministry of Foreign Affairs on it. The mandate of the Committee includes controlling the import and manufacturing of all SALWs; registering and controlling the movement and using of legitimate arms stock; detecting and destroying all illicit and surplus weapons; and permitting exemptions to the Moratorium only in accordance with strict criteria. The Committee has established a 'Framework for implementing the ECOWAS Moratorium. Similarly, the mandate of the PRESCOM is to stop illegal circulation of SALWs; create a Nigeria where everyone would understand the impact of SALW abuse; arrange for safe disposal of excess stockpiles of Small Arms and Light Weapons under state control; and combat illicit accumulation and trafficking of SALW and their ammunition. It fulfills its mandate through surveillance, training and advocacy.

The Office of the National Security Adviser exercises significant control over SALWs in Nigeria. It controls the importation of high calibre weapons and armoured cars including those to be used by private individuals and corporate entities. It issues End-User Certificate for importation of controlled items and products into Nigeria. End-User Certificate is an undertaking by a purchaser/importer that any of the controlled items/products covered by the process transferred from the exporting country is for the sole and lawful use within Nigeria, and that the controlled items/products are not destined for transfer or re-export to any other entity or country, without the prior written consent of the issuing authority, the Office of the National Security Adviser.

The Police are the Central agency responsible for enforcing the regulatory framework for SALWs by issuing licences for non-prohibited firearms (singles and double-barrels), and the licencing of gun dealers. The Department of State Services and Nigeria Customs also deals with issues of SALWs regulation. Agencies such as the National Drug Law Enforcement Agency (NDLEA) are also not left out as they report any suspicious act to the appropriate authorities in discharge of their duties. The Nigeria Security and Civil Defence Corps (NSCDC) registers and monitors private security outfits which occasionally have and utilize licenced firearms. The NATCOM which was set up as a specialized institution for SALWs regulation consisted of all security and intelligence agencies situated in the Ministry of defence. Due to its inaction, the Committee's office was shut down and dissolved by the Ministry in 2012. A key question that will perhaps be asked at this juncture is which institution(s) is solely responsible for containing SALWs proliferation in Nigeria and under what law(s) are they expected to effectively function given the inadequate laws on firearms presently in operation? Despite the Federal Government's efforts towards effective control such as the ban on licencing of all firearms to reduce arms circulation, several amnesty/disarmament programs, collaboration with the international community, symposia to sensitize people on the dangers of SALWs proliferation, the problem still persists. A more practical approach in the fight against proliferation of SALWs may perhaps be more effective and long lasting.

Security agencies adopt intelligence gathering to detect illegal use of SALWs, similar to whistleblowing. The Federal Government tackles corruption through the Whistle Blowing policy it introduced to compensate anybody with useful information for recovering proceeds of corruption. The policy was designed by the Federal Ministry of Finance and approved by the Federal Executive Council on 22 December 2016 (Anya and Iwanger 2019: 35). This policy that has recorded tremendous success since its introduction, has not been extended to other criminal matters, including those related to SALWs.

Conclusion

There is no doubt that proliferation of SALWs in Nigeria is a challenge that concerns not only the government, but also the citizens and corporate entities. Thousands of lives and properties worth millions of naira have been destroyed due to illegal use of SALWs since the emergence of the Fourth Republic in 1999. This underscores the imperative of a holistic approach to tackling the menace of illegal use of SALWs. Evidence abound that some security personnel is complicit in trading and illegal use of SALWs, thereby calling for a collective efforts in tackling the challenge.

Having established that the proliferation of SALWs is growing at an alarming rate and has contributed immensely to the security challenges Nigeria and the entire world is presently facing, it becomes apposite at this point in the chapter to proffer suggestions that will reduce the practice to the barest minimum in Nigeria. First, the National Assembly should give priority to the passage of a bill to establish the National Commission against the Proliferation of Small Arms and Light Weapons, which currently before it. This will form a single, comprehensive and robust legal framework on SALWs which will incorporate International standards for combating proliferation of illegal arms. The Commission sought to be established by the bill will be saddled with the responsibility of ensuring effective implementation of the provisions of the law. This will guarantee successful prosecution and secure conviction of SALWs offenders. The current law on firearms which is the Firearms Act, 1959 has proven to be inadequate or ineffective given its scope, application and the outdated penalties/fines in tackling the current realities on SALWs. Secondly, the whistleblowing policy on corruption should be extended to the fight against proliferation of small arms and light weapons in Nigeria as has been done in kidnapping in some States and trafficking of persons. This will motivate people with useful information to approach the appropriate authorities and report such acts. Since the introduction of the policy in December 2016, there have been proactive information/reporting of corrupt practices. The chapter is hopeful that this will douse to a large extent the illicit trafficking and all forms of dealing in arms when adopted.

Thirdly, relevant security agencies and regulatory institutions should aggressively collaborate with the international community and other relevant agencies to effectively tackle importation of SALWs. Through international collaboration, importation of goods into the country can be properly checked before entry. This collaboration also includes collaboration between security agencies of Nigeria and neighbouring countries to adequately secure the various international borders. Fourthly, the Customs Service and other relevant agencies at the border points should develop effective protocols that would make the inflow and outflow of illicit weapons a herculean task. This can take the form of code of conduct for officers manning the borders, and continuous training for security personnel, customs and immigration officers to adequately secure territorial integrity of Nigeria. Finally, the rehabilitation, reorientation and retraining of law enforcement and security agencies and their personnel is imperative as this will go a long way in effectively addressing, preventing, combating and eliminating the proliferation of SALWs in Nigeria.

Notes

1. The Protocol Against the Illicit Manufacturing and Trafficking in Firearms, their Parts and Components and Ammunitions is a Supplement to the United Nations Convention Against Transnational Organized Crime, 2000. It was adopted by the General Assembly on May 31, 2001.
2. The Convention is the West African sub-regional benchmark for regulating SALW. Cited in Helen Chuma Okoro, 'Proliferation of Small Arms and Light Weapons in Nigeria: Legal Implication' Available: http://nialsnigeria.org/pub/HLelenChumaOkoro.pdf accessed 22 March 2020.
3. See B. E. N. Thom-Otuya, 'Proliferation of Small Arms and Light Weapons in Niger Delta: A Threat to National Security in Nigeria' Available: https://thomotuyaben.files.wordpress.com/2013/01/proliferation-of-small-arms.pdf accessed 22 July 2020.
4. Quoted in Michael I Ogu, 'Proliferation of Small Arms and Light Weapons in Africa: Cause or Effect?' http://paperroom.ipsa.org/papers/paper_33138.pdf accessed 22 July 2020.

References

Abdul'aziz, I. (2011). *Nigeria: Two Police Inspectors Dismissed Over Gun Running*. Available: https://allafrica.com/stories/201111300288.html. Accessed 21 June 2020.

Araromi, M. A. et al. (2017). *Moratorium on Proliferation of Small Arms and Light Weapons and Communal Conflicts in Nigeria*. Being the text of a paper presented at the Nigerian Association of Law Teachers (NALT) Conference held at Nnamdi Azikiwe University Awka, Anambra State from 11th–16th June, 2017.

Anan, K. (2000). *We the People: The Role of the United Nations in the 21st Century*. Geneva: United Nations.

Anya, S., & Iwanger, G. (2019). The Role of Whistle Blowing Policy as an Anti-Corruption Tool in Nigeria. *Journal of Law and Criminal Justice, 7*(1), 35–50.

Eno-Abasi, S., & Sulaimon, S. (2017). *Worries as Proliferation of Small Arms, Light Weapons Burgeons.* Avialable: https://guardian.ng/sunday-magazine/worries-as-proliferation-of-small-arms-light-weapons-burgeons. Accessed 21 June 2020.

Gun Policy. (2016). *Firearm Violence, Gun Control and Small Arms.* Available: http://www.gunpolicy.org/firearms/topic/small_arms_in_nigeria. Accessed 20 June 2020.

Oguche, S. (2013). Revisiting Right to Life in Nigeria: Enthronement or Retreat into Right to Burial. *NJCL, 1,* 1–41.

Oji, G. (2011). *Nigeria: Army of Illegal Arm Dealers.* https://allafrica.com/stories/200812090063.html. Accessed 21 June 2020.

Okeke, V. O. S., & Oji, R. O. (2014). The Nigerian State and the Proliferation Small Arm and Light Weapons in the Northern Part of Nigeria. *Journal of Educational and Social Research, 4*(1), 415–428.

Osoba, O., & Ohene-Asare, S. (2014). *Trafficking of Small Arms and Light Weapons (SALW) in West Africa: Routes and Illegal Arm Caches Between Ghana, Togo, Benin and Nigeria.* Friedrich-Ebert-Stiftung, Regional Security Policy Project West Africa, Regional Office Abuja.

Schroeder, M., & Stohl, R. (2006). *Small Arms, Large Problem: The International Threat of Small Arms Proliferation and Misuse.* https://www.armscontrol.org/act/2006_06/SmallArmsFeature. Accessed 21 June 2020.

Thom-Otuya, B. E. N. (2009). Proliferation of Small Arms and Light Weapons in Niger Delta: A Threat to National Security in Nigeria. *International Journal of Sustainable Development, 2*(5), 57–67.

Usman, E., & Oritse, G. (2017). *Customs Uncovers 1,100 Weapons.* https://www.vanguardngr.com/2017/09/breaking-customs-uncovers-1100-weapons/. Accessed 21 June 2020.

Uwa, O. G., & Anthony, A. B. (2015). Small Arms and Light Weapons (SALW) Proliferation and Problem of National Security in Nigeria. *International Affairs and Global Strategy, 29,* 12–20.

Yahaya, J. U. (2020). *An Overview of the Security Implication of Inflow of Small Arms and Light Weapons: A Nigeria Perspectives.* Available: https://www.researchgate.net/publication/340870416_An_overview_of_the_security_implication_of_inflow_of_Small_Arms_and_Light_Weapons_A_Nigeria_Perspectives. Accessed 21 June 2020.

Shuaibu Abdullahi Danwanka is a specialist in Legislative Drafting, Bill Scrutiny/Analysis, Parliamentary Strengthening, Constitutionalism, Legal Research, Corporate Reconstruction, and Legislative Practice and Procedure. He holds a Doctorate, Master's, and Bachelor Degrees in Law and Barrister at Law (BL) from the University of Jos, Bayero University Kano and Nigerian Law School Lagos respectively. He was a Senior Lecturer in the Law Faculty, University of Jos—Nigeria. In 2008, he joined the erstwhile Policy Analysis and Research Project (PARP)—National Assembly, Abuja—Nigeria as legal expert Legislative Drafting and Deputy Director—Bills and Legislative Drafting, Department of Legislative Support Services, National Institute for Legislative and Democratic Studies (NILDS). Danwanka is a Director, Legal Services National Institute for Legislative and Democratic Studies (NILDS)—National Assembly, Abuja—Nigeria.

CHAPTER 23

Police and the Control of Firearms in Africa

Dawud Muhammad Dawud and Tukur Abdulkadir

INTRODUCTION

Police forces across Africa are challenged more than ever before with task of containing armed related crimes and conflicts that are linked to the growing flow of small arms and light weapons. The major goal of every police service is to ensure safety of every member of society. To achieve this, the police adopt various strategies at national levels and also ventured into collaborative efforts at regional and continental levels to control the illicit possession and use of firearms. Licensing is a major strategy employed by the police to ensure that arms in civilian possession are registered and accounted for. The decision whether a person may possess a firearm rests with the police and must be satisfied that the applicant does not constitute danger to the public safety or to the peace before such licence is granted.

Africa is a continent that suffered and still suffering from arms related violence. Civil wars, terrorism, communal conflicts, violent crimes are all common features in all parts of Africa. From Mali in the west to Libya in the North; from Somali in the East to the DR Congo in the central; in the streets of Johannesburg in South Africa, Lagos in Nigeria and Cairo in Egypt, the story is similar, it's all about crimes and guns. Although the use

---

D. M. Dawud (✉)
Nigeria Police Force, Force Headquarters, Abuja, Nigeria

T. Abdulkadir
Department of Political Science, Kaduna State University, Kaduna, Kaduna State, Nigeria

© The Author(s), under exclusive license to Springer Nature Switzerland AG 2021
U. A. Tar and C. P. Onwurah (eds.), *The Palgrave Handbook of Small Arms and Conflicts in Africa*,
https://doi.org/10.1007/978-3-030-62183-4_23

of unlicensed arms occurs in all parts of the globe, it is concentrated in areas afflicted by armed conflict, violence and organized crime, where the demand for illicit weapons is often highest. While most arms trafficking appears to be conducted by private entities, certain governments also contribute to the illicit trade by deliberately supporting and arming proxy groups involved in insurgencies, political thugs and community militia. The types of arms deals, which are prevalent in Africa and other regions where armed conflict is common, are often conducted in contravention of UN arms embargoes and national laws. In areas where there is no active hostilities and armed conflicts, these arms are used to commits crimes such as armed robbery, kidnapping, assassinations as well as other organized crimes and drug smuggling. The arms are small, lights, easy to maintain and hide which makes its control a huge challenge to the Police.

In most African countries, insufficient national laws and lack of capacity of the police have hampered efforts at licensing all firearms in possession of non-state actors and provide accurate account of the arms in civilian possession. This chapter examines the effort of the police in Africa to license, regulate and control the use of arms with a view to exploring the success and challenges recorded in this regard. To achieve this, this chapter is structured into several parts which comprised Conceptualisation of major terms, factors that precipitate flow of illicit arms in Africa, why Arm licensing, Function of Police Firearm licensing, Arm Licensing and Control in Africa, Police Approach to Arms licensing in Africa, National Laws and Police Powers, Challenges of Arms licensing in Africa and Conclusion.

Conceptualizing Firearms and Arms Licensing

The term *Firearm* is defined differently by different scholars and national legislations. The United Kingdom (UK) Home Office (2016: 3) defined firearm as "a lethal barrelled weapon of any description from which any shot, bullet or other missile can be discharged." The Nigerian firearm act (1990) defines firearm as "any lethal barrelled weapon of any description from which any shot, bullet or other missile can be discharged, and includes a prohibited firearm, a personal firearm and a muzzle-loading firearm of any of the categories and any component part of any such firearm;"

The Tanzanian Arms and Ammunition Act (2007) defines firearm as: (a) every firearm of any description; (b) every air gun and every other kind of gun from which any shot, bullet or other missile can be discharged; (c) every sword, cutlass, spear, pike, bayonet, dagger, fighting iron, flick-knife, gravity knife or other deadly weapon; (d) every gun, pistol or other propelling or releasing instrument or mechanism, from or by which any shell, cartridge, bomb, grenade, or projectile, containing any gas or chemical, could be discharged.

Similarly, the South African Firearm Control Act (2000) defines firearm thus: (a) device manufactured or designed to propel a bullet or projectile through a barrel or cylinder by means of burning propellant, at a muzzle energy exceeding 8 joules; (b) device manufactured or designed to discharge rim-fire, centre-fire or pin-fire ammunition; (c) device which is not at the time capable of discharging any bullet or projectile, but which can be readily altered to be a firearm within the meaning of paragraph (a) or (b); (d) device manufactured to discharge a bullet or any other projectile of 0.22 calibre or higher at a muzzle energy of more than 8 joules, by means of compressed gas and not by means of burning propellant; or (e) barrel, frame or receiver of a device referred to in paragraphs (a), (b), (c). For the purpose of this chapter, Firearm refers to rifles, shotguns and hand guns which are designed to discharge bullet, missile or any projectile.

Firearms Licence: A firearms licence also known as a gun licence or spelt licence in British English is a licence or permit issued by a government authority (typically by the police) of a jurisdiction, that allows the licensee to buy, own, possess, or carry a firearm, often subject to a number of conditions or restrictions, as may be stipulated in the law. The aim of licensing is to create central oversight of weapon possession and use; it is an arm control measure that involves series of activities that may include, for example, the prevention of possession of certain types of weapons either among the general public or restricted access to individuals who are presumed to form a high-risk subset of the population. A record of previous criminal behaviour, for example, is a common factor in the classification of such group. Grip (2017) argues that arm licensing and control involves policies about *who* can own *which* arms under *what* conditions. At the national level, "gun control" measures are aimed at creating central oversight of weapon possession and use, and may include, for example, the prevention of possession of certain types of weapons either among the general public or some individuals who are presumed to form a high-risk subset of the population. Firearm licensing is therefore one of the deliberate policies and programs employed by the state to control arms.

BACKGROUND: STATE POLICING AND ARMS CONTROL IN AFRICA

Around the world, handgun registration and control are acknowledged as the most effective way to minimize arms-related death and trauma. Governments believed that registration of firearms reduces the flow of guns from lawful owner to criminals. Historically, for more than sixty years, registration and owner licensing have been the accepted norm in fields of crime and injury prevention (Alpers 1999). To minimize the destructive effects of the firearms, states create structures for proper governance and monitoring of firearm licensing and registration. These structures vary from one country to another. In Africa, the impact of illicit firearms has been destructive. These arms fuelled conflicts and prolonged wars across the continent. They were used in deadly conflicts in Sudan, Uganda, Sierra Leone, Rwanda, Libya, Angola, the Democratic Republic of Congo, Somalia and other African countries.

They are frequently recycled from country to country, and their ownership is transferred among fighters and war profiteers. The arms are the major facilitators of crime; they are used in killing Millions of lives and causing injuries. As Fleshman (2011) notes, "the more guns we have on the register, the more crimes police can solve and the more traumas we can prevent." Gun control is intimately connected with the social contract between citizens and the state, in which citizens give up their arms in exchange for the protection from the state—and other benefits resulting from political order. This makes arms control a highly political and contested phenomenon, with wide diversity in different national and sub-national contexts. Hence, arms control is connected with state building and order maintenance, in which the state becomes the only legitimate user of armed violence. Arms control is a complicated issue beyond banning or regulating the civilian firearms, as many states allow citizens to own guns for a number of reasons, while ruling out others.

The illicit weapons in circulation originate both from within and outside Africa. They enter the illicit market at virtually every stage of the weapons' life cycle. According to Small Arm Survey and AU (2019), African states have expressed particular concern at the enduring threat posed by the unlicensed craft production of firearms. The illicit conversion of imitation handguns is an emerging development that enables the circulation of lethal illicit handguns at a much reduced cost. Military-grade weapons and ammunition produced in Africa have also found their way into conflict zones. "The crises in the Central African Republic, Libya, and Mali have illustrated the long-term effects of the massive national stockpile diversion that can occur in the context of armed conflict" (Small Arm Survey and AU 2019). Policing is a difficult task, especially in contexts where arms trafficking have become an organized crime posing multiple challenges to the police. There is no easy fix to these multiple challenges. Improving controls at the various stages of the weapons' life cycle will be required to meaningfully counter the threat of illicit arms flows. Although action is required on several fronts, competing priorities and limited resources call for investment in particular areas likely to yield the most benefits. The complex and fluid nature of illicit arms flows on the continent illustrates the need for reliable and timely strategic-level intelligence in order to detect new sources of supply and tackle them effectively. African governments must invest heavily in policing and develop both local and international partnership to prevent and pacify certain types of violent behaviour and minimize the chances of internal. This may reduce the culture of violence and the demand of the arms.

Factors That Precipitate the Movement and Use of Unlicensed Arms in Africa

Africa is devastated by conflicts and violent crimes which culminated into massive insecurity in its entire ramification. There are many factors responsible for the wide spread uncontrolled use of arms in Africa. Some of these factors include:

1. *Weak/Fragile State and Its Institutions*: The quality of every government is measured to some extent by its ability to build strong institutions and leadership embedded on the principles of meritocracy, pragmatism and honesty that implement policies aimed at promoting peace and security for the development of citizenry. Firearms are lethal weapons. They can kill or cause serious injuries to the people or their property. It is the responsibility of the government to regulate and control their use through proper licensing and registrations as well as controlling border/ports to ensure illicit arms are not smuggled. Renner (1997) notes that a case could be made for ignoring the proliferation of military-style small arms. This is because in many countries today, governments are weak, justice is arbitrary, the economy is foundering, and crime is rampant. In these cases, the proliferation of small arms "lights a match to gasoline." The weakness of state in Africa has manifested in such way that the state is unable to provide its basic function of providing security for life and property. States institutions such as the police, the customs and the navy who are responsible to securing land and water borders are so incapacitated and corrupt that they could neither effectively control the flow of illicit arms nor properly license and regulate its illicit use. According to Amnesty International (2016) Easy access to firearms—whether legal or illegal—is one of the main drivers of gun violence. The state has an obligation to maximize the protection of human rights, creating the safest possible environment for the most people, especially those considered to be at the greatest risk. If a state does not exercise adequate control over the possession and use of firearms in the face of persistent gun violence, this could amount to a breach of their obligations under international human rights law.
2. *Internal Conflicts and High Level of Crime*: Internal conflicts and violent crimes are common in Africa. From Johannesburg to Lagos, Cairo to Nairobi, Kinshasa to Mogadishu the story is the same; violent crimes using illicit arms on daily occurrences on the street. The arms fuel conflict and violent crimes; likewise conflict and violent crime trigger the demand for arms by all means. This situation makes illicit arm deals lucrative and formed one of the organized crimes in Africa sometimes with state's institutions involved. Access to illicit firearm also encourages violent crimes such as armed robbery and homicide in Africa: government's statistics across the continent attests to this. According to Fleshman (2011), in

Africa, "more criminals are arming themselves" and "access to firearms has become easier." He further argued that by 2000 the South African government found that homicide, primarily involving firearms, was the leading cause of death among young men aged 15–21 and that gunshots from all causes (murder, suicide and accidents) were the single largest cause of non-natural death in the country. Similarly, Vines (2005) opined that Nigeria's illicit light weapons trade can be traced back to the failure to execute a comprehensive arms collection programme after the 1967–1970 civil war. It has subsequently been fuelled by growing crime, endemic corruption and ethno-religious conflicts. There have also been widespread leakages from government armouries.

3. *Porous Borders*: illegal arms move fast across borders. Because most borders in Africa are poorly control, the arms are usually smuggled from feeder countries (usually countries ravaged by wars and conflict) to the recipient countries by the black marketers. These black marketers have developed underground networks using sophisticated methods for procurements, transportation and sale of arms sometimes with connivance of government corrupt officials at the border points. The porous nature of Africa's borders plays a significant role in proliferation of arms. Unmanned border crossing points and widespread corruption facilitate illicit trafficking and threat to security. Despite the ending of many conflicts in Africa (such as Liberia, Sierra Leone and Rwanda) smuggling and illicit trade in small arms are reported to be on the increase.

4. *Low Cost and Wide Availability*: Sophisticated technology is not usually required to manufacture light arms. This makes it easier for local production and large supplies both legally and illegally through international arms trade. There are well over 600 suppliers around the world with more than 550 million in circulation. Due its large production and easy access in most African countries, it makes its prices relatively affordable to the buyers. They are cheap enough for even the poorest of criminals and insurgent groups to acquire in large quantities. In most cases the arms are illegally trafficked and are sold in open-air markets close to high-demand areas, for instance near artisanal gold-mining sites in northern Niger where miners feel they need guns for self-protection (Pellerin 2017: 8). In some parts of Africa, a Soviet-designed AK-47 assault rifle, coveted for its simplicity and firepower, can be purchased for as little as $6, or traded for a chicken or sack of grain (Fleshman 2011). There is growing evidence of the circulation of imitation firearms across the African continent. Some countries appear to have relatively large regulated markets for imitation weapons. A retailer in Sudan, for instance, declared to UN monitors that on average he sold 1500 blank-firing weapons every year. The wholesale purchase price of each weapon is about USD 9, while the retail price in Sudan is USD 130–150. Converted weapons are sold for USD 200 on the illicit market (UN Security Council-UNSC 2017, paras. 14–17) Similarly accounts were also given by the Nigeria Police officers

(in personal discussion, 2020) that access to cheap firearms that were usually trafficked into the country or stolen from government armouries fuel criminality. An AK-47 rifle is illegally sold at between three hundred and three hundred and fifty Naira (between USD 70 and USD 90) while pump action gun is sold much more lower than that.

5. *Simplicity and Durability*: Small arms are simple, easy to use and maintain. It requires little logistical support and can be in operation for many years. The arm used for decades and the remnants of war can be as effective as new one. Only little training is required to effectively control and use them. Because the arm is light and is extremely durable, it became a weapon of choice for criminals and untrained combatants including children in conflict situation and for committing violent crimes.

6. *Portability and Easy to Conceal*: these categories of arms are portable and can be transported or smuggled from one point to another using vehicles, monocycles or animals. It is easier to conceal the arms in a legitimate luggage or shipments without attracting the attention of law enforcement agents. They are so lightweight and easy to conceal for smuggling and for carrying out operations. Arms are trafficked across Africa using different methods. The portability of the arms makes them suitable for what is called 'Ant trade'. Ant trade refers to the small-scale movement of weapons smuggled across borders in small numbers—usually less than a dozen at a time—the cumulative effect of multiple transfers of this type can be significant and can also fuel crime and conflict (Small Arm Survey and AU 2019). In addition, an emerging trend in the trafficking of firearms parts and components, which are easy to conceal in vehicles or among other commodities also contributed in making arms available.

7. *Theft of Arms from Military and Police Armouries*: one of the major contributors to availability of unlicensed firearms in Africa is thefts of arms from State Security Agents Armouries. In recent times, arms groups in conflict areas in Africa have been able to break Military and Police armouries and looted it. These arms usually find their way into the hands of criminals and civilian easily. Keili (2008) argued that some of the weapons in armed groups' stockpiles are acquired during attacks on police and military armouries. Leakages from poorly constructed and insecure stockpiles are also a chronic problem in West African countries with large numbers of weapons, both during and before and after conflict. Under-resourced security forces may be unable to secure stockpiles properly, and poorly paid individuals may resort to using their official weapons for criminal activities or may rent them out to others to supplement their income.

8. *Culture of Violence*: one of the factors that contribute to massive unlicensed firearms in Africa is the culture of violence. This however varies from one country to another depending on its culture and historical experience. In South Africa for instance, apartheid and the struggle against it has created a "culture of violence" that legitimizes the use of

guns to resolve disputes, further polarizes social relations among races and classes. It also creates a demand for arms that is supplied both legally and illicitly. The cultural significance of the AK-47 to the formerly colonized peoples of Southern Africa is a case in point. After decades of use by anti-colonial and anti-apartheid movements, the powerful weapon has come to be associated with liberation. A silhouette of the gun figures is prominently on the Mozambican flag. Freedom songs from the struggles against minority rule in Namibia, South Africa, Zimbabwe and Angola often extolled virtues of gun and those of the fighters carrying it. In some African countries today, the illicit guns are used to equip brutal insurgencies, criminal gangs and paramilitary militias—paralyzing development efforts and dangerously exaggerating the association between arms and masculinity that is common to many cultures around the world. In some other African countries like Sudan, the culture of brandishing during wedding ceremonies is a mark of pride and has contributed to illicit demand and use of guns by the civilian and fuelled gun-related violence. Replacing the romantic image of guns with an appreciation of their destructive impact, advocates argue, will require a long-term effort to reduce the supply, improve police protection and increase educational and economic opportunities for young men to break their identification with guns and violence.

Why Arms Licensing?

Empirical evidence has shown that availability and accessibility of arms fuels violence and makes simple one complex. Conflicts that are ordinarily regarded as simple, localized and short are prolonged due to the availability of small arms. This is not to suggest any causal relationships between small arms proliferation and conflict but it makes conflicts more destructive and breeds a culture of violence in the post conflict civilian life where firearms become means of dispute settlement. Similarly, police and other security agencies had to also contend with gun-related crimes such as armed robbery and kidnapping that also endangered their lives.

According to Alpers and Wilson (2014), small arms, commonly known as firearms or guns are used to kill as many as one thousand (1000) people each day. Millions more are wounded, or their lives upended when access to development aid, markets, health, education and human rights is disrupted by people with guns. Figures released by Small Arms Survey (2007) estimates that there are more than eight hundred and seventy five million (875,000,000) firearms in the world, 75% of them (approximately 650 million) in the hands of civilian. These guns, in possession of civilian, can hardly be accounted for and cannot as well be regulated in terms of usage and storage. This situation posed a great threat to peace and survival of millions of innocent people especially women and children who are most vulnerable in the world today. Another report by Alper and Wilson (2013) stated that guns outnumbered passenger vehicles' by 253 million, or 29%. Each year about eight million new arms, plus 10–15 billion rounds of ammunition are manufactured-enough bullets to shoot every person in the world not once, but twice. Former UN Secretary General Kofi Annan (2000) opined that "The death toll from small arms dwarfs that of all other weapons systems — and in most years greatly exceeds the toll of the atomic bombs that devastated Hiroshima and Nagasaki. In terms of the carnage they cause, small arms, indeed, could well be described as 'weapons of mass destruction'." Although arms do not create war or conflict, it's a known fact, as evident in many countries in Africa and elsewhere that it fuels civil wars and regional conflicts; it stocks the arsenals of terrorists, drug cartels and other armed groups. It also contributes to violent crime such as armed robbery and kidnapping as well as proliferating sensitive technology.

The proliferation of light weapons in Africa poses a major threat to development due to its availability, low cost and ease of use. These arms are regarded as weapon of choice that "may escalate conflicts, undermine peace agreements, intensify violence and impact of crime, impede economic and social development and hinder the development of social stability, democracy and good governance; noted Ms. Gamba, the former director of the Arms Management Programme of the South African Institute for Security Studies (cited in Alper and Wilson 2013). In Africa, the rate of civilian possession of unlicensed firearms is worrisome. The problem varies from region to region and from one country to another due to historical experiences and geographical location but the impact is similar. Statistics revealed that Central African region has suffered greatly from conflicts and armed violence. Civilian possession of firearms ranges from 1.1 per 100 people in Chad to 19.9 in Equatorial Guinea. In Angola it is estimated that there are 2.8 million privately held firearm. In North Africa, civilian possession of arms is considered above global average; this is due to historical and cultural reasons. Statistics from small arms survey published by Alper and Wilson (2014) in GunPolicy.com estimates Tunisia as having the lowest problem of civilian possession of firearm in the region with an average of 0.1 per 100 persons while Libya records the highest with an average of 15.5 per 100 persons. Egypt and Algeria also record high with 3.5 and 7.6 per 100 persons respectively. In West Africa, the situation is not better than in the other regions. According to Vanguard (2016), the UN report estimates that there about 500 million illicit firearms circulating in West Africa; 70% of this number is believed to be in Nigeria. Another figure released by Small Arms Survey (2007) puts the ration of civilian possession of firearms both licit and illicit in Nigeria at 1.5 per 100. Ghana, Ivory Coast and Senegal also record high with 2.0, 2.4 and 2.0 per 100 respectively. Gambia, Niger and Togo record low with 0.8, 0.7, and 1.0 per 100 respectively. Southern Africa is also ravaged by the scourge of illicit civilian possession of firearms. Data from Small Arms Survey (2007) show high level of civilian gun possession. South Africa and Namibia recorded the highest ration with 6.61 and 12.6 per 100 civilians respectively. At the lowest level in the region is Lesotho and Botswana with 2.7 and 4.9 per 100 persons respectively while Swaziland

Table 23.1 Estimated African sub-regional distribution of civilian firearms, 2017

Sub-Region	Population	Number of civilian held firearms	Civilian-held firearm per 100 population
Africa Total	1,246,505,000	40,009,000	3.2
Eastern Africa	416,676,000	7,802,000	1.9
Middle Africa	161,237,000	4,981,000	3.1
Northern Africa	232,186,000	10,241,000	4.4
Southern Africa	63,854,000	6,012,000	9.4
Western Africa	372,551,000	10,972,000	2.9

Source Adopted from a Joint publication of Small Arms Survey and African Union Commission (2019)

records the ration of 6.4 per 100 persons. All these figures indicated that arms are major threat to security, development and prosperity in the whole of Africa.

In developed societies, tracing the gun is not merely a common Hollywood sub-plot. A gun registry works for real police every day of the week, helping to solve crimes from burglary to murder, from drug-dealing to terrorism. In fact, the Australian Institute of Criminology found that a firearm register aids policing even when it is administratively clumsy and reputedly operating at less than maximum efficiency. Registration helps ensure gun owners are held accountable for their firearms and do not sell them illegally or give them to individuals without appropriate authorization. It will also help ensure that guns are safely stored. Opponents of gun control argue that the registration of firearms will not reduce crime. Claiming that gun registration will not prevent crime is akin to claiming that registering cars does not prevent car theft (Table 23.1).

FUNCTION OF POLICE ARMS LICENSING

The licensing arrangements for firearms cover the granting, renewal and revocation. The police arms licensing process in Africa is similar to the same process in other part of the world; notwithstanding the fact that each country may have some peculiarities based on its national laws. The process involves but not limited to the following functions to ensure that only authorized or licensee possesses or when necessary uses approved firearm and for the purpose of which he/she was granted the licence.

1. *Licensing the Possession of Arms*: this is to ensure that guns in the hands of non-state actors are properly accounted for and are used for the sole purpose of which the licence is granted. In most African countries, arms licence is granted for Hunting, Sports and in some countries like South Africa for self-defence.

2. *Controlling the Movement of Arms*: this process is to ensure that arms are not transferred from authorized to the unauthorized persons or criminal elements that may use them to unleash terror on innocent persons. This process also meant to ensure that guns belonging to deceased licensee is officially transferred to eligible hairs or kept in police armoury for proper accountability.
3. *Licensing the Manufacturers/Merchants dealing in, purchase, removal and storage of arms and explosive*. This is to ensure manufacturers and dealers are properly registered and their activities and premises are subject to police inspection. The arms they produce or trade in are properly numbered and registered with the police. They are also obliged by law to disclose to the police the end users of their arms and these arms are only sold to the persons cleared/certified fit by the police to bear firearms.
4. *Renewal of Licence*: depending on the provision of the national laws, firearms licence holders are usually required to renew their licence after specified period of time. The police will review the conditions of arms licence to decide whether the licensee is still eligible to hold the licence or not. Based on the assessment of the licensing authority, decision will be taken as to renew the licence or not.
5. *Revocation of Licence*: Considerations about public safety are at the heart of the firearms licensing arrangements. The police review the licence conditions periodically to ascertain whether a firearm licence holder violate any. If the police are of the opinion that such licence posed danger to public safety; or the holder is using it for a purpose other than which was issued for, such licence can be revoked. Significantly, it may be terminated if the holder of the licence becomes or is declared unfit to possess a firearm.

ARMS LICENSING AND CONTROL IN AFRICA

The Firearms Programme Policing Capabilities assist Law Enforcement Agencies to solve criminal firearms trafficking that would not otherwise have been solved by tracing the history and ownership of illicit firearms to find the point in the chain of custody at which the firearms were diverted into the illicit chain of supply. (Chande 2019: 3)

The aim of arms licensing system is to ensure that firearms are not distributed to unauthorized persons, or those convicted of serious crime, or those that are prohibited under the law to bear firearms. The prohibition to possess firearms depends on the laws of each individual African country. This is evident in the variety of legislative provisions based on each county's culture, political orientation and risk assessment associated with the civilian possession of firearms. While some countries like Morocco have stringent procedure before a licence is granted others like Namibia adopts a permissive approach with less stringent procedures. Apart from the national laws that regulate the possession of firearms through licensing procedure, there are global and regional efforts in form of international and regional instruments that are geared towards controlling the flow of small arms to prevent the arms from getting into the hands of unqualified non-state actors. The main concern lies in the extent to which the availability of firearms to the general population influences levels of armed violence—including the occurrence of homicides, other types of armed crime.

Global Arms Control Protocol

Over the years, UN member states have periodically highlighted the need for countries to review their national civilian possession of arms laws. However, the focus of regional and international attention and efforts has generally been on combating the transnational illicit trade in small arms, with comparatively little consideration of regulating civilian possession at the national level. In fact, the issue of civilian possession of firearms was expressly removed from the discussion table during the 2001 UN Programme of Action (PoA) deliberations. However, international interest in and attention to the issue of civilian firearm regulation peaked in the mid-1990s with the adoption of a series of resolutions by the Economic and Social Council (ECOSOC) of the United Nations calling for the Secretary General to initiate the exchange of data and other information on the regulation of firearms, including an international study of firearm regulation (ECOSOC 2017, paras. IV: 7–8). Similarly, the July 1997 ECOSOC resolution emphasizes the importance of state responsibility for effective regulation of civilian possession of small arms, and encourages member states to consider regulatory approaches to the civilian use of firearms that include the following common elements such as:

1. Regulations relating to firearm safety and storage;
2. Adopt a licensing system to ensure that firearms are not distributed to persons convicted of serious crimes or other persons who are prohibited under the laws of the respective Member States from owning or possessing firearms;
3. A record-keeping system for firearms (ECOSOC 2017, para. 5).

In the same vein, the 1999 *Report of the UN Disarmament Commission* further encourages states to introduce appropriate national legislation, administrative regulations and licensing requirements defining the conditions under which private citizens can acquire, use and trade firearms. The report urges states to: consider the prohibition of unrestricted trade and private ownership of small arms and light weapons specifically designed for military purposes, such as automatic guns. Similarly, INTERPOL offers unique Policing Capabilities and Protocols to address the modern hybrid threats that are currently facing the world. Some of these Policing Capabilities can be used to implement and to report on the implementation of the Arms Trade Treaty. The INTERPOL Firearms Programme offers to Law Enforcement Agencies worldwide, three unique Policing Capabilities to address the ever present threat of gun crime, terrorism and other forms of organized crime. Chande (2019: 2–3) enumerated the three policing capability instruments as follows:

1. *INTERPOL Illicit Arms Records and Tracing Management System (iARMS)*: this platform provides a centralized system for reporting and querying of Stolen, Lost and Trafficked/Smuggled firearms and enables member countries to share information and trace illicit firearms.
2. *The INTERPOL Firearms Reference Table (IFRT)*: this offers extensive information about firearms makes, models, manufacturer specifications, firearms marking descriptions and a range of information on firearms. Based on the Royal Canadian Mounted Police's (RCMP) Firearms Reference Table, the IFRT has been developed in partnership with the RCMP in order to provide a globally accessible resource of firearm markings, references and images all of which help support law enforcement officers around the world to accurately identify a firearm.
3. *The INTERPOL Ballistics Information Network (IBIN)*: this provides a ballistic network which allows international cross sharing and comparison of ballistic evidence, as part of INTERPOL's Forensic data sharing capabilities to assist transnational investigations. By comparing ballistics evidence, Law Enforcement Agencies are able to link crimes that have been committed in different jurisdictions.

Regional Arms Control

The First Continental Meeting of African Experts on Illicit Proliferation, Circulation and Trafficking of Small Arms and Light Weapons, was held in Addis Ababa in May 2000. Recommendations made included the need for African states to strengthen national legislation, adopt responsible transfer policies, ensure strict control over stocks, destroy surplus stocks, harmonize legislation at the regional level and support regional cooperation to enhance the combating of trans-border crime. Later in December 2000, the Bamako declaration came on board with the African Union, (formerly OAU) member states adoption of common position on proliferation and circulation of small arms. The declaration further recommends member states to harmonize legislation on manufacturing and trading of small arms. It also recommends adoption of common standard in stock keeping as well as licensing of small arms in Africa. Thereafter in 2006, the ECOWAS Convention on Small

Arms and Light Weapons, their Ammunition and Other Related Materials was signed by the 15 ECOWAS heads of state and government in Abuja on 14 June 2006 and entered into force on 29 September 2009 (United Nations Regional Centre for Peace and Disarmament [UNREC] 2014). The convention provides prohibition of possession, use and sale of light weapons by civilians; encourages licensing systems, including the following criteria: minimum age; no criminal record or the subject of a morality investigation; proof of a legitimate reason to possess, carry, or use; proof of safety training and competency training; proof of safe storage and separate storage of ammunition. Also requires limit on the number of weapons a licence may cover; waiting period of at least 21 days; expiration dates on licences and periodic reviews; seizure laws and revocation of licences for contraventions of possession laws; and adequate sanctions and penalties for illicit possession and use (ECOWAS 2006, Article 14).

To further re-enforce the regional efforts, in1998 the chiefs of police from ten countries in the Eastern Africa Region (Kenya, Uganda, Tanzania, Burundi, Rwanda, Ethiopia, Seychelles, Sudan, Djibouti and Eritrea) came together to form the East African Police Chiefs Organization (EAPCO) with the goal of uniting their efforts and sharing resources in the fight against transnational crime in the region. EAPCO targets the proliferation of small arms and light weapons, banditry and cattle-rustling, international car theft syndicates, drug trafficking and money laundering as well as the emerging threat of global terrorism. All these crimes are related to gun use. Similar efforts aimed at creating a united front in controlling arms movements and sharing resources and information were also undertaken by other regional committees of police chiefs. At its 12th Annual General Meeting (2007) held at Lusaka, Zambia from 28 July to 3 August 2007, the Southern African Regional Police Chiefs Cooperation Organization (SARPCCO) established the Regional Coordinating Committee (RCC) on small arms, which meets at least twice a year, and adopts and monitors two-year action plans for implementing the Firearms Protocol. The 2010–2012 action plan includes implementing courses, workshops and seminars on various issues such as law enforcement, train-the-trainers and database management, brokering and marking; marking state and civilian firearms.

Similarly, the West African Police Chiefs Committee (WAPCCO) General Assembly in its July 2012 meeting called for cooperation on small arms, piracy, and terrorism, among other regional security issues. In particular, Niger and Nigeria have been selected to support an anti-crime operation on small arms. Grip (2017: 7) argued that "motivations behind the comparatively extensive regionalization of small arms control in Africa can be summarized in three factors." The first is what liberal institutionalists calls "issue density," i.e. the "fact" that the problem of small arms proliferation is greater in Africa than elsewhere and embedded in many intertwined policy areas, such as governance, security and development. The second factor is the relative weakness of state capacities, for example, weak border controls, in relation to increased cross-border activity. The third factor is the perceived rise of armed non-state actors, causing local and regional conflicts, crime and terrorism. In combination, these motivations are arguably large enough to surpass any resistance against international cooperation. In other words, given the particular challenges posed by small arms, it is in states' material interest to find regional solutions to arms proliferation. For instance, between 2001 and 2006, the joint policing operations between South African and Mozambican police, commonly referred to as "Operations" resulted in the collection and destruction of 46,902 small arms and 24,493,565 rounds of ammunition on Mozambican soil.

POLICE APPROACH TO ARMS LICENSING IN AFRICA

Approach to arms licensing solely depends on the provisions of the national laws of each African country. It is also difficult to make generalization about the legal provision or processes of countries considering differences in history, political system as well as executive structure. One important approach that unites all African countries in terms of granting arm licence to civilian is that the laws are unanimous in treating the matter as "privilege" not a "right." That's civilian possession of firearm is not guaranteed by law. Other important features that are common to the firearm laws in all African countries include:

1. With the exception of Nigeria, where applicants for a firearm licence are not obliged by law to provide reasons for possessing firearm (since the law has made provisions for Hunting and Sporting), applicants for firearm licence elsewhere in Africa must provide genuine reason for possessing firearms.
2. In all African countries, the applicant for firearm licence must pass a background check to consider crime record, mental health, drug addiction, etc.
3. Licensees are required to renew their licence from time to time as may be required by the law.
4. With the exception of Ethiopia, Sudan and Senegal, civilians are prohibited from possessing fully automatic rifles. Therefore, licence to this category of firearm cannot be granted.
5. Licensed firearm vendors are required to make their premises accessible to police for inspection.

National Laws and Police Powers

In all the African countries except Eritrea, subject to the regulations by firearm laws, individuals may obtain firearm licence from the police upon fulfilment of stipulated requirements. Eritrea is the only country in Africa that prohibited civilian possession of all types of firearms. The prohibition is in conformity with the Protocol of the Great Lake Region (GLR) and Horn of Africa (HoA) Article 3 (c) (ii) and Article 5 (b) (iii) and Eritrean Transitional Penal Code Article763. Eretria's exception status has been buttressed as follows: "Understanding the disastrous effects of illicit proliferation of small arms and light weapons (SALW), the State of Eritrea prohibited private ownership of arms. Under Eritrean law, whosoever carries or hides or bargains arms and their parts is punished by law" (Permanent Mission of Eritrea to the United Nations, 1 January 2010).

Licensing laws are one method for closing the "private sale loophole" facilitates responsible gun ownership by requiring a person to obtain a licence before purchasing or acquiring a firearm. Although licensing laws vary from one African country to another, the most comprehensive laws require all gun owners to possess a licence and regularly renew it. The licence may only be issued or renewed after the applicant has undergone a background check and other requirements by law. Civilians who possess arms include collectors, hunters, sports shooters, individuals fearing for their personal security and criminals. Private ownership of firearms, both legal and illegal, accounts for about 75% of the global small arms stockpile. National legislation generally restricts the types of weapons legally available to civilians. In most African countries, the responsibility of granting firearm licence and maintaining records of licenced firearm users and vendor is placed on the police by the law.

Firearms regulation laws and gun control policies also vary among African countries. Depending on the national orientation and the provision of the law, some countries adopt Permissive licensing policy while others adopt Restrictive one. All states in Africa with the exception of (Chad, Namibia, Nigeria and Senegal are operating *Restrictive* policy. Under this licensing policy, the applicant must provide to the Police sufficient reason for allowing him to have a gun rather than the licensing authority being required to show a reason for denying the request. In other words, instead of saying "all but..." members of the prohibited classes may possess firearms; the restrictive system provides that "nobody but..." those who are specifically approved may possess the firearms covered by the system. Newton and Franklin (1969) opined that restrictive licensing attempts to reduce firearms violence by substantially reducing the number of firearms in circulation. This system requires a person seeking to buy a firearm, typically a handgun, provide the licensing authority with evidence of good character and have a valid reason why he needs the firearm.

Permissive arms licensing policy on the other hand allows all but the prohibited categories of persons to acquire guns if they are able to meet licensing requirements. Before an applicant can be denied a licence the police or the administering agency must show that the applicant is a member of one of the groups prohibited to acquire firearm licence under the law. Presently, this policy is operational in four African countries namely Chad, Namibia, Nigeria and Senegal.

Challenges of Arms Licensing in Africa

Controlling the spread of small arms and light weapons in Africa by the police is extremely difficult. The arms are considered "legitimate" weapons that serve a variety of purposes such as policing, national defence and sport shooting. It is practically impossible to place ban on these weapons and their legal trade is difficult to limit given their legitimate uses. It is also important to note that arms production is a huge business that cannot be ignored globally. According to Small Arms Survey (2007) there are a large number of weapons producers around the world. More than 1000 companies operating in approximately 100 states manufacture small arms and ammunition. Accurate data and information on production and movements of these arms is beyond Police control. Only those arms that are officially registered can be accounted for.

The most reliable information about civilian ownership comes from official registration reports. But these are incomplete everywhere in Africa. The more comprehensive information on public gun inventories comes from polling and surveys usually undertaken by NGOs. Unlike official registration data, which only covers legally owned firearms, polling can potentially reveal the approximate total of all guns in civilian hands. Because it relies on voluntary responses to very sensitive questions, however, even polling lacks great reliability. Therefore, firearm licensing in African environment is a challenging task for police due to enormous reasons which include but not limited to the following.

Lack of Capacity and Resources

The effectiveness and consistency with which the licensing arrangements are undertaken by the police depends on the skills of those with responsibility for carrying out the licensing function. Skilled police officers and adequate resources are critical to achieving effective licensing process. Available data revealed that police in Africa do not have sufficient resources to handle current or anticipated future demand nor do they have a structured plan for the long-term resourcing of its licensing arrangements. Skilled manpower and resources are required to undertake correct assessment to determine the suitability of the applicant to possess a firearm. According to Her Majesty's Inspectorate of Constabulary (HMIC) "Gaps in the capacity of a force to undertake efficient and effective licensing arrangements have the potential to let down those involved in the licensing process, and substantially to increase the likelihood that mistakes will be made, thereby compromising public safety" (HMIC 2015). Inadequate training, equipment and resources have always been the bane for poor performance of the police in Africa. The police usually lack the resources to verify the referees, particularly for new licence applications where the police do not have previous knowledge of the applicant. Referees provide essential information to help the police to assess whether there might be any risk to public safety if the applicant is permitted to have access to, or possession of, a firearm.

Absence of Modern Technology

Technology makes things easy and promotes efficiency and accountability. Police in Africa have been less disposed to utilizing the opportunity offered by modern technology to enhance their services. licensing process and record keeping are still manual in most African countries. Presently only few African countries like South Africa have a national police database where all licensees are documented and can be accessed in any part of the country. However even in South Africa the technology is underutilized. Mthethwa, South African Minister of Police (2010), opined that the assessment further pointed out that we have invested in an Information Technology (IT) system that is currently under-utilized, as much of the work is done manually.

In view of the foregoing challenges and the prevailing security situation, it is important that the existing arms licences are properly documented through National Database and using modern technology. In addition, a comprehensive mechanism should be put in place to regulate and monitor the flow of arms into Africa through the creation of regional database. Accurate licensing records are not just important for the purpose of providing data about the number of individuals licenced to possess firearms, they are also important in helping the police to effectively discharge its duty to protect the public from harm.

Weak Public Support

In most African countries, Police–Public Relations is usually weak. Members of the public do not trust the police and they hardly volunteer information to the police. People in possession with unlicensed firearms live in the community. Some of these people may not be eligible to be granted firearm licence and the illicit firearm in their possession posed serious safety threat to the people around them. Public engagement should be considered as a core element of police activity, informing and impacting on every area of policing. A genuine commitment from leadership plays an important role in ensuring that public engagement is effective; generally, police in Africa have had to contend with adverse public perception and an uncooperative attitude from members of the community. It was seen largely as a government apparatus that is anti-people, aggressive and brutal with a poor work ethics. The attitude of the public towards the police is also that of apathy and caution. The general relationship is characterized by suspicion and mistrust. The police are conceived by most people in Africa not as a service organization for the natives but as an instrument of coercion and oppression of the natives.

Corruption in the Public Sector

Corruption has eaten deep into most African societies. Government institutions are often accused of engaging in various forms of corrupt practices,

Police is one of such institutions in Africa where corruption is endemic. Licensing officers are accused of unnecessary delays in processing applications for new or renewal of licence in anticipation of kick back from the applicants. Sometimes the renewal applications will be submitted in good time but the officers will delay the renewal process till the expiry of their certificates. For the police to allow certificate holders to possess firearms unlawfully is a serious failure; arguably, they have colluded in breaking the law. E.N. Mthethwa, South African Minister of Police (2010), laments "during the assessment a number of concerning issues were raised regarding irregularities in the issuing of firearms licences. Some of these include issuing of firearm licences under the old Arms and Ammunition Act. There are also cases where a single firearm is licensed to two different individuals and/or illegally issuing firearms to people who have been genuinely refused licences (such individuals having to pay bribes)." This situation is similar in most African countries with police officials being accused of engaging in all forms of unethical practices and demanding bribes before services are carried out. Ijewereme (2015) observed that in many African states, corruption is a clog in the wheel of progress, as well as a malaise that inflicts every aspect of the society. Corruption drains African countries more than US$140 billion yearly (Ribadu cited in Obuah 2010 and Ijewereme 2015). Corruption deprives enabling environment for potential investors to invest; it distorts public expenditure, increases cost of running businesses, cost of governance and diverts resources from poor to rich nations. The former Nigerian Economic and Financial Crime Commission (EFCC) Chairman, Nuhu Ribadu, claims that the over US$400 billion that had been looted from Nigeria by the leaders is "six times the total value of resources committed to rebuilding Western Europe after the Second World War" (Ademola 2011: 312 cited in Ijewereme 2015). Corruption has derailed meaningful developmental goals, resulting to high rate of insecurity and other social ills. The supply of drugs and SALW can largely be stemmed in a holistic approach by targeting weak law enforcement. By improving border controls, strengthening the police and the judiciary and reducing overall levels of corruption, the working environment of criminal networks can be made much less permissive (UNODC 2007).

State-Sponsored Militias

State-sponsored militias are prevalent in Africa. They are usually established and sponsored by the state or local community to assist the law enforcement agencies in maintaining security. These groups of individual carry firearms that are in most cases not licenced or are used not for the purpose to which licence is issued. In West Africa and other part of Africa, armed vigilante groups are used to re-enforce the local police in coping with the growing security challenges and promote community safety. Such vigilantes are used both in rural and urban areas. In Nigeria for instance, vigilante type of security arrangement is a common practice. But a lot of questions have been raised on the legality, efficiency and legitimacy of their activities. Kialee (2015) argues the government, Multinational Oil Companies (MNOCs) and local communities as key actors involved in arming youth-based vigilante groups in the Niger Delta for purposes that are sometimes contradictory. Community chiefs and local political elites, for instance, may arm vigilante groups not only to provide security for the local populations in the region, but also as a means of consolidating their local authority and power bases as well as demonstrating local power. In this regard, constitutive of broader aspects of community arming patterns, vigilante arming, contributes to the proliferation of Small Arms and Light Weapons (SALW) and militarization of local communities in the Niger Delta.

Similarly, ethnic militias are known to be armed and used by certain governments to conduct proxy wars against its citizens. In Darfur, the Sudanese government through its incorporation of elements of the Janjaweed militia into the state security bodies, such as the Popular Defence Force (PDF), the border intelligence guard, the central reserve police, the popular police have provided arms and ammunition to the Janjaweed Arab militia who perpetrated heinous crimes against humanity in Darfur. These arms cannot be accounted for could be used to commit crimes as the conflict in Darfur draws to an end. In March 2005, Resolution 1591 was passed in an attempt to augment the effectiveness of the sanctions regime. This resolution made provision for targeted travel and financial sanctions and established a Panel of Experts to monitor the implementation of the UN Security Council arms embargo and to report on human rights violations in the Darfur region. Despite this, it is difficult to account for these arms on charge to the militia groups. The report further accused other governments in the region for providing arms to different rebel groups. The Panel of Experts report published in December 2005 indicated that the SLM/A and JEM had received arms, ammunition and equipment from Chad, Eritrea, the Libyan Arab Jamahiriya and non-governmental groups in violation of the arms embargo.

Weak Legal Instruments

Most of the firearm laws in Africa need review to address certain issues. Most provisions in the laws have not reflected the realities of present security challenges in the continent. In firearms licensing, the overarching consideration is public safety at all times. It appears there are still loopholes in addressing some fundamental issues regarding firearm licensing. Issues of licensing locally made guns and the fate of local producers, appeal against the rejection of application or withdrawal of firearm licence, encouragement of declaration of unlicensed firearms, application of technology and provision of independent monitoring and auditing body are some of the gaps discovered in most of the firearm laws in Africa. In Cameroun for instance, despite the fact that most unlicensed firearms are locally made, the law bans all forms of homemade guns thereby making it difficult for people to declare their arms.

According to Amnesty International (2016), The UN has set up international guidelines that states can put in place to incorporate into national laws on firearms control. These international standards recommend prohibiting any possession of firearms without a licence; that states should register all firearms; and that unlicensed possession should be treated as a criminal offence.

To further support the efforts of the law enforcement agencies and to review the national laws for effective control of firearm, the International Association of Chiefs of Police (IACP) (2018) opposes any legislation that would limit or reduce the ability of the national law enforcement agencies to combat the sale of illegal guns. The IACP believes that the ability to trace illegal firearms effectively plays a critical role in law enforcement's ability to protect communities from the scourge of firearms violence. Therefore, the IACP strongly supports efforts to repeal any piece of legislation containing provisions that would weaken law enforcement's ability to trace illegal firearms.

Conclusion: Towards Improved Arm Control and Licensing System in Africa

Firearm is dangerously lethal and needs to be handled with caution. It can endanger lives or cause grievous harm. The way in which the police are required to undertake their firearms licensing responsibilities is set out in the legislative provisions of each country. The aim of arms licensing system is to ensure that firearms are not distributed to persons convicted of serious crime or those that are prohibited under the law to bear firearms. Although there is no reliable data on the number of the arms circulating freely in Africa, it's estimated that about 100 million small arms exist and are responsible for killing and maiming innocent people as well as halting development. There are global, regional as well as national efforts in policing and controlling the movements and use of these arms which include International Conventions and National Laws that empowers the police and other security agents to issue firearm licence through certification and registration of approved vendors, registering all types of arms and the persons possessing them. The main goal is to Limiting civilians' access to inappropriate weapons. Despite these efforts, Police in Africa faces huge challenge in licensing and controlling the possession and use of small arms due to inadequate/obsolete laws, lack of resources and capacity to effectively regulate the trade, flow and use of small arms.

Firearm licensing is one of the important measures taken across Africa in order to ensure protection and community safety. The police, being the government agency responsible for safety and protection of life and property plays significant role in ensuring that only eligible persons that constitute no danger to the public are granted licence to possess or deal in firearm. Despite this effort, it is discovered that gun-related violence and crime are still on the rise in most part of Africa and the police have not been able to guarantee safety through an effective and efficient licensing arrangement. We suggest the following strategies may assist in enhancing the police licensing system thereby improving the community safety and security in Africa.

Public Engagement: Information is a vital raw material for police job everywhere in the world. Arms licensing is one of the critical function of police that requires information to ascertain the applicant's suitability and detect the illicit arms. The police have to work in coordination and partnership with the members of public to generate information on unlicensed arms, illegal firearm vendors and their danger to the society. Engaging members of the public will open the door for voluntary declaration and commencement of genuine process of acquiring licence. Member of the public has great role to play in crime reduction and promotion of public safety. The dangers of keeping unlicensed arms or allowing ineligible persons to keep firearm cannot be over emphasized. However, the issue of trust and confidence building is one of the major issue of concern when it comes to the police–public relations as Nuri and Silva (2011) observes it is only when the police are fully trusted, and it is the foremost duty of the police to work to earn the full public trust, that the community will partner the police in preventing crimes without which the success of policing will be minimal and on the fringes of society. Police in Africa must develop capacity to fully utilize the opportunities provided by the ICT to engage members of the public especially the youth through the social media platforms like Facebook, Twitter and Instagram. Similarly, it is important to note that the task of firearm control is too huge to be left in the hands of police alone; guns are used to commit murder, armed robbery, kidnapping and drugs dealing. They are also used in communal conflicts, religious crises, cattle rustling and banditry. Their destructive effects extend to everybody irrespective of social status. Resources at the disposal of Civil Society Organisations (CSOs), traditional and religious institutions, trade unions, youth and gender-based organizations has to be explored and utilized by the police so that the menace will be tackled collectively.

Legal Review: Despite efforts by most African countries to reviewing their firearm laws, a lot of work is required to making firearm laws relevant to the present security realities. There are emerging issues in arms control relating to background checks and governance arrangement for firearm licensing. Gap exits relating to provisions requiring police forces to make contact with referees before any licence are granted and for the referees to be responsible for misuse/abuse of such arms.

African Parliaments need to provide a strong legal framework within which the holding of firearms by those members of our society who are considered suitable may be appropriately controlled and regulated. For instance, the Ugandan government has undertaken a legislative review process with a view to improving national SALW controls. Its current legislation, the 1970 Firearm Act, lacks proper definitions and has been deemed generally outdated and ineffective. Specifically, the government issued enhanced guidelines for licensing and monitoring firearms in 2002, and later announced that new legislation will be drafted making legal firearms ownership tougher for individuals.

Simplifying the licensing process by deploying adequate resources and relevant Technology: Digitization of the system would reduce bureaucracy, increase transparency, allow applicants to track progress, reduce the variability in the way the police manage the application process and make it much more efficient and effective. Some African countries like South Africa have pioneered the use of technology in simplifying their licensing processes though with some challenges as lamented by the country's police minister. In 2016, the Nigeria's Inspector-General of Police, IGP Solomon Arase urged persons in possession of non-prohibited firearms to immediately obtain or renew their licences before July 2016 by following the process on the requisite weblink of the Nigeria Police Central Information Centre (NCIS) on www.npf.gov.ng. This is also regarded as shift from the cumbersome manual process of firearm licence acquisition in the country. However, this digitalized firearm licence application process in Nigeria is more of rhetoric than practice.

To re-enforce the use of technology in keeping accurate records of licensed firearms and control the movement of arms, in November 2017, Thomas Heston, a public health professor at Washington State University, published a paper suggesting blockchain, (the decentralized ledger technology best known as the backbone for cryptocurrency), could improve gun control without actually requiring the government to change any existing laws on who can or can't own a gun. Blockchain would essentially make up a database to track the manufacture, transfer and purchase of guns. The log would also be "accurate, resistant to hacking, and easily accessible" to vendors, purchasers, and regulators. Every gun owner would have what Heston calls an "electronic gun safe." This wouldn't be a real, physical safe, but a digital one, comparable to a crypto owner's digital wallet. The information in the safe is accessible only through the owner's retina scan, fingerprint, or some other form of biometric data. These safes would contain information about each of the individual's guns, identified through ballistic fingerprinting or micro-stamping. That information would be switched over to a new owner after the gun is sold (and after the purchaser passed the background check).

The electronic gun safe would also contain information about the individual themselves, such as their history of illegal activity, mental health issues or parole status. Heston notes that some nations might include data from an individual's internet browsing history within their electronic gun safe, too. This new technology and many others of its kind, if applied would assist police forces in Africa to improve their arm licensing processes and gun control.

Robust Monitoring and Audit Arrangements: Considerations about public safety are at the heart of the firearms licensing arrangements. Governance does not end with the creation of a structure; it must include effective monitoring, audit and review system. Good monitoring and audit arrangements are an essential part of the government's responsibility to make sure that considerations about public safety are at the heart of the firearms licensing arrangements. "Although a chief officer may delegate some of their responsibilities to selected staff members, they retain oversight, governance and accountability for all firearms licensing decisions made on their behalf" (UK Home Office 2016).

In most African countries, we discovered that there is no independent monitoring and auditing body that periodically review police licensing activities. This allows inefficiency and corruption in the system. It is therefore in public interest and safety that more stakeholder including the parliament and judiciary be involved in monitoring the licensing process. The parliament through its oversight function will play critical role in ensuring adequate resources are appropriated to develop the police capacity in meeting up with the international arms licensing and monitoring standards. Governments in Africa (where such body is not established) should create a body that will be saddled with the responsibility of monitoring and auditing the licensing agency and engage in periodic inspection and review of the firearm records. Monitoring and Auditing promote efficiency and accountability and for Africa to have accurate records of licit arms in the hands of civilians, effective monitoring and auditing mechanisms has to be deployed to ensure that the licensing authorities maintain a transparent system and procedure that will promote public safety and security.

African Firearm Licensing Peer Review System: in a dependent world system, collaborative efforts and multilateralism is a common feature. Like the rest of the world, Africa stands to benefit more if expertise and resources are shared for common good. If illicit firearms are not controlled in one country, all other neighbouring states are at risk. The state collapse in Libya which led to the massive looting of state armouries and subsequent spread of arms into the hands of non-state actors has fuelled armed conflicts in other parts of Africa such as Nigeria and Mali. It is of great advantage if African police forces help and support each other in controlling illicit arms. As a way of ensuring that the day-to-day decisions in this sensitive area of police work are of good quality and remain so, the African Police Chiefs, in consultation with their governments should agree on a system of peer review where a sample of decisions of one police force is evaluated by another. This will provide a measure of independent oversight and provide an opportunity for forces to learn from each other. The problem has to be tackled holistically since any loophole in one African country may have negative effects on other African countries.

Firearms Licensing Course/Capacity Building: the effectiveness and consistency with which the licensing arrangements are undertaken within the police rely upon the skills of those with responsibility for carrying out the licensing function. Gaps in the capacity of a force to undertake efficient and effective licensing arrangements have the potential to let down those involved in the licensing process and substantially to increase the likelihood that mistakes will be made, thereby compromising public safety and security.

Police forces across Africa must acquire sufficient capability and capacity to discharge their licensing obligations relating to effective processing of licence applications and renewal s, contact with applicants' referees; dealing with expired certificates and accurate firearms licensing records. There should be a National Decision Model (as obtained in the UK) that is designed to help staff to make correct decisions, based on a risk assessment framework.

Police Colleges and Academies across the region should initiate and provide extensive firearm licensing courses. The courses should provide training on the theory and practical skills that are required to perform the role of a firearms enquiry and licence officer. This will as well provides the opportunity for firearms licensing offices and staff across Africa to share learning experiences and increase efficiency.

REFERENCES

Alpers, P. (1999, December 1). *Firearm Registration and Owner Licensing—The International Experience; Being a Testimony at California State Assembly Select Committee on Gun Violence*. Glendale, CA.

Alpers, P., & Wilson, M. (2013). *Global Impact of Gun Violence: Firearms, Public Health and Safety*. Sydney School of Public Health. The University of Sydney. www.gunpolicy.org/firearm/region. Accessed 10 November 2019.

Alpers, P., & Wilson, M. (2014). *Guns in North Africa: Small Arms Policy, Firearm Injury and Gun Law*. Sydney School of Public Health. The University of Sydney. www.gunpolicy.org/firearm/region/north-africa. Accessed 10 November 2019.

Amnesty International. (2016). *Gun Violence-Key Facts*. Available: https://www.amnesty.org/en/what-we-do/arms-control/gun-violence/. Accessed 13 May 2020.

Annan, K. (2000, March 27). Freedom from Fear: Small Arms, Report of the Secretary General to the Millennium Assembly of the United Nations; A/54/2000 p. 54. New York, NY: UN General Assembly.

Australian Institute of Criminology. (2012). Research and Public Policy Series no. 116. Available at: http://www.aic.gov.au/publications/rpp/116.

Bamako Declaration on an African Common Position on the Illicit Proliferation, Circulation and Trafficking of Small Arms and Light Weapons. (2000, December). Abuja: ECOWAS Headquarters.

Bashir, M. (2014, June). Small Arms and Light Weapons Proliferation and Its Implication for West African Regional Security. *International Journal of Humanities and Social Studies, 4*(8), 260–269.

Chande, F. (2019). *Interpol Statement; Fifth Conference of States Parties to the Arms Trade Treaty held on 26 August 2019*. Geneva, Switzerland.

Economic and Social Council (ECOSOC). (2017). *Firearm Regulation for Purposes of Crime Prevention and Public Health and Safety*. Resolution 1997/28. New York, the United Nations.

ECOWAS. (2006). *Convention on Small Arms and Light Weapon, their Ammunition and other Related Materials*. Abuja.

Eritrea. (2010). Introduction. In *National Report of Eritrea on Its Implementation of the United Nations Programme of Action to Prevent, Combat and Eradicate the Illicit Trade in Small Arms and Light Weapons in All Its Aspects (UNPoA)*. New York: United Nation.

Federal Government of Nigeria. (1990). Firearms Act. *Firearms Act, Chapter 146, Laws of the Federal Republic of Nigeria 1990*; Section 1. Abuja: Federal Ministry of Information.

Fleshman, M. (2011). *Small Arms in Africa: Counting the Cost of Gun Violence*. https://www.un.org/africarenewal/magazine/december-2011/small-arms-africa. Accessed 20 June 2020.

Grip, L. (2017). *Small Arms Control in Africa*. Academic dissertation of Department of Political and Economic Studies, Helsinki University, Helsinki.

Her Majesty's Inspectorate of Constabulary (HMIC). (2015). *'Targeting the Risk': An Inspection of the Efficiency and Effectiveness of Firearms Licensing in Police Forces in England and Wales*. Available at: www.justiceinspectorates.gov.uk/hmic. Accessed 7 March 2019.

Ijewereme, O. B. (2015, June 4). *Anatomy of Corruption in the Nigerian Public Sector: Theoretical Perspectives and Some Empirical Explanations*. Sage online publications Volume: 5, issue: 2, 4–6. Available: https://journals.sagepub.com/doi/metrics/10.1177/2158244015581188. Accessed 10 May 2020.

International Association of Chiefs of Police. (2018). IACP Firearms Position Paper_2018 (1) Available: https://www.theiacp.org/sites/default/files/201905/IACP%20Firearms%20Position%20Paper. Accessed 10 November 2019.

Karp, A. (2007). Completing the Count: Civilian Firearms—Annexe Online. In Editor? *Small Arms Survey 2007: Guns and the City*. Cambridge: Cambridge University Press.

Keili, F. L. (2008). Small Arms and Light Weapons Transfer in West Africa: A Stock-Taking. In V. Kerstin (Ed.), *The Complex Dynamics of Small Arms in West Africa*. Geneva: The United Nations Institute of Disarmament Research.

Kialee, N. (2015). Arming Community Vigilantes in the Niger Delta: Implications for Peace Building. In I. L. John & L. Tanya (Eds.), *African Frontiers: Insurgency, Governance and Peace Building in Postcolonial States*. Basingstoke, UK: Ashgate Publishing.

Mthethwa, E. N. (2010). "Challenges Affecting the SAPS Firearms Application and Licensing Processes" Being a Remarks at the National Press Club, on 2 November, Sheraton Hotel, Pretoria.

Newton, G. D., & Franklin, E. Z. (1969). Firearm Licensing: 'Permissive v Restrictive.' *Firearms & Violence in American Life*. A staff report submitted to the National Commission on the Causes and Prevention of Violence, Washington, DC: US Government Printing Office.

Nuri, A., & Silva, P. (2011). Aile Polisi (Family Police), Istanbul, Hayat Yayıncılık.

Pellerin, M. (2017). *Beyond the Wild West: The Gold Rush in Northern Niger*. Briefing Paper. Geneva: Small Arms Survey.

Renner, M. (1997). *Small Arms, Big Impact: The Next Challenge of Disarmament* (Paper 137). Washington, DC: World Watch Institute.

Small Arms Survey. (2007). *Guns and the City*. Cambridge: Cambridge University Press.

Small Arms Survey and African Union Commission. (2019). *Weapons Compass: Mapping Illicit Small Arms Flow in Africa*. Gonnet: France.

UN Disarmament Commission. (1999). *Report on Guidelines on Conventional Arms Control/Limitations and Disarmament, with Particular Emphasis on Consolidation of Peace in the Context of General Assembly Resolution 51/45 N*. Available at: www.un.org/disarmaent/wp-content/uploads/2019/09/A-51-182.

United Kingdom Home Office. (2016). *Guide on Firearms Licensing Law*. London: Published by Home Office.

United Nations Office on Drugs and Crime. (2007). Cocaine Trafficking in West Africa: The Threat to Stability and Development. *Report*. http://www.unodc.org/documents/data-andanalysis/west_africa_cocaine_report_2007-12_en.pdf. Accessed 10 October 2019.

United Nations Regional Centre for Peace and Disarmament in Africa (UNREC). (2014). *Trafficking of Small Arms and Light Weapons in West Africa: Routes and Illegal Arms Caches Between Ghana, Togo, Benin and Nigeria*. Abuja: Friedrich Erbert Stiftung.

United Nations Security Council (UNSC). (2017). *Eritrea Report of the Monitoring Group on Somalia and Eritrea Submitted in Accordance with Resolution 2317 (2016)*. S/2017/925 of 6 November.

United Republic of Tanzania. (2001, May 4). Preliminary Provisions. *The Arms and Ammunition Act, Chapter 223, No. 19 of 2007*; Part 1 (Sections 1 and 2). Dar es Salaam: Ministry of Home Affairs.

Vanguard Newspaper. (2016). UN: Nigeria Accounts for 70% of 500 Millicit Weapons in West Africa. Available at: https://www.vanguardngr.com/2016/08/un-nigeria-accounts-for-70-of-500m-illicit-weapons-in-west-africa/. Accessed 25 June 2020.

Vines, A. (2005). Combating Light Weapons Proliferation in West Africa. *International Affairs* (Royal Institute of International Affairs 1944–), *81*(2). Sub-Saharan Africa, pp. 341–360. Oxford University Press.

Dawud Muhammad Dawud is a Nigeria Police Officer and a Doctoral researcher in the Department of Political Science and Defence Studies, Nigerian Defence Academy (NDA), Kaduna Nigeria. His area of research interest is Terrorism, Foreign Policy and Security Sector Reform. He also contributed a Chapter in the Book titled *New Architecture of Regional Security in Africa: Perspectives on Counter-Terrorism and Counter Insurgency in the Lake Chad Basin*, published by Lexington Publishers, Lanham, Maryland, USA.

Tukur Abdulkadir is an Associate Professor and former Head, Department of Political Science at Kaduna State University, Nigeria. He obtained Ph.D. in Political Science from Ahmadu Bello University, Zaria (2015) and MSc in International Relations and Strategic Studies from the University of Jos, Nigeria. His areas of research interest include International Relations, Strategic Studies, Political Islam, Religious Fundamentalism, Terrorism, Democracy and Development.

CHAPTER 24

Civil Society and Arms Control in Africa

Abdulmalik Auwal and Moses T. Aluaigba

INTRODUCTION

One of the dire consequences of the proliferation of Small Arms and Light Weapons (SALWs) worldwide in general and Africa in particular has been heightened security challenges to individuals, societies and states: SALWs provide the main instrument for perpetuating terrorism, insurgencies, civil wars, organized criminal violence, coups d'état, militancy, and robberies, thus posing "great obstacles to sustainable security and development" (Bashir 2014: 260). On average, thousands of people lose their lives daily as victims of SALWs, with many more thousands wounded, displaced, raped or otherwise abused as a result of armed violence. Yet incredibly, the international arms trade is poorly regulated and the binding standards for regulation of arms globally are weakly enforced. Despite growing awareness of the devastating effects of irresponsible arms transfer, many governments continue to approve the export of weapons, munitions and military equipment to parties stoking armed conflicts. The same arms transfer is made to governments known to be perpetrating serious violations of international human rights and humanitarian

---

A. Auwal (✉)
Department of Political Science, Bayero University, Kano, Nigeria

M. T. Aluaigba
Mambayya House, Aminu Kano Centre for Democratic Studies, Bayero University, Kano, Nigeria
e-mail: mtaluaigba.mambayya@buk.edu.ng

© The Author(s), under exclusive license to Springer Nature Switzerland AG 2021
U. A. Tar and C. P. Onwurah (eds.), *The Palgrave Handbook of Small Arms and Conflicts in Africa*,
https://doi.org/10.1007/978-3-030-62183-4_24

laws, and to states where there are institutional and other substantial risks of diversion to unauthorized users (Daniel and Brain 2016).

The weakness and fragile nature of African states and their attendant failure to deliver governance might be considered one of the reasons why these states lack the political will to control SALWs. As a result, a large cache of weapons are illegally in private hands in the region. SALWs kill between 500,000 and 750,000 people annually and are a "contributory factor to armed conflict, the displacement of people, organized crime and terrorism, thereby undermining peace, reconciliation, safety, security, stability and sustainable social and economic development" (Bashir 2014: 261). No wonder a host of African states such as Sierra Leone, Liberia, Rwanda, Burundi, Ghana, Mali, Libya, Guinea, Nigeria, Cote D'Ivoire, Sudan, Niger, etc., have suffered or are still suffering from the menace of the proliferation of SALWs. For instance, from Mali and Libya in Central Sahara to the cancerous plague of the Boko Haram in the West Coast of Africa; from the newly birthed republic of South Sudan, to the Central African Republic's (CARs) Seleka and anti-Balaka bloodshed, the challenge bears identical characteristic especially with regard to the source of their livewire and existence which is easily tied to SALWs. This establishes the fact that the spread of SALWs and the resulting armed conflicts it generates undermine good governance which determines to a large extent, development initiatives in Africa more than in any other continent.

Regional, sub-regional, governmental and non-governmental efforts and mechanism adopted at tackling this menace are numerous. For instance, in 2001, states agreed under the United Nation Programme of Action (UNPoA) to prevent, combat and eradicate the illicit trade in SALWs in all aspects through legislation and administrative procedure. In Africa, all of African Union member states have made a general commitment to control SALWs brokering, while efforts were also adopted by Civil Society Organizations (CSOs) to supplement government's efforts in regulating SALWs through their various activities of advocacy, putting in place development projects that address poverty reduction that will invariably reduce the demand for small arms, providing much needed medical care and support and reach out to the perpetrators through rehabilitation and reintegration (UNREC 2011). Therefore, this chapter examines the role of CSOs in addressing the problem of arms proliferation in Africa particularly small arms with emphasis on measures taken to control the menace.

Proliferation of Small Arms and Its Effects in Africa

It is an established fact that violent conflicts stand as the key instrument used in fueling of the spread of both legal and illegal arms. This is true because in the absence of violent conflicts, the utility of arms will totally diminish to the lowest ebb. Africa has become notorious of violent conflicts. In fact, since the beginning of the twenty-first century, majority of the world's most violent armed conflicts have occurred in sub-Saharan Africa (Ogu n.d.). Surprisingly, virtually all parts of the continent are touched by this dreadful incidence. For instance, in West Africa, there was the Liberian civil war that ended in 1996, the Malian conflict, the civil war in Sierra Leone 1991–2002, the 1967–1970 Nigerian civil war and currently, the lingering Boko Haram insurgency, etc. In Central and horn of Africa, some of the violent conflicts that come to mind include the Sudanese and Ethiopian crises, the protracted conflict in DRC, and the *Al-Shabaab* terrorism in Somalia and the Horn of Africa. In North Africa, the Arab uprising that began in 2010, engulfing Egypt, Tunisia and Libya proved catastrophic. Cases of violent conflicts in Southern Africa worth mentioning include the 40-year old Angolan civil war that ended in 2002, the Ugandan conflict, the Rwandan ultra-violent ethnic crisis, etc.

The conflicts mentioned above were made possible by the quantum of SALWs that have permeated the borders of African states in staggering statistics. These SALWs come in a variety of forms. According to Ayuba and Okafor (2015: 77), SALWs:

> ...include notably firearms and other destructive arms or devices such as an exploding bomb, an incendiary bomb or gas bomb, a grenade, a rocket launcher, a missile, a missile system or landmine. [They] also includes revolvers and pistols with automatic loading; riffles and carbines; machine guns; assault rifles; and light machine guns. Light weapons are portable arms designed to be used by several persons working together in a team and which include notably heavy machine guns; portable grenade launchers, mobile or mounted; portable anti-aircraft cannons; portable anti-tanks cannons, non-recoil guns; portable anti-tank missile launchers or rocket launchers; portable anti-aircraft missile launchers; mortars with a caliber of less than 100 millimeters.

Ayuba and Okafor (2015: 17) further listed the specific versions of SALWs to include Tokarev TT pistols, Makarov PM pistols, AR-70 and AKM-47 assault rifles, RPG-7V1 Mukha "Fly" propelled grenade, 7.62 mm PKMSN-2 machine guns, AK-47 under-barrel grenade launchers, among a variety of other similar arms. These arms flow into Africa in large quantities. Virtually all the African countries are culpable of the act of arms importation. According to the 2017 SIPRI Fact Sheet as compiled by Wezeman et al. (2018), from 2013 to 2017, the three countries with the largest arms import in Africa were Algeria (52%), Morocco (12%) and Nigeria (5.1%). Furthermore, "the top five arms importers in sub-Saharan Africa were Nigeria, Sudan, Angola, Cameroon and Ethiopia. Together, they accounted for 56 percent of arms imports to the sub-region" (Wezeman et al. 2018: 7). These arms were exported to Africa mainly by three world powers including China (55%), Russia (39%) and USA (11%). The interpretation of this is that the large inflow of arms into Africa has served as a sustaining force to the many violent conflicts in the continent. This underscores the non-caseation of protracted conflicts all over Africa because the supply routes of arms remain open without any impediment.

But the question arises: what are the root causes of SALWs proliferation in Africa? Answers to this question vary. Conventionally, countries import arms for the sake of routine internal security. But most often, countries do acquire arms to stem the tide of internal security threat arising from insurrection as the cases of military coups and counter coups in Africa demonstrated. Moreover, the prestige factor can also push a country to accumulate weapons including SALWs in order to either assert its military might in a region or wade off an impending enemy from a neighboring country. Besides these factors, one of the foremost reasons advanced by Ogu (n.d.) for the proliferation of SALWs is Africa's long years of experience with colonial rule and the authoritarian regimes it produced in the continent after independence. SALWs were used to violently maintain the colonial state and this left a violent political legacy that the authoritarian rulers of emerging independent African states inherited from the 1950s to 1960s. As a corollary, the countless intra- and inter-state conflicts generated in post-colonial states of Africa could only be contained or managed by deploying the use of SALWs by importing them massively.

Suffice it to say that the phenomenon of SALWs proliferation in Africa has produced dire consequences in the continent. Foremost among these negative results is the high level of fatalities and material loss that usually accompany violent conflict situations. To illustrate, 100,000 people have been killed by Boko Haram insurgency in Nigeria from 2009 to 2017 (*Premium Times* February 13, 2017). Also, the availability of SALWs has unnecessarily ensured the prolongation of conflicts across Africa by making it difficult for parties in such conflicts to arrive at a negotiated consensus because the parties are confident they can continue to prosecute the conflicts since they have adequate arms. Conflicts in the Democratic Republic of Congo (DRC), Niger Delta, and Mali are some of the cases in mind. Furthermore, increasing inflow of SALWs has instilled a near-permanent state of insecurity in most African countries. This has manifested in form of rampant cases of kidnapping, assassinations, insurgency, armed robbery and the like. In Nigeria, the most populated and one of the economic giants in Africa, the 2015 report of the Nigeria Police indicates an increase in armed robbery cases in 2014 from 1010 to 2129 (The Nigeria Police 2015: 222). This is apart from the increasing wave of kidnapping and adoption of people in the country. Recently, beginning from 2016 up to 2018, Nigeria has suffered the ravaging effects of herdsmen attacks on farming communities around the country and has greatly threatened her national unity. These social upheavals are made possible because SALWs are easily accessible. It must as well be mentioned that proliferation of SALWs in Africa has compelled the affected countries to redirect tremendous resources that would have been used for building infrastructure to managing protracted conflicts. Schnabel (Ayuba and Okafor 2015: 78) has put the cost of conflicts on Africa at approximately US$300 billion from 1990 to 2005. Since 2010, Nigeria has produced over 3.3 million refugees due to insurgency; this number is the highest in the continent. Last but not the least effect is that SALWs proliferation has obstructed the development of democracy in many African states. To illustrate, in Nigeria and Kenya, elections are more often than not, marred by violence where small arms are deployed with unreserved alacrity. Thugs who are employed by politicians rely on SALWs to cause mayhem during electioneering processes. All these culminate into a high state of human rights and outright disregard for the rule of law inimical to the growth of democracy and its institutions.

THEORETICAL PERSPECTIVES ON SMALL ARMS PROLIFERATION IN AFRICA

The incidence of small arms proliferation has created problems that have generated negative consequences in many countries around the world particularly Africa. Arising from this problematic scenario, many theoretical postulations have been generated in an effort to explain the spread of small arms. There is the theory of development as propounded by Seers (1969). According to Seers, the measurement of development can only be realistic if it is based on no indices other than yardsticks that demonstrate the quality of the living standard of individuals in a society. These indices include long life expectancy, good housing, improved nutrition, better schools, adequate supply of food and energy, high level of citizen participation in the political process, etc. In the words of Seers (1969: 5):

> The questions to ask about a country's development are therefore: What has been happening to poverty? What has been happening to unemployment? What has been happening to inequality? If all these three have declined from high levels, then beyond doubt this has been a period of development for the country concerned. If one or two of these central problems have been growing worse, especially if all three have, it would be strange to call the result 'development' even if per capita income doubled.

Therefore, arms proliferation and underdevelopment are twin problems that are common in Africa. This explains the reason why the continent is trailing as far as development is concerned. Moreover, the preponderance of conflicts in Africa is attributable to the incidences of the spread of arms in all its states. These conflicts exacerbate Africa's already ugly refugee condition, destroy existing schools, hospitals and water facilities that are prerequisite for development. So in Seer's (1969) view, development can hardly take place in the midst of these.

Another theory related to the issue of SALWs proliferation in Africa and which this chapter will adopt is conflict theory. Rooted in the philosophy of Karl Marx (1818–1883), the theory posits that coercion and power are tools used in the production of social order in society. Marx conceived society as an arena of competition between fragmented groups that struggle for social and economic resources therein. In order to maintain social order in such a fragmented society, domination by the most powerful who possess immense social, economic and political resources is inevitable. Furthermore, conflict theory holds the view that the existence of inequality in society is necessitated by the control exerted by those who disproportionately own society's resources and acutely defend their advantaged position. In so doing, members of the population in society are not bound by their shared values but rather by the force utilized by the most powerful. Thus, the inequality in society induced by the excessive exercise of power by a few advantaged individuals most likely degenerate and produce conflict. A look at the incidence of SALWs proliferation in Africa will show its direct or indirect interrelation to conflicts in the continent that arise from manipulation of power and domination by a few in African states. Such conflicts as the Liberian war, the Libyan crisis, the conflict in DRC, the Sudanese conflict, etc., are all examples of conflicts based on the dominant role of one group against another.

The structural theory of conflict can also be used to explain the proliferations of small arms and light weapons as a result of tension that arises when groups compete for scarce resources. The theory is built on the thesis that conflict is built into the particular ways societies are structured and organized. It describes the condition of the society and how such condition or environment can create conflict and thus proliferate small arms and light weapons. The Structural conflict theory classifies how certain conditions such as deprivation, political marginalization, social exclusion, economic exploitation, injustices, social exclusion, class inequalities, gender imbalances, racial segregation, among many others, lead to conflict. The theory posits that conflict occurs because of the exploitative and unjust nature of human societies or because of domination of one class by another. One of the critiques of the theory is its one-sidedness of looking at causes of conflict. It, for instance, does not see the bright sides of racial or ethnic diversity and the strength that a society may derive from pluralism. It only sees the flaws. The structural theory thus makes sense only when conflicts are viewed from the broadest possible perspective, and only if the observer opts to ignore alternate (Folarin 2015). As pointed out above, the occurrence of these conflicts in Africa has served as a fertile ground for the proliferation of SALWs in the region.

UNCIVIL SOCIETY AND ARMS PROLIFERATION IN AFRICA: THE FLIP SIDE OF CIVIL SOCIETY

In as much as civil society remains a means to eradicate absolutist rule and create a free society based on the "natural rights" of all human beings (Michael 2019: 390), the uncivil society according to (Annan 1998) are "drivers of conflicts", those who "promote exclusionary policies or encourage people to resort to violence." The idea of uncivil society according to (Ferguson 1995 cited in Michael 2019: 291) is a space "inhabited by the 'savage', the 'primitive', the 'rude', the 'aggressive', or the 'fanatic' other." The uncivil society contains "youth groups, ethnic and sectional militias, vigilantes, paramilitaries, civil security task forces and militant religious groups, secessionist or separatist groups, ethno nationalist-groups to terrorist organizations and groups belonging to organized crime" (Beittinger-Lee 2009). In Nigeria, such groups could be classified into the Bakassi Boys—a vigilante outfit set up by the Abia and Anambra State governments in 1999 to curb criminal activities, the *Egbesu* Boys, the Movement for the Actualization of the Sovereign State of Biafra (MASSOB), Ijaw and Itsekiri Militias, the Oodua People's Congress (OPC) and the *Boko Haram*—a religious sect terrorizing Nigeria and its neighbors in general, using various small arms, IEDs and ammunitions in their possession (Abiodun et al. 2018).

Global survey suggests that violent non-state actors (VNSAS) have become a pervasive challenge to nation-states. In Europe, Jihadist terrorist organizations have carried out dramatic and well-publicized attacks in Madrid and London. In Mexico, drug trafficking organizations are challenging the Mexican state in a particularly brutal manner, and have killed a series of high-ranking security personnel in retaliation for the administration's efforts to disrupt their activities and reduce their power. In the favelas of Rio de Janeiro and Sao Paulo, drug traffickers and, more recently, militias provide rudimentary forms of governance in urban areas where the state is absent. In Albania, Italy and many parts of the former Soviet Union, criminal organizations not only intimidate businesses, corrupt politicians and launder their proceeds, but also engage in a variety of activities that challenge and undermine state sovereignty. In many African countries as well as Central Asia and Afghanistan, warlords are major players in the political system and the economy. In Iraq, insurgents, terrorists, militias and criminal organizations operate in a common opportunity space, intersecting and overlapping in ways that make the restoration of a legitimate and effective central state particularly difficult. In short, these groups, in most cases challenge the state while in some, the state is a passive bystander while they fight one another (Williams 2008: 4).

THE ROLE OF CIVIL SOCIETY IN ARMS CONTROL IN AFRICA

There have been several efforts aimed at curbing or reducing the proliferation of SALWs globally by the United Nations, regional organizations, national governments and CSOs through their varied programmes. Some of these programmes include the UNPoA to prevent, combat and eradicate the illicit trade in small arms and light weapons; the Arms Trade Treaty (ATT); etc. The idea of the ATT initiated by several non-governmental organizations in the 1990s has gradually become accepted by governments, and now by the overwhelming majority of member states in the United Nations. Advocates of ATT seek to prevent such reckless arms trading through the establishment of the highest global standards in a binding international agreement to require states to effectively control all international transfers of conventional arms in their jurisdiction according to strict procedures that ensure maximum respect for established principles of international human rights law, international humanitarian law, socio-economic development, international security and crime prevention.

To demonstrate the nature of the problem of irresponsible conventional arms trading, one could refer to many examples from different countries and continents—as rigorously researched and documented by reputable non-governmental organizations and media. One such example involved the Chinese ship *An Yue Jiang* that sailed in April 2008 toward Zimbabwe to deliver three million ammunition units at the height of grave political tensions and despite a worsening pattern of state-sponsored violence against unarmed civilians in that country. The export was strongly resisted by civil society in several African countries with the support of a global Non-Governmental Organization (NGO) campaign coordinated by the International Action Network on Small Arms (IANSA). Dock workers in South Africa and Angola refused to disembark the shipment, while human rights lawyers began successful national court actions. Religious leaders and parliamentarians protested across the Southern African Development Community (SADC) sub-region, thus, prompting an international outcry by governments which eventually forced the government of China to say it would suspend the munitions shipment and recall the ship. Since there is no global legal instrument with adequate ethical and transparency standards to prevent that sort of irresponsible arms transfer, it is certain that many other such transfers will continue to be authorized by states thus contributing to the destruction of lives and livelihoods in unstable, repressive and conflict-ridden countries. To prevent such situations, and in order to fulfill its promise and purpose as set out in the resolutions of the General Assembly, the ATT must be based on objective universal principles and robust procedures and mechanisms, including the "golden rule" expounded by global civil society: no international conventional arms transfer should be permitted where the weapons, munitions or equipment are likely to be used to commit serious violations of international human rights and humanitarian law, or to undermine social-economic development. Some years after, global civil society commenced the Control Arms campaign to raise public awareness and press governments to accept the idea of a principled ATT (Daniel and Brain 2016).

Indeed, the role of civil society in preventing conflicts and peace-building is indispensable. Ekiyor (2008) is also of the view that civil society's visibility and influence in conflict prevention and peace-building has grown globally and have increasingly become vital forces in discourses, initiatives and programmes that foster peace and security across the world. Specifically, civil society has been instrumental in the re-conceptualization of security from a "state-centered" process to one that is "people-centered." This focus on people-centered security emanates from the belief that fundamentally the sustainable security of states can only be attained through the security of its people. This belief is shared in regions across the world that have experienced open conflicts and civil wars, which have raged communities and brought devastation to the lives of ordinary people. Africa as a region has witnessed various protracted civil wars, ethno-religious conflicts, inter-state conflicts and insurgent uprisings. In fact, it is impossible for state actors to prevent, manage or resolve them without the assistance and involvement of non-state actors. Civil society in particular has been at the forefront of promoting localized peace-building initiatives, initiating reconciliation processes, advocating for adherence to peace agreements and building capacities in peace education. For instance, prior to 1999 in Nigeria, CSOs like Centre for Democracy and Development (CDD), Centre for Alternative Dispute Resolution, Human Right Monitor (HRM), Nigerian Labour Congress (NLC), etc., have acted as whistleblowers and vanguards against authoritarian regimes and democratic threats. CSOs that act as vanguard for democratic restoration and democratic peace such as enhances citizens' participation in the electoral process, agitate demands for transparency and accountability, promote democratic consolidation, lobby and influence government policy formulations, and monitoring the executive, legislatures and the judiciary for accountability and good governance include Campaign for Democracy (CD), Civil Liberty Organization (CLO), Committee for the Defense of Human Rights (CDHR), Transition Monitoring Group (TMG), and Civil Society Legislative Advocacy Centre (CISLAC), among others. The role of civil society in Nigeria is consistent with the experience elsewhere in Africa, Latin America and Asia where, for instance, in the case of South Africa, the African National Congress (ANC) carried a sustained struggle to dismantle the white supremacist government; the Zimbabwe African National Union Patriotic Front (ZANU/PF) which successfully fought the white dominated government of Rhodesia; and the Southwest African People's Organization (SWAPO) which gained power in Namibia (Ataman 2003).

Apart from enhancing conflicts mitigation and management, politically, CSOs play unequaled roles in oiling the wheels of democratic process. These roles are fundamental in virtually all regime types. Under authoritarian regimes, CSOs champion the struggle for the enthronement of people-oriented government. In both the advanced and evolving democracies, CSOs are indispensable. This is because in the established democracies, CSOs anchor the course of populist policies, while in emerging democracies such as the one in Nigeria and many other African states, the existence and functioning of vibrant CSOs are requisite tools in strengthening their democratic heritages. However, despite the unrivaled position of CSOs in society, their efficacy in the African context generally has been obviated by the nature of post-colonial politics fathomed by the elite in their quest to control political power and resources. The unending cycle of this political process in the continent has found solace in the politics of identity and violence (Eyoh 2002: 3) lubricated by political mobilization in the contexts of ethnic and religious cubicles. This phenomenon has truncated the democratization processes of most of the African countries; and in some countries where democracy has managed to survive in the continent; it has done so at the peril of imminent authoritarian reversals. This explains why the conduct of elections in most African countries is usually violently contested culminating into unending political conflicts fueled by the proliferation of SALWs such that 5,994,000 lives have been lost in the last 50 years in the continent (Edeko 2011: 3).

In fact, the problems created by the proliferation of SALWs, demand collective efforts to address them, and this require the concrete effort of civil society to stem the tide of armed violence in which the state and violent non-state actors (insurgents, bandits, militants) are equally culprits. Indeed, the government alone cannot contain this illicit act. This is why CSOs as grassroots oriented bodies and agents of development come in handy. CSOs by their very nature exist as agents of positive change in any society. This partially explains why CSOs are not-for-profit organizations. Civil society therefore, performs functions in furtherance of good governance through policy analysis and advocacy, regulation and monitoring of state performance as well as the action and behavior of public officials. They build social capital that enables citizens to identify and articulate their values, beliefs, civic norms and democratic practices. Civil society mobilizes specific constituencies, particularly the vulnerable and marginalized sections of the masses so that these groups can participate more fully in politics and public affairs. Finally, civil society engages in development work to improve the wellbeing of their communities. Given these avowed creeds of civil society and given that SALWs proliferation is a menace in Africa, the question is, what can CSOs comprising Community Based Organizations (CBOs) and Non-Governmental Organizations (NGOs) do to obviate the consequences of SALWs proliferation in the continent.

Given that CSOs are critical stakeholders in stemming the proliferation of weapons, Aderinwale (2005) has offered two broad-based suggestions regarding the roles that CSOs can play in scuttling the spread of SALWs in Africa. The first suggestion involves the creation of awareness on the scourges of SALWs as conflict propellant in society. This involves respect for the principle of accountability among security agencies as opposed to the culture of impunity, making manifest the international political will and the momentum to support efforts to combat SALWs, denouncing and combating the political, social and economic conditions in Africa that generate the demand for arms, working for the reduction in the demand for arms through measures to consolidate democracy, good governance and respect for human rights and the rule of law. Awareness creation here also implies fostering the reduction of the secrecy associated with decision-making on weapons through holding discussions on small arms to create public awareness about security issues, extensive publicity of messages against SALWs and working to secure the adoption of legislations for disarmament and regulation of firearms circulation. The second suggestion deals with local capacity building. This implies training local community leaders in peace-building and conflict resolution techniques, running awareness-building programmes to help in replacing the culture of violence with that of peace, organizing seminars for senior customs, police and immigration officials on national and international rules governing SALWs proliferation, educating communities about overflows and the forces that facilitate armed conflicts and educating communities on the ideals and virtues of participatory democracy. In order to reinforce Aderinwale's (2005) options highlighted above, CSOs in the various African states, because of their known community-oriented services, can embark on aggressive awareness drive to inform people of the dangers of SALWs and dissuade them from patronizing these arms for usage as means of expressing disenchantment against political authorities.

CHALLENGES OF CIVIL SOCIETY INVOLVEMENT IN THE MANAGEMENT OF SMALL ARMS

Civil society actors may become an important force for peace and security through the following activities: monitoring abuses of power, human rights violations and small arms issues and by increasing public awareness of these issues through advocacy. These actions could put pressure on government authorities to reduce the use of violence, to be more responsive and accountable to its citizens, and to ensure justice and respect for human rights. Civil society can check the power of the state and private sector by playing a type of "watchdog" role (Christine 2012: 5). Civil society actors can at the same time help to reduce mistrust in the security forces by becoming involved in, for instance, SALWs reduction, community policing, peace committee or other very local and community-based activities meant to improve security and conflict prevention capacities. Attempts at curbing Africa from SALWs proliferation by the civil society organizations according to Christine (2012) has its own challenges that consist lack of capacity and political will by civil society organizations to make a positive impact to inform and engage the public, and to engage the state on policy issues. In as much as these civil society actors need to play an important role by promoting peaceful co-existence in societies, they need to be independent, credible, strong and command respect. Another challenge of civil society involvement in the management of SALWs is the occurrences of strain relationship between civil society actors and national government that sometimes causes governments to obstruct the efforts of these actors by limiting their access to information and by limiting or completely barring their participation in security policy development and implementation. There may also be sustainability constraints due to lack or insufficient funding which has restraint and constraint their growth and functioning. Their heavy reliance on donor agencies and countries with little or no local funding capacity. Other challenges of civil society organizations are their lack of internal democracy which makes it difficult for them to learn democratic values and norms within their organization and thus, finds it difficult to adequately inculcate this principle to citizens (Mercy 2012: 7).

CONCLUSION

The danger posed by the raging spread of SALWs in Africa is real and precipitous. Given that Africa has a history of violent eruptions of conflict especially during the anti-colonial struggles and in the post-colonial era due to a variety of authoritarian regimes that were in vogue in virtually all the states in the continent, all stakeholders particularly the CSOs must not relent from taking urgent steps to forestall the ugly consequences of SALWs spread. Although, it is impossible to talk about total eradication of the spread of SALWs especially in Africa where conflicts abound, it is not out of place to emphasize the role of civil society (as well as the state) in mitigating the roots of SALWs proliferation on the continent. Indeed, African leaders have the option of curtailing SALWs proliferation in the continent by reducing violent conflict situations in their countries through good governance and by ensuring strict adherence to democratic tenets in their governance processes. This is because violence comes in handy when people perceive some aspects of alienation, exclusiveness, abuse of human rights, outright disregard for the rule of law, etc., by elected public office holders in the decision-making process. In short, through deliberate policies and strategic actions that reflect the yearnings and aspirations of the mass of Africans by their leaders, violent insurrections will tremendously diminish giving way to lesser number of SALWs in circulation in communities. Despite the prevalence of SALWs proliferation, it does not foreclose the possibility of retracting the nuisance. In order to alleviate the problems created by the spread of small arms in Africa, some suggestions are made.

First, it is important that governments across Africa should provide enabling socio-political environments amenable for CSOs to thrive as viable instruments of positive change in their communities. This can be done by allowing the rule of law to flourish, respect for human rights, press freedom and the likes. These will foster the robustness of CSOs to undertake advocacy and awareness creation activities related to curbing illicit SALWs proliferation. Secondly, CSOs should champion the call for the review of colonial and obsolete laws on firearms in African countries. Most of the laws aimed at addressing the free flow of arms into African states are outdated and colonial in nature without recognizing the present challenges and exigencies in the continent. The onus therefore, rests on CSOs in Africa to pressurize their various legislatures to review their Firearm Acts to conform to current realities in the present spate of SALWs spread is to abate. Third, controlling SALWs proliferation demands collective efforts. Therefore, CSOs can only make effective impact if they work in collaboration with their peers across the world to take collective action and measures against the rise in SALWs spread. Where necessary they can also enter into partnership with genuine sub-regional organizations in Africa. These organizations have great influence economically and politically in their respective sub-regions, so working with them will make quick impact on curtailing the spread of small arms in the entire African regions. Such sub-regional organizations as the Economic Community of West African States (ECOWAS), South African Development Commission (SADC, formerly Southern African Development Coordination Conference, SADCC), East African Community (EAC) and the Arab League are strategic in creating a more formidable force through sub-regional charters and laws against small arms to be adopted by all member countries.

Fourth, it is imperative for African States to work assiduously toward enhancing the capacities of their security agencies particularly the custom services of African countries. The continent of Africa has vast international boundaries that are mostly porous without adequate security personnel guarding vehicular and human traffic across them. This porousness of borders has facilitated the free entry of illegal arms into many African states. To address this and reinforce border security, African countries should improve the capacities of their custom services through personnel training and provision of modern surveillance equipment. These measures will improve monitoring of international borders and dictation of illegal transit of arms. Finally, CSOs in Africa should work toward curbing the proliferation of SALWs in Africa through consistent advocacy, checkmating government actions and inaction to ensure that its policies are in the best interest of the yearnings and aspirations of African masses. In this way, violent conflicts where contending factions utilize arms will be drastically reduced to the extent that the perturbed consequences of arms usage will no longer pose a threat to peace in Africa. In doing this, CSOs in Africa can collaborate and take collective measures similar to the economic efforts made at the sub-regional levels that have culminated into the emergence of economic blocks such as ECOWAS and SADC.

References

Abiodun, T. F., Ayo-Adeyekun, I., Onafowora, O., & Nwannenaya, C. (2018, July-September). Small Arms and Light Weapons Proliferation and its Threats to Nigeria's Internal Security. *International Journal of Social Science and Humanities Research, 6*(3), 34–45.

Aderinwale, A. (2005). Civil Society and the Fight Against the Proliferation of Small Arms and Light Weapons. In A. N. Ayissi & A. Sall (Eds.), *Combating the Proliferation of Small Arms and Light Weapons in West Africa: Handbook for the Training of Armed Security Forces*. Geneva: United Nations Publications.

Annan, K. (1998). *Text of the "Magisterial Lecture."* Delivered by Secretary-General Kofi Annan at the Foreign Ministry of Mexico on 23rd July, 1998.

Ataman, M. (2003). The Impact of Non-State Actors on World Politics: A Challenge to Nation-States. *Alternatives: Turkish Journal of International Relations, 2*(1), 42–66.

Aver, T. T., Nnorom, K. C., & Ilim, M. M. (2014). *The Proliferation of Arms and its Effects on the Development of Democracy in Nigeria*. Retrieved from http://iasir.net/AIJRHASSpapers/AIJRHASS14-196.pdf. Accessed 13 June 2019.

Ayuba, C., & Okafor, G. (2015, March). The Role of Small Arms and Light Weapons Proliferation in African Conflicts. *African Journal of Political Science and International Relations, 9*(2), 76–85.

Bashir, M. (2014, June). Small Arms and Light Weapons Proliferation and its Implication for West African Regional Security. *International Journal of Humanities and Social Science, 4*(8), 260–269.

Beittinger-Lee, V. (2009). *(Un)Civil Society and Political Change in Indonesia: A Contested Arena*. Routledge, Tailor and Francis: London and New York, NY.

Christine, B. (2012). *Small Arms and Light Weapons Control: A Training Manual*. Saferworld: United Kingdom.

Daniel, M., & Brain, W. (2016). *Civil Society and the Drive Towards an Arms Trade Treaty*. A Background Paper, United Nations Institute for Disarmament Research. Retrieved from www.unidir.org. Accessed 18 May 2018.

Edeko, S. E. (2011). The Proliferation of Small Arms and Light Weapons in Africa: A Case Study of the Niger Delta in Nigeria. *Sacha Journal of Environmental Studies, 1*(2), 55–80.

Ekiyor, T. (2008). *The Role of Civil Society in Conflict Prevention: West African Experiences*. United Nations Institute for Disarmament Research (UNIDIR), Disarmament Forum: The Complex Dynamics of Small Arms in West Africa, no. 4, pp. 27–34.

Eyoh, D. (2002, December 8–12). *The Ethnic Question in African Democratization Experiences*. Paper Prepared for Presentation at the 10th General Assembly of Council for the Development of Research in Africa (CODESRIA), Kampala, Uganda.

Folarin, S. F. (2015). *Types and Causes of Conflict, Chapter Three*. Retrieved from eprints.covenantuniversity.edu.ng/3241/1/Folarin%2025pdf.

Ogu, M. I. (n.d.). *Proliferation of Small Arms Light Weapons in Africa: Cause or Effect?* Retrieved from http://paperroom.ipsa.org/papers/paper_33138.pdf. Accessed 14 June 2019.

Mercy, O. A. (2012, February). Civil Society and Democratic Consolidation in Nigeria. *Journal of Emerging Trends in Educational Research and Policy Studies, 3*(1). www.questia.com/library/journal/1p3-3086871741/.

Michael, A. I. (2019). *Corruption, Governance, and Nigeria's Uncivil Society, 1999–2016*. Retrieved from http://CorruptiongovernanceandNigeriasUncivilsociety1999-2016byAbadaandNgwu.Pdf. Accessed 26 November 2019.

Premium Times. (2017). Shocking Revelation: 100,000 Killed, Two Million Displaced by Boko Haram Insurgency, Borno Governor says. Retrieved from https://www.premiumtimesng.com/news/headlines/223399-shocking-revelation-100000-killed-two-million-displaced-boko-haram-insurgency-borno-governor-says.html. Accessed 17 June 2019.

Seers, D. (1969). The Meaning of Development. *IDS Communication 44*. Retrieved from https://www.ids.ac.uk/files/dmfile/themeaningofdevelopment.pdf. Accessed 23 June 2019.

The Nigeria Police. (2015). *The Annual Report of Nigeria Police Force 2015*. Lagos: Department of Research and Planning.

UNREC. (2011). *Regional Initiatives for Disarmament and Non-Proliferation: 2012–2015*. United Nation Regional Centre for Peace and Disarmament in Africa. Retrieved from www.unrec.org/doc/portfolio. Accessed 19 May 2019.

Wezeman, P. D., Fleurant, A., Kuimova, A., Tian, N., & Wezeman, S. T. (2018). *SIPRI Fact Sheet: Trends in International Arms Transfer, 2017*. Retrieved from https://www.sipri.org/sites/default/files/files/FS/SIPRIFS1503.pdf. Accessed 15 June 2019.

Williams, P. (2008). *Violent Non-State Actors and National and International Security, Relations and Security Networks*. Zurich: Swiss Federal Institute of Technology.

Abdulmalik Auwal is an Associate Professor in the Department of Political Sciene, Bayero University, Kano—Nigeria and the immediate past Deputy Dean of the Faculty of Social and Management Sciences, Bayero University, Kano. He is the Secretary General of Fulbright Alumni Association of Nigeria (FAAN) in addition to being a member of Social Science Council of Nigeria (SSCN); Society for Peace Studies and Practice (SPSP); Nigerian Political Science Association (NPSA); among many others. He was a Fulbright Visiting Scholar at the Centre for African Studies, University of Massachussetts, Boston, USA, 2010–2011. Mr Auwal has contributed in several journal articles, book chapters and co-edited conference proceedings in Conflict and Peace-Building; Violence and Security; Civil Society; Democracy and Democratization; Gender; Party Politics and Electoral Process. His areas of research is Political Economy.

Moses T. Aluaigba is an Associate Research Professor at Mambayya House, Aminu Kano Centre for Democratic Studies, Bayero University, Kano—Nigeria. He has authored *Ethnic Conflicts in Nigeria: Insight into the Tiv-Jukun Ethnic Crisis* (2015); edited *Land Resource-based Conflicts in Nigeria* (forthcoming); co-edited *The Nigerian Youth: Political Participation and National Development* (2010); *Corruption, Governance and Development in Nigeria: Perspectives and Remedies* (2012), *Insurgency and Human Rights in Northern Nigeria* (2015) and is the Managing Editor of *Mambayya House Journal of Democratic Studies* (MHJDS). His other contributions on various areas of Political Economy are published as book chapters and as articles in national and international journals. He was a Fulbright Visiting Scholar at the Center for African Studies, Ohio University Athens, USA, 2008–2009. He is also an alumnus of the APSA-Africa Workshop 2013. Dr. Aluaigba is a member of the Nigeria Political Science Association (NPSA), the American Political Science Association (APSA) and the West African Research Association (WARA). His areas of research interest include democracy, democratization in Nigeria, ethnic conflicts, conflict resolution and research methods.

CHAPTER 25

Traditional Institutions and Firearms in Africa: The Politics and Historiography of Small Arms and Conflict Management

Muhammad Sanusi Lawal and Bem Japhet Audu

INTRODUCTION

Traditional institutions in Africa have been in existence since time immemorial. Traditional institutions are those political institutions predating the advent of colonialism in Africa that cater for the economic, social and political aspirations of their people, which today have become part and parcel of our cultural heritage (Aliyu 2012). They are the custodians of the norms and values that guide the African society. The role of traditional institutions in the promotion and preservation of peace, security and harmony cannot be overemphasized. This is largely due to the legitimacy enjoyed by these institutions seen as the custodians of customs and traditions of the people (Ededgoh et al. 2013: 965–966). Traditional institutions partake in ensuring the security of their domain. Traditional institutions usually enjoy a mix of executive, legislative and judicial powers, and command tremendous respect among their people which enable them, discharge a bevy of responsibilities in cultural co-existence and modern state-building. With the advent of colonialism some of these powers were unilaterally usurped by the emergent colonial state: traditional rulers were subjugated and put under the control of the Resident Officer or

---

M. S. Lawal (✉)
Department of Political Science and Defence Studies, Nigerian Defence Academy, Kaduna, Nigeria

B. J. Audu
Department of History and War Studies, Nigerian Defence Academy, Kaduna, Nigeria

© The Author(s), under exclusive license to Springer Nature Switzerland AG 2021
U. A. Tar and C. P. Onwurah (eds.), *The Palgrave Handbook of Small Arms and Conflicts in Africa*,
https://doi.org/10.1007/978-3-030-62183-4_25

District Officer as the case may be. With the attainment of political independence various traditional institutions continued to lose their relevance. The new political leadership saw the traditional rulers as allies to former colonial masters and a stumbling block to the modernization and national building projects of the 1960s and 1970s and therefore some of these governments enacted legislations that abolished traditional institutions altogether—as in Tanzania and Mozambique—while in many other states, traditional institutions were reduced to vestiges of historical, cultural and spiritual value. This systematic neglect has contributed immensely to the deepening security issues facing most parts of Africa today.

Background: Firearms in Africa's Historiography and Politics

Throughout the history of Africa, guns have played important and deadly roles in Africa: as lethal instrument for the capture and subjugation of the continent by European colonial powers. This is well captured through poignant themes such as *guns and the trans Saharan trade* which connotes the dominant place of guns as important articles of trade—and of raids and slavery—between Africa and the Mediterranean world, especially from the sixteenth century. Another theme of interest that abounds in historical account is *gun-slave cycle of the Trans-Atlantic Slave Trade* which conveys the paradox of a fatal repercussion of gun as an instrument of raids, slavery and slave trade. This argument is sustained by the European shipments of firearms to Africa which was accelerated in the late seventeenth and early eighteenth centuries (Curtin 1975: 320–325; Inikori 1977; Richards 1980). This period was represented by an exponential increase in African slave exports. Before this era, the older matchlock musket had proven ineffective in tropical climates and the Catholic Church prohibited their sale to non-Christians. The sale of large numbers of guns and gunpowder to Africans began with Protestant slave traders not bound by Catholic prohibitions (Kea 1971: 186; Wilks 1993: 23; and Northrup 2002: 90–98) although the Dutch were the first to sell large numbers, followed by the English as their participation in the slave trade grew. Fearful of losing their competitive position, the Portuguese quickly followed suit. By the 1680s, the more-reliable flintlock technology was replacing the matchlock technology and firearms became a staple outbound cargo on most slave ships destined for Africa.

By the 1690s, the new flintlock technology was influencing military formations and military strategies along the Lower Guinea Coast, precisely when slave exports from that region began to increase (Kea 1971: 207–213; Thornton 1999: 61–64). Undoubtedly, this began a period of sustained growth in both firearms shipments to Africa and slave exports out of Africa. Between 1680 and 1685, the British Royal African Company shipped only 2615 firearms per year to Africa (Davies 1975: 356). By the end of the eighteenth century, Inikori (1977: 18) estimates that the British were shipping

150,000–200,000 guns per year, and the total for all Europe was 300,000–400,000 guns per year. Eltis and Jennings (1988: 33), estimate a tenfold increase in firearms between the 1680s and the 1780s, increasing from 20,000 to 200,000 guns per year.

The core claim of the *Gun-Slave Cycle* is that the imported gunpowder technology increased the productivity of resources devoted to capturing slaves and marching them to the coast. Firearms played a very significant role in this by giving the captors an advantage. The *Superiority of European Firepower* is another factor which laid the basis for the European "Scramble for Africa" made possible by newly produced weapons such as the Maxim Gun. Even though the flintlocks, percussion muskets, old fashioned muzzle-loaders (also known as Dane Guns), breach-loaders, Bonny gun, Angolan gun, machine guns, revolvers and rifles were popular, especially during the Scramble for Africa their importance in subjugating and colonization of Africa remain cardinal. Africa again witnessed the influx and *Proliferation of Small Arms and Light Weapons* such as the AK-47 assault rifle in parts of post-colonial Africa. This forms the basis for another theme in the history of firearms in Africa, and forms the key objectives of this chapter. Therefore, it is imperative to pose the following questions: what role has the traditional institution in Africa played in the influx, production and proliferation of firearms? How would we explain the changing role of firearms in Africa within the context of the traditional institution? To what extent has the traditional institution's role in Africa efficient in the control of firearms in Africa?

Traditional Institutions, Firearms and War Economy in Africa

Firearms have been in use in Africa for a relatively long period of time and have had a tremendous influence on the course of African history. As noted by Gavin White (1971: 173), "that firearms have had an impact on African history cannot be denied, but the nature of that impact is more questionable". Away from this, it is also difficult to state the exact period firearms became available in Africa, especially sub-Saharan Africa as well as the role played by Arab and European merchants in selling them to Africans.

However, available historical sources indicate that firearms were first introduced to Africa, especially Central Sudan from the northern fringes of Africa in the fifteenth or sixteenth centuries in almost insignificant proportions (Smaldone 1977: 94–107). However, from the nineteenth century, the volume of trade in firearms began to increase but not exponentially. For instance, firearms trade volume and direction were highly localized, even up to the eastern Chad Basin. On the other hand, trade in munitions in the South of the Sahara began much later with greater significance in volume and distribution in the western Central Sudan, especially the Sokoto Caliphate. It is important to note that, although European merchants had been selling firearms on the Guinea coast since the fifteenth century, it was not until the eighteenth century that guns from the South were reported in the Sudan (Smaldone 1977: 94–107).

In spite of limited availability of firearms in Africa before the eighteenth century, traditional institutions showed great interest in the acquisition of firearms for several reasons which include monopoly and military superiority to enemies and rivals as well as royalty. For instance, in 1851 Emir Muhammadu Bello of Katsina (1844–1869) asked Barth to give him two things: "a medicine to increase his conjugal vigor" and some rockets as "a medicine of war" to frighten his enemies (Hull 1968: 63–65). The vizier of Bornu also told Barth, perhaps facetiously, that Shehu Umar would abolish slavery if Her Majesty's Government would supply him with one thousand muskets and four cannon. And in 1889, the Emir of Nassarawa begged H. M. Commissioner Major Claude MacDonald to intercede for him and induce the British Royal Niger Company to sell him modern rifles and ammunition so that he could raid the "pagan tribes" on the southern bank of the Benue River (Smaldone 1977).

These instances support beyond reasonable doubt the argument that the Sudan ic rulers far from demonstrating a fear of military innovations, showed themselves anxious to seize every opportunity to obtain new and advanced weapons. It also goes to show the extent to which the traditional institution in Africa at that time showed interest in the acquisition of firearms which were in limited supply at the time.

Despite the obvious interest of these traditional institutions in the Sudan ic states of Africa in importing firearms, the northern route that linked the central and west African states and northern Africa did not become an important source of guns until the last decades of the nineteenth century, and even then only for Wadai in the east. As shall be seen in this study, for the greater part of the nineteenth century and even beyond, the factors that affected the flow of arms to the most part of the Sahel, including Central Sudan were beyond the control of the traditional institutions in the states of that region, and the "gun-frontier" remained stabilized along the Mediterranean littoral.

Three prominent factors account for the late introduction of firearms in large quantity in Africa south of the Sahara. First, in the 1830 s changing political conditions in North Africa rendered it even more difficult for the Central Sudanic states and their traditional institutions to obtain firearms from the Mediterranean axis which was a major source of firearms through Arab traders. Both the French and Ottoman authorities, the "super powers" operating in the area at that time, proceeded to extend their control over the desert hinterland in the next decades and to regulate the arms trade. In many of the towns and oases of the Algerian desert there existed domestic industries for the manufacture of gunpowder with local materials and imported ingredients like sulfur and saltpeter, and the repair of firearm mechanisms. There was also a limited local trade in firearms and related munitions in the desert hinterland of Algiers; this commerce was, as in the Tripolitan interior, carried on by Tuareg merchants. But as the French progressively extended their control over these areas, they proscribed the trade in firearms and registered those guns that were possessed by the native population. Most of the traffic in firearms was thereby regulated except for a small trade in munitions that emanated from Tunis and Morocco, over which the French had no control.

Secondly, the French annexation of Algiers and the Ottoman reoccupation of Tripoli at that time virtually closed the northern source of firearms to the states of the Central Sudan and so, even though the traditional institutions had expressed the desire to acquire firearms that was not possible due to factors like this. In fact, throughout north Africa the pattern was the same: the Mediterranean powers, Muslim and European alike, regarded the Sudan as a region for economic exploitation and potential conquest, and, not wanting to increase its capacity for military resistance, restricted the trade in munitions to Africa south of the Sahel. Thirdly, local geopolitical conditions also affected the ability of the traditional institutions in Sudanic states to obtain firearms. The Sokoto Caliphate, for instance, was surrounded by hostile states along its northern and eastern frontiers, the most important of which were Zinder, Maradi, Gobir and Bornu. These states took advantage of their strategic location with respect to the North African trade routes to control the irregular supply of munitions and to prevent the shipment of war materials to Sokoto.

By the eighteenth century the Aro traders in present-day South-East Nigeria who were renowned for their slave raiding and trading had started controlling the import of firearms in the area, of which Blunderbusses was among the earliest of such imports. However, the Aro controlled the firearm trade in the Igbo hinterland by denying the communities around of supply of arms in order to maintain their trade interests. In Ibibioland, where Aro had considerable control over land, one way of acquiring land was through payment of a piece of cloth, some case of drinks, salt and a gun (Nwokeji 1995: 84). More so, to form a lineage group out of the established Aro lineages, such lineage was expected to pay some amount of money and one barrel of gunpowder to secure an autonomous lineage group (Nwokeji 1995: 162).

Until the mid-nineteenth century, however, the southern firearms trade was subject to the same limitations as that from North Africa. That is, the traditional institutions in the Sudanic states were denied direct access to the seaborne arms traffic by the commercial monopolies maintained by the forest kingdoms of the Guinea coast. The emirates of the Sokoto Caliphate did eventually gain access to this southern source of guns, but it was due more to British enterprise that broke the coastal monopoly than to the willingness of the forest states to sell munitions in the hinterland.

From the Gold Coast (now Ghana) to the Cameroons, the valuable trade in European was controlled by the coastal kingdoms whose access to these weapons was a principal factor in their local ascendancy. The effectiveness of this restriction by the coastal states of the exportation of firearms to the northern interior was noted by Europeans before the nineteenth century. Simon Lucas, on the basis of testimony from North African traders, reported that:

> Fire arms are unknown to such of the nations on the Niger as the Shereef has visited; and the reason which he assigns for it is, that the Kings in the neighbourhood of the coast, persuaded that if these powerful instruments of war should reach the possession of the populous inland states, their own independence would be lost, have strictly prohibited, and by the wisdom of their measures have effectively prevented this dangerous merchandize from passing beyond the limit of their dominions. (Smaldone 1977: 99)

In Ashanti Kindgom in Northern Ghana, the monarch monopolized the firearms trade and forbade the exportation of munitions to the north. Similarly, in Dahomey the firearms trade was controlled by a royal monopoly. Farther to the east the riparian states of the Niger, Cross, and Nun rivers also monopolized the trade and distribution of firearms purchased from European merchants. Under these conditions, it was virtually impossible for the states of the northern hinterland to obtain a direct access to the southern supply of munitions. In the 1820s, however, the Yoruba states began to acquire firearms. The Ijebu coastal Yoruba who traded with Europeans being the first to so arm themselves. Richard Lander observed at this time that "quantities of muskets are procured from the coast, but they are of comparatively little use to the (Yoruba) people, who know not how to handle them with effect." Thus, during the third decade of the nineteenth century, the southern "gun-frontier" began to move inland from the coast. As Lander's remarks indicate, the number of firearms in the immediate interior increased but did not as yet affect materially the character of warfare. Guns were still scarce in the northern emirates and Bornu, and virtually nonexistent in Nupe, where the Fulani troops were armed only with spears, swords and bows and arrows.

However, by the middle of the nineteenth century most of Yorubaland had been brought within the "gun-frontier" and muskets were the standard weapons of Yoruba warriors. In the early 1850s it was reported that "most of the (Yoruba) people have inferior smooth-bored guns, which are sold to the Guinea Negroes by European traders, and sent off to be sold again in the interior" (Smaldone 1977: 109); yet even by the end of the decade the use of guns had not become general north of Abeokuta. The firearms trade in the Yoruba states was an overland commerce, originating on the coast and being carried largely by traders of Lagos and Ijebu, and after the Ijebu monopoly was broken by the Egba, through Abeokuta. With the Yoruba states engaged in intensive trade competition and internecine warfare after the breakup of the Oyo Empire, the emirates to the north were unable to acquire munitions through this overland route.

After 1830, though, when the Lander brothers opened the Niger River to European trade, European merchant vessels began to bypass the coastal states' commercial monopoly and sell directly on the inland markets. These radically new trading conditions enabled Nupe to emerge after the 1840s as the principal source of munitions for the emirates farther to the north. The Niger mission of 1841 found that gunpowder was being sold in the main

Nupe market at Egga, and so great was the locals' fear of the Nupe army that they told the European visitors that "every Fulatah is armed with a gun." Later, precisely in 1851, Richardson, while in Zinder, was told of South American traders who were exchanging powder and shot for slaves in Nupe. At about this time Nupe began to export muskets and powder to the north; guns and powder were shipped to Kano, and English and American gunpowder to Bornu. Guns from the coast were reported also to be reaching almost all parts of the Sahara. In the l850s and 1860s muskets were selling in Nupe at ten to twelve thousand cowries or about one-sixth the price of slaves.83.

Although the quantity of munitions reaching the emirates of the Sokoto Caliphate was still small, it is evident that a regular trade was developing, and a new class of arms traders was forming alliance with the traditional aristocracy of the Caliphate. By the 1850s the "gun-frontier" had almost absorbed the Yoruba states and had begun to advance through Nupe. The importance of Nupe is that it was the first emirate to fall within this widening zone of gun warfare, and became the main port of entry and distribution of munitions for the northern emirates. During the next decades Nupe itself fell within the "gun-frontier" and the other emirates began to be engulfed by the steadily northward-moving gun belt.

William B. Baikie's establishment of Lokoja in Nupe territory in 1859 further enhanced the position of Nupe as middleman in the arms trade, and their alliance with the traditional institution. Emir Masaba (1841–1850; and 1859–1873) welcomed the British connection and the advantages to be derived from the permanent European trading post in his territory. As one British trader reported of Masaba: "His great-virtue was his attachment to white traders. He gave them every accommodation, encouragement and protection, to facilitate the establishment of trading factories on his part of the 'Kwara'- the native name here for the Niger" (Smaldone 1977: 107). In 1870 Masaba signed a decree officially encouraging the settlement of Lokoja, hoping it would become the most prosperous market at the confluence of the Niger and Benue. By the late 1870s there were four British commercial firms trading regularly up the Niger, and eight or ten steamers did business at Nupe each year. Masaba also sold slaves down the Niger at Idah in exchange for gunpowder, at the rate of one "good male slave" for a small keg.

The British post at Lokoja also served as a diplomatic channel for the emirs of Sokoto (present day northern Nigeria) to establish contact with Britain in the hope of obtaining firearms. Masaba (Year) wrote many letters to the British consuls at Lokoja and Lagos, and to Queen Victoria herself, asking repeatedly for muskets, rifles, powder, and ammunition. Ilorin also opened direct contact with Britain through the consular authorities at Lagos. Emir Abdullahi of Kano (1855–1882) wrote to the English queen through Baikie, requesting a skilled technician to manufacture firearms and ammunition for his army, and offering to pay the expenses of his transportation. Baikie communicated with Gwandu and the Caliph at Sokoto, expressing his desire to open extensive commercial contacts and to sell guns and powder. Baikie also opened Abuja and Zaria to British trade.

The military power of Nupe was expanded considerably under the direction of Masaba. Munitions constituted a large portion of its imports, and by 1871 the army of Nupe was reported to have rockets, 2000 firearms, and 8 cannon, two of them six-pounders. The cannon were mounted and Masaba's gunmen had been trained to fire them by members of the Niger mission. Masaba and his successors enforced a strict monopoly on the arms trade, and prohibited the unauthorized re-export of munitions. According to John Whitford, Masaba forbade "his subjects, on pain of death, to purchase powder or guns, keeping deadly weapons and war material only for his regular army" at Bida. Nupe also supplied its allies with munitions to subdue mutual enemies. In 1878, for example, the traveler Burdo observed canoes "full of arms and ammunition" being sent by Nupe to aid its tributary ally Imaha in an offensive against the "pagan" village of Amara. Moreover Nupe provided Sokoto, Gwandu, Missau, Zaria and Abuja with muskets. Thus, in the 1870s the southern "gun-frontier" began to expand throughout the Sokoto Caliphate.

In the last two decades of the nineteenth century further changes in the commercial situation on the Niger Basin and Benue Trough brought concomitant changes in the nature of the trade in war materials. French commercial competition with Britain on the Niger and Benue became acute after 1880, and by 1884 the *Compagnie Française de l'Afrique Equatoriale* seriously challenged the British trading position. This commercial rivalry was finally resolved at the Berlin West African Conference of 1884–1885, at which Britain was awarded the exclusive right to administer the provisions of the Conference on the lower Niger. In 1886, Sir George Goldie, who bought out the French interests on the eve of the Conference and thereby engineered the British victory, succeeded in obtaining a royal charter for his Royal Niger Company and with it a *de facto* monopoly of European commerce on the Niger and Benue. Trading stations now extended from the Niger delta to the upper reaches of the Benue, thus providing such emirates as Nassarawa, Zaria, Bauchi, Muri and Adamawa with direct access to the arms trade. This marked the beginning of effective colonial control of the geographical area called Nigeria.

Elsewhere in Southern Africa, there was the Shona Chimurenga (rising) of 1896; an example of early resistance to colonialism that involved the use of firearms which were already in circulation in the area. The uprising had occurred as a result of British South Africa company's forced labor, low wages, stock-raiding and taxation policy in Shona Ndebele state of present South Africa (Beach 1979: 418). Although the Shona had become very good at their mining activities, the tax upon their low wages kept growing, while the British South Africa company police regiment kept increasing the tax on the Shona lands and their livestock, failure to pay these increased taxes led to raiding their livestock as a way of ensuring compliance. More so, Europeans increased their farming settlements thereby displacing the local population of their land.

Pockets of unorganized resistance had emerged in 1894. These acts of resistance included a measure of firearm usage by individuals who fired shots on either police regiments enforcing tax collections or raiders (Beach 1979: 419).

From March 1896, organized resistance began in Ndebele especially in areas around Nyandoro, Makoni and Marange. Company misrule had spurred the High priest of Mkwati who organized the people through the cult. The organization of the Shona Chimurenga was conceived and executed secretly. Long swords were used to execute Europeans, there was a feature of firearm use. Although the Chimurenaga uprising was referred to as "night of the long knife" firearms were used extensively. More so, the use of police regiment and imperial troops helped put down the uprising in 1897 (Beach 1979: 420).

Apart from Arab and European merchants who sold firearms in Africa, there is an account of a merchant whose gun running business in East and South African axis transformed firearms trading and led to a wider circulation of arms. Hamed bin Muyharnmed el Murjebi popularly known as *Tippu Tip* was an Arab trader, slave trader, and firearm trader per excellence in the East African coast. The very origin of Tippu Tip was the sound of the guns with which he used to terrify the communities he had traded or fell out with. Angela Downing observed that the people recalled that "This man's guns went 'tip, tip' in a manner too terrible to listen to. The nickname 'Tippu Tip' stuck and has gone down in history." Because of tremendous gunpower, he was able to subdue populations and lords, and claimed the lands that he conquered for his own wealth, and also for the Zanzibari Sultanate. By the 1880s he was said to have above 50,000 guns. He equally served as guide to European explorers in the East Africa (Decker 2015).

The analysis in this section shows the gradual and eventual introduction of firearms in Africa as well as the foundation for changing patterns of gun uses and control in Africa and the role played by the traditional institution. The traditional institution as shown above, to a large extent, played a significant role in the circulation or proliferation of firearms during the pre-colonial era. This role changed with the advent of colonialism. As shown in the next section which focuses on the colonial era, the traditional institution lost control of the circulation of firearms. Rather, the colonialists had total control of the instrument of control of firearms through the enactment of gun license ordinances and policies.

African Traditional Institutions and (Dis)Armament in Africa

The traditional institutions in Africa are equated with rulership with legitimacy driven from tradition. They questioned the rationale for excluding them from the constitution whereas the previous governments included them. They argued that, their exclusion had denied the government the much-needed relationship with the most important sector in the society, the local communities. There are two major schools of thought on this. The abolitionists are one of the two schools and they argued that, there is no place for traditional institutions in government and administration in contemporary Africa. Using Max Weber's threefold categorization of authority, the abolitionists argued that, the raison d'être of traditional institution of rulership is traditional authority, whereas modern governmental systems are based on legal and rational authority (Ekong 1985). They argued that traditional institutions have outlived their usefulness when looked from the premise of third world decolonization, the cold war and globalization, that the modernization theorists saw the decline of traditional institutions powers in the post-colonial African states (Blench et al. 2006).

The other school of thought—which we named the retention school— is made popular by the holders of traditional rulership positions and their supporters. They hold that, the Africa's traditional chiefs and community elders are the true representatives of their people, revered and legitimate, and therefore still useful to politics and administration on the continent (Okonkwo et al. 2019). Concurring to the above position, Sklar (1993: 4) posits that, "the durability of traditional authority in Africa cannot be explained away as a relic of colonial rule." Rather, argues Sklar, the role of local initiative, African agency in the construction of colonial institutions was mainly responsible for the adaptation of traditional authorities to modern systems of government and the legitimacy they continue to enjoy among ordinary people (Vaughan 2000: 4). He used his study on the traditional Yoruba to conclude that, "given the resilience of indigenous political structures and the colossal failure of the Nigerian state, it is essential to re-open the discussion on the role of chieftaincy in colonial and postcolonial Nigerian politics" (Vaughan 2000: 3).

As shown in the previous section, African chiefs had started acquiring firearms before the twentieth century. Most of these firearms were used for purposes such as hunting, status symbols and for protecting croplands. They were used for slave raids as well. But the main uses to which this European technology was put by Europeans were war and state-building. And the control mechanism for the circulation of firearms was now mainly in the hands of the European imperialists to regulate. It was no longer within the jurisdiction of the traditional institution to regulate the use and circulation of firearms under colonialism unlike in the pre-colonial era where emirs and kings had relative control over circulation of firearms given their territoriality. However, the availability of firearms increased, and control measures tightened with the enactment of Gun License ordinances and policies.

The European "civilizing mission" in enhancing imperialism in Africa was impactful. For most parts of Africa, colonialism allowed the educated elites, not just traditional rulers, to own shotguns in the belief that these "civilized" Africans would not want to violently bring down an institution that was responsible for or that enhanced their privileged status. Beyond this, it can be argued that a people who had been made to think they were inferior to Europeans in terms of intelligence would not just get up someday and want to fight a foreign domination they thought was helping them move up the ladder of civilization.43 Also, European political institutions in Africa, whether direct rule as seen in the French colonies or indirect rule as in the British colonies divided Africans across ethnicities and regions, preventing them from forging a common front against imperialism. And the ethnic groups and power structures that imperialism favored generally opposed any subversion of the status quo. As Mahmud Mamdani has noted, indirect rule, which he also refers to as "decentralized despotism," succeeded in British Africa "by tapping authoritarian possibilities in culture, and by giving culture an authoritarian bent.

No doubt, colonialism transformed Africans' encounter with firearms, and posed serious challenges for African chiefs as they struggled tenuously to maintain their legitimacy through the barrel of the gun. For instance, in the first half of the twentieth century, the African gun society—comprising of the colonial officers and local petty bourgeois elements—emerged through the liberalization of firearms controls. In accordance with their social class, Africans could possess different classes of non prohibited firearms, which thus shaped the government's perception of dangers to peace and order. This ordering of Africans fit the established practice of creating differences in order to intensify divisions across social class, region, religion and ethnicity. This led to the interrelatedness of guns, consumer culture and social change. The role of guns in the society became systemic in that firearms were used for numerous economic, social and political purposes in a manner unprecedented. Not only did ceremonial shooting and gun salutes become established elements of public spectacle, but hunting reached its peak of popularity with the availability of firearms.

The political economy of gunpowder and other explosives became extremely common in Africa under colonialism. The international trade in gunpowder became a significant aspect of the African colonial economy. This could be seen through the policies and politics of the gunpowder trade which was a process of maintaining a difficult balance between the economic gains of such trade and public security. The gunpowder imported into most of Africa between the 1920s and 1960 did not go into building empires and fighting wars. The colonial wars to subjugate African states had ended at the time and colonialism fully entrenched. It was deployed primarily for hunting and ceremonial shooting. And, during World Wars I and II, the fecundity of gunpowder in Africa not only became more obvious than ever; it also drove a number of emergency defense and economic policies.

It is important to note here that the European gun culture in Africa enabled the consolidation of the African gun society. Not only were Europeans involved in a different form of ceremonial shooting as part of imperial spectacle that supported the indigenous form, but also the goals and outcomes of game hunting were different and yet sometimes overlapped those of Africans. In establishing the difference between "indigenous" and "imperial" hunting from the perspective of mission, methods, and impact, it is important to understand that the European gun use represented the symbolic domination of the human and natural world. Imperial shooting went beyond killing animals for trophy, sport or meat. It also included rifle shooting, a Europeans-only activity that reinforced the idea of racial superiority. But beyond this, rifle shooting epitomized Europeans' presumed superior masculinity based on the assumption that Africans, given their "lack of intelligence," could not be trusted with the most advanced, non-prohibited firearms. The debate over making rifle shooting a "state leisure" (like polo and horse racing) indicates that such a homogenizing category as "Europeans" needs to be disturbed to emphasize divergent social attitudes and dissimilar understandings of what constitutes safe and profitable leisure.

Also, unlike in the pre-colonial era, colonialism presented a relationship between guns and public disorder. For instance, the mode of operation of the Nigeria Police Force, the efficacy of the arms it used, and its main philosophy, contrasted with the level of indigenous military culture, in order to explicate the failure of armed resistance to imperial rule. What made colonialism successful was access to superior technology of war, as stated earlier, on the part of the colonialists. In other words, colonialism survived and was sustained through the instrumentality of the control of the proliferation of weapons of war such as machine guns. For instance, in Nigeria, major events such as the Enugu colliery shooting of 1949 and the Kano riot of 1953 tested the fundamental principles on which colonial gun society was based. It has been stated that the Enugu incident was as a result of labor agitation and reforms, however, as argued by Saheed Aderonti (2018: 23), it was colonial anxiety informed by the miners' access to explosives. According to him, the twenty-one miners who were gunned down in cold blood by police riflemen would not have died had security reports not indicated that terrorists intended to use mining explosives to undermine the public peace in their quest to radicalize the anti-colonial movement and terminate British rule by force of arms. The nine hundred policemen mobilized to the mines were not there to quell the strike, which was peaceful. Instead, they were dispatched to remove explosives that the colonial intelligence service claimed would be used by enemies of the state to bring colonialism to a halt.

No matter the divergence and convergence of colonial violence in Africa, these examples prove that colonial violence went beyond the confrontation between Africans and the colonialists whether British, French, Germans, Belgians, Italians or Portuguese; it extended to relations among Africans as well. For instance, beyond colonial control, Africans used firearms extensively against each other in inter and intra ethnic conflicts and during the politics of decolonization. There were leading political parties that relied on the use of firearms in driving their demands on the colonialists. In fact, guns became a dominant symbol of political power among most African leaders who had blamed the colonialists for the indiscriminate killing of fellow Africans.

A few examples of colonial violence through the excessive use of firearms will suffice here. For instance, there was the Maji Maji rebellion of 1905–1907 in German East Africa. The rebellion was resistance against German imperialism. The imposition of taxation and brutal methods of collection forced labor on road construction, or European plantations, the replacement of indigenous leaders by alien agents (akidas) all contributed to the rebellion. However, the rebellion had a cultural character, as *Maji* (water medicine) was believed to help neutralize the efficacy of the European bullet from killing people. This motivated the warriors who were sprinkled with *Maji* to carry out direct and organized series of attacks on the Europeans (Iliffe 1967: 495). The arms of these warriors were poisoned arrows and bows. They resisted the German superior weapons of machine guns for many months. The relentless effort to put the rebellion down by Governor Gotzen led to calling on the German empire who sent two cruisers, and 1000 reinforcement from other German-controlled territories to the area. Through arms and economic sabotage of peasants such as the burning of crops, the rebellion was put down.

In Nigeria for instance, the British finally gave up registration of firearms in 1948, meaning Nigerians could possess them without a license but the political volatility in the country following the Enugu colliery shooting focused government attention on arms of precision. A barrage of regulations from the 1950s tightened the possession of arms of precision that featured prominently in partisan political violence. The traditional rulers who were independent in the pre-colonial era, and could negotiate and access firearms for their use now had to apply and obtain licenses from the colonial government. The assumption that holders of shotguns would not use them against the colonial government collapsed in the wake of the alleged radicalization of the labor force in most parts of Africa. By the mid-1950s, the regime of post-colonial Nigerian gun regulation or the Gold Coast (now Ghana) began to unfold as they inched toward independence. This laid the foundation for the violent crises that shook the foundations of most African countries in the post-colonial era.

TRADITIONAL INSTITUTIONS AND PROLIFERATION OF SMALL ARMS AND LIGHT WEAPONS IN POST-COLONIAL AFRICA

It can be argued that the post-colonial state in Africa lost complete control over the regulation of firearms. Even though armed with the constitutional jurisdiction over control of firearms, the state in post-colonial Africa showed a lack of capacity to ensure monopoly or even control of firearms as the period marked an increasing level of proliferation in small arms and light weapons. There was a marked witness of an inherent contradiction in the post-colonial politics of gun control from within the framework of the challenges of nation building. In other words, the proliferation of prohibited arms in post-colonial Africa is both the cause and the consequence of failed political and traditional leadership which has manifested in violent crisis, including wars such as the Sand War of 1963 between Algeria and Morocco over the lands in the Tindouf and Bechar provinces. The Algerian territories were claimed by Moroccan government and this led to heightened tensions between Algeria and Morocco, failure to resolve these issues led to an armed conflict in 1963. There is also the first Sudan civil war between 1955 and 1972 which arose out of demands by South Sudan people for more representation in government and a measure of regional autonomy. The issues involved were not resolved and this led to the Second Sudan Civil War from 1983 to 2005 and culminated in the creation of South Sudan in 2011. However, over 2 million people died during these wars, with many others displaced. A civil war broke out in South Sudan immediately they got independence from Sudan where several hundreds of thousands of people lost their lives through excessive use of arms. Another example is the Nigerian civil war that broke out when the Igbo attempted to secede. There is also the case of the Angolan Civil war that was fought from 1975 and did not end until 2002. It was a liberation war and an extension of the ideological Cold War that was the norm of the 1970s and 1980s.

Arms have also impacted on ethnic and religious relations. For instance, ethnic divisions between the Hutu and Tutsi flared off into a civil war in the East, and Central African region. For instance, between 1993 and 2005, the Burundian civil war was fought by Hutus and Tutsi ethnic groups. The War ended in 2005 with the election of Pierre Nkurunziza. The Rwandan civil war was also fought between 1990 and 1994 between Hutu and Tutsi ethnic groups. The war eventually led to genocide with the killing of over 500,000 to 1 million Tutsi and moderate Hutus.

Terrorist and insurgent activities and separatist movements are also dotted across the continent. For instance, Boko Haram terrorist and insurgent group has continued to undermine the corporate existence of Nigeria, Chad, Niger, Cameroon, while AlQaeda in the Islamic Maghreb operates in Algeria, Morocco, Niger, Mali, Libya. The Islamic State in West Africa Province is also wrecking havoc with violent weapons in Nigeria, Mali, Niger, Chad, just as Al-Shabab is doing the same in Somalia and Kenya. Other terrorist groups operating on the continent include the Lord's Resistance Army in DR Congo, Uganda and South Sudan, and the Salafist Group for Preaching and Fighting (GSPC) in Algeria.

Beyond this, the experience of corruption at all levels, porous national borders, and crises of underdevelopment such as poverty and unemployment have continued to shape the ways Africans use small arms and light weapons to pursue agendas that undermined peace. Traditional institutions too have lost their authority before the people, especially their unconstitutional roles in society has further undermined the institution's instrumentality of control of any kind.

Toward a Paradigm Shift: Traditional Rulers as Agents of Small Arms Control and Conflict Management in Africa

Though the foregoing analyses have evidently demonstrated the role of traditional rulers in armament rather than disarmament; in war-making rather than peacemaking; and in being part of colonial and post-colonial authority rather than civil society, a case can be made for their embedded role in fostering arms control and disarmament, as well as dispute resolution and peace-building on the continent.

In the post-colonial dispensation—particularly, following the institutionalization of democracy in 1990s and beyond, many African traditional institutions have been granted little or no constitutional roles carved out for them at the level of the State. Whereas in the pre-colonial and colonial era, traditional institutions functioned within the limits of colonial dictates. In modern times their duties are outside of State institutions. In any case, traditional institutions have responded to conflicts within their own limit, sometimes collaborating with national institutions to drive conflict transformation. Although they lack the power of sanction, they have often pulled spiritual and communal powers to create avenues for conflict transformation, reconciliation and peace-building. This is because, African chiefs still command tremendous respect among the citizens, as symbols of age-hallowed traditions and custodians of culture—for instance, as agents for alternative dispute resolution.

Traditional institutions have different approaches to conflict resolution and peace-building. Volker (2006) argues that the traditional approaches vary considerably from society to society, and from region to region, from the community to community. A strategy of resolution suitable for one community may not be acceptable for another. The understanding of conflict and peace varies from communities in terms of space and time. In Nigeria, for instance, traditional institutions played specific roles in Disarmament, Demobilization and Reintegration (DDR) process during the Amnesty programme of former President Umar Musa Yar'Adua in 2008 for Niger Delta armed militants, traditional leaders in the area were part of the "Presidential Panel on Amnesty and Disarmament of Militants in the Niger Delta" which was constituted. Their input was critical in understanding the fundamental causes of agitation, modalities for disarmament and they were equally instrumental in identifying militant groups in their domains. Hence, when the amnesty programme was executed, there was a measure of success. Isidore Udoh observed that the amnesty programme in the Niger Delta led to militants surrendering "287,445 rounds of ammunition, 3155 magazines, 1090 dynamite caps, 763 explosives, and 18 gunboats" (Udoh 2013: 66). The intervention of traditional leaders in Nigeria's amnesty programme for militants represents clearly demonstrate their scope of goodwill and respect in society, as an institution that plays a changing role in peace-building. The chiefs liaised with the government to facilitate the procedures of the programme on the one hand, and creating trust between government and militants was crucial to the initial success of the programme.

In Sierra Leone, traditional rulers have participated in the UN-initiated peace process. Here, the government backed by the UN, other regional and international organizations such as the EU and ECOWAS facilitated a three-phased Disarmament, Demobilization and Reintegration (DDR) programme that lasted between 1998 and 2002. Solomon and Ginifer (2008) observed that as a result of the legal pluralism of Sierra Leone which gives allowance for the participation of traditional rulers in the legal system, traditional institutions played a huge role in the process of DDR in post-war Sierra Leone. The aim was to ensure that at the community levels ex-combatants were reintegrated into the communities without fear of recriminations for their roles in the war. When the war officially ended in 2002, the consequences were dire, over 50,000 people were killed and over 2 million more were displaced. A major aspect of the process was the involvement of traditional institutions at all levels. For instance, some of the traditional institutions facilitated the reintegration of ex-combatants into the communities by carrying out ritual cleansing exercises aimed at removing the spirit of evil. This symbolic gesture was crucial to the acceptance of the ex-combatant back to the communities. Furthermore, traditional institutions created the bases of trust between the community, ex-combatants and DDR commission.

It is significant to note that the DDR in Sierra Leone is hailed as an example of a successful process that is a referent point for other conflict situations. Solomon and Ginifer revealed that over 72,490 combatants were disarmed and 71,043 demobilized, with 42,330 weapons and 1.2 million pieces of ammunition were collected and destroyed; and 63,545 former combatants participated in the reintegration segment, including 6845 child soldiers.

The role of African traditional leaders in conflict resolution and peace-building cannot be overemphasized: the traditional conflict resolution mechanism is people-centric, liberal, flexible and restorative by nature, cost-effective, time-saving and a part of the African social system which has been in existence since time immemorial. Over time, it has been proven to be efficient and effective in reconciliation since it improves social relationships by restoring social balance, cohesion and settling conflicts (Choudree 1999) because it is deeply rooted in the traditions and customs of Africa. In the common African traditional setting, the traditional leaders are responsible for executive, legislative and judicial functions, at least informally and within their historical domains. They make laws, execute them and interpret and apply the major laws, customs and traditions of the people for the smooth running of the society. The traditional mechanisms employed by traditional institutions may not necessarily refer to procedural formalities of the judiciary. Rather, the custom is a usage and a practice, which may or may not have social recognition, and whose violation may or may not attract any sanctions. When a custom is found to be useful in maintaining harmony in the society, it becomes established as law. Conflict resolution entails a healing process which should involve all actors and non-actors to rebuild social harmony that was shattered as a result of the conflict.

In most parts of Africa, traditional conflict resolution and peace-building mechanism still prevail at the local level where communities invoke ancestral mechanism to douse tension and execute dialogue on armed conflict which is often sealed with the exchange of gifts among the belligerents, and slaughter animals for communal feast—this contrasts with the signing of formal protocols that are associated with the western models. For example, the Karamoja in Uganda and other pastoralist communities in Kenya look up to their traditional elders to promote conflict resolution, including disarmament (Ndumbell 2001). Traditional leaders in Africa have proved to be consequential mediators drawing huge social capital from the fountains of traditions, culture, communal network and goodwill. For example, in the pastoralist communities of Ethiopia, Kenya, Nigeria, South Sudan and Uganda where cattle rustling is a serious issue, it is the traditional leaders who are called upon by their respective governments to intervene and resolve the problem with the help of other government agencies through jousting and bargaining. The traditional leader is unpredictable; he would often vacillate between extremes of what is traditional and modern. He exercises his powers through manipulation of his divine legitimacy and the use of amulets, charms and protective medicines to ensure victory in solving a difficult social problem; the use of diviners, practitioners and religious leaders to aid him in solving modern problems; the constant mixing of slogans that refer to heroic tribal myths alongside national modernizing propaganda; and the employment of vernacular proverbs to gain the support for the government demands.

It is worth noting that, even though traditional leaders still mediate for peace using customary and traditional laws, the authority exercised by these institutions is hardly backed by laws. The result is that people feel more comfortable seeking redress in a recognized modern court instead of following the customary court which they think apply appropriate sanctions on an offender, or would not permit them (because of communal based African Beliefs), to "cut their required pound of flesh."

THE ROLE OF TRADITIONAL LEADERS IN SUPPORTING LAW ENFORCEMENT AGENCIES TO MOP UP ILLICIT ARMS IN AFRICA

Uncontrolled SALW proliferation in Africa is a factor that has influenced sociopolitical and security issues in the continent. SALW has been used in conflicts over resources, struggle s for political and economic power, violent extremism, radicalization and anti-statism. This was encouraged due to the structural weakness of nearly all the African states. Structural governance weaknesses give room to the proliferation of SALW through illicit sales and trafficking of local and foreign manufactured arms. Controlling the proliferation of arms in Africa requires the participation of traditional leaders. Traditional leaders often played an important role in combating the proliferation of SALW. Most times they are at the forefront of local efforts and at other times are conducting high-level advocacy on the effects of SALW. Traditional leaders can help by informing the relevant agencies of movement of arms within their communities, supporting programmes to combat the social issues and promoting awareness of social strategies of law enforcement. They also assisted in raising awareness for the need to regulate and control arms in the possession of their members for self-defense. Other roles played by traditional leaders in Africa to control the proliferation of SALW are:

a. *Reducing Demand*: Traditional leader offers have the potential to change public attitudes, perception, shape community values and become a public voice against armed violence and social conflict. They engage in activities targeted toward the reduction in demand of SALW through programmes or initiatives that target the demand and reduction through peace education programmes that can lead to broader public awareness of peaceful alternatives to conflict resolution and eventually an attitude change that will lead to voluntary DDR and the dissolution of a culture of violence.
b. *Reducing Availability*: A society with fewer weapons will naturally reduce the risk of them being diverted and employed and will help to restore peace and rule of law. One way is voluntary/destruction programmes in which traditional leaders motivate individuals or groups to voluntarily surrender legal or illegal weapons that are not required for the purpose of community security, or maybe unsafe or unwanted.
c. *Disarmament, Demobilisation and Reintegration*: This involves reaching out not only to the victims of conflicts, but also to the perpetrators of armed violence to submit themselves for DDR, and thus earn acceptability, rehabilitation and reintegration into the society. Traditional leaders often preach the virtue of forgiveness and communal understanding necessary for communities to reconcile in peace. Sustained peace can be achieved using those who hold the trust of the communities and government alike.

Conclusion

As shown in the above analysis, it is difficult to state exactly when firearms started flowing into Africa. However, the paper has demonstrated through records that firearms were in use from the sixteenth century even though in limited supply. However, from the seventeenth to early eighteenth century there was an exponential increase in the supply of firearms to Africa. And this continued through the colonial era to the post-colonial period, causing excessive destruction through wars and other violent conflicts. In all, the traditional institution in Africa, the cradle of a semblance of governance ought to have had a role to play. However, the institution played a significant role in circulation and control only in the pre-colonial period. From the colonial to post-colonial period, they were stripped of almost all powers of control. In some countries in Africa, their role is not even recognized constitutionally even though there is a propensity that they could have been instrumental in curbing the proliferation of small arms and light weapons, given their proximity to the people at the grass root. Thus, the role of the traditional institution in the circulation and control of firearms metamorphosed from total control in the pre-colonial Africa to a total absence of control during the colonial and post-colonial periods. The chapter makes a case for paradigm shift to grant room for traditional rulers to participate actively in the control of illicit arms and conflict management. To restore the glory of traditional institutions, it is argued that African countries should consider hybrid institutions-building that allows room for both traditional agencies and modern democratic institutions to complement each other in providing sustainable mechanism for conflict management, dispute resolution, and management of armed conflict in the continent.

References

Aderonti, Saheed. (2018). *Guns and Society in Colonial Nigeria: Firearms Culture and Public Order*. Bloomington: Indiana University Press.
Aliyu, M. (2012). Chieftaincy in Nigeria: The Role of Traditional Institutions. In U. A. Abdalla (Ed.), *Chieftaincy and Security in Nigeria: Past, Present and Future*. Kano: Kano Emirate Council.
Beach, D. N. (1979). 'Chimurenga': The Shona Rising of 1896–97. *The Journal of African History, 20*(3), 395–420.
Blench, R., et al. (2006). The Role of Traditional Rulers in Conflict Prevention and Mediation in Nigeria, Interim Report Prepared for DFID-Nigeria.
Boege, V. (2006). *Traditional Approaches to Conflict Transformation—Potentials and Limits Berghof Research Center for Constructive Conflict Management—First Launch*. https://www.berghof-foundation.org/fileadmin/redaktion/Publications/Handbook/Articles/boege_handbook.pdf.
Choudree, R. B. G. (1999). Tradition of Conflict Resolutions in South Africa. *African Journal on Conflict Resolution*, SA No. 1.
Curtin, Philip D. (1975). *Economic Change in Precolonial Africa: Senegambia in the Era of the Slave Trade*. Madison: University of Wisconsin Press.
Davies, K. G. (1975). *The Royal African Company*. New York: Octagon Books.
Decker, M. (2015). The 'Autobiography' of Tippu Tip. *Interventions, 17*, 5.
Ededgoh, L. O., Kenechukwu, S. A., & Asemah, E. S. (2013). Arresting Social Insecurity in Nigeria in Nigeria: The Imperative of Indigenous Communication Systems'. *International Journal of Asian Social Science, 3*(4), 951–959.
Ekong, E. E. (1985). Traditional Rulership in Contemporary Nigeria Government System and the Dilemma of Relevance. In A. Oladimeji (Ed.), *Local Government and the Traditional Rulers in Nigeria, Ife*. Ile-Ife, Nigeria: University of Ife Press.

Eltis, D., & Jennings, L. C. (1988). Trade Between West Africa and the Atlantic World in the Pre-Colonial Era. *American Historical Review,* 9(4), 936–959.
Hull, R. W. (1968). *The Development of Administration in Katsina Emirate, Northern Nigeria, 1887–1944.* Ph.D. thesis, Columbia University.
Iliffe, J. (1967). The Organization of the Maji Maji Rebellion. *Journal of African History,* 3, 495–512.
Inikori, J. (1977). The Import of Firearms into West Africa 1750–1807: A Quantitative Analysis. *Journal of African History,* 18(3), 339–368.
Kea, R. A. (1971). Firearms and Warfare on the Gold and Slave Coasts from the Sixteenth to the Nineteenth Centuries. *The Journal of African History,* 21(2), 185–213.
Ndumbell, K. (2001). The Spiritual Dimension of Conflict Resolution Mechanism in African Countries, University of Oslo, Unit for Comparative and International Education, Institute for Educational Research.
Northrup, D. (2002). *Africa's Discovery of Europe: 1450–1850.* New York: Oxford University Press.
Nwokeji, G. U. (1995). *The Biafran Frontier: Trade, Slaves and Aro Society, c. 1750–1905.* Ph.D. thesis, Department of History, University of Toronto.
Okonkwo, C. I., et al. (2019). Traditional Rulers and Community Security in Nigeria: Challenges and Prospects. *International Journal of Innovative Social Sciences and Humanities Research,* 792, 145–159. Assessed @ www.seahipaj.org on 4 July 2020.
Richards, W. A. (1980). The Import of Firearms into West Africa in the Eighteenth Century. *Journal of African History,* 21(1), 43–59.
Sklar, R. L. (1993). The Premise of Mixed Government in African Political Studies. In O. Vaughan (Ed.), *Indigenous Political Structures and Governance in Africa.* Ibadan: Safer Books Ltd.
Smaldone, J. P. (1977). *Warfare in the Sokoto Caliphate: Historical and Sociological Perspectives.* London: University of Cambridge Press.
Solomon, C., & Ginifer, J. (2008). Disarmament, Demobilisation and Reintegration in Sierra Leone. In *DDR and Human Security: Post-Conflict Security-Building in the Interests of the Poor.* A Publication of Centre for International Cooperation and Security, University of Bradford. http://www.operationspaix.net/DATA/DOCUMENT/4024~v~Disarmament_Demobilisation_and_Reintegration_in_Sierra_Leone.pdf.
Thornton, J. K. (1999). *Warfare in Atlantic Africa, 1500–1800.* London: UCL Press.
Udoh, I. A. (2013). A Qualitative Review of the Militancy, Amnesty, and Peacebuilding in Nigeria's Niger Delta. *Peace Research,* 45(2), 63–93.
Vaughan, O. (2000). *Nigerian Chiefs: Traditional Power in Modern Politics, 1890's–1990's.* New York: University of Rochester Press.
White, G. (1971). Firearms in Africa. *Journal of African History,* 12(2), 173–184.
Wilks, I. (1993). *Forests of Gold: Essays on the Akan and the Kingdom of Asante.* Athens: Ohio University Press.

Muhammad Sanusi Lawal is a Senior Lecturer in the Department of Political Science and Defence Studies and Research Fellow at the Yusufu Bala Usman Institute, Zaria and Centre for Defence Studies and Documentation, Nigerian Defence Academy, Kaduna. SM Lawal attended the Ahmadu Bello University where he obtained his BSc in Political Science and MSc in Public Administration in 1994 and 2004. He then obtained his PhD in Defence and Strategic Studies from the Nigerian Defence Academy in 2018. He has published many scholarly articles in local and journals and contributed chapters in local and international book projects. Amongst his prominent contributions are:

1. Lawal, S. M. (2008). Ethno-Religious Conflicts in Nigeria (The Case Study of Kaduna State). *Ahmadu Bello University Journal of Administrative Studies, 6*(2).

2. Lawal, S. M. (2011). Ethnic Violence and Nigeria's National Security. *KADA Journal of Liberal Arts, 5*(1).

3. David, N. A., & Lawal, S. M. (2021). Gender, Counter-Terrorism and Counter-Insurgency in Northeast Nigeria. In U. A. Tar (Eds.), *Routledge Handbook of Counterterrorism and Counterinsurgency in Africa*.

Bem Japhet Audu is a lecturer in the Department of History and War Studies, and Research Fellow, Centre for the Study of Leadership and Complex Military Operations, Nigerian Defence Academy, Kaduna, Nigeria. He earned his Ph.D. in History (International Studies) at the prestigious Nigerian Defence Academy, Kaduna in 2016. He also studied M.A. History (2012) and M.A International Relations and Strategic Studies (2007) as well as B.A. History (2003) at Benue State University, Makurdi. He has published many scholarly articles in local and international journals and contributed chapters in books. One of his notable books is; *Wars and Changing Patterns of Inter-Group Relations in the Middle Benue Valley, c. 1300–1900* (2018).

CHAPTER 26

Customs, Contrabands and Arms Control in Africa

Mubarak Ahmed Mashi and Habu Mohammed

INTRODUCTION

The state—represented by the customs, territorial guards and other security agencies—plays a crucial role in managing national borders, and ensuring the health and safety of citizens. However, due to the porous nature of most African borders, and the weak and failing disposition of most states, the security function of the state is often usurped or undermined. The failure of customs and other border enforcement agencies to control the proliferation of illicit arms, especially small arms and light weapons (SALWs), has contributed to the growing incidence of violent conflicts, arm banditry, cattle rustling and Kidnapping, resulting to deaths, displacement of millions of people, untold hardship, threat of diseases, squalor and underdevelopment across the globe. The massive and widespread proliferation of SALWs has increasingly endangered regional and global security. The spread of SALWs in Africa is alarming, there are about 640 million SALWs in circulation globally, 100 million are in Africa, about 30 million in sub-Saharan Africa and 8 million are found in West Africa alone and Over 70% of about 8–10 million illegal weapons in West Africa are in Nigeria (Abiodun et al. 2015). A great number of these SALWs 59% are in the hands of civilians, 38% are owned by government

M. A. Mashi (✉)
Department of Political Science, Umaru Musa Yar'adua University, Katsina, Nigeria

H. Mohammed
Department of Political Science, Bayero University, Kano, Nigeria
e-mail: hmohammed.pol@buk.edu.ng

© The Author(s), under exclusive license to Springer Nature Switzerland AG 2021
U. A. Tar and C. P. Onwurah (eds.), *The Palgrave Handbook of Small Arms and Conflicts in Africa*,
https://doi.org/10.1007/978-3-030-62183-4_26

armed forces, 2.8% by police and 0.2% by armed groups (Uwa and Anthony 2015). Despite the conventions on arms control, the massive inflow of small arms and light weapons (SALWs) to Africa poses serious challenges to regional security. According to African Union there is estimated influx of about 2100 million SALWs in Africa, an estimated 70 million to 100 million AK47 rifles been produced and are found in the national inventories of at least 58 States. European countries are known to be the principal producers and exporters of these SALWs flowing into Africa (Chelule 2014). As a result, most African states have found it difficult to maintain territorial order. Indeed, African states seem to have lost their monopoly over the control of violence in their territories. The illicit influx of SALWs and the level of its proliferation have reached monumental proportion especially in continents of Africa, Asia and Latin America. The illicit transfer and use of these SALWs has posed serious threat to peace and security in these continents.

The step-up in small arms trade in recent times has been largely eased by the twin trends of globalization and liberalization of the economy. Just as embargo in other areas of economic activity has decreased and eased as part of global trend toward embracing free markets and deregulation, the same is true in relation to the trade in SALWs (Pilbeam 2015). This is so because, globalization has open up markets with little or no economic barriers, where people and goods cross borders frequently, which provides fertile ground for illicit arms transfers by minimizing custom regulations and border control, making trafficking in SALWs easier. This means that, the forces of globalization have made improvement in information and communications technologies, which have made transactions in SALWs to be conducted faster and easier without restrictions.

SALWs proliferation has become a very lucrative venture: globally the earnings from SALWs exports globally stand at US$4bn. The main exporters are Austria, Belgium, Brazil, Germany, Italy and USA, with annual export of USD 100 million, the EU member states produce weapons worth over 550 million Euro and export about 350 million Euro weapons annually (Grip 2017). SALWs producers and exporters are making huge profit, a gain saying among employee of the Russian defense industry is "war is bad, but it pays well" (Amnesty International and Oxfam 2005). This is a result of the physical feature arms, highly destructive, relatively cheap in the production, profitable and easy to operate, as well as being easy to conceal and move with (Oche 2005).

CONCEPTUAL AND THEORETICAL REVIEW OF LITERATURE

Customs

Customs are law enforcement agency charged with the responsibility of ensuring that cross-border influx of goods, people and other means of transport comply with rules and regulations governing customs legislation or international instruments that are empowered to provide. Through the deployment of effective and efficient control measures. Customs contributes to national economic prosperity (through fair and accurate revenue collection), economic development (through trade facilitation), public health and safety (through restriction of illicit trade), and national security (through prevention and detection of smuggling of restricted, prohibited goods) (World Customs Organization 2015). As rightly observed by Adeniji (2018), the central role of customs is to ensuring the economic and political prosperity of a nation. At the economic level, it implies the economic progress and at the political level is it implies protecting the territorial integrity of the nation (Adeniji 2018).

Constitutionally speaking, customs are government agency, established by law that are responsible for the administration of customs law and the collection of duties and taxes. It also has the responsibility for the application of other laws and regulations relating to the exportation, importation and the movement of goods (WCO 2018). Customs are deeply involved in intelligence gathering, monitoring and controlling goods that cross borders, determining the types of goods, origin and transit, generating revenue and administering of trade policies. They are also responsible in the collection of non-oil revenue for the government, public safety and border security, environment and health, consumer protection and trade policy issues (Muktar 2019). Customs have the capability to generate information and conduct analysis on every trade transaction; re-assess revenues; inspect, test, analyze, value and seize goods that are considered as contraband; and detain and question persons—all of which are central competencies at the very heart of customs compliance and enforcement activities. The objective is to ensure the prevention of transnational crime, terrorism and extremism, commercial fraud, suppress cyber-crime, disrupt illicit trade and detect serious non-compliance by traders or their agents such as brokers, licensed premises operators, carriers and freight forwarders (WCO 2015).

The customs have existing laws, rules and regulations that regulate the levying of duties and charges with regard to the importation and exportation, the movement or storage of goods, the import and export procedures and formalities as well as the institutional organization of the agency, that ensure to enforce such rules (Kafeero 2008).

According to Seniora and Poitevin (2010), customs authorities are saddle with the tasks of administering laws governing the import, export and transit of goods, as well as the verification of transport modalities for these goods. They therefore exercise an important role in facilitating the mobility of goods and the means of transport coming in or leaving a particular country (Seniora and Poitevin 2010). Therefore, the customs are responsible in managing and controlling goods including SALWs coming in or going out of a country.

Across the globe, the customs carries out myriads functions that include intelligence and information gathering, combating smuggling; management of maritime; land and aeronautical surveillance; patrols of ports of entry; cargo examination; immigration and emigration processing; passengers and baggage inspection at international land, sea and air border crossing points; cyber monitoring; antidumping measures, valuation, backtracking investigations and undercover programmes (WCO 2015). They also engaged in the enforcement of trade and antidumping policies, in conjunction with other national agencies to ensure quality and do away with illicit weapons and other harmful substances coming into a country.

The tasks of customs differ from country to country, and are often the subject of regular review and changes to ensure their ongoing relevance in a constantly changing world. Traditionally, however, customs has been responsible for implementing a wide range of government policies and programmes, spanning from the collection of revenue, trade compliance cum facilitation, interception of contrabands, protection and preservation of cultural heritage and the enforcement of intellectual property laws (Muktar 2019).

The customs are the second revenue-generating agency after crude oil sector in most African States. For instance, in 2019 Nigerian government generated a sum of 4.6 trillion from oil sector, followed by Nigerian customs with 1.34 trillion (*BusinessDay* 2019). However, they are facing with numerous and multidimensional challenges globally, especially among the less developed countries of Africa, Asia and Latin America. Problems ranging from the poor condition of service, corruption, political interference, absence of intelligence gathering of information, shortage of personnel, obsolete equipments or lack of modern equipments such as surveillance, tracking and scanning devices, making them analogue at this age of globalization. Add to these is lack of coordination between and among African countries and absence of interagency collaboration with the customs and other relevant agencies within countries. These have made customs in Africa backward in discharging their legal duties. While border security challenges, especially of SALWs trafficking, which is increasing unabated more than ever before; the customs lacked the modern techniques, devices and knowledge to confront these challenges effectively. For customs in Africa to effectively control and regulate SALWs trafficking and the smuggling of contrabands, the need for innovative technology devices in line with global best practices is necessary.

Nevertheless, there are many concerns, interests and commitments by African states and governments on how to confront these challenges. In Nigeria for instance, the government have introduced sophisticated scanning, tracking and surveillance devices and salary increment of the customs officer, aimed at improving their conditions of service and enhance its revenue generation and national security.

Small Arms

What constitute small and light weapons have undergone some changes dues to the advancement in technology over time (Honwana and Lamb 1998). As the world continued to advance in the field of science and technology, there is an increasing improvement in the capacity to destroy, kill or maim.

Generally, "small arms" refers to weapons operated by one person; these include revolvers and self-loading pistols, rifles and carbines, sub-machine guns, assault rifles and light machine guns. Light weapons are portable and easy to move weapons, designed for use by several persons serving as a crew, such as heavy machine guns, automatic cannons, howitzers, mortars of less than 100 mm caliber, grenade launchers, anti-tank weapons and launchers, recoilless guns, shoulder fired rockets, anti-aircraft weapons and launchers, and air Defence weapons (SADC Firearms Protocol 2003: Article 1.2).

The United Nations Institute for Disarmament Research classified small arms to include: revolvers and self-loading pistols; rifles and carbines; submachine guns; assault rifles; light machine gun; heavy machine guns; handheld under-barrel and mounted grenade launchers; portable anti-craft guns; portable anti-tank guns; recoilless rifles; portable launchers of antitank missiles and rockets system; portable launchers of anti-aircraft missiles systems; and mortars of calibers less than 100 mm (United Nations Institute for Disarmament Research 2006: 1).

According to The United Nations General Assembly "small arms and light weapons" are any portable lethal weapon that are designed to expel or launch, or may be readily converted to expel or launch a shot, bullet or projectile by the action of an explosive (Heinrich 2006).

Similarly, the ECOWAS Convention (2006) on the control of SALWs provides the following definition: All components, parts or spare parts for small arms or light weapons or ammunition necessary for its functioning; or any chemical substance serving as active material used as propelling or explosive agent (ECOWAS 2006).

Small Arms, are arms used by one person and which include firearms or devices such as explosives, an incendiary bomb or a gas bomb, a grenade, a rocket launcher, a missile system or landmine; revolvers and pistols with automatic loading; rifles and carbines; machines guns; assault rifles and light machine guns (GIABA 2013).

According to Nte (2011), small arms are; smaller infantry weapons, such as firearms that an individual soldier can carry. They are usually limited to revolvers, pistols, submachine guns, shotguns, carbines, assault rifles, rifle squad automatic weapons, light machine guns, general-purpose machine gun, heavy machine guns, smaller mortars, recoilless rifles, rocket launchers medium machine guns and hand grenades. He further stressed that, large mortars, howitzers, cannons, vehicles and larger pieces of equipment cannot be considered small arms (Nte 2011).

Arms Control

Arms control simply connotes the regulation and measures to prevent the production, sales and circulation of arms, with the target of combating security threats. Arms control is created to ensure a legal system, which will distinguish between lawful and illicit production, reposition, development, use, transfer and trade of SALWs. According to the Northern Atlantic Treaty Organisation, arms control generally refers to mutually agreed upon restriction or controls between states on the development, production, transfer, stockpiling, proliferation, deployment and use of small arms, conventional weapons and weapons of mass destruction (NATO 2020).

Arms control can also be viewed as the limitation of arms in circulation through effective mechanisms such as the reduction of the volume of weapons, the categories of weapons or delivery systems, the research and manufacture of certain weapons and deployments of these weapons (Ventura 2018). Arms control can be unilateral but it is usually an agreement between multiple parties. All the treaties regarding nuclear arsenals are strictly arms control, seeking solely limitations in stockpile numbers or technologies. Arms control regimes to thrive three conditions are required: treaty of community coherence, good governance and cooperation of the great powers (Ventura 2018).

There have been many developments in small arms control under the United Nations since the end of the cold war. It will be argued that, this marked the era of small arms control globally (Grip 2017). Therefore, Arms control refers to the agreements between States to ensure decisive restrictions on the production, transfer, deployment, testing and sales of arms.

Small Arms as a Global Phenomenon—A Profiling of Rising Trend in Africa

The entire world is moon-faced with the challenge of SALWs proliferation, these weapons, according to International Action Network on Small Arms (2006) and the Geneva Declaration in (2008) reported that small arms are used to kill as many as 1000 people every day around the globe (Ogu 2014). Every year about eight million new small arms, plus 10–15 billion rounds of ammunition are manufactured, enough bullets to shoot every person in the world twice (Fahrenthold and Kunkle 2009). In the last 40 years, the number of countries producing small arms had doubled, and the majority of these small arms producing companies and exporters are located in European countries of Germany, Russia, Brazil, Belgium, Italy. Others include; Austria, Canada, Iran, Japan, China, Pakistan, Spain and USA whose target is to produce and sell their products (arms) to developing countries, where it will continue to flow and circulate to other neighboring countries (Ogu 2014).

According to the Small Arms Survey, a global center of excellence whose mandate is to generate evidence-based, impartial, and policy-relevant knowledge on all aspects of small arms and armed violence, reports that there are approximately 875 million SALW in the world today (Small Arms Survey 2014). The United Nations estimates that these SALWs are responsible for 350,000–500,000 deaths a year, as well as over a million non-fatal injuries. Not all of these deaths and injuries occur in armed conflicts, since large numbers are as the result of criminal activities and suicides. Regardless of this variation, globally over 90% of civilian casualties resulting from acts of violence can be attributed to SALWs (Pilbeam 2015). Worse still, three-quarters of SALWs in circulation are in the hands of non-state players. They are mainly ethnic militias, insurgents, terrorist, criminal gangs, private military and security companies (ibid.). The fact that these weapons have led destruction of millions of lives, especially women and children, who are considered vulnerable groups in many parts of Africa, unveils the murderous and destructive nature of SALWs. It is also responsible for heinous crimes and armed conflicts globally, increasing terrorism, insurgency and civil wars. For instance, Libya, Syria, Burundi, Ghana, Yemen, Kyrgyzstan, Nepal, Pakistan, Sierra Leone, Cote D'Ivoire, Togo, and Guinea are few of many countries that suffer from this form of "black globalisation" (Malhotra 2011: 11). Other findings show that, there are 640 million SALWs in circulation globally, 100 million are found in Africa and about 30 million are in Sub-Saharan Africa and 8 million in West Africa. The majority of these SALWs about 59% are in the hands of civilians, 38% are owned by government armed forces, 2.8% by police and 0.2% by armed groups (Uwa and Anthony 2015). In 2014, SAS also undertook a review of 11 peace missions deployed in Sudan and South Sudan by the AU and the UN, over a period of 12 years from 2002. In that period, it was estimated that there were at least 22 incidents in which peacekeeping troops lost arms and ammunitions that ends up in the hands of non-state actors. In almost half of these cases, the "losses" were significant—from 50 to 99 firearms and between 2500 and 4999 rounds of ammunition (Alusala 2018).

The results of all these misadventure are that, these arms contributed in the rise of criminal activities, revolts, ethno-religious crisis, communal conflicts, social agitations, kidnapping, arm banditry, cattle rustling, terrorism, insurgency, riots, militancy, political violence, poverty, economic crisis, threats to neighboring countries and unemployment in most African states. The proliferation of SALWs in Africa is destructive one, particularly given its vulnerability as one of the epicenter of conflict globally, between 1990 and 2005, African countries spent over 300 billion dollars on armed conflict equivalent to the sum of international aid that was granted to Africa within the same period (Nte 2011).

Most arms are imported into Africa across land and sea borders, negligence, bribery and corruption among border security agencies like the customs and immigrations, arms dealers, serving and retired military and police officers returning peacekeepers. The inflow of SALWs in the hands of non-state players in Africa has increased the challenges and undermined the ability of governments in Africa to achieve their legal mandate of securing their land and sea borders and ensuring the protection of lives and properties of their citizenry.

The need to regulate and control the influx of SALWs due to their destructive nature emerged in the 1990s from a group of Nobel Peace Laureates, including Mikhail Gorbachev, and Amnesty International; and was led by the former President of Costa Rica, Oscar Arias. The Control Arms

Campaign, a worldwide network that includes non-governmental organizations, such as Amnesty International, Oxfam and Safer World was launched in the year 2006 (Amnesty International, International Action Network on Small Arms and Oxfam 2005). The coalition of these organizations delivered the "Million Faces" Petition-the world's largest photo petition, signed by over one million folks in support of the control and regulation of SALWs across over 160 countries. The United Nations General Assembly adopted the Arms Trade Treaty (ATT) on April 2, 2013 and as of July 31, 2013; more than 80 countries signed the Treaty (ibid.).

Causes and Sources of Small Arms and Light Weapons Proliferations in Africa

The end of the Cold War in 1989 saw the opening of a Pandora's box in many regions of the world. Governments that had been able to depend itself from the opposition found themselves in ferocious fight with non-state players, who found ingenious ways of accessing small arms to confront their local states. The desire to emplace the Cold War surplus weapons and the need to expand production capacity led to the over production of weapons in arms-producing countries. Therefore, the "desire to increase arms exportation as a means of earning foreign exchange" led to the proliferation of SALWs (Naylor 2001). This marked the beginning of arms proliferation not only in Africa, but the rest of the globe.

In West Africa, arms are smuggled into the region, either from one country to another and/or from Europe and America to other African countries, such as Chad, Cameroon, South Africa and the Great Lakes region. Nigeria's borders with Cameroon, Niger, and Chad are well-known routes for arms trafficking (GIABA 2013). Smugglers on these routes employed different tactics and trans-border tricks, often hide weapons in bags of grains, coffins, iced fish cartons, cement bags, paint buckets and under car seats and compartment. Such tactics and strategies are common in many borders within the region where lorries-loaded with arms are successfully trafficked (GIABA 2013). This shows how arms flow to Africa and the strategies and tactics used for the importation and exportation of SALWs.

Across western Africa and the Maghreb, the "Arab spring"—a violent and persistent which swept away several regimes in the Maghreb and Arab countries in Africa most notably, Muammar Gaddafi of Libya and Hosni Mubarak of Egypt and Ben Ali of Tunisia—led to a massive outflow of weaponry which became the weapon of choice in fueling crisis in many countries. The successful overthrow of these erstwhile leaders led to the retention of weaponry in the hands of rebels, insurgents and terrorist groups. In addition, these weapons play an important role in communal and resource conflicts, as well as general criminality (kidnapping, hostage-taking, cattle rustling etc.) in the region. The aftermath of the Arab Spring is that these weapons began to circulate freely from one country to another, and were used in perpetuating instability in those countries. Today, most of the weapons in circulation in Africa were those stolen from the armory of Muammar Gaddafi and smuggled into the country.

In Nigeria for instance and some of her neighboring countries like Niger, Chad, Mali among others, camels and others animals were used in importing arms from Libya, through the Sahara desert which is a vast terrain that has been difficult to surveil or manage.

Another key cause of the proliferation of SALWs is corruption, racketeering and bootlegging among bureaucrats, politicians, security agents and the civilian population. Weapons dealers pay bribes to customs officers, while soldiers, police officers and security forces are known to have sold government weapons to undesirable elements (Ayissi and Sall 2005). A custom officer whose salary is not more than 80,000 naira and his needs are beyond 500,000 to take care of his family, would hardly resist an offer (bribe) of 300–400,000 to compromise his duty. Today most customs officers, as well as subalterns and rank-and-file with lower academic qualification are multi-millionaires, through sharp practices, including the illicit importation of arms, narcotics and contrabands. In 2008, for instance, fifteen Nigerian army officers, including three colonels were arrested as part of the syndicate that stole arms and ammunitions, which includes hundreds of AK-47 rifles, GPMGs and ammunition boxes from the Army Central Ordinance Depot in Kaduna and sold them to militants (GIABA 2013).

Porous borders between African states and vast ungoverned territory constitute a key factor in the proliferation of SALWs. Africa's terrain and demography present a huge challenge in the control of small arms. By virtue of its size, being the second largest continent in the world in terms of land mass, and being the second most populated continent, and given the level of its comatose level of development, make Africa a difficult terrain for border control and demographic management. Also, the sheer size of some of the African countries—such as DRC, Republic of Sudan and Republic of Niger with landmass of 2.345 million Km, 1.886 million Km and 923,763 km respectively—provide challenge in the control of the movement of people, goods and services. The shared boundaries between many weak and failing states provide a safe haven for arms traffickers: Nigeria for instance, has 770 km of shared land border with the Republic of Benin to the west with about 1500 km with Niger to the North, 1700 km with Cameroon to the east, 90 km with the Republic of Chad to the North-east and 850 km maritime border on the Atlantic Ocean. Out-stretched, these tally up to 4910 km of borders, which have to be monitored effectively. Each of these entry points, along with the airports, has been used to smuggling SALWs into the country. Therefore, to effectively monitor these borders is a herculean task. It is also imperative to note that, the three largest sub-Saharan African States, notably Sudan (the continent's overall largest), the Congo DRC (third overall largest) and Chad (fifth overall largest) have been experiencing insecurity, armed conflict and civil wars for long. This perhaps is as a result of their enormous size and the porous nature of their borders, which makes it easy for the influx of SALWs, exacerbating insecurity (Ngang 2007). Based on GIABA report (2013), customs and law enforcement officials revealed that, illicit SALWs are smuggled into Ghana from neighboring countries, such as Cote d'Ivoire and Burkina Faso (GIABA 2013). Arms are also smuggled into Burkina Faso, Mali and Niger from Libya through Sudan, Somalia, Chad and Cameroon. The smuggling routes differ, depending on the country of destination. The officials also assumed that, arms are smuggled into neighboring Togo through airports and land borders, particularly with Benin and Burkina Faso. In Cote d'Ivoire, the northern and western borders remain the major routes for illicit arms trafficking, despite a United Nations restriction. The meeting point of the country's border with neighboring Liberia and Guinea is a notorious transit point (GIABA 2013). There is further speculation among customs and security agencies in the region that arms are smuggled into the Mano River region—Sierra Leone, Liberia, and Guinea-Conakry—through airports, seaports and land borders (see Chapters on MRU and Sierra Leone in this Handbook). Indeed, there is an estimated 150 illicit crossing points to and from Sierra Leone, Guinea and Liberia. The Guinean forest in particular is a notorious transit route for illicit arms into the region (GIABA 2013).

The cultures and traditions of many African countries allow for, and encourage, the ownership and possession of small arms as a means of communal defense, ceremonies, and as symbol of individual display of manhood and bravery. In many cultures in Africa like in Nigeria, Niger, Mali and Chad, weapons are used for traditional ceremonies or "rite of passage." While the Fulanis in northern Nigeria make use of swords, arrows and sticks, the communities of traditional hunters of the west and east carry shotguns and in the south-western part of Nigeria, there is a traditional rite of gun firing at events such as at the traditional burial rites of local dignitaries and harvest festival (Ayissi and Sall 2005: 59). For the sake of prestige, many have now turned to the use of modern weapons like shotguns, revolvers, semi-automatic pistols and even high caliber rifles. Of course, there are gun laws prohibiting such open use arms, but they are hardly respected and can be easily bypassed. This cultural attachment to weapons is prevalent in rural communities, where conservative cultural practices and traditional rituals still have recognition (Ngang 2007). But the lackadaisical attitude of government to effectively address the activities of this customs and traditions, all in the name of promoting and preserving cultural heritage and harmony, has also posed threat to the control of arms, as these arms may later on be transferred to wrong hands, for purposes of ethno-religious violence and crimes (ibid.).

Globalization, which has weakened the territorial borders and sovereignty of many African states: the free movement of goods and people, provides smooth operation of illicit trade in arms by shattering customs regulations and border control. Malhotra (2011), opined that, a small percent of container ships have cargo checks, which ensures the smooth movement of arms. Making bogus documents such as bills of lading and forged end-user certificates, bribing officials at port and borders and concealing arms as humanitarian assistance are common sharp practices in Africa. Malhotra (2011) provides several globalizing actors that facilitate illegal arms trade:

a. Political and economic integration are coupled with little restrictions on migration and movement of persons. This assists the arms dealers to strengthen their illicit business connections and advance with new ones. Arms dealers move freely to various regions, motivated by business expansion or reduced operational risks. In case of arrests, SALWs dealers travel to countries where it is impossible to be extradited. For instance, Abu Salem, a world criminal from India, who besides having criminal records, was involved in providing illegal arms for 1993 serial bomb blasts in India. To escape arrest, he left for Portugal. After 3 years of legal disputes, Indian authorities managed to extradite Abu Salem from Lisbon, Portugal. It was after this case that India and Portugal signed an extradition treaty in 2007.
b. Banking reforms and the movement of capital have aided the black market to spread its trade internationally, utilizing every angle of the well-linked financial market. This also gives rise to offshore markets and tax shelters. An illustration of banking innovation is e-money and e-wallet which allow for large scale transaction in illicit goods without physical exchange of cash. Banks have introduced cards bearing microchips, which are able to store large sums of money. These cards are portable outside conventional channels or can be easily bartered among individuals. In addition to legal tenders, clandestine financial transaction—especially the use of encrypted currencies such as bitcoin—has provided opportunity for arms brokers and merchants to use virtual money to carryout transaction.
c. The linkage of banks with the internet has posed a new challenge in combating illegitimate activities in the financial sector: e-banking has digitized money making it prone to criminality. Even though it has numerous benefits for the world at large, it is misused for money laundering, capital flight, credit card frauds and check kiting. Adding to this, economic integration among regions availsarms brokers with more opportunities to stash their money, by investing in different stock exchanges. Numerous other sharp practices are a by-product of a deregulated financial sector, but money laundering is at the peak. Money Laundering or 'cleansing of money' is an unlawful practice of concealing the point of origin, identity or destination of the funds, when performing a particular financial transaction. The criminals manoeuvre money across borders gaining from banks in countries with disregardful anti-laundering policies.
d. Profound expansion of marketable airline and freight industry (making transport cheaper and easier) assists in increased proliferation of arms in conflict zones. Global junction of airline companies, supply chains, shipping firms makes it tough to supervise unlawful practices in air and sea.

e. The improvement in global communication has been immeasurable. This has improved the ability of arms dealers to communicate internationally through the web at a cheaper and subsidise rate. Arms dealers use 'cloned' cellular phones and unsecured broadband networks to bypass any chances of being traced. Satellite phones are an option in remote areas where other means cannot be operated, providing an uninterrupted channel of contact and reach. In some cases, arms deals are coordinated through wires, where the privilege of anonymity prevails. In 2004, British police arrested more than 50 people in a series of raids to crack down criminals who bought illegal arms from abroad over the internet (Malhotra 2011: 4).

The low price and portability of SALWs; its ease in delivery and concealment as well as maintenance; tactical considerations use in killing and intimidation of people; and their highly effective nature from a combat point of view make SALWs attractive to non-state players who significantly lack the capacity to procure and operate more sophisticated heavy weapons (Jekada 2005). Furthermore, SALWs occupy pride of places, widely used in African conflicts, in particular owing to their "advantages" of being cheap, easy to transport and conceal, simple to maintain and easy to handle (Ndime 2005).

The Flow of Small Arms: Types, Sources, Routes and Destinations of SALWs in West Africa

Arms smuggling is generally more prevalent in areas where militants operate, such as the Niger Delta region of Nigeria, northern Cote d'Ivoire, the Casamance region of Senegal, and the northern regions of Mali and Niger. However, due to porous nature of land borders, all entry points into an ECOWAS country are possible trafficking routes for SALWs (GIABA 2013).

The common SALWs found in West Africa are: AK47 rifles, light machine guns, small bombs, and grenades, rocket launchers, missile systems, firearms, revolvers and automatic loading pistols, assault rifles, landmines and locally made pistols. These arms find their inroads to the region through myriads of routes around the globe into West Africa and other locations of the African continent. Although these illegal routes connect covertly with each other with often-unpredictable stopovers and diversions along the line, there are four known arms trafficking routes in West Africa namely; West Africa, Africa, Middle East and European routes. These illicit arms circle cut across land and sea borders, creeks and footpath (GIABA 2013). These show that, arms are smuggled into and within West Africa, either from one state to another and/or from Europe and other African countries, especially neighboring countries such as Chad, Cameroon, South Africa and the Great Lakes region. For instance, Nigeria shares border with Cameroon, Niger and Chad, which are well-known routes for arms trade. Similarly, illicit arms are smuggled into

Benin Republic from South Africa, Nigeria, Kenya, Ghana, Egypt and Burkina Faso. Other sources are travelers who bring in firearms through illegal transfer before leaving the country. Furthermore, Cote d'Ivoire, Guinea and Liberia are notorious smuggling routes for arms in and out of the three countries and the main countries of origin of these SALWs are USA (41%), Britain (19.5%), Russia (17.5%), France (7%) and China (5%) (GIABA 2013). These are often trafficked illegal pathways within the subregion. Figure 26.1 shows the main pathways, while Table 26.1 shows the dimensions, types, origin and routes of SALWs in West Africa.

The increased proliferation of these SALWs in West Africa and the corresponding increase in their accessibility has also increased the possibility of person especially the unemployed to resort to violence as a means of dispute resolution (GIABA 2013). The availability of weapons thus increases the possibility for violence and violent conflicts in the sub-region and, by extension, hinders development to take place, lead to massive human and physical damages, serious human rights violations, and general instability in the sub-region (GIABA 2013). Consequently, the present day Africa is bedeviled by general insecurity of ethno-religious violence, electoral violence, kidnapping, cattle rustling, arm banditry, arm robbery, insurgency, communal conflicts and militancy. That is why most African states are now suffering from socio-economic crises of unemployment, poverty, corruption, loss of capital and investments, educational and industrial setback, hunger, food insecurity, ballooning internal displacement and refugee debacle.

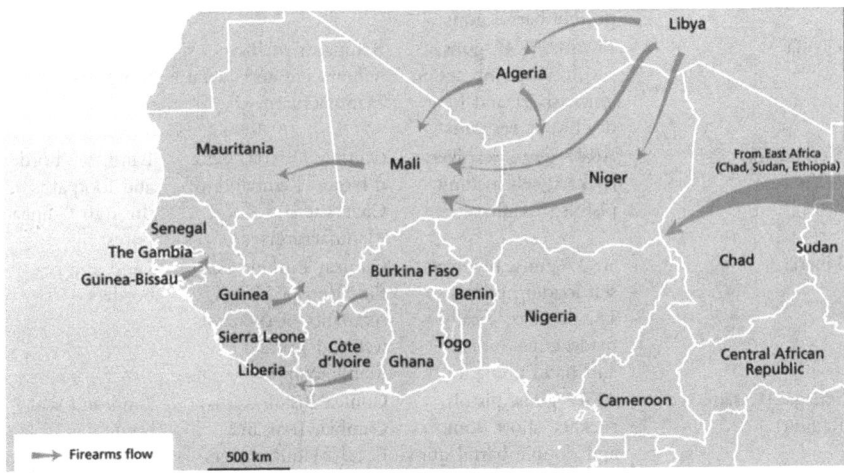

Fig. 26.1 Pathways of illegal proliferation SALWs in West Africa (*Source* United Nations Office on Drugs and Crime [2013: 33])

Table 26.1 Destinations, types, origin and routes of SALWs in West Africa

Country of destination or use	Types of SALWs	Likely countries of origin/suppliers	Means/routes
Niger	AK47 guns, pistols, double barrel, berretta guns	Libya, Chad, Somalia, Sudan, Nigeria, Algeria, Burkina Faso, and Local Manufacturers	Land borders and footpaths
Guinea Bissau	AK47 guns, pistols, double barrel guns	Remnants from the independence struggle, Liberia, Sierra Leone and Local Manufacturers	Land and sea borders
Cote d'Ivoire	AK47 guns, pistols, revolvers, assault rifles	Liberia, Guinea, USA, Britain, Russia, France, China and Local Manufacturers	Land and sea borders
Nigeria (Niger Delta, North East)	Pump action guns, AK47 guns, Revolvers, self-loading guns, Assault rifles, pistols, double barrel guns	Chad, Cameroon, South Africa, Europe, Niger Military and Police officers, Local Manufacturers, Great Lakes region and Russia	Land and sea borders, creeks and air strips
Togo	Ak47 guns, local pistols, and long rifles, pistols, short, long and double barrel guns	Nigeria, Ghana and Local Manufacturers	Land borders, footpaths
Ghana	Pistols, AK47 guns, revolvers, pump action guns, short and long double barrel guns	Remnants of the military-era and Local Manufacturers	Land borders, footpaths
Sierra Leone	AK47 guns, revolvers, rockets, self loading pistols, assault rifles	Guinea, Liberia, Cote d'Ivoire, Remnants of Civil war and Local Manufacturers	Land, sea borders and footpaths through Guinean Forest
Liberia	AK47 guns, revolvers, self loading pistols, assault rifles, locally made guns, mortars and hand grenades	Guinea, Burkina Faso, East Europe, Libya, remnants of the civil war and Local Manufacturers	Land and sea borders
Senegal (Casamance Region)	AK47 guns, pistols, rockets, short, long and double barrel guns	Guinea Bissau, Gambia, Iran and Local Manufacturers	Land and sea borders

(continued)

Table 26.1 (continued)

Country of destination or use	Types of SALWs	Likely countries of origin/suppliers	Means/routes
Gambia	AK47 guns, rockets, short, long and double barrel guns	Local Manufacturers, Iran and Senegal	Land and sea borders
Burkina Faso	AK47 guns, revolvers, self loading pistols, assault rifles and locally made guns	Liberia, Cote d'Ivoire and Local Manufacturers	Land borders and footpaths
Guinea	AK47 guns, local pistols and long rifles, short, long and double barrel guns	Local Manufacturers, Cote d'Ivoire, Sierra Leone and Liberia	Land and sea borders
Cape Verde	AK47 guns, revolvers, assault rifles and double barrel guns	Europe and local manufacturers	Sea borders
Benin	AK47 guns, revolvers, assault rifles, long and double barrel guns	Nigeria, Togo, South Africa	Land and sea borders
Mali	AK47 guns, revolvers, assault rifles, long and double barrel guns	Local Manufacturers, Niger, Libya, Algeria and Mauritania	Land borders

Source GIABA (2013: 16)

CONVENTIONS ON ARMS CONTROL IN AFRICA

The UN came up with some political measures aimed to prevent the influx and diversion of SALWs. One of these measures was the Programme of Action to combat, prevent and to abolish the illegal trafficking of SALWs in all angles and the International instrument to enable states to mark, trace and identify the illicit flow SALWs (UN, 2001 cited in Bromley et al. 2019). On December 24, 2014, the UN adopted the Arms Trade Treaty, a legally binding convention on trade in conventional weapons, including SALW, for the purpose of preventing illicit trafficking and diversion of international arms transfers (Woolcott 2014). Gradually and reliably, the international community is building a structure to distinguish between legal and illegal violence and means of violence, similar to the ones, which exist at national levels. In practical terms, the vast majority of multilateral SALWs control takes place at the regional level. States may use UN agreements as a backdrop for regional implementation, or during regional conference to negotiate their position on global treaties. In both cases, the implementation and practical application of arms control are in states' immediate environments (Grip 2017).

In Africa, there are four arms control agreements, aimed at making the production, possession and transfer of SALWs criminal offenses. This includes:

1. The 2001 Protocol on the control of firearms, ammunition and other related materials in the Southern African Development Community (SADC) Region.
2. The Nairobi Protocol for the Prevention, Control and Reduction of SALWs in the Great Lakes Region and the Horn of Africa (2004), that was signed by 11 East and Central African States.
3. Economic Community of West African States (ECOWAS) Convention on SALWs, adopted on the 14 June 2006 that was signed by 15 members' states.
4. The 2010 Central African Convention for the Control of SALWs, their ammunition, parts and components that can be used for their manufacture, repair and assembling, known as the Kinshasa Convention. Rwanda and the 10 member states of the Economic Community of Central African States, (ECCAS) were also signatories to the Kinshasa convention (Lamb and Dye 2009).

In West Africa alone, there are three regional agreements aimed at preventing illicit trafficking and proliferation of SALWs in West Africa. The first measure has to do with the activities and actions, headed by ECOWAS through its agencies, bodies and committees, that focuses on developing policies against illicit SALWs transactions and creating awareness about the dangers of SALWs. The second measure has to do with the enactment and enforcement of laws and regulations against illegal trade in SALWs by ECOWAS member states. The third has to do with the roles of the civil society organizations, channeling their efforts against illicit trafficking of SALWs in the region and their participation focuses on advocacy, research and international lobbying (GIABA 2013).

The measures used by ECOWAS to reduce the high number of SALWs in circulation in West African region include; the ECOWAS Small Arms Unit and the ECOWAS Small Arms Program (ECOSAP). The Program, in collaboration with the United Nations Development Program (UNDP), helped in strengthening the capacity of national institutions in combating the illicit trafficking in SALWs. At the policy level, most ECOWAS member states have ratified the ECOWAS Convention on SALWs, which came into force on the September 29, 2009. The Convention is the Code for the Implementation of the 1998 Moratorium on the importation, exportation and production of SALWs, adopted in Abuja, Nigeria in October 1998. Specifically, it comes up with institutional procedures and operational mechanisms to be established by ECOWAS member states aimed at achieving the objectives of the Moratorium, the Convention also provides minimum acceptable standards for SALWs regulations in West African region (GIABA 2013).

All these regional agreements covers the illicit manufacture, possession and transfer of SALWs, promote the destruction of surplus weapons stocks and introduce effective control measures weapon stockpiles (Lamb and Dye 2009). But the truth of the matter is that, all of these conventions failed to control the inflows of arms into Africa, due to lack of commitments by the governments, porous borders, lack of proper intelligence gathering and preponderance of corruption among the border security agencies.

The Role of Customs in Curbing Arms Proliferation in Africa

Customs in most African countries are relatively active in terms of arms control in Africa. The customs authorities are responsible for administering laws governing the import, export and transit of goods, as well as the verification of transport modalities for these goods. They therefore fulfill an important role in facilitating the movement of goods and the means of transport coming in or leaving a given country. Nevertheless, their most visible and most developed function involves revenue collection in the sphere of duties and taxes. The customs authorities are also responsible for the detection and prevention of trafficking and can therefore be involved in border monitoring. Border guards or border police are officials in charge of carrying out controls at border posts and surveillance along the border. This involves checking individuals crossing borders to border posts and patrol work to prevent illegal border crossings (Seniora and Poitevin 2010: 6). In Nigeria for instance, the Nigeria Customs Service (NCS) intercepted in July 2017 over 1398 rolls of plain military uniforms and camouflage that were illegally shipped into Nigeria from China at the Lagos port (Adenubi 2017). On July 27, 2018 the Federal Operations Unit of the Nigerian Customs (FOU) Zone C seized a container with registration number MRSU 3040288 carrying military uniforms and 440 pump action rifles along Aba-Port Harcourt road (*Vanguard* 2018). Similarly, in October 2010, thirteen containers containing arms shipped to Nigeria from Iran seized by customs in Lagos, Nigeria; the arms were reported to be heading to the Casamance area through the Gambia (GIABA 2013).

In addition, in September 2017 the Nigeria Customs Service also intercepted 1100 units of pump-action rifles imported into Nigeria through the Tin can Island Port, Lagos (Obiejesi 2017). Furthermore, the anti-smuggling crusade in December 2017, painstakingly intercepted and seized about 2671 pump action rifles, dangerous drugs, foreign rice, and smuggle vehicles among others. Sadly, six of their finest officers lose their lives in the line of duty (*Punch Newspaper* 2017).

In spite of their modest achievement, customs authorities in Africa face with institutional challenges, poor state of equipment, lack of trained personnel to handle hardware and software; and lack of solid national infrastructure to make customs work easier: institutional challenges, attributed to the poor condition of service, which made most of the officers vulnerable to corrupt practices and consequently compromise their official duties. According to McLinden and Durrani (2013), opined that, poor pay and difficult working conditions customs officials in many countries have to contend with as well as very little probability of being caught and it is not surprising that, customs continues to be seen among the most corrupt government institutions (McLinden and Durrani 2013). Goods often flow into the African countries and market without payment of duties and taxes as a result of collusion between importers and customs. This is particularly so in western Africa (Buyonge and Kireeva, n.d.). Apart from these harrowing narratives, there is political interference in the institution by government in power and their allies, contrabands intercepted or confiscated by customs authorities are release base on "order" from the presidency or vested interests.

Furthermore, there is the lack of inter-agency collaboration between the customs and other relevant security agencies such as the immigration, army, police and other para-military in discharging its legal duties. Restrictions on the smuggling of certain goods cannot be a one-man affair; it must be a collective responsibility. Inter-agency rivalry constitutes an inherent challenge of inter-agency cooperation along border country borders.

Porosity of African borders, which has contributed and encouraged transborder crimes, arms trafficking, drug trafficking, illegal transactions such as smuggling of contraband goods like shoes, frozen poultry products, duty non-paid for cars and foreign parboiled rice and many more (Akinyemi 2013). This has encouraged the influx of illegal migrants and cross border criminality, which seemed to be posing serious challenges for the customs to contend. Nigeria for instance, shares 773 kilometres boundary with the Republic of Benin; 1690 Kilometres with the Republic of Cameroun; 1497 Kilometres with Niger Republic; 85 Kilometres with the Republic of Chad and the Republic of Guinea (Salifu, 2013 cited in Olomu et al., n.d.).

There is also shortage of personnel; the numbers of customs personnel in most African States are not adequate to monitor and patrol all the porous borders exploited by arm dealers, their accomplices and other criminal elements. Nigeria for instance, has 1479 illegal routes (*National Daily* 2017). With less than eighteen thousand (18,000) workforce, expected to monitor all the official land borders and sea, illegal routes, revenue generation and security functions in the country (Olomu et al., n.d.). With all these, commensurate result on African borders monitoring is impossible.

Poor State of Equipment, the customs in most African states lacks the basic equipment and modern devices, that could be used to monitor or track down illicit movement of goods and people. Most of the equipments in the agencies are obsolete and outdated and some have none. Hardly, you see customs at borders in Africa using drones, CCTVs, sophisticated scanning devices, monitoring devices and biodata of wanted criminals at their duty post. This also posed a serious challenge. According to Musa (2013), African countries border management system becomes poor and ineffective when it encompasses the problem of patrol vehicles, surveillance helicopters and equipments as well as neglect or non-functioning of intelligence services (Musa, 2013 cited in Olomu et al., n.d.). These are some of the features of African land borders and seaports.

Lack of trained personnel to handle hardware and software; they lack adequately trained personnel that has the capacity to operate both hard and software devices that are vital for the successful operation of the organization. The truth is that, they are not encouraged to attend conferences, workshops on cutting edge technology or even further studies on new trends, which has to do with border control and monitoring, this made some of the personnel are still "analog." The knowledge they acquired from their inception in service is the same knowledge they apply until retirement age, without change in strategy and tactics. Hazen and Horner (2007) further stressed that, border security challenges especially in Africa aggravated due to the fact that, border security agents lack the training, knowledge and resources to perform their duties effectively (Hazen and Horner 2007).

Efforts by African States and Government on Arms Control

There are efforts by African states and government in controlling arms proliferation, through the adoption of global and regional policies on arms control. Yet, this, arms continue to enter Africa.

One of the greatest AU's achievements is the Africa Amnesty Month for the Surrender and Collection of Illicit Weapons in circulation. Launched on September 4, 2017, the event will be observed annually across African continent (AU, 2017 cited in Alusala 2018). African Heads of state and government of the AU ground the amnesty in the 2013 Solemn Declaration, known as Agenda 2063, the Solemn Declaration was drafted to provide a strategic framework for Africa's socio-economic transformation in 50 years to come. There is the silencing the Guns policy, aimed at bringing an end to all the wars, civil conflicts, gender-based violence, violent conflicts and preventing genocide in Africa by the year 2020 (AU 2019). This initiative has been great, it has resuscitated the role of the AU as the key continental player of the efforts undertaken by the RECs and RMs to tackle the challenges of illicit arms circulation and it has shown the commitment of the African Union is in providing effective panacea to the problems affecting African States. For instance, in April 2013, when the UN General Assembly adopted the Arms Trade Treaty (ATT), a multilateral instrument aimed at regulating the US$70 billion international trade in conventional weapons, Africa wholeheartedly supported the adoption, with only three of the AU member states that were not on board with it (Alusala 2018).

At the sub-regional level, effort to control illicit arms flows precedes the "Bamako Declaration." For instance, in 1998, heads of state from the ECOWAS agreed on the Moratorium on the exportation, importation and production of SALWs in West Africa. The moratorium was later transformed into a convention in 2006 (Alusala 2018). Subsequently, negotiations led to the adoption of the ECOWAS Convention on SALWs in 2009, which came into force on September 29, 2009. The Convention has provided a legal and institutional mechanisms at both regional and national levels to combat the illicit trafficking of SALWs. The major objective of the Moratorium is to create an atmosphere conducive to socio-economic development in the sub-region (Mallam 2014).

The Moratorium aims at preventing conflicts in the region; aiding post-conflict reconstructions; and stemming the increasing wave of crime and other security threats in the sub-region, especially with the understanding that the illicit flow and availability of SALWs may lead to violent solutions to problems and their circulation within and across borders facilitates the emergence of new armed groups and new conflicts in the region. The Moratorium prevents the use of untrained civilian militias, ill-disciplined fighters and unaccountable mercenaries. Furthermore, the moratorium aims to promote socio-economic development in general and donor supported development projects in particular as the specific aspects of the Moratorium (Mallam 2014; Badmus 2009).

There is also the National Commissions on SALWs (NATCOMs), which is one of the major initiatives of the Moratorium to regulate and control the illicit import, export and manufacture of SALWs within member states. As contained in Article 4 of the Code of Conduct: "In order to promote and ensure co-ordination of concrete measures for effective implementation of the Moratorium at the national level, member states shall establish National Commissions, made up of representatives of the relevant authorities and civil society organisations" (ECOWAS Code of Conduct 1998). The National commissions will serve as the engines, which the national and regional initiatives revolve. They are to formulate strategies, policies and programs to combat the proliferation of small arms; create awareness on the need to take all illegal weapons in their possession to security forces. They saddled with the responsibility of updating arms registers and transmission to ECOWAS Secretariat and provide appropriate recommendations to ECOWAS Secretariat on exemptions to be granted to the Moratorium for weapons covered by the agreement. Mobilize resource for programme expenditures; Liaise on a permanent basis with ECOWAS and PCASED Secretariats on issues that are important to the Moratorium as well as on the proliferation of SALWs in general (Mallam 2014).

The creation of the National commissions appears to have succeeded in yielding progress especially in terms of compliance by member nations; however, it could be noted that, many of the NATCOMS suffer from weak capacity and a lack of financial and political support. Furthermore, the development of credible regional arms register and database has not materialized; and harmonization of legislation has been very slow. There has also been little progress on a peacekeeping register, with a standoff between PCASED and the United Nations Mission in Sierra Leone (UNAMSIL) in 2003 show casing the challenges (Mallam 2014).

Efforts by ECOWAS have been great, it has succeeded it in destroying surplus or seized illicit SALWs in at least two thirds (ten) of the ECOWAS member states in which more than 85,000 small arms have been collected from armed groups and civilians since 1998 (ibid.).

There are several challenges confronting African countries and regional organizations in their effort to stem the proliferation of small arms. One of the greatest challenges faced by African states and government on arms control is a general lack of transparency in the arms trade, most Sub-Saharan African states consider their arms policies to be highly classified, which makes them difficult to assess. More so, arms traffickers bribe security forces at the borders and checkpoints to ensure easy flow of arms into the region without interception (Mallam 2014). The second challenge is the general insecurity in African States, which makes it easy for SALWs to enter illicit circulation through theft, leakage or re-sale. Thirdly, due to their portable, mobile and affordable features, difficult to monitor or track, small arms are highly attractive to paramilitary and irregular forces and even untrained civilians thereby assisting in their proliferation. There is high demand for SALWs by government forces to counter insurgency and to suppress the emergence domestic separatist groups. On the other hand, insurgent militants and common criminals spend fortunes to acquire small arms to pursue their violent and nefarious activities. Among these outlaws, a number of factors account for their high desirability: their simplicity makes them easy to operate even by people who have had very little or no military training. This explains their use by untrained combatants and even child soldiers, as it was the case in many armed conflicts zones in West Africa (Liberia, Sierra Leone, Code d'Ivoire, Mali and Nigeria). Small arms are abundant, cheap, portable and durable; these weapons are highly desired and profitable commodity and are often sold with little domestic and international regulation by numerous weapons producers, from surplus military stockpiles and by private arms barons (Mallam 2014).

Fourthly, the stealing of arms from armories of the state and diversion from multilateral organization poses a sustainable challenge. For instance, diversions of arms have also been reported in peacekeeping operations, peacekeepers like the soldiers and police in Africa are occasionally relieved of or voluntarily go away with their small arms, during or after peacekeeping operation. Corrupt soldiers or police officers steal or loot state armories, which in most cases end up in the hands of criminal elements (Schroeder and Lamb 2006).

A fifth challenge is lack of sound infrastructure for detecting, apprehending and controlling the inflow of small arms in Africa. In particular, the shortage or lack of cutting-edge technological equipment needed to combat arms proliferation in Africa. For instance, metal detectors are either absent, dysfunctional or woefully inadequate at points of entry into several countries of Africa. Several airports as well as seaports lack scanning devices, which are essential for the detection of contraband goods, including weapons concealed in luggage. The shortage of equipment is compounded by the lack of spare parts, supporting infrastructure and the dependency on external sources of supply. Alusala (2018), further states that, the strengthening stockpile management systems used in most African countries rely on outdated, colonial-era armories for the storage of their weapons. Many of these are dilapidated, making them vulnerable to theft and vandalism. Poorly stored arms and ammunition pose various risks, including unplanned explosions and diversion. As for the former, several African countries have experienced explosions at their munitions storage depots, which have been largely attributable to ineffective stockpile management (Alusala 2018).

While the land transport is less guarded, the worse is the case in other forms of transportation: the evidence for illicit proliferation suggests that air transportation is the preferred means for inter-continental transfers of arms by criminal networks (Griffiths, 2007 cited in Darkwa 2011). Furthermore, the situation at the coastlines is no less precarious: arms are easily trafficked by sea without detection (Keili 2008). Once the arms reach a country within the sub-region, transporting them within and between countries is relatively easy, due in part to the sub-region's porous borders and weak law enforcement mechanisms. The lack of the appropriate equipment at land and seaports has meant that law customs officers face difficulties in identifying and confiscating illicit weapons. Immigration and customs officials at land borders lack the technology to scan cargoes for the detection of arms, making it challenging to address inter- and intra-country transfers by land. Given that large trucks laden with goods criss-cross several countries in the sub-region, it is impractical to expect border personnel to offload each vehicle for inspection (Keili 2008).

Worse still, there is also lack of adequate resources for record keeping; this means that, there is inadequate computerized national databases for the purposes of keeping records. The databases are expected to be compiled using information from the different sectors that are responsible for small arms regulation (Darkwa 2011). The challenge is attributed to the insufficient investment in information storage and recovery systems, the computers are vital in keeping records, but also requited are adequate storage and retrieval systems, that are used to protect records against fire outbreak, power outages, floods, cyber-attacks, etc. Regrettably, the basic backup systems in several offices make it difficult to assure the safety of the data in the event of such unforeseen circumstances (ibid.). There are also serious challenges with computer facilities in some countries in the sub-region that put into question the safety and integrity of data. Where computers exist, there are questions about their effective use and maintenance. Furthermore, SALWs transactions in most Africa States have been difficult to measure and to regulate, because of the inability of the governments to provide statistics or records on the transfer of SALWs into their respective countries.

In addition, structural challenges such as lack of organizational skills, the necessary infrastructure, funds, as well as forces of globalization make the control of SALWs very complex. Among other structural factors are the failure governments to provide the needed support structure for securing lives and property of citizens. It evident that lack confidence in security forces, the inability of security agencies to carry out their duty effectively due to underfunding, understaffing and under-equipping in many African countries informed the tendency by citizens to resort to self-help and acquire arms in order to protect themselves and their property (Mallam 2014). In addition, low salaries/incomes of the custom officers and other border security personnel, had made it possible for personnel to compromise their official duties, by allowing the influx arms and other contrabands into Africa. Weapons dealers bribe customs officers, while soldiers, police officers and security forces are known to have sold government arms to undesirable elements (Ayissi and Sall 2005). The customs in most cases have "divide mindset" at the point of their duties, what they are after is not how to secure the borders from the importation/exportation of goods that are injuries to national security, but rather what they will get in return as kick-back from smugglers and other gun runners. These can be attributed to poor condition of service in the security agencies.

A sixth challenge is the relative lack of political will at local and international levels. The control of small arms appears to be at low priority of most countries in the region. This is largely because, small arms play important role in power politics of most so-called democratic states: politicians resort to arming thugs to intimidate their rivals and "secure" electoral victory. In addition, the proliferation of small arms is driven by active syndicates that are connected to state officials. At the international level, despite the nexus between small arms and other transnational crimes, small arms control has not received the desired attention shown by the international community compared to illegal drug/narcotics trade.

Furthermore, there are the negative effects of some external forces, principally the military industrial complexes "that is, states that deals in the production of weapons, had seriously kicked against ECOWAS" proactive measures on arms control, during the debates in the United Nations. They see ECOWAS measures as shattering their economic interest of weapons production. Thus, the provision of the Convention on dialogue between producers and suppliers has not yielded the desired result and the economic and political instability in each of the member states, which is as a result of SALWs proliferation in the region (GIABA 2013).

Conclusion

The global proliferation of arms compels the international community to come up with measures, to combat the challenges of illicit arms transfer around the world. African states have come up with variety of policies and programs aimed to address the menace, but without commensurate results. This is because of the preponderance of corruption among government officials and border security agencies like customs, and immigrations, porosity of the African land and seaports borders, and the forces of globalization. Consequently, African states are now faced with ethno-religious violence, electoral violence, kidnapping, cattle rustling, arm banditry, arm robbery, insurgency, communal conflicts and armed militancy, where these arms enter.

Generally, although the UN and AU attempted to provide solutions to the lingering arms proliferation in Africa, the phenomenon has continued to unabated in the continent. Therefore, there is the need for the AU to develop an effective regional Customs Union that will oversee a regional protocol and modern devices in line with global best practices for the control of SALWs in Africa. This can be achieved through regional cooperation among African States and there is the need for a key partnership with World Custom Organisation, which can contribute significantly to the AU's efforts to detect illicit arms trafficking in the region. African states should develop systems of tracking and identifying illicit importation of SALWs and to assist member states to secure their land, air and maritime borders. Since poor, obsolete, unstable and redundant stockpiling is one of the contributors of arms circulation, there is the need for effective stockpiling management system, to avoid arms theft. In particular, there is need for urgent implementation of the ECOWAS Convention on SALWs, by developing the guidelines for its implementation.

African states and government should come up with strategic plans that will address the porosity of the borders and the "free" movement of people and goods. This can be achieved through effective monitoring of the land borders, in line with global best practices. In addition, African countries should take punitive action against corruption among governance institutions especially security agencies and lines departments involved in the management of small arms. It has been revealed that the corruptions among personnel are associated with their poor condition of service. Therefore, there is need to improve the condition of service of the security personnel at all levels to discourage them from resorting to corrupt practices. To discourage the support or participation of citizens in small arms proliferation, African governments should improve the socio-economic conditions of their citizens through good governance and democratic development. Addressing unemployment, insecurity (especially human and food security), social exclusion, inequality, poverty and diseases can go a long way in mitigating violence which, in the first instance, generates a veritable condition for the use of illegal arms.

References

Abiodun, T. F., Ifeoluwa, A., Oluwasolape, O., & Chukwuyere, N. (2015). Small Arm and Light Weapons Proliferation and Its Threat to Nigeria's Internal Security. *International Journal of Social Science and Humanities Research*, 6(3), 34–45.

Adeniji, M. (2018). *The Role of Customs Services in Trade Facilitation, Comparison Between Nigeria and Finland*. A Thesis Submitted to the Department of Business Management Centria University of Applied Sciences, Finland. Retrieved from www.sematicsscholar.org/paper/role-of-customs-services-in-trade-facilitation-Adeniji/b736b9929. Accessed 29 June 2020.

Adenubi, T. (2017, August 22). Customs Seizes 1,398 Rolls of Military Uniforms. *The Tribute*. Retrieved from https://tribuneonlineng.com/customs-seizes-1398-rolls-military-uniforms/. Accessed 27 July 2020.

Akinyemi, O. (2013). Globalisation and Nigeria Border Security: Issues and Challenges. *International Affairs and Global Strategy, 11*, 1–7. Retrieved from http://www.iiste.org.

Alusala, N. (2018). *Africa and Arms Control Challenges and Successes*. Retrieved from http://reliefweb.int/report/world/africa-and-arms-control-challenges-and-successes-issues-03-april-2018. Accessed 21 July 2020.

Amnesty International, International Action Network on Small Arms & Oxfam. (2005). *Towards an Arms Trade Treaty, Next Steps for the UN Programme of Action*. Retrieved from http://www.amnesty.org.

Amnesty International & Oxfam. (2005). Towards an Arms Trade Treaty. In A. Ayissi & I. Sall (Eds.), *Combating the Proliferation of Small Arms and Light Weapons in West Africa: Handbook for the Training of Armed and Security Forces*. Geneva: United Nations Institute of Disarmament Research (UNIDIR). Retrieved from http://www.controlarms.org-june-2005. Accessed 11 January 2020.

AU. (2019). *Silencing the Guns by 2020. Towards Peaceful and Secured Africa*. Retrieved from http://au.int/en/flagships/silencing-guns-2020.

Ayissi, A., & Sall, I. (2005). *Combating the Proliferation of Small Arms and Light Weapons in West Africa. Handbook for the Training of Armed and Security Forces*. Retrieved from http://www.unidir.org.

Badmus, I. A. (2009). *Managing Arms in Peace Processes: ECOWAS and the West African Civil Conflict*. Center for African Studies at the University of Porto Panoramic View, Portugal. Retrieved from http://www.africanos.eu.

Bromley, M., Caparini, M., & Malaret, A. (2019). *Measuring Illicit Arms and Financial Flows: Improving the Assessment of Sustainable Development Goal 16*. SIPRI.

BusinessDay. (2019). *Nigeria Generated N4.6trn from Petroleum Tax, Royalties in 11 Months 2019-CBN*. Retrieved from https://businessday.ng. Accessed 29 June 2020.

Buyonge, C., & Kireeva, I. (n.d.). Trade Facilitation in Africa: Challenges and Possible Solutions. *World Customs Journal, 2*(1), 41–54.

Chelule, E. (2014). Proliferation of Small Arms and Light Weapons: Challenge to Development, Peace and Security in Africa. *Journal of Humanities and Social Science, 19*(5), 80–87.

Darkwa, L. (2011). *The Challenges of Sub-Regional Security in West Africa: The Case of the 2006 ECOWAS Convention on SALWs*. Lightning Source UK Ltd: UK.

ECOWAS. (1998, October 31). *Declaration of a Moratorium on Importation, Exportation and Manufacture of Light Weapons in West Africa*. Abuja, Nigeria.

ECOWAS. (2006). *Ecowas Convention on Small Arms and Light Weapons, Their Ammunition and Other Related Materials*. Retrieved from http://www.poa-iss.org.

Fahrenthold, D. A., & Kunkle, F. (2009, November 3). Bullets Are Speeding Faster Out of Gun Shops in U.S. *Washington Post*. Retrieved from http://washingtonpost.com≥politics. Accessed 28 July 2019.

GIABA (Inter-Governmental Action Group Against Money Laundering in West Africa). (2013). *The Nexus Between Small Arms and Light Weapons and Money Laundering and Terrorist Financing in West Africa*. Retrieved from http://www.giaba.org/media/f/613519GIABA%20SALW%20Nexus-final.pdf. Accessed 22 June 2019.

Grip, L. (2017). *Small Arms Control in Africa*. Academic Dissertation Presented to the Department of Political and Economic Studies, Helsinki University.

Hazen, J. M., & Horner, J. (2007). *Small Arms, Armed Violence, and Insecurity in Nigeria: The Niger Delta in Perspective*. An Occassional Paper of the Small Arms Survey. Retrieved from http://www.smallarmssurvey.org.

Heinrich, M. (2006). *Small Arms and Development: The Results of the UN Small Arms Review Conference and Policy Implications*. Retrieved from http://www.ipd.org/i/pdf/IPB-Report-on-small-arms-and-development-pdf. Accessed 11 January 2020.

Honwana, J., & Lamb, G. (1998). *Small Arms Proliferation and Drug Trafficking in Southern Africa: A Conceptual Paper*. Cape Town: Centre for Conflict Resolution. Retrieved from http://ccrweb.ccr.uct.ac.za/archive/staff_papers/guy_small_arms_drugs.html. Accessed 22 July 2019.

International Action Network on Small Arms (IANSA). (2006). *Reviewing Action on Small Arms 2006 Assessing the First Five Years of the UN Programme of Action*. Retrieved from www.international-alert.org/publications/reviewing-action-small-arms-2006. Accessed 28 June 2020.

Jekada, E. (2005). *Proliferation of Small Arms and Ethnic Conflicts in Nigeria: Implication for National Security*. Dissertation for the Award of Ph.D. in International Relations and Strategic Studies, St. Clements University, Somalia.

Kafeero, E. (2008). Customs and Trade Facilitation in the East Africa Community (EAC). *World Customs Journal, 2*(1), 63–71. Retrieved from https://worldcustomsjournal.org. Accessed 4 January 2020.

Keili, F. (2008). *Small Arms and Light Weapons Transfer in West Africa: Stocktaking; The Complex Dynamics of Small Arms in West Africa*. City: United Nation Institute for Disarmament Research.

Lamb, G., & Dye, D. (2009). African Solutions to an International Problem: Arms Control and Disarmament in Africa. *Journal of International Affairs, 62*(2), 69–83. Retrieved from www.jstor.com/stable/24358195. Accessed 27 June 2020.

Malhotra, A. (2011). Globalization and the Illicit Trade of Small Arms and Light Weapons. *Eurasian Review*, 1–11. Retrieved from www.eurasiareview.com/201009017600/globalisation-and-the-illicit-trade-of-small-arms-and-light-weapons.

Mallam, B. (2014). Small Arms and Light Weapons Proliferation and Its Implication for West African Regional Security. *International Journal of Humanities and Social Science, 4*(8), 260–269.

McLinden, G., & Durrani, A. Z. (2013). Corruption in Customs. *World Customs Journal, 7*(2), 3–9.

Muktar, B. (2019). *Challenges of Customs Clearing and Their Implication on International Trade in Ethiopia*. M.A. thesis, Submitted to the Department of Logistics and Supply Chain Management, School of Commerce of Addis Ababa University, Ethiopia.

National Daily. (2017, July 13). Porosity of Borders: Why Nigeria Must Tighten Border Security. *National Daily*. Retrieved from http://nationaldailyng.com/Porosity-of-borders-why-Nigeria-must-tighten-border-security. Accessed 11 January 2020.

NATO. (2020). *Arms Control, Disarmament and Non-Proliferation in NATO*. Retrieved from www.nato.int/cps/en/natohq/topics_48895/htm. Accessed 29 June 2020.

Naylor, R. (2001). The Rise of the Modern Arms Blacket and the fall of Supply-Side Control. In P. Williams & V. Dimitri (Eds.), *Combating Transnational Crimes: Concepts, Activities and Responses* (pp. 29–36). Oxford: Frank Cass Publishers.

Ndime, D. (2005). Cooperation Between States to Combat the Proliferation of Small Arms and Light Weapons. In A. Ayissi & I. Sall (Eds.), *Combating the Proliferation of Small Arms and Light Weapons in West Africa* (pp. 76–84). Switzerland, Geneva: United Nations Institute for Disarmament Research.

Ngang, C. (2007). *Small Arms and Light Weapons, Africa's True Weapons of Mass Destructions: The Role of SALWs in African Sub-Saharan Conflicts and Insecurity*. M.A. Dissertation, Submitted to the European University, Centre for Peace Studies, Austria. Retrieved from https://www.academia.edu/4221688/proliferation_of_small_arms. Accessed 27 April 2019.

Nte, N. D. (2011). The Changing Patterns of Small and Light Weapons (SALW) Proliferation and the Challenges of National Security in Nigeria. *Global Journal of Africa Studies, 1*(1), 5–23.

Obiejesi, K. (2017). Customs Intercepts 1,100 Guns Disguised as 'Wash-Hand Basins'. *The International Centre for Investigative Reporting*. Retrieved from https://www.icirnigeria.org/at-tin-can-port-customs-intercepts-1100-guns-disguised-as-wash-hand-basins/?fbclid. Accessed 2 June 2019.

Oche, O. (2005). *The Proliferation of Small Arms and Light Weapons in Nigeria*. Lagos: FOG Ventures Surulere.

Ogu, M. I. (2014). Civilians, Arms and Endemic Conflicts in Africa. *Journal of Humanities and Social Science, 19*(9), 39–46.

Olomu, B., Oladimeji, A. D., & Adewumi, E. (n.d.). Border Security Issues and Challenges of the Nigeria Customs Service. *International Journal of Latest Research in Humanities and Social Science, 2*(3), 10–19. www.ijlrhss.com.

Pilbeam, B. (2015). The International Arms Trade in Conventional Weapons. In P. Hough, S. Malik, A. Moran, & B. Pilbeam (Eds.), *International Arms Trade in Conventional Weapons* (pp. 134–140). New York: Routledge.

Punch Newspaper. (2017). *Nigeria Customs Generate 1 Trillion Naira Revenue in 2017*. Retrieved from http://punchng.com/customs-generates-n1tn-revenue-in-2017/. Accessed 28 June 2020.

SADC Firearms Protocol. (2003). *Protocol on the Control of Firearms, Ammunition and Other Related Materials*, Article 1.2. Retrieved from http://www.poaiss.org/regionalorganisations/sadc/instruments/sadc%20protocol.pdf. Accessed 11 September 2019.

Schroeder, M., & Lamb, G. (2006). The Illicit Arms Trade in Africa; Global Enterprise. *African Analyst, 1*(3), 69–78.

Seniora, J., & Poitevin, C. (2010). *Managing Land Borders and the Trafficking of Small Arms and Light Weapons*. Group for Research and Information on Peace and Security (GRIP). Retrieved from www.grip.org. Accessed 23 January 2020.

Small Arms Survey. (2014). *Weapons and Markets*. Retrieved from www.smallarmssurvey.org/weapons-and-markets. Accessed 22 May 2018. provide your own date of access.

UNIDIR (United Nations Institute for Disarmament Research). (2006). *Disarmament as Humanitarian Action from Perspective to Practice*. Retrieved from http://www.unidir.org/disarmament-as-humanitarian-action-from-perspective-to-practice-288.pdf. Accessed 27 August 2019.

United Nations. (2008). Geneva Declaration: Dimensions of Armed Violence. *Global Burden of Armed Violence*. Retrieved from www.genevadeclaration.org. Accessed 23 July 2018.

United Nations Office on Drugs and Crime. (2013). *Transnational Organised Crime in West Africa: A Threat Assessment*. Retrieved from http://www.unodc.org.

Uwa, O. G., & Anthony, A. B. (2015). Small Arms and Light Weapons (SALW) Proliferation and Problem of National Security in Nigeria. *International Affairs and Global Strategy, 29*(3), 12–20.

Vanguard. (2018). *Customs Intercepts Container Load of Military Uniforms, Other Items*. Retrieved from https://www.vanguardngr.com/2018/07/customs-intercepts-container-load-of-military-uniforms-other.

Ventura, M. (2018). *Arms Control and Disarmament: Legitimacy, War, and Peace*. M.A. thesis, Presented to the Department of International Studies, Macalester College, Columbia.

WCO (World Customs Organization). (2015). *Compliance and Enforcement Package*. Retrieved from http://www.wcoomd.org. Accessed 1 April 2019.

WCO (World Customs Organization). (2018). *Glossary of International Customs Terms*. Retrieved from www.wcoomd.org. Accessed 29 June 2020.

Woolcott, P. (2014). *The Arms Trade Treaty*. Retrieved from http://www.un.org/law/avl. Accessed 18 January 2020.

Mubarak Ahmed Mashi is a Lecturer at the Department of Political Science, Umaru Musa Yar'adua University, Katsina, Nigeria. His research interest focuses on Security and Political Economy. He has published and presented papers in conferences on the security of internally displaced women and children, rural banditry and cattle rustling and electoral violence in Nigeria.

Habu Mohammed is a Professor at the Department of Political Science, Bayero University, Kano, Nigeria. Prof. Mohammed is biased in Politics of Development, Peace and Conflict Resolution, Federalism and National Question, Civil Society and Democratisation in Africa. He is a co-editor of *Readings in Social Science Research* (2006), editor of *Concepts and Issues in Peace Studies and Conflict Resolution* (2006), co-editor of *Poverty in Nigeria, Causes, Manifestations and Alleviation Strategies* (2008), and author of a book titled: *Civil Society Organizations and Democratization in Nigeria: The Politics of Struggles for Human Rights* (2010), and the editor, *Nigeria's Convulsive Federalism: Flash-Points of Conflicts in Northern Nigeria* (2012); the editor, *The Patterns and Dynamics of Party Politics in Nigeria's Fourth Republic, 1999–2015* (2017). Mohammed served in various Departmental, Faculty and University committees. He has contributed several articles on Nigerian politics and political economy of development in both local and international books and journals. In all, he has more than forty (40) publications thus far; One (1) published book; three (3) edited books on Nigerian Politics; three (3) co-edited books; and more than five (5) technical reports for UNDP, DFID, CODESRIA, CRD, and Mambayya House, among others. He was a Fulbright Visiting Scholar at Programme of African Studies (PAS), Northwestern University, Illinois, USA (2003/2004).

CHAPTER 27

Transport Networks and the Proliferation of Small Arms in Africa

Terzungwe Nyor

Introduction

Peace and security in most African countries have been impeded due to proliferation of small arms and light weapons (SALW). This phenomenon has contributed greatly to the menace of armed robbery, kidnapping, armed banditry, and terrorists' activities. It has also exacerbated inter-communal tensions leading to full-fledge conflicts with attendant consequences of destruction of lives and properties. Movement of Illicit arms from one country to another through transport network is largely successful due to porous borders, thus, making it easy for entry and exit of arms. Moreover, the high level of corruption in most of these countries compounds the tracking and seizure of these illicit arms and cripple efforts made at both state and regional levels to curb insecurity.

Africa has more major armed conflicts than any other continent. In 1998, there were 11 major armed conflicts in Africa, making it the worst. The availability of light weapons alone may not be responsible for these conflicts but there is no gainsaying that it contributes to the outbreak and escalation of such conflicts (Albright 1999). The fact remains that these small arms cannot change location without the impact of transportation, and this is about Africa whose transport networks cut across all the modes and connect to all locations within and outside Africa. It is not surprising then that more than half of the

T. Nyor (✉)
Department of Accounting, Nigerian Defence Academy, Kaduna, Nigeria
e-mail: tnyor@nda.edu.ng

© The Author(s), under exclusive license to Springer Nature Switzerland AG 2021
U. A. Tar and C. P. Onwurah (eds.), *The Palgrave Handbook of Small Arms and Conflicts in Africa*,
https://doi.org/10.1007/978-3-030-62183-4_27

over 700,000 deaths recorded annually from small arms occur in Africa (IRIN 2001).

In the United States' military, small arms are defined as man portable, individual, and crew-served weapon systems used mainly against personnel and lightly armored or unarmored equipment. However, with regard to inventory management, the U.S. Army defines Small Arms and Light Weapons (SALWs) as Handguns, shoulder-fired weapons, light automatic weapons up to and including 12.7 mm machine guns, recoilless rifles up to and including 106 mm, mortars up to and including 81 mm, man-portable rocket launchers, rifle-/shoulder-fired grenade launchers, and individually operated weapons that are portable or can be fired without special mounts or firing devices and that have potential use in civil disturbances and are vulnerable to theft (Alpers 2007). According to the United Nations, *Small arms* include, but not limited to revolvers and self-loading pistols, rifles and carbines, assault rifles, submachine guns, and light machine guns. *Light weapons* are heavy machine guns, hand-held under-barrel and mounted grenade launchers, portable anti-tank and anti-aircraft guns, recoilless rifles, portable launchers of anti-tank and anti-aircraft missile systems, and mortars of calibers of less than 100 mm.

This chapter examines transport network and small arms proliferation in Africa beginning with clarification of key concepts such as transport and transport networks. This is with a view to identifying how transport networks aid small arms proliferation. It highlights lapses in transport networks that makes it possible for easy movement of illicit arms and also reviews measures in place by states and regional groups to tackle it and recommendations in curbing illicit trading of small arms. The study also makes recommendations as to how to curb the proliferation of small arms and light weapons in Africa via transport network.

Conceptual Clarification

Transport

Transport or transportation refers to the movement of humans, animals, goods and or services from one location to another. In other words, transport is the act of moving an object from a point A to a point B. Applied to this chapter, it is the means of moving small arms from point A to point B via various single modes and inter modal network connections. Transport is the means of carrying out activities that require people and material goods to be in different places at different times. It helps in overcoming physical separation for the purpose of economic, social/cultural, and personal activity (Hanson and Giuliano 2016). Transport allows production and consumption of products to occur at different locations. Throughout history, transport has been a spur to expansion as better transport allows more trade and a greater spread of people.

Modes of transport: The means by which passengers and freight achieve mobility is what is termed transport modes. The different modes of transport are air, land (rail, road, and off-road), water, cable, pipeline, and space. The field of transportation can be divided into infrastructures, vehicles, and operations. *Transport infrastructure* consists of the fixed installations, including roads, railways, airways, waterways, canals, and pipelines and terminals such as airports, railway stations, bus stations, warehouses, trucking terminals, refueling depots (including fueling docks and fuel stations), and seaports. Terminals may be used both for interchange of passengers and cargo and for maintenance. *Vehicles* traveling on these networks may include automobiles, bicycles, buses, trains, trucks, helicopters, watercrafts, spacecrafts, and aircrafts; while *operations* deal with the way the vehicles are operated, and the procedures set for this purpose, including financing, legalities, and policies. In the transport industry, operations and ownership of infrastructure can be either public or private, depending on the country and mode (Malhotra and Dash 2011).

Transport Networks

The term *network* refers to the framework of routes within a system of locations, identified as nodes. A route is a single link between two nodes that are part of a larger network. A route can either be tangible route (also referred to as permanent track) such as road and rail, or less tangible routes such as air and sea corridors. Transportation networks are a framework of routes linking locations. Transportation networks represent the structure and organization of transportation infrastructures like roads or train lines through an area. Transportation networks connect the nodes and are significant because they can directly affect the capacity and efficiency of the movement of people and goods (Hanson and Giuliano 2016). The structure of any region corresponds to a network of all its economic and social interactions (Rodrigue and Notteboom 2012). Transport network is the overall system consisting of transport route and mode. Networks are connected through roads and streets, railways, pipes, aqueducts, and power lines.

A transport network, or transportation network is a realization of a spatial network, describing a structure which permits either vehicular movement or flow of some commodity. Examples include but are not limited to road networks, railways, air routes (Rodrigue and Ducruet 2017). Transport network analysis is used to determine the flow of vehicles (or people) through a transport network, typically using mathematical graph theory. It may combine different modes of transport, for example, walking and car, to model multi-modal journeys.

Transport node is a complex network of devices in an area for the functioning and interaction of several types of backbones that serve transit, local, freight and passenger traffic and a set of transport processes. Thus, the concept of transport node includes the process of transportation (the movement of passengers and cargo), technical devices (stations, ports, highways, warehouses, etc.) as well as a means of control and management. The complexity of the transport node is determined by the number and terms of service of its elements (stations, ports, warehouses, intersections, etc.), sizes of operated traffic flow, technological links between the elements and the level of their interaction (Germain et al. 2012). In other words, nodes are the beginning and end points for transportation between geographic areas. Transport nodes are used in conjunction with the transport segments. Transport nodes can be defined as a point that represents one or more of these features: the end of the road; a junction of two or more road segments; a grade separated by intersection; a place where the value of an attribute changes; a small roundabout and a barrier.

TYPES OF TRANSPORTATION NETWORKS AND VULNERABILITIES

Depending on the mode they represent, transportation networks have different configurations:

Air networks. Such networks are commonly a nodal hierarchy articulated around a hub-and-spoke structure, underlining that nodes (airports) are crucial elements. The importance of a node is usually related to the traffic (passengers and freight) it handles and its connectivity (links to other nodes). There is a hierarchy of flows ranging from regional (short distance feeders) to international (inter-hub). Due to its high degree of hobbling, air transportation networks are particularly vulnerable to disruptions at major hubs, while disruptions at smaller hubs will have limited consequences.

Maritime networks. Such networks are a circuitous nodal hierarchy, implying that services are commonly arranged along a sequence of nodes (ports) with inter-range services that loops back to the port of origin. While point-to-point services are reflective of bulk shipping, container shipping is organized between deep sea and feeder services with transshipment hubs acting as the interface. The vulnerability of maritime networks has different considerations depending on if the node is a hub or a gateway. Disruptions at a hub will mostly impact maritime shipping networks while disruptions at a gateway will mostly impact the hinterland (Airriess 2001).

Logistical networks. Such networks are a sequential multi-nodal hierarchy, implying that there are separate networks within networks. A typical logistics sequence is organized along three stages; raw materials and parts, manufacturing, and distribution, each supported by a specific network (manufacturing network, distribution network). They represent sourcing relationships between actors and such networks are vulnerable to disruptions impacting one actor (e.g., a manufacturing plant, a distribution center) and the connected activities (upstream and downstream). This is commonly known as the cumulative effect where a small disruption could result in significant impacts along a supply chain since a product is often made of numerous components and if a part is missing, a supply chain could come temporarily to a halt (Bardi et al. 2006).

Road networks. Such networks are hierarchical meshes, each servicing a different scale. They have no tangible nodes but fixed paths with known capacity. While an interstate highway system is designed to connect a nation or a large region, local streets are only connecting adjacent activities to a wider framework. Because of their mesh structure, road networks are not highly vulnerable to disruptions, unless this disruption is at a wide scale (e.g., a major snowstorm or a hurricane) or impacting a strategic connectors such as bridges or tunnels.

Rail networks. Such networks are a linear nodal hierarchy with nodes related to intermodal yards, train and transit stations. Because of the fixed character of their paths and capacity, they are allocated usage windows during which grouped units circulate. While linear rail networks are vulnerable to disruptions, complex rail and transit networks have a mesh like structure, making them more resilient.

Transportation Networks in Africa

The Trans-African Highway (TAH) is a road network connecting major African cities. The African Union, African Development Bank (ADB), and the United Nations Economic Commission for Africa (UNECA) are the major project donors of the 35,221 miles out of which there are six east-west routes and three north-south routes road network. This network also goes by other names like Trans-African Corridors or Road Corridors. The idea behind the TAH network is the development and better distribution of trade, health, and education by connecting previously inaccessible areas (Monnet 2019). It is made up of the east-west routes and north-south routes as seen below:

East-West Routes

- TAH 1: This highway runs from Cairo to Dakar along the Mediterranean coast then continues down along the Atlantic coast of north-west Africa. TAH 1 is 5366 miles and joins TAH 7 to form an additional north-south route. Among the cities that TAH 1 serves includes Tripoli, Tunis, Algiers, and Rabat.
- TAH 5: TAH 5 runs from Dakar to Ndjamena covering 2794 miles. Also known as the Trans-Sahelian Highway, TAH 5 links west Africa to Sahel. Only 80% of this road is complete. TAH 6: Covering 2622 miles,

TAH 6 connects Ndjamena to Djibouti and continues down through the Sahelian region toward the Indian Ocean.
- TAH 7: TAH 7 (Trans–West African Coastal Road) covers 2490 miles from Dakar, Senegal to Lagos, Nigeria and is 80% complete. TAH 7 joins TAH 1 to form an additional south-north road in the westernmost part of Africa.
- TAH 8: Contiguous to TAH 7 in Lagos, TAH 8 runs from Lagos to Mombasa covering a total 3889 miles. Together with TAH 7, they form the east to west highway of 6381 miles. TAH 8 is complete in Kenya, Uganda, Nigeria, Cameroon, and the Central African Republic (CAR). However, there are missing links in DR Congo thus preventing its complete use.
- TAH 9: TAH 9 is basically complete though parts of it in DR Congo and Angola require repairs. This road runs from Beira to Lobito and is 2189 miles in length.

North-South Routes

- TAH 2: TAH 2 (Trans-Saharan Highway) is 2799 miles between Algiers and Lagos. This road is basically complete with less than 120 miles that require paving. However, due to the security status in the desert, authorities restrict the road's usage.
- TAH 3: The route connects Tripoli, Libya with Cape Town, South Africa through Cameroon, Angola, and Namibia. This route has the most missing links.
- TAH 4: TAH 4 is 6355 miles long from Cairo Pretoria through Sudan, Ethiopia, Kenya, Tanzania, and Zambia. The road is largely complete but parts of it in northern Kenya and Sudan-Egypt border are not safe.

A transport network denotes either a permanent track (e.g., roads, rail, and canals) or a scheduled service (e.g. airline, public transit, train). It can be extended to cover various types of links between points along which mobility can take place. The relevance of a network is related to its connectivity. *Metcalfe's law* states that the value of a network is proportional to the square of connected nodes, so that complex networks are exponentially more valuable than simple networks since they offer a large number of options in connecting locations and as in the case of Africa transport network acting as the major factor behind illegal small arms trade.

The map of Trans-African Highways showing the routes from Cairo to Dakar, Algiers to Lagos, Tripoli to Cape Town, Dakar to Ndjamena, and Cairo to Cape Town through Gaborone, can be seen in Fig. 27.1. Other routes shown on the map are Ndjamena to Djibouti, Dakar to Lagos, Lagos Mombasa, and Beira to Lobito.

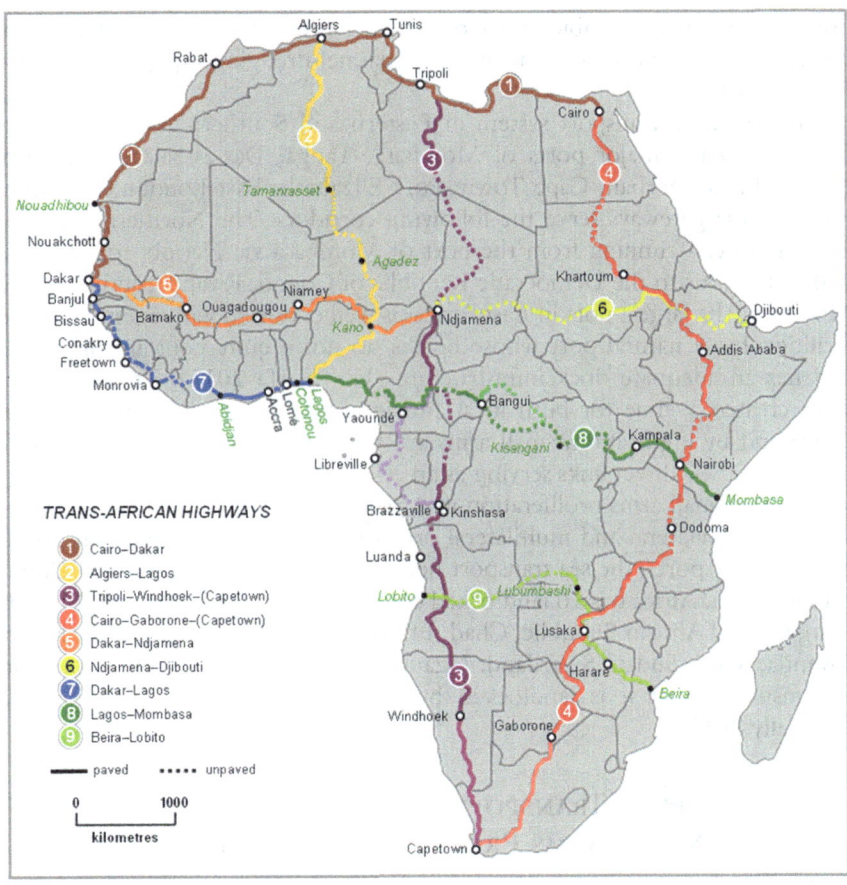

Fig. 27.1 Map of Trans-African highways *Source* Wikimedia Commons, Available: https://commons.wikimedia.org/wiki/File:Map_of_Trans-African_Highways.PNG

Sea Network

The continent of Africa is bounded on the west by the Atlantic Ocean, on the north by the Mediterranean Sea, on the east by the Red Sea and the Indian Ocean, and on the south by the mingling waters of the Atlantic and Indian oceans. The important area is the north-south Corridor in Southern Africa that links Zambia and the southeast Democratic Republic of Congo to the subregion and overseas markets. These are Dar-es-Salaam, Walvis Bay, Beira, and the north-south corridor through Durban. The north-south corridor serves a dual purpose: First, it serves as an intraregional trade route between Zambia (and further southeast, the Democratic Republic of Congo and western Malawi) and its neighbors, Botswana, Zimbabwe, and South Africa, and as a link to the port of Durban for overseas imports and exports. Although the port of Beira in Mozambique is closer than Durban for most Zambian shippers, Durban is more convenient with channel-dredging equipment (World Bank 2010).

The maritime transport system in Eastern and Southern Africa comprises gateways to the major ports of Mombasa, Tanga, Dar-es-Salaam, Maputo, Nacala, Beira, Durban, Cape Town, Port Elizabeth, East London, and other ports. These gateways serve the following corridors: The Northern Corridor in East Africa—running from the port of Mombasa via Nairobi to Kampala, with extensions to the Democratic Republic of Congo, Rwanda, and Burundi. Mombasa, the largest port in East Africa, is well endowed with equipment and facilities, has a natural port whose berths do not require constant dredging, and has an adequate dock infrastructure (UNCTAD 2015). These connections created avenue for both local and international sea network routes in Africa and by implication, small arms are being transported using this mode because of their direct links serving as an evidence that transport networks play vast role in small arms proliferation in Africa.

Through bilateral and multilateral protocols, internal maritime transportation, and dry ports, the sea transport networks also service Landlocked Countries in Africa. Africa has 16 landlocked countries: Botswana, Burundi, Burkina Faso, Central African Republic, Chad, Ethiopia, Lesotho, Malawi, Mali, Niger, Rwanda, South Sudan, Swaziland, Uganda, Zambia, and Zimbabwe. Lesotho is unusual in that it is landlocked by just one country i.e., South Africa (McNally 2017).

How Transportation Network Aid Small Arms Proliferation in Africa

Proliferation is the import, export, acquisition, sale, delivery, movement, or transfer of firearms, ammunition, explosives, and other related materials from or across the territory of one state party to that of another state party, if any one of the states parties concerned does not authorize it (Alpers 2007). It has been estimated that over 100 million small arms and light weapons are circulating in Africa (Atanga 2003). While not being responsible for the multiplicity of ethnic and religious strife, political instability and violent crime that abound in the region, the proliferation of small arms certainly does contribute in no small measure in fueling them (McNally 2017). This proliferation has been facilitated by among other factors, the lengthy, porous and very often poorly policed borders, inefficient border controls, corruption, to mention but few, this assertion proves that transportation is a major player contributing to the success of small arms proliferation in West Africa.

Arms proliferation is made through different transportation means and more especially in West African region where, borders are not be only badly demarcated, but easy to cross and the transport networks are linked altogether via borders which have made these acts very easy in the African Continent. There are evidences of illegal arms transportation through major transport networks. For example, through air borders, This Day Newspaper on 18 September 2013 reported that Nigerian Customs impounded a cargo from the United States, which smuggled Arms concealed in house hold cargo. Also, sometime in June 2009, there were several media reports that security operatives impounded a Ukrainian plane, fully loaded with guns and ammunitions when it made a technical landing at Mallam Aminu Kano International Airport (RadioFreeEurope/Radio Liberty 2009).

Transport via the *water ways* can be evidenced during the first week of August 1999 when Nigerian customs intercepted six nationals of a West African country in a canoe in Lagos with 75,000 rounds of ammunition and bags containing rifles. Hauls by the customs service included 10,000 magazines in Ikeja (31 December 2001), as well as almost equally large hauls in Seme Border Station (February 2002) and at Tabido/Budo in Kwara State in March 2002. The port of Warri in the Niger delta is also regarded as a center for arms smuggling and illegal trading (Ayissi and Ibrahima 2005). The traffickers operate from ships lying at anchor on the high seas, using faster small boats for transfers. These figures represent only a tiny sample of the total numbers of arms and ammunition which enter Nigeria and circulate illegally. In addition, Nigeria's secret service in October 2010 intercepted the shipment of 13 containers filled with rocket launchers, grenades and other explosives and ammunitions. The cargo was said to be on its way to Gambia and had begun its journey from a port in Iran (Onuoha 2012).

Movements of small arms via *land network*. The Small Arms Survey reports that at least 38 different companies are producing small arms in Sub-Saharan Africa. For instance, there are reports that Chadian rebels maintain depots of arms and ammunition in caves in the Tibesti region on the border between Nigeria, Chad and the Niger. These arms are generally transported on camels to border towns and villages in Niger and Nigeria.

Proliferation of small arms in west Africa is majorly through the sea and land borders because the air corridors have standard border security control system caused by the nature of its operation considering international standards. Moreover, where poor land and sea borders' security control is a tradition in Africa thereby increasing the rate of this illicit activities, small arms proliferation. The Trans-African Highway which links all but few African countries contributed majorly in the illegal selling, buying, and transportation of small arms in Africa (Adele and Noel 2008).

A map of transportation network in Africa showing main roads, rail, rivers, lakes, and sea corridors is seen in Fig. 27.2.

Fig. 27.2 Transport network in Africa *Source The Economists*. Avialable: https://www.economist.com/business/2008/10/16/network-effects

ACTIONS TO CONTROL SMALL ARMS PROLIFERATION IN AFRICA

The fight to end small arms proliferation in Africa is not a one country fight but for all the countries involved, and these are some of the reasons for establishing regional organizations such as Economic Community of West African States (ECOWAS). The objective that ECOWAS has set for itself presupposes both "upstream" and "downstream" intervention, from the production and delivery of arms to their final use, from the international manufacturers to local owners and users. These, then, are the general principles set out in the Treaty of ECOWAS and in the 1999 Protocol relating to the Mechanism for Conflict Prevention, Management, Resolution, Peacekeeping, and Security. Efforts to combat the proliferation of small arms are included among them, alongside the Community's other concerns. Provisions that deal exclusively with this problem, and that follow on from these two general instruments, can be found in other ECOWAS legal instruments, namely:

1. The Moratorium on the Importation, Exportation and Manufacture of Light Weapons in ECOWAS member states (referred to as simply the "Moratorium"), adopted on 31 October 1998;
2. The plan of action for implementation of the Programme for Coordination and Assistance for Security and Development in Africa (PCASED), adopted in 1998;
3. The code of conduct for the implementation of the Moratorium, adopted on 10 December 1999 (Ngang 2007).

The Moratorium on the Importation, Exportation and Manufacture of Small Arms and Light Weapons in West Africa

In 1993, the then Malian President Alpha Oumar Konare requested the then United Nations (UN) Secretary-General Boutros, Boutros-Ghali to send a UN mission to observe the effects of uncontrolled SALWs proliferation in his country. By the late 1990s, SALWs control became one of the most important security priorities of a large number of states (ECOWAS 2006b). The search for a feasible and sustainable peace to the internal conflict in Mali led to the adoption in 1998 of the Moratorium on the Importation, Exportation and Manufacture of Small Arms and Light Weapons in West Africa. The broad aim of the Moratorium is to create an environment conducive to socio-economic development in the sub-region. The Moratorium was aimed at preventing conflicts; post-conflict reconstructions; and stems the increasing wave of crime and banditry in the sub-region especially with the understanding that easy access and availability of small arms may lead to violent solutions to problems and their circulation within and across borders facilitates the formation of new armed groups and new conflicts. It also facilitates the use of untrained civilian militias, ill-disciplined fighters, and unaccountable mercenaries. Increase in socio-economic development in general and donor supported development projects in particular is the third objective of the Moratorium (Badmus 2009). Critics of the ECOWAS moratorium, for instance, maintain that neither has it prevented the recycling of weapons from one conflict zone to another, as some states within the region flouted commitments; nor have the wars in the region abated (Berman 2000).

Programme for Coordination and Assistance for Security and Development in Africa (PCASED)

An operational framework was put in place within the context of the Programme for Coordination and Assistance for Security and Development in Africa (PCASED) in 1998 to facilitate implementation of measures associated with the moratorium. PCASED is a regional project of the United Nations Development Programme (UNDP) that is executed by the United Nations Office for Project Services (UNOPS). PCASED predates the Moratorium, as it was originally intended to support the implementation of the UN

Secretary-General's Advisory Mission on the Proliferation of Light Weapons in the Sahel-Sahara sub-region.

However, following the adoption of the Moratorium, the ECOWAS Heads of States and Government requested that PCASED become the central pillar in its implementation. PCASED was expected to support the implementation of the moratorium in nine priority areas, these are: establishing a culture of peace; training programs for military, security, and police forces; enhancing weapons controls at border posts; establishing a database and regional arms register; collecting and destroying surplus weapons; facilitating dialogue with producer suppliers; reviewing and harmonizing national legislation and administrative procedures; mobilizing resources for PCASED objectives and activities; and enlarging membership of the Moratorium (FAS 1999).

Although PCASED face a lot of challenges however it was believed to be very instrumental in the implementation of the West African Moratorium, it was commended by the ECOWAS Authority concerning Natcoms, training of military and security personnel, enhancement of weapons controls at border post, particularly, Benin, Niger, Nigeria, and Mali, and the enhanced coordination between PCASED and the ECOWAS Secretariat. More so, the report also gave credit to PCASED in the areas of arms collection and destruction programs, harmonization of legislations and regional arms register and database (Badmus 2009). Notwithstanding the commendation, PCASED was flooded with a lot of difficulties among others budgetary and financial limitations and technical difficulties plagued its activities.

The Code of Conduct for the Implementation of the Moratorium

In order to assist PCASED, a summit meeting of ECOWAS Heads of State and Government, held on 10 December 1999 in the Togolese capital, Lome, adopted a "Code of Conduct for the Implementation of the Moratorium on the Importation, Exportation and Manufacture of Light Weapons" (ECOWAS 2006a). The code of conduct outlines the institutional arrangements for the implementation of the moratorium. The moratorium has three main instruments: the Moratorium Declaration; the Plan of Action for the Implementation of the Programme for Coordination and Assistance on Security and Development (PCASED)—a UNDP support program—approved in March 1999; lastly, a Code of Conduct, adopted on 10 December 1999,—constitute the main pillars of the ECOWAS strategy to curb the flow of illicit small arms in particular and disarmament in general.

National Commissions (Natcoms)

National Commissions is one of the key initiatives of the Moratorium to deal with illicit weapons proliferation by member states. As contained in Article 4 of the Code of Conduct: "In order to promote and ensure co-ordination of concrete measures for effective implementation of the Moratorium at the national level, Member states shall establish National Commissions, made up of representatives of the relevant authorities and civil society" (ECOWAS 2006a). National commissions are meant to serve as a nucleus around which national and regional initiatives revolve. They are to formulate strategies, policies, and programs to counter the proliferation of small arms; sensitize public on the need to turn in illegally held weapons to security forces; update arms registers and transmission to ECOWAS Secretariat; Provide appropriate recommendations to ECOWAS Secretariat on exemptions to be granted to the Moratorium for weapons covered by the agreement; mobilize resource for program expenditures; liaise on a permanent basis with ECOWAS and PCASED Secretariats on issues relevant to the Moratorium as well as on the proliferation of SALW in general; initiate and develop an exchange of information and experience with the other national commissions (ECOWAS 1999).

Creation of National commissions succeeded in yielding progress especially in terms of compliance by member nations; however, it could be noted that many of the Natcoms suffer from weak capacity and a lack of funds and political support. Moreover, issues that pertain to the development of a credible regional arms register and database have not materialized, and harmonization of legislation has also been very slow. There has also been slow progress on a peacekeeping register, with a stand-off between PCASED and the United Nations Mission in Sierra Leone (UNAMSIL) in 2003 giving an indication of the difficulties.

The Moratorium was later transformed into a convention in 2006 following the signing by ECOWAS member States of the Convention on Small Arms and Light Weapons, Their Ammunition and Other Related Materials, which, inter alia, banned SALW transfers into, from, and through the territories of states parties in order to "prevent and combat excessive and destabilizing accumulation of SALW within ECOWAS" (ECOWAS 2006a).

The transformation was aimed at shifting the focus from mere "moral persuasion" in curtailing the spread of illicit weapons to "enforcement" of the protocol. This, it seeks to achieve by enhancing the capacity of member States through their National Committee on Small Arms and Light Weapons, for the effective control of SALW in their countries. ECOSAP is also engaging and building the capacity of Civil Society Organizations (CSOs) in the sub-region for the same purpose through the West African Action Network on Small Arms (WAANSA) headquartered in Ghana. ECOSAP is also in a strategic partnership with the Media, (through the West African Network of Journalists on Security and Development (WANJSD)) which it engages for the purpose of its advocacy and communication programs in the fight against SALW. ECOWAS provides a humanitarian justification for the convention as it links SALW transfers to international humanitarian law (IHL) and international human rights law—IHRL (Atanga 2003).

Lapses in Transportation that Aid Proliferation of Small Arms in West Africa

Structural problems such as lack of organizational skills, the necessary infrastructure, funds, as well as forces of globalization make the control of SALWs very complex. Among other structural factors are:

a. *Crisis of Governance*: The dilapidation of border control points is compounded by the dispiritedness of the security services personnel. They are generally poorly paid and feel isolated or "abandoned," without proper working tools or proper protection, for example, against attacks by criminals and cross-border traffickers. Lack of adequate welfare and morale constitute a big temptation to service personnel especially when they are offered handsome reward to compromise their duty.

b. *Corruption*: Customs officers are bribed by weapons dealers, while soldiers, police officers and security forces are known to have sold government weapons to criminals (Ayissi and Ibrahima 2005). If the officers and men that are charged with the responsibility of preventing proliferation of illicit small arms and light weapons are found to be collaborators, then the battle is far from being won. Dealers in illicit arms are ready to compromise anybody to pave way for them. So, to succeed in curbing this illegal business that is destructive to safety of lives and property, only trusted officers and men can be used for the fight against proliferation of small arms in the West African sub-region and Africa at large.

c. *Porous Borders*: Another factor is that Africa by virtue of its size, the second largest continent in the world and population, given the level of its development experience persistent problem of border control. Also, due to the sheer size of some of its countries, for instance, Nigeria, has 770 km of shared land border with the Republic of Benin to the west, about 1500 km with Niger to the north, 1700 km with Cameroon to the east, 90 km with the Republic of Chad to the north-east, and 850 km maritime border on the Atlantic Ocean. Out-stretched these tally up to 4910 km of borders which have to be controlled. Each of these entry points, along with the airports, has been used to smuggle arms into the country. One can imagine how tasking it is to effectively control these borders. It is also interesting to observe that all three largest Sub-Saharan countries, namely Sudan (the continent's overall largest), the Congo DRC (3rd overall largest), and Chad (5th overall largest) have been experiencing instability and armed conflict for long. It may well be that their size and their porous borders make it easy for weapons to be smuggled inflaming and protracting violence (Ngang 2007). Similarly, desert and forest regions are extremely difficult to monitor, as are steep slopes. Surveillance of the Senegal-Gambia border, for example, is easier than on the border between Senegal and Guinea (Conakry), in the foothills of the Fouta Djallon massif. West African borders are extremely long and as a result border surveillance is costly.

d. ***Lack of Equipment***: More often than not, the security services personnel at check points are not well equipped to tackle smugglers of small weapons and light arms. They lack modern communication gadgets to enable them connect other officers when they need assistance or reinforcement. There are no scanners at the check points, while surveillance equipment for tracking illegal migration and illicit flow of small arms are either obsolete or non-existent. Security personnel often resort to ransacking vehicles on a sample basis which is not always effective as such an approach is waste of time and energy. Smugglers are often armed with more sophisticated weapons which cannot be matched by what the security personnel are carrying. Some (if not most) of the vehicles used by the security personnel are also not serviceable, while smugglers enjoy the luxury of smart vehicles and drone technology.

e. ***Poor Management of intelligence***: Good intelligence handling is key to success in curbing the spread of small arms and light weapons. Countries within the sub-region needs to share intelligence. As it is now, wanted criminals escape from one country only to make the next neighboring country their safe heaven. There must be collaboration at all levels and echelons of security forces of countries within the sub-region and sensitive information must not be easily divulged.

f. ***Challenges of Globalization***: The forces of globalization bring with it opportunities and challenges, the elimination of state enforced restrictions on exchanges across borders and the increasingly integrated and complex global system of production and exchange that has emerged as a result further complicate the challenge of containing SALWs proliferation. The idea of globalization and its advocate for free market forces with minimum economic barriers and open trade for world development provides ground for illicit trade in arms. By minimizing custom regulations and border control, trafficking of small arms becomes easier. Malhotra and Dash (2011) stressed that, a small percent of container ships have cargo checks, therefore making the arms movement smooth. Faking documents bribing officials and concealing arms as humanitarian aids are common practices.

Conclusion

There exist numerous recorded policies and conventions that have been drafted by ECOWAS and other friendly associations in combating small arms proliferation in Africa, which covers major aspects that when achieved will bring this act down to least possible minimum occurrence in Africa but the problem still lies in the implementation aspect of these policies and conventions. There are too many lapses in the transportation system that will not allow for curbing the proliferation of small arms and light weapons in

Africa. Corruption among officers and men of the different security services charged with the responsibility of stopping this illegal activity is another serious setback to the fight against the spread of illicit arms. Therefore, the following recommends are put forward: First, governments of African countries should intensify surveillance of their borders as well as employ the use of UVS to check illegal movement across their borders. Secondly, scanners should be provided at border crossing points to assist customs in checking of cargoes. This should be done with state-of-the-art technology which should, ideally locally developed and calibrated. Even if scanning devices are sourced from overseas suppliers, there is a need to ensure that the peculiarities of the local terrain are factored into the devices. Thirdly, the ECOWAS free movement protocol—as well as similar facilities in the other regional complexes—should be revisited in order to fine-tune security issues in the protocol. The revised protocol should embed strict restrictions on the movement of small arms and lethal weapons. Thirdly, governments of African countries should establish and strengthen their regional and municipal mechanisms on illegal smuggling of small arms and light weapons. This should be achieved through enhanced regional cooperation and synergies of legal mechanisms and resources.

References

Adele, K., & Noel, S. (2008). Controlling the Transfer of Arms: Progress and Challenges in the African Context. Institute for Security Studies (ISS) Paper 159 Pretoria/Tshwane South Africa.

Airriess, C. A. (2001). The Regionalization of Hutchison Port Holdings in Transportation Business & Management. *Journal of Transport Geography, 9*(4), 267–278.

Albright, M. K. (1999). Speech by Secretary Albright Before the National Association for the Advancement of Colored People (NAACP), New York, (July 13). Retrieved from https://1997-2001.state.gov/statements/1999/990713.html on Jul 5, 2020.

Alpers, P. (Ed). (2007). Report of the Panel of Governmental Experts on Small Arms, UN Document A/70/320, 16 November 2007. Retrieved from www.gunpolicy.org on Oct 10, 2019.

Atanga, L.M. (2003). Tackling Small Arms in Central Africa. Retrieved from https://www.bicc.de/uploads/tx_bicctools/paper29.pdf on Oct 10, 2019.

Ayissi, A., & Ibrahima, S. (2005). Combating the Proliferation of Small Arms and Light Weapons in West Africa; *Handbook for the Trainingof Armed and Security Forces, United Nations* 2005.

Badmus, I. A. (2009). Managing Arms in Peace Processes: ECOWAS and the West African Civil Conflicts. WP/CEAUP/2009. Retrieved from www.Africanos.eu on Oct 5, 2019.

Bardi, E., Coyle, J., & Novack, R. (2006). *Management of Transportation*. Thomson South-Western. ISBN 0-324-31443-4.

Berman, E. (2000). Re-armament in Sierra Leone: One year After the Lomé Peace Agreement. Occasional Paper No. 1, Small Arms Survey, Geneva. BICC, 2002.

ECOWAS. (1999). *Official Journal of the ECOWAS*. Volume 37. Retrieved from http://ecotipa.ecowas.int/wp-content/uploads/2017/07/A.DEC_.1312.99-ESTABLISHING-NATIONALCOMMISSIONS-FOR-THE-CONTROL-OF-THE-PROLIFERATION-AND-ELLICIT-CIRCULATION-OF-LIGHT-WEAPON.pdf on Oct 5, 2019.

ECOWAS. (2006a). Code of Conduct for the Implementation of the Moratorium on the Importation, Manufacture and Exportation of Light Weapons to West Africa. Lome, Togo, 10 December 1999. ECOWAS Executive secretariat 2006, Article 2, 1, 3, 1.

ECOWAS. (2006b). ECOWAS Convention on Small Arms and Light Weapons, TheirAmmunition and Other Related Materials. Retrieved from http://www.poa-iss.org/RegionalOrganizations/ECOWAS/ECOWAS%20Convention%202006.pdf on Oct 5, 2019.

FAS. (1999). Programme for Coordination and Assistance for Security and Development in Africa (PCASED). Published by Federation of American Scientists- FAS. Updated December 21, 1999 Retrieved from https://fas.org/nuke/control/pcased/text/ecowas.htm on July 5, 2020.

Germain, R., Cherenkov, V., Churakova, I., Okrovyakovskiy, E., Krotov, K., Serova, L., & Zyatchin, A. (2012). Supply Chain Management Encyclopedia. Retrieved from http://scm.gsom.spbu.ru/Transport_node.

Hanson, S., & Giuliano, G. (2016). *The Geography of Urban Transportation*. New York: The Guilford Press, 2016. Print.

IRIN. (2001). West Africa: IRIN Focus on renewal of small arms moratorium. June 11, 2001. Retrieved from https://reliefweb.int/report/angola/west-africa-irin-focus-renewal-small- arms-moratorium on July 5, 2020.

Malhotra, N. K., & Dash, S. (2011). *Marketing Research: An Applied Orientation* (6th ed.). Delhi: Pearson-Dorling Kindersley.

McNally, M. G.(2017). Travel Forecasting Glossary 2017. Retrieved fromhttp://www.its.uci.edu/~mmcnally/tdf-glos.html#region on Oct 5, 2019.

Monnet, T (2019). Air transport: which are Africa's most profitable routes? Retrieved from https://www.theafricareport.com/16559/air-transport-which-are-africas-most-profitable-routes/ on Oct 15, 2019.

Ngang, C. K. (2007). *Small Arms and Light Weapons, Africa's True WMDs: The Role of SALW in Conflict and Insecurity in Sub-Saharan Africa*; MA Thesis, European University Center for Peace Studies(EPU), Stadstschlaining, Austria.

Onuoha, F. C. (2012). Small Arms and Light Weapons Proliferation and Human Security in Nigeria. *Handbook for the Training of Armed and Security Forces Article*. Published by the African Centre for the Constructive Resolution of Dispute (ACCORD) Combating the Proliferation of Small Arms and Light Weapons in West Africa.

RadioFreeEurope RadioLiberty. (2009). Nigeria Impounds Ukrainian Plane With Arms OnBoard. Retrieved fromhttps://www.rferl.org/a/Nigeria_Impounds_Ukrainian_Plane_With_Arms_On_Board/1757432.html Oct 15, 2019.

Rodrigue, J-P., & Ducruet, C. (2017). The *Geography of Urban Transportation*. New York: The Guilford Press, 2017. Print.

Rodrigue, J-P., & Notteboom, T. (2012). Dry Ports in European and North American Intermodal Rail Systems: Two of a Kind? *Research in Transportation Business & Management, 5,* 4–15.

UNCTAD. (2015). *Transport and Trade Facilitation Newsletter*, logistics and Trade. Retrieved from http://unctad.org/en/PublicationsLibrary/webdtltlb2015d1_en.pdf on Oct 20, 2019.

World Bank. (2010). The Logistics Performance Index 2010. Retrieved from https://lpi.worldbank.org/international/global/2010 on Oct 20, 2019.

Terzungwe Nyor, Ph. D. is an Accountant and Logistician, a Professor of Accounting, and the present Head of Department of Logistics and Supply Chain Management at the Nigerian Defence Academy, Kaduna. He was Head of Department of Accounting and Management for two consecutive tenures from 2013 to 2017. A man of great interdisciplinary skills and a member of the Institute of Chartered Accountant of Nigeria (ICAN), he is a practicing Company Secretary, a Tax Consultant, a Management Consultant, an Accounting System Designer, an Auditor, and a Researcher. He holds B.Sc. in Accounting from Bayero University Kano (1989), M.Sc. in Accounting also from Bayero University Kano (2008), and Ph.D. in Accounting from the Nigerian Defence Academy (2011). As a Lecturer, Professor Nyor has taught at different undergraduate levels, spanning a period of over twenty (20) years. At postgraduate level, he lectures in the Postgraduate Diploma in Accounting, Postgraduate Diploma in Management, Masters in Business Administration, Masters in Financial Economics, Masters in Security Management, Masters in Disaster and Risk Management, M.Sc. in Accounting, and Ph.D. in Accounting classes till date. He has also delivered lectures and seminars at different training workshops and conferences over time. As a researcher, Prof. Nyor has over thirty five (35) publications to his credit, in both national and international journals. He is a Visiting Professor, an External Examiner, and a member of the NUC and MBTE Accreditation Teams to some Nigerian Tertiary Institutions. His hobbies include travelling, watching football, and swimming.

Multinational Corporations, Trafficking of Small Arms and Intractable Conflicts in Africa

Emmanuel Ukhami and Lassana Doumbia

Introduction

From the inception of Africa, the continent has been characterized by intractable conflict, as a result of proxy wars, inter-community strife, and ethno-religious crisis. Most of these conflicts were/are executed using Small Arms and Light Weapons (SALWs). According to Amnesty International (2014), such violent conflicts continues to accelerate structural poverty and processes of impoverishment across the continent. It has caused untold atrocities, including deaths, sexual violence, displacement, shattered communities and loss of hope for a decent standard of living. Global experts estimated that at least 500,000 people die every year, on average, and millions more are displaced and abused as a result of armed violence and conflict. In terms of the economic cost of war, according to Global Envision, a study has shown that conflicts in Africa cost the continent over $300bn between 1990 and 2005—an amount equivalent to all the international aid received by sub-Saharan Africa in the same period (Global Envision 2007). The implication is that significant percentage of governments revenue in Africa has been used to sponsor the quelling of conflicts. According to Southall (2002), more than 85% of the major conflicts since the Second World War have been in poor countries. During the 1990s, the poorest countries of the world became saturated with arms; some originated from "legal" transfers, and many formed part of the illegal trade. The arms trade destabilized already fragmented countries, making development difficult and blurring distinctions between use for military and criminal purposes. In global relations, according to Francis (2006), the stigma of a "continent at war with itself" had long been attached to Africa. The African Union (2013) admitted that the continent has hosted, and continues to be home to a number of deadly conflicts that jeopardize human, national, and international security and defy efforts to resolve them.

Several African states, such as Central African Republic (CAR), Democratic Republic of Congo (DRC), Libya, Liberia, Sierra Leone, Mali, South Sudan, Sudan, Somalia, and Nigeria have experienced violent armed wars in forms of civil wars or armed struggles, mostly within the boundaries of the state, as a result of ethnic communal identity clash, religious bigotry, struggle for power or distributive justice. According to Barkindo, Omolewa, and Babalola, apart from civil wars, Africa has also witnessed a number of intermittent border and interstate conflicts notable among which are the following: Nigeria-Cameroon dispute over Bakassi Peninsular since the 1970s; Algeria-Morocco conflict over the Atlas Mountains area in October 1963; Eritrea-Ethiopian crisis between 1962 and 1979; Somalia-Ethiopia dispute of 1964–1978 over the Ogaden desert region; Chad-Libya crisis of 1980–1982; Kenya-Somalia border war of 1963–1967 in which Somalia aimed at recovering its lost territories including the northern frontier district of Kenya. Tanzania-Uganda crisis in 1978–1979 (Barkindo et al. 1994). These has led to the proliferation of small arms which include revolvers and self-loading pistols, rifles and carbines, sub-machine guns, assault rifles and light machine guns. Only a very small percentage of these weapons are produced on the continent; the majority is introduced via illegal channels. Although, according to Broga, most of the proliferated uncontrolled arms in circulation in Africa are being trafficked and transferred within the continent, weapons are initially shipped into conflict zones from outside the continent. For example, the UN panel of experts on Sudan identified certain countries, including Ukraine, China, Canada, Israel, Bulgaria, Slovakia, Iran, and Russia as major suppliers of large stockpiles of arms and other material to South Sudan (Broga 2016).

The question of uncontrolled arms, their illicit acquisition and transfer is a recurring security dilemma in Africa. The concentration of most of Africa's estimated 100 million uncontrolled SALWs in crisis zones and other security-challenged environments often exacerbates and elongates conflicts. This brings devastating costs to individuals, families, and communities who experience displacement, erosion of social cohesion and trust, gender-based violence (GBV), injuries and fatalities (Adeniyi 2017). The chapter therefore evaluates the nexus between Multinational Corporations (MNCs), trafficking of small arms and intractable conflicts in Africa. The chapter is divided into seven subsections which include the introduction; conceptual and theoretical framing of Multinationals, conflicts and small arms in Africa; trafficking of small arms in Africa: the role of MNCs and their parent countries; causes of small arms proliferation and intractable conflicts in Africa, and the influence of the MNCs in the value chain; consequences of small arms trafficking and conflict in Africa: *the vicarious liability of MNCS; and* conclusion.

CONCEPTUAL AND THEORETICAL FRAMING OF MULTINATIONALS, CONFLICTS, AND SMALL ARMS IN AFRICA

Who Are the Multinational Corporations?

The globalisation of the international economy, and the spread of MNCs have made them a potent non-state actor in the international system. Spero (1980: 88) on his part defines a multinational corporation as a firm with foreign subsidiaries which extends the production and marketing of the firm beyond the boundaries of any one country. Multinationals do not include large corporation that market their products abroad, they are firms which have sent abroad a package of capital, technology, managerial talent, and marketing skills to carry out production in foreign countries.

Multinational Corporations have broken barriers through global interconnectedness. They operate in both developed and underdeveloped counties. In more recent times, MNCs have grown in power and visibility influencing the decision of state actors both in their home country and host countries. Most top MNCs are headquartered in the USA, Western Europe, and Japan, but they possess an incredible capacity to shape global trade, production and financial transactions across the world (Onwurah and Usman 2016; Agaba and Ukhami 2019). These multinational corporations are capable of destabilizing the economy as well as the politics of weak states (Saleh 2010). This is why the role of MNCs in small arms trafficking cannot be overemphasized. The present intractable conflicts in some African states and regions are as a result of trafficking and proliferation of weapons produced and circulated by the MNCs whose interest is to make huge profit and maintain high power valency in the continent they find themselves. As cited in Cooper (1999), there are a number of ways in which multinationals are actors in the arms trade. First, and most obviously the major defence companies are important actors without whom arms would not be made or sold. It is important to emphasize, however, that arms companies are not simply a response to free market laws of supply and demand. Most are only able to exist because they are adept at lobbying substantial levels of support from domestic governments, in terms of protection for industry subsidies for exports and generosity in the interpretation of national export controls.

Civil MNCs can also be actors in the arms trade, a role that can take a variety of forms. For instance, companies can directly supply either the arms or more usually the finances necessary for participants in internal conflicts to maintain their forces and to acquire new weaponry. In some cases, there are complex links among the private sector activities of large MNCs engaged in primary resource extraction, the global arms trade, and the states and rebel groups engaging in and often profiting from war. For example, in Angola, where cold war tensions had manifested themselves in a long-term civil war, oil MNCs provided huge drilling bonuses and payments to the government. Oil profits were in turn used to purchase arms rather than to fund development projects that would benefit the people of Angola. The government justified its actions by saying that they needed to use the oil money to fight UNITA, the opposition movement. However, the government had other motivations for prolonging the war; arms dealers paid them millions of dollars in commissions to negotiate arms deals. If the war ended, so would the profitable arms deals. In short, the Angolan government found that war itself can be a lucrative business (cited in Cooper 1999). This explains the reason why most MNCs, especially in Africa, determine political, economic and socio-cultural dynamics of states.

Proliferation of Small Arms

Small arms are weapons designed for personal use. It is the most circulated weapons all over the world because of its easy production, durability, and cost. According to ECOWAS (2006), small arms refers to arms used by one person, and which include forearms and other destructive arms or devices such as exploding bombs, incendiary bombs, or gas bombs, grenades, rocket launchers, missiles, missile systems or landmines, revolvers, and pistols with automatic loading, rifles and carbines, machine guns, assault rifles, and light machine guns. The United Nations (2006) highlighted small arms to include: revolvers and self-loading pistols; rifles and carbines; sub-machine guns; assault rifles; light machine guns, heavy machine guns; portable anti-tank guns; recoil-less rifles; portable launchers of anti-tank guns, and rocket systems, anti-aircraft missiles systems; and mortars of calibers less than 100 mm.

There is no universally accepted definition of small arms. Even where some sort of understanding exists, we find that it has been undergoing changes throughout decades. Small arms were generally understood to include personal weapons of troops and limited to 12.7 mm and less calibre even during the Second World War. This traditionally covered man-portable weapons like rifles, pistols, light machine guns, and, in some cases, grenades, etc. As weapons became lighter and more effective, the classification seems to have expanded to include an ever-increasing number and type of weapons. For example, it is believed that by 1983, North Atlantic Treaty Organisation (NATO) had enlarged the original Second World War definition to describe small arms as "all crew-portable direct fire weapons of a calibre less than 50 mm and will include a secondary capability to defeat light armour and helicopters" (Preface to Jane's Infantry Weapons 1992–1993, in Singh 1998).

Small arms and light weapons proliferation is acclaimed to be the major security challenge to people, societies, and states globally, fuelling insurgency, human trafficking and drugs, terrorism, organized crimes, internal insurrections and civil wars, posing obstacles to sustenance of stable peace and security. Many a times, little internal insurrection tends to escalate into larger civil wars and could destabilize a region (Kelvin 2007). This trend especially in sub-Saharan Africa is attributed to the weakness and fragile nature of the states and the failure of government to deliver good governance.

The increasing trafficking of these weapons into Africa has led to high level of conflict in the continent. High concentration and proliferation of small arms has had, and continues to have, devastating consequences on the continent. Belligerents in the conflict areas, for example, Somali, Sudan, and parts of northern Uganda, use the SALWs as the primary tools of violence, causing deaths and injuring thousands of people, among them innocent civilians. In sub-Saharan African countries experiencing violent conflicts, the availability of SALW escalates insecurity and duration of violence. The impact of insecurity and other problems attributed to SALW are also manifested in the neighboring peaceful countries within the region (Nganga 2008).

The Nature and Substance of Conflicts

The word conflict is derived from the Latin word *confligere*, meaning to "strike together." It is to shape together or forces together when you come in contact with someone, it is simply a disagreement. Conflict involves disagreement, clash, collision or a struggle or contest between two or more parties. According to Bakut (2007) conflict is usually used for the range of arguments as tensions and violent conflicts that occur both within and between states. It is the pursuit of incompatible goals or interests by different groups or individuals.

Conflict also means contradiction arising from differences in interests, ideas, ideologies, orientations, beliefs, perceptions, and tendencies. Although conflict is a normal, natural, and inevitable phenomenon in any interactive situation of human life, contradictions exist at all levels of the society be it intra-personal, inter-personal, intra-groups, inter-groups, intra-national, international and institutions. Conflict is not necessarily negative in itself; it is often a by-product of social change and may lead to constructive transformation. It becomes negative when it is intractable.

Conflicts and violence with their multi-dimensional consequences have been an obstacle to progress, political stability, economic prosperity and overall socio-economic development of African countries because of its destructive nature. While conflicts may not always be accompanied by bloodshed, most conflicts in Africa, degenerate into violence, quickly leading to the destruction of lives and properties. Violence provoked by conflicts has often turned the people's intention from creative production to creative destruction (Nnoli 2003). Post-colonial Africa has experienced a spate of conflicts and violence, namely Intra and interstate, ethnic, religious, political and resource control based violence, including structural violence, that is, violence that is expressed in such conditions as poverty, inequality, psychological violence, oppression and social exclusion, which have ravaged one African country after another. National armies have continuously and violently intervened in the political affairs of African countries through bloody coup d'tats, leading in some cases to civil wars. Apart from actual military interregnums, a major development in the style of violence in African countries is the militarization of these conflicts, through the use of SALWs, the involvement of child soldiers and in the struggle for the control of mineral resources, as experienced in the Niger Delta area of Nigeria and the persistent wars between Muslims and non-Muslim groups, especially in the Northern part of Nigeria (Odinka et al. 2012). Apart from Nigeria, countries like Ethiopia, Sudan, Liberia, Somalia, Canada, Burundi, Angola, Sierra Leone, South Africa, and Cote d'Ivoire have suffered greatly from widespread and intense internal conflicts. These conflicts have exploited the myth of national solidarity, undermining the social fabric of these nations and destroying their fragile economies (Alli 2007).

Theoretical Framework—"Intractable Conflict" in Africa

Intractable conflicts are complex in nature, sustained in longevity and permeate wide geography and periods. According to Kriesberg, many conflicts, especially inter-communal or interstate conflicts related to ethnic and religious differences, often sink into self-perpetuating, mutually reinforcing, violent antagonisms. Such conflicts are a longstanding part of human history (Kriesberg 2007). Intractable conflicts are characterized as being protracted, irreconcilable, violent, of a zero-sum nature, total, and highly conflagrating, with the parties involved having an interest in their continuation (Azar 1985, 1990; Bar-Tal 1998; Kriesberg 1998). They are demanding, stressful, painful, exhausting, and costly both in human and material terms (Bar-Tal 1998). Intractable conflicts persist through generations with no end in sight (Vallacher et al. 2010). According to Crocker et al. (2005: 5), an intractable conflict can be defined as a conflict which has "persisted over time and refused to yield to efforts – through either direct negotiations by the parties or mediation with third-party assistance – to arrive at a political settlement."

Protracted social conflict entails a vicious cycle of fear and hostile interactions among the communal contestants (Azar 1990). When societal competition fails to rectify inequalities over time, what begins as a "reasonable" conflict to address perceived social injustice can lead to a shift in the direction of frustration, resulting in violent conflict (Gurr 1970). According to Azar, "inequality in the social structure is largely responsible for overt hostile behaviour, especially in protracted social conflicts. It is the product of political and economic inequality and ideological domination of one social group over another" (Azar 1983: 90).

In Africa, protracted conflicts feed chiefly on the trafficking of small arms. MNCs are argued to be clandestinely involved in aiding and abating the supply of these weapons largely as a result of the elite connivance with MNC, and loopholes in governance infrastructure in African states. Conflicts in Africa always emanate out of the structures that characterize Africans organizational framework. Structures that breeds elitism and inequality, ethnicity and religious bigotry, marginalization and injustice, oppression and exclusion. Mostly, the economic disparity that has led to misappropriation of state resources and its consequences in the African society can best be described by the radical structural conflict theory popularly co-authored by Karl Marx and Friedrich Engels in the "Communist Manifesto" and "Historical Materialism" (Marx and Engels 1977). According to Marx in his Communist Manifesto, "the history of all hitherto existing society, is the history of class struggle." Therefore, the wide economic gap that exist in any given society, including Africa will eventually lead to conflict.

Consequently, Marxists perceive every society to have a base and superstructure. Thus, the base which refers to economic foundation (capitalism, communism, etc.) modifies and is modified by the superstructure which include art, politics, and psychological prospects of both individuals and classes in the society. Since the elites hold the monopoly of power in society, they control the base, superstructure, and ideology. In this manner, exclusion, oppression, and exploitation are initiated in the society (Rawls 1971). The remedy according to Marx is to strip the bourgeoisie of both economic and political power through an action that may lead to social change and revolution.

In Africa, armed inter-communal insurrections are often episodic eruptions of violence, sparked by specific incidents that stoke long simmering antagonisms, anxieties, and aggressions. They can lead to great loss of life and if unchecked can mutate into prolonged warfare between ethnic and regional militias, which in turn can develop into guerrilla armies that threaten the viability of the nation-state. The periodic explosions of genocidal violence in Rwanda and Burundi, for instance, demonstrated most horrifically in the Rwandan genocide of 1994, show the potential destructiveness of inter-communal conflicts abetted by the state and reinforced by the devastations of economic stagnation, as well as the politicization and manipulation of ethnic differences by a cynical and bankrupt political class. Militant or militarized ethnicity is evident in many other countries currently undergoing democratization, as the tensions and twists arising from the competitive politics of democracy often find articulation in the entrenched identities, idioms, and institutions of ethnic solidarity. In Nigeria, for example, democratization has led to the resurgence of ethnic identities and the proliferation of regional and local struggles over the entitlements of citizenship expressed in the language of "indigenes" and "settlers." These struggles have increasingly spilled into the formation of ethnic militias that have wrought havoc on Nigeria's civil society, unleashing periodic convulsions of inter-communal violence (Vickers 2000; Agbu 2004). The DRC war, bred and superimposed on an already ferocious civil war, was fuelled by a mad scramble for the country's vast mineral, forestry, and agricultural resources, and involved Angola, Namibia, and Zimbabwe on the side of the DRC government and Rwanda and Uganda on the side of the rebels (Khadiagala 2006). The destructiveness of these wars was incalculable in the loss of human life and damage to material infrastructure and environmental resources. By the end of 2004, according to several estimates, the war in the DRC alone had claimed a staggering three to four million lives (Institute for Peace and Justice 2005). The nature of African society, being plural, highly heterogenous, trapped in colonial hangover and post-colonial crisis; and taking over by few individual elites who continually create a wide gap between the rich and the poor, has simply led to the need to resort to radical change through taking up arms either against the state or perceived threat to survival. The trafficking and possession of small arms in Africa is simply seen as an easy route to ensure radical structural changes.

The MNCs and arms trade industries take advantage of the domestic structural imbalance in Africa that has led to intractable conflict, to perpetually advance their capitalist tendencies and practices. Manufacturers of weapons know best the link between politics and weapons markets and are therefore often linked to the political instabilities in Africa to take advantage of the weapons business it creates. In a remark to congress, McKinney, a former congresswoman stated that:

> What we do know is that the U.S. Special Forces and U.S funded private military companies have been arming and training Rwandan and Ugandan troops to deadly effect. I think it is appalling that the U.S. taxpayer should be directly assisting the military efforts of Rwanda and Uganda, the aggressors in this tragic conflict and who are confirmed by Amnesty International and Human Rights Watch as the authors of terrible atrocities against Congolese civilians. Our efforts in Africa have amounted to nothing more than bankrolling belligerent and mass murder. (McKinney 2001: 6)

The Control Arms Campaign (CAC), involving Oxfam International, Amnesty International, and the International Network on Small Arms (IANSA) has issued a damning report about countries which should have neither truck nor trade with the Bouts of this world. For example, the United Kingdom (U.K.), Canada, the US, and the European Union (EU) allow companies to circumvent arms regulations by selling weapons components and by sub-contracting the manufacturing of arms. The report details how weapons, including trucks and helicopters, as well as conventional small arms, are being assembled from foreign components under license in countries including Egypt, India, and Turkey. These weapons then end up in African hotspots such as strife-ridden Sudan. As well, they are supplied to police and military in countries such as Somalia, Eritrea, Ethiopia, Kenya, Uganda, Zimbabwe, and Nigeria where, the report says, the arms are used for the killing, subjugation, and displacement of civilians (McCullun 2016).

This influx of arms is the result of the activities of EU–based arms brokers, shipping agents, and associated sub-contractors. They take advantage of loopholes in their own countries—as well as those in unregulated Eastern Europe, Asia, and Africa, where most of the arms trafficking takes place. Even where governments have taken steps to control the activities of brokering and shipping agents, their efforts have often been inadequate, and are frequently undermined by brokers simply stepping over the border into another state with even more loopholes in order to conduct their transactions. In this way, unscrupulous arms dealers have been able to undermine the stated policies of the EU, the United Kingdom (UK) and their partners (McCullun 2016).

Trafficking of Small Arms in Africa: The Role of MNCs and Their Parent Countries

Since the end of the Cold War, Africa has witnessed an outbreak of ethnic, religious, and sectarian conflict characterized by routine massacre of civilians. Hundreds of conflicts erupted just between 1990 and 2000 alone (Boutwell and Klare 2000). These conflicts killed millions of people, devastated entire geographic regions, and left tens of millions refugees. Little of the destruction was inflicted by the tanks, artillery, or aircraft usually associated with modern warfare. Rather most was carried out with pistols, machine guns, and grenades. There are currently about fifteen African countries involved in war, or experiencing post-war conflict and tension. In West Africa the countries include Cote d'Ivoire, Guinea, Liberia, Sierra Leone, Nigeria, and Togo. In East Africa, they are Eritrea, Ethiopia, Somalia, Sudan, and Uganda. In Central Africa, the countries include Burundi, Democratic Republic of Congo, and Rwanda. In North Africa, a war is being waged in Algeria. In Southern Africa, the countries experiencing a war are Angola and Zimbabwe (*Africa Sun News* 2010). Considering the underdeveloped nature and the low technological know-how of the African continent, it is axiomatic to state that the numerous small arms used to carry out some of the conflicts and wars in Africa, are a result of legal and illegal trafficking of these weapons from the technological advanced countries through their MNCs, and supported by their governments. The trafficking and high proliferation of small and light weapons in Africa has further degenerated into more tensions between opposing groups, rather than dousing down tensions.

Although proliferation of small arms generates money for those who manufacture them, African people pay a heavy price due to lack of accountability or international regulations to address the abuses those products cause. According to the Global Facilitation Network Security Sector Reform, nations such as France, Russia, UK, China, and USA, the five permanent members of the United Nations Security Council, together account for 88 percent of the world's conventional arms exports (Bahati 2009). According to Graff, great parts of the developing world are saturated with these light weapons of which the origins can be traced back mainly to the five permanent members of the

Security Council (Graaf 1997). These exports contribute to gross abuses of human rights in Africa and elsewhere. Some of these are legal weapons sales to irresponsible governments who use them to oppress the people. Other supplies are made available to rebel groups by some countries in an effort to overthrow dictatorial regimes which in many cases become worse or as bad as the ousted regime. The United Nations General Assembly resolution subscribes to the idea that the absence of standards in arms sales is one of the contributory factors to conflict, the displacement of people and crimes. It undermines peace, reconciliation, safety and sustainable economic development (Bahati 2009).

More so, arms industries/multinationals have enormously close ties to the governments who are, of course, their main purchasers and subsidizers. According to Bahati (2009), among nations that are culpable is the USA. The U.S. military policies in Africa have promoted dictatorship rather than democracy. The presence of U.S.-made weapons on the African continent has hurt the African people more than it has helped. The USA legally transferred weapons contribute to feeding the illegal arms market which in turn exacerbates conflict situations in Africa. It was U.S.-made weapons that supported the rebel groups RENAMO in Mozambique, UNITA in Angola, RPF in Rwanda, and National Congress for the Defence of the People (CNDP) in the DRC. In the UN experts' report on the crisis in the DRC, S/2008/773, paragraph 28 connects the origin of military uniforms shipment destined to the rebel group CNDP to the USA in these terms: "In October 2008, Rwandan security services seized a shipment of uniforms destined for CNDP at Kanombe airport in Kigali ... The shipment reportedly originated in Boston, Massachusetts, United States" (UN Security Council Report 2008: 10).

In the Rwandan genocide (1994), arms suppliers to the Rwandan Armed Forces before the embargo included France, China, Egypt, Greece, Poland, and South Africa. Uganda is considered to have strongly been the source of arms to the RPF side. Not only state actors were involved in weapons supplies but also private enterprises and multinationals. The French company, DYL signed a multi-million dollar contract to deliver arms to Rwanda (Enuka 2012). Ngang (2007) observed that French companies were undisputed providers of arms to Rwanda. Not only did they carry out direct transfers to the country, they also helped in facilitating weapons deliveries by other countries. Even after the imposition of embargo on arms supplies to Rwanda, many European countries like France were found supplying to Rwanda either to the Hutu side or the Tutsi. Human Right Watch has the record of shipments of small arms into Rwanda through Goma, in Zaire. Zaire did not only help to facilitate deliveries by French through Goma, but also was actively involved in supplying small arms and light weapons to the Hutu group during the genocide.

Arms brokers and shipping agents have shown themselves to be capable of operating regardless of the existence of binding UN or regional arms embargoes. A UN embargo requires all countries to implement prompt and effective measures to enforce the embargo both at the sending and receiving end.

But there is irrefutable evidence that arms brokering and shipping agents are breaking their own laws, especially in the EU (Canada, the USA and other arms peddlers in Asia and Latin America have weaker laws and even weaker enforcement arrangements) (McCullun 2016).

Arms traffickers leave no stone unturned in perpetuating their brisk business. For example, a high profile case, came to light, when in 1998 the UK Company Sandline International (a company closely associated with Executive Outcomes and Diamond Works) arranged the transport of arms from Bulgaria to "rebel" forces seeking to reinstate Ahmed Tejan Kabbah as president of Sierra Leone (McCullun 2016). Furthermore, another UK company, Mil Tec, and its partners are known to have arranged shipments of arms to Rwanda before and during the 1994 genocide. Unfortunately, most governments do not take adequate steps to implement international embargoes; therefore, unscrupulous individuals, agencies, and companies are able to exploit weaknesses and inconsistencies in many national arms export control systems (McCullun 2016). Secret documents from the military archives of the exiled Rwandan armed forces reveal that a UK company, Mil Tec, registered in the Isle of Man, was centrally involved during April to July 1994 using links in Albania, France, Israel, and Italy. Mil Tec is still a major small arms supplier to conflicts in Africa (McCullum 2016). In a taped video interview, a British pilot described how in 1999 and 2000 he flew AK47 assault rifles from Rwanda and Uganda into the rebel-held town of Kisangani in the DRC. He claimed the planes were registered in Swaziland for Planetair and New Gomair. The British pilot said:

> Mostly the stuff we carried were brand new AKs plus the ammunition. They're all packed in plastic and in beautiful condition. It's really quite a standard operation and the Ukrainians are tops at it, supplying both planes and pilots but there's lots of others – Brits, Poles, Canadians, Americans, French, you name it. We know there's a war on but we are not involved because we're just charter pilots. We do about 80-90 hours flying a month (the Ukrainians do a lot more but some of them are not licensed) very easy. Leave the five star hotel they put us up in, do a little hour over there [to Kisangani or Goma] spend a couple more hours on the ground, and hour back in time for dinner. (Amnesty International 2002a, b)

Investigations by governments, non-governmental organisations (NGOs), human rights organizations, and the UN into the 1994 Rwanda genocide show how UK and South African based arms-brokering agents and their network of shipping and other subcontractors in other countries violated the international arms embargo against Rwanda in 1994. As did France's state arms manufacturing firms and the state-owned bank, Credit Lyonaisse; so did the Chinese government who exported a million new machetes (*Pangas*) to fuel the low-tech massacres; as well, the Ukraine and Belarus provided the airlines and crews to fly in the instruments of cruel death and genocide. They all did this by evading inadequate national laws in their home countries, and by easily disguising the routes of their deliveries, choosing to operate where there were loose customs, transport and financial regulations (McCullun 2016).

While Rwanda, Sierra Leone, Liberia, Somalia, and Sudan have received some sense of notoriety in public awareness, hundreds of so-called lesser wars started and continued with the direct support of the arms trade and their scurvy alliance of mercenaries and international corporations from the North. An example that shows the extent and sophistication of these illegal arms gangs can be cited from little-known Congo Republic (oil-rich and dwarfed by the DRC, it is known as Congo-Brazzaville, after its capital city) (McCullun 2016). Fighting among political factions, involving deliberate attacks on civilians, erupted in June 1997 and reached catastrophic proportions by 1999. At least 5000 Congolese civilians were killed and many more injured. The belligerents used small arms and heavier weaponry, including attack helicopters supplied by two West European dealers. Documents found in the offices of the ousted government of the Congo Republic showed that, between June and September 1997, a German arms broker and a Belgian arms trader supplied millions of dollars' worth of military equipment to the forces of the beleaguered President Pascal Lissouba. The German dealer negotiated orders for a wide range of military equipment totalling $42.4 million. Both dealers operated from South Africa where some of the equipment was obtained using companies registered in a number of countries and using Belgian, French, and UK bank accounts. Italian traders supplied the Congo with 15 tonnes of cartridges worth over one billion lire (McCullun 2016).

In the case of Sudan, besides an abundance of decades-old stocks circulating in the region, Sudan's imports of new SALWs before 2010 mostly came from China, and to a lesser extent Iran (Small Arms Survey 2009). According to NISAT-PRIO's database, Sudan has received SALW from a total of 22 countries since 2010, including China, Egypt, Germany, Lebanon, Romania, Russia, Saudi Arabia, Syria, Turkey, the United Arab Emirate (UAE), and Ukraine (NISAT-PRIO Researcher's Database, http://nisat.prio.org/). That said, a few military relationships and their transfers are particularly noteworthy. China's exports to Sudan between 2010 and 2013 were enormous: 26,159 units of artillery (at USD 13.6 million), 1450 grenade launchers/flame throwers, over USD 8 million in military rifles/machine guns, 2650 shotguns and 1268 pistols.

Russia has also provided Sudan with many small arms: at least 285 shotguns and 531 rifles in 2010; 222 shotguns, 210 rifles, and 25 "missiles launchers" in 2011; at least 200 shotguns, 89 pistols, and 319 rifles in 2012; and 381 shotguns and 921 rifles in 2013–2014 (NISAT-PRIO Researcher's Database, http://nisat.prio.org/). Between 2010 and 2011, Thailand exported 57 "grenade launchers/flame throwers" (at USD 332,763), 368 pistols/revolvers (over USD 200,000), 84 shotguns, and 594 military rifles/machine guns (at almost USD 2 million) to Sudan.

In Africa, the sources of SALW proliferation are many and varied of international efforts to curb proliferation tend to concentrate on the manufacture and supply of new weapons, a major pipeline of SALW remains the stockpiles that were pumped into Africa in the 1970s, 1980s and early 90s by the ex-Soviet Union, the USA and their allies to fan proxy intra-state and interstate wars. These leftover weapons have found their way through clandestine networks involving rogue arms brokers, private military companies, shady airline companies, and local smugglers to exacerbate on-going conflicts and facilitate the commencement of new ones in the continent (Abdel-Fatau, 2011 cited in Temitope et al. 2018). 80% of SALW in civilian possession were illegally acquired. Out of the 640 million small arms circulating globally, it is estimated that 100 million are found in Africa about 30 million in sub-Saharan Africa and eight million in West Africa, alone (Jekada 2005; Harzen and Horner 2007). The majority of these SALW about 59% are in the hands of civilians, 38% are owned by government armed forces, 2.8% by police and 0.2% by armed groups. The gun trade is worth $ 4 billion annually, of which up to $ 1 billion may be unauthorized or illicit. Eight million new guns are manufactured every year by at least 1249 companies in 92 countries. Ten to 14 billion units of ammunition are manufactured every year enough to kill (Ibrahim 2005). African countries spent over 300 billion dollars on armed conflict between 1990 and 2005, totalling the sum of international aid that was granted to Africa within the same period. An estimated 79% of small arms in Africa are in the hands of civilians (Ibrahim 2005: 122).

CAUSES OF SMALL ARMS PROLIFERATION AND INTRACTABLE CONFLICTS IN AFRICA, AND THE INFLUENCE OF THE MNCs IN THE VALUE CHAIN

No doubt, the causes of small arms proliferation and intractable conflict in Africa arelargely determined by various factors, which are as a result of the end of cold war, porous borders, low cost of SALWs, poverty, marginalization, and unequal distribution of resources, bad governance, and influence of MNCs. As such, the trafficking of small arms in Africa, which eventually are used in conflict situation, cannot be discussed in isolation of these factors. The origin of arms transfer and proliferation in Africa, is traceable to the cold war era, when the international arena was characterized by arms race as a result of ideological contestation between the USA and the USSR. According to Malam (2014), the surplus arms that were provided during the cold war by the two opposing super powers, were pumped to serve proxy interstate conflict. Massive flow of weapons from Central and Eastern Europe and the loosening control of arms multinational industries, as a result of the collapse of Soviet Union, led to arms transfer into Africa. Following the end of cold war, these arms in circulation lost their way into the hands of illegal arms dealers, security entrepreneurs, ethnic militia groups, private military companies, and local smugglers thereby fuelling on-going wars and facilitating the commencement of new ones in Africa.

One of the principal reasons for the easy trafficking and diffusion of these small arms into Africa is the existence of porous and contested borders in Africa. The laxity of Africa borders has constantly led to uncontrollable dumping of various goods including weapons that has only increased the risk of peaceful coexistence in the continent. According to Ngang (2007), due to the sheer size of some of the countries in Africa, the entry points, along with the airports, has been used to smuggle arms into the country. It is also interesting to observe that all the three largest sub-Saharan countries, namely Sudan (the continent's overall largest), the Congo DRC (3rd overall largest) and Chad (5th overall largest) have been experiencing instability and armed conflict for long. It may well be that their size and their porous borders make it easy for weapons to be smuggled inflaming and protracting violence.

Although the poorest countries struggle to afford major weapons, they could easily and affordably acquire small arms. The AK 47 riffle, for example, can be bought in Africa for a bag of maize which is equivalent to about USD 10 (Southall 2002). More so, the ability to buy these arms at a very low cost from MNCs or through other arms traffickers, with easy maintenance and learning process to use them, has made both the military and non-military individuals to desire to possess them. For instance, children involved in child's soldiering in Africa have access to these small arms and subsequently use them during armed conflict. According to Southall (2002), apart from being cheap and easy to manufacture, small weapons are also readily transported, smuggled, and hidden. To further buttress the point, Malam (2014) said, this explains their use by untrained combatants and even child soldiers as it was the case in many armed conflicts in West Africa, Liberia, Sierra Leone, Cote d' Ivoire and now Mali and Nigeria, among others. Small arms are plentiful, cheap, and durable. These weapons are highly desired and profitable commodity and are often sold with little domestic and international regulation by numerous weapons producers, from surplus military stockpiles, and by private arms dealers.

The control, access, and distribution of natural resources has triggered, sustained, or exacerbated conflicts in many resource-rich countries in Africa. Illicit arms have contributed to the escalation and deadliness of such conflicts in recent years. This includes conflicts over hydrocarbons, mineral deposits, or grazing land. For example, illicit arms are a key factor in the militancy and insecurity in the Niger Delta regions of Nigeria, Katanga areas of DRC, and the gold-rich Tibesti region in Northern Chad. In fact, the gold mines in Tibesti have become a theatre of war fuelled primarily by SALW from Ghaddafi-era SALW stockpiles (Tubiana 2016). Similarly, illicit arms have increased the spate of violence clashes and casualties between herders and farmers in Mali and Nigeria, Bororo in CAR, as well as Barara in Chad. In fact, herdsmen in Sudan and South Sudan openly display SALW, and cattle raids, involving the use of SALW, in rural areas of South Sudan led to over 2000 deaths and 34,000 displacements in Pibor in January, 2012 (BBC News 2012). In neighboring Sudan, the conflict in Dafur began in 2003 when opposition groups who accused the government of wilful neglect of the region took up arms against the state. The crisis is driven by a number of issues, including disagreements over resource control, power struggles, problems resulting from inequalities, and perceived marginalization. Furthermore, the presence of oil, and the recent discovery of large gold deposits in the Jebel Amir Hills of North Darfur, have deepened their crisis (Thomson Reuters Foundation News 2014; Sikainga 2009). MNCs have played a significant role in some of the most destructive civil wars of the developing world. From Colombia, Sierra Leone, Angola, the Democratic Republic of Congo, Azerbaijan, to Myanmar, MNC engagement has aggravated conflict and fed pervasive corruption through the extraction of lucrative natural resources, such as oil and natural gas, timber, diamonds, and other precious minerals. The case of Sudan is yet another example where economic development spurred on by MNC activity has had deadly consequences, benefiting but a few in an impoverished population. For the past fifty years, international oil companies have explored the burning coasts and diverse terrain of the Sudan for precious "black gold" amidst harrowing civil war. Mired in conflict since its independence, it comes as no surprise that MNCs would become embroiled in the dynamics of Sudan's second civil war between the central government in Khartoum and the insurgent Sudan People's Liberation Army/Movement (SPLA/M) from the South. Oilfields were heatedly contested areas of strategic control between warring factions and witness to horrendous human rights violations against civilian populations. The activities of MNCs eventually provided Khartoum with a source of revenue to strengthen its brutal military machine (Patey 2007).

More so, increase radicalization and violent extremism has led to small arms race and the use of illicit arms in Africa. For instance, the radical Tuareg Militia and Al-Qaeda in the Islamic Maghreb (AQIM) in northern Mali have initiated and sustained armed insurgencies because they have access to the use of small arms and light weapons. Boko Haram insurgents in Nigeria have since 2012 proved to have weapons that can match the weapons of the military forces in Nigeria. Al-Shabaab and other similar terrorist groups operating across Africa have increasingly sparked up protracted and intractable violence in Africa. This is as a result of their involvement in the use of weapons to achieve their agenda and the readiness of government to tackle terrorism headlong increase the proliferation of small arms and light weapons in the possession of states and non-state actors.

The inability and failure of governments in Africa to provide basic needs of life to the citizens (such as shelter, good infrastructure and affordable food), ensuring security and equitable distribution of public resources, have led to high level of poverty, unemployment, and suffering. This is responsible for the explosion of small arms in the region. To worsen this menace, African government understands the language of violence than peace. For most unprivileged individuals to get their right in the society, they have to resort to violence. The various amnesty programs in some part of Nigeria, for instance, is a pointer that government shares part of the butty to individuals who have decided to take up arms and perpetuate criminal activities such as armed robbery, piracy, kidnapping, militancy and even terrorism. The amnesty programs have further expanded the tendencies of other law-abiding citizens to be tempted toward violence, resort to criminal activities in anticipation of amnesty and further get a good life. This is a case of rewarding evil with good.

The failure of government in most African countries to provide the needed security is a factor that compel citizens to look for an alternative. Studies indicates that, lack of confidence in security forces, understaffing or sometimes simply the inability of security agencies to carry out their duty effectively in many African countries informed the strong need by citizens to acquire arms in order to protect themselves and their properties from armed violence (Malam 2014). A research conducted in Cote d'Ivoire in 2010 shows that, contrary to common assumptions, state security providers do not perform much better than the rebels. Across Cote d'Ivoire, the population lacks confidence in its security forces. The report indicate that, the deficiencies of the security forces combines with the level of insecurity have encouraged the emergence of a wide range of coping mechanisms, including community self-defense and vigilante groups, which in turn create new forms of insecurity (Small Arms Survey 2011).

Consequences of Small Arms Trafficking and Conflict in Africa: The Vicarious Liability of MNCs

Arms trafficking directly undermines development by eroding security. Conflict and insecurity drive displacement and humanitarian crises, delaying human progress (United Nations 2016). Besides the enormous human cost, armed violence diverts funding away from development and damages infrastructure and industries. Governments are forced to spend larger portions of Gross Domestic Product (GDP) on law enforcement and the military rather than on the delivery of special services. They may also have difficulty in providing services if some areas of the country are rendered inaccessible due to violence. In addition, security is a strong driver to capital flight and inhibitor of domestic resources mobilization (May 2017). The interdependence of small arms control, security, and development suggests that no meaningful development can take place in an atmosphere which is conducive to the production and distribution of small arms. It prevents people from conducting business, leading to reduction in trade and foreign investment. In addition, SALW fuels the illicit trafficking of natural resources such as oil, minerals, and timber (Malam 2014).

In West Africa, for instance, a civil war that started with several hundred insurgents in Liberia in 1989 later triggered fighting in neighboring Sierra Leone, Cote d Ivoire, and Guinea; which led to serious proliferation of small and light weapons in the region, used to carry out the wars. It took more than a decade of effort by the international community—principally through arms embargoes and peacekeeping operations—to stem the fighting. The fighting caused widespread death and destruction, triggered huge refugee flows, and undermined development throughout the region. The cost of conflict in Liberia alone was enormous. By the time the war ended in 2003 the USA had spent more than $430 million in Liberia, mostly on food aid. The regional peacekeeping operation, ECOWAS Monitoring Group (ECOMOG), cost more than $4billion. The United Nations Observer Mission, UNOMIL, cost some $104 million from 1993 to September 1997. Also, UN mission, UNMIL, which peaked at approximately 15,000 personnel, cost several billion dollars from 2003 to 2007 (Stohl and Hogendoorn 2010). No doubt, there can never be development in a conflict-ridden atmosphere. This explains why the continent of Africa is still groping in poverty, backwardness, and economic dependency.

The widespread proliferation of small and light weapons increases the potential for violence and violent conflicts in the West African sub-region. According to Adeniyi (2017), uncontrolled arms do not necessarily cause conflict, but they do exacerbate tension and tip the balance toward violent confrontations. Illicit arms reduce the use and effectiveness of dialogue and negotiated settlement of disputes; uncontrolled arms contribute to the choice of violence to settle disputes. The spread of uncontrolled arms increases mutual suspicion and mistrust, encourages retaliatory measures, and worsens social divides and disagreements among different groups. In South Sudan and CAR, for instance, targeted killings with uncontrolled arms have fragmented communities and countries along ethnic, religious, and political lines.

It is safe to state that in the last two decades (1999s–2010s), millions of lives were lost as a direct result of wars in Africa. For instance, during the period 1983–2005 in DRC, Sudan, and Rwanda combined, between 4.3m and 8.4m people lost their lives due to armed conflict (Adeniyi 2017). The civil war in Sierra Leone, for instance, affected human capital and labour supply substantially, especially in rural areas through casualties, injuries, health, and education deterioration and loss of skills (Kondylis 2008). During conflicts, women and children are often at a more disadvantage position, as they become vulnerable to all kinds of risk. For instance, during the Rwanda crisis alone, Ngang (2007) recorded that Tutsi women were raped at gunpoint, many of whom became pregnant and others infected with HIV/AIDS. It is however, difficult to say with precision the number that died as a result of the use of firearms in the Rwandan conflict, but popular records have it that up to one million lives were claimed.

Armed violence and conflict in any part of the world often leave some individuals displaced from their original habitation. In the case of Africa, which has been a hot bed for violent conflict and the incessant quest to acquire weapons to settle scores, the displacement of people is often not a new thing. Countries and regions affected by violence, such as Somalia, South Sudan, Sudan, CAR, DRC, Lake Chad Basin, and Mali, generally record the highest numbers of

Internally Displaced Persons (IDPs) and refugees in Africa. The Boko Haram insurgency that has ravaged the north eastern part of Nigeria has left so many people internally displaced, homeless, jobless, and hopeless.

From the conspiracy theory perspective, the trafficking of small arms and intractable conflict in Africa, has only succeeded in making the continent poorer and underdeveloped; while the transnational arms merchandise constantly smile to the bank. Ironically, what makes others cry, make other smile. Through the logic of the capitalist arms industries in collaboration with other interested MNCs in conflicts, as far as conflict strive in Africa, their business will continue to survive. This is to say that, there is every possibility for these MNCs that are either specialized in arms production or interest in exploiting the resources of Africa, to instigate violence in Africa, in order to get sales from states and non-state actors or continue in their exploitations. More so, the fact that Africa is the highest conflict-ridden continent, it becomes easy for the continent to be a large market for the multinational arms industries.

Conclusion

The trafficking and proliferation of small arms in Africa has continued to fuel the embers of violence and civil unrest at intra and interstate level within the continent. No conflict of any kind is without a cause and consequence. The study has shown that the end of the cold war led to massive trafficking of weapons across other continents of the world including Africa. The large possession of these weapons in the arsenals of the USA and the USSR during the cold war almost became obsolete at the collapse of the Soviet Union, therefore there was a need to sell them rather than keep or destroy them. These have posed serious security challenge on the Africa continent, and by extension, the entire international system due to the constant demand for them for conflict purpose. The structural imbalance within Africa itself encourages the use of small arms. When there is wide gap between the rich and the poor, bad leadership, marginalization, poverty and unemployment, social and economic injustice, religious intolerance and ethnic divides, what one should expect is violence.

More so, when there is violence and the quest to take up arms, there is always a possibility for the external capitalist arms producers/industries to take advantage of the crisis to sell their arms and to make much profits. Unfortunately, the implication is that, these arms industries most times get the backing of their home countries who collaborate with them to sell arms to needy state and non-state actors. These has led to massive loss of lives and properties, displacement of persons from their habitations, and unresolved rivalry between and among opposing parties.

Though there have been various efforts made by international organizations to prevent the issue of illicit trafficking of weapons, it has not really yielded tangible results. Some of these efforts includes United Nations Programme of Action to Prevent, Combat and Eradicate the Illicit Trade in Small Arms and Light Weapons in All Its Aspects; the Bamako Declaration on illicit proliferation, circulation and trafficking of small arms; and the South African Development Community (SADC) Protocol on firearms, ammunition and other related materials. On the other hand, the United Nations which is supposed to ensure the total eradication of illicit trafficking of arms has not been able to prevent the proliferation of small arms in Africa, especially, in the conflict-ridden regions in Africa. This is not far from the fact that the real suppliers of the arms in Africa are "powerful" countries within the UN, especially the "Big Five" that makes up the United Nations Security Council (UNSC). Consequently, this has prevented the United Nations and the UNSC in particular whose responsibility to maintain peace and stability in the international system to address the issue of arms trafficking in Africa specifically.

Therefore, there is a need to find solutions to every internal and external factor that motivate the trafficking and usage of these small arms that have proliferated all over Africa. First, the United Nations, African Union, and regional economic corporations (RECs) must be ready to weigh the big stick on any defaulting nation and the multinationals that violate the declaration against illegal proliferation of small arms. This can be possible when governments within these organizations take a more pro-active measure in adequately monitoring the inflows of weapons, enforcing sanctions on defaulters and not shielding them when found culpable. Secondly, it is very important to address the internal causes of conflict in Africa. African government must be responsible in addressing high level of poverty, marginalization and unequal distribution of resources in the continent; and this can only be possible through good governance and addressing the scourge of corruption in Africa that has degenerated into intractable conflicts in the continent. This is because when conflicts are prevented, there will be no need for arms purchases from any of the producer/supplier nations or their arms brokers. MNCs will only take advantage of situations in any environment to advance their objectives to make profits. Hence, Africa government must work hard and sincerely to ensure fair distribution of their country's national resources, provide basic amenities for the citizens, avoid creating ethnic and religious disharmony among the citizens to gain political interest.

References

Adeniyi, A. (2017). *The Human Cost of Uncontrolled Arms in Africa: Cross-National Research on Seven African Countries*. Oxfam Research Reports. March.

African Union. (2013). *50th Anniversary Solemn Declaration*. *African Union*, Available from: http://agenda2063.au.int/en/documents/50th-anniversary-solemn-declaration (Accessed 10 February 2015).

AfricanSunNews. (2010). "About Wars and Post-War Conflicts" http://www.africasunnews.com/warshtml.

Agaba, H., & Ukhami, E. (2019). *Issues in International Relations*. Abuja: True Image Global Resources, 2nd Edition.
Agbu, O. (2004). *Ethnic Militias and the Threat to Democracy in Post-Transition Nigeria*. Uppsala: Nordiska Afrikainstitutet Khadiagala.
Alli, W. O. (2007). "The Impact of Globalization on Conflicts in Africa" in Best, S. G., (ed); *Introduction to Peace and Conflict Studies in West Africa*. Ibadan, Spectrum Books Limited.
Amnesty International. (2002a). *The Arab Convention for the Suppression of Terrorism a Serious Threat to Human Rights*. http://web.amnesty.org/library/print/ENG 10RS510012002Dateofaccess?.
Amnesty International. (2002b). *The Terror Trade Times*. www.amnesty.org Date of access?
Amnesty International. (2014). *UN: Final Push Will Bring Landmark Arms Trade Treaty into Force*. http://www.amnesty.org/en/news/un-final-push-will-bring-lan dmark-arms-trade-treaty-force, June 2.
Azar, E. (1983). "The Theory of Protracted Social Conflict and the Challenge of Transforming Conflict Situations," in Zinnes, A.D (ed.) *Conflict and the Breakdown of International Systems*. Denver, CO: University of Colorado.
Azar, E. E. (1985). *Protracted International Conflicts: Ten Propositions. International Interactions, 12*, 59–70.
Azar, E. E. (1990). *The Management of Protracted Social Conflict*. Hampshire, UK: Dartmouth.
Bahati, J. (2009). *Impact of Small Arms Proliferation on Africa*. Washington: AFJN.
Bakut tswak, B. (2007). "The Environment, Peace and Conflict in Africa," in Best, S.G. (Ed.) *Introduction to Peace and Conflict Studies in West Africa*. Ibadan: Spectrum Books Limited.
Barkindo, B., Omolewa, M., & Babalola, G. (1994). *Africa and the Wider World*. Nigeria: Longman Nig. PLC.
Bar-Tal, D. (1998). Societal Beliefs in Times of Intractable Conflict: The Israeli Case. *International Journal of Conflict Management, 9*, 22–50.
BBC News. (2012). *South Sudan Horror at Deadly Cattle Vendetta*. January 16. http://www.bbc.co.uk/news/world-africa-16575153, accessed 13 June 2016.
Boutwell, J., & Klare, M. (2000). *A Scourge of Small Arms*. Cambridge: American Academy of Arts and Social Sciences.
Broga, D. (2016). *Loaded Guns, Smoking Barrels and the Proliferation of Arms in South Sudan*, Iguacu, February 22, http://weareiguacu.com/the-proliferation-of-arms-in-south-sudan/.
Cooper, N. (1999). "The Arms Trade and Militarized Actors in Internal Conflict," in Rich, B.P (ed.). *Warlords in International Relations*. London: Macmillan Press Ltd.
Crocker, C., Hampson, F., & Aall, P. (2005). *Grasping the Nettle: Analyzing Cases of Intractable Conflict*. Washington, D.C.: Institute of Peace Press.
ECOWAS. (2006). *Convention on Small Arms and Light Weapons, their Ammunition and Other Related Materials*. Chapter 1, Article 1 (2), Abuja: June 12.
Enuka, C (2012). "Small Arms Proliferation and Armed Conflicts in Africa: The Case of Rwandan Conflict." *Khazar Journal of Humanities and Social Science*, Nnamdi Azikiwe University, Awka.
Francis, D. J. (2006). *Uniting Africa: Building Regional Peace and Security Systems*. Hampshire: Ashgate Publishing Limited.

Global Envision. (2007, October 11). *War Costs Africa $18bn Annually*. http://www.globalenvision.org/library/3/1778.
Graaf, J. H (1997). Proliferation of Light Weapons in Africa. *Policy Science*, Vol.30, No.3, Springer, https://www.jstor.org/stable/4532407.
Gurr, T. R. (1970). *Why Men Rebel*. Princeton, NJ: Princeton University Press.
Harzen, J., & Horner, J. (2007). "Small Arms, Armed Violence, and Insecurity: The Niger Delta in Perspective." *Occasional Paper*. No. 20 Geneva.
Ibrahim, S. (2005). *Combating the Proliferation of Small Arms and Light Weapons in West Africa*. UN: Handbook for the Training of Armed and Security Forces.
Institute for Peace and Justice. (2005). Peace and Justice. *Update*, 11(1), 1–12.
Jekada, E. K. (2005). *Proliferation of Small Arms and Ethnic Conflicts in Nigeria: Implication for National Security*. Dissertation for the award of the degree of Doctor of Philosophy in International Relations and Strategic Studies, St. Clements University.
Kelvin, L. (2007). *Light Weapons and Intrastate Conflict: Early Warning Factors and Preventive Action*, http://www.unidir.org/pdf/articles.pdf. Retrieved on 18-12-2015.
Khadiagala, G. M. (2006). *Security Dynamics in Africa's Great Lake's Region*. Lynne Rienner Publishers.
Kriesberg, L. (1998). Intractable Conflicts. In E. Weiner (Ed.), *The Handbook of Interethnic Coexistence*. New York: Continuum.
Kriesberg, L. (2007). "Intractable Conflicts, Peace Review," *A Journal of Social Justice*, 5(4), Online: https://doi.org/10.1080/10402659308425753.
Malam, B. (2014). Small Arms and Light Weapons Proliferation and Its Implication for West African Regional Security. *International Journal of Humanities and Social Science*, 4(8).
Marx, K., & Engels, F. (1977). *Manifesto of the Communist Party*. Moscow: Progress.
May, C. (2017). *Transnational Crime and the Developing World*. Global Financial Integrity.
McCullum, H. (2016). "Small Arms: The World's Favourite Weapons of Mass Destruction." *AfricaFiles, At Issue Ezine*, 5.
McKinney, C. (2001). *House of Representatives*. Committee on International Relations, Washington, DC: Subcommittee on International Operations and Human Rights.
Ngang, C. (2007). *Small Arms and Light Weapons: The Role of Small Arms and Light Weapons in Conflict and Security in Sub-Saharan Africa*. Austria: EUCPS.
Nganga, F. (2008). *Effects of Proliferation of Small Arms in Sub-Sahara Africa*. Strategy Research Project.
Nnoli, O. (2003). *Communal Conflict and Population Displacement: An Introduction*. Enugu: PACREP.
Odinka, G. E., Ekok, O. C., Emeka, J. O., & Achu, A. A. (2012). Curbing Multidimensional Violence in Nigeria Society: Causes, Solutions and Methods of Solving This Trend. *Journal of Emerging Trends in Educational Research and Policy Studies (JETERAPS)*, 3(5), 616–623.
Onwurah, C. P., & Usman, H. A. (2016). Globalisation and Multinational Corporations in Africa. In U. A. Tar, E. B. Mijah, & M. E. U. Tedheke (Eds.), *Globalization in Africa: Perspectives on Development, Security and the Environment*. Lanham, MD: Lexington Books.
Patey, A.L. (2007). State Rule: Oil Companies and Armed Conflict in Sudan. *Third World Quarterly*, 28(5), Global Policy Forum.

Rawls, J. (1971). *Theory of Social Justice*. Cambridge: Oxford University Press.
Saleh, D. (2010). *Essentials of International Relations*. Kaduna: Mafolayomi Press Limited.
Sikainga, A. (2009). *The World's Worst Humanitarian Crisis: Understanding the Darfur Conflict*. http://origins.osu.edu/article/worlds-worst-humanitarian-crisis-understanding-darfur-conflict.
Singh, J. (1998). Illicit Trafficking in Small Arms: Some Issues and Aspects. In G. P. Alves (Ed.), *Curbing Illicit Trafficking in Small Arms and Sensitive Technologies: An Action-Oriented Agenda*. Geneva: United Nations Institute for Disarmament Research.
Small Arms Survey. (2009, December). *Supply and Demand—Arms Flows and Holdings in Sudan*.
Small Arms Survey. (2011). *Shadow of War*. Cambridge: Cambridge University Press.
Southall, D. P (2002). *Empty Arms: The Effect of the Arms Trade on Mothers and Children*, BMJ Publishing Group.
Spero, J. E. (1980). *The Politics of International Economic Relations*. London: George Allen and Unwin.
Stohl, R., & Hogendoorn, EJ. (2010). *Stopping the Destructive Spread of Small Arms: How Small Arms and Light Weapons Proliferation Undermines Security and Development*. Centre for American Progress.
Temitope, A. F., Onafowora, O., & Nwannenaya, C. (2018, September). Small Arms and Light Weapons Proliferation and Its Threats to Nigeria's Internal Security. *International Journal of Social Science and Humanities Research*, 6(3). www.researchpublish.com.
Thomson Reuters Foundation News. (2014). *Darfur Conflict*. July 31. http://news.trust.org//spotlight/Darfur-conflict.
Tubiana, J. (2016). *After Libya, a Rush for Gold and Guns: Letter from Aouzou*. Foreign Affairs, https://www.foreignaffairs.com/print/1116879.
United Nations. (2006). *Crush the Illicit Trade in Small Arms, United Nations Conference to Review Progress made in the Implementation of the Programme of Action to Prevent, Combat and Eradicate the Illicit Trade in Small Arms and Light Weapons in all its Aspects*. New York, 26 June–7 July.
United Nations. (2016). "Sustainable Development Knowledge Platform: Goal 16," *United Nations*, accessed September 25, https://sustainabledevelopment.un.org/.
United Nations Security Council. (2008). *From the Chairman of the Security Council Committee in Pursuant to Resolution 1533 (2004) concerning the Democratic Republic of the Congo Addressed to the President of the Security Council*, December 12.
Vallacher, R.R., Coleman, T.P., Nowak, A., & Bui-Wrzosinska, L (2010). "Rethinking Intractable Conflict: The Perspective of Dynamical Systems," *American Psychological Association*. PubMed, Onine: https://www.researchgate.net/publication/44585600.
Vickers, M. (2000). *Ethnicity and Sub-Nationalism in Nigeria: Movement for a Mid-West State*. Oxford: Worldview Publishers.

Emmanuel Ukhami is a candidate for Ph.D. in Defence and Strategic Studies at the Nigerian Defence Academy, Kaduna. He has authored and co-authored books, several journal articles and book chapters in Nigeria and overseas. His major area of research interest includes international politics, security, defence and strategic studies.

Lassana Doumbia is an Army Senior Colonel in Malian Armed Forces, Director General of National Early Warning and Response Center, Mali. He served as Defense Attache in the Embassy of Mali in Abuja, Nigeria, Head of military and security staffs to the Prime minister, consultant for various national and international think tanks, lectures at various institutions and a private University (Sup'Management) in Mali and participated in local and international conferences, seminars, workshops and dialogues. He also participated in the redaction on national DDR strategy. His research interests cut across irregular threats (insurgency, organized crime and terrorism), international relations, security, cooperation and integration. He is a member of scholarly bodies.

CHAPTER 29

Private Security Companies and the Proliferation of Small Arms and Light Weapons in Africa

Jonathan S. Maiangwa and Usman A. Tar

Introduction

Africa is seen as continent of 'anarchy' by the outside world. Abrahamsen (2005), Abrahamsen and Williams (2005) and Abubakar (2017) supported the view as they viewed the postcolonial state with pessimism and argued that it is characterized by political violence; structural imbalances, inequity, social injustices, underdevelopment, corruption and electoral malpractices. The rise in communal, ethnic and regional wars, inter and intra-state armed conflicts, herdsmen-farmers' conflict, terrorism and separatist movements are apt descriptions of the postcolonial state which also fits into the weak state paradigm. The conspicuous failures have, in many contexts, overshadowed the modest achievements attained after independence by many African countries.

A study conducted by the Institute of Security Studies (ISS) in 2011 indicates that most wars in Africa are facilitated by the abuse of small arms and unregulated activities of Private Security Companies (PSCs). Lack of regulations or limited laws against private security firms in some countries has given impetus to 'war merchants' (including governments in some developed countries) and war lords to develop further interest in Africa where laws are flouted and impunity is at its peak. On this premise, the PSCs take

J. S. Maiangwa (✉)
Department of Political Science, University of Maiduguri, Maiduguri, Nigeria

U. A. Tar
Nigerian Defence Academy, Kaduna, Nigeria
e-mail: uatar@nda.edu.ng

© The Author(s), under exclusive license to Springer Nature Switzerland AG 2021
U. A. Tar and C. P. Onwurah (eds.), *The Palgrave Handbook of Small Arms and Conflicts in Africa*,
https://doi.org/10.1007/978-3-030-62183-4_29

undue advantage of governments' insensitivity and lack of measures just to promote their arms trade transactions with both rebels and national armies. This usually happens in circumstances where there are crises and threats to foreign personnel, businesses or national government.

The complex nature of security situation in Africa and the incomprehensive ways in which most states deal with them give no choice for multinational corporations, humanitarian organizations and high-profile individuals to turn to the PSCs for support and defence (Bryden 2006; Crawford 2006; Isima 2009). Scholarly argument in this direction holds that effective and reliable security system is gradually being provided by the private security firms. Foaleng (2007) for example, argued that the PSCs have undergone a rapid growth, because of their capacity to provide guards and police-type security services and is now outnumbering national police forces in some countries.

It is worth noting that PSCs are not only found in developing countries. As their numbers keep growing in the developed countries in the same manner they kept spreading to other parts of the world and building strong connections with the host communities and political elites to facilitate their activities (Barstow 2004; Zarate 1998). Critiques pointed out that in countries where PSCs are prominent, domestic legislation to regulate them are either not available or weak because of certain privileges they enjoy from the elites (Fallah 2007; Gumedze 2007). This may account for their reckless behaviours and criticism of governments that appear not to have been friendly to them. This chapter argues that PSCs are alternative security providers and partly channels through which small arms and light weapons (SALWs) proliferate in Africa. Since the Cold War era, Africa has been the final destination for arms transfer and shipments from the developed world and the scale doubled in the post-Cold War period as a result of burgeoning number of conflicts and increased interest of arms manufacturers, suppliers and defence contractors in the continent. With the swollen numbers of foreign direct investments in Africa, the claims by the multinational corporations and foreign governments over inadequate security for expatriates and their investments dominate African security discourses (Kasali 2011). The situation inadvertently exacerbates anxiety and attention over African security after the 9/11 attacks in the United States (US). However, the thought to promote peace, security and stability in Africa by the international community exerts pressure on the postcolonial states that many African countries embarked on security reforms which culminate into security privatization and security outsourcing with disturbing consequences on African security system (Abrahamsen and Williams 2005; Krahmann 2010).

Furthermore, this chapter argues that PSCs, criminal gangs, militia and terrorist groups are all users of SALWs which simply means that each user has a unique potential of constituting security threat to countries in Africa. Regional groups and the international community have taken this menace very seriously in recent time. The Economic Community of West African States (ECOWAS) security mechanism signed the 1999 Protocol relating to the Mechanism for Conflict Prevention, Resolution, Management, Peacekeeping and Security, it further developed ECOWAS Convention on Small Arms and Light Weapons, Ammunitions and other related materials (Conference ECOWAS Convention on Small Arms and Light Weapons 2006). The Southern Africa Development Community (SADC), Intergovernmental Authority on Development (IGAD), the Economic Community of Central African States (ECCA) and the Arab Maghreb Union (AMU) have all made efforts to tackle SALWs as well as evolved mechanisms to stop the proliferation in their respective regions. The dexterity by the regional organizations has spurred the utilization of the security mechanisms in varying degrees to manage the outbreak of conflicts and spread of SALWs in different countries in Africa. At the level of the United Nations (UN) a Coordinating Action on Small Arms (CASA), centered in the Department of Disarmament Affairs, was created in August 1998 to facilitate and harmonize relevant actions among UN agencies responsible for humanitarian affairs, refugee relief and peacekeeping. Meanwhile it is important to inquire the type of alternative security PSCs provide to Africa. What is the significance of this to African security system? What are the challenges posed by SALW proliferation to African peace? How will the menace of SALW proliferation be checked and tackled in the light of increasing insecurity in African countries? In view of the foregoing this chapter explores the nature of security threats posed to Africa and the involvement of PSCs, security vacuum assumed to be filled by PSCs and how to deal with the menace of SALW in the continent (Olaniyan 2010). Finally, we offer suggestions on how to improve security situation in Africa and reduce the proliferation of SALWs.

Conceptualization of Private Security Companies (PSC) and SALWs

Private Security Companies (PSCs): These are private firms that provide different kinds of services such as intelligence, logistics, support services (supplying of food and arms to the military in war front, and provide escort to humanitarian supplies) protection of facilities, equipment, organizations, institutions or business premises. Other duties include; provision of defence and assistance to humanitarian organizations, provision of security to high-profile individuals such as UN envoys, governments or their representatives. Strom et al. (2010), observed further that PSCs also offer protection to critical infrastructure systems, including industries, utilities, transportation, health and educational facilities. We are also careful in this chapter not to mix up the role of Private Military Security Companies (PMSCs) and PSCs, although sometimes their activities are intertwined as they largely represent an entity (see also, Bryden 2006; Percy 2012). On the other hand, while the latter is concerned with security services the former focuses on combat and sophisticated military operations such as-equipment, training, combat, etc.

Small Arms and Light Weapons (SALWs): These are destructive weapons, hand held fire arms and dangerous devices or apparatuses generally used by anyone who has knowledge or has received some form of military training on how to operate them. SALWs are not limited to security personnel or the military as highlighted above, civilian populations are now large users; most common among militias, terrorists, criminal gangs and individuals. They also use for personal protection and defence. Small arms includes; assault rifles, revolver arms, explosive devices, hand grenades, etc., while light weapons includes; light machine guns, anti-personnel landmines, rockets launchers, missile guided launchers, mortars, shoulder rocket, bombs, anti-tank and anti-aircraft cannons, etc. In their writing, Caleb and Gerald (2015) described SALWs to include: Tokarev TT pistols, Makarov PM Pistols, AR-70 assault rifles (Baretta, Italy), Type 64 assault rifle (Japan), AKM-47 assault rifle (Kalashnikov), General Purpose Machine Guns, (GPMG), Light Machine Guns (UK 59; Rochot Czech), AK-47 under barrel grenade launchers, RPG-42 hand grenades (Soviet), F-1 hand grenades (Soviet), Dynamites explosives (nitropil, dynamite and plastic) and electronic remote detonation devices.

The Evolution and Efflorescence of PSCs in Africa

Scholars have argued that the early period of Post independent Africa was characterized by political instability, military coups and counter coups as well as civil unrest which manifest as banality of power and cult of the 'big man' in African politics (Murithi 2008; Christopher 2006; Reno 1997). The period that later followed was also filled with the overarching success of democracy which has its peculiar challenges; poor governance, corruption, ethno-religious rivalries, terrorism, separatist movements, etc. In the midst of these challenges, military and civilian leaders in many African countries realized the weaknesses of their security arrangements and the enormous threat to their countries both internally and externally (Tar and Bala forthcoming). As a result of that, most leaders resorted to seek for outside help and assistance mainly from private security firms. It is argued that PSCs involvement in African conflicts has been by invitation especially by failed states (Ndlovu-Gatsheni 2007). It is argued that the superior military capability of these companies could have a better impact on the political and security environment of weak countries, which according to Shearer (1998: 9) can stabilize a crisis and coerce a negotiated settlement between government and belligerents. The criticism is that most leaders in some countries are more concerned with their personal safety and how to retain political power instead of the welfare of their citizens. For the sake of their survival they rely on external collaboration with security firms and to some extent prefer them over their security forces. As a result of this, PSCs began to infiltrate weak African states on the pretext of investment and partnership while on the contrary some are agents of developed countries such as the United States and Western Europe (Reno 1997; Crawford 2006; Gatsheni 2007).

In another related development, frequent coups and counter coups in Africa contributed immensely in the evolution and flourishing of PSCs in the continent (Maiangwa forthcoming; Percy 2012). Suspicion and rivalries among political leaders and military leaders' and vice versa eroded trust and created conditions of enmity among the elite groups which increased reliance by both individuals and corporate organizations on private security firms for personal safety. Against this, serious push by governments yielded positive results for the PSCs where they began to be trusted more than the national armies especially by countries constantly affected by unexpected and sudden conflicts, like Angola, Burundi and Congo DR.

Again, it must be noted that countries such as Angola, Mozambique, Liberia, Sierra Leone, Cote d Ivore, Nigeria, Equatorial Guinea, South Sudan and Mali have witnessed the concentration of PSCs in the last couple of years. The PSCs which are described as 'soldiers of fortunes' have established deep root in some of these countries as a result of weak government and institutions. Scholars also argued the growth of PSCs within the context of the Iraqi war where the United States' troops were seen doing less than the PSCs and PMCs (Baker 2011). Because of over saturation in Iraq and Afghanistan some of the PSCs which already have networks in Africa relocated to crisis zones in the continent in order to strengthen their activities and re-affirm the position of their companies which were already successful. A closer look at the growth of the PSCs in Africa reveals that most have a strong attraction to the continent's natural resources and link to poor leadership or unstable regimes as argued by Foaleng (2007) and Ndung'u (2011). Following the wars in Angola, Sierra Leone, Somalia, Congo DR and Mali, PSCs were seen performing most of the security tasks in these countries which also helped to provide stability as well as offer legitimacy to the governments. This is counted as great achievements for the PSCs where they are seen providing stability in conflict ravaged countries. There is no dispute with this, but the most disturbing is where governments completely relinquished the security of their nations to the private security firms and permit them to perform the overall security task of their states (Christopher 2006) and being active in extractive industries.

ARE PSCs ALTERNATIVE SECURITY PROVIDERS?

The US military has a long tradition of utilizing the services of private security companies especially in foreign operations. Zamparelli (1999) observed that, there were over 80,000 private contractors at one time supporting the US military in the Vietnam War, when the military was at Cold War strength. Also, in Afghanistan and Iraq the numbers of US security contractors increased as a result of massive recruitments of immigrant workers searching for job and willing to offer any kinds of services. The most worrisome is that most of them are Africans with military background.

Numerous security contractors have performed diverse tasks which we highlighted in the previous section. Also, in the introductory section of the chapter we sought to find out the type of alternative security the PSCs provide and its significance to African security system. By the way, globalization has reduced the world into a small community that every country is interested in what is happening in other parts of the world once it is assumed to have negative implications on internal affairs of others or the international community. Security generally has become an area of global interest as we can see in the American Global War on terror (GWOT). Africa in recent time is recognized as major scene of GWOT (Mben and Puh 2013). Thus, global focus on Africa is huge as the security concern of the continent continues to increase and attract global attention. Almost everyone in Africa is assumed to be a potential terrorist. With such misgiving and focus on Africa, the presence of defence contractors in Africa doing intelligence gathering, military training, surveillance and reconnaissance increased astronomically after 9/11 (Maiangwa forthcoming).

It is imperative to note that all failed and weak states in Africa relied on alternative security measures offer by defence contractors (Bala and Tar 2020; Maiangwa forthcoming; Tar and Bala forthcoming). PSCs have developed in a very rapid manner that they gain access to political affairs of many countries. Many countries rely on them for their personal security while others look upon them to contain militias and terrorists in their territories. In order to curb the threat and menace of terrorists and militias most governments prefer to outsource the security of their countries to the PSCs whom they describe as reliable, well coordinated and cost effective.

Once more, the use of sophisticated weapons, advanced tactical maneuvers and strategic defence systems which also include the capacity to rapidly deploy destructive weapons with precision by terrorists have forced governments in threatened zones to engage the PSCs. Governments engage the PSCs to provide specialized training for their security forces on counterterrorism and counterinsurgency. It is observed that PSCs have been responsible for intelligence gathering, recruitment into regular armies as well as providing advisory role for armies in countries like Nigeria, Mali and Niger. Recently, defence contractors have been prominent in providing specialized training to members of the Nigerian armed forces to counter the Boko Haram insurgency in northeast Nigeria. Gumedze (2007) contained that PSCs have directly been involved in combat operations in many countries rather than serving as panacea which is assumed to be their cardinal goal, and have thus contributed in small measure to the political destabilization and creation of complex security situation in their host communities.

On the other hand, in South Africa, Raenette (2008) and Smith (2015) stressed that the PSCs have been working in collaboration with the Police force to arrest criminals. Externally South Africa was the largest supplier of PSCs/PMSCs to the US troops in Iraq during the US and allied invasion of Iraq (2003–2010). As such the South African Ministry of Foreign Affairs estimated that 10,000 South Africans, mostly former police officers and soldiers, have been recruited to work in Iraq (*Los Angeles Times* 2007). Gumedze (2007) observed that the recruitment of South Africans by PSCs continues especially because of the expertise that former South African Defence Force

(SADF) members have in security/military-related matters. They used their expertise to earn a living not minding the risk involved especially in a volatile place like Iraq. Messner (2007) observed that the private sector is increasingly utilized to make operations more capable and cost effective, thus reducing the required size-and problems-of interventions.

CHALLENGES OF PSCs AND THREATS OF SMALL ARMS AND LIGHT WEAPONS TO PEACE IN AFRICA

There is no doubt that many actors are involved in protracted conflicts in Africa and, as such, most negotiations on peace settlements produced little result. Disarmament, demobilization and reintegration as post-conflict measures also suffers major setback in many regions because of third party involvement. Somalia, for example provides a good case study of the multiples of actors with diverse interest in regional conflict. PSCs as one of the active actors in African conflicts posed significant security and economic threat to African security and peace. Scholars also argue that autocratic leaders are fond of using PSCs to thwart democratic stability in their countries (Shearer 1998; Viljoen 2007). For example, some leaders at the verge of losing election or after losing election resort to a form of hanky-panky game by engaging the private security firms to intervene in the political affairs of their nation or the national military to destabilize peace in their countries. Cote d'Ivoire under Lawrence Gbagbo and Burundi under Pierre Nkurinziza are clear cases where after the conduct of the 2017 election the latter was reported to have armed some militias (political supporters) alongside the national armies to disperse protesters and attacked opposition leaders using maximum force. The logic behind the strategy was to create instability which will in turn provide opportunity for PSCs's intervention. In Equatorial Guinea it was reported that the defunct Executive Outcome played a crucial role in the coup plot that aimed to topple President Teodoro Obiang Nguema. The main idea behind this was to seize the oil rich of the country, prevent opposition groups and allow foreign companies to operate with less restriction. As we look further Gumedze (2007) identified the challenges to peace in Africa by private security firms from the following points: (with additional information).

1. *Threat to state security*: The presence of PSCs in any country generally is likely to pose a grave danger to such country. For instance, their continue access to critical national security information is a source of danger to the survival of the host country given the fact that information acquired from legitimate activities can be traded with rebels, enemy countries or both.
2. *Involvement in extractive industries which leads to economic exploitation*: in almost every parts of Africa where foreign investment is established PSCs presence are inevitable. For example, Executive Outcome and G4S have significant presence in Angola oil industry, Control Risks and G4S

security companies are very much active in the Niger Delta area in Nigeria.
3. *The pursuit of the agenda and interests of foreign states (powers)*. Their use in disarmament, demobilization and reintegration (DDR) is usually for the interest of their sponsors.
4. *The training of national armies and security forces* e.g. the operation of DynCorp International (US security firm) in Nigeria, Liberia and Sudan.
5. *Unregulated recruitments of African citizens* to serve in their rank in conflict zones like host of Liberian and Sierra Leonean war veterans were recruited PSCs to serve in Iraq and Afghanistan in 2005–2007.
6. *Lack of effective regulatory framework* for their operations in Africa.

During the Cold War era there was great uncertainty in Africa as the two power blocs—the United States and Soviet Union continued to fight proxy wars in developing countries. These superpowers armed both governments and militia groups and deliberately intervened in internal conflict of states. During the long Angolan war, for example the MPLA and UNITA received arm support and training from the two super powers through their agents, the same happened in Liberia where PSCs were accused by the international community of providing protection to rebels in the rich diamond region. Post-colonial Congo DR provide us with another clear example where intervention by major and regional powers caused the plunder of the mineral resources of the country for years unabated. Generally, the activities of PSCs in most crises zones are responsible for the outpouring of small arms and illegal use of weapons against civilian population. Criminal gangs, militias and terrorist organizations are beneficiaries of arms transfer and training from the private security firms who are largely agents of governments from developed countries. In the Niger Delta region of Nigeria, for example for over a decade, communities have continued to experience environmental degradation as a result of pipeline vandalism caused by the activities of militants who received arms in exchange for crude oil from oil thieves. These criminal gangs station their large cargo ships in the deep sea water where stolen crude oil from smaller vessels is transferred into them sometimes under the watchful eyes of the Nigerian security officials (Akinleye 2013). This throw open the debate on whether the state and its officials are neutral in the crime in the Niger Delta. It is estimated that oil thieves steal roughly 20% (or some 400,000 barrels daily) of the nation's crude oil by way of this dangerous practice (Akinleye 2013). The frequency of oil theft is confirmed by the fact that in November 2012, Shell—which produces approximately 40% of all Nigeria's crude oil—shut down one of its pipelines in the Niger Delta after finding six points of theft on its Imo River trunk line (Maiangwa and Agbiboa 2013).

Similarly, the increasing rise in violent insurgencies and transnational crimes are caused by the proliferation of small arms. North Africa has been the major corridors of arms trafficking to the West African region while the Horn of Africa services the Great Lakes region and Southern Africa region. It is argued in many quarters that the increasing wave of Boko Haram attacks in northeast Nigeria and around the Lake Chad basin as well as other terrorist activities in the Sahel region is caused by large cache of weapons that found their way into the regions from North Africa in the wake of the Arab Spring of 2011. Similarly, in Central African Republic the destructive war between Saleka movement and Anti-balaka was greased by SALW used by militias in Libya and Tunisia. Since the use of small arms is not limited to non-state actors many governments in Africa have given defence budget much priority rather than other critical sectors of their economy which would have improved the living condition of their people.

Even though arms procurement is generally advantageous to countries in the north and hampering human capital development in the southern hemisphere, governments in the south would rather spend more to protect their regime instead of investing the teaming populations. There is no clear figure of how much is spent on arm procurement yearly by African countries in any case. However, a survey conducted between 1990 and 2005 gave an approximation of $300 billion (Schnabel 2008). The survey also confirmed that the continent looses almost 15% of its annual Gross Domestic Product (GDP) to conflicts that are fuelled and sustained by SALWs.

With the deteriorating political and security situation in African regions in the post-Cold War era the misuse of small arms continued to cause high death toll, humanitarian catastrophe, population displacement and undermine the security of nations. Most of the world number of deaths are caused by small arms. This is simply because of the low cost and portability of these weapons which are used by all. A hypothesis was made that if 200,000 people are killed per year around the world in 'combat', a reasonable assumption on average during the 1990s, based on the above assumptions, is that 90,000 of them would be civilians killed by small arms and light weapons—nearly four times the estimated landmine casualty rate. The International Committee of the Red Cross (ICRC) estimated that 24,000 people are killed or maimed per year by anti-personnel landmines.

Efforts to Curtail the Menace of SALWS Proliferation in Africa

There are three issues to note in this section: one is that as long as conflicts in developing countries persist, arms supply and shipment will not cease. The second is that the participation of private security companies and mercenaries in African conflicts and security exposes the underbelly of SALWs proliferation by these private security service providers who enjoy a complex network of access to, and diversion of, SALWs in expanding their market and client base. In other words, hiring private security companies and mercenaries could open the flood gate for mass importation of SALWs into African states, thus exacerbating the volume and intensities of conflicts in the continent. Thirdly, prominent manufacturers of arms such as Austria, Belgium, Brazil, Bulgaria,

China, Egypt, France, Germany, Israel, Poland, Romania, Russia, Singapore, South Africa, the United Kingdom, and the United States take up arms production and supply as permanent investment to boost their Gross National Product (GNP) and the enthusiasm to undermine any collective initiative against arms transfer is always exercised by them. This is so clear that their support for PSCs remains unwavering as the supply line continues to persist. It is still doubtful whether countries have implemented the UN arms embargo initiatives of the 1990s and the 2013 measures which text reminded states to take measures against any activity that was in violation of embargoes, including by cooperating with all relevant United Nations entities; making available to sanctions committees all pertinent information on alleged violations and acting on credible information to prevent the supply, sale, transfer or export of small arms and light weapons in contravention of Council embargoes (Security Council resolution 2117 [2013]).

Nevertheless, the UN Security Council document called on States subject to enforce embargoes, including by avoiding the diversion of State-owned or controlled weapons; by enhancing stockpile security and management; and by implementing national weapons-marking programmes, in line with the International Tracing Instrument. It reiterated that United Nations peacekeepers in a country or region subject to a Council-mandated arms embargo could assist the host Government, sanctions committee and relevant experts' group with the implementation and monitoring of compliance with the embargo (Security Council 7036th Meeting 2013).

And because governments are not open about their light weapons sales and shipments to countries confronting security challenges, curbing SALWs has been a difficult task even among UN members. Moreover only few countries expressed interest in curbing SALWs. Sometimes this remains a mere paper work. Most developed countries are yet to demonstrate enthusiasm to curtail arms production and transfer in spite of NGOs (ICRC, International human rights, Amnesty International) collaboration and pressure to curb the spread of military armed equipment after the terrorist attack of 2001 in the United States (Juma 2011). In 1998 at the United Nations Security Council a convincing proposition was made by the United States on SALWs that: States should provide 'full and timely' disclosure of arms shipments into African 'zones of conflict', and they should enact a voluntary moratorium on arms sales 'that could fuel these interconnected conflicts' (http://www.secretary.state.gov/www/statements/1998/). It was further highlighted that:

1. Governments, international governmental organizations, and NGOs should meet to exchange information on regional arms transfers and 'to explore further steps'.
2. UN member-states with relevant expertise should help strengthen the capacity of African governments to monitor and interdict arms flows.

3. The UN should establish a clearinghouse for technical information to facilitate rapid exchange of data on possible violations of UNSC-mandated arms embargoes.
4. All states should enact national legislation regulating exports and making violation of UNSC-mandated embargoes a criminal offense.
5. States should negotiate a global convention against illicit arms trafficking by the year 2000.
6. States should negotiate an agreement 'to restrict' the export of shoulder-fired missiles by the year 2000.
7. States should establish 'an international center to collect and share information on arms transfers' (http://www.secretary.state.gov/www/statements/1998/).

One crucial area that the UN member states have consistently worked upon which is directly related to curbing small arms and violence is sustainable development initiative which is part of the Millennium Development Goals (MDGs). It was realized that when there is an improvement in standard of living of any country the rate at which the citizens will antagonize the government will automatically reduce. In addition, increasing development aid to crises zones was partly identified as a cardinal strategy to curb the spread of incessant conflict which has worked out in many countries. For example, Botswana, post-conflict Rwanda and Sierra Leone received support from donor agencies and governments in millions of dollars to rebuild their nations after the wars. Financial and technical assistance have been used to facilitate the demobilization and reintegration of combatants which paid off as peace has since returned to those countries.

In Africa, efforts by regional organizations (such as ECOWAS, SADC and IGAD) to control the spread of SALWs for years yielded insignificant result as the rush to acquire modern weapons in order to fight violent extremism and oppositions preoccupies the minds of many governments. On the other hand, states on their own have ratified certain agreements, passed legislation defining legal and illegal arms importation and exportation, establish effective control mechanisms, and develop a central contact agency on the issue of fire arms. This has worked out for some considering the reduction of arm purchases which generally shows a drop in defence expenditure in many countries in 2008 and 2009. Meanwhile the most difficult aspect of small arms proliferation within a country is the aspect of weapons in circulation especially from the armory store of security forces. On different account security officials have been accused of complicity and collusion with criminals and militias where they trade fire arms for money. Another means by which arms spread in Africa and constitute a menace to Africa security is lack of drastic measures by governments to take responsibility to truly combat subversion and regulate the activities of PSCs.

Conclusion

This chapter described the intricate nexus between PSCs and the proliferation of SALWs in Africa—this is in the context of weak, contested and collapsing states where elites engage the services of PSCs to ensure regime security and undue advantage in electoral contest. The chapter reveals that PSCs have become preponderant players of national and regional security in Africa (see, Bala and Tar 2020). Thus, we argued that Africa's weak states have largely lost the exclusive monopoly of the use of force, and have to therefore seek partnership with PSCs (Gatsheni 2007; Reno 1997). However, as sovereign entities, African states have not totally relinquished the security space (Crawford 2006; Percy 2012). PSCs constitute both a supporting pillar, and a liability to weak states of Africa: they may serve as the informant and agents of their home states, while some engage in anti-state activities and profiteering, including engaging in the arms trade (Kasali 2011; Bearpark and Schulz 2007). With regard to SALWs, the chapter has revealed that the inflow of small arms have exacerbated the precipitous scenarios in conflict-prone and war-torn countries of Africa.

There are great lessons to be learnt from the explanations and arguments presented most importantly that Africa has been reduced to a battle field where weapons are used by combatants—military, militias, criminals and terrorists indiscriminately. It is also worrisome that most destructive weapons find their way into African markets and are not produced in the continent. For example, the popular Kalashnikov (AK-47) which has become so common in crisis zones and gained notoriety is used by many with less caution. Hence the fact that most of the weapons are not manufactured in Africa it means that the continent is losing hugely and deprived of invaluable revenue resources on regular basis. Without doubt, the beneficiaries of weapons transaction and those who gain much from the violent conflicts in Africa are the countries in the South.

More so now that SALWs has been discovered as lucrative business that can provide easy 'employment' for idle youths in crisis zones or where there are unstable governments everyone is interested and ready to be an undertaker. All kinds of people including women, criminals and militias are engaged in illicit arms trading which are described as 'arms black market' in many African countries today. This enhances quick spread of small arms and broadens the scope of violent crimes and communal conflicts. As argued earlier, government's choice of control is limited as its officials are sometimes part of the illegal arms transaction. It is therefore suggested that governments of African countries should adopt stricter arms control measures in order to curb the menace of arm proliferation.

Consequently, it is worthy to note that misuse of fire arms have recently threatened civilians and states like Mali, Libya, Congo DR, Africa Central Republic, Nigeria, Chad, Cameroon, and Niger. Therefore, countering armed violence does not necessarily mean arms stockpiles or additional recruitment of personnel but ways to negotiate with armed groups and aggrieved members of the society in order to avert conflict which is a medium of arms proliferation. Also, governments should evolve programmes that will improve the standard of living of her citizens in order to distract the youth population from seeing violence as option to their predicaments.

Finally, the illicit use of fire arms has been identified as the cause of human rights violation which leads to killing, rape, arson, robbery, torture and kidnapping, recruitment and use of children to perpetuate violence and population displacement in Africa. In this research, we have identified the PSCs as one key actor in the proliferation of SALWs in Africa, their role as alternative security provider undermines the security of nations. Therefore, governments should be concerned with the activities of the security companies in their countries and regulate their activities. Thus, to curb the menace of SALWs, the following initiatives are emphasized:

1. African countries should evolve policies that would tighten regulation on PSCs and PMSCs activities and curtail outsourcing security matters to private security contractors.
2. Regional organizations should commit financial and technical resources to guarantee implementation of the conventions entered into in order to assist states that are unable to fund implementation measures themselves.
3. There should be strict regulations on the circulation of fire arms in every country so that unauthorized person(s) should not be allowed to carry weapons indiscriminately or use them against innocent civilians.
4. African states should use the platform of the African Union (AU) and regional organizations to negotiate and press on developed countries to control arms shipment and transfer to crisis zones in Africa.
5. African governments should cut down on defence budget and channel more resources on human capital development.
6. Elimination of corruption in the defence sector should be a matter of priority because the most corrupt sector of governance in most countries is the defence sector.

References

Abrahamsen, R. (2005). Blair's Africa: The politics of Securitization and Fear. *Alternatives, 30,* 55–80.

Abrahamsen, R., & Williams, M. (2005). *The Globalisation of Private Security: Country Report: Nigeria.* Aberystwyth: University of Wales Press.

Abubakar, D. (2017). From Sectarianism to Terrorism in Northern Nigeria: A Closer Look at Boko Haram. In Caroline Varin & Dauda Abubakar (Eds.), *Violent Non-State Actors in Africa.* London: Palgrave Macmillan.

Akinleye, A. (2013, January 15). Nigeria's Thieves Say Government Leaves Them No Choice, in: Reuters, Online: www.reuters.com/article/2013/01/15/us-nigeria-oil-theft-idUSBRE90E0D020130115. Accessed 2 May 2020.

Baker, D. P. (2011). Will Global Demand for Private Military Services in Major Conflicts Continue? In Sabelo Gomedze (Ed.), *Merchants of African Conflicts, More Than Just a Pound of Flesh*. Pretoria. Institute for Security Studies (ISS) Monograph 176.

Bala, B., & Tar, U. A. (2020). The Prospects of Counter-Terrorism and Counter-Insurgency in the Lake Chad Basin. In U. A. Tar & B. Bala (Eds.), *New Architecture of Regional Security in Africa. Perspectives on Counter-Terrorism and Counter-Insurgency in the Lake Chad Basin*. Lanham, MD: Lexington Books.

Bala, B., & Tar, U. A. (forthcoming). Private Security Companies and National Security in Africa. In U. A. Tar (Ed.), *Routledge Handbook of Counterterrorism and Counterinsurgency in Africa*. London, New York: Routledge.

Barstow, D. (2004, April 19). Security Companies: Shadow Soldiers in Iraq. *New York Times*.

Bearpark, A., & Schulz, S. (2007). The Private Security Challenge in Africa: Problems and Options for Regulation. In S. Gumedze (Ed.), *Private Security in Africa: Manifestation, Challenges and Regulation*, Monograph No. 139.

Bryden, A. (2006). Approaching the Privatisation of Security from a Security Governance Perspective. In A. Bryden & M. Caparini (Eds.), *Private Actors and Security Governance*. Geneva: Lit & Dcaf Verlag.

Caleb, A., & Gerald, O. (2015). The Role of Small Arms and Lights Weapons Proliferation in African Conflicts. *African Journal of Political Science and International Relations, 9*(3), 77–85.

Christopher, K. (2006). *Corporate Soldiers and International Security-the Rise of Private Military Companies*. New York: Routledge.

Conference on ECOWAS Convention on Small Arms and Light Weapons 2006, Abuja, ECOWAS Commission.

Crawford, A. (2006). Networked Governance and the Post-Regulatory State? Steering Rowing and Anchoring the Provision of Policing and Security. *Theoretical Criminology, 10*(4), 449–479.

Fallah, K. (2007). Regulating Private Security Contractors in Armed Conflicts. In S. Gumedze (Ed.), *Private Security in Africa Manifestation, Challenges and Regulation*. Pretoria, Institute for Security Studies (ISS) Monograph Series No. 139.

Foaleng, M. H. (2007). Private Military and Security Companies and the Nexus Between Natural Resources and Civil Wars in Africa. In S. Gumedze (Ed.), *Private Security in Africa, Manifestation, Challenges and Regulation*. Pretoria, Institute for Security Studies (ISS) Monograph Series No. 139.

Gatsheni, S. J. N. (2007). Weak States and the Growth of the Private Security Sector in Africa: Wither the African State? In S. Gumedze (Ed.), *Private Security in Africa: Manifestation, Challenges and Regulation*. Pretoria, Institute of Strategic Studies (ISS) Monograph Series No. 139.

Gumedze, S. (2007). Regulatory Approaches (If Any) to Private Military and Security Companies in Africa. In S. Gumedze (Ed.), *Private Security in Africa, Manifestation, Challenges and Regulation*. Pretoria, Institute of Strategic Studies (ISS) Monograph Series No. 139. http://www.secretary.state.gov/www/statements/1998/. Accessed 20 May 2020.

Isima, J. (2009). The Global Market Place and the Privatization of Security. *Institute of Development Studies Bulletin, 40*(2), 113–120.

Juma, L. (2011). Privatisation, Human Rights and Security: Reflections on the Draft International Convention on Regulation, Oversight and Monitoring of Private Military and Security Companies. *Law, Democracy & Development, 15*(1), 1–33.

Kasali, M. A. (2011). Analysing the Evolution of Private Security Guards and Their Limitations to Security Management in Nigeria. *African Journal of Criminology and Justice Studies (AJCJS), 5*, 1–2.

Krahmann, E. (2010). *States, Citizens and the Privatisation of Security*. Cambridge: Cambridge University Press.

Los Angeles Times. (2007, October 14). An Exodus of Highly Paid Guns Alarms, Embarrasses Pretoria.

Maiangwa, J. S. (forthcoming). Defence Contractors, Counter-Terrorism and Counter-Insurgency in Africa. In U. A. Tar (Ed.), *Routledge Handbook of Counterterrorism and Counterinsurgency in Africa*. London, New York: Routledge.

Maiangwa, B., & Agbiboa, D. E. (2013). Oil Multinational Corporations, Environmental Irresponsibility and Turbulent Peace in the Niger Delta. *Africa Spectrum*, Online www.africa-spectrum.org. Accessed 2 December 2019.

Mben, P. H., & Puh, J. (2013). 'Gates of Hell': Mali Conflict Opens New Front in War on Terror. Spiegel Online http://www.spiegel.de/international/world/mali-offensive-opens-new-frontin-the-fight-against-terror-a-878750.htm. Accessed 10 June 2020.

Messner, J. J. (2007). Ethical Security: The Private Sector in Peace and Stability Opereation. In S. Gumedze (Ed.), *Private Security in Africa Manifestation, Challenges and Regulation*. Pretoria, Institute for Security Studies (ISS) Monograph Series No. 139.

Murithi, T. (2008). *Pan-Africanism and the Crises of Postcoloniality: From the Organization of African Unity to the African Union*. www.crisesofpostcoloniality. Accessed 20 June 2020.

Ndlovu-Gatsheni, S. J. (2007). Weak States and the Growth of Private Security Sector in Africa: Whither the African States? In S. Gumedze (Ed.), *Private Security in Africa Manifestation, Challenges and Regulation*. Pretoria Institute for Security Studies (ISS) Monograph Series No. 139.

Ndung'u, I. (2011). Human Security and Challenges Related to Private Military and Security Companies in Africa. In S. Gumedze (Ed.), *Merchants of African Conflicts, More Than Just a Pound of Flesh*. Institute for Security Studies (ISS) Monograph 176.

Olaniyan, A. O. (2010). Unorthodox Peacekeepers and Responses in Africa. In S. Gumedze (Ed.), *From Market for Force to Market for Peace: Private Military and Security Companies in Peacekeeping Operations*, Institute for Security Studies Monograph 183.

Percy, S. (2012). Regulating the Private Security Industry: A Story of Regulating the Last War, International. *Review of the Red Cross, 94*(887), 941–960.

Raenette, T. (2008, July). Private and Public Security in South Africa. In S. Gumedze (Ed.), *The Private Sector in Africa: Country Series*. ISS Monograph No. 146. Pretoria: Tshwane, ISS.

Reno, W. (1997). African Weak States and Commercial Alliances. *Africa Affairs, 96*, 165–185.

Schnabel, A. (2008). *The Human Security Approach to Direct and Structural Violence in SPRI Year Book: Armaments, Disarmament and International Security*. London: Oxford University Press.

Security Council 7036th Meeting. (2013). *Security Council Adopts First-Ever Resolution Dedicated to Question of Small Arms, Light Weapons.* www.securitycouncil/ 7036. Accessed 6 May 2020.

Shearer, D. (1998). *Private Armies and Military Interventions: Adelphi Paper 316.* Oxford: Oxford University Press.

Smith, D. (2015, April 4). South Africa's Ageing White Mercenaries Who Helped Turn Tide on Boko Haram. *The Guardian.* https://www.theguardian.com/world/ 2015/apr/14/south-africas-ageing-white-mercenaries-who-helped-turn-tide-on-boko-haram. Accessed 20 June 2020.

Strom, K., Berzofsky, M., Shook, B., Barrick, K., Daye, C., Horstmann, N., & Kinsey, S. (2010). *The Private Security Industry: A Review of the Definitions, Available Data Sources, and Paths Moving Forward.* This Document Was Prepared by RTI International Under Cooperative Agreement Number 2009-BJ-CX-K045 from the Bureau of Justice Statistics (BJS).

Tar, U. A., & Bala, B. (forthcoming). Civil-Military Cooperation: Joint Military/Civilian Operations in Counterterrorism and Counterinsurgency in Northeastern Nigeria. In U. A. Tar (Ed.), *Routledge Handbook of Counterterrorism and Counterinsurgency in Africa.* London, New York: Routledge.

Viljoen, F. (2007). *International Human Rights Law in Africa.* Oxford: Oxford University Press.

Zamparelli, S. (1999). Contractors on the Battlefield: What Have We Signed Up For? *Air Force Journal of Logistics, 23*(3), 11.

Zarate, J.-C. (1998). The Emergence of a New Dog of War: Private International Security Companies, International Law, and the New World Disorder. *Stanford Journal of International Law, 34*(1, Winter), 124–137.

Jonathan S. Maiangwa is a Senior lecturer at the Department of Political Science University of Maiduguri, Borno State, Nigeria. His research interests are in terrorism, counterterrorism/counterinsurgency, local security institutions, private military and security companies, governance and development studies. He published in referred journals and contributed chapters to edited books. He is the author of *The Concept of Terrorism in Africa* (Kaduna, Nigeria: Pyla-Mak Publishers, 2015) which enjoys a wide readership and circulation.

Usman A. Tar is Professor of Political Science and Defence Studies, and Endowed Chair of Defence and Security Studies (26RC Endowment) at the Nigerian Defence Academy. He is the Director of the Academy's flagship Centre for Defence Studies and Documentation, and a member of the Board of Social Science Research Council's African Peacebuidling Network (SSRC/APN), New York, USA. He was formerly Associate Research Fellow at Africa Centre for Peace and Conflict Studies, University of Bradford, UK. He authored several books including *The Politics of Neoliberal Democracy in Africa* (London/New York: I B Tauris, 2009); *Globalization in Africa: Perspectives on Development, Security and the Environment* (Lanham, MD, Lexington Books, 2016); *New Architecture of Regional Security in Africa* (Lanham, MD, Lexington Books, 2020) and *Routledge Handbook of Counterterrorism and Counterinsurgency in Africa* (London, Routledge, 2020). Prof Tar has consulted or consults for the United Nations Development Programme (UNDP), Nigeria; Konrad

Adaneur Stiftung (KAS, German Development Fund); and the Westminster Foundation for Democracy (WFD), Nigeria. Prof Tar is a member of Nigeria's Presidential Think Tank on National Defence and Security, and served as a member of Nigeria's Presidential Committee to review the national defence policy in 2015.

CHAPTER 30

Economics of Armed Violence in Africa: Supply and Demand Sides of Small Arms and Light Weapons Proliferation

Suleiman Sa'ad and Blessing Idakwoji

INTRODUCTION

The proliferation and accumulation of small arms and light weapons across Africa have resulted in conflicts with higher fatalities and increased longevity for conflict. The UN Secretary-General, in a report to the Security Council (S/2008/258), recognized threat posed by SALWS thus:

'Small arms facilitate a vast spectrum of human rights violations, including killing and maiming, rape and other forms of sexual violence, enforced disappearance, torture and forced recruitment of children by armed groups or forces. More human rights abuses are committed with them than with any other weapon'. Current figures indicate that of the 640 million small arms and light weapons circulated globally, an estimated 100 million are located in Africa, 30 million of which are found in sub-Saharan Africa (Small Arms Survey 2019). In the West African region, increase in the number and spread of SALWs has become a phenomenon of major worry. The Small Arms Survey (2018) estimated that about 650 million SALWs circulate the global economy, from this number, it is estimated also that 7 million of these SALWs have their base in West Africa and 77,000 small arms are in the hands of major West African insurgent groups. Still in West Africa, the low price of SALWs makes it easily buyable. For example, pistols are sold in the ranges of N3000 (about US$8), N7000 (about US$19) and 21,000 (about US$58) depending

S. Sa'ad (✉) · B. Idakwoji
Department of Economics, Nigerian Defence Academy, Kaduna, Nigeria
e-mail: ssuleiman@nda.edu.ng

© The Author(s), under exclusive license to Springer Nature Switzerland AG 2021
U. A. Tar and C. P. Onwurah (eds.), *The Palgrave Handbook of Small Arms and Conflicts in Africa*,
https://doi.org/10.1007/978-3-030-62183-4_30

on the type, seller, and area of purchase according to military sources in Nigeria. Meanwhile, noted that conflict areas such as Liberia, Sierra Leone and Guinea-Conakry acquire SALWs easier illicitly than in less conflict areas, and at considerably low prices (Ezell 2000: 9).

The United Nations General Assembly (no reference 2005) defines Small arms as weapons constructed and designed for single use. In other words, weapons meant to be carried and used by an individual to commit a violent act legitimately although with high rate of use illegitimately. This includes, inter alia, revolvers and self-loading pistols, rifles and carbines, sub-machine guns, assault rifles and light machine guns. While Light weapons are constructed and designed for use by more than one person serving as a group of people working on a ship, aircraft, etc., although some may be carried and used by a single person but are originally made for more than one person use. They include, inter alia, general purpose or universal machine guns, medium machine guns, heavy machine guns, rifle grenades, under-barrel grenade launchers and mounted grenade launchers, portable anti-aircraft guns, portable anti-tank guns, recoilless rifles, man-portable launchers of anti-tank missile and rocket systems, man-portable launchers of anti-aircraft missile systems and mortars of a caliber of less than 100 millimetres.

This chapter is premised on the fact that SALWs are often not farfetched in any crisis around Africa, the disperse of these weapons are wide alongside sustainable negative effect on the security of human society and economic development of African. It is based on this that this chapter seeks to critically examine the economics of SALWs in Africa using demand and supply tools to explain the sources and determinants of the proliferations of the SALWs its attendant economic effects within the African countries especially the war prone areas. The chapter is divided into five sections. Section one offers broad introduction and background to the challenges of conflicts and SALWs proliferation in Africa. The second section examines the economics of SALWs where trends of production, availability and international transfers are discussed along with qualities of SALWs, section three critically identifies the sources and the nature as well as the determinants of demand and supply of SALWs in Africa. Meanwhile section four dwells on economic effects of the proliferation of SALWs in Africa. Section five summarizes, concludes and recommends based on the findings of the study.

Framework of Analysis: Demand for and Supply of Small and Light Weapons in Africa

This framework analyses the demand and supply aspects of SALWs in Africa, the conventional analysis of demand and supply of SALWs is analysed from interrelated factors that influences both demand and supply and makes weapon available for end user.

Economist traditionally conceptualizes demand manifestation and aggregation of the willingness and desire of individual supported by means to acquire certain good among possible consumption options. Willingness and desire are treated in this framework as a motivation to acquire weapons while means are treated as economic factors, including money income and price of SALWs. Possible options include the array of weapons available for the consumer to choose based on his motivations to possess them. For example, for personal and group security or for banditry to fight tribal war. The extent to which one's preference for gun ownership can be actualized is in part a function of the price of the weapon, the price of necessary complements (e.g. ammunition, maintenance expenses, time spent on training, even the psychological discomfort of carrying a gun), and the price of acceptable offensive or defensive substitutes (e.g. private security, time devoted to community policing) (David Atwood et al. 2006).

From the demand side, the analyses begin with the motivation and means of holding the arms to the factors determining the willingness of the user (either final or intermediate user) to acquire certain firearms at a given price function of real and relative prices (which can act as a constraint on the realization of preferences). The demand for SALWs consists of some interrelated factors along the chain of transmission that incorporates the motivations and the means to acquire weapons. For example, the framework will explain at each stage of the value chain, what factors influence the flow of weapons? For example, at intermediate or end user point of the value chain, there are some array of factors that influences the choice made by users for personal/group protection different from factors that influence the sponsors of illegal mining, bunkering as well as political groups and government forces. Linking this to supply factors, we can see how these demand factors stimulate movements of weapons at each stage they are traded, stolen from manufacturers stocks or government armoury and smuggled to end users.

On the other hand, supply economist conceptually looks at supply as a willingness and determinations of a producer to offer some bundle of goods for sale at a given market price. In conceptualizing the supply of SALWs, two factors are very important, technology (technology used for manufacturing and sophistications of the weapons) as well as market prices of the weapons. The more sophisticated is a weapon, the more efficient it will be and likely to be more expensive. However, in most cases, fake versions of the sophisticated are also available in the black market.

Supply side of the market looked at the motivations of the supplier either legitimate or illicit to supply SALWs at a given market price. The supply chain starts from the point of production, either legal or illegal production, to legal exports to countries, Theft from manufacturing stocks, Government armouries, Recycling and leakages as well as smuggling to countries and finally to the hands of legitimate end users and illegal uses by criminals. This also consists of interrelated factors along the chain, these array of factors influences the legal and illegal manufacturer as to the types of weapons to manufacture, also how does the demand factors guide the smuggler or legal exporter to the choice of the types of weapons to trade. This also guides the direction of trade for SALWs from origin country of manufacture to final destination country.

The demand and supply framework helps in understanding of the mutual interdependence relationships between economic factors influencing the proliferation of SALWs in Africa, this analysis will help to guide the policy makers in designing suitable policies to combat the proliferations of the SALWs in Africa. For example, in formulating demand-side policies, a bottom-up approach, including demand reduction initiatives like youth empowerment and public enlightenments will be more suitable. On the other hand, tight legislations and control against illegal influx SALWs, which is top-down approach is likely to be more effective way of controlling the supply side of the market. However, it has been suggested that the approach requires a slight shift in traditional arms control and disarmament thinking when applied to policy interventions (Atwood and Jackman 2005: 6–7).

Economics of Small Arms and Light Weapons

This section specifically dwelled on economics dimensions of SALWs in Africa, the section looked at the demand for and supply of SALWs in Africa. It also examines the economic and social consequences of the proliferations of the SALWs. SALWs trading is certainly not a new phenomenon in African continent. However, is fast assuming a debilitating dimension and posing a real threat to the socio-economic well-being of Africans. Proliferations of the SALWs for economic gains and its attendant negative economic consequences is not a new phenomenon to the African continent; it predates the colonial era. In fact, most of the slave trading business during precolonial era were facilitated by the use of Small and Light Weapons (SALW). There were also some isolated cases of cattle rustling, rubbery and intercommunal clashes that used SALW for economic gains or personal protection. After the establishment of colonial dominance over Africa, many independence liberations struggles, like Mau Mau movements and others used locally fabricated and smuggled or stolen SALW to supports their liberation movements. Wairagu and Ndung'u (2003) notes that in 1953, at the height of the Mau Mau uprising, over 660 precision Small arms were stolen or captured from the British troops, the King's African Rifles (KAR) forces. Similarly, the ANC liberation movement in South Africa used SALWs for their independence struggle (Wairagu and Kamenju 2004).

However, the proliferation of Small and Light Weapons (SALW) during that era was not in large scale and the economic damage to the communities was not enormous. Recently, the proliferation of Small and Light Weapons (SALW) has taken a larger economic dimension with the escalation of crises in many African countries such as Burundi, Rwanda, Democratic Republic of Congo (DRC), Nigeria and Libya, among others, SALW plays a significant role in determining the winners of conflicts in sub-Saharan Africa.

With the majority of the fighting being done in small continuous battles and the relative lack of economic prosperity in comparison to the rest of the world, the use of heavy weaponry such as tanks, aircrafts, etc., is limited to governments or significantly large rebel groups. SALW, therefore, play a significant role in the conflicts in many African countries. (Nganga 2005)

Arguably, the economic dimensions of the proliferation of Small and Light Weapons (SALW) and its effects remain inadequately understood and appreciated, it can be analysed from demand and supply factors and their outcomes (Buchanan and Atwood 2002).

Key Features of Small Arms

The key features of SALWs are:

1. *Destructible power/Lethality*: The growing complicacy of SALWs and their extensive spread among states, sub-State groups and civilians give such groups the ability of fire delivery which overwhelms that of national forces. Definitely, with weapons having the ability of firing up to 700 rounds a minute, an individual or small armed group can constitute an extremely large threat to society.
2. *Concealability and Portability*: SALWs can be carried by individuals or light vehicles; they are easily conveyed or smuggled into areas of conflict; and they can be hidden in shipments of legitimate cargo.
3. *Military/police and civilian uses*: SALWs often have legitimate uses for both military and police forces unlike major conventional weapons, which are generally procured only by national military forces.
4. *Low cost and wide availability*: These weapons are produced in mass for military, police and civilian use; there are excess suppliers globally. Furthermore, millions of these weapons are recycled from conflict to conflict; this has led to decrease in price below the cost of manufacture.
5. *Simplicity and durability*: small arms and light weapons have few moving parts unlike major weapons systems which require regular upkeep and maintenance due to their complicated electronics, avionics and propulsion subsystems. With minimal maintenance SALW can remain operational for 20–40 years or more.

In view of the foregoing, SALWs are in high demand throughout conflict zones in Africa: producers and suppliers make brisk business in SALWs. In understanding the market of SALWs, it is critical to first understand the theory of demand and supply of economic commodities generally and like earlier mentioned, small arms and light weapons are economic commodities subject to the forces of demand and supply and which factors determine their supply and demand and also which the law of demand and supply applies.

Trends of Production

The major industrialized countries of the West and the Soviet bloc were the main manufacturers of SALWs from the period of World War II and into the 1950s. It is estimated that between 55 and 72 million SALWs were produced in the 1960s and 1970s under licence in 54 countries in the post-World War II period (1945–1990) (Ezell 2000: 9). A growing number of these SALWs were also manufactured under licence by US and Soviet Cold War allies and a few countries in the developing world. Most of these are still in circulation today, moving with relative ease from one conflict area to another. From the 1980s the manufacturing pattern of small arms began to take a new style. According to Rana (1995: 4), the number of manufacturers of small arms is estimated to have increased by 25% between 1985 and 1995, i.e. to some 300 companies in over 70 countries.

International Transfers

Weapons transfer in the international arena may begin as legal transaction between countries or organizations as part of bilateral sales or military assistance programmes. Although reliable estimates of the percentage of legally transferred weapons which remain in the hands of their original recipients are hard to come by, it is clear that a large percentage of all illicit transfers begin with weapons which were originally transferred legally. There is a range of means where by legally transferred arms can become illegally held arms, including intentional diversion by a government or a private company, the theft or capture of arms stocks by insurgent forces and exchanges between criminal organizations and insurgents. In addition, many countries are either unwilling or unable to effectively monitor the flow of goods across their borders. In some cases, governments or their officials have turned a 'blind eye', for political or economic reasons, to transfers to recipients other than those which are officially declared to national authorities before the export licences are obtained.

Most SALWs involve 'black market' sales, the illicit supply of weapons in defiance of legal sanctions. These networks have developed sophisticated methods for the procurement, transportation and sale of SALWs to willing buyers (Naylor). The international community has so far proven disturbingly unable or unwilling to enforce United Nations embargoes that seek to prevent arms flows into areas of conflict. These are often situations in which fundamental rules of international humanitarian law have been consistently violated. It is widely acknowledged that during and after the break-up of Yugoslavia, a number of countries defied the UN embargo and shipped weapons to forces in Bosnia Herzegovina.

Demand for SALWs in Africa

The demand for Small and Light Weapons in Africa is a derived demand but slightly distinct from the demand for other economic commodities. Demand for SALWs is a function of motivations and means; SALWs are demanded to achieve some purposes include the political, economic, social and cultural reasons such as self-protection and illicit economic motives like cattle rustling, rubbery, illegal mining and bunkering of mineral resources or for political gains including tribal wars and self-protection, they are generally determine by the means to acquire them.

Therefore, the demand for SALWs is not only determined by the individual incomes and price of the SALWs, but mostly, by the motive for the use of such weapons, this is because most end users of such weapons are not the one buying them. So, there is a need to distinguish between the acquirers and possessors/users of weapons, the weapons are being bought by politicians, barons who directly benefit from illegal mining, bunkering of crude oil and fighting tribal wars, It is reported that in a number of rebels groups and gangs—and, of course, in most police and military divisions weapons are made available for the day's (or night's) activities but are then expected to be turned in again (Muggah 2006). Similarly, in many private households, adults acquire weapons but adolescents can take authorized or unauthorized possession of a gun.

The major demanders for SALWs are three sets of actors; the high level of political opportunist and barons; some governments as well as private individuals. High-level opportunist and the baron, the high-level opportunists are the political leaders such as leaders of the Niger Delta Militant groups, Rwandan and DRC rebel groups. By virtue of their position, they recruit the vandals that are the local militants as well as collect profit to the sales of the stolen oil, gold or diamond from Barons to finance the supply of SALWs.

The high-level political opportunist, leaders of militant groups, sometimes highly placed politicians, senior security personnel and traditional leaders who use rebel groups to fight the government and engage in tribal wars. These often use well-established networks and channels also employed for smuggling of other illicit goods. It is this form of trafficking that was partially instrumental in the arming of Hutu and Tutsi warring factions during the Rwandan genocide. This group mostly works closely with the financiers or barons, these are usually foreigners, who normally finance the bunkering and mining operations, supply the militants with weapons (and drugs) for profit motives. They are international syndicates from Eastern Europe, Russia, China and Lebanon, all play roles in financing, transporting of stolen crude oil, diamond and gold and laundering the money associated from the business. It has been suggested that between 1999 and 2001, al Qaeda reaped millions of dollars from the illicit sale of diamonds mined by the Revolutionary United Front (RUF) in Sierra Leone (Dube 2019). Resource profits from illegal mining and bunkering are used for trafficking of SALWs and have enabled rebel groups and terrorist organizations to stay well-armed.

The second group of the demanders of SALWs is the national government who supply hired militias to fight SALWs opposition and rebel groups as well as support opposition groups in its neighbours. Governments sometimes demand supply small arms to supply them to select groups of their own citizens to use against traditional rivals who are also threatening the state (Regehr 2004). However, the supply of weapons to one group by the government can generate new demand from others—for instance the weapons might also be used for other purposes, like cattle raiding, which then prompts neighbouring groups to arm as well (Regehr 2004). Similar pressures to arms occur when states supply arms to political insurgent groups in neighbouring states as part of destabilization tactics related to regional dynamics and competition. In both of these instances, surplus weapons inevitably find their way into economically depressed and socially unstable environments.

Finally, private households also demand SALWs for personal and group protection as well as hunting, this demand is determined by the price of weapons and individual incomes. However, sometimes in many private households, adults acquire weapons for hunting or personal protection, but adolescents can take authorized or unauthorized possession of a gun and inflict irreparable damage to the community.

From the above, the first two categories are the demand for intermediate use and the last category is the demand for final use. The demand for intermediate use does not necessarily depend on the price of SALWs. However, the final demand is determined by economic factors including price of SALWs and individual's income. Figure 30.1 analysed the demand for SALWs in Africa.

Figure 30.1 panel (a) and (b) presents the determinants of the final demand for SALWs in Africa, panel (a) presents the demand for possession of weapons for personal or collective protection and for a culture of hunting, sport

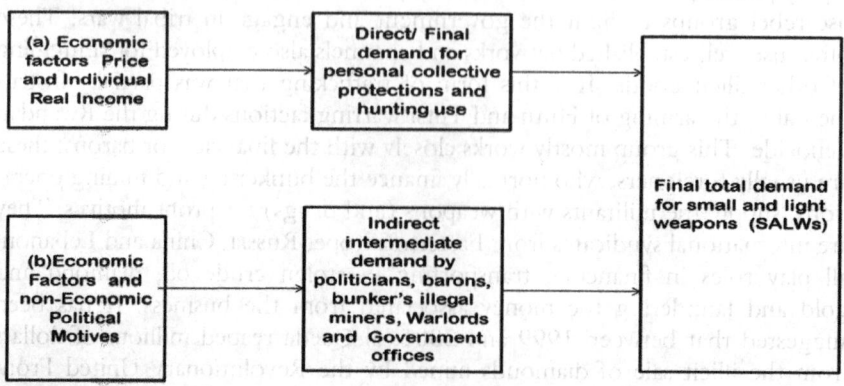

Fig. 30.1 Demand for SALWs in Africa (*Source* Authors [2020])

shooting as well as the pursuit of social status in a society. This kind of demand is considered as final demand. The major determinant for this kind of demand is price of the weapons and the income of the buyer. Prices and incomes directly influence the purchasing power of one's resources. Higher prices reduce purchasing power; lower prices increase it. From figure (a), if the price of weapons goes up, for example, the personal demand reduces, and as price of weapons falls, the demand will rise. On the other hand, as individual real incomes increase, individual demand for personal protection, and individual social status in a society will rise, this will also rise in the culture of hunting, sport shooting by individual, this will ultimately trigger the demand for SALWs which will increases. However, as incomes fall the demand declines. This category of demand is similar to the demand for normal commodities. This kind of demand obeys the law of demand, as price goes up, the quantity demanded declines and as incomes increases. The quantity demanded also increases.

Panel (b), presents the indirect (intermediate) demand for SALWs, under this category, the first two groups who do not demand weapons for their direct use, but the demand weapons to supply them rebel groups, bunkers, illegal miners. The demand under this category is not determined by the price of guns and individual incomes, but by the gains from nefarious activities of the militants and bandits as well as illegal miners and those in the business of illegal bunkering. As the mining and bunkering activities or communal crises escalates, more guns will be demanded irrespective of prices. Under this category, irrespective of the price of weapon, more will be demanded since gains from the use of these weapons are higher than whatever the price of such weapon.

Supply of SALWs in Africa

The major determinant of the supply of SALWs either by licit manufacturers or illegal traffickers is income, income generated from the sales of weapons keeps the business booming. It has been argued that, for instance, the US State Departments licensed over $470 million of light military weapons for export. The Commerce Department, which has jurisdiction over industry-direct sales of shotguns and police equipment, approved an additional $57 million of exports. While these amounts are small in the context of the overall arms trade (estimated at some $30 billion annually), at $100–300 per gun these figures represent enormous quantities of weapons (Grand View Research 2017). It has also been suggested that in 2014, the global arms trade was worth at least $6bilion and ammunition accounted for about 36% of global transfers (Holtom and Pavesi 2017).

Figure 30.2 presents the analysis of the supply of SALWs in Africa. In the analyses of the supply of SALWs, it is important to describe the nature of SALWs as are durable, long-lasting items, start life in both legal and illicit production and finally enter the illicit (and sometimes licit) market. Small arms are traded directly for commodities or for the profits generated by commodity

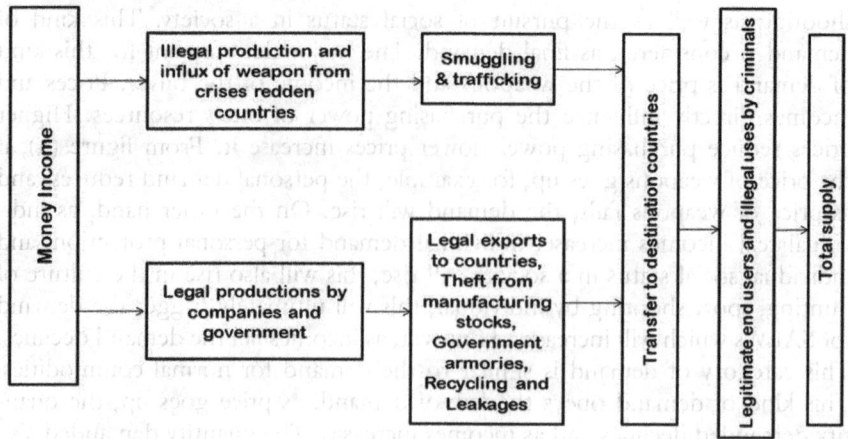

Fig. 30.2 Supply of SALWs in Africa (*Source* Authors [2020])

sales (such as crude oil, gold and diamond from illegal bunkering and mining). Based on this, the most important determinant of supply of SALWs is money income. Most of the licit producers or illegal traffickers do so in most cases for money income, for example, a report shows that the global Small Arms and Light Weapons (SALW) market size was valued over USD 18.70 billion in 2015.

Another aspect of the determinant of the supply of the SALWs in Africa, is the final gains from the use of the weapons, this is related to the indirect demand for SALWs by illegal miners and those engaged in bunkering. Annually, hundreds of thousands of SALWs find its way into the hands of criminals that are engage in nefarious economic activities, these weapons help them to fight security agents and other rival groups. For example, during the 1990s, more than 5 million people were killed due to resource conflicts, and as many as 20 million were displaced from their homes through the use of small arms by rebel forces in resource wars because they are inexpensive, easy to hide, widely accessible. Similarly, in October 2010, barely few months after it received about 20,000 small arms surrendered by Niger Delta militants under the country's Amnesty Program, Nigeria uncovered 13 containers loaded with 107 mm rockets, 120 mm, 80 mm and 60 mm mortars and small arms ammunition at the country's largest seaport (GIABA 2017).

Additional determinant for the supply of SALWs in a country include among others institutional weakness of the government, weak and sometimes corrupt security architecture characterized by inadequate border control mechanisms makes it easy for surplus SALWs from other crises redden neighbouring country to find its way into a peaceful country. Studies suggest that the fall of the Qadhafi government in Libya is among the major contributory factors for proliferation of SALWs in many African countries, including arming the Boko Haram insurgents in Nigeria. The International Crisis group has reported that over 125,000 weapons were in the hands of civilians by the end of the civil war in Libya (ICG 21011; UNSC 2013). Final report of the panel of experts established pursuant to resolution 1973 (2011) concerning Libya. S/2013/99 indicates that other non-state actors were armed with weapons from Libya in at least twelve countries across the Middle East and North Africa (MENA). Similarly, it has been established that due to weak governance structures in Somali, people were used to doing illicit businesses and therefore trade in arms was just normal, the refugees from Somalia brought with them the illicit arms into Kenya (Musoi 2015).

The combination of the demand and supply factors discussed above leads to equilibrium in demand for and supply of SALWs in Africa. The vertical axis indicates the combinations of economic factors such as price of weapons and individual incomes together with non-economic political and social factors, such as rise in political unrest, increase in crimes rate and illegal mining and bunkering that leads to rise or fall in demand or supply of SALWs. The horizontal axis shows the quantity of SALWs demand and supply in response of the economic and non-economic factors. From the demand side, increase in individual incomes, boom in illegal mining and bunkering as well as escalation of crises will bring about appreciable rise in direct or intermediate demand for SALWs, this will shift the demand curve from D_0 to D_1 represented movement from point A to B, shift from D_0 to D_1 will be accompanied by in prices of those weapons. Rise in prices of weapons will be accompanied by increase in smuggling, illegal trafficking and licit supply of such weapons. This will lead to the shift in supply from S_0 to S_1 as represented by point A to B in Fig. 30.3.

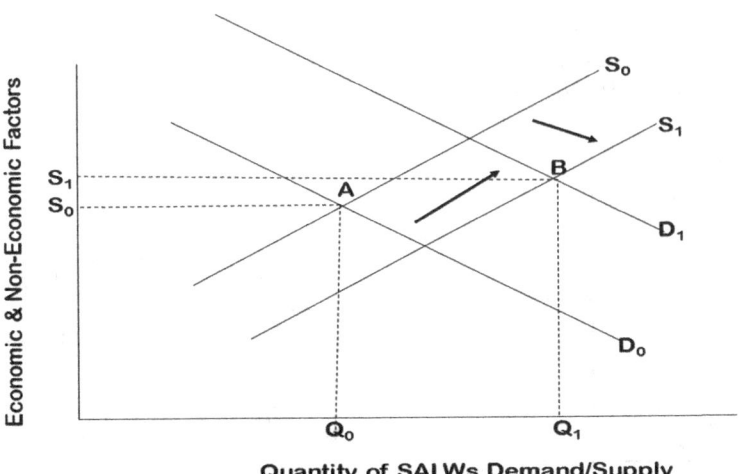

Fig. 30.3 Equilibrium in demand and supply of SALWs (*Source* Authors [2020])

The Economic Trajectories and Consequences of SALWs Proliferation in Africa

The combinations and interplay of the demand and supply factors explained above has some socio-economic consequences in many African countries (Fig. 30.4).

- *Inflow of SALWs*: The first point in the SALWs operation is the influx of the SALWs into a country either through trafficking or legal means, if it is illegally smuggled into a country, arms are smuggled through a complex network that goes hand in hand with the illicit trade of hard drugs, that are mostly needed by criminals as well as illegal miners and those engaged in bunkering to facilitate their nefarious activities. Influence of hard drugs backed by possession of SALWs leads to escalation of crises in a community. SALW plays a significant role in determining the winners of conflicts in sub-Saharan Africa. With the majority of the fighting being done in small continuous battles and the relative lack of economic prosperity in comparison to the rest of the world, the use of heavy weaponry such as tanks, aircrafts, etc., is limited to governments or significantly large rebel groups. SALW, therefore, plays a significant role in the conflicts. They tend to have an impact on the intensity of a conflict as well as the duration of the conflict (Bourne 2006: 223; Biting the Bullet 2006).

In many African countries for example, the Nigeria's Niger Delta militant groups as well as Boko Haram sect are example of two groups that use SALWs to pursue their political and economic motives. The Niger Delta oil rich region alone, there are about one hundred militant groups existed before the federal government's amnesty programme (Asuni 2009: 20). Similarly, the Boko Haram sect also has about three

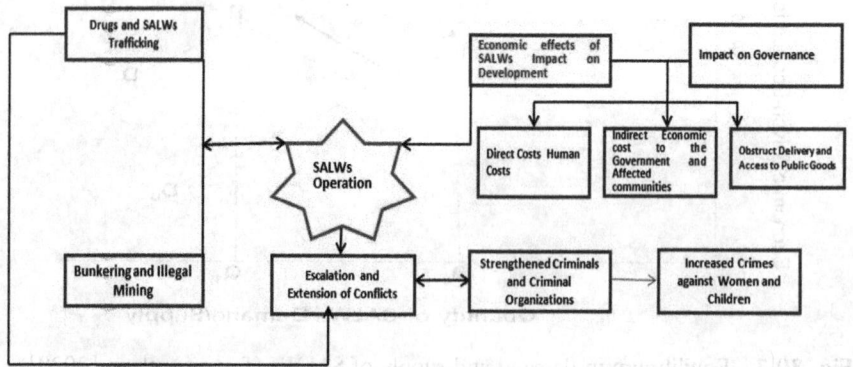

Fig. 30.4 The economic trajectories and consequences of SALWs proliferation in Africa (*Source* Authors [2020])

different factions sometimes fighting each other. In Somalia various warring factions use SALWs to fight each other in competition for supremacy, this leads to escalation of conflict in Somalia. Similarly, the Senegalese rebel *Mouvement des Forces Democtratiques de la Casamance* (MFDC) has been fighting the government for more than twenty years.

- *The escalation of conflicts and violence leads to strengthening of criminals and criminal organizations*: The widespread of SALWs in an area intensifies and escalates conflict and violence in areas, fighting among various criminal groups is very common which will affect civilians living in the area, this causes people to flee the areas of conflict, their means of livelihood will be affected, in the process of moving from conflict redden area to a peaceful area, SALWs trafficking occurs, in most cases those weapons from the internally displaced people falls into the hands of criminals in the new places of refuge, the criminals in turn use them for some criminal activities like rubbery, rapping and other nefarious activities. It has been suggested that many refugees from Somalia and Uganda to neighbouring Kenya enter with SALWs and sale them at giveaway prices to criminals in Kenya who use them for antisocial and human right abuses. The presence of SALW in refugee and internally displaced persons (IDP) camps has been associated with increased intimidation and militarization, in some cases closely linked with attempts to use such camps for recruitment and training of youth for armed groups. In instances where SALW is used to force civilians to actively participate in conflict, not only are their human rights violated but conflicts are further intensified and extended as mentioned earlier (Bourne et al. 2006; *OxResearch* 2007).

- *Social Disintegration and increased crimes against women and children*: The outcome of proliferation of SALWs particularly in a conflict and mining areas leads to social disintegration and human right abuses against women and children. Social disintegration leads to breakdown of laws and order in area, raping and molestation of women and underaged children are very common, some youngsters are conscripted into criminal groups, In north east and south–south of Nigeria, youngsters are recruited into Boko Haram sect and Niger Delta militants, these boys are equipped with SALWs to fight against the security agencies and rival groups. Similarly, the war in Somalia, many adolescents are forcefully conscripted into militant warring factions.

The proliferation of SALWs has more devastating effects on women and children. Although entire communities suffer the consequences of armed conflict, women and girls are particularly affected because of their status in society and their sex. (UN Women 2020). The consequences of SALW proliferation include on women murder, intimidation, rape, torture, sexual abuse, sexual harassment, threats and humiliation, forced prostitution and trafficking of women and girls (Nario-Galace 2014). Increasingly, modern warfare is wreaking havoc on the lives of women and girls, and on the health and educational services that are key to family and community survival and development (UNICEF 2020).

Economic Effects of SALWs on African Economic Development

Proliferations of SALWs in Africa has some devastating economic effect on African continent. The economic effects are both direct and indirect. The direct economic cost of proliferation of SALWs in Africa include loss of billions of dollars revenue accruable to the government which would have been ordinarily used for developmental purpose. In DRC for example, on General Gabriel Amisi Kumba, is noted as among the major actors in illegal gold mining, where SALWs are heavily used, it was estimated by Deutsche Welle (DW), September 2017 that, it's difficult to know how much artisanal gold is smuggled out of the country each year, estimates range from $300 million (252 million euro) to $600 million (DW 2017). The illegal exports not only deprive the government of vital tax income, they also feed corruption and line the pockets of armed groups.

Similarly, in Nigeria's Niger Delta oil rich area and Zamfara state illegal bunkering and illegal mining of gold annually cost the government revenues to the tune of billions of dollars annually. For instance, A special report by the United States Institute of Peace, an independent, nonpartisan institution in 2009 revealed that between 30,000 and 300,000 barrels of oil per day is carted away by oil thieves who operate in Niger Delta and that approximately US$100 billion was lost from illegal oil bunkering between 2003 and 2008. The conflict in Gold rich Zamfara state has been on increase since 2014, over 1000 people have been killed and thousands have been displaced. The crises spread across neighbouring states of Kaduna, Sokoto, Katsina and Kebbi. The illegal miners and bandits use SALWs for their operations, thousands of cattle have been rustled, many farmers have been rendered jobless and their crops destroyed by the bandits. In Zamfara, on 22 February 2020, bandits killed four soldiers and police arrested two Chinese nationals for illegal mining in Zamfara on 27 April. Furthermore, those who sponsor illegal mining also fund banditry and cattle rustling in mining communities in order to incite violence among cattle breeders and herdsmen. Locals from Zamfara revealed that, such conflicts displace people and create opportunities for illegal miners to operate. Many media reports in Nigeria blame the conflicts in the region on rural banditry, without addressing its links to illegal mining. According to a 2015 study, the federal government was losing $13.7 billion in revenue annually because of herder–farmer conflicts in Benue, Kaduna, Nasarawa and Plateau states. The study found that on average these four states lost 47 per cent of their internally generated revenues Mercy Corps (2015). Similarly, throughout the 1990s the RUF mined some $US 25–125 million worth of diamonds each year, of which only $US 1 million is estimated to be legal. The money generated by legal and illegal transfers of such resources not only has enabled rebel groups, terrorists and government forces to stay well-armed.

The rise in illegal mining and bunkering by youth highlights fundamental social, institutional and structural problems in Nigeria's governance system. It reveals the prevailing socio-economic problems in the country, especially the inadequate responses to poverty and poor service delivery by the states. The youth in particular have limited income-generating opportunities, and this is where the sponsors of illegal mining and bunkering recruit their labour force.

Another consequence is the obstruction of delivery and access to public goods. The direct and indirect economic cost of proliferation of SALWs in Africa poses a great challenge to the governments in delivering essential services and fighting terrorism. Annually billions of dollars are expended by various governments to import weapons to fight insurgency and banditry. Defence expenditure, always assumes the highest in annual budget at the expense of education, health and other services. The other side of the coin is that most law enforcement agents in African countries are accused of feeding into the crises in their respective countries, most, of the arms imported by the governments finds its ways into the hand of the terrorist and criminals, similarly, high ranking officers in some countries are accused of participating in illegal mining and bunkering as the case of General Gabriel Amisi Kumba in DRC.

Report by *WikiLeaks* (a US diplomatic cable) on Nigeria equally revealed the involvement of military personnel, politicians (including a late general, retired admiral, generals and a former vice-president) as those not only behind the illicit oil business, but profited from crude thefts. Worst still is that the military is involve in escorting illegally bunkered crude; the foot soldiers are not the only ones who profit; the commissioner of police, the director of the State Security Service, all line up at the governor's door asking for favours (*WikiLeaks* 2010).

Discussion and Conclusion

This chapter used economics tool to unravel the economic dimensions of the SALWs proliferation and its attendant effect in Africa. It has been seen how combinations of demand and supply factors interplay to escalate the proliferations of SALWs in Africa. Due to intercommunal conflicts or economic gains from mining and bunkering of natural resources most African states have become scenes of endemic civil wars (Sierra Leone, Liberia, Guinea-Bissau, Ivory Coast), as well as ethnic and religious crises (Benin, Nigeria, Mali) which have all led to the proliferations of SALWs. This chapter examines the market demand and supply sides of Small Arms and Light Weapons (SALWs) proliferations and their economic implications for regional conflicts and security in Africa. The key determinants of SALWs proliferation identified in the chapter are lethality, portability, concealability, low price and durability. The sources of weapons supply from the case studies are local-made weapons, importation, arms brokers, conflict-to-conflict, arming of militias by governments, misuse by government forces, diversion and theft from state armoury.

On the other hand, the demand determinants identified are incomes, price of weapons and motives for the use of the weapons. The chapter reveals that economic considerations influence SALWs proliferation and conflicts resulting in war economies and the rise of warlords who benefit immensely from the perpetuation violence and criminality. Demand and supply for SALWs in Africa can only be reduced and not completely eradicated. It will be near impossible, in reducing demand and circulation of weapons, government of countries in question should improve the welfare and safety needs of citizens in their respective countries.

A number of conjectures emerge from the analysis presented in this chapter. First, the indiscriminate use of SALWs has more negative than positive economic benefits. With the aid of SALWs billions of dollars revenues annually are lost by the governments through illegal mining and bunkering. Similarly, crops and livestock worth billions are destroyed and rustled in many parts of Africa. The social aspect of the SALWs proliferation shows that, women and youth are the most vulnerable and badly affected by the use of SALWs. Finally, the involvement of security agents and foreigners in financing and equipping rebels and illegal miners makes it extremely difficult task for the government to easily tackle the menace of SALWs in Africa.

From the ongoing, due to the spatial and irreparable nature of the problems associated with the proliferation of SALWs in Africa, there is a need for joint efforts by African governments to tackle the problem. From demand side, local civil societies can be a catalyst of SALWs demand reduction strategies. Secondly, effective synergies between state and local authorities as well as local civil societies will make the demand reduction strategies more effective. In addition, it is recommended that Government of African countries should initiate development programmes that are conflict-sensitive that can make significant contributions to conflict mitigation and demand reduction not development programmes that are poorly conceived and carried out that could provoke conflicts. It is also recommended that the demand and supply sides of SALWs should be strictly regulated to avoid wrongful access by unauthorized persons; destruction of illicit arms; and execution of voluntary weapon collection programmes. Also, Government of affected countries can reduce the availability by reinforcing legislation and enhancing regulatory controls on the entry and exit of arms by enhancing checks on civilian accumulation of weapons and improving the capacity to control and trace weapons market; advocating society arms removal, destruction of surplus arms and undertaking voluntary weapon collection programmes.

REFERENCES

Asuni, J. B. (2009). *Understanding the Armed Groups of the Niger Delta* (Working Paper for *Council on Foreign Relations*). Available: https://www.cfr.org/sites/default/files/pdf/2009/09/CFR_WorkingPaper_2_NigerDelta.pdf. Accessed on 10 July 2020.

Atwood, D., & Jackman, D. (2005). *Security Together: A Unified Supply and Demand Approach to Small Arms Control* (Working Paper). Geneva: Quaker United Nations Office.

Atwood, D., Glatz, A. K., & Muggah, R. (2006). *Demanding Attention: Addressing the Dynamics of Small Arms Demand*. Small Arms Survey Occasional Paper 18 Graduate 47 Avenue Blanc, 1202 Geneva, Switzerland.

Biting the Bullet Project. (2006). *Promoting Effective Global Action on Small Arms: Priorities for the 2006 Un Review Conference.*

Bourne, B., et al. (2006). Implications of Illicit Proliferation and Misuse of SALW in Reviewing.

Bourne, M., et al. (2006). Implications of Illicit Proliferation and Misuse of SALW. In *Reviewing Action on Small Arms 2006: Assessing the First Five Years of the Programme of Action by Biting the Bullet*. London: International Action Network on Small Arms[IANSA], Biting The Bullet Project.

Buchanan, C., & Atwood, D. (2002). *Curbing the Demand for Small Arms: Focus on Southeast Asia*. A Summary Report from the Workshop Held on 26–31 May 2002, Phnom Penh, Cambodia, Centre for Humanitarian Dialogue and Quaker United Nations Office.

Dube, J. (2019). The Africa We Want: Silencing the Guns. *Report for International Action Network on Small Arms*. Available: https://92054894-4da4-47e4-9276-4b6cfef27021.filesusr.com/ugd/bb4a5b_3dea13d5e8ac4a34ad668187d1b692a8.pdf?index=true. Accessed 10 July 2020.

DW (Deutsche Welle). (2017, September). *Democratic Republic of Congo Army General Profits from Illegally Mining Conflict Gold*. Cologne, Germany: Deutsche Welle.

Ezell, V. H. (2000). Report on International Small Arms Production and Proliferation, Institute for Research on Small Arms in International Security, Alexandria VA.

GIABA. (2017). *Nexus Between Small Arms and Light Weapons and Money Laundering in West Africa*. Dakar.

Grand View Research. (2017). *Small Arms & Light Weapons Market, SALW Industry Report 2018–2024*. Available: https://www.grandviewresearch.com/industry-analysis/small-arms-light-weapons-salw-market. Accessed 6 June 2020.

Greene, O., & Kirkham, E. (2009). *Preventing Diversion of Small Arms and Light Weapons: Issues and Priorities for Strengthened Controls*, Biting the Bullet Policy Report, Saferworld and University of Bradford.

Holtom, P., & Pavesi, I. (2017). *Trade Update 2017: Out of the Shadows*. Geneva: Small Arms Survey.

ICG (International Crisis Group). (2013). *Holding Libya Together: Security Challenges After Qadhafi, Middle East/North Africa Report N°115*. Brussels: International Crisis Group.

Mercy Corps. (2015, July). *The Economic Costs of Conflict: Evidence on Violence, Livelihoods and Resilience in Nigeria's Middle Belt*. Available: https://www.mercycorps.org/sites/default/files/2019-11/Mercy%20Corps%20Nigeria%20Policy%20M emo%20Economic%20Costs%20of%20Middle%20Belt%20Conflict.pdf. Accessed 10 June 2020.

Muggah, R. (2006). Completing the Circle: Building a Theory of Small Arms Demand Article in Contemporary Security Policy.

Musoi, Leonard. (2015). Factors Influencing Proliferation of Illicit Small Arms and Light Weapons. In Makadara and Embakasi Divisions, Nairobi East District, Kenya Unpublished Postgraduate Diploma theses, University of Nairobi, Kenya.

Nario-Galace, J. (2014, July 27). *Women's Agency Against Guns.* http://www.isiswomen.org/index.php?option=com_content&view=article&id=1707:women-s-agency-against-guns&catid=22&Itemid=449. Accessed 10 July 2020.

Nganga, C. F. (2005). Effects of Proliferation of Small Arms in Sub-Sahara African Kenya. Strategy Research Project for U.S. Army War College, Carlisle PA, USA.

OXFAM. (2007). *Press Release: 11 October 2007. "Fifteen Years of Conflict Have Cost Africa.* http://www.oxfam.org/en/news/2007/pr071011_control_arms_cost_conflict_africaSwadesh.

Rana. (1995). *Small Arms and Intra-State Conflicts.* New York: United Nations.

Regehr, E. (2004). *Reducing the Demand for Small Arms and Light Weapons: Priorities for the International Community* (Working Paper 04-2, Project Ploughshares, July 2004). www.ploughshares.ca/libraries/WorkingPapers/wp042.pdf. Accessed 10 July 2020.

Small Arms Survey. (2018). Maison de la Paix, Chemin Eugène-Rigot 2E 1202 Geneva, Switzerland.

Small Arms Survey. (2019). *Annual Report 2018.* Available: http://www.smallarmssurvey.org/fileadmin/docs/M-files/SAS-Annual-Report-2018.pdf. Accessed 10 July 2020.

UN Women. (2020). In Focus: Women and Armed Conflict. *UN Women, The Beijing Platform for Action Turns 20.* http://beijing20.unwomen.org/en/in-focus/armed-conflict. Accessed 8 July 2020.

UNICEF. (2020). War Hits Home When It Hits Women and Girls. *UNICEF.* https://www.unicef.org/graca/women.htm. Accessed 10 July 2020.

Wairagu, F., & Kamenju, J. (2004). *Private Security in Kenya.* Nairobi: Oakland Media Services.

Wairagu, F., & Ndung'u, J. (2003). *The Problem of Small Arms and Initiatives for Combating Their Proliferation, Circulation and Trafficking.* In Intermediate Technology Development Group East Africa (ITDG EA). Peace Bulletin, No. 2. Nairobi: ITDG EA.

WikiLeaks. (2010). *Nigeria: Shell Briefs Ambassadord on Oil Gas Issues, Comments on President's Health and High Level Corruption.* Available: https://wikileaks.org/plusd/cables/09ABUJA259_a.html. Accessed 10 July 2020.

Suleiman Sa'ad (Ph.D.) is Associate Professor and former Head of the Department of Economics at the Nigerian Defence Academy. He was also the former Head, Centre for Energy and Environment (CEENDA) in the Academy. He obtained his Ph.D. in Economic from the University of Surrey, United Kingdom. In 2013/2014, Dr. Sa'ad was at the University of Cambridge, United Kingdom as a Visiting Research Fellow. During a sabbatical year at the Kaduna State University in 2017–2018, Dr. Sa'ad pioneered in establishment of the Centre for Energy Studies at the University.

Blessing Idakwoji is a postgraduate student at the Department of Economics, Nigerian Defence Academy. Her research interest includes the economics of violence, economic security and development studies.

CHAPTER 31

Information Communication Technology, CyberSecurity and Small Arms in Africa

Francisca Nonyelum Ogwueleka

INTRODUCTION

Information Communication Technology (ICT) is an umbrella term that includes all technologies for the communication of information. It encompasses any medium to record information (whether paper, pen, magnetic disk/tape, optical disks, flash memory, etc.); technology for broadcasting information (radio, television), any technology for communicating through voice and sound or images (microphone, camera, loudspeaker, telephone to cellular phones) (IGI Global 2019).

Information and Communication Technologies (ICTs) may be viewed in different ways. The World Bank defines ICTs as 'the set of activities which facilitate by electronic means the processing, transmission and display of information' (Rodriguez and Wilson 2000). ICTs 'refers to technologies people use to share, distribute, gather information and to communicate through computers and computer networks' (ESCAP 2000). ICTs can be described as 'a complex varied set of goods, applications and services used for producing, distributing, processing, transforming information (including) telecoms, TV and radio broadcasting, hardware and software, computer services and electronic media' (Marcelle 2000). ICTs represent a cluster of associated technologies defined by their functional usage in information access and communication, of which one embodiment is the Internet.

F. N. Ogwueleka (✉)
Department of Computer Science, Nigerian Defence Academy, Kaduna, Nigeria

© The Author(s), under exclusive license to Springer Nature Switzerland AG 2021
U. A. Tar and C. P. Onwurah (eds.), *The Palgrave Handbook of Small Arms and Conflicts in Africa*,
https://doi.org/10.1007/978-3-030-62183-4_31

A well-functioning information and communication technology sector has been recognized as a critical requirement for economic groswth, hence emphasizing the need to afford every country in Africa with access to this important resource, ensuring African countries are connected to each other and to the rest of the world. Using the key findings from an analysis of ICT in Africa, the report aims to prioritize projects most important to facilitating access to regional telecommunications infrastructure (Akpan-Obong 2009).

Cybersecurity can be defined as the body of technologies, processes and practices designed to protect networks, computers, programs and data from attacks, damage or unauthorized access. Cybersecurity is the technique of protecting computers, networks, programs and data from unauthorized access or attacks that are aimed for exploitation.

Cybersecurity refers to information technology security, focusing on protecting computers, networks, programs and data from unintended or unauthorized access, change or destruction. It is the collection of tools, policies, security concepts, security safeguards, guidelines, risk management approaches, actions, training, best practices, assurance and technologies that can be used to protect the cyber environment and organization and user's assets.

Year over year, the worldwide spend for cybersecurity continues to grow, from 71.1 billion in 2014 (7.9% over 2013), and 75 billion in 2015 (4.7% from 2014) and expected to reach 101 billion by 2018. National cybersecurity is the availability, integrity and secrecy of the information systems and networks in the face of attacks, accidents and failures with the goal of protecting a nation's cyberspace. Cyberwarfare is the use of technology to attack a nation, causing comparable harm to actual warfare (Singer 2016a). Cyberwarfare does not imply scale, protraction or violence which is typically associated with the term 'war' (Green 1981). It is used in a board context to denote interstate use of technological force within computer networks in which information is stored, shared or communicated online. It is also distinct, if closely related to, 'cyber espionage', 'cyber terrorism' and 'cyber crime'. The term and its definition remain the subject of debate and no absolute definition is widely agreed (Green 1981). Cyberwarfare can present a multitude of threats towards a nation. At the most basic level, cyberattacks can be used to support traditional warfare. For example, tampering with the operation of air defences via cyber means in order to facilitate an air attack (Weinberger 2007). Aside from these 'hard' threats, cyberwarfare can also contribute towards 'soft' threats such as espionage and propaganda. Eugene Kaspersky, founder of Kaspersky Lab, equates large-scale cyberweapons, such as Flame and NetTraveler, which his company discovered, to biological weapons, claiming that in an interconnected world, they have the potential to be equally destructive (The Times of Israel 2012).

Conflicts in Africa are constantly evolving. This process is exacerbated by the flow of uncontrolled arms (Adesoji 2017). Three key features have characterized Africa's conflict patterns and trends in the past decade: first, the changing nature of conflict and insecurity. Most current conflicts reflect interwoven causes and triggers, complex networks of transnational actors and processes, as well as their increasing regionalization and internationalization. Second, their spillover effect as they spread, creating a wider radius of impact. Third, their exhibited continuities, as well as new patterns regarding their causes, actors, protraction, and underlying sociopolitical, economic and humanitarian impacts (Adesoji 2017).

A previous report co-authored by Oxfam, Africa's Missing Billions: International arms flows and the cost of conflict, showed how certain processes such as illicit arms procurement, the growth of gun culture, diversion of resources from productive expenditure, etc., were either triggered or sustained by the interaction between conflict/insecurity and uncontrolled arms (Hillier 2007). The report went on to highlight the impact of this interaction on social cohesion, with an emphasis on the tangible and intangible costs of conflicts in Africa (www.oxfam.org). Much has changed since the report was published in 2007. New or renewed conflicts and cases of insecurity have emerged (Libya, South Sudan, Mali, Lake Chad Basin crisis, etc.), while old ones remain protracted (CAR, Somalia, LRA, Eastern DRC, Darfur, Western Sahara). In particular, there has been a surge in incidences of insecurity, as numerous armed conflicts have re-emerged across Africa in the last decade. At present, about twenty-five (25) African states are battling one or more forms of insecurity, such as organized rebellion or civil war, organized crime, violent extremism, ethno-political militancy, secessionist agitations, etc. (www.warsintheworld.com).

Small arms stimulate national wars and other fights, instigating harm to millions of people in Africa. They are small weapons, which are a fraction of much heavier and more deadly weaponry. Studies and reports had shown how these weapons are illegally exported, transported and imported with the involvement of government officials in many countries and smuggled into war zones. These weapons are cheap and so can be bought in small amount.

The production and abuse of small arms is a universal and complicated occurrence that affects people of all tribes and culture. It has been prime source to the increase in violence and due to its effortless accessibility, little price and uncomplicated ability to handle, small arms became the weapons in majority of the dispute today in the world. Many thousand lives are lost each day to small arms aggression and extensive influence that goes beyond their usage in conflict.

Religions for Peace World Assembly Declaration (1984) stated that 'Conventional weapons are also instruments of death and oppression. Halting the spread of militarization and the commercial exploitation of developing countries by trade in arms leading to military and political dependency is a crucial part of our commitment to disarmament'.

In 2018, Small Arms Survey reported that there are over one billion small arms distributed globally, of which 857 million (about 85%) are in civilians hands (Aaron 2018). Illicit flows of small arms and light weapons undermine security and the rule of law. They are often a factor behind the forced displacement of civilians and massive human rights violations (UNODA 2018). There are approximately 640 million small arms in the world, one for every 10 people on earth with nearly 60% of the world's firearms in the hands of private citizens, 8 million new guns manufactured every year by at least 1249 companies in 92 countries, and in every year at least 1 million firearms are stolen or lost worldwide (Small Arms and Light Weapons: Africa 2017). According to the Small Arms Survey (2018), military expenditure in sub-Saharan Africa rose by 47% during the late 1990s, while life expectancy fell from 50 to 46 years. More than 500,000 people are killed by small arms each year.

New technologies in small arms manufacturing and management are often established technologies with a history of application in other industries. Those include the use of non-traditional materials, such as polymers, the use of 3-D printing and modularity in weapon design. These developments in weapon design and production could have consequences for international efforts to address the illicit trade in small arms. The marking, record-keeping and tracing of small arms are affected by new technology applications, such as laser markings, microstamping, automatic information and data collection and tracking technologies. Many of those technologies have the potential to profoundly influence the way weapons are marked and traced, as well as how records of weapons are kept. Innovative ways for governments to address the management of weapons have become technologically feasible. Such technologies have already been put to broad use in commercial sectors such as the parcel business or the food industry (UNODA 2018).

This book chapter will present the ICT, CyberSecurity and Small Arms and Conflict in Africa to guide the understanding of their rising effects in the twenty-first century. It shall provide a background on ICT, CyberSecurity and Small Arms development in Africa by reviewing and discussing existing trends and implications of ICT, CyberSecurity and Small Arms in a violent world.

Conceptual Contours: ICT, Small Arms and CyberSecurity

Information Communication Technology (ICT)

Since the early 1980s, information and communication technology (ICT) has permitted people to participate in a world in which school, work and other activities have been increasingly enhanced by access to varied and developing technologies. ICT tools have helped people find, explore, analyze, exchange and present information—most importantly, without discrimination. When efficiently used, ICT can provide quick access to ideas and experiences from a wide range of people, communities and cultures.

ICTs stand for information and communication technologies and are defined as a diverse set of technological tools and resources used to communicate, and to create, disseminate, store and manage information. These technologies include computers, the Internet, broadcasting technologies (radio and television) and telephony.

ICT had been hailed in many quarters as the solution to many challenging developmental problems. Whether or not it has lived up to this reputation is an ongoing debate. However, it has been observed that ICT has catalyzed developments along unpredicted paths, which has been influenced by erratic events of different scales and actors of various interests.

Generically, ICT may be defined as an extended term for Information Technology, which stresses the role of unified communication and integration of telecommunications computers as well as necessary enterprise software, middleware storage and audio-visual systems enabling users to access, store, transmit, and manipulate information (ITU 2007).

At the most basic level, ICT encompasses all technologies that allow individuals and businesses to interact in the digital world. Internet connectivity, online transactions, hardware, software and cloud computing are just a few to mention. The advancements in this industry fuel the global economy, international trade, communication and services across all sectors.

Information and communication technology has a broader scope than IT and focuses primarily on wireless networks, internet access and other communication channels. ICT includes all of the tools and resources used to create, store, process and exchange information. The objective of any ICT operations strategy is to make an important input to reduction of poverty, increased development and economic growth by increasing the nations role in extending access to ICT infrastructure, inspiring private sector asset, improve good governance and create efficient delivery of public services such as education and health.

While most of the western world may easily conceptualize ICT as an enabler for good governance, many African governments may see it differently. Some observing it as threat to their tight fisted regime as seen in the over 40-day internet outage in Cameroun earlier in 2017, others as both the key to development and as a black hole into which every inefficiency can be blamed and every excuse flushed (Africa News 2017).

Kenya for many years has struggled with the problems concerning the spread of small arms and light weapons (SALW) within its borders and the impact on the security of the country at large. The main regions affected are pastoral regions such as North Eastern Province, upper Eastern province and the North Rift regions. These pastoral communities mainly acquire these arms so as to protect their livestock from cattle rustlers as well as wild animals which is a frequent issue in the pastoral area according to Muchai (2005). Kenya does not manufacture arms but these arms find its way into comes in line with the United Nations Panel on Governmental Commission on Small

Arms defined as 'revolvers and self-loading pistols; rifles and carbines; sub-machine-guns; assault rifles; light machine guns' (UNGA 1997). The most widely used weapon in the North Eastern region as well as other conflict zones in the world is the AK-47 (Automat Kalashnikov 47) which was invented in the Second World War during the invasion of Russia by Germany and was constructed by the one mechanic known as Mikhail Timofeevich Kalashnikov (Blain 2009). AK-47 is mostly preferred because of its ease to master as well as it is easy to operate without much training. Thus, most of the people in the pastoral communities opt to buy the AK-47 for it is cheap and light to carry around the country illegally mostly from its neighbours. Somalia and South Sudan is one such neighbour which has been unstable for many years. The Somali from Somalia has been supplying the pastoral Somali communities in the North Eastern province due to porous border thus making the region prone to conflicts frequently. Most of these pastoral regions are conflict prone due to the presence of small arms and light weapons such as the famous AK-47 and others include G3, pistols, grenades these at the same very efficient.

CyberSecurity

Cybersecurity as a multifaceted field, combines domains as varied as information security, critical infrastructure protection, national security, cybercrime, cyberterrorism and cyberwarfare. Cybersecurity thus encompasses computer security, information security, ICT security, network security and infrastructure protection. Cybersecurity is defined as the proactive and reactive processes working towards the ideal of being free from threats to the confidentiality, integrity or availability of the computers, networks and information that form part of, and together constitute cyberspace (Ogwueleka and Aniche 2020).

Cybersecurity advanced from the confined realm of technical experts into the political limelight. With events such as the discovery of the nuclear-industry sabotaging Stuxnet computer worm, numerous tales of cyber espionage by foreign states, the growing dependence on the 'digital infrastructure' along with the sophistication of cybercriminals and the well-publicized activities of hacker collectives, the impression is created that cyberattacks are becoming more frequent, more organized, more costly and altogether more dangerous. As a result, a growing number of countries consider cybersecurity to be one of their top security issues (Dunn 2012). After 2010, the tone and intensity of the debate changed even further, the latest trend is to frame cybersecurity in strategic-military terms and to focus on countermeasures such as cyber-offence and cyber-defence, or cyber-deterrence (Dunn 2012).

Small Arms and Light Weapons (SALWs)

The proliferation of small arms has an effect on security and the explosive remnants of war exterminate and mutilate both human beings and animals after the end of conflicts. This has been noted to have destabilising effects on social, societal and economic development and is a major challenge to regional and national security. Small arms can be personal weapons that can be operated by only one person, which include revolvers, self loading pistols, rifles, submachine guns and light machine guns. They are also known to be weapons of mass destruction and can cause immense fatality and injury. These weapons are easy to use, it should be hidden and taken care of. Small arms are the key tools of bloodshed in every conflict where the mostly affected ones are the innocent suffer. They cause problems in both countries in conflict and those in peace, and exist after violent conflicts have ended.

According to World Bank, security is a necessity for poor people in all regions of the world and indeed a prerequisite for improving humanity's quality of life. 'Better security and safety...translates into lower vulnerability and thus into more robust production...' Small Arms and Light weapons (SALW) pose huge threat to Africa's sustainable development. Underlying this threat is global trade on SALW and inadequate international technological system to regulate the trade of SALW within and across national boundaries. They posit that West Africa's conflicts in the 1990s were particularly destructive due to the unregulated spread of armaments throughout the subregion. In Eastern Africa, where the AK-47 has become the weapon of choice for insurgents, terrorists, organized criminal syndicates and thugs alike, thousands of deaths have been attributed to the use and misuse of SALW which not only kill and maim, but also undermine all facets of security while diminishing the prospects for economic development. In fact, the Institute for Security Studies of South Africa reports that Africa alone has suffered 5,994,000 fatalities in the last 50 years due to mostly SALW. It is estimated that there are 500 million weapons in circulation worldwide (Ahere and Ouko 2012).

There are over 100 million small arms existing in Africa (SALW 2017). Their effects are devastating. In a vicious cycle, they are both a cause and effect of violence. They not only kill the innocent; they also maim, prolong conflicts, choke development and deepen poverty.

Some of the features of small arms according to Kumar (2008) are its low cost and accessibility, increased availability, easy maintenance and permanence.

i. **Low cost and wide availability**: Small arms are relatively low-tech tools of war, and due to state-driven demand, there are well over 600 suppliers around the world. With more than 550 million in circulation, whether newly produced, liquidated by downsizing militaries or circulated from conflict to conflict. Small arms are inexpensive and easily diffused.
ii. **Increasing lethality**: The increasing availability of rapid-fire military assault rifles, automatic pistols and sub-machine guns and their distribution to non-state actors have given such actors a firepower that often exceeds that of police or military forces. The adoption of newly available technology into shoulder-fired rockets, mortars and light antitank weapons has magnified the presence of warring factions in civil conflicts.

iii. **Simplicity and durability**: Small arms are easy to maintain, require little support and may last several decades. They require almost no training to use effectively, greatly increasing their use in conflicts involving informal militias and children.

iv. **Portability**: The flow of small arms is extremely difficult to track or monitor. Small arms can be carried by a single soldier or light vehicle, are easily shipped or smuggled to areas of conflict and can be effectively cached in legitimate cargo, warehouses or the outdoors, often in the harshest of climates.

v. **Military, police and civilian uses**: Unlike major conventional weapons, small arms cross the dividing line separating military and police forces from the civilian population.

In many countries, there has been a dramatic increase in the number and size of private militias and security firms that, in many cases, are equipped with military-type weapons.

Every country in West Africa has experienced widespread violence in which small arms were a factor. The production of small arms in large number has wide-ranging effects and converges upon many other problems that nations and societies face. At times, these links are incorporated and it is difficult to ascertain if the weapons are the basis of the crisis or an indication of other issues. The knowledge of these connections is an essential first step in promoting transformation.

THE NATURE, SCOPE AND CONSEQUENCES OF SMALL ARMS PROLIFERATION IN AFRICA

Small arms have several negative effects on African countries, from the aspect of development, youth growth, health, crime rate, etc.

The sources of uncontrolled Small Arms Flow in Africa Are

i. *Diversion from state stockpiles*: The diversion of legally acquired arms by African countries is a common source of uncontrolled and illicit arms. This can occur in several forms, including the illegal sale of official arms by corrupt officials to non-state actors. For example, some Nigerian soldiers were arrested in February 2016 for illegally selling arms to Boko Haram members while Ethiopian and Ugandan soldiers serving with the African Union Mission in Somalia (AMISOM) were accused of selling weapons from their stockpiles to traders in Somalia's illicit arms market (Wezeman 2010). Official stockpiles are also diverted through targeted looting of state armoury by armed groups, as was the case with the Séléka rebels in CAR in 2013 (Conflict Armament Research 2015). Similarly, the Libyan military armouries were looted after the fall of Muammar Gaddafi. In other instances, licit arms are also seized by non-state armed groups during raids and battles with state forces, such as in northern Mali.

The diversion of state arms stockpiles is also facilitated by the poor welfare conditions of uniformed personnel, weak governance and a lack of oversight over arms procurement and accountability of weapons (Adesoji 2017). Soldiers in most African countries are underpaid, and their salaries are often delayed for several months. This has reportedly led to riots, sexual violence, looting and involvement in corrupt practices, as has been reported in the DRC, Burkina Faso, Mali and Guinea. In some cases, official acquisitions are either undeclared or unreported by buyers and suppliers in order to bypass extant procedures, thereby complicating official tracing and accountability (Bromley and Holtom 2010). In short, poor stockpile management, and limited transparency and accountability in arms procurement, aid the illegal sale of state weapons by their custodians (http://www.maginternational.org/).

ii. *Black markets and illicit trafficking*: The number of conflicts in Africa illustrates the thriving scope of the illicit arms trade in the continent. Locally made arms and diverted stocks are traded in parallel arms markets. In 2013, Cameroonian security forces arrested a man who was transporting 655 guns to Nigeria, and another 5400 AK-47 rifles were intercepted in Maroua, in the northern region of Cameroon (IRIN 2015). Based on the Small Arms Survey assessment of Libya's illicit arms market, SALW such as heavy machine guns, shoulder-fired recoilless weapons, rocket launchers, anti-tank guided missiles, man-portable air defence systems, grenade launchers and different types of rifles can be bought in online (Small Arms Survey 2016b).

iii. *Poorly regulated local arms production*: Several unauthorized local arms producers exist across Africa, and the limited regulation of their activities contributes to the ready availability of SALW. In Ghana for instance, as of 2005, local gunsmiths have the capacity to produce over 200,000 weapons annually, including pistols, single and double barrel guns, traditional dane guns and pump-action shotguns (Aning 2005). Over 60% of illegal arms in southeast Nigeria are locally made (Nwaiwu 2015). In Mali, locally made weapons are widespread, and are used to commit crimes. This led to the enactment of law 040-50/ANLM to regulate the manufacture, use and trade in locally made weapons, and the promulgation of decree 05-441/P-RM for the enforcement of the law (Bamako 2016).

iv. *External sources*: Although most of the proliferated uncontrolled arms in circulation in Africa are being trafficked and transferred within the continent, weapons are initially shipped into conflict zones from outside the continent. For example, the UN Panel of Experts on Sudan identified certain countries, including Ukraine, China, Canada, Israel, Bulgaria, Slovakia, Iran and Russia as major suppliers of large stockpiles of arms and other material to South Sudan (Broga 2016). The UN-mandated

Somalia and Eritrea Monitoring Group (SEMG) also noted that one of al-Shabaab's supply lines originates in Yemen, with weapons delivered through multiple receiving points on the Somali coast (UN Security Council 2014).

Factors that Drive the Proliferation and Use of Uncontrolled and Illicit Arms in Africa

The first factor is struggle for political power in Africa which often takes violent dimensions, which are underscored by the use of arms in the competition for power. Conflicts often break out when power is manipulated to include or exclude certain individuals, communities, groups, religions or regions (Obi 2009). Those excluded resort to extreme measures such as violent protests or armed rebellion with the use of illicit arms. Illicit weapons were used in electoral violence in various parts of the continent.

Secondly, the worsened economic situation of most African countries in the past 20 years has further eroded their capacity to address pressing developmental challenges such as poverty, unemployment and poor infrastructure. A 2016 World Bank African Poverty Report confirms that poverty levels among Africans are higher than in the 1990s (World Bank 2016). When provided, employment opportunities and infrastructure are mainly concentrated in urban centres or constituencies that are loyal to ruling political parties, thus fuelling or compounding inequality. As such, many deprived or excluded groups express grievances through the use of illicit arms against the state. The widespread poverty and limited economic opportunities in Nigeria's northeast region were exploited by Boko Haram to recruit and radicalize poor, uneducated and vulnerable young people (Tella 2015). For instance, one of the group's recruitment strategies involved the provision of cash loans to potential recruits (Abrak 2016). The underdevelopment of Mali's northern regions, relative to the South, has been identified as a major reason why the Tuaregs decided to bear arms against the Malian state (Adesoji 2017).

Thirdly, the control, access and distribution of natural resources has triggered, sustained or exacerbated conflicts in many resource-rich countries in Africa. Illicit arms have contributed to the escalation and deadliness of such conflicts in recent years. This includes conflicts over hydrocarbons, mineral deposits or grazing land. For example, illicit arms are a key factor in the militancy and insecurity in the Niger Delta region of Nigeria, Katanga areas of DRC and the gold-rich Tibesti region in northern Chad. In fact, the gold mines in Tibesti have become a theatre of war fuelled primarily by SALW from Gaddafi-era SALW stockpiles. Similarly, illicit arms have increased the spate of violent clashes and casualties between herders and farmers in Mali and Nigeria, Bororo in CAR, as well as Barara in Chad. In fact, herdsmen in Sudan and South Sudan openly display SALW, and cattle raids, involving the use of SALW, in rural areas (BBC News 2012).

Fourthly, the growth and activities of religious groups that espouse radical extremist ideologies have contributed to the spread and use of illicit arms in Africa. The existence and possession of SALW by violent extremist groups have negatively impacted security in West, Horn and North Africa. The open display of SALW is a requisite element in the identity of violent extremist groups, and extremist groups appear deadlier as their access to and quantity of SALW increases. For instance, radical Tuareg militias and Al-Qaeda in the Islamic Maghreb (AQIM) in northern Mali have initiated and sustained armed insurgencies because of their access to and use of SALW. Islamist militancy has garnered the most attention as a consequence of the violent attacks of Boko Haram, Al-Qaeda in the Islamic Maghreb, Al-Shabaab and other similar groups operating across Africa (Stephen and Rorisang 2016). Based on UNDP estimates, 24,771 people were killed and 5507 wounded between 2011 and 2015, with most of the fatalities recorded in Nigeria and Somalia (UNDP 2015). The porous border and swathes of 'ungoverned spaces' in the Sahel and West Africa are exploited for the illicit transfer of arms to extremist groups.

Finally, the flow of uncontrolled arms plays a crucial role in the activities of organized crime networks across Africa; they are either the object of illicit trafficking and/or used to protect the infrastructures used for criminal activities. There is a convergence of organized crime, SALW availability and armed conflict, including violent extremism, in places such as the Sahel, Libya and Somalia. Pirates use illicit arms in the Horn of Africa and the Gulf of Guinea region to attack and seize ships and to kidnap crews for ransom. Similarly, South American drugs heading for Europe are trafficked through West Africa and the Sahel, and SALW is used to protect the trafficking routes. A 2013 report by the United Nations Office on Drugs and Crime (UNODC) put the annual cost of drugs trafficked through West Africa at $1.25bn (UNODC 2013). The cost of piracy in the Gulf of Guinea and Somali coast to the global economy in 2015 was $719m and $1.32bn, respectively (Mungai 2016).

The Global Arms Trade Treaty (ATT)

The passage of the ATT in April 2013 and its entry into force in December 2014 are vital steps in tackling the problem of uncontrolled and illicit arms transfer into and within Africa. The ATT is a multilateral treaty that regulates the international trade in, and transfer of, conventional weapons across and within national borders. It is the first internationally legally binding agreement which sets globally common standards for the regulation of the conventional arms trade and prevention of illicit arms trade and transfer (UNODA 2018)

Under the ATT, member states are obliged to:

i. Block arms exports if they breach their international obligations or could be used to commit genocide or war crimes.

ii. Assess the possibility that arms exports would disrupt peace and security or could be used to violate international humanitarian or human rights law.
iii. Submit reports on their implementation of the treaty, detailing their transfer control systems and annual reports on their arms exports and imports.
iv. Establish and maintain a national control system to regulate the export and/or import of arms parts and components, as well as ammunitions or munitions fired, launched or delivered by conventional arms.
v. Take measures to ensure all authorizations for the export of conventional arms, and make available appropriate information on the authorization upon request, to the importing and transit states.
vi. Take appropriate measures to regulate, where necessary and feasible, the transit or trans-shipment of arms and ammunitions of conventional arms under their jurisdiction.
vii. Take measures under their national laws, to regulate brokering taking place under their jurisdiction for conventional arms.

It will be challenging to break the cycle of illicit trade of small arms. The illegal small arms trade is a global occurrence, but mainly at concentrated areas of armed conflict. The kinds of weapons in circulation ranging from firearms (such as pistols and light machine guns), to mortars and rocket-propelled grenades have become the weapons of choice for the majority of regional conflicts taking place today. The weapons which enter the illegal trade originate from both within and outside Africa. Weapons trafficking across borders in Africa is the primary source of illicit arms. In the vast majority of cases, sophisticated organizations and networks are made up of criminals, corrupt security officials and returning peacekeepers, who are usually the ones who specialize in moving weapons across African borders. The mode of trafficking can range from large convoys carrying a significant amount of weapons and ammunition, or the so-called 'ant trade' in which the weapons are smuggled across borders in smaller numbers, but at a high rate. The lay of the land also makes a big difference.

In some parts of Africa, the production of homemade arms, known as 'craft weapons' is big business, producing everything from rudimentary pistols to sophisticated assault rifles. In Ghana, for example, craft weapons are involved in 80% of gun-related crimes, according to the Ghana Police Service, while Sierra Leone and Ivory Coast ranked domestic craft weapons production as the most significant source of illicit arms. The illegal arms trade also hinders development across the continent.

Destabilizing the Continent—The illicit weapons trade in small arms has been at least partially blamed for the persistence of wars across the African continent. Currently, approximately 30 million firearms are being circulated through Africa. This is compared to an estimated 84 million in Europe. However, the number of firearms is less important than how they are being used. The transfer of weapons between countries can be linked to the increase in conflict in bordering regions by the same armed groups, with conflicts frequently seeming to follow the flow of arms. The conflict which took place in Congo and the conflict in Libya have all aided the proliferation and acquisition of small arms in the region, example, violence has broken out in Liberia before moving towards Sierra Leone, Ivory Coast and eventually Guinea.

Illegal weapons have also been traded online in Libya. The regular monitoring and analysis of new sources of illicit weapons, gaining a better understanding of the demand factors which drive illicit arms flows, and increasing joint border initiatives are just some of the recommendations made in the latest study by the Small Arms Survey (2016b).

SMALL ARMS: A TOOL IN CONFLICT, DEVELOPMENT, HEALTH AND CRIME

Small arms and conflict: The SALW problem can be seen consisting of three independent dimensions: availability, misuse and demand. SALW has many uses beyond their primary functions as weapons of war. As a consequence, conflict and insecurity, and includes both the direct costs (death and injuries in conflict) and the indirect costs (post-conflict insecurity, intercommunal tensions, etc.) of SALW proliferation and use. Although the presence or proliferation of SALWs does not cause the conflict that are evident around the world, they contribute to their level of violence and make the resolution of these conflicts more difficult. SALW is used both by government forces (military and police) and by non-state actors (guerrillas, ethnic militias, self-defence units, violent criminals, etc.) engaged in conflicts against each other or against the state, or in violent criminal activities. Of the 49 armed conflicts since 1990, all but three relied on SALW as the only instrument of war, and only one, the 1991 Persian Gulf War, was dominated by heavy weapons (Klare 2012; SALW Training Manual 2012). Modern small arms, especially assault rifles like the Soviet/Russian AK-47 and the US made M-16 have played an especially conspicuous role in recent conflicts, accounting for anywhere between 35 and 60% of all the deaths and injuries in warfare since 1990. In 2009, South Sudan experienced a major spike in armed violence, causing 2500 deaths and displacing 350,000. The violence reached crisis point, with the Government of Southern Sudan, almost exclusively preoccupied with countering perceived Northern aggression at the expense of security and governance issues closer to home (McEvoy and LeBrun 2010).

Small arms and development: Sustainable development is a combination of economic growth and social progress that meets the needs of the present without compromising the ability of future generations to meet their own needs. It is also undeniably linked to the problems of small arms and armed violence. Small arms affect development in the most basic way because they are the tools of conflict. During conflict, physical and human resources are destroyed; transit routes or fertile areas are blocked and diverted; and sometimes national industries are corrupted or taken over by armed groups. Foreign investors and aid agencies are discouraged from proceeding with essential projects and support. All of this undermines halts or prevents development. In Darfur, for example, security deteriorated rapidly in 2005 as armed forces terrorized civilians. Many development organizations withdrew thousands of personnel who had been delivering critical basic services to displaced citizens. The cost of conflict on African development was approximately $300 billion between 1990 and 2005, according to new research by Oxfam International, IANSA and Saferworld. The report shows that on average, a war, civil war or insurgency shrinks an African economy by 15%. The continent loses an average of around $18 billion a year due to armed conflict.

Half of the countries emerging from war resume conflict partially due to inadequate post-conflict development and reintegration programs and the availability of arms supports this regression. In post-conflict societies, large numbers of former combatants flood the job market only to discover a lack of economic opportunities. Ex-soldiers, typically still armed, often turn to crime as the only means of survival (SALW 2016).

Small arms and health: Community health is affected by the production and wrong use of small arms. Violence leads to injury; injury requires care and when there is widespread injury, it is all too easy for health care systems in African countries to turn out to be besieged. Nursing the armed violence fatalities avert medical resources from ill patients or persons in need of medical attention. In many conflict zones, the transportation routes for the distribution of food and medicine are insecure due to the threat of small arms, and sanitation and water purification systems break down, leading to epidemic of diseases such as cholera. The costs of the medical care are high. Also, the health workers, hospitals, ambulances and clinics can be targets of small arms.

Small Arms and Youth: Children are susceptible to the propagation and abuse of small arms. They are defenceless to armed attacks and kidnapping or injury. The influence of what they see during violent times makes them to learn to use guns and also become a combatant. This can have impact of a nation's development. The ordeal that armed violence causes ruins family organizations and destroys the provision of basic services children depends on, such as education, proper health care, etc. Nothing functions well even education, as schools cannot function properly and can be targets for armed groups seeking child recruits. Other things such as children displacement from their homes come from conflicts creating diseases, brutality, military recruitment and sexual attack.

In at least 20 countries around the world, children are direct participants in war. Denied a childhood and often subjected to horrific violence, hundreds of thousands of children are serving as soldiers, often for non-state armed groups. These young combatants participate in all aspects of contemporary warfare (SALW 2016). They wield AK-47s and M16s on the front lines of combat, serve as human mine detectors, participate in suicide missions, carry supplies and act as spies, messengers or lookouts. Some of these children are abducted while at school and coerced into service, an activity made easier by weakened family and social structures, and, of course, fear of their abductors who are wielding their own weapons. Moreover, when there are few employment opportunities available, the option of serving a militia or army and belonging to something is more appealing than it otherwise would be. In the trend of using child soldiers, one sees the tragic intersection of small arms proliferation and the challenges of development.

The United Nations Children's Fund (UNICEF) and many others have launched programs to help adolescents learn about the danger of small arms and alternatives to gun violence in many countries across Africa. The projects combine basic gun safety education with leadership development, vocational training and conflict-resolution techniques to give boys and girls real alternatives to lives of violence and fear (SALW 2016).

Small arms and gender: The large number of small arms is one of the factors to gender inequality and brutality against African women. In conflict and post-conflict regions, women and girls suffer from a variety of harmful effects related to the threat and misuse of small arms (DFAIT 2008; SALW 2012). At the use of guns, sexual violence such as rape, sexual slavery and forced impregnation is obtainable. In the course of the armed conflict in eastern Democratic Republic of Congo (DRC), tens of thousands of women and girls were raped and sexually assaulted by well-armed combatant forces. In the Dadaab refugee camp in northern Kenya, 75% of reported rapes and sexual assaults occurred at the hands of armed assailants (SALW 2016). Women also become the breadwinner of their families when their husbands die or critically injured during war. Women are affected by the damage to health, education and other social services. In time of peace, women are also the target to violence and harassment, even in their homes. A gun increases the chance of death by 12 times compared to other means of violence. Every six hours in South Africa, a woman is shot dead by her current or former partner. Women in many countries have taken on strong leadership roles in combating gun violence through awareness-raising and gun collection programs, by lobbying governments for gun law reform, and contributing to a number of creative and courageous initiatives (SALW 2016).

Small arms and crime: Small arms are used in different ways for criminal activities by both individuals and organizations. It is easy to obtain and use forcefully. Armed crime is frequent in municipals and some African countries. The young men are the actually the main users and victims of small arms in criminal acts. The fatality and wounds of affected people by the misuse of small arms impair, downgrade the number of skilled people, among other things. This can be eradicated by the creation of job opportunities, creating awareness of types of crime and implications of the use of small arms.

The Role of ICT in the Proliferation of Small Arms in Africa

The rapid movement of small arms across the world is increasingly difficult to trace and has long-lasting effects on human security. Often small arms become available in a region for valid and legal reasons related to national security, peacekeeping or law enforcement. In fact, much of the trade in arms is legitimate and accounted for; it is a well-established and prosperous industry. Like other industries, it has become increasingly globalized. Most weapons are now assembled from components sourced from many countries. The result of this rapid global expansion is that weapons, their parts and ammunition are more easily diverted from their intended destination. They may end up in countries that have few controls over how they will be used. Surplus or poorly guarded military weapons find markets in war-torn or post-conflict nations, or are stolen and end up in the hands of non-state armed groups or terrorists. Illicit brokers are able to manipulate the inconsistencies and loopholes between national arms trade laws. Small arms can cross from state to private owners many times over (SALW 2016).

Small arms remain in existence for many years after entering a region and have an efficient existence of many decades. Small arms change the motivations of a conflict instantaneously. They are deadly and intended to kill. They can transform a simple argument into a tragedy, and be used against civilians seeking to protect themselves. Some countries at peace still have high level of small arms violence and their presence is an acknowledged means through which domestic violence occurs.

Small arms and light weapons are responsible for the majority of battle-related conflict deaths with an estimated seventy (70) to ninety-two (92) per cent of all direct conflict victims are killed with firearms. Large numbers of men, women, older people and children die indirectly from the effects of armed conflict on the economy, ruined health and security infrastructures, disease and famine. Many people are made refugees or are displaced, injured or abused. Arms fuel conflict. Conflict fuels instability and poverty. Violence does not necessarily begin with a weapon, but it increases dramatically when weapons are present, particularly in already volatile environments rife with poverty, mistrust or injustice. Some of the small arms are guns of different categorises, grenades, etc.

The small arms propagation has been overwhelming in Africa, where machine guns, rifles, grenades, pistols and other small arms have killed and displaced many civilians across the continent. It has been used in deadly conflicts in African countries such as Uganda, Rwanda, Sudan, Sierra Leone, Angola, Congo, Somalia, etc. These arms are often recycled from country to country, and their ownership is transferred among fighters, security forces and war profiteers.

In central and eastern Africa, many lives have been lost through conflict and its related effects. The irregular warfare that has been common there in recent decades is well served by these kinds of weapons, which are easily available and sometimes cost less than food items. In 1994, an intra-ethnic conflict in Rwanda left more than 800,000 people murdered, mostly with small arms, including machetes. An estimated 300,000 civilians have also lost their lives the same way in Burundi. However, the foreign supply of arms to both governments and rebel groups continues to grow in illicit, ungoverned or poorly controlled transactions. The small arms that are already in the subregion move easily across borders, the borders between Cameroon, Chad and the Central African Republic have been identified specifically as areas of high proliferation (SALW 2016).

Small arms are widely available in southern Africa. Civil and interstate conflicts drive demand for small arms and create a pool of weapons that can be used to commit violent crime as well as fuel conflict. Most were transferred there during the Cold War, but some others originate from within the region. South Africa maintains a sizable arms production industry. There is also another aspect to the issue here, that is, the cultural significance of the AK-47 to the formerly colonized peoples of southern Africa. After decades of use by anti-colonial and anti-apartheid movements, the powerful small arms have come to be associated with liberation. For example, the silhouette of a gun is featured on the Mozambican flag. Freedom songs from the struggles against minority rule in Namibia, South Africa, Zimbabwe and Angola often extolled the virtues of the AK-47, and those of the fighters carrying it. Recognizing the problems posed by its proliferation, many countries are involved in coordinated action, mainly within the framework of the Southern African Development Community (SADC).

The estimated 8 million small arms that are circulating throughout western Africa play a central role in fostering instability (Michael 2011; SALW 2017). Demand for small arms in West Africa is motivated by weak governance, insecurity and poverty. The supply comes mostly from external sources. They have been used in armed robberies, intra- and inter-communal feuds, local wars, armed insurrections, armed rebel activities and terrorism. They are used to facilitate drug trafficking, smuggling and other such crimes. Overall, small arms maintain a general state of fear. As a result of the armed conflict in the region, many people have been killed, many others displaced or made refugees and property.

ICT-Driven Counter Small Arms and CyberSecurity Policy in Africa

Following the contours of challenges confronting Africa's distinctive digital cultures, it is easy to recognize that cybersecurity and cyber resilience are not simply technical problems that respond to advanced technical solutions as the case in advanced nations attempt to suggest (Fischer 2014). Contrarily and by comparing data on ICT penetration measured by the proportion of mobile phone subscription in the country and its population to its GDP per capita for countries like Mali, Malawi and Madagascar on one end of digital penetration ranking in Africa and Ethiopia at the other end. The correlation between ICT penetration and economic growth becomes skewed revealing the unique and unprecedented case of African ICT and Cybersecurity ecosystem inherently shaped by political footprints (ITU 2016) (Table 31.1).

Available data shows that conflicts in Africa represent a significant percentage of global conflicts. In a 2015 report on conflict, violence and extremism in Africa, the Institute for Security Studies (ISS) noted that 52% of global armed conflict incidents in 2014 occurred in Africa, despite Africa having only 16% of the world's population. Eleven (11) statistics collated from the Heidelberg Conflict Barometer show that 87 of the 236 global

Table 31.1 Countries with ongoing conflicts or incidences of Insecurity in Africa

Country	Civil war or rebellion	Violent extremism and/or terrorism	Interstate conflict	Organized crime	Ethno-political militancy	Secessionist agitation
Algeria		Y				
Angola						Y
Burundi					Y	
Cameroon		Y				
CAR	Y				Y	
Chad		Y			Y	
Congo DR	Y			Y	Y	
Côte d'Ivoire	Y				Y	
Djibouti	Y					
Egypt	Y					
Ethiopia					Y	Y
Eritrea			Y			
Libya	Y	Y		Y	Y	Y
Mali	Y	Y			Y	Y
Mauritania				Y		
Niger		Y		Y		
Nigeria	Y				Y	Y
Senegal						Y
Somalia	Y	Y			Y	
South Sudan	Y				Y	Y
Sudan	Y	Y			Y	Y
Tunisia		Y				
Uganda	Y					Y
Western Sahara						

(*Source* Adesoji 2017)

high-intensity conflicts between 2011 and 2015 took place in Africa. Africa's security situation is fluid, and conflicts occur at varying degrees of intensity. As indicated in Figs. 31.1 and 31.2, between 2013 and 2015, an average of 22 new and ongoing wars was recorded annually.

Figure 31.1 shows the conflicts in Africa disaggregated by their intensity from 2011 to 2015, while Fig. 31.2 is the high violent conflicts in Africa 2013–2015.

Most conflicts in Africa occur at the sub-state level, and are fought using uncontrolled arms. This is because these conflicts are primary among non-state

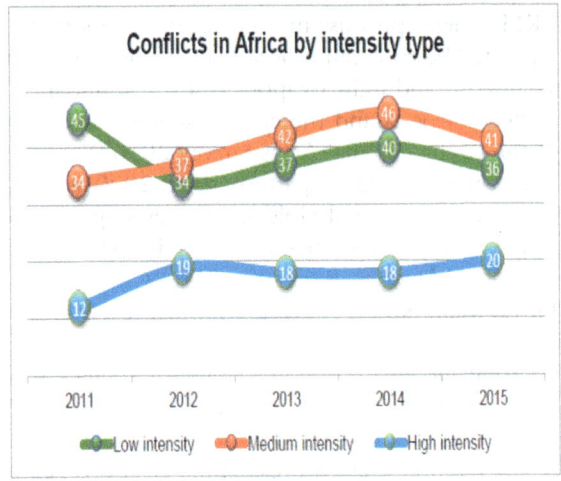

Fig. 31.1 Conflicts in Africa by their intensity, 2011–2015 (*Source* Heidelberg conflict barometer, 2011–2015)

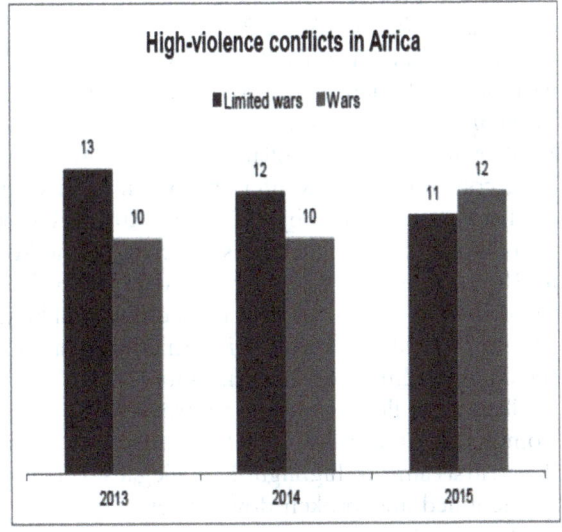

Fig. 31.2 High-Intensity Conflicts in Africa 2013–2015 (*Source* Heidelberg conflict barometer, 2013–2015)

actors, or between non-state actors and national governments. Since non-state actors (including militias, warlords and extremist groups) have no legal authority to purchase or bear arms, they resort to illicit means of arms acquisition. While it is important to note that intra-state conflicts are not necessarily caused by small arms, the fundamental implication of illicit circulation of arms in conflict zones is the heightened risk of higher and more deadly levels of violence. Uncontrolled access to weapons encourages violence instead of dialogue. It creates a false sense of entitlement among competing interests that 'might is right'. Such a mindset results in protracted conflicts. For instance, the proliferation of firearms across Somalia is a major cause of instability in the country; weapons such as the Duska 108 mm heavy machine gun and the PKM general-purpose machine gun are reportedly sold in Mogadishu's Bakara market. The root cause of Somalia's unending conflict cannot be attributed to small arms and light weapons, yet the abundance of illicitly purchased uncontrolled weapons and the ease of acquisition are key factors in the protraction of the conflict (Small Arms Survey 2016b).

Another emergent pattern since 2000 is the rise in political violence in the form of electoral violence, protests against long-term leaders and constitutional crises. This has occurred in around fifteen (15) African countries including Algeria, Burundi, CAR, Côte d'Ivoire, DRC, Egypt, Ethiopia, Libya, Mali, Niger, Nigeria, South Africa, South Sudan and Sudan. The nexus between uncontrolled arms and political violence is evident in the level of electoral violence, as politicians either seek to forcefully attain or hold on to power. For instance, Charlotte Osei, Ghana's Electoral Commission (EC) Chair, noted that the proliferation of illegal small arms constituted a danger to the country's 2016 presidential elections (Citifmonline 2016). The use of small arms and light weapons was responsible for over 800 deaths recorded during the post-electoral violence that erupted after the 2011 presidential elections in Nigeria (Adele 2012).

An analysis of Africa's illicit arms flows has revealed the extent of the illegal weapons trade across the continent. The study, entitled *Weapons Compass: Mapping Illicit Small Arms Flows in Africa*, which was compiled by the Small Arms Survey in collaboration with the African Union (AU) Commission, comes just weeks after the AU met to outline its ambitious goal of a total ceasefire in Africa by 2020. The African Union Master Roadmap of Practical Steps to Silence the Guns in Africa by the Year 2020 was conceived back in 2016. However, with just one year left before the deadline, turning this vision into reality is looking increasingly unlikely. The latest report aims to provide valuable background information to assist with the implementation of the AU's roadmap (Small Arms Survey 2016b).

Illicit arms flows continue to promote conflicts in many African countries, from petty crime to insurgencies and terrorist activities. The data collected in the analysis aims to highlight how illegal small arms and ammunition flows can be identified and broken down, providing entry points to intercept and halt the trade.

CyberSecurity Strategies and the Control of Small Arms in Africa

To design and implement a secure cyberspace, some stringent strategies have been put in place. The major strategies employed to ensure cybersecurity include Creating a Secure Cyber Ecosystem, Creating an Assurance Framework, Encouraging Open Standards, Strengthening the Regulatory Framework, Creating Mechanisms for IT Security, Securing E-governance Services and Protecting Critical Information Infrastructure.

Strategy 1—Creating a Secure Cyber Ecosystem: The cyber ecosystem involves a wide range of varied entities like devices (communication technologies and computers), individuals, governments, private organizations, etc., which interact with each other for numerous reasons. This strategy explores the idea of having a strong and robust cyber ecosystem where the cyber devices can work with each other in the future to prevent cyberattacks, reduce their effectiveness, or find solutions to recover from a cyberattack. Such a cyber ecosystem would have the ability to built into its cyber devices to permit secured ways of action to be organized within and among groups of devices. This cyber ecosystem can be supervised by present monitoring techniques where software products are used to detect and report security weaknesses.

A strong cyber ecosystem has three symbiotic structures, namely Automation, Interoperability and Authentication. *Automation* eases the implementation of advanced security measures, enhances the swiftness and optimizes the decision-making processes. *Interoperability* toughens the collaborative actions, improves awareness and accelerates the learning procedure. There are three types of interoperability, which are Semantic (i.e., shared lexicon based on common understanding), Technical and Policy (important in assimilating different contributors into an inclusive cyber-defence structure). *Authentication* improves the identification and verification technologies that work in order to provide security, affordability, ease of use and administration, scalability and interoperability.

Strategy 2—Creating an Assurance Framework: The objective of this strategy is to design an outline in compliance with the global security standards through traditional products, processes, people and technology. To cater to the national security requirements, a national framework known as the *Cyber security Assurance Framework* was developed. It accommodates critical infrastructure organizations and the governments through 'Enabling and Endorsing' actions. *Enabling* actions are performed by government entities that are autonomous bodies free from commercial interests. The publication of 'National Security Policy Compliance Requirements' and IT security guidelines and documents to enable IT security implementation and compliance is done by these authorities. *Endorsing* actions are involved in profitable services after meeting the obligatory qualification standards. The structure that has been produced through such association between industry and government, comprises of the standards, guidelines and practices. These parameters help the owners and operators of critical infrastructure to manage cybersecurity-related risks.

Strategy 3—Encouraging Open Standards: Standards play a significant role in defining how we approach information security-related issues across geographical regions and societies. Open standards are encouraged to enhance the efficiency of key processes, enable systems incorporations, provide a medium for users to measure new products or services, organize the approach to arrange new technologies or business models, interpret complex environments and endorse economic growth.

Strategy 4—Strengthening the Regulatory Framework: The objective of this strategy is to create a secure cyberspace ecosystem and strengthen the regulatory framework. A 24X7 mechanism has been envisioned to deal with cyberthreats through National Critical Information Infrastructure Protection Centre (NCIIPC). The Computer Emergency Response Team (CERT-In) has been designated to act as a nodal agency for crisis management. Some highlights of this strategy are to promote research and development in cybersecurity; develop human resource through education and training programs; encourage all organizations, whether public or private, to designate a person to serve as Chief Information Security Officer (CISO) who will be responsible for cybersecurity initiatives; establish a cybercommand as a part of strengthening procedure for the cybersecurity of defence network and installations; and effective implementation of public–private partnership is in pipeline that will go a long way in creating solutions to the ever-changing threat landscape.

Strategy 5—Creating Mechanisms for IT Security: Some basic mechanisms that are in place for ensuring IT security are link-oriented security measures, end-to-end security measures, association-oriented measures and data encryption. These methods differ in their internal application features and also in the attributes of the security they provide. *Link-Oriented Measures* delivers security while transferring data between two nodes, irrespective of the eventual source and destination of the data. *End-to-End Measures* are a medium for transporting Protocol Data Units (PDUs) in a protected manner from source to destination in such a way that disruption of any of their communication links does not violate security. *Association-Oriented Measures* are a modified set of end-to-end measures that protect every association individually. *Data Encryption* defines some general features of conventional ciphers and the recently developed class of public-key ciphers. It encodes information in a way that only the authorized personnel can decrypt them.

Strategy 6—Securing E-Governance Services: Electronic governance (e-governance) is the most treasured instrument with the government to provide public services in an accountable manner. Unfortunately, in the current scenario, there is no devoted legal structure for e-governance and law for obligatory e-delivery of public service in Nigeria. And nothing is more hazardous and troublesome than executing e-governance projects without sufficient cybersecurity. Hence, securing the e-governance services has become a crucial task, especially when the nation is making daily transactions through cards.

Strategy 7—Protecting Critical Information Infrastructure: Critical information infrastructure is the backbone of a country's national and economic security. It includes power plants, highways, bridges, chemical plants, networks, as well as the buildings where millions of people work every day. These can be secured with stringent collaboration plans and disciplined implementations. Safeguarding critical infrastructure against developing cyberthreats needs a structured approach. It is required that the government aggressively collaborates with public and private sectors on a regular basis to prevent, respond to and coordinate mitigation efforts against attempted disruptions and adverse impacts to the nation's critical infrastructure.

CRISIS OF REGULATION OF UNCONTROLLED SPREAD OF ARMS IN AFRICA

The problem of uncontrolled arms, as well as their illicit acquisition and transfer, is a recurring security challenge in Africa. While they do not directly cause conflict, their concentration in crisis zones often sustains or prolongs them. Uncontrolled arms also fuel civil wars, empowering non-state armed groups to launch attacks against governments and local communities. For instance, in DRC, conflict and insecurity are fuelled by the continued inflow of illicit small arms. Notwithstanding a subsisting UN arms embargo, illicit arms are traced to stockpiles from past conflicts and new supplies from a variety of sources in the Great Lakes region. For instance, the Democratic Forces for the Liberation of Rwanda (FDLR) reportedly received different types of small arms from Tanzania by boat in June 2008, March 2009 and November 2009 (Bromley and Holtom 2010). The Council of Foreign Relations puts the annual monetary value of the illicit arms trade at $1bn (Council on Foreign Relations 2013). This represents between 10 and 20% of global trade in SALWs and the use of these weapons continues to have devastating consequences on individuals, families and communities across Africa, where over 100 million small arms are estimated to be in circulation as shown in Table 31.2.

Table 31.2 Legal and illegal spread and possession of firearms in Africa

Country	Privately owned firearms (licit and illicit)	Civilian firearms possession per 100 population
Algeria	1,900,000	7.6
Angola	2,800,000	17.3
CAR	40,000	1.0
Côte d'Ivoire	400,000	2.4
DRC	800,000	1.4
Ghana	2,300,000	8.55
Libya	900,000	15.5
Mali	143,000	1.1
Mozambique	1,000,000	5.1
Nigeria	2,000,000	1.5
South Africa	3,400,000	6.61
South Sudan	3,000,000	28.23
Sudan	2,000,000	5.5
Somalia	750,000	9.1
Uganda	400,000	1.4

Source Gun policy portal, Available www.gunpolicy.org

COOPERATION AMONG ARMED FORCES AND SECURITY FORCES IN COMBATING THE PROLIFERATION OF SMALL ARMS IN AFRICA

The excessive and uncontrolled accumulation of small arms has led to the emergence of groups of armed individuals operating across and beyond state borders: rebel movements, private militias, terrorists, drug traffickers, arms dealers, etc. In some cases, this proliferation of armed groups undermines the authority of the state and its ability to guarantee the safety of its citizens. Everyday experience in West Africa shows that the proliferation of small arms is a catalyst for crises and armed violence and helps to destabilize governments and states, in particular as a result of the

activities of subversive movements, guerrilla campaigns, terrorism, drug trafficking, civil wars and other attacks on fundamental rights and human dignity. Consequently, it has become vital for all West African states to curb the proliferation of small arms.

With the aim of combating the proliferation of small arms and light weapons, the heads of state and government of the Economic Community of West African States (ECOWAS) declared a moratorium on the importation, exportation and manufacture of small arms and light weapons on 31 October 1998. In enforcing the West African moratorium on small arms, the armed forces and security forces will be the key to any campaign aimed at halting the proliferation of small arms and light weapons. The way in which the armed forces and security forces organize, cooperate and conduct themselves will prompt the local people to comply with the law in general, and in particular the law on the monitoring and regulation of small arms (Yacubu 2003).

The government has a heavy responsibility in monitoring the proliferation of small arms and light weapons. The prime responsibility is connected with the fact that increased circulation of illegal weapons diminishes the government's credibility, owing to its inability to curb the phenomenon and combat the major crime that inevitably results. The second responsibility relates to the issue by the government of permits to buy weapons. In fact, in a system where citizens feel properly protected by the state, there is no need for individuals to apply for permits to buy weapons for reasons of protection. Citizens who acquire weapons for sports purposes do not need to own a weapon personally. A weapons monitoring centre can be set up where interested citizens can borrow weapons for a time and return them after use.

Other responsibilities of the government include the strengthening of regulations on possession of weapons; the acquisition of modern equipment for detection of arms and ammunition; the provision of all necessary equipment to the armed forces and security forces for monitoring the proliferation of small arms; a survey of local arms and ammunition manufacturers so as to monitor their production and sales; the outlawing of all traditions and cultures which encourage the display of firearms; suspension of the issue of permits to buy weapons to individuals; and creation of public awareness of the dangers posed by the proliferation of small arms and light weapons.

Conclusion

The propagation of small arms and their negative consequences have become major concerns underlying a number of national, regional and international initiatives. These arms come from many sources, and are acquired legally by the armed forces and security forces, which end up in the hands of criminals as a result of theft or illegal sale. One of the most alarming factors promoting the proliferation of small arms is the role of tradition and culture, especially in the form of the ceremonial and ritual use of such weapons, but the introduction of good governance and transparency in the management of public affairs can help to eradicate the scourge of small arms proliferation.

Africa should break this vicious cycle with any religious leaders. Religious leaders are the successor of powerful religious and moral traditions that know it is greatly erroneous to overflow populations with small arms. They know about the devastation of death, the shattering of families and the orphaning of children by small arms. They know that children are supposed to be in schools but are being stocked with guns instead of books, paper and pens. Working together, religious leaders can use their moral authority to call their communities to work together for the reduction of these lethal weapons.

Light weapons proliferation is a serious problem in West Africa. A regional moratorium on imports of small arms and light weapons has not worked and UN arms embargoes on Sierra Leone, Liberia and Côte d'Ivoire have had limited impact. The Economic Community of West African States is currently drafting a new binding legal instrument aimed at controlling flows in West Africa but this will only succeed if the heads of state and government seriously adopt it. This needs to include greater compliance of UN sanctions, international reform of the End User Certificate system, mapping the spread of artisan production and an examination of ammunition imports to West Africa. Better control of ammunition imports in particular may assist the combat of light weapons proliferation as well as the comprehensive destruction of weapons from disarmament efforts. The illicit weapons trade in Africa is increasingly transnational and it requires regional and international cooperation and support to combat it.

Governments should control the arms trade and agree that illicit trade in small arms must be curbed. A first step is to reduce and monitor the legal trade, whose high volume helps to mask illegal transfers. To increase transparency, all nations should report imports and exports, public and private. These transfers of small arms should be disclosed in a form parallel to the UN's existing register of major conventional arms (this is being discussed regionally in Africa and globally at the UN).

A bolder step would be direct monitoring of flows by Interpol, the UNand/or a new agency. Methods could include assistance to border services, short-notice inspections, on-request inspection teams or even challenge-inspection, as used with unwilling states under the Chemical Weapons Convention. Development agencies have begun supporting customs/border officials. In West Africa, UNDP/PCASED is helping to develop procedures such as checking of cargo manifests, flight plans and inspection.

Control of arms brokers is rising on the international agenda, with Secretary-General Annan calling, in his *Report on Africa*, for 'more effective measures to punish the continent's arms traffickers' who exploit gaps in national systems and lack of global controls. A recent NGO report (Wood and Peleman 1999, *The Arms Fixers*, PRIO rept. 3/99) throws light on their murky, lucrative world.

New global norms should be promoted. Tackling illicit arms trade and restricting international transfers are important but limited steps towards global goals. A much bigger challenge is the problem of domestic manufacture, possession and movement.

States and communities should enforce strict regulations on firearms, and then push for new higher standards and norms, at least in their region, so that their security is not undermined by weak laws in neighbouring jurisdictions.

Moving ahead, no small arms should be in criminal hands, police and the military should have an essential minimum and civilians should have only licensed guns for legitimate needs, properly registered, marked and safely stored, with international trade under strict control. Steps can be taken now towards these still-distant goals. The control of small arms is a key piece of the interlocking puzzles of sustainable human development and sustainable human security. Without it, neither can be solved. Development agencies, in partnership with governments, civil society and local communities, can be agents of change by working in the ways described above and others yet to be discovered.

The real solution to the small arms problem is, ultimately, rising global levels of human security and development. When people are free, have the means to achieve their human potential, and realize that conflict can be resolved justly without violence, then resentment and revenge will become as rare as guns. With an integrated agenda of human security and human development, we can gradually build respect for life, overcome poverty and raise the physical, intellectual and spiritual standards of our communities and our world (Dorn 2000).

REFERENCES

Aaron, K. (2018). *Estimating Global Civilian HELD Firearms Numbers. ECOWAS Convention on Small Arms and Light Weapons, Their Ammunition and Other Related Materials* (pp. 1–1). http://www.smallarmssurvey.org/fileadmin/docs/T-Briefing-Papers/SAS-BP-Civilian-Firearms-Numbers.pdf. Accessed on 20 September 2019.

Abrak, I. (2016, May 9). Boko Haram Using Cash Loans to Recruit Members in Face of Crackdown. *The Guardian*. https://www.theguardian.com/global-development/2016/may/09/boko-haram-loans-recruit-members-crackdown-nigeria-traders-spy. Accessed 20 September 2019.

Adele, B. J. (2012). Electoral Violence and Nigeria's 2011 General Elections. *International Review of Social Sciences and Humanities, 4*(1), 205–19.

Adesoji, A. (2017). *The Human Cost of Uncontrolled Arms in Africa Cross-National Research on Seven African Countries* (pp. 36). Oxfam Research Report. www.oxfam.org.

AEFJN. *Small Arms in Africa.* http://www.aefjn.org/index.php/arms-361.html?file=tl_files/aefjn-files/publications/Fact%20Sheets%20EN/120521-SALW-Factsheet-eng.pdf. Accessed 18 July 2019.

Africa News. (2017). *Cameroun: Internet Shutdown Costs $1.39m*. Club of Mozambique Newsletter. https://clubmozambique.com/news/cameroon-internet-shutdown-costs-1-39m/. Accessed 10 August 2019.

Ahere, J., & Ouko, M. (2012). Information Communication Technology (ICT) in combat of Small Arms and Light Weapons. *Horn of Africa Bulletin, 24,* 10.

Akpan-Obong Patience Idaresit. (2009). *Information and Communication Technology in Nigeria: Prospects and Challenges for Development* (pp. 69). Peter New York: Lang Publishing. https//books.google.com.ng.

Aning, E. K. (2005). *The Anatomy of Ghana's Secret Arms Industry*. https://works.bepress.com/kwesi_aning/17/. Accessed 13 July 2019.

BBC News. (2012, January 16). *South Sudan Horror at Deadly Cattle Vendetta.* http://www.bbc.co.uk/news/world-africa-16575153, Accessed 13 June 2019.

Bromley, M., & Holtom, P. (2010). *Arms Transfer to the Democratic Republic of the Congo: Assessing the System of Arms Notification 2008–10* (p. 3). SIPRI Background Paper. https://www.sipri.org/sites/default/files/files/misc/SIPRIBP1010a.pdf. Accessed on 13 July 2019.

Buchanan-Clarke, S., & Lekalake, R. (2016). *Violent Extremism in Africa: Public Opinion from the Sahel, Lake Chad, and the Horn* (pp. 4–7). Afrobarometer Policy Paper No. 32. http://afrobarometer.org/sites/default/files/publications/Policy%20papers/r6-afropaperno32-violent-extremism-in-ss-africa-en.pdf.

Citifmonline. (2016, September 27). *Illegal Arms, Unemployment Threatens Peaceful Polls—EC Chair.* Citifmonline. http://citifmonline.com/2016/09/07/illegal-arms-unemployment-threatens-peaceful-polls-ec-chair/. Accessed 13 June 2019.

Conflict Armament Research. (2015). *Non-State Armed Groups in the Central African Republic.* http://www.conflictarm.com/car_publications/NONSTATE_ARMED_GROUPS_IN_CENTRAL_AFRICAN_REPUBLIC.pdf. Accessed 18 July 2019.

Council Decision 2011/428/CFSP. http//eur-lex.europa.eu. Accessed 15 July 2019.

Council on Foreign Relations. (2013, June 25). *The Global Regime for Transnational Crime.* http://www.cfr.org/transnational-crime/global-regime-transnationalcrime/p28656. Accessed 18 September 2019.

Declaration of a Moratorium on Importation, Exportation and Manufacture of Light Weapons in West Africa. Bureau of Political-Military Affairs Washington, DC, October 30, 1998. https://2001-2009.state.gov/t/ac/csbm/rd/6688.htm. Accessed 15 August 2019.

Department of Foreign Affairs and International Trade, Canada (DFAIT). (2008). *The Effects of Small Arms and Light Weapons Proliferation and Use.* www.international.gc.ca/arms-armes/isrop-pris/research-recherche/conventional-conventionnelles/krause2000/section5.aspx?view=d. Accessed 10 September 2019.

Dorn, W. (2000). Small Arms, Human Security and Development. *Development Express, 5,* 1999–2000. https://walterdorn.net/38-small-arms-human-security-and-development. Accessed 10 August 2019.

Economic and Social Commission for Asia and the Pacific (ESCAP). (2000). *Are ICT Policies Addressing Gender Equality.* https://www.unescap.org. Accessed 16 June 2019.

Fleshman, M. (2011). *Small Arms in Africa. Counting the Cost of Gun Violence.* Africa Renewal. https://www.un.org/africarenewal/magazine/issue/december2011. Accessed 20 September 2019.

Green, J. A., (1981). *Cyber Warfare: A Multidisciplinary Analysis.* London. https://worldcat.org. Accessed 18 June 2019.

Herby, in Boutwell & Klare. (1999, July 20). *Light Weapons and Civil Conflict* (p. 199). Routman and Littlefield. UNICEF Press Rrelease.

Hillier, D. (2007). *Africa's Missing Billions: International Arms flows and the Cost of Conflict.* Oxfam Briefing Paper, 107. http://policy-practice.oxfam.org.uk/publications/africas-missing-billions-international-arms-flows-and-the-cost-of-conflict-123908. Accessed 14 June 2019.

Hon. Lloyd Axworthy, address to UN Security Council, Sept. 24, 1999.

IGI Global. (2019). *Information and Communication Technology (ICT).* Accessed 18 June 2019.

IRIN. (2015, February 21). *Arms Smuggling to Boko Haram Threatens Cameroon.* http://www.irinnews.org/news/2014/02/21. Accessed 8 August 2019.

ITU. (2007). *Measuring the Information Society 2007: ICT Opportunity Index and World Telecommunication/ICT Indicators.* Geneva: ITU. Accessed 4 August 2019.

ITU (International Telecommunication Union). (2016). *Measuring the Information Society Report 2016.* International Telecommunication Union, Geneva Switzerland. Accessed 18 July 2019.

Klare, M. (2012). *Small Arms Proliferation and International Security.* Five College Consortium, Peace World Security Studies program. http://pawss.hamshire.edu/topics/smallarms/index.html. Accessed 18 July 2019.

Kumar, S. (2008). Small Arms and Light Weapons: A global Threat to Human Security and Development. *The Indian Journal of Political Science, 69*(4), 789–790.

Marcelle, G. (2000). *Gender, Justice and ICTs.* http://www.un.org/womenwatc hdaw/csw/marcello.htm. Accessed 18 July 2019.

McEvoy, C., & LeBrun, E. (2010). *Uncertain Future: Armed Violence in Southern Sudan, Human Security Baseline Assessment (HSBA)* (p. 20). Working Paper. www.smallarmssurveysudan.org/pdfs/HSBA-SWP-20-Armed-Violence-Southern-Sudan.pdf.

Mungai, C. (2016). *Another Twist from Oil Price Crash.* http://mgafrica.com/article/2016-05-03-trends-in-piracy-2015-report. Accessed 18 July 2019.

Nwaiwu, C. (2015, October 27). *60% of Illegal Arms in S/East Produced Locally—Presidential Committee, Vanguard.* http://www.vanguardngr.com/2015/10/60-of-illegal-arms-in-seast-produced-locally-presidential-cttee/. Accessed 8 August 2019.

Obi, C. (2009). *Nigeria's Niger Delta: Understanding the Complex Drivers of Violent Oil-Related Conflict.* African Development, Africa Development, Council for the Development of Social Science Research in Africa, *XXXIV*(2), 103–128.

Ogwueleka, F. N., & Aniche, A. D. (2020). Information and Communication Technology, Cyber Security and Counterterrorism in Afica. In *Routledge Handbook of Counterterrorism and Counterinsurgency in Africa* (p. 155). Routledge. ISBN 9781351271929.

Religions for Peace World Assembly Declaration. (1984). *Small Arms and Light Weapons: Africa—A Resource Guide for Religions for Peace* (p. 3). Religion for Peace, African Council of Religious Leaders. https://controlarms.org.

Rodriguez, F., & Wilson, E. (2000). *Are Poor Countries Losing the Information Revolution?* mfoDevWorking Paper. Washington, DC: World Bank. Accessed 20 September 2019.

Singer, P. W. (2016a). *Cybersecurity and Cyberwar: What Everyone Needs to Know.* https//.www.cybersecurityandwar.com. Accessed 18 August 2019.

Singer, P. W. (2016b). *Cybersecurity and Cyberwar: What Everyone Needs to Know.* https//worldcat.org. Accessed 18 July 2019.

Small Arms and Light Weapons. (2016). *Africa: A Resource Guide for Religions for Peace* (p. 5).

Small Arms and Light Weapons: Africa. (2017). A Resource Guide for Religions for Peace. A Publication of the Religious for Peace African Council of Religious Leaders Under The Norwegian Ministry of Foreign Affairs. New York. pp 4–5. https://rfp.org, http://religiousforpace.org/initiatives/violent-conflict

Small Arms and Light Weapons Control—A Training Manual. (2012). *Module Three: South Sudan Peace Fund and Canadian Department of Foreign Affairs and International Trade (DFAITJ)*. Accessed 18 August 2019.

Small Arms and Light Weapons at United Nations Office for Disarmament Affairs (UNODA). www.un.org/disarmanent/convarms/SALW/. Accessed 13 June 2019.

Small Arms Survey. (2016a). *Definitions of Small Arms and Light Weapons*. http://www.smallarmssurvey.org/weapons-and-markets/definitions.html. Accessed 13 July 2019.

Small Arms Survey. (2016b, April). *The Online Trade of Light Weapons in Libya*, Dispatch number 6, 2016. Accessed 13 June 2019.

Small Arms Survey. (2016c, October). *Measuring Illicit Arms Flow: Somalia*. Research Notes, Number 61. http://www.smallarmssurvey.org/fileadmin/docs/H-_Notes/SAS-Research-ResearchNote-61.pdf. Accessed 18 August 2019.

The Times of Israel. (2012, June 6). www/timesofisrael.org. Accessed 8 August 2019.

UNDP. (2015). *Preventing and Responding to Violent Extremism in Africa: A Development Approach*. http://www.undp.org/content/dam/undp/library/Democratic%20Governance/Local%20Governance/UNDP-RBA-Preventing-Extremism-2015.pdf. Accessed 8 July 2019.

UNGA. (1997, August 27). *Report of the Panel of Governmental Experts on Small Arms*. General and Complete Disarmament: Small Arms; Note by the Secretary-General: A/52/298 (III) (p. 11). New York, NY: United Nations General Assembly.

United Nations Office for Disarmament Affairs (UNODA). (2018). *Small Arms Report*. Accessed 12 July 2019.

UNODC. (2013). *Transnational Organized Crime in West Africa: A Threat Assessment*. http://www.unodc.org/documents/data-and-analysis/tocta/West_Africa_TOCTA_2013_EN.pdf. Accessed 18 August 2019.

UN Security Council. (2014). *Report of the Monitoring Group on Somalia and Eritrea Pursuant to Security Council Resolution 2111(2013)*. S/2014/726 of 13 October. Accessed 8 July 2019.

Weinberger, S. (2007, October 4). *How Israel Spoofed Syria's Air Defense System*. http://www.smallarmssurvey.org. Accessed 18 August 2019.

Wezeman, P. (2010). *Arms Flow and the Conflict in Somalia*. SIPRI Background Paper. http://books.sipri.org/files/misc/SIPRIBP1010b.pdf. Accessed 8 July 2019.

Wood, B., & Peleman, J. (1999). *The Arms Fixers: Controlling the Brokers and Shipping Agents* (Basic Research Report 99.3, p. 139). Oslo: International Peace Research Institute.

World Bank. (2016). *Poverty in a Rising Africa*. http://www.worldbank.org/en/region/afr/publication/poverty-rising-africa-poverty-report. Accessed 20 July 2019.

Francisca Nonyelum Ogwueleka is a Professor of Computer Science in Nigerian Defence Academy, Kaduna-Nigeria. She is currently the Dean of Faculty of Military Science and Interdisciplinary Studies. Her research focuses on big data, artificial intelligence, cloud security, data mining techniques, steganography, penetration testing solutions and information security. She has nine published books, two book chapters and ninety-two original articles in international and national journals. She is a member of numerous professional bodies, editorial board and conference technical program committee. She has been a keynote speaker and conference session chair in several international and national conferences. She has received many academic and professional awards. Professor Ogwueleka is an external examiner for PhD dissertation and M.Sc. thesis evaluation for national and international universities. She was a resource person for the development of Nigeria Undergraduate Curriculum in CyberSecurity and Information Technology programs for National Universities Commission.

Part IV

National Experiences

CHAPTER 32

Central African Republic: The Contagion of Identity-Linked Sectarian Violence, Internally Displaced Populations (IDPs) and Small Arms Proliferation

Wendy Isaacs-Martin

INTRODUCTION

The conflict that began in the north-east of the country has since 2013 engulfed the entire country deteriorating into strong identity patterns (Wendy Isaacs-Martin 2016). The conflict was presented as a binary conflict of Christian vs Muslim, brought about by misinterpreting the sociopolitical realities of the CAR but equally a convenient ideology for the various factions by reducing the conflict to two 'ethnic and religious' coalitions (Isaacs-Martin 2017). This argument disintegrated once the violence escalated along with the number of armed groups operating in the villages and suburbs of Bangui. During this period large national stockpiles of weapons were stolen and Séléka obtained much of those stockpiles in Bangui, although they claimed to purchase weapons from markets in Sudan and Chad too. Due to the constant change of allegiances between armed groups, within coalitions and the missions undertaken by the international organisations problematises recording the 'supply and route' of weapons (Conflict Armament Research 2015). Many arms originally transferred from China, Iran and Europe to the governments of CAR and Sudan, among other African countries, are now held by Séléka and anti-Balaka forces. In such an arms-charged environment conflicts arise out of simple disputes due to a lack of effective resolve-oriented institutions (Ayittey 2003; Broodryk and Solomon 2010).

W. Isaacs-Martin (✉)
Archie Mafeje Research Institute, University of South Africa, Pretoria, South Africa

© The Author(s), under exclusive license to Springer Nature Switzerland AG 2021
U. A. Tar and C. P. Onwurah (eds.), *The Palgrave Handbook of Small Arms and Conflicts in Africa*,
https://doi.org/10.1007/978-3-030-62183-4_32

Nyerere, ex-prime minister and president of Tanzania once argued that Africa was hamstrung by three persistent issues of corruption, political instability and the lack/decline of physical infrastructure (Ayittey 2003). Africa struggles to attract significant investment beyond developmental assistance exacerbating conflict that threatens civilians. Yet the security institutions serve not the population but government leadership where the population are regarded as the enemy (Ayittey 2003). The military no longer fulfils its original mandate and opportunistic government personnel act egregiously towards the population, looting and razing villages and assaulting civilians, in their personal capacity and on flimsy reasons as seen in Ghana, Nigeria, Sudan, Mauritania, Liberia, Ethiopia and the Central African Republic (CAR). Such behaviours undermine the state institutions and destroy civilian trust in the government that forces people to join armed groups for protection and resources. The persistence of the war economy allows for all three factors to be on a continuous cycle, namely issues of identity politics that divides regions within a state, the movement of people to areas in which they are unwelcome and vulnerable, and thirdly the persistence of SALWs in which to perpetuate conflict and fear. Winning the 'war' is secondary to sustaining profit and the more individuals involved, and its increasing benefits, sustains the conflict.

The proliferation of SALWs in Africa is supported by commercial ventures originating in Asia, Europe and North America that is hinged on the political and social instability in countries such as CAR. The post-Cold War and the proliferation of weapon development and production resulted in a surplus of weapons, but this was coupled with the decrease in governmental military sizes and an environment in which to recuperate costs. These industries, often private enterprises, sustained through contracts to produce innovative weaponry, require funding. Various governments compete to distribute their surplus outdated weapons to conflict zones in Africa. This is further complicated by middlemen who also sell weapons to various warlords and non-state actors. Many states have the capability to replicate many of the weapon designs due to its simplicity; this is most notable of the AK-47 and AK-74. Accessibility to weapons is not restricted to the armaments distributed by state institutions and external stakeholders but also within communities. People manufacture their own crude artisanal weapons that may not render the firepower of automatic weapons but remain equally lethal, raises the 'violent breakdown of society' (Boutwell and Klare 1998). Post-conflict environments remain unstable due to 'unregistered' firearms and a fear of the authorities translates into few casualties, who are overwhelmingly young and vulnerable, being reported (Arya 2002).

There are twenty-seven international organisations globally and have undertaken over 100 peace missions as well as ad hoc coalitions that culminate in demobilisation, disarmament and reintegration (DDR) programmes (Berman 2019). DDR programmes are often repeated in the same countries such as the CAR with limited success. The lack of funding from stakeholders and contradicting ideologies often delay and reduce expectations in negotiations. Disarmament timelines are problematic as weapons remain in circulation.

The CAR has a population of approximately 4.5 million (United Nations 2017) and comprised of more than 80 ethnic groups and almost half the population located in the rural areas. Since independence in 1960 the country has experienced political conflict and poor leadership. An environment plagued with armed state and non-state actors has led to cycles of displacement. The conflict in 2013 saw the coalition militia of Séléka change the political dynamic forcing Bozizé from power. In turn it has been argued that the anti-Balaka forces that challenged the Séléka received support from Bozizé. The violence enacted by these two coalition forces led to attack on civilians rather than armed combatants (Wendy Isaacs-Martin 2016). In response civilians began attacking each other based simply on religious affiliation creating an environment of increased displacement and insecurity. Violent conflict occurred in each of the sixteen prefectures, including the city of Bangui which is an autonomous commune. Apart from vast numbers of CAR refugees into neighbouring states there are also high volumes of IDPs.

CAR is indicative of a region in perpetual conflict between various groups that engage in complex, at often contradictory, alliances. These multiple conflicts have led to the decline in state power, the erosion of national security and sovereignty and surely has led, as Onuoha (2006) has alluded to in other states in Africa, to political, economic, social and cultural changes. The country remains 'chronically underfunded' exacerbating the chronic social and political instability (Gauthier 2018). One of the criticisms is the reluctance of donors to honour their commitments, only 36.5% (Gauthier 2018). As such more areas, especially since 2017, territory previously not affected by the instability, have now been engulfed in the violence and IDPs. Gauthier (2018) asserts that 70% of the country is controlled by militias and other armed groups.

While ethnicity—and identity conflicts—are not the primary reason for conflicts, there become an auxiliary factor. Persistent conflict in a region creates insecurity among the civilian population. Civilians tend to form self-defence groups within their communities and these tend to be arranged along ethnic and regional identities. Often this comes about as a result of attacks by armed groups like militias, ex- and currently soldiers. These groups, using SALWs, attack certain areas and populations giving the impression that they are supporting or defending a particular ethnicity. This is compounded by self-defence units formed in the villages and suburbs in the urban areas along ethnic lines and therefore seek assistance from particular armed groups in order to access arms and other resources. These self-defence groups arise from continuous assaults from criminals, neighbouring villagers or ex-soldiers. To maintain access to the resources provided by larger armed groups many self-defence units find themselves drafted into assisting with conflicts directed against civilians. This rouses issues of ethnic and identity-linked tensions.

Ethnic tensions are not the reason for conflicts but rather a secondary consequence. Conflict arises due to economic constraints, opportunism and access to perceived resources in a particular area. Often, groups are pushed from a particular area as it is located close to areas that are rich in natural resources. This expulsion of people from their ancestral land is often perceived to be along ethnic lines but often the demographics are not considered. Bandits target people regardless of their identity and herders and pastoralists target each other due to resources that exist beyond the concept of ethnicity. Often, politicians and 'strongmen' are themselves protagonists in these conflicts, financing many of the SALWs and the fighters.

Tensions also arise between humanitarian organisations and 'factional leaders' as although once welcomed to assist themselves and the affected population, the attention to the humanitarian work grants legitimacy to the government through negotiation where militias now demand that they be negotiated with ultimately leading to extortion and threats. In 2017 CAR had the most attacks on humanitarian workers, 1/3 of attacks globally.

Usurpation of government leadership by the Séléka, although short-lived, illustrated how conflict continues even once peace initiatives are attended and agreed upon by all attendant parties. While elections and an interim-leader were meant to quell the conflict and reduce ethnic tensions it has largely failed in its efforts.

The data used in this chapter taken from the United Nations World Population Prospects and the Internal Displacement Monitoring Centre. It illustrates the movement of civilians within the sixteen prefectures and civilian fatalities in 2017. The research findings are aimed at demonstrating that even when peace initiatives are negotiated and in place conceived and implemented over a number of years, the proliferation of SALWs creates and leaves behind an insecure environment for civilians. The movement of the population illustrates that conflicts escalate and are not confined to particular prefectures but rather spread across the country. It also encourages armed groups from neighbouring countries to take advantage of the vulnerability of the population but equally state forces contribute to the insecurity of the prefectures (Isaacs-Martin 2015).

The rise of conflict in various regions across the globe can be attributed to availability and portability, 'global deluge of surplus' SALWs (Boutwell and Klare 1998). Lightweight and requiring little training 'emboldens belligerents', children to adults, to use these weapons to threaten communities with violence ranging from assaults to mass murder and genocide.

This chapter highlights some of the ways in which SALWs are central to the ongoing violence, political and social destabilisation of states and regions, and particularly insecurity for rural and urban populations. The chapter is divided into two areas of discussion; the first part will focus on the degree of internally displaced population movements in the CAR. IDP movements would not occur to such an extent without the use of SALWs that elevate the level of insecurity in communities. The second part will describe the proliferation of SALWs in Africa and its impact on communities, societies and regions.

The aim of the chapter is to *assert that the persistence of armed groups in a failing state leads to an increase in SALWs, greater insecurity and displacement and inevitably identity conflicts*. The conclusions reached are that firstly, the disarmament, demobilisation and reintegration programmes are overwhelmingly ineffective due to continued conflict. Secondly that large movements of people add to the insecurity as the economy is severely undermined as well as their incomes; it also leads to increased ethnic tensions due to the competition for limited resources. Finally the movement of IDPs also leads to more conflicts, and criminal activity, creating a cycle of insecurity and poverty.

Literature

Small arms as the 'weapon of choice' contribute to the destruction of villages, communities, societal norms and laws and legitimate national and regional economies which Boutwell and Klare (1998) refer to as the 'failed state syndrome'. SALWs are used to indiscriminately kill and maim non-combatants. As the majority of people injured are not combatants NGOs and governments tend to view SALWs proliferation *locus standi* as either a criminal issue, a conflict prevention/resolution issue or a relief/development issue that required 'different remedial policies and different priorities' (Lumpe 1999). The focus is on the oversupply of weapons but there is minimal emphasis on establishing controls of distribution, accountability in terms of transfer or transparency. Alternative arguments exist for a supply and demand approach in conflict-prone countries (Muggah 2010). Easy access to powerful weaponry has changed war dynamics from inter-nation to intra-nation composed of varied actors with 'little to no formal training' and 'few compunctions' of observing the rules of war.

A 'small army can take over a country…with a few hundred machine guns' and combatants include official militias and paramilitary gangs (Boutwell and Klare 2000), 'children and teenagers' (Boutwell and Klare 1998) engaging in 'terrorising' and the 'routine massacre' of civilians.

State forces, are one of the mediums, supplying weapons, a staple of armed conflicts, to insurgents that are used to terrorise civilians. Unlike SALWs, there is greater armament control in terms of the sale of nuclear weaponry, jets and tanks as these are expensive and almost exclusively used by national military forces. Governments providing arms to foreign insurgents 'is a major source of small arms proliferation' that are intended to covertly 'destabilise and topple [other] governments' (Lumpe 1999: 158). The small weapons trade, including agents, is vast making the control of such transactions complex. Declining military sizes led to excess weaponry sold to black market agents including manufacturers that employ covert transactions. SALWs are often distributed by regional networks of permissive government agencies, 'false end-user documents and paid-off customs officials' and dealers (Boutwell and Klare 1998;

Hartung 2001). Easily obtained and distributed to untrained and unprofessional actors leads to many conflicts and should be comparative to major conventional systems of weaponry.

Several treaties exist to negotiate this proliferation. As the proliferation continues these treaties have marginal effect. Signatories to these treaties doesn't translate into ratification. Legal parameters should be equally scrutinised as that of illegal trade. There are several treaties and embargoes with different foci meant to counter the sociopolitical and economic realities caused by SALWs. These include the UN Small Arms Conference and the UN Special Session in 2002, a follow-up to the World Summit for Children in 1999, to provide measures on eliminating SALWs and diminish the effect of these weapons on children (Stohl 2002). The Convention on Certain Conventional Weapons (CCW) of 1983 had 125 state signatories along with the Arms Trade Treaty (ATT) of 2014 was a global treaty to establish common standards for governments on arms transfers with 92 state signatories (Gillis 2017). Obstacles to institutions wanting to control the supply and access of small arms is largely due to the effective lobbying of influential groups such as the National Rifle Association, governments who manufacture arms, those distributing and arming groups globally, curtail any implicit restrictions (Arya 2002: 991). Sanctions such as arms embargoes are often ignored and mostly ineffective in Africa due to government complicity and limited application (Stohl and Tuttle 2009; Vines 2007). UN embargoes are either mandatory or voluntary; voluntary symbolic embargoes are an expectation that states will cease supplying arms while mandatory embargoes prohibit any sales. Hartung (2001: 88) argues that these treaties and embargoes require a series of stricter laws and regulations, transparency, public education, innovative diplomatic and economic initiatives. Since the 1990s there has been a plethora of multi- and bilateral conventions and agreements to control the SALWs trade (Muggah 2010). Many embargoes are compromises, and effectively watered down, and are employed only against one or two armed groups while ignoring many others. Small arms are not well-regulated although it is argued that the majority are sold and transferred legally unlike the ammunition trade (Gillis 2017: 83). The vast caches of SALWs are due to their 'low cost and wide availability, lethality, portability and concealment and military and civilian uses' (Boutwell and Klare 1998: 16). Over one thousand companies in one hundred countries manufacture SALWs (Kinsella 2006) and the trade in illicit arms are solely for economic gain (Collier and Sambanis 2002).

Adding to this complexity of potential disarmament agreements with armed groups is that civilians possess approximately three quarters of the global SALWs with 30 million in Africa alone (Muggah 2010: 221). There is also 'craft production' also known as artisanal weapons (Stohl and Tuttle 2009: 20) that are localised makeshift crude weapons that can add '200 000 new weapons a year'. As Muggah (2010: 221) asserts '...arms used in Africa are increasingly produced in Africa...to devastating effect'. Overwhelmingly disarmament programmes fail due to commitment failures by stakeholders, lack of financial resources to implement these initiatives and these limits translate into timeous implementation complexities. Disarmament efforts cannot be limited to the supply chain alone but should include a broad spectrum approach that includes the causes, not limited to the results, of arms proliferation. While these programmes call for peaceful reintegration within society for combatants and socio-economic development, the reality is that many are poorly funded and instituted at the end of peace negotiations (Pouligny 2004). Yet, DDR programmes never explore the reason behind the individual motivation to possess weapons. The lack of economic opportunities and the forced reintegration of combatants into communities must dovetail the international expectations to control and restrict the supply of arms to civilians. Without economic development and individual financial sustainability, there is little incentive to surrender weapons that currently serve as a medium for survival. Instead weapons are recycled, leading to further conflicts and criminal activity further harming conflict-prone states.

Due to SALWs, warfare has transformed from national-ordered conflicts to 'volatile, anarchic forms of violence… engaged in calculated terror' (Hartung 2001: 80). Genocides are often possible due to the distribution of SALWs to militias, paramilitaries and gangs. The Rwandan and Balkan genocides were preceded by the distribution of SALWs by the governments (Boutwell and Klare 2000; Weiss 2003). The large number of people murdered and displaced by these conflicts was not inflicted by the artillery of modern warfare but with guns, grenades and mortars—such as AK-47s, AK-74s, FALs, M16s and Uzis, weapons with immense fire rates of firepower between 600 and 1000 rounds per minute, where poorly trained but deadly combatants, can render large number of casualties—estimated between 60 and 80% civilians. The ease of these weapons is obtained, particularly as surplus from other conflicts, also leads to an increase in localised conflicts.

Conflict-affected and fragile states are vulnerable to organised crime (Gillis 2017; Vorrath 2014). The trade in natural resources and drugs due to the lack of security and porous borders has repercussions beyond the originally affected state. However these are scaffolded events, where initially violent actors assisted in destabilising the region, it is the organisation of criminal activity that is dependent on patronage networks that are located within the state as seen in Sierra Leone and Liberia (Vorrath 2014).

The proliferation of small arms leads to the social degradation of communities (Boutwell and Klare 1998; Stohl 2002). Conflict undermines the bonds within society and inflames identity crises—be it religious, ethnic and racial. Often the violence occurs because weakened ineffective state institutions fail to control and eliminate it. A functionalist position is that institutions exist to fulfil the needs of society (Castoriadis 1997). Without these institutions societies, they argue, are unable to function effectively. In impoverished weak states, even with strong regimes, institutions are undermined, manipulated and eventually fail. Rather institutions become empty shells and exist simply for political leaders to populate with their supporters who often share regional and ethnic affiliation. Due to the fragility of state institutions, bureaucrats utilise the resources for their own benefit and corruption becomes widespread. The lack of effective institutions in securing the country leads to a rise in banditry and other forms of violence, such as genocide, intercommunal conflicts and the displacement of people. A decline in income and economic opportunities expedites armed group recruitment (Collier 1998; Fjelde 2015; Reno 2009) and farming is the overall occupation during the pre-war period.

The ease of accessing weapons has transformed conflict from interstate to intercommunal that draws in a varied group of actors namely government troops, state and non-state militias, village self-defence units (Gerlach 2010; Mkutu 2006), youth criminal gangs and civilians (Hartung 2001). This transforms the conflict from the traditional state armed forces to local communities, 'blurring the lines of conflict' encompassing 'multiple warring parties' with little to no formal training that destroys society (Boutwell and Klare 1998: 15). This allows for war to move away from ethical approaches to violating any rules of armed conflict that overwhelmingly occurs from SALWs. The movement and exchange of these weapons are not dependent on 'formal authority but on shared interests and ongoing relationships'—instead it relies on economic organisation that is often 'part of more general military relationships' that lend to 'longer-term investments in mutually beneficial' interactions that are non-hierarchically organised that should not be regarded as a market but as a network(Kinsella 2006: 100).

Boutwell and Klare (1998) argue that the use of SALWs in conflict occurs mainly in impoverished countries that are also confronted with large waves of IDPs and refugees. These weapons, regardless of how they were retrieved, 'contributes to a culture of violence and criminality that undermines the stability of the state' and social cohesion (Boutwell and Klare 1998: 18). Kinsella (2006) asserts that a network of economic organisation is facilitated by the small arms trade by opting for a social network analysis approach. Further he argues that it should not be assumed that the partnerships are located primarily in ideological or political interests, but rather they are built upon economic, military and other interests that maintain this infrastructure. This has led to a growth in warlordism presenting new forms of power structures in conflict-ridden societies (Hartung 2001; Reno 1999). Reno (1997) argues that warlordism presents new economic modes for communities, and particularly youth and unemployed soldiers, under the direction of a violent autocratic individual. Notions of human rights and democracy are of little interest in such social environments (Hartung 2001) but rather the economic advantages and safety provided by the militias directed by the warlord (Collier et al. 2009; Isaacs-Martin 2015; Reno 2009). Warlordism demonstrated that the proliferation of conflict does not require the support of the nation but rather accessing a country's mineral wealth can finance participation in the conflict and simultaneously enrich warlords and other key leaders.

These ethnic conflicts are also hinged on cattle raids that are escalating across the continent particularly in Central Africa, North Eastern Africa, West

Africa and the Horn of Africa; while these go back centuries, they have become commercialised through the use of SALWs. A series of political decisions by colonial administrators, post-independent governments and localised strongmen that resulted in land alienation and restricting pastoralists from accessing water and pasture increased competition and vulnerability (Wendy Isaacs-Martin 2016). Rather than the intercommunal rustling the trend has escalated in violence and destruction and has 'become embedded in wider criminal networks serving national and regional black markets...[depleting] the communities of their cattle and their livelihoods' where pastoralists provide the 'largest market for small arms from local circulation' (Mkutu 2007: 35). Cross-border attacks involving large groups of combatants serve to also finance conflicts and have moved away from the historical patterns of cattle raids, a customary practice among pastoralists sanctioned and mediated by elders. In conjunction with these raids are attacks on hospitals, schools and other services which are raided, razed and workers attacked and robbed (Isaacs-Martin 2015; Mkutu 2006, 2007).

As ethnic groups straddle borders in Africa small arms are transported unhindered. As many areas where the violence erupts are in remote and marginalised areas absent of state security. The escalation of conflict in these areas results in them becoming no-go areas and hinders development and aid. Aid is often distributed with the assistance of warlords, giving them greater power in the area and influence among agencies (Wendy Isaacs-Martin 2016).

It is worthy of note that continuous conflicts escalate the breakdown of social cohesive communities into single identity units facilitates violence creating the balance of power in communities and societies. Therefore, victims can also be perpetrators in a cycle of violence also in retaliation by communities of initial victims. The cultural respect given to the elderly, and care for children, has evaporated and violence perpetrated against everyone. There are few mechanisms to deal with multisided conflicts such as those in the Democratic Republic of Congo (DRC) and the CAR (Hartung 2001). The nature of conflict has changed (Gillis 2017). Identity structures, and communal relationships, are destroyed when children take on adult roles and responsibilities due to the absence of parents and elders, often killed in the many ongoing conflicts (Stohl 2002). Adolescents were often ignored by aid support programmes (Stohl 2002: 18) exposing them to economic hardship and isolation. Often those who are armed combatants developed a reliance on narcotics and psychological problems (Vorrath 2014). Failed states cannot provide food or employment, the threat of infectious diseases due to the collapse of public services (Patrick 2006).

The greatest issue brought on by the proliferation of SALWs is the ethnic, religious and regional tensions that are raised. Where communities have existed for centuries, and identity has been fluid among groups, the tension created by attacks against specific communities and villages raises and magnifies, even creating, new sociopolitical situations. Regardless of efforts of peace negotiations, treaties and socio-economic development, countries are at best separated into community zones of heterogeneous identities.

State Structures, Political Leadership and Displaced Populations

The CAR is long mired by poor governance, illiberal politics, historical grievances and economic deprivation. In Africa the state is often the primary source of violence but this is complicated by external stakeholders and internal strongmen who also inter into the conflict for various reasons ranging from accessing natural resources, political leadership access and reinforcing 'traditional' power structures.. Musah (2002) argues that many African states are a shell lacking popular legitimacy so leaders rely on a 'clique of sectional/regional political heavyweights' (Musah 2002: 916) popularly known as strongmen or warlords. Armed groups under the leadership of a strongman can begin conflict with only a small number of weapons. Securing the natural resources allows the use of profits to purchase additional light weapons (Boutwell and Klare 2000). To increase the number of 'reliable' fighters many groups including state-controlled and non-state forces alike use child soldiers. Unlike adults, child soldiers do not question leadership and tend to be more dependent on commanders as many have been forcibly removed from their families and support structures.

Increased banditry (zaraguinas) in the CAR illustrates an increase in available weapons. Much of the violence has also come from pastoralists and herders, while these conflicts have existed for centuries and there have always been parameters to these conflicts. Mkutu (2006: 48) argues that the last two decades have seen a 'transformation of raiding into large-scale armed conflict...[and] raiders in armies of 100-500 people'. In the CAR the violence between pastoralists and herders has increased in the north along the border with Chad. As the two groups are linked to different ethnic identities, this is termed part of the ethnic conflict which it was not originally and is to a large extent still linked to accessing land and water rather than ethnic differences. However these attacks lead to displaced populations.

Many of the villages are attacked by state and non-state armed actors in the CAR, assaulting and robbing villagers eventually razing the area destroying crops. Many are forced to live in the forests hiding from combatants. As many IDPs and refugees are moving from rural areas to new development areas around camps or villages, agricultural activities are abandoned and supply chain economic activities take precedence. Due to the ethnic distribution in the CAR the ethnic and sectarian violence is characterised by brutality, 'where minor disputes escalate quickly into major bloodbaths' and the ease of weaponry prolongs social tensions (Boutwell and Klare 2000: 52). Once conflicts cease, criminal violence often increases as former combatants retain their weapons and even weapons entering from neighbouring regions (Stohl and Tuttle 2009). The movement of the population leads many to seek security in camps located in the various prefectures.

Camps inevitably become militarised as armed fighters, including current and ex-soldiers hide among the civilian population indirectly threatening non-combatants (Stohl 2002). Many fighters refuse to surrender their weapons in these camps as they refuse instructions other than commanders. Fleeing families often are forced to surrender their possession, livestock and land at gunpoint by other civilians. Being dispersed and displaced inevitably forces people together in terms of security. Without access to their land, regions become militarised as civilians are forced to obtain weapons and find alternative incomes. So there is a dynamic between insecurity and mobility. Forced displacement results in a changing ethnic composition of a particular location. Due to the insecurity created by the proliferation of SALWs IDPs settle in camps and in the surrounding areas and often become part of the village structure. Without the state able to provide security due to its failing or ineffective institutions many IDPs relocate permanently to new areas increasing populations in these areas drawing more IDPs and refugees. This indirectly creates commercial opportunities for greater migration but simultaneously greater competition and resentment. The CAR has experienced escalating ethnic tensions in the displacement camps as well as the surrounding areas often based on autochthonous issues but also fear of other ethnic groups bringing armed combatants.

Due to ongoing violence in the CAR many of the camps and the surrounding villages are heavily militarised due to a large number of SALWs. Social life is located in violence and intimidation and leads to an escalation of weapons. Economic growth within a particular location leads to more armed groups, state and non-state, arriving so that they can benefit by extorting the population. Environments of high insecurity lead to communities forming along lines of ethnic identities and strongmen utilise these tensions by which to assert themselves claiming to represent specific populations.

The ease with which weapons can be accessed leads to the 'development of cultures of violence' in communities (Stohl 2002: 21). Arms are used to 'cultivate influence, reinforce authority, and symbolise value' that traps 'whole societies in an endless cycle of war' and for those, particularly children, that are only familiar with the use of weaponry as a control mechanism, it becomes the medium of conflict resolution (Stohl 2002: 21). However, children involved directly in the conflict as combatants are ostracised by their families and communities, making it impossible for them to return home or leave the armed groups. In the CAR adult fighters are welcomed back as they may receive opportunities from the peace agreements as well as stipends as part of a militia. Women and children do not receive such financial assistance from negotiations and are usually the parties negatively affected by the war.

The control, supply and possession of firearms directly impact on the mortality rate. In conflict situations, it is the non-combatants, overwhelmingly women and children, who are casualties and also 'suffer the psychological and social burdens' due to small arms violence (Arya 2002: 990; McIntyre and Weiss 2003). Even when peace negotiations are concluded and a region is no longer contested, small arms violence continue as the weapons remain in circulation. This behaviour supports Muggah (2010: 217)argument that 'second generation armed violence prevention' investigates supply and demand.

The movement of populations leads to social disintegration that will take decades to reorganise. Social interaction changes from traditional structures to levels of intimidation on account of SALWs. All the prefectures of CAR continue to be affected by violence, the growth of armed groups and coalitions and IDPs. This leads to immense distrust within communities. Many civilians believe that conflict is the result of political elites seeking power (Vinck and Pham 2010). There is an overwhelming belief that peace is difficult to achieve in CAR and this is directly attributed to the manner in which politics plays out. Rather than using the ballot box, in perhaps which many know they will be unsuccessful, they instead turn to weapons and violence against civilians.

'Lethal material' regarded as armoured vehicles and weapons are lost to attacks on secured sites monitored and utilised by 'peacekeepers in non-UN missions' (Berman 2019). As an example he states that in simple five attacks on these missions resulted in 1000 SALWs and 1 million rounds of ammunition lost. Accountability and oversight are rarely exercised as the focus is on economics and development.

Sectarian Violence, Internally Displaced Populations (IDPs) and SALWs Proliferation

Ethnic composition varies greatly across prefectures possibly influenced by persistent displacement. Perceived lack of security is reinforced by frequent exposure to persistent violence particularly as it increases with the availability of SALWs. These acts of violence include killings, sexual violence, beatings and pillaging all committed by armed groups (Vinck and Pham 2010). Part of the need to leave their homes, sometimes families, is linked to fear of potential violence, as well as the threat of abduction, being forced to work often in mining and participate in killing their families, villagers when taken by armed groups. The latter is often experienced by children. Therefore, entire families often flee insecure areas and move to camps and urbanised areas (Fig. 32.1).

The estimated number of people internally displaced within the CAR is 426,000 out of a total population of just under five million (United Nations 2017). This number only represents people within CAR seeking security not refugees fleeing conflicts in neighbouring countries such as the DRC, South Sudan or Cameroon or CAR refugees fleeing across the national borders. This is not to state there are no foreigners included in IDP numbers but that those added were resident in the CAR.

To demonstrate the scale of the displacement the data reveals the movement of the populations within each of the sixteen prefectures and Bangui, an autonomous commune. The displacement within the administrative capital of Bangui represents 8% of the population, approximately 58,700 out of 734,000.

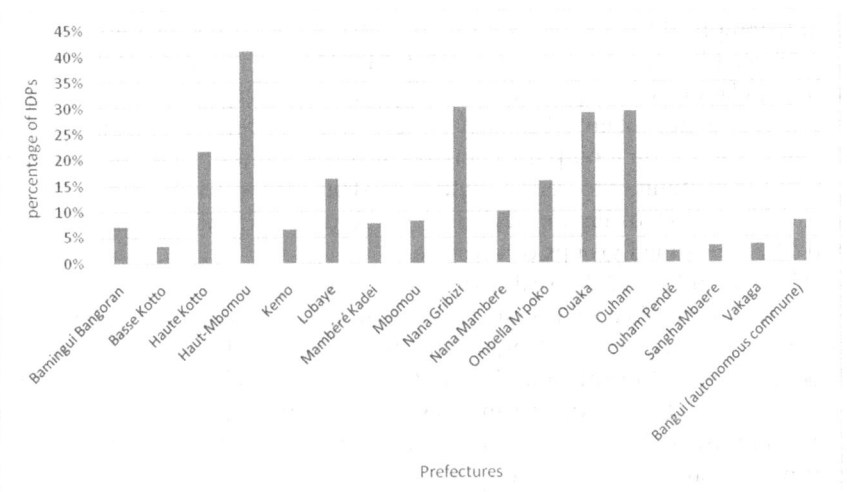

Fig. 32.1 Internally displaced persons in the Central African Republic (CAR) in 2017 (*Source* Internal displacement Monitoring centre: Central African Republic. www.internal-displacement.org)

The highest percentage of displacement happened in the Haut-Mbomou prefecture, 41.12% of the population, approximately 15,700 inhabitants out of 38,184. This is closely followed by three prefectures namely Nana Gribizi, Ouham and Ouaka with 30.11% (26,300 out of 87,341), 29.38% (82,500 out of 280,772) and 28.92% (64,800 out of 224,076), respectively. For the total of four prefectures around a third of the population has been displaced due to violence and insecurity. Haute-Kotto prefecture also experienced displacement of 21.72%, 15,100 out of 69,514 of the population effectively.

Several prefectures demonstrated displacement of approximately 10% of their regional population. Nana Mambere prefecture experienced displacement of 10.13%, 18,700 out of 184,594, OmbellaM'poko had 15.92%, 48,400 out of 304,025 and Lobaye prefecture 16.44%, 35,200 out of 214,137 approximately. Other prefectures with just under 10% displacement were BaminguiBangoran, Kemo, MambéréKadei, Mbomou with 7.02% (2700 out of 38,437), 6.57% (6500 out of 98,881), 7.66% (22,200 out of 289,688) and 8.29% (11,000 out of 132,740), respectively.

Other marginal displacements occurred in four prefectures namely Basse-Kotto, OuhamPendé, Sangha Mbaere and Vakaga, with 3.29% (6700 out of 203,889), 2.24% (7300 out of 325,567), 3.23% (2900 out of 89,871) and 3.46% (1300 out of 37,595), respectively. Similarly the administrative capital of Bangui that saw displacement of 8%, 58,700 out of 734,000. Although these percentages seem low in comparison to the other prefectures the numbers displaced are still significant. With a combined approximate amount of 3,353,311 people displaced this results in severe socio-economic disintegration. What the data depicts is that IDPs are a national problem and experienced in every prefecture in the CAR. This creates a scenario in which vast populations of people are unemployed, taken away from their ability to create economic sustainability such as agriculture. These movements lead to a decline in agricultural output forcing populations to move to centres for security and opportunities to generate income. Many are forced into low wage jobs and easily exploited. Figure 32.2 depicts the data on fatalities between 2017 and 2018 by armed groups on civilians.

The data in Fig. 32.2 reveals that were casualties in almost every prefecture. The highest number of casualties were in Ouaka (334), and lesser fatalities in prefectures such as Bangui (46), Basse-Kotto (71), Haute-Kotto (67), Mbomou (64), OuhamPende (73) and Ouham (54). There were no fatalities in Vakaga and OmbellaMpoko and this could be due to the isolation of several prefectures particularly a lack of transport networks and this is affected by rains that wash away temporary roads.

That civilian deaths remain high in CAR after the elections demonstrates that the state forces still cannot offer security for the civilian population. It also illustrates that militias have not agreed to the peace agreements although peace

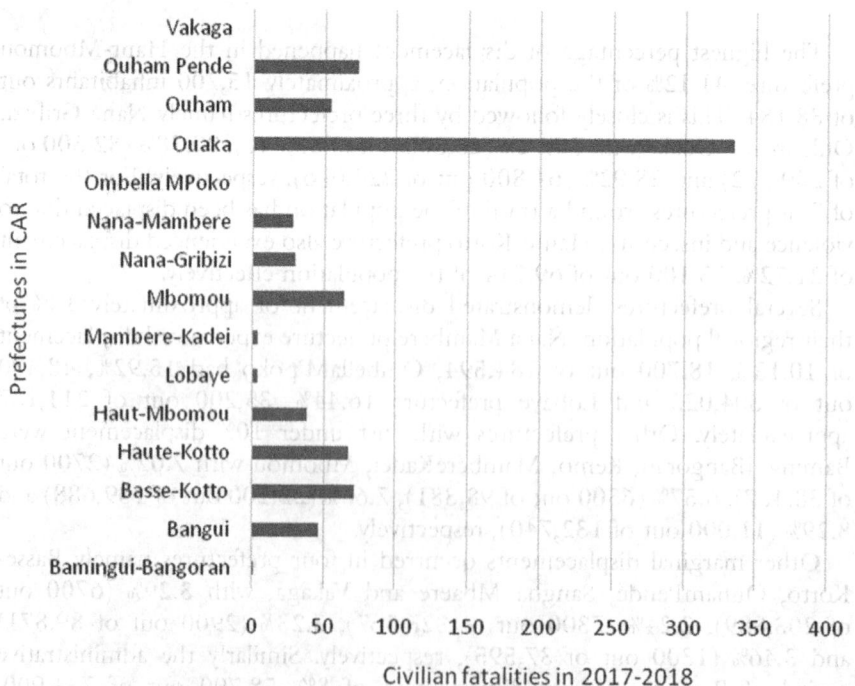

Fig. 32.2 Civilian and deaths by armed groups between 2017 and 2018 (*Source* United Nations, World population prospects 2017 Revision. https://esa.un.org/unpd/wpp/)

agreements do not include all armed groups and some continue to fight, when they cannot secure their financial interests, and escalate insecurity in villages and towns. The deaths can also be attributed to the criminal behaviour of fighters seeking to supplement their income beyond the stipends by robbing and extorting civilians.

It should be noted that although the United States is shown to export large volumes of weapons globally including the CAR no information of US manufactured weaponry is captured by the Conflict Armament Research in any of its data. Similarly, limited data appears to exist on Western European manufactured weaponry and perhaps this could reveal a slight prejudice in terms of the literature and its findings. Heavy emphasis appears to be on weaponry from countries that are not considered 'favourable' according to the West such as China, former Soviet bloc countries (Bulgaria, Czechia), Russia and Iran. The only mention of a Western European country is that vehicles were recovered but no actual weaponry. The reality seems rather unlikely considering the volumes of weapons exported from Western Europe and North America annually that not a single weapon of origin was located in the CAR.

What was noted was that the move into Bangui by the Séléka coalition in 2013 was joined by the military assistance of the Sudan. Apart from weapons Sudan also provided personnel particularly mercenaries who remained with the Séléka forces providing tactical training and information. However, fighters tend to be a motley crew and militias are comprised of various individuals seeking enrichment, access to resources, protection, security and even bloodlust.

Type 82-2 hand grenades are the most widespread item used in the CAR and has been recovered from the Séléka, anti-Balaka, several armed groups and civilians. By February 2017 Russia had sent nine planes stocked with weapons and personnel to train the national armed forces in CAR and to secure mining projects, although this is not included in the table, it demonstrates the willingness to void the arms embargo to suit the interests of UN Security Council members. The majority of weapons and ammunition that have been recovered were SALWs in and around Bangui reveals heavy fighting between armed groups and civilians. From the data it can be gleamed that there are attempts by Russia, China and the United States to export large quantities of armaments to the CAR with China even including anti-aircraft missiles which has been met with reluctance from other members of the Security Council (Ross 2018).

The findings reveal that the preponderance of available weapons, particularly the volume that has been recovered, illustrate a sociopolitical environment plagued by potential criminality, civil violence and disobedience and a reluctance to participate in proper negotiation to address differences. This behaviour escalates the number of IDPs in the country further destabilising the state and the role of administrative institutions in correcting the social malaise.

What Is Peculiar About CAR?

Although IDPs movements occur within the state, displaced people find themselves without access to state institutional support and resources. There is also little security offered by the government apparatus. What is apparent is that 2017 was a period of post-peace negotiations in which elections were held and conflict between government forces and non-state armed groups were to have ceased. What Figs. 32.1 and 32.2 reflect is the high level of insecurity in the CAR in the period when the country was in 'peaceful transition'.

IDPs often find themselves in locations where they are required to share limited resources and space with armed combatants. Often these combatants disguise that they were fighters and many NGOs report that some even refuse to surrender their weapons unless ordered to do so by commanders. This raises tensions in the camps and surrounding areas between groups and people bind together along lines of ethnicity. Many civilians, while obviously desiring peace and the potential programmes put in place to reduce political violence against them, many do not trust disarmed former combatants (Vinck and Pham 2010). Due to continued violence, instability and insecurity the population is paranoid and fearful. The lack of reliable information due to continued destruction of infrastructure means that many people do not have access to radios, the most common form of information within CAR.

Both tables illustrate that the national movement of civilians in which every prefecture is affected means that the economy has been severely disrupted and with continued uncertainty there is unlikely to be any form of real peace and social development. As the data is confined to 2017 this illustrates that even though politically with a new president the country remains dangerous and unstable. Armed groups, including criminals, target civilians forcing them to flee their villages and often prefectures.

This is a country that has experienced four coups and several failed attempts including that of 2013 that introduced a religious dimension to the conflict. Although this claim was eventually used by armed groups in order to draw support from external stakeholders and those seeking political power. It led to several rebellions in various prefectures creating cycles of displacement that continue at present. The tables demonstrate that even once conflict seizes in terms of political interests for elites financing the violence, the effects on the civilian population continue due to the large number of weapons that are easily available. The insecure environment forces people to seek those that share ethnic identities coupled with SALWs.

The data on the SALWs is not complete and often much information cannot be corroborated. However the information released by the Small Arms Survey and the Conflict Armament Research reveal a disturbing picture of conflict globally but particularly in the CAR. What is apparent is that while earlier media releases have placed emphasis on a binary conflict located within the borders of the country often without knowledge of the historical sociopolitical reality of this particular nation-state. Earlier information

Table 32.1 Weapons and ammunition of origin located in the Central African Republic during the period 2000–2017

Country of origin	Year manufactured	Type of weaponry recovered
China	2000–2001	7.62 × 54R mm ammunition
	2002–2006	Type 82-2 hand grenades
	2006–2007	82 mm HEAT recoilless rifle
	2008–2011	rockets
		Type 56-2 assault rifles
		Type 82-2 hand grenades
		PP93 60 mm mortar and mortar rounds
		12.7 × 108 mm ammunition
		DZPIC-40 40 mm RPG rockets
		7.62 × 54R mm ammunition
		9 × 19 mm ammunition
		7.62 × 39 mm ammunition
		QLZ-87 35 mm grenade launchers
		Type 69 40 mm HEAT RPG rockets and propellant charges
Iran	2000–2002	7.62 × 39 mm ammunition
	2003–2004	12.7 × 108 mm ammunition
	2000–2007	12.7 × 108 mm ammunition
		7.62 × 54R mm ammunition
Sudan	2013	7.62 × 39 mm ammunition
		Karaba light tactical vehicles
		82 mm mortar rounds
		60 mm mortar rounds
		Khawad 12.7 × 108 mm machine guns
		120 mm mortar rounds
		7.62 × 51 mm ammunition
		Makhtar 7.62 × 54R mm general purpose machine gun
UK	2007	5.56 × 45 mm L15 and L16 tracer ammunition
Czechia	2000–2010	PZ-59 7.62 × 54R mm ammunition
		9 × 19 mm sub machine gun ammunition
Belgium	2008	12.7 × 99 mm ammunition

(continued)

presented only allayed to an environment of ex-soldiers, the national army (FACA) and non-state armed actors led by former government employees and regional strongmen (French 2015). Later developments would demonstrate that fighters from neighbouring states such as Chad, the DRC and Sudan were engaged in assisting CAR fighters (Isaacs-Martin 2017).

Table 32.1 (continued)

Country of origin	Year manufactured	Type of weaponry recovered
Bulgaria	2001	FSQSD3 fuses 30 mm UBGL grenades
	2002	
	2006–2008	RHU-HEF 30 mm grenades
	2009	RHE-F 40 mm UBGL grenades 40 mm under barrel grenade launcher VOG-25 40 mm grenade
Germany	2012	MAN KAT-1 military trucks
South Africa		Milkor-1 grenade launchers
Russia	2017	*although not part of seizure the following were donated by Russia: AK-47 assault rifles Sniper rifles Machine guns Grenade launchers
Spain, Italy and Cameroon	2012	Anti-Balaka and civilians; 12 gauge shotgun shells

Sources Compiled from source material of the Conflict Armament Research (2015) and Ross (2018). Weapons of origin used in the CAR during the period 2000–2014. Information derived from the Conflict Armament Research (Conflict Armament Research 2015)

Research would later illustrate that apart from fighters from neighbouring states assisting the conflict, weaponry would also accompany certain groups (Conflict Armament Research 2015). The Sudan has been highlighted as a state that has supplied weaponry to FACA but also to the Séléka under the leadership of Djotodia. Often these conflicts are continuous and armed groups simply splinter and form under new leaders in order to achieve their objectives while at the same time claiming to espouse a particular ideological slant to receive external financial support. While not the scope of this chapter, research has shown that anti-Balaka sympathisers such as ex-president Bozize have asked for assistance from CAR citizens now resident in Europe. Former warlords involved in conflicts in other neighbouring countries have also entered into the conflict and terrorised the population. What is apparent is that while new actors enter conflict, old actors maintain their presence and form new alliances.

The Séléka coalition presents a new perspective in the CAR conflict. While the formation, re-formation and dissolution of armed groups are not a new development in CAR, the coalition to form a mega-militia is. While groups coalesce, in areas of identity to an extent, the overwhelming rationale is to acquire access to better weapons, resources such as food and stipends, the ability to extort resources from civilians to supplement meagre stipends. Access to weapons is easier within the coalitions and this was demonstrated by the findings of the Conflict Armament Research. Table 32.1 presents the weapons and ammunition recovered from conflict areas within the CAR. The information provides demonstrates findings before and after the UN arms embargo imposed on the country in 2013. However the embargo has been lifted to allow Russia to send weapons into the country due to a disagreement with France over using recycled weapons recovered from Somalia (Ross 2018).

The majority of weapons and ammunitions were located in Bangui from Séléka fighters. This would suggest that the militia has access to a vast cache of weapons and thus is able to draw more fighters. However the findings offer much speculation as it is difficult to assume that the countries of origin are necessarily directly exporting weapons to the militia. It has been stated that the end-user agreements are also being violated as in the case of China and Sudan. Much of the weapons shipped to the Sudan have been found in the CAR suggesting that end-user agreements are not being upheld. Secondly shotgun ammunition, which the Conflict Armament Research located among anti-Balaka and civilians alike, suggest that the countries of origin such as Spain and Italy are not necessarily in contractual agreement with militias or even the government. It does suggest that ammunition, and the weapons, are being smuggled across the borders of Cameroon and perhaps other neighbouring countries. The creation of artisanal weapons suggests that ammunition can be used without the need for the manufacturers weapons per se.

The adopted 2006 ECOWAS Convention, implemented in 2009, requires that all member states keep strict tally on the usage of SALWs they take into missions and operations and to report to the ECOWAS commission on the behaviour of their personnel, considered the most active peacekeepers globally. However, to date this has never been implemented among the member states. Similarly, the 2010 Kinshasa Convention adopted in 2017, equally is a small arms convention for the Economic Community of Central African States (ECCAS) and its eleven member states to maintain records of SALWs used in their missions. Apart from the ideological and philosophical positions of International Organisations (IOs), there are also stakeholders and lobby groups that themselves have their own agendas that can undermine and hamper any attempts to restrict weapon movement, distribution and disarmament (Arya 2002). Similarly persistent peace treaties and cycles of DDR programmes lead to donor fatigue and 'institutional decay' and 'crumbling infrastructure' and as Ayittey (2003) noted 'black elephants' such as international airports, cathedrals, monuments and conference centres. Although the Conflict Armament Research initiative do highlight that much information on weapons cannot be corroborated and there is much speculation regarding its movements, it should be noted that it is overwhelmingly former 'soviet' and 'communist' countries that appear to be the source of the weapons and ammunition and little on countries in Western Europe and North America although these are the largest global exporters of arms.

However apart from the purchase of SALWs a large proportion of weapons, although the data is imperfect, can be attributed to seizures, theft, road blocks, threats and attacks on various sites also compounded by corruption and ill-discipline (Berman 2019). Throw such means hundreds of weapons and thousands of small arms are lost through fixed site attacks and patrols. Even arms that are recovered by peacekeepers are stolen again and often the personal effects of peacekeepers are taken as well. Airdrops are another opportunity in which weapons are intercepted over long periods. Apart from the UN there is no financial incentive to report on weapon losses that includes vehicles and 'lethal material'. Yet it is not necessarily all coercive, there are instances where, to counter certain behaviours or actions, weapons are given to state and non-state actors alike by peacekeepers even when UN embargoes are in place but official policy allows it. In CAR the EU Force (EUFOR)RCA provided riot material to the national police. Peacekeepers also sell and trade their weapons, fuel and rations, when participating in ad hoc missions in the DRC, in the CAR.

According to (Berman 2019) a large proportion of weapons used by non-state forces are obtained from peacekeepers 'fixed sites, patrols and convoy movements'. Peace operations deployed to the CAR include the AU-MISCA mission (2013–2014), CEMAC-FOMAC (2003–2008), SEN-SAD/SEN-SAD (2001–2003), ECCAS-MICOPAX (2008–2013), EU-EUFOR Tchad/RCA (2008–2009) and (2014–2015), EU-EUMAM-RCA (2014–2015), (2015–2016), EU-EUTM/RCA (2016–present). All of these peacekeeping missions were armed and often militias deliberately target these troops. It is argued that the EU forces and NATO were able to assist the Bosnia and Herzegovina government to recover 10,000s weapons from civilians such an effective method can be applied to other conflict zones globally. However the resources and funds needed are prohibitive and questions must be asked regarding physical proximity of the Balkans in comparison to African and Asian states.

Overall the United States is among the largest exporter of weapons, in 2015 according to Holtom and Pavesi (2018) accounted for 33% of global exports. The CAR accounted for 7% of those deliveries. Coupled with these exports in 2015, the UN Comtrade noted that Zambia exported US $49m 'worth of small arms' to CAR. Yet in 2018, France, Britain and the United States put a hold on weapons donated from China to the CAR when the country approached the UN for an exemption as the weapons were for the national armed forces. Specific concern was that the weapons would be unescorted to the CAR and that many weapons such as anti-aircraft technology, rockets and missiles were not needed. However these weapons were backed by the EU military training mission and MINUSCA due to the constant attacks by armed groups in CAR (France-Presse 2018).

Nonetheless the proliferation of arms and the ease with which they can be obtained by militias and civilians alike raises concerns on peace processes and stabilising the CAR in future. The ease with which criminal activity can be facilitated with arms, the salience of identity conflicts leaves the application of complex methods in correcting these developments. Yet there is little emphasis or will to facilitate effective and long-term peace processes and little financial assistance from many powerful states. As earlier stated often IOs often have conflicting ideological and philosophical position straining their ability to render effective solutions that do not offer piecemeal solutions.

Conclusion

There is much discussion on the need to implement liberal democratic processes and respect for human rights in countries plagued by SALWs. However changing political and social circumstances without offering alternative economic opportunities is short-sighted and will eventually fail as no alternatives are offered to former combatants or civilians who were victims of violence and therefore insecurity. In the CAR the state lost control over the security apparatus through corruption and poor management limiting its ability to maintain the integrity of its borders or the well-being of its citizens. Without security and political and administrative control armed violence and crime escalated throughout the country. This led to displacement that undermines possible economic and social development for decades.

This facilitates an environment of increased weapons demand; those involved in criminal activity, those seeking to defend themselves and those who are unable to secure an income due to the economic collapse. This results in an unsecure environment that is incredibly difficult to change. Weaponry also creates a war economy, which is a distorted economy located in violence and displacement, for participants where many of the commodities traded are precious minerals, lumber, narcotics, people and weapons. It is difficult to create sustainable and equitable development for citizenry in such an environment as that is not its intended purpose—rather its purpose is predatory, temporary and mobile. In an environment of insecurity the SALWs serve as a curse and a saviour. While it has resulted in the loss of life, property and family structure it has also provided civilians with the perceived notion that they can protect themselves and maintain access to economic lifelines in new locations such as boomtowns.

Boomtowns are created of displaced populations and specifically around refugee sites. These sites are often loci of identity politics and the prejudice, and fear, towards those of different ethnic and cultural identities are heightened. This is often a direct result of the state armed forces and the militias who attack civilians. All armed groups, state or non-state, often hide their intentions behind a veneer of ideology that is conveniently linked to ethnic and cultural affinities. This so-called allegiance allows these groups to indirectly justify their behaviour, extortion and violence against civilians of different identities. However, this is often a characteristic gleamed from government forces. This behaviour from armed groups transfers to the society in general who become sensitised to identity politics and practice the divisions that permeate the country and lead to civil violence that resulted in Muslims fleeing to neighbouring regions. Like most violence that targets particular groups it spills across into other identities creating an environment of fear and distrust that takes years, even decades, to overcome. This is further complicated by the consistent supply of armaments into the affected space.

SALWs have undermined the political structures and institutions of the CAR due to persistent coups. It provided those seeking access and maintaining control with the ability to secure power without using the ballot. It excludes the need to gain support from the population and competing against contenders. Also, those who cannot be assured of success opt to utilise conflict as a way to gain economic traction. Often the post-Cold War environment has resulted in traditional clients seeking alternative sources of income often encouraged by external stakeholders. Often not seeking access to political power many of these regional leaders have resources to purchase SALWs but also the allegiance of those residing there. As many living in the rural areas are farmers or unemployed youth, many join armed groups not out of a desire to support political ideology but rather to secure protection, weapons and stipends. These individuals who are not trained fighters are able to use SALWs and expected to assault and kill other villagers and raze their crops and properties.

Such behaviours are often transferred to children who can easily use SALWs are often expected to kill their families and other community members. Without the ability to return many are forced to become fighters and cannot leave these militias. This limits their ability to seek alternative employment as they mature or return to their villages. Due to the distrust of civilians living under potential threat of violence many move to camps supervised by NGOs which are themselves problematic areas. Many camps are equally insecure spaces as they behave as zones of ethnic hostility and militias often hide among the civilians intimidating and threatening people.

The proliferation of SALWs will continue to result in IDPs as the destroyed economy makes it difficult for society to restructure a legitimate economy in which civilians, and even former fighters, can participate. What confronts the CAR, like many of her neighbours, is the lack of conflict resolution mechanisms that would prevent effectively minor disputes from developing into wars and humanitarian disasters. The vast amount of weapons in the CAR from external suppliers and regional stakeholders such as the Sudan makes peace an impossible task as new groups enter into the war economy seeking riches. The vast number of external actors seeking exacerbate the conflict in the CAR will continue to destabilise the country and effectively the region and serve to benefit stakeholders that are external to the violence. Solving such complexities require commitment from various governments in the region and the continued violence will only in apathy if numerous peace agreements do not render effective results.

REFERENCES

Arya, N. (2002). Confronting the Small Arms Pandemic: Unrestricted Access Should Be Viewed as a Public Health Disaster. *BMJ: British Medical Journal, 324*(7344), 990.
Ayittey, G. (2003). Economic Impact of Africa's Conflicts. In E. E. Uwazie (Ed.), *Conflict Resolution and Peace Education in Africa* (pp. 39–56). Minneapolis, MN: Lexington Books.
Berman, E. G. (2019). *Beyond Blue Helmets*. Retrieved from Geneva, Switzerland.
Boutwell, J., & Klare, M. (1998). Small Arms and Light Weapons: Controlling the Real Instruments of War. *Arms Control Today, 28*(6), 15.
Boutwell, J., & Klare, M. T. (2000). A Scourge of Small Arms. *Scientific American, 282*(6), 48–53.
Broodryk, A., & Solomon, H. (2010). From War Economies to Peace Economies in Africa. *Scientia Militaria, 38*(1). https://doi.org/10.5787/38-1-77.
Castoriadis, C. (1997). *The Imaginary Institution of Society*. Cambridge: MIT Press.
Collier, P. (1998). *The Political Economy of Ethnicity*. Washington, DC: World Bank.
Collier, P., Hoeffler, A., & Rohner, D. (2009). Beyond Greed and Grievance: Feasibility and Civil War. *Oxford Economic Papers, 61*(1), 1–27. Retrieved from http://www.jstor.org/stable/25167719.
Collier, P., & Sambanis, N. (2002). Understanding Civil War: A New Agenda. *The Journal of Conflict Resolution, 46*(1), 3–12. Retrieved from http://www.jstor.org/stable/3176236.
Conflict Armament Research, C. A. R. (2015). *Non-State Armed Groups in the Central African Republic: Types and Sources of Documented Arms and Ammunition*. Retrieved from https://www.conflictarm.com/car_publications/NONSTATE_ARMED_GROUPS_IN_CENTRAL_AFRICAN_REPUBLIC.pdf from Conflict Armament Research https://www.conflictarm.com/car_publications/NONSTATE_ARMED_GROUPS_IN_CENTRAL_AFRICAN_REPUBLIC.pdf.
Fjelde, H. (2015). Farming or Fighting? Agricultural Price Shocks and Civil War in Africa. *World Development, 67*, 525–534.
France-Presse, A. (2018). *France, Britain, US Put UN Hold on Chinese Arms Deliveries to Central African Republic*. Retrieved 16 November 2019.
French, H. W. (2015). The Looting Machine: Warlords, Oligarchs, Corporations, Smugglers, and the Theft of Africa's Wealth. *Foreign Affairs, 94*(4), 150–155. Retrieved from < Go to ISI >://WOS:000356128900018.
Gauthier, A. (2018). *The Future of Central African Republic is Still at Risk*.
Gerlach, C. (2010). *Extremely Violent Societies: Mass Violence in the Twentieth Century World*. New York: Cambridge University Press.
Gillis, M. (2017). *Disarmament: A Basic Guide* (3rd ed.). New York: United Nations. http://www.un.org/disarmament/HomePage/ODAPublications/AdhocPublications/PDF/Basic%5FGuide-2011-web.pdf. Accessed April 2018.
Hartung, W. D. (2001). The New Business of War: Small Arms and the Proliferation of Conflict. *Ethics & International Affairs, 15*(1), 79–96.
Holtom, P., & Pavesi, I. (2018, August). The 2018 Small Arms Trade Transparency Barometer. In *Briefing Paper*. Geneva: Small Arms Survey.
Isaacs-Martin, W. (2015). The Motivations of Warlords and the Role of Militias in the Central African Republic. *Conflict Trends, 2015*(4), 26–32. Retrieved

from http://0-search.ebscohost.com.oasis.unisa.ac.za/login.aspx?direct=true&db=awn&AN=1121940&site=eds-live&scope=site.

Isaacs-Martin, W. (2016). Political and Ethnic Identity in Violent Conflict: The Case of Central African Republic. *International Journal of Conflict and Violence, 10*(1), 26.

Isaacs-Martin, W. (2017). The Séléka and Anti-Balaka Rebel Movements in the Central African Republic. In C. Varin & D. Abubakar (Eds.), *Violent Non-State Actors in Africa: Terrorists, Rebels and Warlords* (pp. 131–161). Cham, Switzerland: Palgrave Macmillan.

Kinsella, D. (2006). The Black Market in Small Arms: Examining a Social Network. *Contemporary Security Policy, 27*(01), 100–117.

Lumpe, L. (1999). Curbing the Proliferation of Small Arms and Light Weapons. *Security Dialogue, 30*(2), 151–164.

McIntyre, A., & Weiss, T. (2003). Exploring Small Arms Demand: A Youth Perspective. *Institute for Security Studies Papers, 2003*(67), 11.

Mkutu, K. A. (2006). Small Arms and Light Weapons Among Pastoral Groups in the Kenya-Uganda Border Area. *African Affairs, 106*(422), 47–70.

Mkutu, K. A. (2007). Impact of Small Arms Insecurity on the Public Health of Pastoralists in the Kenya-Uganda Border Regions. *Crime, Law and Social Change, 47*(1), 33–56.

Muggah, R. (2010). Rethinking Small Arms Control in Africa: It Is Time to Set an Armed Violence Reduction Agenda: Analysis. *Conflict, Security & Development, 10*(2), 217–238.

Musah, A. F. (2002). Privatization of Security, Arms Proliferation and the Process of State Collapse in Africa. *Development and Change, 33*(5), 911–933.

Onuoha, G. (2006). Contextualising the Proliferation of Small Arms and Light Weapons in Nigeria's Niger Delta: Local and Global Intersections. *African Security Studies, 15*(2), 108–114.

Patrick, S. (2006). Weak States and Global Threats: Fact or Fiction? *Washington Quarterly, 29*(2), 27–53.

Pouligny, B. (2004). *The Politics and Anti-Politics of Contemporary Disarmament, Demobilisation and Reintegration Programs/ Les Anciens Combattants d'aujourd'hui Désarmement, Démobilisation et Réinsertion.* Retrieved from France.

Reno, W. (1997). African Weak States and Commercial Alliances. *African Affairs, 96*, 165–185.

Reno, W. (1999). *Warlord Politics and African States.* Boulder: Lynne Rienner Publishers.

Reno, W. (2009). Explaining Patterns of Violence in Collapsed States. *Contemporary Security Policy, 30*(2), 356–374.

Ross, A. (2018). *How Russia Moved into Central Africa [Press Release].* Retrieved from https://www.reuters.com/article/us-africa-russia-insight/how-russia-moved-into-central-africa-idUSKCN1MR0KA.

Stohl, R., & Tuttle, D. (2009). The Challenges of Small Arms and Light Weapons in Africa. *Conflict Trends, 2009*(1), 19–26.

Stohl, R. J. (2002). Under the Gun: Children and Small Arms. *African Security Studies, 11*(3), 17–25.

United Nations. (2017). *World Population Prospects: The 2017 Revision.* Retrieved 22 June 2018.

Vinck, P., & Pham, P. (2010, August 3). Building Peace, Seeking Justice: A Population-Based Survey on Attitudes About Accountability and Social Reconstruction in the Central African Republic. In *Seeking Justice: A Population-Based Survey on Attitudes About Accountability and Social Reconstruction in the Central African Republic*.

Vines, A. (2007). Can UN Arms Embargoes in Africa Be Effective? *International Affairs, 83*(6), 1107–1121.

Vorrath, J. (2014). *From War to Illicit Economies: Organised Crime and State-Building in Liberia and Sierra Leone*. Berlin: Stiftung Wissenschaft und Politik/German Institute for International and Security Affairs.

Weiss, T. (2003). A Demand-Side Approach to Fighting Small Arms Proliferation: Feature. *African Security Review, 12*(2), 5–16.

Wendy Isaacs-Martin is a research associate with the Archie Mafeje Research Institute at the University of South Africa. She has published in several peer reviewed journals and book chapters on the themes of identity and conflict in Africa. Currently she is working on a narrative on the future of state formation. Her research on scapegoating, identity formation and maintenance, and violence is viewed through the lens of nation-state ideologies and state-formation theories.

CHAPTER 33

Egypt: Arab Spring, Regime Crisis and the Proliferation of Small Arms

Audu Nanven Gambo

Introduction

The phenomenon of globalization has not only eroded the traditional borders between countries of the world, but has also made the world pretty transparent for easy comparison by citizens in different locations. The information, communication and technology (ICT) components of the forces of globalization have opened up the world stage for close and critical scrutiny by citizens of different countries. The traditional notion of sovereignty as is widely acknowledged by scholars of International Relations has largely been compromised on account of the growing wave of globalization. There is hardly any significant development in any part of the globe that is not known to other parts of the world in a matter of minutes. Citizens can easily compare their socio-economic and political condition with those of their counterparts in other countries. This is the context in which we can make sense out of the development widely referred to as "Arab Spring" which engulfed some Arab countries (Tunisia, Egypt, Libya, Yemen and Syria). The unprecedented phenomenon started in Tunisia on 18 December 2010 and, like the harmattan wildfire, quickly spread to some Arab states leading to the ouster of regimes in some, while stoking intensely violent conflicts in others. Before the Arab Spring, many of the countries that were affected by this development were under undemocratic or authoritarian rule and Egypt in particular had been under authoritarian rule since 1952. The Arab Spring was indeed a much welcome relief to those Arab

A. N. Gambo (✉)
Department of Political Science, University of Jos, Jos, Nigeria

© The Author(s), under exclusive license to Springer Nature Switzerland AG 2021
U. A. Tar and C. P. Onwurah (eds.), *The Palgrave Handbook of Small Arms and Conflicts in Africa*,
https://doi.org/10.1007/978-3-030-62183-4_33

countries that have been under the throes and weight of undemocratic regimes and the consequent denial of citizens' fundamental rights and freedoms.

The Arab Spring which emerged in January 2011 when a disgruntled Tunisian young man set himself ablaze in a town square in protest against excesses of local government officials and set the tone for regime collapse in Tunisia ignited mass revolt in the Maghreb region and elsewhere. The Arab Spring has far-reaching implications for the sociopolitical order of Egypt. Egyptian society had for the greater part of her post-independence life, remained under authoritarian rule until the Arab Spring had liquidated the foundation of unrepresentative government in 2011. Egypt had existed between 1922 and 1952 as a constitutional monarchy (Ernest 2015). When Abdel Nasser took over power in 1952 through a carefully staged coup against King Farouk, he changed from monarchy to a republic even as Egypt remained under authoritarian rule. Authoritarianism continued to be the core defining characteristic of the Egyptian political system until 11 February 2011 when the authoritarian system was overthrown through popular uprisings. An authoritarian political system is inevitably characterized by absence of consensus-driven social order and this breeds a fertile environment for antagonism between citizens and the government. This condition creates a context for frictions often expressed violently. More often than not, the demand for small arms and lightWeapons (SALWs) becomes pretty high. The prevailing authoritarian climate in Egypt fuelled the motivation for acquisition of arms by non-state actors in particular for engaging with security agencies (Osman 2013). The demonstration effect of the violent uprising in Libya in 2011 increased the demand for SALWs in Egypt. The collapse of critical institutions of governance such as the executive, legislative, judicial, bureaucracy and security apparatuses had far-reaching implications for social and political order and stability of Egypt. It is in this context that one can underscore the link between Egyptian uprisings and the one in Libya.

The erstwhile President Hosni Mubarak who came to power in 1981 following the assassination of his boss, Anwar Sadat, was the first casualty after intense and widespread protests against his authoritarian rule. Following the overthrow of Hosni Mubarak's regime in 2011, Egypt for the first time in the history of her existence as a sovereign state, had the opportunity to democratically constitute a government headed by President Mohamed Morsi, a frontline member of the Muslim Brotherhood (MB) in 2011. This historic development in Egypt was widely greeted with effusive outpouring of joy and relief across the country. The MB in particular was thrown into frenzy when Mohamed Morsi was declared the elected President of Egypt. The secular activists were not excited by this development because they never expected the victory of the MB. Nonetheless, the secular political community in Egypt accepted the outcome of the process with an equanimity of mind. Many had expected that there would be considerable improvement in their socio-economic condition under the Muslim Brotherhood-affiliated Mohamed Morsi regime. Many others had expected significant improvement of the comatose security environment in Egypt to enable them pursue their legitimate means of livelihoods. No sooner had Mohamed Morsi sworn into office than citizens started hoping for immediate delivery of social services. The rising expectations of Egyptians could not be met because of the depth of the mess bequeathed to the newly sworn in President.

It is against the background of the foregoing that the chapter analyses the nexus between Arab Spring and regime crisis in Egypt and how this in turn fuelled small arms and light weapons proliferation in the country. The contention here is that the proliferation of SALWs in Egypt is a direct fall out of the interplay between the phenomena of Arab Spring and regime crisis. Arab Spring which started in Tunisia on 18 December 2010 and spread to Egypt on 25 January 2011 had plunged the regime in Egypt into profound crisis situation thereby weakening the foundation of effective governance. Once effective governance had taken a flight, the sociopolitical space in Egypt got inundated with SALWs most of which were believed to originate from Libya. This unhealthy development had led to rapid deterioration of the security environment in Egypt including the rise in insurgency and terrorism in the Sinai Peninsula. The chapter is structured into five sections. Section one provides the introductory remarks. Section two dwells on conceptual clarifications. Section three examines the phenomenon of Arab Spring and how this has stoked regime crisis in Egypt. Section four explains how the regime crisis in Egypt has catalyzed the proliferation of SALWs in Egypt. Section five concludes the chapter with some prescriptions in terms of how to arrest the small arms and light weapons proliferation in Egypt for improved security environment in Egypt.

CONCEPTUAL CLARIFICATIONS

Three key operative concepts embodied in the title of the chapter are worth clarifying to help readers comprehend the sense they are used here. These are "Arab Spring," regime crisis and SALWs proliferation. The "Arab Spring" is an expression popularly used to describe the spate of violent uprisings that took place in some North African states of Tunisia, Egypt and Libya spilling over to some Arab states of Yemen, Bahrain, Lebanon and Syria. Danjibo (2013) describes the expression "Arab Spring" as a term used to "designate popular revolutions that have taken place in the Arab world to liberate and liberalize the states, ensure change of autocratic governments, and institute socioeconomic and political reforms." Arab Spring in the context of Danjibo's view could be fundamentally described as pro-democracy movements motivated and fuelled by the collective desire of the Arab world to be governed by their consent. The underlying belief here is that a democratically established government is guided by the principles of constitutionalism, rule of law, accountability, transparency, due process and respect for the fundamental rights and freedoms of citizens. It was generally an expression of widespread discontentment with the living condition of people of the affected countries in autocratic systems. Tsuwa and Otsapa (2016: 407) have observed that "the Middle East and North Africa regions are characterized by insecurity, poverty, weak states, underdevelopment, absence of social justice, lack of accountability and transparency in public life, youth unemployment, poor infrastructure, and environmental hazards." A confluence of all these factors has given rise to general feeling of discontentment across the Egyptian society and the consequent violent expression of same. Before the Arab Spring, many countries in North Africa and Middle East (MENA) were governed under authoritarian political system characterized by denial of fundamental human rights and freedoms, unelected representatives in government, lack of participation by people in the governance process on account of denial of access, insensitivity and unresponsiveness of government to the popular aspirations and expectations of citizens, etc. The legitimate demand of citizens for democratic freedom is likened to Sekou Toure's contention that Guineans would "prefer poverty in freedom to opulence in slavery." The Arab Spring is therefore popular uprising and revolts targeted at establishing a healthy, productive, tolerance, prosperity and rule of law conscious society in the Middle East and North Africa.

A crisis is viewed as a situation where there is a perception of threat, heightened anxiety, expectation of possible violence and the widespread belief that any action will have far-reaching consequences for the social order (Shlaim 1988; Charles 1969). A crisis is one of the critical stages in the progression of conflict along the continuum and has its own distinguishing features such as sudden eruption of unexpected events caused by previous, but badly managed conflict. Charles (1969: 414) notes that "a crisis is unanticipated (surprise) actions by the opponents, perception of great threat, perception of limited time to consider possible available response options and perception of disastrous consequences from inaction." The following can be distilled as the defining characteristics of crisis:

i. It is unanticipated: This simply means that people do not have a premonition of what is about to befall them. Here, there is element of surprise;
ii. Perception of great threat arising from the unanticipated actions of the opponents;
iii. Perception of limited time available to carefully and critically consider all possible available response options; and
iv. Perception of disastrous consequences from inaction.

A crisis situation arises when policy makers are under intense pressure to articulate appropriate response to sudden development that has far-reaching implications for the status quo social order. This development could be social or natural in nature. It is instructive to note that even individuals do experience crisis from time to time. For instance, a man is driving in his car and is suddenly commanded to stop and the next thing is a rifle pointed at him by an armed robber. This is a typical crisis situation because the man in question never had a premonition about his travail. There is not much time available for him to critically think through possible alternatives for responding to the threat. His not doing anything in response to the threat could have disastrous consequence for him. He could be killed by the armed robber or he could have his car snatched away by the armed robber or both could happen to him. Sovereign state actors in the international system do encounter crisis situation in the course of their interaction with one another. The Cuban missile crisis of October 1962—a nuclear stand-off involving the United States of America and the defunct Union of Soviet Socialist Republic (USSR) is a good example. The defunct Soviet Union had placed strategic offensive missiles in Cuba as a base to launch missiles offensive against the United States of America (USA). The United States of America responded with a Naval quarantine (Allison 1971). The 13 days crisis had imposed on the United States of American government under John F. Kennedy intense pressure to respond in order to avoid disastrous consequences.

By extension, "regime crisis" in the context of this chapter is viewed as sudden and unanticipated challenges that overstretch the responsive capacity of the sociopolitical order in place. Regime crisis in most cases is an expression of loss of trust and faith in the governing entity. To put it more explicitly, regime crisis is the point at which citizens cultivate the feeling that the governing authority has lost the right to rule on account of consistent failure to meet their aspirations and expectations. Indicators of regime crisis are sudden withdrawal of tangible and intangible support from the political system, rebellious political behaviour of citizens, attacks on public institutions and officials. When confronted with this sudden change in the political behaviour of citizens, government mobilizes its instruments of coercion with a view to extinguishing the rebellious behaviour of citizens. This leads to active confrontation between a coalition of various interest groups in the society and the law and order institutions of government. This was how the situation played out in Egypt when a multitude of Egyptians aggregated and took over the historic *Tahrir* Square to demand for the liquidation of former President Hosni Mubarak's authoritarian government. The popular uprisings which started on 25 January 2011 continued until February when Hosni Mubarak had to throw in the towel on the advice of top military officers. The massive clampdown on the protesting citizens at the *Tahrir* Square had failed to weaken the resolve of the protesters to cause the dissolution of Hosni Mubarak's undemocratic government. The more frequent the attacks against the protesters, the more the anti-government protests grew in resilience and potency.

Finally, SALWs as one of the operative concepts to be clarified in this chapter could be understood in the context of Economic Community of West African States' (ECOWAS) conception. According to the ECOWAS' (2006: 197) Convention on SALWs, light weapons consist of portable arms designed to be used by several persons working together in a team and which include notably heavy machine guns; portable grenade launchers, mobile or mounted;

portable anti-aircraft cannons; portable anti-tank cannons, non-recoil guns; portable anti-tank missile launchers or rocket launchers; portable anti-aircraft missile launchers; and mortars with a caliber of less than 100 millimetres. Similarly, it defines small arms as arms used by one person and which include notably firearms and other destructive arms or devices such as an exploding bomb; an incendiary bomb or gas bomb; a grenade; a rocket launcher; a missile; a missile system or landmine; revolvers and pistols with automatic loading; rifles and carbines; machine guns; assault rifles; and light machine guns. All these put together constitute what is popularly referred to in the literature as SALWs. The proliferation or spread of these weapons within or across borders is determined by two fundamental factors. These are the supply side or push factors such as willing sellers, profitability are porous borders; and the demand side or what may also be referred to as pull factors such as crimes, violence, conflicts, unrests, etc. (Simon and Akintunde 2015). The proliferation of SALWs is one of the key drivers of instability in most societies that have not found an effective cure for this deadly social phenomenon. Most Third world societies are particularly vulnerable to this phenomenon because of their inability to effectively articulate strategies for curbing the spread.

The chapter utilizes frustration-aggression as analytical framework. The choice of this theoretical framework of analysis is predicated on the nature and character of the uprisings in some countries in the Middle East and North Africa. The self-immolation by Mohamed Bouazizi on 18 December 2010 was obviously a response to the frustrating ordeal the 26-year old was made to go through. He was driven by frustration and a sense of abuse of dignity to engage in self-immolation as an expression of dissatisfaction with the sociopolitical order in Tunisia. This act of self-immolation became the genesis of what is today widely referred to as "Arab Spring." Frustration-aggression theory was developed by Dollard et al. (1939) in a monograph they published on the theme of aggression. The three scholars noted in their monograph that aggressive behaviour by individuals or groups is an expression of frustration fuelled by the existing socio-economic and political order in a given political community. Aggressive behaviour is motivated by intense feelings of frustration caused by consistent denial of opportunity of meeting one's needs in the society. Individuals and groups who are habitually denied opportunities of satisfying basic needs soon begin to develop the tendency to react angrily or violently to the source of the denial. Aggressive or violent behaviour is motivated by extreme feelings of helplessness in a frustrating context. Hindering goal seeking behaviour as contended by Ho-won (2011), could in a fundamentally sense elicit violent attack on the blocking source or its surrogate. Violent behaviour is closely associated with a group's persistent inability to achieve its goal. The state legitimacy is widely challenged when traditional authority norms are not sufficiently and strongly responsive to the inherent needs of persons in the society (Ho-won 2011). The Egyptian state was trapped in this dilemma when it proved grossly incapable of providing welfare and security to citizens when the popular uprisings began in January 2011.

Frustration-aggression as a theoretical framework is not without its limitations in terms of explanatory utility. It is not always true to attribute violent behaviour to frustration. Frustrated individuals or groups may convert such experience into something more constructive, for instance playing some games that may provide relief to them from the emotional and psychological anguish associated with frustration. A frustrated individual or group may choose to move away from the goal blocking source rather than expressing aggressive or violent behaviour. Managing frustration is in some cases, a learned behaviour (Ho-won 2011) and so experiences of individuals and groups with deep sense of discontent can influence their attitude towards the blocking source. Individuals and groups may choose to resign to fate rather than giving violent expression to intense feelings of frustration.

The frustration-aggression thesis is further elaborated by Gurr (1970) in his highly rated book titled "Why Men Rebel." Gurr (1970: 210) notes that people who are experiencing frustration often feel the need to behave rebelliously because of the belief that they stand a chance of relieving their discontents by doing so. The phenomenon of Arab Spring fits into this theoretical framework in the sense that the uprisings, revolts and demonstrations that characterized the developments in the affected countries in the Middle East and North Africa were responses to decades of catastrophic governance, widespread poverty, unemployment, severe hunger, denial of rights and freedoms, deprivation, disempowerment, exclusion from the mainstream sociopolitical processes and a host of other debilitating conditions. A confluence of all these factors has induced violent political behaviour across some Middle East and North African countries. The deeply entrenched culture of authoritarianism in the Middle East and North Africa has only succeeded in breeding fertile ground for the eruption of violence in the age of globalization.

Arab Spring and Regime Crisis in Egypt

Egypt has established a reputation for being politically unstable since her independence from the British in 1922. After gaining independence, Egypt started as a constitutional monarchy under King Farouk from 1922 to 1952 when a military coup led by Colonel Gamal Abdel Nasser ended the monarchy. Authoritarian republic was instituted in place of constitutional monarchy, with Abdel Nasser as the Head of State. King Farouk was widely known as one of the famous richest men in the world, famous for his spending sprees, gargantuan appetite and endless procession of mistresses (Martin 2005). The Egyptian military in particular, were distrustful of King Farouk who was addicted to pleasure seeking and with sparse time for state affairs. Cairo, the capital of Egypt as observed by Martin (2005: 31) remained "in ferment, a cauldron of conspiracy, assassination, rioting and press agitation, where communists, nationalists, royalists and Muslim extremists competed for ascendancy." It was in the midst of all these mounting and threatening domestic sociopolitical conditions that a section of the military led by Colonel Gamal

Abdel Nasser, got King Farouk on the 26 July 1952 to sign an act of abdication and to proceed on exile. Once in total control of power, the Revolutionary Command Council (RCC) clamped down heavily on rival opposition groups such as the MB, and ultra-nationalists. The monarchical system was ultimately abolished in June 1923 and proclaimed Egypt a republic (Martin 2005).

The legacy of authoritarianism was for a long time a key defining element of the Egyptian political system. From 1922 to 2011, there had been no credible, free or fair democratic electoral contest for political power in Egypt. This was the context in which the Arab Spring or revolution or uprising as variously described by the western press and scholars, permeated the Egyptian society to bring about some fundamental changes in the country's political system. The Arab Spring which began on 18 December 2010 in Tunisia, was a spontaneous uprising against the erstwhile Tunisian President Zine El Abidine Ben Ali. It all started when a 26-year-old fruits and vegetables vendor, Mohamed Bouazizi, was unjustly harassed by the Tunisian local government officials in company of security and law enforcement agencies when he wanted to sell his goods in the countryside of Sidi Bouzid in Tunisia. Apparently, Mohamed Bouazizi did not have the police permit to sell his commodities. When local officials unleashed the police on Bouazizi to hand over his wooden cart, he vehemently refused and this fetched him a slap from a policewoman. The young man was filled with indignation at the inhumane treatment meted out to him by the unsmpathetic policewoman. He felt so dehumanized that he matched in front of a government building, bathed with petrol and set himself ablaze. The news of this self-immolation quickly spread within and outside Tunisia using various media, including social media and this stoked the mass protests, revolts and demonstrations against the government of President Ben Ali, by then one of the longest-serving sit tight leaders in Africa. This scary development pushed President Ben Ali to flee to Saudi Arabia where he later died.

The Arab Spring soon spread to some Middle East and North African countries such as Egypt, Libya, Yemen, Syria, Bahrain and a host of others. While the effect of the Arab Spring was far reaching in Libya in the sense that Col. Muammar Ghaddafi was killed in the process, in other affected Arab and North African countries, the leaders were pressured into stepping aside to bring about a new sociopolitical order expected to meet the developmental aspirations of their citizens. In the case of Syria, the violent conflict ignited by the protests between government forces and protesting citizens is still raging with scant promise of ending soon. Scholars (Adetula 2011; Adejo 2011; Ogunsanwo 2014; Onuoha 2011; Idahosa 2011) have attributed the uprisings or revolts to economic stagnation, domination, exploitation, denial of fundamental rights and freedoms, repression, corruption, chronic poverty, unemployment, declining economic fortunes, exclusion and a host of other factors. A close and critical scrutiny of these drivers or enablers of the Arab Spring would reveal the entrenched culture of authoritarianism and bad governance which has failed to bring equitable and sustainable development and prosperity to the affected societies straddling between North Africa and the Middle East. The Arab Spring is therefore an expression of mass discontent with the prevailing socio-economic and political condition of the countries in question.

Authoritarian rule has come to be closely associated with the Arab world. Many or nearly all regimes in the Arab world are authoritarian with scant consideration for rule of law, fundamental human rights and freedoms of citizens, constitutionalism and due process in the pattern of governance. Consequently, the majority of the people are not only excluded from the governance process but are also robbed of the tangible benefits of habitual loyalty to the state. The dilemma of the Arab world is that globalization has contracted the world into a village and made it quite transparent that everybody can see through the affairs of any society. Happenings in one corner of the village are quickly brought to public consciousness through both conventional and new social media. The enormous sacrifice made by Mohamed Bouazizi when he set himself ablaze in front of government building in Tunisia was a fundamental statement on the lamentable socio-economic and political condition of citizens in the Arab world fuelled by decades of authoritarian rule. Citizens in most MENA are economically and politically disempowered and this makes such societies inherently combustible. This is the context in which the Arab Spring or uprisings can be comprehended.

The authoritarian Egyptian regime like anywhere else cannot but be hopelessly and helplessly vulnerable to mass discontent and collective action. The same factors that stoked the uprisings in Tunisia and other affected countries were present in Egypt. The demonstration effect of the uprising in Tunisia quickly resonated in Egypt because of the combustible socio-economic and political environment just waiting for a trigger. Authoritarian regime in Egypt was facing serious crisis of legitimacy in view of the massive loss of faith in the capacity and capability of the system to meet the developmental aspirations of citizens. Lack of trust in the Hosni Mubarak government that has consistently failed to bring about significant progress in the socio-economic and political condition of the people had already weakened the responsive capacity of the regime. A combination of crisis of legitimacy and weak capacity of government institutions to respond to the challenges of development robbed the authoritarian regime of the support and emotional attachment of citizens. The Tunisian experience simply provided impetus for the crisis in Egypt. A coalition of activists of various persuasions took advantage of the development in Tunisia to give expression to their long-standing desire to bring about regime change in Egypt.

The popular *Tahrir* square in Cairo which has historically served as an incubator of progressive ideas, was effectively occupied as protesters using the potent new social media to mobilize for collective action, converged on it to articulate strategies on the most effective way to engage the embattled authoritarian regime. The popular uprisings against the authoritarian regime of Hosni Mubarak would not have been effective and successful without the skillful and astute use of the new social media such as Facebook, Twitter, YouTube and several others. The Egyptian youth effectively used the new social media to broadly mobilize for collective action against Hosni Mubarak's regime. As Danjibo (2013) correctly observes, Egyptian youth were reminded of the incident of June 2010 when the Egyptian police beat Khaled Said to death. The memory of this inhumane treatment meted out to Khaled Said leading to his untimely death fuelled citizens' sense of anger and the resolve to terminate the authoritarian regime in Egypt at the time. The new social media therefore played a very critical role in the 2011 uprisings in Egypt. The protest which started on the 25 January 2011 continued to gain momentum as more and more people expressed support for the civil disobedience and collective action. Meanwhile, the weak authoritarian government of Hosni Mubarak faced intense pressures over how to respond to the sudden collective action. Lacking capacity for engaging the protesters in constructive dialogue, the regime quickly employed the use of brute force, albeit in futility to bring the situation under control. There was massive clamp down on the protesters with several persons killed in the process. It was estimated that about 800 lives (Danjibo 2013) were lost in the Egyptian 25th January Revolution. The regime did not quite appreciate the strong resolve of the protesters by trusting in the efficacy of brute force to extinguish the flaming arrows of mounting opposition. The more the killings, the more the protest gathered momentum as thousands of citizens continued to identify with the opposition. The opposition to Hosni Mubarak's regime continued until 11 February 2011 when the military advised former President Hosni Mubarak to step down and which he did without further delay. The advice became necessary in view of the obvious futility of the use of state instruments of coercion to quell the uprisings. It was partly to save the image of the security personnel who were clearly overwhelmed by the domestic revolts and partly to provide soft landing for the embattled Hosni Mubarak.

Hosni Mubarak's acceptance to step down as the head of the embattled regime created in the minds of the protesters a sense of relief and belief that the revolts had succeeded. This was a fundamental fallacy in the sense that a successful revolution should sweep away all the structures of the old order to allow new and progressive structures to be put in place. In other words, mere stepping aside of Hosni Mubarak who had been in power for 30 years was not enough to provide relief to the long oppressed and disempowered Egyptians. One would have expected and rationally so that the process of framing a new constitution for Egypt would follow immediately. All the interest groups in Egypt should have had the opportunity provided by the new development to make key inputs in terms of their expectations, aspirations and preferences. A new constitution that reflects the genuine and legitimate aspirations of citizens would have been the culminating point of victory for the agitators. The civic actions led to regime change in Egypt but with no clearly defined foundation for the kind of society Egyptians would want to have in place to guarantee them decent survival. In a sense, the revolts against authoritarian rule had yielded limited result. Mere regime change was obviously not enough to bring about a new society that places the welfare of people first before any other things.

REGIME CRISIS AND SMALL ARMS AND LIGHT WEAPONS PROLIFERATION IN EGYPT

The regime crisis in Egypt was so profound that effective governance became illusive while the crisis lasted. While the regime of Hosni Mubarak was contending with the challenges generated by the collective civic actions, Libya was plunged into wave of intense disorder. Pro-government forces and anti-government militias locked up horns in what turned out to be a full-scale civil war. Colonel Muammar Ghaddafi had drawn disadvantaged minority ethnic groups from neighbouring countries and enlisted them into the national army to broaden his support base. He trained militants from neighbouring states either to engage their home governments in a fight or to integrate them into his national army. After the civil war in Libya in 2011, the regime change and the consequent challenges posed to the responsive capacity of the National Transitional Council (NTC), Libya became temporarily a society without effective government to discharge the legitimate functions of the state. Many anti-government protesters got engaged in illicit arms transactions as there was no strong and effective government to regulate such deals. Nichols (2017), quoting from a 94 page report of the United Nations Group of Experts (UNGE), notes that "while arms trafficking from Libya to Egypt represents a challenge primarily for Egypt's internal security in particular in relation to armed groups in the Sinai, some of the materials appear to have crossed Egypt to further destinations, including the Gaza strip." This is no doubt a fragment of credible evidence in support of the claim that there was influx of SALWs into Egypt as a result of the uprisings in Libya.

In every post violent conflict society, illicit weapons circulate freely in the hands of non-state actors who use them to pursue sinister agenda considered to be at odd with collective aspirations. This is fundamentally so because there is no organized and effective public authority to enforce laws. This was the situation in Libya after the 2011 popular uprisings that brought about regime change in the oil rich North African country. The NTC had not sufficient responsive capacity to speedily tackle the post 2011 security challenges in Libya and therefore could not have taken concrete steps to halt the proliferation of SALWs. One of the destinations of weapons from Libya was Egypt. There was massive influx of weapons from Libya following the overthrow and subsequent killing of Muammar Ghaddafi. Smuggled weapons include automatic and sniper rifles, heavy projectiles, rocket propelled grenades, grad rockets and anti-air craft ammunition (*Independent Newspaper*, April 2012). The smuggling of arms from Libya into Egypt is partly attributed to the disorder created by the popular uprisings and the weak capacity of the regime to articulate appropriate responses to the challenge. The smuggled SALWs further fuelled the violence in different parts of Egypt including terrorism and insurgency infested Sinai Peninsula (see Chapter 27 in this volume).

It is instructive to note that SALWs proliferation in Egypt is demand-driven and this simply implies that the demand for SALWs is high in societies with considerable records of varying crimes, widespread violent conflicts, riots, unrests and many other factors. An entrenched culture of bad governance in any society such as Egypt could serve as a pull factor for the proliferation of SALWs. The pervasive climate of insecurity in Egypt especially during the popular uprisings was a strong motivation for widespread availability of SALWs. Citizens' loss of trust and faith in government could breed a sense of insecurity and the consequent response to this expressed by growing demand for the deadly SALWs. It is hardly debatable that Egypt was and is still contending with insurgency and terrorism in Sinai Peninsula. Where there is insurgency or terrorism, criminal behaviour becomes very common because the insurgents or terrorists do engage in resource mobilization drive to sustain their anti-establishment project.

CONCLUDING REMARKS

It is quite clear from the foregoing that Egypt is contending with numerous security challenges believed to have been generated by decades of bad governance and worsened by the popular uprisings that led to regime change. The capacity of the embattled Hosni Mubarak's regime had declined considerably and this made Egypt helplessly permeable to smuggled arms from Libya. The volume of SALWs coming into Egypt helped to exaggerate the security challenges including terrorism and insurgency in Sinai Peninsula. The security environment in Egypt has worsened since the popular collective civil action against the regime of Hosni Mubarak widely perceived as weak, corrupt, lacking legitimacy and capacity to provide adequately for the security and welfare of Egyptians. The pull factors such as crimes, violent conflicts, terrorism and insurgency, unrests, etc., have considerably grown the demand for SALWs in Egypt. Most Egyptians have lost faith in the capacity of the state to meet their security need and this has provided motivation for citizens to seek to provide security for themselves through acquisition of SALWs. Conscious and active mobilization of citizens to support the Egyptian state in tackling the multitude of security challenges will no doubt refuel their trust and confidence in the state once more. Good governance driven by transparency, accountability, constitutionalism, efficiency, due process, rule of law and many other factors can help to stem the rising tide of insecurity in Egypt and this may diminish the demand for SALWs by citizens. Once there is remarkable improvement in the security environment, the motivation for SALWs acquisition will be lost.

References

Adejo, A. M. (2011, May–August). Salient Aspects of Nigeria-Libya Relations. *Nigerian Journal of International Affairs, 37*(2), 1–16.

Adetula, V. A. O. (2011, May–August). Markets, Revolts, and Regime Change: The Political Economy of the Arab Spring. *Nigerian Journal of International Affairs, 37*(2), 17–47.

Allison, G. T. (1971). *The Essence of Decision Explaining the Cuban Missile Crisis*. Boston: Little, Brown and Company.

Charles, F. H. (1969). International Crisis as a Situational Variable. In J. N. Rosenau (Ed.), *International Politics and Foreign Policy: A Reader in Research and Theory*. New York: Free Press.

ECOWAS Convention. (2006). *ECOWAS Convention on Small Arms and Light Weapons, Their Ammunition and Other Related Materials*. Abuja: ECOWAS Commission.

Danjibo, N. D. (2013). The Aftermath of the Arab Spring and Its Implication for Peace and Development in the Sahel and Sub-Saharan Africa. *Strategic Review for Southern Africa, 35*(2), 16–34.

Dollard, J., Miller, N., Doob, L., Mowrer, O., & Sears, R. (1939). *Frustration and Aggression*. New Haven: Yale University Press.

Ernest, A. U. (2015). Politics in Egypt. In C. O. Chris & I. M. Alumona (Eds.). *Comparative Politics: An African Viewpoint*. Enugu: Rhyce Kerex Publishers.

Gurr, R. T. (1970). *Why Men Rebel*. New Jersey: Princeton University Press.

Ho-won, J. (2011). *Understanding Conflict and Conflict Analysis*. Los Angeles: Sage.

Idahosa, O. (2011). Responsibility to Protect and the Libyan Conflict. *Nigerian Journal of International Affairs, 37*(2), 91–102.

Independent. (2012). *Police Find Prohibited Firearms and Ammunition Northeast of Cairo, Egypt*. http://www.egyptindependent.com/news/rpg-and-ammunition-found-falyed-news-2. Accessed 17 July 2019.

Martin, M. (2005). *The Fate of Africa: From Hopes of Freedom to the Heart of Despair*. New York: Public Affairs.

Nichols, M. (2017). *Libya Arms Fueling Conflicts in Syria, Mali and Beyond*. reuters.com/article/us.libyaarms-un-idUSBRE93814Y2013. Accessed 15 July 2019.

Ogunsanwo, A. (2014). Arab Spring and Contemporary Challenges in Nigeria. In C. N. Nwoke & O. Ogaba (Eds.), *Contemporary Challenges in Nigeria, Africa and the World*. Nigeria Institute of International Affairs: Lagos.

Onuoha, B. (2011). Transnational Oil Corporations and the Arab Spring. *Nigerian Journal of International Affairs, 37*(2), 67–90.

Osman, T. (2013). *From Nasser to Muslim Brotherhood*. New Haven, CT: Yale University Press.

Shlaim, A. (1988). *The US and Berlin Blockade, 1948–1949: A Study in Crisis Decision Making*. Berkeley: California University Press.

Simon, G. U., & Akintunde, B. A. (2015). Small Arms and Light Weapons Proliferation and Problem of National Security in Nigeria. *International Affairs and Global Strategy, 29*, 13–32.

Tsuwa, J. T., & Otsapa, S. E. (2016). The Arab Spring, Unsecured Libyan Weapons and Boko Haram Insurgency in Nigeria. In C. C. C. Osakwe (Ed.), *Leadership and Complex Military Operations*. Kaduna: Nigerian Defence Academy.

Audu Nanven Gambo is a Professor of International Relations and Strategic Studies in the Department of Political Science, University of Jos, Nigeria. He holds a Ph.D. degree in International Relations and Strategic Studies from the University of Jos. He was the Director of Centre for Conflict Management and Peace Studies, University of Jos between 2010 and 2015. He was a Fulbright Fellow for the Study of United States Foreign Policy at the University of South Carolina in 2006. He was also a Visiting Scholar at the University of Amsterdam, Netherlands, in 2011. His scholarship focuses on national defence, conflict and peace studies, foreign policy and security studies and he has published nationally and internationally in these areas. Among his recent publications is *Peace Architecture for Jos city, Nigeria* (2013), published by John Archers Publishers in Ibadan.

CHAPTER 34

Ethiopia: Political Volatility and Small Arms Proliferation

Roy Love

INTRODUCTION

In a seminal account of the acquisition of firearms in Ethiopia from the fifteenth century, Richard Pankhurst describes them as playing

> a decisive role in Ethiopian history, revolutionising the nature of war, determining the outcome of many a battle, profoundly influencing the balance of power both internally and externally, … the quest for arms and experts to handle them being moreover a major factor influencing the country's foreign policy and almost all efforts at rapprochement with other lands. (Pankhurst 1968a)

His words are as relevant to the situation of Ethiopia in the Horn today as they had been in the past and reflect a regrettable continuity in the incidence of conflict in the region, mirrored in the preamble to the 2004 Nairobi Protocol on the Prevention, Control and Reduction of Small Arms in the region which refers to the

> problem of the proliferation of illicit small arms and light weapons in the Great Lakes Region and the Horn of Africa and the devastating consequences they have had in sustaining armed conflict and armed crime, degrading the environment, fuelling the illegal exploitation of natural resources and abetting terrorism and other serious crimes in the region. (Nairobi Protocol 2004)

R. Love (✉)
Centre for Lifelong Learning, University of York, York, UK
e-mail: roylove439@btinternet.com

© The Author(s), under exclusive license to Springer Nature Switzerland AG 2021
U. A. Tar and C. P. Onwurah (eds.), *The Palgrave Handbook of Small Arms and Conflicts in Africa*,
https://doi.org/10.1007/978-3-030-62183-4_34

It is notoriously difficult to measure the prevalence of small arms with any degree of accuracy in countries like those in the Horn of Africa, especially on private ownership. The last report by the Small Arms Survey to do this was in 2017 and placed Ethiopia among the lowest of 178 countries as measured by guns per 100 population (Small Arms Survey 2007a), though it nevertheless amounted to an estimated 377,000, as against 69,000 with law enforcement agencies. This, however, overlooks guns per household and regional variations where populations in poor, remote highland areas are likely to own fewer firearms than will those closer to urban centres, larger markets or in conflict prone zones, where the ratio will increase substantially.

The chapter begins with a brief account of the parallel histories of conflict in Ethiopia and growth in the acquisition and use of small arms. This is followed by a summary of agreements and legislation on arms control within Ethiopia, in the region, and internationally, and a conceptual section analysing the impact of a proliferation of small arms and light weapons in a region such as the Horn of Africa. A regional overview then precedes a section on three broad geopolitical differences across Ethiopia: highland, pastoral and borderland, followed by a brief consideration of women and children as perpetrators of armed violence in Ethiopia. The concluding section draws together the significant challenges faced by the Ethiopian government in this area, stressing the elimination of the demand for weapons as the only successful strategy in the long run.

The Historical Legacy of Firearm Prevalence in Ethiopia and the Horn

By the fifteenth century, firearms were being sought by most Abyssinian monarchs, in part for internal purposes and in part to combat the growth of Turkish and Arab influence along the borders of Sudan in the west and north, and in the coastal regions of the Red Sea and the Somali hinterland in the east. James Bruce in his visit to Gondar in 1770 mentioned "*a sister's son of the Ras*" who "*commanded one third of the troops of Tigre, which carried fire-arms, that is about 2,000 men*" (Bruce 1790). The speed of acquisition remained slow, however, until the early nineteenth century when a prolonged period of internal conflict accelerated the demand for firearms. By the second half of the century, after the fall of Tewodros in 1868, firearms were critical to the rise of emperors Yohannes IV and Menelik II, including the latter's expansion south, and to the abilities of each to resist Italian intrusion and the growing influence of France and Britain along the coastal regions. Prior to the battle of Adua in 1896, for example, Menelik was estimated variously to have acquired between 60,000 and 100,000 rifles, while during 1899–1900, he imported a further 65,000 rifles and five million rounds of ammunition, mainly from France and Russia (Pankurst 1968b), and by 1903 had an estimated 320,000 riflemen under his command (Tegenu 1996) (Fig. 34.1).

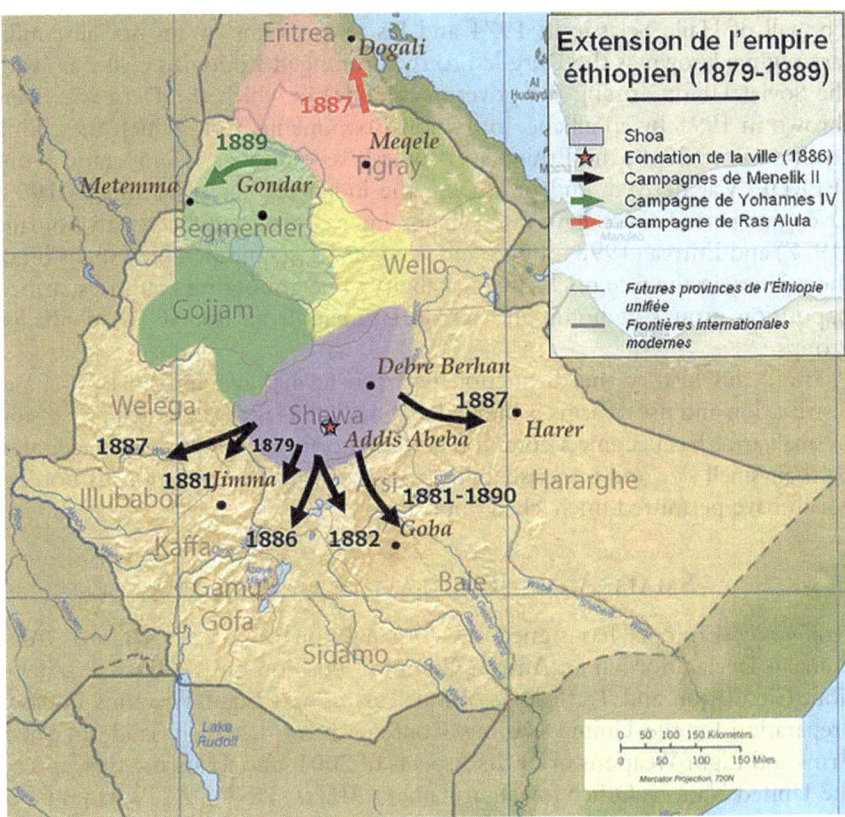

Fig. 34.1 Expansion of Abyssinia under Emperor Menelik II (*Source* File_Ethiopia_shaded_relief_map_1999,_CIA. University of Texas Libraries, Perry-Castañeda Library Map Collection, available https://legacy.lib.utexas.edu/maps/ethiopia.html)

Large supplies of arms also underpinned the consolidation by Ras Tafari Makonnen (later Haile Selassie I) of his position as regent in the early twentieth century and as Emperor from 1930, though not without difficulties, as the various European colonial powers now well entrenched along the country's borders gave their own rival interests priority in considering how many arms they would sell to Ethiopia (Marcus 1987). In May 1935 Britain joined France in an embargo against arms sales to both Italy and Ethiopia, a decision clearly to Ethiopia's greater detriment. There then followed the 1936–1941 Italian occupation, British and Ethiopian defeat of the Italians in 1941, various regional rebellions, and Western support in the Cold War period during which Ethiopia purchased some half a billion dollars' worth of arms from the USA (Stohl and Grillot 2009). Throughout this earlier period there was also a tradition of *shifta*, or armed bandit groups in the remoter parts of the country.

The fall of Haile Selassie in 1974 and his replacement by the socialist military regime known as the Derg led to the prolonged Ethiopian civil war (with the Soviet Union arming the government side) in which the Derg was overthrown in 1991 by an alliance of regional opponents, from which the ruling coalition until 2019, the Ethiopian Peoples' Revolutionary Democratic Front (EPRDF) was derived, and producing the independence of Eritrea in 1993. Over this period there have been major international conflicts with Somalia (1977) and Eritrea (1998–2000), and, since 1991, a considerable expansion of the military in the face of chronic instability in neighbouring countries, armed opposition groups at home and terrorist threats from Somali-based jihadist groups.

In all this history the distinction between formal and informal purchase, distribution and use of arms is blurred and has left a legacy in which possession of small arms has become a common cultural norm, their prevalence facilitated by their small size and imperishability, together with the long porous borders which have permitted unchecked importation.

Small Arms Regulation in Ethiopia

Regionally, Ethiopia has signed the Organisation of African Unity (OAU) Bamako Declaration on an African Common Position on the Illicit Proliferation, Circulation and Trafficking of Small Arms and Light Weapons 2000 as preparation for the United Nations Conference on the Illicit Trade in Small Arms and Light Weapons in All Its Aspects of 2001, and following this, agreed the United Nations Office for Disarmament Affairs (UNODA) Programme of Action to Prevent, Combat, and Eradicate the Illicit Trade in Small Arms and Light Weapons in All Its Aspects (Programme of Action) also of 2001. As a follow-up, UNODA also produced an International Instrument to Enable States to Identify and Trace, in a Timely and Reliable Manner, Illicit Small Arms and Light Weapons (International Tracing Instrument or ITI). In its most recent report to UNODA, in 2008, the Ethiopian government reported that from May 2006 to February 2007, more than 20,000 surplus SALW stocks from the National Police Force were destroyed.

The country is also committed to the Nairobi Protocol for the Prevention, Control and Reduction of Small Arms and Light Weapons in the Great Lakes Region, the Horn of Africa and Bordering States of 2004, and of the Regional Centre on Small Arms in the Great Lakes Region, the Horn of Africa and Bordering States (RECSA) which was established in June 2005 to oversee the implementation of the Nairobi Protocol.

In 2012, Ethiopia also signed the United Nations Office on Drugs and Crime 2001 Protocol against the Illicit Manufacturing of and Trafficking in Firearms, Their Parts and Components and Ammunition, supplementing the United Nations Convention against Transnational Organized Crime.

Table 34.1 provides a short summary of the law requiring arms regulation across the Horn of Africa for three indicative categories, from which it is clear

Table 34.1 Indicative data on Arms Regulation in the Horn of Africa

Regulation	Countries
Civilian gun Regulation	
Record of the acquisition, possession and transfer of privately held firearm be in an official register	Ethiopia, Eritrea, Djibouti, Sudan, South Sudan
Record of the acquisition, possession and transfer of privately held firearm **not** required for an official register	Somalia
Gun dealer record keeping	
Licenced firearm dealers not required to record on behalf of a regulating authority	Ethiopia, Eritrea, Sudan, South Sudan
No information	Djibouti, Somalia
Regulation of arms brokers	
Activities of arms brokers and intermediaries not specifically regulated	Ethiopia, Eritrea, Djibouti, Sudan, Somalia
Activities of arms brokers are intermediaries **are** specifically regulated	South Sudan

Source https://www.gunpolicy.org/firearms/region/ accessed 12 November 2019
Data from 2018 report for 2017

that in most cases the requirement for regulation in various forms is already in statute. This is not the same as practice, however, and in most cases the administrative capacity for enforcement is extremely limited. In two of the countries, South Sudan and Somalia, there is also a high level of firearm and ammunition smuggling. Each borders on Ethiopia with inevitable suggestions of a two-way flow as regional tensions change.

Domestically, the Criminal code of the Federal Democratic Republic of Ethiopia (2005), Articles 481, Prohibited Trafficking in Arms, 808 Control of Arms and Ammunition, and 809, Carrying and Use of Prohibited Arms, all carry penalties. There have also been Regional proclamations on registration of firearms, implemented at zonal level, such as the Misrak Gojjam Zone in Amhara region where Debre Markos is the zonal capital, though no recognised arms tracing and tracking procedures are conducted (Alpers and Wilson 2019).

The series of anti-government protests across the country beginning in 2016, in which the authorities claimed that firearms were used by protesters, prompted an official announcement that new legislation to control the flow of illicit arms and weapons into the county was being drafted, which would consolidate and add to existing laws, and in January 2018 the final draft of the new Proclamation was announced by the Minister of Defence stating that it "will give directives and a legal base towards the use of arms by guiding the identification of the sale of each and every firearm in the country" (Tsegaye 2018). This was overtaken by the appointment of Abiy Ahmed as Prime Minister in April 2018 and appointment of a new cabinet, and in February

2019 a new Ministry of Peace in collaboration with the Office of the Attorney General announced a new draft bill to regulate firearms (Abrham Yohannes 2019). This would fill "gaps not covered by existing laws and practices and create consistent system" (un-numbered opening paragraph) and requires the Federal Police Force (the Supervising Institution) to "register and administer all firearms in the country by their serial number with information technology system" (Section 18 Firearm Registration System). It also provides the Institution with enforcement powers to "organize a national firearm control business unit under it and enforce and control the enforcement of this proclamation", and to "give license to use firearm in accordance with this proclamation and control illegal use of firearm" (Section 22, Paragraphs 1 and 2).

Effective implementation, of course, depends upon adequate policing and administrative resources, in addition to the considerable problem in Ethiopia of eliminating the incentives to hold arms.

A Conceptual Note: Relation Between Availability of SALWs and the Frequency and Severity of Conflict

It is generally claimed that the recent record of conflict in the Horn, within and between countries, has produced an unprecedented proliferation of SALW, allowing them to become more widespread, more readily available and more likely to be used in interpersonal, intergroup and anti-state disputes. Yet, whether or not possession of guns in itself leads to an increase in either the number of conflicts or their magnitude rather than a change in the format of conflicts that would have occurred in any case, is unclear. A number of factors peculiar to the region are relevant.

First, is the complex role of structural economic change in the process of economic development, and the accompanying ideological stance of the state. For example, the impact of encroachment by agricultural land on traditional animal grazing rights, whether by peasant farmers or large-scale schemes, has created conflict between settled groups and pastoralists, and among pastoralists themselves in competition for reduced grazing land, making it more likely that small arms, having become widely available and affordable, will be used by either side, perhaps even more readily when the weapon is an AK-47 rather than the traditional spear or curved *gile* knife of the Afar people which requires physical contact.

Second, has been the legacy of state formation following the postcolonial settlement in Somalia and the ending of imperial rule in Ethiopia, with both contributing to a number of interstate conflicts, often involving disputable and poorly policed, state boundaries. These have created chronic levels of insecurity among border populations, often pastoralists, to a degree that has prompted unprecedentedly high levels of small arms possession, for defence and offence, across recent generations. In this particular, the boundary heritage in the Horn is quite different from that of most other African countries where the 1884–1885 Berlin Conference was an important determining factor in setting the international boundaries that generally prevail today (Zoppi 2013).

Third, is the specific historical juncture of 1991 when in Ethiopia the introduction of ethnic Federalism by the incoming coalition, dominated since then until early 2018, by the Tigre Peoples' Liberation Front (TPLF), led to the appearance of armed opposition parties such as the Oromo Liberation Front(OLF) and continuing insurgency by the Ogaden National Liberation Front (ONLF), both feeding on regional discontent. Also in 1991 was the collapse of central government in Somalia, thus permitting the creation both of armed ethnic rivalries, such as Somali National Alliance and Somali National Front (leading to the self-declared independence of Somaliland replicating the borders of former British Somaliland), and radical Islamist groups such as *al Ittihad*, and *al Shabaab*. These have not only all sought supplies of arms but have prompted national governments to augment their own supplies, at times also providing arms to opposition groups in neighbouring states. Illegally sourced arms have included seepage from official supplies, haphazard disposal following conflict and regular smuggling.

Fourth, is a problem of perception. Where there is little factual evidence, then in situations such as the above, there is more likely to be a perception that gun ownership has increased rather than fallen, and therefore that one's own family or community should also be arming up thus contributing to an internal "arms race" in which opposing parties competitively build up their military arsenals with increasingly sophisticated weapons (Vinci 2009).

Fifth, and finally, there is the nature of the regional market in the supply and price of small arms. Prices tend to be significantly cheaper where there is conflict in neighbouring countries; and where the price of weapons is lower the greater is the risk of civil war. Regulatory ineffectiveness, transport costs, the porosity of borders and high levels of military expenditure in neighbouring countries are all significant in bringing prices down (Small Arms Survey 2007a, Ch8). All these have been, and continue to be, present in Ethiopia, whose own level of military expenditure will have affected the price of small arms among its neighbours. Where borders are porous and trade barriers ineffective, as in the Horn, then a classical market equilibrium will emerge (Killicoat 2007). The absence of state regulation does not mean anarchy: informal and cultural understandings create trust between purchasers and sellers in an illicit supply chain. This may come from clan, ethnic or extended family connections, or from the knowledge by each party of the consequences of cheating. Multiple informal means of transferring money internationally, such as variations on the *hawala* process are well known and are also based on mutual trust. In these ways market inefficiencies of asymmetric information and risk of price exploitation are minimised.

Regional Overview: Porous Borders and a Single Market in the Horn

In the Horn of Africa sources of supply are varied and extensive, and in the past have often come from the collapse or defeat of one of the region's armed forces, an effect that tends to be highest in the immediate aftermath of the end of conflict. The collapse of Siad Barre's government in 1991, for instance, left many soldiers with only their weapons to sell or trade in exchange for safe passage through militia or warlord-controlled territory. The fall of the Derg in the same year in Ethiopia produced a similar flow of weapons traded for cash by defeated government forces. In each case the initial origins of many of the weapons lay with earlier support from the Soviet Union and the USA to the armed forces of governments in the region. In Gambella during the period when southern Sudanese opposition had bases there, arms were often exchanged for food and clothing, thereby contributing to the severity of later conflict between local Anyuak and incoming Nuer refugees from Sudan (Feyissa 2010).

Following the inconclusive 1998–2000 war with Ethiopia, the Eritrean government was accused of supplying arms and logistic support to Ethiopian insurgent groups such as the ONLF operating from Somalia as well as to *al Shabaab* to strengthen its ability to counter Ethiopian armed forces in Somalia (UN Report 2011). Further south, in the borderlands between Somalia and northern Kenya, the role of the border town of Garissa on the Kenya side as a major transit town for Somali refugees, overland trade from Kenya and livestock trekked from south east Ethiopia and southern Somalia *en route* to Nairobi and its large Somali community, has also turned it into a key centre for arms arriving by camel and truck in transit either from or to Somalia, while Nairobi itself is a major hub for transacting deals in small arms.

A second major source is across the Red Sea from where the principal supplies are from Yemen by small dhows and the Makran coast of Iran for larger shipments by ocean going dhows, in each case often entering Somalia through harbours in Puntland, in some instances destined for local units of Islamic State of Iraq and Levant (ISIL), and involving sums of as much as US$260,000 over a ten-month period (UN Report 2017a). Much of the money for payment of these shipments has come from *al Shabaab*'s control over charcoal exports to Yemen and the Gulf States, from taxing trade, such as in livestock and *khat*, as it passes through their control, and from illicit international money transfers from diaspora supporters in Europe and the USA. Across the Horn there have also been significant legal inflows of arms from the USA and Europe, especially after 9/11, the invasion of Iraq, and concerns over *al Qaeda*, and, more recently, with ISIS and its variants, plus relations with Iran. Arms have also been coming from China (Conteh-Morgan 2017), and although in Somalia systems for management and logging of imported material at Halane Central Armoury in Mogadishu, and in the distribution and tracking of weapons are in place operationally they have remained weak and vulnerable to manipulation (UN Report on Somalia 2017). Other suppliers have been Russia, Israel and South Africa. This steady inflow of state acquisition of arms from international sources is itself a significant contributor to the proliferation of small arms and light weapons (SALW) in the Horn, creating both a reaction by opponents to increase their own arms arsenals and through loose accountability and failure to track what subsequently happens to these arms. Various private security firms operating in the area, under contract to national and regional governments or to international corporations and organisations, also add to the regional proliferation of arms.

Finally, Ethiopia has had its own arms industry since the 1980s, in the form of the Homicho Ammunition Engineering Industry and the Gafat Armament Engineering Industry, producing AK-47s and light machine guns and ammunition, both having been established with assistance from North Korea. They are now under the ownership of what was until recently the military controlled parastatal, Metals and Engineering Corporation (METEC), but over the years the suspicion of continued support from North Korea has raised the risk of UN sanctions being breached (Berger 2014), though sunk capital dependency and favourable prices encourage continuing links (Ramani 2018). Over the years it is likely that many of these weapons will have passed into unregistered private hands. In November 2018, following the radical change of government of that year, senior officials of METEC were arrested under suspicion of corruption, including the use of merchant ships for arms transfers from Iran to Somalia (Ethiopia Observer 2018).

Weapons are therefore extensively found in the hands of governments, of groups committed to armed opposition, of militias, local warlords and assorted bandits such as pirates operating off the coast of Somalia, of private security guards and of the numerous pastoralist, agro-pastoralist and remote minority ethnic groups that inhabit the dry lowlands of the peripheral lands of the Horn. Widespread availability, supported by illicit networks of supply crossing poorly policed and widely porous interstate borders, provide a ready resource for any disaffected group which, for whatever reason, wishes to arm itself.

The Pattern of Small Arms and Light Weapons Prevalence in Ethiopia Today

Although ownership of small arms is widespread across the country there are important regional differences based upon geography and history which require individually nuanced policy measures for their possible regulation or eventual reduction. These may be defined broadly as the traditional Amhara and Tigre highlands to the north of Addis Ababa which gradually drop down south through what is now the Oromia region to an eventual broad crescent of pastoralist lowlands, and borderlands. The last two often overlap in the case of Ethiopia, while within each of them are numerous ethnic, and at times, faith-based differences. These are now taken in turn.

HIGHLAND ETHIOPIA

While international attention often tends to focus on conflicts close to border zones, the prevalence of small arms in the highland regions of Amhara, large parts of Oromia, Tigray and Beni-Shangul-Gumuz is also high. Precise data is scarce but local estimates for East Gojjam Zone (in the loop of the Blue Nile as it leaves Lake Tana—see Fig. 34.2) range from 60% of households with at least one weapon to the "majority" of households (Birhan 2016). Although this region is not in close border proximity to conflicts in neighbouring countries the history of the struggle against the previous socialist regime, culminating in its overthrow in 1991, is well within living memory for many adults, and the longer history of rival claims to power and resistance to colonial occupation has created a culture in which possession of a rifle or, as is more common today, an AK-47, has become a symbol of masculinity

Fig. 34.2 Horn of Africa with major urban centres (*Source* https://globalbiodefense.com/wp-content/uploads/2013/05/horn_of_africa_map.jpg)

and household protector. This has also come through to the younger generation, facilitated by the relative ease by which such weapons may be obtained, and often expressed by firing into the air at weddings, funerals and other festive occasions, accompanied by songs of war, heroism and patriotism. The pattern recurs in other highland *woredas* such as Armacheho situated between Gondar and the Sudan border, and Samre near Mekele in Tigray region (Maru 2008). Warrior culture is common in many other societies, of course, but in the Ethiopian context the ready availability of firearms and ammunition, their relatively recent use in regional conflict, and the additional aspect of a culture of revenge and vendetta where local neighbours fall out, has meant that their use to settle scores has significantly increased (ibid.). Over the four-year period 2004–2007 in East Gojjam Zone, for instance, 190 deaths by firearms were recorded (Birhan 2016). Even churches often have firearms to protect their religious contents and during external ceremonies.

A number of Federal Regions have an arms registration requirement, though few are up to date. An example is the Amhara regional state proclamation 44/2001 as implemented in the Debre Marcos Zone in 2007, where the Zone Militia Office registered a total of 35,489 small arms, of which about 11,253 were owned by police and militia while some 24,236 were privately owned (Birhan 2016). It is likely, however, that many multi-weapon households registered only a single weapon. The primary routes by which illicit weapons reach these central highland areas are (See Fig. 34.2) from Sudan via North Gondar, from South Sudan via Gambella on the border to the west of Addis Ababa, with traders sometimes even using public transport, and through Afar in the eastern semi-desert lands bordering the Red Sea coast between Djibouti and Massawa, often passing through several intermediate markets on the way (Birhan 2016). In the eastern highlands generally, roughly between Addis Ababa and Mekele, the commonest imported source is from the various ports and small harbours on the coasts of the Red Sea and Gulf of Aden. Until the fall of the Derg in 1991 and parallel collapse of government in Somalia, the principal illicit arms traders were members of the Somali Hawiyya clan, travelling via the neighbourhood of Harar and on further east into the upper Awash valley. More recently, Argobba agro-pastoralists of the latter region, which borders on the highland escarpment at one of its closest points to the coastal regions of Djibouti and Somaliland, have been a principal source, often reaching the highland market of Shoa Robit on the principal road north from Addis Ababa to Mekele, and from there via a number of minor markets as far south as proximity to Adama (Nazareth), on the the principal land and rail route from Addis Ababa to Djibouti (Gebre 2009). Another route to the upper Awash is the corridor via Togo-Wuchalle from Somaliland and the port of Berbera among other harbours. With the renewal of diplomatic relations between Ethiopia and Eritrea in 2018 the possibility of new routes via Assab and other harbours along the Eritrean Red Sea coast emerges.

Pastoralist Lowlands

According to the World Bank in 2016 there were some 12 million pastoralists in Ethiopia (World Bank 2016). Precise figures are hard to obtain, given mobile lifestyles in arid regions often remote from any state authorities. In Ethiopia they are scattered in a low-lying, semi-desert crescent between the eastern and southern highland escarpments of central Ethiopia and the porous borders of Eritrea, Djibouti, Somaliland (Hargeysa and Berbera towns in Fig. 34.2), Somalia, northern Kenya and South Sudan.

Much has been written about an increased prevalence of arms and readiness to use them among pastoralists across this region, whether by the Afar of Eritrea and Ethiopia, the Issa of Djibouti and north west Somalia, Ogadeni and Borana in Somali region of Ethiopia, the Turkana and Rendille of northern Kenya, the Shilluk and Murle of eastern South Sudan and the Missiriya and Dinka Ngok of Abyei and others. Firearms come into use in conflict between neighbouring groups, perhaps in dispute over access to a watering hole or to grazing land as a result of changes in climate or in land use. The latter may include occupation of land by agro-pastoralists, large-scale commercial farming or for oil drilling and ancillary services. In the last of these an additional problem can be land registration by urban or local speculators and exclusion from former grazing land. Lying behind the proximate causes of dispute are often issues relating to past grievances or to a history of confrontation and endemic mistrust between clans or groups which override traditional modes of mediation. Regular episodes of cattle rustling by groups of young men, restless to assert themselves or as a means of obtaining a bride price, add to the frictions. Where there may once have been one firearm in a pastoralist household, there is now often one per adult male usually an AK-47 (ibid.), and inter-clan conflicts are now more likely to involve fatalities than before, as injury can be caused without the need for a physical encounter. This, in turn, leads to more revenge killings and an increased social propensity for a cycle of violence to continue.

Some groups are geographically closer to the highlands than they are to the borders of neighbouring countries. One such is the Karrayu of the Upper Awash Region of Ethiopia, between Dire Dawa and Addis Ababa, for whom the ready availability of small arms has changed the dynamic of disputes with neighbouring communities over transhumance and grazing rights. As indicated above, ownership of an AK-47, has become a matter of pride and a symbol of manhood among young Karrayu men, and to which young boys in the clan aspire. The case of the Karrayu is typical and, given their location in the upper Awash valley, there is a ready source of imported small arms from the same routes as that of the eastern highlands of Shoa region as indicated in the previous section (Gebre 2009). Elsewhere, other examples include Issa encroachment on the Afar in the lands between Djibouti and the Awash River (Yasin 2010), or recently along part of the Somali-Oromo regional border (roughly a line east of Harare running irregularly south to the

North East corner of Kenya) within Ethiopia where the activities of a paramilitary group, known as Liyu, sponsored by the Somali Regional State of Ethiopia, has contributed to the generation of a substantial refugee population in the area of tension (BBC 2017; Africa News 2018). Such chronic conditions of repeated conflict and aggression in the midst of poverty is a driving force for the emigration of many young people to larger towns and cities in the search for independence and employment, but where their poor education and desperation renders them vulnerable to the ploys of traffickers and other exploiters.

Border Regions

Much of the Eastern and Southern border regions of Ethiopia are desert and semi-desert, while the Western border with Sudan and South Sudan has intermittent agricultural zones, such as at Gambella and Humera, where the Baro and Takazze rivers cross into Sudan. To the North the largest part of the border area with Eritrea is a continuation of highland Tigray in Ethiopia, except as it nears the Sudan border. As already observed, the vast dryland border regions to the south and east are sparsely populated, mainly by pastoralists, and often distant from facilities such as schools, hospitals and other public services. Many border regions are remote, poorly policed and open to firearms smuggling from any direction. They have also witnessed recent and past conflict: along the length of the Eritrean border during the 1999–2000 war; the Djibouti border where Issa groups have expanded into Ethiopian Afar territory; the Somali border across which Somalian armed forces entered Ethiopian territory in 1977; the more recent threat from *al Shabaab* which controls pockets close to the Ethiopian border in south Somalia (Indermuehli 2017). In Gambella, on the west of Ethiopia, bordering now with Southern Sudan, the resident Anywaa people have been for decades in recurring conflict with the Nuer across the border (Markakis 2011), and during the imperial period were supplied with guns by the state (Feyissa 2010). This combination of porous borders and recent histories of violent conflict has produced a situation where weapons are readily available, mostly affordable and their possession endemic.

Both the demand for weapons and their availability are closely linked to the wider pattern of informal cross-border trade, especially in livestock trekked from the southern Somali region of Ethiopia via southern Somalia (Baidoa region) to Garissa in Northern Kenya for transhipping to Nairobi (Tesfaye and Amaha 2018; Mahmoud 2010) and small livestock from the northern part of the same region for shipment to Yemen, Saudi Arabia and the Gulf States. Herders and traders have long carried weapons for personal protection and to be dependent on clan networks for security, but a growth in large-scale commercialisation of cattle rustling to meet the demand for beef in Nairobi has intensified this (Opongo 2016). At the same time, other unregistered trade, such as electrical goods, routinely cross in one direction while human traffickers and people smugglers cross in the other on their way to the labour markets of the same group of countries. The magnitude and spatial dispersion of these informal markets in the region work against easy solutions to the largely uninhibited flow of illicit weapons, particularly where intergovernmental cooperation can be constrained by ongoing conflict on the ground, loss of state control over some areas, lack of capacity or effective governance on one or both sides, and the ability of traffickers to divert to alternative routes.

Who Are the Users?

One of the principal advantages of small arms, in trading, storage and use in conflict, is their portability in terms of weight and dimensions, which means that although most bearers and users are men, reflecting dominant cultural patterns, there have been many instances where women and children have also been fighters, both in regular armies, especially when under pressure, and within insurgency groups. This occurred on all sides of the prolonged battle to depose the socialist regime in Ethiopia between 1976 and 1991, and in the case of women, was a matter of pride in the Eritrean Peoples' Liberation Front during this period, when 30% of members were women and 15% were fighters (Firebrace and Holland 1984). Women, too, play a key role in *al Shabaab* as combatants and recruiters, facilitated by their low profile in markets and urban settings (Nordiiska Afrikainstitutet 2017), while in many other cases, such as the OLF in Ethiopia women are ideologically committed and will contribute in a variety of ways, including the storage and movement of weapons behind the scenes. (Oromo Nederland 2017; Williams 2015).

Children, too, are often involved, though in such circumstances, it is impossible to quantify the number of child combatants because of lack of birth documents and different cultural understandings both of what constitutes a child and what its role in different activities might be. The UN has reported the recruitment of children into *al Shabaab* (United Nations Report of the Secretary-General 2017) and for many children from impoverished households in such cases the opportunity to wield a weapon can be a mark of status and pride, while for their recruiters the child's immature moral sensibility can be manipulated and an armed adult opponent may hesitate before shooting a child (Love 2015). All sides in past Ethiopian conflicts have been accused of recruiting child soldiers (Child Soldiers International 2001).

Conclusion and the Future

Chronic regional instability and conflict in Ethiopia since the overthrow of Haile Selassie in 1974 reinforced an existing widespread culture of arms possession as an identifier of power and status, especially among younger men across Ethiopia and the region, and of security among family, clan and ethnic communities. To this has been added years of conflict in the neighbouring states of Somalia, Sudan and South Sudan. Plus, all the complexity of proximity to the geopolitics of the Middle East, where Yemen, for instance is only some 30 km from Djibouti.

Prospects for the future are mixed, though not without hope. The election in 2018 by the then ruling party in Ethiopia, the EPRDF, of a new Prime Minister, Abye Ahmed, from the Oromo group in the coalition, marked a radical change from the largely Amhara and Tigre dominated rule of the previous hundred years; a change not only in its ethnic implications but also in the more liberal policies immediately implemented. These included the freeing of most political prisoners, unbanning of opposition groups until then classified as "terrorist", renewing diplomatic relations with Eritrea, appointing a woman President, Sahle-Work Zewde, and a new mixed gender Cabinet. On 16 November a range of senior figures in the army-run industrial conglomerate, METEC, were arrested on charges of corruption.

Threats, remain, however. While addressing a rally in Addis Ababa on 23 June 2018 a hand grenade was thrown from within the crowd at the Prime Minister, and on 17 August a petrol tanker and truck stopped by police in an outer suburb were found to be carrying numerous small arms, while on 28 October an overturned oil tanker on a rural road from Sudan had also been carrying a load of small arms. The greatest number of illegal arms imports are from Sudan, a concern that the Ethiopian authorities have taken up with their Sudanese counterparts, and some recent success in reducing the total from all sources has been reported (Yonas 2019). In the meantime, serious internal regional ethnic-based conflicts continue, such as those on the borders of the Oromo–Somali regions and in Benishangul-Gumuz against Amhara and Tigre residents (ECADF Ethiopian News and Views 2019), highlighting the challenges faced by the new government in controlling ethnically based tensions in the run-up to the then intended 2020 national elections while at the same time avoiding a return to the oppressive tactics of the preceding regime. The role of the military will also be crucial. In the longer term the growing threat to livelihoods from climate change must also be factored in.

Taken together, although there is much optimism about the change of government, especially in a general context of rapid economic growth, there is also fear that the ethnic nature of the Federal regions, and continued inequalities, real or imagined, may erupt into a new era of violent opposition (Fisher and Meressa 2019), possibly even threating the viability of Ethiopia as a state, not helped by the late 2020 conflict in Tigray Federal State. Additionally, the reluctance of sections of the OLF to surrender their arms as now required by the government is an indication, together with the incidents reported in the previous paragraph, of the enormity of the task facing the Ethiopian government in implementing control over the proliferation of small arms and light weapons in the country.

REFERENCES

Abrham, Y. (2019). *FDRE Firearms Control and Administration /draft/ Proclamation*. https://chilot.me/2019/05/fdre-firearms-control-and-administration-draft-proclamation/. Accessed 12 November 2019.

Africa News. (2018). *Ethiopia's Somali Regional Politics: New Leader, Abdi Illey Charged, Liyu Police*. http://www.africanews.com/2018/08/30/ethiopias-somali-regional-politics-new-leader-abdi-illey-charged-liyu-police/. Accessed 3 December 2018.

Alpers, P., & Wilson, M. (2019, 16 April). *Ethiopia—Gun Facts, Figures and the Law*. Sydney School of Public Health, The University of Sydney. GunPolicy.org. https://www.gunpolicy.org/firearms/region/ethiopia. Accessed 13 May 2019.

BBC. (2017). *What Is Behind Clashes in Ethiopia's Oromia and Somali Regions?* https://www.bbc.co.uk/news/world-africa-41278618. Accessed 25 May 2018.

Berger, A. (2014, November). *Is Ethiopia Violating UN Sanctions Against North Korea?* 38North. See https://www.38north.org/2014/12/aberger12 2314/. Accessed 7 May 2018.

Birhan, A. T. (2016). *Regulating Proliferation and Misuse of Small Arms in Eastern Gojjam Zone of Amhara Regional State*. MA Thesis, Institute for Peace and Security Studies, School of Graduate Studies, Addis Ababa University.

Bruce, J. (1790). *Travels to Discover the Source of the Nile* (p. 70). Selected and Edited by C. F. Beckingham. Edinburgh University Press 1964.

Capital. (2019, May 15). *New Gun Law Makes 21 the Age Limit for Gun Possession*. Accessed 12 November 2019.

Child Soldiers International. (2001). *Child Soldiers Global Report 2001—Ethiopia*. Available at http://www.refworld.org/docid/498805fc2.html. Accessed 12 June 2018.

Conteh-Morgan, E. (2017, April 19). *China's Arms Sales in Africa*. Oxford Research Group. https://www.oxfordresearchgroup.org.uk/Blog/chinas-arms-sales-in-africa. Accessed 26 May 2018.

ECADF Ethiopian News and Views. (2019, May 3). *Dozens Killed in Ethnic Clashes in Ethiopia, Regional Official Says*. https://ecadforum.com/2019/05/03/dozens-killed-in-ethnic-clashes-in-ethiopia-regional-official-says/. Accessed 6 May 2019.

Ethiopia Observer. (2018, November 10). *Senior Military and Intelligence Officers Arrested*. https://www.ethiopiaobserver.com/2018/11/10/senior-military-and-intelligence-officers-arrested/. Accessed 14 November 2018.

Federal Democratic Republic of Ethiopia, Proclamation No.414/2004. The Criminal Code of the Federal Democratic Republic of Ethiopia (came into force in 2005).

Feyissa, D. (2010). The Anywaa's Call for the Rigidification of the Ethio-Sudanese Border. In D. Feyissa & M. V. Hoehne (Eds.), *Borders and Borderlands as Resources in the Horn of Africa*. Eastern Africa Series. Suffolk, UK: James Currey.

Firebrace, J., & Holland, S. (1984). *Never Kneel Down: Drought, Development and Liberation in Eritrea*. Nottingham, UK: Spokesman.

Fisher, J., & Gebrewahd, M. T. (2019, January). 'Game Over'? Abiy Ahmed, the Tigrayan People's Liberation Front and Ethiopia's Political Crisis. *African Affairs*, 18(470), 94–207.

Gebre, A. (2009). *Inter-Group Conflict, the Role of Pastoral Youths and Small Arms Proliferation in Nomadic Areas of Ethiopia: The Case of the Karrayu and their Neighbours in the Upper Awash Valley Region*. Addis Ababa: OSSREA.

Indermuehli, J. (2017, October). *Al Shabaab Area of Operations in Somalia.* https://www.criticalthreats.org/analysis/al-shabaab-area-of-operations-october-2017. Accessed 18 May 2018.

Killicoat, P. (2007). *Weaponomics: The Global Market for Assault Rifles.* Policy Research Working Paper 4202. Washington DC: World Bank.

Love, R. (2015). Child Soldiers. In F. F. Wherry & J. B. Schor (Eds.), *Sage Encyclopedia of Economics and Society.* Washington: Sage.

Mahmoud, H. A. (2010, September). *Livestock Trade in the Kenyan, Somali and Ethiopian Borderlands.* Chatham House Briefing Paper.

Markakis, J. (2011). *Ethiopia: The Last Two Frontiers.* Eastern Africa Series (pp. 220–225). Milton: James Currey.

Marcus, H. G. (1987) *Haile Sellassie I: The Formative Years 1892–1936.* Red Sea Press edition (1996), Lawrenceville, USA and Asmara, Eritrea p. 101.

Maru, M. T. (2008). Arms Control and Arms Traditions in Ethiopia. *Arms Control: Africa* (Vol 1-Issue 4), published by the Arms Management Programme (AMP) of the Institute for Security Studies (ISS). (https://hornaffairs.com/2015/09/20/arms-control-traditions-ethiopia/. Accessed 16 April 2018.

Nairobi Protocol for the Prevention, Control and Reduction of Small Arms and Light Weapons in the Great Lakes Region, the Horn of Africa and Bordering States. 2004, United Nations Programme of Action Implementation Support System: Regional Organisations. New York, NY: Regional Centre on Small Arms / United Nations Office for Disarmament Affairs.

Nordiiska Afrikainstitutet. (2017, March 10). *Women Militants Often Go Unnoticed.* http://nai.uu.se/news/articles/2017/03/10/110150/index.xml. Accessed 19 May 2018 at 14.52.

Opongo, E. (2016). *Report on the Nexus between Illicit SALW Proliferation and Cattle Rustling.* Ethiopia, Kenya, Somalia, South Sudan and Uganda. Nairobi: Regional Centre on Small Arms and Light Weapons. https://recsasec.org/wp-content/uploads/2018/08/cattle-rustling-pdf.pdf. Accessed 20 April 2019.

Oromo Nederland. (2017). *The Role of Women in the Oromo National Liberation Movement.* See http://www.oromonederland.org/news/the-role-of-women-in-the-oromo-national-liberation-0movement/. Accessed 1 June 2018.

Pankhurst, R. (1968a). The History of Firearms in Ethiopia Prior to the Nineteenth Century. *Ethiopia Observer, 11*(3), 202–225.

Pankhurst, R. (1968b). *Economic History of Ethiopia* (pp. 602–603). Addis Ababa: Haile Sellassie I University Press.

Ramani, S. (2018, January 6). North Korea's Military Partners in the Horn of Africa. *The Diplomat.* https://thediplomat.com/2018/01/north-koreas-military-partners-in-the-horn-of-africa/ Accessed 27 June 2018.

Small Arms Survey. (2007a). *Guns and the City.* http://www.smallarmssurvey.org/publications/by-type/yearbook/small-arms-survey-2007.html. Accessed 10 May 2018 at 14.54.

Small Arms Survey. (2007b). *What Price the Kalashnikov? The Economics of Small Arms* (Ch 8). http://www.smallarmssurvey.org/fileadmin/docs/A-Yearbook/2007/en/full/Small-Arms-Survey-2007-Chapter-08-EN.pdf Accessed 12 May 2018 13.45.

Stohl, R., & Grillot, G. (2009). *The International Arms Trade* (p. 19). Hoboken, NJ: Wiley.

Tegenu, T. (1996). *The Evolution of Ethiopian Absolutism: The Genesis and the Making of the Fiscal Military State, 1696–1913.* Sweden: Upsalla University.

Tesfaye, A., & Amaha, N. (2018). A Review on Cross-Border Livestock Trade Across Dry Land Borders of Ethiopia: The Trends and Implications. *Journal of Scientific and Innovative Research*, 7(2), 36–42. Available Online at www.jsirjournal.com.

Tsegay, J. (2018). *Ethiopia Drafts New Proclamation to Control Illicit Flow of Arms, Weapons*. See http://www.afro105fm.com/afrofm.com/2018/01/10/ethiopia-drafts-new-proclamation-to-control-illicit-flow-of-arms-weapons/. Accessed 27 May 2018 at 16.14.

United Nations. (2011). *Report of Monitoring Group on Somalia and Eritrea*. http://www.un.org/ga/search/view_doc.asp?symbol=S/2011/433. Accessed 10 May 2018.

United Nations. (2017a, November). *Report on Somalia of the Monitoring Group on Somalia and Eritrea*. (https://www.un.org/ga/search/view_doc.asp?symbol=S/2017/924. Accessed 7 May 2018.

United Nations. (2017b). *Report of the Secretary-General on Children and Armed Conflict (A/72/361-S/2017/821) issued on 24 August 2017*. Somalia. https://childrenandarmedconflict.un.org/somalia/. Accessed 19 May 2018.

United Nations Security Council. (2017, December 26). *Report of the Secretary-General on Somalia*.

Vinci, A. (2009). *Armed Groups and the Balance of Power: The International Relations of Terrorists, Warlords and Insurgents* (p. 59). LSE International Studies. London: Routledge.

Williams, K. (2015). *Women in Armed Groups Are More Than Just an Exotic Novelty*. Inclusive Security. https://www.inclusivesecurity.org/2015/06/29/women-in-armed-groups-are-more-than-just-an-exotic-novelty/. Accessed 31 May 2018.

World Bank. (2016, October). *Empowering Ethiopia's Pastoral and Agro-Pastoral Communities*. http://www.worldbank.org/en/news/feature/2016/10/11/empowering-ethiopias-pastoral-and-agro-pastoral-communities. Accessed 12 May 2018.

Yasin, Y. M. (2010). Trans-Border Political Alliance in the Horn of Africa: The Case of the Afar-Issa Conflict. In D. Feyissa & M. V. Hoehne (Eds.), *Borders and Borderlands as Resources in the Horn of Africa*. Eastern Africa Series. Suffolk, UK: James Currey.

Yonas A. (2019, February 2). Ethiopian Government Urges Sudan to Tighten Border Control. *The Reporter*, 23(1169). https://archive.thereporterethiopia.com/sites/default/files/Pdf%20Archive/reporter-issue-1169.pdf. Accessed 3 March 2019.

Zoppi, M. (2013). The OAU and the Question of Borders. *Journal of African Union Studies*, 2(1 and 2), 43–62. London and Abuja: Adonis & Abbey.

Roy Love is an economist who has published regularly on Ethiopia and the Horn of Africa since 1979 and has lectured at the Universities of Addis Ababa, Botswana, Lesotho and Sheffield Hallam (in the UK). He has also in recent years been engaged in consultancy on African projects, including Ethiopia, for the European Union, World Bank, UK Department for International Development and USAID. He is currently attached, as associate staff, to the Centre for Lifelong Learning at the University of York in Britain, with current research on the economics of modern slavery in Ethiopia and the Horn of Africa.

CHAPTER 35

Libya: The Proliferation of Small Arms Post-Ghaddafi

Dauda Abubakar and Sharkdam Wapmuk

INTRODUCTION

The chapter focuses on Small Arms and Light Weapons (SALWs) proliferation in post-Ghaddafi Libya. It argues that SALWs proliferation, within and from Libya, in the post-Ghaddafi era has affected not only the security environment in Libya, but also its neighbouring countries, the Sahel and beyond. Before the 2011 "revolution" or "revolt" and later the civil war from 2014, the Libyan government under Muammar Ghaddafi had created huge arms and ammunition depots throughout Libya, however, domestic arms trade was tightly regulated and to some extend the government prevented the widespread illicit arms trade within Libya and beyond its borders (Marsh 2012; Adetula 2011). The Libyan revolution of 2011, however, led to the capture and looting of a wide range of arms and munitions by Non-State Actors (NSA) who had no control over its distribution and usage. While Libya's rival governing factions held significant quantities of weapons and ammunition, substantial quantities proliferated from Libya and many found their way into the domestic black market, the Sahel and beyond into the hands of Violent

D. Abubakar (✉)
Department of Political Science and Africana Studies, University of Michigan-Flint, Flint, MI, USA
e-mail: dauda@umich.edu

S. Wapmuk
Department of Defence and Security Studies, Nigerian Defence Academy, Kaduna, Nigeria

© The Author(s), under exclusive license to Springer Nature Switzerland AG 2021
U. A. Tar and C. P. Onwurah (eds.), *The Palgrave Handbook of Small Arms and Conflicts in Africa*,
https://doi.org/10.1007/978-3-030-62183-4_35

Non-State Actors (VNSA) such as militia's, terrorists and anti-government forces. Another dimension to the SALWs proliferation in Libya is the emergence of web trafficking (Jenzen-Jones and McCollum 2017). The internet as a marketing platform for SALWs has made accessibility easier.

SALWs are wielded and abused by diverse actors around the world, including individuals, state militaries, NSA and VNSA. Small arms are weapons that can be carried by an individual and includes revolvers and self-loading pistols, rifles and carbines, sub-machine guns, assault rifles, and light machine guns (Jacqmin 2017: 4). Light weapons can be carried by a small group of people, or transported by a small vehicle. They include heavy machine guns; grenade launchers; recoilless rifles; portable launchers of anti-tank missile and rocket systems; portable launchers of anti-aircraft missile systems; mortars of calibres of less than 100 mm (Jacqmin 2017: 4). In Libya, as in other parts of the world, widespread availability, relatively low cost and ease of concealment and transport make SALWs appealing to violent individuals and groups. The proliferation of SALWs in fragile contexts, which often lack functioning governance structures like border controls, often catalyzes or exacerbates violent conflict (Chivvis et al. 2012). This was the scenario in post-Ghaddafi era. The effect of SALWs proliferation in Libya has not only been domestic, but has transcended its borders into neighbouring countries and beyond. SALWs trafficking from Libya, especially during 2012–2013, provided arms to VNSA in Mali, Nigeria, Algeria, Chad, Egypt, Niger, Tunisia, the Sudan, Central African Republic (CAR), and even to Gaza and Syria. The ease with which armed groups were able to obtain weapons of different types that were previously rare or unavailable significantly enhanced their military capacity.

The 2011 Libyan Civil War was widely portrayed as an ideal example of a popular uprising overthrowing a corrupt dictatorship with the aim of establishing basic human rights and democracy (Adetula 2011). At the same time, the international intervention in the war was presented as an ideal model of humanitarian intervention under the pretext of "Responsibility to Protect" (R2P). The unfolding events in the aftermath of these events confirmed that these notions were gross over simplifications of the realities in Libya. Indeed, there were deep historical, structural, cultural, and political factors leading to the uprising in Libya beyond simple narrative of a struggle for freedom and democracy; and the intervention of foreign forces in the ensuing civil war was the result of complex motives and long-standing hostilities rather than pure humanitarianism. In short, the 2011 Libyan Civil War cannot be understood without a thorough examination of the history and politics of Libya. Likewise, the foreign intervention in that war can only be explained in the context of the historical relationships between the Libyan state under Muammar Ghaddafi and the other states involved in the conflict. Beyond the historical context of post-independence politics, power and ideological issues in Libya, this chapter focuses on the proliferation of SALWs.

In the light of large-scale proliferation of SALWs in post-Ghaddafi Libya, several questions can be raised in this chapter. What were the factors that propelled Ghaddafi to amass and store large quantities of arms and ammunition in Libya? To what extent did the collapse of Ghaddafi's regime in Libya lead to the proliferation of SALW within and beyond Libya? What are the major effects of proliferation of SALWs on the domestic security of Libya and the other states in Africa? The chapter, which seeks answers to these questions, is divided into five sections. Following section one, which introduces the chapter; section two examines domestic contestations, external threats, and the amassment of SALWs in Libya under Ghaddafi. Section three assesses the effects of SALWs proliferation in post-Ghaddafi's Libya on Africa states. Section four discusses efforts at curbing SALWs proliferation in Libya, and section five is the conclusion.

AUTHORITARIAN RESILIENCE, GLOBAL "ROGUE POLITICS" AND STATE COLLAPSE: A CONCEPTUAL FRAMING OF THE LIBYAN CONUNDRUM

In his work, *The End of History?* Francis Fukuyama *represented the end of history as* "mankind's ideological evolution and the universalization of Western liberal democracy as the final form of human government" (Fukuyama 1989). This followed the emergence of a unipolar world with the United States as the unrivalled global power at the end of the Cold War. However, the application of Fukuyama's statement is, to an extent, controversial with regard to the number of non-democratic regimes that demonstrated "authoritarian resilience" at least before the "hope and disappointment that accompanied the 2011 Arab uprisings" and foreign interventions that destabilize the Middle East, and to some extent, North Africa (Kesici 2019). The emergence of the United States as the global superpower did not only mark the decline of support for authoritarian and dictatorial regimes in some parts of the world including Africa, but also the redefinition of its relationship with states that later turned and were termed as "rogue states", "rentier states", and "collapsed states" (Merelli 2018).

In order to explain the stability or otherwise of authoritarian regimes, Albrecht and Schlumberger (2004: 371) coined the term "authoritarian resilience" as a basis for understanding the sustenance of an authoritarian regime. They argued that the stability of an authoritarian regime depends on its legitimacy and ability to repress its population. Authoritarian resilience is an umbrella term, containing multiple theories used to explain sustenance of authoritarian regimes. Authoritarianism is a form of government characterized by strong central power and limited political freedoms. Definitions and typologies of authoritarianism are not without contestations among scholars. One of the most commonly used definitions is that of Juan Linz. According to Linz, typology of authoritarian systems revolves around four characteristics, namely, "limited political pluralism, legitimacy based on emotion, no extensive or intensive political mobilisation as well as constrains on the mass public, and formally ill-defined executive power" (Linz 1964). Authoritarian states might contain supposedly democratic institutions, such as political parties, electoral management bodies, conduct elections, and have legislatures. However, they serve to entrench authoritarian rule and rulers in such states.

Some studies have focused on the underlying reasons for authoritarian regime resilience in the Arab World. For instance, Benjamin Smith argues that "the most durable regimes are either highly authoritarian or highly democratic" (Smith 2004). The study also demonstrated that many long-lasting authoritarian regimes are situated in the Middle Eastern and North African region, and that these countries share a great deal of commonalities such as their religion, language, and customs, as well as natural resources, particularly oil. The reasons for the durability of their regimes may differ; however, the capacity of the state's political system and ability to withstand internal and external shocks to a large extent is a crucial factor in explaining authoritarian regime stability. Another explanation provided for authoritarian resilience is the existence of support by the external powers. During the Cold War, Non-Western and Western powers, particularly USSR (now Russia) and the United States played major roles in authoritarian regime stability around the world by offering financial assistance, education, arms, military training, and technical support were given to numerous regimes across the world.

Thus, to understand authoritarian resilience in Libya, it is necessary to look beyond the failure to achieve the prerequisites of democracy. Rentier State Theorists have argued that resource wealth is one of the key factors in explaining authoritarian resilience. For instance, Paul Cipriani argues that "states that derive the majority of their revenue from rent tend to be both stable and authoritarian" (Cipriani 2012). According to Cipriani's position, Libya under Ghaddafi was a rentier state which obtains a significant portion of its income from renting its natural resources to external buyers. In this regard, Dirk J. Vandewalle notes that for Ghaddafi, legitimacy was *bought* by ensuring that the regime's distributive largesse was applied to a wide segment of Libyan society. However, despite its rentier politics, Libya has experienced considerable instability in spite of its oil wealth. The reasons are not farfetched. In addition to demonstrations by opposition, Libya under Ghaddafi had a frosty relationship with the West which earned the regime internal sympathy. Libya under Ghaddafi was frowned as a state sponsoring terror. This followed the bombings of a German discotheque in 1986 and Pan Am flight 103 over Lockerbie, Scotland by terrorists, which the United States responded through air raids and imposing economic sanctions against Libya.

Authoritarian rule under Ghaddafi in Libya began with the overthrow of the monarchial dynasty of King Idris (Sidi Muhammad Idris Al-Mahdi As-Sanusi) through military coup led by Colonel Ghaddafi on 2 September 1969. Ghaddafi, who took over power at the age of twenty-seven, initially enjoyed support both locally and internationally when he toppled the King. Though oil was discovered in Libya in the late fifties, King Idris who had allowed most of the profits to be siphoned into the coffers of the oil companies denied the citizens the good life (Campbell 2013). The US and European companies had huge stakes in the lucrative petroleum and banking sectors (Adejo 2011). Following the takeover of power, the Revolutionary Command Council of Libya commenced series of political and economic measures, which ushered radical changes in Libyan society. In 1977, Ghaddafi renamed the state, the *"Jamahiriya"*—that is *"State of the Masses"* (Adejo 2011: 4). After the United States' actions against Libya in the 1980s, the country enjoyed a relatively peaceful time until the civil war broke out in 2011. Despite privatizing some portions of the economy, Ghaddafi maintained a firm grip upon all political discourse in the state. Libya enjoyed higher per capita income than most African countries. With a population of about 7 million, an area of 1.8 million square kilometres, Libya in 2009 had the highest HDI in Africa and the 4th GDP (PPP) per capita in Africa. But this support eventually faded. A façade democracy was established by Ghaddafi and his rule was largely unchallenged for almost forty-two years. Although Ghaddafi came to power by promoting "sovereignty of the people", it can be argued that the emergence of a patronage system caused considerable damage both to Libya's "already weak state bureaucracy", and to the legitimacy of Ghaddafi's government in the eyes of Libyan people. The Libyan regime was technically turned into some form of one-party rule dominated by family members. To secure his rule and wade off opposition, Ghaddafi continued to amass and stockpile huge quantity of weapons, particularly SALW, in different regions. These weapons to a large extent were responsible for helping Ghaddafi to maintain state control, retain and enforce his power for so long. The amassment of huge supply of arms created the potential for SALW to proliferate if the state collapsed, and eventually that was what happened. Following the collapsed of Col. Gaddafi's regime, the state went from exercising control over SALW stockpiles, to distributing them, to losing control as the NTC rebels, supported by NATO. In his work, *"State Collapse and Social Reconstruction in Africa"*, Stephen Riley outlines three characteristics that characterize state collapse in Africa. First, he notes that the state loses its ability to rule throughout its land. This essentially means that the citizens in large areas of the state do not recognize the current government. Secondly, he states that there is an economic decline of the state. Thirdly, he posits that the state declines into violent conflict. The scenario above was exactly what eventually played out in Libya.

The Arab Spring, which swept through the Arab world in 2011, did not spare Libya. Reactions to the development had been disparate with most Western democracies generally supporting protesters demonstrating for expanded freedom and broader participation in authoritarian regimes. Some scholars have argued that the range of international reactions to the protests, uprisings, and revolutions associated with the Arab Spring demonstrated hypocrisy (Adejo 2011; Adetula 2011). World powers that had supported the authoritarian regimes, suddenly took a different turn denouncing these regimes. For instance the French Foreign Minister, Alain Juppe, a Symposium on the Arab Spring, at the Arab World Institute in Paris, 16 April 2011, argued that: "For too long we thought that the authoritarian regimes were only bastions against extremism in the Arab world. Too long, we have brandished the Islamits threat as a pretext for justifying to an extent turning a blind eye on government which were flouting and curbing their country's development" (cited in Adejo 2011: 13).

The Libyan case drew the greatest form of practical intervention from the Western nationals acting under the notion of the Responsibility to Protect (R2P) Libyans, and a chorus from the rest of the world. The Libyan uprising had the backing of North Atlantic Treaty Organization (NATO), the UN Security Council Resolution 1973 created a Libyan no-fly zone on 17 March 2011 and many members of the international community including the Arab League, and the African Union (AU) recognized the anti-Ghaddafi, National Transitional Council (NTC). In Libya, there were ethnic, religious, ideological, and oil-related contestations that account for the collapse of the authoritarian resilient regime of Ghaddafi, however, the existence of small arms played a major role as well. The killing of Muammar Ghaddafi, and subsequent developments in Libya, particularly the inability of the NTC and rebel forces to control the flow of SALWs led to large quantities of SALWs proliferation beyond the Libyan borders into other states in Africa.

Domestic Contestations, External Threats, and the Amassment of SALWs in Libya Under Ghaddafi

Muammar Ghaddafi emerged as the Libyan leader following a bloodless military coup that deposed King Sayyid Muhammad Idris bin Muhammad al-Mahdi as-Sennusi in 1969. After gaining power, Ghaddafi began amassing a significant arsenal of SALWs to serve as deterrent to internal and external threats. Ghaddafi had to reorganize the governance system in Libya after two failed coup attempts. Accordingly, the Council of Ministers was shuffled to include more members of the army—Revolutionary Command Council (RCC), and Ghaddafi was made Chairman of the RCC, Minister of Defence, and Prime Minister of Libya (Siebens and Case 2012). His regime was also characterized by domestic riots and demonstrations, most of which were suppressed by state security. As noted by El-Katiri (2012: 1), Libya cannot be regarded as a homogeneous country in terms of ethnicity or ideological precepts. While tribalism had always been an issue of concern in Libya during the Gaddafi era, it was contained by Ghaddafi's authoritarian and manipulation of different groups. Benghazi was the site of multiple riots and attempted uprisings throughout Ghaddafi's rule; the most recent were series of public demonstrations in 2009, held in memory of the 1993 massacre of rioting prisoners at Abu Salim prison, many of whom had been Islamists from Benghazi (Becker 2011). With his self-professed pan-Arabism, pan-Africanism, and anti-capitalism, Ghaddafi did not exactly have excellent relationship with Western, Arabian, and some African countries. Libya's conflict with Chad over the Aouzou Strip, which Ghaddafi claimed rightfully belonged to Libya brought him into confrontation with Nigeria. His support for violent actors such as Idi Amin, Charles Taylor, and Foday Sankoh, among others, undermined internal security and brought about unprecedented violence in Uganda, Liberia, and Sierra Leone (Tar and Wapmuk 2017: 258). His association with anti-government forces and to his association with terrorism led to the deterioration in his relations with the US and Western countries.

Ghaddafi's reputation was worsened by Libya's involvement in a number of terrorist attacks. These included the bombings of a German discotheque in 1986 and Pan Am flight 103 over Lockerbie, Scotland by terrorists (Stewart 2011). Ghaddafi was fingered as the master minder and the United States responded to the terrorist bombings of 1986 by deepening its existing economic sanctions against Libya. It also launched an air-raid against targets in Tripoli and Benghazi. Unfortunately, the victims of the bombing were largely civilians, a situation which ended earning domestic sympathy and support for Ghaddafi, and even drew condemnation by fellow African countries. The frosty relationship with the West was maintained until in 1999, when the two suspects in the bombing were turned over to Scottish authorities, and in 2003, Libya accepted responsibility for its role in the attack and agreed to pay damages to the victims' families (Siebens and Case 2012). The UN sanctions were lifted soon thereafter, and at the end of 2003, Libya announced that it would cease its pursuit of WMD and advanced missile technology. These moves allowed Libya to normalize relations with the United States, and the United States lifted its sanctions against Libya in 2004.

During the regime of Muammar Ghaddafi, Libya imported huge amounts of weapons, particularly SALW. This is presented in the Table 35.1.

The stockpile was largely for the military, which was responsible for helping Gaddafi to retain and enforce his power for so long. Despite a UN arms embargo on Libya from 1992 to 2003, and again from February 2011, Ghaddafi maintained several multi-million dollar arms contracts to successfully consolidate his arsenal. According to Sivaram and Karasik (2012: 1) Libya spent close to US$30 bn on weapons alone between 1970 and 2009 and most of these arms came from the USSR. Other countries that sold arms to Libya include Austria, Bulgaria, France, Germany, and Italy. Interestingly, Libya also imported military planes worth US$375m, just under US$135m in small guns, and UA$115m in electronic equipment from the EU between 2005 and 2009 (Sivaram and Karasik 2012: 1). Figure 35.1 captures the eight top arms exporters to Libya, from 1970 to 1991.

Before 2011, Ghaddafi distributed his arms and ammunition depots throughout Libya. Ghaddafi was distrustful of his army and scattered part of his weapons stocks throughout Libya, with many weapons stocked in the south-western Sebha region. The weapons cache included assault rifles, mines, shells, and surface-to-air missiles. According to Marsh (2012), "this approach was likely intended to employ a 'people's war' strategy where after an invasion arms would be distributed to the militias and the general population". From

Table 35.1 Transfers of major conventional weapons to Libya, 1951–2008 (In Million US$)

	King Idris Era	Ghaddafi Regime up to UN/EU embargo		UN/EU embargo era	Post-embargo era	Total	
	1951–1969	1970–1980	1981–1992	1993–2004	2005–2008	1951–2008	%
USSR/Russia	0	17,832	6862	0	0	24,694	75
France	6	2554	576	0	0	3136	10
Italy	0	431	828	0	0	1267	4
Czechoslovaka	0	396	546	0	0	943	3
UK	225	181	83	0	0	487	2
Brazil	0	360	29	0	0	389	<1
USA	103	227	0	0	0	329	<1
Yugoslavia	0	113	186	0	0	298	<1
Ukraine	–	–	–	145	145	290	<1
West Germany	0	5	160	0	0	165	<1
North Korea/Other	0	0	0	11	0	11	<1
Total	336	22,198	9316	156	151	32,009	100
Libya's Global rank	67	2	10	81	70	15	
Arms imports per capita/year	25 US$	890 US$	250 US$	2 US$	6 US$		

Source SIPRI Arms Transfer Database cited in Derek Lutterbeck (2009) Arming Libya: Transfers of Conventional Weapons Past and Present, Contemporary Security Policy, 30:3, p. 506

the beginning of the Libyan conflict, unguarded arsenals became easily accessible to looters, rebels, and others wishing to traffic them, including tribes, al-Qaeda in the Islamic Maghreb (AQIM), as well as Sudanese, Chadian, and Tuareg mercenaries that participated in the Libyan conflict (Ammour 2012). As at 2010 the Libyan armed forces were relatively weak with an estimated 76,000 regular personnel. The government had "400,000–1,000,000 firearms under its control at the beginning of the war" (Marsh 2012: 6).

In an effort to defeat the protesters at the onset of the Libyan civil war, Ghaddafi resorted to the strategy of increasing his stockpile of weapons through armed purchases from Belarus, and China (Shaw and Mangan 2014). This was just before the UN's second embargo in 2011. During the Cold War, Ghaddafi also amassed arms to prepare himself for the possibility of a proxy war being fought in Africa. To some extent this explains, Ghaddafi's government's solidarity with the USSR, and later Russia. Even though the revolution ended the regime of Ghaddafi in Libya, it also signified the end of a strong centralized government that had enjoyed absolute control over its territories,

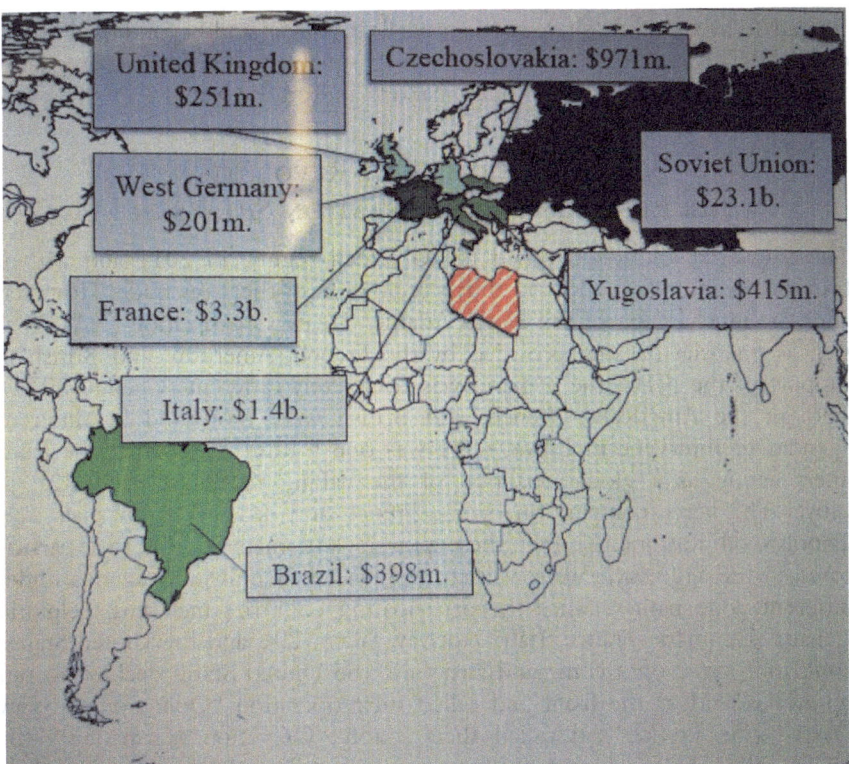

Fig. 35.1 Top eight arms exporters to Libya, 1970–1991 (*Source* SIPRI Arms Transfer Database 2015)

a control which also extended to the wider region and had a destabilizing influence on other states, particularly following the proliferation of SALWs in post-Ghaddafi era. Since the dead of Ghaddafi, arms smuggling out of Libya to Egypt, Tunisia, Algeria, and the Sahel has increased (Lacher 2013).

Before the 2011 revolution, the availability of small arms and light weapons among civilians was "almost non-existent" and "unheard of" because the Libyan government under Muammar Ghaddafi kept weapons proliferation in check (Jenzen-Jones and McCollum 2017; ARES 2016). Moreover, the Libyan report on the Implementation of Programme of Action to Prevent, Combat and Eradicate the Illicit Trade in Small Arms and Light Weapons submitted to the UN states clearly that Small Arms and Light Weapons could not be possessed by civilians without authorization. Such permits were only granted to members of the armed forces, police officers, judicial officials, and prosecutors (Libya Report 2010). The situation was to change with the Libyan revolution of 2011, which directly resulted in a massive increase of SALW proliferation in Libya; a situation which the UN Security Council's new arms embargo on Libya could not stem the tide. On the contrary, the revolution created an avenue for a sharp rise in arms flows within and beyond the borders of Libya. This reality is reflected in both the quantity of arms being regularly traded overtly and covertly in open markets and on the web.

POWER VACUUM, POST-REVOLUTION, AND THE EFFECTS OF PROLIFERATION SALWs IN LIBYA

The Libyan revolution deposed the Ghaddafi regime in 2011 and with it brought to an end, the Libyan state's regulation of the arms trade. However, after the intervention of the North Atlantic Treaty Organization (NATO) as well as financial backing provided by the French, American, and British in support of the NTC, the scenario was completely different (Chengu 2014). Though the Americans, French, and British were motivated by different agendas to intervene in Libya, there was one feature that united the front liners acting as a global coalition of the willing to enforce the R2P in Libya. The fierce competition by the French and other Western allies over Tripoli's oil was intense that these powers and many others that participated in the aggression were willing to pursue their individual agenda under different code names. Since the participating countries including Belgium, Canada, Denmark, France, Italy, Norway, Spain, UK, and the United States, could not agree on a command structure, the United States decided to put up AFRICOM as the front and called their operation "Operation Odyssey Dawn", the French had called their action "Operation Harmattan", the British called their involvement "Operation Ellamy", and Canada termed their involvement "Operation Mobile". When the United States decided to give up its dominant role and to place the operation in the hands of NATO, it was named as "Operation United Protector". In his work, *Global NATO and the Catastrophic Failure in Libya*, Horrace Campbell submitted that the NATO intervention in Libya was a grave misadventure that left the country in a destabilized and chaotic state. After the NATO backed NTC overran Libya, fierce conflict over the control of state power, territories, and resources only continued unabated. Thus, the country became the largest ungoverned space in the world (Campbell 2013). Among the problems resulting from Ghaddafi's removal is the power vacuum in Libya, which made post-Ghaddafi Libya to become almost ungovernable. Essentially, military power became diffuse and commands bastardized to the extent that national military was considered little more than just one among hundreds of militias. Although the members of the opposition had declared a National Transitional Council (NTC) to serve as the interim authority in Libya in 2012, the rebel factions did not consider it a legitimate governing force. In effect, while the NTC had international recognition, it lacked total internal control. The situation was worsened with the defection of many troops from the military. Military stockpiles were therefore raided, and SALWs made their way into the hands of NSA and private sellers. From a virtually non-existent domestic market, the revolution and its aftermath paved the way for a large illicit arms trade to emerge.

The power vacuum created by the exit of the Libyan strong man—Muammar Ghaddafi created a chaotic situation that later degenerating into the 2014 civil war (Chivvis and Martini 2014). The situation coupled with the decline of oil prices in the international market; worsen the economic standing of Libya. Thus, the black market economy became a dynamic source of resources for the militias. Libya slowly transitioned into a major illicit trafficking hub of arms, antiquities, drugs, migrants, and fuel (Shaw and Mangan 2014). By that time, the resurgence of illicit arms flows had seen black market sellers emerge and consolidate in densely populated areas across Libya, including Tripoli and Misrata, as well as in smaller towns in closer proximity to the ongoing fighting. In larger towns and cities, firearms were traded openly or semi-openly in marketplaces (ARES 2016). The numbers of killings involving SALWs are devastating. Estimates of Libya's body count show that 2011 recorded the highest dead with 50,000, while 2825 and 1523 people were killed in 2014 and 2015, respectively, and up to August in 2016, about 902 deaths have been recorded (Adeniyi 2017: 19). The huge arsenals of uncontrolled arms in the possession of NSA, and increasing reports of clashes with pro-government forces, suggests that unarmed civilians will continue to be victims of uncontrolled arm. The effects of SALWs proliferation in post-Ghaddafi Libya were not only on the domestic security within Libya, but also on several other countries and regions. In essence the consequences of SALWs proliferation in post-Ghaddafi Libya are both internal and external.

Internally, the proliferation of small arms has made the Libyan security environment more unpredictable. The use of the internet as site for sales has made access to SALWs easier for citizens. Under Ghaddafi, access to the internet was limited, but after the revolution this strict system has changed and more people are able to use this service. An online black market, in particular on social media, allows inhabitants to advertise weapons for sale. When the internet restrictions disappeared, individuals and arm traders quickly realized the opportunity, provided by the unrestricted internet, to broaden the illegal weapons market. Owing to the weak security environment, especially during the civil war, individuals in Libya resorted to obtaining small arms to protect their families and themselves. SALWs used by militia groups and individuals, further intensify the conflict in Libya. These illegal weapons may be bought by terrorist organizations, which can further deteriorate the security situation within the country. According to Jaeger (2017: 83) the failure of the NTC in Libya to unite all relevant stakeholders under the common objective of national reconstruction created a fertile ground for the growth of a powerful ideological doctrine, which offered the radical people in Libya a consistent belief system amidst the never-ending conflict between the warring militias. This aided the Islamic state in Libya to gain a foothold in October 2014. The role of ISIS and Anshar al-Sharia has decreased, however, some of the weapons in Libya aided the terrorist activities in other parts of the world.

The Impacts of SALWs Proliferation from Post-Ghaddafi's Libya on Other Africa States

The proliferation of arms from Libya has had an severe effect on conflicts in some parts of Africa namely Mali, Niger, Tunisia, Algeria, Egypt, Central African Republic, Nigeria, the Sudan, and Somalia, significant quantities were also trafficked to Turkey, Syria, and beyond. This is captured in Fig. 35.2.

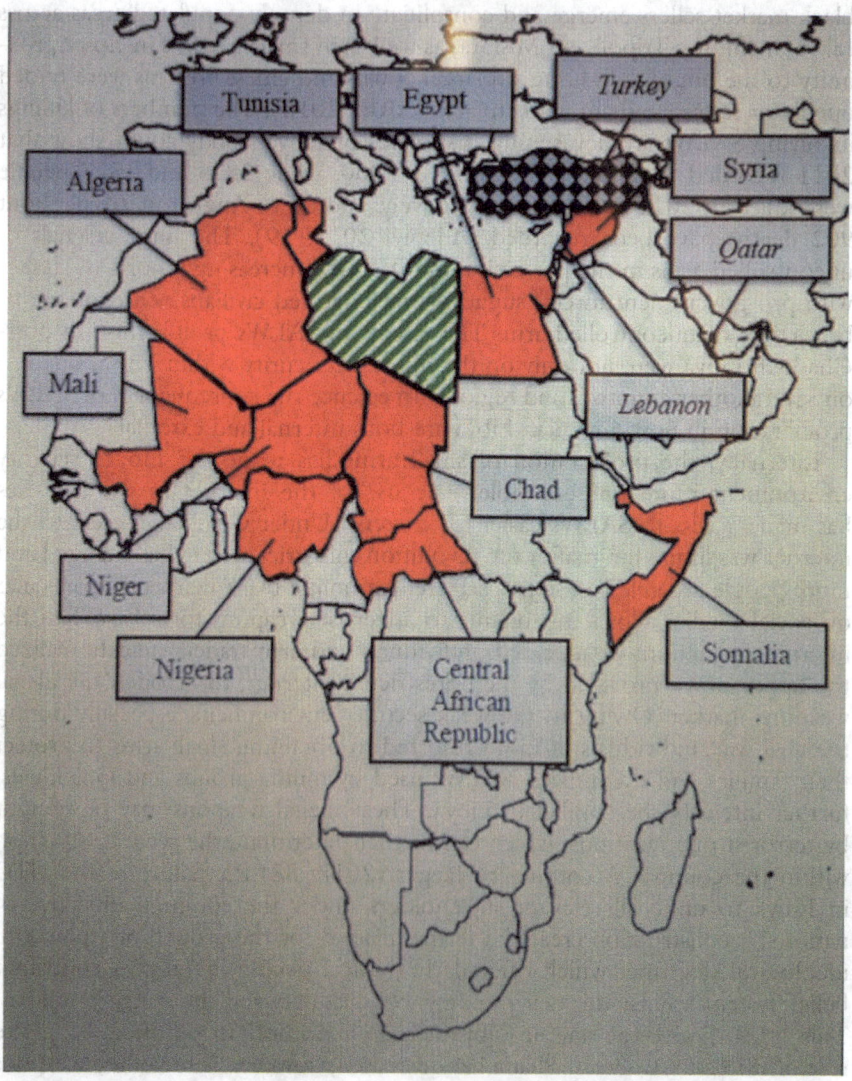

Fig. 35.2 States with confirmed Libyan SALWs proliferation (*Source* SIPRI Arms Transfer Database 2015)

These arms have proliferated into the hands of VNSAs including terrorists groups. However, in this section of the chapter, we shall examine the effects of SALWs proliferation in the post-Ghaddafi era on other African countries. Specifically, we will limit ourselves to Mali and Nigeria. The 2015 UNSC panel report stated that "arms originating from Libya have significantly reinforced the military capacity of terrorist groups operating in different parts of the region of the Sahel".

The Impact of SALWs Proliferation from Libya on Mali

The weapons proliferation from Libya had an effect on the conflict in Mali. Many ethnic Tuareg fighters that left Libya during and after the 2011 conflict drove across the desert to northern Mali. They took with them arms that had not previously been common such as anti-tank weapons, mortars, and heavy machine guns. The Tuaregs that left Libya joined with local Tuareg separatists and in January 2012 started a rebellion. In not more than three months the Malian government had lost control of large areas of northern Mali. In its 7 February 2013 edition, the New York Times Magazine stated that the Malian armed forces were overwhelmed by their opponents' armaments. According to the Small Arms Survey of 2015, the weapons from Libya addressed the scarcity previously being experience of heavy machine guns, 23 mm canon, and associated ammunition. According the Malian Foreign Minister, quoted in Anders (2015: 176) "All of a sudden we found ourselves face to face with a thousand men, heavily armed". Anders (2015) further argued that the availability of SALWs from Libya emboldened the Tuaregs to begin a rebellion in Mali. According to the 2014 UNSC panel report a "wide range of Libyan materiel" including SALWs that had been definitively traced to Libya were reported to have been trafficked into Mali via Niger; via Algeria; and via Tunisia and then Algeria. Clearly, Libyan arms played an important role in the conflict in Mali in 2012, however, that is not to say that the weapons from Libya were the only veritable sources of conflict in Mali. Reports state that some weapons were also obtained from the defeat of Malian armed forces who abandoned arms depots. The warring Tuaregs made it clear that it rejected the government in Bamako and wanted to create an independent state of Azawad led by the National Movement for the Liberation of Azawad (MNLA). To address the threat posed by the Tuareg, the French government launched Opération Serval in January 2013. The operation involved 5000 French troops, plus aircraft, and armoured vehicles. With the involvement of the French troops, working with the Malian army, Arms flows to northern Mali were reduced, but not totally eliminated.

The Impact of SALWs Proliferation from Libya on Nigeria

The Boko Haram, known as Jama atu Ahlis Sunna Lidda a Waati Wal Jihad (in Arabic—meaning people committed to the prophet's teaching and jihad) is an Islamic terrorist group operating mainly within Nigeria. Boko Haram intensified its operations since 2011, gaining momentum from the porosity of Nigeria's borders and instability in Mali. After 2011, Boko Haram tactics became more sophisticated and it started using suicide bombers, suggesting that it was receiving assistance from some elements of the international jihadist movement. The bombing of the UN building in Abuja on 24 August 2011 marked the departure of the group's exclusive focus on domestic attacks. In 2012, the Boko Haram intensified violence in the middle belt. Since then, the Boko Haram graduated to kidnapping, some of which attracted international attention and outcry for the release of the victims. First was the Chibok girls and later the Dapchi girls. Boko Haram uses this strategy to negotiate for the release of its members and demand for ransom.

The Boko Haram is not only believed to have links to al-Qaeda in the Islamic Maghreb (AQIM), but also obtained weapons from Libya (Basar 2012). SALWs proliferation from Libya to Nigeria is believed to bse trafficked through Niger and Chad (UNSC 2014: 37; Adelaja 2014). The Nigerian authorities have argued that the Boko Haram terrorism has been waged with the support of weapons proliferated from Libya and the porous region of the Sahel. This position has been affirmed by the former Nigerian Head of State, President Olusegun Obasanjo, who said that the killing of Muammar Ghaddafi and the destabilization of Libya resulted in the mass proliferation of SALWs. He also argued that the Libyan civil war produced many uncontrolled, trained, and armed militants who continue to fuel violence in the region, including the atrocities committed by Boko Haram in Nigeria. In addition, in August 2012, the Minister of State for Defence, Mrs. Olusola Obada also said that Libyan weapons that had found their way into Nigeria were in the possession of the Boko Haram. Recently, the Nigerian President, Muhammadu Buhari also said that the Fulani Herdsmen, who have been involved in mass killing of farmers in the middle belt region of Nigeria, were trained and use SALWs obtained from Libya. While the Nigerian authorities continue to point to Libya as a source of SALWs, particularly the hands of criminal elements including the Boko Haram and Fulani Herdsmen, the reality, however, is that the quantity of arms which may have come from Libya is unknown. That notwithstanding, the while SALWs may not be the cause of insecurity in Nigeria, the case of Boko Haram in North shows that such weapons used by VNSA further intensify instability in fragile regions of Africa.

Addressing the Proliferation of SALWs in Post-Ghaddafi Libya Through Implementation of International Instruments

The international community has at its disposal legal instruments that seek to address the proliferation of SALWs and which apply to the case of Libya post-Ghaddafi. These instruments have delivered varied successes over the years. Some of the major instruments are discussed here. At the regional and multilateral level, instruments have been established over the past two decades to address the illicit trade in and misuse of small arms. The Arms Trade Treaty (ATT) adopted by the UN General Assembly in April 2013 is significant. It the first binding treaty under international law on the international trade in conventional weapons. The ATT obliges States Parties to control among other things the export, import, and transit of the conventional weapons defined in the treaty, including small arms and light weapons as well as their ammunition. Secondly, the International Ammunition Technical Guidelines (IATG) and the International Small Arms Control Standards (ISACS) developed by the UN is worth noting here. These are two sets of voluntary, practical guidelines on the management and control of ammunition and small arms.

The concerns generated by the trafficking of SALWs to VNSAs including terrorist groups in various parts of the world, among other related issues at the international level, prompted the UN Security Council to adopt a resolution on small arms for the first time in 2013 (UNSC 2013). This resolution, which was updated in 2015, focuses on the illicit transfer, destabilizing accumulation and misuse of small arms. The resolution further calls for better coordination within the UN, and encourages the implementation of UN arms embargoes, including by means of measures relating to the safe and secure storage and disposal of small arms and ammunition. To match words with action, a special trust fund was created to facilitate the implementation of UN arms embargoes. Specifically, the United Nations Trust Facility Supporting Cooperation on Arms Regulation (UNSCAR) that was established in 2013 has a dedicated fund aimed at promoting the implementation of the UN Programme of Action on Small Arms and the ATT, as well as coordinating assistance and cooperation. Regulation of SALWs proliferation will not be complete without the role of customs and border control measures. In this light, the World Customs Organization (WCO) adopted a Small Arms and Light Weapons Strategy in 2015, with a view to assisting its 181 members in combating the illegal cross-border transfer of arms and their parts (Parker and Green 2012). Another major achievement at the global level towards addressing the problem of illicit proliferation of SALWs is formal recognition of the connection between peace and sustainable development in the 2030 Agenda for Sustainable Development adopted in September 2015. Achieving the SDGs by 2030 requires significant reduction of illicit arms flows. Sustainable Development Goal 16 (SDG16) thus addresses the underlying causes of fragility, and the need to promote peaceful, just and inclusive societies (Parker and Green 2012).

African states also established a National Commission on Small Arms dedicated to policy guidance, research, and monitoring of efforts to address the illicit trade in small arms. This is in accordance with the commitment in Paragraph II.4 of the UN Programme of Action to Prevent, Combat and Eradicate the Illicit Trade in Small Arms and Light Weapons in All Its Aspects (UNPoA). Subregional bodies have keyed into the struggle to address the challenges posed by SALWs proliferation. Since 2017, the Economic Community of Central African States (ECCAS) and the Economic Community of West African States (ECOWAS) have put in place conventions for the control of small arms, their ammunition, parts, and components. Such policies that have been initiated to regulate the proliferation of SALWs include ECOWAS Moratorium on Importation, Exportation and Manufacture of Light Weapons in West Africa, ECOWAS Small Arms Control Programme (ECOSAP), Small Arms Transparency and Control Regime in Africa (SATCRA), West Africa Action Network on Small Arms (WAANSA), among other national policies.

To what extent has Libya keyed into the global and regional instruments on SALWs? Under the regime of Ghaddafi, Libya as member of the League of Arab States had adopted the Arab Model Law on Weapons, Ammunitions, Explosives, and Hazardous Material in January 2002. As a member of the African Union, Libya adopted an African Common Position to take to the Conference to Review the UN Programme of Action to Prevent, Combat and Eradicate the Illicit Trade in Small Arms and Light Weapons in All Its Aspects (UNPoA), in June 2006. Libya is also a signatory of the Geneva Declaration on Armed Violence and Development in 2007 (GDAV 2006). The Geneva declaration was a diplomatic initiative aimed at addressing the linkages between armed violence and development. However, Libya signed, but did not ratify the UN Arms Trade Treaty (UNODA 2013). Libya signed and ratified the UN Protocol against the Illicit Manufacturing of and Trafficking in Firearms, Their Parts and Components and Ammunition has been signed and ratified by Libya (UNGA 2001). On 21 July 2001, Libya committed to a consensus decision of the UN to adopt, support, and implement the UN Programme of Action to Prevent, Combat and Eradicate the Illicit Trade in Small Arms and Light Weapons in All Its Aspects.

Under the terms of its 2001 commitment to the UN small arms Programme of Action, Libya has submitted one or more national reports on its implementation of the UNPoA (Parker and Green 2012). However, in terms of global ranking of commitment to the UN small arms Programme of Action Implementation Monitor (PoAIM Phase 1), Libya ranked 142 among 159 Member States by Small Arms Survey (UNGA 2001). One of the issues observed in National Reports of Libya submitted to the UN from 2001 to 2010, were that a National Point of Contact to deal with issues relating to the UNPoA has not been designated; secondly, a history of substantive cooperation with civil society in support of UNPoA activities was not apparent; and thirdly, that Funds for UNPoA implementation have not been donated by Libya to other UN Member States. However, Funds for UNPoA implementation have been provided to Libya by other UN Member States (UNODA 2015). According to the United Nations Register of Conventional Arms, Libya has not declared its small arms exports in one or more annual National Reports on Arms Exports (UNODA 2011). The Wassenaar Arrangement on Export Controls and Conventional Arms and Dual-Use Goods and Technologies does not list Libya as a Participating State. On the whole, the issue of SALWs proliferation in post-Ghaddafi Libya is no doubt complex, which requires a multifaceted approach to address. Evidently, the situation in Libya requires strengthening of state institutions, security sector reform, border control and cooperation with neighbouring countries, and the international community to stem the tide of SALWs proliferation from Libya. As part of its security reform programmes, the national government should take stock of all weapons at its disposal and to bring same under central control, while a programme of buy-back should be initiated to mop up weapons in the hands of civilians. The government should also revisit the regulation of internet activities so as to check the sales of SALWs through the internet, a trend which emerged following the demise of the Libyan strong man—Muammar Ghaddafi.

Conclusion

In this chapter, we focused on SALW proliferation in post-Ghaddafi Libya. We argued that SALW proliferation from Libya in the post-Ghaddafi era has affected not only the security environment in Libya, but also several countries within and beyond the African continent. The chapter highlighted the situation of SALWs amassment under the regime of Muammar Ghaddafi, and also, the revolution and subsequent civil war which created a vacuum with major implications in terms of governance and security. What came out clearly in the chapter is that after the death of Ghaddafi, the security environment deteriorated within Libya and led to mass proliferation of SALW within and beyond Libya. SALWs became widely available to civilians due to their availability at black markets and sales on the internet. Libya indirectly influences other countries security environment, causing a spill-over effect within the continent. The chapter also discussed the impact of SALW proliferation for other African countries, with specific focus on Mali and Nigeria. The chapter concludes on the note that the existence of global and regional legal instruments is not enough to curtail the proliferation of SALWs in fragile regions of the world. Libya as a member of the UN is a signatory to a number of international instruments, some of which it has not ratified. The situation in Libya is no doubt complex, given its fragile political and security environment. While the control of SALWs in Libya in post-Ghaddafi requires internal regulation, security sector reforms, and implementation of an arms buyback initiative, the role regional and international cooperation as well as strong border control must be emphasized. A model arms for development initiative should be considered for Libya. A combination of these and other well thought out strategies will go a long way in addressing the proliferation within and beyond Libyan.

REFERENCES

Adejo, A. M. (2011). Salient Aspects of Nigeria-Libya Relations. *Nigerian Journal of International Affairs, 37*(1), 1–16.

Adelaja, T. (2014). How Nigeria's Leaky Borders Aid Insurgents. *National Mirror Newspaper*, Nigeria. Retrieved from http://nationalmirroronline.net/new/how-nigerias-leaky-borders-aid-insurgents/ on 23 December 2020.

Adeniyi, A. (2017). *The Human Cost of Uncontrolled Arms in Africa: Cross-National Research on Seven African Countries*. Retrieved from https://www.oxfam.org/sites/www.oxfam.org/files/file_attachments/rr-human-cost-uncontrolled-arms-africa-080317-en.pdf on 6 January 2020.

Adetula, V. O. A. (2011). Markets, Revolts, and Regime Change: The Political Economy of the Arab Spring. *Nigerian Journal of International Affairs, 37*(2), 17–47.

Albrecht, H., & Schlumberger, O. (2004). "Waiting for Godot": Regime Change Without Democratization in the Middle East. *International Political Science Review, 25*, 371–392.

Ammour, A. L. (2012). *The Sahara and Sahel After Gaddhafi*. CIDOB Notes Internacionales, No. 44. Barcelona: Barcelona Centre for International Affairs. Retrieved from http://www.cidob.org/en/content/download/30335/360460/file/NOTES+44_A%C3%8FDA_ANG.pdf on 23 December 2020.

Anders, H. (2015). Expanding Arsenals Insurgent Arms in Northern Mali. In G. McDonald, et al. (Eds.), *Small Arms Survey 2015 Weapons and the World* (p. 176). Cambridge: Cambridge University Press.

ARES. (2016, April 8). *Small Arms & Light Weapons Traded Via Social Media Platforms in Libya*. Geneva: Small Arms Survey, Armament Research Services.

Basar, E. (2012). *Report Update: Unsecured Libyan Weapons—Regional Impact and Possible Threats*. Retrieved from http://www.cimicweb.org/ on 6 August 2018.

Becker, J. (2011). Events of Two Years Ago Sparked Current Uprising in Libya. *Global Post*. Retrieved from http://mobile.globalpost.com/dispatch/news/regions/middle-east/110311/prison-massacre-2-years-ago-sparked-current-uprising-libya.

Campbell, H. (2013). *Global NATO and the Catastrophic Failure in Libya*. New York: Monthly Review Press.

Chengu, G. (2014). *Libya: From Africa's Richest State Under Gaddafi, to Failed State After NATO Intervention*. USA: Global Research. Retrieved from http://www.globalresearch.ca/libya-from-africas-richest-state-under-gaddafi-to-failed-state-after-nato-intervention/5408740.

Chivvis, S. C., Crane, K., Mandavalle, P., & Martini, J. (2012). *Libya's Post-Gaddafi Transition: The Nation-Building Challenge*. New York: Cambridge University Press.

Chivvis, S. C., & Martini, J. (2014). *Libya After Gaddafi: Lessons and Implication for the Future*. Washington, DC: Rand Corporation.

Cipriani, P. (2012). *Oil Wealth and Regime Stability in Light of the Arab Spring*. Retrieved from https://graphitepublications.com/wpcontent/uploads/2013/04/Oil-Wealth-and-Regime-Stability-in-Light-of-the-Arab-Spring.pdf on 23 December 2020.

El-Katiri, M. (2012). *State Building Challenges in Post-Revolution Libya*. USA: Army War College.

Fukuyama, F. (1989). *Have We Reached the End of History? RAND Corporation*. Retrieved from https://www.rand.org/pubs/papers/P7532.html on 16 January 2020.

GDAV. (2006, June 7). Geneva Declaration. *Geneva Declaration on Armed Violence and Development*. Geneva: Geneva Declaration on Armed Violence and Development Secretariat.

Jacqmin, D. (2017, June 23). *The Proliferation of Small Arms and Light Weapons: Definitions and Challenges*. Brussels: Group for Research and Information on Peace and Security.

Jaeger, L. (2017). Islamic State in Libya. In C. Varin & D. Abubakar (Eds.), *Violent Non State Actors in Africa: Terrorists, Rebels and Warlords* (pp. 75–105). Switzerland: Palgrave Macmillan.

Jenzen-Jones, N. R., & McCollum, I. (2017). *Web Trafficking Analysing the Online Trade of Small Arms and Light Weapons in Libya* (Working Paper No. 226). Geneva: Small Arms Survey, Graduate Institute of International and Development Studies. Retrieved from http://www.smallarmssurvey.org/fileadmin/docs/F-Working-papers/SAS-SANA-WP26-Libya-web-trafficking.pdf on 23 December 2020.

Kesici, Z. (2019). *Authoritarian Regime Stability: A Comparison Between Libya and Saudi Arabia*. Retrieved from https://medium.com/@zeykes/authoritarian-regime-stability-a-comparison-between-libya-and-saudi-arabia-1ee13a18ce80#_ftn19 on 16 January 2020.

Lacher, W. (2013). Fault Lines of the Revolution: Political Actors, Camps, and Conflicts in the New Libya. *SWP Research Paper*.

Libya Report. (2010). *Report of the Libyan Arab Jamahiriya on Implementation of the United Nations Programme of Action to Prevent, Combat and Eradicate the Illicit Trade in Small Arms and Light Weapons in All Its Aspects Submitted Pursuant to General Assembly Resolution 64/50*. Report 1032867E.

Linz, J. J. (1964). An Authoritarian Regime: The Case of Spain. In E. Allard & Y. Littunen (Eds.), *Cleavages, Ideologies and Party Systems*. Helsinki: Academic Publishers.

Lutterbeck, D. (2009). Arming Libya: Transfers of Conventional Weapons Past and Present. *Contemporary Security Policy*, 30(3), 505–528.

Marsh, N. (2012). Brothers Came Back with Weapons the Effects of Arms Proliferation from Libya. *Prism*, 6(4), 49–96.

Merelli, A. (2018, March 17). *American Support for Authoritarian Rule Has Dropped for the First Time in 23 Years*. Retrieved from https://qz.com/1228323/american-support-for-authoritarian-rule-has-dropped-for-the-first-time-in-23-years/ on 16 January 2020.

Parker, S., & Green, K. (2012, August 1). Findings—Table 3: Reporting States by Rank and Score. *The Programme of Action Implementation Monitor (Phase 1): Assessing Reported Progress*. Geneva: Small Arms Survey, the Graduate Institute of International and Development Studies, Geneva.

Shaw, M., & Mangan, F. (2014). *Illicit Trafficking and Libya's Transition: Profits and Losses: United States Institute for Peace*. Retrieved from https://www.usip.org/sites/default/files/PW96-Illicit-Trafficking-and-Libyas-Transition.pdf on 6 December 2019.

Siebens, J., & Case, B. (2012). *The Libyan Civil War: Context and Consequences*. Special Report. THINK International and Human Security.

Retrieved from http://www.thinkihs.org/wp-content/uploads/2012/08/Siebens-Case-LibyaSReport-2012.pdf on 23 December 2020.

SIPRI Arms Transfers Database. (2015). *Stockholm International Peace Research Institute*. Retrieved from http://www.sipri.org/databases/armstransfers on 20 January 2020.

Sivaram, A., & Karasik, T. (2012). An Arms Buyback for Libya? *INEGMA Special Report No. 16*. Dubai: Institute for Near East & Gulf Military Analysis (INEGMA).

Smith, B. (2004). Oil Wealth and Regime Survival in the Developing World, 1960–1999. *American Journal of Political Science, 48*(2), 232–246.

Stewart, S. (2011, March 23). Libya's Terrorism Option. *STRATFOR Global Intelligence*. Retrieved from http://www.stratfor.com/weekly/20110323-libyas-terrorism-option.

Tar, U. A., & Wapmuk, S. (2017). The Revolutionary United Front, Liberian Warlords and Civil War in Sierra Leone. In C. Varin & D. Abubakar (Eds.), *Violent Non State Actors in Africa: Terrrorists, Rebels and Warlords* (pp. 251–275). Switzerland: Palgrave Macmillan.

The Arms Trade Treaty (SR 0.518.61). *The Interpretative Declaration for the ATT*. Retrieved from https://www.newsd.admin.ch/newsd/message/attachments/38163.pdf on 6 August 2018.

UNGA. (2001, July 20). Programme of Action to Prevent, Combat and Eradicate the Illicit Trade in Small Arms and Light Weapons in All Its Aspects. *United Nations General Assembly*. New York, NY: UN General Assembly.

UNGA. (2001, May 31).United Nations Protocol Against the Illicit Manufacturing of and Trafficking in Firearms, Their Parts and Components and Ammunition. *UN General Assembly Resolution 55/255*. New York, NY: UN General Assembly.

United Nations SC. (2014). Final Report of the Panel of Experts Established Pursuant to Resolution 1973 (2011) Concerning Libya (pp. 30–32). New York: United Nations, S/2014/106, 2014.

UNODA. (2011, October 21). National Reports on Small Arms Exports. *United Nations Register of Conventional Arms—The Global Reported Arms Trade*. New York, NY: United Nations Office for Disarmament Affairs.

UNODA. (2013, April 2). Towards entry into force. *Arms Trade Treaty*. New York, NY: United Nations Office for Disarmament Affairs.

UNODA. (2015, September 11). PoA-ISS Country Profiles. *UN Small Arms Programme of Action (UNPoA)—Implementation Support System*. New York, NY: United Nations Office of Disarmament Affairs.

UNSC. (2013, September 26). *Security Council Adopts First-Ever Resolution Dedicated to Question of Small Arms, Light Weapons*. Retrieved from https://www.un.org/press/en/2013/sc11131.doc.htm on 6 January 2020.

Dauda Abubakar received his Ph.D. from the University of Wisconsin-Madison. He taught at the University of Maiduguri in the Department of Political Science where he was also the Head of Department; and coordinator of Graduate programmes. From 2003 to 2009, Dr. Abubakar taught in the Department of Political Science at Ohio University-Athens, United States. He is a tenured faculty in the Department of Political Science and African Studies at the University of Michigan-Flint; and also the Chair of Africana Studies Department. He is the co-editor (with Caroline Varin) of *Violent Non-State Actors in Africa: Terrorists, Rebels and Warlords* (Palgrave

Macmillan, 2017); and has contributed numerous chapters to edited volumes on Africa and global politics. His current research agenda examines the intersection of identity politics, securitization, and intervention in postcolonial Africa.

Sharkdam Wapmuk is an Associate Professor in the Department of Defence and Security Studies, Nigerian Defence Academy (NDA) Kaduna. He served as consultant for international organizations and think tanks, lectures at various institutions in Nigeria and participated in local and international conferences, seminars, workshops, and dialogues. His research interests cut across the thematic fields of Afro-Asian relations, security, cooperation, and integration. His articles have been published in local and international journals and books. He is a member of scholarly bodies, including the Nigerian Political Science Association (NPSA) and Nigerian Society of International Affairs (NSIA).

CHAPTER 36

Mali: The Ecology of Insurgency, Terrorism and Small Arms Proliferation

Jude Cocodia

INTRODUCTION

Captivated by the majesty of Mali during his visit in 132, Ibn Battuta, a fourteenth-century North African geographer wrote: "There is complete security in the country" (see Cheref 2012: 1). Once considered the model of democracy and security in West Africa, much of Mali today is a cesspit of anarchy as governance fails progressively and increasingly ungovernable areas continue to expand. The growing anarchy is captured by the increasing number of conflicts that have spread from the north of the country to the central regions. While Islamist jihadists groups compete and cooperate to fill the vacuum created by the government's absence in the north of the country, state policies that promote horizontal inequality among ethnic groups have exacerbated communal tensions in the central regions of the country.

The recycling of weapons left over from the cold war, which alone would have been unable to feed the militarisation impelled by these crises, got a huge boost with the influx of weapons from Libya following the fall of Muammar Qaddafi and the non-securitisation of his huge and sophisticated weapons stockpile. These weapons became the bane of instability in the region from 2012 and fed rebellions across the Sahel in what has been termed the "arc of instability" with Mali and Niger right at the middle (see Alexander 2016: 4). Mali's geographical position in this volatile region, and the instability within

---

J. Cocodia (✉)
Department of Political Science, Niger Delta University, Wilberforce Island, Nigeria

© The Author(s), under exclusive license to Springer Nature Switzerland AG 2021
U. A. Tar and C. P. Onwurah (eds.), *The Palgrave Handbook of Small Arms and Conflicts in Africa*,
https://doi.org/10.1007/978-3-030-62183-4_36

its borders, coupled with its porous borders (a problem shared by most African states) has seen it serve as a major destination and transit hub for Small Arms and Light Weapons (SALWs).

A major part of Mali's problem stemmed from the civil war in Libya in 2011 and the country's porous borders which have ensured the proliferation of SALWs in the country (Alexander 2016; Haugegaard 2017; Marsh 2017; Cocodia 2018). Though the north of Mali has been home to organised crime syndicates and jihadists (Leboeuf 2014), events from 2011 took this to an entirely new level such that involvement in organised crime is seen as a norm and the rivalries between syndicates and the communities that support them have become intensely violent. This has paved way for the increased militarisation of the area and the abundance of SALWs therein.

This chapter discusses the issue of SALWs in Mali through looking at the factors that have shaped this phenomenon. The chapter begins by examining the evolution of insurgency in Mali that centres mainly around Tuareg rebellions and then focuses on the drivers of terrorism in the country. Finally, this chapter examines the factors responsible for the proliferation of SALWs in Mali.

THE ECOLOGY OF INSURGENCY IN MALI

Prior to the political landmark coup d'état of 2012, much of the ethnic restiveness in Mali and rebellions had been among the minority Tuaregs of northern Mali. Three major reasons account for this. First was the feeling of racial/cultural superiority of the Tuaregs who were of Berber descent over the black sub-Saharan Africans in the south who held political power (Keys 2013: 3). Second was the feeling of irredentism among Tuaregs who had been split, during the colonial era, into states in West (Mali, Mauritania, Niger) and North Africa (Algeria) and so pushed a cause of unification of the Tuareg nation—Azawad (Keys 2013: 3). Third was the severe underdevelopment of the north and the lack of government presence there (Devon 2013: 1–3; Cocodia 2017: 51).

In accordance with the first reason, the Tuaregs of northern Mali who were granted some form of autonomy during French colonial rule, found it difficult to be subservient to the rule of the black sub-Saharan Africans who were immersed into colonial mainstream governance and so dominated the corridors of power in the postcolonial era. With Mali having its independence in September 1960, "the Tuareg began to push forward their dream of establishing Azawad" (Devon 2013: 2). By 1962, the Tuaregs carried out their first rebellion (Alfellaga) which began with small hit and run attacks on government forces. The rebellion was crushed by the end of 1964 due to the Tuaregs lacking a unified leadership, a well-coordinated strategy and coherent strategic vision. The end of the rebellion saw the Tuaregs condemned to harsher repressive measures that alienated them from the central government situated in Mali's south (Devon 2013: 3, Cocodia 2017: 52).

The restiveness of the Tuaregs also derived from the bid to unite all Tuaregs under the state of Azawad. The Tuaregs had suffered the same fate of the Somalis who, by virtue of colonial partitioning, had been split into Djibouti, Ethiopia and Kenya, and the Kurds who, through the same means, became minorities in Iran, Iraq, Syria and Turkey. The Tuaregs had learned from their crushing defeat in 1964 that, if future rebellions were to have any chance of succeeding, there ought to be unity and cohesion in pushing this cause. Consequently, the second Tuareg rebellion in 1990, was under the banner of the Azawad People's Movement (MPA). This time, the government of Mali was compelled to negotiate an agreement—the National Pact of 1992. By 2011, the Tuaregs formed the Movement for the Liberation of Azawad (MNLA) to counter the United States' bid to strengthen the Malian government's control of the north. This move by the Tuaregs was also fuelled by the perception that developments in northern Mali were security-oriented rather than economic (Kisangani 2012; Neelakantan 2013). The MNLA incorporated returning Tuareg mercenaries who had fought in Libya in support of Muammar Qaddafi, and they brought with them their combat experience and sophisticated weapons. It was the MNLA that began the assault on Mali in 2013 from which the country is yet to recover.

Finally, the underdevelopment of the north incensed the feeling of marginalisation and ethnic sentiments in the region. The autonomy granted the Tuaregs by France during the colonial era ensured the south of Mali became the target of French modernisation and development. So development was lopsided in the country in favour of the south and his lopsided pattern continued after independence (Keys 2013; Cocodia 2017). As a result, much of Tuareg agitations derived from this lopsided development. Yet, surprisingly, especially with the third wave of democracy (1990–2010), Mali was seen as a model democracy in Africa (see Allen 2013: 8). This was in spite of the thriving cartels, illicit drug trade, human trafficking, porous borders, ethnic tensions, poor governance and restiveness that pervaded the north. While the urban towns like Bamako, Gao and Timbuktu portrayed signs of democratic freedoms on which Mali was judged, its Saharan and Sahelian reaches showed signs to the contrary. But as noted by Stephen Harmon (2014: 71), "observers saw only what they wanted to see."

The Tuaregs have largely been at the centre of insurgencies in Mali. Prior to 2012, Mali had experienced two Tuareg rebellions—1962–1964 and 1990–1991. The Tuareg's demand for a sovereign state dates back to the colonial era under French rule despite the degree of autonomy enjoyed (Lode 2002: 59; Devon 2013: 1). With Mali's independence in 1960, the Tuaregs began to push forward their dream of establishing the state of Azawad. This met with stiff repression from the government and culminated in the first Tuareg rebellion. The second rebellion was an expression of dissatisfaction with the government's poor management of the drought that ravaged northern Mali through the 70s and 80s and brought extreme hardships especially to the Tuaregs (Lode 2002: 56; Meredith 2006: 276). The 2012 crisis that plagues

Mali till date largely owes its existence to Tuareg dissatisfaction (Cocodia 2018: 127).

The tendency of the Tuareg's towards conflict has also been fuelled by irredentism of which secession is conceived as an avenue to achieve. Then again is the feeling of cultural superiority to the black sub-Saharans who hold political power within the country. In addition to these factors is the fact that the Tuaregs perception of marginalisation is justified. Marginalisation of the Tuaregs was the result of poor governance which was due either to weak state institutions, or a deliberate perpetuation of horizontal inequality by the black majority (Bourgeot 1990: 146; Tandoğan and Bouacha 2017: 315). Tuareg restiveness in Mali exemplifies the argument of Deiwiks et al (2012: 289–290) that "in cases where regions have a distinct ethnic identity, perceived ethnic discrimination through economic disadvantages may trigger or reinforce ethno-nationalist grievances thus increasing the risk of secessionist conflict."

The rise of the MNLA, whose membership consists of Tuareg mercenaries with combat experience from Libya also contributed to the instability and political fragility of the Malian state. Compounding issues still is the fact that these mercenaries returned with their sophisticated weapons and still bear strong links to the arms market in Libya which is currently Africa's hub for the trade in illegal weapons. As noted by Stewart Patrick (2013: 1).

> Colonel Muammar al-Qaddafi, the deposed Libyan leader had filled well over a thousand arms depots. The collapse of his regime left behind miles of unsecured warehouses filled with rockets, machine guns, ammunition and antiaircraft systems,... Within hours after Qaddafi's death on October 20, 2011, Tuareg fighters from Mali that had served as his mercenaries were speeding home with pickup trucks full of weapons from the dictator's warehouses. By January 2012, a United Nations report warned that governments in the Sahel were struggling to address a spike in weapons proliferation, organised crime and terrorism.

A report by Devon Maylie and Drew Hinshaw (2011) notes too that the stretch of desert between Libya and West Africa ranks among the world's principal smuggling routes. While the Tuaregs, by virtue of their knowledge of the desert dominate this trade, militants from the local Tuareg tribe run the trafficking of arms.

With the Tuaregs access to Libya's weapon's stockpiles their knowledge of the desert, tendency towards violent confrontation, and the porous borders of Mali, the northern regions of the country remain rife for the proliferation of SALWs (Cheref 2012). The impact of the Tuaregs on this landscape is best captured in the phrase; "What the Tuareg do after the fall of Qaddafi will determine the security and future of the Sahel" (Jamestown Foundation 2011). Soon after the fall of Qaddafi, the Malian Prime Minister at the time of the 2012 crisis explained, "all of a sudden, we found ourselves face to face with a thousand men, heavily armed" (Marsh 2017: 82).

The Ecology of Terrorism in Mali

Though the lack of governance in areas in the north had served Tuareg militant groups and other terror groups like Al Qaeda in the Islamic Maghreb (AQIM) well, there were other factors that attracted terror groups to the region. Prominent among these were, the proximity of Mali to Libya which had become a major source of SALWs with the deposition of Muammar Qaddafi, and the decrepit state of the Malian armed forces that made it unable to impose security in the region. As a result, the northern part of Mali witnessed a huge growth in organised crime, drug cartels, trafficking in cocaine, humans, firearms and other illicit merchandise. The Tuaregs could not have been solely in charge of, or been the sole beneficiaries of these illegal trades. So, the situation in Mali was attractive to people and groups—the so-called "merchants of conflict"—who made a living out of instigating conflict and spreading terror. The presence of these terror groups in the region has bolstered the proliferation of SALWs (Fig. 36.1).

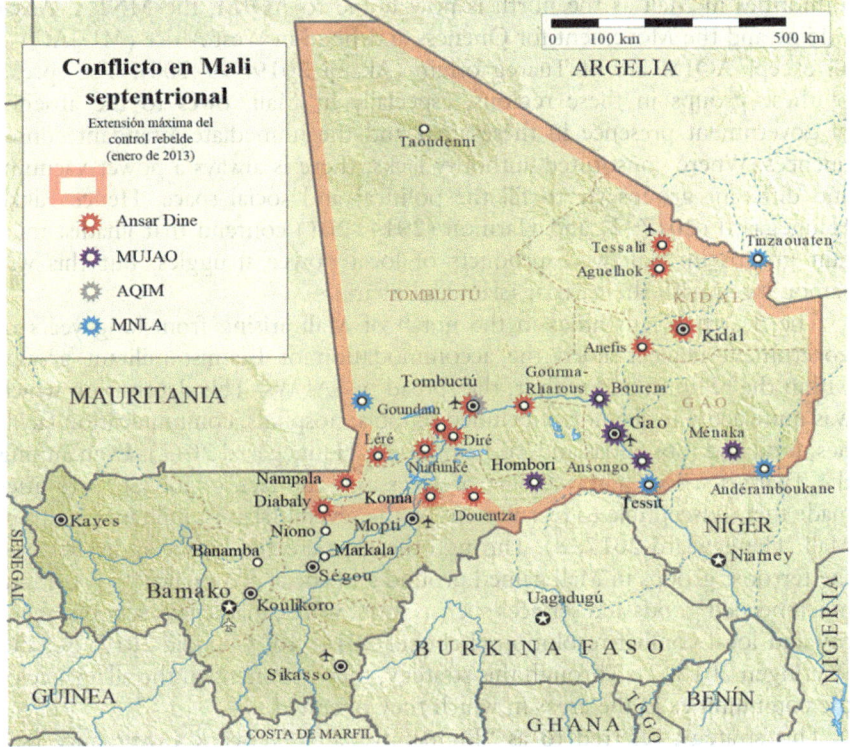

Fig. 36.1 Conflict in the north and central regions of Mali (*Source* The organisation for world peace)

Due to the porous borders of countries within the Sahara and the Sahel, what happens in one country easily affects its neighbours. The ability of AQIM, having been decimated in Algeria, to get a foothold in Mali is a good case in point. It should be known that AQIM is of Algerian origin, but having been decimated there, its remaining members sought refuge in the plains of northern Mali (Bøås 2014: 2–3; Harmon 2014: 60–61). Laurence Ammour (2013: 6) contends that mobility and adaptability are key to the survival of terrorist groups. Robin Hardy (2019: 256–261) contends that when jihadists in one territory have taken a beating, the surviving fighters simply relocate to other geographies. Considering then the successes of international and national efforts against Islamic militancy in other parts of the world, the defeat of the Islamic State n the Levant (ISIL) in the Middle East for example, it means that many of these jihadists will end up in Africa's Sahara-Sahel and either join forces with the terror groups in the region or form new ones. If this happens, then the proliferation of SALWs will be almost impossible to surmount, and the fragile security in the Sahel will be closer to total collapse.

The spread of terrorist groups is one of the major challenges facing the authorities in Mali as the north is now home to AQIM, the MNLA, Ansar Eddine and the Movement for Oneness and Jihad in West Africa (MUJAO)—all except AQIM are of Tuareg origin (Akanji 2019: 99–100). The spread of these groups in these regions, especially in Mali, owes to the absence of government presence in these areas and the immediate attendant consequences. Where constituted authority lacks, there is always a power vacuum, and different groups vie to fill the political and social space. Hence Rikke Haugegaard (2017: 2) and Harmon (2014: 201) contend that jihadist militant groups in Mali were products of local power struggles, but this was camouflaged with the garb of Islam and Sharia.

The dearth of amenities in the north of Mali arising from long years of government neglect aided the accommodation of Islamist militant groups within the regions, and with it, the spread of SALWs. This deprivation which was quite acute in the north included schools, hospitals, communication facilities, food and jobs (Bøås and Torheim 2013; Haugegaard 2017). Even among the Tuaregs whose aim was one of secession, the lack of job opportunities made them susceptible to recruitment by the several Islamist militant groups in Mali (Haugegaard 2017: 8). Through the gaps created by social deficiencies, the terrorist groups in Mali gained ground and social acceptance by providing much needed goods and services such as food, water, medicines, schools' security and local conflict resolution (Leboeuf 2014: 46; Cocodia 2017: 56; van Wieringen 2018: 2). Through this strategy, they commanded the allegiance of the communities in the areas in which they operated.

This strategy, referred to as "Bigmanity" and Network Governance (see Utas 2012), consists of a group attracting followers through its ability to assist people or communities. They provide protection and social security for these followers and in turn earn their loyalty. Building power is based on amassing wealth and redistributing it with astutely calculated generosity. Beyond the

Bigmanity syndrome to secure loyalty, AQIM and other terrorist groups in Mali such as the Ansar Edine and the MUJAO also employ some form of social integration. In addition to providing economic incentives which is important for recruitment, AQIM members also marry locals to develop lasting relations and they reinvest ransom in the local economy (Kühne 2013: 6; Haugegaard 2017: 8). Similarly, Morten Bøås and Liv Torheim (2013: 420) contend that "the AQIM strategy was a careful and gradual one of integration and penetration into the local communities based on a combination of military, political, religious, economic and humanitarian means." The combined strategy of bigmanity and social integration secured a solid base for these terror groups within the communities from which they operated. With these terror groups firmly established in the area, it is inevitable that Mali would be a transit and destination hub for SALWs.

Proliferation of SALWs in Mali

It is a known fact that West Africa lacks the capacity to produce its own weapons. This implies that most of the guns in circulation are from outside the subregion. A report by the United Nations Office on Drugs and Crime (UNODC) (n.d.) contends that, despite the decline in active conflicts, many countries in West Africa are still affected by the presence of terror groups. Prior to the deposition of Muammar Qaddafi in 2011, much of the weapons in the Africa, were vestiges of the cold war. Weapons trafficked during those years did not disappear instead they continued to be recycled and found their way to groups looking to start a revolution (UNODC, n.d.). With the 2011 civil war in Libya, the influx of weapons into Africa's Sahel ballooned and Mali was directly affected by virtue of its proximity, its well-established drugs and arms smuggling trade, and the return of Tuaregs who had fought in Qaddafi's army and who were willing to join local forces to start a rebellion. Compounding these issues was the presence of Islamist jihadist groups exploiting the vacuum of governance of Mali's northern region and priming for territory and territorial expansion (Bleck and Michelitch 2015: 600–601). There is also evidence that local officials have either been complacent or stoked the problem of abundance of SALWs (Marsh 2017). The prevalence of these factors ensured that Mali has remained a hub for SALWs. Making this problem seem irredeemable is the fact that prominent Malian state officials have either been complacent in curbing, or contributed to the exacerbation of these issues that have collectively been responsible for the superfluity of SALWs in Mali.

The Drug and Criminal Networks

A major connecting factor in the issue of conflict, terrorist groups, ethnic tensions and SALWs in Mali are the smuggling and drug trafficking gangs. So important are their presence in Mali that they have close ties with terrorist groups and state officials (Rao 2013: 4). While some experts contend that there is some fusion between trafficking gangs and jihadist groups (Alexander 2016: 7; Haugegaard 2017: 1–2), others contend that this link is overrated (International Crisis Group 2018a: 2). The latter position may not be far fetched considering that the drug and arms smuggling cartels are largely of (Christian) South American origin (Kühne 2013: 6), while the Islamic militants are of Arab and Tuareg extraction. Irrespective of this identity variance, they have a common interest in wealth, influence and power and achieving them is what matters. The smuggling cartels procure weapons and ammunition for the Islamist militants. The militants in turn facilitate the free passage of smuggled goods through the areas they control (Harmon 2014: 201; Haugegaard 2017: 4). The ICG (2018a: 1) observes that:

> Traffickers have adapted and forged closer ties to the region's various armed groups, including in some cases jihadists. Major traffickers maintain relations with both Malian authorities ... and political and military groups in the north; indeed often trafficking networks are embedded in, or overlap with, those groups, who themselves depend on trafficking to finance their operations and to buy weapons.... 'However' rivalries among trafficking networks sometimes provoke confrontation between armed groups.

In concurrence with this view, Lacher (in Haugegaard 2017: 9–10) states that:

> Organised crime is one of the root causes of the current conflicts in Mali but it also functions as an opportunity to combat poverty and unemployment. Organised crime is closely linked to national and local politics as local criminals try to buy political influence through donations and food packages to villages; some even run for local or national elections.

That drug traffickers are allies of jihadists and state officials explains why the government has turned a blind eye, and why international efforts at curbing this phenomenon have been wary. In as much as the drug cartels remain a salient part of Mali's politics, along with their issues, the country will always suffer the influx of SALWs.

Islamist militant groups benefit from these transnational smuggling groups. This much is adduced to by the United Nations Security Council (UNSC) in Resolution 2322 when it states that terrorist groups benefit from Transnational Organised Crime (TOC) and the trafficking of arms, drugs and persons (UNSC 2016). However, the mix of Islamist militants into this complex relationship has made the impact less desirable. This is aptly captured by Anouar Boukhars (2015: 1) who observes that:

> There has been a marked intensification of conflict across the Sahara and the Sahel. This has created a new normal, where ethnic tensions are reinforced, religious divisions are more pronounced and crises are less local. The current

conflicts in Mali, for example show this having been deeply shaped by a cross-section of Saharan radicalised militants that mix with transnational smuggling networks and independence movements.

Drug trafficking in Mali yields enormous profits and this has attracted other groups into the trade. The resulting competition and the inflow of arms across the Sahel has militarised smuggling with traffickers using heavy arms and militias to protect or intercept convoys (Haugegaard 2017: 3–4; ICG 2018b: 1–2). Drug money has caused disputes among communities that spiral into protracted feuds because criminal groups increasingly fall back on their communities for support. For this reason, drug trafficking is generating a level of violence that is unparalleled in the region and the weapons circulating have exacerbated the progressive militarisation of trafficking networks whose rivalries fuel political and intercommunal tensions (International Crisis Group 2018a).

State Policies and Horizontal Inequality

The repeated droughts in the north of Mali, coupled with government's neglect and retrogressive policies in the region, have ensured limited economic opportunities in the area. Many in the countryside, especially among Tuareg youths welcome employment in organised crime as a means of survival. The result is the criminalisation of the Tuareg culture. Winrich Kühne (2014: 6) holds that the North's steady drift towards crime and terrorism was as the result of the disastrous state policies that fuelled ethnic dissent between groups of the north instead of policies aimed at forging unity and integration (also see Tandoğan and Bouacha 2017: 315). The tendency of the government to focus on the country's gold-rich south-west has allowed drug traffickers, militiamen and jihadists to flourish in central and northern regions (*The Economist*, 2019: 1). Due to the ripple effects of the lapses of the Malian government, the 2016 Seventh Annual Report of the Inter-University Centre for Terrorism Studies contends that the first of two factors that contribute to Mali's lingering instability is the failure of the government to find suitable political solutions for its internal security concerns (Alexander 2016: 13).

The intensification of conflict across the Sahel encircles much of Mali and this has spread to the central region of the country where violence escalates at an alarming rate. The violence in this region owes to the state's lack of legitimacy and the growth of Jihadist militia, self-defence militia and banditry. The increase in these militarised groups has led invariably to an upsurge in the availability of SALWs (International Crisis Group 2016). Incongruous government policies or weak political will, or both, festered ethnic strife in the region and this has been a major reason for the failure of the implementation of the 1992, 2006 and 2015 peace deals (Gold 2013: 1; Cocodia 2017: 61). The instability in the north has spread to the central regions which now witnesses violent conflicts between the Dogon and Bambara against the Fulani. The

Dogon and the Bambara accuse the Fulani of trespassing on their farmlands and destroying their crops in feeding their animals. The Fulani accuse both groups of stealing their cattle. Coincidentally, leaders of these groups agree that the growing mutual mistrust is fanned by outside influences (Al Jazeera News 2019). A report by *The Economist* (2019: 1) corroborates this view:

> Recent violence in Mali has an element of inter-ethnic rivalry that did not previously figure so strongly. The country's most powerful jihadist group, *Jama'at Nasr al-Islam wal Muslimin*, has concentrated recruitment efforts on the Fulani ethnic group, many of whom are impoverished, disenfranchised, semi-nomadic herders. Fulani relations with two primarily farming-focused groups in central Mali, the Dogon and the Bambara, are becoming increasingly strained. In the past two years Dogon and Bambara militiamen, claiming to be anti-jihadist, have massacred hundreds of Fulani men, women and children. In response, Fulani groups have armed and now carry out their own killing sprees.... The murders are part of a cycle of tit-for-tat attacks that are also often linked to conflicts about land or theft of cattle. The government has done little to resolve them.

Supporting this claim, an Al Jazeera June 2013 report states that reprisal attacks involving the Dogon and the Fulani in the Mopti region of Mali left approximately 180 people, inclusive of 24 children, dead. Despite appeals from the government, the militia groups on both sides refused to lay down their weapons (Thomas-Johnson 2013).

Human Rights Watch (2018: 1) concurs with the above and states that: "The violence pitted ethnically aligned self-defence groups against communities accused of supporting Islamist armed groups." The International Crisis Group (2018b: 1) explains that local communities and the government of Mali employed ethnic militias to fight the jihadists. This strategy aggravated intercommunal feuding and arguably played into the hands of the jihadists. The government's support for the Dogon and Bambara militias and the Jama'at Nasr al-Islam wal Muslimin support for the Fulani has fuelled the conflict in central Mali (*The Economist* 2019). The growing demand for firearms to sustain this level of conflict has fostered the supply of SALWs.

The Fall of Muammar Qaddafi vs Local Shenanigans

As has been stated above, a lot of Tuaregs who fought in Muammar Qaddafi's army returned home after the war and they came with weapons and as well trained fighters. This was the beginning of the direct impact of the War in Libya on Mali. Michelle Nichols (2013) states that weapons from Libya were being transported through southern Tunisia, southern Algeria and northern Niger to destinations such as Mali. These transfers from Libya qualitatively enhanced the military capacity of non-state opposition groups by supplying weapons that had previously been unavailable or in short supply (Marsh 2017: 79).

The 2016 Seventh Annual Report of the Inter-University Centre for Terrorism Studies avers that the continuing flow of combatants and weapons from Libya is the second of two factors that contribute to Mali's lingering instability (Alexander 2016: 13). Records show that between the 2011 when Qaddafi was ousted and 2013, huge caches of heavy and light weapons that were trafficked from Libya, ended up in Mali. The evidence is seen in the 2012 rebellion of the MNLA, and the push of the Islamist militants in the same year that saw AQIM over much of northern and central Mali. Nicholas Marsh (2017: 82) states:

> Mali offers the most clear-cut case of weapons proliferation from Libya having an effect upon conflict. Hundreds of ethnic Tuareg fighters left Libya during and after the 2011 conflict and drove across the desert to northern Mali, and took with them arms .... They joined with local Tuareg separatists and in January 2012 started a rebellion. Within three months the government had lost control of large areas of northern Mali. The Malian armed forces were said to have been surprised by their opponents' armaments..... The Malian Foreign Minister explained that "All of a sudden we found ourselves face to face with a thousand men, heavily armed."

The demand for these weapons got even higher given the influx of Islamic militants to the area, the increasing militarisation of the drug trade and rising ethnic tensions leading to frequent violent intercommunal clashes. Though records show that a very limited amount of weapons came in from Libya from 2015 onward, but as earlier stated, once trafficked, weapons do not just evaporate, they are recycled. Libya may no longer be the major source of SALWs in Mali, but events there in 2011 set the stage for Mali's current crisis which began a year later.

Mali has been marching increasingly towards anarchy since 2012, and the weapons from Libya alone, especially now that supply has trickled, cannot feed the rising number of conflicts and high level of militarisation of the drug/arms trade. The UNODC (n.d.) report indicates two avenues through which the bulk of SALWs in Mali are sourced from local security officials. The report states:

> Criminals seem able to get what they need from the local security forces, buying or renting weapons from corrupt elements in the police and military. The imports that do occur are not made through underground arms brokers, but rather through mainstream commercial channels, and then directed though corrupt officials or complicit governments to criminals and rebel groups.... Flows from corrupt security officials remain strong because few states in the sub-region have records of all the weapons they possess, and thus cannot detect when some disappear. Accounting for ammunition is even weaker, and sales of odd rounds supplement the meagre incomes of police and soldiers in many parts of the sub-region. Where soldiers and police cannot part with their weapons indefinitely, they may rent them to the very people they are meant

to be combatting.... These sales can occur across borders, as can be seen in seizures crossing from Guinea into Mali. Once stolen, the weapons and ammunition were transported to Mali in civilian trucks, often secreted under local produce. Malian Customs officials report having seized Kalashnikov-pattern assault rifles, PK-pattern machine guns, RPG-7 rocket launchers and various types of ammunition.

While corrupt officials who collude with smugglers or jihadists or both have become a viable source for the abundance of weapons in the public domain, the conquest of military bases by militants was an even more potent source. Remembering that Mali had a fractured army that was low in morale, records of lost battles at the hands of militants abound (see Harmon 2014: 177). Again, Marsh (2017: 82) argues that beyond 2013, arms from Libya were not the most important source sustaining the abundance of arms. He notes that:

> An analysis of tons of material seized by French troops based in Mali shows that the main source of arms and ammunition for opposition fighters was from the Malian armed forces. 'Each' defeat of the Malian army allowed the opposition forces to seize arms depots abandoned by the fleeing soldiers, and this started a cascade whereby each capture of weapons and ammunition strengthened the fighters and allowed them to capture more depots.

Marsh (2017: 83) holds that there is a third factor fuelling proliferation of arms in Mali. He contends that when French intervention stemmed the rebel capture of Mali military bases, and intercepted trafficking from Libya, the various militia were compelled to raise funds and purchase arms from illicit regional markets. One of such markets is in Gao, and guns from the cold war era (still preferred two decades later) and newer ones mostly of Chinese manufacture are common items (see UNODC, n.d.).

Therefore, the "Qaddafi factor" was a major contributor to the proliferation of SALWs in Mali from 2011 to 2013, but beyond this period, the acquisition of weapons from the Malian security services, however procured, sustained the easy availability of these firearms with the country. This indicates that state failure, has been the larger culprit for the proliferation of firearms in Mali.

Conclusion

The opening remark of an *Al Jazeera* report states: "The crisis in the Sahel, particularly Mali, has presented ... a challenge unseen since the breakout of the war in the Western Sahara in the 1970s" (Zoubir 2012: 1). Mali is certainly descending into anarchy as the north and central regions are riddled with conflict as the state confronts Islamist militant groups, rival drugs and arms smuggling gang battle for control and relevance in the trade, and ethnic animosity builds and violent conflicts become more frequent between the Dogon and Bambara against the Fulani. The climate is rife for the proliferation of SALWs.

It is obvious that the issue of SALWs in Mali is a combination of local, continental and extra-continental forces. Getting the issue of local governance right will largely control the influence of the other two. The shortage of governance in the northern regions encouraged rebellion from neglected groups and allowed gun runners, drug smugglers and crime syndicates thrive and become influential in government. The later inclusion Islamic militants to this mix, and their strategy of plugging the gap in governance and commanding allegiance from local groups through the provision of basic amenities compounded the problem of the Malian government ever regaining control of this area. Putting all these factors into one pot was bound to brew weapons proliferation. With these factors already playing out in Mali's north, the porous borders of the country and its proximity to Libya ensured that the fallout from the deposition of Qaddafi was huge.

The influx weapons from Libya aided the rebellions of the insurgent Tuareg groups of the north that further destabilised Mali. It also made the availability weapons to Islamic militants in the country easy. And with the army of Mali fractured, each defeat suffered, added to the weapons arsenal of these insurgent groups. With these insurgents well-armed, taking sides in local conflict in order to spread chaos and further destabilise the country became possible. Consequently, the instability in the north of the country spread to the centre as the Islamic militants armed the Fulani herders. The argument is made that this would not have been possible had the government not initially taken sides through supporting the Dogon and Bambara (agrarian) ethnic groups in disputes with the Fulani. These feuds took on catastrophically violent dimension with the influx of SALWs through the support of the militant groups.

Mali now has to contend with crime syndicates from Central, North and West Africa, drug smugglers from South America and gun runners from as far flung places as China. With a government that is weak and seems content governing a fraction of its territory, SALWs proliferation in Mali is an issue to contend with today and for the long term. If the government of Mali is to fix this problem, they have to begin with their internal politics and policies.

REFERENCES

Akanji, O. O. (2019). Sub-Regional Security Challenge: ECOWAS and the War on Terrorism in West Africa. *Insight on Africa, 11*(1), 94–112.

Al Jazeera News. (2019, August 24). *Mali in Crisis: The Fight Between the Dogon and the Fulani.* https://www.aljazeera.com/programmes/talktojazeera/inthefield/2019/08/mali-crisis-fight-dogon-fulani-190822125317990.htm. Accessed 22 September 2019.

Alexander, Y. (2016, March). *Terrorism in North Africa and the Sahel in 2015.* Seventh Annual Report of the Inter-University Centre for Terrorism Studies.

Allen, N. D. F. (2013). Misreading Mali's Collapse: Governance, Foreign Aid, and Political Instability in Emerging Democracies. *Journal of Public and International Affairs, 24,* 7–28.

Ammour, L. (2013). *Capitalising on Conflict-Unresolution in North Africa and Sahel: Newfound Land Grabbing Opportunities for Jihadism*. Brussels: Studia Diplomatica, Egemont Institute. https://www.academia.edu/5326013/CAPITALIZING_ON_CONFLICT-UNRESOLUTION_IN_NORTH_AFRICA_AND_SAHEL_NEW FOUND_LAND_GRABING_OPPORTUNITIES_FOR_JIHADISM. Accessed 29 September 2019.

Bleck, J., & Michelitch, K. (2015). The 2012 Crisis in Mali: Ongoing Empirical State Failure. *African Affairs, 114*(457), 598–623.

Bøås, M. (2014). Guns, Money and Prayers: AQIM's Blueprint for Securing Control of Northern Mali. *CTC Sentinel, 7*(4), 1–9.

Bøås, M., & Torheim, L. E. (2013). The International Intervention in Mali: "Desert Blues" or a New Beginning? *International Journal, 68*(3), 417–423.

Boukhars, A. (2015, April) *Rethinking Security Across the Sahara and the Sahel*. FRIDE, Policy Brief. https://carnegieendowment.org/2015/04/08/rethinking-security-across-sahara-and-sahel-pub-59719. Accessed 18 October 2019.

Bourgeot, A. (1990, October–December). Identité Touarègue: De l'Aristocratie à la Révolution. *Études rurales, 120*, 129–162.

Cheref, A. (2012, July 25). Al Qaeda Allies Take Control After Tuareg Uprising in Mali. *The National*. https://www.thenational.ae/al-qaeda-allies-take-control-after-tuareg-uprising-in-mali-1.579688. Accessed 25 September 2019.

Cocodia, J. (2017). Nationalist Sentiment, Terrorist Incursions and the Survival of the Malian State. In C. Varin & D. Abubakar (Eds.), *Violent Non-State Actors in Africa: Terrorists, Rebels and Warlords* (pp. 49–75). Cham, Switzerland: Palgrave Macmillan.

Cocodia, J. (2018). *Peacekeeping in the African Union, Building Negative Peace*. London: Routledge.

Deiwiks, C., Cederman, L.-E., & Gleditsch, K. S. (2012). Inequality and Conflict in Federations. *Journal of Peace Research, 49*(2), 289–304.

Devon, D.-B. (2013, February 1). The Crisis in Mali: A Historical Perspective on the Tuareg People. *Global Research*. www.globalresearch.ca/the-crisis-in-mali-a-historical-perspective-on-the-tuareg-people/5321407. Accessed 16 September 2014.

Gold, R. (2013, February 13). Initiatives for Peace in Northern Mali in the 1990's—LessonsLearned. *A Contrario*. http://acontrarioicl.com/2013/02/13/initiatives-for-peace-in-northern-mali-in-the-1990s-lessons-learned/. Accessed 4 October 2014.

Hardy, R. (2019). Countering Violent Extremism in Sub-Saharan Africa: What Policy Makers Need to Know. *World Affairs, 182* (Fall), 256–272.

Harmon, S. (2014). *Terror and Insurgency in the Sahara-Sahel Region: Corruption, Contraband, Jihad and the Mali War of 2012–2013*. Surrey, UK: Ashgate.

Haugegaard, R. (2017). Sharia as 'Desert Business': Understanding the Links Between Criminal Networks and Jihadism in Northern Mali. *Stability: International Journal of Security and Development, 6*(1), 1–15.

Human Rights Watch. (2018, May 30). *Mali: Events of 2018*. https://www.hrw.org/world-report/2019/country-chapters/mali. Accessed 18 October 2019.

ICG (International Crisis Group) (2016, July 6). *Central Mali: An Uprising in the Making?* https://www.crisisgroup.org/africa/west-africa/mali/central-mali-uprising-making. Accessed 3 November 2019.

ICG (International Crisis Group). (2018a, December 13). *Drug Trafficking, Violence and Politics in Northern Mali*. https://www.crisisgroup.org/africa/sahel/mali/267-narcotrafic-violence-et-politique-au-nord-du-mali.Accessed 18 October 2019.

ICG (International Crisis Group). (2018b, June 12). *The Niger-Mali Border: Subordinating Military Action to a Political Strategy*. https://www.crisisgroup.org/fr/africa/west-africa/mali/261-frontiere-niger-mali-mettre-loutil-militaire-au-service-dune-approche-politique. Accessed 18 October 2019.

Jamestown Foundation. (2011, September 16). What the Tuareg Do After the Fall of Qaddafi Will Determine the Security Future of the Sahel. *Terrorism Monitor, 9*(35). https://www.refworld.org/docid/4e7861382.html. Accessed 8 October 2019.

Keys, D. (2013). *Mali: The History Behind the World's Newest Conflict. Aspen Institute Italia*. www.aspeninstitute.it/aspenia-online/system/files/inline/keys-ing_080413.pdf. Accessed 7 September 2019.

Kisangani, E. F. (2012). The Tuaregs' Rebellions in Mali and Niger and the U.S. Global War on Terror. *International Journal on World Peace, 29*(1), 59–97.

Kühne, W. (2013, August). West Africa and the Sahel in the Grip of Organised Crime and International Terrorism–What Perspectives for Mali After the Elections? Sicherheit Und Frieden (S F) / Security and Peace, Policy Brief.

Kühne, W. (2014). West Africa and the Sahel in the Grip of Organized Crime and International Terrorism—Why the UN, EU and Germany Should Prepare for a Long Stay. *Sicherheit Und Frieden (S F) / Security and Peace, 32*(2), 113–118. Retrieved December 21, 2020, from http://www.jstor.org/stable/24234176.

Leboeuf, A. (2014, June). The Sahel States—Part of the Problem, Part of the Solution. In C. Barrios & T. Koepf (Eds.), *Re-mapping the Sahel: Transnational Security and Challenges and International Responses*. European Union Institute for Security Studies (Report No. 19). https://www.iss.europa.eu/content/re-mapping-sahel-transnational-security-challenges-and-international-responses. Accessed 5 October 2019.

Lode, K. (2002). Mali's Peace Process: Context, Analysis and Evaluation. *ACCORD*, Issue 13, 56–63.

Marsh, N. (2017). Brothers Came With Weapons: The Effects of Arms Proliferation from Libya. *Prism, 6*(4), 79–96. https://cco.ndu.edu/Portals/96/Documents/prism/prism_6-4/6-Marsh.pdf?ver=2017-05-12-110302-900. Accessed 13 October 2019.

Maylie, D., & Hinshaw, D. (2011, November 12). Alarm Over Smuggled Libyan Arms: Weapons Flow Amplifies al Qaeda Fears, Says Niger Leader; Clash With Traffickers. *The Wall Street Journal*. https://www.wsj.com/articles/SB10001424052970203537304577031892657376080. Accessed 6 April 2019.

Meredith, M. (2006). *The State of Africa: A History of Fifty Years of Independence*. London: Free Press.

Neelakantan, M. (2013, May 2). Creating Lasting Peace in Mali: Why Current Security Efforts Will Be Unsuccessful in Northern Mali's Conflict. *Foreign Policy Journal*. www.foreignpolicyjournal.com/2013/05/02/creating-a-lasting-peace-in-mali/. Accessed 10 May 2019.

Nichols, M. (2013, April 13). Libya Arms Fuelling Conflicts in Syria, Mali and Beyond: UN Experts. *Reuters*. https://www.reuters.com/article/us-libya-arms-un/libya-arms-fueling-conflicts-in-syria-mali-and-beyond-u-n-experts-idUSBRE93814Y20130409. Accessed 20 October 2019.

Patrick, S. M. (2013, January 29). *Collateral Damage: How Libyan Weapons Fueled Mali's Violence.* Council on Foreign Relations. https://www.cfr.org/blog/collateral-damage-how-libyan-weapons-fueled-malis-violence. Accessed 17 August 2015.

Rao, S. (2013, January 25). *Helpdesk Research Report: Conflict and Stabilisation in Mali and the Sahel Region.* Government and Social Development Resource Centre. https://issat.dcaf.ch/Learn/Resource-Library2/Policy-and-Research-Papers/Conflict-and-Stabilisation-in-Mali-and-the-Sahel-region. Accessed 14 September 2019.

Tandoğan, M., & Bouacha, Omar. (2017). The Algerian Security Approach Towards the Sahelian Region: Case of Mali. *Türkiyat Mecmuası, 27*(1), 305–325.

The Economist. (2019, July 3). *A New Round of Violence in Mali.* https://www.economist.com/the-economist-explains/2019/07/03/a-new-round-of-violence-in-mali. Accessed 18 October 2019.

Thomas-Johnson, A. (2013, June 13). What's Behind Mali Massacre and How to Stop Escalating the Violence. *Al Jazeera News.* https://www.aljazeera.com/news/2019/06/mali-massacre-escalating-violence-190613133110169.html. Accessed 22 September 2017.

UNODC (United Nations Office for Drug and Crime. (n.d.). *Firearms Trafficking in West Africa.* https://www.unodc.org/documents/toc/Reports/TOCTAWestAfrica/West_Africa_TOC_FIREARMS.pdf. Accessed 18 October 2019.

UNSC (United Nations Security Council). (2016). *Resolution 2322.* https://www.un.org/en/ga/search/view_doc.asp?symbol=S/RES/2322%282016%29. Accessed 22 September 2017.

Utas, M. (2012). Introduction: Bigmanity and Network Governance in African Conflicts. In M. Utas (Ed.), *African Conflicts and Informal Power: Big Men and Networks* (pp. 1–34). Uppsala, Sweden: Nordic Africa Institute; London and New York: Zed Books.

van Wieringen, K. (2018). *Building an Islamic State in the Sahel: The Case of Jihadist Governance in Northern Mali.* Netherlands: University of Utrecht.

Zoubir, Y. (2012, November 25). Algeria and the Sahelian Imbroglio: Preventing War and Fighting Terrorism. *Al Jazeera Report.* https://scholar.google.com/scholar?hl=en&as_sdt=0%2C5&as_vis=1&q=Algeria+and+the+Sahelian+Imbroglio%3A+Preventing+War+and+Fighting+Terrorism&btnG=. Accessed 22 September 2017.

Jude Cocodia is a Senior Lecturer and Acting Head of the Department of Political Science, Niger Delta University, Nigeria. He has a Ph.D. from the University of Nottingham, UK (2016). He is a recipient of the International Peace Research Association Foundation award and an Associate Fellow of the Higher Education Academy, UK (2016). He is the Secretary to the Nigeria Political Science Association South–South Zone. His research interests are in the areas of Peace, Conflict, Security and Democracy in Africa. His publications include *Peacekeeping in the African Union: Building Negative Peace* (Routledge, 2018). Outside academics, Jude worked with Everyone Counts International Charity, a London-based NGO as the Project Coordinator in Yenagoa, Nigeria (2011–2012) and London, UK (2013–2016).

CHAPTER 37

Nigeria: Militancy, Insurgency and the Proliferation of Small Arms and Light Weapon

Freedom Chukwudi Onuoha, Joachim Chukwuma Okafor, and Osinimu Osebeba Femi-Adedayo

Introduction

Since independence in 1960, Nigeria has leveraged its enormous human and material resources to promote regional peace, stability and integration, particularly in the West African subregion (Ogunnubi 2017; Seteolu and Okunye 2017; Odigbo et al. 2014; Ojakorotu and Adeleke 2017). In the last two decades, however, Nigeria's ability to play to its leadership strength and aspiration in Africa has tremendously declined (Lyman 2019; Sule et al. 2017). The outbreak of multiple violent security threats coupled with the failure of political leadership and governance has not only weakened the capacity of Nigeria to provide security within its territory, but also gradually draining its ability to contribute to regional peace and security. Notable among the violent threats are banditry, Boko Haram insurgency, kidnapping, armed robbery, cattle rustling, oil theft, militancy, communal conflicts, sea piracy, ethno-religious crisis, and herdsmen–farmer conflicts. A common denominator in

---

F. C. Onuoha (✉) · J. C. Okafor
Department of Political Science, University of Nigeria, Nsukka, Nigeria
e-mail: freedom.onuoha@unn.edu.ng

J. C. Okafor
e-mail: Chukwuma.okafor@unn.edu.ng

O. O. Femi-Adedayo
Centre for Strategic Studies and Research, National Defence College, Abuja, Nigeria

© The Author(s), under exclusive license to Springer Nature
Switzerland AG 2021
U. A. Tar and C. P. Onwurah (eds.), *The Palgrave Handbook of Small Arms and Conflicts in Africa*,
https://doi.org/10.1007/978-3-030-62183-4_37

the manifestation and exacerbation of these violent threats in Nigeria is the proliferation of small arms and light weapons (SALWs).

The media in Nigeria is awash with frightening reports of sophisticated SALWs seized by security operatives almost on a daily basis. For instance, it was reported that a total of 21,548,608 arms and ammunition were smuggled into Nigeria at the close of 2017 (Adenubi 2018). The intricate connection between proliferation of SALWs and prevalence of violent criminality is a thread in the web of insecurity in Nigeria. Although it is difficult to estimate the precise quantity of illicit SALWs circulating in Nigeria at any point in time, there is a consensus that SALWs proliferation has become both a cause and consequence of insecurity in Nigeria (Aghedo and Osumah 2015; Onuoha 2011). Nowhere is this nexus more evident than in the outbreak of militancy in the oil-rich Niger Delta and insurgency waged by the Boko Haram in the Northeast. These two forms of violent conflicts that manifest in two extreme parts of the country are draining Nigeria financially, materially and militarily.

This chapter, therefore, examines the dynamics of militancy in the Niger Delta, Boko Haram insurgency in the Northeast and proliferation of SALWs in Nigeria. Its main objective is to highlight how the nature of militancy and insurgency is connected with, and exacerbated by, proliferation of SALWs and how this feed into the "security crisis" that has engulfed Nigeria in the form of escalation of violent criminality. It will equally reflect on the various responses of the Nigerian government to the threat of militancy and insurgency vis-à-vis the proliferation of SALWs.

Conceptual Clarifications

Given the tendency for concepts to elicit varying interpretations in discourse like this, matters of conceptual clarification are pertinent. For the purposes of aiding clarity to the approach taken in this chapter, a working definition of the key concepts will be adopted.

Militancy

Militancy as a concept has continued to elicit different definitions, partly due to differences in the nature, operations, objectives and factors behind the emergence of such groups in a society. For instance, Akwash and Nweze (2013: 254) define militancy as "the use of terror by political thuggery as a means of overthrowing a government in power or of forcing that government to change its policies. All these could be manifested in the form of sabotage, assassination, kidnapping, etc." It is pertinent to mention that while state response to militant groups can lead the so-called militants to engage in extreme violence, it is doubtful if militancy is ever oriented towards overthrowing a government in power as implied in the above definition.

For the purposes of this chapter, militancy is defined as a form of organised struggle that combines disruptive agitation and violent acts embarked upon by a group in a region, community or enclave of a state to force authorities to address their professed demands concerning perceived or real instances of marginalisation, subjugation or exploitation over the nature and pattern of value appropriation in their society. Such resistant struggle may seek to achieve clear objectives of extracting concessions for the well-being of their community who they claim to be pursuing their interests. The cause of their violent mobilisation may be religious, political, ideological, economic, social or environmental. Unlike terrorism, the resort to violence in militancy is seldom indiscriminate and its ultimate motive is not to cause morbid fear. It also differs from insurgency in that militant actors do not overtly seek to govern a specific territory by overthrowing a regime or seceding from a state.

Insurgency

As with militancy, the term insurgency does not lend itself to a universally accepted definition. O'Neill (1990: 13), for instance, defines insurgency as a "struggle between a non-ruling group and the ruling authorities in which the non-ruling group consciously uses political resources (organisational expertise, propaganda, and demonstrations) and violence to destroy, reformulate, or sustain the basis of legitimacy of one or more aspects of politics". Although insightful, this definition overlooks the fact that insurgency seeks radical change to the existing political or social order through the use of sustained violence and political disruption.

Insurgency is seen here as "a protracted violent conflict in which one or more groups seek to overthrow or fundamentally change the political or social order in a state or region through the use of sustained violence, subversion, social disruption, and political action" (Moore 2007: 3). This definition clearly reveals the multifaceted character of insurgency. It posits that insurgency is a protracted struggle carried out through the application of sustained violence or subversion, to achieve the goal of undermining the legitimacy of government or replacing the existing power structure in a state. The ultimate goal of an insurgency is to challenge the existing government for control of all or a portion of its territory or extract political concessions in sharing political power. The Boko Haram insurgency fits into this conceptual frame. Although the group originally began as a non-violent Islamic sect, it over time transformed into a network of loose and flexible cells that conduct guerrilla and terrorist acts. Progressively, its insurgent silhouette manifested with the seizure and administration of several communities in the Northeast of Nigeria.

Proliferation of Small Arms and Light Weapons

The usage of the expression SALWs proliferation is ubiquitous in media, academic, policy and security circles. For all the attention that the concept has received, there is the absence of clear and universally accepted definition. To better comprehend what constitutes SALWs proliferation, it is logical to explain what is SALWs. An often-cited definition of SALWs holds that small arms include revolvers and self-loading pistols, rifles and carbines, sub-machine guns, assault rifles and light machine guns. Light weapons include heavy machine guns, hand-held under-barrel and mounted grenade launchers, portable anti-aircraft guns, portable anti-tank guns, recoilless rifles (sometimes mounted), portable launchers of anti-aircraft missile systems (sometimes mounted), and mortars of calibre less than 100 mm. Ammunition and explosives include cartridges (rounds) for small arms, shells and missiles for light weapons, mobile containers with missiles or shells for single-action anti-aircraft and anti-tank systems, anti-personnel and anti-tank hand grenades, landmines and explosives (UN Report of the Panel of Government Experts on Small Arms 1997).

Given the above understanding of SALWs, Ekemenah (2013) defines proliferation of SALWs as the illegal acquisition and circulation of arms and ammunitions of different types (usually small, light and medium) and from one degree to another (at the local, state or national scale). Proliferation of SALWs is defined here as a situation of heightened increase in the rate of illicit acquisition, transfer, circulation, storage and use of arms and weapons by individuals and groups within and across a geographic space with destabilising effects on peace, security, stability and development. At the centre of SALWs proliferation is the portability of these objects, making it possible for them to be easily acquired, transferred, concealed, maintained, stored and deployed by users. Thus, they can be easily transferred from one individual or group to another or transported from one location to another with very little chances of being detected. The very portability of SALWs significantly contributes to the ease of its availability, and the ease of its availability embolden disgruntled groups to take to violence or criminality in the form of militancy and insurgency. In turn, the modus operandi of militancy and insurgency feeds into the demand for SALWs which precipitates SALWs proliferation, especially in states with lax laws, weak security establishments, porous borders and corrupt institutions.

Militancy in the Niger Delta and the Proliferation of Small Arms and Light Weapons

Since crude oil was first discovered in Oloibiri in 1956, the Niger Delta region has played a pivotal role in the politics, economics and security of Nigeria. Geopolitically, the region comprises nine states of southern Nigeria: Abia, Akwa-Ibom, Bayelsa, Cross River, Delta, Edo, Imo, Ondo and Rivers. The region's estimated 37.2 billion barrels of proven oil reserves and 188 trillion standard cubic feet of natural gas are the largest hydrocarbon deposits in Africa (Onuoha 2016a). Despite the vast wealth created by its petroleum, however, much of the Niger Delta region is characterized by widespread poverty, youth unemployment, political underrepresentation and environmental degradation. These forces have contributed to recurrent outbreaks of violence in the region.

Since the precolonial period, the region has witnessed a series of conflicts in the form of protests by indigenous people demanding compensation as well as control of the oil wealth. It is pertinent to remark here that resistant movements and violent mobilisation in the Niger Delta have a long-standing history, dating back to the 1960s when Isaack Adaka Boro formed his Niger Delta Volunteer Force that declared the Niger Delta Republic on February 23, 1966. Since then, protests over environmental degradation caused by oil industry and marginalisation of the region by the Nigerian state have trailed the region (Onuoha 2008). For instance, in October 1990, the Ogoni Bill of Rights was presented to the Nigerian government and people. The Ogoni Bill of Rights among other things demanded for the right to use a fair proportion of the economic resources in Ogoni land for its development and the right to protect their environment. In October 1999, the Movement of the Survival of the Ijaw Ethnic Nationality in the Niger Delta (MOSIEND) also presented the Izon people charter which among other things demanded for the right of the Ijaw to control their natural resources. On December 1998, a meeting held by Ijaw youths in Kaiama, Bayelsa state, established the Ijaw Youth Council (IYC) and made the famous Kaiama Declaration. The ten-point resolution in the Declaration, among other things, asserted the right of the Ijaw people to ownership and control of their lives and resources, affirming that:

> All land and natural resources (including mineral resources) within the ijaw territory belong to ijaw communities and are the basis of our survival. We cease to recognize all undemocratic decrees that rob our people/communities of the right to ownership and control of our lives and resources, which were enacted without our participation and consent. These include the Land Use Decree and the Petroleum Decree, among others. (Kaiama Declaration 1998)

The Kaima Declaration by the IYC marked a curtain raiser in organised agitation for the control of, and access to, oil resource of the Niger Delta. It heralded threats by youths to shut down all oil wells in Ijaw land and called on companies to suspend further business relations with the State and Federal Governments over the issue of oil exploitation and its related consequences for the environment. The main aim of the agitators was to own, control and manage the mineral resources, especially oil, found in the Niger Delta in a manner that preserves their environment. This demand led to a confrontation between activists and Multinational Oil Companies operating in the region as well as the Federal Government. The struggle which started as a peaceful protest metamorphosed into armed conflict few years after the killing on November 10, 1995 of a renowned activist and playwright in the region, Ken Sara-Wiwa and eight other Ogoni men leading the struggle for environmental justice in the region.

Following the return to democracy in 1999, a new wave of protests characterised by violent militancy began in 2003. Violence during this period grew out of the political campaigns in 2003 (Ajodo-Adebanjoko 2017). As they competed for office, politicians in Rivers State manipulated the Niger Delta Vigilantes (NDV), led by Ateke Tom, and the Niger Delta People's Volunteer Force (NDPVF), led by Alhaji Asari Dokubo. They used these groups to advance their aspirations, often rewarding gang members for acts of political violence and intimidation against their opponents (Ajodo-Adebanjoko 2017; Bekoe 2005). State-orchestrated campaign against the NDPVF led to the arrest of Asari Dokubo in 2005 for treason. The vacuum created by his arrest gave rise to the emergence of other groups like the Movement for the Emancipation of the Niger Delta (MEND), Martyrs Brigade, Niger Delta Freedom Fighters (NDFF), Niger Delta Militants (NDM) and the Coalition for Militant Action (COMA) in the Niger Delta, among others (Onuoha 2008).

Mr. Dokubo was arrested in 2005 after he declared in a newspaper interview that the Niger Delta should secede from the Nigerian federation. While in detention, these new militant groups began to make various demands which included, among others, the unconditional release of Asari Dokubo; payment of compensation for protracted years of environmental degradation; upward review of the 13% derivation to oil-bearing communities to 50%; provision of employment opportunities for the youth from the region; and the provision of infrastructural facilities. These tensions erupted into violent armed struggle in 2006 when militants began bombing of critical oil installations, kidnapping expatriate oil workers, engaging in oil theft and gunfight with security forces (Onuoha 2008). To compel government to heed to their demands, these groups embarked on sabotage of oil installations (including pipeline vandalisastion), guerilla warfare and kidnapping of foreign oil workers.

As shown in Fig. 37.1, year 2006 had the highest incidents with 2753

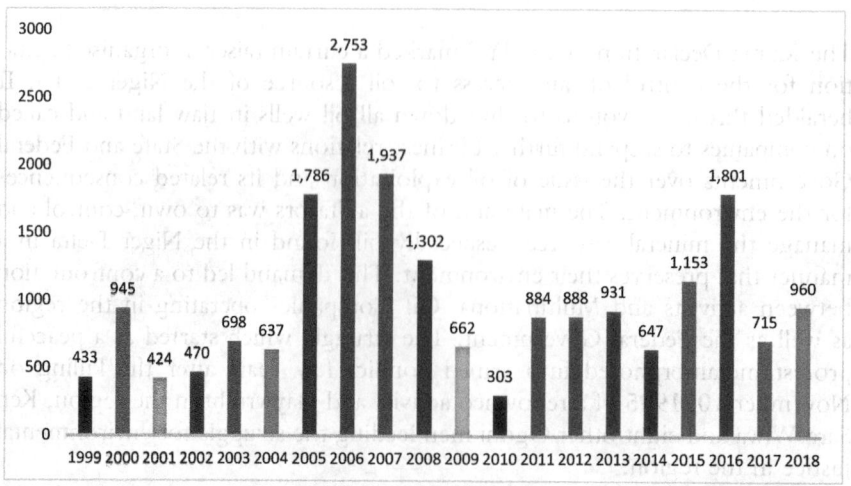

Fig. 37.1 Trend of pipeline vandalisation in the Niger Delta region, 1999–2018 (*Source* Authors' compilation from NNPC Annual Statistical Bulletin for the various years)

cases of oil pipeline vandalisation. This was followed by 2007 and 2016, with 1937 cases and 1801 cases, respectively. The high rate of pipeline vandalisation between 2005 and 2008 is directly related to the wave of insecurity in the Niger Delta that ensued from militant increased attacks in protest over the detention of Asari Dokubo. Another related factor was the emergence of more sophisticated groups like MEND, whose leader, Henry Okah, was arrested on gun-running charges in Angola in 2007 and then transferred to Nigeria but never convicted. The decrease in the level of vandalisation recorded between 2009 and 2010 is attributed to the granting of amnesty to militants on August 2009 by President Umaru Musa Yar Adua and the subsequent award of contracts to ex-militants for pipeline surveillance in the region. Notwithstanding, sporadic attacks continued into 2010 and increased from 2011 partly due to the arrest of Henry Okah in South Africa over links with the car bombing of the Nigerian Independence Day parade in Abuja that killed about 25 people. The high rate of pipeline vandalism recorded in 2015 and 2016 is not unconnected with President Mohammed Buhari's threat to terminate the amnesty programme as well as the cancellation of all pipeline surveillance contract on assumption of office in 2015 (this point is elaborated upon in later part of this section).

In the bid to sustain their violent onslaught on oil installations and security posts, militants acquired weapons through various means. For instance, militant groups traded stolen crude oil for sophisticated arms and ammunition around sea edges (Bestman 2007). These weapons are brought into the delta through Nigeria's porous maritime borders. Weapons in circulation in the region included pistols, revolvers, hunting rifles, craft weapons, pump-action shotguns and (light) machine guns such as Beretta 12S and AR-70, MAT 49, Sten MK 2, Czech Model 26 and Model 59 (Rachot), MG 36, Tokarev TT and Marakov PM pistols, AK-47, the German G3, the Belgian FN-FAL, the Czech machine guns and the Serbian RPGs, which mostly supplied by illegal dealers and sellers (Bestman 2007). These foreign made weapons contributed in swelling the underground market for weapons in Nigeria, and Warri became the "hub of the gun trade" in the Niger Delta (Ojudu 2007).

Some weapons available to militant groups come from local fabrication. Locally manufactured SALW is commonly used by armed groups in the Niger Delta, owing to the fact that they are generally less regulated and substantially cheaper than imported weapons sold on the black market (Duquet 2011). In July 2017, for instance, operatives of the Joint Task Force (JTF) in the Niger Delta code-named Operation Delta Safe, uncovered a local arms manufacturing hideout in Arhavwarien Kingdom in Ughelli South, Delta State. Items recovered from the arrested suspects included 13 short barrel local made guns, five double barrel local made guns, 10 locally made pistols, three live cartridges, one empty cartridge and two rounds of 7.62 millimetre special ammunition (Oyadongha and Erunke 2017).

In addition, a significant portion of weapons possessed by militants are acquired after attacks on police and military outposts. In June 2015, for instance, about 30 militants attacked the Marine Police Base at Eyo Edem Beach in Calabar, killing two policemen and looted the armoury. Sometimes when militants do not get arms forcefully by raiding security posts, they obtain it clandestinely through corrupt security personnel. Militants have historically been able to bribe their way into the pockets of unscrupulous state and security officials to receive or traffic weapons in the region. For example, a Major and five other soldiers of the Nigerian Army were convicted in November 2008 of selling over 7000 arms (valued at over N100 million) to the Niger Delta militants. These arms, including AK-47 rifles, GPMGs and ammunition boxes, were stolen from the depots of the Nigerian Army in Kaduna (Iriekpen 2008).

Successive Nigerian government responded to the wave of insecurity initially with the reinforcement of military operations and later with cosmetic development initiatives, like the establishment of development agencies or commissions as well as the Ministry of the Niger Delta. Efforts to contain explosive militant attacks on oil installations in the region failed until 2009, when then President Umaru Musa Yar'Adua offered amnesty, vocational training and monthly cash payments to nearly 30,000 militants, at a yearly cost of about $500 million (Onuoha 2016a). This amnesty exercise saw some 26,808 militants surrendering their arms and ammunition. Weapons recovered during the disarmament process included 2760 assorted guns, 287,445 ammunitions of different caliber, 18 gun-boats, 763 dynamites, 1090 dynamite caps, 3155 magazines and several other military accessories, such as dynamite cables, bullet-proof jackets and jack-knives. The large quantity of sophisticated arms and ammunition surrendered by Niger Delta militants in the amnesty programme revealed the alarming level of loose weapons in Nigeria.

The amnesty programme brought relative peace to the region, and petroleum exports increased from about 700,000 barrels per day (bpd) in mid-2009 to about 2.4 million bpd in 2011. Several ex-militant leaders such as Asari Dokubo, Gen. Ebikabowei "Boyloaf", Victor Ben, Ateke Tom and Government Ekpumopolo (alias Tompolo) were rewarded with lucrative contracts to guard pipelines. Despite the programme's early success, however, tensions resurfaced in June 2016, when President Muhammadu Buhari terminated the ex-militants' pipeline security contracts and commenced prosecution against the former militant leader, Tompolo, for contract fraud. President Buhari's government took over power in 2015 under the auspices of the All Progressive Congress (APC) after defeating the Peoples Democratic Party and upstaging the sitting President Goodluck Ebele Jonathan who hails from the Niger Delta and the first from the region to occupy the coveted seat. There were allegations that President Jonathan and his PDP government treated the Niger Delta militants with levity. President Buhari also cuts funding for the amnesty programme by around 70% in the 2016 budget, citing corruption.

With these developments, coupled with the government's ongoing failure to properly address local grievances in the Delta region, it was hardly a surprise when new militant groups emerged in 2016 with various demands. These include the Adaka Boro Avengers (ABA), Asawana Deadly Force of Niger

Delta, (ADFND), Concerned Militant Leaders (CML), Ekpeye Liberation Group (ELG), Joint Niger Delta Liberation Front (JNDLF), Niger Delta Avengers (NDA), Niger Delta Greenland Justice Mandate (NDJM), Niger Delta Red Squad (NDRS), Red Egbesu Water Lions (REWL) and Ultimate Warriors of Niger Delta (UWND), among others. Renewed attacks on oil installation by the NDA and other smaller groups contributed to the increase in the incidents of pipeline vandalisation in 2016 (see Fig. 37.1). The result is that oil production declined from 2.2 million barrels per day (bpd) to the two decades low of 1.4 million bpd (Onuoha 2016a).

President Buhari's administration initially responded with aggressive military operations with different code names such as *Operation Delta Safe*. The military operations vowed to use proportional force to dislodge criminals and militant groups threatening the peace and stability of the region. Several lives have been lost including those of militants and security operatives, as well as innocent civilians caught in the crossfire between militants and security forces. The military counteroffensive is taking place on water as well as land, leading to the destruction of militants' camps and recovery of weapons. For instance, the raid by soldiers of *Operation Delta Safe*, on militants camp at Saraba Creek in August 2019 led to the recovery of 9 AK-47 rifles; 20 AK-47 magazines; 3G magazines; 1 FN rifle; 4HK 21 MGs; 1 FN magazine; 1 container of gunpowder; 1 G3 MG; 3 GPMGs; 2 G3 magazines; 1145 rounds of 7.62 mm metal link; 2, 485 rounds of 7.62 mm ball cartons; 370 rounds of 7.62 mm special ammunition and 1356 rounds of 7.62 mm NATO (Utebor 2016).

While militarisation or sustenance of military deployments over the years have recorded modest achievement in the fight against pipeline vandalism, cultism and other criminal acts in the region, it has failed to restore sustainable peace in the region. The need for civil dialogue and constructive engagement has remained compelling. Therefore, in June 2016, President Buhari's administration began engaging the Niger Delta militants in talks in order to end the spate of destruction of crude oil facilities in the region. His combination of carrot and stick approach in the region has only served to maintain peace of the graveyard. Thus, the prevalence of SALWs and government's failure to address the root causes of SALWs proliferation appear to have given fillip to the sustenance of militancy in the Niger Delta.

BOKO HARAM INSURGENCY AND THE PROLIFERATION OF SMALL ARMS AND LIGHT WEAPONS

As the wave of militancy receded in the Niger Delta following the commencement of the amnesty programme in 2009, the tide of insurgency dramatically escalated in Nigeria's Northeast following a short-lived uprising by the Boko Haram Sect in July 2009. The group formally known as the *Jama'atu Ahlissunnah Lidda'awati wal Jihad* (People Committed to the Propagation of the Prophet's Teachings and Jihad), was then led by Mohammed Yusuf. The five-day confrontation resulted in the death of over 800 people, mostly members of the Boko Haram Sect. It ended on July 30, when the military captured the group's leader, Mohammed Yusuf, in his residence in Maiduguri and handed him over to the Police. Yusuf was later killed extrajudicially in Police custody (Onuoha 2010). The group, which promotes an extreme form of Islamist fundamentalism and opposes Western-style education, went underground and later adopted Yusuf's hard-line deputy, Abubakar Shekau, as their new spiritual leader.

Under Shekau's brutal leadership, the Boko Haram was transformed into a clandestine organisation that adopted the strategy of terrorism and insurgency from 2010 henceforth. It has sustained a deadly insurgency that overwhelmingly targeted civilians, earning it in 2014 the infamous title of the "world's deadliest terrorist organisation" (Institute for Economics and Peace 2015). In the Northeast region, Adamawa, Borno and Yobe States are the hardest hit by the insurgency, although the group has equally mounted attacks in other enclaves such as Bauchi, Gombe, Jigawa, Kaduna, Kano, Kogi, Niger, and Plateau States, and the FCT, Abuja. In 2014, Boko Haram emerged as a regional security threat, following its intensification of cross-border attacks in Cameroon, Chad and Niger. Later that year, it started taking control of territories in Nigeria's Northeast and proclaimed a caliphate in August 2014 (Ukwu 2014).

By early January 2015, the insurgents controlled about 20,000 square miles of territory in Nigeria—an area the size of Belgium. It hoisted its flag in 13 Local Governments in Borno State and several other towns and villages in neighbouring states of Adamawa and Yobe States. In March 2015, Shekau pledged allegiance to the Islamic State in Iraq and Syria (ISIS), effectively becoming the *Wilāyat al-Islāmiyya Gharb Afrīqiyyah* or Islamic State in West Africa Province (ISWAP). However, disagreement over doctrine, ideology, targets and tactics caused a major split in its leadership in August 2016, leading to the emergence of at least three factions (Onuoha 2016b). One faction still being referred to as Boko Haram is led by Abubakar Shekau. The other faction, the ISWAP, was initially headed by the ISIS-appointed Abu-Mus'ab al-Barnawi, the son of Mohammed Yusuf. There is speculation of the existence of a third faction led by Mummur Nur, although thought to align with the ISWAP group (Onuoha and Ugwueze 2020). However ISWAP's leadership has changed in the intervening three years. In 2018 an internal dispute reportedly led it to execute Nur, and in March 2019, it announced that Abu Musab had been replaced by another (albeit unrelated) al-Barnawi, Abu Abdallah (International Crisis Group 2019).

Irrespective of the schism within the terrorist organisation, the tactics employed by the factions are those of insurgency, terrorism and guerrilla warfare. Their violent tactics have evolved over time from poorly planned and open confrontations with state security forces to targeted assassinations, drive-by shootings, use of improvised explosive devices (IEDs), ambushes and raiding of military bases and remote communities. Boko Haram and the rival

ISWAP splinter group have shown the ability to mount well-coordinated and audacious attacks on civilian, military and humanitarian targets.

The SBM Intelligence (2019: 3) noted that at its peak in 2014, the Boko Haram insurgency saw an average of 25 attacks monthly. Since 2015, however, the group's attack rate has continued to decline. As shown in Fig. 37.2, the number of attacks rose in 2017, declined in 2018 and is obviously rising again in 2019. This fluctuation is influenced by several factors including but not limited to offensive military operations by Nigerian troops acting under Operation Lafiya Dole and the Lake Chad basin Multinational Joint Task Force (MNJTF), and the insurgents' tactics of withdrawing into enclaves to avoid military advances until pressure from government forces eases, after which the terrorists re-emerge to launch new attacks (SBM Intelligence 2019; Onuoha and Oyewole 2018).

Notwithstanding, a factor of notable significance in the group's violent attacks is their acquisition and use of sophisticated SALWs. It has been argued that Boko Haram fighters now have more sophisticated arms and weapons than the Nigerian military, including possession of sophisticated drones capable of giving them battlespace advantages (Mac-Leva and Ibrahim 2019; Searcey 2019). As with Niger Delta militants, the insurgents acquire such weapons through diverse channels, notably cross-border trafficking, looting of armouries, purchase from corrupt security forces and patronage of black market.

Cross-border trafficking entails the movement of arms and weapons across borders of sovereign States. In this wise, Boko Haram's access to sophisticated weapons is made possible by Nigeria's porous borders with Cameroon (1690 kilometres) in the east, Niger (1497 kilometres) in the north, Benin (773 kilometres) in the west and Chad (87 kilometres) in the Northeast. Most

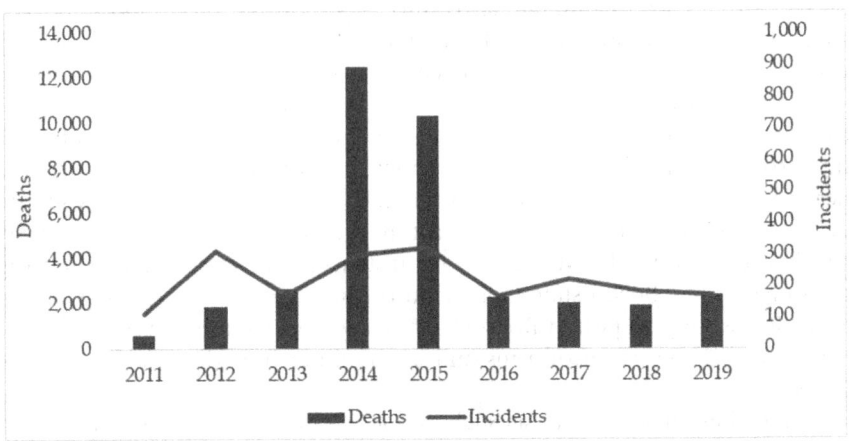

Fig. 37.2 Incidents and casualties from the Boko Haram insurgency, 2011–2019 (*Source* Allen 2019)

of these border areas are either mountainous, desert plains or in the jungle, while almost all are not clearly demarcated and easily penetrable without detection. The volume of traffic in contrabands and small arms is high and largely undetected. Irrespective of their geographic nature, a common feature of the nation's borders is its porosity. With over 1499 irregular (illegal) and 84 regular (legal) officially identified entry routes into Nigeria, criminal groups take advantage of this porous borders to smuggle SALWs into Nigeria (Ojeme and Odiniya 2013).

Cross-border arms trafficking increased in the wake of the Arab uprising or *Arabellion*. With the outbreak of the Libyan revolt, traffickers, mercenaries and terrorist groups acquired heavy weapons and transported them back to the Sahel region (see Chapters 8 and 35 in this Handbook). They were either surreptitiously obtained by posing as President Maummar Gaddafi's supporters or indirectly purchased from mercenaries who had acquired these arms from Libyan depositories. Libyan arms first obtained by Al Qaeda in the Land of Islamic Maghreb (AQIM) have been transferred to non-state armed groups such as Boko Haram, emboldening and enabling them to mount more deadly attacks. Thus, the audacity of Boko Haram grew with the proliferation of weapons in the Sahara-Sahel region.

The porous borders in Adamawa, Borno and Yobe States make it possible for the insurgents to acquire and smuggle SALWs into Nigeria. In Adamawa State, there are about 25 illegal routes into Nigeria from neighbouring countries. Also, Maiduguri-Damaturu axis, Gomboru-Bama corridor and Abadam-Baga corridor have over 250 routes that have link with the Republic of Cameroon, Chad and Niger (Oliver 2014; Musa 2013). Smuggling networks in these axes and corridors who are familiar with the terrains serve as the agents for the smuggling of assorted materials including SALWs. In addition to patronising the elaborate smuggling networks, Boko Haram has been able to rely on its own devises to smuggle arms into Nigeria using these poorly policed routes, adopting various concealment methods such as the use of specially crafted skin or thatched bags attached to camels, donkeys and cows where arms are concealed and moved across the borders. Its members are known to connive with corrupt state officials and merchants involved in cross-border trade to help stuff their arms and weapons in goods that are transported via heavy trucks, trailers and lorries. Given the huge size of the goods loaded on these vehicles, very little or no scrutiny is conducted on them by security and border officials. In May 2013, for instance, military forces arrested top personnel of the Borno state Command of the Nigeria Customs Service, for allegedly assisting suspected Boko Haram insurgents to smuggle several trucks loaded with large cache of arms and ammunition into the country (Kwaru 2013).

The raiding of security posts such as police and military bases to loot their armoury is also a notable source of weapons acquisition. Data in Table 37.1 vividly illustrate that each time Boko Haram and ISWAP overpowered a

Table 37.1 Some reported cases of Boko Haram attacks and looting of security posts in Nigeria

Date	Location	Security post attacked	Nature of weapons looted
September 4, 2019	Gajiram (Borno State)	A military base in Gajiram and Police divisional headquarter in the Lake Chad area	The ISWAP captured six four-wheel drive vehicles, cache of weapons and ammunitions, a military pickup truck, four-wheel drive trucks, an armoured car, an armoured personnel carrier and large transport truck
August 14, 2019	Gubio (Borno state)	Nigerian Army base at Gubio	The ISWAP fighters captured 4 technical vehicles, a mortar gun, an artillery piece and an Otokar Cobra armoured vehicle
June 12, 2019	Kareto (Borno state)	Nigeria Army's 158th Battalion stationed at Kareto	Heavy military equipment such as gun trucks, rocket launchers were looted by the insurgents
May 22, 2019	Gubio (Borno State)	Nigerian Army base at Gubio	The insurgents made away with a crew-cab type pickup truck, 2 dozen assault rifles, one rocket-propelled grenade launcher, 3 machine guns and 20 ammunition boxes
April 27, 2019	Biu (Borno State)	Mararrabar Kimba Army base	The insurgents looted some heavy machine guns and 3 armoured personnel carriers
March 27, 2019	Miringa (Borno State)	Miringa Military base	The insurgent carted away 2 armoured personnel carriers, cache of weapons and ammunitions

(continued)

Table 37.1 (continued)

Date	Location	Security post attacked	Nature of weapons looted
January 24, 2019	Geidam (Yobe State)	81 Division Task Force Brigade in Jilli, near Geidam,	The insurgents took hold of 2 armoured tanks, 5 four-wheel drive vehicle and cache of weapons and ammunitions
November 18, 2018	Metele (Borno State)	An Army base in Metele	The insurgents burnt down the Army base and carted away two T-72 tanks, 2 armour personnel carriers, 2 gun trucks, armoured tanks and cache of weapons in the base
November 18, 2018	Gajiram (Borno State)	An Army base at Gajiram	A Military truck was captured by the insurgents
December 26, 2018	Baga (Borno State)	A Naval base and a Multinational Joint Task Force (MNJTF) outpost in the fishing town of Baga	The Boko Haram insurgents carted away many gun trucks, multiple rocket launchers, cache of weapons, equipment and vehicles

Source Compiled by the authors

military base, they seized caches of assault rifles, thousands of rounds of ammunition and military grade weapons which they often use in later attacks. In the case of attack on Metele in November 2018, over 100 Nigerian soldiers were allegedly killed by Boko Haram insurgents who also carted away large stock of weapons. In its fight against Boko Haram, Nigeria's military has consistently appeared less equipped than its adversaries. However, there are suspicion that the insurgents often attack military bases when they receive new or upgraded weapons, stoking suspicion of sabotage. Thus, preventing unexpected battle losses of arms and ammunition to Boko Haram insurgents is now a major strategic concern for military authorities in Nigeria.

Another means the insurgents have used to obtain SALWs is buying from corrupt state security forces. Poor accountability and weak audit mechanisms have ensured pilfering and diversion of arms from military and police armouries in Nigeria. The role of corruption is not only evident in weak stockpile management, it is also manifest in the activities of some unscrupulous security personnel. Because corruption is endemic and systemic in Nigeria, some morally depraved officers sell arms to the insurgents. In September 2016, the military confirmed that some officers are selling arms and ammunition to Boko Haram, indicating the corruption bedevilling the country's counterinsurgency operations (VOA 2016). Hence, the connivance and complicity of state officials contribute to Boko Haram access to weapons and overall proliferation of SALWs.

In addition, Boko Haram is able to purchase weapons from arms traffickers operating within Nigeria. In July 2013, for example, an ex-Niger Delta militant, Anietie Etim and four others who allegedly specialised in buying arms in Bakassi Peninsula for supply to the Boko Haram insurgents were arrested by the Police (Okwe 2013). The gang carefully constructed a special tank in the booth of an Audi salon car where they conceal arms for shipment to the north. Conceivably, some of the earlier weapons used by Boko Haram, particularly AK-47, where sourced from the black market.

With the prevalence of violent criminality in almost every parts of Nigeria, weapons are readily available and in high circulation in the underground market. In 2017, for instance, it was estimated that the average cost of an illegally acquired AK-47 on the black market in Nigeria was about $1292 compared to Afghanistan where it could cost as little as $600 (see Fig. 37.3).

In the light of the foregoing, it is reasonable to argue that the Boko Haram insurgency festered because of the capacity of the group to acquire SALWs through clandestine means, in particular, smuggling and raid of military installations. In addition, SALWs constitute a weapon of choice because of the ease with which they can be acquired, carried and transported by militants. Finally, the culpability of state officials has enabled the Boko Haram Sect to gain access to steady stockpile of small arms. Thus, the state and its personnel constitute,

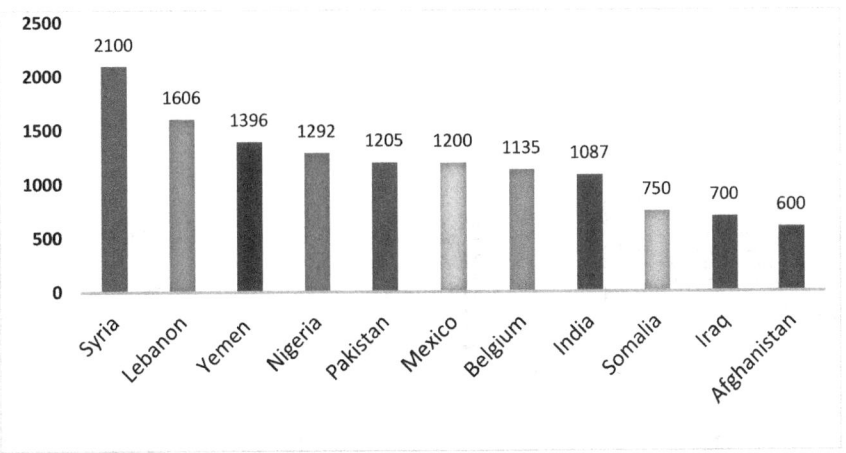

Fig. 37.3 Average cost of an illegally acquired AK-47 on the black market in US dollars (*Source* Adapted from Global Financial Integrity [2017: 14])

by default, *agent provocateur* in enabling Boko Haram to access SALWs, seize territory and sustain clandestine battle success.

Consequences of Militancy, Insurgency and Proliferation of SALWs

The consequences of militancy, insurgency and the proliferation of SALWs on Nigeria's national security are enormous. The obvious consequence of the triadic forces in Nigeria is depredation of human security. Although the problem of SALWs availability is not new, its proliferation in the last decade has helped stoke a wave of violent conflict and lubricate the wheels of crimes in Nigeria. As earlier noted, violent conflicts and crimes could be both causes and consequences of SALWs proliferation. When SALWs are used in violent conflicts and crimes human security is compromised, resulting in death, deformation, destruction and displacement of persons (Fig. 37.4).

SALWs proliferation has fuelled violence in different parts of Nigeria such as militancy and insurgency, leading to the prolongation of conflicts, forced population displacement, disruption of peace, devastation of livelihoods and emasculation of economic viability. In turn, the persistence of these armed violence feed into the dynamics of SALWs circulation in the larger society, perpetuating the cycle and culture of violence.

The ease of their availability played a huge role in the intensity and resurgence of militancy in the Niger Delta much as it has equally underpinned the audacity and resiliency of Boko Haram insurgency. A common outcome is the lethality of these spate of armed violence. While no fewer than 10,000 people

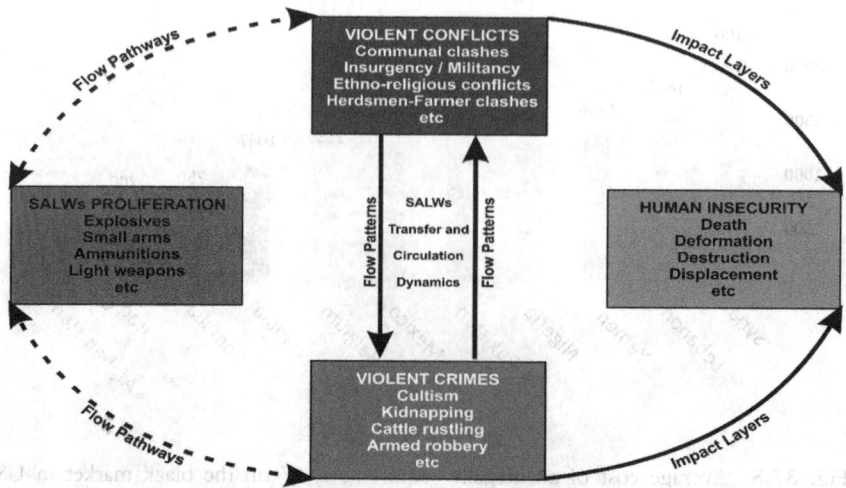

Fig. 37.4 SALWs proliferation, armed violence and human (in)security dynamics (*Source* Onuoha and Ezirim [2020: 76])

were killed in the Niger Delta crises between 1999 and 2007 (Isiguzo 2007), the decade-long insurgency by Boko Haram has killed some 30,000 people (Reuters 2019). It is important to note that not all the deaths were as a result of the use of SALWs.

As a result of militancy and insurgency as wells as other conflicts involving the use of SALWs, Nigeria is faced with the herculean task of responding to a fluctuating but always high number of internally displaced persons (IDPs). The United Nations High Commission for Refugees (UNHCR) estimates the Boko Haram insurgency has displaced 2.4 million people and put more than seven million at risk of starvation (UNHCR 2018). The full scale and impact of internal displacement in Nigeria are unclear, due to among other factors, poor methodologies of collecting and collating reliable data. Situations of forced displacement further undermine human security at the individual and community levels.

The impact on human security is also evident in material and financial losses associated with armed violence. For instance, Nigeria's oil production plummeted from 2.2 million bpd in 2014 to about 1.1 million bpd in May 2016 due to resurgence of militancy (Onuoha 2016a). Similarly, the Boko Haram insurgency has caused about $9 billion worth of damage in Nigeria (Ibukun 2016). The loss of property compounds the problem of poverty, deprivation and vulnerability of the affected population.

SALWs proliferation not only feeds into the dynamics of militancy and insurgency, but also sustains the intensity and lethality of other violent crimes that undermine human security in Nigeria. A recent compilation by Mac-Leva and Ibrahim (2019) of deaths caused by violent groups in Nigeria between January and September 2019 shows that Boko Haram killed 370, representing 16.70% of 1950 Nigerians killed in the last nine months. The report further showed that bandits killed twice as much (875 persons), which is equivalent to 47.50%. Cultists, armed robbers, kidnappers and other groups ended the lives of 705 (36.15%) in parts of the country (see Fig. 37.5). Familiarity with the modus operandi of these groups reveals that the possession of sophisticated SALWs is behind their brazen audacity. There is equally the challenge of fluidity and permeability of criminal livelihoods in the economy of violence in Nigeria. Cultists, pirates and hoodlums have in the recent past swelled the ranks of militants in the Niger Delta, much as it is very likely that bandits, armed robbers, kidnappers and cattle rustlers are within Boko Haram fold.

Furthermore, the proliferation of SALWs as both a cause and consequence of violent conflicts like militancy and insurgency has resulted in deep fracturing of kinship and family structures. Besides the direct physical harm often resulting in death, many more are left injured, permanently disabled and traumatised. The Boko Haram insurgency has turned thousands of women into widows, and has created over 75,000 orphans (Ibukun 2016). Thus, for every person killed or injured in conflicts and crimes involving the use of SALWs, there are many more who must cope with the psychological, physical and economic effects that endure in its aftermath.

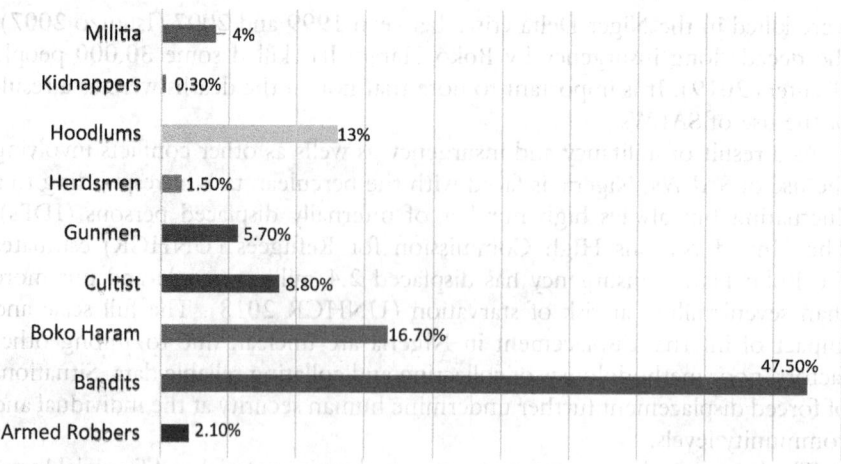

Fig. 37.5 Killings by violent groups in Nigeria, January to September 2019 (*Source* Adapted from Mac-Leva and Ibrahim [2019])

EFFORTS AT COMBATING MILITANCY, INSURGENCY AND THE PROLIFERATION OF SALWs

The prevalence of militancy and insurgency as well as their connections to SALWs proliferation is an enduring security challenge in Nigeria. The Nigerian governments have adopted strategic, legislative, prosecutorial, institutional, political and military measures to combat militancy, insurgency and the proliferation of SALWs in the country. These interventions are too numerous and space constraint does not warrant exhaustive treatment of them. But a few are worth highlighting.

In terms of strategic effort, the adoption of national strategic guidance documents reflects effort to take a holistic response to the wave of insecurity in Nigeria, including the threat of SALWs. The national security guidance documents encompass frameworks that help define the epistemic and textual conceptualisation of national security in Nigeria, including contemplating on the responsibilities of statutory apparatuses tasked with security provisioning. In relation to militancy, insurgency and SALWs proliferation, the National Security Strategy (ONSA 2014a) and National Counter Terrorism Strategy (NACTEST) stand out (ONSA 2014a, b). First published in 2014, the NSS is a guidance document which in broad terms, outlines the national security concerns of Nigeria and corresponding strategies to deal with them. The updated NSS (ONSA 2019: 10) clearly recognises that "proliferation of SALWs aid non-state actors like Boko Haram terrorists and armed bandits, while undermining state monopoly of instruments of coercion. The threats posed by proliferation of SALWs are of such magnitude that a security strategy which contemplates the monitoring of their flow and use is required". Also, the NACTEST (ONSA 2014b: 32) stipulates that the "the Nigerian government through the ONSA should develop a comprehensive border security system capable of tackling the recurring security challenges stemming from the porous borders of the nation". Inflow of SALWs from Nigeria's porous borders is one of the prominent challenges contemplated in this provision.

In relation to legislative and prosecutorial efforts, the Nigeria government enacted the Terrorism Prevention Act (TPA) 2011 (as amended) as legal framework for combating terrorism and activities of other violent groups that may adopt terrorist tactics (Federal Republic of Nigeria 2011, 2013). Some suspected militants and insurgents or their corroborators have been successfully tried and convicted against the provisions of this legislation. As at February 2018, for instance, more than 200 people have been convicted in Nigeria on charges related to their involvement with the Boko Haram (Reuters 2018). In order to limit criminal's access to SALWs, Section 9 of the TPA prohibits "the direct or indirect supply, sale and transfer of arms, weapons, ammunitions, military vehicles and equipment, paramilitary equipment, spare parts and related material, technical advice, assistance or training related to military activities" that will benefit violent non-state armed actors (VNSAs) such as militants, insurgents and terrorists.

Political approach to cubing militancy and insurgency vis-à-vis proliferation of SALWs have come largely in the form of amnesty programme and back-door negotiations with VNSAs. When it became obvious that militarised response to militancy has failed to guarantee stability in the Niger Delta region, President Yar'Ádua's administration resorted to the implementation of the PAP, which has a disarmament, demobilisation and reintegration (DDR) component. The initiative brought relative peace in the region, evidenced by sudden increase in the volume of petroleum exports from about 700,000 bpd in mid-2009 to about 2.4 million bpd in 2011. But the amnesty programme has failed to address the underlying causes of militancy which accounts for the resurgence of violence in the region. Yet, the experience of the Niger Delta has informed government efforts to negotiate with the Boko Haram insurgents for a similar amnesty. Several efforts to woo the insurgents into a negotiated settlement has failed, but a notable development is back-door negotiations that have led to the release of Boko Haram captives such as the abducted Chibok schoolgirls and Dapchi school girls in prisoner swap and ransom deals. Meanwhile ransom paid to these terrorist help to fund their operations, including the procurement of SALWs. Another intervention is the conception and delivery of rehabilitation programme for ex-Boko Haram militants under the Operation Safe Corridor programme. The defectors programme provides the only mechanism for Boko Haram fighters to leave the battlefield, but its implementation is fraught with several challenges (Onuoha 2020; Felbab-Brown 2018; Ogbogu 2016).

The military approach entails the use of kinetic or coercive apparatus of the Nigerian state in offensive, defensive and proactive postures to prevent, deter, pre-empt, repel and respond to the disruptive, subversive and destructive activities of hostile elements such as militants and insurgents. Successive Nigerian governments have deployed military operations with different code names against militants and insurgents, with a view to deterring, degrading and defeating them, including interdicting and neutralising their access to SALWs. Since the early 1990s, there have been sustained military deployments to achieve security in the Niger Delta region (Obasi 2005). For instance, the *Operations Hakuri I* and *Hakuri II* were set up in the late 1990s with the mandate of protecting lives and property—particularly oil platforms, flow stations, operating rig terminals and pipelines, refineries and power installations in the Niger Delta (Omeje 2006). In September 2003, a JTF code-named *Operation Restore Hope* was set up to deal with the conflicts in the region. This operation was later replaced with *Operation Pulo Shield*, launched on January 9, 2013. On 22 June 2016, the military scrapped the *Operation Pulo Shield* and replaced it with *Operation Delta Safe*. The operation was mandated to tackle the persistent security challenges in the Niger Delta region, including SALWs proliferation. Despite the sustenance of military operations and exercise such as *Operation Crocodile Smile* since 2017 in the region, there is recurrent incidents of oil theft, sea banditry and actual or threatened militant attacks on oil infrastructure. It is apparent that kinetic approach has not achieved the desired results, underpinning government continuation of the PAP beyond the five years initially slated for its termination.

As with militancy in the delta region, the Boko Haram insurgency has equally elicited aggressive military response from successive Nigerian governments. Starting with *Operation Flush* which was deployed to quell the July 2009 revolt, the government later deployed *Operation Restore Order* on June 8, 2011 to secure Maiduguri and check the frequency of attacks by the Boko Haram. However, as the insurgency grew in intensity and spread, *Operation Restore Order* was disbanded on May 15, 2013, and the operation transferred to the Nigerian Army and christened *Operation BOYONA*. Following a strategic review of the military operations in the Northeast and the creation of a new Division 7 of the Nigerian Army, *Operation BOYONA* was replaced with *Operation Zaman Lafiya* in August 2013. On July 19, 2015, the military launched *Operation Lafiya Dole* as a new codename to tackle activities of Boko Haram. Other operations were equally deployed to complement the kinetic responses such as *Operation Crackdown*, initiated in May 2016 to clear the remnants of the Boko Haram sect in Sambisa Forest and *Operation GAMA AIKI*, activated in June 2016 by the MNJTF to clear the insurgents operating in the northern part of Borno state (Iroegbu 2016). Notwithstanding these multi-pronged military operations, the insurgents have proven resilient as evidence by continued attacks on remote communities, humanitarian convoy, IDP camps and military bases in the Northeast.

These operations have so far not yielded the desired result of defeating the insurgents. In fact, they appear to have made the Boko Haram less monstrous in the eyes of the people. Consequently, of recent the government has focused attention on the utility of non-kinetic approach which involves dialogue and amnesty for repenting militants under "Operation Safe Corridor". It has equally resorted to back-door channel of negotiation and use of ransom payment and prisoner swap to secure the release of persons abducted by the insurgents. Like the military approaches, these measures have yielded minimal success.

Conclusion

The threat of militancy and insurgency have had a far-reaching impact on the economy, security, peace and development of Nigeria. Underpinning the scope and scale of devastation by these violent conflicts is the proliferation of SALWs. Although the proliferation of SALWs is not a direct cause of militancy and insurgency, it is nonetheless a factor in their intensity and longevity. It has equally fed into the lethality of other violent crimes in Nigeria with devastating impact on human security. The most important overarching result of this review is that porosity of borders and complicity of state actors are facilitating militants' and insurgents' access to SALWs. Militants and insurgents have also raided armouries of security forces to increase their weapon stockpile. Hence, breaking the vicious cycle of SALWs circulation remains a major challenge to peace and security in Nigeria.

Going forward, renewing the social contract between the Nigerian state and the citizens, especially in marginalised communities, should be prioritised by the government. This will require greater attention in addressing the development challenges confronting these marginalised communities by providing basic amenities such as road, potable water, affordable healthcare and employment opportunities. This will earn their support for the government. Thus, government at all levels—federal, state and local—need to strengthen institutions and processes of governance to enhance social provisioning for its citizens who are becoming increasingly frustrated over governance failure, thereby resorting to armed violence such as militancy and insurgency that stoke demand for SALWs.

The Nigeria government needs to evolve a new approach to border management, one that includes an integrated mix of installation of border situation awareness infrastructure, deployment of trained and dedicated border officials, and more importantly, execution of development interventions. In particular, border communities need to be accorded special attention through proper identification and implementation of targeted developments interventions to earn their goodwill in order to support government's efforts at combating criminality, including arms trafficking. In this way, these land and riverine communities that have for long been neglected by successive administrations will be empowered and integrated into the fight against criminality and trafficking of SALWs. Such development interventions will enable security and law enforcement agencies to gain the trust and confidence of border communities, thereby boosting their commitment to sharing information with security agents on activities along the borders.

Also, the Nigerian government should implement robust accountability mechanisms to block black market racketeering or arms leakages in the security sector. This would require conduct of regular and comprehensive verification exercises to ensure that government arms held by security and law enforcement officials do not slip into the hands of criminals. In addition, mechanisms for ensuring motivation and reward for committed security officers is as important as the imposition of stringent sanctions against depraved officers aiding and abetting arms smuggling. To this should be added the imperative of enhanced collaboration between security and intelligence agencies in the country and between them and their international counterparts to ensure effective tracking and interdiction of arms smuggling operations across national borders.

Furthermore, installation of high-tech electronic and surveillance equipment for security agencies at the nation's borders (land, sea and air) to maintain effective border domain awareness will assist in curtailing the nefarious activities of militants and insurgents. Beside national frontiers, government should invest in the procurement and deployment of powerful mobile scanners and surveillance gadgets in strategic high-ways for scanning mobile conveyances in order to detect and intercept arms, weapons and explosives trafficking. This will equally require bespoke capacity building for security agents to improve their awareness, skills and knowledge of border management as well as modus operandi of militants, insurgents and other criminals involved in arms trafficking. Training in intelligence collection, analysis and dissemination is equally critical in plugging leaky borders.

Measures to prevent weapons inflow should be marched with national efforts at mopping existing arms in circulation. The proposed establishment of a National Commission on the Control of Small Arms and Light Weapons (NatCom) should be fast-tracked to lead in this effort such that the NatCom can evolve a national arms control strategy (NACS) to guide the mopping up of SALWs circulation and mapping of local arms fabrication for effective regulation in the country.

REFERENCES

Adenubi, T. (2018). 21 Million Guns, Ammo Smuggled into Nigeria—Investigation. *Tribune*. http://www.tribuneonlineng.com/21-million-guns-ammo-smuggled-nigeria-investigation/. Accessed 6 January 2019.

Aghedo, I., & Osumah, O. (2015). The Insurgency in Nigeria: A Comparative Study of Niger Delta and Boko Haram Uprisings. *Journal of Asian and African Studies*, 50(2), 208–222.

Ajodo-Adebanjoko, A. (2017). Towards Ending Conflict and Insecurity in the Niger Delta Region: A Collective Non-Violent Approach. *African Journal on Conflict Resolution*, 17(1), 9–27.

Akwash, F., & Nweze, A. (2013). Terrorism, Militancy and the Nigerian State. In O. Mbachu & U. M. Bature (Eds.), *Internal Security Management in Nigeria: A Study in Terrorism and Counter-Terrorism*. Kaduna: Medusa Academic Publishing Ltd.

Allen, N. (2019). How Boko Haram Has Regained the Initiative and What Nigeria Should Do to Stop It. *War on the Rocks*. https://warontherocks.com/2019/12/how-boko-haram-has-regained-the-initiative-and-what-nigeria-should-do-to-stop-it/. Accessed 25 December 2019.

Bekoe, D. (2005). Strategies for Peace in the Niger Delta. *Peace Brief*. United States Institute of Peace. https://www.usip.org/publications/2005/12/strategies-peace-niger-delta. Accessed 6 June 2019.

Bestman, W. (2007). Weapons of War in the Niger Delta. *Terrorism Monitor, 5*(10), 8–10.

Duquet, N. (2011). Swamped with Weapons: The Proliferation of Illicit Small Arms and Light Weapons in the Niger Delta. In C. Obi, & S. A. Rustad (Eds.), *Oil and Insurgency in the Niger Delta: Managing the Complex Politics of Petro Violence* (pp. 136–149). London: Zed Books.

Ekemenah, A. (2013). National Security and the Menace of Weapon Proliferation in Nigeria. *BusinessWorld*. http://businessworldng.com/web/articles/284National-Security-and-the—Menace-of-Weapon—Proliferation\inNigeria/Page1.htm. Accessed 1 May 2014.

Federal Republic of Nigeria. (2011). *The Terrorism Prevention Act*. Abuja.

Federal Republic of Nigeria. (2013). *The Terrorism Prevention Amendment Act: Explanatory Memorandum*. Abuja.

Felbab-Brown, V. (2018, May). In Nigeria, We Don't Want Them Back. *Brookings*. https://www.brookings.edu/research/in-nigeria-we-don't-want-them-back/. Accessed 3 February 2019.

Global Financial Integrity. (2017). *Transnational Crime and the Developing World*. https://secureservercdn.net/45.40.149.159/34n.8bd.myftpupload.com/wp-content/uploads/2017/03/Transnational_Crime-final.pdf. Accessed 4 March 2018.

Ibukun, Y. (2016). Nigeria's Boko Haram Caused $9 Billion in Damage Since 2011. *Bloomberg*. https://www.bloomberg.com/news/articles/2016-04-04/nigeria-s-boko-haram-caused-9-billion-in-damage-since-2011. Accessed 9 May 2016.

Institute for Economics and Peace. (2015). *Global Terrorism Index*. New York: Institute for Economics and Peace.

International Crisis Group. (2019, May 16). *Facing the Challenge of the Islamic State in West Africa Province, Africa Report N°273*. https://d2071andvip0wj.cloudfront.net/273-facing-the-challenge.pdf. Accessed 10 June 2019.

Iriekpen, D. (2008, May 6). Revealed: Why FG Opted for Secret Trial of Okah. *Thisday*.

Iroegbu, S. (2016, September 11). With 10 Major Security Operations Across the Country, Military Stretched Too Thin. *Thisday*, p. 1.

Isiguzo, I. (2007, August 6). Niger Delta: One Story, Many Sides. *Vanguard*.

Kaiama Declaration. (1998). *Being Communique Issued at the End of the All Ijaw Youths Conference which Held in the Town of Kaiama this 11th Day of December 1998*. http://www.unitedijaw.com/kaiama.htm#Kaiama.

Kwaru, M. (2013, May 29). Boko Haram: Senior Customs Personnel Arrested Over Arms Importation in Borno. *Peoples Daily*.

Lyman, P. (2019, July 27). How Nigeria May Become a Strategic Failure to the World. *Thisday*.

Mac-Leva, F., & Ibrahim, H. (2019, September 22). Bandits Kill More Nigerians Than Boko Haram, Robbers, Kidnappers, Cultists, Others. *Daily Trust*. https://www.dailytrust.com.ng/bandits-kill-more-nigerians-than-boko-haram-robbers-kidnappers-cultists-others.html. Accessed 28 September 2019.

Moore, S. (2007). *The Basis of Counterinsurgency*. Joint Urban Operations Office, US Joint Forces Command.

Musa, S. (2013). *Border Security, Arms Proliferation and Terrorism in Nigeria*. http://saharareporters.com. Accessed 11 April 2014.

O'Neill, B. (1990). *Insurgency and Terrorism: Inside Modern Revolutionary Warfare*. Washington, DC: Brassey.

Obasi, N. (2005). The Military and Management of Conflicts in the Nigeria Delta. In A. G. Adedeji & I. S. Zabadi (Eds.), *The Military and Management of Internal Conflict in Nigeria* (p. 122). Abuja: National War College.

Odigbo, J., Udaw, E. J., & Igwe, A. (2014). Regional Hegemony and Leadership Space in Africa: Assessing Nigeria's Prospects and Challenges. *Review of History and Political Science*, 2(1), 89–105.

Ogbogu, J. (2016). Nigeria's Approach to Terrorist Rehabilitation. *Counter Terrorist Trends and Analysis*, 8(4), 16–21.

Ogunnubi, O. (2017). Effective Hegemonic Influence in Africa: An Analysis of Nigeria's 'Hegemonic' Position. *Journal of Asian and African Studies*, 52(7), 932–946.

Ojakorotu, V., & Adeleke, Adewole. (2017). "Nigeria and Conflict Resolution in the Sub-regional West Africa: The Quest for a Regional Hegemon? *Insight on Africa.*, 10(1), 37–53.

Ojeme, V., & Odiniya, R. (2013, June 19). Nigeria Has Over 1,499 Illegal Entry Routes—Interior Minister. *Vanguard*. https://www.vanguardngr.com/2013/06/nigeria-has-over-1499-illegal-entry-routes-interior-minister/. Accessed 24 June 2014.

Ojudu, P. (2007). Combating the Proliferation of Small Arms and Light Weapons in West Africa. In *Handbook for the Training of Armed and Security Forces*. Geneva: United Nations Institute of Disarmament Research (UNIDIR).

Okwe, J. (2013, July 27). Ex-Militant, 4 Others Arrested for Arms Supply to Boko Haram. *Thisday*, p. 57.

Oliver, G. (2014). *Arms Smuggling to Boko Haram Threatens Cameroon*. Retrieved from https://reliefweb.int/report/cameroon/arms-smuggling-boko-haram-threatens-cameroon. Accessed 2 December 2014.

Omeje, K. (2006). *High Stakes and Stakeholders: Oil Conflict and Security in Nigeria*. Aldershot: Ashgate.

ONSA (Office of the National Security Adviser, Nigeria). (2014a). *National Security Strategy*. Abuja: ONSA.

ONSA (Office of the National Security Adviser, Nigeria). (2014b). *National Counter Terrorism Strategy*. Abuja: ONSA.

ONSA (Office of the National Security Adviser, Nigeria). (2019). *National Security Strategy*. Abuja: ONSA.

Onuoha, F. C. (2008). The Transformation of Conflicts in the Niger Delta. In H. A. Saliu, I. O. Taiwo, R. A. Seniyi, B. Salawu, & A. Usman (Eds.), *Nigeria Beyond 2007: Issues, Perspectives and Challenges* (pp. 263–283). Ilorin: Faculty of Business and Social Sciences, University of Ilorin.

Onuoha, F. C. (2010). The Islamist Challenge: Nigeria's Boko Haram Crisis Explained. *African Security Review, 19*(2), 54–67.

Onuoha, F. C. (2011). Small Arms and Light Weapons Proliferation and Human Security in Nigeria. *Conflict Trends, 1,* 50–56.

Onuoha, F. C. (2016a). *The Resurgence of Militancy in Nigeria's Oil-Rich Niger Delta and the Dangers of Militarization Report* (pp. 1–9). Doha: Aljazeera Centre for Studies.

Onuoha, F. C. (2016b, October 27). *Split in ISIS-Aligned Boko Haram Group, Report.* Al Jazeera Centre for Studies.

Onuoha, F. C. (2020). Dilemma of Voluntary Surrender to State Security Forces by Boko Haram Recruitment in Nigeria. *African Journal of Terrorism and Insurgency Research, S1*(1), 199–218.

Onuoha, F. C., & Ezirim, G. E. (2020). Small Arms Proliferation. In C. Varin & F. C. Onuoha (Eds.), *Security in Nigeria.* London: Bloomsbury.

Onuoha, F. C., & Oyewole, S. (2018). *Anatomy of Boko Haram: The Rise and Decline of a Violent Group in Nigeria.* Doha: Al Jazeera Centre for Studies.

Onuoha, F. C., & Ugwueze, M. (2020). Special Operations Forces, Counter-Terrorism, and Counter-Insurgency Operations in the Lake Chad Area. In U. A. Tar & B. Bala (Eds.), *New Architecture of Regional Security in Africa: Perspectives on Counter-Terrorism and Counter-Insurgency in the Lake Chad Basin* (pp. 267–293). London: Rowman & Littlefield.

Oyadongha, S., & Erunke, J. (2017, July 4). Troops Uncover Local Arms Manufacturing hideout in Delta. *Vanguard.* https://www.vanguardngr.com/2017/07/troops-uncover-local-arms-manufacturing-hideout-delta/. Accessed 9 August 2018.

Reuters. (2018, February 19). *Nigeria Convicts 205 Boko Haram Duspects in Mass Trials.* https://www.reuters.com/article/us-nigeria-security/nigeria-convicts-205-boko-haram-suspects-in-mass-trials-idUSKCN1G3253. Accessed 6 July 2018.

Reuters. (2019, September 23). *Targeting Militants, Nigeria to Require ID Cards in the Northeast.* https://www.defenceweb.co.za/security/national-security/targeting-militants-nigeria-to-require-id-cards-in-the-northeast. Accessed 3 October 2019.

SBM Intelligence. (2019, October). *Stalemate: Boko Haram's New Strategy Means Fewer Attacks*.https://www.sbmintel.com/wp-content/uploads/2019/10/201910_Boko-Haram.pdf. Accessed 10 November 2019.

Searcey, D. (2019, September 13). Boko Haram Is Back: With Better Drones. *The New York Times.* https://www.nytimes.com/2019/09/13/world/africa/nigeria-boko-haram.html. Accessed 23 September 2019.

Seteolu, B., & Okunye, J. (2017). The Struggle for Hegemony in Africa: Nigeria and South Africa Relations in Perspectives, 1999–2014. *African Journal of Political Science and International Relations, 11*(3), 57–67.

Sule, S. A., Darshan, R. S., & Sani, M. (2017). The Influence of Leadership Personality on the Nigeria's Hegemonic Decline in West Africa. *The Social Sciences, 12*(2), 2293–2298.

Ukwu, C. (2014, August 25). Boko Haram Declares Gwoza Caliphate. *Daily Independent.* http://allafrica.com/stories/201408251173.html. Accessed 28 September 2014.

UN Report of the Panel of Government Experts on Small Arms. (1997). https://www.sipri.org/sites/default/files/research/disarmament/dualuse/pdf-archive-att/pdfs/un-report-of-the-panel-of-governmental-experts-on-small-arms.pdf. Accessed 4 January 2018.

United Nations High Commission on Refugees. (2018, February 1). *UNHCR and Partners Seek US$157 Million to Aid Boko Haram Displaced*. https://www.unhcr.org/5a7184f34.html. Accessed 4 May 2019.

Utebor, Simon. (2016, August 24). JTF Kills Two Avengers, Arrests Three Militants. *Punch*.

Voice of America. (2016, September 4). *Nigerian Military: Some Officers Selling Arms to Boko Haram*. https://www.voanews.com/africa/nigerian-military-some-officers-selling-arms-boko-haram. Accessed 14 June 2017.

Freedom Chukwudi Onuoha is Senior Lecturer in the Department of Political Science, University of Nigeria, Nsukka. He is also the Coordinator of the Security, Violence and Conflict (SVC) Research Group at the University. Prior to joining the University, Dr. Onuoha worked for over a decade as a Research Fellow at the Centre for Strategic Research and Studies, National Defence College, Nigeria. Dr. Onuoha received his Ph.D. from the University of Nigeria, Nsukka, with specialty in political economy. He has published extensively in the broad area of security and strategic studies, covering diverse subject as terrorism, maritime security, radicalisation, violent extremism, kidnapping, civil-military relations, infrastructure protection, election and globalisation, among others. His recent co-edited books include *Security in Nigeria: Contemporary Threats and Responses* (Bloomsbury, 2020) and *Internal Security Management in Nigeria: Perspectives, Challenges and Lessons* (Palgrave Macmillan, 2019).

Joachim Chukwuma Okafor is Lecturer in the Department of Political Science, University of Nigeria, Nsukka, and a doctoral student in International Relations with research interest in Global Environmental Governance, Peace, Security and Strategic Studies, Governance, Foreign Policy Analysis, Energy Politics and International Political Economy. He obtained his B.Sc. degree from Ebonyi State University, Abakaliki, and M.Sc. degree from University of Ibadan, Nigeria. He has published widely in reputable journals and books.

Osinimu Osebeba Femi-Adedayo is a Research Fellow with the Centre for strategic Research and studies, National Defence College, Abuja. She is a graduate of English Language and International studies from Benue state University Makurdi, Benue State and Nigerian Defence Academy, Kaduna, respectively. Her research interests include but not limited to Conflict Analysis and Management. Other area of interest centre around leadership structure, nation building and Governance.

CHAPTER 38

Niger Republic: Small Arms and Asymmetric Warfare in a Volatile Neighborhood

David Omeiza Moveh

INTRODUCTION

The proliferation of small arms and light weapons (SALWs) have posed serious threats to security and stability in Africa; as they have over the years been the primary tools and enablers of violence and conflict on the continent. While in conflict situations, SALWs are often used to commit a wide range of human rights violations, including mass killings, forced displacements, gender-based violence, and attacks on peacekeepers and humanitarian workers, SALWs have also aggravated intercommunal conflict and competition over natural resources, as well as a wide range of criminal activities and new forms of asymmetric warfare in Africa. Since the early 2000s, SALWs have significantly contributed to the expanding ambitions, and capacities of insurgent and terrorist groups in most parts of Africa. Indeed, with the increasing activities of terrorist groups such as AL Qaeda in the Islamic Maghreb (AQIM), Islamic State and Boko Haram, as well as the emergence of counterterrorist operations such as the Sahel G5, the Multinational Joint Task Force (MNJTF), the Sahel region has for instance become a theater of globalized security concerns where the traditional lines between domestic and foreign affairs have increasingly become blurred.

The republic of Niger is significantly implicated in a dyad of SALWs proliferation and asymmetric warfare in the form of terrorism and counterterrorism;

D. O. Moveh (✉)
Department of Political Science and International Studies, Ahmadu Bello University, Zaria, Nigeria

© The Author(s), under exclusive license to Springer Nature Switzerland AG 2021
U. A. Tar and C. P. Onwurah (eds.), *The Palgrave Handbook of Small Arms and Conflicts in Africa*,
https://doi.org/10.1007/978-3-030-62183-4_38

such that the country has become a key western counterterrorist ally. Apart from hosting French troops as part of its Trans Sahara Counter-Terrorism Initiative, the United States built a $100 million drone base in Niger in 2017 to monitor and respond to terrorist activities across the Sahel. Similarly, Germany also built a military outpost in Niger to support the U.N. mission in Mali. Yet, in spite of the increasing international counterterrorist initiatives in the country, Niger continued to record terrorist attacks largely from groups operating from without, particularly along its western and southern borders. Indeed, the increasing "externalities" of terrorism confronting Niger resulted in the United Nations Development Program's (UNDP) categorization of the country as one of the "spill over" countries for conflicts from neighboring countries like Mali and Nigeria.

This chapter examines the externalities of terrorism and counterterrorism in Niger within the dyadic context of SALWs proliferation and asymmetric warfare. Two major features to the externalities of terrorism and counterterrorism in Niger are identified and elaborated on. First, the chapter demonstrates that most of the terrorist acts in Niger, particularly; from 2012 have been from terrorist groups based in neighboring countries which have taken advantage of the porous borders and access to SALWs to regroup and recruit new members. Secondly, it is also noted that given the transnational nature of terrorism in the Sahel as a whole, the counterterrorist responses adopted in Niger have essentially involved international partnerships as well as membership of regional multinational counterterrorist commands: Sahel G.5 and the Multinational Joint Task Force against Terrorism. The chapter is divided into six sections. Following this introduction is an examination of the concepts and dyad of SALWs proliferation and asymmetric warfare. The third section examines the concepts of terrorism and counterterrorism as a typical example of asymmetric warfare. In the fourth section, the security dilemma engendered by the proliferation of SALWs and asymmetric warfare in Niger is examined, while the fifth section examines the nature of the externalities of terrorism and counterterrorism in Niger. Lastly, the sixth section is the conclusion of the chapter.

SALWs and Asymmetric Warfare: A Dyadic Context

SALWs and asymmetric warfare have become central issues in the fields of international politics, strategic studies and peace and conflict management; particularly, in the post-Cold War era. Indeed, with the end of the Cold War, traditional interstate wars have increasingly given way to internal and asymmetric conflicts across the globe; and these conflicts have been fueled essentially by illicit or poorly regulated arms sales. The African Union (AU) and Small Arms Survey-SAS (2019), for example notes that "while the causes of conflicts in Africa as a whole and the factors driving them have changed, the use of SALWs has been a common feature of these conflicts." Hence, the germane question of what constitutes SALWs, and how they influence conflicts has attracted political and scholarly attention.

The term small arms is often used conterminously with light weapons in the description of weapons designed for individual use. According to the United Nations (1997) small arms are those weapons that can be carried by an individual for personal use, and light weapons are those designed for use by several persons serving as a crew. They include, inter alia, revolvers and self-loading pistols, rifles and carbines, sub-machine guns, assault rifles and light machine guns. Thus, what is generally understood as SALWs is determined essentially by the criterion of portability. That is, weapons that are portable for use by an individual or a small group of individuals.

Available data on SALWs show that out of the 640 million circulating globally, an estimated 100 million are found in Africa with about 30 million in sub-Saharan Africa and eight million in West Africa (*The Guardian* 2018). Most of these arms were shipped to Africa during the Cold War to equip anti-colonial fighters, newly independent states and superpower proxy forces alike. The collapse of the Soviet Union also resulted in a new flood of SALWs entering Africa as manufacturers put additional millions of surplus Cold War-era weapons on the international arms market at cut-rate prices. Furthermore, SALWs have also been seized or stolen from government forces or looted from state armories. A wide range of locally manufactured SALWs such as pistols and Improvised Explosive Devises (IEDs) are also an essential part of the SALWs in circulation in Africa. Boko Haram has for example severally carted away arms after attacking the military bases in Nigeria and Niger. The group is also known to have had a base in Bauchi state, Nigeria where they manufacture IEDs. By 1999, the Red Cross estimated that in the Somali capital of Mogadishu alone, the city's 1.3 million residents possessed over a million guns. Similarly, in July 2001 the US government estimated that SALWs are fueling conflicts in 22 African countries that have taken 7–8 million lives. Thus, since the end of the Cold War, SALWs and asymmetric warfare have become dyadic. Indeed, the fact that SALWs are relatively cheap, easy to handle, transport and conceal have made them attractive for irregular warfare, terrorism, and criminal activities.

The proliferation of SALWs and the escalation of asymmetric warfare is a major feature of the security challenges confronting Africa in general and Niger republic in particular. These conflicts essentially in the form of terrorism and counterterrorism, and other forms of insurgent activities are asymmetrical in the sense that they are characterized by an imbalance in the military capacity of warring parties and the increasing involvement of non-state entities. Asymmetric warfare is thus, a war between belligerents whose relative military power and strategy or tactics differ significantly. It is typically a war between a standing professional army and a terrorist organization, an insurgency, a militia, or resistance movement who often have the status of unlawful combatants. Thus, while African states and their western allies have continued to leverage on a military industrial complex, terrorist organizations and other unconventional belligerent groups have taken advantage of the proliferation of SALWs to engage in an asymmetric warfare by unleashing attacks against civilians and state establishments.

It is also noteworthy that the dyad of SALWs and asymmetric warfare tend to be cyclical. Unlike heavy weapons systems, which can be costly to acquire and operate and comparatively easy to decommission and monitor, the end of a war does not necessarily bring an end to the use of SALWs. Indeed, "the durability of SALWs ensures that once they are present in a country they present a continuous risk; especially in societies where there are large accumulations of weapons. They frequently outlast peace agreements and are taken up again in the post-conflict period" by criminal gangs, vigilantes, dissidents, and individuals concerned about personal security (Muggah and Bachelor 2002). Hence, the need for deliberate programs on disarmament.

In spite of the consensus that SALWs have been central in the prosecution of post-Cold War conflicts, changes in the level of arms proliferation and level of conflicts have not been perfectly correlated. Indeed, theories on the dyadic relationship between SALWs proliferation and asymmetric warfare are yet to be fully developed. However, revisions of the security dilemma theory provides a useful context for the understanding of this dyad. The security dilemma theory in international relations describes a relationship between two or more actors; where a mutual mistrust and fear of each other's military motives may exacerbate or even cause a state of military tension which may escalate into war. The concept of security dilemma was first used by Herz (1951) in reference to a "structural notion in which the self-help attempts of states to look after their security needs results in rising insecurity for others; as each interprets its own measures as defensive and the measures of others as potentially threatening". "Security dilemma" was particularly useful in explaining the arms race between the US and the Soviet Union during the Cold War. Proponents of the security dilemma theory argue that the concept of security dilemma is not necessarily tied to a specific historical era. Instead, they suggest that it reflects the fundamental nature of international life where state actors strive for peace and stability but end up in military conflict. While the concept of security dilemma developed within the context of interstate relations, the theory has been successfully applied in intrastate conflicts. Posen (1993) for example asserts that the way anarchy promotes security dilemma dynamics in the international arena is the same way it is relevant to intrastate conflicts: "An emerging anarchy grows within the state putting sub-state factions in the same dilemma as states in the international system" (Posen 1993: 24). Similarly, Hill (2004: 14) argues that the anarchical intrastate milieu can probably be even more delicate than the international because individuals are more susceptible in relation to states. Indeed, the preponderance of "non-state internal security threats" which have been characteristic of the post-Cold War era has diminished the tendency of a security dilemma within the international system. Instead, SALWs have increasingly become associated with the potential for violence and even the outbreak of civil war among other insecurities in domestic settings.

Still within a revision of the theory of security dilemma, the dyad of SALWs proliferation and asymmetric warfare also accentuates the widely perceived paradox of the contemporary strategic environment where military superiority may actually accentuate the threat of nuclear, biological, chemical and, generally speaking, and perfidious attacks (Geib 2006). Indeed, direct attacks against civilians, hostage-taking, and the use of human shields—practices that have long been outlawed in armed conflicts—have seen a revival in recent conflicts in which the far "weaker party" has often sought to gain a comparative advantage over the militarily superior enemy by resorting to such practices as a matter of strategy (Geib 2006).

Terrorism and Counterterrorism: A Conceptual and Historical Overview

As one of the major forms of asymmetric warfare, terrorism has attracted significant political and scholarly attention. Yet, the concept has proven rather difficult to conceptualize; as a lot of confusion and inexactitudes have continued to trail the discourse on the subject. Indeed, as a highly emotional and subjective concept, terrorism has defied a commonly acceptable definition for a number of reasons which includes: disputes over the perpetrators (who is a terrorist?), and their motives (what constitutes acts of terrorism?), the difficulty in distinguishing terrorism from other forms of asymmetric warfare like guerilla warfare, fight for independence, irredentism, etc. and the pejorative and rather indiscriminate use of the term by politicians and the media to discredit certain individuals or groups. Yet, defining the concept of terrorism is not only critical toward developing sufficient understanding of the phenomenon but also to deal with it effectively.

The term "terrorism" originates from the Latin word "terrere" which means "to frighten." Generally, terrorism may be defined as the premeditated use or the threat to use violence by individuals or groups toward the achievement of a political or socio-economic objective. According to the United States Department of defense terrorism is the calculated use of unlawful violence or the threat of violence to inculcate fear; intended to coerce or to intimidate governments or societies in the pursuit of goals that are generally political, religious, or ideological. Laqueur (1996) defines terrorism as the illegitimate use of force to achieve a political objective by targeting innocent people."

In his own submission, Bjorgo (2005) sees "terrorism as a set of methods of combat rather than an identifiable ideology or movement which involves the premeditated use of violence against noncombatants in order to achieve a psychological effect of fear on others and not necessarily the immediate targets". Hoffman and Reinares (2016) in their submission identify three major features that define terrorism. Firstly, is that it is an act of violence that produces widespread disproportionate emotional reactions such as fear and anxiety which are likely to influence attitudes and behavior. Secondly, the violence is systemic and rather unpredictable and is usually directed against symbolic targets. Thirdly, the violence conveys messages and threats in order to communicate and gain social control. In their study which examined 109 definitions of terrorism Schmid and Jongman (1988) provide a very useful guide on the concept of terrorism. They found 22 frequently used "definitional elements" in the conceptualization of terrorism as indicated in Table 38.1.

As indicated in Table 38.1, the most critical element in the definition of terrorism is violence and the use of force. Other crucial elements include: political motives and the emphasis on fear and terror. For the purposes of this chapter therefore, terrorism is thus, seen as an anxiety-inspiring method of repeated violent action, employed by (semi-) clandestine individual, group or state actors, for idiosyncratic, criminal, or political reasons, whereby—in contrast to assassination—the direct targets of violence are not the main targets (Weinberg et al. 2010). The immediate human victims of violence are generally chosen randomly (targets of opportunity) or selectively (representative or symbolic targets) from a target population, and serve as message generators.

Table 38.1 Frequencies of definitional elements in 109 definitions of terrorism

S/No	Definitional element	Frequency %
1	Violence, force	83.5
2	Political	65
3	Fear, terror emphasized	51
4	Threat	47
5	Effects (psychological) and reactions (anticipated)	41.5
6	Victim-target differentiation	37.5
7	Purposive, planned and systematic, organized action	32
8	Method of combat, strategy, tactic	30.5
9	Extra-normality, in breach of accepted rules, without humanitarian constraints	30
10	Coercion, extortion, induction of compliance	28
11	Publicity aspect	21.5
12	Arbitrariness, impersonal, random character, indiscrimination	21
13	Civilians, noncombatants, neutrals, outsiders as victims	17.5
14	Intimidation	17
15	Innocence of victims emphasized	15.5
16	Group, movement, organization as perpetrator	14
17	Symbolic aspect, demonstration to others	13.5
18	Incalculability, unpredictability, unexpectedness of occurrence of violence	9
19	Clandestine, covert nature	9
20	Repetitiveness, serial, or campaign character of violence	7
21	Criminal	6
22	Demands made on third parties	4

Source Schmid and Jongman (1988: 5–6)

It is apparent from the foregoing conceptualization that terrorism predates the Cold War and the asymmetric conflicts following from that era. Indeed, the use of violence and the threat of violence for the realization of political and socio-economic objectives is as old as mankind. Early zealots refer essentially to a member of a Jewish sect noted for its uncompromising opposition to Rome. They were an aggressive political party whose concern was for the national and religious life of the Jewish people. The Sicarii, was a first-century Jewish group and one of the earliest, organized groups of assassins which murdered their enemies and collaborators in a campaign to oust their Roman rulers from Judea. They used small daggers (sicae) hidden in their cloaks to stab people in crowds, then melt quietly away in the throng. Similarly, the Hashhashin were a secretive sect that was active in Iran and Syria from the eleventh to the thirteenth centuries. The group also employed violence in taking down political and financial rivals alike before their organization fell in the mid-1200s. Many etymological studies on the origins of terrorism however, trace the modern use of the term back to the aftermath of the French Revolution and Maximilien Robespierre's "reign of terror" which saw more than 20,000 people being sent to the guillotine between 1792 and 1794 (Greene 2017). Other notable examples of drastic "state terrorism" include Nazi Germany, Stalinist Soviet Union, and communist China. All these cases were similar in the sense that the threat and use of violence represented a critical part of state policy. From this incipient stage as an essential part of state policy, terrorism has evolved within the international system as a whole; blurring the distinction between domestic and international affairs; to include violent acts and strategies by non-state actors toward the realization of a bewildering range of ideological, religious, or political goals.

In his work on the history of international terrorism, Rapoport (2004) identified four major waves of modern international terrorism. The first wave Rapoport (2004) notes was the period of the "anarchist" which began in Russia in the 1880s and lasted until the 1920s. The "anarchist" wave of terrorism grew out of the deep dissatisfaction of anarchists with the slow reforms of societies and a realization that the attempts of revolutionaries to ignite uprisings toward changing the social order through various writings were inefficient. Anarchists viewed societies as being chained by various conventions and sought acts of terror to destroy these conventions. The high point of the first wave of terrorism Rapoport (2004) notes began in 1890s and it continued even beyond the first wave—until 1940. Rapoport further describes this period as the "Golden Age of Assassinations" during which one major European minister or Head of state was assassinated every 18 months. The first period of international terrorism also witnessed the first multilateral attempts toward countering terrorism; particularly after the assassination of US President William McKinley in 1901. However, such attempt failed as states were unable to forge consensus for joint action. The second wave of international terrorism as identified by Rapoport was the period of the anti-colonial struggles which began in the 1920s following the signing the Treaty of Versailles ending the First World War and ended in the 1960s. The principle of self-determination during the second wave was crucial in breaking up defeated empires and it provided a foundation for new kind of terrorist organizations. Examples include the Irish Republican Army and the various Jewish organizations that operated against British forces in the Palestine. During the "anticolonial" wave of terrorism it became common place for supposed "terrorists" fighting against colonial powers to be called "freedom fighters." Following the end of the second wave, the third wave began in the 1960s with the rise of the new left and continued through to the 1980s. The occurrence of "new left terrorism" Rapoport notes was stimulated by the Vietnam War which supposedly; proved that modern states were vulnerable to relatively unsophisticated weapons and tactics. That is, to SALWs and asymmetric conflicts. The increasing dissatisfaction among young people was seen to have given rise to the emergence of groups such as the Red Army Faction in the Western part of Germany, Italian Red Brigades, and French Action Directe. The targets of the third wave of terrorism was remarkably similar to those of the first wave of international terrorism: prominent targets became very popular again. Rapoport's (2004) notes that the "new left" wave of terrorism produced some "700 hijackings, 409 international kidnapping incidents involving 951 hostages from 1968 to 1982, assassination of high-ranking officials including the prime ministers of Spain and Jordan amongst others." The third wave of international terrorism also witnessed much more international cooperation in counterterrorism activities. The UN for instance adopted for the first time major conventions in 1963, 1970, and 1971 which outlawed hijacking and hostage taking aboard airlines. Lastly, the fourth wave of terrorism according to Rapoport (2004) is characterized by the rise of extremist religious movements which emerged in 1979 and continues until the present times. In 1979 three events signaled the commencement of religious wave of terrorism: The Iranian Revolution, the Soviet invasion of Afghanistan, and the beginning of a new Islamic century. The "religious" wave of terrorism gave prominence to suicide terrorism and was also characterized by the attempt to cause mass casualties to the general populace. The terrorist groups operating in most parts of Africa such as Boko Haram, AQIM, and the Janjawee of Southern Sudan fall with this category due to their main objective of doing away with western civilization and the restoration of classical Islam.

Rapoports categorization of the different waves of international terrorism is no doubt controversial particularly given the subjectivities surrounding the concept of terrorism. While the anarchists, the anti-colonialist and other categories he referred to as terrorists might have been seen as such by mainstream political establishments, many of these so called terrorist groups never saw themselves as such. Indeed, many anti-colonialists for instance were not only seen as freedom fighters, but also as liberators of the indigenous populations from colonial subjugation and exploitation. Yet, the four-pronged categorization by Rapoport succinctly captures the salience of terrorism within the international system as a concept that has oscillated in meaning, reflecting ideas contextually specific to the time period and location to which it is being applied.

Since terrorism involves the premeditated use of violence in the pursuit of socio-economic, political, religious, or any other ideological goals, counterterrorism generally implies actions and measures taken against terrorism. It incorporates military tactics and techniques, law enforcement, and intelligence in the efforts to combat or prevent terrorism. Given the highly sophisticated nature of international terrorism, international finance and multilateral cooperation have also become critical elements in counterterrorism strategies. However, the impact of multinational cooperation in checking the proliferation of SALWs—the weapons of choice for the terrorist groups in Africa as a whole has been quite insignificant due to the porosity of borders.

SALWs and Asymmetric Warfare: The "Security Dilemma" in Niger Republic

The Republic of Niger, is a landlocked country in the Sahel named after the Niger River. Niger is bordered by Libya to the northeast, Chad to the east, Nigeria to the south, Benin to the southwest, Burkina Faso and Mali to the west, and Algeria to the northwest. The country covers a land area of about 1,270,000 km², making it the largest country in the Sahel region. Over 80% of its land area lies in the Sahara Desert to the north; and the country's population of about 21 million lives mostly in clusters in the far south and west of the country.

Niger has been affected by the general security challenges in the Sahel, as well as crisis and conflicts in neighboring states, such as Libya, Mali, and Nigeria. These neighboring countries have also served as sources of SALWs to militant groups operating in Niger as indicated in Table 38.2 and Fig. 38.1.

As indicated in Fig. 38.1, Niger has been a major transit route for the trafficking of SALWs. Indeed, most of the SALWs in Niger are trafficked across

Table 38.2 Types, sources and estimated number of SALWs in Niger Republic

Country of destination or use	Types of SALWs	Countries of origin/suppliers of SALWs	Estimated no. of SALWs in circulation	Means/routes of transfers of SALWs
Niger	AK 47Riffles, Pistols. Short, long and double barrel guns, and Kalashnikov rifles	Libya, Chad, Somali, Sudan, Nigeria, Mali, Algeria, Burkina Faso, and local manufacturers	117,305	Land borders and foot paths

Source Adapted from Intergovernmental Action Group Against Money Laundering-GIABA (2013)

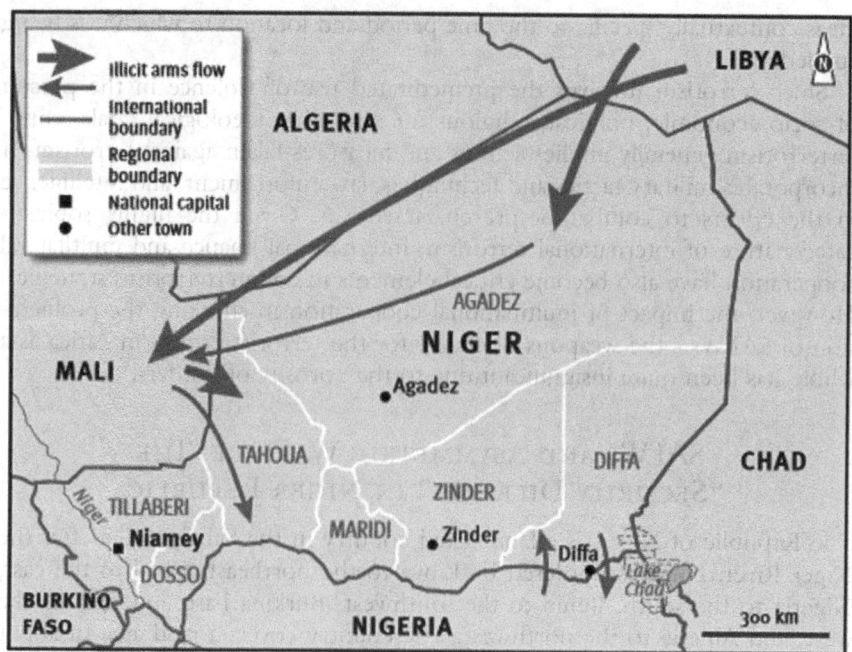

Fig. 38.1 Trafficking routes of illicit SALWs in Niger Republic (*Source* Tessieres [2017])

land borders from neighboring countries in the Sahel. While trafficking in contraband including SALWs has for long been a way of life for the countries in the Sahel as a whole, the civil war in Libya particularly unleashed a significant quantity of SALWs flows into Niger. Niger's borders with other countries such as Mali and Nigeria have also served as major trafficking routes of SALWs. Indeed, the inability of the Nigerien government to effectively police its vast borders has ensured that the illicit trade in SALWs has thrived; with local tribe leaders, terrorist recruits, and criminal groups at the center of this illicit trade.

In addition to being a major transit route for SALWs, corruption and the activities of terrorist groups has also ensured that Niger served as a source of SALWs. In 2013, for example, it was reported that a senior Nigerien officer sold a number of Type 56-1 assault rifles after removing their serial numbers to Boko Haram (Tessieres 2017). Similarly, in 2015 a network of members of the security forces diverted ammunition; mainly 7.62 × 39 mm, which they sold to local armed bandits. Terrorists attacks on Nigerien security facilities have also resulted in the theft of SALWs. For instance, in June 2016 Boko Haram attacked the southern town of Bosso and its military camp, killing 32 members of the security forces and seizing significant quantities of SALWs (Tessieres 2017). In the northwest of the country several attacks on security facilities also resulted in Nigerien materiel being diverted to Mali. For instance, in October 2016 an unidentified armed group of ten people from Mali attacked the Tassara refugee camp and killed 22 members of the security forces and took several vehicles, 5 hand-guns, 29 AK-type assault rifles, 2 general-purpose machine guns, and a 12.7 mm heavy machine gun (Tessieres 2017).

Given the generally amorphous nature of trafficking activities and the illicit trade in SALWs, it is difficult to generate reliable baseline data on the quantity of licit and illicit SALWs in Niger. However, the AU and Small arms survey (2019) estimates that over a hundred thousand SALWs are held by civilians in Niger. Indeed, the extensive nature of the proliferation of SALWs was a major factor that resulted in establishment of the national commission for the collection and control of illicit arms in the republic of Niger. Suffice it to say that the proliferation of SALWs in Niger has been associated with an increase in the activities of terrorist groups in the country; and in the face of the extensive international counterterrorist response, an asymmetric warfare has ensued; creating a "security dilemma" where both terrorist organizations and government forces are engaged in a war of attrition.

SALWs AND THE EXTERNALITIES OF TERRORISM AND COUNTERTERRORISM IN NIGER

As earlier noted, one of the major features of terrorism and counterterrorism in Niger is the strong externalities associated with both phenomenon in the country. Indeed, most of the terrorist acts which have been committed in Niger have been from groups based outside the country and the major counterterrorist initiatives adopted in the country have also essentially involved international and regional cooperation. Evidence gathered in the course of this chapter suggests that there are three major terrorist groups that have been active in Niger republic from 2013 to 2017. These are: Boko Haram, Islamic State, and Al Qaida in the Islamic Maghreb (AQIM). These groups have also employed different SALWs in their operations as indicated in Table 38.3.

Table 38.3 Terrorists organizations and types of SALWs used in Niger Republic (2013–2017)

Terrorist organization	Type of SALWs used in attacks	Attacks	Killed	Injured	Hostages
Boko Haram	AK 47 Rifles, Type 56 assault rifles, IEDs	46	807	208	35
Islamic State	AK 47 Rifles, IEDs	3	21	10	4
Al Qaida (AQIM)	AK 47 Rifles	1	3	0	0
Total	Not available	50	831	218	39

Source Roser et al. (2008: 14)

Table 38.3 indicates that Boko Haram which is based in Nigeria along Niger's southern border has been the most active terrorist group in Niger. Out of a total of about 50 major terrorist attacks between 2013 and 2017, Boko Haram alone was responsible for 46 of these attacks and the major type of SALWs used in these operations were AK 47 riffles and IEDs.

The Boko Haram insurgency began in 2009 when the jihadist rebel group Boko Haram started an armed rebellion against the Nigerian state. Since 2009 the group emerged as the deadliest insurgency Nigeria has witnessed in its post-independence history. The violent activities of the group are concentrated in Nigeria's north-eastern region; particularly in Borno state along the border with Niger. From neighboring towns in Borno state, Boko Haram has severally crossed into Niger's southern border to the Diffa region to launch attacks. Indeed, the border between the Diffa region and Nigeria is largely symbolic since the ethnic groups along both sides are the same with families often divided between the two countries. The Nigerian currency (Naira) which is accepted everywhere in the city of Diffa also facilitated Boko Haram's initial use of Niger as a rare base to source supplies. Between 2009 and 2015, Niger served as a primary transit and recruitment point for the terrorist group. In an interview granted at the rehabilitation and resettlement camp in Goudoumaria, Aboubacar for example noted that he was 22 when Boko Haram first showed up near his home on the shore of Lake Chad in 2013. He recalled, how a Boko Haram commander handed him one million Nigerian naira (about $6250), which was an astronomical sum in a country where the average income is about $400 a year. The money he noted was an investment in his family's goods-trading business, with two major strings attached: He had to supply the militants with whatever supplies they needed; including SALWs, and he would have to join them whenever they needed foot soldiers (Bearak 2008). Thus, Boko Haram has also been a major player in the proliferation of SALWs in Niger. Apart from arming new recruits in the country, the group is also one of the major beneficiaries of the influx of SALWs coming into Niger from Libya.

Along its western border with Mali, Niger has also been contending with terrorist attacks; where an umbrella of Al-Qaida-affiliated groups and Islamic State affiliates in the region have expanded their operations into the border regions of Burkina Faso and Niger. Unlike in its southern border where Boko Haram and ISIS attacked civilian and military targets using SALWs, the terrorist attacks by AQIM along Niger's western border almost exclusively focused on security forces. The first suicide attacks in Niger along the border with Mali took place in May 2013, when two simultaneous attacks were carried out against a military camp and the French Areva uranium facility in the Agadez region, killing 24 people. The attacks were jointly claimed by the Movement for Unity and Jihad in West Africa and Al Moulathamoun; two break away factions of Al Qaeda in the Islamic Maghreb which has mainly been active in Mali. Indeed, the Jihadist groups present since the 2012 crisis in Mali exploited local unrest and the weak presence of the state in northern Mali to launch cross-border attacks against the Nigerien army. In 2017 gunmen on pick-up trucks and motorcycles coming from Mali killed 13 gendarmes and wounded five more in an attack on their base in western Niger. The assailants crossed over the border from Mali and drove up to the village of Ayorou, about 40 km (25 miles) inside, before springing their attack (*Guardian* 2018). Still in 2017 four members of the US army were killed along with five Nigerien soldiers in an ambush along Niger's western border with Mali. In an interview on the terrorist threats from Niger's western border, the Nigerien minister of defense noted thus: "certainly, this is an existential threat to us. Terror groups are still strong around us and their stated intention is to establish a caliphate and bring our country onto its knees" (Ahmed 2018). Niger has thus, been a melting point where Al Qaeda, ISIS, and Boko Haram; all armed with various types of SALWs have converged to move the country from the 51st to the 16th position in the last two editions of the Global Terrorism Index (Peter 2018).

In response to the externalities of the terrorist activities in Niger republic, the country has adopted several counterterrorist initiatives and has also become active in several counterterrorist operations. Niger's laws criminalize acts of terrorism consistent with international instruments. In 2011, Niger established a legal framework enabling stronger responses against terrorist threats, notably through a reform of the criminal legislation, as well as the creation of an anti-terrorism specialized judicial unit. Nigerien law enforcement and security services have since the reform of its legal frameworks against terrorism been actively engaged in detecting, deterring, and preventing acts of terrorism on Nigerien territory. However, the country continues to suffer from insufficient manpower, funding, and equipment. Apart from the creation of the specialized judicial unit, to deal with cases of terrorism, counterterrorist investigations in Niger are primarily the responsibility of the Central Service for the Fight against Terrorism, an interagency body comprising representatives from Niger's National Police, National Guard, and Gendarmerie.

In addition to its domestic counterterrorist initiatives, Niger has also had extensive counterterrorist operations with international partners. The country's long and vast borders; through which trafficking of SALWs has continued, made effective border security a challenge. However, through the US Global Security Contingency Fund, a joint interagency program between the US Departments of Defense, Justice, and State, Niger developed a Draft National Border Security Strategy and corresponding Implementation Plan. As part of a broader counterterrorism strategy, the United States also worked with the Government of Niger to improve its capacity to employ forensic investigative tools. The US Federal Bureau of Investigation and the Department of Defense collected the biometric information of more than 1300 terrorism detainees and digitized more than 600 terrorism-linked fingerprint records. With this development Niger became the only country in the Sahel region where terrorist suspects are identified systematically in a biometric enrollment initiative.

Still as part of its regional counterterrorist initiatives, Niger, Burkina Faso, and Mali signed an accord creating the Liptako-Gourma authority in early 2017 to direct security operations in the Tri-Border Region where ISIS-GS and AQIM are active. In mid-2017, the Liptako-Gourma authority was folded into the G-5 Sahel Joint Force, a military effort fielded by Burkina Faso, Chad, Mali, Mauritania, and Niger, to address security threats in the region. Niger also deployed an infantry battalion to the UN Multidimensional Integrated Stabilization Mission in Mali as part of efforts to forestall the advance of the extremist groups.

Along its southern borders, Niger conducted joint patrols with Chad and Nigeria and increased its cooperation with Lake Chad Basin Commission member countries to fight Boko Haram and ISIS-WA. In 2012, the Multinational Joint Task Force against Boko Haram was reorganized by the countries of the Lake Chad basin commission including Niger and mandated to counter the Boko Haram terrorist. However, cooperation under the umbrella of the MNJTF has been characterized with ineffectiveness particularly, as a result of the failure of the regional security complex to fully take shape. This failure was essentially manifested in the lack of an effective command structure for the MNJTF. While the MNJTF initially struggled to demonstrate its effectiveness from 2012 to 2015 due largely to the lack of political will by the Nigerian government, since 2016, a more definite commitment by the Nigerian government to the MNJTF and improved regional coordination has severely diminished Boko Haram's ability to hold territory and carry out cross-border attacks.

Conclusion

This chapter examined the nature of terrorism and counterterrorism in Niger republic within the dyadic context of the proliferation of SALWs and asymmetric conflicts. Two major fetures to the nature of terrorism and counterterrorism in Niger are identified and elaborated on. First, the chapter argued that most of the terrorist acts in Niger, particularly; from 2012 have been from terrorist groups based in neighboring countries which have taken advantage of the proliferation of SALWs and porous borders to regroup and recruit new members in Niger republic. The case of Boko Haram which is based in north-eastern Nigeria, along Niger's southern border and Al Qaida in the Islamic Maghreb which operates along Niger's western border with Mali is illustrative. Secondly, it is also noted that given the transnational nature of terrorism in the Sahel as a whole, the counterterrorist responses adopted in Niger have essentially involved international partnerships as well as membership of regional multinational counterterrorist commands particularly, the Sahel G.5 and the Multinational Joint Task Force against Terrorism.

Yet, in spite of the several counterterrorism initiatives introduced in Niger two major challenges still exist. First, the vast, porous, and unpopulated border regions of the country has continued to serve as routes for the smuggling and proliferation of SALWs. Indeed, this accentuates the need for effective border patrol as critical component of the counterterrorism strategy in Niger. Secondly, the Sahel as a whole has, in many respects become an ideal environment for extremist groups to penetrate given the fragile conditions of many of the states in the region as well as the plethora of local conflicts that can be exploited. Thus, the inability to guarantee efficient public services to the populations of the Sahel as a whole has also made the people of Niger vulnerable to terrorist recruitment and indoctrination. This situation is compounded by the ecological challenges of desertification and climate change which accentuate already fragile conditions. In order to effectively deal with the issues of terrorism in Niger, a comprehensive regional strategy for mopping up SALWs as part of the counterterrorist initiative is crucial. Such a counterterrorist strategy must also aim to address the socio-economic, political, and ecological challenges of the entire Sahel region.

REFERENCES

African Union and Small Arms Survey. (2019). *Weapons Compass: Mapping Illicit Small Arms Flow in Africa*. Retrieved from http://www.smallarmssurvey.org/about-us/highlights/2019/highlight-au-mapping.html. 24/10/2019.

Ahmed, I. (2018). *Official: Niger Is Facing Existential Threat*. Retrieved from https://www.voanews.com/africa/official-niger-facing-existential-threat. 29/10/2019.

Bearak, M. (2008). *Boko-Haram Brought Terrorism into Niger*. Retrieved from https://www.washingtonpost.com/news/world/wp/2018/11/20/feature/boko-haram-brought-terror-to-niger-can-a-defectors-program-bring-peace/?noredirect=on&utm_term=.2cb370b3c83f. 12/10/2019.

Bjorgo, T. (2005). *Root Causes of Terrorism*. London: Routledge.

Geib, R. (2006). *Asymmetric Conflict Structures*. Retrieved from https://www.icrc.org/en/doc/assets/files/other/irrc_864_geiss.pdf. 13/9/2019.

GIABA. (2013). *Annual Report*. Dakar: GIABA.

Greene, A. (2017). Defining Terrorism: One Size Fits All. *International and Comparative Law Quarterly*, 66(2), 124–141.

Herz, J. H. (1951). *Political Realism and Political Idealism: A Study in Theories and Realities*. Chicago: University of Chicago Press.

Hill, S. M. (2004). *United Nations Disarmament Processes in Intra-State Conflict*. New York: Palgrave Macmillan.

Hoffman, B., & Reinares, F. (2016). *The Evolution of the Global Terrorist Threat: From 9/11 to Osama Bin Laden's Death(eds)*. New York: Columbia University Press.

Laqueur, W. (1996). Postmodern Terrorism. *Foreign Affairs*, 75(5), 24–36.

Muggah, R., & Bachelor, P. (2002). *Development Held Hostage: Assessing the Effects of Small Arms on Human Development*. Retrieved from https://gsdrc.org/document-library/development-held-hostage-assessing-the-effects-of-small-arms-on-human-development/. 30/10/2019.

Peter, J. (2018). *Niger on the Frontline of the War Against Terrorism*. Retrieved from https://thehill.com/opinion/national-security/357828-niger-is-on-the-frontlines-of-the-war-against-terrorism. 12/9/2019.

Posen, B. (1993). The Security Dilemma and Ethnic Conflict. *Global Politics and Strategy, 35*(1), 27–47.

Rapoport, D. C. (2004). *Four Waves of Modern Terrorism—Attacking Terrorism: Elements of a Grand Strategy*. Washington, DC: Georgetown University Press.

Roser, M., Nagdy, M., & Ritchie, H. (2008). *Terrorism*. Retrieved from https://ourworldindata.org/terrorism/. 20/2/2019.

Schmid, A. P., & Jongman, A. J. (1988). *Political Terrorism: A New Guide to Actors, Authors, Concepts, Databases, Theories and Literature*. New Brunswick, NJ: Routledge.

Tessieres, S. D. (2017). *Measuring Illicit Arms Flows: Niger* (Small Arms Survey Briefing Paper).

The Guardian. (2018). *Influx of Small Arms and Light Weapons*. Retrieved from https://www.pressreader.com/nigeria/the-guardian-nigeria/20180222/282471414342517. 13/8/2019.

United Nations. (1997). General and Complete Disarmament: Small Arms Item 71 (b), (A/52/298). Official Record. New York. Retrieved from UN.org: http://www.un.org/depts/ddar/Firstcom/SGreport52/a52298.html. 12/8/2019.

Weinberg, L., Pedahzur, A., & Hirsch, H. (2010). The Challenges of Conceptualizing Terrorism. *Terrorism and Political Violence, 16*(4), 777–794.

David Omeiza Moveh is a Senior Lecturer in the Department of Political Science and International Studies, Ahmadu Bello University, Zaria, Nigeria. Moveh's research interest are in the areas of Insurgencies and counter insurgencies, elections management, party politics and the democratization process in Africa. Moveh has published extensively in local and international journals. He is also presently coordinating a research network in the areas of peace and conflict management in Africa.

CHAPTER 39

South Africa: Xenophobia, Crime and Small Arms Proliferation

Dorcas Ettang

INTRODUCTION

South Africa has had a long history with arms, and by its first democratic elections in April 1994, it had been identified as one of the top ten arms manufacturers in the world (Human Rights Watch 2000). The Apartheid government developed a strong domestic arms industry in addition to building and strengthening its national defence force. In addition to its highly militarised state, it was able to develop a wide range of military hardware including nuclear bombs, rockets, launchers, grenades and various light and heavy machine guns including pistols and assault rifles (Robinson 1995). Robinson (1995) noted that during Apartheid, the South African government participated in the illegal manufacturing, sales and purchase of Small Arms and Light Weapons (SALWs) due to its isolation from the international arena. The Armaments Corporation of South Africa (ARMSCOR), South Africa's Department of Defense acquisition agency, sold arms to repressive governments (Haiti and Burma), fragile countries (Sudan and Somalia), and also smuggled weapons to Iraq in exchange for crude oil; and supplied ammunition and automatic rifles, grenades and grenade launchers to Rwanda prior to the 1994 genocide (Robinson 1995). It also developed various military hardware, including 9 mm guns and nuclear weapons (Robinson 1995). In post-1994 South Africa,

D. Ettang (✉)
School of Social Sciences, University of KwaZulu-Natal, Pietermaritzburg, South Africa
e-mail: ettang@ukzn.ac.za

© The Author(s), under exclusive license to Springer Nature Switzerland AG 2021
U. A. Tar and C. P. Onwurah (eds.), *The Palgrave Handbook of Small Arms and Conflicts in Africa*,
https://doi.org/10.1007/978-3-030-62183-4_39

however, many gun manufacturers had to close their businesses due to the influx of illegal SALW displacing locally made SALW (Keegan 2005).

The Apartheid era was characterised by the accumulation of SALWs as nationalist groups armed themselves for violent clashes. The end of the Cold War—which occurred four years before the end of the Apartheid era in South Africa—also resulted in the influx of arms to the African continent, resulting in their circulation within South Africa. Thus, in developing their caches, liberation armies had access to these weapons. SALWs thus gained dominance in the Apartheid era, continuing even after Independence in 1994.

In South Africa's current democratic dispensation (post-1994), the threat of SALWs continues to affect communities. As will be discussed subsequently, xenophobic attacks and crime in South Africa are linked to the proliferation of SALWs. These weapons have contributed to high levels of insecurity in communities. There has been a rapid increase in the use of illegal firearms to carry out violent criminal activities throughout the country. Over ten years, the seizing of illegal possession of firearms and ammunition has increased mainly from 2009/2010 to 2017/2018, while noting that a significant decrease was noted from April 2018 to March 2019 (see Fig. 39.1). This could be attributed to increased efforts at stopping the spread of these SALWs through police efforts and civil society and community involvement.

Taking a provincial focus, Fig. 39.2 shows the provinces with the highest number of illegal possessions of firearm and ammunition seized during police operations and intelligence-led investigations between March 2018 and April 2019. KwaZulu-Natal (KZN), Gauteng and the Western Cape make up the

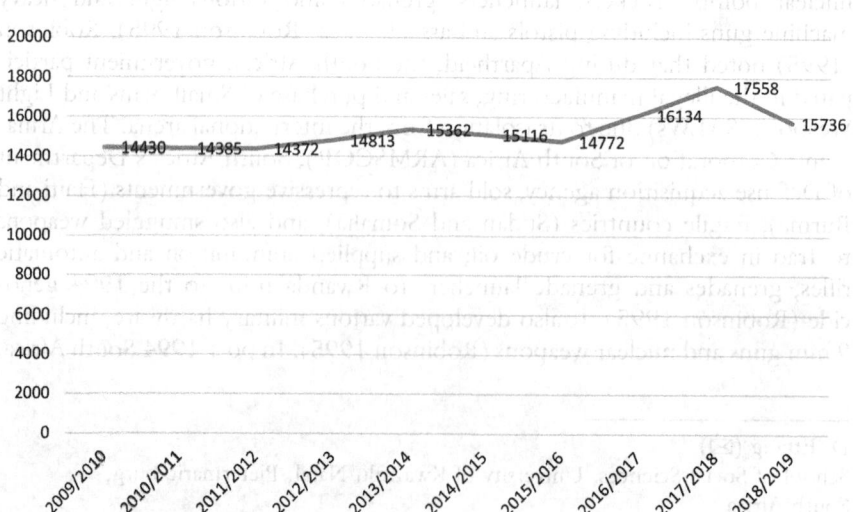

Fig. 39.1 Illegal possession of firearms and ammunition: trend over ten years, SAPS (2019)

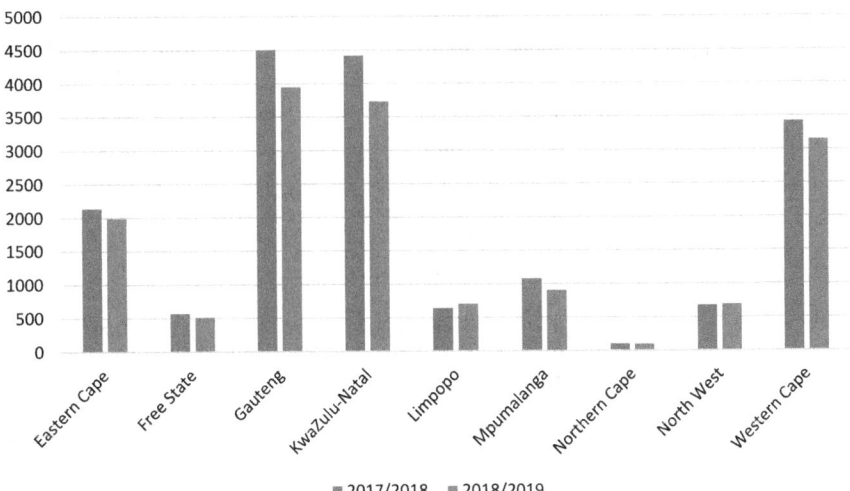

Fig. 39.2 Illegal possession of firearms and ammunition by province for 2017/2018 and 2018/2019 (*Source* SAPS [2019])

top three provinces; they also make up the most populous of the nine provinces.

This is why authors like Shaw and Gastrow (2001), wrote that South Africa sits as one of the most violent countries in the world when it comes to crimes, including rape and armed robbery. The idea behind the violence is the clear intention to hurt or harm someone. For the United Nations, the definition of violence against women is: "any act of gender-based violence that results in, or is likely to result in, physical, sexual or psychological harm or suffering to women, including threats of such acts, coercion or arbitrary deprivation of liberty, whether occurring in public or private life" (OCHCR 1993: 2). This is relevant in the case of South Africa with its high rate of femicide. Noting that there is no commonly agreed-upon definition of femicide, the United Nations Office on Drugs and Crime (UNODC 2019) identifies the following as constituting femicide, namely: intimate partner violence, honour-related killings, killings as a result of sexual orientation and gender identity, and violence during armed conflict. South Africa sits at fourth in the top ten countries with high rates of femicide (see Table 39.1).

According to McEvoy and Hideg (2017), South Africa was one of 23 countries that experienced high violent death rates in 2015 and 2016 with a minimum of 20 deaths per 100,000 persons. They also reported that crime claimed as many victims as those in high-intensity conflict countries in proportion to their population (McEvoy and Hideg 2017). Acknowledging the limitations and inconsistencies in data which leads to the undercounting of the number of homicide victims in the twentieth century, the UNODC Global Study on Homicide (2019), points out that South Africa still has a high rate

Table 39.1 Highest femicide rates in the world

Rank	Location	Femicide rate per 100,000 women
1	Honduras	32.7
2	Jamaica	15.5
3	Lesotho	15.4
4	South Africa	12.5
5	Guinea Bissau	11.1
6	Haiti	10.6
7	El Salvador	10.6
8	Trinidad and Tobago	10.5
9	Côte d'Ivoire	10.3
10	Iraq	9.1

Source WHO (2016: https://www.who.int/healthinfo/global_burden_disease/estimates/en/)

of homicide in the world with 36 per 100,000 of the population based on data collected until the end of March 2018. Homicide here is defined as the killing of another human being, with murder and manslaughter categorised as unlawful homicides. These high levels of violence have earned it the most violent country in the world according to Interpol in areas of assault, robbery, violent theft and murder (Abdi 2011).

Despite this, the country continues to contribute to the prevention of trafficking of illegal SALWs and regulating the use of legal SALWs. The South African National Conventional Arms Control Committee (NCACC), enacted by the National Conventional Arms Control Act NCACA No. 41 of 2002, has shown its commitment to international efforts at curbing the spread of illicit arms by disposing all "state-held redundant, obsolete, unserviceable and confiscated semi-automatic and automatic weapons of a calibre up to and including 12.7 mm by destruction" (Meek and Stott 2004: 1). This decision gained support through its ratification by the South African Cabinet and becoming official government policy (Meek and Stott 2004: 1). In its White Paper on Defence (1996), the country stated its commitment to strengthening international and regional efforts in containing and preventing the proliferation of SALWs among others, including weapons of mass destruction. It also ratified the Arms Trade Treaty (ATT) in 2014.

Furthermore, it has played a vital role in adopting the 1998 Southern Africa Regional Action Programme on Light Arms and Illicit Trafficking in cooperation with the European Union, which focuses on information sharing, developing appropriate policy and enhancing capabilities for enforcement (HRW 2000). South Africa is also part of the Southern African Regional Police Chiefs Co-operation Organisation (SARPCCO), a SADC organ focused on regional police cooperation on cross border priorities including terrorism, illegal weapons and explosives and human trafficking. In addition to this is its commitment to the SADC Protocol of 2001 that is focused on preventing and combating the illicit manufacturing of SALWs in order to regulate illegal movements of SALWs and prevent their movement across borders.

South Africa's interest in SALWs proliferation emerged in 1992–1993 with the realisation that unlicensed SALWs and former Mozambican weapons were flowing into the country from places like Mozambique as a result of their shared borders (Small Arms Survey 2001). Thus, various efforts to limit the movement of illegal weapons into the country has included the closing of 107 out of 117 international airports and developing radar facilities to monitor flights over Botswana, Namibia, Southern Zambia and Angola (HRW 2000).

This chapter brings a national and grassroots perspective to the fight against SALWs proliferation. It examines the causes and manifestations of SALWs in communities, especially in the context of crime and xenophobic attacks. It also looks at the outcomes and impact of the availability of SALWs on communities and South Africa's stability as a whole. While South Africa is part of various global and regional programmes and efforts, much more work is needed by a myriad of actors including the government and relevant law enforcement and security institutions to curtail SALWs proliferation within its borders and manage the impact this has on criminality and violence. This chapter, therefore, concludes with implications for policy and practice. The lethality of these weapons calls for a more robust and holistic response.

South Africa's Experience with SALWs

The term "firearm" has been defined under South Africa's Firearms Control Act (2000: 8) as "a device manufactured or designed to propel a bullet or projectile through a barrel or cylinder by means of burning propellant, at a muzzle energy exceeding 8 joules (6 ft-lbs)". According to SAPS 2018/2019 annual crime statistics, SALWs include high-calibre firearms, pistols, revolvers, ammunition, shotguns and AK-47s (SAPS 2018). Homemade guns are also in circulation, which includes the Zip Guns, makeshift guns used by gangs because they are easy to build and difficult to trace (Petersen 2015). Firearms are the most used instruments in committing murder nationally (Figs. 39.2 and 39.3). It was also the most common instrument used for attempted murder and robberies at both residences and businesses (SAPS 2019).

These SALWs are found all across the country. The proliferation of these weapons in South Africa is also due to the remnants from the Apartheid era where weapons were accumulated and kept for private use. The South African government according to Robinson (1995) was also known to have accumulated over time a large stockpile of weapons, including assault rifles, machine guns and rocket launchers, from forces like the South West African People's Organisation (SWAPO), the African National Congress (ANC) and from Communist-backed groups in Angola and Mozambique. The uncertainty of the early post-apartheid South Africa in 1995 resulted in legally owned SALWs being stockpiled into private collections and illegal SALWs

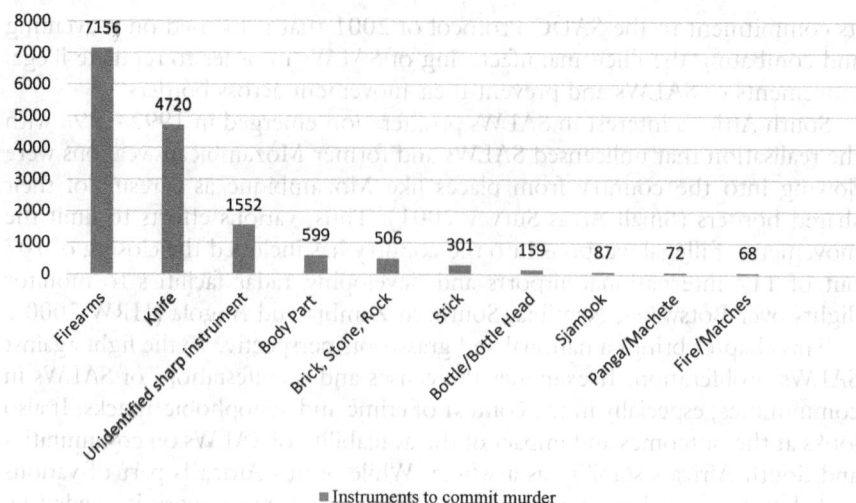

Fig. 39.3 The ten most common instruments used nationally to commit murder 2018/2019 (*Source* SAPS [2019: https://www.saps.gov.za/services/april_to_march2018_19_presentation.pdf])

being smuggled into the country by the ANC (Robinson 1995). Shaw and Gastrow (2001) note that the available weapons were reportedly smuggled in from Angola and the Democratic Republic of Congo (DRC) but are also from local arms stockpiles from the apartheid days.

Beyond the apartheid remnants, these illegal firearms have been identified as coming from three primary sources: fraud and corruption where unfit individuals obtain firearm licenses; guns smuggled in from different countries and the loss or theft of firearms from licensed owners and the state (SAPS 2015/2016). Firearms usually are legal or illegal, and Kirsten (2007) notes that virtually every illegal firearm begins as a legal weapon. The loss or theft of firearms from licensed owners and the state is the most common source of illegal SALWs in the country. Chetty (2000) noted an increase in the loss or theft of illegal firearms from 15,309 in 1994 to 30,220 in 1998. According to the SAPS Crime Statistics (2015/2016), an average of two guns is lost or stolen from police per day while 20 guns on average are stolen or lost from civilians. In response to written parliamentary questions, police minister Bheki Cele noted that 500 firearms and 10,765 rounds of ammunition were lost by officials who took these home with them while some of these were lost while they were off duty (Timeslive 2019). According to Smillie (2019), the police estimate that 450,000 gun owners own guns with expired licenses.

Police officers have also engaged in the sale of police-issued firearms. For example, in 2015, 2400 guns scheduled for destruction were stolen and sold to gang lords in the Western Cape by a law enforcement officer who was later sentenced to 18 years in prison (Mzantsi 2016). After ballistic testing,

888 of these weapons were linked to 1066 murders (261 of them being child victims from the age of 1 to 18), with more than 1100 of these weapons yet to be recovered (Ryklief 2017). In 2017, 33 firearms went missing from two police stations in Cape Town (Dolley 2017a). Guns have gone missing in police stations in areas plagued with gang violence like Mitchell Plains and Bellville South in Cape Town (Dolley 2017b). These lost and stolen firearms are used in gang hits, taxi violence and politically motivated attacks (Dolley 2017a).

The trade in SALWs is a multi-billion dollar enterprise, and essentially, SALWs trafficking has become a lucrative business for those involved. Corruption through bribes allows law enforcement and border officials to gain financially from supporting and protecting these non-state groups. The case of illegal gun trade by a police officer and his accomplice in the Western Cape saw them make about 2 million rands from their illegal activities (Mzantsi 2016). In KwaZulu-Natal, two police officers were arrested for selling police-issued weapons and ammunition, including bulletproof vests and pepper spray (Singh 2017).

South Africa continues to face a significant security challenge in the proliferation and illicit trafficking of SALW. This cannot be examined in isolation of regional factors, where speaking of the Southern African region, Interpol's regional bureau for Southern Africa put the number of SALWs circulating the region at 4 million (HRW 2000). In the absence of recent statistics, these are significantly higher. These weapons circulating the Southern African region have existed since the struggles for decolonisation (HRW 2000). The weak arms management and control mechanisms in South Africa's neighbouring countries contributes to the difficulty in tracking the illicit movement of SALWs into the country. Porous borders in the Southern African Development Community (SADC) region have contributed to the proliferation of these weapons. Also, these weapons are easily hidden, thus making it difficult to find, and smugglers have become rather tricky in their approaches. According to an HRW (2000) report, smugglers are ahead of authorities, hiding weapons in different places including modified petrol tanks. In addition to porous borders, the following also contribute to the proliferation of SALWs: use of various transit routes, poor intelligence and collaboration between law enforcement officials and the presence of criminal syndicates and arms traffickers.

In sum, the foregoing reveals that South Africa's experience with SALWs goes back to pre-independence, therefore making the problem highly challenging and persistent. It also reveals the problem that illegal weapons possession poses to individual security. As long as these weapons are in the wrong hands (including rogue security officials), they will be easily used to perpetrate extreme levels of violence to innocent victims. Identifying and understanding the source and movement of the weapons will contribute to providing solutions.

Understanding Xenophobia and Crime in South Africa

Human migration has shaped Africa's political and economic landscape for decades. It can simply be defined as the movement of people from one place to another permanently to settle in the new location. Migrants have been attracted to South Africa for many reasons, including a desire to escape from poverty, underdevelopment, various forms of persecution and insecurity, while others have moved for job or economic opportunities. Migrants in South Africa come from countries like Zimbabwe, Pakistan, Malawi, Nigeria, DRC, Bangladesh, Somalia, Ethiopia and other developed countries. Xenophobia has emerged as an outcome of migration, and it continues to put the lives of migrants at significant risk. Various community leaders and organisations have used Xenophobia in building political and economic support by capitalising on the emotions and frustrations of the population (Misago 2017), thereby showing how persistent this threat has become.

The South African Human Rights Commission (SAHRC 1999: 12) defines Xenophobia as "the irrational fear and deep dislike of non-nationals". Individuals based on their nationality are attacked both physically and otherwise. Various reasons have been identified for the rise of Xenophobia and xenophobic violence. These include poor service delivery, competition for jobs and other scarce resources; foreigners taking the jobs of locals away by accepting lower pay; the sexual exploitation of women by foreigners; the high crime rates in the country and foreign shop owners driving out local businesses due to their cheap and affordable products. Foreigners are, therefore seen as a threat to the physical and economic life of many South Africans. For example, Abdi (2011) noted that the relationship between Somalis and South Africans in townships are because of the structural inequities in the country post-apartheid, these inequities are characterised by high rates of violent crimes and a widening chasm between those who have and those who do not. Skweyiya (2017) brings in the idea that South Africans are not educated on what African countries like Nigeria and Zimbabwe provided for the country during the Apartheid era, which involved providing safety for South African leaders and fighting for the country's freedom.

Xenophobic violence in South Africa has become familiar over time and according to Misago (2017), it has become a daily occurrence. Since 1994, tens of thousands of people have been killed, harassed or attacked because they are foreigners (Misago, Freemantle and Landau 2015). Attacks have occurred in Limpopo, the Western Cape, KwaZulu-Natal, Free State and Gauteng provinces. Attacks occurred in 1995, 1998 and 2008 in Gauteng; 2000 and 2009 in Cape Town; 2015 in Limpopo and 2008 and 2015 in KwaZulu-Natal. In 2008, violence spread from Gauteng to other provinces including Durban in KwaZulu-Natal and Cape Town in the Western Cape. Key violent episodes point out the link between SALWs and xenophobic violence. During the violent clashes against foreigners in September 2019, there were 90 arrests in Gauteng and 20 arrests in KwaZulu-Natal, and some of those arrested were because of possession of unlicensed firearms although none were arrested for xenophobic attacks (Maeko 2019). In relation to this, the police spokesperson Vish Naidoo stated that most of the arrests were related to public violence, and there is no crime called xenophobia (Maeko 2019). A review of empirical and evidence-based research does not show the link between illegal firearms use as contributing or being used to carry out xenophobic attacks, however one can conclude based on the examples below that illegal arms and weapons will feature in these attacks no matter what (xenophobic violence, crime, public disorder) they are defined as. For example, in September 2019, a Zimbabwean national gave his account of a mob arriving armed with guns, sticks and other dangerous weapons asking them to leave Mandela section, in Katlehong, Johannesburg (Seleka 2019). In another account, the mob opened fire with guns, and the migrants left their home empty-handed (Seleka 2019). In 2013, after the looting of 19 foreign-owned shops in Diepsloot, 38 suspects were arrested, four of them for their possession of unlicensed firearms, public violence and housebreaking and theft (Bauer 2013). Based on the SAPS 2018/2019 crime statistics, the causative factors of murder and attempted murder did not present xenophobia as a variable (see Fig. 39.4).

The examples mentioned above speaks to the ongoing debate and public narratives on whether xenophobic violence is occurring in South Africa or if attacks on foreigners can be grouped under broader crime and violent activity. Statements by key political actors have argued that Xenophobia does not exist, but attacks on migrants are a reflection of the violence in society. For

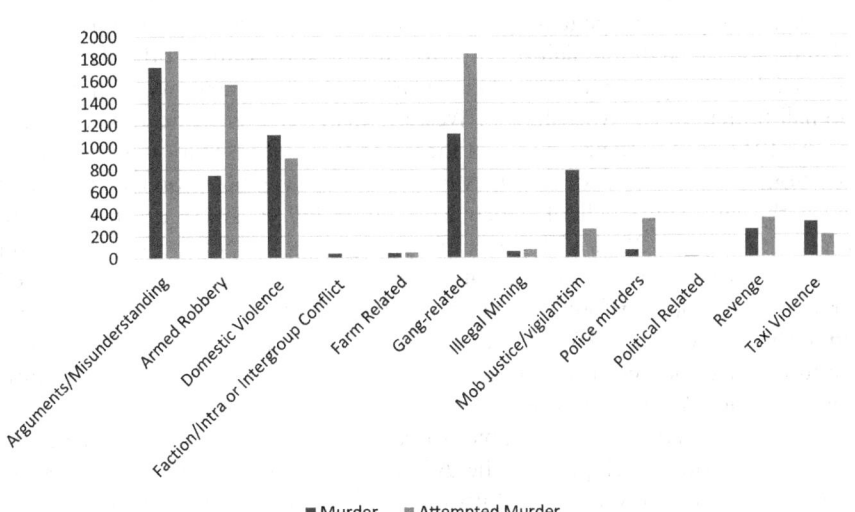

Fig. 39.4 Causative factors of murder and attempted murder (April 2018–March 2019) (*Source* SAPS [2019: https://www.saps.gov.za/services/april_to_march2018_19_presentation.pdf])

instance, in his address to members of the SA Students Congress (SASCO) at the Tshwane University of Technology (TUT), ANC Secretary-General Ace Magashule termed the violence in September 2019 as acts of criminality and tribal clashes and not xenophobic in nature (Madia and Somdyala 2019).

As long as the narrative persists that xenophobic violence does not exist and the act is clouded by the idea of public violence and crime in South Africa, the link between illegal firearms and xenophobic attacks will remain weak. It can be argued that criminality has increased, particularly when it targets foreigners and their businesses and property. Gastrow (2015) writes that statistics on business robberies show that foreign nationals make up a disproportionate number of victims. Also, she notes that while crimes like robbery generally involve the threat or direct use of force, in the case of foreigners these robberies include murder and armed assault with intent to inflict grievous bodily harm (Gastrow 2015).

Migrants, mainly of African descent, have been attacked both verbally and physically including being beaten, stabbed, shot, burnt alive or hijacked. Their homes and businesses have been looted, destroyed and burnt during these attacks. They have been displaced and are forced to run from their homes when these attacks occur. The police have also been involved in perpetrating these crimes by assisting looters to raid shops and steal goods, and prominent political actors have verbally incited anti-foreigner sentiments and actions. In some instances, state agents have actively protected perpetrators accused of anti-foreigner violence (Misago 2017). Thus authors like Abdi (2011) and a report from Human Rights Watch (2008) show that the insecurity migrants face is triggered further by the role of the media, government officials and the police in "migrant scapegoating" (Misago 2017), an idea where migrants are blamed for the systemic failures of government and political officials to meet the needs of citizens and keep their promises. In his interviews with migrant Somali traders in the townships of Western Cape, Gauteng and Eastern Cape, Abdi (2011) noted their feelings of incessant fear and insecurity. According to the Somali Association of South Africa (SASA), over 600 Somalis have died since the late 1990s, all of which have rarely led to arrest or any form of prosecution (Abdi 2011). This example portrays the lack of accountability and a culture of impunity as since 1994, very few perpetrators have been charged or convicted for anti-foreigner violence, and efforts to set up special courts after the 2008 and 2015 violence failed to materialise (Misago 2017). The impunity that perpetrators enjoy within communities is evidence that anti-foreigner violence will continue.

Data collected on xenophobic threats and violence by *Xenowatch*, a monitoring tool developed by the African Centre for Migration & Society (ACMS) at the University of Witwatersrand, shows the trajectory of xenophobic violence from January to September 2019 (See Table 39.2). Xenophobic violence has emerged in the following forms: murder, displacement, physical assault and shops looted (Xenowatch 2019).

Table 39.2 Categories of victimisation of xenophobic violence from January to September 2019

Category of victimisation	Total (January–September 2019)	September 2019
Total number of incidents	68	28
Persons killed	18	12
Displacement	1449	800+
Physical assaults	43	14
Shops looted	147(+2) in the absence of accurate statistics, +2 refers to two or more shops	49+

Source Xenowatch (2019)

According to the Global Study on Homicide by the United Nations Office on Drugs and Crime (UNODC 2019), people are killed more from crime than terrorism and armed conflict combined. While 89,000 people were recorded to be killed from armed conflict and 26,000 from terrorism in 2017, 464,000 people were killed through crime (UNODC 2019). Returning to the broader discussion on criminality in South Africa, crime has become very common in the country. While foreigners are victims of criminal activity through looting and murder, crime affects South Africans as well. Masuku (2002) distinguishes between two categories of individual crime: interpersonal violent crime, which includes murder, attempted murder, serious and common assaults; and, secondly, violent property crime, which includes all other categories of crimes like armed robbery, car hijacking and common robbery. Shaw and Gastrow (2001) identify three categories of crimes, namely: violent interpersonal crime, which covers murder, assault and rape; property crime including theft and burglary where the victim is absent during the committing of the crime and violent property theft, which includes armed robbery where there is contact with the victim. More recently, there has been an increase in crime through cash-in-transit heists with about 140 cash-in-transit heists occurring in the country since January 2018, with 460 heists in 2006 alone (Pijoos 2018). It has increasingly become prevalent in South Africa as seen through the daily news reports, although many of these remain unreported.

Drawing from these reports, crime is widespread and negatively affects South Africa's social and security landscape. Significant gaps in police response to crime have further exacerbated the situation. South Africa was noted to have violent severe crime levels than countries like Brazil and Argentina and as having the highest murder rates in the world according to data released by Interpol in 1997 (Shaw and Gastrow 2001). Authors like Shaw (1997) and Shaw and Gastrow (2001) posit that crime has been identified as one of the main reasons for emigration. The rise in crime has been attributed to various factors, ranging from unemployment, poverty and structural inequalities in the country to other factors like the ineffective judiciary and inadequate policing. According to a report by the Small Arms Survey (2013), there is a strong correlation between high levels of inequality and high levels of armed violence thus requiring better national policies to address and reduce levels of inequality. Citing the report by Synovate (2010) and the study on Kenya by Kyalo (2015), one can argue that in the case of South Africa, high levels of unemployment, the unchanging gap between the rich and the poor has resulted in high levels of desperation among individuals and groups thus leading to increasing crime rates and the arming of individuals.

Figure 39.5 shows that murder steadily increased from 2012/2013 to 2018/2019 (SAPS 2019). The data (not shown) also shows that while there was an increase in attempted murders and robbery with aggravating circumstances, there was a decrease in sexual offences, assault with the intent to inflict grievous bodily harm, common assault and common robbery. Linked to this, is the threat of gang violence, which has become a significant source of insecurity in provinces like the Western Cape (Dolley 2017a).

Beyond the physical harm and violence from crime, the impact of violence has created feelings of fear, uncertainty and anxiety in many communities. Regular news headlines of crime and violence have increased public fear and frustrations for many citizens. For instance, in interviews with residents in Gauteng, Western Cape and the Eastern Cape provinces from 2007 to 2009; Abdi (2011) noted high levels of crime during the night and day; lack of safety in the community and a feeling of uncertainty of the next hit, crime or attack. The high levels of crime have contributed to the culture of violence birthed from Apartheid. This culture of violence as examined by various authors (Hamber 1998; Power 2017; Mncube and Harber 2013) has been attributed

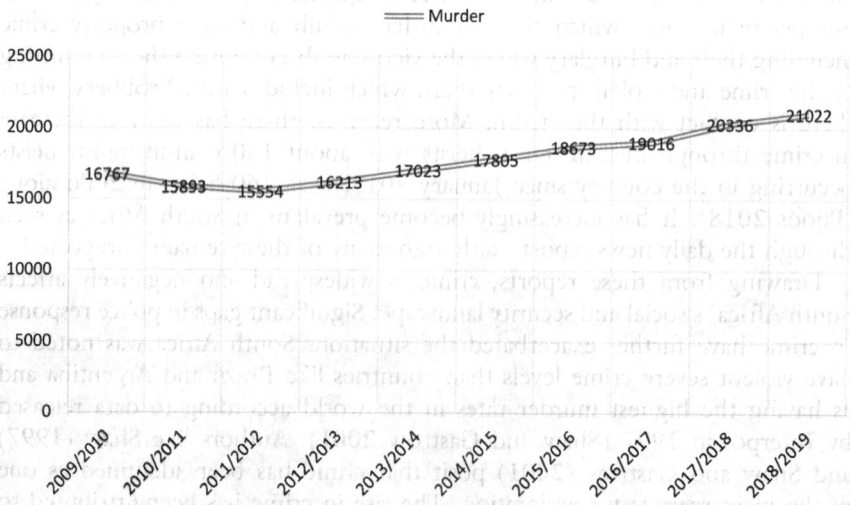

Fig. 39.5 South Africa murder statistics April 1, 2018–March 31, 2019 (*Source* SAPS [2019: https://www.saps.gov.za/services/april_to_march2018_19_presentation.pdf])

to the era and legacy of Apartheid where violence, brutality, repression as a form of oppression and retaliation were played out. Drugs and alcohol are identified as also contributing to this culture of violence (Abdi 2011). The role of alcohol mainly shows that in over 70% of assault cases, both offenders and victims were under the influence of alcohol (Shaw and Gastrow 2001). This requires a broader discussion on how to limit the influence of alcohol and drug use in communities.

A strong link between crime and xenophobia is that they both speak to the structural challenges in South Africa, namely high levels of unemployment, poverty and entrenched inequality. Abdi (2011: 698) notes this relationship when he states that: "violence against migrants is part and parcel of an accepted and generalised violence that is disproportionately affecting poor black South Africans in informal settlements and some areas of the township…" There must, however, be a distinction between xenophobic-related attacks and crime, as failing to do so will simplify or diminish the threats against foreigners. Government response to xenophobia and related violence can, therefore, be termed as "denialism", where xenophobia is seen as a crime, which then requires minimal and sustained interventions or policy changes by the government according to Misago (2017). It is essential to make a distinction between general crime and xenophobic violence.

The previous analysis of xenophobia and crime in South African reveals that the nature of violence has become complicated as attacks do not only affect locals but foreigners as well. What the previous statistics and information present are that responses to criminal activity and violence must take into account the characteristics of the victims, that they can either be locals or foreigners and the latter sometimes being worse off. The role of political stakeholders, security officials and the media are essential in shaping the discourses on xenophobia and crime and how to resolve these. Worthy of note is the role of SALWs as a propellant of violent activities, as well as the disturbing trend of how criminals quickly access these arms to perpetuate their nefarious activities. The following section deals with the impact of SALWs in crime and xenophobia in South Africa.

IMPACT OF SALWS ON CRIME AND XENOPHOBIA

Authors have established that firearms are increasingly available in South Africa (e.g. Shaw and Gastrow 2001). The increasing number of these firearms has also resulted in increased violence and crime (National Crime Prevention Strategy 1996; Abdi 2011; Shaw and Gastrow 2001; HRW 2000). Masuku (2002) thus notes that firearms are used in most crimes reported to the police. For instance, by 1998, 85% of all robberies were committed with firearms, up from 76% in 1996 (Shaw and Gastrow 2001). Firearms have been used in rape; for example, guns were used in 40.9% of rapes of adult women reported to the police in Gauteng Province in 2003 (Abrahams et al. 2010). Firearms are the leading cause of death in political violence (Robinson 1995). These arms are also used in domestic violence, hijackings and other criminal ventures. Thus, firearms-related crime has been a central feature of South African society, as evidenced by the annual rate of firearm deaths. McEvoy and Hideg (2017) report that South Africa has one of the top firearms by death rates in the world. Authors like Azrael and Hemenway (2000) note that the presence of a gun in a household has a high chance of being used against a family member than in providing protection.

It is challenging to know the exact number of arms in circulation in South Africa, although estimates put it at 5 million (Robinson 1995). Masuku (2002) reports that an estimated 3.7 million licensed firearms are in private use with about half a million illegal firearms in circulation. While these numbers are not accurate and are dated, it is clear, however, that illegal SALWs are available across the country and have been used in various criminal activities. Abdi (2011) notes the abundant availability of guns in townships. A year after its Independence, Robinson (1995) writes that South Africa has one of the most armed population in the world with murder rates more than five times that of the United States.

According to Kirsten (2007), there are more SALWs in the hands of civilians than with state agencies. Firearms contribute to intimate partner violence, putting mostly women at risk of death or injury by their partners. Therefore, while men remain the primary victims of gun violence, women are most vulnerable as their intimate partners use guns to hurt, control, intimidate and sometimes kill them. Some men, who committed intimate femicide where firearms are used, usually commit suicide after the killing or within a week of the murder (Abrahams et al. 2010). South Africa has the highest reported global rate of females murdered by shooting in a country, not in war (Abrahams et al. 2010).

Worth noting is the use of legal firearms to commit crime and violence. In a community-based sample of adult men, licensed firearms were used in 74.4% of murders and unlicensed guns in 25.6% (Abrahams et al. 2010). After a homicide, legal firearms have also been associated with suicide increasing the risk for suicide by seven times (Abrahams et al. 2010). The use of firearms in crime and xenophobic attacks always ensures a lethal outcome. Hostility geared towards foreigners has contributed to the rise in murder, injury, looting, threats of mob violence, displacement and destruction of property (Misago 2017) and SALWs are used in most instances. Gang violence has been linked to the illegal trade of SALWs, both contributing to insecurity in the Western Cape Province (Dolley 2017a). Private security firms are also getting a hold of these illegal weapons through legitimate and illegitimate means (Dolley 2017b). Citing a study conducted by Minaar (2008), Berg and Gabi (2011: 15), note that a significant issue with regards to the use and regulation of firearms in the security industry was the weak monitoring of firearms as they were issued to "untrained, unqualified and unlicensed staff". Berg and Gabi (2011) in their study, also noted the incidences of illegal private security companies and illegal training centres which affected the credibility and work of private security firms in general. Private Security Industry Regulatory Authority (PSIRA) spokesperson Siziwe Zuma could not rule out the possibility that criminals obtained accreditation with PSIRA as a way to access weapons (Dolley 2017c). In an incidence, some of the firearms previously seized from shooters outside a city centre strip club were later confiscated from The Security Group (TSG), in Bellville on July 12, these weapons belonging to its sister group Eagle VIP Security (Dolley 2017c).

A wide range of authors has written on human security and SALWs noting that the trade and transfer of illegal SALWs have negative implications on the security of individuals and their human rights (Abass 2010; Kumar 2008; Abrahams et al. 2010). These SALWs have gotten into the wrong hands, and in some instances, government arms are stolen regularly. For instance, police raids around Cape Town in 2017, found illegal SALWs in gang hotspots, stashed in vehicles or on various suspects (Dolley 2017a). A young 14-year-old primary school student was arrested for illegally possessing a firearm after a murder in an area highly known for gang violence (Dolley 2017a). What has therefore emerged is a highly securitised and insecure society, one where the illegal possession of firearms occurs even with the younger generation. The SAPS 2017/2018 annual crime report highlights that illegal weapons have been confiscated in schools (SAPS 2018). Human security has therefore suffered from the presence of SALWs as their availability, ease of production and failure to curb their proliferation create an atmosphere of insecurity. With the presence of these arms, high levels of crime and the inability of law enforcement institutions to provide adequate and speedy responses, many citizens are left to arm themselves for protection. Therefore, the fear in communities is further triggered by the realisation that firearms are readily available and can be used to carry out violent attacks on innocent and unarmed individuals, including security officials.

From the preceding discussions, it is evident that the increasing presence of SALWs and the high murder rates in the country puts the security of its citizens at constant risk. Beyond the availability of SALWs, the South African government has to contend with illegal drug trafficking, human trafficking and the presence of crime syndicates fuelling and financing these illicit ventures. These criminal organisations in the country were estimated to be about 800, with over 12,000 suspects involved (Shaw and Gastrow 2001). These and the preceding sections show that SALWs and its proliferation has implications on policy and security in South Africa, as will be discussed in the following section.

POLICY AND SECURITY IMPLICATIONS ON SALWs AND CRIME

SALWs affects all aspects of society, and so its response requires a holistic response, bringing in non-governmental organisations, the private sector and the community in addition to core stakeholders like the SAPS, government and intelligence institutions. This holistic approach requires solutions that focus on the supply, demand and availability of these weapons. Furthermore, they should pay attention to how the non-proliferation of SALWs can be achieved by ensuring stringent gun-licensing programmes, regularising arms destruction and improving mechanisms to manage the entry, acquisition and circulation of these weapons in and out of the country. According to a press release by the Parliamentary Portfolio Committee on Police (2018), the Committee noted that the following key actions are needed in effectively addressing the rise in the proliferation of SALWs. These include: diverting resources to the Directorate for Priority Crime Investigation's (DPIC) specialised unit focusing on illegal firearms; increasing activities and operations to address gun smuggling by crime syndicates; enforcing stricter arms control measures in SAPS, gun shops, stations and the South African National Defence Force (SANDF); increasing cooperation with SADC countries in curbing the proliferation and inflow of high-calibre automatic firearms in the region and carrying out an extensive and in-depth review of the National Firearms Registry turn-around strategy and forensic audits in the licensing of firearms, permits and authorisations (Parliamentary Portfolio Committee on Police 2018). These recommendations speak to the need for stricter regulations on the ownership and sale of guns in the country but also of the need for a multi-level and multi-actor engagement from the national to the grassroots level. In discussing the different stakeholders and their responsibilities below, this section highlights ongoing efforts to address SALWs and identifies ways to improve and address it.

Legislative Framework Implementation

South Africa has robust legislative frameworks in place, and these include the FCA. Replacing the 1969 Arms and Ammunitions Act (1969), the Firearms Control Act of 2000 was created for various reasons, one of which was to "prevent the proliferation of illegally possessed firearms and, by providing for the removal of those firearms from society and by improving control over legally possessed firearms, to prevent crime involving the use of firearms" (2000: 10). It was also created to establish a comprehensive and useful system to manage and control firearms; enforce relevant legislation; ensure punishment for illegal use; and more importantly guarantee the rights of its citizens to life and integrity as outlined in the constitution (Firearms Control Act 2000: 10). The Act also states the use of background checks to investigate the criminal history of applicants and check regular license renewals to ensure that applicants are fit to own a firearm and if they still have that firearm in their possession. It also allows the Minister to impose certain conditions like conducting ballistic testing of any firearm handed into determine if it is linked to a crime (Kirsten 2007).

While the Act has been used successfully in reducing firearm-related incidents, all its provisions must be fully implemented in order to see a significant reduction in firearm homicides. According to the Small Arms Survey (2013), there is a definite link between the partial implementation of the FCA and reduced firearm homicides thus purporting that better or full implementation will produce more positive results. This view is shared by Gun Free South Africa (GFSA) as they claim that the FCA has reduced gun deaths by 50% over ten years (Smillie 2019). The Firearms Control Amendment Bill passed in 2018 seeks to amend and further strengthen the FCA. The Amendment calls for a wide range of changes including inserting and changing definitions, penalties for late renewals of firearms, and amending the Criminal Law Amendment Act 1997 (No. 105 of 1997) so as to provide for minimum sentences in cases where firearms were used in murder, rapes and robberies and for the illegal possession of firearms.

Responses from the South African Government to SALW Proliferation

At the core of SALWs proliferation in South Africa is how the government and its relevant institutions can commit resources and enhance their capacities to curb the proliferation of arms. While SALWs has played an integral role in South Africa's history of apartheid and conflict between groups, the current threat focuses on the role of SALWs in existing high levels of criminality and violence in both rural and urban areas. This is exacerbated by the culture of violence that permeates society in general.

Two key government institutions are worth noting in highlighting South Africa's efforts at addressing SALWs proliferation outside its borders. Firstly, at the Ministerial level, the NCACC has highlighted national focus and commitment to reducing SALWs. Its principal mandate is to oversee the control of trade in conventional arms and the offering of foreign military assistance, thus ensuring that trade in all weapons is regulated through the issuing of permits and applications for registration with the Chief Directorate Conventional Arms Control (CDCAC). Issuing of permits are therefore needed for the development, marketing, manufacturing, exporting, importing, transferring of firearms, ammunition and other weapons, all of these permits are referred for extensive review and scrutiny before approval. Secondly, its Department of International Relations and Cooperation (DIRCO), has within it, a Directorate on Disarmament and Non-proliferation and its main area of work focuses on national, regional and international arms control including negotiations at the regional and international level.

As a way for governments to control the pool of illegal SALWs in a country, firearms amnesty has been used to collect and destroy legal and illegal firearms. According to the National Commissioner of SAPS, 110,000 firearms and 1 million ammunition were destroyed between the periods of 2012–2015 (SAPS 2015). As another example, the firearms amnesty of 2005, was used to collect 100,006 firearms, 53,435 of these were illegal, and the other 33,823 weapons were surrendered by people who unlawfully possessed these weapons through failure to register, negligence and the possession of a deceased's firearm (Kirsten 2007). In addition, the police recovered 17,665 of these weapons from crime scenes (Kirsten 2007). In April 2019, over 30,000 firearms were destroyed by the police in Gauteng, many of these weapons were seized and surrendered to the state, with the last destruction exercise taking place in 2016 (Farber 2019).

The Parliamentary Portfolio Committee on Police unanimously approved another firearms amnesty on the 23 October 2019 with the committee proposing that the starting date for amnesty be moved from December 1, 2019 to May 2020 to ensure that necessary administrative processes are in place. In addition, the committee has requested that those with expired firearms licenses are allowed to apply for new licenses during the amnesty period. Based on the previous examples, firearm amnesty programmes should be regularised, and weapons should be collected and destroyed frequently to avoid them returning into circulation. Firearms amnesty programmes have proved to be successful in communities in countries like the United Kingdom, Australia, United States, Ghana and South Africa as guns and ammunition have been brought in by various members of the community. Taking various forms like gun buy-back schemes or exchange programmes, these weapons have been successfully collected in Disarmament, Demobilization and Reintegration (DDR) programmes in Sierra Leone and Liberia.

Firearms amnesty should be used regularly in communities, as according to Kirsten (2007), it will allow firearm owners to hand in unwanted, licensed firearms. This can be done through community policing structures and in working with community leaders and neighbourhood watch structures. Community engagement is pivotal in the firearms amnesty programmes because of their commitment and involvement in surrendering arms, and registering their firearms contributes to fighting crime and removing their presence in the community. Based on past lessons, amnesty programmes can be successful in South Africa as long as there is sufficient internal communication on the new firearms legislation; it covers both legal and illegal weapons collection; ensures that incentives are made available for criminals, and the amnesty conditions like names, identity numbers, addresses and ballistic testing requirements are lessened (Kirsten 2007). Meek (1998) thus notes that achieving successful amnesty programmes requires proper timing and duration, clear conditions for amnesty, location of hand-in points, clarity on objectives, communication and publicity; incentives and internal organisational planning and capacity.

The established connection between firearms and violence requires efforts to focus on both legal and illegal weapons. For instance, while illegal firearms are used in violent crime, legally owned weapons are the leading risk factor for the murder of intimate partners (Abrahams et al. 2010). Much effort is also required in limiting the shift of legal to illegal weapon status. The main reason for this is to reduce gun-related deaths in the country, particularly those from illegal arms. Kirsten (2007) proposes that the diversion of legal guns into the illegal market requires strengthening controls over civilian possession;

improving the management of stockpiles and placing restrictions on the types of firearms that civilians can own.

Community Engagement and Ownership in Preventing SALW Proliferation

Public involvement is vital to curbing the spread of illegal weapons. Gould and Lamb (2004) note that civilians have more than six times as many guns as the South African police and military, thus showing that citizens contribute to the illegal SALWs proliferation. Community awareness and involvement are essential in preventing violent crime and curbing the spread of illegal arms. Sensitisation campaigns to build and encourage civic responsibility where they help to report the move or sale of illegal guns, as with other vices such as drugs is integral to the success of curbing SALWs proliferation. Within townships and high-risk areas, residents should be informed and educated on the FCA, on how to be responsible gun owners and on the need to remove illegal firearms from circulation.

Police have successfully confiscated firearms through tip-offs (SAPS 2018) as well, thus proving that community engagement is pivotal. In the Western Cape Province, the community safety department offered 10,000 rands to reports that lead to the confiscation of illegal weapons and has set up a hotline for this initiative (Chambers 2019). When offering the first 10,000 to an anonymous individual, former Member of the Executive Council (MEC), Community Safety Alan Winde, noted the importance of community reporting on storage locations of weapons in order to remove them as a threat to safety, while emphasising the commitment to ensuring the anonymity of those who report (Chambers 2019).

Neighbourhood watches are present throughout communities in South Africa to protect from crime. They are essential in any security framework because they are made up of the members of the community. In South Africa's case, their role has become particularly important due to the budget cuts in SAPS and projected cuts of 19.3 billion expected between 2020 and 2023 (Dawood 2019). The budget cuts which will lead to the removal of 23,617 positions (Dawood 2019) will require the role of neighbourhood watches. Neighbourhood watches are important in reducing the spread of SALWs by reporting locations of these weapons and related suspicious activity.

The South Africa Police Service and Managing SALW Proliferation and Preventing Crime

The South African Police, under the leadership of the Minister of Police, is responsible for the management and control of SALWs. It is responsible for the Central Firearms Register where it controls the manufacture, possession, import and export of SALWs. The role of police investigations and intelligence operations have successfully contributed to the seizure of SALWs. Amnesty can be successful if it is complemented with regular intelligence operations, according to Gun Free South Africa's (GFSA) Adéle Kirsten (Smillie 2019). This view is supported by the SAPS 2017–2018 annual report, which states that firearm seizures occur mainly during crime combating, crime prevention and stop/search operations (SAPS 2018). According to its annual report, anyone found with an unlicensed firearm and or ammunition during police and intelligence operations is arrested, and the incident is recorded (SAPS 2019). SAPS has carried out stings including Operation Sethunya in 2003. This operation, which was conducted with the extension of the 2005 Amnesty Programme, focused on curbing the proliferation of firearms. It was seen as the most extensive police effort to address the presence of illegal SALWs in the country.

Since the start of the Operation, 2 834 guns (including AK-47's, R-5 and Uzi submachine guns) and 36,919 rounds of ammunition were confiscated from criminals throughout Gauteng province, and 8899 firearms and 81,150 rounds of ammunition were seized throughout the province (Hosken 2003). In another operation, triggered by information received by a police informant, police seized two arms caches, which included explosives, narcotics, 15 rifles and close to 1000 police-issued 9 mm and R-5 ammunitions (Hosken 2019). For future operations, more resources should be diverted to intelligence gathering, which can be used to track illegal activities, weapons and their usage. Hosken (2003) noted that through intelligence gathering during Operation Sethunya, police were tracking the whereabouts of 14,000 illegal guns currently circulating in Gauteng.

Rapid and regular destruction of these weapons is equally important to avoid it getting into the wrong hands and reducing the chances of its sale by police officers. A significant challenge with the Firearms Amnesty of 2005 was the lack of storage facilities for weapons and lengthy wait periods before weapons were destroyed, with one police station having several thousand weapons in safe storage in May 2006, more than a year after the amnesty (Kirsten 2004). This challenge has been raised again with the recent decision in October 2019 by the Police Minister and the Parliament's Police Portfolio Committee to carry out another firearms amnesty programme. The question is if the police have the capacity and logistical requirements to store and destroy these firearms (Smillie 2019). Furthermore, the legal representative of the SA Gun Owners Association—Martin Hood noted that the police would be overstretched in storing and carrying out individual ballistic testing of these weapons (Smillie 2019).

Police efforts have become more focused and decentralised in response to community needs in high-risk areas. In Cape Town, Neighbourhood Security Teams (NST) made up of law enforcement officials have been deployed to high-risk areas, with the main aim of being visible and actively involved in community security. They have been successful in various instances, including confiscating illegal weapons, drugs and carrying out searches. For example, in the Leiden area of Cape Town, the Delft Neighbourhood Safety Team (NST) discovered six firearms while on patrol after approaching three suspects to perform a search (Staff Reporter, *IOL News* 2019). These initiatives in various communities have reduced the number of deaths and resulted in decreased gang threats and general insecurity.

Non-governmental Organisations and Their Fight Against SALW

Non-governmental organisations in South Africa are involved in contributing to efforts to prevent SALWs effects on society. They are involved in raising public awareness on the effects of small arms and its impacts on society, they have called for transparency and accountability in government's highly lucrative arms trade and transfers, galvanised public support for gun control and have protested against organised violence. In South Africa, non-governmental organisations working on SALWs are either part of global networks or are locally established. For example, the International Action Network on Small Arms (IANSA), launched in The Hague, Netherlands has a South African chapter. In another example, the South African based Gun Control Alliance was launched in 1999, which represents over 450 organisations, institutions and individuals. This alliance coordinated by GFSA is focused on building an alliance to implement stricter gun controls in the country.

A prominent organisation in the fight against illegal SALWs is the GFSA, a non-profit organisation formed in 1995 created with the main aim of reducing gun-related violence in South Africa, plays a vital role in the fight against SALWs proliferation. Among its many activities which include running campaigns and policy engagement, it runs the Gun Free Zone project (GFZ) in order to create safe spaces and increase debate on the danger of weapons and how to defend oneself without a gun.

Two other important organisations include the Gunowners Association of South Africa (GOSA) and the South African Gunowners Association (SAGA), both focusing on ensuring accountability and transparency in the use and ownership of firearms. Both organisations advocate for the responsible use of firearms and are engaged in various processes to ensure that the rights of legal arms owners are protected. SAGA has engaged in protests, contributes to national debates on arms matters, participates in policy development and helps shape political discourses on SALWs. GOSA has been involved in litigation on behalf of their members, and engaging with key political stakeholders and coordinating public outreach programmes. Kirsten (2007) noted that more partnerships are needed between government and civil society organisations such as Gun Free South Africa (GFSA) and the South African Gunowners Association (SAGA).

Businesses are also part of the nation-wide gun control alliance in South Africa because they have become targets of criminal activity as well. The private sector can contribute to firearms control as they can ask customers to declare firearms, search customers and have safes to store firearms. The private sector is also involved in developing firearms and ammunition. By the mid-1960s, there were an estimated 1000 private sector firms involved in domestic arms production processes in South Africa; thus the Armaments Production Board (APB) was created to coordinate arms production in the private sector. They must be held accountable, and more research is required on their role in contributing to reducing SALWs proliferation in South Africa.

While the government has acted in many ways to curtail and reduce the proliferation of SALWs in the country, some challenges continue to inhibit any efforts at success. Corruption is a significant challenge as police officers are involved in the proliferation of SALWs by selling guns while working with crime syndicates and stealing criminal dockets. As of September 2017, SAPS in the Western Cape Province is considering a wide range of measures to prevent smuggling of police guns to criminals, and these include a national audit of all firearms at the 151 police stations in the province and a tracking system to quickly find every single police gun (Dolley 2017b).

Taking the preceding analysis of programmes, legal frameworks and stakeholders into account, it can be deduced that South Africa has identified avenues to reduce the spread of SALWs in the country, many of which have produced positive results. Efforts need to be channelled towards strengthening these broad ranges of initiatives and increasing resources and efforts at intelligence gathering, curbing corruption and destruction of weapons. Firearm-related crime levels are significantly higher, which shows the need for doubling of efforts in crime prevention.

Conclusion

South Africa's stability and security depend significantly on its ability to curb the spread and availability of SALWs. National responses have included recovering lost, stolen and illegally sold guns through search and seizure operations, destruction of firearms and tracking their movement. Future efforts will benefit from regular destruction of firearms, regular collections of weapons that are voluntarily surrendered and providing amnesty to willing individuals. Gun regulation is equally important such that manufacturers, traders and owners of firearms are granted firearm certificates and permits authorising them to own these weapons. Regular accounting and audits of police caches and stockpiles are essential. Furthermore, gun destructions must be audited as well to avoid theft.

The security of both migrants and South Africans are essential, and efforts are needed to curb the spread of SALWs in exacerbating human insecurity in these communities. While Xenophobia must be addressed by reducing inequality, ensuring even development, providing jobs, improving public services, developing infrastructure and improving intergroup relations and cohesion; the role of SALWs in contributing to xenophobic violence and crime requires an urgent response. In addressing Xenophobia, the South African government should engage more with migrants in understanding their experiences and challenges. In realising that they contribute significantly to its economy and growth, it is crucial to acknowledge these and improve police and judiciary systems to protect them from violent crimes. Prosecutions of perpetrators are also very important.

The South African government must manage internal insecurity while improving efforts to secure their borders. Furthermore, it must continue to improve the socio-economic lives of its citizens including providing of basic needs and services, preventing and limiting the abuse of government funds and resources, addressing the high levels of unemployment, inequality and poverty all of which propel individuals to engage in criminal activities.

REFERENCES

Abass, A. (2010). *Protecting Human Security in Africa*. London: Oxford University Press.

Abdi, C. M. (2011). Moving Beyond Xenophobia: Structural Violence, Conflict and Encounters with the 'Other' Africans. *Development Southern Africa, 28*, 691–704. https://doi.org/10.1080/0376835X.2011.623916.

Abrahams, N., Jewkes, R., & Mathews, S. (2010). Guns and Gender-Based Violence in South Africa. *South African Medical Journal, 100*(9), 586–588. Retrieved June 15, 2018, from Scielo South Africa.

Azrael, D., & Hemenway, D. (2000). In the Safety of Your Own Home: Results from a National Survey on Gun Use at Home. *Social Science and Medicine, 50*, 285–291. https://doi.org/10.1016/s0277-9536(99)00283-x.

Bauer, N. (2013, May 28). Diepsloot: Crime, Xenophobia—Or Both? *Mail and Guardian*. Retrieved from https://mg.co.za/article/2013-05-28-diepsloot-crime-xenophobia-or-both. Accessed 20 November 2019.

Berg, J., & Gabi, B. (2011). *Regulating Private Security in South Africa Context, Challenges and Recommendation* (APCOF Policy Paper). Retrieved from http://apcof.org/wp-content/uploads/2016/05/No-3-Regulating-Private-Security-in-South-Africa_-Context-challenges-and-recommendations-Julie-Berg-and-Vavariro-Gabi.pdf.

Chambers, D. (2019, March 28). Western Cape Pays First R10,000 Reward to Gun Informant. *Timeslive*. Retrieved from https://www.timeslive.co.za/news/south-africa/2019-03-28-western-cape-pays-first-r10000-reward-to-gun-informant/.

Chetty, R. (2000). *Firearm Use and Distribution in South Africa*. Pretoria: The National Crime Prevention Centre.

Dawood, Z. (2019, September 5). Pinetown Neighbourhood Watch Members Come Under Fire from Robbers. *IOL*. Retrieved from https://www.iol.co.za/dailynews/news/kwazulu-natal/pinetown-neighbourhood-watch-members-come-under-fire-from-robbers-31897017. Accessed 23 November 2019.

Dolley, C. (2017a, November 14). Hunting Rifles, Drugs and Child Suspects: What Seizure of Guns in Cape Town Reveals. *News24*. Retrieved from https://www.news24.com/SouthAfrica/News/hunting-rifles-drugs-and-child-suspects-what-guns-seized-in-cape-town-reveals-20171114. Accessed 12 June 2018.

Dolley, C. (2017b, September 12). EXCLUSIVE: 'Plan' Implemented to Crack Down on Cops Smuggling Guns to Criminals. *News24*. Retrieved from https://www.news24.com/SouthAfrica/News/exclusive-plan-implemented-to-crack-down-on-cops-smuggling-guns-to-criminals-20170912. Accessed 14 June 2018.

Dolley, C. (2017c, July 19). Gang Bosses Exploit Private Security Loophole to 'Legally Intimidate' Rivals—Sources. *News24*. Retrieved from https://www.news24.com/SouthAfrica/News/gang-bosses-exploit-private-security-loophole-to-legally-intimidate-rivals-sources-20170719.

Farber, T. (2019, April 17). Gauteng Police Destroy More Than 30,000 Seized and Surrendered Guns. *Timeslive*. Retrieved from https://www.timeslive.co.za/news/south-africa/2019-04-17-gauteng-police-destroy-more-than-30000-seized-and-surrendered-guns/. Accessed 25 November 2019.

Firearms Control Act No. 60, 2000, s.145 (South Africa).

Gastrow, V. (2015, February 2). Soweto Xenophobia and the Foreign Cowboy. *Daily Maverick*. Retrieved from https://www.dailymaverick.co.za/opinionista/2015-02-02-soweto-xenophobia-and-the-foreign-cowboy/. Accessed 20 November 2019.

Gould, C., & Lamb, G. (2004). *Hide and Seek: A Report on the Southern Africa Research Programme on Small Arms and Light Weapons*. Pretoria: Institute for Security Studies.

Hamber, B. E. (1998). Dr Jekyll and Mr Hyde: Violence and Transition in South Africa. In E. Bornman, R. Van Eeden, & M. Wentzel (Eds.), *Violence in South Africa* (pp. 349–370). Pretoria: Human Sciences and Research Council.

Hosken, G. (2003, September 3). *Police Seize Thousands of Illegal Firearms*. Retrieved from IOL, South Africa. https://www.iol.co.za/news/south-africa/police-seize-thousands-of-illegal-firearms-112274. Accessed 14 June 2018.

Hosken, G. (2019, June 23). Cops Seize Nearly 1000 Rounds of Ammunition Hidden in Couches in Pretoria Flat. *TimesLive*. Retrieved from https://www.timeslive.co.za/news/south-africa/2019-06-23-breaking-cops-seize-nearly-1000-rounds-of-ammunition-hidden-in-couches-in-pretoria-flat/. Accessed 20 November 2019.

HRW. (2000, October 1). South Africa: A Question of Principle, Arms Trade and Human Rights. *Human Rights Watch*. Retrieved from https://www.hrw.org/reports/2000/safrica/index.htm#TopOfPage. Accessed 2 June 2018.

HRW. (2008, May 22). South Africa: Punish Attackers in Xenophobic Violence: Government Should Protect Victims to Ensure Justice. *Human Rights Watch*. Retrieved from https://www.hrw.org/news/2008/05/22/south-africa-punish-attackers-xenophobic-violence. Accessed 4 June 2018.

IOL. (2019, August 30). Neighbourhood Safety Officer Uncovers Cape Woman Carrying a Lethal Weapon in Her Panty. *IOL*. Retrieved from https://www.iol.co.za/capeargus/news/neighbourhood-safety-officer-uncovers-cape-woman-carrying-a-lethal-weapon-in-her-panty-31533758. Accessed 23 November 2019.

Keegan, M. (2005). *The Proliferation of Firearms in South Africa 1994–2004*. Gun Free South Africa. Retrieved from https://africacheck.org/wp-content/uploads/2013/03/The-Proliferation-of-Firearms-in-South-Africa-1994-2004.pdf. Accessed 6 December 2019.

Kirsten, A. (2004). *The Role of Social Movements in Gun Control: An International Comparison Between South Africa, Brazil and Australia* (Research Report No. 21). Centre for Civil Society, University of KZN, Durban.

Kirsten, A. (2007). *Simpler, Better, Faster: Review of the 2005 Firearms Amnesty* (pp. 1–14). Pretoria: Institute of Security Studies.

Kumar, S. (2008). Small Arms and Light Weapons: A Global Threat to Human Security and Development. *The Indian Journal of Political Science, LXIX*(4), 787–800. Retrieved November 20, 2019, from JSTOR.

Madia, T., & Somdyala, K. (2019, September 4). 'This Is Not Xenophobia, Thugs Are Taking Chances', Says Magashule on Gauteng Unrest. *News24*. Retrieved from https://www.news24.com/SouthAfrica/News/magashule-on-gauteng-violence-this-is-not-xenophobia-thugs-are-taking-chances-20190904. Accessed 25 November 2019.

Maeko, T. (2019, September 6). Attacks Point to 'Deeply Entrenched' Xenophobic Attitudes. *Mail and Guardian*. Retrieved from https://mg.co.za/article/2019-09-06-00-attacks-point-to-deeply-entrenched-xenophobic-attitudes. Accessed 20 November 2019.

Masuku, S. (2002). Prevention Is Better Than Cure: Addressing Violent Crime in South Africa. *South African Crime Quarterly*, 2, 5–12. https://doi.org/10.17159/2413-3108/2002/v0i2a1078.

McEvoy, C., & Hideg, G. (2017). *Global Violent Deaths 2017: Time to Decide: Small Arms Survey*. Geneva: Graduate Institute of International Studies.

Meek, S. (1998). *Buy or Barter: The History and Prospects of Voluntary Weapons Collection Programmes*. ISS Monograph No 22. Pretoria: Institute for Security Studies.

Meek, S., & Stott, N. (2004). *A guide to the destruction of small arms and light weapons: the approach of the South African National Defence Force*. Geneva: United Nations Institute for Disarmament Research.

Minnaar, A. (2008). The Impact of Firearms' Controls on the South African Private Security Industry. *Acta Criminologica*, 21, 100–123. Retrieved from https://hdl.handle.net/10520/EJC28988.

Misago, J. P. (2017, March 1). Xenophobic Violence in the 'Rainbow Nation'—South Africa. *Aljazeera*. Retrieved from https://www.aljazeera.com/indepth/opinion/2017/03/xenophobic-violence-rainbow-nation-170301075103169.html. Accessed 12 June 2018.

Misago, J. P., Freemantle, I., & Landau, L. B. (2015). *Protection from Xenophobia: An Evaluation of UNHCR's Regional Office for Southern Africa's Xenophobia Related Programmes*. UNHCR.

Mncube, V., & Harber, C. (2013). *The Dynamics of Violence in South African Schools*. Pretoria: UNISA.

Mzantsi, S. (2016, June 21). Former Top Cop Gets 18 Years for Illegal Gun Trade. *Cape Times. IOL News*. https://www.iol.co.za/capetimes/news/former-top-cop-gets-18-years-for-illegal-gun-trade-2037039. Accessed 12 June 2018.

National Crime Prevention Strategy. (1996). Pretoria: Government Printers.

OCHCR. (1993). *Declaration on the Elimination of Violence Against Women*. General Assembly Resolution 48/104 of 20 December 1993.

Parliamentary Portfolio Committee on Police. (2018, May 16). *Committee Recommends These Gun Control Measures Be Prioritised* [Press Release]. Retrieved from https://www.parliament.gov.za/press-releases/committee-recommends-these-gun-control-measures-be-prioritised.

Petersen, T. (2015, July 28). Cape Town Boy, 12, Killed While Playing with Homemade Gun. *News24*. Retrieved from https://www.news24.com/SouthAfrica/News/Cape-Town-boy-12-killed-while-playing-with-homemade-gun-20150728. Accessed 14 June 2018.

Pijoos, I. (2018, May 29). MAP: 140 Heists and Counting—Tracking the 'Dangerous' Surge in 2018 Cash-in-Transit Robberies. *News24*. Retrieved from https://www.news24.com/SouthAfrica/News/map-140-heists-and-counting-tracking-the-dangerous-surge-in-2018-cash-in-transit-robberies-20180529. Accessed 13 July 2018.

Power, T. (2017). School Violence. In F. Veriava, A. Thom, & T. F. Hodgson (Eds.), *Basic Education Rights Handbook—Education Rights in South Africa*. Braamfontein: Section27.

Robinson, T. (1995). South African Arms: Old Tricks of a New Trade. *Bulletin of the American Academy of Arts and Sciences, 48*(8), 11–21. https://doi.org/10.2307/3824953.

Ryklief, N. (2017, July 9). Get Guns Off Streets and Destroy Them: Opinion Piece. *IOL News*. Retrieved from https://www.iol.co.za/capetimes/opinion/get-guns-off-streets-and-destroy-them-10208258. Accessed 12 June 2018.

Seleka, N. (2019, September 10). Xenophobia: Agony, Grief and Fear Stalks Shelter Set Up for Foreign Nationals in Katlehong. *News24*. Retrieved from https://www.news24.com/SouthAfrica/News/xenophobia-agony-grief-and-fear-stalks-shelter-set-up-for-foreign-nationals-in-katlehong-20190910. Accessed 20 November 2019.

Shaw, M., & Gastrow, P. (2001). Stealing the Show? Crime and Its Impact in Post-Apartheid South Africa. *Daedalus, 130*(1), 235–258. Retrieved June 12, 2018 from JSTOR.

Singh, K. (2017, October 30). KZN Cop Arrested for Allegedly Selling Police Guns, Ammo to Criminals. *News24*. Retrieved from https://www.news24.com/SouthAfrica/News/kzn-cop-arrested-for-allegedly-selling-police-guns-ammo-to-criminals-20171030. Accessed 12 June 2018.

Skweyiya, K. (2017, March 22). Why Xenophobia Happens in South Africa [Blog Post]. *Huffington Post*. Retrieved from https://www.huffingtonpost.co.za/kholisa-skweyiya/why-xenophobia-happens-in-south-africa_a_21897362/.

Small Arms Survey. (2001). *Profiling the Problem*. Geneva: Graduate Institute of International and Development Studies.

Small Arms Survey. (2013). *Trend Lines: Armed Violence in South Africa*. Geneva: The Graduate Institute of International and Development Studies.

Small Arms Survey, Geneva. (2013). *Small Arms Survey 2013: Everyday Dangers (Small Arms Survey)*. Cambridge: Cambridge University Press. https://doi.org/10.1017/CBO9781107323612.

Smillie, S. (2019, September 17). Cele's Gun Amnesty, 'A Massive Exercise'. *IOL News*. Retrieved from https://www.iol.co.za/saturday-star/news/celes-gun-amnesty-a-massive-exercise-33120372. Accessed 20 November 2019.

South African Human Rights Commission. (1999). *Fourth Annual Report*. Retrieved from https://www.sahrc.org.za/home/21/files/Reports/Annual%20Reports/4th%20annual_report98_99.pdf. Accessed 22 November 2019.

South African Police Service. (2015, July). SAAPS Destroys 14382 Firearms. *Police*, p. 3. Retrieved from https://www.saps.gov.za/resource_centre/publications/police_mag/police_mag_july2015.pdf. Accessed 22 November 2019.

South African Police Service. (2018). *Annual Crime Report 2017/2018*. Retrieved from https://www.saps.gov.za/services/annual_crime_report2019.pdf. Accessed 21 November 2019.

South African Police Service. (2019). *Crime Statistics: Crime Situation in Republic of South Africa 12 Months (April to March 2018–2019) PowerPoint Presentation*.

Retrieved from https://www.saps.gov.za/services/april_to_march2018_19_presentation.pdf. Accessed 21 November 2019.

Timeslive "500 Police Firearms Vanished After Cops Took Them Home". (2019, October 30). *TimesLive*. Retrieved from https://www.timeslive.co.za/news/south-africa/2019-10-30-500-police-firearms-vanished-after-cops-took-them-home/. Accessed 25 November 2019.

United Nations Office on Drugs and Crime. (2019). *Global Study on Homicide*. United Nations.

World Health Organization. (2016). *Disease Burden and Mortality Estimates*. Retrieved from https://www.who.int/healthinfo/global_burden_disease/estimates/en/. Accessed 21 November 2019.

Xenowatch. (2019). *Factsheet 1: Incidents of Xenophobic Violence in South Africa: January–September 2019*. African Centre for Migration and Society. Retrieved from http://www.xenowatch.ac.za/wp-content/uploads/2019/10/Factsheet-1-Xenohopbic-violence-incidents-in-SA_-Jan-Sept-2019.pdf. Accessed 25 November 2019.

Dorcas Ettang is a Senior Lecturer in Political Science in the School of Social Sciences, University of KwaZulu-Natal, Pietermaritzburg, South Africa. She teaches undergraduate and postgraduate modules while supervising Masters and Ph.D. students in Political Science, International Relations and Conflict Transformation and Peace Studies. She holds a Ph.D. in Conflict Transformation and Peace Studies from the University of KwaZulu-Natal, South Africa and a Masters in Political Science from the University of Windsor, Canada. She has previous experience as a Programme Officer and Analyst with the African Centre for the Constructive Resolution of Disputes (ACCORD) in Durban, South Africa. Her areas of research include conflict prevention, peacebuilding, identity politics, migration and non-violence with a grassroots focus. She has published in journals including *Africa Development, Journal of African Elections, Communicatio* and *Gender and Behaviour*.

CHAPTER 40

Sierra Leone: Civil War, Democratic Collapse and Small Arms Proliferation

Sharkdam Wapmuk

INTRODUCTION

The proliferation of Small Arms and Light Weapons (SALWs) is an immediate security challenge to individuals, societies and states across the world. SALWs fuel civil wars, organised criminal violence and terrorist activities. The case of Sierra Leone presents the stark reality of the role that small arms played in fueling the rebellion led by violent non-state actors, particularly the Revolutionary United Front (RUF) leading to complete breakdown of law and order, democratic collapse and civil war. Sierra Leone is one of the many countries that depicted the nature of the post-Cold-War security environment in Africa. The end of the Cold War did not exactly bring about the much-expected peace to the global environment. Instead, it had other indirect and unforeseen effects on African insurgency groups who were exposed to an illicit international market for SALWs. The RUF and other rebel groups in Sierra Leone, fought for the control of diamond fields and other mineral-rich areas, and used that economic leverage to access the international market for SALWs. The availability of blood diamonds which were sold to buy weapons made it lucrative for the RUF to invade Sierra Leone, backed by the governments of Libya, Burkina Faso and Charles Taylor's National Patriotic Front of Liberia (NPFL) in 1991 (Berman and Labonte 2006). The RUF terrorised

S. Wapmuk (✉)
Department of Defence and Security Studies, Nigerian Defence Academy, Kaduna, Nigeria

© The Author(s), under exclusive license to Springer Nature Switzerland AG 2021
U. A. Tar and C. P. Onwurah (eds.), *The Palgrave Handbook of Small Arms and Conflicts in Africa*,
https://doi.org/10.1007/978-3-030-62183-4_40

civilians and engaged in gruesome killings, looting, raping and torture waged by undisciplined militia, which included child soldiers.

While SALWs were not directly the cause of the conflicts in Sierra Leone, they were prosecuted with the use of highly lethal small arms and light weapons (Oluwadare 2014). The conflict had its roots in a complex mix of historical dynamics, failed democratic experiments, bad governance as well as "greed and grievances" that played out in Sierra Leone (Blank 2012). The post-independence era had been characterised by corrupt governments that alienated the country's youth and destroyed basic institutions, including education, parliament, the police and the civil service. This dissatisfaction led to support for the rebels in the early years of the war. With the backing of Charles Taylor, then President of Liberia, the Revolutionary United Front (RUF) which crossed the border from Liberia, with the prime objective of capturing state power and controlling the diamond mines, began attacking civilians. By the time the war was declared over, more than 70,000 people died, over two million were displaced and 500,000 refugees were forced into neighbouring countries in the West African subregion, thousands had been mutilated or raped, and an estimated 10,000 children had been abducted to be child soldiers. The proliferation of SALW ensured that the war in Sierra Leone was not only prolonged, but the trail of dead and properties destroyed confirm the destructive nature of SALWs and their categorisation as weapons of mass destruction.

The chapter, which examines the crisis leading to democratic collapse, civil war and the proliferation of SALWs in the context of Sierra Leone, is divided into five parts. Following the introduction, the second section discusses the historical dynamics, failed democratic experiments and civil war in Sierra Leone. The third section examines the supply and impacts of SALW on Sierra Leone during the civil war. Section four is titled addressing SALWs proliferation in post-conflict Sierra Leone. The fifth section is the conclusion.

HISTORICAL DYNAMICS, FAILED DEMOCRATIC EXPERIMENTS AND CIVIL WAR IN SIERRA LEONE

The history of the territory that later became known as Sierra Leone was to change in 1787 when 400 freed North American slaves were settled in the city of Freetown. Originally, the name was derived from "Serra Lyoa" (meaning Lion Mountains), a name first used by Pedro da Cintra, a Portuguese explorer in 1462. Though the British had justified the takeover of the interior of Sierra Leone on the grounds of outlawing slavery, the presence of rich deposits of diamond and other mineral resources, proved to be a better explanation seeking control of the ports and hinterland, and collaboration with local chiefs (Tar and Wapmuk 2017: 255). It wasn't long before the British took over the political economy of the area, thus redefining the social and cultural relations of the ethnic population. The former slaves, known as Creoles, who had vantage position and background in education also became politically and historically dominant in the affairs of Sierra Leone. Beginning from this period to independence in 1961, the population, ethnic composition and the socio-economic and political landscape of the entire society were altered. Against the backdrop of its diluted historical dynamics, the people of Sierra Leone were not exactly united at independence, a situation which was further compounded by subsequent failure of democratic experiments in the country and perpetuation of state of underdevelopment in the post-independence era. State managers that took over power in the post-independence era, failed to practice good governance and reposition the country on the path of development, rather, attention shifted to the consolidation of state power (Sesay 1999). Milton Marga of Sierra Leone People's Party (SLPP) became Sierra Leone's first Prime Minister after independence in 1961. However, in 1967, the All People's Congress (APC), a party which was formed out of the SLPP in 1957, won the elections and its leader, Siaka Stevens who was the Prime Minister (1967 and 1968–1971), formed a new government and later became the country's first President (1971–1985). Sierra Leone was transformed into a single-party state during his rule and his regime was also accused of massive corruption. Post-colonial Sierra Leone experienced democratic rule interrupted by a series of military juntas that seized power through coups with the excuse of fixing the damage done by politicians. In the years that followed failed democratic experiments, domestic politics became increasingly characterised by mistrust of opposition, massive corruption, mismanagement and intermitted violence that led to a weak civil society, lack of popular participation in governance, and poor performance of important state institutions including, the education sector (Abdullah 2004). By 1991, an entire generation of dissatisfied youth, became easy targets for recruitment to join RUF in a rebellion that was initially claimed by the RUF aimed at liberating the state from corruption and misrule, and to promote social justice for all. This grave scenario paved the way for the entry of the rebel groups, armed with illicit weapons.

The RUF, led by Army Corporal Foday Sankoh had received external support from the governments of Libya and Burkina Faso and Charles Taylor's National Patriotic Front of Liberia (NPFL) (Berman and Labonte 2006). Its activities were sustained through the capture, control, exploitation and sale of mineral wealth, particularly the diamonds, mined in the Eastern Kono district. President Momoh could not stop the rebel force as the Sierra Leone Army (SLA) had insufficient supplies, ammunition and food. The relationship between the Liberian warlords and the RUF in Sierra Leone, as well as availability of blood diamonds enabled endless access to SALWs in order to wage their vicious war (Hironaka 2005). Armed with these weapons, the RUF engaged in killing, looting raping and torturing of civilians, especially young men and women who refused forceful conscription. Their mark became characterised by recruitment of child soldiers, cutting off the hands and feet of men, women and children. The grave situation in Sierra Leone attracted international outcry against the crimes being committed by the rebel groups against humanity. Dwindling domestic support as well as lack of international recognition compelled the RUF and other rebel groups to passively embrace negotiation, this awakened hope of ending the war.

The government's efforts at finding peace led to the adoption of a new constitution providing for a multiparty system in September 1991. However, this did not pacify the rebels that continued to unleash destructions of lives and properties. Apparently as a result of frustration due to government's failure to deal with the rebels, Army officers led by Captain Valentine Strasser, staged a coup and ousted President Joseph Momoh in 1992. The coup was not well received by international community and under international pressure; Strasser announced plans for the first multiparty elections since 1967. Strasser himself was ousted in military coup led by his defense minister, Brigadier Julius Maada Bio in January 1996. It was in February of the same year that Ahmad Tejan Kabbah was elected president. With the help of Executive Outcomes (EO), a defense contractor based in South Africa, the government was able to temporarily push back the rebel forces and later signed a peace accord (Abidjan Accord) with Sankoh's rebels in November. The deal was short lived as President Kabbah was deposed by the army in May 1997. The coup led by Major Johnny Paul Koroma, who was in prison and awaiting the outcome of a treason trial, had the support of the Armed Forces Revolutionary Council (AFRC). President Kabbah had to flee to Guinea to seek international support. Kabbah secured asylum in Nigeria; his choice of Nigeria was eminent—Nigeria lobbied within ECOWAS and elsewhere to negotiate a ceasefire and facilitate Kabbah's return to power.

Johnny Paul Koroma and his junta aligned with the RUF and established an Armed Forces Revolutionary Council (AFRC), chaired by himself and with Sankoh as Vice-Chair. It was at this point that the Nigerian led ECOWAS Monitoring Group (ECOMOG) intervened in June 1997 and again in February 1998 to drive out the rebels and reinstate Kabbah as President. Even so, the RUF and AFRC fighters retreated into the bush, resorting to guerrilla tactics. The RUF continued to receive support from Liberia and Burkina Faso. The alliance between the RUF and AFRC fighters was short-lived as mistrust and disregard for the command chain weakened the partnership. There is no doubt that the fractionalisation of the fighting forces exacerbated the level of violence in the country. It increased the personalisation of power in the RUF and AFRC. An environment that was characterised by proliferation of SALWs in hands of rebels, militias, and regular army, civilians became easy targets of a proxy war of anti-government resentment. Amputations, public and gang rape, and summary executions all increased (Marks 2013). The reports of violence in 1998 followed the path of the RUF–AFRC's retreat out of the capital into the North and East of the country. The disastrous six January siege of Freetown the following year saw a return and increase in the violence. In just two weeks, in the month of January 1999, the RUF–AFRC forces committed over 1000 reported human rights violations (Kabbah 2012). The RUF–AFRC forces also embarked on vicious practice of deliberate mutilation, whereby parts of the body inter alia, arms, lips, noses, hands, breasts, and legs were amputated and eyes gouged out. According to Human Rights Watch, this was deliberately done to Sierra Leoneans "so that they could not vote" (Human Rights Watch 1998). When the rebel and former army forces were again pushed back into the provinces, they remained in territorial control of almost 80% of the country (Kabbah 2012). There is no doubt that the failure of governance as well as democratic experiments in Sierra Leone's post-independence era and the civil war provided the context for further proliferation of SALWs in the country.

THE SUPPLY AND IMPACT OF SALWS ON SIERRA LEONE DURING THE CIVIL WAR

Sierra Leone's war was fought primarily with small arms and light weapons. According to Amnesty International, the International Action Network on Small Arms, and Oxfam International (2006) about 25,000 small arms, 1000 light weapons, and almost a million rounds of ammunition were handed in during the various disarmament processes for rebel forces and pro-government militias between September 1998 and January 2002. This was before the resumption of fighting following the collapse of the Lomé peace process. According to the Report of the Panel of Experts Appointed in relation to Sierra Leone, and, Small Arms Survey (2000), the weapons submitted by the rebels included 496 pistols; 4000 AK-47 rifles from China, the Soviet Union, and Eastern Europe; 1072 AK-74 rifles; 940 G3 rifles from Germany, seized from peacekeeping units or re-exported from third countries; 440 FN-FAL rifles—originally from Belgium; 451 SLR rifles; 140 machine guns from China; 217 grenade launchers; 1855 grenades; 45 mortars (Report of the Panel of Experts 2000a). A major issue is that these SALWs flowing into the hands of the rebels were not manufactured in Sierra Leone and more so that the state lacked the capacity to manufacture them. Furthermore, the weapons were being accessed underan UN arms embargo that was imposed in May 1997. The embargo was later amended in June 1998 to permit the sale of weapons to the Sierra Leonean government. It was also in October 1998 that the Economic Community of West African States (ECOWAS) Moratorium on the production, procurement, and sale of small arms and light weapons in the subregion was adopted (ECOWAS 1998). Though the Moratorium is a non-legally binding agreement, it seeks to prevent weapons imports, unless all ECOWAS member states agree to make an exception (Report of the Panel of Experts 2000a).

Despite the existence of arm embargo, the rebels in Sierra Leone who had enough resources from "blood diamonds" to pay for SALWs were able to access them aided by weak international controls, porosity of the borders, the roles of middlemen or brokers, and the collapse of internal government controls. According to Small Arms Survey (2000), while transfers of weapons came from Ukraine, Bulgaria and Slovakia, among others, countries that served as supply lines in providing weapons to the RUF were Burkina

Faso, Niger, and Liberia, Libya, Côte d'Ivoire and Guinea. In addition, the Small Arms Survey (2000: 17) argued that air cargo companies from the UK, Senegal and Belgium carried weapons to Sierra Leone. The RUF had access to diamond money, which was used to buy weapons of choice, particularly the AK 47. The Small Arms Survey (2000: 15) notes that the RUF was earning an estimate of US$30m and US$125m a year from diamond sales and most of the trade in diamonds was going through Liberia. Former President Charles Taylor played a major role not only in providing military training for the RUF, but also in ensuring constant supplies of weapons, ammunition and food through the Liberian border into RUF territory in Sierra Leone. Small Arms Survey (2000: 14) insists that SALWs were sent from "Liberia to the RUF between May 1997 and February 1998, and again in late 1999. Libya under Muammar Ghaddafi also provided weapons to the RUF, with Libyan transport aircraft flying the cargo to Burkina Faso and then Liberia". Burkina Faso was the first arrival point for many of the weapons supply for the RUF, which were supplied through Liberia. Liberia and Côte d'Ivoire were said to have provided direct flights of military equipment to the RUF. Apart from these, the RUF also obtained a number of weapons from within Sierra Leone, which it looted from defeated government troops that abandoned weapons, ECOMOG forces and UN peacekeepers (Small Arms Survey 2000: 14).

SALWs in the hands of the RUF, other rebel groups, the CDF and even government soldiers, had destructive impact in Sierra Leone. Millions of Sierra Leoneans were killed and displaced as a result, and unquantifiable worth of property destroyed. SALWs were used to grossly violate human rights and maintain a general state of fear, insecurity and instability. During the civil war in Sierra Leone, SALWs become the most potent weapons of mass destruction. The availability of SALW empowered the RUF and other rebel groups and provided them the leverage to turn dangerous and vicious, even within a relatively short period of handling the weapons. The relative lack of sophistication and the near-uncomplicated processes for handling these weapons made them the weapons of choice for the rebels. Furthermore, the proliferation, continued supply and recycling, made the weapons relatively easily available thereby aiding the prolongation of the war, and underlining the viciousness of the RUF rebels in the use of the weapons. According to Keili (2008) "The civil war in Sierra Leone where SALW was the main engine of violence saw some 50,000 people killed, 30,000 had their limbs amputated, and 215,000–257,000, women were victims of sexual violence". The danger in the possession of these weapons, especially for the untrained is that, "SALW are particularly prone to rights abuse, as they are easy to maintain, manipulate and are deadly". Musah (2001) further argues, "the SALW facilitated wars led and executed by people other than the military, in many instances child combatants. These civilians-turned combatants usually benefit from the very minimal, if any, combat training and are hardly aware of international human rights laws. As a consequence the civilians- women, the elderly and children- constitute legitimate targets during the war".

Even though most of the civil war atrocities were committed by the RUF and AFRC rebel forces, violations were also committed by government forces and the Civil Defence Force (CDF). The CDF was initially known to use mostly hunting rifles in defending their communities. However, according to the Report of the Panel of Experts (2000a), when they were disarmed, CDF members also handed in some assault rifles, including AK-47s and G3s. Report of the Panel of Experts (2000a: 17) also stated that the "CDF recruited child soldiers and engaged in torture, ill-treatment, and extra-judicial executions of captured rebel combatants and civilians suspected of collaborating with rebel forces". Apart from weapons obtained from illegal sources, the government also provided guns to CDF militias. SALWs proliferation during the Sierra Leonean war was not limited to the RUF. Following the breakout of RUF rebellion in 1991, some friendly governments donated weapons to support the government of Sierra Leone. Examples included Guinea and Egypt that donated ammunition while Nigeria also provided 2500 rifles. Weapons, including SALWs, were procured by the government from Romania, Russia and Ukraine (Small Arms Survey 2000: 22). The implication is that irrespective of the sources, they added to a number of SALWs proliferation in Sierra Leone during the war. The circulation of SALWs did not appear to have waned after the civil war. A recent study conducted by the Small Arms Survey and the African Union (AU) Commission found that while most of the illicit small arms were obtained from other countries, Sierra Leone ranked domestic craft production as the most significant source of illicit arm in circulation in the country (Small Arms Survey and AU 2018). The craft manufacture of small arms, which is the production of weapons outside of state control, by hand, in small quantities, and with a reduced capability, is an important source of small arms proliferation, not receiving adequate attention by the government of Sierra Leone.

The availability of SALWs procured from sales of blood diamonds to fuel the war made it difficult to bring it to an end. As captured in Table 40.1, GIABA noted that from 2000 to 2006, illicit funds acquired from unrecorded

Table 40.1 Estimate of illicitly acquired funds from unrecorded diamond export in Sierra Leone, 2001–2006

S/No.	Year	Official Record (USD)	Unofficial Estimate (USD)	Difference (USD)
1	2001	26 Million	250 Million	224 Million
2	2002	42 Million	250 Million	208 Million
3	2003	76 Million	250 Million	174 Million
4	2004	127 Million	250 Million	123 Million
5	2005	142 Million	250 Million	108 Million
6	2006	125 Million	250 Million	125 Million

Source GIABA (2013) Annual Report, p. 26

exports of diamond in Sierra Leone may have been used to fund the purchase of SALWs in Sierra Leone.

According to GIABA, an estimated USD250–300 million worth of diamonds were produced in Sierra Leone between 2001 and 2006. This means that country received about USD1.5 billion (calculated at the rate of USD$250 million per year) during the period. With a total of USD538 million officially recorded, a balance of USD$962 million is estimated to have been illicitly acquired by various groups and individuals. It noted that though it is difficult to ascertain the exact amount used for purchase of SALWs, the high rebel activities necessitated that a substantial percentage of the amount could be spent on illegal arms deals.

Several regional and international bodies such as the UN and ECOWAS as well as UK played major roles in seeking peace in Sierra Leone. These included the ECOWAS Monitoring Group (ECOMOG) with about 13,000 soldiers—staffed with principally Nigerian soldiers and two UN operations—United Nations Mission in Sierra Leone (UNAMSIL) and United Nations Observer Mission in Sierra Leone (UNOMSIL)—with an authorised strength of more than 20,000 men. The entry in 1997 of ECOMOG led by Nigeria in Sierra Leone was significant in driving the rebels out of Free Town and later reinstatement of Kabbah to power in 1998, before UN peacekeepers arrived. However, according to Amnesty International (1998), the ECOMOG did not take inadequate measures to protect civilians. When the arms embargo on the Sierra Leonean government was lifted in 1998, the UK became the biggest arms supplier to the Sierra Leone government, particularly since it began training the Sierra Leone armed forces.

As from July 1998, the Security Council set up the UN Observer Mission in Sierra Leone (UNOMSIL) and United Nations Mission in Sierra Leone (UNAMSIL) to monitor the peace and disarmament process (Olonisakin 2008). This intervention on the part of the international community could not prevent the rebels from continued attacks. Negotiations had to be opened, culminating in the Lomé Agreement, which provided for power-sharing agreement between the government and RUF in a government of national unity under Kabbah as president and Sankoh as Vice-President and head of the Commission for the Management of Strategic Mineral Resources, National Reconstruction and Development (CMRRD). The reality as to why Sankoh's and RUF agreed to participate in the government of national unity became clearer when, under his leadership as Chairman of the CMRRD, he did nothing to stop the flow of diamonds to Liberia. The security situation worsened as Sankoh used his position to engage in illicit trade in diamonds and purchase of more SALWs to continue waging RUF's senseless war. The RUF also attacked UNAMSIL repeatedly, and kidnapped about 500 peacekeepers in May 2000 (Olonisakin 2008). It took the combined efforts of ECOWAS, UNAMSIL, the Sierra Leone Army, and a British intervention to successful defeat of the RUF. This paved the way for the conclusion of the Abuja Cease-Fire Agreement and the restoration of democracy in the country (Kabbah

2012). Sankoh was subsequently arrested and a Special Court for Sierra Leone was established to try him and fellow combatants. Sankoh died before he could be tried by UN-backed war crimes court.

Addressing SALWs Proliferation in Post-conflict Sierra Leone

In 1996, the Sierra Leonean government created a Ministry for Reconstruction, Resettlement and Rehabilitation, which was later renamed the National Commission for Reconstruction, Resettlement and Rehabilitation (NCRRR). The Commission had a department that was charged with the Disarmament, Demobilisation and Reintegration (DDR) of various armed groups that participated in the civil war. In July 1998, the department was reorganised and renamed as the National Commission for Disarmament, Demobilisation and Reintegration (NCDDR). The Commission comprised of the President of the Republic, the Ministers of Information, Finance, Defence and the Interior, a representative from the donor community, the Special Representative of the United Nations Secretary General, the Commander of UNAMSIL, the head of the RUF, and the head of the AFRC. In addition, three Technical Committees (TCs) were established to provide technical input for a successful DDR. The committees included, first for disarmament and demobilisation (comprising the NCDDR's Executive Secretariat, UNAMSIL and UNICEF), second for awareness and information, and third for reintegration (the NCDDR's Executive Secretariat, UNAMSIL, UNICEF, the UNDP and donor representatives.

Components of the DDR included disarmament, demobilisation and reintegration of the many armed groups, particularly child soldiers as well as armed forces reform. In terms of disarmament, which is of particular interest to this article, a total of 45 reception centres were established across the country. The supervision of these centres was done by first, the ECOMOG forces and later the UNAMSIL (NCDDR 2002). By February 2004, when the government announced that disarmament and rehabilitation of more than 70,000 civil war combatants was officially completed, a total of 42,330 weapons and more than 1.2 million rounds of ammunition were collected and destroyed (NCDDR 2004). A number of programmes also formed component of the DDR in Sierra Leone. Of particular interest are the Community Arms Collection and Destruction Program (CACD) and Arms for Development. Under the CACD, which involved the collection of weapons through police campaigns, and with support from the UNDP and UNAMSIL, more than 9000 weapons were collected and destroyed. The Arms for Development Programme (AFD) was run by the UNDP, the government's Interim Commission for the Proliferation of Small Arms and Light Weapons, the police, the DDR/Community Development section of UNAMSIL, the German Technical Cooperation International Services (GTZ) and grassroot communities. Financial reward of 20,000 dollars was given to each area declared weapons free. However, the money was to be invested in the development programmes chosen by the community itself. The AFD programme, funded by Canada, the Netherlands, Norway and the United Kingdom, began with pilot projects in 2003 in four chiefdoms (Weiss 2005). According to Weiss (2005), the AFD programme involved five phases. While phase I, was mainly public awareness, consists of preparatory activities whereby sensitisation is done at the district level, phase II focused on capacity building and mobilisation. A Project Management Committee (PMC) is formed from community members and representatives, and a coordinating unit of that committee is chosen, to be comprised of one chief one elder, one woman, one youth and a respected community member. The third phase entailed arms collection, and the fourth phase is certification. The fifth phase is the development phase, where communities begin implementing a project with the money they have been given as a reward for being certified arms-free. During all phases, capacity building and mobilisation are ongoing in preparation for the development project. Since the close of Sierra Leone's DDR programme, the Arms for Development extension of the CACD programme dominated the post-conflict landscape. Despite the DDR programme in the post-war, GAIBA report indicated that by 2010, the estimated number of SALW in circulation in Sierra Leone was still high vis-à-vis other West African countries (Table 40.2).

Table 40.2 Estimates of West African SALW in or out of circulation (2000–2010)

Name of country	SALW in circulation	SALW seized	SALW surrendered	SALW lost
Benin	135,505	1800	–	–
Burkina Faso	83,913	–	–	–
Cape verde	12,188	–	–	–
Cote d'ivoire	10,000	–	1000	–
	458,677			
Gambia	136,850	–	28	–
Ghana	100,000	3387	–	–
Guinea	130,884	61	–	–
Guinea Bissau	25,000	–	–	1270
Liberia	166,117	–	27,000	–
			61,918,000	
Mali	174,752	–	–	–
Niger	117,305	28	12,432	–
			30,000	
Nigeria	2.5 million	3732	20,000	140
			1257	7000
Senegal	263,714	–	8000	–
Sierra Leone	49,785	–	9237	–
			6165	
			30,000	

Source GIABA 2013 Annual Report, p. 22

The establishment of the Sierra Leone National Commission on Small Arms is no doubt a major step towards addressing the proliferation of SALWs in post-conflict Sierra Leone. Since the end of the civil war, private gun ownership of any kind was illegalised in Sierra Leone. This work continues with the National Commission for the Proliferation of Small Arms and Light Weapons (NCPSALW), which later introduce a national legislation on the monitoring and movement of small arms. This legislation culminated in the establishment of the Sierra Leone National Commission on Small Arms through an Act of Parliament in 2010. The creation of the Commission was in compliance with the 2006 ECOWAS Convention on Small Arms and Light Weapons. The Commission was tasked with the responsibility of regulating and supervising the manufacture, trade and use of small arms and light weapons, their ammunitions and other related materials. In specific terms the objectives of the commission are stated as follows:

a. set in place programmes of action to prevent, combat and eradicate the illicit manufacture, trade and use of small arms and light weapons in all its aspects;
b. educate and sensitise the public and provide information on the dangers associated with the illicit manufacture, trade and use of small arms and light weapons;
c. ensure that obligations under the ECOWAS Convention are complied with;
d. establish and maintain an Arms Register for transmission to the ECOWAS Secretariat;
e. provide appropriate recommendation to the ECOWAS Secretariat on exemptions to be granted under the Convention;
f. mobilise resources for programme activities of the Commission;
g. advise the Minister on the formulation of policies and strategies as contained in the Convention and any other relevant international conventions to which Sierra Leone is a party;
h. receive and study periodic reports from the Sierra Leone Police on the registration and licensing of arms; and
i. Perform any other functions related to the object of the Commission.

Apart from working on the domestic legislation on SALWs, Sierra Leone has also keyed into the global and regional instruments on SALWs. In June 2006, as a member of the African Union, Sierra Leone adopted an African Common Position to take to the Conference to Review the UN Programme of Action to Prevent, Combat and Eradicate the Illicit Trade in Small Arms and Light Weapons in All Its Aspects (UNPoA), held in June 2006 (African Union 2015; African Union/UNODA 2005). Sierra Leone adopted the ECOWAS Convention on Small Arms and Light Weapons, their Ammunition and other Related

Materials, in June 2006 (ECOWAS/UNODA 2006). The convention stipulates strict controls on the transfer, manufacture, possession and security of small arms and light weapons. Sierra Leone also signed the Geneva Declaration on Armed Violence and Development, a diplomatic initiative aimed at addressing the interrelations between armed violence and development, in 2006. It signed and ratified the United Nations Arms Trade Treaty (UNODA 2013). The country has also signed and ratified the United Nations Protocol against the Illicit Manufacturing of and Trafficking in Firearms, their Parts and Components and Ammunition (UNGA 2001a).

Furthermore, on 21 July 2001, Sierra Leone committed to a consensus decision of the United Nations to adopt, support and implement the UN Programme of Action to Prevent, Combat and Eradicate the Illicit Trade in Small Arms and Light Weapons in All Its Aspects (UNGA 2001a). In its UN small arms Programme of Action Implementation Monitor (PoAIM Phase 1), the Small Arms Survey scored Sierra Leone against its commitments to the PoA, then ranked it at No. 49 among 159 Member States (Parker and Green 2012). Under the terms of its 2001 commitment to the United Nations small arms Programme of Action, Sierra Leone has submitted national reports on its implementation of the UNPoA (Cattaneo and Parker 2008). Sierra Leone has designated a National Point of Contact to deal with issues relating to the UNPoA. In National Reports of Sierra Leone submitted to the UN from 2001 to 2010, a history of substantive cooperation with civil society in support of UNPoA activities was apparent. Funds for UNPoA implementation have not been donated by Sierra Leone to other UN Member States (UNODA 2015). However, funds for UNPoA implementation have been provided to Sierra Leone by other UN Member States. According to the United Nations Register of Conventional Arms, Sierra Leone has not declared its small arms exports in one or more annual National Reports on Arms Exports (UNODA 2011). The Wassenaar Arrangement on Export Controls and Conventional Arms and Dual-Use Goods and Technologies does not list Sierra Leone as a Participating State (Hayner 2007).

Despite the efforts by the Sierra Leonean government in the aftermath of the civil war in addressing the proliferation of small arms and light weapons including the establishment and operation of the Commission, the UNDP technical committee argues that Sierra Leone, particularly its border territories are still exposed to threats from the influx of small arms (Weiss 2005). The estimated total number of guns, both legal and illegal, held by civilians in Sierra Leone as of 2007 was estimated at 34,000 (Karp 2007). This number was estimated to have risen to 35,000 in 2017 (Karp 2018). In a 2007 comparison of the number of privately owned guns, Sierra Leone ranked at No. 160 out of 178 countries (Karp 2007). In light of these challenges, according to the UNDP, if funding can be allocated for education and empowerment, specifically focusing on the borders, the demand for guns could be reduced short-run and perhaps eliminated in the long run. In 2013, Sierra Leone established a Firearms Licensing Bureau and Arms Registry within the premises of the National Commission on Small Arms. The Commission also launched the marking and computerisation of all weapons in order to facilitate easy tracing of such weapons in the event of criminal activities. Furthermore, the country reported that all weapons owned by Army and Police forces were marked. On Monday 4 June 2018, members of the Sierra Leone Commission on Small Arms declared that they had destroyed 4773 weapons collected by the Arms for Development (AfD) (Milton 2018). While the marking of weapons of the military has posed any challenge for the commission, not all citizens embraced the issuance of Firearms Licenses eligible citizens for crop and cattle protection, sports and hunting purposes, which started in 2016. The issuance of firearms licenses has witnessed low turnout because people have been suspicious and fear retribution by the government (Milton 2018). Consequently, the Commission had to go directly to small farmers and hunters in rural communities to assure them of government's sincerity and openness of the process. While the Sierra Leonean government is making efforts in addressing SALW proliferation in the country, the number of weapon destroyed as of 2018 are far below the number estimated in 2007. The multiple sources of SALWs in Sierra Leone as well as actors involved, most of who continue to escape the searchlight of the state authorities, make control of SALWs in the case of Sierra Leone quite a huge and complex task.

Conclusion

In this chapter, we examined the proliferation of small arms and light weapons in the context of Sierra Leone. We argued that during the civil war, the availability of SALWs purchased mostly with money from trade of blood diamonds were used by mostly violent non-state actors such as the RUF and other rebel groups in Sierra Leone to fight a civil war. The rebellion led to truncation of democratic rule in the country, instability and eventual state collapse. The proliferation and continued supply of SALWs, to not only the RUF, but also AFRC rebel forces and CDF, aided the prolongation of the war. In the post-civil war era, Sierra Leone, supported by external partners such as UNDP, has initiated programmes aimed at addressing the proliferation of SALWs. The programs, particularly the Community Arms Collection and Destruction Program (CACD) and Arms for Development (AFD), have yielded varying successes across the country. In addition, the establishment of Sierra Leone National Commission on Small Arms in 2010 and commitment to regional and international instruments on SALWs are no doubt part of the government's efforts towards checking the proliferation of SALWs in post-conflict Sierra Leone. That notwithstanding, Sierra Leone is not completely weapons free as issues of poverty, illiteracy, unemployment and civilian faith in guns-for-protection are still endemic (Weiss 2005; Small Arms Survey and AU 2018). Furthermore, borders are porous and SALWs proliferation regulations are weak and susceptible to internal and external abuse. The chapter concludes on the note that current efforts towards addressing the challenges posed by the proliferation of SALWs will only work if conditions that lead their demand and proliferation are eliminated. The Mano River Union strategy for cross-border security and monthly security meetings between Sierra Leone, Côte d'Ivoire, Liberia and Guinea has been underscored as an example of good practice (Florquin et al. 2019). However, funding remains a huge challenge for ensuring effective border controls. Accordingly, the government needs to adequately fund traditional security operations, ensure better regulation of borders and infrastructural development in rural areas. In addition, the government should also ensure adequate funding of education to reduce the number of illiterate young people, create youth agricultural empowerment initiatives, continues demobilisation for ex-combatants and sustainability of the Arms for Development programme. These suggestions could go a long way in stemming the flow of illegal small arms and light weapons in Sierra Leone.

References

Abdullah, I. (2004). Bush Path to Destruction: The Origin and Character of the Revolutionary United Front (RUF/SL). In A. Ibrahim (Ed.), *Between Democracy and Terror: The Sierra Leone Civil War* (pp. 41–65). Dakar: CODESRIA.

African Union. (2015). *Member States of African Union: A United and Strong Africa*. Addis Ababa: African Union.

African Union/UNODA. (2005). Windhoek Common Position. In *United Nations Programme of Action Implementation Support System: Regional Organisations*. New York, NY: African Union/United Nations Office for Disarmament Affairs.

Amnesty International, Sierra Leone. (1998, November 1). *1998: A Year of Atrocities Against Civilians* (AI Index: 51/022/1998).

Berman, E. G., & Labonte, M. T. C. (2006). Sierra Leone. In E. G. Berman & M. T. C. Labonte (Eds.), *Twenty-First Century Peace Operation*. Washington, DC: US Institute of Peace Press.

Blank, G. (2012). Both Greed and Grievance: Explaining Violence in Sierra Leone's Civil War. *Journal of History and Diplomatic Studies, 9*, 115–136.

Cattaneo, S., & Parker, S. (2008). Reporting, NPCs and NCAs, 2002 to 2008. In *Implementing the United Nations Programme of Action on Small Arms and Light Weapons: Analysis of the National Reports Submitted by States from 2002 to 2008*. Geneva: United Nations Development Programme.

ECOWAS. (1998, October). ECOWAS Declaration of a Moratorium on the Importation, Exportation and Manufacture of Small Arms and Light Weapons in West Africa.

ECOWAS/UNODA. (2006). Convention on Small Arms and Light Weapons, Their Ammunition and Other Related Materials. In *United Nations Programme of Action Implementation Support System: Regional Organisations*. New York, NY: Economic Community of West African States Secretariat/United Nations Office for Disarmament Affairs.

Florquin, N., Lipott, S., & Wairagu, F. (2019). *Weapons Compass: Mapping Illicit Small Arms Flows in Africa*. Geneva: Small Arms Survey.

GIABA. (2013). *The Nexus Between Small Arms and Light Weapons and Money Laundering and Terrorist Financing in West Africa*. Dakar: GIABA.

Hayner, P. (2007). *Negotiating Peace in Sierra Leone: Confronting the Justice Challenge*. Geneva: The Centre for Humanitarian Dialogue.

Hironaka, A. (2005). *Never-Ending Wars: The International Community, Weak States, and the Perpetuation of Civil War*. Cambridge: Harvard University Press.

Human Rights Watch. (1998, July 29). *Human Rights Watch condemns atrocities in Sierra Leone*. Retrieved December 23, 2020 from https://www.hrw.org/news/1998/07/29/human-rights-watch-condemns-atrocities-sierra-leone.

Kabbah, A. T. (2012). *Two Decades of Conflict and Democracy in Sierra Leone: A Personal Experience*. Tshwane: Institute for Security Studies.

Karp, A. (2007). Completing the Count: Civilian Firearms—Annexe Online. In *Small Arms Survey 2007: Guns and the City*. Cambridge: Cambridge University Press.

Karp, A. (2018). *Civilian Firearms Holdings, 2017: Estimating Global Civilian-Held Firearms Numbers*. Geneva: Small Arms Survey.

Keili, F. (2008). Small arms and light weapons transfer in West Africa: A stock-taking. Disarmament Forum. Retrieved December 23, 2020 from http://www.ssrnetwork.net/uploaded_files/4508.pdf.

Marks, Z. (2013). Sexual Violence Inside Rebellion: Policies and Perspectives of the Revolutionary United Front of Sierra Leone. *Civil Wars, 15*(3), 359–379.

Milton, B. (2018, June 5). *Sierra Leone News: Small Arms Comm. Explains License and Weapon Marking Process*. Retrieved January 21, 2020, from https://awoko.org/2018/06/06/sierra-leone-news-small-arms-comm-explains-license-and-weapon-marking-process/.

Musah, A. (2001, July). Africa: The Political Economy of Small Arms and Conflicts. *DPMN Bulletin, VIII*(1).

NCDDR (Executive Secretariat) Government of Sierra Leona. (11/2002). *The DDR Programme: Status and Strategies for Completion*. Retrieved March 6, 2020, from http://siteresources.worldbank.org/SIERRALEONEEXTN/Resources/ddr_status.pdf.

NCDDR. (2004).*(Executive Secretariat) Government of Sierra Leona (11/2002) The DDR Programme: Status and Strategies for Completion*. Retrieved December 23, 2020 from http://siteresources.worldbank.org/SIERRALEONEEXTN/Resources/ddr_status.pdf.

Olonisakin, F. (2008). *Peacekeeping in Sierra Leone: The Story of UNAMSIL*. London: Lynne Rienner Publishers.

Oluwadare, A. J. (2014). The Impact of the Proliferation of Small Arms and Light Weapons on West African States: An Analysis of the Sierra Leone Civil War. *Journal of Studies in Social Sciences, 7*(2), 189–209.

Parker, S., & Green, K. (2012). Findings—Table 3: Reporting States by Rank and Score. In *The Programme of Action Implementation Monitor (Phase 1): Assessing Reported Progress*. Geneva: Small Arms Survey, the Graduate Institute of International and Development Studies, Geneva.

Report of the Panel of Experts Appointed Pursuant to Security Council Resolution 1306. (2000a). Paragraph 19, in Relation to Sierra Leone S/2000/1195, 20 December 2000, para. 173.

Report of the Panel of Experts Appointed Pursuant to Security Council Resolution 1306. (2000b). Paragraph 19, in Relation to Sierra Leone, op. cit., paras. 167–168.

Sesay, A. (1999). Paradise Lost and Regained? The Travails of Democracy in Sierra Leone. In D. Olowu, A. Williams, & K. Soremekun (Eds.), *Governance and Democratisation in West Africa*. CODESRIA: Dakar.

Small Arms Survey. (2000). *Re-Armament in Sierra Leone: One Year After the Lomé Peace Agreement* (Occasional Paper 1).

Small Arms Survey and African Union. (2018). *Country Responses to the Questionnaire on Mapping Illicit Arms Flows in Africa*. Geneva: Small Arms Survey.

Tar, U. A., & Wapmuk, S. (2017). The Revolutionary United Front, Liberian Warlords and the Civil War in Sierra Leone. In C. Varin & D. Abubakar (Eds.), *Violent Non-State Actors: Terrorists, Rebels and Warlords* (pp. 251–275). Cham: Palgrave Macmillan.

UNGA. (2001a). United Nations Protocol Against the Illicit Manufacturing of and Trafficking in Firearms, Their Parts and Components and Ammunition. In *UN General Assembly Resolution 55/255*. New York, NY: UN General Assembly.

UNGA. (2001b). Programme of Action to Prevent, Combat and Eradicate the Illicit Trade in Small Arms and Light Weapons in All Its Aspects. In *United Nations General Assembly*. New York, NY: UN General Assembly.

UNODA. (2011). National Reports on Small Arms Exports. In *United Nations Register of Conventional Arms—The Global Reported Arms Trade*. New York, NY: United Nations Office for Disarmament Affairs.

UNODA. (2013). Towards Entry into Force. In *Arms Trade Treaty*. New York, NY: United Nations Office for Disarmament Affairs.

UNODA. (2015, September 11). PoA-ISS Country Profiles. *UN Small Arms Programme of Action (UNPoA)—Implementation Support System*. New York, NY: United Nations Office of Disarmament Affairs.

Weiss, T. (2005). *Perpetrating power: Small arms in post-conflict Sierra Leone and Liberia*. Pretoria: Institute for Security Studies.

Sharkdam Wapmuk is an Associate Professor in the Department of Defence and Security Studies, Nigerian Defence Academy (NDA) Kaduna. He was formally a Senior Research and Head of Department at the Nigerian Institute of International Affairs (NIIA), Lagos. He served as consultant for international organisations and think tanks, lectures at various institutions in Nigeria and participated in local and international conferences, seminars, workshops and dialogues. His research interests cut across the thematic fields of Afro–Asian relations, security, cooperation and integration. His articles have been published in local and international journals and books. He is a member of scholarly bodies, including the Nigerian Political Science Association (NPSA) and Nigerian Society of International Affairs (NSIA).

CHAPTER 41

Somalia: State Collapse and the Proliferation of Small Arms and Light Weapons

Mala Mustapha and Haruna Yerima

INTRODUCTION

The prevailing existence of anarchy and lawlessness in the Horn of Africa creates a major problem for the proliferation of Small Arms and Light Weapons (SALWs) in Somalia. In recent years, some studies were conducted largely by think-tank outlets than from scholars to examine the dynamics of proliferation of SALWs in the Horn of Africa particularly in Somalia. Notably, the Regional Centre on Small Arms (RECSA) Report on illicit SALWs and fragility situation in Somalia; the Bonn International Center for Conversion (BICC); and the International Crisis Group, and the United Nations Institute for Disarmament Research (UNIDIR), among others, have examined how conflict dynamics and fragility situation in the region has intricately led to intense proliferation of SALWs in Somalia (Whiteheads 2006). This chapter, therefore, synthesizes and reviews the major contents of these works to examine the conceptual nexus between Somali's complex descent to anarchy and fragmentation—resurgence of warlordism, deep clannism and violent Jihadism and proliferation and diffusion of SALWs. This is against the backdrop of the fact there are few and scanty literature on the proliferation of SALWs on Somalia particularly among Somali studies scholars. Thus, the aim of this chapter is to

M. Mustapha (✉)
Department of Political Science, University of Maiduguri, Maiduguri, Nigeria
e-mail: mmustapha@live.com

H. Yerima
Department of Public Administration, Ahmadu Bello University, Zaria, Nigeria

© The Author(s), under exclusive license to Springer Nature Switzerland AG 2021
U. A. Tar and C. P. Onwurah (eds.), *The Palgrave Handbook of Small Arms and Conflicts in Africa*,
https://doi.org/10.1007/978-3-030-62183-4_41

contribute to the existing literature and policy discourse on the proliferation of SALWs in Somalia.

In Somalia, fragile security situation—not least the existence of "ungovernable spaces"—provides the contestable spaces among different armed groups for the proliferation of illicit SALWs. According to the Global Peace Index (GPI) 2019 Report, Somalia alongside Afghanistan, Syria, South Sudan, Yemen and Iraq are ranked as the least peaceful countries (GPI Report 2019). The key drivers of volatility in Somalia include violent conflict by violent non-state actors and militarization of conflict spaces as a result of proliferation of SALWs. This has resulted into deepened insecurity and weakened the state capacity to curb the menace of proliferation of SALWs. For more than 20 years, Somalia has no properly functioning government. Its leaders have been driven by internal clan rivalries and leadership squabble. Regional and global efforts of state-building in post-Barre era Somalia led to the establishment of the Transitional National Government (TNG) in 2000 and lasted until 2004. Somalia was governed by the TFG from October 2004 to August 2012, with the support of international and regional actors. However, a slow but positive progress has been made to move Somalia out of the woods to a stable state. Yet, the country continues to experience a great deal of deepening insecurity characterized by legitimacy crisis. The proliferation of illicit SALWs remains a major challenge to building a peaceful Somalian state (Fergusson 2013). Despite many sanctions, arm embargoes and existing local and international disarmament mechanisms against arms trade in Somalia, the business of illicit arms trade continued to thrive and the country remains a microcosm of illicit SALWs paving the way for the emergence of numerous transnational terrorist groups (Koigi 2018). Farah et al. (2005: 10) argued "the illegal trade in SALWs has become a way of life and a source of livelihood for many Somalis".

The chapter is divided into five main sections: Section one offers a background to the conflict in Somalia. It traces the historical trajectory of state collapse and the emerging ungovernable spaces that provided the enabling environment for the proliferation of SALWs in the country. Section two examines the dynamics of illicit arms flows into Somalia in the midst of the protracted conflict focusing on the multidimensional sources of arms supplies. Section three discusses the local, regional and global intersections in the dynamics of arms flows to Somali. Section four examines the national, regional and the international mechanisms put in place for arms control and disarmament. Finally, section five offers a conclusion.

Somalia: Mapping the Historical Trajectory of State Collapse and Emerging Contested Spaces

The collapse of the Somali state and the accompanying proliferation of SALWs were underpinned by myriad of factors (Fig. 41.1) shows the vastness of the Somali state. Tar and Mustapha's (2017) study attributed the dynamics of

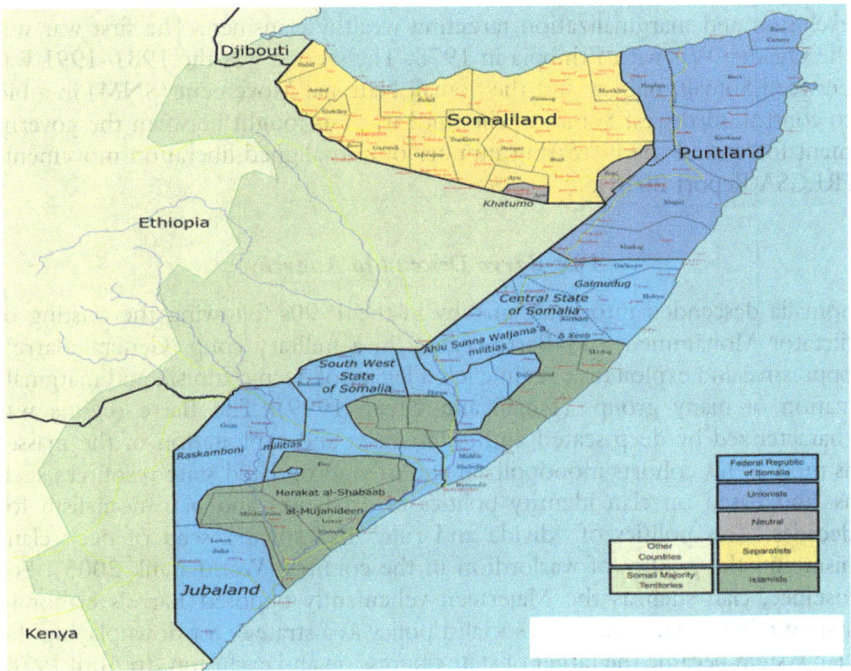

Fig. 41.1 Political map of Somalia (*Source* Google Map [2019])

state collapse, the resurgence of warlordism and later Islamist insurgency in Somalia to the following factors: first was the deep-rooted postcolonial fragmentation of the Somaliland into factitious clan-based politics. Clannism and clan cleavages are major sources of conflict. It serves as a fault line for social divisions, fuel endemic violence over scarce resources and struggle for power and platform for the mobilization of militia (World Bank 2005). Second, was the institutionalization of repressive and dictatorial policies by General Barre's regime, which led to the polarization and exclusion of other segments of the Somali society. The third factor is the rise of violent terrorism from the radical Islamist group Al-Shabaab.

PostColonial Complex Social Formation and Fragmentation

The end of colonialism in 1960 has led to the fragmentation of Somaliland based on divergent colonial entities (Tar and Mustapha 2017). The distinct political and economic traditions between the southern region and Somaliland to the north became a major source of discontent and division. In 1969, Major General Siad Barre ended the established postcolonial democracy through military coup. However, under Barre's rule, Somalia experienced numerous armed conflicts largely fomented by disenchanted Somalis in diaspora backed by foreign powers to challenge Barre's authoritarian, and repressive politics of exclusion and marginalization targeting wealthy clansmen. The first war was the Ogaden War with Ethiopia in 1978. The second was the 1981–1991 war between Somali military and the Somali National Movement (SNM) in a bid to control northwest Somalia. The third war was fought between the government forces and the increasing number of clan-aligned liberation movements (RECSA Report 2018).

Post-Barre Descend to Anarchy

Somalia descended into total anarchy in the 1990s following the ousting of dictator Mohammed Siad Barre regime in a military coup. General Barre's oppressive and exploitative regime left a legacy of deep clannism and marginalization of many groups (Ismail and Green 1999). The Barre regime was characterized by deep-seated authoritarianism and exploitation of the masses as most of his cohorts monopolized and misappropriated state resources such as land based on clan identity politics of predation and patrimonialism for decades. This politics of "divide and rule" had sown a seed of deep clannism and the politics of warlordism in the country (World Bank 2005). For instance, clan such as the Majerteen vehemently opposed Barre's elaborate system of patronage and state socialist policy as a strategy for downplaying the clan system became the target of state oppression and exclusion. In April 1978, Barre's loyalist in the military foiled an attempted military coup masterminded by senior military officers of the Majerteen origin. The escaped coup plotters later formed a clan-based rebel movement known as the Somali Salvation Democratic Front (SSDF) with the support of Ethiopia and launched attacks across Somalia. Subsequently in 1981 the Isaaq clan also formed their own rebel movement known as Somali National Movement (SNM) targeting the overthrow of Barre. In 1987, the Hawiye clan also formed the United Somali Congress (USC) in Italy. Furthermore, in 1989 the Ogadeni-led Somali Patriotic Movement was formed following the detention of General Gabyo the highest-ranking military officer of Ogadeni descent by Barre forces. Face with coterie of emerging rebel movements, Barre's government became hollow and lost absolute legitimacy. By 1991, the Somali state crumbled into failed state with multitude of competing clan-based warlords drummed up for inter-clan war that engulfed the country to fill the vacuum of its unoccupied political spaces (Tar and Mustapha 2017).

Rooted in, and driven by, clan-based intense competition for power and control of scarce resources, the ensuing violent conflicts unabatedly led to the collapse of institutions of governance that ushered in the incubation of radical Islamist groups such as Al-Shaabab. This emerging contested conflict spaces plunged Somalia into prolonged years of violent conflict characterized by warlordism, terrorism and state collapse (Menkhaus 2003). In this scenario, the proliferation and use of SALWs, led to escalation of conflict and state collapse in Somalia.

State Collapse and the Incubation of Radical Islamist Group

The collapse of the state opened up the space for the emergence of a radical Islamist movements struggling for the establishment of theocratic Islamic State in Somalia, among which were *Al Itihad Al Islamiya*, the Islamic Courts Union (ICU) and the subsequent resurgence of Al-Shabaab in 2006 (Jones et al. 2016). The rise of Al-Shaabab in Somalia has exacerbated the problem of anarchy and lawlessness. The exact origin of Al-Shaabab is a subject of huge debate among scholars. A number of radical elements pulled from numerous clans such as Sheik Hassan Dahir Awey who fought Ethiopia under Siad Barre regime in the 1970s founded the group and commanded the military wing of the *Al Itihad Al Islamiya* and later took the mantle of leadership of the ICU. In 2006, Awey handed over leadership of the group to Aden Hashi Ayro, a young Somali militant who was later killed by US airstrike in 2008. Subsequently, Ahmed Abdi Godane took over the military command of Al-Shaabab and was later killed by the US military in September 2014 (Menkhaus 2004). Al-Shaabab emerged to represent a broad spectrum of violent terrorism initiated and implemented by the loose coalition of the Somali's diverse groups in the light of the state's collapse that followed the demise of former dictator General Siad Barre (Tar and Mustapha 2017).

The rising trend of terrorist attacks in Somalia and across the Horn of Africa is largely linked to Al-Shaabab. Towards the end of the year 2007, Al-Shaabab rising wave of terrorist activity became frequent due to deep-seated corruption in the Somali security sector—poor condition of service for the police, low morale and obsolete equipment. This is furthermore compounded by the alleged infiltration of the Somali Police and the Army by the jihadist and militia elements (Tar and Mustapha 2017). Bruton Bronwyn (2015) argues that Al-Shabaab's main ambition is to overthrow an unpopular, Western-backed government to establish the radical brand of Islam and forcefully expel peacekeeping troops out of Somalia. But its recent sporadic attacks across the Horn of Africa indicates that the jihadist group is gradually tilting towards a pragmatic approach—alternating between populist and terrorist tendencies committed to violence. For instance, in 2013, the group internationalized its terrorist activities with the attack of Westgate Mall in Kenya and later Garissa University killing more than 147 students. These attacks beyond the shores of Somalia demonstrated that the group has joined the global jihadi expansionist ambition funded by Al-Qaeda (Bronwyn 2015). However, by 2011 Al-Shaabab began to lose ground due to high-level military offensive from the Africa Union (AU) sponsored African Union Peacekeeping Mission in Somalia (AMISOM). Though, the AU-backed military campaign has weakened the group capability, it still remains an existential threat to the war-torn Somalia and the volatile Horn of Africa region.

State Fragility and the Dynamics of Proliferation of SALWs

An empirical study by the Regional Centre on Small Arms (RECSA) in 2008 on state fragility in Somalia indicates that there is an intrinsic link between state collapse and the rapid proliferation of illicit Small Arms and Light Weapons (SALWs). Since the eruption of violent conflict in the 1960s, Somalia has witnessed a pervasive proliferation of SALWs. Particularly in the post-Barre regime the proliferation of illicit SALWs, has dominated the conflict spaces across the country with an estimated 550,000–750,000 weapons in the hands of the civilians. Of these figures, only 14,000 arms are legally acquired (Philip et al. 2019). One of the major consequences of the illicit flow of SALWs includes deepening clan-based conflict and self-defence militias, the resurgence of violent terrorism from Al-Shabaab and other forms of criminality.

Despite efforts put in place by the Somali Government to address fragile security situations, however, the challenges of continued proliferation of SALWs, weak governance institutions, clan-based politics, the emergence of violent non-state actors—terrorist and radicalized groups such as Al-Shaabab has undermined the recovering of the failed Somalian state (Whiteheads 2006). The level and dynamics of heavy presence of illicit SALWs in Somalia could be attributed to the following myriad of factors: weak governance institution, porous borders, resurging violent extremism, deepening clan-based politics and poverty and radicalization of the youth by terrorist groups such as Al-Shaabab.

- Weak governance institutions and state capacity, this relates to the institutionalization of corruption, neo-patrimonialism and pervasive culture of impunity and disregards to the rule of law. The problems of patronage and corruption have undermined the state's capacity to foster effective and efficient security mechanism and border control measures that will control the inflow of illicit arms into Somalia.
- The dysfunctional nature of the state institutions paved the way for border porosity. Somalia's porous borders with Kenya and Ethiopia are the main conduits for smuggling of arms.
- As a consequence of weak state institutions, numerous "ungoverned spaces" are captured by the emergence of terrorist groups such as Al-Shaabab demanding the establishment of theocratic Islamic state—the Caliphate. This led to the massive influx of illicit weapons from transnationally affiliated actors backing Al-Shaaba's destabilization of Somalia.
- Clan-based politics and conflict is another key driver for illicit arms flow into Somalia.
- Poverty and youth radicalization into violent extremist groups is identified as a factor for the proliferation of small arms and arms black markets throughout Somalia. High rate of abject poverty coupled with youth

unemployment provides fertile ground for the massive recruitment of the youth into Al-Qaeda affiliate Al-Shaabab and into criminal gangs (RECSA Report 2018).

Crosscutting Connections in Proliferation of Illicit SALWs: Local Dynamics, Regional Trends and Global Intersections

Apparently, persistent armed conflicts and the prevailing state of insecurity in Somalia have been fuelled by access to illicit SALWs by civilian and violent armed groups emanating from local and transnational sources. For instance, violent non-state actors in Somalia such as Al-Shaabab, Hawadle, Hizbul Islam, Rahanweyn Resistance Army and Ras-Kamoni to mention some few have received large cache of arms and ammunitions from local and transnational sources (Small Arms Survey 2014). In 2003, a study by the United Nations Institute for Disarmament Research (UNIDR) and the European Union (EU) on the state of proliferation of SALWs in the Horn of Africa indicates that there are three main trajectories in the dynamics of proliferation of SALWs in Somalia namely: Regional SALWs proliferation, State-Level SALWs proliferation and Local-Level SALWs proliferation.

Regional SALWs Proliferation: Porous Border, Illicit Arms Trade and "Ungoverned Spaces"

The 2003 survey by the UNIDR and EU shows that the international arms trade is a significant source for the proliferation of SALWs in the Horn of Africa, particularly Somalia. Most weapons illicitly emanate from EU member countries in which weapons worth millions of dollars were exported into the Horn of Africa. Related to the arms trade is how years of poverty and underdevelopment has led to the cultivation and resurgence of terrorist groups and international criminal organizations in Somalia. The emergence of these groups in the Somali "ungoverned spaces" has added to the SALWs proliferation pressures by aiding the illicit trade and compounding the security threats in the region. This could be largely attributed to border porosity in the Horn, which allows the quick and easy diffusion of supplies of weapons across the region (Mbugua 2013).

Similarly, the long-standing border disputes between Ethiopia and Eritrea has also been a major factor of SALWs proliferation in the region. This conflict that began since 1998 has led to massive acquisition of armaments that spilled over into neighbouring states like Somalia (Farah et al. 2005). The SALWs proliferation caused by the Ethiopian–Eritrean conflict is a good example of the entangled nature of supply and demand factors as the conflict. Somalia was driven by the SALWs proliferation and diffusion (Whiteheads 2006).

The sources of arms inflow have received the attention of scholars and policy practitioners. Some studies on Somalian arms dynamics (Koigi 2018; Wezeman 2010) have traced external sources of arms inflows—in particular countries such as Eriteria and Djibouti as key players in the massive shipment of illegal arms to Somalia violent non-state actors and across the Horn of Africa. These countries have and other regional players have become a conduit for illicit arms that are transported from Yemen's Houthi territory which eventually find their way to Northern Somalia's Awdal province (Koigi 2018). This transnational proliferation of illicit arms in Somalia is further compounded by the origination of SALWs from, Libya, Iran and United Arab Emirates through arms traffickers (Small Arms Survey 2014).

State-Level Proliferation of SALWs: Dysfunctional Governance and Informalization of Security

The UNIDIR (2003) Report revealed that one of the major dynamics of state-level SALWs proliferation across the Horn of Africa manifests in form of arms transfer from state to non-state actors. In Somalia governance deficit has created the room for insecurity and lack of protection. As a result, a form of local decentralization of security emerged out of state control in which arming militia; nomadic pastoralists and clans through an informal security arrangement is widely considered as a way for securitization. This has further resulted in a key way for the proliferation of arms. Other factors that deepened the pace of the proliferation of SALWs pressure in Somalia and the Horn of Africa at large include: poor security of national SALWs stockpiles, poorly coordinated disarmament initiatives and the domestic weapon production capability of the Somali state. As a result of massive import of illicit weapons coupled with dysfunctional governance structure in Somalia, insufficient control of the nation's stockpile and failure to coordinate disarmament programmes have also contributed to the proliferation of SALWs across Somaliland (Whiteheads 2006). Another factor of SALWs proliferation at the state level has been the domestic manufacturing capabilities of states within the Horn of Africa such as Somalia to produce locally produced weapons local factories and Blacksmiths to local consumers. Although, locally manufactured weapons are mostly of poor quality, but their heavy presence adds to the proliferation pressure as it allows almost any individual to purchase a firearm (Gebre-Wold and Masson 2002).

Local Dynamics in the Proliferation of SALWs: State of Anarchy and Clan-Based Conflict

The collapse of Somalia after the fall of Siad Barre in 1991 saw the massive dispersing of large stockpiles of weapons that had been amassed for the creation of a "greater Somalia". The state of anarchy and total collapse of the Somali state led to the local proliferation of weapons in which many weapons were locally traded in exchange for safe passage home, food, or shelter. Furthermore, the ensuing clan-based politics have heightened the level of insecurity and increased the level of proliferation pressure within Somalia (Whiteheads 2006).

Another consequence of the state collapse in Somalia is the resurgence of clan-based politics and armed conflict. Darryl Whiteheads (2006) argues that the prevailing state of anarchy that has followed the collapse of the Somali government created clan-based contested spaces—the power struggle among the various clans for access to state power and scarce resources, which resulted into, armed conflict and added pressure in the proliferation of SALWs. Rooted in deep-seated postcolonial dynamics of inter-clan mistrust, animosity and the power struggle that ensued among the various clans—the feeling of exclusion and marginalization from the process of government provided the fertile ground for different clans to arm themselves in an attempt to provide for their own security (Paffenholz 2003).

Multi-Level Mechanisms for Arms Control and Disarmament

In recent years, there have emerged a significant number of global, regional and local initiatives that aimed at tackling the proliferation of SALWs across the Horn of Africa and beyond (Whiteheads 2006). The international responses to the violent conflict in Somalia have included a whole range of efforts aimed at controlling arms flow. The United Nations 1992 arms embargo prohibits arming or supplying arms to non-state actors. The UN allowed the international community to supply weapons only to the Transitional Federal Government and AMISOM (Wezeman 2010). Similarly, the EU and member states have adopted a wide array of policy responses to the SALWs problem in the Horn of Africa particularly in Somalia. The establishment of an EU Code of Conduct on Arms Exports in 1998 setting out standards for EU members arms sales for non-EU countries. Such policies have brought greater scrutiny to the export of SALWs and made arms trade to areas involved in conflict much more difficult (Benson 2001).

At the regional level, the Nairobi Declaration of 2000 under the aegis of IGAD? and the subsequent Protocols of that agreement on arms control has so far remains the most impeccable laid out plan for ensuring political action, legislative measures and civil society involvement in combating the challenges posed by SALWs across the Horn of Africa and the Great Lake region. Through the Declaration, a regional intergovernmental mechanism and the Nairobi Secretariat now the Regional Centre for Small Arms of the Great Lakes Region and the Horn of Africa, or RECSA, was formed in order to coordinate the responses of the governments in the region (Whiteheads 2006). Member states with the inclusion of the Seychelles, agreed the Nairobi Protocol for the Prevention, Control and Reduction of Small Arms and Light Weapons, in the region, which entered into force as legally binding.

Other provisions of the Protocol include safe disposal, transfer of SALWs and brokering. The member states unanimously agree to cooperate in terms of mutual legal assistance, law enforcement and transparency, information exchange and harmonization (Whiteheads 2006). As of 2005 only Kenya and Uganda had taken steps to implement the national plans of action as addressed within their Nairobi Declaration commitments.

In the 2000s, there have been multitudes of concerted efforts by national and grassroots actors as well as NGOs that focus on addressing the challenges of the proliferation of SALWs in Somalia. These multilevel local initiatives aimed at capacity building of grassroots actors for tackling the misuse of Small Arms and Light Weapons. To achieve this objective, in January 2014, the Federal Government of Somalia hosted a Weapons and Ammunition Management (WAM) workshop in Mogadishu, in collaboration with the UNDP, the United Nations Institute for Disarmament Research (UNIDIR), the United Nation Mine Action Service (UNMAS), the United Nations Assistance Mission in Somalia (UNSOM) and RECSA, with the aim of reviewing the scope of existing WAM activities and identifying WAM capacity-building requirements. The WAM focuses on five key areas of disarmament namely: arms control and stockpile management, import, export and transit, tracking and brokering, public awareness and education and legislative measures (RECSA 2018).

NGOs and local community-based organizations have built the capacity of grassroots actors and created awareness for understanding the challenges posed by SALWs in the country. Table 41.1 illustrates the multilevel approaches to arms control in Somalia.

Conclusion

This chapter highlighted the interface between state collapse—the prevalence of ungoverned spaces and resurgent violent non-state actors within the Somalian state and the proliferation of SALWs. It argued that the collapse of the Somali state nurtured the emergence of numerous violent non-state actors including the violent jihadi group Al-Shaabab. The disintegration of the state and the resurging armed groups created the safe haven for massive inflow of illicit arms in Somalia. The fractured governance structure bequeathed by the state collapse and ensuing quasi-statehood status of the Federal Government of Somalia as a result of its "semi-autonomous" administrative structures and lack of governance capacity has continued to undermine efforts for stabilization and disarmament. Thus, the lack of central government to coordinate governance and the failed attempts to establish a transitional government has paved the way for numerous clashes among the various clans and warlords. This "ungovernable" situation in Somalia has allowed illicit SALWs to flow locally from regional sources unchecked and deepened the risks of arms supply to non-state actors.

Table 41.1 Existing mechanisms for arms control

Level	Mechanism	Policy Objective
International Actors	• Partial lifting of arms embargo on Somalia • Capacity building for Somali government, to manage weapons (through UN bodies UNDP, UNIDIR, UNMAS and UNSOM) the EU, NGOs and bilateral partners • Financial and logistics support for the government to fight the militant group, Al-Shabaab (AMISOM of the AU)	• Build government capacity to fight the militant groups • Enhance the authority and legitimacy of the Somali state • To reduce insecurity violence and
National		

(continued)

Table 41.1 (continued)

Level	Mechanism	Policy Objective
Policy Initiative	• Provisional Constitution • Government policies • State institutions (government, military and security apparatus) • Fighting Al-Shabab • Specific illicit SALWs reducing measures (a) Reconcile warring clans (b) Encouraging disarmament (c) Abolition of illicit SALWs markets (d) Policy act on licencing of arms (e) Built (with the help of development partners) arms storage facilities (f) Training government officials good governance (g) Raising awareness on the dangers of illicit SALWs (h) Granting amnesty to militias and rehabilitating them (i) Training police and army	• Governance toll • To fight corruption, security sector reform and promote good governance • Promoting authority, capacity and legitimacy of the state • To promote state security • To control and reduce trade and diffusion of illicit SALWs
Local Actors	• CSO (Neighbourhood Watch) • Local development NGOs: Coalition for Grassroots Women Organizations (COGWO)	• To stop violence, promote political dialogue • Support (DDR) for former armed groups • Support alternative livelihood including women empowerment

Source Somalia Report by RECSA (2018)

In spite of several national, regional and international arms control initiatives, most security challenges that bedevilled the Somalian state are intricately tied to the proliferation of SALWs. The problem of fragile governance institutions, lack of security sector reform, absence of post-conflict reconstruction programmes by external donors to stem the tide of poverty and underdevelopment, lack of a centrally coordinating mechanism and lack of international cooperation on a mechanism to control the flow of SALWs particularly control of illicit arms transfer to Somalia profoundly remain the major obstacles to peacebuilding and disarmament. There is the need for coherent and concerted efforts at the national, regional and global level to evolve and mainstream a robust disarmament, demobilization and reintegration (DDR) and security sector reform (SSR) mechanisms into the post-conflict peacebuilding interventions projects in Somalia. This will help address the challenges arms supplies to violent non-state actors in the country. Furthermore, tackling the problems of SALWs inflow in Somalia and in the Horn of Africa will require both international and regional efforts of tackling the key drivers of conflict not least the socio-economic and political inequalities, poverty and marginalization that allowed violent armed groups to feast.

REFERENCES

Benson, W. (2001). *Light Weapons Controls and Security Assistance: A Review of Current Practice*. London: International Alert and Saferworld.

Bronwyn, B. (2015, April 3). Al-Shabab Crosses the Rubicon in *Foreign Affairs*. http://www.atlanticcouncil.org/insight-impact/in-the-news/bruton-al-shabaab-crosses-the-rubicon/. Accessed on 13 January 2020.

Farah, I., Ahmad, A., & Omar, D. (2005). Small Arms and Border Controls in the Horn of Africa: The Case of Malkasufta, Ethiopia; Mandera, Kenya; and Bula Hawa, Somalia (Eds.). In *Controlling Small Arms in the Horn of Africa and the Great Lakes Region: Supporting Implementation of the Nairobi Declaration, African Peace Forum and Project*, p. 10. Ploughshares. http://www.ploughshares.ca/libraries/Control/APFO-PPSmallArmsPub05.pdf. Accessed on 13 January 2020.

Fergusson, J. (2013). *Somalia: A Failed State Is Back from the Dead*. http://www-indepdendent-couk.cdn.amproject.org/v/s/www.independent.co.uk/news/world/africa/somalia-a-failed-state-is-back-from-the-dead-8449310.html?amp=&usqp=mq331AQCKAE%3D&amp_js_v=0.1#aoh=15734769631427&referrer. Accessed on 13 January 2020.

Gebre-Wold, K., & Masson, I. (2002). Small Arms in the Horn of Africa: Challenges, Issues, and Perspectives. *Bonn International Center for Conversion*, Brief 23. http://www.bicc.de/publications/briefs/brief23/brief23.pdf. Accessed on 13 January 2020.

Global Peace Index (GPI) Somalia Report. (2019). https://reliefweb.int/report/world/global-peace-index-2019. Accessed on 13 January 2020.

Google Map. (2019). *Political Map of Somalia*. https://www.google.com/search?q=Map+of+Somalia&oq=map+of+som&aqs=chrome.0.69i59j0j69i57j0l5.3998j0j8&sourceid=chrome&ie=UTF-8.

Ismail, A. I., & Green, R. G. (1999). The Heritage of War and State Collapse in Somalia and Somaliland: Local-Level Effects, External Interventions and Reconstruction. *Third World Quarterly, 20*(1), 113–127.

Jones, G. S., Liepman, M., & Chandler, N. (2016). *Counterterrorism and Counterinsurgency in Somalia: Assessing the Campaign against Al-Shaabab*. Santa Monica, California: Published by RAND Corporation.

Koigi, B. (2018). *The Dangerous and Mutating Arms Trade in the Horn of Africa*. Online at https://www.fairplanet.org. Accessed on 17 October 2019.

Mbugua, K. (2013). Drivers of Insecurity in Somalia: Mapping Contours of Violence. *Occasional Paper*, Series 4, no. 3. Nairobi, Kenya: International Peace Support Training Centre IPSTC.

Menkhaus, K. (2003). State Collapse in Somalia: Second Thoughts. *Review of African Political Economy, 30*(97), 405–422.

Menkhaus, K. (2004). *Somalia: State Collapse: Collapse and the Threats of Terrorism*. Oxford: Oxford University Press.

Paffenholz, T. (2003). *Community-Based Bottom-Up Peace-Building*. Uppsala: Life & Peace Institute.

Philip, A., Wilson, M., & Rossetti, A. (2019). *Somalia—Gun Facts, Figures and the Law*. Sydney School of Public Health, The University of Sydney. Gun Policy at: http://www.gunpolicy.org/firearms/region/somalia. Accessed on 13 January 2020.

Regional Centre on Small Arms (RECSA) Report. (2018). *An Assessment of Illicit Small Arms and Light Weapons Proliferation and Fragility Situation in Somalia*. https://recsasec.org/2018/08/16/report-on-illicit-small-arms-and-light-weapons-proliferation-and-fragility-situations-somalia/. Accessed on 13 January 2020.

Small Arms Survey. (2014). "Feeding the Fire: Illicit Small Arms Ammunition in Afghanistan, Iraq and Somalia. *Issue Brief, 8,* 12.

Tar, A. U., & Mustapha, M. (2017). Al-Shaabab: State Collapse, Warlords and Islamist Insurgency in Somalia. In C. Varin & D. Abubakar (eds.), *Violent Non-State Actors in Africa: Terrorists, Rebels and Warlords*, 227–300. Switzerland, Palgrave Macmillan.

UNIDIR Report. (2003). *Implementing the United Nations Programme of Action on Small Arms and Light Weapons: Analysis of the Reports Submitted by States*. https://unidir.org/files/publication/pdfs/implementing-the-united-nations-programme-of-action-on-small-arms-and-light-weapons-analysis-of-the-reports-submitted-by-states-in-2003-320.pdf. Accessed on 13 January 2020.

Wezeman, P. (2010). Arms Flows and the Conflict in Somali. *SIPRI Background Paper*. https://www.sipri.org/sites/default/files/files/misc/SIPRIBP1010b.pdf. Accessed on 10 January 2020.

Whiteheads, D. (2006). SALW Proliferation Pressures, The Horn of Africa and EU Responses. *A Background Paper, Prepared for the Project European Action on Small Arms and Light Weapons and Explosive Remnants of War*. https://books.google.com.ng/books?id=9TXoSxhOOCoC&pg=PA10&dq=Darryl+Whitehead+SALW+proliferation+the+horn+of+Africa+and+EU+responses&source=bl&ots=_1AKVjhEC9&sig=ACfU3U089vFWwdq. Accessed on 13 January 2020.

World Bank. (2005). *Conflict in Somalia: Drivers and Dynamics*. Available at: http://www.siteresources.worldbank.org/INTSOMALIA/Resources/conflictinsomalia.pdf. Accessed on 10 January 2020.

Mala Mustapha is a Reader and Head at the Department of Political Science University of Maiduguri, Nigeria. He obtained his MA in International Politics and Security Studies at Bradford University UK in 2003 and awarded a Ph.D. in Conflict Resolution and Peace Studies by the University of Central Lancashire UK in 2013. His research interests are the security in the Lake Chad region, the Horn of Africa and regional security in Africa focusing on themes of resource conflicts, political economy, globalization and human security, democracy and democratization in Africa and terrorism studies. Recently his research focuses on internal displacements (refugee/IDP), humanitarian crisis and counterterrorism and counterinsurgency studies in the Northeast part of Nigeria and Somalia. He has published widely in peer-reviewed journals and books including the *Review of African Political Economy* and *CODESRIA*. Since 2019 Mustapha has been a Senior Research Fellow at the Centre for Democracy and Development (CDD), Abuja, Nigeria.

Haruna Yerima is an Associate Professor at the Department of Public Administration, Ahmadu Bello University, Zaria, Nigeria. He obtained Ph.D. in Public Administration from the University of Maiduguri. Dr. Yerima has worked as a distinguished lecturer at the Ramat Polytechnic Maiduguri. He was a member of Nigeria's Federal House of Representatives (2003–2007) representing Biu-Shani-Kwayakusar Federal Constituency. Yerima has published extensively on governance, public sector management, public policy, public service and democracy. He is a member of the Nigerian Political Science Association.

CHAPTER 42

Uganda: Protracted Conflict, Insurgency and SALWs Proliferation

David Andrew Omona and Samuel Baba Ayegba

Introduction: Background to Protracted Conflicts and Insurgency in Uganda

Located in East Africa, Uganda has been an epicentre of conflicts during much of her postcolonial history. Most of the available literature on the formative years of Uganda's postcolonial period indicates that the first two years of Uganda's independence were years of progress and cordial relationship among the political elites (Rubaihayo 2006; Karugire 1980; Kabwegere 1994; Mutiabwa 2010). Rubaihayo (2006: 24), in particular, notes that soon after independence the government of Uganda embarked on transforming the Ugandan society from the colonial vestiges to a productive and free society. Social services, infrastructure, trade and commerce were developed following Uganda People's Congress' (UPC's) manifesto to fight ignorance, disease and poverty.

To address this agenda, the independence government under the leadership of Apollo Milton Obote built schools, hospitals, roads and established parastatal bodies. Agriculture was boosted being the backbone of the economy

---

D. A. Omona (✉)
Department of Governance and Public Administration, Uganda Christian University, Mukono, Uganda

S. B. Ayegba
Department of Defence and Security Studies, Nigerian Defence Academy, Kaduna, Nigeria

and livelihood of many people; cooperative societies were set to promote agricultural production and marketing of farm produce. Besides, government institutions were developed with competent and effective public service. The political astuteness shown by the UPC government within the few years of independence made some members of the Democratic Party (DP) and the Kabaka Yeka (KY) to cross over to the ruling party (Omona 2015: 39–40). Although political analysts like Karugire (1980), Kabwegere (1994), and Mutiabwa (2010) blame this act for the erosion of democratic governance in Uganda, I believe it was a right gesture so to help break down barriers between the different political and ethnic groups in Uganda at the time. Given the smooth takeoff, Mutiabwa (2010: 29–35) argues, such a vibrant independent Uganda made a local artist to compose a song in praise of Obote.

However, the problems that the independent government got embroiled in so far exceeded their capacity to handle. While some of these conflicts were inherited from the colonial government, others were failures to take appropriate decisions by the political elites at the time. For example, as the excitement of independence and glamorous take-off was still being celebrated, the age-old Bakonzo and Bamba resentment of the Batoro imperialism in Rwenzori region flared into a conflict (Omona 2015: 17). This made the Bakonzo and Bamba to organize the famous Rwenzururu Movement. As this was going on, another conflict erupted in Eastern Uganda between the Bagisu and Sebiny, and also the Bagisu and Bakedi over border demarcation (Khanakwa 2012: 3). In Ankole, the Bairu started to resent the Bahima suppression (Doornbos 1971: 2). On the religious frontier, the Protestant and the Roman Catholic religious rivalry re-surfaced (Mutiabwa 2010: 7; Omona 2015: 17–18).

Worse still, the first challenge ensued from the army in January 1964 when the army mutinied demanding for higher pay and more rapid promotion. Unlike the governments of Kenya and Tanzania that responded to similar demands by disciplining their army and instituting tight control, Apollo Milton Obote accepted the demands of the mutineers, increased their salary and promoted officers including Iddi Amin Dada (Byrnes 1992: 22). This made the military to become a major constituency in brokering power.

Then from 1965 to 1970, the turmoil reached a heightened level as the country became a scene for multiple deep-rooted conflicts that were seeking to tear the country apart. Although many commentators blamed these unfortunate events on the British colonial administration, the independence political leadership's greed for power, personal character, and myopic judgement were also to blame (Odoi 2009: 12). The independence regimes' leadership skills were tested by the implementation of the 1962 constitution, the balancing of power within the coalition government, and unification of the different ethnic and racial groups. Furthermore, bridging the development gaps between the regions, handling religious rivalries, taming the characters of some leaders and their constituencies became a challenge. The confusion these series of challenges set worked negatively to disorganize the achievements the independent government made in the two years of independence (Omona 2015).

In regard to the 1962 constitution, which Othman Haroub and Maria Nassali (2002: 9) likened to a negotiated treaty, two major issues of conflict stood out. Firstly, the 1962 constitution's accord of federal status to Buganda and semi federal status to the kingdoms of Ankole, Bunyoro Kitara and Toro and somewhat the district of Busoga while leaving the non-kingdom areas to be governed following unitary system brought suspicions (Mutiabwa 2010: 25). The people from the non-kingdom area saw this as creation of states within a state. The special position this constitution gave to Buganda became a source of anxiety and conflict between Buganda and the people from other parts of Uganda. The people from other parts of Uganda argued that since the British used the Baganda as their agents to colonize other parts of Uganda and consequently concentrated to develop Buganda at the expense of other parts, such special position given to Buganda would increase their dominance and arrogance (Omona 2015). Secondly, as Rubaihayo (2010) argues;

> The other most politically explosive…was the implementation of the constitutional provision which required a referendum to be held within two years of independence to determine the wishes of the people of Bugangaizi, Singo, Buhekula, and Buyaga whether they wanted: 1) to stay under the jurisdiction of Buganda or; 2) transfer their allegiance to Bunyoro Kitara Kingdom or; 3) form a separate district. (Rubaihayo 2010: 24–25)

Unfortunately, the result of the referendum actually became the source of disintegration of the Uganda People's Congress (UPC) and KY alliance. The friction it brought between Obote and Kabaka Edward Mutesa II-King of Buganda, coupled with the ideological and ethnic struggle for supremacy within the ruling party led to the infamous 1966 constitutional crisis and its antecedent effects. As these unfortunate events were unfolding, the protagonists' seeking for support from the military made the army to become arbiter in political conflicts in Uganda to date. Besides, this single event created an insurgent group within Buganda who identified with the Kingdom and started to fight the government of the time. As Haroub and Nassali (2002: 11) have argued, the 1966 crisis culminated into the suspension of the 1962 constitution, the introduction of the pigeon hole Interim Constitution of 1966 and then the Republican Constitution of 1967. The deposition and exile of the first president of Uganda, and the declaration of a state of emergency depicted a deeply polarized political atmosphere in Uganda. These happenings did not help to solve the situation, but created more chaos.

To make matters worse, the attempt of Obote to ally with the Socialist Block coupled with a rift between him and the army commander was used to ferment the 1971 coup that saw Iddi Amin Dada coming to the political limelight (Adhola 2012). Although Amin's coming to power was highly welcomed by the Baganda and a few other people who were anti-Obote, the Ugandans who went into exile decided to form insurgent groups like the Uganda Freedom Fighters (UFF) of Professor Yusuf Lule, Kikosi Maalum (KM) of Apollo Milton Obote though coordinated by David Oyite Ojok, and Front for National Salvation (FRONASA) of Yuweri Kaguta Museveni.

Those who were excited with Amin's ascendancy to power's disappointment came when the attempted rebel invasion of 1972 made them to see Amin's true colours. Starting with the Acholi and Lan'gi army officers, and other civilians and religious leaders in key positions like Archbishop Janani Luwum, Amin tried to weed all people suspected to be in opposition to him (National Resistance Council [NRC] 2004: 17). Since a sizable number of the officers in his army came from the West Nile, it set the Acholi and Lan'gi against the people of West Nile thus making them to retaliate latter after the overthrow of Amin in 1979. With the parliament dissolved and the constitution suspended, Amin ruled by decree. In the confusion that ensued, the insurgent groups that were based in Tanzania used dubious propaganda to discredit Amin's regime, and at times kill which were all blamed on Amin. In his book showing the mastered seed, Yuweri Kaguta Museveni (2007) did argue that while in Tanzania they used to carry out clandestine activities in Uganda.

The ascendance of Amin to the political echelon brought the Muslims who felt disenfranchised during much of Uganda's history to the limelight, thus leading to Muslim–Christian conflict (Odoi 2009: 236). At the international level, the expulsion of Asians and Israelis, and the turbulent relationship with Kenya and Tanzania isolated the Amin regime greatly. However, Amin's ardent campaign for Third World liberation won him friendship from some African and Arab leaders (Mutiabwa 2010). Although the overthrow of Amin's government in 1979 brought a sigh of relief, the arrogance that the Uganda National Liberation Army (UNLA) soldiers came with returned Uganda into chaos. Mass murder, looting, and rape of women that came to define the state led to emergence of insurgent groups like the "Oyoro Boys" who eventually transformed into the Uganda National Rescue Front I (UNRF I) under the leadership of Moses Ali and Former Uganda National Army (FUNA) under the leadership of Major General Isaac Lumago in the West Nile region of Uganda. At the political level, the failure of the coalition government to work out proper administrative modalities led to four presidents ruling Uganda within a span of two years starting with Professor Yusuf Lule, Godfrey Binaisa, Paul Muwanga and Milton Apollo Obote (Omona 2015). Lamenting such rapid change of government, the religious leaders in Uganda wrote a letter to President Nyerere that reads in part;

> As soon as it (*the UNLF*) had seized power, among all other things we were promised peace, stability, and security; "never again Uganda shall be ruled by the power of the gun" ...*but*...the development which have taken place within the UNLF government have not been very promising. For three times the UNLF has changed government within a period of less than two years-thus we realize instability still lives with us. Shooting and killing have continued as in the times of Amin at times even worse. We have seen families being exterminated; father, mother, and children all killed on the same day. (Nsubuga et al. 1980: 1)

The above quotation is a clear testimony that the hope of many people who celebrated the fall of Amin was not met. What the liberators promised was not realized as such they started to regret because of the events that were unfolding. Thus, prior to sending the above letter to President Nyerere, the religious leaders had drawn the attention of President Binaisa on the worsening situation in Uganda (Nsubuga et al. 1980). This degenerating situation was also echoed by a statement issued by the Bishops and clergy of the Church of Uganda (CoU) that met at Makerere University from 16 to 19 June 1980 (Wani 1980). Although in the letter to President Nyerere the religious leaders suggested that;

> The present government should use all possible means in its capacity to fight insecurity, not to wait until they were elected into power as one of the members of the military commission said *(published in the Uganda Times of Monday September 1, 1980)*: "if the UPM is voted in power it will ensure total security for all Ugandans within its first two weeks in office". (Nsubuga et al. 1980: 1)

The interesting campaign catchphrase from the Uganda Patriotic Movement's (UPM's) candidate, Yuweri Kaguta Museveni in the quotation of the church leaders, was that "if the UPM is voted into power it will ensure total security...within its first two weeks in office". It may mean the UPM's candidate was either the source of insecurity or he knew the people who were creating the insecurity that he could easily deal with them or negotiate with them to stop such acts. However, nothing was done to address this situation. Instead, the situation continued to degenerate further. Citing the example of Lebanon, the religious leaders suggested peacekeeping forces from the UN, Organisation of African Unity (OAU) or the Common Wealth countries to be set up, but nothing in line with their suggestion was put in place to address the emergency (Omona 2015).

Another setback occurred soon after the December 1980 election that brought Obote to the presidency for the second time. The controversy surrounding the result of the election led to the emergence of many insurgent groups to challenge the victory of the UPCs candidate. Outstanding among these insurgent groups were the Peoples' Redemption Army (PRA) that metamorphosed into National Resistant Army/Movement (NRA/M) of Yuweri Kaguta Museveni after merging with Professor Yusuf Lule's Uganda Freedom Fighters (UFF), the Freedom Democratic Movement of Uganda (FEDEMU) of George Nkangwa, the Uganda Freedom Movement (UFM) of Andrew Lutakome Kayira, the Vumbula of Kakoza Mutale and Uganda National Rescue Front of Moses Ali (RLP 2014: 86–89). The pressure exerted by these insurgent groups coupled with the power struggle within the UNLA eventually led to the military coup that saw General Tito Okello Lutwa taking over government in 1985. General Lutwa was also overthrown by Museveni in 1986 after the failed Nairobi peace agreement (RLP 2014: 89–90). The tumultuous event that ensued did not only shutter the UNLA administration but also brought animosity at local levels between the Acholi and Lango since the Lan'gi saw the Acholi as the source of their woes (Omona 2015).

The period between 1986 and 2011 saw the emergence of many kinds of conflicts that pitched different insurgent groups against the NRA government

(Omona 2015). Among these were: the more than twenty armed insurgent groups like the Uganda People's Democratic Army (UPDA) led by Odongo Latek, Uganda People's Front/Army (UPF/A) of Otai Peter commandeered by Major General Moses Eregu *aka* Hitler, the Ninth October Movement (NOM)/Force Obote Back Again (FOBA) of Peter Otai, National Army for the Liberation of Uganda (NALU) of Amon Bazira, The Holy Spirit Movement/Army (HSM/A) of Alice Auma Lakwena. Others were: The Lord's Resistant Army (NRA) of Joseph (Kibanja et al. 2012), the National Democratic Alliance (NDA) of Major Hebert Itongwa and Allied Democratic Forces (ADF) of Jamal Mukulu, to mention a few, all emerged to contest the National Resistance Movement's (NRM) hold to government. The various inter/intra clan conflicts, land conflicts and cattle rustling (Omona 2015) added to this list of conflicts. Though most of these conflicts have been contained militarily, the conflicts they generated at the local level lived on.

In view of the above, whereas each of the conflicts and insurgency had their peculiar grievances, Marximino Ngabirano (2010) sees the nature of conflicts in postcolonial Uganda to be Religious and regionalism expressed between the religious groups and the different regions of Uganda. Samwiri Karugire (1980), agreeing with Ngabirano adds ethnicity on the list. Ngabirano (2010) observes:

> For example, the first years of independence up to 1967, the conflict factor in was mainly between Protestants against Catholics, and the central region dominating the political life. Between 1967 and 1971, the centre of conflict became Protestant against Catholics and domination of the Northern region. During the rule of Amin Dada (from 19771 to 1979), the issue of conflict shifted to Muslims against Christians and Northern domination against other regions. From 1979 to 1986 the issue of conflict turned to Protestant against Catholics and the Northern region still dominated the army and some key political positions. Yet from 1986 to date the Protestant and Catholic factor still remains and while regional domination has shifted to Western region. (Ngabirano 2010: 61)

Then, on his part, Karugire (1980) asserts:

> At the time of independence, Ugandan politics had become polarized along religious lines. Secondly, regionalism or ethnic nationalism had assumed a fundamental character while, at the same time, a national institution such as the National assembly was no more than a forum of district delegates. The Ugandan army was ethnically unbalanced. And the then government which took over the control of the Uganda at independence was itself composed of an artificial alliance, and the partners in that alliance had a history of mutual antagonism. (Karugire 1980: 49)

Although the analysis of Ngabirano and Karugire are valid, differences in region, ethnicity and religion are not bad in themselves but rather the way people use these differences is that which bring about problems. Some of the hotspots of the conflicts in Uganda could be seen in Fig. 42.1.

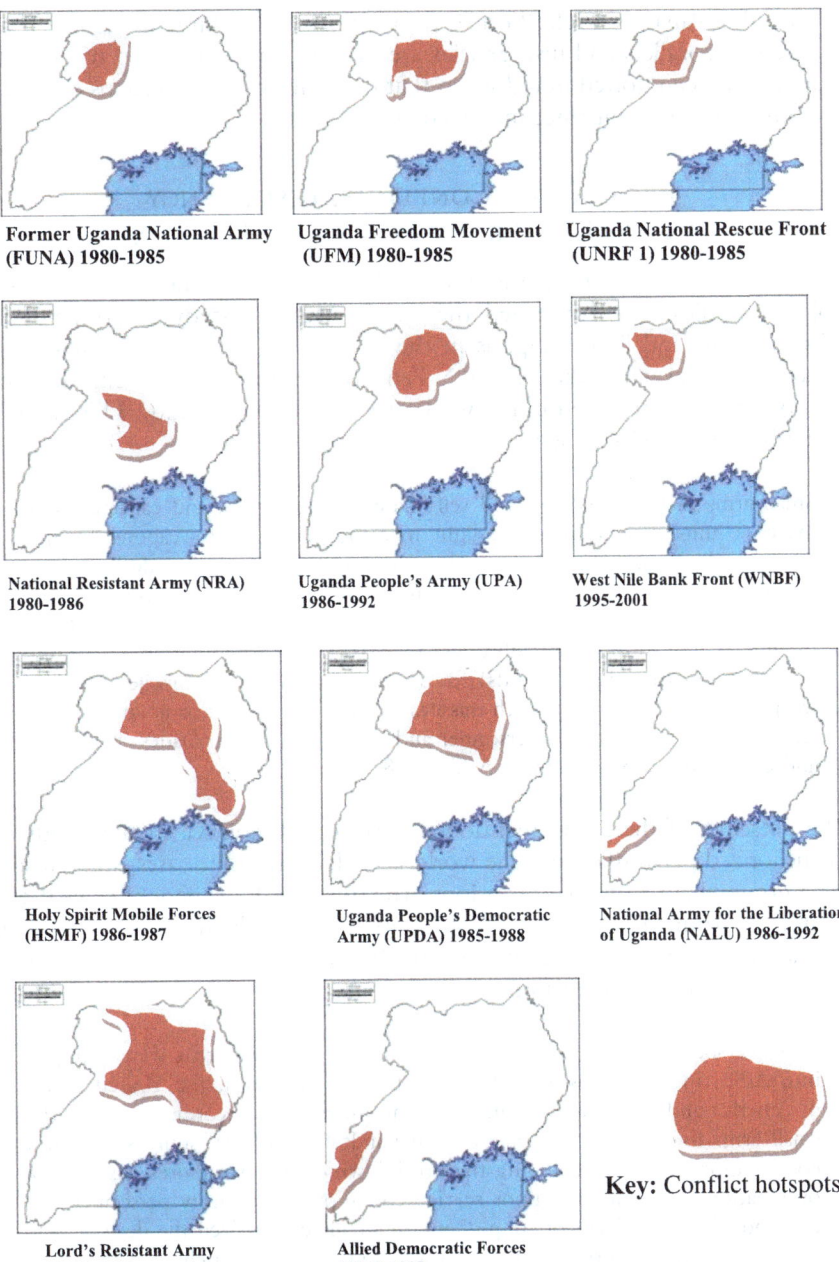

Fig. 42.1 Maps of Uganda showing some of the Postcolonial Conflict Hotspots (*Sources* Adopted from Ogenga, Otunu (2002), Causes and Consequences of the War in Acholiland, ACCORD, p. 15; cf. Omona, A. D. (2015), Management of postcolonial intrastate conflicts in Uganda: A case of northern Uganda, Nairobi: Kenyatta University—Ph.D. Thesis, p. 26)

The above map is a reflection of theatres of a few insurgent groups. If all the sites of conflicts and insurgencies are marked, the whole map of Uganda would have been dotted in red given that different insurgent groups emerged to contest government since independence.

Protracted Conflicts, Insurgency and SALWs Proliferation in Uganda

Over the years, scholars in the field of international relations, history and political studies have concerned themselves with the study of proliferation of small arms and light weapons in the world. A lot of literature has been generated from such studies. The UN Panel of Experts on Small Arms description of SALW, as reflected in the work of Edward Mogire (n.d.: 1) is candid. According to the UN Panel:

> Small arms include revolvers and self-loading pistols, rifles and carbines, sub-machine guns, assault rifles and light machine guns. Light weapons, include heavy machine guns, hand-held under-barrel and mounted grenade launchers, portable anti-aircraft guns, portable anti-tank guns, recoilless rifles (sometimes mounted), portable launchers of anti- aircraft missile systems (sometimes mounted), and mortars of calibre less than 100 mm. Ammunition and explosives includes cartridges (rounds) for small arms, shells and missiles for light weapons, mobile containers with missiles or shells for single-action anti- aircraft and anti-tank systems, anti-personnel and anti-tank hand grenades, landmines and explosives. (UN Document A/52/298, 199)

The presence of the above-mentioned weapons of violence in the hands of unauthorized persons around the world is evident. In some cases, some insurgent groups have in their possessions arms that are far superior to what the sitting government's army has. Writing about the proliferation of SALWs in Africa, Nna et al. (2012) quoting from Musah's (2002) study on small arms and light weapons proliferation contends that:

> A major source of its proliferation remains the stockpiles that were pumped into Africa in the 1970s and 1980s by the Soviet Union, the United States of America and their allies to fan proxy interstate wars. According to him, the small arms found their way into civilian hands from official sources due to a combination of factors including the breakdown of state structures, lax control over national armories and poor service conditions for security personnel. He contends that the advent of coup d"etat gradually emphasized the decisive role of weapons as the surest route to power and personal enrichment and their proliferation increased with the entry of junior officers in the political arena. He further contends that the proliferation of weapons is socially- oriented because the issues involved revolve around social relationship, values, beliefs, practices and identities. (Nna et al. 2012: 32)

Whereas the observation of Nna et al. (2012) is a general picture of the situation in Africa, in the case of Uganda, proliferation of SALWs started before the British colonial administration has been set and became more available as a result of the cycle of conflicts since the country got political independence from Britain. While the 2003 survey of Small arms estimates about 630,000–950,000 small arms in Uganda, or 3–4.5 small arms per 100 persons (Pinto et al., n.d.: 2), a 2007 news report by Vision Reporter (17 March 2007) puts the figure to 400,000. The reduction in the number SALWs in circulation could be attributed to a massive disarmament that took place between 2003 and 2007. Unfortunately, though, there is no official statistics of current figures of SALWs in private hands.

Both external and internal factors could explain the proliferation of SALWs in Uganda. The external factors that aided proliferation of small arms, in particular, started way back before British administration was established in Uganda. This was mainly as a result of the invasion of Turko-Egyptian forces into Sudan and eventually northern parts of Uganda and ivory poachers from Ethiopia who exchanged guns for ivory with the local people. By the time the British extended their influence into Acholi, for example, there were more than 1500 firearms in the possession of the local people (Omona 2015: 190; Behrend 1999: 17). Around the same time, the engagement of Ethiopian ivory poachers with the Karamojong pastoralists who supplied the pastoralists with guns in return for ivory (Ralston 2013: 6), afforded the opportunity for the local people to acquire firearms, which others used for selfish purposes. Whereas firearms were introduced in the Kingdom areas of Ankole, Buganda and Bunyoro at almost the same, the only difference was that in these areas the use of firearms was the preserve of the Kings, leading chiefs and their standing army.

One of the greatest external factor that led to SALWs proliferation into Uganda was as a result of the conflicts in neighbouring countries like Sudan, South Sudan, DRC, Rwanda, Burundi and Somalia. Given Uganda's porous borders, the influx of refugees from these countries since the early 1950s made a large number of guns to find their ways into the county. In the case of Sudan, when in the 1960s the Sudanese refugees came to Uganda, the Anyanya rebels of Sudan were using Uganda as a launch pad to recruit and train their forces. During the protracted conflicts that pitched Sudan's People's Liberation Movement/Army (SPLM/A) against the government of Sudan, apart from Uganda becoming a conduit through which arms enroot to Sudan were passing, the rebel SPLM/A was using Uganda as a recruitment and training ground for their forces. These and the other guns that were captured during attacks on the enemy are being sold cheaply to civilians in Uganda which in the process made guns to became easily available in the hands of the local people. Besides, during the LRA operations in northern Uganda, the turns of SALWs supplied in support of the LRA by the Sudan Government have increased the number of guns in the hands of the local people (Omona 2009).

As in the case with arms from Sudan and South Sudan, the conflict in the DRC, Rwanda, Burundi and Somalia has pumped a lot of SALWs into Uganda. The porous borders have facilitated this easily over the years. Some of these arms end up remaining in the hands of local people when after a fight some of the wielders of the firearms are killed and or, in the process of trying to escape they throw the guns which the civilians land on it. During the invasion of Rwanda by the Rwanda Patriotic Front (RPF), Uganda was a launch pad. That meant some of the guns were procured through Uganda and others ended up becoming available to the local people.

In as far as the internal factors are concerned, SALWs stared being common in the communities in the Rwenzori subregion when after independence in 1962 the relationship between the Bakonzo/Bamba and the Batoro flared into a fully-fledged fight (Omona 2015: 17, 64–68). The fight the ensued during the tough periods made each party to acquire firearms, which even after the cessation of hostilities were not handed to rightful people who are to keep instruments of violence. The 1964–1966 constitutional crisis opened up the avenue for more small arms in the hands of the local people in Uganda. This time around it was right in the capital city, Kampala, that the Baganda forces loyal to King Edward Mutes II fought against the Uganda Army (Refugee Law Project [RLP] 2014: 73–74). Shortly after this crisis when government of Obote was overthrown by the army in 1971, a lot of guns of all sorts became available to the local people. The insurgent groups that were formed to fight the hold of Amin to power armed some local people who were not supposed to be in possession of such firearms. During some failed attacks, the guns that were thrown by the running insurgent groups or by the government forces who were killed were recovered by the local population, who could not report them to the government for fear of being taken to be rebels.

Whereas during the presidency of Amin, in most parts of Uganda it was rare to see soldiers wielding guns in the open, but the people who were not convinced that he was the right president easily acquired firearms to fight him. This situation became worse, with the overthrow of Amin in 1979. Many of the soldiers ran to their villages with guns and started using it the way they wanted, including for robbing innocent people. Others used it to organize rebellion in the West Nile subregion, the case of UNRF I, and FUNA (RLP 2014: 117–120). All these aided the proliferation of SALWs greatly in that subregion. Apart from recruiting the local people into the rebel ranks that made guns to be available to the local people, the guns that some of the government forces leave in the barracks during attacks or thrown by running soldiers were taken by the local population for their own security, as was the case in Karamoja.

The same trend continued during the reign of the four successive presidents: Professor Lule, Godferry Binaisa, Paul Mwanga, and Obote. The insurgent groups that emerged to challenge the presidency of Obote in the early 1980s opened up the flood gates of SALWs flow in central, northern and parts of western Uganda as the NRA/M of Museveni, the UFM/A of Kayira and UNRF I of Moses Ali were fighting the UPC government (Omona 2015: 79–81, 83–89). It became fissionable to wield guns given that even teenagers were recruited as fighters. The overthrow of Obote for the second time in 1985 and General Tito Okello Lutwa in 1986 compounded the state even further. The emergence of the UPA and FOBA in eastern Uganda, the UPDA, HSA/M, LRA and others in Northern Uganda (Omona 2009), several insurgent groups in central Uganda, and the NALU and ADF in western Uganda further became avenues for SALWs proliferation. Since small arms became largely available and can easily be used to enrich those who have them, some security personnel have resorted to hiring them to thugs and robbers at a fee.

The Effects of Protracted Conflicts, Insurgency and SALWs Proliferation on Peace, Security and Development in Uganda

Given the easy accessibility, as Badmus (2005) observes, the proliferation of SALWs has become so widespread that not only do they threaten security across the world but also undermine the peace and stability of innocent civilians. To this end, the UN Security Council assert that:

> The destabilizing accumulation and uncontrolled spread of small arms and light weapons in many regions of the world increases the intensity and duration of armed conflict, undermines the sustainability of peace agreements, impedes the success of peace building, frustrates efforts aimed at the prevention of armed conflict, hinders considerably the provision of humanitarian assistance and compromises the effectiveness of the Security Council discharging its primary responsibility for the maintenance of international peace and security. (United Nations 2001: 31)

Indeed, as noted above, the availability of weapons in the possession of rebels, combatants and private individuals who use them for wrong purposes impedes the alternative conflict resolution strategies and instead, increases insecurity and further protracted conflict in the country as well as frustrating efforts of peacekeeping and peacebuilding operations in rebuilding and reconstructing of the societies that have been devastated by conflict (Sunday 2011; Stemmet 2001). Man-portable Air Defense Systems (MANPADS), which are light weapons that are commonly referred to as shoulder-fired anti-aircraft missiles, when in the hands of criminals, terrorists and other non-state actors, also pose a potential danger to commercial aviation around the world (Chelule 2014: 81).

From 1988 up to 2006, millions of people in northern Uganda region in the districts of Gulu, Kitgum, Pader, Lira, Apach, Adjumani and their environs, were greatly displaced by war given that arms went in the hands of rebel groups. As a result, many children whose parents were killed were also orphaned and forced to work at an early age and become heads of households (Omona 2009). The Small Arms and Light Weapons that are easily available in the hands of rebels, criminal gangs and those not legally authorized to possess them, have been a source of insecurity in the civilians in the region. As a result, many lives have been lost to violence of SALW (Religions for Peace 2004). Besides, millions of people have sustained injuries, and others are maimed thus causing misery to the community. Such is a direct violation of human rights in the context of the right to live and freedom from slavery. The threat of use of small arms economy has made many in Uganda to lag far behind in terms of personal development because whatever is put is destroyed by such senseless fights. Given the constant fear and insecurity people fail to engage in economic and gainful activities thus making them to continue in a vicious circle of poverty. For, many people flee from their homes to other places as refugees and internally displaced persons and migrants crossing the border into the neighbouring districts and countries. As a result, it led to the interruption of humanitarian assistance for the needy.

In Uganda as elsewhere in the world, the World Bank found that the use of small arms by rebels and criminals negatively affect the economy which includes the private wealth being divested which doubles during an armed conflict, and that the cost of civil war is approximated at 60% of its annual gross domestic product. An armed conflict is very expensive and drains a country's resources and thus impoverishes the populace (Pinto, Olupot-Olupot, and Neufeld, n.d.: 2–4). The proliferation of small arms and light weapons, given their availability and ease in operation, maintenance and easy portability has given rise to child soldiers where the rebels give children weapons to carry and use them in fighting. In the case of Uganda this started with the NRA bush war, which was copied by other rebel groups like the HSF and HSM, LRA, and UPA. Some of the children have been killed in conflict, seriously injured or maimed, permanently disabled and others have been left with serious psychological trauma. Unfortunately, some of these child soldiers are girls who serve as "wives" to the combatant (UNICEF 2007).

In the Karamja subregion, the proliferation of SALWs has been characterized by, among others: surging of violent crime, retardation of development, emergence of conflicts between the Karamojong and other tribes like the Teso, Lango, Sebei, Bagisu and Turkana. Others have decided to organize themselves into militias/armed gangs and participate in cattle rustling and poaching. The health effects of SALWs proliferation around the country is evident. A lot of people are nursing wounds as a result of attacks by gang stars or insurgent groups. The unfortunate situation is that most of the victims have failed to meet their own health costs.

SALWs Control and Prevention Strategies in Uganda

The Government of Uganda has overtime taken steps aimed at curbing SALWs proliferation, which has been blamed for fueling protracted conflicts and insurgency in the country. Accordingly, this chapter shall briefly outline some of these measures in this section. The range of measures deployed to try to regulate the spread of SALWs, fall into three main categories namely reduction, preventative and coordination strategies. All the categories are fused into the National Policy of Small Arms and Light Weapons (2010), as well as NAP (2004–2009).

Small Arms Mapping Exercise: The Government of Uganda in past facilitated an agenda embarked on a comprehensive mapping of SALWs holdings at the National level. The initiative integrated vital governmental organizations, institutions, local authorities and civil society organizations, with emphasis on significant roles for: The Uganda National Focal Point on Small Arms and Light Weapons; Regional Task Forces; District Task Forces; and other minor structures (Uganda National Focal Point 2007). The National Focal Point, with backing from SaferAfrica and Saferworld in partnership with Centre for Conflict Resolution (CECORE), Oxfam GB, People with Disability (PWD) and Uganda Joint Christian Council (UJCC) embarked on a study on the actual level of the challenge and impact of SALWs proliferation on national security in the country. The aim was to recognize and appreciate the nature and degree of small arms spread in terms of supply and demand influences; the prevailing capability and funds obtainable to tackle Small Arms problems, attitudes and consequences of proliferation on Ugandan people (Saferworld 2008). According to the Uganda National Focal Point [NFP] (2007), the outcome of the study brought to the fore the following areas:

Policy on Small Arms and Light Weapons: International SALW transfer control guidelines will be of crucial importance particularly for the states that are most affected by illicit SALWs. In Uganda, the Great Lakes Region and Horn of Africa, and many other parts of Africa, unrestrained transfers and trafficking signifies a major source of supply for illicit SALWs that have persisted to drive and prolong conflicts, such as the insurgency by the Lord's Resistance Army Northern Uganda. The problem is compounded by lack of capacity for countries of the region to monitor and control transfers, making them conduits for further illicit transfer. There was necessity to appraise the law and integrate present realities predominant in Uganda in line with the subregional and internationally approved procedures. Thus, the review of legislation was commenced in the year 2010. A vibrant and all-inclusive national policy on Small Arms, Light Weapons, ammunition and explosives was acknowledged as an urgent prerequisite to administer the National Action Plan and offer procedures to prevent, control and manage the proliferation, illegal ownership and misuse of SALWs. In response to this finding, a Firearms Policy and guiding principle for evaluation of regulation were approved by Government in October 2010 and this formed the foundation for the review of SALWs legislation (Gun Policy, n.d.).

l Firearms Stockpile Management: There was demand to create a central electronic database for national recordkeeping, control of national stockpile, investigations and information sharing at national, regional and international levels. This system was developed in line with international best practices (Kytömäki and Yankey-Wayne 2006). In particular, attention was given to stockpile management issues in conformity with the national policy and RECSA Best Practice Guidelines on Stockpile Management. RECSA's principle objective is to ensure the efficient and effective implementation of the Nairobi Declaration and Nairobi Protocol, which relate to the prevention, control, and reduction of illicit small arms. Most of RECSA's funding comes from external donors, in particular (but not limited to) the EU, Japan, and the United States. For the year ending June 2010 RECSA members contributed less than 3% of the organization's operating funds, with most dues-paying members being in arrears. RECSA, created in 2005, has its origins with the Nairobi Declaration of March 2000, and the Nairobi Secretariat was created to assist its ten signatories to attain their objectives. Focus is on security of stock, management of captured and seized stocks, surplus and obsolete stock, disposal and destruction, national recordkeeping, licensing criteria and procedure. This helps to reduce the influx of illicit arms into countries such as Uganda (United Nations Office on Drugs and Crime 2011).

Capacity Building and Training: Training for national points of contact on the Arms Trade Treaty (ATT) (which establishes common standards for the international trade of conventional weapons and seeks to reduce the illicit arms trade) and UNPOA and other related Arms Control Instruments and to develop the capacity of nation states to strengthen their response to the illegal trafficking of firearms by improving the capacity and awareness of small arms control instruments. A training programme on international, multilateral and regional arms control instruments, monitoring tools, and roles and functions of national points of contact was initiated and completed in collaboration with partner agencies such as the Small Arms Survey, United Nations Institute for Disarmament Research (UNIDIR) and Stimson Center. Key areas requiring skills development and training identified under the small arms mapping exercise are arms management and disarmament competences for intermediate and senior management personnel; expert investigation skills on national level such as ballistic experts, forensic investigation, record keeping and firearm crime associated investigation, as well as resource mobilization. Consequently, series of capacity building programmes were carried out targeting specifically Uganda Peoples' Defence Forces (UPDF), Uganda Police Force (UPF), Uganda Prison's Service (UPS), Internal Security Organisation (ISO) and Uganda Wildlife Authority (UWA) (Uganda Human Rights Commission 2014).

National Co-ordination Instruments: As part of the small arms mapping exercise, a national coordination mechanism was put in place to consolidate synchronization and execution of events in line with the National Focal Point by creating lower structures that were responsible for grassroot implementation at Regional, District, Sub-county and lower stages. Accordingly, the lower structures were accountable for the coordination and implementation of the National Action Plan as directed by the National Focal Point, and also functioned as the coordination mechanism between the National Focal Point, implementing institutions and communities (Uganda National Focal Point, n.d.). The *Uganda Police Force*—is in charge of licensing of civilian (including PSOs) imports, exports and transit, enforcing Firearms Act, investigation of breaches, border control, distribution of SALWs to police, SPCs, LDUs, PSOs and other militia, and security provision to SALWs in transit. The *Uganda Peoples' Defence Force*—is the main procurement authority for state SALWs and enforcement role where national security and/or territorial integrity is threatened such as role in trafficking enforcement operations and border security, and security provision to arms in transit, stockpile management and security of SALW held by the state. On its part, the *Intelligence Services (ESO and ISO)*—is responsible for the organization of intelligence on illicit SALWs trafficking and deployed at all border posts. *Uganda Revenue Authority*—primary responsibility for revenue collection (Customs), law enforcement section responsible for countering illicit trafficking, including of SALWs, verifies and administers paperwork at border posts, ensuring compliance of entry/exit permits. *Immigration*—is the organ responsible for controlling the movement of people into/out of Uganda, as well as for the limited direct responsibility for controlling movement of SALWs. The *Civil Aviation Authority*—responsible for managing the day-day-day operations of Uganda's aerodromes. It is also mainly concerned with air safety, security issues are within mandate, inter-agency coordination between the various state and commercial entities on security, and other issues responsible for approving flight plans, and monitoring and controlling air traffic (Saferworld 2008).

Civil Society: Civil Society Organisations were identified as central in the struggle against Small Arms Proliferation, especially in their roles in field of research, advocacy, lobbying and resource mobilization, which is extremely recognized both internationally and nationally. Many civil society organizations and institutions in the region and within Uganda are undertaking specific research aimed not only at establishing the nature and magnitude of the problems caused by SALWs but also at informing policy related to this issue. The IRG is one such organization. Since 1994, the IRG has been working to encourage a more focused and sustained exploration of alternative security structures and disarmament measures for the Greater Horn subregion. The IRG's programmes are designed to stimulate indigenous research and analysis on national and regional security and peacebuilding issues and to bring the results of that research to the attention of interested civil society and government policymakers through a series of roundtables, workshops and conferences. Each year the IRG holds a Regional Conference on Sustainable Peace and Human Security, bringing together participants from various fields of expertise from across the Greater Horn to provide an overview of issues relating to its three programme themes—security sector reform, the proliferation of SALWs and the establishment of a regional security architecture (Griffiths-Fulton 2002). The need for carrying the populace along in the fight against SALWs proliferation cannot be overstated. Hence, massive public awareness and education programmes were organized for various segments of the society and other major stakeholders geared towards their involvement in combating proliferation of Small Arms and its associated problems (Barnes 2006).

Uganda National Action Plan (NAP) 2004–2009: The National Action Plan was a five-year programme (2004–2009) meant to regulate the execution of the national action to address the problem of Small Arms and Light Weapons proliferation in Uganda. The NAP focused activity on three key result areas namely control and management of existing stocks of small arms, reduction of excess volumes of SALWs and prevention of proliferation of small arms. The key result areas were later condensed into 11 broad thematic areas on which action has been focused: Building institutional framework; Review of National Policy and Legislation; Stockpile management; National awareness and education programme; International and regional cooperation and information exchange; Border control and refugees; Human development planning, connecting projects on small arms and development; promoting police community relations, as well as training and capacity building; Research, this entails conducting action-oriented research; Critical areas of support— data collection and analysis on firearms; material backing for law enforcement agencies etc., and consolidation of collaboration with Civil Society Organizations. The execution of NAP was supported by Government of Uganda, development Partners and Civil Society Organizations under the coordination of the Uganda National Focal Point. The implementation of the NAP was carried out with many Government Ministries *and* agencies *including*: Ministry of Defence (UPDF), Ministry of Internal Affairs (Police, Prisons, Immigration), Presidents Office (ISO, ESO), Office of the Prime Minister, Ministries of Transport and Communications; *and* Local Government. Furthermore, it included Justice and Constitutional Affairs; Foreign Affairs, Trade and Industry; Finance, Planning and Economic Development; Education and Sports; Information; Gender and Social Development; and related establishments such as Uganda Wild Life Authority, Uganda Revenue Authority, as well as civil society organizations. These institutions similarly made up the NFP structures at lower level and were liable for the execution of the NAP (Uganda National Focal Point, n.d.).

The issues the study of the NAP laid bare were critical to attending to the concerns of SALWs proliferation, only if due attention were given to it. However, the NAP focused activity on three key result areas namely control and management of existing stocks of Small Arms, reduction of excess volumes of Small Arms and Light Weapons, and prevention of SALWs proliferation. These areas were condensed into eleven (11) comprehensive thematic areas on which action was focused. The thematic areas are, namely: building institutional framework; review of National Policy and Legislation; Stockpile management; National awareness and education programme; international and regional cooperation and information exchange; and border control and refugees. Others are human development planning, linking initiatives on small arms and development; promoting police community relations; training and capacity building; research (action-oriented research in vital areas of support—data collection and analysis on firearms); material support for law enforcement agencies etc. (Uganda National Focal Point, n.d.).

The Uganda National Action Plan 2011–2015: Following lessons learned from the implementation of NAP (2004–2009), the Government of Uganda noted some oversights and made recommendations intended to develop a more cautious and comprehensive application of NAP. Thus, NAP 2011–2015 was built on the accomplishment of the previous implementation period, adopting success stories and addressing the oversights identified within that period. Accordingly, NAP was developed through a comprehensive consultation process involving a range of stakeholders and actors whose involvement and perception of SALWs issues was considered as significant and critical to the process. The review process undertook several stages that included desk review of the performance of the NAP, stakeholder discussions with key implementing institutions and consultations with implementing structures. The mission of NAP 2011–2015 was to coordinate efforts to prevent, combat and eradicate the proliferation of illicit small arms and light weapons, through comprehensive, integrated and coordinated approaches, while the key objectives of the plan were to prevent, and control and reduce the proliferation of Small Arms and Light Weapons. More so to enhance the capacity of the NFP in management of SALWs; educate and sensitize the community on Small Arms issues; and getting a cross-section of stakeholders to contribute to the SALWs control process (Uganda National Focal Point, n.d.).

The scope of NAP activities includes, among others, prevention, control and reduction of proliferation of illicit stocks, reducing dependency on SALWs through public awareness and education, and establishment of economic alternatives and improving border controls including cross-border cooperation between Uganda and her neighbours. It also includes strengthening the cooperation with RECSA, Regional and subregional Bodies (EAC, IGAD, ICGLR, and EAPCCO) and other National Focal Points within the region; and strengthening the human and structural capacity of the populace. NAP implementing institutions include the Ministry of Defence, UPDF, Ministry of Internal Affairs-Police, prisons, Immigration, Presidents Office—ISO, ESO, Office of the Prime Minister, Ministry of Transport and Communications, Ministry of Local Government, Ministry of Justice, Foreign Affairs, Trade and Industry, Finance, Planning and Economic Development, Education and Sports. With the firearms policy firmly entrenched, the NAP 2012–2017 was put in place a sustainable SALWs strategy presents a new direction in the efforts to combat, prevent and eradicate the problem of Small Arms proliferation with the NFP at the forefront of coordinating these measures in Uganda (Uganda Country Self-Assessment Report 2017).

Bilateral and Multilateral Strategies: The Government of Uganda has carried out other sundry bilateral and multilateral actions aimed at controlling the spread of SALWs in the country. For instance, in early 2002 the Government of Uganda signed a Memorandum of Understanding (MoU) with the Government of the Republic of Sudan to enable cooperation between the two states, with the intent of restoring security in their border regions, thereby, boosting transborder collaboration for purposes of combating SALWs proliferation. Under the terms of the MoU, the Government of Sudan permitted the UPDF into its territory to hunt down the rebels of the Lord's Resistance Army (LRA) which has continued to wage lethal insurgency that has destroyed the Northern part of Uganda. Though it has not altogether stopped the operations of the rebel group, this cross-border collaboration has assisted in the recovery of huge cache of arms from the LRA (Uganda Country Report 2003). In the same vein, about 124 guns were recovered in a gun recovery operation from the districts of Napak, Amudat, Nakapiripirit, and Moroto, parts of Teso, Bugisu, Sebei, 1600 bullets and military gear in September 2013 (GunPolicy.org, n.d.).

Furthermore, in 2016, the Government of Uganda, through the relevant coordinating agencies. For instance, in Lira district, a directive was issued for those in possession of illegal firearms to surrender them or face the full force of the law; the directive follows apprehensions over a high proportion of firearms that were believed to be in the hands of wrong people in the district, which was once a war-torn area. Also, by April 30, 2016, all firearms in civilian's possession must have been registered; this was an attempt by the ministry of Internal Affairs to crack down on illegal small arms. Thereafter, unregistered firearms were declared illegal, as the government made concerted efforts to control small arms and light weapons owned by civilians and maintain proper national control over government stockpiles of all small arms in Uganda. This exercise led to the destruction of an estimated 6000 small arms and weapons collected by police in a nationwide drill (Kugonza 2016). In a bid to discourage the boom in small arms business, the Government in April 2017, increased license fees for individuals and companies importing firearms into the country. Estimates of non-tax revenue (NTR) rates tabled before Parliament by the finance ministry show that gun importers and owners were taxed Shs five million each. Besides, any company which seeks a permit to acquire or import a firearm pays Shs 1 million per year, which a private security company also pays Shs 200,000 for an application to import or acquire firearms (Eyotaru 2017).

International Collaborations: In addition the United Nations Programme of Action (UNPOA), Uganda is signatory to the Bamako Declaration on an African Common Position on the Illicit Proliferation, and Circulation and Trafficking of Small Arms and Light Weapons. And also the Nairobi Declaration on the Problem of the Proliferation of Illicit Small Arms and Light

Weapons in the Great Lakes Region and Horn of Africa. These agreements confirm governments efforts to deal with the conundrum of the proliferation of illicit SALWs through regional cooperation. The Nairobi Declaration action plan "Agenda for Action" sets out the strategy and framework for comprehensive action. State Parties under the Nairobi Declaration have adopted a Draft Regional Protocol for the Prevention, Control and Reduction of Small Arms and Light Weapons which when ratified by the States Parties will provide the legal force to reinforce the Nairobi Declaration (Bamako Declaration 2000).

Challenges of SALWs Control and Prevention in Uganda

Arms management and control systems remain inadequate to eradicate the outflow of arms from legal government stocks into illegal ownership. Thus, efforts should be targeted at consolidating arms management and control systems to guarantee greater accountability and security for all SALWs owned and regulated by government (United Nations Office on Drugs and Crime 2019). As noted above, the Government of Uganda has been making concerted efforts to curb SALWs proliferation, with the aim of end protracted conflicts and insurgency in the country. Unfortunately, measures taken thus far have not yielded the desired outcome, owing some challenges. Some of the challenges mitigating against SALWs proliferation include among others the activities of non-state actors, inadequate funding of arms recovery programme, weak firearms legislation, lack of a coordinated approach for Disarmament, Demobilization and Reintegration (DDR), low awareness among Civil Society Organizations of the Problems Associated with Small Arms Proliferation. These challenges are discussed subsequently.

The Activities of Violent Non-State Actors (VNSAs): Regulation is also hampered by the involvement in illicit proliferation of non-state or sub-state actors operating outside the state system. These include ethnic and dissident groups, private commercial concerns, terrorist groups, rebel movements, irregular forces, private security companies and mercenaries. As mentioned earlier, the instability Uganda has experienced has throughout its post-independence history remains a major factor that fueled the activities of non-state actors who are the defining factor in SALWs proliferation in the country. For instance, following the overthrow of Idi Amin in 1979, soldiers deserted their barracks, and the population were able to gain access to these unprotected weapons, that remain in circulation despite repeated efforts to recover some of these "disappeared" weapons (Reliefweb 2006). In addition, during the LRA operations in northern Uganda, the cache of SALWs supplied in support of the LRA by the Sudan Government have amplified the quantity of weapons in the hands of non-state actors (Omona 2009). Such non- and sub-state proliferation has seriously undermined the state's traditional monopoly over the legitimate use of force to provide internal security and defense from external threats.

Inadequate Funding of Arms Recovery Programmes: Funding is a key component in any SALWs control and prevention programme. In Uganda, the collection and destruction of large stocks of surplus and illicit SALWs was undertaken by the National Focal Point programme with backing from the United Nations Development Programme, which assisted in the establishment of a comprehensive weapons collection, stockpile management and destruction programme for the country. However, assessment of the project revealed that the issue of inadequate funding, was a major concern that threatened the project. There are limited resources to implement NAP activities, leading to high dependency on donor funds (Saferworld 2008). According to a Ugandan Parliamentary Committee (2015) report on Defence and Internal Affairs, inadequate financing of SALWs control programmes and the lack of a separate budget line for SALWs initiatives will cause Uganda to linger behind other countries in the region, while drawing other stakeholders back.

Weak SALWs Legal Framework: Whereas earlier on Uganda has carried out a legislative review process with a view to enhancing national SALWs controls, nothing concrete has been done to effect it. To an extent, the current legal framework in use, is, the 1970 Firearm Act—as amended in 2005 (Kamwesiga 2016: 34), lacks proper descriptions and is largely considered obsolete and ineffective. For instance, while the government issued improved rules for licensing and monitoring firearms in 2002, and later announced that new legislation will be drafted rendering legal weapons ownership harder for people, the amended law seems not to have aided the stringent process of possessing firearms. Yet, Uganda's consent to the UN Firearms Protocol necessitates it to implement provisions on proscription of illicit SALWs activities. In this regard, the government announced in early April 2005 plans to carry out a survey of legally owned guns and to launch a voluntary weapons collection programme. The government also reviewed principles and administrative processes for import, export, shipment and transport of SALWs and explosives, national SALWs manufacturing, and stockpile management (Eyotaru 2017). In advancing SALWs legislation and policy, Uganda has followed the Best Practice Guidelines approved by signatories to the Nairobi Declaration and has endeavoured to incorporate a broad range of civil society actors and stakeholders in this process (Regional Centre on Small Arms and Light Weapons 2005). In addition, legal control frameworks must differentiate between genuine handlers of weapons categories such as state security forces, and the illicit (illegal) proliferation that takes place outside the state system (e.g. transfer of state-held arms to non-state users (Sagramoso 2001). Notwithstanding, the relationship between armed conflict over the control of resources and the trafficking in SALWs render legislation further problematic to execute; proceeds from the exploitation of natural resources are used not only for maintaining armies but also for personal enrichment and building political support. Thus, leaders of armed groups involved in exploitation are reluctant to give up control over these resources, or the SALWs that make control possible (Bannon and Collier 2003).

Porous Borders: Porous borders contribute to the influx of illegal Small Arms into Uganda. Insecurity in border areas and the inability of border control systems to manage Uganda's border are notable issues facilitating the movement of small arms into the country. Similarly, cross-border conflicts, crime and insecurity, particularly along Uganda's borders with South Sudan, Kenya and DRC, are of grave-concern (Uganda National Focal Point 2007). For instance, cross-border conflicts and cattle raiding are major concerns in border areas, mostly in the Northern and North Eastern regions. Refugee movements further aggravate this situation across Uganda's porous borders with DRC and Sudan, which makes effective policing and control of movements especially tough. In addition, the absence of well-defined entry points along the borders makes controls very problematic, this coupled with weak border surveillance and poor staffing, combine to further weaken customs and immigration control systems. Lastly, the regional nature of arms trade between Uganda and its neighbours, the lack of robust joint-border collaboration and intelligence sharing between countries in the region, militate against small arms control strategies in Uganda (Uganda National Focal Point 2007).

Lack of Coordinated Approach for Disarmament, Demobisation and Reintegration (DDR): A prerequisite for post-conflict recovery is social reintegration, which was therefore the central component of the project approach. The Amnesty Act of 2000 provided amnesty to all individuals willing to abandon rebellion and peacefully rejoin society without fear of retribution, as well as created the Amnesty Commission to monitor and coordinate demobilization, reintegration, and resettlement of reporters (persons receiving Amnesty such as ex-combatants and collaborators. The Uganda DDR programme helped implement the agreed demobilization and repatriation of LRA and ADF rebels, while assisting the social and economic reintegration of former rebels and collaborators. A total of 28,800 ex-rebel beneficiaries were targeted by the project, with secondary benefits extending to families and communities. The project worked to consolidate peace, reconciliation, and security, particularly in the northern regions. The specific targets of the project were demobilization and repatriation of LRA members including assembly, food, shelter, medical care, registration, information, sensitization, and transfer to Uganda, reinsertion of cases of local reporters along with provision of basic items. It also involved cash grants, and interim care to facilitate re-entry of reporters, socio-economic support for 28,800 reporters, including counseling, education and other services, with an emphasis on the needs of women, children, and the disabled. While the LRA and ADF have not completely demobilized during the lifetime of the project, the project did see significant progress in demobilization and reinsertion (Borzello 2007).

Although this process has helped many returnees to manage the transition to civilian life, it is marked by a number of problems demobilization is haphazard, with a significant number of returnees going home without reporting to the authorities. Reception centres suffer from the failure to standardize counselling, go-home packages; length of stay and overall approach, reintegration is complicated by massive displacement of populations; returnees are often reintegrated into IDP camps where the situation is one of squalor and insecurity. Even though the community in general welcomes home returnees, stigmatization is common. Giving packages or skills training to returnees can cause resentment among civilians, and the emphasis on returnees as children and victims sought to distort the effectiveness or reintegration. Thus, while many returnees are profoundly disturbed by their experience, others have adapted to bush life and even grown to enjoy it. The challenge with the way DDR is being handled is that, there is the risk of ex-combatants refusing to turn in their arms completely, if they entertain any form of fear with the entire DDR process. Some may want to sell these arms to survive or go back altogether to the bush to continue the conflict, thereby reinforcing the circle of illicit SALWs proliferation (Borzello 2007).

Limited Involvement of CSOs in Arms Transfer Programme: In Uganda, there seems to be little official prospect for civil society to examine the exercise of the GoU in handling international transfers of arms. Though, civil society has been involved in the development of policy on international SALWs transfers, with representation on the National Focal Point and the SALWs, Policy Drafting Committee, as well as through public consultations on the draft policy document, as Uganda has some mechanisms for public scrutiny of its policy and practice on international SALW transfer controls. Yet, these are limited, the GoU should provide more detailed publicly available information on its policy and practice, create more opportunities for public scrutiny, strengthen formal mechanisms of oversight and pro-actively respond to and engage with parliament and civil society on SALWs issues. The involvement of CSOs could go a long way to help in raising public awareness on the issues of SALWs proliferation across the country (Saferworld 2008).

Conclusion

Small Arms and Light Weapons (SALWs) proliferation and misapplication can intensify insecurity and undermine development in any society. In countries not at war, the ready availability of illicit SALWs renders the countries less safe by snowballing crime, social disintegration, while making the resort to violence more likely and more lethal. The presence of weapons of violence in the hands of unauthorized persons around the world is evident. In some cases, some insurgent groups have in their possessions arms that are far superior to what the sitting government's army has. Given the easy accessibility of SALWs, its proliferation has become so widespread that not only do they threaten security across the world but also undermine the peace and stability of innocent civilians.

The chapter reveals that the use of small arms by rebels and criminal gangs negatively affect national security and the economy of nations. In the case of Uganda, external factors that aided proliferation of small arms, in particular, started way back before British administration was established in Uganda. This was mainly as a result of the invasion of Turko-Egyptian forces into Sudan and eventually northern parts of Uganda and ivory poachers from Ethiopia who exchanged guns for ivory with the local people, and became more available as a result of the cycle of conflicts since the country got political independence from Britain. The post-independence phase began with the NRA bush war, which was copied by other rebel groups like the HSF and HSM, LRA, and UPA, resulting in wanton destruction of lives and property. The greatest external factors that led to SALWs proliferation in Uganda is strongly linked with series of conflicts neighboring countries such Sudan, South Sudan, DRC, Rwanda, Burundi and Somalia.

Given Uganda's vast porous borders, the influx of refugees from these countries since the early 1950s made a large number of small arms to find their ways into the county; small arms sold cheaply to civilians in Uganda and in the process guns, in particular became easily available in the hands of the local people. This has continued fuel insurgency and insecurity the country with attendant consequences for national security and sustainable development in the country. Besides, millions of people have sustained injuries, others have been, while violation of human rights has become the order of the day. More importantly, the SALWs proliferation has continued to threat the national economy, with many Ugandans are lagging behind in terms of personal development, as the people to persist in a vicious circle of poverty. In a bid to stem the tide of SALWs proliferations, the Government of Uganda has overtime taken steps intended to curb SALWs proliferation, which has been held responsible for fueling protracted conflicts and insurgency in the country.

However, measures taken thus far have not yielded the desired outcome, owing to some teething challenges such as porous boarders through which more SALW enter the country, lack of coordinated approach for DDR in the region, and weak SALWs legal framework in the country, among others. Firstly, to break the influx of illicit SALWs which has fueled protracted conflict in Uganda, there is need to implement a robust and timely disarmament programmes in Uganda. For, a badly managed disarmament programme can result in the unrestrained proliferation of weapons retained by ex-combatants, who could easily be persuaded to sell or retain some of their weaponries when volunteering for demobilization. The international community should support the government to follow through on promises to begin registering weapons held by private individuals and public organizations, as well as attending to the needs of ex-combatants volunteering for demobilization before they become tired of waiting and resorting to alternate means of safeguarding their livelihoods, thereby jeopardizing the entire peace process.

Secondly, despite drafting of a comprehensive weapons collection, stockpile management and destruction programmes, the National Focal Point is experiencing shortage of funds for its implementation; thus, requiring external financial support to push through the laudable objectives of the programme. Thirdly, there is a need for a robust and harmonized SALWs legislation in Uganda. Support the Government of Uganda should seek external technical support for developing national legal and administrative procedures on SALWs possession, use, manufacture and sale, taking into cognizance appropriate international and regional obligations. Fourthly, the Government of Uganda should reform existing police, custom and immigration training in the country, with added provision for capacity building in border control and surveillance, with emphasis on SALWs monitoring and certification. Fifthly, although the vital role of civil society in SALWs action is continually documented, civil society remains undeveloped in Uganda; most CSOs lack information about advancement in executing regional and international SALWs obligations required to hold their governments responsible. Hence, international support intended at firming the accountability role of civil society in monitoring national institutions are urgently needed.

References

Adhola, Y. (2012, September 3). *Amin Takes the 'Throne' as Obote Is Overthrown*, Monday. Retrieved from https://www.monitor.co.ug/SpecialReports/uganda at50/Amin-takes-the-throne-as-Obote-is-overthrown/1370466-1493416-kke443/index.html. Accessed 30 June 2020.

Badmus, I. A. (2005). Small Arms and Light Weapon's Proliferation and Conflicts: Three Africa Case Studies. *Nigerian Journal of International Affairs, 3*(2), 61–104. Shomolu, Lagos: PrintServe, Ltd.

Bamako Declaration. (2000). *Bamako Declaration on an African Common Position on the Illicit Proliferation, Circulation and Trafficking of Small Arms and Light Weapons.* Retrieved from https://www.un.org/en/africa/osaa/pdf/au/cap_smalla rms_2000.pdf. Accessed 14 June 2020.

Bannon, I., & Collier, P. (Eds.). (2003). *Natural Resources and Violent: Conflict, Options and Actions.* Washington, DC: The World Bank.

Barnes, C. (2006, September). *Agents for Change: Civil Society Roles in Preventing War and Building Peace* (Issue Paper 2). Amsterdam: European Centre for Conflict Prevention.

Behrend, H. (1999). *Alice Lakwena & the Holy Spirits: War in Northern Uganda, 1985–97.* Oxford: James Curry Publishers/Fountain Publishers.

Borzello, A. (2007). The Challenge of DDR in Northern Uganda: The Lord's Resistance Army. *Conflict, Security & Development, 7*(3), 387–415. Oxford: Routledge.

Byrnes, R. M. (Ed.). (1992). *Uganda a Country Study.* Washington, DC: Library of Congress.

Chelule, E. (2014). Proliferation of Small Arms and Light Weapons: Challenge to Development, Peace and Security in Africa. *IOSR Journal of Humanities and Social Science (IOSR-JHSS), 19*(5), Ver. V, 80–87, e-ISSN: 2279-0837, p-ISSN: 2279-0845. Available from www.iosrjournals.org.

Doornbos, M. R. (1971). *Regalia Galore: The Decline of Ankole Kingship* (ISS Occasional Papers).

Eyotaru, O. (2017). *Uganda: Why Govt Raised Firearm Licenses.* Retrieved from https://allafrica.com/stories/201704210359.html. Accessed 16 June 2020.

Griffiths-Fulton, L. (2002). Small Arms and Light Weapons in the Horn of Africa. *The Ploughshares Monitor, 23*(2, Summer). Retrieved from https://ploughshares.ca/pl_

publications/small-arms-and-light-weapons-in-the-horn-of-africa/. Accessed 4 July 2020.

GunPolicy.org. (n.d.). *International Firearms Injury Prevention and Policy*. Retrieved from https://www.gunpolicy.org/firearms/topic/firearms_in_uganda. Accessed 24 June 2020.

Haroub, O., & Nassali, M. (2002). *Towards Political Liberalisation in Uganda: A Report of the Uganda Fact-Finding Mission*. Kampala: Fountain Publishers.

Kabwegere, T. (1994). *Politics of State Formation and Destruction in Uganda*. Kampala: Fountain Publishers.

Kamwesiga, K. P. (2016). *Small Arms Proliferation and Homegrown Terrorism in the Great Lakes Region: Uganda's Experience*. M.A. dissertation, Naval Postgraduate School, Monterey.

Khanakwa, P. (2012). *Inter-Communal Violence and Land Rights: Bugisu-Bugwere Territorial Boundary Conflict* (MISR Working Paper No. 6). Makerere Institute of Social Research.

Karugire, S. K. (1980). *Political History of Uganda*. Nairobi: Heinemann Educational Books.

Kibanja, G. M., Kajumba, M. M., & Johnson, L. R. (2012). Ethno-Cultural Conflicts in Uganda: Politics Based on Ethnic Division Influences Tensions. In D. Landis & D. A. Rasita (Eds.), *Handbook of Ethnic Conflict: International Perspectives* (pp. 403–435). New York, Dordrecht, Heidelberg, and London: Springer.

Kugonza, D. (2016). *Guns Destroyed*. Retrieved from https://www.kfm.co.ug/news/guns-destroyed.html. Accessed 23 June 2020.

Kytömäki, E., & Yankey-Wayne, V. (2006). *Five Years of Implementing the United Nations Programme of Action on Small Arms and Light Weapons: Regional Analysis of National Reports*. Geneva, Switzerland: United Nations Institute for Disarmament Research.

Mogire, E. (n.d.). *The Humanitarian Impact of Small Arms and Light Weapons and the Threat to Security*.

Museveni, Y. (2007). *Sowing the Mustard Seed: The Struggle for Freedom and Democracy in Uganda*. London: Macmillan.

Musah, A. F. (2002). Privatization of Security, Arms Proliferation and the Process of State Collapse in Africa. *Development and Change, 33*(5), 911–933.

Mutiabwa, P. (2010). *Uganda Since Independence: A History of Unfulfilled Hopes*. Kampala: Fountain Publishers.

National Resistance Council. (2004). *Uganda Index*. Avaialbe from http://www.mongabay.com/history/uganda/uganda-the_national_resistance_council.html. Accessed on 2 February 2018.

Ngabirano, M. (2010). *Conflict and Peace Building: Theological and Ethical Foundation for a Political Reconstruction of the Great Lakes Region in Africa*. Kampala: Uganda Martyrs University Book Series.

Nna, N. J., Pabon, B. G., & Nkoro, F. (2012). Arms Proliferation and Conflicts in Africa: The Sudan Experience. *IOSR Journal of Humanities and Social Science (JHSS), 4*(4), 31–39. ISSN: 2279-0837, ISBN: 2279-0845.

Nsubuga, E., et al. (1980). A Letter by Four Religious Leaders of Uganda to His Excellency President Julius Nyerere of Tanzania on Insecurity and the Coming Elections in Uganda, UCU Archive, box 120.2, Folder/Title: Ministry of Internal Affairs, Pm3/7(a).

Odoi, T. F. (2009). *Politics, Ethnicity and Conflict in Post-Independence Acholiland, Uganda 1962–2006*. Ph.D. thesis, University of Pretoria, Pretoria.

Ogenga, O. (2002). *Causes and Consequences of the War in Acholiland*. ACCORD.

Omona, A. D. (2009). Northern Uganda Peace Process: Why the Parties Have Failed to Agree. *Jesuit Journal of Social Justice in East Africa, Issue 01/09* (pp. 64–73). Hekimani: Nairobi.

Omona, A. D. (2015). *Management of Postcolonial Intrastate Conflicts in Uganda: A Case of Northern Uganda*. Ph.D. thesis, Kenyatta University, Nairobi.

Pinto, D. A., Olupot-Olupot, P., & Neufeld, V. (n.d.). *Health Implications of Small Arms and Light Weapons in Eastern Uganda*.

Ralston, L. (2013). *Less Guns, More Violence: Evidence from Disarmament in Uganda*. WGAPE-WBpdf.

Refugee Law Project. (2014). *Compendium of Conflicts in Uganda: Findings of the National Reconciliation and Transitional Justice Audit*. Kampala: Refugee Law Project.

Regional Centre on Small Arms and Light Weapons (RECSA). (2005). *Best Practice Guidelines for the Implementation of the Nairobi Protocol*. Nairobi: RECSA. Retrieved from http://www.poa-iss.org/RegionalOrganizations/RECSA/Nairobi%20Best%20Practice%20Guidelines.pdf. Accessed 13 June 2020.

ReliefWeb. (2006). *Uganda: Extinguishing the Fire of Small Arms*. Retrieved from https://reliefweb.int/report/uganda/uganda-extinguishing-fire-small-arms. Accessed 15 May 2020.

Religions for Peace 777 United Nations Plaza, 9th Floor, New York, NY 10017. (2004). http://religionsforpeace.org/initiatives/violent-conflict/disarmament. Accessed 19 May 2013.

Rubaihayo, P. (2006). Obote the Nationalist: His Vision Enabled Buganda to Remain Part of Uganda. In O. R. Anguria (Ed.), *Apollo Milton Obote: What Others Say*. Kampala: Fountain Publishers.

Rubaihayo, P. (2010). *A Short Treatise on Uganda Peoples Congress (UPC)*. Available from https://www.upcparty.net/upcparty/roots_rubaihayo.htm. Accessed on 19 December 2020.

Saferworld. (2008). *Uganda and International Small Arms Transfers: Implementing UN Programme of Action Commitments*. Retrieved from https://www.files.ethz.ch/isn/90985/Uganda_USformat.pdf. Accessed 25 June 2020.

Sagramoso, D. (2001). *The Proliferation of Illegal Small Arms and Light Weapons in and Around the European Union: Instability, Organised Crime and Terrorist Groups*. UK: Centre for Defence Studies, Kings College, University of London.

Small Arms Survey. (2003). *Small Arms Survey 2003: Development Denied*. Geneva: Graduate Institute of International Studies.

Stemmet, A. (2001). Regulating Small Arms and Light Weapons, the African Experience. Published in *African Security Review*, 10(3), 2001. Accessed 20 March 2013.

Sunday, E. (2011). The Proliferation of Small Arms and Light Weapons in Africa: A Case Study of the Niger Delta in Nigeria. *Sacha Journal of Environmental Studies*, 1(2), 55–80.

Uganda Country Report. (2003). *Reporting on the Implementation of the United Nations Programme of Action to Prevent, Combat and Eradicate the Illicit Trade in Small Arms and Light Weapons in All Its Aspects*. Retrieved from https://www.un.org/disarmament/convarms/salw/programme-of-action/. Accessed 23 June 2020.

Uganda Country Self-Assessment Report. (2017). *African Peer Review Mechanism (APRM)*. Retrieved from http://npa.go.ug/wp-content/uploads/2017/09/UGANDA-COUNTRY-SELF-ASSESSMENT-REPORT-DRAFT-May-2017.pdf. Accessed 14 June 2020.

Uganda Human Rights Commission. (2014). Report the Human Rights Committee on the 17th Annual Report of the Uganda Human Rights Commission, 2014.

Uganda National Focal Point. (2007). *Mapping the Small Arms Problems in Uganda: The Development of Uganda's National Action Plan*.

Uganda National Focal Point. (n.d.). *Mapping the Small Arms Problems in Uganda: The Development of Uganda's National Action Plan*.

Ugandan Parliamentary Committee. (2015). *The Report of the Committee on Defence and Internal Affairs on the Ministerial Policy Statement and Budget Estimates for the Fiscal Year 2015/2016*. Retrieved from http://parliamentwatch.ug/wp-content/uploads/2015/04/DIA-2-Ministerial-Policy-Statement-and-Budget-Estimates-for-the-Fiscal-Year-201516.pdf. Accessed 12 May 2020.

UN. (2001). *Council Makes Presidential Statement on Importance of, Responsibilities for, Addressing Question of Small Arms, Press Release SC/7134*. Available from https://www.un.org/press/en/2001/SC7134.doc.htm. Accessed 19 December 2020.

UNICEF. (2007). *Small Arms Exhibit*. Available from http://www.unicef/smallarms/exhibit. Accessed 15 May 2019.

United Nations Office on Drugs and Crime (UNDOC). (2011). *Technical Guide to the Implementation of the Protocol Against the Illicit Manufacturing of and Trafficking in Firearms, Their Parts and Components and Ammunition, Supplementing the United Nations Convention Against Transnational Organized Crime*. Vienna: United Nations Office on Drugs and Crime.

United Nations Office on Drugs and Crime (UNDOC) (2019). "The Illicit Market in Firearms". Doha Declaration: Education for Justice. Retrieved: https://www.unodc.org/documents/e4j/Module_04_-_The_Illicit_Market_in_Firearms_FINAL.pdf. (Accessed on 12th May, 2020).

Vision Reporter. (2007, March 17). 400,000 Small Arms in Uganda. Retrieved from https://www.newvision.co.ug/news/1168887/400-arms-uganda. Accessed 30 June 2020.

Wani, S. (1980, June 16–19). A Statement from the Bishops and Clergy of the Church of Uganda Meeting at Makerere, UCU archive, Box 120.2, Folder/Title: Ministry of Internal Affairs, Pm3/7 (a).

David Andrew Omona is a Senior Lecturer and Head of Department of Governance and Public Administration at Uganda Christian University, a National Coordinator for Religious Leaders' Justice and Peace Network, a Researcher, Transitional Justice Fellow and a Trainer of Trainers in Peacebuilding and Conflict Resolution in the East and Greater Horn of Africa. He holds a Ph.D. in Political Studies/International Relations and Diplomacy, M.A. International Relations and Diplomacy, M.A. Theology, B.A. with Education, and several specialized Diplomas and Certificates. He has done extensive research on conflicts in Africa, the Great Lakes Region and Uganda in particular. His current research interest is in Transitional Justice, Peacebuilding and conflict resolution, and Ethics. He has done collaborative research with people from across the world and still looks forward to getting researchers to collaborate within his areas of expertise.

Samuel Baba Ayegba is a Lecturer in the Department of Defence and Security Studies, Nigerian Defence Academy, Kaduna, and a research fellow at the Centre for Defence Studies and Documentation (CDSD), Nigerian Defence Academy, Kaduna. He is currently a Doctoral candidate in Defence and Strategic Studies, Nigerian Defence Academy, Kaduna. His thesis title is *Gender and violent extremism in Nigeria*. His area of specialization includes Security and Strategic Studies, Gender Studies, Environmental Politics, Peace and Conflict Studies.

Part V

Regional Perspectives

CHAPTER 43

West Africa: Regional Control of Small Arms and Light Weapons Proliferation

*Oluwafisan Babatunde Bankale
and Chukwuzitara Juliet Uchegbu*

Introduction

Many Member States of the Economic Community of West African States (ECOWAS) have experienced conflicts where the weapons of choice were smallarms and light weapons (SALWs), which are available to non-state actors through illicit proliferation. Implication of the illicit circulations of SALWs in the region is that various violent conflicts have been intense and long-lasting with far-reaching consequences to peace, security and development in West Africa (SALWs Annual Progress Report 2015).

The trend in the movement of illicit SALWs across the region, given the various sources of proliferation have proved to be more complicated with challenges faced from managing porous borders, local craft production, national stockpile leakages, activities of illegal brokers, insurgency and terrorism among others in West Africa. With this prevalence, small arms continue to play significant roles in securing access to external supply of weapons to meet the internal demands of crimes and violent armed conflicts in many West African countries as it was in Liberia and Sierra Leone (Darkwa 2011). The circulation of these weapons in the region further offers high premium in the hands of violent non-state actors attracting huge profit because of the purpose they serve.

O. B. Bankale (✉)
Economic Community of West Africa States, Abuja, Nigeria

C. J. Uchegbu
National Defence College, Abuja, Nigeria

© The Author(s), under exclusive license to Springer Nature Switzerland AG 2021
U. A. Tar and C. P. Onwurah (eds.), *The Palgrave Handbook of Small Arms and Conflicts in Africa*,
https://doi.org/10.1007/978-3-030-62183-4_43

Their impact, aside from loss of lives and livelihoods, extends to their usage in perpetrating transnational criminal activities such as drug and human trafficking, illegal mining of minerals, cross-border smuggling, piracy and money laundering in West Africa (Aning and Amedzrator 2016).

The menace of SALWs proliferation, because of the devastation in the region, has attracted attention and laudable support from the global and continental levels down to the regional. Most of this support comes through the ECOWAS Commission which has the mandate to assist the President of the Commission in coordinating the implementation of SALWs issues (ECOWAS Convention 2006). In West Africa, the primary concern is to eradicate the illicit proliferation of SALWs because of their extensive use in the region's internal conflicts.

ECOWAS, beyond the mandate of integration, has further expanded its agenda for regionalised approaches to curb persisting violent conflicts with particular attention on addressing the scourge of SALWs in West Africa. These efforts consolidated the gains of ECOWAS intervention in armed conflicts with the endorsement of the 1999 Protocol on Conflict Prevention, Management and Resolution as part of the collective responsibility of Member States identified in the 1993-revised ECOWAS treaty (Sesay and Akoni 2010). The initiatives however, targeted the adoption of a collective approach through regionalised decisions, declarations and mechanisms to tackle the impact upsurge of the Cold War such as the proliferation of SALWs affecting its Member States. Although confronted with varying degrees of challenges such as weak governance and insufficient resources, these developments have helped in curbing new sources of violent instabilities that are localised within countries with regional dimensions.

The proliferation and indiscriminate handling of SALWs compelled ECOWAS to initiate efforts towards addressing the grave dangers of unprecedented circulation of SALWs in the region. In this regard and resulting from various consultations, Badmus (2009), observed that the signing of *ECOWAS Moratorium on the Importation, Exportation and Manufacture of SALWs on 31 October 1998* and the institutionalisation of the *ECOWAS Small Arms Control Programme (ECOSAP)* set the pace for ECOWAS achievements to manage arms in peace processes and in non-conflict situation in Member States.

This approach served as the bedrock and take-off point for *The 2006 ECOWAS Convention on Small Arms and Light Weapons, Their Ammunition and Other Related Materials* offering comprehensive strategy towards combating illicit flow of SALWs in West Africa. Supported by the fifteen (15) Member States of ECOWAS (Benin Republic, Burkina Faso, Cape Verde, Cote d'Ivoire, Gambia, Ghana, Guinea Bissau, Guinea, Liberia, Senegal, Sierra Leone, Mali, Togo Niger and Nigeria), with the exit of Mauritania in 2000 in West Africa, these achievements along with other regional preferences, continued in building confidence of Member States.

While creating credible and effective platforms towards reducing and resolving tensions in West Africa, the approach offers more coherent and progressive strategies to structural stability and long-term development through partnership and international collaboration at continental and global levels. A good example is the ECOWAS/European Union Small Arms Projects on Border Communities' Intervention for the Implementation of the Pilot Weapons Collection Programmes in West Africa (SALWs Annual Report 2015). In addition, the approach mobilises resources to enhance the capacity of governments and their agencies to exercise have legal controls on weapons' flow and possession and promoting wider awareness and involvement of civil society on the threat that illicit SALWs pose to peace and development within their countries and across national frontiers.

It is in the light of the foregoing, that this chapter in six sections presents: first, an introduction, secondly, conceptual explications and thirdly, the complexities and dynamics of SALWs in West Africa. The fourth section covers various ECOWAS regional efforts undertaken to combat the proliferation of SALWs in West Africa. The fifth section enumerates the challenges at national and regional level to actualising effective control of SALWs in West Africa. The sixth section is the concluding part and proposes way forward towards eradicating illicit small arms within Member States in the ECOWAS region.

Conceptualising the Control of SALWs: A Regional Security Perspective

The concept *Small Arms and Light Weapons* emerged referring not to firearms alone but to include; clubs, knives and machetes and to those weapons covered by the United Nations (UN) Register of Conventional Arms. *Small arms* also refer to artisanal, hand-made or home-made weapons as included by the United Nations (1997) Report of the Panel of Experts on Small Arms and Light Weapons. Small arms as firearms are easily accessed and purchased and are not difficult to use. Therefore, the spread and illegal use of small arms began with the sudden increase in their numbers beyond those needed for legitimate security of state.

The ECOWAS Convention (2006) lists small arms as follows: 'firearms and other destructive arms or devices such as exploding bomb, an incendiary bomb or a gas bomb, a grenade, a rocket launcher, a missile, a missile system or landmine; revolvers and pistols with automatic loading; rifles and carbines; machine guns, assault rifles and light machine guns. It also identifies light weapons as follows:' heavy machine guns; portable grenade launchers, mobile or mounted; portable anti-tank cannons, non-recoil guns; portable anti-tank missile launchers or rocket launchers and mortars with a caliber of less than 100 millimetres'.

These developments, principally facilitated by the rapid improvements in the science and technology of weaponry and their miniaturisation further increased the availability of SALWs in diverse locations, particularly in Africa. To this effect, previously classified weapons known as *medium* weapons such as explosive missile projectors, US M72 and the Russian RPG7 among others are now effectively considered as individual *light weapons*. Added to these, are the traditional man portage small arms, including the popular Soviet-built AK-47 assault rifles, automatic rifles, machine guns, shoulder-fired missiles and rocket systems, light mortars, to mention but a few. Since small arms require little training in operating them, they became overwhelming weapons of choice in the prosecution of post-Cold War violent conflicts in Africa (Ogwu 2006). The growing use of SALWs in African conflicts led to their classification as either *licit* or *illicit*, gaining popularity after the Cold War describing their *origin*, *destination* and *usage*. While arguing that the function to which these weapons are used, does not define their status as licit or illicit, it accepted that their usage for illegal and criminal acts changes the status of these weapons automatically.

The factors surrounding the possession, destination and utilisation of SALWs constitutes their characterisation in many instances as proliferation of SALWs (Hazen and Horner 2007). The proliferations of SALWs therefore are best monitored, by adopting the life cycle approach which monitors these weapons from the manufacturing stage through to the stage of possession, domestic and international transfers, storage (stockpiling) and final disposal (destruction) as part of small arms life cycle. These measures include SALWs marking, record keeping, and tracing interventions at several stages as control mechanisms. In this regard, control efforts confront series of problems that include the remarkable longevity of small arms, which if stored carefully, several decades may pass before the original weapon becomes unusable, as it were in cases of the weapons transported into African continent after the Cold War. This circulation process extends widely beyond state control because small arms are easy to conceal and their lightness in weight facilitates transportation across international borders (Berman and Maze 2012).

Conceptually, the approach for *control* offers a more coherent and progressive framework for addressing the supply of, and demand for illicit weapons in West Africa as a region. In a broader context, small arms have multiple functions in West Africa; their usage in the provision of security by the State, authorised individuals and as symbols of power in some traditional governance structures across the region. Thus, controlling illicit SALWs ensures that individuals or groups hold weapons and ammunition for approved purposes, which, in the judgement of relevant authorities, can be used without inflicting any harm. Although, they serve as status of wealth and the coming of age of young men in most African cultures including in West Africa, their usage in dehumanising circumstances to induce fear and commit crimes, certainly remains a threat to both individuals and State institutions in various communities across the region (Darkwa 2011).

In this context, Acharya (2014) also presented a glance at post-independence Africa's regional interactions by arguing that the frictions of geography, culture, linguistic, politics, religion and economics surrounds the complexities shared within a region. These linkages attracted the search for appropriate mechanisms in form of regional bodies to enable neighbouring

States cope with overwhelming issues that cut across regional dimension like the proliferation of SALWs. The adoption of a regional approach therefore followed the general acknowledgement that problems of SALWs are not exclusively domestic and national affairs, but that they also pose complex multi-country and regional implications. The regional approach according to Ogwu (2006) thus, offers the best possible means of addressing the overall implications of SALW proliferation through global public policy. The measures are critical to the practical cross-border cooperation tailoring down the benefits to national, regional, continental and global needs of peace and security. Thus, a national-cum-regional approach favours more effective and workable efforts to combat illicit trafficking of SALWs.

The importance of a regional security approach was clearly demonstrated in the movement of weapons from Liberia to Sierra Leone. These two countries, with Guinea, neighbouring them were under pressure with local opposition groups resulting to massive movement of SALWs across State borders. This reality is best captured by the concept of security regionalisation. Fawcett (2003) explains that security regionalisation as 'a concentration of activity, collective action and problem solving at local level'. Hettne (2008) underscores the point citing the increasing regional cooperation in peacekeeping operations since the end of the cold war. He observes that, 'Post sovereign political rationality assumes that solutions to problems of security must be found in transnational structures'. The various initiatives in the EOWAS space, some of which are cited in this chapter, further attest to the acceptance of security regionalisation in the region. The circulation and trafficking of SALWs across ECOWAS Member States, incurred huge humanitarian consequences with refugees and rebels operating across their borders. Thus, cross-border demand for these weapons attracted anticipated profits, and this was aided by non-existent or ineffective national laws regulating brokering and trafficking of small arms across porous state lines. In view of these realities, various regional-based projects, targeted weapons collection and destruction to enhance information sharing, coordination and cooperation to handle the proliferation of SALWs while managing conflicts among ECOWAS Member States. As explained by Sesay and Akoni (2010), successful ECOWAS Conflict Prevention, Management and Peacemaking initiatives in Liberia, Sierra Leone, Guinea Bissau, Cote d'Ivoire, Mali and the Gambia were also structured towards achievable SALWs reduction strategies through a regional approach. This collective endeavour provided among other initiatives the platform for (2006) *ECOWAS Convention on Small Arms and Light Weapons, Their Ammunition and Other Related Materials* with the political and institutional will of ECOWAS for effective control of SALWs in West Africa (Agneketom 2008).

Complex Dynamics of Small Arms in West Africa

The primary concern in West Africa over the wide spread availability of SALWs remains the complexities surrounding extensive illegal use of small arms and the threat that these weapons pose to fragile States in the region. With the phenomena featuring among the 'heterogeneous' communities and ethno-cultural groups across West Africa, the dynamics associated with the circulation of illicit SALWs are interconnected with multi-causal and multi-dimensional effects of weak governance institutions, structure and practice, poverty and underdevelopment in the region. Small arms hence, serve as first-hand weapons in the reaction to these challenges through intra- and inter-communal feuds, local wars, armed insurrections, rebel activities, militancy, insurgency that are prevalent in West Africa.

It is important to acknowledge that these complex dynamics have followed three distinct trajectories facilitating the proliferation of small arms in West Africa. The first of these is *the acquisition dynamics* following trends in estimated projections of types and number of SALW circulating in the hands of unauthorised persons across the region. This estimation in the number of theft/looting of police and military stockpiles, or international transfer made through legal acquisition or illicit trafficking constitutes the pattern of small arms acquisition in ECOWAS Member States. In West Africa, the acquisition of small arms revolves in their circulation through routes and caches mainly from Nigeria, Benin, Togo, Ghana to Cote D'Ivoire, Liberia, Sierra Leone, Guinea and to Guinea Bissau, The Gambia, Senegal and then from Mali, to Burkina Faso, Niger and back to Nigeria from the Northern part of the region. However, current trends of circulation are influenced by the crisis in the Sahel region with the nature of insecurity and political instability experienced in neighbouring countries surrounding Mali (as shown in Fig. 43.1).

The flow of SALWs into West Africa can be traced to the existence of long and insecure borders on land and on the sea. International borders and routes where small arms move from one country to another, existed since independence and were created to meet several needs, such as illegal migration and the cross-border smuggling of minerals and cash crops. The West Coast of Africa according to Ikoh (2013), serves as smuggling routes for firearms smugglers, sailing through the Gulf of Guinea which confirms that Nigeria's porous borders on both land and sea edges allows for gun smuggling from countries like Cameroon and Equatorial Guinea using speed-boats and ferry at the high seas and seashores. Following the aftermath of the Civil Wars in the Mano River region, there is still continuous recycling of small arms in West Africa that defines the purpose of weapon acquisition across the region (SALWs Annual Report 2015).

The second trajectory is the *possession dynamics* involving the size of state stockpiles and weapon possession pattern among organised criminal groups within West Africa. The capturing of state stockpiles of SALWs in West Africa especially where warring factions steal weapons as it were in the cases of

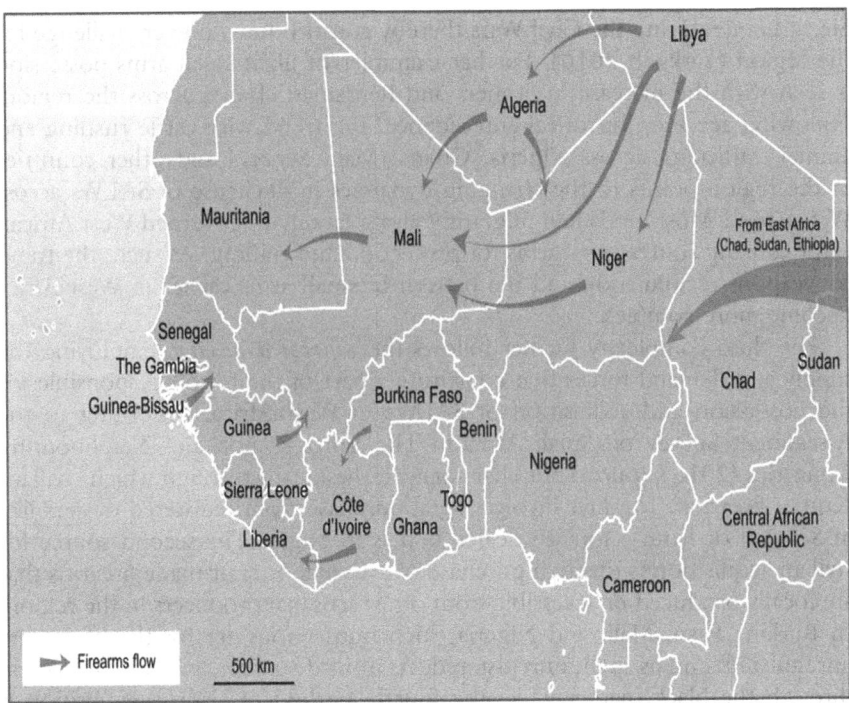

Fig. 43.1 Movements of SALWs in West Africa (*Source* UNODC, TOC in West Africa)

National Patriotic Front of Liberia and the Revolutionary United Front (RUF) of Sierra Leone remains significant to the proliferation dynamics of SALWs in West Africa. Thus, some of the weapons in the possession of 'armed groups stockpiles' were stolen during attacks on police and military armouries because of poorly constructed and insecure stockpiles contributing to the chronic problem of SALWs proliferation in West Africa (Keili 2008). These complexities, in the possession of weapons within the region, has become significant following incessant attacks on state security agencies and military forces by insurgent and terrorist groups. For instance, in Mali, the Tuareg Nationalist Movement for the Liberation of Azawad (MNLA), Al Qaida in the Islamic Maghreb (AQMI), Movement for Unity and Jihad in West Africa (MUJAO) and Ansar al Dine Movements all invaded military and state security stockpiles. Furthermore, Boko Haram terrorist attacks on the Nigerian Military and Multinational Joint Task Force (MNJTF) confirms that the trend is commonplace as a route to possess weapons by violent non-state actors in West Africa (Agneketom 2014).

The situation became more deplorable with the conscription of women, girls and particularly children by Boko Haram terrorist group to bear arms as it was in cases of child soldiers recruited by rebel groups in Liberia and

Sierra Leone during the Civil Wars thereby constituting a bigger challenge for the region (Yarkpeh 2016). Further examples of illicit small arms possession is seen with the increase in farmers and herdsmen clashes across the region. Following age long historical antecedence, the trend with cattle rustling and animal trafficking across Nigeria, Ghana, Mali, Senegal and other countries in the region points to the changing dynamics in illicit use of SALWs across West Africa. Most herdsmen migrating along largely ungoverned West African cattle grazing routes carry arms for protection and trading. As such, the trend of weapons recirculation and the pattern of small arms caches in West Africa become more complex.

The third complexity further follows the *market dynamics*, employing the supply and demand forces that constitute a part of the factors responsible for the possession and acquisition of SALWs in West Africa. According to the Assessment Survey on Small Arms in The Sahel Region and Neighbouring Countries (2016), four trends characterised the means through which civilians acquire firearms. The first involves legal purchase from registered dealers like in Senegal or from a foreign dealer as it is in Niger. The second source for civilian acquisition is through purchase of artisanal or craft-made firearms that are locally produced or accessible from other artisanal producers in the region. In Burkina Faso, Mali, and Nigeria, such transactions are for the most part unregulated, and as such, unregistered. As a third source, civilians have access through the black market while the fourth method of civilian acquisition is from donation or as inheritance.

The dynamic complexities are stretched by caches of artisanal craft manufacturers in the region, predominantly in Ghana and Nigeria with skills of artisanship which predated colonial era. This provides access to SALWs for performing sociocultural rites in some of these countries where, in addition, owning a gun among some ethnic groups like Akan, Gonja and Dagombas ethnic groups is a status symbol (Ohene-Asare 2014). In Togo, weapons craft production major transformation is limited to the repairs of weapon parts though blacksmiths also produce for agricultural purposes. The Republic of Benin, is also noted for skills in local arms manufacture which produce guns for hunters and people desiring arms for personal protection (Moussou 2014). In Nigeria, craft production spreads across the country with more manufacturing in Awka, Anambra state serving as reference to its popular tag, 'Awka-made'. With an artisanal history of blacksmith skills in gun making transferred through several generations, Awka is regarded as the centre point for gun production, bombs (*Ogbunigwe*, in *Igbo language of Southeastern Nigeria*), gunpowder, repairs of weapon parts and for acquiring craft production skills in Nigeria (Uchegbu 2015). Other places like Kuru and Barkin Ladi in Plateau state, Aba and Onitsha in the Southeast region, Benue state and the Niger-Delta region with Eleme in Rivers State and Awka Ibom states are notable areas of local craft production in Nigeria (Onuoha 2012). These put together, provided opportunity for increasing cooperation and control at the regional level, which offers the best approach to successful implementation of SALWs recovery and destruction in West Africa.

ECOWAS Approach to Controlling SALWs in West Africa

ECOWAS Member States have adopted many initiatives at the regional, continental and global levels in view of controlling SALW in West Africa. One pioneering effort in that regard was Organisation for African Unity/African Union (OAU/AU) Bamako Declaration that developed out of the need for a common '*African Approach*' against SALWs proliferation at the July 2001 UN Small Arms Conference in New York. In light of episodes of armed conflict, armed violence and cross-border movement of illicit SALW in West Africa, ECOWAS tailored effective strategies, structured towards meeting the political and institutional dynamic needs of both Member States and the ECOWAS Commission in West Africa. These initiatives followed in-depth analyses of the nature, scale, distribution and impact of the circulation of SALW across West African porous border areas. Hence, ECOWAS initial strategy to checkmate the spread of small arms in the region began with the signing of *Moratorium on the Import, Export and Transfer of Small Arms and Light Weapon* in West Africa by the Conference of Heads of State and Government in Abuja on 31 October 1998. In the views of Badmus (2009), ECOWAS Moratorium represented a fundamental step and comprehensive strategy towards addressing SALW proliferation in West Africa.

The Moratorium served as the cornerstone for disarmament efforts in Sierra Leone resumed in March 1998 with the ECOWAS Monitoring Group (ECOMOG) intervention and the restoration of the Sierra Leone People's Party (SLPP) government. During this early period, the Disarmament and Demobilisation and Reintegration (DDR) processes were rendered impossible due to the unwillingness of the warring parties to commit to the peace process. Many combatants left the country for Liberia or Côte d'Ivoire with their weapons (Miller et al. 2006).

The first phase of the DDR programme, marked by international governmental and non-governmental support, was prepared in April 1998, and was to be implemented by the Government of Sierra Leone with the support of ECOWAS and UNDP targeted at all who belonged to armed groups and participated in the civil war following the coup of 25 May 1997. A low-key disarmament process continued, meanwhile, bringing in a further 2600 combatants during what is now referred to as the interim phase, from May 2000 to 17 May 2001. The third phase of DDR was undertaken between 18 May 2001 and 6 January 2002, and came about as a result of the intensive and concerted efforts of ECOWAS and the UN to bring the peace process back on track.

The approach with the Moratorium as a strategy came into existence following three key central objectives. ECOWAS first objective was aimed at preventing conflicts in the region, while the second objective targeted implementing post-conflict reconstruction and stemming the increasing wave of crime and banditry in the region. The third objective for adopting the approach was to promote socio-economic development of member states. These objectives were premised on the rationale that meaningful control of SALW in West Africa centred on the position that conditions for development in any State are largely dependent on governments maintaining adequate level of security within their States. It was in this direction that ECOWAS with the *Security First Approach* in West Africa invested in a more effective law and order mechanism such as *Security Sector Reform* under appropriate international monitoring.

The approach also targeted presenting functional substitutes in form of development strategies for the roles weapons play by replacing them with incentive schemes during arms collection in the region. The strategy with the Moratorium, further driven by the initiative of the *Programme for Coordination and Assistance for Security and Development* (PCASED) in 1999, was in alignment with ECOWAS vision towards effective control of SALWs through its security-first approach paradigm. Despite numerous setbacks, the need for a great deal of creativity and results that were somewhat less beneficial than anticipated for ECOWAS, the process has proven to have gained some level of achievements in the control of SALW in West Africa. Example of these weapon collections were the voluntary exercises in Sierra Leone and Liberia after the Civil Wars (Miller et al. 2006). This model and various arms collection and destruction interventions provided directions on the policy and legal framework for ECOWAS especially with the training of military and security personnel, enhancement of weapons controls at border posts in Benin, Niger, Nigeria and Mali.

ECOWAS, in its fight against SALWs proliferation in West Africa, declared a Moratorium as the world's first regional small arms framework of its kind to address various conflicts in its region through control of illicit proliferation. Despite this giant leap, the voluntary nature of the Moratorium created challenges to ECOWAS because it lacks the power of sanction and its monitoring mechanism, is inadequate. An enhanced mechanism through *ECOWAS Convention on Small Arms and Light Weapons, Their Ammunition and Other Related Materials* entered into force in 2009 as a '*Holistic Approach*' to the control of SALW in the West African region (Agneketom 2014). Through implementation of the Convention and related normative frameworks, the following were identified as been of major interest; capacity building through training, provision of equipment, development of Standard Operating Procedures (SOPs) manuals, guides, sensitisation and advocacy materials among others as the road map to weapons collection in West Africa. The Convention's initiatives and measures to control SALW in the region include the broad areas of: (1) Capacity building of National institutions (2) Harmonisation of Legislation (3) Data Management (4) Arms Marking and Tracing (5) International transfers (6) Brokering (7) Stockpile management

(8) Border Controls (9) Awareness-raising campaigns (10) DDR and Recovery of Arms (11) Cooperation and Assistance.

The adoption of a Convention brought PCASED came to an end in 2003 and was replaced with the ECOWAS Small Arms Programme (ECOSAP) in 2006 to drive a five-year priority action plan for the implementation of the Convention at the regional level targeting national needs on SALWs. Provisions of the Code of Conduct to the Moratorium in 1998, provided mandate for establishment of National Commissions of Small Arms and Light Weapons Control (NATCOM) with significant participation and influence of the Civil Society under the West African Action Network on Small Arms (WAANSA) which assisted member states in sensitisation, mobilisation and engagement with their parliaments for the pupose of resource mobilisation (Badmus 2009). In turn, ECOSAP was wound up in 2011 and replaced by the African Union-European Union (AU-EU) Small Arms Project in 2014 as part of international cooperation and assistance in the ECOWAS Convention. However in 2015, a new ECOWAS-EU Arms for Development Project, referred to earlier was launched as a better targeted intervention to meet the peculiar challenges of West Africa. See table on the next page.

As a result of the advancement of the ECOWAS region relative to the other RECs, it was only able to participate in two components of the AU-EU project namely, Arms Marking and the cross-cutting Promoting Gender Mainstreaming Survey. ECOWAS Member States participation was on a pilot basis that included Burkina Faso, Cote d'Ivoire Ghana and Mali and they drew down funds to start the arms marking through the purchase of marking machines and training for identified professional in the Member States.

The ECOWAS sustains its achievements with international cooperation as a '*Holistic Approach*' to the control in West Africa by rendering assistance towards addressing common issues relating to inventory management, appropriate sites and recordkeeping based on current international best practices in physical safety and stockpile management. At national levels, the approach, among other things, required the establishment of national monitoring mechanisms; national legislation against violations of international arms embargoes; national small arms collection, destruction programmes; and civil society participation backed by the indispensable role of parliament to guarantee institutionalisation of this approach as stipulated in the Convention.

Through partnerships with international stakeholders, ECOWAS interfaces with myriad of actors providing expertise and funds to implement the provisions in the instruments. For instance, in 2016, the European Union Support to ECOWAS Regional Peace, Security and Stability Mandate Programme (ECOWAS-EU PSS Project) under the 10th European Development Fund (EDF) came on stream. Before its formalisation process, a component on practical disarmament aimed at implementation of the various provisions of the Convention and other international frameworks to which the region has obligations to pursue the fight against the proliferation of SALW was included. Implemented on a pilot basis, the project captioned *Arms for Development*

Project running in the Mano-River Union (CI, Liberia, Guinea, Sierra Leone) and in two Sahel Countries (Niger and Mali), with the inclusion of Nigeria in 2016 (Table 43.1).

Table 43.1 ECOWAS/EU arms collection project

Selected ECOWAS States	Strategy	Indicators	Milestones
Cote d'Ivoire (in Guiglo, Man, Danane, Touba and Odienne Regions)	Sensitisation campaign awareness of the communities on SALW and conduct of needs assessment mission	Handing over of illicit arms for community projects	Five (5) identified sites and five (5) indicated containers for weapon storage in the country
Guinea (Security personnel from Lola, Yomou, Macenta, Gueckedou, Kissidougo, Beyla and Nzerekore)	Sensitisation campaigns on the dangers of illegal retention and illicit circulation of small arms communities	Validation of communication strategy to ensure effective implementation of small arms collection project	Four (4) identified sites and four (4) indicated containers for weapon storage in the country
Liberia (in Maryland County, River Gee County and Grand Gedeh County)	Sensitisation and awareness campaign in local communities to bring back weapons in exchange of development project	Identifying and executing development projects to serve as hub for weapon collection	Three (3) identified sites and three (3) indicated containers for weapon storage in the country
Sierra Leone (in Kenema, Kailahun, Kono and Koinadugu Districts)	Sensitisation and awareness-raising campaigns on Knowledge of SALW control in local communities	Adoption of communication strategy and community sensitisation programmes on the dangers of SALWs	Twelve (12) identified sites and five (5) indicated containers for weapon storage in the country
Niger (Abala, Banibangou, Inates, Gorooul, Tilia and Tchintabaraden)	Communication strategy, high-level sensitisation and awareness campaign on the dangers of SALW and community outreach initiatives	Resulting voluntary weapons hand over at the common border (Tahoua, Tillabery, Maradi) of Niger with Nigeria and with Mali	Six (6) identified sites and five (5) indicated containers for weapon storage in the country
Mali (Mopti, Gao and Bamako)	Sensitisation activities and advocacy in the regions	Country-wide economic benefits resulting from adequate response to the SALW problem	Twenty (20) identified sites and five (5) indicated containers for weapon storage in the country

(continued)

Table 43.1 (continued)

Selected ECOWAS States	Strategy	Indicators	Milestones
Nigeria (Six (6) Geo-Political Zones)	Sensitisation and implementation of Survey in two Geopolitical areas of the South East and South-South Zones	Mobilise nationwide ownership and support for the comprehensive National Survey on strategies for combating SALW proliferation in Nigeria	Development of a National SALW Action Plan

Source Small Arms Annual Report ECOWAS-EU Small Arms Project (2015)

It is worthy to note that the collaboration with EU encouraged ECOWAS to support enhancement of the capacities and strategies for practical communities' disarmament with support from the United Nations Development Programme (UNDP). In all, the programme created awareness on the socio-economic impact (such as youth unemployment, loss of livelihood, internal displacement and depleted education and health systems among others) as major factors increasing the proliferation of SALW in West Africa.

CHALLENGES TO MANAGING SALW IN WEST AFRICA

Although, efforts in controlling SALW in West Africa have attained significant achievements, these efforts are still faced by numerous challenges as follows:

a. Non-integration of the Parliament in the signing and ratification of instruments: The primary responsibility for the implementation of *The ECOWAS Convention on Small Arms and Light Weapons, Their Ammunition and Other Related Materials* as a legally binding instrument lies with the ECOWAS Member States through parliamentary actions to domesticate the convention at national level. In some Member States, parliamentarians have slowed down domestication of this instrument because of the legislative bureaucracies encountered in the passage of the bill in the Parliament. For instance, Nigeria, the host state of ECOWAS Commission, has delayed in the establishment of a NATCOM despite the persisting security challenges as a result of the wide spread of illicit small arms in the country. Thus, there is the absence of national annual budget, while other Member states including Nigeria also experience lack of policies to prioritise the marking of arms. Parliaments are key for sustainability especially by annually making budgetary allocations for project implementation.
b. Corruption: the challenge of corruption in the fight against illicit proliferation of SALWs is most noticeable at the border posts where officials

receive bribes to allow smugglers carry large caches of arms in or out of a country. It is also seen when security officers 'hire' out weapons to criminals. This ties up with the justice system where state officials turn the other eye in not arresting smugglers, or in not carrying out diligent prosecution.

c. Political Will: ECOWAS Member States are confronted with the issue of trust and transparency in executing SALWs control projects in the region on one hand and political will at the highest levels of decision-making on the other hand. Political will can be measured by a number of indicators including, ratification and domestication of international legal instruments, implementation of activities, their funding and engagement in regional and global discussions.

d. Impact of Violent Conflicts in West Africa: Poverty and underdevelopment are results of conflicts. In addition, the worst affected people, namely, women, children, the aged are displaced, traumatised creating humanitarian crises. In recent times, the outbreak of diseases like the Ebola Virus in Guinea, Sierra Leone and Liberia have heightened challenges to effective control of SALWs within post-conflict states in the region.

e. Lack of financial resources: Insufficient financial resources is one major challenge impeding implementation of the decisions to control the proliferation of SALWs and often times, ECOWAS SALWs projects are sponsored by donors with states finding it difficult to raise their counterpart contribution (Bankale 2016). This lack of financial resources affects every level of project implementation leading to a slowdown in implementation of activities.

f. Limitations surrounding the control of SALW in West Africa encourage the resurgence of criminal elements, insurgents and terrorist groups moving across the region (Onuoha 2013). The prevalence exacerbated by the laxity of institutions responsible for border control and lack of technological equipment for border management created opportunity for the expansion and easy movement of SALWs by these groups. For instance, while Niger Republic disarmed the Tuareg ex-combatants coming in from Libya, in Mali the returnees were in possession of their arms, which facilitated Tuareg nationalist movement, MNLA in taking the lead in over-running the Malian military forces. Similar to the above in the Lake Chad Region, Boko Haram insurgents attacked and confronted both the Nigerian Military and Multi-National Joint Task Force (MNJTF), these explains why the challenge of SALWs recycling among non-state actors cannot be underestimated.

CONCLUSION

Despite these efforts, there is still a great deal of ground to be covered towards the effective and efficient coordination of the fight against the illicit proliferation of SALWs. For instance, it is still hard to see how effective DDR operations have been in the region and this hampers progress in the control of SALWs in the region. The failure of disarmament in Niger, Nigeria, Senegal and other countries further requires increased capacity in information technology for instance through development and use of database and data analyses. These calls for proactivity based on an effective early warning system to improve focus on prevention of SALWs proliferation in Member States and their movement across the region. It is therefore vital to institutionalise strategic plans that will establish knowledge sharing practices between stakeholders among Member States. Thus, innovative research can bridge the gap between policy and practice by establishing new approaches to small arms control initiatives executed by ECOWAS following research findings on SALWs in Member States.

This chapter reveals that SALWs proliferation and inefficient control regime in West Africa have fueled and exacerbated the conflicts that occurred in the region. In the region, there were instances where exportation of not only arms and rebels occurred, but also of more complex situation of volunteer fighters which distibalised the region. In addition, the increase in intra-state violence, with the crucial trend in the emergence of new non-state conflict actors, and growing connections between local, national and regionalised conflicts across West African states moving from Mali to Niger and Nigeria remains worrisome. These new trends in turn, have had wider ramifications for the geography of conflict transnationalisation, prompting responses from regional bodies like ECOWAS to address the emerging trajectories through holistic and comprehensive regional frameworks.

Understanding how best to curb current patterns of SALWs proliferation within the West African region requires that more needs to be done in harnessing States' capacities in various activities to control SALW. Thus, expanding upon existing knowledge regarding illicit SALWs globally should be at the core in the areas of measuring data on quantities, types and values of SALW in Member States. Yet measuring and monitoring the values and volumes of illicit SALWs flow can provide important baselines of information to combat illicit SALW proliferation at national and regional in West Africa. These will enhance ECOWAS strategies towards balancing its policy initiatives and control measures with research findings and the collation of current data on SALW in the region. Hence, public data concerning legal firearms in the hands of government forces and illicit weapons in possession of civilians can be made available on statistical estimations to meet real demands of SALW control in West Africa.

References

Acharya, A. (2014). Global International Relations (IR) and Regional World: A New Agenda for International Studies'. *International Studies Quarterly, 58*(4), 647–659.

Agneketom, C. (2008). *Political and Institutional Dynamics of the Control of Small Arms and Light Weapons in West Africa*. United Nations Institute for Disarmament Research (UNIDIR), Disarmament Forum-The Complex Dynamics of Small Arms in West Africa Number 4.

Agneketom, C. (2014). *An Appraisal of Terrorism, Armed Violence and SALWs in West Africa and the Implementation of Sub-Regional Control Instrument*. Economic Community of West African States (ECOWAS) Directorate of Peacekeeping and Regional Security, Abuja-Nigeria: A Paper Presentation at the National Consultative Forum on the Proliferation of Small Arms in Nigeria 2–4 June 2014.

Alemika, E. (2011). Privatisation of Security, Arms Proliferation and Electoral Violence in Nigeria. In L. Olurode & A. Jega (Eds.), *Security Challenges of Election Management in Nigeria*. Independent National Electoral Commission and Friedrich-Ebert Stiftung, Abuja, Nigeria.

Aning, K., &Amedzrator, L. (2016). Critical Perspectives on Transnational Criminality in West Africa. *Journal of Military and Strategic Studies, 17*(2), Centre for Military, Security and Strategic Studies, University of Calgary, Canada.

Badmus, I. (2009). Managing Arms in Peace Processes: ECOWAS and the West African Conflicts; Centro De Estudos Africanos Universidade do Porto.

Bankale, O. B. (2016). *Paving the Way to Silencing the Guns in Africa*. Institute for Peace and Security Studies (IPSS).

Berman, E., & Maze, K. (2012). *Regional Organizations and the UN Programme of Action on Small Arms (PoA)* (2nd ed.), Published by Small Arms Survey, Graduate Institute of International and Development Studies, 47 Avenue Blanc, 1202 Geneva Switzerland.

Buzan, B. (2003). *Regions and Powers: The Structure of International Security*, 6–26, 40–65, 397–437. Published by Cambridge University Press.

Darkwa, L. (2011). *The Challenge of Sub-Regional Security in West Africa*. The Case of The 2006 ECOWAS Convention on Small Arms and Light Weapons Disscission Paper 69 Nordiska Afrika institutet, Uppsala.

Declaration on the Moratorium on the Importation, Exportation and Manufacture of Light Weapons and Its Code of Coduct. (1998). ECOWAS Commission, Abuja.

ECOWAS Convention on Small Arms and Light Weapons, Their Ammunition and Other Related Materials, 2006, Abuja.

Fawcett, L. (2003). The Regionalisation of Security: A Comparative Analysis. In J. Prantl (Ed.), *Effective Multilateralism*. St Antony Series. London: Palgrave Macmillan.

Hazen, J. M., & Horner, J. (2007). *Small Arms Survey*. Geneva: Graduate Institute of International Studies.

Hettne, B. (2008). Security Regionalisation in Theory and Practice. In H. G. Baruch et al. (Eds.), *Globalisation and Environmental Challenges: Hexagon Series on Human and Environmental Security and Peace* (Vol. 3). Berlin, Heidelberg: Springer.

Ikoh, M. U. (2013). Organised Crime in the Gulf of Guinea with a Focus on Nigeria. In Alemika, Friedrich Ebert Stiftung (Eds.), *The Impact of Organised Crime on Governance in West Africa*. Regional Office Abuja, Nigeria.

Keili, L. (2008). Small Arms and Light Weapons Transfer in West Africa: A Stock-Taking. In *The Complex Dynamics of Small Arms in West Africa*. A Publication of the United Nations Institute for Disarmament Research (UNIDIR), Disarmament Forum, Volume Four (4).

Miller, D., Ladouceur, D., & Dugal, Z. (2006). From Research to Road Map: Learning from the Arms for Development Initiative in Sierra UNIDIR United Nations Institute for Disarmament Research Geneva, Switzerland.

Moussou, T. (2014, December). *Routes and Illegal Arm Catches in Benin in 'Trafficking of Small Arms and Light Weapons in West Africa: Routes and Illegal Arm Catches Between Ghana, Togo, Benin and Nigeria*. Regional Security Policy Project in West Africa; Published by Friedrich Ebert Stiftung and United Nations Centre for Peace and Disarmament (UNREC).

Ogwu, J. (2006). Small Arms Recovery; Global, Regional and Sub-Regional Initiatives. In A. Sesay & A. Simbine (Eds.), *Small Arms and Light Weapons Proliferation and Collection in the Niger Delta*, Nigeria.

Ohene-Asare, S. (2014). *Routes and Illegal Arm Caches in Ghana*. In S. Asoba & R. Glokpo (Eds.), *Trafficking of Small Arms and Light Weapons and Illegal Arm Caches Between Ghana, Togo, Benin and Nigeria*. Published by Friedrich Ebert Stiftung (FES) and United Nations Centre for Peace and Disarmament (UNREC).

Onuoha, F. C. (2012). *Small Arms and Light Weapons Proliferation and Human Security in Nigeria*. Published by African Centre for Constructive Resolution of Dispute (ACCORD).

Onuoha, F. C. (2013). *Porous Borders and Boko Haram's Arms Smuggling Operations in Nigeria*-Al Jazeera Center for Studies Report Published on 8 September 2013.

SALWs Annual Report. (2015). ECOWAS/EU Small Arms Project; Forward by the Resident Representative, UNDP Nigeria in the Annual Progress Report.

Sesay, A. (2014). *Peace and Stability Operations: Nigerian Lessons Learned Series' Volume 1 Nigeria in ECOMOG: Background to Interventions*. Publication of the Centre for the Study of Complex Operations and National Security Affairs (CCONSA), Nigerian Defence Academy, NDA, Kaduna, Nigeria.

Sesay, A., & Akonai, R. I. (2010). Where are the Leaders of the Regional Grouping? African Union, Regional Economic Communities and Maintenance of Regional Security. In O. C. Eze, C. Anigbo, & C. Dokubo (Eds.), *Nigeria's Security Interest in Africa*.

Uchegbu, C. J. (2015). *Effects of Small Arms and Light Weapons Proliferation on Human Security: A Case Study of Anambra State, Nigeria*. Centre for Peace and Strategic Studies, University of Ilorin, Kwara State, Nigeria.

United Nations. (1997). Report of the Panel of Experts on Small Arms and Light Weapons.

United Nations Office for Drug and Crime (UNODC): Report on *Transnational Organised Crime in West Africa- Flow of Fire Arms in West Africa*.

Yarkpeh, P. M. (2016). *Factors Influencing the Use of Child Soldiers in Armed Conflicts: Perspectives on Liberia and a Way Forward for Future Wars*. A Master's Thesis Presented to the Faculty of the U.S. Army Command and General Staff College, Published in Fort Leavenworth, Kansas.

Oluwafisan Babatunde Bankale was the Head of Policy Advocacy in the Small Arms Division of the ECOWAS Commission and Representative of the President of the Commission on the International Advisory Board on Small Arms for 7 years (2006–2012); Adviser on Advocacy/Gender and Head of the National Programme Advisory Unit at the United Nations Population Fund's Nigeria Country Office (2001–2006); Chief Executive/Editor-in-Chief between 1999 and 2001 at Sketch Press Limited.

Since 2006, Mr. Bankale has been providing policy advice to stakeholders at national, regional and global levels in the fight against proliferation of Small Arms Light Weapons (SALW); 1993–2001 Mr. Bankale was Consultant to various UN agencies including the UNDP, UNICEF, UNAIDS among others. He has advised governments, intergovernmental organisations on public policy in thematic areas as varied as education, democracy and good governance, gender equity/equality, conflict prevention, management and resolution, poverty eradication, sustainable human development, population, reproductive health/rights, media/communication. Mr. Bankale is alumnus of the University of Ife, University of Ibadan, where he is currently enrolled as a Ph.D. student, the University of Wales, Cardiff and the United Nations University.

Chukwuzitara Juliet Uchegbu is a candidate for Ph.D. in Defence and Strategic Studies at the Nigerian Defence Academy, Kaduna. She had worked with the civil society as a Programme Officer with the West Africa Action Network on Small Arms (WAANSA) in Nigeria before joining the National Defence College (NDC), Nigeria as a Research Fellow at the Centre for Strategic Research and Studies, NDC.

CHAPTER 44

Lake Chad Basin: Transnational Insurgency, Counter-Insurgency and the Proliferation of Small Arms

Bashir Bala and Usman A. Tar

INTRODUCTION: INSURGENCY AND COUNTERINSURGENCY IN THE LAKE CHAD BASIN

The proliferation of Small Arms and Light Weapons (SALWs) is a protracted security challenge to human, food and national safety and an immediate obstacle to the sustenance of economic growth, security and development (Stohl and Hogendoorn 2010). It is one of the most fundamental hurdles to peace and security in West Africa as it has continued to fuel small wars, inter-communal clashes and transnational insurgencies with heavy human and material casualties (Malam 2013). In Africa, the scourge of SALWs has assumed a precipitous dimension with the rate of transborder criminalities aiding and abetting the illicit trafficking in arms and insurgents' finances which have persisted in compounding the security challenges faced by states and regional efforts. In West Africa, the weak government structures, ineffective border policing strategies couple with lack of compliance in the stipulations of various regulations and protocols of SALWs control and management have

---

B. Bala (✉)
Doctoral Researcher in Strategy and Security Studies, University of Exeter, Exeter, UK

U. A. Tar
Centre for Defence Studies and Documentation, Nigerian Defence Academy, Kaduna, Nigeria
e-mail: uatar@nda.edu.ng

© The Author(s), under exclusive license to Springer Nature Switzerland AG 2021
U. A. Tar and C. P. Onwurah (eds.), *The Palgrave Handbook of Small Arms and Conflicts in Africa*,
https://doi.org/10.1007/978-3-030-62183-4_44

heightened the inflow of SALWs in virtually most parts of the region. Similarly, the incessant farmers–herders conflict, unmanned porous borders and the loosening of control and administration of sophisticated weapons during the Libyan uprising have saturated the charged security environment in the Lake Chad Basin (LCB).

The existing precarious security situation in the LCB has been altered and exacerbated by the spate of lethal attacks and waging influence in the circulation of SALWs by transnational terrorism and insurgency of Boko Haram and its splinter group, Islamic State in West Africa Province (ISWAP). The insurgency in the region has resulted in one of the most devastating humanitarian crises in human history evident from near-collapse of socio-economic and political lifelines. For example, The Report of the United Nations Security Country Secretary General on the Situation in the LCB (2017) revealed that about 10.7 million across the region are in need of humanitarian assistance with 0.6 million children need life-saving assistance and 2.7 million children need psychosocial support. The report further estimates that displacement dynamics in the region is still complex due to the recent development in the return of internally displaced persons. An estimated 2.4 million people have been displaced as a result of attacks by Boko Haram and national and subregional military operations conducted in the LCB. As the situation deteriorated and affected the agricultural productivity of the LCB, the report affirms that about 515,000 children are expected to suffer from severe acute malnutrition in 2017, most of them (approximately 450,000) in north-eastern Nigeria. Due to destruction of hospitals and other medical health services delivery centres estimated to stand around 201 health centres (about 40% of health facilities) in North East Nigeria, there is high risk of disease outbreaks. In the Diffa region of the Niger, an outbreak of hepatitis E affected more than 1100 people and killed at least 36 in 2017, and more than half the population does not have access to health-care services or potable water.

In the light of the foregoing, Boko Haram and ISWAP transnational insurgency have thus crippled the needed permissive environment for peace and security in the LCB. The insurgency is fueled by the availability of sophisticated SALWs that has continued to proliferate and circulate among various insurgent groups in the LCB. Attempts were made at both international, national, regional and subregional levels to prevent, combat and eradicate the illicit transfer of these weapons. At the UN level, a Conference on the Illicit Trade of Small Arms and Light Weapons in All its Aspects was convened seamlessly in July 2001 to consider steps that could be taken to address the issue. One of the key decisions taken during the Conference resulted in the creation of the Programme of Action (PoA) to Prevent, Combat and Eradicate the Illicit Trade in Small Arms and Light Weapons in All Its Aspects…

This alone brought together several binding commitments of member states to eradicate SALWs proliferation. At the regional level, the ECOWAS Moratorium on the Importation, Exportation and Manufacture of Small Arms and Light Weapons (established in 1998) which was later replaced with ECOWAS Convention on SALWs was implemented. At the subregional level, several cross-border patrols and ad-hoc security arrangements to checkmate illegal transfer of arms was done by West African states. Equally, at the national level, LCB member states established National Commissions for the Control of SALWs and all these efforts were made in recognition of the huge security impasse that insurgency has subjected the region to. Notwithstanding these concomitant efforts at various levels of governance, the proliferation of SALWs has continued to heighten the tempo of insurgency and affect the pace as well as momentum of an effective counterinsurgency in the LCB which is a new regional security complex that seats adjacent the West Africa Regional Security complex (Tar and Mustapha 2017; Bala and Tar 2020). This chapter therefore proceeds to engage existing realities in the proliferation, control and management of SALWs as well as the cross-border insurgency and counterinsurgency in the LCB. The chapter first examines the conceptualization of transnational insurgency, counterinsurgency and SALWs. The chapter then discusses the propellants of SALWs as they relate to insurgency and counterinsurgency. It further prescribes some measures for combating the proliferation of SALWs for effective counterinsurgency in the LCB. The chapter finally provides some concluding remarks.

Conceptualization: Transnational Insurgency, Counterinsurgency and Proliferation of SALWs

Transnational Insurgency

Transnational Insurgency is defined as the conduct of armed opposition groups whose soft and hard operations are not limited to the geographic territory of a country they challenge (Salehyan 2007, 2011). The common dynamic of transnational insurgent group is the maneuverability affords the group not to confine to the geographic area of any state but straddle national boundaries. This conception buttressed Gleditsch's (2007) assertion that several contemporary civil wars are displaying the transnational character of cross-border insurgencies as actors, resources sustaining them and attacks span national boundaries. This ability has incapacitated states to implement effective counterinsurgency measures against transnational insurgencies and this corroborated the argument by Kilcullen (2006). The author projects the relevance of classical counterinsurgency to provide the best fit for overcoming the strategic challenges of transnational insurgency. For instance, the Afghan government and U.S/NATO coalition forces have been facing difficulties in dealing with Taliban and Al-Qaeda insurgent despite several years of counterinsurgency operations in Afghanistan because of the groups' ability to slip into Pakistan. In Africa also, the transborder dynamic is demonstrated by the conflict in the Darfur region of Sudan as the Darfurian rebels operate in East Chad where they share ethnic kinships with locals, source their supplies and recruit fighters within the refugee camps. This transnational dynamics of insurgency in relation to ethnic ties augmented Malet's (2013) argument that transnational insurgencies are further motivated by the ethnic ties with neighbouring states that provide cross-border safe heaven.

The phenomenon was also viewed by Sandler et al. (2009) as the incident where the masterminds, foot soldiers, victims and the intended instigated audience are from more than one or two countries. The author cited instances of transnational insurgent attacks to include the case of a midair hijacking of a plane that leaves Athens bound for Cairo and is made to fly to Algiers and the kidnappings of foreign workers in Iraq in 2004. Other examples include the attack on the World Trade Center towers at New York on 9/11 as the victims were from ninety different countries and the mission was planned and financed abroad; the terrorists were foreigners, and the targeted audience was global. This is equally the main argument advanced by D'Amato (2018) that the transnationality of insurgent organizations with ethnic and nationalistic ties present formidable complications on the part of the counterinsurgents. The mobility, strategic and political cost of operating beyond national boundaries imposed limitations on counterinsurgency. The limitations range from the necessity of recognizing international boundaries by the military and police forces when conducting counterinsurgency and the inability of weak neighbouring states to control their borders against insurgents seeking them as safe heavens. Other limitations include the transnational ethnic communities that straddle borders use by insurgents to establish foreign sanctuaries and the mass migration of refugees into neighbouring countries which provide the insurgent groups with recruits and supplies (Salehyan 2010).

The challenges of overcoming transnational insurgencies are surmountable and require the blinding of offensive strategies and defensive mechanisms. Thus Staniland (2005) suggests embracing a containment strategy and a defensive strategy that encompasses border defenses with aggressive propaganda and international intelligence cooperation for success in countering transnational insurgencies. Since transnational insurgencies are generated by certain causes that range from ethnonationalism, structural determinism, social injustice, religious fundamentalism and extremism as well as anti-capitalism (Sandler et. al. 2009), overcoming them would require certain tasks beyond military approach but intelligence and human-driven measures. Salehyan (2010) proposes the interrelated tasks to be carried out by the government forces to include (1) Destroy insurgents in their area of domination through the appropriate application of offensive actions and sound field intelligence; (2) dominate the area and protect civilian populations from insurgent attacks; and (3) carry out humanitarian intervention projects to win over the "hearts and minds" of the population.

Counterinsurgency

Counterinsurgency is defined by the US Army-Marine Corps Counterinsurgency Field Manual (FM 3-24) as a "military, paramilitary, political, economic, psychological, and civic actions taken by a government to defeat insurgency" (Petraeus and Amos 2006: 1–2). This definition is too specific given the broader perspective of contemporary counterinsurgency. Thus, the U.S. Government (2012) provides a better conceptualization by situating the concept within the integration of integration and synchronization of political, security, legal, economic, development and psychological activities to establish a comprehensive approach aimed at defeating insurgents and winning public confidence on the government. On the peripheral conception, this definition strongly suggests that there is an interlink between insurgency and counterinsurgency as both require political and military action (Hammes 2006). The political approach requires building effective institutions for good governance and provision of efficient social services in areas that are cleared by the military (Fitzsimmons 2008; Egnell 2010; Qazi 2010; Berman et al. 2011). The military approach stressed the need for simultaneous offensive actions to neutralize or destroy insurgent armed formations and place the population as a priority in the fight between counterinsurgents and insurgents (Shultz 1979; Hoffman 2006; Sewall 2006; Findley and Young 2007). There is also the selective implementation of economic reform that needs to be undertaken to create healthy economy after the insurgents have been separated from the populace (Byman 2006; Branch 2010; Branch and Wood 2010; Jensen 2010). Current counterinsurgency operations in the LCB demonstrated the need for a holistic approach to containing the protracted Boko Haram insurgency. The military actions are yielding result though with collateral damages and the recent political commitment on the part of the regional and subregional powers are also satisfactory, but economic reforms are still at the lowest ebbs.

Small Arms and Light Weapons

SALWs are defined in different international and regional instruments, conventions and also in national statutes and treaties (Chuma-Okoro 2011). The most widely acceptable definition of SALWs is the one provided by the 1997 report of the United Nations Panel of Governmental Experts on Small Arms. The Report defines small arms in general terms as the weapon designed for personal use and may be handled by one person and light weapons are "used by several persons or a crew and may be transported by two or more people, a pack animal, or a light vehicle" (UNGA 1997: 25). The United Nations General Assembly defines small arms and light weapons as any portable, easily collapsible, easily stripped and assemble lethal weapon design to expel or launch, and may be readily converted to expel or launch a shot, bullet or projectile by the action of an explosive (UNGA 1997; The International Tracing Instrument 2005; Chelule 2014).

The ECOWAS Convention on Small Arms and Light Weapons, their Ammunition and other Related Materials of 2006 as the West African subregional instrument for regulating SALWs proliferation provides the categorization of small arms to inlcude (1) firearms and other destructive arms or devices such as an exploding bomb, an incendiary bomb or a gas bomb, a grenade, a rocket launcher, a missile, a missile system or a mine; (2) Revolvers and pistols with automatic loading; (3) rifles and carbines; (4) machine guns; (5) assault rifles; (6) light machine guns. The benchmark instrument further categorizes light weapons to include (1) heavy machine guns; (2) portable grenade launchers, mobile or mounted; (3) portable anti-aircraft cannons; (4) portable antitank cannons, non-recoil guns; (5) portable anti-tank missile launchers or rocket launchers; (6) portable anti-aircraft missile launchers; (7) mortars with a calibre of less than 100 millimetres. SALWs in general are best fit for intrastate conflict wage through guerilla warfare, they are easy to transfer, conceal, they are also durable and relatively inexpensive, require minimum standard of maintenance and they are used for mobile and covert operations (Dhanapala 2002).

The proliferation of SALWs is attributed to weak national regulation and governance structure, as well as the growing influence and expansion of Private Security and Military Companies (PMSCs) as their services contributes to the increasing demand for SALWs in every area they operate (Bala and Tar 2021). This assertion was further grounded by scholars such as Boutwell and Klare (2000), Bolton et al. (2012) and Holtom (2012) in their various works examining the scourge of small arms and the private networks in their proliferation. The various areas through which the PSMCs contribute in SALWs proliferation was captured by Makki et al. (2001) as (1) Arms brokering and transportation activities (2) Violations of UN arms embargoes (3) Impact on human rights and humanitarian law (4) Driving demand for small arms. In the LCB, the cross-border dynamics and ramifications of the Boko Haram (Agbiboa 2017) and ISWAP insurgencies have altered the security environment and paved way for the conducive flow of illicit arms and ammunitions.

"Thorns on the Flesh of Counterinsurgency": The Propellants of Small Arms and Light Weapons in the Lake Chad Basin

Farmers–Herders Conflict

The current social tension and political instability generated by farmers–herders conflict since the droughts of 1970s and 1980s is a factor that fuels the proliferation of SALWs in the LCB and is attributed to two influencing factors. First is the changing patterns of resource use and increasing conflictual competition for scarce resource and secondly, the breakdown of just mechanisms in administering scarce resource and conflict resolution/management (Hussein et al. 1999). Phenomenal changes in socio-economic, climatic and security conditions in different ecological zones make farmers attractive to the shift. The rise of cultivation elsewhere due to exhaustion of soils to compensate for low yields in the sub-humid zones has attracted farmers fanning the embers of competition for the pooled resources. Access to security, facilities and infrastructure are partly responsible for this migration that resulted in the shift of farming systems from intensive cultivation to shifting cultivation. The many years of pastoral migration and the shifting nature of farming systems encroached into several cattle routes use by cattle herds which result in patchy overgrazing with tendencies for conflict over scarce resource (Blench 1997).

Events in history suggest that nomadic and semi-nomadic herders like Fulbe have been migrating to different parts of Africa, and also cementing relationships with sedentary farming population in West Africa. However, because farmers and pastoralists deal with conflicting means of livelihood (crop farming versus animal rearing), they often encounter bloody frictions which may spiral into protracted conflicts. Therefore, the contacts between farmers and pastoralists have taken various forms ranging from coexistence to cooperation, competition and conflicts over the use of fresh water and land as the shared natural renewal resources commonly known as Common-Pool Resources (CPRs) (Cabot 2017). Civil wars and genocides are given more prominent attention than conflict over access to livelihood resources such as land and fresh water (Straus 2012). Forecasts from available projections also indicate more irregular precipitation and rising temperatures as the effects of climate change that could aggravate land degradation and heightened the patterns of droughts. This situation is believed to result in decreasing rate of food production and declining availability of water thereby making climate change to put a strain in the complex relation between farmers and herders. Due to the perceived importance of fresh water and land as object of the conflict between farmers and herders, there is the possibility of an escalation of violence over scarce resource and thus a further destabilization of security in the region (Cabot 2017).

Related to the aforementioned likelihood of the resource conflict are the changes on the socio-economic structure of the Sahel in relation to the process of colonization and decolonization which changed the modalities of dealing with scarce resource (Herrero 2006). The changes include the sedentarization of pastoralists in settlements, the unjust allocation of lands belonging to pastoralists to investors and wildlife conservation groups, imposed land grabbing, misconception equating pastoralism with ineffective tenure system and land degradation as well as the false narrative that perceived mobile pastoralism needs to be controlled or abolished to contain the growing threats to security. These changes in modalities have significant political and policy implications (Little 2013). The implications prominently include the likelihood of escalation of the farmers–herders conflict in a window of widespread tension and political dislocation (Herrero 2006). The genesis of the migration problem fuelling the conflict is that Fulani herdsmen loitre their cows into the fields for grazing during growing season allowing their herds to eat and damage crops which otherwise provoke farmers within local communities as their crops, livestock and other vegetal resources are destroyed. This situation particularly triggers conflict of resource control owing to the need for the maintenance and development of vegetal resources as strength of local communities (Ofem and Inyang 2014).

Since nineteenth century, migration of Fulani pastoralists from ecological zones in West and Central Africa to Northern part of Nigeria particularly within the general shores of the LCB brought them in close contact with farming communities in the LCB. The transhumance movements are caused by the effects of climate change and in search for vital pasture. The Northeast and Northwest parts of Nigeria provide two pastoral corridors prominent for farmers and herders conflict (Ahmadu and Yusof 2010) and thus the intensifications of SALWs proliferation in the regions. In Nigeria for instance, the current scale of attacks and reprisal attacks between Fulani nomadic pastoralists and ethnic Birom Farmers where variegated calibres of SALWs are brandished is a pointer to the increasing circulation of SALWs courtesy of farmers–herders conflict. The availability of modern weapons in the hands of both farmers and herders couple with the fragility of ecosystem have increased the intensity and incidence of the conflict (Hussein et al. 1999).

For example, in Nigeria, the fierce clashes between farmers and herders in the Northeast and Northcentral states of Plateau and Benue in 2014 and 2015 spread to other parts of Nigeria with increase in fatality rates recorded in Delta, Oyo, Ekiti and Zamfara States (Genyi 2019). The intensification and expansion were largely driven by the modern weapons in the hands of authorized persons within those areas particularly the nomadic population. The accessibility and availability of illicit small arms have also added a complex dimension to the conflict where low-scale cattle rustling has now transmogrified into a large-scale activity involving banditry and wanton destruction of lives and property (Schroeder and Lamb 2006). The gradual involvement of dispossessed cattle herders and other "criminals of opportunity" into rustling and the abundant cattle routes in the shores of LCB all aggravated the scale of insecurity in the LCB.

Undoubtedly, the current trend of SALWs proliferation and circulation in the LCB witnessed a peak in occurrence with the illicit flow of these weapons in the hands of both herders, farming communities and ethnic militias. Similarly, in the Niger's shores of the LCB, there is prevalence of increasing weapon ownership where nomadic communities are armed, security presence is low and the level of armed banditry has gained ground compared to other parts of the country (Baca 2015). The army, Gendarmerie, and Garde Nationale make regular seizures of arms and ammunitions along the shores of the LCB. The weapons confiscated include AK-type rifle, converted blank-firing handguns, assault rifles, RPGs, and general-purpose machine guns (Baca 2015).

Porous Borders

Security practitioners, scholars and even international organizations like the UN Security Council (UNSC) have held the view that border is the first line of defense against terrorist movements and insurgent activities and the last line of defensive shield of a country's territorial integrity. Nigeria and particularly its shores of the LCB remain the epicentre of cross-border organized crimes that the extended and porous borders make the country an exit, transit and entry routes of SALWs (Moses and Ngomba 2017). In the LCB, Nigeria shares mountainous and jungle border of 1690 kilometres with Cameroon in the East, a border of 1497 kilometres with Niger in the North, a border of 773 kilometres with Benin in the West and a border of 87 kilometres with Chad in the North East. This long stretch of porous borders further buttressed the expansion of Boko Haram insurgency in the LCB which provide wide expanse of operating spaces for terrorist activities (Onuoha 2013).

Several African countries provide the platforms upon which these weapons are routed, transited and exited to destinations of circulation and violence. The countries identified as entrance routes include Cameroon, Chad, Benin, Gabon, Guinea Bissau, Niger, Liberia and South Africa (Hazen and Horner 2007). The former Minister of Interior, Abba Moro who is now a serving Senator was referenced by Onuoha (2013) as disclosing that there are over 1499 irregular (illegal) entry routes into Nigeria and thus facilitating the illicit transnational arms smuggling. For example, in the shores of the LCB, Adamawa state has approximately 25 irregular routes into Nigeria from the neighbouring countries of Cameroon, Chad and Niger. These leakages and routes provide insurgents and arms smugglers with unhindered window of SALWs trafficking and thus making 70% of about eight million SALWs in West Africa to find way into Nigeria (Onuoha 2013). Therefore, it is safe to state that there is hardly any country in the world that can effectively control and monitor activities on inflow and outflow of items in such extensive borders particularly the northeast border (Adamawa, Borno and Yobe States) (Nte 2011).

Notwithstanding cross-border patrols and various transnational cordon and search operations by cross-border security agencies like the police, custom and immigration services, Nigeria borders along the LCB axis are porous. The porosity of the borders have given rise to illicit arms trafficking thereby fuelling the proliferation of SALWs (Okeke and Oji 2014). Limited numerical strength, overstretched nature of responsibilities, poor administrative and logistics equipment challenge the discharge of effective duties and obligations on the parts of the police, customs and immigration officials as well as the navy for maritime security of coastal areas and waterways (Hazen and Horner 2007). Therefore, SALWs are circulated in line with the operational loopholes of military and security agencies in addition to local manufacturing as a conduit pipe of SALWs proliferation in the LCB. For example, the Defense Industries Corporation of Nigeria (DICON) is the Nigeria's SALWs-manufacturing industry and the only authorized producer of arms and ammunition in the country. DICON produces different calibres of rifles, pistols, sub-machine guns, shotguns, prototypes of a Nigerian brand of the AK-47 named OBJ-006 after former president Obasanjo, grenades and various ranges of bullets and cartridges (Nte 2011). The local manufacturing output even though benefits the police and local security agencies, the legal SALWs acquired for various security agencies by the Nigerian government sometimes eventually are picked up by insurgent and criminal groups (Okeke and Oji 2014).

Boko Haram insurgent group has been using various networks and lifelines to smuggle arms to sustain its insurgency against the LCB member states. Onuoha (2013) in an article on porous borders and Boko Haram's arms smuggling operations, outlines the various ways through which arms trafficking by the group is eased and perpetual. These ways include the use of nomadic pastoralists to conceal and move around arms in aspecially crafted skin bags mounted on cows, donkeys and camels. Other ways include the use of merchants by the insurgent group to stuff arms and ammunitions in bags containing foodstuff transported in lorries, trucks and other heavy-duty vehicles as well as stuffing arms in empty petrol and sewage tankers for cross-border transportation of arms. By implication, the easy access to the exiting and transiting of these weapons and munitions makes it easier for militia and criminal groups to escalate weapon ownership in the LCB LCB (Achumba et al. 2013). The porous borders have also made it undetected for massive influx of migrants from neighbouring countries who in most cases aid and abet insurgency and banditry beyond Nigeria's orbit and unto the shores of the LCB (International Crisis Group, 8 March 2017).

Looting from National Stockpiles

Events unfolding in the theatre of insurgency and counter-insurgency in Nigeria in particular and LCB in general point to the emerging looting of national stockpiles of arms and munitions by insurgents during several reprisal attacks on military bases and police stations. Clothia (2015) summed the scenario by arguing that Boko Haram has waged a protracted insurgency against the state and has continued to overrun many police stations and military units and formations, thus giving the insurgents large cache of arsenals. These arsenals include Armoured Personnel Carriers (APCs), Rocket-Propelled Guns (RPGs), grenades, assault rifles and pickup trucks. Current trend in attacks reveals that Boko Haram and ISWAP attacks aimed at overpowering and dislodging military bases are mostly carried out to satisfy the need for seizing arms and rounds of ammunitions that the insurgents could use for subsequent attacks (Reinl 2019). This is further informed by the insurgents' operational need to sustain the tempo of their attacks and inflict further casualties on the military and civilian population around the LCB. For example, the attack of Month? 2019 in Metele by the ISWAP witnessed the insurgents carting away the entire armoury of the invaded army unit: four battle tanks, gun trucks, sniper rifles, field artillery and armored vehicles. This exploit raised the insurgents' morale and firepower due to quantum of equipment captured and battle success through element of surprise.

Boko Haram's quest for procuring arms and ammunitions recently witnessed a burst considering how some of the group's arms supply networks have been cut down and their tactics reduced to suicide bombing and attacks on isolated target areas of interest. It was on record that, the heavy military operations and the renewed effort of the reinvigorated subregional security force—MNJTF incapacitated the group's capacity to procure arms from external sources. The group thus resorts to looting and seizures since 2016. A report by Small Arms Survey captured that, on 3 June 2016, Boko Haram attacked the military base of Bosso in the Diffa region of Niger. During the attack, the group deployed superior firepower on the troops with 10 pick-up vehicles and motorbikes, transporting more than 100 combatants. The Boko Haram foot soldiers enveloped the camp and attacked by lunching craft rockets, assault rifles, light machine guns, and RPG-7 rocket launchers, as well as vehicles mounted with light weapons. The attack and the heavy logistic materials the group carted away with were evidenced by the video released by the *Wilayat Gharb Afriqiyah* which captured the preparation, planning and actual conduct of the attack as well as the significant cache of military materiel. In the last quarter of 2019, there has been a trend of sustained increase in attacks in Borno states particularly along the shores of the LCB where Boko Haram insurgents stormed military bases and loot weapons. ISWAP is more prominent nowadays for carving a combative niche for itself in the fringes and large swathes of LCB (*The Guardian*, 17 January 2019). The attack on Rann in which more than 8,000 refugeees fled into Cameroon and Niger while heavy calibres of arms were looted is instructive of the insurgents' renewed resolve to amass SALWs and heavy *technicals* that would continue to give them an operational edge against the counterinsurgents.

The Repercussions of the "Arab Spring"

The Arab Spring, in particular, the Libyan Uprising of 2011 uprising which led to the demise of Ghaddafi regime let loose huge stockpiles of arms and ammunitions on the West African and Sahelian plains. Suddenly, states in these regions were compelled to contend with a heightened "viral load" of SALWs in regions, with implications for rise in insurgency and criminality in the regions. The collapse of Libya and the loosening of its stockpiles or abandonment of national armouries and other weapons depots, posed threats of strategic importance to neighbouring states (Allen 1999; Musah 2002; Vinci 2006). One of such threats is the proliferation of SALWs that find their way into the hands of militias, rebel groups, insurgent movements and other violent actors (Danczuk 2nd, 2016). During the Libyan uprising, unaccountable firearms and light weapons were made readily available and thus the conflict environment was replete by a widespread accessibility to SALWs (Strazzari and Tholens 2014). It was estimated that there was in excess of 125,000 SALWs in the hands of militias by the end of the first period of the conflict and other non-state actors were armed with SALWs from Libya in at least twelve countries across the Middle East and North Africa (MENA) (Bowsher et al. 2018).

During the first phase of the Libyan uprising, national armouries were both ordered or declared opened and looted by mercenaries, Taureg fighters and other rebel forces and most of these weapons were neither traced nor recovered (Onouha 2013). Some of the weapons from Libya include SAM-7 anti-aircraft and anti-tank missiles, assault rifles, general-purpose machine guns, rocket-propelled grenade launchers, mortar launchers and related ammunition, as well as a small number of MANPADS (Small Arms Survey 2018). Majority of the weapons looted during and since the 2011 uprising that overthrew long-serving ruler Muammar Gaddafi were later smuggled into Niger, Chad, Mali and Nigeria, among other African countries (*Anadolu Agency*, 20 January 2015). The government loss of control over the huge stockpiles in 2011, Niger in the LCB was the first to suffer the consequences of materiel proliferating across the region as large convoys of these weapons were intercepted in the North part of Niger (Small Arms Survey 2018).

Likewise, terrorist groups like AQIM procured the weapons and transported them across the LCB and Sahel region to groups such as Ansar Dine, Boko Haram and MUJAO (Onuoha 2013). These groups even replenished their stocks of arms and munitions frequently by sending members into Libya with shopping list to procure materiel using criminal trafficking networks (Small Arms Survey 2018). In 2014, the second phase of the uprising erupted after a prolonged insurgency with different rebel groups emerging and fuelled by SALWs proliferation and unhindered circulation. The insurgency and counterinsurgency between the democratically elected Council of Deputies, known here as the Libyan government, and the Islamist government of the General National Congress brought in another wave of SALWs availability (Bowsher et al. 2018). For example, the illicit arms trafficking from Libya to Niger in 2013 and 2014 was massive and was therefore contained by Operations Serval and Barkhane that neutralized three tonnes of materiel, small arms, and light weapons, including MANPADS, being transported by terrorist and criminal elements in a six-vehicle convoy in northern Niger (Small Arms Survey 2018).

By implication, the availability of SALWs due to the outbreak of conflict in Libya proliferated the mass stockpiles of arms to opposition rebellious groups and armed insurgencies thereby posing threat to the peace and stability of neighbouring countries (Strazzari 2014). Taking into account the regional and international dynamics of SALWs proliferation, Strazzari and Tholens (2014), articulated the process of fragmentation among splintered insurgencies that blocked the efforts to build conflict resolution mechanisms and saturation of local armed conflicts to be the main implications of Libyan uprising. The AQIM's vast criminal networks of arms trafficking in the Sahel and LCB in particular has further created a permissive grounds under which insurgencies are armed, replenished and sustained with SALWs thereby emboldening their operational capacity. This enabled them to carry-out large-scale attacks against military and civilian targets (Onuoha 2013).

Measures for Addressing the Proliferation of SALWs in the Lake Chad Basin

Full Compliance to the ECOWAS Moratorium/Convention on Small Arms

The ECOWAS Moratorium on the Importation, Exportation and Manufacture of Small Arms and Light Weapons (established in 1998), was a roadmap for implementing an effective control of the spread of SALWs in the subregion. The Moratorium enumerated the roles of the various critical stakeholders and relevant implementation strategies to achieve its mandate. The stakeholders include the various National Commissions for the Control of SALWs, civil society organizations, national lawmakers, media and the private sector comprising of manufacturers, suppliers and contractors of SALWs in and out of the sub region (Okereke 2008. On 14 June 2006, the fifteen Heads of State and government from the West Africa signed the ECOWAS Convention on small arms, which replaces the 1998 ECOWAS Moratorium (Coulibaly 2008). The replacement of the Moratorium into a Convention Convention on small arms and light weapons and their ammunition and other related materials was necessitated by the escalating proliferation of SALWs in the subregion. The shift was also informed by the need to attain the objectives of the 2001 United Nations Programme of Action (UNPoA) to Prevent, Combat and Eradicate the Illicit Trade in Small Arms and Light Weapons in All Its Aspects (Alusala 2008). The Convention covers areas such as:

> (1) A ban on international small arms transfers except those for legitimate self-defence and security needs, or for peace supporting operations. Exemption requests are submitted to the ECOWAS Executive Secretary by Member states for approval; (2) A ban on transfers of small arms to non-state actors; (3) Regulation of artisan (or local) arms manufacturers. (4) Member states to create an inventory of the arms made by these local manufacturers; (5) Member states are required to establish national databases or registries of all small arms in their jurisdiction; (6) Encourages dialogue between the sub-region and arms suppliers; (7) Regulation of small arms possession (8) Management and security of stockpiles. (Coulibaly 2008: 4)

The Moratorium that was initially adopted was not even adopted at the national level by most countries In spite of the political declaration, ineffective government structures and unceasing flow of SALWs in the subregion all contributed in undermining the implementation of the Moratorium. The fact that it was declared, full implementation was optional and not binding on signatories and this lack of enforceable sanctions marred the effectiveness of the Moratorium (Coulibaly 2008). Furthermore, lack of effective mechanisms for ensuring communication and information exchange on cache of arms procured by receiving countries resulted in poor transfer and accountability on arms flow all impaired the goals of the Moratorium (Berkol 2007). While the implementation of both the Moratorium and now the Convention are fraught with challenges, the ECOWAS needs to improve its institutional and policy instruments for controlling the import and export of SALWs. Since the implementation of the Convention is faced with resistance by even member states of LCB as stated by Aning and Bah (2009), ECOWAS needs to formalize forcible sanctions on countries that lag behind implementation and compliance. The first step should be the compelling need for countries to domesticate the Convention and reflect it in their national legal system and mainstream its provisions in dealing with the scourge of SALWs proliferation.

Border Security

Recent events in the LCB particularly the transnational insurgency of Boko Haram and ISWAP aided by porous borders, has points to the phenomenal rise of violent conflicts which calls for strengthening the existing legal and political protocols for border control (Ayuba and Okafor 2014). It is important to note that, various protocols and regulations where implemented at both regional and subregional levels to achieve border management. For example, the 1999 ECOWAS Protocol relating to the Mechanism for Conflict Prevention, Management and Resolution, Peacekeeping and Security and The ECOWAS Convention on Small Arms and Light Weapons of 200612 under Article 22. All these instruments stipulated the relevance and modalities of effective border control (Lamptey 2013).

As discussed above, several subregional efforts have been initiated to curb, prevent and control the proliferation of SALWs across the national borders of member states, a position well affirmed by however, recent transnationalization of crimes and insurgencies particularly around the LCB calls for effective response that could help to checkmate the illicit flow of arms. The domestication of various Conventions and Protocols on arms control by national governments is necessary to complement the effort of the subregional security and arms control architecture. Governments in the LCB could also consider the fortification of national borders with sufficient strength of military and other security agencies that would deploy sophisticated equipment in the monitoring and evaluation of cross-border movements. Furthermore, the establishment of the West African Police Chiefs Committee with the main objective of strengthening cooperation among ECOWAS' member states police forces to prevent cross-border banditry and illicit arms, human and financial trafficking, is a step in the right direction. However, efforts must be made by member states to ensure proper funding of the activities of the establishment and provide the needed capacity-building mechanism for overcoming operational gaps in border control. Similarly, Addo (2006) suggests the establishment for a Joint Cross Border Patrol Task Force, donation of vehicles and ensure effective information sharing among the countries in the LCB. The formation of this transnational border patrol will be a step in the right direction. However, there is the need for effective resources and manpower commitment by all LCBC member states to ensure the full implementation of such effort. This will help to ensure compliance with acceptable standards in cross-borders patrols by national armies, customs, immigrations and other security agencies. The effort, if well-intentioned and implemented, it will provide a common ground upon which national border patrol teams will have first-hand and accurate information on outcomes of events at the various borders.

Inter-agency Cooperation

Interagency cooperation is important in the vital role to ensure effective border control and management for curbing illicit arms trafficking networks in the LCB. Detzi and Winkleman (2016) quarried the lack of effective interagency construct in West Africa's LCB which has given rise to platforms under which violent extremist groups facilitate their arms trafficking and thus obtain streams of funding. Interagency rivalry and lack of coordination of information gathering, sharing and as well as communication gaps are common features of the Nigerian security architecture (Udounwa 2013), so also the LCB member states. The lack of frequent border patrols set by the member states is a peculiar challenge that speaks to the seeming lack of cooperation by the various police forces. The Multinational Joint Task Force (MNJTF) which was reinvigorated to combat cross-border banditry and transnational insurgency and terrorism, has been struggling with unhealthy competition and political relevance among the Troops' Contributing Countries (TCCs). These challenges therefore require a subregional standardized effective mechanism that would harness the roles of the various military and security stakeholders for ease of command and control in subregional security effort. A common subregional framework to address areas of interface such as policy coordination, intelligence sharing, integration of resources, and joint planning and conduct of operations among the member states must be implemented and compliance ensured. Furthermore, the establishment of a subregional information sharing and ICT capacity building Centre for the border patrol forces in the LCB would be an effective measure towards addressing the unaccountable transfer of arms in region. This would help in providing forces with tracing abilities and thus, according to Parker (2011), giving the various LCB states the needed capacity to respond appropriately to tracing requests.

Civil Society Advocacy

Civil Society is one of the forces at the forefront of entrenching and sustaining democratic values in Africa (Gyimah-Boadi 1996) and serves as vanguard of the call for defense and security in the LCB (Auwal 2020; Nwosu 2020; Nwosu and Auwal 2020). No doubt, the civil society has become part of the critical stakeholders in regional security decision-making processes of ECOWAS even though it is challenging to transform local-level civil society engagement into a large-scale regional involvement (Makumbe 1998; Olonisakin 2009). Contrariwise, Hearn (2001) held a view that donor agencies subvert the efforts of most civil societies by providing them peanuts not to challenge the prevailing condition but to ensure the sustenance of status quo. Despite this reality, still new democratic waves have ensured the empowerment of civil society engagement with the local communities, the state, the subregion and the international community on control of SALWs proliferation (Coulibaly 2008). For example, the West Africa Network on Small Arms (WAANSA) as a regional network of the International Action Network on Small Arms (IANSA) has been campaigning for the control of SALWs through the adoption of an Arms Trade Treaty (ATT) by the West African countries. The civil society organizations in the LCB have been alarmed by the use of sophisticated SALWs and the lethality of Boko Haram and ISWAP attacks. In the face of the insurgency, several civil society organizations have been at the frontline providing humanitarian relief assistance to the victims as well as issuing policy briefs on the control of arms and the insurgency. The activities of these organizations usually come with cost implication and the funding has to be outsourced and many a times does not use to be forthcoming. This suggests the need for effective funding streams to finance the advocacy as well as the practical engagement cum collaborations of the civil society organizations in a bid to raise awareness on the negative impacts of SALWs circulation and proliferation in the LCB.

Also, the Centre for Democracy and Development (CDD), a civil society organization based in Abuja and London, has worked on the management and control of small arms in Nigeria and across West Africa. Under its SALWs programme, the CDD recently a stakeholder dialogue to engage critical stakeholders of a workable mechanism for monitoring and control the flow of SALWs. The CDD dialogue literature states thus

> Against the backdrop of fragile security, local manufacturing and the circulation of illegal guns, grenades and rocket launchers that have ripped communities apart while fuelling terrorism, in Nigeria. These weapons, described as small arms and light weapons (SALWs) are in dense possession of unauthorized non-state actors. For this reason the government of Nigeria has initiated several interventions in addressing the proliferation of Small Arms and Light Weapons; in April 2013, The Federal Government set up the Presidential Committee on Small Arms and Light Weapons, PRESCOM. The Nigeria Firearms Act of 1959 is also before the national assembly for review. The country has also committed to several regional and international treaties including the implementation of the UN's Arms Trade Treaty (ATT), ECOWAS Convention on Small Arms and Light Weapons, their ammunition and other related materials amongst several others. However, the implementation of these frameworks remains a challenge; for instance, Nigeria as well as Gambia remains the only member states without a functional National Commission on Small Arms as stipulated under the article 24 of ECOWAS Convention on SALW. It is within this purview that the Centre conveyed [sic] a stakeholder's forum to propose series of actionable efforts to

address various aspects of preventing and solving the proliferation of small arms and light weapons. (CDD 2020)

Thus, the CDD—like many civil society organizations across Africa—is acutely conscious of government's effort in addressing the menace of SALWs, and seeks to provide a forum for constructive engagement. It is imperative to that CSOs avail themselves for partnership with state authorities, rather than seeking to supplant or replace them. They also initiative their own programmes that are complementary the efforts of the host states.

Conclusion

Proliferation of SALWs is one of the most plaguing threats to the peace and security of West Africa as it has continued to conflagrate inter-communal clashes and cross-border terrorism and insurgency. The human suffering and material loss cause by Boko Haram terrorism and insurgency and that of ISWAP in the LCB are instructive to evidence the calamitous impacts of SALWs proliferation and circulation. The subregion has continued to wallow in abject poverty caused by disruption of agricultural activities that have been the mainstay of the LCB's economy as a result of protracted insurgency. Over the years, Boko Haram and ISWAP insurgency has been propelled by the availability of SALWs getting into the hands of various VNSAs in the sub region. The farmer–herders conflict has transmogrified into a large-scale activity involving armed banditry and destruction of lives and properties as well as kidnapping for ransome which has been providing streams of funds for illicit procurement of SALWs in the subregion. The illicit circulation of these weapons in the hands of nomadic and farming communities amd ethnic militias in the subregion coupled with the low-security presence in remote areas as staging areas for the transfer of SALWs has altered the dynamics of proliferation in both demand for and accessibility to SALWs. Porous borders crisscrossing the various unmanned intersections along the shores of LCB where member states share similar international boundaries has provided the avenues through which SALWs are illegally transferred and circulated. By implication, porous borders have aided the availability of and accessibility of SALWs in the LCB. The loosening of national stockpiles and looting of various calibres of arms and munitions as spoils of war from Libyan uprising have given the needed sophistication in arms holding to the various insurgent groups in the subregion. The combined effect of the forces that propel proliferation of SALWs in the LCB is the high stake of insecurity the subregion has been reduced to and the various routes opened to illicit dealings in SALWs. Certain measures to prevent, combat and eliminate the proliferation of SALWs are therefore expedient to implement at international, regional and national levels. The full implementation and compliance of the ECOWAS Convention on SALWs Importation, Exportation and Manufacturing is a step in the right direction towards addressing the menace.

ECOWAS needs to formalize the full implementation of and ensure compliance with the ECOWAS Moratorium on the Importation, Exportation and Manufacture of Small Arms and Light Weapons. Possibly, The ECOWAS needs to liaise with the LCBC to ensure the formalization of sanctions on nations found wanting in the implementation politics and processes of this Moratorium. It is also important to consider the fortification of national borders by ensuring effective deployment of military, customs, immigrations and other security agencies with the requisite complements and equipment to carry out the task of border control and management in the LCBC member states. Cross-border joint task force patrols as well as robust civil society advocacy on the implication of SALWs proliferation to the attainment of peace and development in the LCB will be expedient. These transnational patrols should also be complemented with efficient interagency cooperation that will provide the needed platforms for transnational information and intelligence sharing processes.

References

Achumba, I. C., Ighomereho, O. S., & Akpor-Robaro, M. O. M. (2013). Security Challenges in Nigeria and the Implications for Business Activities and Sustainable Development. *Journal of Economics and Sustainable Development,* 4(2), 79–100.

Addo, P. (2006). *Cross Border Criminal Activities in West Africa: Options for Effective Responses* (Kofi Anan International Peacekeeping Training Centre [KAIPTC], Paper No. 12).

Agbiboa, D. E. (2017). Borders That Continue to Bother Us: The Politics of Cross-Border Security Cooperation in Africa's Lake Chad Basin. *Commonwealth and Comparative Politics,* 55(4), 403–425.

Ahmadu, H. J., & Yusof, R. (2010, December 1–2). *The Dynamics of Resource Conflict: Lessons from Nigeria and Malaysia.* In The Third International Conference on International Studies (ICIS 2010), Hotel Istana Kuala Lumpur. College of Law, Government and International Studies, Universiti Utara Malaysia, Sintok, pp. 1–15. ISBN 9789832078456.

Allen, C. (1999). Warfare, Endemic Violence & State Collapse in Africa. *Review of African Political Economy,* 26(81), 367–384.

Alusala, N. (2008). ECOWAS Small Arms and Light Weapons Convention: Examining Implementation. *Arms Control: Africa,* 1(4), 14–15.

Anadolu Agency. (2015, January 20). Boko Haram Using Weapons Looted from Libya: Diplomat, Ambassador Dangor Told AA. Retrieved November 4, 2019, from https://www.aa.com.tr/en/world/boko-haram-using-weapons-looted-from-libya-diplomat/82491.

Aning, K., & Bah, S. A. (2009). *ECOWAS and Conflict Prevention in West Africa: Confronting the Triple Threats.* New York: New York University, Centre on International Cooperation.

Auwal, A. (2020). Participatory Security in Africa (Chapter 11). In U. A. Tar (Ed.), *Routledge Handbook of Counterterrrorism and Counterinsurgency in Africa.* London and New York: Routlegde Publishers.

Ayuba, C., & Okafor, G. (2014). *The Role of Small Arms and Light Weapons Proliferation in African Conflicts*. Available at: https://ssrn.com/abstract=2484743 or http://dx.doi.org/10.2139/ssrn.2484743.

Baca, M. W. (2015). Farmer-Herder Clashes Amplify Challenge for Beleaguered Nigeri's Security. *Global Observatory*. Retrieved November 15, 2019, from http://theglobalobservatory.org/2015/07/farmer-herder-nyeri.

Bala, B., & Tar, U. A. (2020). Emerging Architecture for Regional Security Complex in the Lake Chad Basin: The Multinational Joint Task Force in Perspective (Chapter 7). In U. A. Tar & B. Bala (Eds.), *New Architecture of Regional Security in Africa: Perspectives on Counterterrorism and Counterinsurgency in the Lake Chad Basin*. Lanham, MD: Lexington Books.

Bala, B., & Tar, U. A. (2021). Private Security Companies and National Security in Africa (Chapter 40). In U. A. Tar (Ed.), *Routledge Handbook of Counterterrrorism and Counterinsurgency in Africa*. London and New York: Routlegde Publishers.

Berkol, I. (2007). *Analysis of the ECOWAS Convention on Small Arms and Light Weapons and Recommendations for the Development of an Action Plan*. A Special Publication of Groupe de recherche et d'information sur la paix et la sécurité (GRIP).

Berman, E., Shapiro, J. N., & Felter, J. H. (2011). Can Hearts and Minds Be Bought? The Economics of Counterinsurgency in Iraq. *Journal of Political Economy, 119*(4), 766–819.

Blench, R. (1997). *Aspects of Resource Conflict in Semi-Arid Africa*. London: Overseas Development Institute.

Bolton, M., Sakamoto, E. E., & Griffiths, H. (2012). Globalization and the Kalashnikov: Public-Private Networks in the Trafficking and Control of Small Arms. *Global Policy, 3*(3), 303–313.

Boutwell, J., & Klare, M. T. (2000). A Scourge of Small Arms. *Scientific American, 282*(6), 48–53.

Bowsher, G., Bogue, P., Patel, P., Boyle, P., & Sullivan, R. (2018). Small and Light Arms Violence Reduction as a Public Health Measure: The Case of Libya. *Conflict and Health, 12*(1), 29. https://doi.org/10.1186/s13031-018-0162-0.

Branch, D. (2010). Footprints in the Sand: British Colonial Counterinsurgency and the War in Iraq. *Politics and Society, 38*(1), 15–34.

Branch, D., & Wood, E. J. (2010). Revisiting Counterinsurgency. *Politics and Society, 38*(1), 3–14.

Byman, D. L. (2006). Friends Like These: Counterinsurgency and the War on Terrorism. *International Security, 31*(2), 79–115.

Cabot, C. (2017). Climate Change and Farmer–Herder Conflicts in West Africa. In *Climate Change, Security Risks and Conflict Reduction in Africa* (pp. 11–44). Berlin, Heidelberg: Springer.

CDD (Centre for Democracy and Development). (2020). *What We Do*. Available: https://www.cddwestafrica.org/what-we-do/. Accessed 21 June 2020.

Chelule, E. (2014). Proliferation of Small Arms and Light Weapons: Challenge to Development, Peace and Security in Africa. *Journal of Humanities and Social Science, 19*(5), 80–87.

Chuma-Okoro, H. (2011). Proliferation of Small Arms and Light Weapons in Nigeria: Legal Implications. *Law and Security in Nigeria*, pp. 255–313.

Clothia, F. (2015, January 26). Boko Haram Crisis: How Have Nigeria's Militants Become so Strong? *BBC News*. https://www.bbc.com/news/world-africa-30933860. Accessed 5 November 2019.

Coulibaly, M. (2008). *From Moratorium to a Convention on Small Arms: A Change in Politics and Practices for the 15 Member Countries of the Economic Community of West African States (ECOWAS)*. A Special Publication of Oxfam International.

D'Amato, S. (2018). Terrorists Going Transnational: Rethinking the Role of States in the Case of AQIM and Boko Haram. *Critical Studies on Terrorism, 11*(1), 151–172.

Danczuk, L. J., 2nd. (2016). The Global Spread of Arms: The Link Between State Collapse, Small Arms Proliferation, and Global Conflict. *Military Review, 96*(5), 42.

Detzi, D., & Winkleman, S. (2016). Hitting Them Where It Hurts: A Joint Interagency Network to Disrupt Terrorist Financing in West Africa. *Studies in Conflict and Terrorism, 39*(3), 227–239.

Dhanapala, J. (2002). Multilateral Cooperation on Small Arms and Light Weapons: From Crisis to Collective Response. *Brown Journal of World Affairs, 9*, 163.

ECOWAS Convention on Small Arms and Light Weapons, Their Ammunition and Other Related Materials. (2006, June 14). Retrieved November 8, 2019, from http://www.iansa.org/regions/wafrica/documents/CONVENTION-CEDEAO-ENGLISH.PDF.

Egnell, R. (2010). Winning 'Hearts and Minds'? A Critical Analysis of Counter-Insurgency Operations in Afghanistan. *Civil Wars, 12*(3), 282–303.

Findley, M. G., & Young, J. K. (2007). Fighting Fire with Fire? How (Not) to Neutralize an Insurgency. *Civil Wars, 9*(4), 378–401.

Fitzsimmons, M. (2008). Hard Hearts and Open Minds? Governance, Identity and the Intellectual Foundations of Counterinsurgency Strategy. *Journal of Strategic Studies, 31*(3), 337–365.

Genyi, G. A. (2019). The Nigerian State and the Farmers-Herders Conflict: A Search for Peace in a Multi-ethnic Society. *FUDMA Journal of Politics and International Affairs, 2*(1), 229–244.

Gleditsch, K. S. (2007). Transnational Dimensions of Civil War. *Journal of Peace Research, 44*(3), 293–309.

Gyimah-Boadi, E. (1996). Civil Society in Africa. *Journal of Democracy, 7*(2), 118–132.

Hammes, T. X. (2006). Countering Evolved Insurgent Networks. *Military Review*, p. 150.

Hazen, J. M., & Horner, J. (2007). *Small Arms, Armed Violence, and Insecurity in Nigeria: The Niger Delta in Perspective* (p. 83). Geneva: Small Arms Survey.

Hearn, J. (2001). The 'Uses and Abuses' of Civil Society in Africa. *Review of African Political Economy, 28*(87), 43–53.

Herrero, S. T. (2006). Desertification and Environmental Security: The Case of Conflicts Between Farmers and Herders in the Arid Environments of the Sahel. In *Desertification in the Mediterranean Region: A Security Issue* (pp. 109–132). Dordrecht: Springer.

Hoffman, B. (2006). Insurgency and Counterinsurgency in Iraq. *Studies in Conflict & Terrorism, 29*(2), 103–121.

Holtom, P. (2012). Prohibiting Arms Transfers to Non-State Actors and the Arms Trade Treaty. *The United Nations Institute for Disarmament Research (UNIDIR) Resources*, pp. 1–18.

Hussein, K., Sumberg, J., & Seddon, D. (1999). Increasing Violent Conflict Between Herders and Farmers in Africa: Claims and Evidence. *Development Policy Review, 17*(4), 397–418.

International Crisis Group (ICG). (2017, March 8). *Fighting Boko Haram in Chad: Beyond Military Measures* (Report 246/The Boko Haram Insurgency). Retrieved November 14, 2019, from https://www.crisisgroup.org/africa/central-africa/chad/246-fighting-boko-haram-chad-beyond-military-measures.

Jensen, S. (2010). The Security and Development Nexus in Cape Town: War on Gangs, Counterinsurgency and Citizenship. *Security Dialogue, 41*(1), 77–97.

Kilcullen, D. (2006). Counter-Insurgency Redux. *Survival, 48*(4), 111–130.

Lamptey, A. A. (2013). *Rethinking Border Management Strategies in West Africa: Experiences* (Policy Brief 12). A Special Publication of the Kofi Anan International Peacekeeping Training Centre, Ghana.

Little, P. D. (2013). Reflections on the Future of Pastoralism in the Horn of Africa. Pastoralism and Development in Africa: Dynamic Change at the Margins. In A. Catley, I. Scoones, & J. Lind (Eds.), *Pastoralism and Development in Africa: Dynamic Change at the Margins*. London and New York: Routledge.

Makki, S., Meek, S., Musah, A. F., Crowley, M., & Lilly, D. (2001). *Private Military Companies and the Proliferation of Small Arms: Regulating the Actors* (Biting the Bullet Briefing Papers. Briefing 10). London: British American Security Information Council (BASIC), International Alert and Saferworld.

Makumbe, J. M. (1998). Is There a Civil Society in Africa? *International Affairs, 74*(2), 305–317.

Malam, B. (2013). Small Arms and Light Weapons Proliferation and Its Implication for West African Regional Security. *Journal of Social Sciences—Sri Lanka, Special Issue on Proceedings of 2nd International conference on Social Sciences 2013* (ICSS 2013). Faculty of Social Sciences, University of Kelaniya, Sri Lanka.

Malet, D. (2013). *Foreign Fighters: Transnational Identity in Civil Conflicts*. Oxford: Oxford University Press.

Moses, J. M., & Ngomba, J. (2017). Small Arms and Light Weapons Proliferation in the Early 21st Century: The Nigerian Case. *International Journal of Development and Sustainability, 6*(11), 1638–1652.

Musah, A. F. (2002). Privatization of Security, Arms Proliferation and the Process of State Collapse in Africa. *Development and Change, 33*(5), 911–933.

Nte, N. D. (2011). The Changing Patterns of Small and Light Weapons (SALW) Proliferation and the Challenges of National Security in Nigeria. *Global Journal of Africa Studies, 1*(1), 5–23.

Nwosu, B. (2020). Civil Society, Counterterrorism and Counterinsurgency in Africa (Chapter 35). In U. A. Tar (Ed.), *Routledge Handbook of Counterterrrorism and Counterinsurgency in Africa*. London and New York: Routlegde Publishers.

Nwosu, B., & Auwal, A. (2020). Civil Society, Counterterrorism and Counterinsurgency in the Lake Chad Basin (Chapter 15). In U. A. Tar & B. Bala (Eds.), *New Architecture of Regional Security in Africa: Perspectives on Counterterrorism and Counterinsurgency in the Lake Chad Basin*. Lanham, MD: Lexington Books.

Ofem, O. O., & Inyang, B. (2014). Livelihood and Conflict Dimension Among Crop Farmers and Fulani Herdsmen in Yakurr Region of Cross River State. *Mediterranean Journal of Social Sciences, 5*(8), 512.

Okeke, V. O. S., & Oji, R. O. (2014). The Nigerian State and the Proliferation Small Arm and Light Weapons in the Northern Part of Nigeria. *Journal of Educational and Social Research,* 4(1), 398–415.

Okereke, C. N. E. (2008). Implementing the ECOWAS Convention on Small Arms and Light Weapons: Challenges and Prospects. *Arms Control: Africa,* 1(4), 11–14.

Olonisakin, F. (2009). ECOWAS and Civil Society Movements in West Africa. *IDS Bulletin,* 40(2), 105–112.

Onuoha, F. C. (2013). Porous Borders and Boko Haram's Arms Smuggling Operations in Nigeria. *Al Jazeera Center for Studies,* 8. https://studies.aljazeera.net/en/reports/2013/09/201398104245877469.html.

Parker, S. (2011). *Improving the Effectiveness of the Programme of Action on Small Arms Implementation Challenges and Opportunities.* A Special Publication of UNIDIR United Nations Institute for Disarmament Research Geneva, Switzerland.

Petraeus, Lt. Gen. David H., & Amos, Lt. Gen. James F. (2006). "FM 3-24 Counterinsurgency," Marine Corps Warfighting Publication No. 3-33.5. Washington, DC: Department of the Army.

Qazi, S. H. (2010). The 'Neo-Taliban'and Counterinsurgency in Afghanistan. *Third World Quarterly,* 31(3), 485–499.

Reinl, J. (2019, April 19). How Stolen Weapons Keep Groups Like Boko Haram in Business. *GlobalPost,* electronic article. https://www.pri.org/stories/2019-04-19/how-stolen-weapons-keep-groups-boko-haram-business. Accessed 3 November 2019.

Salehyan, I. (2007). Transnational Rebels: Neighbouring States as Sanctuary for Rebel Groups. *World Politics,* 59(2), 217–242.

Salehyan, I. (2010). *Transnational Insurgencies and the Escalation of Regional Conflict: Lessons for Iraq and Afghanistan.* Carlisle Barracks, PA: Army War College Strategic Studies Institute. https://apps.dtic.mil/dtic/tr/fulltext/u2/a515804.pdf.

Salehyan, I. (2011). *Rebels Without Borders: Transnational Insurgencies in World Politics.* Cornell: Cornell University Press.

Sandler, T., Arce, D. G., & Enders, W. (2009). Transnational Terrorism. *Global Crises, Global Solutions,* 2, 516–562.

Schroeder, M., & Lamb, G. (2006). The Illicit Arms Trade in Africa. *African Analyst,* 1(4), 69–78.

Sewall, S. (2006). Modernizing US Counterinsurgency Practice: Rethinking Risk and Developing a National Strategy. *Military Review,* 86(5), 103.

Shultz, R. (1979). Coercive Force and Military Strategy: Deterrence Logic and the Cost-Benefit Model of Counterinsurgency Warfare. *Western Political Quarterly,* 32(4), 444–466.

Small Arms Survey. (2018, January). At the Crossroads of Sahelian Conflicts, Insecurity, Terrorism, and Arms Trafficking in Niger, Report. Retrieved November 6, 2019, from http://www.smallarmssurvey.org/fileadmin/docs/U-Reports/SAS-SANA-Report-Niger.pdf.

Staniland, P. (2005). Defeating Transnational Insurgencies: The Best Offense Is a Good Fence. *The Washington Quarterly,* 29(1), 21–40.

Stohl, R., & Hogendoorn, E. J. (2010). *Stopping the Destructive Spread of Small Arms How Small Arms and Light Weapons Proliferation Undermines Security and Development.* A Special Publication of the Centre for American Progress.

Straus, S. (2012). Wars Do End! Changing Patterns of Political Violence in Sub-Saharan Africa. *African Affairs,* 111(443), 179–201.

Strazzari, F. (2014). Libyan Arms and Regional Instability. *The International Spectator, 49*(3), 54–68.

Strazzari, F., & Tholens, S. (2014). 'Tesco for Terrorists' Reconsidered: Arms and Conflict Dynamics in Libya and in the Sahara-Sahel Region. *European Journal on Criminal Policy and Research, 20*(3), 343–360.

Tar, U. A., & Mustapha, M. (2017). The Emerging Architecture of a Regional Security Complex in the Lake Chad Basin. *Africa Development, 42*(3), 99–118.

The Guardian International Edition. (2019, January 17). Thousands Flee North-East Nigeria After Devastating Boko Haram Attack. https://www.theguardian.com/global-development/2019/jan/17/thousands-flee-north-east-nigeria-after-devastating-boko-haram-attack-rann-cameroon-bodo. Accessed 2 November 2019.

UN Security Council. (2017, September 7). *Report of the Secretary-General on the Situation in the Lake Chad Basin Region*. https://reliefweb.int/sites/reliefweb.int/files/resources/N1726743.pdf.

United Nations General Assembly (UNGA). (1997). Report of the Panel of Governmental Experts on Small Arms. A/52/298 of 27 August.

United Nations General Assembly (UNGA). (2005). *International Instrument to Enable States to Identify and Trace, in a Timely and Reliable Manner, Illicit Small Arms and Light Weapons* ('International Tracing Instrument'). A/60/88 of 27 June.

Udounwa, S. F. (2013). *Boko Haram: Developing New Strategies to Combat Terrorism in Nigeria*. A Research Paper Submitted to the United States Army War College in Partial Fulfillment of the Requirements of the Master of Strategic Studies Degree. The U.S. Army War College.

U.S. Government. (2012). *Guide to the Analysis of Insurgency*. file:///C:/Users/DELL/Downloads/713599.pdf.

Vinci, A. (2006). The "Problems of Mobilization" and the Analysis of Armed Groups. *Parameters, 36*(1), 49–62.

Bashir Bala Doctoral researcher in Defense and Security Studies at the University of Exeter, UK, and a Captain in the Nigerian Army. Bala graduated from the Nigerian Defense Academy (NDA), commissioned at the Royal Military Academy Sandhurst, United Kingdom, and thereafter, attended Shijiazhuang Mechanized Infantry Academy for Basic and Advanced Special Operations Courses, China. Capt. Bala is a Research Fellow, Centre for Defense Studies and Documentation, Nigerian Defense Academy (NDA). He is now a Doctoral Candidate for Ph.D. Strategy and Security Studies at the University of Exeter, United Kingdom. Formerly, a tactical commander in several critical Counter-Insurgency Operations in the Northeast region of Nigeria. He is the Co-author of *Insurgency and Counter-Insurgency in Nigeria: Perspectives on the Nigerian Army Operation Against Boko Haram* (Nigerian Defense Academy Publishers, 2019) and co-editor of *New Architecture for Regional Security in Africa: Perspectives on Counter-Terrorism and Counter-Insurgency in the Lake Chad Basin* (Lanham, MD, Lexington Books, USA). He has published widely on terrorism, insurgency, CT-COIN, security and development, cattle rustling and armed banditry.

Usman A. Tar is Professor of Political Science and Defense Studies, and Endowed Chair of Defense and Security Studies (26RC Endowment) at the Nigerian Defense Academy. He is the Director of the Academy's flagship Centre for Defense Studies and Documentation, and a member of the Board of Social Science Research Council's African Peacebuidling Network (SSRC/APN), New York, USA. He was formerly, Associate Research Fellow at Africa Centre for Peace and Conflict Studies, University of Bradford, UK. He authored several books including *The Politics of Neoliberal Democracy in Africa* (London/New York: I.B. Tauris, 2009); *Globalization in Africa: Perspectives on Development, Security and the Environment* (Lanham, MD: Lexington Books, 2016); *New Architecture of Regional Security in Africa* (Lanham, MD: Lexington Books, 2020); and *Routledge Handbook of Counterterrorism and Counterinsurgency in Africa* (London: Routledge, 2020). Prof Tar has consulted or consults for the United Nations Development Programme (UNDP), Nigeria; Konrad Adaneur Stiftung (KAS, German Development Fund); and the Westminster Foundation for Democracy (WFD), Nigeria. Prof Tar is a member of Nigeria's Presidential Think Tank on National Defense and Security, and served as a member of Nigeria's Presidential Committee to review the national defense policy in 2015.

CHAPTER 45

The Manor River Region: Volatility and Proliferation of Small Arms and Light Weapons

Uchenna Simeon

INTRODUCTION

Like existing geographical formations in Africa—the Sahel, Gulf of Guinea, Great Lakes, Lake Chad Basin, Horn of Africa and Sub-Saharan Africa among others—the Mano River (MR) Basin is a familiar terrain located geographically in West Africa. Etymologically, MR region originated from the Mano River also referred to as Bewa or Gbeya River that rises in the Guinea Highlands on the northeast region of a Liberian enclave known as Voinjama (*Encyclopaedia Britannica* 2020). The significance of the nomenclature "Mano" revolves not only around the formal and natural boundary between Sierra Leone and Liberia but because "Mano" is located within a district previously identified as Kailahun Luwa, an area between present-day Liberia and Sierra Leone (Wathinote 2017). With over 90 miles (145 km) of the Liberian–Sierra Leone border created by MR and the offshoot, known as Morro, which equally drains a basin of 3185 square miles (8250) square km), the Mano River, via the Liberia Gola National Forest, follows a 200-mile (320 km) south-westerly course and discharges into the Atlantic at Maco Salija, Sierra Leone (*Encyclopaedia Britannica* 2020). Reminiscent of many African states, the atmospheric condition within the Manor River region is characterized by days of good equal rain and sun that guarantee better working atmosphere in all industries.

U. Simeon (✉)
Department of Political Science, Federal University, Lafia, Nigeria

© The Author(s), under exclusive license to Springer Nature Switzerland AG 2021
U. A. Tar and C. P. Onwurah (eds.), *The Palgrave Handbook of Small Arms and Conflicts in Africa*,
https://doi.org/10.1007/978-3-030-62183-4_45

In terms of natural resource endowment, the region is abundantly gifted and is among the best tourists' destinations for all seasons in Africa and the world (Libseib 2014). For instance, with about 30% of global production, Cote d'Ivoire remains a major producer of cocoa representing about a third of total export value; Guinea has the world's largest reserve of bauxite in addition to possessing and exporting significant quantities of iron ore, gold, diamond, oil and coffee; Liberia on its part is a major exporter of rubber recording two-thirds of total exports and also exports diamonds, gold and iron ore while Sierra Leone is a major exporter of diamonds recording about 60% of total exports in addition to cocoa (*Interdiagnostix* 2015).

Semblances in history, colonial heritage in addition to certain political and economic dynamics are among the basic features and attributes far from border linkages that define the countries of MR region, a development that has made it virtually impossible to extricate them (Ettang et al. 2011). Commonality in tribal make up, dialect and traditions with family ties stretching into neighbouring countries as well as unregulated and recurrent passage through the borders are part of the traits shared by the Mano river countries (*Interdiagnostix* 2015). Yet, these countries share a history of violent conflict making them susceptible to fragility and volatility. From 1989 to 2011, the MR region has been an arena of brutal conflict and uncertainties. Violent conflicts as well as political instability have enveloped the Manor River region countries. Beyond the Sierra Leonean, Liberian and Ivoirean civil wars, the MR region witnessed conflict escalation between countries as a result of porous borders. Suffice it to state that there are varied interpretations of the character and pattern of the violent conflicts across the region, nevertheless, the rate of recurrence of regional spill-over from internal conflicts underscores the close level of interconnectivity between countries in the region (Marc et al. 2015).

Beyond the existence of protracted conflict in the MR region, the nonexistence of democratic dividends, gross violation of citizens' rights, crisis of governance and pervasive sleaze which created an opportunity for renegade militias and warlords to plunder and commit all manner of atrocities were common structural and institutional challenges faced by the Manor River countries (International Peace Academy 2002). In spite of the relative peace that returned to the region, abject poverty still persists among the vast majority of the populace (Jorgel and Utas 2007).

Apart from Sierra Leone and Cote d'Ivoire, border and family ties extend the neighbouring countries, creating opportunities for people to traverse the border easily and frequently (*Interdiagnostix* 2015); the result is that for many years now, there is transborder movement of armed insurgency as the conflict in one country spills into another (Cobb 2002). As Silberfein and Conteh (2006) succinctly noted, violence in one country ended up stimulating an analogous occurrence in another country until the whole MR region became enmeshed in crisis. So disturbing is the unfolding scenario in the region that the countries are either beneficiaries of an international peacekeeping operation/peacebuilding mission or victim of internal governance challenges (*Interdiagnostix* 2015).

The heightened catastrophes experienced in the MR region has not only created a volatile political environment but also led to the proliferation SALWs facilitated by porous and unregulated borders. The spread of SALWs has no doubt become one of the difficult security issues confronting the MR region and by extension, the African continent. Out of the global 640 million SALWs in circulation, 100 million are estimated to be domiciled in Africa with Sub-Saharan Africa recording about 30 million while West African subregion alone has eight million (*The Guardian* 2018). Within the countries of MR region, Afolabi and Idowu (2018), noted that for more than two decades, SALWs proliferation triggered violence, conflicts and social disruptions. The UN Secretary General (2003) on his part, noted that violent conflicts occasioned largely by unencumbered small arms trafficking acquired constantly with earnings from unauthorized utilization of natural resources has led to an increase in the activities of mercenaries that traverse borders ready to fight for the highest bidder or what Keili (n.d.) described as "Mercenaries of Fortune". The dangers, scale and magnitude of the SALWs proliferation particularly in the developing world are so monumental and frightening that the United Nations argues that the proliferation of SALWs around the globe continues to pose a systemic and pervasive threat to long-term socio-economic development of many states especially the developing ones (*UN Chronicle* 2011). It is in the light of the foregoing that this chapter sets out to interrogate how the intersection of volatility and the spread of SALWs in the MR region have contributed in shaping and reinforcing the violent conflicts and instabilities experienced in the area.

Conceptual Clarification

Two basic concepts form the conceptual thrust of this chapter, namely volatility and proliferation of SALWs.

Volatility

The concept "volatility" means different things to different people. The origin of the word is traced to the Latin verb "volare" which, when translated in English, means "to fly". Literally, the word volatility denoted a noun employed to describe birds particularly "wild fowl or other winged creatures such as butterflies" (Merriam Webster Dictionary 2020). Towards the end of the sixteenth century, the usage was stretched to describe objects that were so light that they seemed eager to fly. From there, the application of the concept was broadened to include vapours and gases and during the early seventeenth century, volatile became applicable to things and individuals that are prone to sudden change as some gaseous substances whereby volatility was used to describe how quickly a substance will vaporize, that is, turn into gas or vapour (Merriam Webster Dictionary 2020).

Volatility in the political context denotes a situation when it appears that political life is faster-moving, more unpredictable and more unstable than ever before, leading to electoral shocks, policy surprises and even regime change (The Alan Turing Institute 2020). A United States think tank, Fund For Peace, which measures on yearly basis, the condition of a state at a stipulated period using Fragile States Index, has come up with twelve conflict risk indicators accounting for cohesion, economic, political, social and cross-cutting factors (Fund for Peace 2019) The twelve indicators spread among the afore-mentioned factors include: Cohesion indicators (security apparatus, factionalized elites and group grievances); Economic factors (economic decline, uneven economic development as well as human flight and brain drain); Political indicators (state legitimacy, public services including human rights and rule of law); Social indicators (demographic pressures as well as refugees and internally displaced persons) and Cross-cutting factors characterized by external intervention (Fund for Peace 2019). For instance, the bloody civil war in Syria triggered by the Arab Spring has made the country one of the most volatile and chaotic countries in the world.

In a related development, using the Criminality Index designed by Verisk Maplecroft consultancy firm, countries where there is widespread prevalence of drug trafficking, kidnapping, extortion, robbery and other activities that involve or lead to violence are adjudged dangerous because according to the firm, countries where political systems are volatile help to create a climate where violence is prevalent as can be seen in the Middle East, Africa and Latin America (Martin 2016). For instance, with the prevalence of Boko Haram terror group mainly in the north-eastern part of Nigeria and militancy in the Niger Delta region, Nigeria has been classified as a volatile country on the basis of this Criminality Index; Pakistan is also not left out following the prevalence of political and religious tensions as well as terrorist activities in that country (Martin 2016).

Finally, with particular reference to the Manor River Union countries of Guinea, Liberia and Sierra Leone, a former Assistant Secretary General of the United Nations for Political Affairs, Ibrahima Fall, averred that the overall security situation in West Africa remains volatile as insecurity and instability can spread in addition to the plight of refugees and internally displaced persons (*UN News* 2001). Fall drew reference from the fighting in neighbouring Liberia which had the capacity of stimulating disastrous spill-over effects in Sierra Leone thereby underscoring the dire need for a collaborative framework in confronting the crisis within the subregion. Other factors fuelling insecurity and instability according to Ibrahima Fall include escalating tensions across states borders triggered by acute underdevelopment and political crisis coupled with additional challenges posed by the need to protect children in armed conflicts, address illicit trafficking in arms, the desire to reintegrate demobilized soldiers as well as the promotion of peace, justice and national reconciliation in many countries across West Africa (*UN News* 2001).

Small Arms and Light Weapons (SALWs)

Based on Article 1 (9) of ECOWAS Convention on Small Arms and Light Weapons, transfer or proliferation of SALWs refers to any movement of SALWs, ammunition and other related materials from or through the territory of a state (ECOWAS 2006). However, drawing from the dichotomy between licit and illicit arms as observed by Darkwa (2011), depending on a change of jurisdiction, ownership, designation and location, the proliferation of SALWs can be licit or illicit depending on legal interpretation. According to him, legal proliferation arises when the production and assemblage of SALWs conform to the laws operating at national, regional and international levels and vice versa when the reverse is the case.

The concept of SALWs defies common interpretation. The UN Panel of Government Experts in its recommendation aver that SALWs represent those weapons just below those covered by the United Nations Register of Conventional Arms ranging from clubs, knives and machetes (International Peace Bureau 2020). Based on the international instrument in the aftermath of the 2006 UN Review Conference on Small Arms, any man-made transportable fatal weapon that has the ability of ejecting or firing, and intended to force out or fire, or may be gamely transformed to push out or fire a shot, by the action of an explosive excluding antique SALWs or their replicas are regarded as SALWs (United Nations 2006). On its part, the definition offered by the Economic Community of West African States (ECOWAS) added firearms in the category of small arms and other destructive arms or devices such as an exploding bomb, an incendiary bomb or a gas bomb, a grenade, a rocket launcher, a missile, a missile system or landmine as contained in Article 1 (2) of the ECOWAS Convention in addition to ammunition as provided for in Article 1 (3) as well as other related materials as captured in Article 1 (4) (*Weapons Law Encyclopedia* 2020). Article 1 (11) of the ECOWAS Convention defines SALWs to cover ammunition and other related materials (ECOWAS 2006).

While there are myriad of definitions of SALWs, however, an indispensable feature of SALWs is their portability as the proposal from the 1997 UN Panel of Government Expert states, weapons with the capacity of launching a shot with the circumstance that the unit or system may be transported by a pack animal or a light vehicle, moved by an individual or a small number of people, or fall on the list of SALWs (Small Arms Survey 2020). Since they are not expensive to acquire, easily moveable as well as and do not require special skills to handle, SALWs are often especially baneful having become very striking for irregular warfare, terrorism and criminal activities (International Peace Bureau 2020; Global Policy Forum 2020). Prolonged armed conflict, emergence of armed groups, human trafficking, gender violence and piracy have all been identified as part of the challenges arising from illicit proliferation of SALWs with far-reaching repercussions on the developmental needs of the society (North Atlantic Treaty Organization 2017). According to UN

Table 45.1 Classifications of small arms and light weapons (SALWs)

Small arms	Light weapons	Ammunition and explosives
Firearms	Heavy machine guns	All components, parts or spare parts for small arms or light weapons or ammunition necessary for its functioning, or any chemical substance serving as active material used as propelling or explosive agent such as:
Exploding bomb	Hand-held under-barrel	
An incendiary bomb or a gas bomb	Mounted grenade launchers	
	Portable anti-aircraft guns	
A grenade	Portable anti-tank guns	
Rocket launcher	Recoilless rifles	
A missile	Portable launchers of anti-tank missile and rocket systems	
A missile system or landmine		
Revolvers and pistols with automatic loading	Portable launchers of anti-aircraft missile systems	Cartridges (rounds) for small arms
Rifles and carbines	Mortars of calibres of less than 100 mm	Shells and missiles for light weapons
Machine guns		
Assault rifles and light machine guns	120 mm mortars	Mobile containers with missiles or shells for single-action anti-aircraft and anti-tank systems
	Single-rail-launched rockets	
		Anti-personnel and anti-tank hand grenades
		Landmines
		Explosives

Source Author's compilation adapted from ECOWAS. (2006). *ECOWAS Convention on Small Arms and Light Weapons, Their Ammunition and Other Related Materials*. Retrieved from http://www.poa-iss.org/RegionalOrganizations/ECOWAS/ECOWAS%20Convention%202006.pdf; Small Arms Survey. (2020). *Definitions of Small and Light Weapons*. Retrieved from http://www.smallarmssurvey.org/weapons-and-markets/definitions.html; United Nations. (2006, June 26–July 7). International Instrument to Enable States to Identify and Trace, in a Timely and Reliable Manner, Illicit Small Arms and Light Weapons. *United Nations Conference to Review Progress Made in the Implementation of the Programme of Action to Prevent, Combat and Eradicate the Illicit Trade in Small Arms and Light Weapons in All Its Aspects*. Retrieved from https://www.un.org/events/smallarms2006/pdf/international_instrument.pdf

Secretary General (2003), some of the ills associated with the availability of SALWs include rise in the ill-treatment of kids and as well as emergence of child soldiers. Table 45.1 illustrates the various classifications of SALWs.

Background on the Manor River Union

The Origin of MRU

The MRU is a regional institution that has the goal of enhancing cooperation in economic matters among member states. Its membership is drawn from the four Mano River countries of Liberia, Sierra Leone, Cote d'Ivoire and Guinea. At its formation, its membership was limited to Liberia and Sierra Leone (the two countries that signed the Declaration) but later enlarged on 25 October 1980 and 15 May 2008 following the accession of Republics of Guinea and Cote d'Ivoire respectively. The resolve at regional cooperation within the Mano River region dates back to 1967 when Liberia and Sierra Leone opened deliberations on the feasibility of forging closer links in trade and economic cooperation (Conteh 1975). In furtherance of the determination to attain this goal, a joint statement on mutual economic cooperation was issued by the Governments of Liberia and Sierra Leone in 1971 followed by the establishment of a joint Ministerial Committee for Economic Cooperation which met in May 1971 (Tschirgi 2002).

At the May 1971 meeting, a Committee of Experts was appointed to examine the principles and criteria for cooperation (Mano River Declaration and Protocols to the Declaration, 1973 cited in Conteh 1975). In 1972, the two governments sent a request to the United Nations Development Programme to mount a Joint United Nations Conference on Trade and Development (UNCTAD), United Nations Industrial Development Organization (UNIDO) as well as Food and Agricultural Organization (FAO) Mission for the purpose of assessing the potentials for cooperation between the two countries (UNECA 2000). Another meeting was held in January 1972 in the Sierra Leonean capital, Freetown where the philosophy of regional cooperation was reiterated. To kick start the process of cooperation, three permanent working sub-committees of the Committee of Experts were constituted to fashion out the details of future cooperation in the fields of trade, industry and agriculture; transport and communication as well as education and training (Conteh 1975; UNECA 2000).

Relying on the findings of the Joint UNCTAD/UNIDO/FAO Mission, a Joint Ministerial Committee made recommendations that resulted in the Mano River Union Declaration on 3 October 1973 at Malema, in the Pujehun District, Southern Province of Sierra Leone with the resolve to establish a Customs Union in two phases (UNECA 2000). The first Six Protocols to the Declaration were signed by William Tolbert of the Republic of Liberia and Dr. Siaka Stevens of the Republic of Sierra Leone at Bo in Liberia (Wathinote 2017; Conteh 1975). This development did not only provide the legal basis for the MRU but also outlined the key aims and objectives of MRU, marshalling the essential characteristics of the programmes of economic cooperation and dedicated the member states to the programme while simultaneously, serving as a reference point for the resolution of any differences that may arise in the course of the implementation (Conteh 1975).

Barely 15 years after its formation, one of the founding members, Liberia, was engulfed in a civil war and two years later, the co-founder, Sierra Leone followed suit. As fallout from the wars that ravaged the two countries, mistrust and suspicion pervaded the atmosphere within the organization thereby putting a wedge on the wheel of progress previously attained (Keili, n.d.). Arising from continual brutal conflicts in the region, a mechanism of civil society organizations was developed in the early 1990s aimed at conflict management and peacebuilding (International Peace Academy 2002). This initiative no doubt led to the establishment of the Mano River Union Civil

Society Forum in 1994, through the initiative of International Alert, a British-based non-governmental organization as a platform for the development of peace and mediation between warring parties in the region (International Peace Academy 2002). Furthermore, in 2000, the 15th Protocol to the Manor River Declaration was signed with aim of guaranteeing the preservation of peace, security and stability among the member states.

To address the myriad of security challenges confronting member states, a mechanism for the monitoring of common boundaries was instituted (Poole and Mohammed 2013) through the creation of Joint Security Committee as well as Joint Border Security and Confidence Building Units. However, it is one thing to sign a peace agreements and another to either conform to it or even to muster the political will to implement same. Analysts and observers have alluded to the breaking of peace agreements by warring parties a case in point being the failure of Charles Taylor of Liberia to honour over a dozen of peace agreements he entered into (*The Perspective* 2001). An atmosphere of mutual suspicion, mistrust and deceit characterized by accusations and counter-accusations pervaded the formal efforts at conflict resolution. For instance, while Guinea and Sierra Leone accused Liberia of sponsoring rebellion (in the case of Sierra Leone, the Revolutionary United Front, RUF) against their governments, Liberia in return accused Guinea of supporting Liberians United for Reconciliation and Democracy (LURD) which was desirous of overthrowing the Taylor-led government in Liberia (*The Perspective* 2001).

The Structure and Dynamics of MRU

As a regional body first fashioned along a Custom Union, the MRU was founded with the aim of strengthening the capacity of the member states to integrate their economies and coordinate development programmes particularly with regard to the expansion of trade, development of productive capacity/industry, agriculture, promotion of joint development projects, natural resources, gradual development of a common policy and cooperation regarding harmonization of tariffs and regulations concerning customs, transport and communications, monetary and financial cooperation as well as other aspects of the economic and social life of the member states with a view to ensuring a fair distribution of the benefits from economic cooperation (Wathinote 2017).

In a bid to actualize its mandate and set objectives, the Second Protocol to the Manor River Declaration contains the provisions for the institutions and structures of the MRU. They comprise the Summit or Assembly of Heads of State and Government which is regarded as the supreme institution of the MRU, the Union Ministerial Council which meets at least once a year and comprises the Ministers of Finance and Economic Affairs of the Member States; the Union Standing Committee, the Sub-Committees, the

Union Secretariat as well as such other organizations, bodies, departments and services as contained in the Manor River Declaration and its Protocols or by the Union Ministerial Council (United Nations—Treaty Series 1974).

The Summit or Assembly of Heads of State and Government

This is the highest decision-making organ of the MRU and it is made of the Heads of State and Government of the Member States.

Union Ministerial Council

This institution is made up of Ministers of the Member States in charge of Economic Cooperation, Finance, Planning, Education, Development, Trade, Industry, Agriculture, Transport, Communications, Energy, Natural Resources as well as Works. Meanwhile, attendance to its meetings is open to other Ministers when matters of interest to them form part of the agenda. Its meetings are conducted once a year and decisions at such meetings are arrived at by consensus and resolutions which may be by recommendations to the Heads of States regarding addition of Protocols to the MRU Declaration as well as resolutions for action by Union Secretariat or by Governments (United Nations—Treaty Series 1974). The Union Ministerial Council also has the responsibility for the establishment, on ad hoc basis, the Working Groups drawn from senior officers and other professionals charged with the task of reviewing, on daily basis, activities in certain sectors or areas (United Nations—Treaty Series 1974). Beyond the Working Groups, the MRU Document empowers the Union Ministerial Committee to appoint Liaison Officers to oversee particular projects in which they have expertise. In addition, the Liaison Officers provide the basic data needed by the Union Secretariat to undertake certain studies within its mandate (United Nations—Treaty Series 1974).

The Union Standing Committee/Technical Commissions

This structure of MRU comprises top-ranking professional officers of agencies of Governments saddled with the responsibility for reviewing matters peculiar to their various sectors (trade and industry, agriculture, forestry and fisheries, transport, communications and power; education, training and research as well as finance and administration) based either on their initiative or as directed by the Union Ministerial Councillor upon request by the Secretary General. up immediately before the ordinary meetings of the Union Ministerial Council with the aim of preparing the agenda for Union Ministerial Council's meetings (Wathinote 2017; United Nations—Treaty Series 1974). Its meetings are conducted once a year with provision for special sessions as the need arises.

The Union Secretariat

This organ of MRU which serves as the administrative hub derives existence from the Sixth Article of the Manor River Declaration. It is headed by a Secretary General assisted by a Deputy Secretary General. The Secretary General has responsibility for the appointment of Directors to function as Secretaries to the Union Sub-Committees. The condition of service as well as the duties of all the officials of the Secretariat are determined and governed by the Manor River Declaration as well as the rules and regulations guiding the condition of service of staff of the MRU as authorized by the Union Ministerial Council (United Nations—Treaty Series 1974). As international staff and due to the sensitive nature of the task carried out by the Secretariat, the officials including the Secretary General are expected to eschew conduct capable of interfering with their positions in the performance of their duties.

VIOLENT CONFLICTS IN THE MANOR RIVER REGION

From 1989 to 2011, violent conflicts prosecuted through the deployment of SALWs enveloped the countries of the MR region threatening not only peace and security in the affected states but also their continued existence. In the Manor River region, though richly endowed with natural resources with great potentials for peace and development, yet, the region is bedevilled by an avalanche of obstacles and challenges that render its fragile institutions and countries vulnerable to political instability, economic and humanitarian crises as well as armed conflicts (Darkwa 2011). Some member states of the MRU such as Liberia, Sierra Leone, Cote d'Ivoire and Guinea, have for decades been enveloped by violent conflicts and political strife. The civil wars which started in Liberia and spread to Sierra Leone through to Cote d' Ivoire coupled with the crisis in Guinea, got escalated due to ungoverned borders within the subregion.

In Liberia, due to the ideological differences and the struggle for control over natural resources mainly timber, iron ore and gold, the National Patriotic Front of Liberia (NPFL), (formed in 1983 and comprised a few Libyan-trained rebels led by Charles Taylor), invaded Liberia from Cote d'Ivoire, thereby kick-starting a multidimensional war against Doe's Armed Forces of Liberia and other armed groups and splinter militias in what is regarded as the first Liberian Civil War, notorious today for being one of Africa's bloodiest civil conflicts in the post-independence era that claimed more than 200,000 Liberia lives (Momodu 2016; Peace Insight 2017). Between December 1989 and mid-1993, the NPFL was lurked in armed confrontation with government forces and other ethnic militias loyal to Samuel Doe. The ensuing violent conflict that characterized this period created civilian casualties with the NPFL being responsible for the massacre of thousands of Liberians who opposed his rebellion (Momodu 2016). The main targets of the offensive were the Krahn and Mandigo ethnic groups that supported the Doe government (Momodu

2016). The high civilian death toll prompted the Economic Community of West African States (ECOWAS) to deploy troops to Liberian capital, Monrovia but regrettably, rather than ameliorate the situation, their presence aggravated the situation. On 9 September 1990, Samuel Doe was finally assassinated by a rebel group, the Independent National Patriotic Front of Liberia (INPFL) led by Prince Johnson which had been waging a separate war against the government of Samuel Doe (Momodu 2016).

In 1991, violent upheavals in Liberia transcended its boundaries as the Revolutionary United Front (RUF) of Sierra Leone supported by Charles Taylor invaded Sierra Leone and in reaction to the aggression, refugees from Liberia (comprising mainly of former soldiers of Krahn extraction loyal to Samuel Doe) as well as Mandingoes were organized into the United Liberation Movement for Democracy (ULIMO) by both Guinea and Sierra Leone (Jorgel and Utas 2007). The outcome was the intensification of the conflict which lasted till 1996 following the negotiation of a ceasefire. The ceasefire eventually paved a way for elections in 1997 in which Charles Taylor was elected President.

The successful transition to civil rule did not however solve the problem as groups opposed to Taylor ganged up against him with the formation of Liberians United for Reconciliation and Democracy (LURD) (Jorgel and Utas 2007). Taylor's counter-offensives notwithstanding, by early 2002, the LURD rebel forces had out-manoeuvred the government forces and effectively carried out raids that evaded government strongholds (Momodu 2016). Like a hydra-headed monster, by early 2003, another group of rebels, Movement for Democracy in Liberia (MODEL) supported by the government of Cote d'Ivoire emerged in the southern part of the country to challenge the Taylor-led government. Violent campaigns against the government became intensified such that by May 2003, Taylor's government could only control one-third of the entire country. As an array of rebel forces advanced towards Monrovia, closing in on the capital city amid bloodshed, an intervention by the subregional body ECOWAS became imperative and as such, former Ghanian President, John Kufor, then ECOWAS Chairman initiated a peace move in Accra that would usher in a negotiated agreement that would forestall further bloodletting.

Regrettably, by July 2003 while the peace talks were on in Accra, the LURD rebels laid siege on Liberia's capital, Monrovia and subsequent bombardment left over one thousand civilians dead with many more displaced. A ceasefire was however announced by LURD on 29 July 2003 paving the way for ECOWAS troops mainly from Nigeria to move to Monrovia as peacekeepers. Cognizance of the fact that his government could no longer withstand the onslaught against it, Charles Taylor resigned as President of Liberia on 11 August 2003 and fled Liberia to Nigeria on exile. As a prelude to ending the catastrophe, the Accra Comprehensive Peace Agreement (CPA) was announced on 18 August 2003 clearing the coast for the formation of the National Transition Government of Liberia under the leadership of Gyude Bryant. As part of the peace accord, Liberia's first post-civil war national election was scheduled for 2005 and eventually, Ellen Johnson Sirleaf won the election thereby becoming Liberia's twenty-fourth President as well as the first woman to lead the country (Momodu 2016; Jorgel and Utas 2007). As part of the efforts towards reforming the system, Sirleaf established the Liberian Truth and Reconciliation Commission (LTRC) to examine crimes committed in the country between 1979 and 2003 (Jorgel and Utas 2007).

In Sierra Leone, 23 March 1991 marked a turning point in the country's political history with the eruption of a civil war subsequent upon a fierce attack launched against the country with the help of fighters from the RUF of Liberia. Though it is conventionally believed that diamond was the driving behind the crisis, nonetheless, the Sierra Leonean catastrophe was a product of varied interactions between structural problems that escalated grievances among the people and consequently led to the emergence of RUF (Jang 2012). In the ensuing melee, in May 1997, Ahmad Tejan Kabbah government was toppled by the Armed Forces Revolutionary Council (AFRC) made up of the rebellious members of the Sierra Leonean Army (referred to as ex-SLA) (Small Arms Survey 2005a). Sequel to pervasive denunciation of the military incursion into Sierra Leonean politics, Nigerian troops under the umbrella of ECOMOG reinstated Tejan Kabbah in March 1998. Beyond the siege on Sierra Leonean capital, Freetown by the AFRC-RUF coalition in January 1999 that resulted in more than 5000 deaths as well as the capture of some 500 UN peacekeepers in May 2000 by RUF, the Sierra Leonean civil war was quite notorious for sheer scale of human rights violations and use of child soldiers (Small Arms Survey 2005a). Nevertheless, following the military intervention by the British government aimed at suppressing rebellion, the civil war that lasted for ten years ended in January 2002 with features of cruelty and viciousness in the conflict still lingering in the minds and bodies of the populace (Jang 2012).

As part of the muddled and complex regional cataclysm that originated in Liberia between the late 1980s and early 1990s, Guinea was also engulfed in civil strife. The civil wars that enveloped Liberia and Sierra Leone during the 1990s had negative implications for the relationship between Guinea and the two (Global Security 2020a). On its part, though Guinea was not engulfed by civil war, nevertheless, political instability in the neighbouring countries had adversely affected the country especially the *Guinee Forestiere*, (part of Guinea that shares boundary with Sierra Leone Liberia and Cote d'Ivoire) which became a victim as a result of transborder armed attacks and the influx of refugees (Jorgel and Utas 2007). From September 2000, thousands of Guinean villagers and close to 500,000 Sierra Leonian and Liberian refugees were affected by border attacks carried out by Guinean dissident group from the military, RFDG with the backing of Sierra Leone's RUF and Liberia (Ploughshares 2014). A brutal attack against Guinea between late 2000 and early 2001 left 1000 Guineans dead with more than 100,000 displaced (Global Security 2020a).

Following the incessant attacks, a youth militia *Jeunes Volontaires* was formed between 2001 and 2002 to protect Guinea from external aggression (Jorgel and Utas 2007). While members of the youth militia did well by warding off attacks, nonetheless, they became willing tools for recruitment into various illicit activities including drug trafficking as a result of the failure of the government to settle them (Jorgel and Utas 2007). Sandwiched by war torn countries, Guinea became exposed to serious security and developmental challenges mainly refugee crisis and displacements. Beyond the refugee crisis, Guinea which at that time was a member of the United Nation Security Council acted in violation of the arms embargo imposed on Liberia by engaging in illicit supply of arms, providing a base for the recruitment of various armed groups in both Liberia and Sierra Leone as illustrated by the recruitment of Guineans into the LURD and the country serving as base for the recruitment of RUF of Sierra Leone (HRW 2003; Child Soldiers International 2008).

In Cote d'Ivoire, entrenched cleavages gyrating around ethnicity, nationality and religion have been blamed for the violent conflict in that country as politicians cashed in on these incompatibilities to strengthen their monopoly on power and in the process, lured the country into a civil war (Ogwang 2011). Suffice it to state that the country was divided along religious lines between Christians and Muslims who were predominantly found in the south and north respectively, however, under the strong leadership of its first President, Felix Houphouet Boigny, the two religious groups were united (Global Security 2020b). Meanwhile, with the emergence of Henri Bedie in 1993 as the President of the country, the north/south divide was reinforced following Bedie's commitment to "*Ivoirite*", a slogan that differentiated the "real" south from the "foreigners" in the north (Peace Insight 2017). This pattern of leadership which triggered marginalization and retaliation resulted in the alignment of political affiliations with both regional and ethnic identities, a development that continued even when Bedie was overthrown on 25 December 1999 by the military led by General Guei in what is known as the country's first military coup till the emergence of Laurent Gbagbo who exploited these differences to aspire to perpetuate himself in office (Peace Insight 2017; Global Security 2020b).

The apprehension in the country however escalated when Alassane Quattara of *Reassemblement des Republicairies* (RDR) party was barred from contesting the election scheduled for 2000 on the ground that his mother hailed from Burkinafaso following a verdict handed down by the country's Supreme Court handpicked by Guei which had declared that all candidates for the election had to have two Ivoirian parents without holding another country's nationality (Peace Insight 2017). Arising from this chequered development, Quattara and his RDR supporters boycotted the election leaving Guei and Gbagbo of the Front Populaire Ivoirien (FPI) as the contestants. The country was engulfed by another crisis as the electoral process got truncated by Guei who not only disbanded the Electoral Commission on the allegation of fraud but also declared himself winner after early results indicated that Gbagbo was leading (Peace Insight 2017). Guei's reign was however, short-lived as widespread protest involving gendarmes and soldiers forced him on exile, paving the way for Gbagbo to take over the leadership of the country. Normalcy did not return to the country notwithstanding as the supporter of Allassane Quattara embarked on protests pressing for the conduct of fresh elections resulting in violent confrontations between forces loyal to Quattara and the Gbagbo led government (Peace Insight 2017).

In 2002, army officers of northern extraction led Guillaume Soro, staged another coup and gained control of the northern part of the country thereby sparking the civil war in which hundreds were killed and thousands displaced (Essa 2011). The catastrophe was however relaxed in 2004 and following the Ouagadougou Agreement of 2007, Gbagbo was named the President while Soro became the Prime Minister with an outline on security sector reform as well as the dismantlement of the buffer zone as a way of reconciling the warring factions which was however impeded by unnecessary procrastination (Peace Insight 2017). On 8 November 2010, another presidential election was held in the country with Allassane Quattara declared the winner but his major challenger, Laurent Gbagbo who assumed power in 2000 rejected the outcome on the allegation that the poll was rigged in the northern part of the country (Purefoy 2011). As a result, Gbagbo refused to relinquish power and was sworn in as President, leading to violent clashes that lasted for five months between the supporters of both Gbagbo and Quattara in which 3000 people lost their lives (Peace Insight 2017). Eventually, in April 2011, with the support of France and the UN, Gbagbo's forces were subdued and Quattara was sworn in as President (Peace Insight 2017).

The foregoing revelations have shown that violent conflicts in one country replicated itself in a neighbouring state until the whole Manor River region became engulfed in cataclysm stimulated by porous borders. The manner in which the civil wars in Liberia and Sierra Leone did not only result in the death of 200,000 and 70,000 people respectively but ended up facilitating the influx of 750,000 and 500,000 refugees into the territories of their neighbours (International Peace Academy 2002) vividly illustrates this. The sociopolitical and economic lives of the Manor River populace were grossly affected due to difficult violent conflicts and constant collapse of Peace Agreements to the extent that between the 1980s and 1990s, the subregion suffered political and economic decline of monumental magnitude (Ettang et al. 2011). The ensuing sociopolitical and economic challenges got so entrenched that even till date, instability and fragility have persisted in the subregion such that the institutions of governance became so much interfered with to the extent that the government has failed in its primary responsibility of providing security and other auxiliary duties (Ettang et al. 2011).

While the proximity of these countries has created opportunities for trade and economic cooperation, social integration, tourism and even religious pilgrimage, on the other hand, it has endangered security and hampered development. Worthy of note is that the unregulated borders have created unhindered access for all manner of people and their activities that cut across territorial boundaries.

Volatility and the Proliferation of Small Arms and Light Weapons in the Manor River Region

In the MR countries have experienced various degrees of armed conflict as a result of which their very existence, sociopolitical and economic development, peace, security and stability have become threatened. Struggle for scarce resources, bad governance, high levels of poverty, the competition for economic and/or political power among the elites etcetera have been identified as some of the factors fuelling these armed hostilities (GIABA 2013). Violence in one country ended up stimulating a similar phenomenon in a neighbouring state until the entire region became engulfed by catastrophe; a pattern facilitated by porous borders manifesting in the flow of weapons, the movement of former combatants and the transnational exploitation of resources (Silberfein and Conteh 2006). The existence of large stockpiles of arms from preceding conflicts, weak arms control mechanisms, long and porous national borders, established smuggling routes, inadequate cooperation among national border security officials, the informal modes of trade as well as easy movement of cash across borders have been identified as some of the developments facilitating and sustaining the illicit trafficking and proliferation of SALWs (GIABA 2013). Arising from the spread of SALWs in the Manor Region, there is a rise in the activities of mercenaries who move across borders and willing to fight for the highest bidder (UN Secretary General 2003).

During the Civil Wars in Liberia, SALWs were deployed by both the two rebel groups (LURD and MODEL) on one hand and the Armed Forces of Liberia (AFL) in collaboration with pro-government groups. Self-loading pistols, M72 AB2 automatic rifles, FN FAL rifles, AKM and AK-47 assault rifles, M-16 rifles, SKS rifles, PKM light machine guns, RPK and RPD machine guns and Chinese M-60 type 7.62 mm light machine guns (Table 45.2) were among the small arms in the cache of the LURD and MODEL rebel fighters (UN Security Council 2003). Despite sanctions, Liberia was awash with weapons as the UNSC Panel of Experts documented several companies as having violated the arms embargo by delivering weapons to Liberia and its neighbours including Cote d'Ivoire (UN Security Council 2003). On the side of Taylor-led government, the UNSC Panel of Experts Report concluded that weapons were obtained from Zastara (arms manufacturer) in Serbia in 2002 using a false Nigerian end-user certificate. This is in addition to a false Guinean end-user certificate from Belarus was obtained as well as another fake Ivorien end-user certificate that was detected (UN Security Council 2003). Often times, Liberia witnessed the transhipment of weapons from Eastern Europe every two to three weeks via Nigeria and Libya (Global Witness 2003).

Table 45.2 Proliferation of SALWs in liberian civil war

Weapon type	Model	Calibre (mm)	Recipient	Country of origin	Mode of proliferation
Self-loading pistols	–	–	LURD, MODEL	–	Seizure from government forces; shipment through Guinean border
Automatic rifles	M72 AB2	–	LURD, MODEL	–	
Rifle	M-16; SKS, FN FAL	–	LURD, MODEL	–	
Assault rifles	AKM, AK-47	–	LURD, MODEL	100 Yugoslavia AKM, 56 Chinese made AK-47	
Light machine gun	PKM, M-60	–	LURD, MODEL	–	
Machine gun	RPK, RPD	–	LURD, MODEL	–	
Shell	RPG	–	LURD	–	
Mortar	–	81	LURD	United Arab Emirate	Shipped from Iran to Guinea then to LURD; Leaked from Guinean stockpiles

Source Author's compilation adapted from Brabazon, J. (2003, February). *Liberia, Liberians United for Reconciliation and Democracy (LURD)* (Briefing Paper No. 1). Armed Non-State Actors Project. Royal Institute of International Affairs. Retrieved from http://www.chathamhouse.org/sites/default/files/public/Research/Africa/brabazon_bp,pdf; Global Witness. (2003, March 31). *West Africa Arms Trafficking and Mercenary Activities Supported by the Liberian Government and Logging Companies*. Retrieved from https://www.globalwitness.org/en-gb/achive/west-african-arms-trafficking-and-mercenary-activities-supported-liberian-government-and/; Small Arms Survey. (2005b, April 26). *Liberia*. Retrieved from http://www.smallarmssurvey.org/fileadmin/docs/D-Book-series/book-01-Armed-and-Aimless/SAS-Armed-Aimless-Part-2-09-Liberia.pdf; UN Security Council. (2003, April 24). *Report of the Panel of Experts Concerning Liberia (S/2003/498)*. Retrieved from https://reliefweb.int/report/liberia/report-panel-experts-concerning-liberia-s2003498

Though the LURD rebel forces captured weapons and ammunition from government forces like the over 100 likely Yugoslav-made AKM assault rifles, nevertheless, a large number of the weapons caches delivered to the rebel group were sighted near the Guinean border containing several hundred newly packaged Chinese-made type 56 AKM assault rifles, hundreds of pallets of various 7.62 mm calibre ammunition stamped 2001 and 2002 as well as probably thousands of RPG shells suggesting the unlikelihood of the weapons being seized from the government security forces (Brabazon 2003). For instance, some of the 81 mm mortar rounds deployed by LURD rebel fighters during the June–July 2003 attacks on Monrovia were shipped from Iran to Guinea and smuggled to LURD (Human Rights Watch 2003 as cited in Small Arms Survey 2005b). Besides, mortar ammunition manufactured by the United Arab Emirate suspected to have been deployed by the LURD was alleged to have leaked in some way from Guinean stockpiles (Human Rights Watch [HRW] 2003). For LIMA armed militia and MODEL rebels, Cote d'Ivoire provided the needed support (UN Security Council 2003).

Worthy of note here is that in total violation of UN sanctions, Liberia played a destabilizing role in West Africa by not only engaging in arms importation but also supporting mercenaries in neighbouring Cote d'Ivoire and Sierra Leone (Global Witness 2003). The Ivorian Popular Movement of the Great West (*Mouvement Populaire Ivoirien du Grand Ouest-MPIGO1*) and Movement for Justice and Peace (*Mouvement pour la justice et la paix* MJP2) rebel forces in Cote d'Ivoire received support from Liberia by way of arming, training and deployment while mercenaries were deployed in Sierra Leone to destabilize the country (Global Witness 2003). The overflow of refugees as well as armed fighters in Liberia to its neighbours made it thorny to isolate the Liberian crisis as armed youths from Liberia, Sierra Leone, Guinea and Cote d'Ivoire who had become accustomed to a life of conflict, banditry and lawlessness identified with armed groups in Liberia and western Cote d'Ivoire thus, creating a vicious circle of violence within the sub-region (UN Security Council 2003).

In Sierra Leone, the outbreak of the civil war undoubtedly triggered the emergence of armed groups comprising the Revolutionary United Front (RUF), Civil Defence Force (CDF), Armed Forces Revolutionary Council (AFRC) and West Side Boys (WSB) (Small Arms Survey 2005). Though the leader of RUF Foday Saybana Sankoh denied receiving arms from countries like Libya, Liberia and Burkinafaso (FAS 2020), yet, available data suggest that the rebel group was a recipient of support, guidance and weapons from Taylor-led NPFL government including large supplies of small arms and ammunition delivered in June 2000 (*Encyclopedia* 2020). Also, during the RUF-led invasion of Sierra Leone in March 1991, of the about 2,000 troops that launched the offensive, 1600 were sent by Charles Taylor while 360 were fighters from RUF (Rashid 2016). Furthermore, Taylor's NPFL supplied trucks, 4 × 4 vehicles, AK-47s and rocket-propelled grenades deployed for the operation (Rashid 2016). Burkina Faso, Cote d'Ivoire, Libya and Gambia, were widely reported to have provided the RUF with an avalanche of small weapons and other military equipment including AK-47 assault rifles of Chinese, Soviet and Eastern European origin, Belgian FN-FALs, German G3s and British Lee-Enfield no. 4s as well as sub-machine gun s that include German Sten and Israeli Uzi (Table 45.3) (Berman 2000; *Encyclopedia* 2020). Also, a substantial quantity of weapons used by the RUF came through government sources. According to a former Sierra Leonean Supreme Council member, Col K.S. Mondeh, troops and officers of the Sierra Leonean Army sometimes sold

Table 45.3 Proliferation of SALWs in Sierra Leonean civil war

Weapon type	Model	Calibre (mm)	Recipient	Country of Origin	Mode of proliferation
Assault rifle	AK-47	–	RUF; CDF; Sierra Leonean Armed Forces	Soviet, Eastern European, China	Arms provided by Burkinafaso, Cote d'Ivoire, Liberia and Libya; 1000 AK-47 s shipped by China
Rifle	FN-FALs; G3; Lee-Enfield	–	RUF; CDF	Belgium; Germany; Britain; Nigeria	G3s turned in by Gbethis (local militia from Gbinty) after disarmament; 2500 rifles supplied by Nigeria
Self-loading rifles	–	–	CDF	–	–
Hunting rifles	–	–	–	–	–
Machine gun	–	–	Sierra Leonean Armed Forces	China	50 machine guns shipped by China
Automatic grenade launcher	–	–	Sierra Leonean Armed Forces	China	Supplied by China
Grenade	–	–	Sierra Leonean Armed Forces	China	Supplied by China
Anti-aircraft gun	Twin barrelled, wheeled	–	–	–	10 twin barrelled wheeled anti-aircraft gun supplied
Mortar	–	60; 82; 120	–	Nigeria	Direct supply from Nigeria

(continued)

weapons to the RUF in addition to weapons confiscated from troops after abandonment (Mondeh 2000 cited in Berman 2000). Peacekeeping troops from both ECOMOG and UNAMSIL were also victims of arms seizure by the RUF. For instance, the RUF confiscated hundreds of weapons from Guinea, Kenya and Zambian troops (when about four hundred Zambian soldiers were

Table 45.3 (continued)

Weapon type	Model	Calibre (mm)	Recipient	Country of Origin	Mode of proliferation
Ammunition	–	7.62	–	Nigeria; Egypt	Nigeria supplied a considerable number; Egypt supplied 1500 rounds per box free of charge

Source Author's compilation adapted from Berman, E. G. (2006, December). *Re-armament in Sierra Leone: One Year After the Lome Peace Agreement* (Occasional Paper No. 1). Small Arms Survey. Retrieved from https://www.files.ethz.ch/isn/87844/2000-12-OP1_Re-armament%20Sierra%20Leone%20English.pdf; Small Arms Survey. (2005a, April 26). *Sierra Leone*. Retrieved from http://www.smallarmssurvey.org/fileadmin/docs/D-Book-series/book-01-Armed-and-Aimless/SAS-aArmed-Aimless-Part-2-14-Sierra-Leone.pdf

captured and dispossessed of their weapons) during the UNAMSIL hostage crisis of May 2000 (Berman 2000; Jonathan 2000).

From 18–21 May 2001, at Port Loko and Kambia districts, a total of 1728 RUF and CDF combatants handed over a range of heavy and light weapons comprising anti-aircraft battery and motars, AK-47s, AK-58s, FN rifles, rocket-propelled grenade s well as other small arms and ammunition in their stockpiles (Relief Web 2001). For the AFRC rebel group, Malians in ECOMOG helped the group to access weapons (Berman 2000). On the side of the Sierra Leonean government, based on responses Eric Berman obtained from Conteh on 2 June 2000 at Sierra Leonian capital Freetown, China was reported to have shipped about 1000 AK-47 type rifles and ammunition in addition to 50 machine guns and a number of automatic grenade launchers and grenades (Table 45.4) (Berman 2000). Also, Eric Berman obtained responses from Gottor on 3 June 2000 at Freetown Sierra Leone, indicating that ten twin-barrelled, wheeled anti-aircraft guns and an assortment of 60 mm, 82 mm and 120 mm mortars were supplied to the Sierra Leonian government while Egypt supplied ammunition free of charge to Sierra Leone which comprised 80 boxes of AK-47 ammunition (1500 rounds of 7.62 mm per box) (Berman 2000). Furthermore, some 2500 rifles in addition to a considerable number of ammunition were supplied by Nigeria (Berman 2000).

On the Guinean side, suffice it to state that Guinea is one of the countries within the Manor River region that was not enveloped by civil strife, nevertheless, tension mounted following the 1996 army mutiny and the 2000–2001 transborder violent attacks by rebels aided by neighbouring Liberia. In addition, it is pertinent to note that with over one million refugees from war-ravaged neighbouring countries that entered Guinea, the country became a

Table 45.4 Proliferation of SALWs in Guinean conflict

Weapon type	Model	Calibre (mm)	Recipient	Country of origin	Mode of proliferation
Assault rifle	AK-47; SKS	–	Young Volunteers	Guinea	Distributed by Guinean Army
Hunting rifle	–	–	Young Volunteers	Guinea	Supplied by Guinean Army
Shot gun	Gauge	–	Young Volunteers	Guinea	Guinean Army; illegal small arms production workshop in Guinea
Carbine	–	–	Young Volunteers	Guinea	Illegal small arms workshop in Guinea
Pistol	TT30	–	Young Volunteers	Guinea	Illegal small arms workshop in Guinea
Revolver	–	–	Young Volunteers	Guinea	Illegal small arms workshop in Guinea
Craft pistol	–	–	Young Volunteers	Guinea	Illegal small arms workshop in Guinea
Surface-to-air missile	SA-7/Strella-2	–	Guinean dissidents (RFDG)	Liberia	Through sponsorship by Charles Taylor of Liberia and Liberian fighter

Source Author's compilation adapted from Brabazon, J. (2003, February). *Liberia, Liberians United for Reconciliation and Democracy (LURD)* (Briefing Paper No. 1). Armed Non-State Actors Project. Royal Institute of International Affairs. Retrieved from http://www.chathamhouse.org/sites/default/files/public/Research/Africa/brabazon_bp.pdf; Small Arms Survey. (2005c, April 26). *Guinea*. Retrieved from http://www.smallarmssurvey.org/fileadmin/docs/D-Book-Series/book-01-Armed-and-Aimless/SAS-Armed-Aimless-Part-2-07-Guinea.pdf

victim of humanitarian crisis that paved the way for the penetration of armed groups into the country. More importantly, the significant involvement of President Conte of Guinea in conflict in Liberia via championing of Liberia rebels contributed to escalating tensions between the communities of the Forestiere region, an area bordering Liberia, Sierra Leone and Cote d'Ivoire (International Crisis Group 2003) as well as the presence of LURD rebels and Sierra Leonean Kamajors in refugee camps located in Guinea (UNSC 2003) was a key factor that destabilized the country as Charles Taylor cashed in on this development to sponsor transborder attacks by RUF, Liberian fighters and Guinean dissidents known as the Movement of the Democratic Forces of Guinea (Reassemblement des forces democratiques de Guinee, RFDG) between 2000–2001 (International Crisis Group 2003). In an effort to repel the 2000–2001 attacks by RFDG, RUF and Liberian fighters, President Conte of Guinea recruited an estimated 7000–30,000 volunteers that fought alongside the Guinean military assisted by LURD (International Crisis Group 2003).

Suffice it to state that accurate and precise information regarding the quantities and calibres of arms supplied to the Young Volunteers by the Guinean army, nevertheless, during the 2000–2001 attacks at Gueckedou region in the southwestern area of Guinea, 70% of 2380 volunteers surveyed were armed and equally took part in the operation (Berman and Florquin 2005). Also, in clear violation of ECOWAS moratorium on the manufacture, import and export of small arms by member states, Guinea through its Defence Ministry, used a private mining and trading company, *Societe Katex Mine Guinee* (Katex Mine Guinea Company or Katex Mine) as a broker for the procurement of military hardware (HRW 2003). To that effect, an end-user certificate was issued by the Defence Ministry for the procurement of 60,060 mortar rounds including 60 mm calibre (HRW 2003). Also, despite the fact that 222 weapons were seized in 2000–2003 as reported by the Ministry of Security, nonetheless, data released by in 2003 by the Republic of Guinea indicated that small weapons such as AK-47s and SKS assault rifles, hunting rifles, 12 gauge shotguns, carbines, Makarov, TT30 pistols, revolvers and craft pistols were discovered (Small Arms Survey 2005c). Light weapons were equally in use as nine SA-7/Strella-2 surface-to-air missiles were reported to have been confiscated from the Guinean dissidents by LURD (Brabazon 2003). Furthermore, the same information from the authorities in Guinea attest to the confiscation of 52 craft 12-gauge shotguns by the Anti-Crime Brigade of Guinea between 2001 and 2003 confirms the operation outfits for illicit manufacturing of SALWs (Small Arms Survey 2005c). Lastly, while it is difficult to ascertain the number and calibre of weapons either confiscated by the Guinean authorites or through voluntary surrender, nevertheless, weapons such as MAT 49, PPSh 41 and PPS 43 sub-machine guns, Mannlicher 1895 and Springfield M1903 rifles, Ruger rifle of the 1980s, SKS-pattern rifles as well as 13 firearms seized from one individual in March 2019 (Desmarais 2020).

Finally, in Cote d'Ivoire, sequel to over a decade of political instability and violent conflict—especially, the skirmishes in September 2002 that pitted the *Forces Novelles* rebel movement that controlled northern part of the country against government forces that retained control of the south—the number of weapons and ammunition in possession of the government and its opponents skyrocketed well above the pre-war levels (Anders 2014). Despite an arms embargo imposed on Cote d'Ivoire in November 2004 by the UN Security Council, the supply of ammunition to both parties to the conflict was not interrupted as significant quantities of ammunition for both Western-standard and Eastern Bloc-standard weapons were imported by the government in its effort to crush the rebellion (Table 45.5), while Sudanese ammunition arrived Cote d'Ivoire at the peak of the conflict in the early 2011 (Anders 2014). Suffice it to state that Cote d'Ivoire had been into arms importation since the 1990s for its defense and security needs; however, the crisis in neighbouring Liberia contributed to the extant stockpile as assault rifles and other small arms deployed in Liberian civil war found their way into Cote d'Ivoire: Machine guns, sub-machine guns, automatic and semi-automatic rifles as well as pistols

Table 45.5 Western-standard ammunition calibre and related arms in Cote d'Ivoire

Calibre (mm)	Type of weapon	Models
5.56 × 45	Assault Rifle	FAMMAS F-I, MI6A1; MI6A2; SG540; SG543
7.5 + 54	Bolt-action riffle	MAS-36; MAS-36/51
	Semi-automatic riffle	MAS-49/56
	General-purpose machine gun	MAC FM Mle. 1924/29; AA-52
7.62 + 51	Automatic rifle	FN FAL 50.00
9 + 19	Pistol	Beretta 92F; MAB PA-15; MAC Mle. 1950
	Sub-machine gun	Gevarm D4; MAT-49; MPS-AS
12.7 + 99	Heavy machine gun	M2HB

Source Anders, H. (2012, June). *Identifying Sources: Small-Calibre Ammunition in Cote d'voire*. Geneva: Small Arms Survey, Graduate Institution of International Development Studies (p. 14). Retrieved from http://www.smallarmssurvey.org/fileadmin/docs/c-special-reports/SAS-SR21-Coted'Ivoire.pdf

are some of the small arms and light weapons that featured considerably during the violent conflict in the country (Anders 2014) (Table 45.6).

Table 45.6 Eastern Bloc-standard ammunition calibres and related arms in Cote d'Ivoire

Calibre (mm)	Type of weapon	Models
5.45 + 39	Assault riffle	ASK–74
7.62 + 39	Pistol	TT-33
	Sub-machine gun	PPS-43
7.62 + 39	Automatic rifle	AK, AKS, AKM, AKMS, Type 56, 56-1, 56-2, Type 81-1; V2.58p, V2.58 V
7.62 + 54 R	General-purpose machine gun	PKM
	Sniper riffle	DSVD
12.7 + 108	Heavy machine gun	DSHKM
14.5 + 114	Heavy machine gun	KPVT

Source Anders, H. (2012, June). *Identifying Sources: Small-Calibre Ammunition in Cote d'voire*. Geneva: Small Arms Survey, Graduate Institution of International Development Studies (p. 14). Retrieved from http://www.smallarmssurvey.org/fileadmin/docs/c-special-reports/SAS-SR21-Coted'Ivoire.pdf

MRU's Architecture for Small Arms Control and Conflict Resolution

It is undisputable the fact that the principal aim and fundamental objective of creating the MRU is to promote economic cooperation and foster peace, security and stability among the member states. After the armed conflicts that engulfed the region for years, efforts were initiated and geared towards reviving the MRU. To this end, and as part of the strategies towards resolving conflicts and guaranteeing border security in the region, the member countries of MRU adopted, on 19 May 2000, the 15th Protocol to the MRU Declaration aimed at social integration and economic development which assigned to the Secretariat, an intergovernmental role in conflict prevention and peacebuilding (Small Arms Survey 2012; Keili, n.d.). The 15th Protocol to the MRU Declaration captioned: *Cooperation on Defence, Security, Internal Affairs and Foreign Affairs* sanctioned the establishment of a joint security and technical committees with the mandate of monitoring and investigating border security as well as related issues in addition to certain mechanisms put in place for ensuring effective implementation of the programme including the one on early warning (Small Arms Survey 2012). In May 2008, as part of the efforts towards repositioning the Union to deliver on its mandate, a resolution was passed by the Summit of Heads of State and Government that authorized the Secretariat to commence the revival, growth, socio-economic development and integration of the subregion within the parameter of four pillars: institutional revitalization and restructuring focusing on the MRU Secretariat as well as the Public Sector of Member States; peace and security; economic development and regional integration as well as social development (Wathinote 2017).

On 10 December 2008, a mini Summit was held at Sierra Leonean capital, Freetown, to tackle security, agriculture and financing of the MRU Secretariat (Keili, n.d.). To achieve the objectives of the 15th Protocol to the MRU Declaration, efforts were geared and intensified towards implementing the resolutions. To this end, in November 2011, series of meetings were held with small arms forming part of the agenda (Small Arms Survey 2012). Moreover, a framework was adopted in January 2012 for cross-border cooperation which was followed by the creation in March 2012, of "Joint Border Security and Confidence Building Units" in five identified borders by the Secretariat to further sustain peace, security and stability (Keili, n.d.; Small Arms Survey 2012). The foregoing protocol which relaxed security measure across inter-state borders, had implications for the proliferation of SALWs in the region.

Moreover, the MRU works in concert with other intergovernmental organizations at the subregional, regional, continental and global levels. For instance, to confront the threats posed by transborder movement of armed groups, arms and illicit trafficking in the subregion, the MRU works in conjunction with ECOWAS and United Nations Office for West Africa and Sahel (UNOWAS)

(UNOWAS 2019). Using the instrumentality of UN Security Council Resolutions 2000 of 2011, 2062 of 2012 and 2066 of 2012, the MRU is being assisted since 2009 by UN through the later's operations in the four MRU countries comprising United Nations Missions in Liberia (UNMIL), United Nations Integrated Peacebuilding Mission in Sierra Leone (UNIPSIL), United Nations Operations in Cote d'Ivoire (UNOCI) and United Nations Country Team in Guinea (UNCT) (UNOWAS 2019). Also, in furtherance of its efforts at containing cross-border threats occasioned by the escalation of violent conflicts and political strife including civil hostilities, in June 2013, Ministers from Liberia, Sierra Leone, Cote d'Ivoire and Guinea alongside the MRU Secretary General, ECOWAS President as well as UN and African Union (AU) converged at the Senegalese capital, Dakar to deliberate on joint security threats such as illicit trafficking of SALWs and transborder movement of armed groups (Lazuta 2013). As a follow up to the resolutions adopted in the Dakar meeting, a steering Committee made up of MRU, ECOWAS and UN was set up to midwife the evolution of the strategy for cross-border security within the subregion (UNOWAS 2019).

Suffice it to state that the machineries so far put in place to enhance border security and curtail the unregulated movement of arms and armed groups constitute a step in the right direction; however, for these measures to yield positive result, the prevailing sociopolitical and economic conditions in the four Manor River countries that predispose people to violent conflicts must be addressed. The reason is not far-fetched. When the prevailing conditions at home are not favourable, the attendant frustration can trigger violent conflicts which transcend national boundaries with possible spill-over effects. Furthermore, while it is arguable that some success stories have been recorded in the management of insecurity and control of the proliferation of SALWs, nonetheless, new security challenges are still unfolding with the tendency of undermining the progress already recorded. Such security challenges being experienced relate to increasing apprehension over maritime security in Liberia and Sierra Leone, transnational organized crime, the urgent need for total overhaul of the security sector in all the MRU countries as well as the possibility of the discovery of oil in Liberia and Sierra Leone (Keili, n.d.). As the political instability and the atmosphere of uncertainty continue to pervade the Manor River region, it is arguable that beyond the unregulated borders which has made possible the unrestrained movement of armed groups and SALWs, nonetheless, worthy of note is that such uncontrolled movements were triggered by prevailing socio-political and economic challenges in the countries within the subregion which constitute the primary drivers of insecurity and spread of SALWs.

Post-conflict Reconstruction, Disarmament, Demobilization and Reintegration (DDR)

The world over, post-war reconstruction programmes following cessation of hostilities are usually geared towards securing a lasting peace by disarming, demobilizing, reintegrating former combatants into the civil society via an instrument known as Disarmament, Demobilization and Reintegration (DDR). The case is not different in the Manor River region countries as there have been coordinated programmes at post-conflict reconstruction via DDR. In Liberia, between December 2003 and November 2004, the UNMIL disarmed over 100,000 former combatants through disarmament, demobilization, reintegration and rehabilitation (DDRR), programmes, nevertheless, the programme was not totally successful as not only less than 28,000 guns were retrieved but also there was no apt and ample reintegration for those demobilized (Paes 2006). In Sierra Leone, after three phases of problematic engagement after the end of the civil war in 2002, 72,500 combatants comprising 24,000 RUF, 37,000 CDF and 11,500 SLA were disarmed by the UNAMSIL with a total of 46,435 weapons and 1 million munitions registered (Knight 2008). Despite this success, difficulties such as mistrust, insufficient and apt funding, lack of regional approach to the DDR, lack of corresponding emphasis on the needs of the victims, lack of proper coordination as well as the obscurity in the reintegration programme, several cases of ceasefire violations, accusations and counter-accusations and long-lasting hostilities threatened the process (Knight 2008).

According to data obtained from the Republic of Guinea by Small Arms Survey, between September 26 and November 2003, the Guinean government, supported by the United States, destroyed 21,906 obsolete SALWs as well as 89,889 rounds of ammunition which include AK-47s, portable anti-tank guns as well as 278 strela-2 surface-to-air missiles (Small Arms Survey 2005c). As of March 2004, though an estimated 2000 child soldiers were demobilized and reintegrated into the Guinean population (Child Soldiers International 2004; UNICEF 2003), nevertheless, there is uncertainty over the fate of their weapons as statistics on the number of weapons handed to the volunteers or the ones retrieved from them is lacking (Small Arms Survey 2005c). Furthermore, the presence in Guinea of former LURD rebels whose number cannot be ascertained despite Guinean government's denial of their existence poses serious challenge bothering on how to disarm and demobilize them (International Crisis Group 2003). In Cote d'Ivoire, following numerous abortive attempts at DDR, however, from 2012 through to 2015, a strategy was finally designed to address the aspirations of 74,000 former combatants from both sides and in August 2012, arising from the establishment of national programme on DDR, 69,506 ex-combatants including 105 women keyed into the project with a total of 43,150 armaments including 14,121 weapons were retrieved in the process (Ehlert 2017; ONUCI 2017). With about 95% of the target population reintegrated based on statistics from the government, nonetheless, amidst fear of retaliation by the government, former fighters on the side of Gbagbo and former *Forces de Securite* (FDS), many of them handed in one weapon instead of all the weapons in their custody thus, leaving a large quantity of arms and ammunition that cannot be accounted for (Ehlert 2017). Suffice it to state that there were efforts towards DDR in the aftermath of these violent conflicts that led to the illicit spread of SALWs, some of these weapons are still in circulation within the region.

Conclusion

This Chapter examined the nexus between volatile political situation and the proliferation of SALWs in the Manor River region. A region with potentials for socio-economic and political development regrettably became enveloped by armed conflicts for over two decades. What started as a rebellion against the government in Liberia went beyond the country and spread to neighbouring Sierra Leone, Guinea and Cote d'Ivoire until the entire region was engulfed in a cataclysm. The ensuing volatile political situation triggered by violent conflicts, political instability and governance deficit heightened and facilitated by porous borders gave rise to the illicit spread of SALWs that not only fuelled the armed conflicts but also prolonged the conflicts thereby threatening peace, security and stability in the region. Despite efforts at DDR, following the formal cessation of hostilities, the region is still a den of SALWs that continue to pose serious threats to peace, security and stability of the entire region and even beyond because in so many cases, while disarmament and demobilization were pursued with vigour, however, the reintegration process was not sufficiently executed. To consolidate on the relative peace, security and stability experienced in the region, a regional security framework was created to control the proliferation of SALWs considered as the key driver of armed conflicts in the region. Through the instrumentality of MRU, the 15th Protocol to the MRU was adopted with mechanisms for border monitoring and enhancement of defense and security defense needs of member states. To this end, the Joint Security Committee as well as Joint Border Security and Confidence Building Units were created. Incidentally, while some progress has been in these areas, more still needs to be done. The failure of key actors to demonstrate sufficient political will and commitment towards achieving the avowed goals constitutes a bane as suspicion, mistrust and deceit that characterized the past still persist. As a panacea, there should be collaboration at the national, subregional, regional and global levels at mopping up these arms and preventing their continued spread as well as pursuing with vigour, the process of fully reintegrating the former combatants into the civil society. Most importantly, because prevention will always be a better option than cure, all the actors (state and non-state) in the Mano River region should always opt for timely and peaceful settlement of disputes rather than resort to armed confrontations. In addition, all the prevailing sociopolitical and economic conditions that threaten security should be addressed as they constitute the bedrock of violent conflicts across the Manor River region.

REFERENCES

Afolabi, D. S., & Idowu, H. A. (2018, October). Mano River Basin: An Evaluation of Negotiation and Mediation Techniques. *Conflict Studies Quarterly* (25), 3–19. Retrieved from https://doi.org/10.24193/csq.25.1.

Anders, H. (2014, June). *Identifying Sources: Small-Calibre Ammunition in Cote d'Ivoire*. Small Arms Survey. Retrieved from http://www.smallarmssurvey.org/filead min/docs/c-special-reports/SAS-SR21-Coted'Ivoire.pdf.

Berman, E. G. (2000, December). *Re-armament in Sierra Leone: One Year After the Lome Peace Agreement* (Occasional Paper No. 1). Small Arms Survey. Retrieved from https://www.files.ethz.ch/isn/87844/2000-12-OP1_Re-armament%20Sierra%20Leone%20English.pdf.

Berman, E. G., & Florquin, N. (2005, May). Armed Groups and Small Arms in ECOWAS Member States (1998–2004). In N. Florquin & Eric G Berman (Eds.), *Armed and Aimless: Armed Groups, Guns, and Human Security in the ECOWAS Region Small Arms Survey* (pp. 224–388). Retrieved from https://reliefweb.int/sites/reliefweb.int/files/resources/IFC130FAE95B841 FC12570D80047D5BA-Full%20Manuscript.pdf.

Brabazon, J. (2003, February). *Liberia, Liberians United for Reconciliation and Democracy (LURD)* (Briefing Paper No. 1). Armed Non-State Actors Project. Royal Institute of International Affairs. Retrieved from http://www.chathamhouse.org/sites/default/files/public/Research/Africa/brabazon_bp,pdf.

Child Soldiers International. (2004). *Child Soldiers Global Report 2004—Guinea*. Retrieved from https://www.refworld.org/docid/49880658c.html. Accessed 21 December 2020.

Child Soldiers International. (2008, May 20). *Child Soldiers Global Report 2008—Guinea*. Retrieved from https://www.refworld.org/docid/486cb104c.html. Accessed 25 June 2020.

Cobb, C. (2002, May 24). *Cycle of Conflict in Mano River Threatens S. Leone Peace—Analyst*. Retrieved from http://allafrica.com.

Conteh, C. M. (1975). The Mano River Approach, Intereconomics, ISSN 0020-5346, Verlag, Weltarchiv, Hamburg, vol. 10, iss. 4, pp. 102–106. Retrieved from https://www.econstor.eu/bitstream/10419/139179/1/v10-i04-a08-BF02929598.pdf; http://dx.doi.org/10.1007/BF02929598.

Darkwa, L. (2011). *The Challenge of Sub-Regional Security in West Africa: The Case of the 2006 ECOWAS Convention on Small Arms and Light Weapons* (Discussion Paper 69). Retrieved from http://nai.diva-portal.org/smash/get/diva2:478514/FULLTEXT01.

Desmarais, N. (2020, April). *Arms Monitoring in Guinea: A Survey of National Forensic Services* (Briefing Paper). Small Arms Survey. Retrieved from http://www.smallarmssurvey.org/fileadmin/docs/T-Briefing-Papers/SANA-BP-Forensics-Guinee.pdf.

ECOWAS. (2006). *ECOWAS Convention on Small Arms and Light Weapons, Their Ammunition and Other Related Materials*. Retrieved from http://www.poa-iss.org/RegionalOrganizations/ECOWAS/ECOWAS%20Convention%202006.pdf.

Ehlert, F. (2017, October 4). *Disarmament, Demobilization and Reintegration in Cote d'Ivoire: Lessons Identified for Security Sector Reform*. Retrieved from https://issat.dcaf.ch/share/Blogs/ISSAT-Blog/Disarmament-demobilization-and-reintegra tion-in-Cote-d-Ivoire-Lessons-Identified-for-Security-Sector-Reform.

Encyclopedia. (2020). *Revolutionary United Front (RUF).* Retrieved from https://www.encyclopedia.com/politics/legal-and-political-magazines/revolutionary-united-front-ruf. Accessed 26 June 2020.

Encyclopaedia Britannica. (2020). *Mano River.* Retrieved from https://www.britannica.com/place/Mano-River. Accessed 21 June 2020.

Essa, A. (2011, April 1). *Cote d'Ivoire: The Forgotten War?* Retrieved from https://www.aljazeera.com/indepth/features/2011/04/20114116296998447.html.

Ettang, D., Maina, G., & Razia, W. (2011, January). *A Regional Approach to Peacebuilding—The Mano River Region.* African Centre for Constructive Resolution of Disputes (ACCORD). Retrieved from https://www.eldis.org/document/A70912.

FAS. (2020). *Footpaths to Democracy: Toward a New Sierra Leone.* Retrieved from https://fas.org/irp/world/para/docs/footpaths.htm. Accessed 26 June 2020.

Fund for Peace. (2019, April 10). *Fragile States Index 2019.* Retrieved from https://fundforpeace.org/2019/04/10/fragile-states-index-2019/.

GIABA. (2013). *The Nexus Between Small Arms and Light Weapons and Money Laundering and Terrorist Financing in West Africa.* Retrieved from https://www.giaba.org/media/f/613_519_GIABA%20SALW%Nexus-final.pdf.

Global Policy Forum. (2020). *Small Arms and Light Weapons.* Retrieved from https://www.globalpolicy.org/security-council/index-of-countries-on-the-security-council-agenda/small-arms-and-light-weapons.html. Accessed online 22 June 2020.

Global Security. (2020a). *Guinea Conflict.* Retrieved from https://www.globalsecurity.org/military/world/war/guinea.htm. Accessed online 22 June 2020.

Global Security. (2020b). *Ivory Coast Conflict.* Retrieved from https://www.globalsecurity.org/military/world/war/ivory-coast.htm. Accessed online 22 June 2020.

Global Witness. (2003, March 31). *West Africa Arms Trafficking and Mercenary Activities Supported by the Liberian Government and Logging Companies.* Retrieved from https://www.globalwitness.org/en-gb/achive/west-african-arms-trafficking-and-mercenary-activities-supported-liberian-government-and/.

HRW. (2003, November 3). *Weapons Sanctions, Military Spending, and Human Suffering: Illegal Arms Flows to Liberia and the June–July 2003 Shelling of Monrovia* (A Human Rights Watch Briefing Paper). Retrieved from https://www.hrw.org/legacy/backgrounder/arms/liberia/liberia_arms.htm.

Inter Diagnostix. (2015, April 30). *The Mano River Union.* Retrieved from http://www.interdiagnostix.com/car-rta/mano-river-union.

International Crisis Group. (2003, December 19). *Guinea: Uncertainties at the End of an Era* (Africa Report No. 74). Retrieved from https://www.crisisgroup.org/africa/west-africa/guinea-uncertainties-end-era.html.

International Peace Academy. (2002, June 14). *Civil Society Perspectives from the Mano River Union.* An International Peace Academy Africa Program Civil Society Dialogue, Millenium Hotel, UN Plaza New York.

International Peace Bureau. (2020). *Small Arms and Light Weapons.* Retrieved from http://www.ipb.org/small-arms-and-light-weapons/. Accessed online 22 June 2020.

Jang, S. Y. (2012, October 25). *The Causes of the Sierra Leone Civil War.* Retrieved from http://www.e-ir.info/2012/10/25/the-causes-of-the-sierra-leone-civil-war-underlying-grievances-and-the-role-of-the-revolutionary-united-front/.

Jonathan, M. (2000, May 9). Can the UN Force Restore Peace? *BBC News.* Retrieved from http://news.bbc.co.uk/2/hi/Africa/742196.stm.

Jorgel, M., & Utas, M. (2007). *The Mano River Basin Area: Formal and Informal Security Providers in Liberia, Guinea and Sierra Leone.* Retrieved from http_webbrapp.ptn.foi.se_pdf_4072057f-bbf5-408e-8baf-6da5101622f7.pdf.
Keili, F. L. (n.d.). *Cross Border Cooperation as an Example of How to Converge Security and Development in the Mano River Union.* Retrieved from https://www.oecd.org/swac/events/cross-border%20co-operation%20in%20the%20MRU.pdf. Accessed online 22 June 2020.
Knight, W. A. (2008). Disarmament, Demobilization and Reintegration and Post-Conflict Peace Building in Africa: An Overview. *African Security, 1*(1, August), 24–52. Retrieved from https://www.tandfonline.com/doi/full/10.1080/19362200802285757.
Lazuta, J. (2013, June 30). *Mano River Countries Tackle Cross-Border Arms.* Retrieved from https://www.voanews.com/africa/mano-river-countries-tackle-cross-border-arms.
Libseib. (2014, November 11). *Welcome to the Mano River Union Countries in Africa.* Retrieved from https://libseib-wordpress.com/2014/11/11/welcome-to-the-manor-river-union-countries-in-africa/.
Marc, A. Verjee, N., & Mogaka, S. (2015). *The Challenge of Security and Stability in West Africa.* Retrieved from https://gsdrc.org/document-library/the-challenge-of-stability-and-security-in-west-africa/. Accessed online 21 June 2020.
Martin, W. (2016, December 1). *The 13 Most Dangerous Countries in the World.* Retrieved from https://www.independent.co.uk/news/world/politics/most-dangerous-countries-in-the-world-criminality-index-97450266.html.
Merriam Webster Dictionary. (2020). *Definition of Volatile.* Retrieved from https://www.merriam-webster.com/dictionary/volatile. Accessed online 22 June 2020.
Momodu, S. (2016, July 25). *First Liberian Civil War 1989–1996.* Retrieved from http://www.blackpast.org/gah/first-liberian-civil-war-1989-1996.
North Atlantic Treaty Organization. (2017, May 22). *Small Arms and Light Weapons (SALW) and Mine Action (MA).* Retrieved from https://www.nato.int/cps/en/natohq/topics_52142.htm.
Ogwang, T. (2011, April 1). *The Root Causes of the Conflict in Ivory Coast.* Retrieved from https://www.africaportal.org/publications/the-root-causes-of-the-conflict-in-ivory-coast/.
ONUCI (United Nations Operation in Cote d'Ivoire). (2017, July 2). *Disarmament, Demobilization and Reintegration of Ex-combatants in Cote d'Ivoire.* Retrieved from https://onuci.unmissions.org/en/disarmament-demobilization-and-reintegration-ex-combatants-c%C3%B4te-d%E2%80%99ivoire.
Paes, W. (2006). The Challenges of Disarmament, Demobilization and Reintegration in Liberia. *International Peacekeeping, 12*(2, August), 253–261. Retrieved from https://www.tandfonline.com/doi/abs/10.1080/1353310500066537.
Peace Insight. (2017, September). *Liberia: Conflict Profile.* Retrieved from https://www.peaceinsight.org/conflicts/liberia/.
Ploughshares. (2014, February 25). *Armed Conflicts Report—Guinea.* Retrieved from https://www.justice.gov/sites/default/files/eoir/legacy/2014/02/25/Guinea.pdf.
Poole, M., & Mohammed, J. A. (2013). *Border Community Security: Mano River Union Region.* Retrieved from https://rc-services-assets.s3.eu-west-1.amazonaws.com/s3fs-public/MRU_bordercommunitysecurity_ConciliationResources.pdf.

Purefoy, C. (2011, April 5). *What Is Causing the Conflict in Ivory Coast?* Retrieved from http://edition.cnn.com/2011/WORLD/africa/04/03/ivory.coast.explainer/index.html.

Rashid, I. (2016, May). Chapter 8 Sierra Leone: The Revolutionary United Front. *The Journal of Complex Operations.* Retrieved from https://cco.ndu.edu/News/Article/780201/chapter-8-sierra-leone-the-revolutionary-united-front/.

Relief Web. (2001, May 22). *UNAMSIL Press Briefing.* Retrieved from https://reliefweb.int/report/guinea/unamsil-press-briefing-22-may-2001.

Silberfein, M., & Conteh, A. (2006, September 1). *Boundaries and Conflict in the Mano River Region of West Africa.* Retrieved from http://journals.sagepub.com/doi/abs/10.1080/07388940600972685.

Small Arms Survey. (2005a, April 26). *Sierra Leone.* Retrieved from http://www.smallarmssurvey.org/fileadmin/docs/D-Book-series/book-01-Armed-and-Aimless/SAS-aArmed-Aimless-Part-2-14-Sierra-Leone.pdf.

Small Arms Survey. (2005b, April 26). *Liberia.* Retrieved from http://www.smallarmssurvey.org/fileadmin/docs/D-Book-series/book-01-Armed-and-Aimless/SAS-Armed-Aimless-Part-2-09-Liberia.pdf.

Small Arms Survey. (2005c, April 26). *Guinea.* Retrieved from http://www.smallarmssurvey.org/fileadmin/docs/D-Book-Series/book-01-Armed-and-Aimless/SAS-Armed-Aimless-Part-2-07-Guinea.pdf.

Small Arms Survey. (2012, April 12). *15th Protocol to the MRU Declaration: Cooperation on Defence, Security, Internal Affairs and Foreign Affairs.* Retrieved from http://smallarmssurvey.org/tools/no-poa/profiles-of-regional-organizations/Africa/mru.html.

Small Arms Survey. (2020). *Definitions of Small and Light Weapons.* Retrieved from http://www.smallarmssurvey.org/weapons-and-markets/definitions.html. Accessed online 22 June 2020.

The Alan Turing Institute. (2020). *Political Volatility.* Retrieved from https://turing.ac.uk/research-projects/political-volatility/. Accessed online 22 June 2020.

The Guardian. (2018, February 22). *The Influx of Small Arms, Light Weapons.* Retrieved from https://guardian.ng/opinion/the-influx-of-small-arms-light-weapons/.

The Perspective. (2001, August 30). *Can Mano River Countries Achieve Peace.* Retrieved from www.theperspective.org/mru.html. Accessed online 23 June 2020.

Tschirgi, N. (2002). Making the Case for Regional Approach to Peace-Building. *Journal of Peacebuilding and Development,* 1(1), 25–38. In D. Ettang, G. Maina, & W. Razia. (2011, May). *A Regional Approach to Peacebuilding—The Mano River Region* (Policy and Practice Brief). Iss. 006.

UN Chronicle. (2011, December). *The UN Role and Efforts in Combating the Proliferation of Small Arms and Light Weapons,* Vol. XLVIII, No. 4. Retrieved from https://unchronicle.un.org/article/un-role-and-efforts-combating-proliferation-small-arms-and-light-weapons.

UNICEF. (2003, November 4). *Guinea: A Window on West Africa's War-Weary Children.* Retrieved from https://www.unicef.org/media/media_15421.html.

United Nations. (2006, June 26–July 7). *International Instrument to Enable States to Identify and Trace, in a Timely and Reliable Manner, Illicit Small Arms and Light Weapons. United Nations Conference to Review Progress Made in the Implementation of the Programme of Action to Prevent, Combat and Eradicate the Illicit Trade in*

Small Arms and Light Weapons in All Its Aspects. Retrieved from https://www.un.org/events/smallarms2006/pdf/international_instrument.pdf.

United Nations Economic Commission for Africa: Subregional Development Centre (SRDC/WA) for West Africa. (2000). *Consultancy Report on the Revitalization of the Mano River Union Secretariat Freetown-Sierra Leone*. Retrieved from https://repository.uneca.org/bitstream/handle/10855/3276/Bib-26787.pdf?sequence=1.

United Nations—Treaty Series. (1974). *The Mano River Declaration 1*. Retrieved from https://wits.worldbank.org/GPTAD/PDF/archive/MRU.pdf.

UN News. (2001, December). *West Africa: Amid Progress, Region Remains Volatile, Security Council Told*. Retrieved from https://news.un.org/en/story/2001/12/23362-west-africa-amid-progress-region-remains-volatile-security-council-told.

UNOWAS. (2019, November 25). *Support to Mano River Union*. Retrieved from https://unowas.unmissions.org/support-mano-river-union.

UN Secretary General. (2003, March 18). *Unless Adequately Addressed, Proliferation of Small Arms, Mercenaries Will Continue to Pose Severe Threat to West Africa, SG Says*. Retrieved from https://reliefweb.int/report/liberia/unless-adequately-addressed-prolifeartion-small-arms-mercenaries-will-continue-pose.

UN Security Council. (2003, April 24). *Report of the Panel of Experts Concerning Liberia (S/2003/498)*. Retrieved from https://reliefweb.int/report/liberia/report-panel-experts-concerning-liberia-s2003498.

Wathinote. (2017, April 10). *Presentation of the Mano River Union (MRU)*. Retrieved from https://www.wathi.org/debat_id/organisations-regionales/wathinote-organisations-regionales/wathinote-presentation-of-the-mano-river-union/.

Weapons Law Encyclopedia. (2020). *2006 ECOWAS Convention*. Geneva Academy of International Humanitarian Law and Human Rights. Retrieved from http://www.weaponslaw.org/instruments/2006-ecowas-convention. Accessed online 22 June 2020.

Uchenna Simeon a Lecturer in the Department of Political Science, Federal University, Lafia, Nasarawa State, Nigeria. His research interests include international affairs, security, peace and conflict studies as well as defense and strategic studies. Prior to his foray into academia, Uchenna had worked in various capacities in the organized private sector in Nigeria which include Hallmark Bank PLC (defunct), Nigerian Association of Small and Medium Enterprises (NASME) Abia State Chapter, Ecobank Nigeria PLC, Fidelity Bank PLC and Oceanic Bank International PLC (defunct). He is a member of the Chartered Institute of Bankers of Nigeria (CIBN) and a registered student of the Chartered Institute of Administration.

CHAPTER 46

Southern Africa: Regional Dynamics of Conflict and the Proliferation of Small Arms and Light Weapons

Pamela Machakanja and Chupicai Shollah Manuel

Introduction

The Sustainable Development Goals (SDGs), adopted along with the 2030 Agenda for Sustainable Development acknowledges that "there can be no sustainable development without peace, and no peace without sustainable development". Thus, SDG 16 aims to "Promote peaceful and inclusive societies for sustainable development, provide access to justice for all and build effective, accountable and inclusive institutions at all levels". SDG 16 acknowledges the links of development with peace and governance, and thus the role that violence, conflict, state fragility, corruption and poor governance can play in undermining development. Globally, according to the United Nations Commodity Trade Statistics Database (UN Comtrade 2019) the international small arms trade was worth at least USD 6.5 billion in 2016, a 13% increase compared to 2015. Small arms ammunition remains the largest category, with exports worth USD 2.6 billion in 2016. Such glaring statistics show the severity and proliferation of SALW hence resulting in direct negative effects on the aspirations of the SDGs and that of AU and SADC.

The proliferation of such SALWs in Southern Africa is redefining bilateralism, crime, bordering and regional integration ecosystem. Notably, South Africa is battling with dealing with xenophobia and violence, while Mozambique is struggling to deal with terrorism in Cabo Delgado which are a manifestation of the shifting dynamics of conflicts which part are necessitated

P. Machakanja (✉) · C. S. Manuel
College of Business, Peace Leadership and Governance, Africa University, Mutare, Zimbabwe

© The Author(s), under exclusive license to Springer Nature Switzerland AG 2021
U. A. Tar and C. P. Onwurah (eds.), *The Palgrave Handbook of Small Arms and Conflicts in Africa*,
https://doi.org/10.1007/978-3-030-62183-4_46

by SALW, Crime in South Africa involving gun robbery and xenophobia, the proliferation of SALW in twenty-first century has witnessed the increase use of these available small arms by terrorist, militants, killer herdsmen and criminal gangs to engage in political, economic and sociocultural benefits. Besides the high-level loss of lives and properties, it also witnessed an increase in sexual violence from raping of innocent victims, sexual slavery to forced marriage. SALW proliferation in the SADC (Mozambique, DRC, Zimbabwe as examples) today, creates a negative perception of security, preventing foreign direct investments, puncturing the notion of ease of doing business, while increasing lack of confidence in government and its security apparatus.

There is a growing trend in Africa of terrorism which has strengthened terrorist organisations' weapons acquisition patterns and this has also increased incidences of terrorist attacks in Africa. Organised crime has been witnessed in Kenya where terrorist group such as Al-Shabab was involved in the bombing and killings of civilians and tourists in hotels and shopping malls. A report from Aljazeera (2019) noted that this was not the first time the Sub-Saharan African nation has been attacked. In August 1998, the al-Qaeda bombed the US embassy in the central Nairobi, killing more than 200 people and wounding thousands. In September 2013, Al-Shabab gunmen attacked the capital's high-end Westgate shopping mall in a three-day siege that killed 67 people. Al-Shabab, which is linked to al-Qaeda, has launched a number of other attacks across the country in recent years; targeting churches and setting up landmines along the Kenya-Somalia border. In 2015, the gunmen killed 147 students at Garissa University: the worst attack on Kenyan soil since the 1998 US embassy bombing. SALW has increased the complexity of crime and terrorism globally while the case from DRC where there is conflict financing and militarisation of extractives is as example of the deep-rooted challenges Africa is dealing with on silencing the guns.

Conceptualising Small Arms and Light Weapons (SALWs)

While there is no universally accepted definition of small arms and light weapons, the United Panel of Governmental Experts at the United Nations General Assembly (UNGA) (1997) considers portability as a defining characteristic of SALW. In this paper, we adopted a definition of SALWs as any portable lethal weapon that expels or launches, is designed to expel or launch, or may be readily converted to expel or launch a shot, bullet or projectile by the action of an explosive (Small Arms Survey 2013). This is a normative definition, however, for the purposes of further conceptualising SALWs, we also included some portable weapons range which are peculiar to Southern Africa such knives, machetes, knob carries to those covered under that United Nations Register of Conventional arms. In addition, the Southern African Development Community (SADC) through the Protocol on the Control of Firearms, ammunition and other related weapons define "small arms" as weapons which include machine guns, sub-machines guns, pistols, automatic and assault rifles and light weapons as designed for use by groups of persons including heavy machine guns, automatic cannons, howitzers, mortars of less than 100 mm calibre, grenade launchers, anti-tank weapons and launchers, recoilless guns, rocket launchers, anti-aircraft and air defence weapons (SADC Protocol, Article 1, 2001; United Nations General Assembly 2017).

In the context of the Sustainable Development Goals (SDGs), adopted in 2015, SDG 16, Target 16.4 focuses on identifying and reducing illicit financial and small arms flows, through strengthening recovery and return of stolen assets and combating all forms of violent crime. Thus, violence and the proliferation of illicit small arms are correlated in the sense that they reinforce each other in impeding the achievement of positive peace, justice and sustainable development hence UN member states are urged to commit themselves to reduce the proliferation of illicit arms and financial flows by 2030 (UNGA 2015; 2018: 7).

The danger of small arms and light weapons lies in the fact that they are cheap, are easily accessible, making their circulation and/or transportation clandestine and fluid. In Southern Africa the proliferation of small arms and light weapons correlates with the persistent high levels of protracted violent conflict which has resulted in high death rates, casualties and untold suffering on innocent civilians. The trade of small arms and light weapons are disruptive in the sense that they are discreet, secretive and least transparent than the trade of any other conventional weapons. Global statistics estimate the total number of SALW to be at 875 million of which 650 million likely to be used recklessly by civilians. It is also estimated that over 1000 companies in about 100 countries are engaged in the production of small arms with 30 of the 100 countries being major producers (Small Arms Survey 2018). The SADC Protocol on the Control of Firearms, ammunition and other related weapons recognise the destabilising nature of SALW as they perpetuate instability, human insecurities and untold suffering (SADC 2001).

In the context of SALW, it is important to note that it affects state and regional security hence the need for collective defence by the SADC region. The notion of state security recognises the right of all people to protection against all forms fear, intimidation, harm and/or violence manifesting from the use of small arms. Thus, the state has the responsibility to protect human citizens from the proliferation of small arms and light weapons which militates against the fulfilment of one's potential to live in peace and achievement of sustainable development as envisioned in the African Union 2030 and 2063 developmental agenda (African Union, Agenda 2063).

It is also important to note that security transcends borders and at this juncture, regionalism plays an important function in conceptualising manifestation of SALWs in the SADC region. In our attempt to conceptualise the notion of regional security and integration against SALW, the concept of "Regional Security Complex" becomes paramount. Our understanding of these concepts come from the concept of "Regional Security Community"

(RSC) propounded by Buzan and Waever (2003). The understanding of regionalism is that a group that sees itself as marginalised at home might develop a stronger sense of its identity, and thereby its dissatisfaction, by observing a comparable struggle in other states. Groups that already are discontented might learn from conflicts elsewhere how they can become less vulnerable or more autonomous and metamorphose into a non-state actor status (Buzan and Waever 2003: 29–30). Regional security complex theory' highlights threat, conflict, security and defence; "security community" emphasises conflict avoidance and management, avoidance of war and assurance of peace which also provides a rationale for studying regional dynamics of SALW in SADC countries. This school of thought therefore, suggests that regionalism signals to outside powers that a shift has taken place from political dependency of states to autonomy of collectively enhanced actors and the growth of a raised level of diplomacy and exchange in the management of security. In that regard, fighting SALW is no longer the sole duty of one sovereign state but a collective defence responsibility. The balancing rock for the regional security complexes are made to persist by constraining antagonisms and conflicts that are specific among their member states and also by behaviour of states enhancing amity among them (Buzan and Waever 2003). Geophysical closeness and historical and cultural affinities such as colonial history, cultural similarities and inter-marriages as well as cold war experiences may also be contributing factors in regional amity in the SADC region. While there may be some shades of antagonism or conflict and affinity or friendship, the idea of solidarity and collectivism overcome difference in dealing with the adages of proliferation of SALWs in the SADC Member States.

Conflict and Proliferation of SALWs in Southern Africa

Since the turn of independence for many African states in the1960s, Southern Africa has remained with the residues of endless conflicts due partly to the proliferation of SALWs. A historical analysis of conflicts in Southern Africa in the post-colonial era illuminates the proliferation of SALWs as the chief cause of protracted conflicts in the region: uncontrolled stockpiles of small arms flooded the southern African region (Onslow and van Wyk 2013). Conflict and armed struggle in Southern Africa are always intractable, and sometimes some peace agreements are short lived due to proliferation of small arms and light weapons. For example, Mozambique's opposition party, the Mozambique National Resistance (RENAMO) embarked on massive killings and re-insurgency in Northern Mozambique at the beginning of 2013 and hence reversed the gains of the long standing 1992 Rome Peace Agreement (Regalia 2017). Part of the problem stems from the fact that a staggering figure of about 5–6 million SALWs were imported to Mozambique during the civil war of 1979–1992 (Leaõ 2004; Aird et al. 2002). Despite the presence of the UN Peacekeeping Mission (ONUMOZ) to deal with issues of Disarmament,

Demobilization and Reintegration (DDR) in Mozambique, there is evidence that after 21 years of signing a Peace Agreement, conflict broke out again in Mozambique in 2013 (Mozambique, National Report on United Nations Plan of Action on SALWs 2016; Reid and Wimpy 2013). The opposition party-initiated attacks in Gorongosa and Muxungue the main base for the opposition and northern part of Mozambique targeting railway lines, trucks and civilians.

Uncontrolled arms in Southern Africa are both a source and cause of endemic conflicts in South Africa in the form of xenophobia, "resource war" in DRC and terrorist violence in Kenya by extremist groups such as Al-Shabaab. In DRC, militarisation of mineral extraction accounts for most of the conflicts in Kivu where it is estimated that there are more than 1100 types of minerals. The recruitment of child soldiers by a rebel group called M3, the Mai Mai militias and the Banyarwandan community militias in DRC to fight against the DRC government are underpinned by the availability of cheap and uncontrolled SALWs. Thus, due to armament transfers and militarisation, armed conflict in the DRC played out with so much destruction to human life, loss of business and caused daunting levels of poverty hence the perpetuation of the conflict. For example, in Beni in DRC, around 600 Congolese have died since 2014, and 64 bodies with gunshot wounds were recovered by local officials after rebels attacked the village in August 2016 (Gaffey 2016).

In 2018, Zimbabwe had a catastrophic bombing at the White City Stadium in Bulawayo where the ruling national political party, the Zimbabwe African National Union–Patriotic Front (ZANU PF) was holding its rally (The Zimbabwe Mail, 23 June 2018). The bombing injured 49 people while there were 6 casualties at the stadium. The individual(s) who launched the bomb remain unknown despite the investigations by the security personnel. This dilemma confirms in part the challenges and developing problems of proliferation of arms and light weapons in Zimbabwe which is also real in many other jurisdictions in Africa. Similar incidents of conflict are evident in Kenya where cattle rustling and fights with pastoralists at community level is rampant. For example, Mulinzi and Kurantin (2016), observes that widespread proliferation of small arms is contributing to alarming levels of armed crime, in the northern part of Kenya, which exacerbates armed cattle rustling and conflicts in these pastoralist areas. Tribal wars and conflicts who are largely involved in proliferation of small arms includes Samburu, Pokot, Turkana, Borana, Rendille, Somali and Gabbra, who are basically pastoralists and mainly keep cattle, camels, goats, sheep and donkeys. Other tribes in these areas include Teso, Njemps, Marakwet, El Molo, Tugen, Elkony, Kiprign, and Orma. Armed violence is found most frequently in the pastoralist and cross-border areas in the North Rift, north-eastern and parts of the eastern and coastal provinces. Kenya's lack of capacity at and in between border checkpoints, as well as proximity to countries experiencing varying levels of conflict, contributes to a steady flow of arms in and out of the country. Similarly, Wepundi et al. (2012) argued that, small arms play a significant role in determining the winners and losers of conflicts, and in the commission of crimes. Other than legitimate use by state personnel for security management, illicitly transferred small arms in private hand carry higher risk of misapplication for incendiary conflict and criminality against communities and innocent people. They increase the severity of conflicts and extend their duration. One of the major impacts of illicit small arms is the displacement of people, which is not only confined to hotspots of electoral violence in the central Rift Valley in the Horn of Africa.

REGIONAL DYNAMICS OF SALWs AND GOVERNANCE IN SOUTHERN AFRICA

The SADC region is bound by a familiar history of colonialism, post-colonial crises of governance and wars that ravaged the continent during that era were more inter-state and regional. However, it is interesting to note that intra-state conflicts such as communal violence and civil wars, spawned by underlying internal contradictions, have also evolved by died a natural death. It is important to underscore the regional architecture for SALWs governance and its evolution in the SADC region. Regional security is a key agenda of member states of the Southern Africa Development Commission (SADC). The SADC Treaty informed by Articles 21 and 22 and the Finance and Development Protocol (FIP) lays the foundation and call for cooperation by member states in specific areas for the advancement of trade, industry, finance, investment and regional integration. Ideally, regional cooperation provides the platform for developing a regional economic and security bloc. However, in the context of the Southern African region, the history of violent protracted conflict characterised by rampant illicit proliferation and trafficking of SALWs remains a serious threat to effective economic and security regionalisation (Stohl and Myerscough 2007). While there are a myriad of factors contributing to the proliferation of SALWs across the African continent including weak governance institutions and lack of a robust border control mechanisms have led to the advent of black market trading and smuggling in small arms (Nganga 2008).

One can trace back the roots of this regional initiative to colonial Frontline States that were put in place to deal with colonialism and later with cold war. When the SADC was formed, there was a consensus among the Member States to come up with the Southern African Regional Police Chiefs Co-operation Organisation (SARPCCO) whose primary operational mechanism in southern Africa is the prevention and fighting of cross-border crime, including the trafficking of weapons'. In addition, one can point out that the Interpol subregional bureau with its secretariat in Zimbabwe, SARPCCO is essentially a regional mechanism through which small arms and light weapons can be controlled and enforced. This gives southern African police chiefs direct access to Interpol's resources and expertise, and therefore a unique capacity for combating crime across borders and throughout the region.

SARPCCO as a regional framework is able to disseminate relevant intelligence and information to the appropriate bodies across the region and coordinate joint-enforcement strategies to combat transnational crime that involves illicit trade on SALWs. Just like the SADC Protocol on firearms, SARPCCO demonstrates that there is both the capacity and the will in the SADC to coordinate law enforcement and to combat cross-border crime and promote peace and regional stability. However, SARPCCO cannot entirely be a proxy for a regional anti-terrorism programme. For one, the DRC is not a member of SARPCCO, though an important member of SADC. Beyond that, combating terrorism in southern Africa goes beyond merely law enforcement. Financial instruments, national defence and national security agencies, and national legislatures will all be required to play important roles. Still, there are already important instruments in place that can be built upon in the creation of a regional anti-terrorism strategy.

Another key regional framework through which SALWs is regulated and governed is through the Southern African Development Community (SADC) 1 Protocol on the Control of Firearms, Ammunition and other Related Materials in August 2001 means that countries in the region are now faced with the significant challenge of implementing its numerous broad provisions. The primary objective of the SADC Protocol is to prevent, combat and eradicate the illicit manufacturing of firearms, ammunition and other related materials. According to Institute of Security Studies (ISS) (2003), the SADC Protocol of 2001 also seeks to regulate the import and export of legal small arms and thus curb the transit of these weapons into, and within, the region. In addition, the Protocol aims for the harmonisation of national legislation across member states on the manufacture and ownership of small arms and light weapons. Thus the SADC Protocol "marks a further significant development in the efforts of the states of Southern Africa to tackle the scourge of small arms and light weapons".

The regional governance architecture of SALWs also gained impetus in the year 2000 when the African leaders also committed themselves through the Bamako Declaration which also has a bearing on peace and security for the SADC countries. The Bamako Declaration compels Member States to combating the illicit proliferation, circulation and trafficking of small arms, light weapons and landmines at the subregional and continental levels. In essence, the Bamako Declaration echoes an African Common Position on the Illicit Proliferation, Circulation and Trafficking on Small Arms and Light Weapons (Bamako Declaration) adopted in December 2000. The ISS report of 2003 noted that the Declaration was developed to: "promote measures aimed at restoring peace, security and confidence among, and, between Member States with a view to reducing the resort to arms; promote structures and processes to strengthen democracy, the observance of human rights, the rule of law and good governance, as well as economic recovery and growth; and importantly, to promote comprehensive solutions to the problem of the illicit proliferation circulation and trafficking of small arms and light weapons that, include both control and reduction, as well as supply and demand aspects; that are based on the coordination and harmonization of the efforts of the Member States at regional, continental and international levels and which involve civil society in support of the central role of governments".

GOVERNANCE AND INSTITUTIONS FOR PEACE AND SECURITY

The SADC as an institution of regional governance and developmental body expanded group of member states and a broader agenda of regional integration, covering issues such as trade, transport, infrastructure peace and security, corruption, governance, hence the SADC Protocol of Firearms. Vanheukelom and Bertelsmann-Scott (2016), note that decision-making in SADC rather than being monopolised by the country chairing the Summit or the Organ for Politics Defence and Security (hereafter the Organ), (SADC's two key decision-making bodies in terms of peace and security), decision-making within SADC as regards for peace and security matters happens on the basis of consensus. Therefore, cooperation on matters of SALWs come with a sense of collectivism in the SADC region. In addition, the Ministerial Committee preparing and coordinating the work of the Organ is also a collective effort which in this case provide a framework through which Member States will be guided in preventing the effects of SALWs in the region (Desmidt 2017). For example, an Extra-Ordinary SADC Troika met in Harare on 20 May 2020 to deliberate on the Mozambique conflict in Cabo Delgado that was attended by Botswana, Mozambique, Zambia and Zimbabwe (SADC News, May 2020). These governance institutions further demonstrate the availability of regional powers and governance which also play a critical role in dealing with SALWs in the SADC (Saurombe 2012). One limitation that Nathan (2016) observed is that despite the SADC relatively strong protocols on security and democracy and elections, it operates on the pillars of absolute sovereignty and solidarity, principles which are also in SADC's protocols, and member states are unwilling to surrender any measure of sovereignty.

The Bamako Declaration emphasises the need to "enhance the capacity of Member States to identify, seize and destroy illicit weapons and to put in place measures to control the circulation, possession, transfer and use of small arms and light weapons; promote a culture of peace by encouraging education and public awareness programmes on the problems of the illicit proliferation, circulation and trafficking of small arms and light weapons, involving all sectors of society; institutionalise national and regional programmes for action aimed at preventing, controlling and eradicating the illicit proliferation, circulation and trafficking of small arms and light weapons in Africa. While, the SADC Member States are bound by other pieces of laws and policies as well as the continent wide frameworks such as the African Union Peace and Security Council (AU-PSC) and its Peace and Security Architecture (PSA) together with the AU's Vision to Silence the Gun by 2020, we will zero on more on the above discussed framework by the SADC.

Regional Initiatives and Agreements for Combatting SALWs in Southern Africa

Recognising that many challenges that the continent is facing because of the continued proliferation and illegal of SALWs to perpetuate heinous human rights violations and criminal activities the 28th Ordinary Session of the Assembly of the Union, held in January 2017, adopted the African Union (AU) Master Roadmap of Practical Steps to Silence the Guns in Africa by Year 2020 (AU Roadmap) (AU 2016). This was done through the signing of a memorandum of agreement whose mandate is to scale up cooperation and commitment among AU member states to tackle the trafficking of illicit small arms and light weapons and violent conflicts. The AU roadmap recognises that while the nature, causes and actors of many violent conflicts on the continent have changed the widespread availability and illegal use of small arms and light weapons has created new complex emergencies whose effects perniciously result in untold suffering, loss of life and disruption of all efforts to achieving positive peace on the continent. Informed by the small arms survey of 2019 the African Union has managed to systematically map out the routes used to traffic illicit small arms across the porous borders of those countries that are prone to illicit flows (Florquin et al. 2019). Despite these progressive efforts consolidating efforts towards creation of regional economic blocks to boost Africa's developmental agenda on trade and economic remains an aspiration because of the weak border controls, corrupt leadership and fragile governance systems that exacerbate multiple insecurities.

As demonstrated by Hennop et al. (2011) and Berman and Maze (2016), an integrated regional framework for SALWs policies is necessary in many SADC countries have weak domestic gun regulatory systems in addition to having porous borders which facilitate illicit movement of small arms and light weapons. As such, SADC has made tremendous efforts in addressing the security threats of SALWs through the establishment of progressive subregional agreements. Two instruments are worth considering here. (a) the Nairobi Protocol for the Prevention, Control and Reduction of Small Arms and Light Weapons signed in 2004, by eleven states in the Great Lakes Region and the Horn of Africa; (b) the Protocol on the Control of Firearms, Ammunition and Other Related Materials in the Southern African Development Community (SADC) region which came into force in 2004.

SADC Firearms Protocol

The SADC Firearms Protocol requires each member state to:

- Enact national legal measures to ensure proper controls over the manufacturing, possession and use of firearms and ammunition;

- Promote legal uniformity and minimum standards as to the manufacture, control, possession, import, export and transfer of firearms and ammunition;
- Ensure the standardised marking of firearms at the time of manufacture;
- Destroy surplus, redundant or obsolete state-owned firearms and related materials;
- Become party to international instruments relating to the prevention, combating and eradication of illicit manufacturing of, excessive and destabilising accumulation of, trafficking in, possession and use of firearms, ammunition and other related materials;
- Establish as criminal offences the illicit manufacturing, possession, trafficking and use of firearms, ammunition and other related materials;
- Establish national inventories of firearms held by security forces and other state bodies and to enhance their capacity to manage and maintain their secure storage; and
- Develop and improve transparency in firearms accumulation, flow and policies relating to civilian owned firearms and to establish national firearms databases to facilitate the exchange of information on firearms imports, exports and transfers.

The SADC Firearms Protocol commits member states to standards relating to, inter alia, the coordination of procedures for the import, export and transit of firearms shipments. The SADC region has recently begun to address the topic of arms transfer controls and the problems that occur when there are minimal national regulations to control the legal, and to curtail the illicit, transfer of weapons. This will help the SADC to institute measures, laws and policies harmonised to the Protocol in regulation firearms manufacturing and trade.

Impact of Proliferation of SALWs on and Regional Economic Cooperation and Security in Southern Africa

The proliferation of SALWs come with a plethora of human and economic costs in the SADC region. SALWs cause deaths, increase internal displacement, fan terrorism, xenophobia, cut down on smooth trade and business, undermine peace and security as well as derailing economic progress which will be discussed in detail. One of the fundamental impacts of SALWs in the SADC region is devastating development of intractable conflicts and notable genocidal conflicts or ethnic-based conflicts such as the Matabeleland genocide in Zimbabwe. Such conflicts are characterised by the fact that they involve the massive use of hate and hateful speech, they spread with extremely high speed, cause immense displacement of people, create an atmosphere of fear and confusion, have a high death toll within relatively short periods and are fought without the use of sophisticated and heavy weapons. The catalyst of all these man-made human catastrophes is small arms and light weapons (SALWs).

According to the Small Arms Survey (2018), the continent's armed forces and law enforcement agencies hold less than 11 million small arms. Among the 40 million civilian-held firearms in Africa, 5,841,200 are recorded as being officially registered, while 16,043,800 are unregistered, with the status of the remainder remaining unclear (Small Arms Survey 2018).

Table 46.1 illustrates the regional distribution of arms held by civilians but these do not take into account those that are acquired by clandestine actors using illicit means; such difficulties in establishing the exact figures of SALWs also permeates down to the problems associated with gun licensing and possession. Given the complexity associated with national regulation relating to possession of SALWs, many citizens and organisations who own guns through "black market" will refuse to report to the state. In addition to municipal regulation of guns which is the prerogative of the state, African states are part of regional and international governance systems that seek to foster management of arms and weapons through coordinated activities and strategies.

There are also some economic costs that come with proliferation of SALWs. For example, statistics by the World Bank indicates how an economy affected by civil war and proliferation of SALWs declines by around 2.2% per annum relative to its underlying growth path (Reference required here). As Paul Collier observes, even after a decade of civil war, a state will have a 20% lower income than it would have had under peaceful conditions (Collier 1999). The SADC region experienced rapid economic decline and crisis of security as a result of conflicts in the region. This was compounded by the heavy proliferation and exploitative nature of SALW which impacted negatively on trade, development, regional security and its integration. This is because SALWs are often used as instruments to organise and mobilise the illegal trafficking and plundering of a country's mineral and natural resources. The looting of mineral assets as well as of precious renewable natural resources helps the

Table 46.1 Estimated African subregional distribution of civilian firearms, 2017

UN subregion	Population	Number of civilian-held firearms	Civilian-held firearms per 100 population
Africa total	1,246,505,000	40,009,000	3.2
Eastern Africa	416,676,000	7,802,000	1.9
Middle Africa	161,237,000	4,981,000	3.1
Northern Africa	232,186,000	10,241,000	4.4
Southern Africa	63,854,000	6,012,000	9.4
Western Africa	372,551,000	10,972,000	2.9

Source Small Arms Survey (2018)

rebels to finance their war efforts, not to mention the destruction of institutions and social capital, crystallising in mistrust and the disrespect for social and legal norms, and provoking continued misuse of SALWs (Heinrich 2006).

As Heinrich (2006) points out compared to other developing regions, conflicts in Africa are among the most enduring in the world and the devastating human toll accounting for all conflict-related deaths in Africa. In addition, Africa accounts for over eight million refugees and displaced persons due to protracted violent wars Sub-Saharan Africa in particular remains the most adversely affected by massive proliferation, trafficking and illegal use of SALWs, a situation which perpetuates the fuelling of the protracted armed violent conflicts, poverty and underdevelopment. In the context of SADC, case evidence on the proliferation of SALWs in protracted violent conflicts and wars in Angola, Mozambique, Zimbabwe and Democratic Republic of Congo continue to spark refugee flows, due to the depressed economic situations which spark cycles of cultures of violence and impunity which in turn deter investors from doing business in the conflicted and unstable environments (Bromley and Holton 2010). Even countries such as Kenya, Rwanda and South Africa that are no longer involved in violent conflict remain on the radar of experiencing some of highest mortality and morbidity rates in the region due to uncontrolled use of small arms and light weapons to perpetuate armed criminality.

The rampant and lethal illegal use of SALWs impacts negatively on the trade and development of already weak and fragile economies as it blocks investment forcing countries to divert the meagre economic resources attempting to intervene thereby increasing military expenditure and hyperinflation. SALWs also exacerbate illicit financial flows through fraudulent trade deals which deprives the already weak developing countries. This leads to human rights violations through perpetuation of mass killings, forced displacement, sexual violence on women and children in addition to forced recruitment of children into armed criminal crimes. This leads to vicious cycles of violence and stagnation of development.

From a gender perspective the proliferation of SALWs in the Southern African region has created inequitable and exclusive forms of trade and development as most men have the monopoly over the violence that manifest from the illicit and exploitative nature of SALWs. For example, Gender-Based Violence (GBV) has increased in DRC. Gender-based violence (GBV) is widespread especially in conflict situations in North Kivu in DRC. It is estimated that about 45.6% of African women have experienced GBV, compared to 35% globally. The DRC's Ministry of Gender estimates that there were 15,645 cases of sexual violence in 2012, with women, girls and boys constituting 98% of survivors (UNFPA 2013). In conflict situations, GBV is generally associated with armed groups and combatants who use SALWs to humiliate, intimidate, displace and traumatise individuals and communities. For instance, earlier this decade DRC became known as the world's rape capital, with an estimated 48 women raped per hour by rebels and Congolese soldiers at the height of violent conflict in 2013 (Bradley 2013). But statistics barely reveal the contribution of uncontrolled arms to GBV in Africa Again, just in a day on 23 June, almost 5000 people were forced to flee their homes in North Kivu province, due to ongoing fighting between two armed groups in Mweso town. Attackers looted schools where people had fled to.

As a result, this conflict is inextricably linked to underdevelopment as foreign direct investment is demobilised to other countries, while illicit financial flows also become the order of the day. One direct impact of uncontrolled SALWs is the recruitment of child soldiers in armed struggle in DRC and displacement of persons in Cabo Delgado in Northern Mozambique. In addition, as of July 2016, the total figure of DRC refugees in neighbouring countries was estimated at 450,474, while the number of registered refugees in Congo was put at 387,963 (UNHCR 2016). Child soldiers have also been on the rise.

Manifestation of SALWs at Community Level: Case of Machete Wars in Small Scale Mining Areas in Southern Africa

The Southern African region continue to suffer from significant levels of illegal and illicit use of SALWs to perpetuate terrorist activities resulting in high-level of loss of human life, human rights violations and traumatic human suffering. Experience from the field indicate that while Zimbabwe is well known as a country with some the largest pure gold deposits in the world ranging from 65 to 95%, with Manicaland one of the third largest provinces in the country accounting for pure hard rock deposits ranging from 72 to 96% (United Nations Industrial Development Organization 2018). The pervasive informality of the artisanal gold mining popularly known as "makorokoza" meaning illegal, informal, unregulated and uncontrolled give rise to serious competition among the gold panners or miners. The turf wars that characterise much of this informal mining leads to the illicit acquisition of small arms such as machetes, spears, shovels and catapults which are used as defense mechanisms against mafia miner competitors as well as tools used to clear the bushy areas where mining takes place. Experience from the field indicates how the small-scale artisanal miners are caught between hard rock and space in the sense that possession of these small arms makes a difference between life and death, striking a fortune and poverty. For them to survive the brutality of the mining jungle where those who get gold deposits from the mining shafts have to protect themselves and the precious mineral from being stolen by bullies who prey on anyone emerging out of the mining shafts with the precious mineral (Zenda 2019). As such, artisanal mining in Zimbabwe makes it incredibly attractive to illicit actors who are willing to sacrifice human lives over the precious and lucrative mineral. Thus, machetes in particular are not only used to fend off marauders, but are frequently used to settle off disputes over ownership of mining shafts and savage revenge attacks against artisanal gang rivals. A field interview with one of the artisanal miners who survived a machete attack but had his knee permanent damaged indicated that the idea is to ferociously attack your enemy such that even if they survive they would be unable to mobilise reinforcements because the machete would have settled the bitter grudge.

Similarly, a number of foreign-sponsored militia groups including the Ugandan-based Allied Democratic Forces (ADF), the Democratic Forces for the Liberation of Rwanda (FDLR) and the Lord Resistance Army (LRA) and the M23 continue to destabilise the peace and security in the eastern Democratic Republic of Congo, committing serious human rights violations and atrocities through assassinations, hacking and beheading of local community leaders, civilians including women and children with machetes while plundering mineral sources to fuel war economies (Bureau of Counter Terrorism 2013). This is compounded by the fact DRC is a vast country which shares borders with nine countries namely: Angola, Burundi, Central African Republic, The Republic of the Congo, Rwanda, South Sudan, Tanzania, Uganda and Zambia many of which have their fair share of protracted violent conflicts spanning decades. Apart from weakening regional security the porous borders pose a serious threat and insecurity of small arms and light weapons trafficking spreading throughout the region (Alusala 2015; Berman and Maze 2016).

Conclusion

In conclusion, the proliferation of SALWs in the SADC region is visible due to increasing levels of human insecurity, conflict in countries like Mozambique and DRC which are more inclined to natural resources. Despite all these challenges that range from humanitarian crisis through economic decline and poverty to compromised regional security and stability, the SADC has a number of frameworks in place to respond to SALWs. For example, the SADC Protocol on Firearms and the Bamako Declaration are legally binding instruments that can be used to promote coordination among Member States in the SADC region to combat illicit trade in small arms and light weapons. Despite the presence of regional frameworks and governance systems in place, the SADC Members States still suffer from reliable information, statistical data and analyses are critical to understanding the extent, nature and impact of illicit small arms proliferation; identifying and developing relevant and effective measures to deal with the issue; and monitoring and evaluating their impact. This calls for the need to raise awareness about the dangers and consequences of uncontrolled trade in small arms among governments, companies and civil society realising that there is no quick fix to the multiple complex challenges of illicit arms flows and their consequential effects. Emphasis should be on the human security, public health and economic costs of small arms trade which far outweigh the economic benefits. To enhance efforts of the African Union peace and security roadmap AU member states need to show serious political will and commitment to tackle the scourge of illicit SALWs flows. There is need to diligently follow the practical steps outlined in the AU roadmap including building and strengthening the capacity of AU member states in managing small weapons stockpiles, record keeping, monitoring, tracking and destruction of illicit weapons which cause a threat to human security. This calls for increased regional cooperation among Sub-Saharan governments, security–sector organisations and partner organisations in exchanging intelligence information in the field of prevention of armed crime and illicit cross-border trafficking in SALWs. Evidence from different Mozambique and the DRC reveal the need for coordinated innovative and proactive approaches to combat the trafficking and proliferation of small arms and light weapons and the atrocious human right violations and killings, displacements affecting innocent civilians and communities.

While recognising the global and regional efforts to tackle illicit SALWs flows, measuring progress towards achieving SDG goal number 16 remains a challenge because the secretive nature of this phenomena, its complexity, multifaceted and context-specific nature. It therefore becomes imperative that in order to enhance counterterrorism emanating from smuggling of SALWs requires the creation and strengthening of a multifaceted border security system which includes information sharing and cooperation aimed at countering trafficking of SALWs. Through regional cooperation governments of violent prone countries like the DRC need to seriously cooperate through signing peace and security agreements with neighbouring countries such as the Central African Republic, Uganda, Rwanda and South Sudan to counter the proliferation of SALWs through the porous borders. Given that many of the violent conflicts are a manifestation of youth disenchantment, weak leadership, bad governance and faulty development policies for economic recovery to increase employment opportunities and create alternative livelihoods for ex-combatants, women and youth it becomes imperative that countries in Sub-Saharan Africa take account of the anti-developmental effects of criminal violence which is fuelled by SALWs.

References

African Union (AU). (2016). *Master Roadmap of Practical Steps to Silence the Guns in Africa by Year 2020*. Lusaka Master Roadmap 2016.

African Union Commission. (2015). *African Union Agenda 2063: The Africa We Want*. Retrieved from http://www.agenda2063.au.int. Accessed 13 November 2019.

Aird, S., Efraime, B. J., & Errante, A (2002). *Mozambique: The Battle Continues for Former Child Soldiers* (Youth Advocate Program International Resource Paper). Youth Advocate Program.

Aljazeera. (2019, November 23). ISIL Is Not Dead, It Just Moved to Africa. Opinion by Rashid Abdallah.

Alusala, N. (2015). *Assessment Report on Cross-border Small Arms and Light Weapons Trafficking Between the Democratic Republic of the Congo and the Republic of Burundi*. London: Action on Armed Violence. December.

Berman, E., & Maze, K. (2016, May). *Regional Organizations and the UN Programme of Action on Small Arms* (PoA), (2nd edn.). Handbook. Geneva: Small Arms Survey.

Bradley, M. (2013, November 13). *Sexual and Gender-Based Violence in the Democratic Republic of Congo: Opportunities for Progress as M23 Disarms? Africa in Focus*. https://www.brookings.edu/blog/africa-in-focus/2013/11/13/sexual-and-gender-based-violence-in-the-democratic-republic-of-the-congoopportunities-for-progress-as-m23-disarms/. Accessed 28 October 2019.

Bromley, M., & Holtom, P. (2010). *Arms Transfer to the Democratic Republic of the Congo: Assessing the System of Arms Transfer Notifications, 2008–10* (SIPRI Background Paper). Signalistgatan 9, Solma, Sweden. Retrieved from: http://www.sipri.org/sites/defaults/files/files/misc/SIPRIBP1010a.pdf. Accessed 3 November 2019.

Bureau of Counter Terrorism. (2013). *Chapter 2, Country Reports: Africa Overview*. Retrieved from http://www.2009-2017.state.gov/j/ct/rls/crt/2013/224820.htm. Accessed 2 November 2019.

Buzan, B., & Waever, O. (2003). *Regions and Powers*. Cambridge: CUP.

Collier, P. (1999, April). *Doing Well Out of War*. Retrieved from: http://www.worldbank.org/research/conflict/papers/econagendas.pdf, 24 October 2019.

Desmidt, S. (2017). *Understanding the Southern African Development Community Peace and Security: How to Fight Old and New demons?* Political Economy Dynamics of Regional Organisations (PEDRO) Paper Series. European Centre for Development Policy Management.

Florquin, N., Lipott, S., & Wairagu, F. (2019) *Small Arms Survey: Weapons Compass: Mapping Illicit Small Arms Flows in Africa*. Report January 2019.

Gaffey, C. (2016, August 15). DR Congo: Ugandan Rebels Blamed for Beni Massacre, Killing at Least 30. *Newsweek*. http://europe.newsweek.com/dr-congo-ugandan-rebels-blamed-beni-massacre-killing-least-30-490304?rm=eu. Accessed 29 June 2020.

Heinrich, M. (2006). Small Arms and Development: The Results of the UN Small Arms Review Conference 2006. *International Peace Bureau*. Zurich, Switzerland. Retrieved from http://www.ipb.org, 25 October 2019.

Hennop, E., Jefferson, C., & McLean, A. (2011). *The Challenge to Control South Africa's Borders and Borderline*. Pretoria: Institute for Security Studies.

ISS. (2003). *Implementing the Southern Africa Firearms Protocol: Identifying Challenges and Priorities* (ISS Paper 83).

Leaõ, A. (2004). Civilian Firearms. *Hide and Seek: Taking Account of Small Arms in Southern Africa*. Pretoria: Institute for Security Studies.

Mozambique. (2016). Manufacture. *National Report of Mozambique on Its Implementation of the United Nations Programme of Action to Prevent, Combat and Eradicate the Illicit Trade in Small Arms and Light Weapons in All Its Aspects (UNPoA)*. New York NY: Perman.

Mulinzi, M., & Kurantin. N. (2016). Challenges of Proliferation of Small Arms and Light Weapons in Northern Region of Kenya. *Journal of African Foreign Affairs*, 4(2), 65–85.

Nairobi Protocol. (2004). *Nairobi Protocol for the Prevention, Control and Reduction of Small Arms and Light Weapons in the Great Lakes Region and the Horn of Africa*. Retrieved from http://www.poaiss.org/RegionalOrganizations/RECSA/Nairobi%20Protocol.pdf. Accessed 2 November 2019.

Nganga, F. C. (2008). *Effects of Proliferation of Small Arms in Sub-Saharan Africa*. US Army War College, Carlisle Barracks, Pennsylvania 17013.

Onslow, S., & Van Wyk, A.-M. (2013). From the Nuclear Laager to the Nonproliferation Club: South Africa and the NPT. *South African Historical Journal, 67*(1), 32–46.

Regalia, S. (2017). The Resurgence of Conflict in Mozambique. Ghosts from the Past and Brakes to Peaceful Democracy (IFRI, Sub-Saharan Africa Program).

Reid, I. D., & Wimpy, C. (2013). Defining Opposition: An Interview with Afonso Dhlakama of RENAMO. Ufahamu: *A Journal of African Studies, 37*(1), 375–393.

SADC. (2001). *Declaration Concerning Firearms, Ammunition and Other Related Materials in the Southern African Development Community*. Retrieved from http://www.sadc.int/files/4113/5292/8379/Declaration_concerning_Firearms_Ammunition_and_other_related_materials2001.pdf. Accessed 1 November 2019.

SADC Communique. (2020, May 20). *Communiqué of the Extraordinary Organ Troika Plus Republic of Mozambique Summit of Heads of State and Government Harare—Zimbabwe*. https://www.sadc.int/news-events/news/extraordinary-sadc-organ-troika-plus-republic-mozambique-summit-heads-state-and-government-held-harare-zimbabwe/. Accessed 5 July 2020.

SADC Protocol. (2001). *Protocol on the Control of Firearms, Ammunition, and Other Related Materials in the Southern African Development Community (SADC) Region*.

Saurombe, A. (2012). The Role of SADC Institutions in Implementing SADC Treaty Provisions Dealing with Regional Integration. *PER, 15*(2).

Small Arms Survey. (2013). *Small Arms Survey*. Cambridge University Press.

Small Arms Survey. (2016, May 25). *Definitions of Small Arms and Light Weapons*. Retrieved from http://www.smallarmssurvey.org/weapons-and-markets/definitions.html. Accessed 28 October 2019.

Small Arms Survey. (2018). *Global Firearms Holdings Database*. Geneva: Small Arms Survey. Retrieved from: http://www.smallarmssurvey.org. Accessed 28 October 2019.

Small Arms Survey and the African Union (AU). (2018). *Country Responses to the Questionnaire on Mapping Illicit Arms Flows in Africa*. Geneva. Small Arms Survey. Retrieved from http://www.smallarmssurvey.org. Accessed 28 October 2019.

Stohl, R., & Myerscough, R. (2007, May). Sub-Saharan Small Arms: The Damage Continues. *Current History, 106,* 230.

The Zimbabwe Mail. (2018, June 23). *8 Injured in Assassination Plot on Zimbabwe's President*. Retrieved 7 November 2019.

UN Comtrade (United Nations Commodity Trade Statistics Database). (2019). *Small Arms Survey. UN Comtrade Database*. Accessed 10 November 2019.

UNFPA. (2013, November 6). *Act Now, Act Big to End Sexual Violence in the Democratic Republic of the Congo*. http://www.unfpa.org/press/act-now-act-big-end-sexual-violence-democratic-republic-congo. Accessed 1 July 2020.

UNHCR. (2016). *DRC Regional Refugee Response: Regional Overview*. http://data.unhcr.org/drc/regional.php. Accessed 29 June 2020.

United Nations General Assembly (UNGA). (1997). General and Complete Disarmament: Small Arms. A/52/298 of 27 August.

United Nations General Assembly (UNGA). (2015). *Transforming Our World: The 2030 Agenda for Sustainable Development*, Resolution 70/1 of 25 September. A/RES/70/1 of 21 October.

United Nations General Assembly (UNGA). (2017). Resolution 71/313 of 6 July. A/RES/71/313 of 10 July.

United Nations General Assembly (UNGA). (2018). *Outcome Document of the Third United Nations Conference to Review Progress Made in the Implementation of the Programme of Action to Prevent, Combat and Eradicate the Illicit Trade in Small Arms and Light Weapons in All its Aspects*. A/CONF.192/2018/RC/3of 6 July.

United Nations Industrial Development Organization (UNIDO). (2018, April). *Follow the Money: Zimbabwe: A Rapid Assessment of Gold Supply Chains and Financial Flows Linked to Artisanal and Small—Scale Mining in Zimbabwe*. Retrieved from http://www.globalinitiative.net. Accessed 10 October 2019.

Vanheukelom, J., & Bertelsmann-Scott, T. (2016). *The Political Economy of Regional Integration in Africa—The Southern African Development Community* (SADC). Maastricht: ECDPM.

Wepundi, N., Kabuu, M., & del Frate, A. (2012). A Study by the Small Arms Survey and Kenya National Focus Point on Small Arms and Light Weapons with Support from the Ministry of Foreign Affairs of Denmark Special Report June 2012. enlargethispage-24pt

Zenda, C. (2019, January). In Zimbabwe's Gold Wars, Miners Wield Machetes for Safety. *News/Magazine*. Retrieved from: http://www.trtworld.com/magazine/in-zimbabwe-s-gold-wars-miners-wield-machetes-for-safety-229933. Accessed 7 November 2019.

Pamela Machakanja is a Professor of Peace, Leadership and Security Studies and the Dean in the College of Business, Peace Leadership and Governance at Africa University, Africa University, Zimbabwe. She holds a Ph.D. in Peace, Conflict and Security Studies from the University of Bradford in the United Kingdom, a Master of Arts degree in Peace and Conflict Resolution, a Diploma in Research Methods in Social Sciences and a Diploma in Leadership and Policy Development all from the University of Bradford in the United Kingdom. She also holds a Masters degree in Educational Psychology and a Bachelor of Education degree from the University of Zimbabwe; a Diploma and Advanced Diploma in Negotiation Skills from the International Negotiation Academy in South Africa. Her expansive multidisciplinary research interests include peace and conflict issues, gender equality, state capture and corruption, human security and the rights of vulnerable groups including minority groups; democratisation processes in post-conflict transitional societies, gender and post-colonial discourses, and transitional justice processes. Prof Machakanja has written three books, fourteen book chapters and twenty-four journal articles in international peer-reviewed journals. Over the years Pamela has developed skills in innovative competency-based curriculum development that integrate technological content knowledge that facilitate innovative e-pedagogical models in peace, human rights, gender and development.

Chupicai Shollah Manuel is a Ph.D. Candidate in Governance and Political Transformation, with a Master in Peace and Governance, Master in Intellectual Property Law and Bachelor of Social Sciences in Sociology and Economics. Currently affiliated to Africa University as a Lecturer in the area of Peace and Security, Governance, Human Rights and International Relations.

INDEX

A
Abeokuta, 522
Abia State, 236
Abnormal States, 78, 80
Absence, 63, 96, 98, 99, 116, 121, 164, 171, 192, 248, 249, 328, 347, 433, 454, 502, 535, 542, 594, 689, 708, 710, 727, 761, 766, 779, 825, 875, 899, 921
Abuja, 124, 228, 238, 239, 326, 362, 363, 486, 524, 554, 752, 783, 786, 917, 942
Abyssinia, 722, 723
Acquired Immium Deficiency Syndrome (AIDS)/(HIV/AIDs), 92, 188, 402, 601
Acquisition, 5, 19, 44, 127, 128, 134, 189, 209, 230, 268, 331, 340, 367, 373, 374, 376, 383, 385, 393, 394, 396, 404, 440, 447, 495, 520, 574, 586, 655, 659, 666, 669, 671, 708, 718, 721, 722, 729, 772, 780, 787, 788, 819, 834, 869, 914, 984, 995
  of SALWs, 7, 50, 147, 194, 268, 303, 309, 378, 432, 916
Actors, 3, 6–9, 11, 25, 33, 41, 48, 50, 57–60, 73, 97, 99, 103, 107, 114, 115, 117–122, 133, 134, 138, 140, 141, 150, 161–165, 167, 170, 171, 175, 179–181, 187, 189, 194–196, 220, 223, 228, 230, 239, 252, 259, 268, 271, 295, 296, 299, 303, 304, 307, 310, 312, 324, 328, 331, 345, 347, 373–375, 393, 397, 401, 403, 412, 414, 419–421, 430, 431, 433, 441, 444, 445, 447, 454, 456, 458–461, 464, 474, 484, 487, 492, 496, 508, 511, 532, 548, 571, 587, 594, 599, 602, 615, 617, 633, 637, 640, 649, 651, 653, 654, 659, 666, 682, 683, 685–688, 690, 697, 698, 700, 702, 708, 711, 717, 740, 745, 779, 794, 797, 806, 808, 809, 823, 827, 828, 847, 859, 864, 868–872, 875, 889, 895, 897, 898, 909, 915, 919, 922, 923, 929, 937, 976, 991, 993, 995
  in conflicts in Africa, 142
Adaka Boro Avengers (ABA), 784
Aden Hashi Ayro, 867
Advocacy, 106, 405, 469, 502, 510–513, 534, 554, 579, 893, 918, 942, 944
Afghanistan, 6, 7, 49, 76, 199, 507, 613, 616, 791, 810, 864, 929
Africa's
  development, 385
  experience, 24, 25, 823, 825
  merchants, 35
  terrains of conflicts, 19
  top, 446
  topography, 150
  ungoverned spaces, 11, 162–164, 170, 171, 181
  weapons, 274

African
  borders, 19, 63, 114, 116, 172, 190, 273, 293, 416, 539, 556, 581, 658
  Commission on Nuclear Energy (AFCONE), 127
  countries, 1, 2, 6, 9, 12, 22–26, 31, 35, 42, 49, 60, 61, 100, 118, 119, 121, 127, 128, 151, 172, 196, 211, 213, 216, 230, 231, 233, 273–276, 278, 285, 286, 289, 291, 292, 295, 296, 309, 327, 346, 350, 358, 366, 373, 378, 386, 394, 416, 420, 436, 440, 474, 475, 478–480, 482, 487, 488, 490, 491, 494–496, 503, 504, 507–509, 512, 513, 529, 535, 542, 545–548, 550, 555, 556, 559–562, 567, 575, 582, 589, 590, 593, 597, 600, 609–612, 617, 620, 621, 628, 630, 631, 636, 638, 641, 642, 648, 654–656, 660–662, 666, 681, 713, 714, 726, 743, 745, 751, 755, 805, 826, 856, 909, 935, 938, 942
  democracies, 25
  Development Bank (ADB), 571
  economy, 276, 278, 279, 660
  elites, 24, 379
  National Congress (ANC), 509, 630, 823, 828
  Nuclear-Weapons-Free-Zone Treaty.. See Pelindaba Treaty
  Sahel region, 18
  societies, 29, 75, 117, 118, 302, 367, 374, 377, 378, 385, 400, 490
  states, 2, 19, 24, 30, 81, 87, 95, 114, 118, 126, 127, 189–191, 196, 201, 215, 231, 235, 236, 239, 249, 270, 275–277, 286, 301, 302, 312, 324–326, 346, 374, 386, 413, 414, 416, 419, 436, 440, 441, 443, 444, 446, 448, 459, 476, 485, 491, 502–504, 506, 509, 511–513, 520, 526, 527, 533, 540, 542, 545, 547, 548, 551, 554, 556, 557, 559, 561, 562, 587, 591, 612, 617, 620, 641, 649, 670, 672, 690, 754, 762, 805, 923, 929, 951, 986, 993; and government, 196, 388, 448
  Subregional distribution, 33
  traditional institutions, 525, 531
  Union.. See African Union (AU); Organisation of African Unity (OAU)
Africanistan.. See Failed states
African Union (AU), 31, 33, 61–63, 89, 116, 120, 124–128, 180, 201, 209, 464, 476, 479, 545, 557, 562, 571, 586, 603, 621, 666, 744, 754, 804, 813, 853, 857, 859, 867, 917, 974, 983, 990, 991, 997
  report, 135, 138, 159
AFRICOM, 748
Age
  distribution, 377
Agents
  of SALWs, 219, 642
Agitators, 456, 716, 781
Agrarians, 210
Agreements, 100, 115, 128, 129, 272, 307, 324, 374, 403, 412, 458, 462, 509, 544, 553, 554, 619, 686, 691, 694, 699, 702, 722, 806, 889, 897, 958, 986, 991, 997
Air
  networks, 570
AK-47, 33, 100, 193, 231, 235, 291, 295, 346, 375, 376, 379, 418, 420, 458, 478–480, 503, 519, 547, 652, 653, 655, 659, 660, 663, 783, 784, 791, 823, 838, 851, 853, 912, 935, 965, 967, 969, 971, 975
Akwa Ibom, 237, 362, 916
Albania, 57, 103, 507, 595
Alexander the Great, 69, 74, 76, 90
Ali Modu Sheriff, 117
al Ittihad, 727
Al Jazeera, 178, 770, 772
Alpha Oumar Konare, 577
Al Qaeda in the Islamic Maghreb (AQIM), 167, 179, 233, 384, 438, 599, 657, 746, 752, 765–767, 771, 788, 803, 810, 813, 814, 816, 915, 938

Al-Shabaab, 25, 26, 56, 197, 231, 233, 388, 413, 417, 419, 436, 438, 503, 599, 656, 657, 867, 868, 987
al Shabaab, 727, 728, 733, 734
Al-Sharaha, 384
Alternative security providers, 610, 613
Amasi, Gabriel, 122
Ambazonia, 20
American
  Global War on terror (GWOT), 614
Ammunition
  and explosives, 192, 413, 456, 780, 886, 891
  in Africa, 116, 234
  manufacturing capacities in Africa, 31
Amnesty
  International, 399, 405, 477, 493, 540, 545, 546, 585, 592, 595, 618, 851, 854
  program, 128, 295, 456, 531, 599, 600, 636, 638, 784, 785, 795, 836, 838
Anambra, 294, 361, 362, 507, 916
Anarchy, 609, 727, 761, 771, 772, 806, 863, 866, 867, 870, 871
Angola, 49, 55, 89, 137, 142, 253, 254, 256, 257, 270, 274, 278, 305, 307, 310, 311, 325, 346, 440, 475, 480, 481, 503, 508, 572, 588, 590, 591, 593, 594, 599, 613, 615, 662, 663, 783, 823, 824, 994, 996
Annan, Kofi, 23, 100, 220, 400, 410, 458, 481
Ansar al Dine, 167, 179, 915
Anti-Balaka, 179, 397, 502, 617, 681, 683, 695, 698, 699
Anwar Sadat, 708
An Yue Jiang, 508
Apartheid, 289, 307, 385, 479, 480, 819, 820, 823, 824, 826, 830, 831, 835
Arab
  merchants, 519, 525
  spring, 118, 150, 273, 546, 617, 707–710, 712–715, 743, 937, 954
Architecture, 8, 12, 26, 54, 63, 114, 251, 448, 636, 894, 940, 941, 988–990

Areas Affected, 357
Armed
  banditry, 42, 83, 99, 101, 196, 201, 224, 239, 266, 273, 295, 306, 562, 567, 934, 943, 967
  conflicts; in Nigeria, 25, 32, 54, 99, 101, 114, 134, 191, 218, 232, 235, 266, 276, 278, 293, 295, 345, 357, 359, 362, 364, 387, 413, 440, 442, 460, 474, 496, 502, 533, 559, 586, 598, 601
  forces, 2, 8, 25, 26, 29, 31, 41, 58, 138, 172, 173, 177, 196, 232, 271, 365, 381, 397, 401, 430, 431, 445, 466, 467, 540, 545, 595, 597, 614, 660, 670, 671, 688, 695, 700, 701, 728, 733, 746, 747, 751, 765, 771, 772, 854, 855, 968, 993
  groups, 26, 56, 58, 104, 117, 118, 122, 138, 192, 193, 227, 229, 252, 265, 266, 268, 273, 307, 309–311, 374, 376, 379, 387, 393, 396–398, 401, 435, 440, 443, 446, 460, 479, 481, 540, 545, 558, 559, 577, 597, 620, 627, 631, 639, 640, 654, 659, 660, 662, 669, 670, 681–686, 688, 690–692, 694–696, 698, 700–702, 717, 740, 768, 770, 783, 788, 813, 855, 864, 869, 872, 874, 875, 898, 915, 917, 955, 960, 963, 967, 970, 973, 974, 994, 995
  robbery, 50, 52, 53, 101, 168, 224, 229, 237, 238, 273, 276, 326, 362, 442, 459, 460, 474, 477, 480, 481, 494, 504, 567, 600, 777, 821, 829
  violence, 9–13, 18, 20, 32, 99, 102, 103, 193, 230, 236, 238, 303, 347, 362, 385, 388, 401, 421, 431, 433, 440, 442, 476, 481, 484, 501, 510, 534, 544, 585, 600, 620, 659, 660, 670, 692, 701, 722, 754, 792, 793, 797, 830, 858, 917, 987
Arms
  and ammunitions; Act, 834

and crime, 151, 364, 548, 661, 831
brokers, 6, 98, 104, 126, 219, 549, 593–597, 603, 641, 672, 725, 771, 932
control, 2, 4, 6, 8, 11, 12, 17, 19, 42, 46, 60, 61, 96, 105–107, 115, 120–123, 125, 128, 201, 326, 354, 366, 396, 403, 404, 406, 421, 430, 460, 476, 486, 493, 494, 527, 531, 540, 543, 544, 553, 555, 557, 559, 561, 600, 620, 630, 722, 834, 835, 839, 864, 871–873, 875, 892, 899, 923, 940, 965; and disarmament, 6, 11, 115, 122, 128, 404, 531, 578, 630, 699, 864, 872, 875, 892; in Africa, 2, 42, 60, 105, 106, 120, 122, 123, 125, 201, 326, 366, 396, 403, 421, 475, 486, 494, 553, 557, 620
economy, 18, 117, 128, 890
embargo, 57, 101, 125, 126, 128, 193, 335, 421, 474, 492, 594, 595, 601, 618, 619, 669, 672, 686, 695, 699, 745, 747, 753, 851, 854, 871, 873, 919, 932, 963, 965, 971
exporters; to Libya, 745, 747
flows in Africa, 12, 58, 437
for Development Programme (AFD), 855, 859, 860
licencing/licensing, 359, 460, 473–475, 482–485, 487, 488, 490, 491, 529, 592, 632, 672, 834, 896, 993; in Africa, 125, 474, 475, 477, 482, 483, 487, 488, 490, 493, 494, 496
manufacturing Industries, 117, 167, 935
monopoly, 34, 122, 430, 431, 435, 445, 447, 524
proliferation; in Africa, 3, 4, 6, 8, 9, 11, 12, 17–19, 28, 29, 32, 33, 41–46, 49, 52, 54–56, 61–64, 69–71, 77, 84, 86, 89, 91, 95, 97–100, 102, 106, 107, 113–122, 125, 126, 128, 134, 139, 140, 145, 146, 150, 151, 189, 193, 195, 201, 203, 209, 218–220, 225, 230, 233, 239, 268, 294–296, 311, 324, 326, 330, 335, 339, 346, 354, 356, 358, 359, 366, 384, 400
regulation, 128, 466, 484, 560, 592, 724, 725
Trade; legislations, 114; Treaty (ATT), 123, 336, 396, 403–405, 507, 508, 546, 557, 657, 686, 753, 822, 892, 942
use in Africa, 119, 324, 519
Aro traders, 521
Asawana Deadly Force of Niger Delta (ADFND), 785
Ashanti Kindgom, 522
Asymmetric warfare, 803–807, 811, 813
Atlantic
  Chattel Slavery, 70, 71, 74–76, 78, 81, 83, 84, 86, 88, 90
  killing, 71, 86
  slave trade, 214, 301, 518
Audit, 492, 495, 496, 790, 834, 840
  arrangements, 495
Australia, 74, 78, 245, 247, 251, 260, 274, 437, 836
Authoritarian, 504, 509, 512, 527, 707, 708, 710, 711, 713, 715, 716, 741–744, 865
Authoritarianism, 708, 713, 714, 741, 866
Automation, 137, 667
Availability, 5, 52, 54, 57, 99–102, 117, 194, 196, 200, 201, 203, 231, 233, 258, 266, 268, 294, 295, 306, 312, 324, 326, 336, 373–375, 379, 386, 393–395, 400–402, 418, 420, 421, 431, 432, 439, 454, 461, 479, 480, 484, 504, 520, 526, 527, 534, 551, 558, 567, 577, 589, 628, 642, 648, 652, 653, 655, 657, 659, 660, 684, 686, 692, 718, 729, 731–733, 740, 747, 751, 755, 769, 772, 773, 780, 792, 823, 832–834, 840, 847, 849, 852, 853, 859, 889, 890, 900, 911, 914, 928, 933, 934, 938, 943, 956, 987, 990, 991
Azawad People's Movement (MPA), 763
Azwadi, 273
Azzawad, 178, 179

B

Bahrain, 709, 714
Bakassi Boys, 507
Balaka Movement, 417
Balasange, 227
Balmo Forest, 229
Baltics, 24
Bamako Declaration, 8, 60, 62, 95, 121, 403, 464, 485, 557, 603, 724, 896, 917, 989, 990, 996
Banditry, 42, 83, 99, 101, 138, 141, 150, 156, 177, 196, 201, 224, 235, 236, 239, 266, 273, 295, 296, 306, 325, 355, 356, 363, 379, 411, 412, 433, 438, 441, 442, 486, 494, 539, 545, 551, 562, 567, 577, 629, 640, 641, 688, 690, 769, 777, 796, 918, 934, 936, 940, 941, 943, 967
Banking, 549, 743
Banya Malinge, 198
Battle of Dien Bien Phu, 71
Beijing Declaration, 395, 404
Belgians, 86, 88, 528, 596, 783, 967
Belgium, 29, 270, 286, 312, 437, 540, 544, 617, 697, 748, 786, 851, 852, 968
Benin, 9, 152, 155, 167, 212, 302, 313, 347, 356, 419, 547, 548, 551, 553, 556, 578, 580, 641, 787, 811, 856, 910, 914, 916, 918, 935
Biafran Science group, 293
Black market, 34, 117, 126, 127, 150, 266, 268, 273, 276, 294, 312, 339, 549, 620, 629, 632, 655, 685, 689, 739, 749, 755, 783, 787, 791, 798, 868, 916, 988, 993
Blood diamond, 89, 254, 847, 849, 851, 853, 859
Boko Haram, 21, 34, 56, 57, 89, 99, 117, 134, 167, 170, 225, 232, 233, 238, 273, 278, 295, 325, 345, 356, 358, 361, 362, 365, 379, 383, 384, 394, 413, 420, 433, 435, 436, 438, 441, 456, 458, 459, 502, 530, 599, 617, 638, 639, 654, 656, 657, 752, 786–796, 812–816, 915, 922, 928, 931, 932, 936–938, 942, 943, 954
  insurgency, 26, 47, 122, 200, 202, 229, 235, 238, 239, 275, 278, 291, 325, 355, 356, 365, 387, 420, 440, 443, 503, 504, 507, 602, 614, 636, 777–779, 786, 787, 791–793, 796, 814, 928, 931, 935, 936, 940, 942, 943
Bomb, 44, 87, 114, 200, 220, 225, 238, 239, 268, 288, 293, 295, 339, 362, 363, 377, 388, 453, 455, 458, 464, 474, 481, 503, 543, 549, 550, 588, 712, 819, 911, 916, 932, 955, 956, 987
Bonny, 301, 519
Border, 9, 54–56, 138, 164, 165, 173, 188, 338, 414, 415, 540, 548, 798, 814, 848, 851, 859
  management, 47, 63, 64, 556, 797, 798, 922, 940
  regions, 233, 420, 733, 814, 817, 896
  security; management, 189, 201
Borderland, 11, 189, 190, 202, 203, 722, 728, 729
  in Africa, 11, 188–190, 193, 194, 197, 200–203
  security; in Africa, 187, 189, 193
Borno State, 117, 239, 278, 358, 365, 786, 788–790, 796, 814, 937
Boutros-Ghali, 577
Bozize, Francois, 198, 683, 698
Brazil, 13, 33, 48, 254, 540, 544, 617, 746, 829
Brazzaville, 85, 596
Britain, 29, 175, 180, 232, 253, 254, 286, 293, 300, 523, 524, 551, 552, 700, 722, 723, 887, 901, 968
British, 75, 120, 177, 302, 303, 324, 363, 456, 475, 518, 520, 521, 523, 524, 527–529, 550, 595, 630, 713, 723, 727, 748, 810, 848, 854, 880, 881, 887, 900, 958, 962, 967
Buganda Kingdom, 29, 211, 881, 887
Buhari, 168, 278, 358, 752, 783–785
Burkina Faso, 152, 155, 171, 179, 212, 224, 266, 276, 346, 387, 438, 440–442, 548, 551–553, 574, 655, 811, 814, 816, 847, 849, 850, 852, 856, 910, 914, 916, 919, 967
Burundi, 21, 54, 100, 128, 152, 156, 165, 168, 197, 198, 203, 212, 218, 270, 271, 276, 290, 311, 374, 381,

387, 394, 442, 446, 486, 502, 545,
574, 590, 591, 593, 613, 615, 630,
663, 664, 666, 887, 888, 901, 996

C

Cairo, 473, 477, 571, 572, 713, 715, 930
Cambodia, 103, 224, 255, 305, 336, 402
Cameroon, 20, 24, 31, 59, 116, 137, 153, 157, 171, 212, 223, 224, 231, 233, 275, 276, 278, 330, 336, 346, 356, 413, 416, 438, 442, 503, 521, 530, 546–548, 550, 552, 572, 580, 586, 620, 655, 663, 664, 692, 698, 699, 786–788, 914, 935, 937
Campaign for Democracy (CD), 509
Canada, 231, 245, 247, 251, 260, 381, 437, 544, 586, 590, 592, 595, 655, 748, 856
Capacity
  and resources, 489, 496
  building; and training, 8, 892, 894, 895, 918
Cape Verde, 25, 152, 155, 553, 856, 910
Capitalism, 69, 70, 72–79, 83, 84, 88, 91, 215, 249, 289, 591
Casablanca, 85
Categories, 96, 115, 165, 209, 210, 254, 258, 287, 296, 393, 455, 474, 479, 488, 544, 724, 810, 829
  SALWS, 6, 134, 245, 376, 394, 414, 415, 431, 432, 634, 891, 898
Catholic Church, 518
Cattle rustling, 134, 224, 225, 233, 234, 276, 295, 296, 358, 362, 363, 379, 414, 420, 433, 441, 494, 533, 539, 545, 546, 551, 562, 630, 633, 640, 732, 733, 777, 884, 890, 916, 934, 987
Causality, 377, 382
  of conflicts; in Africa, 377, 379, 382
Causative factors, 234, 246, 827
Causes, 81, 83, 136, 271, 296, 305, 309, 312, 325, 422, 478, 506, 511, 531, 603, 649, 660, 732, 753, 768, 795, 930, 991

of proliferation, 3, 79, 81, 82, 191, 193, 230, 307, 312, 454, 503, 587, 597, 687, 785, 792, 823
of SALWs, 3, 19, 79, 82, 191, 193, 197, 307, 312, 454, 460, 503, 597, 785, 792, 804, 823
CEDAW, 395, 404
Central
  Africa, 18, 54, 61, 62, 116, 123, 128, 139, 145, 153, 157, 168, 198, 199, 218, 387, 417, 441, 442, 481, 530, 554, 593, 688, 934
Central African Republic (CAR), 2, 12, 21, 23, 25, 55, 58, 59, 119, 120, 168, 171, 179, 198, 203, 212, 218, 223, 232, 235, 276, 374, 387, 397, 418, 442, 443, 446, 476, 502, 572, 574, 586, 598, 601, 617, 649, 654, 656, 663, 664, 666, 670, 681–684, 689–702, 740, 750, 996, 997
Centre, 108, 379, 384, 396, 457, 684, 941
  for Alternative Dispute Resolution, 509
  for Democracy and Development (CDD), 131, 509, 942, 943
Chad, 12, 21, 31, 47, 115, 116, 118, 119, 125, 137, 153, 157, 176, 179, 191, 198, 200, 210, 212, 218, 223, 232, 234, 270, 273, 276, 278, 325, 330, 336, 346, 356, 374, 381, 387, 413, 419, 420, 438, 440, 442, 446, 481, 488, 492, 519, 530, 546–548, 550, 552, 556, 574, 575, 580, 598, 601, 617, 620, 649, 656, 663, 664, 681, 690, 697, 740, 744, 752, 786–789, 811, 814, 816, 922, 929, 935, 938, 951
Challenges
  and solutions, 4, 161, 171, 189, 324, 487
  of globalization, 8, 34, 273, 560, 581
  of PSCs, 611, 612, 615
  of SALWs, 2–4, 7, 8, 34, 61, 64, 89, 90, 115, 116, 120, 134, 151, 162, 171, 187, 189, 201, 203, 207, 218, 220, 245, 257, 260, 267, 276, 303, 388, 400, 420, 421, 438, 446, 447, 453,

454, 458, 470, 501, 511, 540, 542, 544, 545, 547, 559, 581, 618, 628, 641, 754, 793–797, 805, 811, 815, 817, 825, 840, 847, 859, 864, 868, 871, 872, 875, 888, 891, 897, 900, 901, 909–911, 914, 916, 921, 922, 927, 935, 940, 942, 954, 955, 974, 991, 996, 997
of the proliferation, 3, 4, 6, 8, 9, 64, 89, 99, 115, 116, 120, 128, 134, 150, 151, 189, 201, 203, 207, 219, 220, 225, 239, 245, 260, 266, 273, 286, 324, 339, 354, 356, 438, 447, 454, 459, 470, 487, 529, 544, 547, 561, 611, 628, 641, 661, 754, 825, 840, 859, 864, 868, 872, 875, 891, 897, 910, 955, 974, 987
Characteristics, 47, 48, 52, 55, 135, 151, 189, 207, 209, 213, 215, 239, 327, 331, 332, 334, 350, 354, 413, 414, 432, 741, 743, 831, 957
of crisis, 710
Characterization
of conflicts in Africa, 135, 139, 144
Chibok, 239, 358, 752, 795
China, 18, 33, 48, 120, 127, 137, 181, 187, 231, 254, 256, 274, 361, 414, 503, 508, 544, 551, 552, 555, 586, 593, 594, 596, 618, 633, 655, 681, 695, 697, 699, 700, 728, 746, 773, 809, 851, 968, 969
Circles, 74, 87, 190, 462, 779
of arms proliferations, 45
Civil
Liberty Organization (CLO), 509
society; involvement, 511, 871; Legislative Advocacy Centre (CISLAC), 509
war; in Sierra Leone, 601, 848, 852, 858, 859, 968
Civilian, 18, 34, 42, 55, 58, 59, 115, 126, 134, 138, 175, 179, 181, 189, 191, 196, 200, 218, 225, 227, 230, 232, 233, 271, 272, 324, 326, 330, 335, 336, 339, 346, 366, 381, 396, 397, 400–402, 414, 432, 439, 445, 457, 465, 473, 474, 479–481, 483,

484, 486–489, 493, 496, 508, 539, 545, 547, 558, 559, 577, 589, 592, 593, 596, 597, 599, 612, 616, 617, 620, 621, 637, 639, 642, 649, 654, 660, 662, 663, 670, 672, 682–687, 691, 692, 694–696, 698–702, 725, 745, 747, 749, 755, 772, 785–787, 806–808, 813, 814, 824, 832, 836, 837, 848–850, 852–854, 858, 859, 868, 869, 882, 886–890, 893, 896, 899–901, 916, 923, 930, 936, 938, 960, 961, 984, 985, 987, 993, 996, 997
firearms, 33, 59, 119, 138, 196, 439, 476, 482, 484, 486, 670, 993
Civil Society Organisations (CSOs), 494, 502, 507, 509, 510, 512, 513, 579, 891, 893, 894, 897, 900, 902, 942, 943, 957
Clan-based conflict, 868
Classifications, 116, 212, 475, 588, 912
of SALWs, 956
Cocaine, 169, 305, 339, 412, 415, 416, 765
Code of conduct, 471, 558, 577, 578, 871, 919
Cold War, 6, 7, 18, 20, 24, 31, 32, 41, 48, 77, 81, 90, 187, 194, 268, 272, 275, 287–289, 292–294, 296, 304, 307, 325, 347, 381, 397, 442, 526, 530, 544, 546, 588, 593, 597, 602, 610, 613, 616, 617, 632, 663, 723, 741, 742, 746, 761, 767, 772, 804–806, 809, 820, 847, 910, 912, 913, 986, 988
tensions, 293, 588
Collective Amnesia, 71, 75, 80, 84, 92
Colombia, 255, 437, 599
Colonial, 20, 29, 30, 70, 71, 75, 83–85, 88, 90, 163, 170–174, 177, 180, 181, 189–191, 194, 197, 198, 209, 211, 214–216, 270, 285, 286, 288, 291, 293, 300, 303, 306, 307, 312, 324, 325, 378, 385, 480, 504, 512, 517–519, 524–529, 531, 535, 592, 630, 663, 689, 723, 730, 762, 763, 810, 865, 879, 880, 887, 916, 952, 986, 988
structures, 173

Colonialism, 71, 72, 80, 81, 83, 90, 163, 171–174, 207, 213, 214, 288, 302, 456, 517, 524–528, 865, 988
Committee for the Defense of Human Rights (CDHR), 509
Communal, 1, 2, 19, 25, 49, 53, 76, 188, 194, 219, 230, 234, 235, 266, 275, 290, 296, 306, 330, 331, 339, 348, 351, 355, 356, 361, 363, 385, 438, 441–443, 454, 473, 494, 531, 533, 534, 545, 546, 548, 551, 562, 567, 586, 590, 591, 609, 620, 630, 635, 689, 761, 777, 988
  violence, 32, 361, 988
Community engagement, 836, 837
Comparative, 4, 5, 9, 686, 807
Complex, 54, 96, 113, 114, 150, 188, 197, 217, 253, 333, 345, 348, 352, 476, 480, 560, 569, 571, 572, 580, 581, 588, 590, 610, 614, 617, 638, 647, 649, 668, 683, 685, 700, 726, 740, 755, 768, 805, 816, 848, 859, 863, 913, 916, 923, 928, 929, 933, 934, 962, 996
  dynamics, 379, 914
  emergencies, 19, 20, 49, 285–296, 991
Comtrade data, 437
Concentration, 165, 305, 308, 309, 414, 440, 613, 669
  of SALWs, 202, 275, 586, 589, 913
Conceptual, 51, 107, 135, 430
  clarification, 207, 208, 267, 412, 455, 568, 709, 778, 953
  parameters, 326
  review, 267, 540
Conceptualizing, 43, 375, 629, 985
Concerned Militant Leaders (CML), 785
Conflict
  and insecurity, 3, 19, 279, 600, 649, 659, 669, 899
  and proliferation, 3, 134, 151, 162, 374, 480, 533, 539, 545, 549, 587, 597, 642, 688
  and SALWs, 11, 136, 139, 767, 886, 889
  and small arms, 11, 28, 97, 98, 150, 586, 587
  and violence, 589, 639
  hotspots in Africa, 35, 885
  in Africa, 1, 4, 11, 28, 34, 62, 87, 134, 135, 139, 148, 151, 167, 270, 296, 299, 303, 377, 379, 383, 415, 420, 459, 478, 587, 589, 591, 595, 597, 600, 602, 603, 615, 620, 648–650, 655, 664, 665, 804, 912, 994
  incompatibility, 22, 963
  in Sahel, 168, 768, 769, 811
  management, 2, 3, 7, 23, 101, 531, 535, 804, 957
  prevention, 406, 685, 973
  resolution, 151, 445
  trends; in Africa, 20, 648
  zones in Africa, 187, 631, 682
Congo, 49, 57, 62, 70, 153, 157, 210, 246, 311, 337, 381, 547, 572, 593, 596, 599, 659, 662, 995, 996
Congo war, 381
Consequences, 6, 18, 28, 46, 47, 78, 85, 95, 100, 101, 119, 133, 150, 151, 172, 180, 181, 188, 191, 201, 248, 249, 265, 268, 270, 299, 325, 328, 331, 339, 340, 345–347, 378, 393, 394, 401, 402, 405, 416, 439, 501, 504, 505, 510, 512, 513, 532, 567, 570, 587, 589, 591, 599, 610, 630, 638, 639, 650, 669, 671, 710, 711, 721, 727, 749, 766, 781, 792, 868, 891, 901, 909, 913, 938, 996
  of violence, 102
Construction, 4, 71, 277, 526, 529
  of Conflict, 11, 98
Constructivist feminist, 97
Contestations, 289, 365, 379, 380, 385, 440, 741, 744
Contested spaces, 434, 864, 871
Continental question, 80, 81, 84, 89
Contours, 265, 663
  of conflicts, 151
Contrabands, 11, 60, 191, 196, 460, 541, 542, 547, 556, 559, 561, 788, 812
Control
  and disarmament, 115, 531, 630
  and prevention, 61, 124, 891, 897, 898

of firearms, 494; in Africa, 61, 519, 525, 529, 535
of SALWs; in Africa, 60, 62, 539, 562, 911, 913, 942; proliferation in Africa, 19, 46, 60, 562
Controlling, 63, 99, 103, 106, 115, 228, 402, 463, 469, 477, 484, 486, 489, 493, 496, 512, 521, 533, 541, 557, 559, 630, 672, 735, 848, 871, 893, 896, 912, 917, 921, 940, 990
Conventional weapons, 405, 544, 553, 557, 631, 649, 657, 753, 892, 985
Conventions, 60, 128, 540, 554, 581, 621, 686, 754, 809, 810, 857, 931
on arms control; in Africa, 123, 553
Cooperation, 6, 61, 126, 127, 199, 406, 445, 462, 464, 544, 556, 562, 582, 672, 734, 753–755, 810, 811, 813, 816, 822, 834, 858, 875, 895–897, 913, 916, 919, 930, 933, 940, 941, 944, 956–958, 964, 965, 973, 988, 990, 991, 997
Copper, 215, 253, 255
Corruption, 25, 43, 52, 56, 113, 134, 196, 219, 228, 250, 252, 260, 266, 273, 296, 339, 346, 354, 454, 460, 470, 478, 490, 491, 496, 530, 542, 545, 547, 551, 555, 561, 562, 567, 574, 580, 582, 599, 603, 609, 612, 621, 640, 682, 688, 699, 701, 714, 729, 735, 784, 790, 824, 825, 840, 849, 867, 868, 874, 921, 983, 990
and terrorism, 169, 812
Côte d'Ivoire, 6, 55, 82, 118, 119, 152, 155, 166, 210, 212, 218, 335, 394, 402, 414, 436, 437, 439, 442, 502, 666, 822, 852, 860
Counter insurgency, 26, 559
Counterterrorism, 26, 614, 803–805, 810, 811, 813, 815–817
Countries, 8, 19–23, 33, 34, 56, 58, 100, 117, 126, 139, 149, 180, 201, 245, 305, 385, 414, 503, 509, 535, 540, 542, 544–551, 555, 559–561, 567, 574, 576, 579–581, 586, 587, 589–598, 601–603, 609–621, 629, 632, 637, 641, 642, 649, 650, 652–656, 659–664, 682, 684–686, 688, 689, 692, 695, 698, 699, 701, 707–710, 712–715, 717, 722, 724–727, 730, 732, 734, 739, 740, 742, 744, 745, 748, 749, 755, 766, 767, 788, 804, 811, 812, 814, 816, 819, 821, 824–826, 829, 834, 836, 847, 848, 851, 853, 858, 864, 869–871, 883, 887, 890–892, 898–901, 910, 911, 913, 914, 916, 923, 930, 935, 936, 938–940, 952–954, 956, 957, 960, 962–965, 967, 969, 973–975, 985–987, 989, 991, 994–997
Coup D'etat, 22
Craft production, 195, 476, 686, 853, 909, 916
Crime, 1, 2, 8, 18, 23, 42, 51, 52, 79, 80, 136, 152, 168, 169, 193, 257, 277, 334, 354, 384, 387, 412, 421, 430–432, 474, 541, 545, 556, 558, 561, 574, 577, 589, 594, 616, 620, 637, 648, 649, 654, 655, 657, 658, 660, 661, 663, 664, 666, 671, 687, 701, 712, 718, 724, 762, 765, 769, 773, 792, 793, 797, 820, 821, 823, 826–834, 836–838, 840, 849, 855, 890, 892, 899, 900, 909, 912, 918, 935, 940, 962, 974, 983–985, 987–989, 994, 997
in South Africa, 663, 820, 828, 829, 831, 834, 837, 983, 984
Criminal, 2, 122, 137, 147, 152, 188, 196, 228, 328, 334, 401, 545, 549, 553, 556, 559, 586, 600, 610, 616, 619, 632, 639, 653, 657, 659, 661, 672, 685, 687, 688, 690, 695, 700, 701, 718, 752, 769, 785, 788, 793, 795, 803, 805, 806, 808, 812, 815, 820, 825, 829, 831–834, 839–841, 847, 859, 869, 890, 900, 910, 912, 914, 922, 936, 938, 955, 984, 991, 992, 994, 997
Code Act, 466
networks, 23, 116, 560, 689, 938
Criminality, 1, 2, 116, 188, 224, 228, 233, 234, 238, 324, 328, 335, 354, 376, 379, 380, 384, 400, 430, 442, 458, 549, 556, 688, 695, 778, 780, 791, 797, 868, 937

and violence, 118, 366, 434; in Africa, 384, 443, 546, 642, 823, 828, 829, 835, 954, 988, 994
Crisis, 89, 101, 139, 181, 200, 358, 460, 529, 545, 546, 585, 586, 592, 594, 599, 601, 602, 612, 613, 620, 621, 628, 636, 649, 654, 659, 668, 669, 709, 711, 715, 717, 763, 764, 771, 772, 777, 778, 811, 814, 848, 864, 881, 888, 914, 952, 954, 960, 962, 963, 967, 969–971, 993, 996
of regulation, 188, 669
Critical, 60, 63, 248, 250, 253, 256, 395, 396, 400, 489, 493, 510, 531, 611, 615, 617, 628, 631, 648, 652, 660, 661, 667–669, 707, 708, 710, 714, 716, 722, 782, 798, 807–809, 811, 817, 894, 895, 913, 939, 941, 942, 990, 996
perspective, 96, 98, 104, 107
Critical Security Studies (CSS), 162, 163
Cross-border, 7, 8, 56, 188, 194, 198–200, 202, 209, 306, 441, 487, 540, 580, 733, 753, 786–788, 815, 816, 860, 899, 910, 913, 914, 917, 929, 930, 932, 935, 936, 940, 941, 943, 944, 973, 974, 987–989, 997
Cross-cutting, 61, 919, 954
Cultists, 433, 456, 793
Cultural, 102, 350, 351, 354, 355, 517, 518, 529, 542, 548, 568, 633, 663, 683, 689, 690, 694, 701, 724, 727, 734, 740, 762, 764, 848, 986
dominance, 102
Culture, 527, 528, 531, 533, 534, 548, 578, 634, 649, 650, 663, 671, 691, 713, 714, 718, 730, 731, 734, 769, 828, 830, 835, 868, 912, 990, 994
of violence; in Nigeria, 355, 688, 792
Cult violence, 442, 443
Customs, 517, 532, 539–542, 545, 547, 548, 555, 556, 560–562, 575, 580, 582, 596, 672, 685, 742, 772, 788, 893, 899, 941, 944, 958
and SALWs proliferation; in Africa, 43, 753, 935, 944
Cyber
ecosystem, 664, 667, 668

security; policy, 648, 663; strategies, 667

D

Dakar, 571, 572, 974
Darfur, 49, 57, 90, 179, 492, 599, 649, 660, 929
Darwinism, 81
Dass, 76
Deaths, 17, 18, 20, 21, 23, 34, 203, 232, 254, 268, 290, 295, 345, 397, 460, 539, 544, 568, 585, 589, 598, 617, 653, 659, 662, 666, 694, 695, 731, 749, 793, 821, 832, 835, 836, 839, 962, 992, 994
de facto, 524
Defence Industry Corporation of Nigeria (DICON), 34, 468, 935
Demand, 106, 211, 227, 307, 308, 327, 347, 386
and supply; cycle, 418; of SALWs, 510, 534, 559, 628, 630, 631, 633, 634, 637, 638, 641, 642, 659, 780, 869, 912, 916, 923
for SALWs, 194, 196, 218, 271, 361, 559, 629, 630, 633–637, 642, 780, 797, 932
Demobilization, 122, 307, 421, 615, 616, 619, 795, 836, 855, 875, 899, 901, 975, 976
Demobilization, Disarmament and Rehabilitation (DDR), 448
Democratic, 23–25, 535, 561, 562, 615, 701, 710, 714, 742, 763, 819, 820, 848, 849, 851, 859, 880, 941, 952
collapse, 25, 847, 848
Republic of Congo, 31, 547, 573, 574, 580, 586, 591, 593–596, 598, 599, 601, 630, 633, 640, 641, 649, 655, 656, 661, 666, 669, 670, 689, 692, 697, 700, 824, 826, 887, 888, 899, 901, 984, 987, 989, 994–997
Democratic Republic of Congo.. *See* DRC
Democratic Republic of Congo (DRC), 55, 100, 101, 115, 119, 122, 126–128, 165, 196, 218, 223, 224,

275, 276, 290, 329, 386, 387, 440, 475, 504
Demography, 350, 352, 547
  and conflict, 352, 684
Dependency, 72, 75, 85, 211, 215, 304, 559, 601, 649, 729, 895, 898, 986
Dependent Urbanisation, 211, 215
Deprived Actor (DA), 303
Destinations, 167, 238, 717, 770, 935, 952
  of SALWs, 436, 550, 552
Development, 23, 54, 79, 91, 213, 275, 276, 304, 351, 374, 458, 482, 486, 541, 543, 544, 547, 551, 558, 562, 571, 577, 579–581, 586, 588–590, 594, 599–601, 612, 617, 619, 621, 628, 642, 650, 651, 653, 654, 658–661, 668, 672, 673, 682, 685, 687, 689–692, 696–698, 700, 701, 707–710, 713–716, 726, 743, 744, 753, 754, 763, 780, 781, 784, 795, 797, 815, 835, 839, 840, 849, 856, 858, 860, 874, 880, 882, 890, 892, 894, 895, 900, 901, 909–911, 918, 920, 921, 927, 928, 931, 934, 944, 952–954, 957, 958, 960, 963, 965, 970, 973, 976, 983, 985, 989, 992–994, 997
Deviance Theory, 136
Diamond.. *See* Sierra Leone
DICON Act, 935
Dimensions, 48, 215, 383, 448, 551, 630, 631, 641, 656, 659, 734, 804, 816, 910
  of social change, 353
Disarmament, 101, 103, 126, 127, 406, 469, 531, 533, 578, 615, 616, 630, 649, 672, 682, 685–687, 784, 795, 806, 836, 851, 854, 855, 864, 870, 872, 874, 875, 887, 892, 893, 901, 917, 919, 921, 923, 968, 975, 976
Disarmament, Demobilisation and Reintegration (DDR), 6, 7, 17, 97, 126, 128, 293, 296, 398, 531, 532, 534, 616, 682, 687, 699, 795, 897, 899–901, 917, 919, 923, 975, 976, 987
Disarmament in Africa, 122, 533, 611, 615, 672, 686, 870, 875

Disarmament measures, 125, 893
Displaced populations, 458, 684, 690, 701
Disruption, 275, 328, 362, 417, 570, 571, 668, 669, 779, 792, 943, 953, 991
Disruptive Behaviour Disorder (DBD), 329
Distribution, 25, 116, 219, 246, 251, 308, 406, 416, 440, 519, 522, 523, 570, 571, 597–600, 603, 653, 656, 660, 685, 690, 699, 724, 728, 739, 917, 958, 993
  of civilian firearms, 33; SALWs production, 4. *See also* Mapping
Diversifiers, 210
Diversions, 56, 59, 122, 550, 559
Djibouti, 120, 126, 152, 156, 197, 199, 212, 442, 486, 572, 664, 725, 731–733, 735, 763, 870
Domestic, 31, 47, 54, 82, 106, 145, 395, 520, 559, 587, 592, 598, 600, 610, 658, 662, 672, 713, 716, 739–741, 744, 745, 748, 749, 752, 803, 806, 809, 815, 819, 832, 840, 849, 853, 857, 870, 890, 912, 913, 991
Drivers, 714, 762, 864, 974
  conflicts; in Africa, 506, 528, 712, 875
Drug network, 767
Drug smuggling, 169, 474, 767, 772
Drug trafficking, 99, 168, 191, 199, 306, 311, 328, 337, 339, 411, 414–416, 418–421, 441, 443, 486, 507, 556, 663, 670, 767, 769, 833, 954, 963
Duration, 836, 889
  of conflicts in Africa, 141, 589, 638, 988
Dutch, 86, 518
Dutch disease, 246, 248, 256
Dwarfing, 276, 596
Dynamics
  of conflicts, 151, 197, 806, 983
  of SALWs, 207, 778, 792, 848, 863, 864, 869, 870, 911, 914–916, 938, 943, 986, 988
  SALWs, 634, 793, 864, 868

DynCorp International, 616
Dysfunctional, 421, 559, 868, 870

E

Early urbanisers, 210
East Africa, 136, 139, 145, 150, 165, 166, 212, 271, 302, 387, 417, 418, 420, 442, 525, 529, 574, 593, 879
East African Community.. *See* EAC
East African Community (EAC), 62, 512
Eastern Africa, 31, 33, 59, 116, 138, 152, 156, 166, 196, 271, 414, 443, 482, 486, 653, 662, 688, 993
East-West routes, 214, 571
Ebola, 92, 922
Ecology
  of insurgency; in Mali, 762
  of terrorism; in Mali, 765
ECOMOG, 364
Economic, 1, 2, 19, 34, 54, 85, 113, 180, 188, 202, 208, 220, 227, 246, 260, 276, 277, 308, 336, 350, 412
  development, 48, 55, 91, 164, 266–268, 277–279, 346, 443, 448, 460, 541, 558, 577, 594, 599, 628, 653, 687, 689, 726, 894, 954, 965, 973
  effects, 256, 628, 640, 793
  exploitation, 506, 521, 615
Economic and Financial Crime Commission (EFCC), 491
Economic Community of Central African States (ECCAS), 62, 123, 554, 699, 700, 754
Economic Community of West African States.. *See* ECOWAS
Economic geography, 246, 247
Economic performance, 267
Economics, 248, 630, 641, 692, 780, 786, 912
  of SALWs, 628
Economic trajectories, 265, 638
Economist Magazine, 248
ECOWAS, 9, 55, 56, 61, 62, 114, 121, 123, 128, 201, 219, 400, 412, 417, 419, 455, 463–465, 486, 512, 513
  approach, 917

  convention, 464; on SALWs, 43, 44, 114, 554, 557, 562, 928, 943
  moratorium, 82, 463, 469, 577, 754, 910, 917, 928, 939, 944, 971
  protocol, 56, 61, 201, 359, 576, 582, 610, 940
  Secretariat, 121, 558, 578, 857
ECOWAS/EU, 911
  Arms Collection Project, 920
ECOWAS Monitoring Group (ECOMOG), 601, 850, 852, 854, 855, 917, 962, 968, 969
Effects, 58, 95, 101, 133, 151, 187, 196, 200, 202, 203, 213, 220, 239, 245, 306, 312, 340, 346, 348, 421, 432, 459, 561, 650, 652–654, 661, 662, 696, 700, 769, 780, 839, 847, 881, 914, 933, 934, 954, 974, 983, 991, 996, 997
  of SALWs, 294, 356, 399, 534, 577, 628, 631, 639, 640, 741, 749, 751, 839, 890, 990
Efflorescence, 25, 269, 291, 357
  of PSCs in Africa, 612
Egbesu Boys, 507
E-governance, 667, 668
Egypt, 31, 35, 116, 127, 152, 154, 179, 193, 210, 211, 270, 274, 275, 291, 346, 398, 436, 437, 442, 473, 481, 503, 546, 551, 592, 594, 596, 618, 664, 666, 707–709, 711, 713–718, 740, 747, 750, 853, 969
Electoral violence, 232, 295, 361, 441–443, 551, 561, 656, 666, 988
Elite, 2, 24, 25, 42, 53, 357, 365, 509, 526, 590–592, 610, 613, 620, 692, 696, 879, 880, 954, 965
  power struggle, 31, 383
Emperor Menelik, 723
Empirical dimensions, 54
English, 81, 86, 518, 523, 953
Environment, 7, 50, 55, 105, 125, 133, 134, 136, 139, 193, 197, 208, 213, 224, 225, 258, 268, 277, 306, 309, 326, 328, 330, 332–335, 348, 350, 352, 375, 378, 385, 388, 400, 415, 444, 477, 491, 506, 512, 541, 553, 577, 586, 603, 612, 634, 648, 662, 668, 681–684, 688, 691, 695–697,

701, 702, 708, 709, 715, 718, 739, 749, 755, 781, 807, 817, 847, 850, 864, 928, 932, 937, 953, 994
Environmental, 23, 54, 165, 188, 307, 335, 351, 354, 416, 592, 616, 710, 779–782
Environmental experience, 329, 330, 616
Equilibrium, 727
of SALWs, 637
Equipment, 44, 219, 249, 257, 268, 278, 308, 311, 338, 414, 489, 492, 501, 508, 513, 542, 543, 555, 556, 559, 560, 568, 574, 581, 596, 611, 618, 635, 671, 745, 789, 790, 795, 798, 815, 852, 867, 918, 922, 935, 936, 940, 944, 967
Eritrea, 54, 57, 115, 126, 153, 156, 191, 197, 199, 212, 218, 270, 307, 325, 442, 446, 486, 487, 492, 586, 592, 593, 656, 664, 724, 725, 728, 731–733, 735, 869
Eritreans, 288, 733, 734, 869
Erosion, 224, 287, 356, 388, 435, 683, 880
of social cohesion, 385, 586
Essentialist feminist, 96
Estimate, 33, 42, 138, 177, 189, 203, 233, 258, 266, 303, 346, 384, 480, 481, 518, 519, 540, 544, 545, 548, 574, 585, 586, 592, 597, 614, 616, 617, 627, 632, 635, 640, 653, 657, 658, 662, 663, 669, 687, 692, 716, 722, 730, 746, 749, 778, 780, 791, 793, 805, 811, 813, 824, 832, 833, 840, 848, 852–854, 856, 859, 868, 887, 896, 914, 928, 953, 975, 985, 987, 993–995
Ethiopia, 8, 12, 24, 28, 31, 54, 115, 116, 126, 137, 153, 156, 191, 197–199, 210, 212, 218, 233, 234, 270, 271, 275, 276, 286, 288, 302, 307, 325, 387, 398, 442, 446, 486, 487, 503, 533, 572, 574, 586, 590, 592, 593, 664, 666, 682, 721–729, 731–735, 763, 826, 866–869, 887, 901
Ethnic conflict, 217, 397, 459, 515, 528, 663, 688, 690

Ethnicity, 75, 82, 151, 173, 217, 252, 253, 288, 309, 364, 385, 527, 591, 683, 684, 696, 744, 884, 963
Eurasia, 24, 359
Euro-American civilisation, 74, 76, 78, 86
Europe, 24, 41, 43, 60, 69–72, 75, 76, 79, 83, 120, 137, 168, 194, 214, 215, 245, 247, 274, 287, 292, 302, 304, 305, 307, 339, 362, 384, 414–417, 439, 507, 519, 546, 550, 552, 553, 587, 593, 597, 612, 633, 657, 658, 681, 682, 695, 698, 699, 728, 851, 965
European colonial powers, 29
European merchants, 519, 522, 525
Evaluation, 105, 114, 367, 371, 891, 940
Evolution, 47, 71, 79, 82, 84, 92, 189, 302, 323, 612, 741, 762, 974, 988
Expansion, 23, 47, 69, 79, 90, 188, 211, 219, 294, 454, 549, 568, 662, 722–724, 767, 922, 932, 934, 935, 958
Exportation, 123, 276, 326, 463, 464, 466, 521, 522, 541, 546, 554, 557, 561, 577, 578, 619, 670, 754, 923, 928, 943, 944
Exporters, 88, 134, 137, 540, 544, 745, 747
of arms, 274, 699
of SALWs, 170, 540
Exposition, 396, 433
External influence, 352
Externalities, 815
of terrorism, 804, 813
External sources, 2, 81, 559, 655, 663, 870, 937
External threats, 741, 744, 897
Extortion, 257, 684, 701, 808, 954

F
Facebook, 494, 716
Factors, 25, 26, 60, 82, 99, 105, 113, 114, 128, 141, 168, 175, 197, 200, 218, 233, 247, 248, 256, 266, 267, 272, 296, 304, 310, 333, 334, 350–352, 354, 364, 377, 378, 382,

418, 421, 422, 445, 460, 474, 477, 479, 486, 520, 559, 597, 629–631, 634, 637, 659, 661, 666, 671, 682, 710, 712, 713, 715, 718, 726, 740, 742, 764, 765, 767, 769, 771, 773, 778, 787, 793, 825, 827, 829, 864, 932, 954, 965, 986
  to SALWs, 1, 3, 54, 64, 77, 174, 181, 187, 191, 194, 197, 218, 219, 303, 347, 504, 560, 580, 628, 629, 631, 634, 636–638, 740, 762, 767, 804, 825, 864, 870, 887, 912, 916, 988
Failed states, 11, 22, 48, 49, 57, 161, 198, 200, 203, 441, 443, 444, 612, 685, 689, 866
Falgore forest, 229
Fall.. *See* Muammar Qaddafi
Family Interaction, 329, 330
Farmer–herder, 168
  crisis, 235, 443
Farmers-herders conflict, 1, 25, 53, 168, 358, 412, 418, 441, 458, 928, 932–934
Fatalities, 21, 168, 233, 237, 346, 384, 400, 504, 586, 627, 653, 657, 660, 684, 694, 732
Features, 55, 72, 78, 133, 135, 136, 190, 191, 287, 327, 386, 412, 415, 465, 473, 487, 556, 570, 648, 668, 710, 807, 813, 952, 962
  of SALWs, 631
  of small arms, 559, 631, 653
Felix Houphouet Boigny, 963
Femicide, 103, 401, 821, 822, 832
Feminist, 96, 98, 103, 217, 398
Fight, 55, 106, 126, 187, 202, 203, 234, 252, 273, 278, 292, 293, 329, 331, 336, 379, 380, 384, 395, 454, 465, 468, 486, 507, 526, 546, 576, 580, 582, 588, 616, 619, 629, 633, 636, 639, 641, 649, 695, 717, 770, 785, 790, 797, 807, 816, 823, 839, 859, 873, 874, 879, 881, 888, 890, 918, 919, 921–923, 931, 953, 954, 965, 987
  against SALWs, 60, 61, 464, 470, 579, 634, 823, 839, 894
Financial flows, 169, 985, 994, 995

Finland, 247, 251, 260, 437
Firearms, 11, 29, 33, 42, 44, 57, 102, 106, 114, 121, 127, 135, 166, 167, 177, 194, 258, 267, 294, 295, 300–303, 326, 330, 347, 354, 394, 396, 400, 401, 411, 454, 455, 459, 462, 464–470, 473–485, 487–495, 497, 503, 510, 512
  in Africa, 58, 138, 519, 520, 525, 670, 993
  licence, 469, 475, 483, 495
  licensing course, 469, 483, 492, 493, 495, 496
Firearms Act, 457, 465–468, 470, 893, 942
Firearms data, 119, 439, 992
Flow
  of SALWS, 85, 134, 170, 194, 199, 200, 311, 312, 744, 868, 875, 910, 914, 939, 942
  of weapons, 178, 225, 399, 597, 629, 728, 965
Foday Sankoh, 849
Forces, 540, 547, 558–561, 578–581, 587, 589, 594–596, 599, 600, 610, 612, 614, 619, 627, 629–632, 636, 640, 641, 653–655, 659–662, 669–671, 681–685, 690, 691, 694–696, 700, 701, 707, 714, 717, 728, 744, 745, 749, 762, 766, 767, 771, 773, 780, 782, 785–788, 790, 792, 797, 805, 810, 812–814, 823, 850–853, 855, 859, 866, 883, 887, 888, 897, 898, 901, 915, 916, 922, 923, 929, 930, 938, 940, 941, 943, 960, 961, 964, 966, 967, 971, 992
  of social change, 352, 353
Forest management, 227, 230, 231, 233
Forests
  and ungoverned spaces, 11, 225, 229, 231, 657, 748, 868, 869, 872
Fragile, 22, 120, 165, 173, 197, 218, 325, 502, 589, 590, 740, 752, 755, 766, 817, 819, 864, 868, 875, 942, 960, 991, 994
Fragile state(s), 22, 165, 259, 441, 443, 444, 446, 477, 687, 914, 954
Fragmentation, 30, 57, 176, 312, 386, 863, 865, 938

France, 18, 29, 47, 48, 72, 87, 127, 137, 170, 171, 174, 175, 177, 179, 180, 246, 254, 274, 286, 293, 381, 437, 551, 552, 593–595, 618, 699, 700, 722, 723, 745, 746, 748, 763, 964
Francophone
  African, 293
French, 30, 71, 86, 163, 173, 520, 521, 524, 527, 528, 594–596, 748, 751, 762, 763, 772, 804, 814
  annexation, 521
Frustration-Aggression Theory, 46, 53, 712
Fulani, 173, 174, 362, 385, 522, 548, 769, 770, 772, 773, 933, 934
Fulani Herdsmen, 325, 456, 459, 752
Functional institutions, 248, 250
Funtua, 238
Future, 6, 71, 90, 92, 114, 133, 135, 188, 287, 305, 307, 311, 327, 331, 334–337, 374, 383, 384, 388, 489, 659, 667, 700, 735, 763, 764, 838, 840, 957

G
Gajiram, 789, 790
Gamba, Virginia, 100
Gambia, 152, 155, 212, 481, 552, 553, 555, 575, 856, 910, 913, 914, 942, 967
Gao, 178, 763, 772, 920
Garamba forest, 227
Gatling Gun, 76, 77
Gender
  and SALWs Proliferation, 994
  and violent conflicts, 101, 557
  perspectives, 106, 406, 994
Gendered
  dimensions, 399, 405
  impact, 396
Gendering
  SALWs, 95
Generations, 92, 188, 267, 328, 335, 590, 659, 726, 916
Geographical, 23, 63, 77, 133, 136, 164, 165, 172, 174, 178, 190, 304, 308, 337, 364, 481, 524, 668, 732, 761, 951
Geopolitics, 46–48, 162, 174, 175, 521, 780
Geo-spatial Dynamics, 362
Germans, 86, 528
Germany, 29, 48, 246, 274, 286, 381, 437, 540, 544, 596, 618, 652, 698, 745, 746, 804, 809, 810, 851, 968
Ghaddafi, 162, 167, 168, 175–181, 598, 714, 717, 739–749, 751–755, 852, 937
Ghana, 521, 522, 529, 545, 548, 551, 552, 579, 655, 658, 666, 670, 682, 836, 856, 910, 914, 916, 919
  National Commission on Small Arms (GNCSA), 19, 754, 857, 859, 942
Global, 539, 540, 542, 544, 549, 553, 557, 561, 562, 585, 587, 588, 614, 627, 635, 636, 651, 657, 658, 664, 669, 672, 673, 686, 699, 700, 741, 748, 753–755, 829, 847, 857, 864, 871, 875, 910, 913, 922, 930, 952, 953, 963, 973, 976, 997
  actors, 162, 163, 170, 171, 180, 181, 823
  Arms Control Protocol, 484
Global Arms Trade Treaty (ATT), 461, 657
Global intersections, 864
Globalising Agenda, 84
Globalization, 8, 10, 34, 69, 187, 188, 194, 202, 207, 273, 290, 378, 412, 418, 430, 526, 540, 548, 560, 561, 580, 581, 613, 707, 713, 715
Global phenomenon, 73, 219, 447, 544
Global system, 41, 50, 92, 219, 581
Gold, 167, 215, 232, 253–255, 311, 312, 769
Gorji, 227
Governance, 533, 535, 544, 562, 589, 591, 597, 603, 612, 621, 637, 641, 651, 655, 659, 663, 671, 690, 708–710, 713–715, 717, 718, 734, 740, 744, 755, 761–767, 773, 777, 797, 848, 849, 851, 866, 868, 870, 872, 874, 875, 880, 910, 912, 914,

929, 931, 932, 952, 964, 965, 976, 983, 988–991, 993, 996, 997
in Southern Africa, 988
Government, 518, 520, 525–527, 529, 531, 533, 539, 541, 542, 545–548, 555–557, 559–562, 578, 580, 582, 585, 587–589, 592–597, 599, 600, 603, 609–614, 616–621, 629, 631–634, 636, 638–642, 649–651, 659, 661, 663, 666–673, 681, 682, 684–689, 696, 697, 699–702, 708–711, 714–718, 722, 724, 725, 727–729, 731, 735, 739, 741, 743, 744, 746, 747, 751, 755, 761–764, 766, 768–771, 773, 778, 779, 781, 782, 784, 785, 787, 794–798, 805, 807, 812, 813, 816, 819, 823, 828, 831, 833, 835, 839–841, 847–855, 858–860, 864, 866–868, 871–873, 879–884, 886–889, 893, 896–898, 900–902, 911, 917, 918, 923, 927, 929–931, 936, 938–940, 943, 957–967, 969, 971, 975, 976, 984, 987, 990, 996, 997
stockpiles, 122, 896
Great Lakes Region, 8, 61, 62, 89, 124, 125, 128, 165, 197, 290, 381, 438, 439, 442, 546, 550, 552, 554, 616, 669, 721, 724, 871, 891, 897, 991
Greed, 848, 880
in Africa, 306
in SALWs Proliferation, 303
Growth, 8, 23, 26, 41, 81, 86, 87, 99, 100, 113, 114, 188, 195, 208, 210, 211, 213, 215, 216, 219, 232, 238, 247–251, 254, 256, 270, 324, 351, 374, 383, 385, 388, 400, 415, 419, 454, 505, 511, 518, 610, 613, 648, 649, 651, 654, 657, 659, 664, 668, 688, 691, 692, 722, 733, 735, 749, 765, 769, 841, 927, 973, 986, 989, 993
Gubio, 789
Guinea, 117, 119, 152, 154, 155, 157, 218, 230, 338, 346, 412, 416, 418, 502, 518, 519, 521, 522, 545, 548, 551–553, 556, 580, 593, 600, 613, 615, 655, 659, 772, 850, 852, 853, 856, 860, 910, 913, 914, 920, 922, 951, 952, 954, 956, 958, 960–963, 966–971, 974–976
Guinea Bissau, 307, 412, 416, 552, 822, 856, 910, 913, 914, 935
Guinean conflict
and SALWs, 970
Gulf
of Aden, 117, 119, 125, 166, 731
of Guinea, 119, 384, 413, 417, 439, 442, 443, 657, 914, 951
Gun culture, 101, 113, 118, 303, 386, 527, 649
Guns
and implications, 385
in Nigeria, 360, 385, 456, 528, 548, 783, 916
plan of action, 62, 63, 577
Guns-for-slaves, 171
Gun-Slave Cycle, 518, 519

H
Haile Selassie, 723, 724, 734
Haushofer, Karl, 47
Haut-Mbomou, 693
Health, 26, 100, 106, 480, 539, 541, 571, 601, 611, 640, 641, 651, 654, 660–662, 710, 890, 921, 928, 996
Herder/farmer, 234, 598, 640, 656, 770, 928, 932–934, 943
Herdsmen militancy, 234–236, 984
High intensity conflicts
in Africa, 17, 665
Highland Ethiopia, 730
Highway robbery, 237, 361
Historical legacy
of firearm, 722
Historiography, 174, 209
and politics, 518
of SALWs, 518
Homemade guns, 360, 492, 823
Hong Kong, 247
Horizontal inequality, 761, 764, 769
Horn, 117, 193, 197, 657, 721, 722, 726, 727, 729, 869, 894
of Africa, 8, 23, 25, 26, 47, 61, 62, 124, 165, 197, 198, 202, 218, 277, 384, 413, 417, 419, 438, 439, 443, 488, 503, 554, 616,

657, 689, 721, 722, 724, 725,
    728, 730, 863, 867, 869–871,
    875, 891, 897, 951, 988, 991
Hostage taking, 225, 236, 361, 362,
    364, 441, 443, 459, 546, 807
Humanitarian, 54, 548, 579, 581, 610,
    611, 617, 632, 649, 658, 684, 702,
    740, 767, 787, 796, 803, 808, 889,
    890, 913, 930, 932, 942
  crisis, 20, 188, 200, 276, 287, 386,
    399, 600, 922, 928, 960, 970,
    996
Human Right Monitor (HRM), 509
Human Rights Watch, 592, 770, 819,
    828, 851, 967
Human security, 96, 162–164, 175, 179,
    193, 236, 258, 327, 332, 412, 448,
    662, 673, 792, 793, 797, 833, 996
Hutu, 197, 290, 530, 594, 633

I

Idah, 523
Iddi Amin Dada, 880, 881
Identity, 24, 81, 98, 101, 131, 197,
    213, 217, 233, 295, 336, 338, 355,
    364, 374, 378–380, 383, 385, 400,
    446, 509, 549, 586, 657, 681–684,
    687, 689, 698, 700, 701, 764, 768,
    821, 836, 866, 986
IDPs and refugees, 387, 691
  in Africa, 387, 691
IFRT.. *See* INTERPOL
Illegal, 6, 42, 58, 113, 116, 117, 120,
    121, 128, 166, 174, 188, 194, 201,
    219, 224, 227, 231, 270, 292, 294,
    311, 339, 347, 359, 374, 376, 396,
    411, 415, 416, 418, 419, 432, 454,
    462, 463, 469, 470, 477, 488, 513,
    534, 539, 548–551, 553–556, 561,
    562, 572, 574, 575, 580–582, 586,
    593, 594, 596, 597, 603, 616,
    619, 620, 629, 630, 633, 635–638,
    640–642, 654, 655, 658, 659, 666,
    670–672, 686, 721, 726, 735, 749,
    753, 764, 765, 780, 783, 788,
    819–825, 827, 828, 832–839, 853,
    854, 858, 860, 864, 870, 891, 892,
    896–899, 909–912, 914, 920, 929,
    935, 942, 970, 991, 993–995
Illicit, 194, 308, 346, 400, 414, 415,
    432, 439, 507, 542, 543, 547, 553,
    554, 556–558, 560, 567, 575, 579,
    581, 586, 597, 602, 633, 635, 637,
    663, 666, 727, 728, 731, 734, 765,
    780, 804, 847, 849, 853, 895, 897,
    898, 910–914, 916–918, 923, 934,
    943, 963, 965, 971, 973, 985,
    988–991, 993–996
  arms market, 60, 64, 654, 655
Illicit arms, 61, 64, 383–386, 393, 394,
    439, 539, 540, 548, 550, 557, 562,
    567, 568, 580, 582, 598, 599, 601,
    620, 637, 642, 649, 654–659, 666,
    669, 672, 686, 717, 725, 731, 739,
    748, 749, 753, 813, 822, 864, 868,
    870, 872, 875, 892, 920, 932, 935,
    938, 940, 941, 955, 985, 996
  in Africa, 63, 383, 533
  transfer, 395, 436, 533, 540, 561,
    657, 875
Illicit SALWs, 62, 63, 95, 101, 196,
    199, 414, 417, 432, 547, 554, 558,
    778, 812, 813, 863, 864, 868, 869,
    872, 874, 891, 893, 897, 898, 900,
    901, 909, 911, 912, 914, 997
Impact, 8, 9, 18, 20, 60, 72, 118, 163,
    172, 175, 193, 211, 219, 325, 346,
    352, 375, 379, 475, 480, 481, 511,
    512
  of Gun Trafficking, 419
  of SALWs, 6, 8, 46, 388, 750–752,
    831, 839, 848, 851, 891, 942,
    943, 992, 994
  of SALWs proliferation, 189, 194,
    750, 943
Imperialism, 71, 72, 75–77, 79, 81, 85,
    88–90, 302, 526, 527, 529, 880
Implementation, 60, 61, 63, 105, 106,
    116, 117, 126, 128, 219, 267, 278,
    293, 340, 403–405, 462, 468, 470,
    485, 492, 511, 553, 554, 558, 562,
    577, 578, 581, 618, 621, 658,
    666–669, 687, 724, 726, 753–755,
    769, 795, 797, 835, 858, 880, 881,
    892–895, 901, 910, 917–922, 931,
    939–944, 957, 973

1020   INDEX

Implications, 4–6, 25, 41, 54, 60, 114, 135, 139, 151, 188, 189, 198, 207, 216, 218, 250, 256, 269, 273, 277, 279, 385, 387, 430, 440, 454, 614, 641, 650, 661, 708, 710, 735, 755, 823, 833, 913, 933, 937, 938, 962, 973

Importation, 9, 114, 146, 172, 214, 292, 300, 301, 463, 464, 466, 468, 469, 471, 503, 541, 546, 547, 554, 557, 561, 562, 577, 578, 619, 641, 670, 724, 754, 928, 939, 943, 944, 967, 971

Incidences, 233, 238, 308, 309, 340, 362, 420, 441, 466, 505, 649, 664, 832, 984

Incidents, 18, 100, 167, 169, 188, 236–238, 346, 417, 460, 545, 591, 664, 735, 782, 785, 796, 810, 829, 834, 987

and casualties, 787

Incubation, 866

Industrial revolution, 74, 76–79, 88, 213

Informalization
of security, 870

Information Communication Technology (ICT), 354, 494, 647, 648, 650–652, 662–664, 707, 941
and SALWs, 12; in Africa, 361, 647, 650
operations strategy, 651

Infrastructure, 4, 91, 118, 137, 195, 210, 216, 225, 231, 249, 257, 258, 265, 277–279, 310, 384, 438, 460, 504, 555, 559, 560, 569, 574, 580, 591, 592, 599, 600, 611, 648, 651, 652, 656, 657, 662, 667–669, 688, 696, 710, 796, 797, 840, 879, 933, 990

Insecurity, 8, 19, 42, 50, 55, 56, 85, 91, 96–98, 101, 115, 119, 125, 176, 179, 181, 187, 190, 193, 196, 201–203, 210, 215, 232, 234, 236, 239, 259, 266, 269, 272, 277–279, 285, 286, 296, 312, 324, 346, 388, 400, 406, 417, 422, 439, 453, 460, 477, 491, 504, 547, 551, 559, 562, 567, 589, 598, 600, 611, 649, 656, 663, 664, 683–685, 691, 693, 695, 696, 701, 710, 718, 726, 752, 778, 783, 784, 794, 806, 820, 826, 828, 830, 832, 833, 839–841, 852, 864, 869–871, 873, 883, 889, 890, 899–901, 914, 934, 943, 954, 974, 996

in Africa, 10, 19, 453, 559, 611, 664

Institution, 3, 5, 10, 12, 17, 18, 23, 33, 48–50, 53, 55, 76, 77, 84, 96, 107, 114, 117, 162, 199, 207, 216, 219, 220, 224, 227, 238, 250, 251, 259, 265, 270, 271, 324, 347, 348, 351, 352, 356, 362, 374, 404, 411, 412, 415, 422, 429, 445, 447, 469, 471, 477, 491, 494, 505, 517, 519, 520, 523, 525, 526, 530, 531, 535, 556, 640, 726, 868, 884, 956, 958, 959, 990

Institutional, 51, 114, 116, 118, 121, 173, 216, 219, 502, 541, 554, 555, 558, 578, 636, 641, 696, 794, 894, 895, 913, 917, 940, 952, 973

framework on SALWs, 461

Institution-building, 23, 465, 535, 895

Instruments, 28, 43, 63, 123, 125, 172, 207, 208, 220, 225, 257, 259, 268, 379, 396, 403, 438, 458, 459, 461, 462, 464, 465, 484, 485, 512, 522, 541, 576, 578, 595, 649, 711, 716, 753–755, 794, 815, 823, 824, 857, 859, 888, 892, 919, 921, 922, 931, 940, 989, 991–993, 996

Insurgency, 1, 23, 25, 26, 42, 113, 117, 118, 218, 224, 235, 239, 266, 273, 276, 357, 365, 434, 438, 442, 443, 453, 454, 504
and militancy, 238, 551
and terrorism, 99, 125, 188, 266, 709, 718, 909, 941
in Uganda, 879, 886

Intensity, 20, 54, 83, 151, 271, 272, 304, 305, 310–312, 324, 361, 374, 415, 420, 441, 458, 459, 638, 652, 665, 792, 793, 796, 797, 821, 889, 934

Inter-agency cooperation, 556, 941, 944

Inter-communal, 113, 296, 306, 459, 567, 591, 659, 663, 688, 689, 771, 914, 927, 943
  tension, 113, 295, 324, 567, 659, 769
  violence, 99, 591
Intergovernmental Authority on Development (IGAD), 128, 611, 619, 871, 895
Inter-group relations, 234, 589
Internal conflicts, 21, 48, 82, 99, 139, 196, 356, 477, 577, 587, 590, 616, 722, 910, 952
Internally Displaced Persons (IDPs), 276, 277, 387, 602, 691, 692, 696, 793
  and SALWs, 200, 688, 691, 702, 793
  in CAR, 200, 602, 683, 690, 692, 694, 696
Internally Displaced Populations (IDPs), 683, 685, 688, 690–692, 694, 695, 702, 793
International, 6, 32, 42, 56, 58, 63, 82, 96, 106, 453, 458, 459, 461, 468, 471, 484, 513
  conflicts, 28, 724
  instrument, 462, 465, 541, 553, 724, 755, 815, 859, 955, 956, 992
  law, 190, 209, 268, 435, 436, 753
International policy, 402–404
International transfers, 465, 507, 628, 632, 672, 900, 912, 914, 918
INTERPOL, 485
INTERPOL Ballistics Information Network (IBIN).. *See* INTERPOL
Interstate, 571, 589, 590, 597, 648, 663, 664, 726, 806, 886
Interstate Defence and Security Committee (ISDSC), 19
Interstate war, 21, 32, 42, 307, 397, 597, 886
IQ, 334, 335
Islamic, 238, 239, 291, 325, 383, 749, 752, 766, 768, 771, 773, 779, 810, 813, 867, 868, 928
  countries, 773, 815
  State in West African Province.. *See* ISWAP

Islamic Maghreb, 167, 233, 384, 599, 657, 746, 765, 788, 803, 813, 814, 816, 915
Islamic State in Iraq and Syria (ISIS), 26, 345, 728, 749, 786, 814, 815
Islamic State in West Africa Province (ISWAP), 26, 200, 345, 394, 786–789, 928, 932, 936, 937, 940, 942, 943
Italian, 52, 528, 723
Italy, 29, 137, 170, 171, 286, 381, 437, 507, 540, 544, 595, 698, 699, 723, 745, 746, 748, 866

J
Jama'atu Ahlissunnah Lidda'awati Wal Jihad (JAL), 200, 785
Janjaweed, 379, 492, 810
Japan, 69, 78, 81, 247, 254, 381, 437, 544, 587, 892
Jihad, 167, 179, 438, 752, 766, 785, 814
Johannesburg.. *See* South Africa
Jonathan, Goodluck Ebele, 784

K
Kabaka Yeka (KY), 880, 881
Kabila, Joseph, 122, 198
Kaduna, 225, 237, 238, 358, 363, 547, 640, 784, 786
Kamuku, 225
Kamuku forest, 226, 237
Kanem-Bornu Empire, 29
Kareto, 789
Kebbi State, 295, 640
Kenya, 1, 2, 8, 31, 47–49, 116, 121, 134, 137, 153, 156, 165, 191, 197, 199, 210, 212, 223, 224, 233, 234, 239, 275, 295, 331, 337, 346, 388, 413–418, 442, 443, 486, 504, 530, 533, 551, 572, 586, 592, 637, 639, 651, 661, 728, 732, 733, 763, 830, 867, 868, 872, 880, 882, 899, 968, 984, 987, 994
Kidandan, 237
Kidnapping, 50, 52, 53, 76, 83, 170, 172, 196, 218, 224, 236, 237, 257,

266, 273, 276, 277, 295, 296, 325,
326, 336, 339, 358, 361–363, 383,
417, 438, 441, 443, 454, 459, 470,
474, 480, 481, 494, 504, 539, 545,
546, 551, 561, 567, 600, 621, 660,
752, 777, 778, 782, 810, 930, 943,
954
Kilimanjaro, 136
Killings, 1, 34, 175, 266, 269, 276, 361,
362, 364, 385, 443, 459, 601, 692,
716, 732, 749, 803, 821, 848, 984,
986, 994, 997
in Nigeria, 134, 794
King
Ibanichuka of Okrika, 302
Jaja of Opobo, 302
Koko of Brass, 302
Nana of Olomu, 302
King Leopold, 70
Kjellen, Rudolf, 47
Koroma, Johnny Paul, 850
Kumbi Saleh, 209
Kuyanbana, 225
Kyrgyzstan, 545

L

Lack, 3, 18, 19, 31, 35, 50, 63, 73, 79,
89, 92, 99, 121, 164, 165, 172,
180, 196, 197, 202, 214, 218, 219,
230, 233, 248, 250, 252, 259, 260,
277, 306, 307, 309, 328, 333, 334,
337, 388, 395, 398, 405, 406, 432,
443, 454, 461, 474, 489, 493, 502,
511, 529, 531, 542, 550, 555–561,
579–581, 593, 600, 609, 610, 619,
631, 638, 655, 660, 672, 681, 682,
686–688, 692, 696, 702, 710, 715,
734, 740, 762, 765, 766, 769, 816,
828, 830, 838, 849, 852, 870, 872,
875, 891, 897–899, 901, 902, 918,
921, 922, 927, 939, 941, 975, 984,
987, 988
Lake Chad Basin (LCB), 816, 928, 929,
931, 932, 934–938, 940–944
Lapses, 769
in transportation, 568, 580, 581
Late urbanisers, 210

Law enforcement agencies, 42, 58, 138,
196, 266, 271, 483, 485, 491, 493,
533, 714, 722, 798, 894, 895, 993
Leadership succession, 27
League of Arab States (LAS), 123, 754
Legacy, 172, 173, 197, 306, 324, 504,
714, 724, 726, 831, 866
Legal
arms sales, 270
instrument, 87, 508, 576, 672, 753,
755, 922
review, 494
Legal framework, 234, 454, 494, 795,
815, 840, 898, 901, 918
on SALWs, 402, 454, 461, 470, 840,
898, 901
Legislation, 8, 11, 55, 60, 96, 128, 233,
239, 366, 404, 406, 421, 460, 465,
468, 474, 484, 485, 488, 493, 494,
502, 510, 518, 540, 558, 578, 579,
610, 619, 630, 642, 722, 725, 795,
815, 834, 836, 857, 891, 892, 894,
895, 897, 898, 901, 919, 989
Legislative framework, 834
Legislature, 509, 512, 742, 989
Legitimacy, 2, 19, 24, 31, 42, 49, 51,
55, 310, 325, 364, 419, 420, 431,
434, 443, 446, 492, 517, 525–527,
533, 613, 684, 690, 712, 715, 718,
741–743, 769, 779, 864, 866, 873,
874, 954
Lethality, 70, 95, 187, 195, 235, 259,
336, 393, 401, 432, 457, 631, 641,
653, 686, 792, 793, 797, 823, 942
Liability, 620
of MNCs, 587, 600
Liberia, 6, 24, 31, 48, 55, 82, 101,
118, 122, 128, 143, 152, 155, 166,
198–200, 212, 218, 224, 255, 270,
273, 275, 291, 305, 310, 311, 325,
326, 338, 346, 379, 394, 398, 399,
402, 420, 442, 458, 478, 502, 548,
551–553, 559, 586, 590, 593, 596,
598, 600, 601, 613, 616, 628, 641,
659, 672, 682, 687, 745, 836, 848,
850, 852, 854, 856, 860, 909, 910,
913–915, 917, 918, 920, 922, 935,
951, 952, 954, 956–958, 960–965,
967–971, 974–976

INDEX 1023

Liberian Civil War, 312, 503, 960, 966, 971
Libya, 12, 18, 21, 23, 49, 55–58, 76, 115, 118–120, 122, 143, 152, 154, 163, 168, 174–181, 200, 219, 224, 266, 270, 273–275, 336, 346, 359, 361, 384, 386, 398, 406, 418, 438–440, 442, 446, 473, 475, 476, 481, 496, 502, 503, 530, 545, 546, 548, 552, 553, 572, 586, 617, 620, 630, 636, 649, 655, 657, 659, 664, 666, 670, 707–709, 714, 717, 718, 739–755, 761–765, 767, 770–773, 811, 812, 814, 847, 849, 852, 870, 922, 937, 938, 965, 967, 968
 and proliferation of SALWs, 175, 636, 740, 747, 752, 753, 755, 762, 937, 943
Libyan Civil War, 163, 291, 740, 746, 752
Libya SALWs
 on Mali, 751, 755, 763, 770
 on Nigeria, 752, 814
Licensing, 57, 125, 469, 473–475, 477, 488, 489, 492–497, 834, 892, 893, 898
 merchants, 483
 of arms, 474, 480, 482, 483, 487, 857, 874
Light weapons, 17, 42, 43, 49, 61, 62, 70, 86, 89, 99–101, 114, 117, 135, 139, 162, 192, 209, 258, 330, 335, 336, 354, 376, 413, 414, 456, 465, 468, 478, 486, 503, 506, 529, 530, 535, 542, 543, 567, 568, 574, 580–582, 588, 593, 594, 599–601, 610–612, 617, 618, 627, 628, 631, 636, 649, 652, 662, 666, 670–672, 690, 708, 709, 711, 712, 717, 718, 722, 729, 735, 740, 747, 753, 754, 771, 778, 780, 803, 805, 848, 851, 857, 860, 871, 886, 889, 890, 895, 896, 909, 911, 931, 956, 969, 971, 972, 985, 988, 989, 991, 994, 996
Literature, 3, 4, 6, 8, 10, 11, 13, 49, 83, 163, 200, 247, 302–304, 348, 352, 355, 396, 398, 434, 685, 695, 712, 863, 879, 886, 942
Litigation, 839

Local arms production, 166, 231, 312, 655
Local blacksmiths, 18, 146
Local crafts, 293, 909, 916
Local dynamics, 28, 869, 870
Local production, 6, 7, 29, 33, 34, 122, 325, 478
Local Shenanigans, 770
Logistical, 23, 44, 208, 225, 448, 479, 838
 networks, 570
Logistics, 398, 570, 611, 873, 935
Lokoja, 523
Lome.. *See* Togo; ECOWAS, protocol
Looting, 58, 90, 230, 252, 309, 310, 312, 339, 387, 496, 654, 655, 682, 739, 787, 789, 827, 829, 832, 848, 849, 882, 914, 936, 937, 943, 993
Lord Curzon, 190
Lord Resistance Army (LRA), 198, 291, 346, 397, 420, 649, 887, 889, 890, 896, 897, 899, 901, 996

M

Machete Wars, 995
Machine guns, 43, 44, 100, 114, 135, 162, 165, 192, 200, 209, 231, 258, 267, 268, 291, 338, 376, 393, 411, 413, 418, 455, 503, 519, 528, 529, 543, 550, 568, 586, 588, 593, 596, 612, 628, 652, 653, 655, 658, 662, 666, 685, 697, 698, 711, 712, 729, 764, 772, 780, 783, 789, 805, 813, 819, 823, 851, 886, 911, 912, 932, 934, 937, 938, 956, 965–969, 971, 972, 985
Mackinder, Halford, 47
Madagascar, 31, 120, 137, 153, 156, 212, 664
Maji Maji
 rebellion, 528
Malawi, 137, 153, 156, 210, 212, 224, 437, 442, 573, 574, 664, 826
Mali, 7, 21, 23, 31, 32, 95, 103, 115, 116, 118, 119, 122, 137, 152, 155, 166, 167, 171, 173, 176–180, 210, 212, 218, 230–235, 266, 273, 275, 326, 336, 346, 361, 387, 394,

420, 435, 436, 438–443, 473, 476, 496, 502, 504, 530, 547, 548, 550, 553, 559, 574, 577, 578, 586, 598, 599, 601, 613, 614, 620, 641, 649, 655–657, 664, 666, 670, 740, 750–752, 755, 761–773, 804, 811–816, 856, 910, 913–916, 918–920, 922, 923, 938
Malignant anxiety, 336, 337
Management
  of armed violence, 797
  of intelligence, 581
  of small arms, 511, 562
  of violent conflicts, 535
Managing, 539, 541, 713, 893, 913, 997
  SALWs, 8; in West Africa, 539, 909, 913, 921
Manifestation, 778, 983
  of SALWs, 307, 628, 823, 985, 995, 997
Mano River Basin, 89, 90, 338
Manor River
  region, 951, 952, 960, 964, 969, 974–976
  Union, 954, 956
Manufacture, 5, 18, 122, 127, 214, 231, 239, 254, 275, 294, 411, 447, 463–468, 478, 489, 495, 520, 523, 544, 554, 558, 593, 596, 598, 629, 631, 651, 655, 670, 672, 682, 686, 772, 805, 837, 851, 853, 857, 858, 902, 916, 971, 989, 992
Manufacturing, 570, 571, 592, 595, 629, 632, 650, 783, 835, 916, 942, 943, 989, 991, 992
  of SALWs, 9, 469, 629, 823, 870, 898, 912, 935, 971
Map, 572, 573, 575, 865, 886, 918, 991
  of Uganda, 886
Mapping
  of conflicts, 139
  of SALWs and conflict, 11
  SALWs production, 4
Marginal, 686, 693
  elites and citizens, 19, 163
Marginalisation, 19, 597, 602, 603, 763, 764, 779, 781

Maritime, 356, 411, 413–415, 417, 418, 421, 434, 435, 541, 547, 562, 574, 580, 783, 935, 974
  networks, 570
Marxian, 80
  circles, 69, 74
Marxist conflict, 52
Marx, Karl, 79, 80, 87, 91, 505, 591
Masaba, 523, 524
Masculinity, 528, 730
  and gun culture, 101, 527
Masina, 211
Mass media, 327, 329–331, 348, 351, 366
MASSOB, 507
Materials, 10, 87, 89, 135, 208, 214, 215, 246, 253, 267, 273, 364, 460, 464, 520, 521, 524, 554, 570, 574, 579, 603, 611, 650, 717, 788, 857, 858, 918, 931, 937, 939, 942, 955, 989, 992
Mauritania, 152, 155, 179, 387, 553, 664, 682, 762, 816, 910
Maxim gun, 76, 77, 519
Measures, 9, 50, 59–61, 64, 107, 115, 125, 127, 224, 227, 230, 232, 239, 251, 259, 269, 326, 334, 340, 374, 383, 385, 394, 399, 402–406, 463, 468, 475, 493, 502, 510, 512, 513, 522, 526, 541–543, 553, 554, 558, 561, 568, 577, 578, 594, 601, 610, 614, 615, 618–621, 652, 656, 658, 667, 668, 672, 686, 729, 743, 753, 762, 794, 797, 798, 806, 811, 834, 840, 854, 868, 871, 872, 874, 891, 893, 896, 897, 901, 912, 913, 918, 923, 929, 930, 943, 954, 974, 989–992, 996
Mechanism(s), 2, 8, 9, 12, 17, 42, 53, 61, 63, 106, 114, 116, 120, 121, 125–128, 176, 228, 336, 352, 366, 448, 462, 464, 474, 490, 496, 502, 508, 520, 526, 532, 533, 535, 544, 554, 558, 560, 582, 600, 610, 611, 619, 636, 668, 689, 691, 702, 790, 795, 798, 825, 834, 864, 868, 871, 873–875, 892, 893, 900, 910, 912, 918, 919, 930, 932, 938–942, 957, 958, 965, 973, 976, 988, 995

INDEX 1025

Media, 1, 20, 102, 175, 225, 286, 287, 331, 339, 351, 354, 355, 361, 494, 508, 575, 579, 640, 647, 696, 714–716, 749, 778, 779, 807, 828, 831, 939
Mediterranean, 442, 518, 520, 521, 571
Mediterranean Sea, 136, 573
Memphis, 209
Mercenaries, 7, 8, 32, 34, 83, 118, 119, 235, 273, 310, 325, 336, 337, 359, 361, 558, 577, 596, 617, 695, 746, 764, 788, 897, 938, 953, 965, 967
Merchandise, 602, 765
  of death, 69, 71, 89
Merton, Robert K., 51
Metcalfe's law, 572
Methods, 9, 79, 135, 136, 173, 214, 257, 340, 396, 478, 479, 527, 529, 632, 668, 672, 700, 788, 807
Mfecane, 211
MICA, 468
Middle Africa, 31, 33, 59, 116, 138, 196, 271, 414, 482, 993
Middle East, 25, 199, 268, 274, 287, 328, 416, 550, 637, 710, 712–715, 735, 741, 742, 938, 954
Militancy, 42, 52, 54, 134, 196, 224, 232–236, 238, 239, 266, 277, 306, 355, 358, 384, 442, 453, 454, 456, 459, 501, 545, 551, 562, 598, 600, 649, 656, 657, 664, 766, 777–781, 785, 792–797, 914, 954
Militant(s), 28, 49, 57, 128, 178, 197, 200, 225, 277, 291, 295, 325, 340, 356, 365, 397, 420, 433, 438, 440, 456, 506, 531, 547, 550, 559, 591, 616, 633, 635, 636, 638, 639, 717, 752, 764–766, 768, 769, 771–773, 778, 779, 782–785, 787, 791, 793, 795–798, 811, 814, 867, 873, 984
Militarization, 114, 232, 303, 335, 356, 374, 385, 386, 448, 492, 590, 639, 649, 785, 864, 984, 987
Military, 5–7, 11, 13, 25, 28, 34, 41–44, 49, 55–58, 76, 77, 81, 83, 84, 86, 89, 91, 99, 102, 105, 118, 120, 122, 124, 126, 135, 180, 189, 194, 200, 218, 224, 225, 228, 229, 232, 233, 237, 253, 256, 257, 259, 269, 272, 278, 288, 292, 300–302, 304, 305, 308, 311, 312, 324, 332, 336, 340, 359, 362, 363, 374, 378, 381, 384, 386, 397, 404, 414, 420, 429–431, 435, 438, 440, 445–448, 457, 459, 463, 476, 479, 484, 501, 504, 518, 520, 521, 524, 528, 545, 552, 555, 559, 561, 568, 578, 586, 590, 592, 594–600, 611–615, 618, 620, 628, 631–633, 635, 641, 649, 650, 652–654, 659, 660, 662, 672, 682, 685, 686, 688, 695, 698, 700, 711, 713, 716, 724, 727, 735, 740, 742, 744, 745, 748, 751, 767, 768, 770–772, 783–791, 794–796, 804–807, 811, 812, 814, 816, 819, 835, 837, 849, 850, 852, 859, 865–867, 874, 880, 881, 883, 896, 914, 915, 918, 922, 928, 930, 931, 935–938, 940, 941, 944, 962, 963, 967, 970, 971, 994
Millennium Development Goals (MDGs), 324, 327, 619
Minority, 663, 717, 729, 762, 763
  of SALWs, 104
Mobutu Sese Seko, 198
Modern technology, 63, 220, 490
Modes, 567, 568, 688, 732, 965
  of transport, 569
Mohamed Bouazizi, 712, 714, 715
Mohamed Morsi, 708, 709
Mohammed Abubakar, 236
Mohammed Ali Pasha, 211
Mohammed Ibn Chambas, 165, 400
Mohammed Siad Barre, 728, 865–867, 870
Mohammed Yusuf, 785, 786
Monitoring, 96, 105, 114, 116, 121, 125, 165, 228, 231, 326, 337, 367, 475, 492, 494–496, 509–511, 513, 541, 542, 555–557, 562, 601, 603, 618, 659, 667, 671, 672, 684, 693, 754, 794, 828, 832, 857, 892, 893, 898, 902, 918, 919, 923, 940, 942, 958, 973, 976, 996, 997
Monopoly, 520–522, 529, 540, 591, 620, 794, 897, 963, 994
  of arms, 34, 430, 431, 435, 445, 524
Monrovian, 85, 961, 967

Moratorium, 62, 82, 463, 464, 469, 554, 557, 558, 577–579, 618, 670, 672, 851, 917–919, 939, 944
Movement for Unity and Jihad in West Africa (MUJAO), 167, 179, 438, 766, 767, 915, 938
Movements, 530, 575, 609, 612, 629, 630, 663, 670, 694, 696, 700, 709, 769, 781, 810, 866, 867, 897, 899, 915, 934, 940
  of SALWs, 56, 684, 699, 823, 915, 934, 937, 974
MPLA, 312, 616
Muammar al-Qaddafi, 761, 763–765, 767, 770, 771, 773
Muammar Gadhafi, 119
Muammar Ghadafi, 122
Muammar Qaddafi, 58
Mubarak, Hosni, 275, 546, 708, 711, 715–718
Muhammadu Bello, 520
Mujahiddeens, 273
Mujahidin, 76
Multilateral, 2, 6, 8, 60, 312, 412, 461, 553, 557, 559, 574, 657, 753, 809, 811, 892, 896
Multi-level mechanisms, 871
Multinational corporations.. *See* MNCs
Multinational Corporations (MNCs), 586–588, 590, 593, 597–599, 602, 603
  and arms trade, 587, 592
Municipal, 9, 12, 268, 465, 582, 661, 993
Musa Yar'adua, 128, 456, 531
Museveni, Yoweri Kaguta, 289, 881–883, 888
Muslim Brotherhood (MB), 291, 708, 714
Myanmar, 255, 599

N

Namibia, 31, 35, 116, 121, 137, 154, 157, 212, 325, 381, 414, 442, 480, 481, 484, 488, 509, 572, 591, 663, 823
Narratives, 556, 740, 827, 828, 933
  of SALWs, 75, 80

National, 518, 531, 533, 539–542, 553–555, 558, 560, 561, 578, 586, 587, 590, 595, 603, 610, 613, 615, 618–620, 631, 632, 634, 648, 649, 652, 653, 657, 658, 660, 662, 666, 667, 669, 671, 672, 681, 683, 685, 687, 689, 692, 694–696, 700, 717, 726, 727, 729, 735, 748, 749, 754, 755, 766, 768, 780, 792, 794, 798, 813, 819, 823, 827, 830, 834, 835, 839, 840, 854, 858, 864, 870, 872, 873, 875, 884, 886, 891–894, 896, 900–902, 911, 913, 919, 921, 923, 927–932, 936–944, 954, 955, 962, 965, 974–976, 987, 989, 990, 992, 993
  legitimacy, 24, 60, 474, 484, 485, 488
Security Adviser (ONSA), 34, 469, 794
National Commissions, 558, 578, 579, 929, 939
  on SALWs (NATCOMs), 121, 558, 578, 919
National Commissions of Small Arms and Light Weapons Control (NATCOM), 558, 578, 579, 798, 919, 921
National Focal Points (NFP), 96, 121, 891, 894–896
National laws, 463, 465, 474, 482–484, 487, 493, 662
National security, 56, 115, 163, 224, 235, 236, 239, 265, 267–269, 415, 420, 429, 447, 448, 454, 541, 561, 586, 615, 652, 653, 662, 667, 792, 794, 870, 891, 893, 900, 901, 965
National stockpiles, 59, 432, 681, 870, 936, 943
National Union for the Total Independence of Angola (UNITA), 312, 588, 594, 616
Nature
  of SALWs proliferation, 187, 218, 259, 346, 357, 361, 804, 869
  of violent conflicts, 357, 589, 778, 991
Nature Perspective, 334

Need, 534, 542, 546, 558, 562, 579, 581, 582, 592, 600, 602, 603, 633, 648, 660, 671, 692, 699, 701, 702, 713, 718, 732, 753, 771, 785, 797, 806, 834, 837, 840, 875, 894, 901, 917, 918, 928, 931, 933, 936, 940, 942, 954, 959, 974, 985, 990, 996, 997
of SALWs, 308, 309, 545, 642, 814, 817, 834, 840, 913, 939
Neocolonialism, 72, 302
Neo-imperial, 71, 72, 75, 76, 79, 83–88, 90
Nepal, 545
Netherland, 86, 248, 437, 839, 856
Network, 5, 9, 23, 35, 41, 42, 47, 60, 61, 199, 201–203, 268, 294, 310, 311, 351, 359, 384, 416, 441, 443, 485, 491, 533, 546, 560, 567–572, 574, 575, 595, 597, 613, 617, 632, 633, 638, 647–649, 651, 652, 657, 658, 668, 669, 685, 687–689, 694, 729, 733, 768, 769, 779, 788, 812, 839, 932, 936–938, 941, 942
New World Order, 289
Niger, 12, 21, 48, 115, 118, 137, 152, 155, 171, 173, 176, 179, 210, 212, 223, 224, 233, 238, 266, 326, 330, 336, 346, 347, 356, 361, 362, 374, 387, 394, 413, 419, 420, 436, 438, 481, 486, 502, 522–524, 530, 546–548, 550, 552, 553, 574, 575, 578, 580, 614, 620, 664, 666, 740, 750–752, 761, 762, 770, 786–788, 804, 805, 811–817, 852, 856, 910, 914, 916, 918, 920, 922, 923, 928, 934, 935, 937, 938
Niger Delta
 militancy, 89, 225
 militants, 57, 295, 433, 438, 531, 550, 636, 639, 784, 785, 787, 793
Niger Delta Avengers, 25, 459, 785
Niger Delta Greenland Justice Mandate (NDJM), 785
Nigeria
 and Botswana, 251
Nigerian civil war, 32, 82, 292, 385, 503, 530

Nigerian Labour Congress (NLC), 509
Nigeria Police, 361, 478, 504, 528
Nigeria Police Force (NPF), 236, 358, 528
Nigerien Movement for Justice, 167
Niger Republic, 200, 225, 278, 556, 805, 811–813, 815, 816, 922
Nile, 386, 730, 882, 888
Nkrumah, Kwame, 87, 92
Non-Governmental Organisations (NGOs), 10, 100, 461, 489, 507, 508, 510, 546, 595, 618, 685, 696, 702, 872–874
Non-state, 545, 546, 655, 662, 669, 688, 690, 691, 697, 700, 701, 770, 788, 805, 825, 898
 armed personnel, 178
 conflicts, 20, 21, 34, 346, 923
Non-state actors (NSA), 4, 8, 11, 41, 48, 52, 57, 118, 134, 164, 165, 167, 187, 189, 194, 195, 220, 228, 230, 239, 259, 268, 271, 293, 295, 296, 304, 347, 373–375, 393, 397, 401, 403, 412, 414, 419–421, 429–431, 446, 454, 456, 458, 460, 461, 464, 474, 482, 484, 487, 496, 509, 545, 587, 599, 602, 617, 637, 653, 654, 659, 666, 682, 683, 700, 708, 717, 739, 740, 748, 749, 794, 809, 864, 868–872, 875, 889, 897, 909, 915, 922, 937, 939, 942, 986
Nordic region, 24
North Africa, 12, 63, 123, 139, 141, 150, 152, 154, 167, 200, 212, 233, 274, 416, 442, 481, 503, 520, 521, 593, 616, 637, 657, 710, 712, 713, 715, 741, 762, 938
North America, 24, 69–72, 74, 75, 78, 81, 83, 85, 88, 90, 120, 292, 359, 362, 417, 682, 695, 699, 848
North Atlantic Treaty Organisation (NATO), 544, 588, 700, 743, 744, 748, 785, 929
 intervention, 177, 180, 181, 748
Northern Africa, 31, 33, 59, 116, 138, 196, 271, 415, 482, 520, 993
North-South routes, 214, 571, 572
Nupe, 522–524
Nurture Perspective, 335

Nyerere, 682, 882, 883

O

Obote, Apollo Milton, 289, 879–883
Ogbunigwe, 293, 916
Ogunmola, 302
Oils, 215, 542, 588, 599, 600, 615, 616, 633, 636, 638, 640, 641, 717, 732, 735, 742, 744, 748, 749, 777, 780–785, 793, 796, 819, 952, 974
On-Sided
  conflicts, 21
Oodua Peoples Congress (OPC), 507
Operation
  BOYONA, 796
  Flush, 796
  Restore Order, 796
Operation Barkhane, 179, 938
Operation Delta Safe, 783, 785, 796
Operation Harmattan, 748
Operation Linda Nchi, 25
Ore, 253, 952, 960
Organisation of African Unity.. *See* Organisation of African Unity (OAU)
Organisation of African Unity (OAU), 85, 118, 124, 127, 485, 724, 883, 917
Organised crime, 23, 42, 51, 52, 60, 99, 125, 168, 169, 220, 230, 266, 326, 376, 384, 393, 430–433, 438–441, 443, 453, 459, 474, 476, 477, 485, 502, 506, 589, 649, 657, 664, 687, 762, 764, 765, 768, 769, 935, 974, 984
Origin, 79, 86, 197, 248, 364, 375, 525, 541, 549, 552, 553, 570, 594, 597, 630, 695, 697–699, 766, 768, 867, 912, 953, 966–970
  of SALWs, 167, 551, 552, 811
Oromo, 289, 732, 735
Ownership, 7, 8, 102, 150, 152–154, 224, 246, 252, 295, 338, 395, 400, 440, 457, 476, 483, 484, 488, 489, 495
  of conflicts in Africa, 143, 662
Oyo Alafinate, 211

P

Pakistan, 437, 544, 545, 826, 929, 954
Palliative, 24, 105
Paradigm shift, 7, 150, 327, 535
Paradoxical, 197, 246, 356
Pastoralist lowlands, 356, 729, 732
Pathways.. *See* Routes
Patronage, 24, 35, 73, 117, 165, 172, 251, 252, 260, 270, 687, 743, 787, 866, 868
Patterns, 4, 51, 133, 151, 213, 215, 260, 338, 350, 351, 354, 435, 492, 525, 648, 681, 689, 734, 923, 933, 984
  of SALWs, 443, 923
  of Ungoverned Spaces, 435
Peace, 9, 25, 61, 64, 81, 101, 106, 128, 196, 197, 202, 203, 247, 266, 294, 324, 339, 340, 352, 378, 393–396, 402, 458, 459, 462, 467, 473, 502
  and security, 23, 395, 511, 540, 567, 589, 658, 777, 797, 889, 913, 927, 928, 943, 960, 973, 989, 990, 992, 996, 997
  and security architecture, 120, 990
  in Africa, 440, 513, 615
  Research Institute Oslo.. *See* PRIO
Peacebuilding, 3, 9, 395, 403, 410, 448, 508–510, 531–533, 875, 889, 893, 952, 957
Peace-keeping, 230, 463, 464, 952
Peace Research Institute Oslo (PRIO), 12, 13, 20
  conflict trends in Africa, 21
Peculiar, 61, 150, 173, 198, 260, 323, 482, 612, 726, 884, 941, 959, 984
Peer Review System, 496
Pelindaba Treaty, 127
Personality, 11, 198, 327, 332–334, 340, 348, 349, 351
Phenomena, 45, 47, 49, 83, 84, 133, 162, 207, 208, 238, 323, 396, 709, 914, 997
Phenomenon, 19, 50, 83, 99, 119, 162, 198, 201, 203, 207, 209, 237, 245–248, 259, 260, 300, 307, 324, 338, 348, 377, 420, 435, 436, 444, 446, 456, 458, 461, 476, 504, 509, 562, 567, 589, 627, 630, 671, 707,

709, 712, 713, 762, 768, 807, 813, 930, 965
Pipeline, 257, 277, 362, 569, 597, 616, 668, 782–785, 796
Piracy, 52, 119, 165, 266, 273, 411, 412, 417, 419, 421, 441–443, 486, 600, 657, 777, 910, 955
Pokot, 28, 295, 987
Polarization, 27, 865
Police, 524, 525, 528, 540, 545, 547, 550, 555, 556, 561, 578, 580, 592, 597, 614, 631, 633, 635, 640, 641, 653, 654, 659, 672, 714, 716, 731, 735, 747, 771, 783, 786, 788–791, 812, 815, 820, 824, 825, 827–829, 831, 833, 834, 836–838, 840, 855, 867, 894, 895, 902, 914, 915, 935, 936, 941, 988
   approach, 474, 487
   armouries, 479, 559, 790, 915
   arms licensing, 487
   powers, 487
Police Act, 467
Policy, 3, 4, 6, 10, 13, 20, 39, 43, 47, 77, 82, 87, 96, 98, 104, 106, 107, 120, 121, 124, 125, 164, 224, 228, 304, 359, 396, 415, 422, 454, 465, 466, 470, 486, 488, 509–511, 524, 541, 554, 557, 630, 667, 700, 710, 721, 729, 754, 779, 809, 822, 823, 831, 833, 839, 864, 866, 870, 871, 873, 874, 891–895, 898, 900, 913, 918, 923, 941, 942, 954, 958
Policy implications, 124, 304, 933
Political
   economy, 11, 70–73, 75, 78, 82, 83, 85, 89–92, 113–115, 213, 225, 260, 309, 527, 848; of SALWs, 70, 71, 89, 90, 92, 309
   implications, 216, 708, 933
   instability, 288
   volatility, 529, 954
Political elite, 216, 270, 364, 365, 379, 383, 492, 610, 692, 879, 880
Political factionalism, 27
Political instability, 42, 54, 56, 270, 287, 324, 377, 397, 454, 561, 574, 612, 682, 683, 914, 932, 952, 960, 962, 971, 974, 976

Political leadership, 63, 518, 690, 777, 880
Political Map
   of Somalia, 865
Politics, 6, 7, 20, 24, 44, 47, 71–74, 77, 79–81, 89, 151, 168, 172, 190, 197, 216, 251, 265, 288, 290, 292, 325, 329, 351, 352, 365, 509, 526–529, 561, 587, 591, 592, 612, 682, 690, 692, 701, 740, 742, 768, 773, 779, 780, 804, 849, 865, 866, 868, 871, 884, 912, 944, 962
Poor border, 47, 56, 63, 64, 116
Poor forest, 230
Population, 9, 33, 59, 85–87, 91, 92, 103, 115, 136, 138, 139, 167, 172–174, 191, 196, 198, 208, 210, 212, 215, 227, 228, 232, 233, 236, 238, 256, 271, 275, 291, 305, 307, 324, 326, 336, 339, 351, 355, 366, 377, 380, 383, 386, 388, 402, 418, 432, 434, 439, 446, 475, 482, 484, 492, 506, 521, 524, 525, 547, 580, 599, 600, 616, 617, 621, 654, 663, 664, 670, 671, 682–684, 690–694, 696, 698, 701, 702, 722, 726, 733, 741, 743, 745, 792, 793, 808, 810, 811, 817, 821, 826, 832, 848, 888, 897, 900, 928, 930, 931, 933, 934, 936, 975, 993
Porosity, 114, 116, 165, 179, 189, 416, 556, 561, 562, 727, 752, 788, 797, 811, 851, 868, 869, 935
Porous borders, 42, 47, 99, 114, 120, 134, 150, 151, 164, 176, 203, 224, 233, 239, 266, 273, 347, 417, 420, 421, 454, 460, 478, 547, 555, 556, 560, 567, 580, 597, 598, 652, 657, 687, 712, 724, 728, 732, 733, 762–764, 766, 773, 780, 787, 788, 795, 804, 816, 825, 868, 887, 888, 899, 901, 909, 914, 917, 928, 934–936, 940, 943, 952, 964, 965, 976, 991, 996, 997
Portability, 33, 150, 151, 208, 209, 258, 259, 268, 292, 417, 420, 421, 431, 432, 479, 550, 617, 631, 641, 654, 684, 686, 734, 780, 805, 890, 955, 984

Portugal, 29, 286, 300, 437, 549
Portuguese, 75, 76, 86, 90, 300, 518, 528, 848
Post-Cold War, 610, 682, 702, 804, 806, 912
  Africa, 84, 87–90, 290, 294, 610
Post-colonial, 531, 534, 592, 610, 616, 726, 762, 849, 865, 871, 986, 988
  Africa, 32, 64, 308, 519, 529, 589
  SALWs proliferation, 306, 986
  state in Africa, 42, 174, 382, 504, 529
Postcolonial conflict hotspots, 885
Post-conflict, 558, 577, 615, 659–662, 806, 848, 856, 875, 899, 918, 922, 975
  Sierra Leone, 326, 855, 857, 859
Post-conflict reconstruction, 99, 975
Potential, 521, 534, 568, 591, 601, 610, 614, 648, 650, 656, 673, 686, 692, 695, 696, 702, 743, 806, 889, 957, 960, 976, 985
  ungoverned spaces, 166
Poverty, 11, 19, 26, 28, 54, 55, 72, 92, 128, 151, 188, 190, 194, 196, 199, 202, 203, 210, 215, 231, 232, 246, 252, 253, 256, 276, 277, 286, 287, 296, 299–301, 303–309, 312, 326, 327, 333, 340, 347, 361, 378, 384, 387, 388, 393, 400, 404, 416, 418, 421, 422, 445, 460, 502, 530, 545, 551, 562, 585, 590, 597, 599, 601–603, 641, 651, 653, 656, 662, 663, 673, 685, 710, 713, 714, 733, 768, 780, 793, 826, 829, 831, 841, 859, 868, 869, 875, 879, 890, 901, 914, 922, 943, 952, 965, 987, 994–996
Power vacuum, 748, 749, 766
Pre-colonial, 29, 84, 171, 173, 211, 303, 456, 525, 526, 528, 529, 535, 781
Presidential Committee on Small Arms and Light Weapons (PRESCOM), 457, 468, 469, 942
Prevention strategies, 831
Principles, 528, 576, 709, 810, 891, 892, 957, 990
  of SALWs, 126, 898

Private Military and Security Companies (PMSCs), 120, 125, 611, 932
  in Africa, 119, 120, 614, 621
Private Military Companies (PMCs), 259
Private security, 7, 105, 374, 385, 386, 469, 609, 610, 612, 613, 615–617, 621, 629, 729, 832, 833
Private Security Companies (PSCs), 7, 12, 58, 120, 138, 196, 271, 609–621, 832, 896, 897
Production, 4–7, 29, 31, 33, 34, 42, 52, 70, 73–75, 91, 114, 116, 121, 122, 127, 134, 137, 145, 150, 163, 166, 194, 211, 213, 214, 217, 219, 231, 250, 251, 268, 269, 276, 277, 285, 294, 305, 308, 312, 359, 378, 404, 416, 436, 447, 454, 476, 478, 489, 519, 540, 543, 544, 546, 553, 554, 557, 561, 568, 576, 581, 587–589, 600, 602, 618, 628, 629, 635, 649, 650, 653–655, 658, 660, 663, 671, 672, 682, 785, 793, 833, 840, 851, 853, 870, 880, 909, 916, 933, 952, 955, 970, 985
Program, 532, 534, 542, 558, 561, 577–579, 599, 638, 642, 648, 660, 661, 668, 784, 795, 806, 815, 894, 919
  for Coordination and Assistance (PCASED), 463, 558, 577–579, 672, 918, 919
Proliferation
  in Africa, 546, 555, 559, 562, 568, 574, 576, 581, 597, 617, 638, 654
  of SALWs, 1, 17, 41, 42, 47, 50, 53, 54, 56, 60, 61, 63, 64, 115, 116, 121, 133–135, 140, 144, 150, 162, 168, 170, 171, 174, 175, 187–191, 194–197, 200, 201, 203, 207, 218, 219, 230, 234, 245, 246, 251, 257, 265, 267, 275, 276, 278, 279, 286, 287, 291–294, 296, 299, 300, 302, 303, 307–309, 311, 312, 324, 330, 345–347, 351, 354, 356, 359, 361, 362, 364, 367, 373, 393, 394, 399, 400, 415–417, 419, 421, 422, 430, 453, 455,

457, 458, 461, 463, 465, 466, 468, 470, 546, 547, 554, 558, 611, 620, 621, 628, 630, 636, 639–642, 659, 682, 684, 689, 691, 702, 740, 747, 752–755, 762, 764–766; in Africa, 43, 51–54, 193, 219, 220, 239, 246, 257, 271–273, 278, 292–296, 306–309, 312, 327, 504, 513, 534, 539, 546, 547, 554, 558, 579, 611, 620, 621, 628, 630, 636, 640–642, 682, 684, 806, 811, 869–871, 886, 887, 910, 988; in Libya, 438, 636, 740, 747, 752, 753, 755, 762, 937; in Mali, 232, 762, 764, 767, 772; in Nigeria, 454, 456, 460, 470, 471, 636, 752, 778, 792, 794, 797; in Somalia, 639, 863, 864, 868–870, 872, 875; in West Africa, 8, 9, 417, 554, 754, 910, 911
of small arms, 6, 9, 12, 18, 28, 29, 41, 46, 121, 220, 326, 330, 336, 383, 394, 399, 453, 454, 458, 464, 502, 519, 529, 535, 558, 559, 561, 567, 568, 574–576, 579–581, 586, 588, 589, 593, 599, 602, 603, 616, 652, 670, 671, 687, 709, 712, 717, 718, 722, 729, 735, 749, 778, 803, 847, 855, 858, 859, 868, 886, 887, 890, 894, 895, 900, 927, 943, 985–987, 997
Propellant, 475
of SALWs, 510
Protocols, 2, 8, 60, 150, 201, 331, 354, 403, 460, 471, 485, 533, 574, 871, 927, 940, 957, 959, 990
Protracted conflict, 134, 503, 504, 590, 615, 666, 864, 886, 887, 889, 891, 897, 901, 933, 952, 986, 988
Psychological, 11, 50, 105, 216, 238, 323, 325–329, 332, 340, 367, 402, 591, 629, 689, 691, 713, 793, 807, 808, 821, 931
effects, 335; of SALWs in Africa, 340
trauma, 339, 890
Psychology, 323, 327, 328, 331

of violence, 324, 326, 590
Public sector, 10, 460, 490, 973
Public support, 490, 839
Putin, Vladimir, 246

Q
Queer Ladder Theory (QLT), 51, 52

R
Rabat, 209, 571
Racial capitalism, 77, 78
Radical Islamist group, 727, 865, 866
Radicalization, 113, 529, 868
and extremism, 383, 533, 599, 868
Rail, 137, 569, 572, 575, 731
network, 214, 571
Rape/raping, 83, 102, 105, 218, 224, 276, 326, 328, 363, 394, 397, 399, 401, 402, 405, 621, 627, 639, 661, 821, 829, 831, 848–850, 882, 984, 994
Rate, 44, 49, 50, 52, 219, 237, 238, 248, 296, 351, 358, 383, 523, 550, 575, 617, 619, 628, 637, 654, 658, 691, 769, 780, 783, 787, 805, 821, 822, 832, 854, 868, 927, 933
of conflict, 48, 952
Rational actor (RA), 303
Ratzel, Friedrich, 47
Reasons, 42, 46, 57, 104, 105, 133, 139, 141, 210, 246, 252, 253, 257, 260, 272, 293, 325, 334, 388, 454, 476, 481, 487, 489, 502, 504, 520, 576, 598, 632, 633, 662, 667, 671, 682, 690, 742, 762, 807, 808, 826, 829, 834
for conflicts in Africa, 144
Rebellion, 19, 51, 53, 58, 174, 175, 232, 234, 252, 253, 255, 256, 266, 273, 296, 304, 305, 309, 310, 350, 374, 382, 383, 397, 529, 649, 656, 664, 696, 723, 751, 761–763, 767, 771, 773, 814, 847, 849, 853, 859, 888, 899, 958, 960, 962, 971, 976
Rebels, 51, 53, 57, 59, 117, 119, 122, 126, 166, 177, 179, 200, 252, 256, 257, 273, 294, 310, 339, 345, 401,

546, 575, 592, 600, 610, 615, 616, 633, 642, 654, 743, 746, 848, 850–852, 854, 887–890, 896, 899, 900, 913, 923, 929, 960, 961, 967, 969, 970, 975, 987, 994
Red Cross, 33, 100, 805
Refugees, 23, 56, 167, 200, 326, 346, 386, 387, 393, 504, 593, 602, 637, 639, 662, 663, 683, 688, 690–692, 728, 848, 887, 890, 894, 895, 901, 913, 930, 954, 961, 962, 964, 967, 969, 994, 995
Regime crisis, 709, 711
  and SALWs; in Egypt, 709
  in Egypt, 709, 713, 717
Regime security, 361, 620
Regional, 42, 43, 60, 61, 96, 106, 125, 162, 199, 201, 295, 302, 323, 412, 419, 430, 441, 448, 459, 461–463, 473, 484, 493, 502
  and continental efforts, 122, 910, 913, 917, 990
  arms control, 123, 485, 892
  distribution; of SALWs, 271, 687, 893
Regional Centre on Small Arms (RECSA), 124, 724, 863, 866, 868, 869, 871, 872, 874, 892, 895, 898
Regional control, 892
Regional dynamics, 634, 986, 988
Regional initiatives, 8, 61, 123, 558, 579, 988
Regional instruments, 403, 459, 461, 464, 465, 484, 754, 857, 931
Regional overview, 722, 728
Regional prevalence, 954
  of SALWs, 442, 785
Regional trends, 869
Regulation, 4, 312, 328, 329, 337, 406, 466, 467, 484, 510, 529, 540, 541, 543, 548, 554, 559, 581, 593, 596, 598, 609, 621, 655, 657, 671, 672, 686, 724, 725, 727, 729, 748, 755, 798, 832, 834, 840, 859, 891, 897, 927, 932, 940, 958, 960, 992, 993
  of SALWs in Africa, 60, 546, 554
Regulatory, 9, 42, 125, 190, 460, 463, 469, 471, 484, 642, 668, 727, 991

Reintegration, 96, 502, 531, 532, 534, 615, 619, 660, 685, 687, 855, 899, 900, 975, 976
Relative deprivation, 308, 418
RENAMO, 594, 986
Renewal, 482, 497, 731, 835, 933
  of licence, 466, 483, 491, 834
Resolution, 23, 54, 81, 181, 193, 257, 395, 403, 406, 460, 461, 463, 464, 508, 531–535, 551, 594, 618, 637, 659, 661, 685, 691, 702, 753, 766, 781, 889, 932, 938, 957–959, 973, 974
Resource, 23, 25, 42, 52, 87, 114, 195, 245, 255, 418, 441, 460, 465, 476, 486, 489, 494, 496, 509
  curse, 245, 701
  curse & SALWs, 257, 701
  wars, 11, 50, 53, 188, 245, 246, 251, 253, 254, 256, 257, 260, 636, 987
Revocation, 482
  of licence, 466, 483, 486
Revolutionary United Front (RUF), 633, 640, 847–855, 859, 915, 958, 961–963, 967–970, 975
Ribadu, Nuhu, 491
Ritual killing, 224
Road, 137, 215, 228, 229, 249, 529, 569, 572, 699, 731, 735, 797, 918
  network, 214, 569, 571
Robbery, 79, 121, 134, 154, 218, 295, 337, 339, 363, 467, 551, 562, 567, 600, 621, 777, 821, 822, 828–830, 954, 984
  and firearms act, 467
Rogue politics, 741
Role, 6, 19, 43, 44, 48, 57, 74, 76, 79, 97, 98, 101–106, 120, 122, 134, 138, 162–164, 170, 171, 175–177, 180, 181, 198, 215, 217, 246, 247, 249, 250, 252, 253, 258, 272, 302, 326, 332, 346, 348, 366, 383, 384, 395, 396, 398, 399, 404, 415, 436, 478, 490, 502, 508, 511, 512, 517, 519, 525–527, 531, 532, 534, 535, 539, 541, 546, 555, 557, 561, 574, 587, 599, 611, 614, 615, 621, 630, 638, 651, 657, 659, 663, 668, 671,

716, 726, 728, 734, 735, 744, 745, 748, 749, 751, 753, 755, 780, 790, 792, 822, 828, 831, 835, 837, 839, 840, 847, 852, 893, 902, 919, 941, 967, 973, 983, 987, 990
of ICT, 12, 651, 662
Root causes, 3, 19, 63, 81, 82, 197, 296, 325, 422, 503, 768, 785
Routes, 19, 56, 190, 196, 213, 273, 338, 454, 503, 521, 546, 548, 550, 551, 556, 569, 572, 574, 596, 657, 660, 731, 732, 734, 764, 788, 811, 817, 914, 916, 933–935, 943, 965, 991
of SALWs, 193, 551, 552, 812, 817, 825, 935
Rugu, 225
Rugu Grazing reserve, 229
Rural banditry, 233, 235, 355, 356, 379, 433, 438, 441, 443, 640
Russia, 18, 33, 48, 76, 82, 120, 127, 177, 181, 187, 231, 246, 254, 274, 381, 503, 544, 551, 552, 586, 593, 596, 618, 633, 652, 655, 695, 698, 699, 722, 729, 742, 746, 809, 853
Russia-Africa summit, 127
Rwanda, 21, 25, 54, 57, 121, 126, 127, 153, 156, 197, 198, 203, 212, 218, 254, 270, 271, 275, 286, 290, 311, 325, 381, 385, 387, 398, 402, 440, 442, 458, 475, 478, 486, 502, 530, 554, 574, 591–596, 601, 619, 630, 662, 663, 819, 887, 888, 901, 994, 996, 997

S
SADC Firearms Protocol, 268, 543, 991, 992
Safana-Batsari, 229
Sahara Desert, 136, 165, 178, 547, 811
Sahel, 23, 90, 125, 163, 165, 167, 171, 173, 176–180, 197, 224, 384, 437, 439, 441, 443, 520, 521, 571, 578, 617, 657, 739, 747, 751, 752, 761, 764, 766, 767, 769, 772, 788, 803, 804, 811, 812, 815–817, 914, 916, 920, 933, 938, 951, 973
Saleka movement, 617

SALWs
and asymmetric warfare, 803–807, 811
and conflict, 11, 34, 139, 163, 533, 539, 545, 589, 590, 627, 628, 630–632, 638, 639, 641, 657, 659, 661, 687, 767, 792, 793, 797, 803–805, 811, 816, 835, 848, 859, 863, 868, 869, 871, 875, 887, 889, 890, 897, 898, 900, 901, 909, 910, 912, 913, 917, 922, 934, 937, 938, 943, 953, 960, 970, 976, 983, 986
and crime, 833
and development, 543, 642, 653, 753, 780, 797, 900, 901, 909, 911
and gender, 11, 404, 803, 994
and health, 460, 641, 890, 921
and state, 445, 767, 806, 847, 866
and youth, 642, 660, 997
control; in Uganda, 871, 891, 895, 897, 898, 902
control and regulation, 3, 176, 402, 406, 546
control in Africa, 444, 525
effects in Africa, 502, 534, 628, 640, 741, 890
in Africa, 3, 8, 11, 17, 33, 43, 46, 47, 51–54, 58, 60, 62–64, 134, 135, 145, 150, 162, 167, 193, 194, 218–220, 239, 246, 257, 258, 260, 271–273, 275, 276, 278, 292–296, 302, 306–309, 312, 327, 354, 414, 453, 504, 510, 511, 513, 534, 539, 554, 579, 611, 620, 621, 628, 630, 636, 640–642, 682, 684, 806, 811, 869–871, 886, 887, 910, 911, 913, 942
in circulation, 18, 86, 194, 218, 512, 539, 545, 554, 805, 811, 856, 887, 953, 976
in civilian hands, 271, 539, 545, 597, 832, 850, 868
in conflict, 89, 98, 347, 394, 441, 533, 639, 659, 688, 793, 803, 871
in Egypt, 596, 853

in Libya, 175, 617, 636, 659,
739–741, 744, 747–749, 755
in Mali, 232, 577, 598, 656, 740,
751, 762, 767, 771–773
in Nigeria, 99, 170, 198, 200,
232, 275, 292, 355–357, 359,
361, 454, 456–458, 460, 465,
469–471, 539, 628, 636, 752,
778, 792–794, 797, 805, 934,
942
in Niger Republic, 811, 813, 816
in Pre-Colonial Africa, 525, 526, 528
in Somalia, 273, 639, 863–866,
868–872, 875
in Southern Africa, 503, 663, 983,
985, 986, 988, 989, 991, 992,
995
in the Lake Chad, 47, 789, 922, 928,
939
in the Niger Delta, 232, 239, 456,
492, 524, 531, 550, 598, 633,
656, 778, 783, 785, 793, 796
in West Africa, 9, 57, 167, 199,
417, 457, 464, 539, 545, 546,
550–552, 554, 557, 580, 627,
663, 754, 909–915, 917, 918,
921–923, 935
legal perspective, 455
Manor River region, 952, 960, 969,
974, 976
on African, 6, 279, 610, 640, 654,
847
proliferation, 54, 96, 107, 233, 326,
340, 354, 355, 366, 461, 512;
from Libya, 547, 637, 739,
740, 751, 752, 755, 761, 770,
771, 814, 922, 937, 938, 943;
in Africa, 19, 46, 54, 60, 139,
150, 151, 291, 300, 323, 340,
366, 430, 435, 436, 438–442,
445–447, 456, 503–506, 546,
554, 558, 611, 620, 621, 628,
630, 636, 639–642, 659, 682,
684, 689, 691, 702, 740, 741,
811, 869, 886, 911, 994; in
South Africa, 525, 820, 822, 834,
994; in Uganda, 887, 889
proliferation in Africa, 19, 46, 54,
60, 139, 150, 151, 291, 300,
323, 340, 366, 430, 435,
436, 438–442, 445–447, 456,
503–506, 555, 559, 562, 568,
574, 576, 617, 638, 654
proliferation in Nigeria, 355, 357,
361, 469, 547, 636, 639, 755,
792, 794, 797, 816, 921, 935
regulation; in Ethiopia, 724
smuggling, 42, 167, 168, 187, 196,
199, 338, 359, 542, 547, 548,
550, 551, 629, 633, 637, 747,
764, 767, 772, 788, 791, 817,
834, 910, 914, 935, 965, 997
trafficking, 7, 61, 63, 95, 193, 201,
203, 274, 347, 416, 420, 469,
542, 639, 740, 825, 935
Sankoh, Foday, 745
Satellisation, 75
Scenario, 11, 20, 32, 34, 86, 92, 149,
193, 325, 347, 381, 430, 440, 441,
443, 445, 446, 505, 620, 668, 694,
740, 743, 748, 849, 866, 936, 952
Sea network, 573, 574
Second World War, 71, 77, 188, 253,
491, 585, 588, 652
Sectarian violence, 194, 230, 275, 690,
692
Security
dilemma, 49, 586, 804, 806, 807,
811, 813
implications, 189, 233, 833
Security paradox, 50, 518, 807
Security posts, 783, 784, 788–790
Séléka, 179, 654, 683
Séléka militia, 683
Senegal, 117, 152, 155, 210, 274, 326,
481, 487, 488, 550, 552, 553, 572,
580, 664, 852, 856, 910, 914, 916,
923
Severity, 726, 728, 983, 988
Sexual violence, 97, 102, 192, 193, 203,
230, 394–405, 421, 585, 627, 655,
661, 692, 852, 984, 994
Shifta, 723
Siad Barre, 290, 728, 865–867, 870
Sierra Leone, 7, 12, 25, 31, 49, 55,
82, 89, 101, 118, 119, 122, 128,
143, 152, 155, 198, 200, 218, 224,
254–257, 270, 273, 275, 291, 295,

305, 310–312, 325, 326, 338, 339,
346, 379, 382, 394, 397, 398, 420,
421, 440, 442, 475, 478, 502, 503,
532, 545, 548, 552, 553, 559, 579,
586, 590, 595, 596, 598–600, 613,
619, 628, 633, 641, 658, 659,
662, 672, 687, 745, 836, 847–849,
851–860, 910, 913–918, 920, 922,
951, 952, 954, 956–958, 960–964,
967, 969, 970, 974–976
Simplicity, 559, 682
and durability, 432, 479, 631, 654
Singapore, 247, 437, 618
Slave-gun cycle, 301
Slavery, 70, 75, 79, 83, 102, 105, 300,
394, 397, 399, 518, 520, 661, 710,
848, 890, 984
Small
arms, 529, 530, 535, 539, 540,
542–544, 546–548, 559–562,
567, 568, 572, 574–579, 581,
582, 586–590, 592–600, 602,
603, 609, 612, 616–620, 627,
628, 630–632, 634, 636, 649,
650, 652–654, 658–663, 666,
669–673, 685–689, 691, 699,
700, 708, 709, 711, 712, 717,
718, 722, 724, 726–729, 731,
732, 734, 735, 740, 747, 749,
753, 754, 780, 788, 791, 805,
813, 847, 848, 851, 853, 857,
858, 860, 868, 887, 892, 894–
896, 899–901, 909, 911, 912,
914, 916–921, 923, 931, 932,
934, 938, 939, 942, 955, 956,
965, 969–971, 973, 983–986,
988–991, 993–996
Small arms.. *See* SALWs
a tool, 421, 659
bill, 468, 921
flow in African, 29, 654
proliferation, 3, 6, 12, 28, 32, 54, 97,
98, 103, 104, 106, 107, 189,
191, 220, 276, 311, 326, 335,
339, 374, 384, 439, 453, 458,
459, 480, 486, 505, 533, 534,
539, 546, 547, 554, 558, 579,
611, 620, 621, 628, 630, 636,
639–642, 659, 682, 684, 689,

691, 702, 726, 740, 741, 752–
755, 762, 764–767, 772, 778,
780, 791–795, 797, 804–806,
811, 813, 814, 816, 817, 820,
822, 825, 834, 840, 848, 850,
851, 857, 859, 860, 863, 864,
868–872, 875, 886–890, 894,
910–913, 919, 921–923, 929,
932, 935, 937, 939, 940, 943,
953, 955, 965, 966, 968, 970,
973, 974, 976, 983, 984, 986,
988, 992–994, 996, 997
survey, 12, 13, 33, 41, 56, 58,
103, 116, 117, 135, 137, 138,
167, 189, 191, 196, 231, 266,
327, 338, 339, 401, 403, 406,
414, 480, 481, 489, 544, 575,
596, 600, 627, 649, 650, 655,
659, 666, 671, 696, 722, 727,
751, 754, 804, 813, 823, 829,
851–853, 858, 859, 869, 870,
892, 937, 938, 955, 962, 967,
971, 973, 975, 985, 993
Social
change, 213, 349–353, 355, 357,
527, 589, 591
influence, 350
transformation, 349, 350, 355, 398,
557, 589
Social cohesion, 113, 266, 267, 356,
385, 388, 586, 649, 688
Social disintegration, 335, 639, 692, 900
Social formation, 73, 75, 865
Socialisation, 348–350
Social reconstruction
in Africa, 743
Socio-economic, 8, 52, 54, 72, 79, 81,
89, 99, 150, 202, 203, 207, 211,
213, 216, 219, 220, 226, 236, 245,
286, 305, 385, 387, 388, 411,
419–421, 460, 462, 507, 551, 557,
558, 562, 577, 589, 630, 641, 687,
689, 693, 712, 715, 807, 809, 811,
817, 849, 875, 899, 918, 921, 928,
932, 933, 953, 973, 976
Sokoto, 211, 347, 363, 521, 523, 524,
640
Sokoto Caliphate, 29, 303, 519, 521,
523, 524

1036 INDEX

Somalia, 7, 12, 20–23, 25, 28, 32, 47, 49, 57, 58, 101, 118, 119, 122, 126, 128, 142, 153, 156, 167, 191, 193, 197–200, 203, 218, 233, 234, 270, 271, 275, 276, 286, 290, 291, 296, 346, 359, 374, 379, 384, 386, 387, 413, 417–420, 435, 439, 440, 442, 443, 446, 475, 503, 530, 548, 552, 586, 590, 592, 593, 596, 601, 613, 615, 637, 639, 649, 652, 654, 656, 657, 662, 664, 666, 670, 699, 724–729, 731–733, 735, 750, 819, 826, 863–873, 875, 887, 888, 901, 984
Somali militias, 294, 866, 867
Sources
  of SALWs, 193, 291, 292, 294, 436, 596, 811, 859
  of SALWs in Nigeria, 359, 811
  of weapons in Africa, 8, 146, 582, 633
South Africa, 524, 546, 550, 552, 553, 572–574, 590, 594, 596, 614, 618, 630, 653, 661, 663, 666, 670, 698, 729, 783, 819–823, 825–827, 829–837, 839, 840, 850, 935, 984, 987, 994
  police service, 837
  with SALWs, 823, 825
South African, 525, 595, 614, 826, 829, 831–834, 837, 839, 840
  government, 478, 819, 823, 833, 840, 841
Southern
  Africa, 12, 31, 33, 59, 90, 116, 138–140, 154, 157, 211, 271, 302, 325, 442, 480–482, 503, 524, 573, 574, 593, 616, 663, 825, 983–989, 993, 995
  Europe, 17
Southern African, 29, 123, 165, 196, 825, 986, 988, 994, 995
Southern African Development Community (SADC), 62, 123, 128, 403, 419, 508, 512, 554, 603, 611, 619, 663, 822, 823, 825, 834, 983–986, 988–993, 996
South Sudan, 18, 21, 24, 49, 57, 90, 115, 118, 119, 134, 136, 142, 153, 156, 168, 218, 232–234, 271, 275, 276, 374, 379, 385–387, 394, 398, 401, 402, 417, 439, 443, 446, 502, 530, 533, 545, 574, 586, 598, 601, 613, 649, 652, 655, 656, 659, 664, 666, 670, 692, 725, 731–733, 735, 864, 887, 888, 899, 901, 996, 997
Southwest African People's Organisation (SWAPO), 509, 823
Soviet, 632, 659, 695, 699, 810, 967, 968
Soviet-designed
  AK-, 33, 100, 193, 478
Soviet Union, 42, 55, 76, 194, 272, 287, 289, 292, 293, 296, 507, 597, 602, 616, 711, 724, 728, 805, 806, 809, 851, 886
Spain, 29, 35, 137, 170, 171, 286, 437, 544, 698, 699, 748, 810
Spanish, 86
Spatial pattern, 150
Spread, 539, 549, 568, 579, 581, 582, 587, 601, 611, 618–620, 627, 631, 639, 640, 649, 651, 653, 657, 670, 672, 684, 707, 709, 712, 714, 761, 766, 769, 773, 796, 820, 822, 826, 837, 840, 889, 891, 896, 911, 914, 917, 921, 934, 939, 953, 954, 960, 965, 974, 976, 992
  of guns, 380
Standard, 123, 126, 194, 210, 328, 355, 421, 461, 463, 468, 470, 485, 493, 496, 501, 505, 507, 508, 522, 554, 575, 585, 594, 595, 619, 621, 657, 667, 668, 672, 673, 686, 780, 871, 892, 932, 941, 971, 972, 992
State
  collapse, 47, 49, 188, 198, 203, 386, 433, 496, 741, 743, 859, 864–866, 868, 871, 872
  failure, 49, 53, 57, 63, 64, 77, 85, 433, 435, 447, 772
  fragility, 11, 115, 308, 447, 868, 983
  monopoly, 48, 444, 445, 794
  policing, 475, 761, 769, 809
  stockpiles, 230, 436, 654, 914
  structures, 690, 886
State-based
  conflicts, 20, 21, 34
State Collapse Theory, 48

State fragility, 11, 115, 308, 447, 868, 983
States, 518, 520–523, 539, 540, 542, 544, 546, 547, 551, 553, 554, 558, 559, 561, 562, 568, 572, 574, 577–579, 586–589, 599, 602, 610, 613, 614, 616, 618–621, 631, 634, 640, 641, 652, 657, 658, 670, 672, 683, 684, 686, 687, 692, 697, 699–701, 709, 717, 727, 735, 740–744, 747, 750, 762, 768, 770–772, 780, 786, 806, 809, 811, 817, 834, 838, 851, 869–872, 881, 891, 896, 910, 913, 916, 918–923, 927, 928, 930, 934, 936, 937, 939–944, 953–956, 958–960, 971, 973, 976, 986, 988–992, 997
of Africa, 29, 340, 504, 520, 620
State-sponsored militias, 491
Stealing, 233, 237, 330, 339, 559, 770, 840
Stockpile management, 126, 230, 559, 560, 655, 790, 872, 892–895, 898, 901, 918, 919
Stockpiling, 58, 64, 468, 544, 562, 912
Strategic/Strategy, 43, 48, 60, 61, 63, 75, 76, 81, 89, 91, 92, 115, 128, 129, 163, 175, 178, 199, 202, 215, 225, 250, 251, 253, 265, 278, 305, 331, 378, 394, 397, 398, 429, 447, 448, 473, 512, 521, 531, 557, 562, 571, 578, 579, 599, 614, 615, 619, 652, 667–669, 711, 722, 746, 752, 753, 762, 766, 767, 770, 773, 786, 790, 794, 796, 798, 804, 805, 807, 808, 815, 817, 831, 834, 854, 860, 866, 895, 897, 910, 917, 918, 920, 921, 923, 929, 930, 937, 974, 975, 989
Strictu sensu, 254
Structural Adjustment Programmes, 88
Structural imbalance, 8, 19, 25, 592, 602, 609
Structure, 526, 527, 553, 560, 569–571, 590, 591, 637, 661, 667, 668, 688–692, 701, 702, 709, 716, 740, 748, 779, 793, 816, 836, 870, 872, 886, 891, 893–895, 912–914, 927, 932, 933, 939, 958, 959, 989

and dynamics, 4, 5, 958
Sub-regional, 754, 891, 931, 940, 941, 961, 973, 976, 988, 991
protocols, 60
Sub-regional distribution, 59, 196, 271, 482, 993
Sub-Saharan Africa, 24, 86, 136, 137, 170, 171, 176, 177, 202, 210, 230, 234, 246, 258, 266, 273, 274, 278, 303, 325, 382, 502, 503, 519, 539, 545, 559, 575, 585, 589, 597, 627, 630, 638, 650, 762, 805, 951, 953, 984, 994, 997
Substance, 387, 441, 443, 464, 542, 543, 589, 953, 956
Sudan, 28, 31, 49, 54, 55, 57, 101, 116, 119, 137, 152, 154, 179, 197, 199, 200, 218, 219, 224, 231, 232, 266, 270, 273–276, 278, 288, 291, 311, 325, 346, 379, 381, 388, 394, 398, 401, 439, 440, 442, 446, 475, 478, 480, 486, 487, 502, 503, 519–521, 530, 533, 545, 547, 552, 572, 574, 580, 586, 589, 590, 592, 593, 596, 598, 599, 601, 616, 655, 656, 659, 662, 664, 666, 670, 681, 682, 695, 697–699, 702, 722, 725, 728, 731, 733, 735, 740, 750, 810, 811, 819, 887, 896, 897, 899, 901, 929
Supply, 520–522, 534, 549, 559, 571, 590, 597, 601, 617, 618, 629, 632, 634–637, 663, 685–687, 690, 691, 702, 712, 727–729, 743, 770, 771, 791, 795, 814, 834, 848, 851, 852, 859, 869, 871, 872, 891, 909, 937, 963, 971
of SALWs, 307, 312, 628–630, 633, 635–637, 770, 859
Supply and demand, 100, 587, 631, 685, 692, 869, 891, 916, 990
Syria, 76, 122, 179, 219, 545, 596, 707, 709, 714, 740, 750, 763, 786, 809, 864, 954

T
Tafari Makonnen, 723
Tahrir Square, 711, 715. *See also* Arab, spring

Taliban, 76, 929
Tangible capital, 248, 249
Tanzania, 1, 31, 32, 116, 136, 137, 153, 156, 191, 199, 210, 212, 224, 275, 311, 486, 518, 572, 669, 682, 880, 882, 996
Taxonomy
 of arms control, 115
Technical commissions, 959
Technology, 5, 63, 70, 115, 133, 188, 194, 208, 220, 257, 267, 268, 330, 336, 350, 478, 481, 490, 492, 495, 518, 519, 526, 528, 542, 557, 560, 581, 582, 587, 629, 647, 648, 650, 651, 653, 667, 700, 745, 911
Terrorism, 2, 18, 23, 25, 42, 53, 54, 79, 83, 86, 88, 99, 100, 116, 125, 134, 150, 151, 165, 167, 168, 172, 188, 196, 197, 199–201, 234, 238, 266, 276, 290, 306, 325, 326, 354, 393, 400, 413, 418, 430, 434, 438, 442, 454, 473, 482, 485–487, 501–503, 541, 545, 589, 599, 600, 609, 612, 641, 648, 663, 664, 670, 709, 718, 721, 745, 752, 762, 764, 769, 779, 786, 795, 803–805, 807–811, 813, 815–817, 822, 829, 865–868, 928, 941–943, 955, 983, 984, 989, 992
Terrorist, 2, 23, 25, 26, 49, 51, 56, 57, 83, 100, 137, 165, 167, 170, 188, 190, 194, 199, 202, 203, 218, 220, 224, 272, 273, 295, 328, 336, 376, 379, 394, 397, 413, 414, 417, 420, 431, 434, 436, 438, 441, 453, 458, 459, 481, 528, 530, 545, 546, 567, 599, 610, 612, 614, 617, 618, 620, 640, 641, 653, 662, 666, 670, 718, 724, 735, 740, 742, 745, 751–753, 766–768, 779, 787, 788, 794, 795, 803, 804, 807, 810–817, 847, 864, 867–869, 889, 897, 915, 922, 930, 934, 935, 938, 954, 984, 987, 995
 organizations, 138, 164, 177, 223, 329, 506, 507, 616, 634, 749, 786, 805, 810, 813, 984
The Ego, 327
Theft, 559, 560, 568, 616, 629, 641, 671, 699, 770, 777, 782, 796, 812, 822, 827, 829, 840, 914
 of arms, 2, 122, 562, 632, 824
The Id, 327
Theoretical, 11, 43, 46, 54, 64, 71, 81–83, 96, 98, 163, 303, 304, 310, 412, 413, 430, 434, 505
 review, 540
Theoretical dimensions, 45
Theoretical framing, 135, 375, 377, 586, 587, 590, 712, 713
Theoretical matrix, 46
Theory, 569, 591, 602, 631, 712, 806, 807, 986
 of capitalism, 72
Theory of Deviance, 50, 51
The Super ego, 328
Threat, 539, 548, 592, 610, 612, 614, 615, 627, 630, 631, 651, 653, 660, 661, 668, 689, 692, 702, 710, 711, 733, 735, 744, 751, 778, 783, 786, 794, 797, 807–809, 815, 820, 826, 828, 830, 835, 837, 867, 890, 901, 911, 912, 914, 938, 953, 986, 988, 996, 997
 of SALWs, 54, 794, 820
 to state security, 181, 615
Threshold Terminologies, 430
Tigray, 288, 730, 731, 733
Timbuktu, 178, 763
Togo, 9, 152, 156, 167, 191, 481, 545, 548, 552, 553, 593, 910, 914, 916
Trade, 518–524, 527, 540–542, 544, 548–550, 553, 554, 557, 559, 561, 568, 571–573, 581, 586–588, 592, 596, 597, 600, 610, 619, 620, 630, 635, 637, 638, 649–651, 653, 655, 657, 658, 662, 666, 669, 672, 685–688, 700, 727, 728, 733, 739, 748, 753, 754, 763, 764, 767, 769, 771, 772, 783, 788, 812, 813, 825, 832, 833, 835, 839, 852, 854, 857, 859, 864, 869, 871, 874, 879, 892, 899, 957–959, 964, 965, 983, 985, 988–994, 996
 in SALWs, 58, 95, 124, 187, 188, 274, 338, 347, 376, 402, 404, 414, 415, 462, 502, 507, 540, 554, 669, 812, 813, 825, 864
Traditional, 523, 526, 529, 532, 533, 548, 630, 634, 648, 655, 667, 688,

INDEX 1039

690, 692, 702, 707, 712, 726, 729, 732, 803, 804, 860, 897, 912
leaders, 531–534, 633
rulers, 237, 362, 517, 518, 526, 529, 531, 532, 535
Traditional institutions, 11, 366, 517, 518, 520, 521, 525, 526, 530–532, 535
and proliferation of SALWs, 519
Trafficking
of SALWs, 9, 61–63, 95, 201, 203, 274, 417, 469, 485; in Africa, 61, 420, 553, 554, 558, 634, 753, 797, 811, 815, 825, 913, 974, 988, 997
routes, 18, 384, 439, 550, 657, 812
Trans African Highway (TAH), 571–573
Transformation, 9, 19, 76, 79, 89, 208, 210, 211, 235, 269, 302, 349–351, 355, 358, 398, 457, 531, 557, 579, 589, 654, 690, 916
Transition Monitoring Group (TMG), 509
Transnational crime, 2, 11, 411, 412, 417, 419–422, 486, 541, 561, 616
in Africa, 411–413, 415, 416, 418, 419, 616
Transnational insurgency, 928, 929, 940, 941
Transport, 10, 26, 117, 189, 192, 193, 213, 214, 257, 354, 438, 479
infrastructure, 26, 215, 569
network, 11, 214, 567–569, 572, 574, 576, 694; in Africa, 26, 117, 230, 567, 568, 571, 572, 574–576
node, 569, 570
Transportation, 56, 98, 179, 188, 215, 219, 478
network, 478; and vulnerabilities, 570; in Africa, 11, 26, 215; of SALWs, 188, 189, 192, 193, 219, 354, 438, 567, 568, 574
Treaty, 127, 189, 201, 202, 405, 461, 544, 546, 549, 553, 576, 657, 658, 686, 753, 881, 910, 959
Trend(s), 20, 22, 23, 133, 150, 151, 168, 188, 209, 210, 215, 218, 238, 253, 267, 336, 365, 366, 383, 419, 436, 438, 447, 454, 479

in Africa, 18, 21, 23, 133, 151, 253, 436, 557, 628, 648, 650
of production, 436, 447, 628, 632
of proliferation, 18, 151, 238, 447, 454, 458, 589, 628, 661, 755, 869, 909, 914, 934
of SALWS, 151, 168, 188, 267, 365, 419, 454, 458, 628, 755, 831, 888, 916, 934
Tuareg, 173, 174, 177–179, 202, 232, 233, 520, 656, 746, 751, 762–771, 773, 922
militia, 34, 179, 202, 233, 599, 657, 765
Tudun Wada, 229
Tunisia, 143, 152, 154, 210, 212, 274, 275, 291, 346, 398, 416, 425, 442, 481, 503, 546, 617, 664, 707–709, 712, 714, 715, 740, 747, 750, 751, 770
Turko-Egyptian, 887, 901
Tutsi, 88, 197, 290, 530, 594, 601, 633
Twitter, 494, 716
Types
of conflicts in Africa, 17, 20, 113, 117, 139, 140, 277, 290, 382, 506, 628
of SALWs, 145, 457, 551, 552, 811, 813–815, 914, 923
of SALWs in Africa, 3, 8, 41, 43, 51, 53, 135, 162, 219, 294, 923
Tyranny, 707

U

Uganda, 8, 12, 29, 31, 32, 47, 49, 54, 57, 116, 119, 126, 127, 137, 153, 156, 165, 191, 198, 212, 218, 233, 234, 254, 275, 289, 291, 295, 325, 335, 381, 417, 420, 439, 440, 442, 475, 486, 530, 533, 572, 574, 586, 589, 592–595, 639, 662, 664, 670, 745, 872, 879–902
Uganda Joint Christian Council (UJCC), 891
Uganda National Action Plan (NAP), 891, 894, 895, 898
Uganda Police Force (UPF), 892, 893

Ukraine, 33, 231, 273, 437, 586, 595, 596, 655, 746, 851, 853
Uncivil society, 506
Uncontrolled, 54, 99, 119, 203, 223, 225, 230, 231, 272, 308, 374, 380, 384–387, 394, 400, 435, 438, 440, 458, 462, 477, 586, 601, 648, 654, 655, 657, 665, 666, 669, 670, 749, 994, 995
   SALWs, 203, 272, 308, 394, 400, 462; in Africa, 203, 308, 394, 477, 533, 577, 586, 752, 974, 986, 987, 996
Underdevelopment, 48, 79, 91, 92, 114, 214, 232, 248, 270, 285, 286, 324, 378, 388, 400, 505, 530, 656, 849, 869, 875, 995
   in Africa, 79, 91, 92, 214, 324, 505, 539, 609, 710, 762, 763, 826, 914, 922
Undergoverned spaces, 430, 433
Unemployment, 26, 48, 52, 91, 188, 196, 215, 219, 231, 246, 256, 277, 309, 336, 361, 388, 393, 418, 460, 505, 530, 545, 551, 562, 599, 602, 656, 710, 713, 714, 768, 780, 829–831, 841, 859, 921
Ungoverned
   forests, 223, 230, 233, 239
   spaces, 2, 11, 56, 57, 162–168, 170–172, 174–177, 180, 181, 228, 231, 305, 308, 365, 419, 420, 430, 433–435, 444, 447; in Africa, 11, 163, 170, 171, 174, 225, 657; in Nigeria, 228
Ungoverned spaces(UGS), 2, 11, 56, 57, 162–165, 167, 168, 170, 225, 229, 305, 308, 365, 419, 420, 433–435, 444, 447
Unguwan Bilya, 237
Union of Soviet Socialist Republic (USSR), 293, 597, 602, 711, 742, 745, 746
Union Secretariat, 959, 960
United Kingdom (UK), 13, 18, 38, 48, 68, 127, 170, 180, 381, 437, 474, 497, 593, 595, 596, 612, 697, 746, 748, 852, 854

United Nation Programme of Action (UNPoA), 403, 462, 502, 507
United Nations Children's Fund (UNICEF), 358, 374, 640, 661, 855, 890, 975
United Nations Institute for Disarmament Research (UNIDIR), 8, 9, 115, 863, 870, 872, 873, 892
United Nations Mission in Sierra Leone (UNAMSIL), 558, 579, 854, 855, 968, 969, 975
United Nations Office for West Africa and Sahel (UNOWAS), 165, 973, 974
United Nations Security Council (UNSC), 7, 18, 20, 57, 58, 60, 193, 478, 492, 594, 618, 656, 695, 744, 747, 753, 889, 934, 965, 967, 971, 974
United Nations (UN), 7, 17–19, 23, 99, 119, 120, 125, 126, 150, 166, 167, 189, 192, 219, 226, 227, 239, 259, 270, 347, 356, 363, 396, 397, 403, 404, 421, 456, 464, 478, 481, 484, 493, 507
   arms control, 484; in Africa, 105, 475, 507, 544, 553, 561
   Arms Trade Treaty, 402, 404, 461, 546, 553, 557, 753, 754, 858, 942
   firearms protocol, 126, 455, 898
   programme, 126, 128, 404, 507, 602, 753, 754, 857, 858, 896
   protocol, 462, 754
United States (US), 18, 33, 48, 68, 187, 268, 292, 503, 587, 594, 601, 610, 613, 618, 640, 695, 700, 711, 741, 748, 763, 815, 832, 836, 886, 892, 954, 975
   arms transfer, 610, 618
   military, 568, 594, 641, 742, 743, 748, 804
Unlicensed, 18, 294, 456, 474, 476, 477, 479, 481, 490, 492–494, 823, 827, 832, 838
   arms in Africa, 474, 477, 494, 827
UN Programme of Action to Prevent, Combat and Eradicate the Illicit

INDEX 1041

Trade in Small (UNPoA), 754, 857, 858, 892, 896, 939
UN Secretary General, 23, 458, 481, 627, 953, 956, 965
Urban dynamics, 11, 207, 216–218, 220
Urbanisation
  in Africa, 207, 209, 215, 216
Urbanscapes, 215
Users, 32, 44, 103, 259, 268, 374, 395, 399–401, 456, 483, 488, 502, 576, 610, 612, 629, 633, 651, 661, 668, 734, 780, 898

V

Vandalisation, 782, 783
Video-games, 101
Vietnam War, 613, 810
Violence, 528, 529, 534, 540, 545, 548, 551, 553, 557, 562, 580, 589, 598–602, 609, 619, 621, 627, 639, 640, 642, 648, 649, 653, 654, 659–662, 664, 666, 673, 681, 683, 684, 687–693, 695, 696, 701, 702, 710, 712, 713, 718, 722, 732, 745, 752, 754, 769, 770, 778–782, 792, 793, 795, 797, 803, 806–809, 811, 821–823, 825–833, 835, 836, 839, 840, 847, 849, 850, 852, 858, 865, 867, 873, 874, 886, 888, 890, 900, 917, 923, 933, 935, 952–955, 965, 967, 983–985, 987, 988, 994, 997
  in post-colonial Africa, 32, 589
Violent
  conflict, 34, 56, 96, 101, 102, 106, 107, 114, 115, 117, 124, 134, 162, 164, 194, 202, 203, 268–270, 273, 275–279, 285, 286, 289, 290, 293, 295, 296, 323, 345–347, 354, 362, 363, 375, 386, 438, 459, 502–504, 512, 513, 535, 539, 551, 557, 585, 589, 590, 601, 620, 653, 665, 683, 707, 714, 717, 718, 733, 740, 743, 769, 772, 778, 779, 792, 793, 797, 864, 866, 868, 871, 909, 910, 912, 922, 940, 952, 953, 960, 963, 964, 971, 972, 974, 976, 985, 991, 994–997
extremism, 1, 18, 23, 25, 26, 113, 232, 306, 365, 533, 599, 619, 649, 657, 664, 868
extremist groups, 657, 868, 941, 987
extremist wars, 32
films, 101
non-state actors (VNSAs), 599, 659, 708, 717, 739, 809, 864, 868–872, 875, 897, 909, 915
reproduction, 98
scenarios, 32, 740, 743. *See also* Non-State Actors (VNSAs)
Violent conflict, 535, 539, 551, 557, 585, 589, 590, 601, 620, 653, 665, 683, 707, 714, 718, 733, 740, 743, 769, 772, 778, 779, 792, 793, 797, 864, 866, 868, 871, 909, 910, 912, 922, 940, 952, 953, 960, 963, 964, 971, 972, 974, 976, 985, 991, 994–997
  in Africa, 277, 290, 296, 345, 386, 535, 539, 551, 557, 585, 590, 601, 620, 665, 871, 909, 910, 912, 922, 940, 974, 985, 991, 994
Violent non-state actors (VNSAs), 31, 34, 118, 430, 433–435, 448, 507, 599, 740, 751–753, 795, 897, 943
Volatile Neighbourhood, 803
Volatility, 248, 529, 864, 952–954

W

War, 1, 11, 19–21, 23, 28, 29, 31, 41, 42, 55, 70–73, 76–79, 81, 83–86, 88, 90, 92, 99, 101, 113, 115, 134, 187, 188, 194, 198, 218, 219, 245, 246, 251–257, 260, 270, 273, 279, 285–287, 289–296, 300–302, 304–307, 309, 310, 312, 324, 329, 338, 339, 354, 386, 393, 395, 397, 398, 412, 413, 418, 442, 458, 473, 475, 478, 481, 492, 501, 508, 520, 521, 524, 526, 528–530, 532, 540, 552, 585, 586, 588, 591–593, 595, 598–601, 609, 611, 613, 616, 617, 628, 629, 637, 642, 648, 649, 652,

653, 656, 657, 659–662, 682, 685,
688, 691, 701, 702, 717, 724, 728,
731, 733, 739, 740, 743, 745, 746,
749, 755, 762, 767, 770, 772, 805,
806, 813, 832, 848, 850–855, 857,
859, 866, 889, 890, 900, 901, 917,
943, 954, 957, 960, 962–964, 967,
968, 971, 975, 986, 993, 994, 996
economy, 71, 118, 119, 268, 269,
302, 309, 310, 339, 359, 366,
519, 682, 701, 702
in Sierra Leone, 421, 503
of liberation, 80, 85, 530
War economy
in Africa, 519, 682, 701, 702
Warlordism, 253, 688, 863, 865, 866
Warlords, 47, 117–119, 166, 218, 254,
258, 273, 310, 326, 397, 507, 642,
666, 682, 688–690, 698, 728, 729,
849, 866, 872, 952
Weak, 2, 6, 17, 42, 48, 55, 59, 114,
120, 121, 165, 167, 190, 197, 219,
220, 233, 250, 260, 265, 328, 337,
347, 374, 401, 402, 441, 444, 453,
459, 460, 490, 539, 547, 558, 560,
579, 610, 612, 613, 620, 637, 655,
663, 672, 715–718, 728, 746, 749,
769, 773, 780, 790, 814, 825, 828,
832, 849, 851, 859, 868, 897, 899,
901, 910, 914, 927, 930, 932, 965,
988, 991, 994, 997
Weak states, 2, 18, 48, 161, 164, 259,
339, 443, 444, 587, 609, 614, 620,
687, 710, 743, 764, 868
Wealth, 29, 52, 53, 78, 89, 102, 215,
217, 245, 246, 249, 251–255, 260,
270, 295, 311, 312, 364, 400, 438,
460, 525, 688, 742, 766, 768, 780,
781, 849, 890, 912
Weapons
and ammunition, 18, 413, 465; in
CAR, 476, 520, 524, 532, 543,
560, 611, 629, 635, 636, 658,
662, 671, 672, 695, 699, 717,
739, 745, 753, 754, 768, 771,
772, 783, 789, 790, 795, 819,
825, 835, 851–853, 857, 891,
912, 931, 938, 939, 956, 966,
971, 976, 984, 985

in post-colonial Africa, 529
transfer, 544, 574, 586, 594, 632,
655, 657, 659, 746, 795, 851,
928, 955, 990, 992
Weapons for development (WfD), 103
Weapons of Mass Destruction (WMD),
100, 164, 220, 326, 339, 414, 453,
454, 458, 481, 544, 745
West Africa, 530, 539, 545, 546,
550–552, 554, 557, 559, 571, 574,
575, 577, 580, 593, 597, 598, 600,
627, 653, 654, 657, 663, 670, 672,
689, 761, 764, 767, 773, 805, 814,
910–912, 914–919, 921–923, 927,
933, 935, 939, 941–943, 951, 954,
967, 973
countries, 575, 856, 909, 942
Western, 5, 49, 70, 71, 73, 88, 91,
167, 170, 180, 273, 337, 438, 519,
533, 546, 548, 651, 714, 723, 733,
741, 743–745, 748, 804, 805, 810,
814–816, 888, 967
Western Africa, 31, 33, 59, 116, 138,
152, 155, 271, 414, 416, 443, 482
Western African, 196, 198, 520, 524,
554, 556, 572, 574, 578–581, 601,
616, 627, 670, 777, 823, 848, 856,
909, 917, 918, 923, 931, 937, 940,
942, 953, 961
What Africans
must do, 90
WikiLeaks, 641
Women
and children, 105, 189, 199, 203,
217, 220, 230, 236, 275, 276,
402, 404, 405, 480, 545, 601,
639, 691, 722, 734, 770, 849,
994, 996
and girls, 97, 102–106, 336, 394–398,
401–404, 416, 639, 640, 661
and violence, 402, 404, 661, 722,
831, 832, 852, 994
World, 2, 4, 7, 48, 71, 75, 77, 79, 80,
83, 84, 89, 126, 151, 167, 187,
188, 201, 214, 218, 235, 247, 254,
270, 272, 276, 301, 304, 307, 311,
332, 333, 347, 397, 458, 478, 482,
494, 505, 508, 518, 526, 528, 542,
544, 546, 547, 549, 561, 580, 581,

586–588, 592, 593, 599, 601, 602, 609, 610, 614, 617, 631, 632, 638, 648–653, 659, 660, 662, 664, 672, 673, 684, 686, 707, 709, 712, 713, 715, 740–744, 748, 749, 753, 755, 764, 766, 786, 819, 821, 822, 829, 832, 847, 886, 889, 890, 900, 918, 935, 952–954, 975, 994, 995
World Bank, 231, 574, 647, 653, 656, 732, 865, 866, 890, 993

X

Xenophobia, 826, 827, 831, 840, 984, 987, 992
Xenophobic violence, 831, 983

Y

Yar'adua, Umaru, 295
Yargamji, 229
Yemen, 49, 117, 231, 387, 545, 656, 707, 709, 714, 728, 733, 735, 864, 870
Yorubaland, 522
Youth, 28, 117, 238, 256, 277, 309, 331, 355, 377, 379, 382, 383, 386, 388, 494, 620, 621, 630, 639, 641, 642, 654, 660, 688, 702, 710, 716, 769, 780–782, 848, 849, 856, 860, 868, 921, 963, 967, 997
Youth bulge, 11, 374, 377, 380, 382, 384, 388
YouTube, 716

Z

Zambia, 153, 156, 210, 212, 274, 486, 572–574, 700, 823, 990, 996
Zamfara state, 236, 640, 934
Zaria, 363, 524
Zimbabwe, 24, 31, 35, 116, 137, 153, 157, 193, 210, 212, 275, 325, 381, 385, 442, 480, 508, 573, 574, 592, 593, 663, 826, 984, 987, 988, 990, 992, 994, 995
Zindiq, 365
Zones, 549, 559, 586, 613, 614, 616, 618–621, 631, 649, 652, 655, 660, 669, 682, 689, 700, 702, 722, 730, 733, 921, 932, 934
 of violence, 1, 363, 619, 660, 666
Zulu Kingdoms, 29